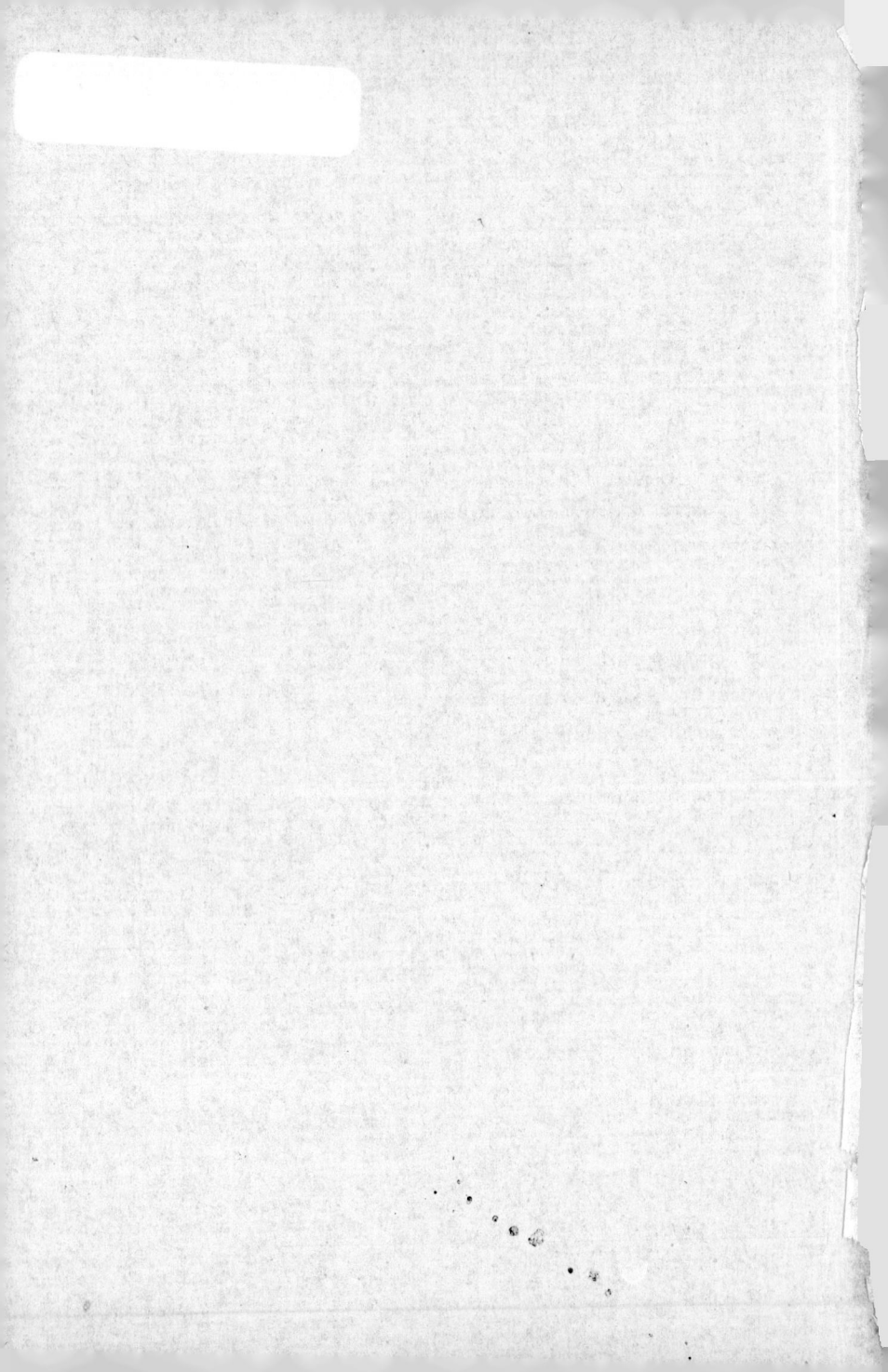

Bhagavad Gita

DECODED

satsanghs delivered to Swamis, Ananda Samajis, Satsanghis and members of the Nithyananda Sangha all over the world.

Bhagavad Gita

DECODED

by

His Holiness

Paramahamsa Nithyananda

with the original Sanskrit texts, transliteration,
English translation

NITHYANANDA
UNIVERSITY
PRESS

All meditation techniques, practices and procedures described or recommended in this book, are suitable for practice only under the direct supervision of an instructor, trained and ordained by Paramahamsa Nithyananda. Further, you should consult with your personal physician to determine whether those techniques, practices and procedures are suitable for you in relation to your own health, fitness and ability.

This publication is not intended to be a substitute for a personal medical attention, examination,diagnosis or treatment. Should any person engage in any of the techniques, practices or procedures described or recommended in this book, he would be doing so at his own risk, unless he has received a personal recommendation from his own physician and from an instructor trained and ordained by Paramahamsa Nithyananda.

Bhagavad Gita Decoded (English)

Published by Nithyananda University Press

First printing: January 2015, 10,000 copies

ISBN: 978-1-60607-160-1 (softcover)

A portion of the proceeds from the sale of this book will be towards supporting charitable activities.

Printed in India at
PrintOGraph,
124 Sultanpet, Bangalore 560053, India. Tel: + 91 80 22877398

Table of Contents

Bhagavad Gītā: A Background

vasudeva sutaṁ devaṃ kamsa cānūra mardanam I

devakī paramānandaṁ kṛṣṇam vande jagad gurum II

'I salute unto you Bhagavān Kṛṣṇa,
Guru (master) of the world,
son of Vasudeva, supreme bliss of Devakī,
destroyer of Kamsa and Cāṇūra'

Srīmad Bhagavad Gītā is the ultimate sacred scripture of yoga, *Yogaśastra* and the pristine glory of the Vedic culture, the eternal living tradition called *sanātana-dharma*. It belongs to the whole Universe for it is delivered to the Universe by the source and embodiment of Universe. We salute and bow down to Bhagavān Śrī Kṛṣṇa, who spoke the Bhagavad Gītā out of His infinite love and compassion for all beings.

Whenever unrighteousness, *adharma* becomes predominant and *dharma*, righteous living declines and the Yoga of Enlightenment is lost, *Parabrahma* Kṛṣṇa, the Supreme Consciousness appears again and again to revive this sacred yoga, to protect and to enrich the devoted beings; and destroys *adharma* to re-establish the pure and everlasting *dharma*—the Science of Enlightenment. *dharma saṁsthāpanārthāya sambhavāmi yuge yuge*—this is Śrī Kṛṣṇa's promise and the essence and spirit of the Gītā.

Gītā is also called *Brahmavidyā*—the Knowledge of Brahman, the supreme absolute truth; it is *Jīvan Mukti Vijñāna*—the Science of

Living Enlightenment. As with all scriptures, it is the knowledge and experience that is transmitted verbally as *Śri Kṛṣṇārjuna Saṁvād*, an intimate dialogue between Master of the world, *Jagadguru* Lord Śrī Kṛṣṇa and His dear devotee and disciple, Arjuna. It is called *śruti* in Saṃskṛit, meaning something that is heard.

Gītā, as Bhagavad Gītā is generally called, translates literally from Saṃskṛit as *'Sacred Song of God'*. Unlike the *Vedas* and *Upaniṣads*, which are stand alone expressions of Truth, the Gītā is written into the greatest Hindu epic, the Mahābhārat, called a *purāṇa*, an ancient historical happening. It is part of the recorded history of the greatest tradition, the paramount civilization in all its Divine grandeur and its human complexity, so to speak.

As a scripture, Gītā is *Gītāśastra*, the essence and the most important part of the ancient knowledge base of the Vedic tradition, which is the expression of the experiences of great sages. *Vedas* and *Upaniṣads,* the foundation of *śruti* literature, arose from the insight, vision and the consciousness of completion of these great sages when they were raised into a no-mind state of *Advaita* (non-duality). These are as old as humanity, as eternal as truth, and the first and truest expressions in the journey of man's search for truth.

Unlike the *Vedas,* which were revealed to the great Sages or the *Upaniṣads,* which were the teachings of these great Enlightened Eages, Gītā is part of the great Bhārata's (India's) history narrated by Śrī Veda Vyāsa or Śrī Kṛṣṇa Dvāipāyana Vyāsa, one of the great Enlightened Sages and the compiler of all scriptures and hymns. Gītā is scribed by Śrī Ganeṣa, the elephant God who embodies pure wisdom and joyful spontaneity. It is narrated as the direct expression of the Divine Himself. It is because of Bhagavān Śrī Kṛṣṇa's direct presence that the Mahābhārat and jeweled in it, the Bhagavad Gītā is the indisputable authority of the greatest revelation of Truth. The Gītā is the sacred text incarnation of the Absolute Divine.

No other epic or part of an epic has the special status and space of the Gītā. No other book but the Gītā gives a scientific, systematic, applied science of living joyfully in completion, while empowering the human action-field with authenticity to evolve into a responsible Divine play-field.

Called the royal supreme knowledge and the royal secret of secrets—*rājavidyā rājaguhyaṁ* (9.2), this one sacred book conveys the essence of knowledge contained in all written and oral vedic truths to enrich the simplest to complex humans at all planes. It holds within itself the direct key to every possible human enquiry, the solution to every dilemma of emotions, and the sublime righteous path and goal of every quest of rising or falling civilizations for every age, time or geography. As a consequence of the presence of the Gītā, the Mahābhārat epic itself is considered a sacred Hindu scripture.

Gītā arose from the super consciousness of Śri Kṛṣṇa, the Supreme God, the complete Incarnation *Purṇāvatār*, and is therefore considered *Gītāśastra*—the essential scripture, knowing which, one is liberated from all incompletions, *yaj jñātvā mokṣyase asubhāt* (9.1) and *Gītopaniṣad*—the essence of all Upaniṣads, the purest and highest knowledge to be ever known and cognized because it gives the direct experience of the Self— *pavitram idam uttamam pratyakṣāvagaṁ dharmyaṁ* (9.2).

MAHĀBHĀRAT IS THE STORY OF YOUR LIFE

Mahābhārat, literally meaning the great Bhārata, is a grand narration about the nation and civilization, which is now known as India. It was then a nation ruled by king Bhārata and his descendants.

dharme cārthe ca kāme ca mokśe ca bharatarśabha /
yadihasti tadanyatra yannehasti na tatkvachit //
~ *Mahābhārat, Ādi Parva 56.33* ~

'O Scion of Bharat race, whatever *dharma* (righteousness), *artha* (economic growth), *kāma* (pleasure) and *mokṣa* (liberation) exist in this text is found elsewhere, but what is not found in this text does not exist elsewhere.'

Look into your life! Your whole life is nothing but the Mahābhārat War. The Mahābharāt should be read again and again to understand the intricacies of life, the complications of life, and the ability to handle life.

The true story of this perfectly recorded epic is about two warring clans, Kauravas and Pāṇḍavas, closely related to one another. Dhṛtarāṣṭra, the blind king of Hastināpur and father of the 100 Kaurava brothers was the brother of Pāṇḍu, whose children were the five Pāṇḍava princes. It is a tale of strife between cousins and ultimately between *dhārmic* and *adhārmic*, righteous and unrighteous civilizations.

Since Dhṛtarāṣṭra was blind, Pāṇḍu was made the king of Hastināpura. Pāṇḍu was cursed by a sage that he would die if he ever entered into a physical relationship with his wives. He therefore had no children. Vyāsa says that all the five Pāṇḍava children were born to their mothers Kuntī and Mādri through the blessing of divine beings. Pāṇḍu handed over the kingdom and his children to his blind brother

Dhṛtarāṣṭra and retired to meditate in the forest.

Kuntī, who is the embodiment of *tapas*, spiritual penance, had received a boon when she was still a young unmarried adolescent, that she could summon any divine power at will to father a child. Before she married, she tested her boon. The Sun god, Sūrya appeared before her. Karṇa was born to her as a result. In fear of social reprisals, she cast the newborn away in a river. Yudhiṣṭra, Bhīma and Arjuna were born to Kuntī after her marriage by invocation of her powers, and the twins Nakula and Sahadeva were born to Mādri, the second wife of Pāṇḍu.

Yudhiṣṭra was born to Kuntī as a result of her being blessed by Yama, the god of death, *dharma* and justice, Bhīma by Vāyu, the god of wind, and Arjuna by Indra, god of all the divine beings. Nakula and Sahadeva, the youngest Pāṇḍava twins, were born to Mādri, through the Divine Aśvini twins.

Dhṛtarāṣṭra had a hundred sons through his wife Gāndhārī. The eldest of these Kaurava princes was Duryodhana. Duryodhana felt no love for his five Pāṇḍava cousins. He made many unsuccessful attempts, along with his brother Duśśāsana, to kill the Pāṇḍava brothers. Kuntī's eldest son Karṇa, whom she had cast away at birth, was found and brought up by a chariot driver in the palace, and by a strange twist of fate, joined hands with Duryodhana.

Dhṛtarāṣṭra gave Yudhiṣṭra one half of the Kuru kingdom on his coming of age, since the Pāṇḍava prince was the rightful heir to the throne that his father Pāṇḍu had vacated. Yudhiṣṭra ruled from his new capital Indraprastha, along with his brothers Bhīma, Arjuna, Nakula and Sahadeva. Arjuna won the hand of princess Draupadī, daughter of the king of Pāñcāla, in a *svayaṁvara*, a marital contest in which princes fought for the hand of a fair damsel. In fulfillment of their mother Kuntī's desire that the brothers share everything equally, Draupadī became the wife of all five Pāṇḍava brothers.

Duryodhana persuaded Yudhiṣṭra to join a gambling session, where his cunning uncle Śakunī defeated the Pāṇḍava king. Yudhiṣṭra lost all that he owned—his kingdom, his brothers, his wife and himself, to Duryodhana. Duśśāsana shamed Draupadī in public by trying to disrobe her. The Pāṇḍava brothers and Draupadī were forced to go into exile for fourteen years, with the condition that in the last year they should live incognito or *ajyāta vāsa*.

At the end of the fourteen years, the Pāṇḍava brothers tried to reclaim their kingdom. In this effort they were helped by Śrī Kṛṣṇa, the king of the Yādava clan, who is the eighth divine incarnation of Lord Viṣṇu. However, Duryodhana refused to yield even a needlepoint of land, and as a result, the Great War, the War of Mahābhārat ensued. In this war, various rulers of the entire nation that is modern India aligned with one or the other of these two clans, the Kauravas or the Pāṇḍavas.

Kṛṣṇa offered to join with either of the two clans. He says, 'One of you may have Me unarmed. I will not take any part in the battle. The other may have my entire Yādava army.' When the offer was first made to Duryodhana, he predictably chose the large and well-armed Yādava army, *Nārāyaṇī Senā*, in preference to the unarmed Kṛṣṇa. Arjuna joyfully and gratefully chose his dearest friend, his life mentor and his Guru, Kṛṣṇa, *Nārāyaṇa*, to be his unarmed charioteer!

Amidst The Warfield, Appears The Song Of God

Oṁ pārthāya pratibodhitāṁ bhagavatā nārāyaṇena svayaṁ
vyāsena gratitāṁ purāṇa muninā madhye mahābhāratam /
advaitāmṛta varṣiṇīṁ bhagavatīṁ aṣṭādaśā'dhyāyinīṁ
amba tvām anusandadhāmi bhagavadgīte bhavadveṣiṇīm //

'Oṁ, I meditate upon you, *Bhagavad Gītā*,
the affectionate Divine Mother,
showering the nectar of *advaita*, non-duality and
destroying rebirth, incorporated into the midst of
Mahābhārat of eighteen chapters by sage Vyāsa, the
author of the purāṇas and imparted to Arjuna by
Bhagavān Nārāyaṇa, Himself.'

~ *Invocation Verse of Bhagavad Gītā*

Bhagavad Gītā appears in the heart of Mahābhārat in Bhīṣma Parva, the sixth chapter of its eighteen chapters. Veda Vyāsa, the narrator, in glorifying the Gītā sings, 'the one who drinks the water of Ganges (the sacred river for Hindus) attains liberation, what to speak of the one who drinks the nectar of Gītā? Gītā is the essential nectar of the Mahābhārat, *bhāratamṛta sarvasvam* as it is directly spoken by Nārāyaṇa, Bhagavān Kṛṣṇa Himself.'

The armies assembled in the vast field of Kurukṣetra, now in the state of Haryana in modern day India. All the kings and princes were related to one another, and were often on opposite sides. Facing the Kaurava army and his friends, relatives and teachers, Arjuna was overcome by remorse and guilt, and wanted to walk away from the battle out of total powerlessness unbecoming an invincible warrior among warriors.

Śrī Kṛṣṇa's dialogue with Arjuna on the battlefield of Kurukṣetra out of His utmost concern and love for him and humanity is the content of Bhagavad Gītā. Of its seven hundred and forty-five (745) verses, Bhagavān Śrī Kṛṣṇa sings the Gītā in six hundred and twenty (620) verses responding to Arjuna's fifty-seven (57) enquiries. Śrī Kṛṣṇa persuades Arjuna to give-up his powerlessness unfitting an *Ārya*—the spiritually evolved one who understands human life and urges him to raise himself again as *Parantapa*—the conqueror of enemy, and take up arms and vanquish his enemies.

'They are already dead,' says Śrī Kṛṣṇa, 'All those who are facing you have been already killed by Me. Go ahead and do what you have to do. That is your responsibility. Do not worry about the outcome. Leave that to Me.'

Gītā is the ultimate practical teaching on the inner science of spirituality that expresses as outer victory and success in life now and after. It is not, as some scholars incorrectly claim, a promotion of violence. It is about the impermanence of the mind and body, and the need to go beyond the mind, ego and logic.

Being blind with self-doubt, king Dhṛtarāṣṭra does not participate in the war. His minister Sañjaya uses his power of clairvoyance bestowed by Veda Vyāsa to 'see' and relate to king Dhṛtarāṣṭra the goings on the battlefield. It is in Sañjaya's voice that we hear Gītā, the dialogue between Śrī Kṛṣṇa and Arjuna.

All the Kaurava princes as well as all their commanders such as Bhīṣma, Droṇa and Karṇa were killed in battle. The five Pāṇḍava brothers survived as winners and became the rulers of the combined kingdom.

This dialogue sung between Śrī Kṛṣṇa and Arjuna is a dialogue between man and God or *Nara* and *Nārāyaṇa* as they are called in Saṃskrit.

Arjuna's questions and doubts are those of each one of us. Nara Arjuna is the leader, the embodiment of responsibility representing the whole humanity that is burdened with the sufferings born from self-doubt, self-hatred and self-denial of its innate natural state of liberation, *mokṣa.* Only Nārāyaṇa as Śrī Kṛṣṇa can sport a divine smile on His face and sing the nectars of *Advaita*—space of infinity (non-duality) and *Sāṅkhya Yoga*—knowledge of completion in the midst of the waging world war.

Only Bhagavān, one possessed with infinite powers, infinite knowledge, infinite renunciation, and infinite riches, fame and beauty can declare the imperishable and eternal nature of the Self; and also give the direct experience of the Self to Arjuna in *Viśvarūpa Darśan Yoga* and culminate it with *Mokṣa Sannyāsa Yoga*—the yoga of liberation.

The answers of the Divine, Śrī Kṛṣṇa, transcend time and space. Śrī Kṛṣṇa's message is everlasting and joyfully performed, and is as valid today as it was on that fateful battlefield over five thousand years ago. The science of Gītā is the eternal technique of living in completion; the song of Gītā is the eternal life-enriching nectar, having no expiry date, time or age!

Introduction To Bhagavad Gītā Decoded

Bhagavad Gītā Decoded book is not a commentary or a modern interpretation on the *Bhagavad Gītā*. It is the re-speaking, the revival of the supreme secret of the Gītā from the consciousness of the rare living incarnation, Paramahamsa Nithyananda, who embodies the very science and experience of the Gītā. A pure, absolute revelation of the happening of Gītā presented in its original spirit and body language that only an Enlightened being can radiate through the inexpressible energy veiled within His expressed words. To read this book is to obtain an insight that is rare. It is not mere reading; it is an experience; it is meditation.

He takes the reader through a inner world tour while talking on each verse. It is believed that each verse of Gītā has seven levels of meaning. What is commonly rendered is the first-level meaning. Here, an Enlightened Master, an Incarnation takes us beyond the common into the uncommon, with equal ease and simplicity.

The power of the Living Master's words, the confidence and energy of Enlightenment, the space of Advaita that He radiates can directly become the experience in us, when we authentically study this book. The absolute truths of life are to be listened and internalized from the direct source, the living presence of those truths, who can also transmit the experience unto us.

His Holiness Paramahamsa Nithyananda explains the inner metaphorical meaning and the deep spiritual insights of the Mahābhārat and the Bhagavad Gītā:

Understand, this whole history is such a beautiful happening. Mahābhārat is actually your life!

Every character in the Mahābhārat teaches so much! We don't need to go anywhere for our life success or fulfillment or for anything else that we may desire. We don't need to study any other book to learn the human psychology or the science of living and leaving. Whether we seek righteous living—*dharma*; or we want to learn business or administration, economy or abundance—*artha*; or we want to create the best rich lifestyle—*kāma*; or we want to be a leader and want the enriching life of being enlightened—*mokṣa*, for all these purposes, we don't need anything other than the Mahābharāt!

Study each character. We will not find any more characters in our life than the characters described in the Mahābharāt! Any character we see in our life is mapped to Mahābharāt's one character. They are either half or full representation of some character. To know how to handle them and even handle yourself, just see how Śrī Kṛṣṇa handles them and handle them the same way.

The Mahābharāt war is a representation of life as it was lived in that age. Vyāsa, its author is an unbiased historian who recorded the whole history as it happened without trying to apply any makeup. People ask whether the Mahābharāt war happened at all!

Let me tell you this: If the Mahābharāt was a story and not history, Vyāsa should receive multiple Pulitzer prizes for his highly creative work! The Mahābharāt is the longest literary work in the whole world with hundred thousand Saṃskṛit verses—the longest poem ever written with such delicate harmony of unmatched poetic perfection. It is larger than the Greek epics. Vyāsa had no computer, no tape recorder with speech-to-text capabilities. He dictated and Lord Ganeṣa wrote it down!

The Mahābharāt is like an ocean. It has at least 10,000 stories woven into it. All of these are seamlessly woven into the main text even though each is an independent event. Just imagine the effort required to create hundreds of thousands of characters and maintain the integrity of these characters throughout the epic without the help of editors. Do you think anyone could do it today?

Because it is impossible to create such a work of fiction, one needs to accept this as a compilation of true incidents that reflect the lifestyle in what is referred to as Tretā yuga, third quarter of Time, in our scriptures. This is how people behaved then and how people behave now. What happened then repeats itself now, again and again!

The Great War of Mahābhārat is the fight between the positive and negative thought patterns of the mind called the *saṁskāras* or the root thought patterns—meaning the deep identity or the earliest memory you carry and create about you and others. Please understand, don't think you carry only the identity about you, you also carry an identity of the world inside you and look at the world only through that. That is what I call root thought pattern—the identity through which you see you and the world.

The positive thought patterns are the Pāṇḍava princes and the negative thought patterns are the Kaurava princes. Kurukṣetra or the battlefield is the body. Arjuna is the individual consciousness and Śrī Kṛṣṇa is the enlightened Master, the supreme consciousness driving and guiding the individual consciousness.

The various commanders who led the Kaurava army represent the major incompletions of root patterns and conflicting patterns that the individual consciousness faces in its journey to Enlightenment or liberation, *mokṣa*. Bhīṣma, the grand patriarch of the Kuru clan who embodies *dharma*, represents the pattern of parental and societal conditioning. Droṇa, the teacher of both the Kauravas and the Pāṇḍavas, represents the conditioning from teachers who provide knowledge including spiritual guidance.

Śakuni, the maternal uncle of Duryodhana embodies the pattern of self-hatred, which is cunningness personified. Karṇa represents the restrictive influence of good deeds such as charity and compassion done out of incompletion from the pattern of feeling deprived. Finally Duryodhana represents the ego or the self-denial pattern, which is root of the root patterns and is the last to fall.

Parental and societal conditioning has to be overcome by rebelling against conventions. This is why, traditionally, those seeking the path of enlightenment are required to renounce the world as Sannyāsi and move away from civilization. This conditioning does not die as long as the body lives, but its influence drops.

Droṇa represents all the best knowledge one imbibes and the teachers one encounters, who guide us but are unable to take us through to the ultimate flowering of enlightenment. It is difficult to give them up since one feels grateful to them. This is where the Enlightened Master, the incarnation steps in and guides us.

Karṇa is the repository of all good deeds and it is his good deeds that stand in the way of his own Enlightenment. Śrī Kṛṣṇa has to take the load of Karṇa's *puṇya,* his meritorious deeds, before he could be liberated. The Enlightened Master guides one to drop one's attachment to good deeds arising out of what are perceived to be charitable and compassionate intentions. He also shows us that the quest for and the experience of enlightenment is the ultimate act of compassion that one can offer to the world.

Finally one reaches Duryodhana, one's ego or root-pattern, the most difficult to conquer as it leads one to self-destruction. One needs the full help of the Master here. It is subtle work and even the Master's help may not be obvious, since at this point, sometimes the ego makes us deny and disconnect from the Master as well.

The Great War was between 180 million (18 crore) people—110 million on the Kaurava side representing our negative root patterns and conflicting patterns (saṁskāras) and 70 million on the Pāṇḍava side representing our positive patterns. The War lasted 18 days and nights. The number eighteen (18) has a great mystical significance. It essentially signifies our ten (10) senses that are made up of five *jñānendriya*—the senses of perception like taste, sight, smell, hearing and touch, and five *karmendriya*—the senses initiating action like speech, bodily movements, etc., added to our eight (8) kinds of thoughts like lust, greed, etc. All eighteen need to be dropped for self-realization, completion or liberation, *mokṣa*!

Mahābhārat is not just an epic history. It is not merely the fight between good and evil. It is the dissolution of both positive and negative *saṁskāras* (root patterns) that reside in our bio-memory or body-mind system, which must happen for the ultimate liberation. It is a tale of the path of living advaita, the process of powerfully living, radiating enlightenment and causing enlightenment for humanity.

Gītā Belongs To The Whole Universe

Mahābhārat is the living legend. Bhagavad Gītā is the manual for Enlightenment.

Understand, the Gītā is not just for the people who worship Kṛṣṇa or who worship Śiva or who worship Arjuna or who worship Buddha or Mahāvira. Gītā is spoken by the Cosmos through Kṛṣṇa. That is why Vyāsa is using the word ***Bhagavān*** for Śrī Kṛṣṇa throughout the Gītā. So, it is universal. Nobody can claim it or own it as it is given by the Universe to the human society, to the whole civilization. It is not a personal property of anybody; not even the personal property of Hindus. Once it is delivered, it belongs to the whole world!

The essence of the whole Bhagavad Gītā is the Master awakening responsibility in the disciple. That is why everywhere the Gītā talks only about responsibility!

Through '*karmaṇy ev'ādhikāraste mā phaleṣu kadācana* (2.47)—you have the right to work, but never to the outcome of the work', through '*tvakvottiṣṭha parantapa* (2.3)—Giving up your powerlessness, arise, O Parantapa' and through '*uddhared ātmanā'tmānaṁ* (6.5)—raise yourself by yourself', Śrī Kṛṣṇa is awakening the responsibility in Arjuna—Guru is awakening the responsibility in all of us through the awakening of Arjuna, the hero of Gītā.

When you study the Gītā, you will find that Arjuna's logic seems to be very intelligent. He does not want to fight. But Kṛṣṇa emphasizes the intelligent ones need to enter into the fight from the space of *advaita* (non-duality), with the power and joy of feeling responsibility.

Only to a close friend with whom you can open your heart can your struggles be opened. Only when you are able to respect somebody more and more by knowing his struggles and conflicts, by knowing the success he achieved, you become a friend to him. But, by knowing somebody's struggles and conflicts, if you start judging him, there is no friendliness. It is an envious relationship waiting to vomit enmity. It is a seed sown with poison.

Here, Kṛṣṇa shares Gītā to His own closest dearmost friend, Arjuna, who is beyond any envy or incompletion, to whom He can really show *viśvarūpa* (cosmic form) and reveal all His dimensions, with whom He has a freedom to just say, 'Do not yield to this degrading impotence of powerlessness,' 'Do it Kaunteya! O son of Kuntī, just do it,' '*nānuśocitum arhasi* (2.25)—Do not grieve for the body,' and '*mat-karma-kṛn mat-paramo mad-bhakaḥ* (11.55)—Do My work! Be My devotee! Always undividedly think of Me, you shall enter into Me.'

Finally Kṛṣṇa goes to the extreme of saying, '*sarva dharmān parityaja mām ekaṁ śaraṇaṁ vraja* (18.66)—Give up all your concepts and ideas about *dharma*, about right and wrong. Just surrender to Me. I will liberate you.'

To say these words of surrender what an intimate understanding, what a feeling connection, what a space of completion between Master-disciple, beloved-friend should have been there between Kṛṣṇa and Arjuna. Kṛṣṇa summarizes His Gītā saying drop your life at My feet. I will not cheat you, I will think for you. I will see to it you achieve the ultimate—*mokṣayiṣyāmi mā śucah*—I will liberate you, do not fear or worry!

Like Arjuna many thousand years ago, you are here on the warfield of your life in a dialogue with the living Enlightened Master, the rare living

Incarnation in this book.

This is a tremendous opportunity to resolve all life questions, to complete with root thought patterns and to clear all self-doubts by listening into the Master's words and allowing His energy to rewrite your future! This is an extraordinary possibility to awaken your true nature, to arise with your inner powers, and to cause your highest reality—with the Master driving your Self into the absolute victory of life—Living Enlightenment, Living Advaita.

yatra yogeśvaraḥ kṛṣṇo yatra pārtho dhanurdharaḥ |
tatra śrīrvijaya bhūtir dhrūvā nītir matirmama || 18.78

'Wherever there is Yogeśvara Kṛṣṇa, the Master of
all mystics, and wherever there is Pārtha (Arjuna),
the supreme carrier of bow and arrow, there will
certainly be opulence, victory, extraordinary powers,
and morality. That is my opinion.'

Foreword: Bhagavad Gītā And The Four Tattvas

The Great 'Why'

The *Bhagavad Gītā* opens with the great 'WHY', reflecting the personal crisis that we all face at some point of our lives.

We are drawn into the protagonist Arjuna's life at a crucial moment, when the renowned young prince is getting ready for a bloody battle against a huge army consisting of his own family, cousin and teachers. Struggling with fears, a misconstrued sense of duty and an awakening consciousness, the young prince is caught in the dilemma of his life.

Even after five thousand years, Arjuna's dilemma is still alive in humanity's experience of life. Our questions are hardly different from Arjuna's...

- Why are we here?
- Why do we do what we do in our lives?
- Why don't we find fulfillment, even after years of working for success in the world?
- Why do more and more challenges await us, even after we solve and overcome numerous challenges?
- How can we become spiritually mature and integrated individuals? Why is this path even required?

This '*Why*?' can be answered in a very simple way—You are here to manifest your ultimate Possibility!

But each one of you has to discover your own answer to this '*Why*'. Any other answer can only be an inspiration for you to discover your *own* answer. We can only move when we have the ability to handle this great '*Why*'. Whether you know it or not, only your deepest conviction about your '*Why*', only your deepest clarity about your purpose, can give you the inspiration, energy and courage to face life.

This great 'Why' is the seed of God himself! This seed is put inside you when you are sent to planet Earth, so that you do not rest until you become a tree and bear fruit. Please understand, every seed has an energy called *vīrya*, which does not rest till it produces more seeds. Even if you eat the seed, you cannot destroy it, because that *vīrya* still goes into your body and does its job in some other way! The question 'Why' is the *vīrya* put into your very DNA structure to help you realize yourself.

This is the journey that Arjuna undertakes through the Gītā. Under the compassionate guidance of the enlightened master Kṛṣṇa, Arjuna faces and realizes the meaning of the great 'Why', to become a realized soul.

Just like Arjuna, you too will not be able to rest until you realize the meaning of the great 'Why' for you.

Just as Kṛṣṇa addresses Arjuna's questions, Paramahamsa Nithyananda addresses the readers' questions and doubts, guiding us on the path of transformation, refusing to give up on us until we discover our full potential and live like Gods on earth. As you read this book, you will find the presence of Paramahamsa Nithyananda guiding you to discover your own unique yet universal path to realization.

Life Is Expansion

The Art of Listening

Through the entire opening chapter of the Gītā, it is Arjuna who continuously speaks, while Kṛṣṇa listens, listens and listens!

Only an intelligent man will allow the other person to speak. We all continuously speak to each other, but a 'real' conversation does not happen. We simply carry out simultaneous monologues with each other. We are polite enough to pretend that we are listening, so that we will, in turn, be heard. You need intelligence to allow the other person to speak. You need intelligence to listen!

When you listen to others, you listen to yourself. And when you don't listen to others, you also don't listen to yourself. Are you getting it? Only when you listen to you, you will be able to listen to others. When you listen to others, you will also listen to YOU! Because any listening that happens, happens from the space of completion. Please understand, you can only listen when you are complete. If there is any incompletion in you, you will not be able to listen.

What is incompletion? For example, you are sitting here right now, hearing me speak, but you are not listening to me, you are thinking—'I have not done this, I have not done that, this has not happened, that has not happened, I am restless'–that is incompletion. If you have such incompletions inside, be very clear, you will not be listening to me. You may be sitting here out of compulsion or some other reason, but you will not be listening to me. And when you don't listen, more and more incompletions happen. It is a vicious circle.

If you *listen*, especially to the words that come out of the space of completion of an enlightened being, you will suddenly see that the energy of those very words goes and changes your inner space.

See, when you come to me and tell me about your problems, I give you my authentic listening. That is why you suddenly feel light; you suddenly feel that all your problems are not big anymore. It is the power of listening. Listening awakens your intuition. Listening awakens your innermost intelligence. Listening is GOD!

By His very listening, Kṛṣṇa is able to heal the restlessness in Arjuna, the incompletions in Arjuna. Kṛṣṇa is showing us the power of His completion, the power of His listening. He just listens while Arjuna empties himself. He allows Arjuna to speak into His pure listening. Now, the real Gītā can start!

Arjuna's Root Pattern

Please understand, when Kṛṣṇa listens to Arjuna, He is interested in Arjuna's real problem, not what Arjuna is complaining about. And He is not interested in just expressing what He knows. He allows Arjuna to speak into His listening, so that He can go to the root of the problem and address the issue. He knows that once He allows Arjuna to express his problems, Arjuna himself can find a solution to them. And as Arjuna continues to speak, he exposes the root of his problem—his root thought pattern.

Let me define root thought pattern.

> The first strong cognition you receive in your life, which influences you to continue to function based on the same cognition, is a root thought pattern! It is the pattern you develop when powerlessness takes you over for the first time in your life. Your pure cognition is imbalanced and your mind is born!

Listen! The way you behave, feel and respond, all come from this root thought pattern. It is the limiting cognition that happens in you and fills you at a very young age, overpowering you. Sometimes it is fear, sometimes it is greed, sometimes it is jealousy and sometimes it is the decision to prove yourself. Sometimes, it is just plain confusion and worry!

Throughout the initial chapters of the Gītā, Arjuna is operating out of his root thought pattern—his parental and societal conditioning—struggling with all the dos and don'ts that he learnt from society. The moment he sees that the enemy he has to fight are his own extended family, he is overcome by powerlessness and refuses to fight, lamenting, '*svajanam, svajanam*!'—my people, my people! The bonds of family were rooted in his very identity, and to Arjuna, to cut these bonds was to destroy himself! This was Arjuna's dilemma.

It is here that the Gītā begins, as Kṛṣṇa finally begins to speak.

In the succeeding chapters of the Gītā, Kṛṣṇa compassionately guides Arjuna, releasing him from his root thought pattern, guiding him to completion, and leading him to the ultimate knowledge—the knowledge of the Self, *ātmajñāna*. Arjuna is re-established in *jīvanmukti*, Living Enlightenment; the space of living Advaita.

Understanding The Essence Of Kṛṣṇa's Teachings Through The Four Tattvas

The essence of Kṛṣṇa's teachings in the Gītā can be understood through four simple but powerful Universal principles, the four *tattvas—Integrity, Authenticity, Responsibility and Enriching.* These four principles awaken the four innate great powers within us.

Let me define these principles.

Integrity (sampūrti) is you fulfilling the word and thought you give to yourself and to others, and experiencing a state of '*pūrnatva*'—completion with yourself and with life.

Authenticity (śraddha) is you being established in the peak of your capability, and responding to life from who you perceive yourself to be for yourself, who you project yourself to be for others, and, what others expect you to be for them.

Responsibility (upāyanam) is living and responding to life from the truth that you are the source of, and therefore, you are responsible for all happenings in and around you.

Enriching (āpyāyanam) is you taking responsibility with integrity and authenticity, that you are committed to continuously enriching, which is expanding yourself and life, in and around you.

Any problem or conflict you have in your life can be handled very practically, efficiently and skillfully with these four principles. I can say with my entire experience that these four principles are the essence of all spiritual scriptures! They are the essence of life.

These four spiritual principles awaken four great inner powers in you. Each *tattva* is the key to unlock a corresponding power in you. Now, I will reveal these four inner powers that manifest when Kṛṣṇa's message is internalized and lived.

Tattvas, Your Keys To Four Inner Powers

Listen! You actually have the power to simply manifest the reality of your choice!

Whether you know it or not, whether you believe it not, in each one of you is an enormous potential energy that expresses as four great powers.

To be able to unlock these great powers inside you, you must first understand a little more about yourself. They are related to the four major dimensions of your life—your words, your thinking, your emotions, and your living. When you awaken your peak possibility in each of these dimensions, it becomes a great power and support in your life.

These four inner powers are...

The power of words or *vāk śakti*. The power of words will be available to you when you practice Integrity.

The power of thoughts or *mano śakti.* The power of thinking will be open to you when you practice Authenticity.

The power of feeling or *prema śakti.* The power of feeling will be possible when you practice Responsibility.

The power of living or *ātma śakti.* The power of living will be established in you the moment you Enrich others.

Now, I will summarize Kṛṣṇa's teachings through these *tattvas* and their powers.

Integrity—The Strategy For Success

Listen!

Your words are your life. Integrity is the key that unlocks the power of words.

We all know honesty. Honesty is more like ethics, morality. But with the *tattva* of integrity, you are taking a step deeper than honesty. With honesty, you only have to honor the words that you give to others. With integrity, you also have to honor the words that you give to yourself. Honesty is not integrity. Integrity is honesty also.

It is very unfortunate that society teaches you to honor the words that you give to others, but forgets to teach you to honor the words that you give to yourself. The words you give to yourself are as important as—or more important than—the words you give to others. Because the flow of your life—the amount of contentment that you feel in your life, the degree of fulfillment that you feel in your life and the experience of fulfillment that you feel in your life—everything depends on the words that you have given to you!

Please understand, the words you give to yourself form the bone structure of your life. If you commit with yourself that you will become a doctor and you don't honor that word, and you don't even bother to complete that word inside your heart, then that word hangs inside you as a broken commitment given by you! Integrity is you not carrying the hangover of the commitments you have made, either to yourself or to others.

When you break the commitments you give to you, you lose self-confidence. The more commitments you give and break, the more your self-confidence is lost. You lose confidence in you! When you break the commitments you give to others, it takes away their confidence in you. When you break the words you have given to yourself, you lose confidence in yourself. When you don't honor the words you give, and don't even bother to complete with them, the broken commitments that hang in your heart take away your self-confidence in life!

This is what happens to Arjuna on the battlefield.

Arjuna is a kṣatriya by birth, a warrior, a Pāṇḍava prince. When the Pāṇḍavas decide to wage war against their Kaurava cousins, Arjuna is perfectly aware that this includes a large part of his extended family! Yet he makes the decision to fight as per his *dharma*, as per his path as a *kṣatriya*. But when he enters the battlefield, he only sees 'friends', 'teachers', 'uncles' and 'relatives' leading the army, not the evil men who snatched away his kingdom and publicly insulted his brother and wife! Caught in the clutches of his parental conditioning, Arjuna instantly becomes powerless and decides to leave the battlefield.

By trying to escape from the battle, Arjuna falls completely out of integrity with his *dharma* as a warrior; he has slipped from his *dharma.* As a kṣatriya, he should have fulfilled the words he gave to himself, to his family, and to his Master; and he should have had the courage to face his decision of waging war against the Kauravas. Otherwise, he should not have taken the decision for war! But by becoming powerless and preparing to leave the battlefield, Arjuna is out of integrity with his *dharma*. This is what happens when you function out of your root pattern. You fall out of integrity with the words you give to yourself and others, and the root pattern takes over your response to life!

Understand, taking responsibility for your words is practicing *dharma*, the right living. In Mahābhārat, *dharma* is defined as—'This is the essence of *dharma*. Do not do unto others that which would cause pain when done to you.'

The only way to come out of lack of integrity is through completion.

Through His dialogues with Arjuna on *sāṅkhya yoga* and *karma yoga*, the nature of life and the purpose of action, Kṛṣṇa helps Arjuna find the right understanding to complete with the limiting cognition created by his root thought pattern. Kṛṣṇa teaches Arjuna two key concepts—*Nityam* (the nature of the Eternal) and *na tvam śocitumarhasi* (the pointlessness of grieving). By revealing to Arjuna the truth about his true eternal self, Kṛṣṇa helps him with the right understanding to go beyond all the arguments of his logic and complete with his root pattern.

Arjuna then awakens his power of words that brings him the spontaneous intelligence and the clarity to use the right words to verbalize his real self-doubts. His initial powerless words of grief such as, '*katham bhiṣmamahaṁ saṅkhye dronaṁ ca madhūsudana* (2.4)—O Madhūsudana, how can I oppose Bhīṣma and Drona in the battle who are worthy of my worship?', now turn into words of enquiry such as, '*sthitaprajñasya kā bhāṣā samādhistaye keśava* (2.54)—what are the descriptions of the steady one who is merged in the awareness of truth and wisdom? How does he speak, how does he sit and how does he walk?'

Now, Arjuna is ready for the next lesson—Authenticity, the power of thinking.

Discover Your Peak Capacity Through Authenticity

With authenticity, you open the power of thinking in you!

When you unlock the power of thinking, you will be able to spontaneously focus your thoughts to achieve your highest potential.

Kṛṣṇa now initiates Arjuna into the path of authenticity in

action and the path of knowledge in renunciation in *Karma Yoga* and *Jñāna-karma-sannyāsa Yoga. 'Yogaḥ karmasu kauśalam*—Yoga is authenticity in action,' declares Kṛṣṇa.

karmaṇy evādhikāras te mā phaleṣu kadācana |
mā karmaphala hetur bhur mā te saṅgo'stv akarmaṇi || 2.47

yoga-sthaḥ kuru karmāṇi saṅgaṁ tvaktvā dhanañjaya |
siddhy-asiddhyoḥ samo bhūtvā samatvaṁ yoga ucyate || 2.48

The entire teaching of *Bhagavad Gītā* can be summarized in these two verses. Nothing more can be said or ever needs to be said about why and how one should perform.

Kṛṣṇa says, 'You have the right only to work, but never to the results of that work. Let not the outcome be your motive; but do not move into inaction. Do what you have to do with a complete inner space centered on yoga. Be balanced in success and failure. Evenness of mind is yoga.'

He emphasizes again and again to be complete in yoga and drop all attachments—'Act without attachment. Do not worry about the success and failure in results of your actions. Surrender yourself to the wisdom of completion.'

I am going to share an important concept here.

Listen! You don't have just a single identity, as you imagine. You have four identities!

Please understand, what you consider as *you* has four dimensions.

1. *Mamakāra*—what you believe as you or *inner image.*
2. *Ahaṁkāra* —what you project to others as you or *outer image.*
3. *Anyakāra*—what others believe as you or *others' image.*
4. *Svānyakāra* —what you believe life to be for you or *life image.*

All these identities put together is YOU.

Authenticity is nothing but keeping your four identities in tune and being at the peak of all four dimensions of you.

Usually, what you think as you—your *mamakāra, inner image* is always less than what you are, and what you project as yourself to others—your *ahaṁkāra, outer image* is always more than what you are. For example, you may experience yourself as a very fearful person, but you will always project yourself as strong and powerful. Rarely, some people have a high *mamakāra*, but they project a low *ahaṁkāra* to others. And many times, the *others' image* or *anyakāra* that others have about you will be completely different from both your *mamakāra* and your *ahaṁkāra*!

When one identity is fighting with another identity, how can your thinking be focused? All your energy is going to be used in reconciling your fighting identities. When all your identities or 'images' are in tune, all your thinking will be aligned in one direction. Your thinking becomes clear and sharp, like a laser beam. You will awaken the power of thinking.

Authenticity is not just you living at what *you think* as your peak, or what *you project* as your peak, but also at what *others think* as your peak and what *you experience* life to be for you. Only when you stretch yourself to others' image and expectations about you, you express extraordinary capacities and miracle powers.

Every time you raise yourself and stretch yourself to fulfill others' *anyakāra*, you achieve completion. You achieve fulfillment. You achieve union. Liberation from your individual identity happens to you only when you raise yourself to others' *anyakāra*. When you stretch yourself to others' *anyakāra*, liberation from *ahaṁkāra* and *mamakāra* happens!

You may think, 'I am responsible for what I feel as me, and what I project as me to others. But why should I take responsibility for others' expectations about me?'

As long as you think that you are stretching just because of others' expectation, you will carry continuous irritation, agitation and heaviness. Understand this important truth—It is YOU who is sitting in the inner consciousness of those who have expectations about you, and making them expect things from you!

Listen: when you are not ready to listen to your own heart and expand, the Divine helps you by creating the same expectation in others, so that you can expand! It is some part of you which is suppressed by you, which wants to realize itself, that goes and sits in another's heart and becomes their expectation about you, so that the suppressed part is realized!

At the root of *mamakāra* is your *jīva*—your soul, in which all of us are one. If you suppress it in one body, it simply comes out in another body. When you are suppressing your expectations (*mamakāra)* about you in your own body, it simply comes out as *anyakāra* in another's body. Nobody else is forcing you. It is your own expectation about you, giving you one more chance! Now, it is no more somebody else's *anyakāra*. You are simply expanding to fulfill your own *mamakāra* and *ahaṁkāra*.

Others' expectation about you is nothing but a reminder, another chance that Bhagavān (Divine) gives you to realize yourself. When you realize that this is also your own expectation about you, you will have fulfillment!

The *Bhagavad Gītā* is the manifestation of Arjuna's suppressed longing to realize his own divine self. With authenticity, Arjuna discovers his power of thinking. He is now able to dive deeper into his suppressed thoughts and allows them to surface in Kṛṣṇa's Divine presence!

In the early chapters, Kṛṣṇa shares His *anyakāra* for Arjuna. He urges Arjuna to realize his eternal blissful *self.* He gives him an intellectual understanding of this truth. Through the chapters of *Jñana-karma-sannyāsa Yogaḥ* and *Sannyāsa Yogaḥ,* Kṛṣṇa guides Arjuna on the ways to achieve this.

Kṛṣṇa gives the ultimate winning strategy of life to Arjuna—to stand up with the courage of authenticity in all his actions—*yogaḥ karmasu kauśalam.* He urges Arjuna to devote himself to yoga to expand himself to his peak energy. Kṛṣṇa then deepens Arjuna's understanding by revealing to him the deeper truths of death, renunciation and *sannyāsa*.

Once this understanding has settled in Arjuna, Kṛṣṇa leads him to the next *tattva*, Responsibility, the power of feeling.

Responsibility—Waking Up To Your Highest Possibility

Kṛṣṇa's teachings in the next chapter, *Dhyāna Yoga*, can be summarized in these words—'Look in' and 'Take responsibility to raise yourself'.

Listen! Responsibility is the key that awakens the power of feeling. The power of feeling is unlocked when you recognize yourself as a leader and take responsibility for everything in and around you!

Here, Kṛṣṇa teaches Arjuna the techniques to go beyond the mind and senses and become liberated. He guides Arjuna to rise to the level of *Īśvaratva*, leadership consciousness and become like Himself.

That is why Kṛṣṇa says,

uddhared ātmanātmānaṁ nātmānaṁ avasāyadet |
ātmaiva hy ātmano bandhur ātmaiva ripur ātmanaḥ || 6.5

'You are your own friend; you are your own enemy. Evolve yourself through the Self and do not degrade yourself.'

By this Kṛṣṇa means—if you know the technique of how to raise yourself by yourself, you are the friend of your Self. If you let yourself down, you are the enemy of your Self!

> Listen: Responsibility means thinking, feeling, acting and cognizing life from the truth that YOU are the source of everything; therefore, you are responsible for all happenings inside you and around you.

I know the big question you will all have now! You must be thinking,

'How can I be responsible for everything happening around me? I can be held responsible for what is happening inside me. How can I be held responsible for what is happening outside me? For example, if an accident happens in my life, how can I be responsible?'

Everybody asks this question. Let me answer you.

- A person who does not feel responsible even for his own actions is an animal. He lives at a very low level of consciousness!
- A person who feels responsible for his own actions is a human being. He lives at the middle level of consciousness.
- A person who takes responsibility even for others' actions is Divine. He lives in leadership consciousness, *Iśvaratva*.

Please understand, only when you feel that you are responsible for everything happening in and around you, you will start looking into the truth and start seeing the possibility for a solution. Only when you take responsibility will you even find the solution!

Listen. When you take responsibility, the higher energies express through you. Even if you take one step towards responsibility, the Cosmos takes a thousand steps towards you, taking responsibility for you. When you are in the space of responsibility, both your inner space and your outer space support you. The whole Universe supports you, because the Universe experiences its fulfillment through the cognition of those who feel responsible.

Take responsibility in every situation. When you don't feel responsible, you are a drop in the ocean. When you feel responsible, you are the ocean in a drop! When you take responsibility, *Īśvaratva*, leadership consciousness starts happening in you.

The power of feeling is nothing but your ability to realize yourself as the source of all the happenings in your life. This understanding gives you tremendous control over your own life and gives you the power to be a positive influence in the life of others.

With responsibility, life happens to you. But life always demands your expansion, because expansion is the natural flow of life. The more you engage with life, the greater the expansion that will be demanded of you. When you take responsibility for whatever is seen and experienced by you, that which is unseen and un-experienced by you takes responsibility for you! If you take responsibility for the known part of God and the world, the unknown part of God and the world takes responsibility for you. When God takes responsibility for you, you are God. You are an Incarnation!

Kṛṣṇa guides Arjuna to realize Kṛṣṇa consciousness through the *tattva* of responsibility. Kṛṣṇa's teaching of responsibility culminates in *Viśvarūpa Darśan,* where He blesses Arjuna with a glimpse of His Cosmic dimension, His infinite expansion—a foretaste of Arjuna's own Enlightenment.

Listen.

Your expansion frightens you. Whenever bigness is demanded of you, whenever you feel you are being 'forced' to expand, you shrink even further into your comfort zone. Your tiredness, your weakness, your powerlessness all these are nothing but the resistance you have to seeing your own bigness!

That is what becomes of Arjuna after *Viśvarūpa Darśan*, the fear of expansion overtakes him. But being devoted to Kṛṣṇa, the embodiment of Cosmos, Arjuna responsibly expands and awakens his Enlightenment with the next *tattva* of enriching, the power of living. Kṛṣṇa assures him after the *darśan* that only by taking the responsibility to enrich others—by doing His work, by being undividedly devoted onto Him, can Arjuna expand himself into his highest possibility—*mad-karma-kṛn mad-paramo mad-bhaktaḥ* (11.55)!

Enriching With Enlightenment

We now come to the fourth *tattva*—enriching. Enriching means infusing all these three *tattvas* continuously, in your life and others' lives!

You may ask, 'I can understand why I should enrich myself. But why should I enrich others?'

Listen. Life happens to you with others! The purpose for which you are born is for enriching yourself and others. When you operate from this understanding, you are most alive, you are at your peak and living enlightenment.

Enriching is the key that unlocks the power of living in you!

Please understand, every relationship you experience is just one dimension of you. It is your son who makes you a father, it is your wife who makes you a husband, it is your followers who make you a leader. Each significant relationship in your life is one dimension of you. And unless you fulfill all your dimensions, how can you be fulfilled?

Again and again, the ego forgets, the *ahaṁkāra* forgets, that all its joy comes only when it stretches itself to others' *anyakāra* (expectations), not when it fights with others' *ahaṁkāra*! You very conveniently forget this important fact and take life happening to you with others for granted. You think, 'My brother has to behave like a brother! My father has to behave like a father! My teacher has to behave like a teacher,' without taking the responsibility or understanding that you should also fulfill your role! Why should the teacher enrich the student, if the student does not take the responsibility of enriching the teacher?

Kṛṣna beautifully enriches Arjuna—'If you don't do *yajña* (enriching sacrifice) and give back to the Divine for what you receive, you are a thief!—*yo bhuṅkte stena eva saḥ* (3.12).' It means that anything you receive from the Cosmos without enriching in return, is stolen!

Please understand, enriching means taking responsibility for everyone. I tell you, when you take responsibility for others, extraordinary powers start flowing through you! When you start enriching others, the whole Cosmos starts expressing through you. Whenever you enrich others, the energy that flows through you is cosmic energy. If you want to taste and experience cosmic energy, just start enriching others! The excitement you feel, the freshness you feel and the readiness, the joy and the inspiration that happens in you is all Cosmic energy, pure Cosmic energy.

Just see Bhagavān Śrī Kṛṣṇa! He is the ultimate embodiment of enriching. His very presence is enriching. Throughout the Gītā, He takes responsibility for Arjuna's inauthenticity, for Arjuna's confusion, without giving up on him. The entire Gītā itself is the manifestation of His enriching expression. *Bhagavad Gītā* is Lord Kṛṣṇa's gift to the world, enriching generations with its timeless truths. Lord Kṛṣṇa blesses Arjuna and humanity with the ultimate tools to look inward and explode in Divine Consciousness.

Again and again, Kṛṣṇa beautifully says—'To know your Self is to know God.'

What Kṛṣṇa says is true for everyone. Whether you accept it or not, any idea that you have about yourself, other than the understanding that *you are God*, is low self-esteem! What you are lacking is just the awareness of the truth. Once you realize the truth that *you are God*, there is no difference between you and Kṛṣṇa. You are enlightened.

Kṛṣṇa is so compassionate that He expresses the whole Bhagavad Gītā just to prove this. That is what Kṛṣṇa came to prove. He has no need to prove that He is God. His mission is to prove that *you are God*! His mission is to enlighten Arjuna and through Arjuna, the rest of humanity. Kṛṣṇa's expression is the ultimate enriching, because he takes responsibility even for your enlightenment! That is why He concludes the *Bhagavad Gītā* with the importance of completing with one's root patterns and joyfully surrendering to Life.

Kṛṣṇa showers Himself on Arjuna, waking him up to the experience of the Whole. He simply says, 'Drop everything and surrender onto Me. Drop everything you know as *dharma*, whatever you think you know as life, just drop it! I will liberate you from all sinful reactions. Do not worry.'

sarvadharmān parityajya mām ekaṁ śaraṇaṁ vraja |
ahaṁ tvām sarvapāpebhyo mokṣayiṣyāmi mā sucaḥ || 18.65

The Enlightened Master is nothing but concentrated Life! When you drop your conflicts, your root patterns and surrender to His wisdom, He liberates you. This is the ultimate enriching!

Tattvas, The Natural Flow Of Life

Please understand, these four *tattvas* are the very nectar pot of spirituality. They exist in our very DNA. They are the natural flow of life and they can solve any problem.

When you live these *tattvas*, you will find that

- *With Integrity, the innate intelligence to expand is straightened and the space of positivity is awakened in you.*
- *With Authenticity, life continuously oozes in you. You experience the space of possibility.*
- *With Responsibility, you awaken to your true nature. Īśvaratva—leadership consciousness blossoms in you.*
- *With Enriching, you establish your Existence into everything and ultmately experience yourself as Brahmanyam Bahuputratām—the favorite inheritor of the Cosmos!*

These four Universal principles will continuously inspire, encourage and make you experience your ultimate possibility. When you live these *tattvas*, you will constantly expand and fulfill the very purpose for which the *Bhagavad Gītā* was delivered!

Mahābhārat, The Personification Of Gīta

To fully internalize the message of the *Bhagavad Gītā*, calls for a deeper insight into its genesis. We must go back into its great origin—the Mahābharāt.

Mahābharāt is the physical, visual presentation of the Bhagavad Gītā. All the principles of life that are explained in the Gītā are portrayed in the personified form of characters in the Mahābharāt. All the principles that Śrī Kṛṣṇa teaches in the Gītā, the Mahābharāt is a movie of those life principles.

Mahābhārat is a book where the personification of each quality appears as one character. You live so many different experiences in your life. You carry so many parts—one part of you is integrity, one part of you is authenticity, another part is responsibility and some part of you is enriching. One part of you is self-doubt, some part of you is self-hatred and another self-denial. One part of you is knowledge, one part of you is compassion, one part of you is violence, one part of you is cunningness, and one part of your is penance (tapas), one part of you is the pure silence. *When all these parts are fully awakened in you, you are full bloomed, then you are Kṛṣṇa!*

The celebration of life is Śrī Kṛṣṇa. He is the purnāvatar, the most powerful and complete Incarnation, the embodiment of pure love and compassion. Śrī Kṛṣṇa is the personification beyond any personality who never gives up on people, even those who are hypocrites and *adhārmic*! He can simply enter into any multi-layered personality and joyfully play to handle them as they are.

If you understand the Mahābharāt, you will understand the complexity of personalities or the complexity of you. You will never have hatred or denial to some part of you or towards some part of others. You will understand how to handle the whole life as it is.

Pañca Pāṇḍavas or the five sons of King Pāṇḍu are the embodiment of the great powers that come from the four *tattvas* of life.

- Yudhiṣṭra is embodiment of Integrity—the power of words, *vāk śakti.*
- Bhīma is embodiment of Authenticity—the power of thoughts, *mano śakti.*
- Arjuna is embodiment of Responsibility—the power of feeling, *prema śakti.*
- Sahadeva is embodiment of Enriching—the power of living, *ātma śakti.*
- Nakula is embodiment of causing reality for others.

Kuntī is the mother of Pañca Pāṇḍavas, she is the embodiment of *tapas,* penance. *Tapaḥ* aligns with the different powers of Nature and gives birth to integrity, authenticity, responsibility and enriching. Kuntī connects with the power of nature—Sūrya (son god), Yama Dharma (god of time, justice), Vāyu (wind god), Indra (king of gods) and Aśvini Kumaras (divine physicians of gods) and gives birth to Pāṇḍavas.

Listen, Yudhiṣṭra is Integrity! Integrity is born from Kāla, Yama Dharma, the lord of time, righteousness. Who is the most integrated being in the Cosmos? Yama Dharma! As the son of time, Yudhiṣṭra never misses time and is integrated to *dharma*. That is why Yudhiṣṭra, also glorified as Dharmarajā, the king of *dharma*, is the embodiment of integrity.

Next, Bhīma is the embodiment of authenticity. He is the physiology of peak possibility! Most authentic being is Vāyu, the wind energy! Bhīma is the son of Vāyu, authenticity. His whole life is an ideal of constantly expanding with strength of authenticity without any tiredness or powerlessness.

Arjuna is the embodiment of responsibility, the space of leadership! Indra, the king of the gods is the most responsible person in the universe. So, Arjuna is the son of responsibility. Arjuna is also Nara, who embodies the responsibility of *Nārāyaṇa* Himself! The tradition says that Kṛṣṇa and Arjuna are incarnations of *Nara-Nārāyaṇa*, meaning they are the same energy that expresses as *Paramatmā* and *Jīvatmā*—super consciousness and its reflection on body. In Vaiśnava tradition, Viṣṇu expresses himself as *Nārāyaṇa* and *Nara*. In Śaiva tradition, we call them as *Paśupati*; pure soul and the soul that reflects on the body. The pure soul is *Pati* and the reflection of the soul on the body is *Paśu*. Pure soul is *Nārāyaṇa* and the soul that reflects on the body is *Nara*. So, *Nara* Arjuna is just the very own reflection of *Nārāyaṇa*.

Nakula and Sahadeva, the Aśvini Kumāras are the most enriching beings, the greatest doctors. Understand, doctor's profession is the best enriching profession. They are sons of the greatest healers who are the greatest enrichers! Even when the enemy, Duryodhana comes to Sahadeva, he blesses him saying, 'You start the war on this day, you will be successful!' That level of enriching! Enriching even the enemy! Nakula went on being a catalyst for everyone to realize the reality for others. He is such an amazing support for Yudhiṣṭra, Arjuna, Bhīma and Sahadeva, for everyone.

All these five Pāṇḍavas won the game of life only when they listened to their Guru, Śrī Kṛṣṇa. Otherwise, at uncountable times the Pāndavas were in the jaws of death and would have been killed or died! It is their association with the Guru, the *satsang*—association with Truth that saves them again and again! I tell you, whoever you may become, never miss the association of a living Guru.

Understand, Māhabhārat is actually your life. It is nothing but the story of all incompletions. Your body is the earthly kingdom that is attacked by your incompletions—the root patterns of self-doubt, self-hatred and self-denial that weigh you down, and forbid the *tattvas* to manifest as your great powers.

In the warfield of your life, stand the Kauravas—Dhritarāṣṭra, Śakuni and Duryodhana along with Bhīsma (the great grandfather) and Karṇa (the eldest of Pāṇḍavas). Dhritarāṣṭra is the self-doubt in you. Duryodhana is the self-denial in you. Śakuni is the self-hatred in you. Karṇa is the charity and compassion in you. Bhīsma is the *dharma* in you, the undying righteousness. But because of the wrong association with self-denial, both your charity and righteousness turn powerless and give up their pure inner space.

Self-doubt, Dhritarāṣṭra joins with self-destruction, Gāndhāri and gives birth to self-denial patterns—the Kauravas: Duryodhana and his brothers. Self-denial is born from self-doubt and assisted by self-hatred, Śakuni. Self-doubt is blind like Dhritarāṣṭra; self-hatred is cunning like Śakuni; self-denial is stupid like Duryodhana.

Understand, let me explain the roots of all root-patterns—*self-doubt, self-hatred and self-denial.* These are the most powerful patterns that make you powerless.

Look in!

The thought of what you really want from life is enough to put you in depression. Because, when you think about something you really want to achieve, self-doubt is the first and foremost pattern that comes up in you. The pattern of doubting—'*Will I get it? Will I be able to make it? Do I deserve it?*' The whole of Dhritarāṣṭra's life is this root-pattern of self-doubt. You can see all his actions and reactions are out of this one root-pattern.

Second, self-hatred happens because of the incompletions of earlier failures. You cunningly cheat yourself saying, '*Earlier I tried this same thing ten times, but it failed miserably! Now how is it going to be successful? I will fail again*! ' The whole of Śakuni's life and his actions are, '*I will not make it!*'—the root-pattern of self-hatred!

This self-hatred immediately makes self-denial erupt out! You just give a life-sentence to you saying, '*No! I cannot make it*!' This deep self-denial pattern erupting out is end of life! If you see the whole life of

Duryodhana, it is a deep, painful reaction of his stupid conviction that he is a failure and he cannot make it. So, constantly he has to prove himself only by destroying others, never by creating on his own reality.

When all these three root-patterns of self-doubt, self-hatred and self-denial gather together, what happens? That is what happens to the Kauravas. Don't allow what happened to the Kauravas happen to you!

Understand, your body is the kingdom which integrity, Yudhiṣṭra inherits. Integrity should be the *yuvarāja* (crown prince) ruling you. But self-denial or Duryodhana tries every possible way to destroy integrity (Yudhiṣṭra), authenticity (Bhīma), responsibility (Arjuna) and enriching (Nakula and Sahadeva). But, the power of the Guru, Śrī Kṛṣṇa again and again protects integrity, authenticity, responsibility and enriching.

When you start the war of your life, integrity (Yudhiṣṭra) never looks like he is going to win the war with self-denial patterns (Duryodhana). But, when you complete with these root-patterns, you cause what you want as reality in your life. You rewrite your future!

You will see that finally it is only Dharmarāja Yudhiṣṭra who is coronated as the king of kings and rules over extraordinary opulence and vast abundance with his brothers! I tell you, even if you have thousands of self-doubts about integrity and authenticity, stand with these Truths. Then, Guru's grace will always be with you. Kṛṣṇa's grace is always with the Pāṇḍavas because they embody the pure qualities of *tattvas.*

All Incarnations land on planet Earth just to tell you this one Truth: your self-denial, self-hatred, self-doubt patterns are not truth or fact. That's all! You are more than what you believe as you; because what you believe as you is framed by your root-patterns. No one can take away what you want from your life.

The great hope, the great news, which is the Truth is—you are not an ordinary being as you perceive yourself to be because of your root-patterns. Complete all these three root-patterns with the power of the four *tattvas* and rewrite your future as you want to create it!

This is the essence of the *Bhagavad Gītā* and the four *tattvas.*

Carry integrity, authenticity, responsibility and enriching; you will always have the Guru's grace on you. When Guru is on your side, you can win any war of life and create the ultimate reality of your life. When you carry the inner space of Pāṇḍavas in your very being and live the four *tattvas* sincerely, you will always have the grace, protection and powers of Śrī Kṛṣṇa!

When you surrender to the master of Masters, Śrī Kṛṣṇa, what you lack will be showered on you and what you have will be protected for you—*yoga-kṣema vahāmy ahaṁ* (9.22)!

CHAPTER

1

Arjunaviśāda Yogaḥ

Sāstras, Stotras, Sūtras

Life will always be a mix of the Good and the bad, the Divine and the evil. Choosing one over the other does not enrich. We need to complete and go beyond both!

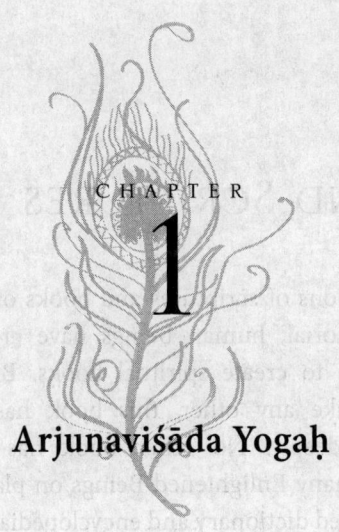

Beyond Scriptures

There are millions of scriptures and books on planet Earth. From time immemorial, human beings have created scriptures and still continue to create spiritual books. But *Bhagavad Gītā* is incomparable. Unlike any other, this book has penetrated human consciousness so deeply. No other book has contributed to the preparation of so many Enlightened Beings on planet Earth. *Bhagavad Gītā* is the unabridged dictionary and encyclopedia of spirituality.

Spiritual literature can be classified into three categories. First we have *śāstras*: *Sāstras* give us clarity about the goal of human life. They give intellectual understanding about the ultimate truth of man and God.

Śāstras are the scriptures which guide us to have the right cognitions of life. They logically and intellectually answer all major questions so that we can be logically convinced to follow the ultimate path. There are many examples. The *śṛutis* and *smṛtis* of *sanātana-hindu-dharma*, the sacred scriptures such as the *Vedas* and *Upaniṣads*, the guidelines such as the *Manusmṛti* and *Itihās*, and the great epics, historical happenings such as *Rāmāyaṇa*, *Mahābhārat*, are *śāstras*.

The second category of literature is *stotra*. It is the expression of someone who has realized the ultimate Truth; who has had the glimpse of divine love. When such a person expresses his joy, the expression is *stotras*. When we worship and surrender ourselves to the Divine, the form of expression is *stotras*, devotional compositions.

The literature from the heart is *stotras*; literature from the head is *śastras*. The third type of literature, called *sūtras*, gives us techniques to realize the state of uniting with the Divine.

Śāstras give us intellectual understanding, *stotras* give emotional feeling connection, *Sūtras* give the being level experience. *Śāstras* are like signboards, intellectual scriptures that explain the basics of life. They alone cannot lead us to enlightenment; although they can take us to an Enlightened Master. *Stotras* enrich us to surrender to the Divine. The glory of the Divine is expounded on by the *stotras*. *Sūtras* give us techniques to achieve devotion or Enlightenment.

Stotras are spoken from the level of emotion, feeling. *Sūtras* mean the technique that helps us achieve the goal of the *śāstras* and the *stotras*.

People who are intellectually oriented, need *śāstras*—intellectual scriptures. They do not do anything unless they are intellectually convinced. We cannot say that because of this attitude, they should not seek spirituality, the path of living the highest potential and expanding with peak possibility. Listen, we should look at man with more compassion. We can't put faith as the main criterion to enter into spirituality, then we are refusing spirituality to almost 90% of humanity. We should create a system through which we can reach and enrich every individual with the science of completion and creation.

Our *Vedic* seers created *śāstras*—the absolute science of living in completion while creating our peak possibility. They logically taught us the path and the goal—*why* we are asked to do *what* we do, why we need spirituality in our day-to-day living. All these major questions are proven logically in *śastras* and the conclusions are given. Understand, *śāstras* completely take away our doubts. Doubt is a devil. Once a doubt enters our mind in the form of self-doubt, self-hatred and self-denial, we can't sleep, we can't rest until we clear and complete with it. *Śāstras* help us get rid of these doubts intellectually, scientifically!

Unless we have complete intellectual clarity, complete cognition, our belief will be a pseudo belief; anyone can shake our faith as it will be rooted in self-doubt. Our cognition is not complete cognition till the *śāstras* of integrity, authenticity, responsibility and enriching become the basis of our cognition. Till then our cognitions are nothing but confusions, self-doubts. Our faith does not have a strong base, it is like a building without a foundation. It will collapse. The same will happen to us if we don't have the base of *śāstras*.

A person asked the great Master Vivekananda, 'Master, what is the importance of *Vedas* and why should we study the scriptures?' Vivekananda said, 'If you study the scriptures, all your faith and sincerity will become so strong that nobody will be able to shake you.' Otherwise, any fool can tell us that what we are doing is superstitious and we can start thinking, 'Am I really doing superstitious things? Am I really following the right path?' We will start having doubts about ourselves.

We may think we believe in something; but our faith or belief is not deep enough, not authentic enough. We are not integrated to our words, and we are not authentic to our thinking and actions. Unless we have the deep foundation of *śāstras*, not only we will not be able to believe in anything, we will be doubting and hating our very own self! We will not be authentic and integrated to the truth.

Understand, even our emotions are not so deep. We think we have love, we think we believe. I see all kinds of people who say they believe in what they think. One man said, 'Oh Master, I love the whole world.' We can always say *Vasudaiva Kuṭuṃbakaṁ*—the world is my family. Again and again, I tell people that to love the world is easy, but to love your wife is very difficult! The problem is that we are not in tune with our own family. This is because we don't have the right cognition of completion, without which our faith can be shaken by anybody. *Śāstras*, the science of Living Enlightenment, gives a powerful base of the *'great why of life'* so that all our cognitions, all our faith can enter into our being and start creating our possibilities.

DEVOTION IS AUTHENTICITY WITH GOD

Bhakti, devotion, is just an alchemy process. It is as if a touchstone has touched us. Rāmakṛṣṇa says beautifully, 'If a touchstone touches any metal it becomes gold; just a touch of the stone is enough for any metal to be converted into gold.'

Devotion is a touchstone. The moment devotion touches us, we become God, we become Divine. The problem is, we never allow devotion to touch us; we never allow devotion to penetrate our being. We think we want God, but we are continuously afraid of the Divine. We may think we want the Divine, but as long as it is superficial, as long as it is under our control, things go well. The moment the devotion enters our being, and starts the process, we say, 'No, no, not that much. I think that is too much for me!' We stop at a certain point.

A small story:

> A guy lived as an atheist. One day he fell from a cliff and was hanging on to a small branch. Slowly, the branch also started giving way.
>
> The man started shouting, 'Oh God! I never believed in you, but now I do. Please save me!'
>
> A booming voice from heaven said, 'Oh my son, don't worry. I will save you. Just let go of the branch and I will save you.'
>
> Immediately the man responded, 'Is there anybody else out there who can save me?'

Our faith is just an inauthentic show. Until we have an intellectual conviction about life, God is just one more choice; just one more shop like Walmart; it is Spiritual mart. This is our relationship with God. We remember God only when we need something. When things go well according to our chosen route, then God is great, else throw away the God.

Our faith is pseudo if it is not life transforming. We do not allow devotion to work on us. *Śāstras* give us that intellectual clarity, that completion cognition. All the great devotional people like Caitanya, Rāmānuja and Mādhva had a strong intellectual base of this science. Caitanya Mahāprabhu was a great *Nyayaika* philosopher of logic. It is only when you reach the peak of logic, can you fall into the valley of love; only then you are qualified to fall in love. All great Masters and devotees who reach the peak of intellect have a strong *śāstras* base.

Next are the *stotras. Stotra* means expressing our experience, our

deep love or devotion to our Master or God. Many people ask, 'Swamiji, why does Hinduism have idol worship?' Listen. Hinduism does not have idol worship. We don't worship the idol; we worship through the idol. When we stand in front of the idol, do we say, 'Oh stone! Give me a boon. Oh stone! Please save me?' No! We say, 'Oh God, please save me.' We don't worship the idol; we worship through the idol. So we are not doing idol worship. In *Vaiśnavism*, the devotional stream of Hinduism, there is a beautiful word *Arcāvatār*. This means the idol worshipped in the temple is the Incarnation of God, it is not just a stone.

Incarnation means the Divine descending on planet Earth, just like the ten Incarnations of Viṣṇu. All these idols are like these ten Incarnations. Just like these Incarnations, the stone, the idol that we worship to relate with God is called *Arcāvatār*.

When we stand in front of the idol and pour our heart out through verses, this enriching expression is what is *stotras*. All the songs written by great devotees like the Alvars, Nayanmars, Mīrā and Caitanya, are *stotras*. People ask me, '*Swamiji,* sometimes I don't feel like chanting these *stotras*. Should I do it mechanically even if I don't like doing it?' I say, 'Do it with integrity and authenticity. You may feel it is a mechanical exercise for one or two days. But, it will become your being once you start enjoying the meaning and experiencing what you express. It will become your feeling that enriches you deeply.' The reason I allow these *stotras* to be chanted is this—I can see thousands of people, when they have feeling connection with the Divine, they flower and become enlightened. So, when you express your heart, it becomes *stotra*.

Understand, in *Vedic* tradition, even God is a stepping-stone for Enlightenment. All the forms and names of the Gods, everything is used for attaining Enlightenment, for *nirvikalpa samādhi,* for *living advaita.* When the devotion, the feeling connection is awakened in you, you automatically go towards enlightenment.

Next are the *sūtras*. *Sūtras* give us the technique to reach enlightenment. *Sāstras* are from the intellectual level. *Stotras* are from the emotional level. *Sūtras* are from the being level.

Please understand, learning *śāstras* means bringing integrity and authenticity to our mind. Going around and practicing *śāstras* is living authenticity and being responsible. Being in integrity with the Master or God is feeling connection and being enriched with Enlightenment.

When integrity comes through the *head*, it is intellect, *śāstra*. When it comes through your *heart*, it is *stotra*. When it comes through your *being*, it is *sūtra*.

When authenticity expresses through our *head*, it is power of *śāstra*, the knowledge weapons to fight our patterns, our dilemmas. When authenticity expresses through our *heart*, it is love, *stotra*. When authenticity expresses through our *being*, it is meditation, *sūtra*.

Listen. There are three kinds of human beings: head oriented, heart oriented and being oriented. To fulfill everyone, our enlightened sages have created three kinds of literature—*śāstras*, *stotras* and *sūtras*. *Bhagavad Gītā* is the only book that is a combination of *śāstras*, *stotras* and *sūtras*, with something more!

Gītā* is *śāstra; it gives a clear intellectual understanding about life, death, soul, about the '*great why of life*' as well as the '*what of life*,' the do's and don'ts, rules and regulations. Very few books give reasons *why* we should or should not do something. *Gītā* is the only book I know that gives a strong intellectual base, intellectual clarity, a complete cognition about *why* and *what* we should do.

No other religion has as many scriptures as Hinduism. Within the Vedic literature, our Masters have chosen three books called *prasthāntraya* that are the ultimate authorities in spirituality. They are *Brahma Sūtra*, *Upaniṣads* and *Bhagavad Gītā*. Veda Vyāsa, the lord of Enlightened Masters, is the compiler of all the *Vedas*, who wrote the *Brahma Sutra* and also authored the *Mahābhārat*. He is responsible for all the methods and expressions of enlightenment science or *jīvan muktī vijñāna*. Many enlightened Masters taught what is known as *Upaniṣad*. However, *Gītā* is directly from *Bhagavān*, God Himself, from a *Pūrṇāvatār*—a perfect, complete Incarnation, Śrī Kṛṣṇa.

KṚṢṆA, THE PŪRṆĀVATĀR

Among the Incarnations, Bhagavān Śrī Kṛṣṇa is considered *pūrṇa*, complete, a full Incarnation. Why is Śrī Kṛṣṇa considered the only perfect, complete Incarnation, a pūrṇāvatār? Why can't He be just one more Incarnation? Still He is the one being ruling the whole Hindu consciousness and the largest worshipped being! The most worshipped Incarnation on planet Earth is Śrī Kṛṣṇa. Only Kṛṣṇa can be called the most worshipped being.

First, let us understand why Incarnations come to planet Earth. Śrī Rāmakṛṣṇa Paramahamsa recounts beautifully:

There was a beautiful paradise with many trees and varieties of flowers and fruits. Three friends were walking near this paradise that had a big wall around it. One of them climbed the wall and peeped inside.

> He cried out, 'Oh, my God! Such a beautiful place!' He jumped into the garden and started enjoying the fruits. The second man climbed the wall and saw the garden. He too felt it was beautiful, but he had a little bit of courtesy.
>
> He turned and said to the third man who was below, 'Dear friend, there is a beautiful paradise below. Come, I am going in.' Saying this, he jumped over the wall and started enjoying the fruits.
>
> The third man climbed the wall and saw the paradise. He saw his two friends and understood the level of joy and bliss that they were enjoying.
>
> Then he said to himself, 'Let me go down and tell all the people about this beautiful paradise. I will bring them all to enjoy this garden.'

An Incarnation is someone who descends to enrich the world about the blissful place that He experienced. The man who descends from Divine to express the bliss of that Divinity is an Incarnation. The person who returns to planet Earth to tell you and enrich you about Divinity and to also make you realize what He has experienced, is an Incarnation.

An enlightened spiritual Master is a person who creates a formula to reproduce his inner world experiences. Scientists create formulae for the outer world, whereas a Master creates a formula to recreate the experience of the inner world. Meditation techniques are these formulae.

An Incarnation is a person who can directly give the experience *without* even using the formula! All these great Incarnations come down to planet Earth to make people realize that—they too are Divine, that they too are God; to tell and enrich people that the other side is beautiful. 'There's a very big paradise. Come, let us go and enjoy. Come, join me,' they say.

Why is Kṛṣṇa a perfect Incarnation? He has all the qualities needed to push human beings to divinity, to the space of completion. It is Śrī Kṛṣṇa who is responsible for all the good things we have in our lives. Please understand, it is Kṛṣṇa who is responsible for anything good, anything joyful, and anything auspicious in our lives. The science of living life out of completion and joy—living life out of completion will lead to enlightenment in whatever we are doing without renouncing—this science is introduced to the world for the first time by Śrī Kṛṣṇa.

Understand, till Śrī Kṛṣṇa all Incarnations were teaching only the science of leaving, renouncing the world if one wanted Enlightenment. But it is Śrī Kṛṣṇa who gave this science of living in the space of completion, *pūrṇatva*; that you don't need to renounce anything; wherever you are, you will be radiating life and enjoying life.

The person who can push human beings to divinity, to the space of completion is called *Jagadguru*—the Guru who awakens. He is the teacher, the Master of the whole Universe.

Jagadguru is a person who can enrich the whole world, all types of human beings at all levels. The Universe is a place with all types of human beings who are at all levels of experience and maturity. Kṛṣṇa can enrich and help people from all levels to experience divinity, to reach the ultimate, to realize the truth, to be complete.

The life of Śrī Kṛṣṇa, *pūrṇāvatār* is an example of living in the space of completion, *pūrṇatva*. He has not done anything out of incompletion. He has done everything out of completion and He has done everything, which we think will be done only out of incompletion!

This science of completion is the most sacred secret revealed by Śrī Kṛṣṇa in the *Bhagavad Gītā*, which is the most powerful *rājavidyā rājaguhyaṃ*, royal sacred knowledge and royal sacred secret. This royal sacred science of completion keeps us eternally in love with life, eternally experiencing life.

Please understand, some religions teach what completion *is*; some religions show us what completion *is not,* some religions show us the effect of incompletion. **This science of completion is the essence of all religions, the essence of vedic knowledge, the source of the knowledge of Vedic tradition.**

Let me define Completion.

Completion means living and acting without any hangover of the past incidents, words, actions or memories. Not having a hangover does not mean that you will not remember your past at all. When you are in completion, you will remember past incidents and actions, but they will no longer have the power to cause pain or anger or guilt in you anymore.

Completion! Please listen; I am giving you another definition of Completion.

Completion is nothing but reclaiming the bits and pieces you threw away in unconsciousness. Listen. The parts of you, bits of you, pieces of you that you shared or threw them with so many things and people in your life unconsciously; reclaiming all those parts back and becoming complete with you, is Completion.

Listen. There are intellectual, emotional being-level people. Incarnations, such as Śaṇkara, Buddha strongly appeal to intellectual people. It is difficult for emotional people to relate to them. We can't imagine Buddha singing and dancing with a flute or Śaṇkara doing *rās-līlā!* Emotional people relate to Mīrā, Caitanya Mahāprabhu, Āndāl who are always singing, dancing and celebrating.

People who are at the being level straightaway want the experience; they cannot relate to the intellectual or emotional Incarnations. They are neither ready to analyze nor ready to believe. A person ready to analyze goes to *śāstras*. A person ready to believe is drawn to *stotras*, but a person who wants straight experience, instant coffee, instant experience, can neither wait for *śāstras* nor *stotras*. He straightaway wants the technology, the applied science. For him, Śiva, Mahādeva who created the *vijñana-bhairava-tantra*, is the answer. All the great meditation techniques He deliveres are for being-oriented people. *Śāstras* are like the main theory, the basic science. *Sūtras* are applied science. They give straight answers.

Of course, when I say we go through the *stotras*, we need to 'intranalyze' them, which is analyzing the truth for the sake of internalizing it, not for the sake of rejecting it. Please be very clear, when we go through the *purāṇas*—the epic historical happenings, we need to understand the spirit and truth of the *purāṇas*. There is a big difference between fact and truth. *Purāṇas*, our epics are truths and facts also. All *Purāṇas* of *sanātana-dharma* are history, not mythological stories. *Purāṇas* have been wrongly translated as mythological stories or high stories. They are not high stories, they are histories—they are HIS stories. They are the true history of *Bhārata*. They are showing us, leading us to the truth. Only truth can lead us to the Truth. So while understanding *stotras* we should understand and intranalyze the spirit and truth of the *stotras*.

Listen! Śrī Kṛṣṇa can relate to people at all three levels. The way that He is born, the way He expresses all powers and completion from His birth, and the way He expresses such beautiful, sweet romance! If you are intellectual, He gives you the *Gītā*, He is *Gītā Kṛṣṇa*. If you are emotional, have *Rādhā Kṛṣṇa*, the beloved of Rādhā! He can sing and dance; He can play; He can give you the ultimate emotional fulfillment. Understand, making each one feel that he belongs to them, is the basic need for the romance to happen. Kṛṣṇa was able to do that! And He has the ability to handle all the anger and jealousy of people who were not able to raise themselves to His level. At the being level, you straightaway want the technology of enlightenment. Again, He offers the truth, *Dhyāna Yoga,* the path of meditation, in the *Gītā*.

When you see the way He radiates knowledge, love, romance, intelligence and strategy planning; *only* He can be called as *pūrṇāvatār*. The word *pūrṇāvatār* can be given only for Śrī Kṛṣṇa. Śrī Kṛṣṇa is the unimaginable expression of ultimate Consciousness.

Kṛṣṇa is complete fulfillment. He is such an embodiment of completion. The very life of Kṛṣṇa is a technique that leads you to enlightenment. The body language of an enlightened person is a *sūtra*, a technique. Kṛṣṇa is the being whose body language straightaway leads you to enlightenment. Understand that Śrī Rāma will lead you to *dharma*, righteousness. If you follow what Śrī Rāma did, you will have *dharma*, but with Kṛṣṇa, you will straightaway have *mokṣa*, liberation!

The power of Kṛṣṇa's presence and the amount of opposition that He has to go through due to His pure love, His pure energy, His pure intelligence. Even after creating His own kingdom at Dvārikapuri, the sacrifice that He does to establish *dharma*, the way He lives *dharma* and protects *dharma*! And He is such a powerful strategy planner that when needed He even escapes from the war field as *Raṇachoḍa*. The space of completion that Kṛṣṇa holds and the space from which He operates! **Please understand that when you operate from the space of completion, whatever you do is *Līlā*—a divine play. It is not boring life!**

Kṛṣṇa is the first Incarnation who demonstrates the concept of *Līlā* on planet Earth; the first Incarnation who demonstrates that life can be lived from the space of completion; life can be lived from the space of joy. Kṛṣṇa is the embodiment of joy, embodiment of bliss, embodiment of life!

When we experience the being of Kṛṣṇa, when we understand Kṛṣṇa, His very being is a technique; His very life is a technique! That is why there is a beautiful word in the *Bhāgavatam* (Hindu epic glorifying devotion) called *Līlā Dhyāna*. Just remembering the *Līlā*, the playful pranks of Kṛṣṇa, is *dhyāna*, meditation. No other Incarnation is given the word, *Līlā Dhyāna*. No other Incarnation is praised like this. Just remembering His acts is meditation! Just remembering His *Līlā*, divine acts, we are led to completion and liberation!

An Incarnation's *Līlā* or pastimes always leads you to completion. Your past always leads you to incompletion. If you constantly remember what you did when you were a child, you will be in more and more incompletion. If you constantly remember what Śrī Kṛṣṇa did when He was a child, you will be more and more in the space of completion. Remembering the Incarnation's pastimes, *Līlā Dhyāna* creates more and more completion and the higher space.

'You Cannot Forget Me', says Kṛṣṇa

The great sages were once disturbed by the singing and dancing of the gopikas, cowherdesses who are Kṛṣṇa's playmates. They thought, 'We sages are sitting with closed eyes trying to meditate with long faces for a long time and nothing is happening. These gopikās are so happy singing and dancing! What is really happening in that place?' So they went to Kṛṣṇa's birthplace, Vrindāvan to see what was happening.

They came down to see the gopikās, but the gopikās did not receive them well, nor did they care to listen to what the sages had to say. They were happy, completely fulfilled, in total completion in their remembrance of Kṛṣṇa.

The sages asked, 'What is this? We are great sages. We have come all the way to see you and you are not even receiving us properly.'

One gopikā asked, 'Sages? Who are they?'

'We meditate on His feet in our heart,' explained one of the sages.

The gopikās said, 'Meditate on His feet? We are playing

with His entire form! Come, we will show you. You say you are trying to remember Him. We are trying to forget Him! He is so much in our being. We are unable to do our work. He has completely filled up our inner space!'

Many people ask, '*Swamiji*, should we remember you? Should we take you as our Master?' I tell them, 'Never make that mistake. If I am your Master, you will not be able to forget me! That is the real scale to know if I am your Master or not.'

If you must remember me with effort, then I am not your Master. Forget me. Carry on doing your work. Carry on with your life. If you must remember something consciously, with effort, it is ugly. Only when you can't forget, only then, devotion happens in you. These gopikās say, 'We are unable to forget Him.'

Let me define *bhaktas*, devotees.

***Bhaktas* are the ones who experience completion out of the emotion which happens due to the higher consciousness *līlā* or pastimes.** I tell you, they are the only people who understand the amount of completion that bhakti (devotion) can bring in our system. It is altogether a different channel!

Kṛṣṇa also appeals to the being level people who are continually aspiring, seeking an experience straightaway. Just by His will, Kṛṣṇa can give the experience of enlightenment, etenal bliss to Arjuna. He can give the Divine experience of Advata, infinity to Arjuna, by just showing him His Cosmic form, *Viśvarūpa darśan*. Kṛṣṇa shows that He is in everybody, that everybody is in Him. Whether we are intellectually oriented, emotionally oriented or being level oriented, we can find our completion in Kṛṣṇa.

When intellect ripens, it becomes intelligence; when emotion ripens, it becomes devotion; when our being ripens, we become enlightened, complete. All these three enlightenment spaces of completion—being, devotion and intelligence—express at their peak in Kṛṣṇa. Hence, Kṛṣṇa can fulfill and complete every being. That is why He is called *Jagadguru*, Master of the whole Universe.

Just through His logic, He has not convinced us about His greatness. The way Kṛṣṇa handles every moment of His life, the way He lives every moment of His life, the way He holds Himself, the way He expresses Himself, He has stolen our hearts. Kṛṣṇa is the Lord of our hearts!

> One man in India said to me, 'I am a *jagat guru*.' I was surprised! I wondered, 'What is this? It is like having a small hotel on the roadside and naming it the Sheraton!'
>
> I asked him, '*Jagat guru*? What do you mean by that word? Do you know the qualifications of a *Jagad guru*?'
>
> He said, 'I have one disciple and his name is Jagat. I am his guru!'

So understand: *Jagat Guru* does not mean just the Guru of one person named Jagat. *Jagat Guru* leads the whole Universe into the Divine Consciousness.

Kṛṣṇa is the *Jagadguru*. Kṛṣṇa appeals to every being. He has created keys to open all the locks. He has created methods to give the spiritual experience to the whole of humanity, to people who have come, people who are here, and those yet to come. He has created the technology even for the future generations. He is *nitya-ānanda*, eternal bliss. *Gītā* is the ultimate scripture—*śāstra*, *stotra* and *sūtra*.

Kṛṣṇa is beyond scriptures. We can't speak about any dimension of Kṛṣṇa. He is the Whole! I can say that whenever we try to describe any of His dimensions, the words look so futile. His is endowed with *ananta-kalyān-guṇa*, His innumerable spiritual energies and infinite auspicious qualities.

When Kṛṣṇa says,

nainaṃ chindanti śastrāṇi nainaṃ dahati pāvakaḥ |
na cainaṃ kledayanty āpo na śoṣayati mārutaḥ || 2.23

'Weapons do not cleave, nor fire burns the Ātman.
Water does not wet It and wind does not dry It'

When He talks about the basic truths of life and spirituality, it is *śāstra*. He is giving intellectual knowledge of completion.

When Arjuna says,

namaḥ purustād atha pṛsthatas te
namo'stu te sarvata eva sarva |
ananta-vīryāmita-vikramas tvaṃ
sarvaṃ samāpṇoti tato 'si sarvaḥ || 11.40

'Oh Lord, I bow down to you from the front, from behind, from all sides; You are infinitely mighty, pervading everything, you are the Ultimate'

Arjuna is expressing the *stotra*; he is praising the Lord with his devotion.

Krṣṇa says,

yaṁ yaṁ vāpi smaran bhāvaṁ tyajaty ante kalevaram |
taṁ taṁ evaiti kaunteya sadā tad-bhāva-bhāvitaḥ || 8.6

'Whatever your state of thought is when you leave this body, absorbed in that thought, that alone you attain, without fail, O Arjuna!'

Here Krṣṇa provides Arjuna the technique, the most powerful *sūtra* that helps anyone attain and create his reality as what he wants to.

Bhagavad Gītā is the only complete scripture that combines the wisdom of *śāstras*, the depth of feeling connection of *stotras* and the practical reality of *sūtras*. It is a means to enlightenment for all, delivered by the Master of masters, by the Incarnation of incarnations, *Bhagavān* Śrī Krṣṇa.

ARJUNA'S DILEMMA AND FOUR IDENTITIES

In this first chapter of *Gītā*, *Arjunaviśāda Yogaḥ*, we see Arjuna, the most courageous fighter amongst the Pāṇḍava princes, the darling of all his teachers, and the close friend of Krṣṇa, in deep dilemma, deep incompletion.

Arjuna is both the *yogi* and the *kṣatriya*. As a *yogi*, he is deeply spiritual, centered and complete within himself, and deeply aware and integrated to his moral and ethical obligations. As the *kṣatriya*, Arjuna is the warrior leader, empowered with responsibility, ready to avenge, ready to impose order and control for protecting and upholding *dharma*; he is the typical *kṣatriya* prince.

Only with enlightenment, is it possible to continuously, consistently proceed with both these personalities of inner completion as a *yogi* and outer responsibility to enrich as a warrior leader without faltering. Arjuna falters as he faces his enemies on the battlefield of the great Mahābhārat War. His dilemma unfolds!

Arjuna's dilemma is such that he is now able to be neither a *yogi* nor a *kṣatriya*. Known as *parantapa*, the destroyer of enemies, as *vijaya*, the undefeatable warrior and as *dhanañjaya*, the unconquerable archer, the winner of wealth, *Nara* Arjuna, the best among men, loses his detachment as a *yogi*. In turn, he loses his courage as a *kṣatriya*, a warrior hero. He loses his space of completion and falls into such deep grief that bewilders his mind, *bhramatīva ca me manaḥ* (1.30) and burns his sense coverings, *tvak caiva paridahyate* (1.29).

He sees his enemies and identifies himself with them. In front of him are his mentors, family and friends, his *svajanam*. They are his extension, his lineage and his inner identity. He can no longer pretend with his outer identity that he is the ultimate warrior, the *kṣatriya*, who can dispassionately dispatch them to death.

Arjuna's dilemma is the dilemma of humanity. It represents the collective root patterns of humanity. It is an internal conflict between *what we feel as us*, what we feel we can actually do, our inner identity—*mamakāra*; *what we project* as us to others, what we feel we want to actually do, our outer identity—*ahaṁkara*; *what others think and perceive* as us—*anyakāra*; and *what we think about life and others* or what we perceive as our value systems and beliefs, our *svānyakāra*.

Please listen. You don't have just one identity, as you imagine. You have four identities. At all times you carry four identities or dimensions together.

Your own expectation about you is *mamakāra* or Inner Image. It is the inner idea and the experience you carry about yourself like—*I am healthy, I am ugly, I am intelligent, I cannot tolerate hard work, I love people etc.* But, the idea you carry about you is always less than what you project yourself to be for others!

The second identity is how you show or project yourself to others called *ahaṁkāra* or Outer Image. Unfortunately, what you project is always far more than what you believe yourself to be.

The third identity you carry is the image that others have about you, how others expect you to be, called *anyakāra* or Others' Image. How others perceive you may be different from how you project yourself to them, because people create their opinion about you from the subtle signals you give them, rather than what you openly project. Humans are intelligent enough to catch even what you don't say or especially what you don't say!

And the fourth identity is very subtle, because it is not directly related to you. It is how you experience life to be for you and what you expect others to be, called *svānyakāra* or Life Image. For example, you may feel—*life is lonely, life is complicated or life is sacred or life is scary, or life and people are always showering me with everything*! Please understand, this is also your identity, because it defines the exact experience you will be receiving from the people and situations from life!

Please listen!

Living in your peak capacity in all the four identities, aligning your life to all the four dimensions, and expressing your peak potential in all these four, is Authenticity, *Śraddha!*

It is the confusion, the non-alignment between all these identities that is responsible for all our dilemmas, our inauthenticies, our sufferings, everything. What is the only obstruction for this alignment? Our root thought patterns!

Understand, I am defining root thought pattern.

The first attack of any strong emotion happening in us and imbalancing our whole cognition, giving birth to our mind—the pattern we develop from that moment, is root thought pattern. The root thought pattern is the source of our every response to life.

Arjuna understood his *kṣatriya* code of conduct and responsibility very well. This code demanded that he cannot turn down a righteous challenge to fight. This *kṣatriya* code was not only his *ahaṁkāra* or outer image—how he showed himself to others, but also the *anyakāra* or others' image also—how his clan expected him to be. However, his own feeling about him, his *mamakāra* was based on his deep-rooted attachment to his clan and lineage that proved stronger than his *ahaṁkāra*, what he perceived and projected to be his responsibilities. These doubtful feelings were far stronger than code of his conduct, and overpowered even his outer image, which he projected as the most powerful and responsible warrior on the face of Earth!

In effect, Arjuna's life image or *svanyakāra* became seeing life as a cause of just the opposite of auspiciousness; clearly saying how he perceives his life, he cries out, '*nimittāni ca paśyāmi viparītāni keśava* (1.30)—I see only causes of misfortune, O Keśava!'

With all these non-aligned four identities, Arjuna is unable to stand any longer on the warfield. His powerless inner image, a deep self-doubt about himself that arise from his root patterns, make him derive power from his people, *svajanam* and identify himself only through them.

Arjuna's root thought patterns were primal. His self-doubts were self destroying. They related to survival issues, identity issues that totally imbalanced his whole cognition and made him powerless. By his killing clan members, he was in effect destroying a part of himself. No code of conduct was worth that destruction. Arjuna's incomplete part of *mamakāra*, his inner identity which was his own idea about himself overpowered all his other identities. That was his dilemma, the root of his incompletions and his self-doubt, the root of his root patterns.

Each of us is caught in such a dilemma and powerlessness at one time or the other. We are taught to follow certain societal rules and regulations on which our identity is built upon. As long as our basic desires, born out of our inner identity, *mamakāra*, are in tune with our outer identity, *ahaṁkāra* that we project, we have no problems, no confusion, and no dilemma. We are authentic! We are complete! However, our dilemmas start when, what we seek and the path we need to follow to achieve them, violate these rules and regulations. And what we truly seek to realize is rooted in our *mamakāra* which we have not been ready to listen to, which we are constantly suppressing.

Everyone, without exception, has incompletions, the patterns of innate fear, guilt for violating the rules and regulations of religion, philosophy and society. That guilt is sin. And we fear that unknown and unseen forces will rise against us to punish us for these violations. Desire versus guilt is our dilemma, always.

In almost all cases, if the root patterns of desire are strong enough, desire wins. Rules and regulations can wait, we say. Worst come worse, we can always work out some means of appeasing these godly forces. We think, after all, what are temples and priests for? Such is the genesis of religious guidelines and societal regulations. Some religions are based only on such guidelines, without any intelligent reasoning to support the regulations. It is almost as though they are established so that we break them and feel guilty. Once we feel guilty, we are caught.

No! I tell you, the first quality one should see before taking up any religion or lifestyle is—in that philosophy ask, '*What is the introduction given to you about you?*' Whether to practice a religion or a philosophy or not, the scale should be the first line, 'What is the introduction you are given about you,' how that philosophy cognizes you!

Gītā Introduces You to Yourself as Whole

Understand, there are four kinds of religions or philosophies—philosophy that encages you; philosophy that enslaves you; philosophy that engages you; and philosophy that enriches you. The philosophy that encages you makes you animal. You are neither useful to others nor useful to you. All philosophies that make you fanatic, that encage you, are terrorist philosophies. When you are encaged, you become fanatic.

Next, come the enslaving philosophies where the introduction about you is completely enslaving. They do not make you a terrorist, but you become a slave. Ideologically, you do not have freedom, independence. You are no more fresh. Then come the philosophies that engage you. They tend to convince you with dialogue. The more and more you get engaged, the more and more you get attracted.

Then come the philosophies that enrich you. For that, I will give the example of the traditions of *Aghoris*, the tradition of *Advaitis*, the tradition of *Yogis* and *Siddhas*. *Yoga, Siddha, Aghori*, and of course *Vedānta, Sāṅkhya Yoga*—all these philosophies are very powerful, enriching philosophies. Because *Vedānta* introduces yourself to your Self as '*amṛtasya pūtrāḥ*—children of immortality' with a beautiful declaration of completion:

Oṁ pūrṇamadaḥ pūrṇamidaṁ pūrṇāt pūrṇamudacyate /
pūrṇasya pūrṇamādāya pūrṇameva avaśiṣyate //

It means, '*Out of the Whole, came out the Whole.*
Even if the Whole is removed from the Whole,
the Whole remains as Whole.'

Please understand, humas because of the societal upbringing with rules and regulations, with do's and don'ts suffer a gap between the inner image, *mamakāra* and outer image, *ahaṁkāra*. **The gap between the inner image and outer image creates a deep self-doubt. This self-doubt is Arjuna's dilemma!** So, understand, whenever the gap between the inner image and outer image is established in us, we suffer with self-doubt. This self-doubt leads to self-hatred and then to self-denial!

Some philosophies teach us that we are the sinners, which is self-denial. Some philosophies teach that we are the slaves; that we are supposed to be the followers. This is nothing but self-hatred. These philosophers exploit our root thought pattern of self-doubt by introducing our Self to our self as sinners. In the spiritual sense, there is no such thing as sin; nothing that is totally good or bad. When you become truly complete, you realize that there are no sins.

Vedānta is the only honest, integrated, authentic, responsible, and enriching philosophy which does not exploit our self-doubting pattern and which reminds us—*even when we feel that we are removed from the Whole, we remain as Whole.* Even when we have self-doubt, understand we are the Self! Even when you have self-doubt, you are Self. Self-doubt is only *self* doubt.

This should be the scale, the introduction we should be given about us to ourselves. What kind of an introduction a philosophy gives to us about us, only based on that we can classify that philosophy; whether it is encaging or enslaving or engaging, or enriching philosophy. The whole *Vedānta* system is all about enriching.

The whole *Bhagavad Gītā Śastra* is all about enriching. It is the greatest enriching philosophy that introduces *you* to yourself as the Self!

Please listen. Whatever happens to us happens as a result of natural laws or *dharma*. ***Dharma* means the natural law of the Cosmos.** Morality, ethics, orders, and rules and regulations vary from time to time. They change by geography, from country to country, and from society to society. But the science of completion, living *adviata* (non-duality), living with the four spiritual principles of life, the *dharma* of integrity, authenticity, responsibility and enriching self and others—is an absolute principle.

Patañjali (the founding father of yoga) declares this *dharma* as, '*sārvabhaumya vratah*,' it is universal! Completion makes us realize the space of *advaita*, that we are deeply connected and in oneness with the Whole and only then true compassion flowers. The realized ones flow with this realization of *advaita*, constantly giving life to this *dharma*. When one has compassion for humanity, for every living being, the same compassion that one feels for oneself, one can do no harm to another. There can be no sin. And therefore, there is no guilt either.

Arjuna's progress on this path of *dharma*, unto his self-discovery to re-establish himself in the space of Completion is the path of Bhagavad Gītā. That can also be our path of *dharma*, if we internalize the message of the *Gītā*. When there is no conflict between—what we feel as us, what we wish to be for us and for others; what we project ourselves to be, and what others feel about us and wish from us, then we have no dilemma, no incompletion! When we are complete with our root thought patterns and we act in total completion, we have no dilemma. We are established in the space of completion, living Advaita.

Please understand, all of us are born with pre-existing desires. This is called *prārabdha karma*, those desires that we choose to complete when we take birth. They carry their own energy for completion in that lifetime.

The trouble is that the time between death and the next birth is quick and painful. The body-mind system lapses into unconsciousness, a coma, as the energy leaves matter (the body). As the energy enters another piece of matter, another body-mind, the memory of *prārabdha karma* is erased. Therefore, when we are reborn in another body, we no longer remember why we were born or with what desires and purpose we have chosen this birth. This non-remembrance of our 'great why,' our true desires and purpose creates the self-doubt in us. This is the root cause of our dilemma. This is the root of our root pattern!

Incarnations and enlightened beings choose a conscious birth out of their energy of completion with full awareness of their reason for birth. They know what they are here for. They have no confusion, no dilemma, no patterns. Arjuna is not at that stage, nor are most of us.

Fortunately, it is possible to become aware of our *prārabdha karma*, our opening balance of desires. We can then work towards their completion during each life without accumulating more karma in this lifetime. *Āgāmya karma* is the 'current account' of desires that we accumulate this lifetime. By exhausting the *prārabdha*, the incompletions that we brought with us to complete and by not accumulating more *āgāmya*, we reduce the overall 'account' of total karmas that we collect over millions of births.

This total account is called *sañcita karma.*

These *karmas* or unfulfilled desires are also referred to as *saṁskāras* or *mūla vāsanas*, the root thought patterns stored in our unconscious space, stirring up these desires. They are also called *vāsanas* or conflicting patterns, which in turn create the desires and store them as incomplete memories. These three words can be used interchangeably for all practical purposes, although they do have separate deeper meanings. By understanding the nature and types of *saṁskāras* or *mūla vāsana, vāsana* and *karma*—root patterns, conflicting patterns and incompletions that we carry over into this birth, we can work towards their completion. Then, our stock of root patterns diminishes.

In the Inner Awakening program, these *karmas* are directly addressed. The participants learn and get initiated into the science of completion, *pūrṇatva* to live with the four sacred life principles, *catur tattvas—integrity, authenticity, responsibility, and enriching*. They experientially learn to complete with their *saṁskāras*, root thought patterns; what motivates their behavior, '*why they do what they do*,' how to complete these *karmas*. We begin to understand our opening balance of desires in this life, the *karmas* we accumulate during this lifetime and how to complete and release them while alive and how to create our own reality by living Enlightenment, *jīvan mukti*.

This science of completion and creation is also the process of yoga, the *Yogaśāstra* that Kṛṣṇa takes Arjuna through in these eighteen chapters of *Bhagavad Gītā*. These teachings are not meant for Arjuna alone. They are meant for us, so that we complete with our dilemmas and self-doubts, drop everything and surrender to Existence, and experience the ultimate truth of Enlightenment, liberation, *mokṣa*.

The *Gitopaniṣad*, the science of Kṛṣṇa Consciousness, is the science of completion, *pūrṇatva* which is the science of Eternal Bliss, *Nityānanda*.

Planet Earth Is A Battlefield

1.1 *Dhṛtarāṣṭra said: O Sañjaya, assembled on this righteous holy land of pilgrimage at Kurukṣetra, what did my sons and those of Pāṇḍu, eager and ready to fight, do?*

1.2 *Sañjaya said:*
O King, seeing the Pāṇḍava army in full military formation,
Duryodhana went to his teacher, and spoke the following words.

1.3 *My teacher, behold the great army of the sons of Pāṇḍu,*
Expertly arranged by your intelligent disciple, the son of Drupada,

1.4, 1.5, 1.6 *Many are the heroes and mighty archers equal to Bhīma and Arjuna in war; Yuyudhāna, Virāta, and the great warrior Drupada, Dṛṣṭaketu, Cekitāna, and the heroic king of Kāśī; Also Purujit, Kuntibhoja, and the great man Śaibya; the valiant Yudāmanyu, the formidable Uttamauja, the son of Subhadrā, and the sons of Draupadī, all great warriors.*

1.7 *Best of the Brāhmaṇas, let me tell you, who are the powerful*
warriors on our side—the generals of my army,
for your information, I mention them.

It is significant that a blind man gave the opening statement of this great scripture. Not only had he lost the power of sight, but also the power of insight, the wisdom to distinguish between right and wrong.

Dhṛtarāṣṭra's brother Pāṇḍu handed over to him his throne, as well as the care of his five children. From the point of view of any righteous person, these five Pāṇḍava princes were Dhṛtarāṣṭra's responsibility as well. However, the separation born out of the self-doubt in Dhṛtarāṣṭra's mind was clear when he said, 'My sons and the sons of Pāṇḍu.'

'What are they doing?' he asked Sañjaya plaintively, 'These sons of mine, the hundred Kaurava princes, and those five sons of Pāṇḍu, the Pāṇḍava princes?' He claimed no ownership or responsibility of the Pāṇḍava princes or concern for their welfare. His concern was for his own sons.

Dhṛtarāṣṭra is the embodiment of self-doubt which is always blind! His attachment to his sons, especially the crown prince Duryodhana, had blinded his powers of reasoning. Whatever his son did received his endorsement. From early adolescence, Duryodhana had been plotting to kill his Pāṇḍava cousins. Although Dhṛtarāṣṭra pretended ignorance of his son's evil deeds, he was aware of what his son was up to. Even when Duryodhana and his brother Duśśāssana went to the extreme of disgracing Draupadī, the wife of Pāṇḍavas, trying to disrobe her in public court, Dhṛtarāṣṭra seemed powerless to act. When Duryodhana finally refused to give the Pāṇḍavas even a needlepoint of land, still Dhṛtarāśṭra kept quiet, ensuring that blood would be shed.

Dhṛtarāśṭra was fully aware that he was non-integrated and inauthentic, following the evil path of *adharma* and that it would result in the destruction of his clan. Yet he seemed powerless to act otherwise. Dhṛtarāśṭra's tale is common to humankind. Often, we follow wrong paths even though we know it is wrong, we go out of integrity and authenticity almost as if under a hypnotic spell of doubting ourselves. *Gītā*, therefore, begins from this premise of blinding self-doubting pattern, the primal pattern that invokes all other patterns in us!

Mahābhārat is not merely the fight between good and evil. Far from that, it is about our root patterns, our inner conflict in being unable to do the right thing, not being courageous enough to stand for what is right, and not taking responsibility to be complete. It is about the lack of awareness, clarity and courage to follow the path of righteousness, *dharma* of integrity, authenticity, responsibility, and enriching. It is a fight between good and evil within us, not merely outside of us. It is actually a fight between the completions and incompletions within us, between possibilities and patterns within us.

Kṛṣṇa, the Superconscious, constantly looms over our being, eternally reminding us of our space of highest positivity, possibility, divinity and enlightenment with His tremendous patience and infinite compassion. Yet we ignore this divine call within us, caught in self-doubting illusion that what we choose instead will make us happy.

Listen. I tell you, all wars between countries are nothing but triggering the collective root patterns of that society. Whether it is war at home, or war in the communities, or war between the countries, the root pattern is responsible.

Incompletion at the level of a single individual piles up and becomes the incompletion at the level of society. Incompletion in the level of society piles up and becomes the incompletion in the level of large communities. Incompletion in the level of large communities piles up and becomes the incompletion in the level of the whole country. Incompletion in the level of countries leads to and causes wars.

War is the result of incompletions. Whether it is war between you and *you,* or war between a country and country, it is the result of incompletions, which is there in a single human being. Kurukṣetra war is the ultimate war of the collective root patterns of humanity itself.

Dhṛtarāṣṭra refers to Kurukṣetra, the site of this world war, as a holy land or place of righteousness, *dharmakṣetra.*

dharmakṣetre kurukṣetra samavetā yuyutsavaḥ |
māmakāḥ pāṇḍavāś caiva kim akurtava sañjaya || 1.1

People ask, 'How can a battlefield be called a holy land?' If you study the history of humanity, you find that it has always been a battlefield. Whether these wars were morally guided or misguided is a matter of opinion. What is right for one need not be right for another.

Listen! Mahābhārat beautifully says, 'Let the fight be in *kurukṣetra*!' In Saṃskṛit, *kurukṣetra* means space of creation. *Kuru* means doing. Let the fight be in the space of creation. The whole place of fight should *not* be with the lowest realm, but with the highest realm! So, you will always be in the middle. In the fight itself, you will always be in the middle, and in the end you will be at the peak.

Look into your life. Now all your fight is, 'Will I lose this job or not?' 'What will happen if I fall sick, if I am alone?' 'What will happen if I become bankrupt?' 'What will happen if this happens, that happens?' Then you console yourself, 'All that will not happen! Don't bother!' This is the fight you always do! Shift from the zone of fight into positive creation.

Listen! You are fighting in the wrong zone of your life. For example, if you are all the time afraid of becoming bankrupt, decide, 'I am going to be a billionaire.' So, in your inner space the fight will be about—will you become a billionaire or not. You may have millions, but the fight will no more be of self-doubting thoughts of bankruptcy or not. Let the fight always be in *kurukṣetra*, the zone of creation, not in the zone of destruction. All your worrying, all your thinking, all your basic cognition is, 'Will I lose this job or not?' Even in your nightmare dreams, you will only be worried about, 'Will I lose this job or not?' No! Always let your fight be, 'Will I become CEO or not?' not 'Will I lose this job or not?'

Shift the battlefield onto the land of creation! Let *kurukṣetra* be the battlefield—*dharmakṣetre kurukṣetra*. Please listen! The fight in your life, if it is in the field of creation, you are living in *dharma*. If it is in the field of failure, you are living in a*dharma*. This is the meaning of this first *śloka* (verse) of the *Gītā*.

Practically every century, if not every decade, there have been battles in some part of the world. Almost all were created out of the belief that one party was morally right and the other wrong. In that sense, each battle was fought to restore righteousness, as believed by both parties. So, in that sense every battlefield was a holy site according to someone's belief, restoring the highest values and beliefs. In the case of Dhṛtarāṣṭra, he had an additional reason. He implicitly recognized the divinity of Śrī Kṛṣṇa, whose mere presence on this battlefield conferred upon it the mantle of *dharma*. Wherever Kṛṣṇa was, that was where *dharma*, righteousness would prevail. Even in his confused state of doubtful thinking, there was enough clarity in Dhṛtarāṣṭra's mind to acknowledge the supremacy of Śrī Kṛṣṇa. This revealed itself in his choice of words. It was as if, at one level, Dhṛtarāṣṭra knew that the fate of his Kaurava clan was sealed.

Listen. Life is a fight till you are enlightened. But, let your fight be in *kurukṣetra*, the field of creation, not in the field of losing. Don't be constantly fighting with, 'Will I get heart-attack and die?' 'Will my health collapse?' 'Will others leave me?' 'Will I become bankrupt?' No! The ground on which the battle happens decides your existence and expansion. Let your visualization be—'Will I become CEO or not?' 'Will I become yogi or not?' 'Will I become jñani or not?' 'Will I become rich or not, leader or not?' 'Will I become enlightened or not?'

I tell you, if your fight is in the direction of *kuru*, you will win the game very easily with least or no stress. It does not take more than forty-eight hours to convince yourself to shift the battleground. You just need to complete some of the self-doubts that you got from your elders, family and societal conditioning. Complete with them! So, all you need to do is just shift your core visualization, your core cognition, your core energy.

Change the battlefield and enter the energy-field of *dharma*, led and controlled by Śrī Kṛṣṇa, immediately you will experience so much of completion. Kṛṣṇa is the epitome of *dharma* (righteousness), and Kṛṣṇa was on the side of the Pāṇḍavas, then how could they lose? The tragic fate of Dhṛtarāṣṭra was that he knew that the destruction of his clan was inevitable, and yet his self-doubts had turned into self-denial, making him powerless and deny the obvious path of *dharma*.

Listen. The moment you change the battlefield from *adharma* to *dharma*, you may even become enlightened; because it is your default parking spot that decides whether you are enlightened or not. Otherwise you ARE enlightened! You just need to remember and reclaim it. The best way to remember and reclaim it is to complete with your self-doubting patterns and shift the battlefield itself. See, now your battlefield is—'any one day I am going to become bankrupt. Let me delay it as much as possible!' Instead, let it be—'any one day I am going to become the richest being. Let me do it as early as possible!'

So, your goal should be your parking spot, default parking spot. You can take your car wherever you want, but finally you will park where it belongs; your garage. Same way, your mind can go wherever it wants, but end of the day it should come and parking spot of your goal, not your accident spot. Accidents may or may not happen, but accident spot cannot be the parking spot. In your life, bad things may or may not happen, but that is not the spot where you should park yourself. Listen, your parking spot should be the spot of creation, the field of Kurukṣetra.

Kauravas were fighting all the time with their insecurities and lost everything. Pāṇḍavas were fighting all the time to create *Indraprastha*, the land of creation. So, Pāṇḍavas were living *dharma*. Kauravas were living in their self-denial, self-hatred and self-destructive mentality, *adharma*.

Please listen, if you think, 'Any one day I am going to become bankrupt. Let me do whatever I want to delay it,' then you are living in *adharma*.

Shift the battlefield. Shifting the battlefield itself is victory! Because, your whole energy will be flowing in that direction. Only if you know you are going to make it, only if you don't doubt yourself, you will even take the risk of investing in it, whether it is your time, energy, money, emotions, anything; investing happens only when you know you are going to make it. I tell you, the moment you complete with your self-doubts and your battlefield changes, your strategy, your understanding and your whole expression will also change.

Sañjaya was Dhṛtarāṣṭra's minister and charioteer. By the grace of sage Vyāsa, Sañjaya was given the power to see what was going on in the battlefield, to faithfully convey to king Dhṛtarāṣṭra and queen Gāndhāri the tragic happenings therein. His third eye or centre of intuition was opened, and not only could he see what was happening at a faraway location, but he had the power of intuition as well, to know what would unfold.

Please listen! Your life is nothing but seeing. Seeing is your life. If you can see something through the eyes, you can experience it with your physical body. If you can see something with your mind, you can understand it with your mental body. If you can see something with your consciousness, you can control it, as the Lord of it. We are all blind in one sense or another, and Dhṛtarāṣṭra represents the majority of mankind in this aspect. Blindness in this case is not only the physical inability to see. It essentially represents the inability and the absence of desire to discriminate between right and wrong. It represents the non-integrity to separate completion from incompletion.

We can all be like Sañjaya, with our third eyes open instead of being blind like Dhṛtarāṣṭra. This is one of the messages of *Gītā*. Whether you are blind or have physical eyes, you continue to see through your inner eyes. Dhṛtarāṣṭra blinded by his self-doubts, saw only his sons, who represent his incomplete identity. Listen. The third eye is not just an eye; it is the very source of consciousness. Third-eye is nothing but conscious-seeing. Consciously seeing our incompletions, our inner conflicts is the first step in opening the third eye, the energy center located between the eyebrows. Third eye can be awakened with right thinking.

Let me define right thinking, the thinking based on *dharma*.

Aligning all your thinking based on the cognition of the four principles—*tattvas* of integrity, authenticity, responsibility and enriching is right thinking.

Again, it is interesting the way Sañjaya started his description of the proceedings.

Before the War...

Duryodhana was the crown prince, and for all practical purposes the king as well, since his father was both blind and powerless to stop him. Duryodhana saw the soldiers of the Pāṇḍava army arrayed in front of him. There were many ways he could have responded to the sight. As the person who single-handedly instigated this war, Duryodhana could have gloated, that surely he would vanquish his cousins. As a measure to reassure himself and his army, Duryodhana could have roared out in anger and in defiance. Yet, after seeing the army he chose to approach his teacher and mentor, Droṇa, one of the commanders of the Kaurava army, to seek his blessings.

The move was to ensure that any blame for the outcome of the war would fall on Droṇa's shoulders; it was to hold him responsible more than to seek reassurance or blessings.

This is how most people act when they go forward with a plan of action, knowing fully well that it is wrong and can lead to serious consequences. They find something or someone else to blame. Blaming somebody else will only make you feel more and more powerless, more and more incomplete. Duryodhana understood well the modern management concept of delegation. Like many managers today, he delegated so that he could abdicate responsibility. It is very unfortunate that human beings are taught from the beginning to put the responsibility on others.

Duryodhana, aware that there was no hope to win the war, yet his greed for power and wealth blinded him to a point where he could not face reality as it IS. Please understand, sometimes we believe what IS. The reality, the creation IS and we are seeing it. Most of us always feel, 'It is there. I am seeing. So I am caught! I don't know what to do!' Duryodhana also was caught in his greed patterns and wished to change what IS, the reality so that he could control the outcome.

Please listen. We are not seeing what IS. We are only seeing what we want. We create what we want. When Duryodhana cognized, 'It is there! I am seeing and I need to control it,' he already lost the game! He was fighting a losing war! He was feeling powerless! He put all the blame on what IS, 'It is there! What can I do?'

What is Responsibility? Responsibility means living and responding to life from the truth that you are the Source of, and therefore responsible for all happenings in and around you.

Listen. There are only two types of human beings on planet Earth—those who feel responsible for everything and those who don't feel responsible for anything.

People who feel responsible become leaders. People who don't feel responsible become slaves. There are some people who don't feel responsible even for their actions. Duryodhana is one of them. He could not take responsibility for the situation as it was, since he was caught in his root patterns. He was not planning for success, he was only planning to hold others responsible, if he fails. All he could do was turn to his mentors and tell them they were responsible for ensuring his success.

Duryodhana was blunt in his message to Droṇa on the battlefield. Not a typical warrior, Droṇācārya was a *brāhmaṇa*, a scholar, and learned his skills of archery and warfare from his father, sage Bharadwāj. Drupad, the prince of Pāñchāla, was a fellow disciple, and he once had insulted Droṇa, turning him away from his court. Droṇa became the teacher of the Pāṇḍava and Kaurava princes. Droṇa later avenged Drupad by having Arjuna capture him, as part of Pāṇḍava's *gurudakṣina*, and also released Drupad. Drupad, mortified at his capture, went into penance to please Lord Śiva and sought a child, Dṛṣṭadyumna, who ironically, became disciple of Droṇa. Well aware of the intent of Dṛṣṭadyumna's birth, Droṇa still accepted him as a disciple. Dṛṣṭadyumna became the Commander-in-Chief, *senāpatī* of the Pāṇḍava army, and Droṇa was the opposing Commanders in Kaurava army.

Duryodhana then started praising the strength of the great Pāṇḍava warriors, such as Bhīma and Arjuna. Next, he explained to Droṇa about the great Kaurava warriors. Duryodhana was no longer a disciple addressing his master, but was berating Droṇa's lack in foresight in training his potential killers, who now led the opposing army and then pacified him by listing him at the head of his own great warriors.

At one level, as a kṣatriya, Duryodhana did not have respect for Droṇa, a *brāhmaṇa* scholar; he felt that a *brāhmaṇa* had no business engaging in warfare. However, knowing the unmatched warrior skills of Droṇa, Duryodhana had no choice but to keep him on his side; it would have been too dangerous had Droṇa taken sides with Pāṇḍavas. At another level, he had no trust in Droṇa. He always felt that Droṇa was partial to the Pāṇḍava princes, that Arjuna was his favorite, and that Droṇa held Kṛṣṇa in great esteem.

Duryodhana is embodiment of self-denial. His whole life was filled with deep inner conflict and painful reactions as he was fully convinced that he is a failure, the feeling of '*I cannot make it!*' So, constantly he has to prove his failures to himself by destroying others, never creating anything by himself. He had no sense of guilt going to war against his brothers, as he desperately wanted to keep the kingdom for himself and did not believe that he would be safe as long as the Pāṇḍava princes were alive.

Listen. If you are suffering with greed, your root pattern will be fear. If you are suffering with insecurity, your root pattern will be worrying. Understand, once the patterns are formed they act in a completely different way so that we can never discover them. Duryodhana's inner identity, *mamakāra* was rooted in deep fear and insecurity born from self-denial. Self-denial was Duryodhana's root pattern. And his outer identity, *ahaṁkāra*, the image he projected to others, was greed to possess, which led to anger, hatred, violence, and ultimately his destruction. His problem was not one of doing right or wrong. His pattern was might is right. Whatever he did was right, according to him. He was not a man given to deep thinking.

Please listen, all incompletions boil down to just two patterns—violence and fear. Both are one and the same. When fear comes, violence comes. When violence comes, fear comes. That's all!

Understand, I am defining incompletions.

Incompletions are nothing but not looking at the fact and trying to pervert it, interpret it, manipulate it. All your plans to manipulate, pervert and exploit is incompletion.

Duryodhana tried to pervert, manipulate, push and pull as he wanted to possess and conquer everything. But victory remains as victory wherever *dharma* is, wherever Kṛṣṇa is.

However, Duryodhana had no trust in many of the great warriors who had taken his side. Please understand, all distrust, all doubting others is self-doubt. This is the rule of thumb. When you are in incompletion driven by your root pattern, you will never be able to trust anybody. You will go on doubting others and you. All self-doubting is not having the right reason or adequate reasons. Duryodhana did not have right or adequate reasons for his action to wage the war. So, he constantly kept on doubting and distrusting others. He knew that many, especially Droṇa, Bhīṣma, and Kṛpa, who were also the teachers of the Pāṇḍava princes, did not want to fight the Pāṇḍava army. He knew that they were compelled from a moral standpoint to fight for him and not as directed by their consciousness. This was the source of his conflict, uncertainty, and incompletions.

Duryodhana's root pattern of self-denial was steeped in deep fear of survival. His pattern of self-doubting, *ātma saṇdeh* led to self-denial, *ātma droḥa*, leading to his self-destruction, *ātma hatyā*. I tell you, the worst killer is the self-doubting pattern. The one who doubts himself and doubts others is already in hell. Hell is sponsored by the people who doubt themselves and others. It was also strange that at the beginning of the war Duryodhana chose to go to Droṇa, and not Bhīṣma, his great grandfather and Commander-in-Chief.

Droṇa was a subject of the king, to whom Duryodhana could talk abrasively. Bhīṣma, on the other hand, was his great grandfather, the one who had given up his chance to be king to fulfill his own father's moral obligations, and to satisfy his father's lust. Duryodhana could not have said the same words to Bhīṣma at this stage of the war.

Ego Needs Support

1.8 *Your goodself, Bhīṣma, Karṇa, Kṛpa, who are ever victorious in battle, an even so Aśvatthāma, Vikarṇa and the son of Somadatta.*

1.9 *Many other heroes there are who are prepared to lay down their lives for my sake; all are well-equipped with different weapons, and well experienced in warfare science.*

1.10 *The strength of army of ours, protected by Bhīṣma, is invincible whereas the strength of their army carefully protected by Bhīma is limited.*

1.11 *Stationed in your respective divisions on all strategic fronts, all of you must give full protection to Grandfather Bhīṣma.*

1.12 *Bhīṣma, the mighty patriarch of the Kuru dynasty, their glorious grandsire, then blew upon his conch loudly, roaring like a lion and Duryodhana was joyful.*

Duryodhana was a coward by nature. Cowardice is the smell of inauthenticity. Courage is the fragrance of authenticity. He was inauthentic as his *mamakāra*, what he perceived as himself, was much lower than his *ahaṁkāra*, what he projected as himself to others.

Understand, when one is in denial, suffering is naturally going to be there. His root pattern of self-denial, of deep fear and insecurity had always made him feel threatened by the fact that his Pāṇḍava cousins especially Arjuna and Bhīma were far more superior, physically stronger and skilled than him.

Duryodhana felt secure only when surrounded by cronies. His strength and valor arose from the feeling of being supported by his clan and the army around him. On the positive side, Duryodhana was an extremely generous friend who gave his all for the sake of someone he trusted. This quality had attracted strong men like Karṇa to him who swore undying loyalty. Even though Karṇa knew that Arjuna was his own brother, all he could say to his mother Kuntī was that she would finally be left with five sons, implying that one of her sons, either Arjuna or Karṇa, would perish in the war. Such was the loyalty that Duryodhana evoked in his friends.

Duryodhana now rightly went on to claim that there were a number of people, who were great warriors, who would willingly lay down their lives for him. He then began to boost his own morale by saying that the power of the Kaurava army led by Bhīṣma was immense, whereas the Pāṇḍava army with Bhīma as one of the commanders was limited in power. Duryodhana's reference to Bhīma alongside Bhīṣma was due to the fear pattern that he had, of the oath that Bhīma had taken—to break Duryodhana's thigh and drink his blood to avenge the insult to Draupadī. Duryodhana knew that the only factor that could prevent it would be the protection of Bhīṣma.

Duryodhana then addressed the Kaurava army, exhorting them to support their Commander-in-Chief, Bhīṣma. In response, Bhīṣma blew his conch like a lion, making Duryodhana joyful. Bhīṣma was the first Kaurava Commander-in-Chief and Duryodhana wanted to make sure that the entire Kaurava army was committed to his leadership. Bhīṣma, the greatest warrior either side had known, was leading the Kaurava army. Duryodhana wanted to take no chances that his past hatred towards Bhīṣma would affect his assembled supporters. Though he knew that Bhīṣma and even Droṇa would have gone with the Pāṇḍava princes and Kṛṣṇa, had it not been their strong bonds of duty, he could not afford to antagonize them.

The Qualities of Dharma

Bhīṣma is the embodiment of *dharma*, righteousness. He is the Pitāmaḥ, the greatfather of Mahābhārat, the grand sire and patriarch of the Pāṇḍavas and Kaurava clan. Bhīṣma was born to Gaṅgā as

Devavṛata. He was the only surviving son of eight sons whom Gaṅgā had given birth to. So, Gaṅgā, the sacred most river energy is the great grandmother of Mahābhārat. When Bhīṣma's father king Śāntanu wanted to marry Satyavatī, a daughter of a fisherman, Devavṛata swore to remain as a *brahmacāri*, never to marry, so that his stepmother Satyavatī's children could have access to his father's throne. Satyavatī was the grandmother of both Pāṇḍu and Dhṛtarāṣṭra. Bhīṣma was highly respected for his valor and sagacity. It is one of the greatest ironies of Mahābhārat that wise men like Bhīṣma and Droṇa chose to be on Duryodhana's side, knowing fully well that whatever path Duryodhana was following was not only morally incorrect, but also against *dharma*, the cosmic law.

In the highest spiritual sense there is no right or wrong morally. Everything is neutral. Bhīṣma and Droṇa were not ordinary people, they were highly matured souls, adept in living the scriptural truths. Moreover, they were fully aware that Kṛṣṇa is a divine Incarnation, and the very fact that Kṛṣṇa sided with the Pāṇḍavas was a clear indication to them as to how the war would unfold. As great warriors themselves, they had no fears about their own deaths; and more importantly they had no guilt, no incompletions about what they had embarked upon.

Great men like Bhīṣma, Droṇa, and Kṛpācārya, trusted their inner space. Duryodhana was their prince and they were committed to him. Not attached to result of the war, they were certain that Duryodhana would perish and they would too, along with him. In fact, at one point in the war when Kṛṣṇa was greatly angered at the rout that Bhīṣma was causing in the Pāṇḍava army, Kṛṣṇa got down from Arjuna's chariot that He was driving and advanced menacingly towards Bhīṣma. Bhīṣma instantly laid down his arms, joined his palms in prayer to the advancing Kṛṣṇa who was wielding a chariot wheel as His *sudarśana cakra*, the divine discus weapon on His finger, and greeted Him. 'Lord, it will be the greatest blessing for me to die at Your hands.'

To these great warriors, dying on the battlefield was the duty of a *kṣatriya*, a warrior. They weren't concerned with the righteousness of

Duryodhana's motives. Their integrity transcended the moral rights and wrongs established by society and religion.

What is morality? In a given society, in a given era, morality is generally the accepted standards of what is desirable and undesirable, what is considered right or wrong conduct and good or bad behavior of a person, a group or an entity. Morality is about good and bad, right and wrong. It changes from time to time, era to era. When time changes, all this changes!

Please understand, integrity is not morality or ethics of the society.

Integrity is a spiritual value. Integrity is you fulfilling the word and thought you give to yourself and others, and experiencing a state of pūrṇatva, completion with yourself and others.

Integrity is not ethics. Ethics is different, integrity is different. Morality and ethics vary from time to time. Integrity is absolute. These warriors disapproved of Duryodhana's insult of the Pāṇḍava princes and Draupadī in the court but did not protest. They disapproved of Duryodhana's instigation of this war and yet took his side, knowing fully well that what lay ahead was destruction.

Flow with Nature

This was not foolishness or resignation from the powerless space. This was surrender to the inevitable, surrender to the Divine. At the level of their consciousness, these great Masters allowed Nature to take its own course. To relax and allow whatever happens to happen is the sure sign of an evolved spirit. Ordinary humans have the freedom to think, choose and act. As a result, they think they are in control of their destinies. In a sense they are; they make their decisions and act upon them. But it is their unconscious root patterns that drive them to all these decisions.

A cycle is created as the root thought patterns lead to certain incomplete actions and those incomplete actions in turn mold their mental set-up and lead to more and more incompletions. Yet, a human has the choice to break out of this cycle of incompletions and live in freedom. This freedom is the space of completion. And the science of completing with this incomplete cycle of root patterns is the science of completion, *pūrṇatva*. This is the *dharma* taught in the *Gītā* scripture.

Listen! There are two ways to live life.

One is to accept the world and life as it is, as we perceive it without any resistance being complete, to see the reality as IT IS—what in Saṃskṛit is termed *Sṛṣṭi Dṛṣṭi*. The other way is to try to make circumstances evolve according to our viewpoint, to create the reality as we want to see, called *Dṛṣṭi Sṛṣṭi*. The first attitude, one of acceptance out of completion brings happiness; the second, one of resistance, brings suffering. No one can change the world according to his viewpoint. It is an exercise doomed to encounter failure. At best, we can transform ourselves, that's all. And when we *do* transform ourselves, we are also empowered with the great inner powers to create the reality as we want, for ourselves and others!

No revolution has ever succeeded in bringing about any significant, positive change. Revolutionaries who claim that they are against dictatorship become dictators themselves. That has always been history. Ironically, an Enlightened Master has no such freedom. He is a faithful channel of the universal energy, *Parāśakti*, the Divine Existence. Every move, every thought is at the behest of the Divine. An Enlightened Being is beyond choice; He is in complete surrender to the Divine.

Bhīṣma was of pure divine origin, the son of Gaṅgā. Gaṅgā is the embodiment of pure inner space. Bhīṣma had the gift of icchā-mṛtyū, self-willed death. His *dharma*, his integrity and authenticity were the standard for his era. Yet Bhīṣma kept quiet when Draupadī was attempted to be disrobed and insulted. Because he had the wrong association with self-denial, Duryodhana and being in integrity to his huge vow to always protect the kingdom's royal seat, he did not act when Duryodhana denied the Pāṇḍavas even a patch of land the size of a needle tip.

He chose to fight for Duryodhana. However, when Duryodhana requested him to lead the Kaurava army, Bhīṣma told him that the Pāṇḍava princes were as dear to him as Duryodhana was, and while he would wage war against their army, he could not take their lives. This was the condition under which Bhīṣma agreed to fight against the Pāṇḍava army on Duryodhana's behalf.

Yet, in this instance, Bhīṣma's compassion for Duryodhana overcame his distaste for his actions and behavior. Bhīṣma understood the desperate fear running through Duryodhana's mind, and he felt the need to reassure him. In response to these exaggerated claims of Duryodhana, Bhīṣma blew his conch as a sign of resounding affirmation of whatever had been said by Duryodhana. Sañjaya said that Bhīṣma's conch sounded like the roar of a lion, coming from the oldest and the bravest of all the warriors assembled on the battlefield. It was also an affirmation of Bhīṣma's own support to the Kaurava prince and the signal for the war to begin. Bhīṣma's conch was a celebratory signal, seeking victory.

The War Begins

1.13 *Conches, bugles, trumpets, drums, and horns all suddenly sounded; Their combined sound renting the skies.*

1.14 *Then, seated on a magnificent chariot drawn by white horses, both Mādhava (Kṛṣṇa) and Arjuna sounded their divine conches.*

1.15 *Hṛṣikeśa (Kṛṣṇa) blew on His conch, the Pāñcajanya; Dhanañjaya (Arjuna) sounded the Devadatta and Vṛkodara (Bhīma) sounded his mighty conch called Pauṇḍra.*

1.16, 1.17, 1.18 *King Yudhisṭra, the son of Kuntī, blew his conch, the Anantavijaya; Nakula and Sahadeva blew the Sughośa and Maṇipuṣpaka. That great archer, the king of Kāśī, the great fighter Śikhaṇḍi, Dṛṣṭadyumna, Virāṭa and the invincible Sātyaki, Drupada, the sons of Draupadī, and the others, such as the mighty-armed son of Subhadrā, all sounded their conches.*

Conches, called *śankha* in Saṃskṛit, are the shells of mollusks that live in the sea. From time immemorial, Hindu scriptures have referred to the use of conches during ritualistic, devotional and celebratory occasions. In general, a conch is blown to signify obeisance to the Divine, or in celebration of an auspicious, victorious occasion.

Each of the great warriors in the Mahābhārat war had his own conch with its unique sound signature. Most of the great warriors also had their own chariot flags and their weapons, especially their bows, had great spiritual significance. It is said that Arjuna's presence in any part of the battlefield would be known by the sound of his conch and the twang of his bow!

When Bhīṣma blew his conch in support of Duryodhana, the response was tumultuous on both sides. Every warrior on the battlefield took out his conch and blew his signature note. Of all the sounds that emanated at that moment, a few were heard above the rest. Kṛṣṇa sounded His Pañcajanya, the conch of Viṣṇu, which drowned out all other sounds. It was the victorious announcement for all that the Divine was already present with the Pāṇḍava army.

Vyāsa, through Sañjaya, attributes divinity only to Kṛṣṇa's conch, not to anyone else's. He refers to Kṛṣṇa as *Mādhava*, and later as *Hṛiṣīkeśa*. *Mādhava* signifies that Kṛṣṇa is an Incarnation of Viṣṇu, the husband of Lakṣmī, goddess of wealth and fortune. In this context, it signifies that whoever Kṛṣṇa sides with would be invincible. Kṛṣṇa is then referred to as *Hṛiṣīkeśa*, controller of the senses, the superconscious, who has created the māyā, the illusion that is this great war of Mahābhārat. Vyāsa implies that all that happens is a creation of Kṛṣṇa. For what purpose? He alone knows. The Divine truly has no purpose. The Divine IS, that's all.

Kṛṣṇa was Arjuna's charioteer. Arjuna's chariot and his bow, Gāṇḍīva were a blessing from Agnī, the fire god. The chariot was capable of traversing all three worlds. The chariot flew the flag of Hanumān, the monkey god, the close confidante, disciple of Lord Śrī Rāma, the earlier Incarnation of Viṣṇu or Kṛṣṇa. Hanumān had blessed Bhīma that he would be with the Pāṇḍava princes at all times, and he himself would ride upon Arjuna's chariot flag. Wherever Hanumān is, Śrī Rāma is present. So Arjuna is accompanied not only by Śrī Kṛṣṇa, but also by His earlier Incarnation Śrī Rāma! Arjuna and the Pāṇḍava princes were twice blessed! Arjuna is referred to as Dhañanjaya, winner of wealth, in reference to his ability to generate the wealth needed by his brother Yudhishṭra.

Not to be outdone, Bhīma, also called Vṛikodara blew on his conch Pauṇḍra, a fearsome sound that invoked dread amongst the Kaurava army. Bhīma was feared by his enemies for his strength and anger. The other three Pāṇḍava princes, Yudhiṣtra, Nakula and Sahadeva and then by the great warriors, Drupada, Virāṭa, Sātyaki, Śikhaṇḍī, Dṛṣṭadyumna, Abhimanyu and others followed, all blowing their conches in celebration of their impending victory.

Each of these warriors had a great history. Yudhiṣṭra, the eldest of the Pāṇḍava princes, was born to his mother Kuntī through the grace of Yama, the god of justice and death, and was universally known as *Dharmarāja*, the king of truth, as he was established in *dharma*, an embodiment of integrity with the power of words, never known to tell a lie. Nakula and Sahadeva embodied enriching, the power of living who were born to Mādri, the second wife of Pāṇḍu, through the grace of the Aśvini Kumāras, celestial beings.

Drupada, the king of Pāñchāla, was the father of Dṛṣṭadyumna and Draupadī, wife of the Pāṇḍavas. Virāṭa was the king in whose kingdom the five Pāṇḍava princes and Draupadī spent a year in hiding. His daughter married Abhimanyu, Arjuna's son by Subhadrā, Kṛṣṇa's sister. Śikhaṇḍi was born as Bhīṣma's nemesis, when Ambā, a princess whom Bhīṣma captured as a bride for his stepbrother Vicitravīrya, immolated herself to be reborn to avenge her shame.

It is as if Sañjaya, the narrator of the war, repeatedly tries to impress upon the blind king Dhṛtarāśṭra the caliber of the Pāṇḍava warriors. Sañjaya specifically refers to these warriors as '*aparājita*', invincible, ever victorious in whatever task they undertook, implying that they would be victorious in this war.

It is significant that Bhiṣma's conch, sounded by him as the Commander-in-Chief of Kaurava army, to signify the war opening, was responded to by Kṛṣṇa, and not by Dṛṣṭadyumna, the Pāṇḍava Commander-in-Chief, or any of the other Pāṇḍava princes. Kṛṣṇa's was a response of victory, not a reaction to the challenge issued by Bhiṣma.

Law of Cosmos is Responsibilism

Understand, if you feel that you are not responsible, you react. If you feel that you are responsible, you respond. When all your actions are responses and not reactions, you are a *karma yogi*; no karma binds you—you are living in completion and expressing completion. The cosmic vibration of Kṛṣṇa's *Pañcajanya* conch was a declaration of His responsibility for everything in and around Him, an acceptance of the fact that whatever was thrown at the Pāṇḍava army was being accepted by Him, Divinity Incarnate.

Kṛṣṇa, as the Superconscious guide of the Pāṇḍavas, the five embodiments of *dharma*, absolves them of any incompletions, any guilt or wrongdoing by taking upon Himself the responsibility for everything happening and is to happen.

The biggest question we have in our mind is, 'How can I be responsible for everything happening around me? I can be held responsible for what is happening inside me. How can I be held responsible for what is happening outside me? For example, if an accident happens in my life, how can I be responsible?' Everybody asks this question! Let me answer you.

Listen: there is an important difference between being the cause for something, and being responsible for it! Sometimes you may not be the reason for a certain happening, but if it is affecting *your* life, you ARE responsible for that happening. For example, you may not be the cause of political corruption in your country, but as a citizen of the country, you ARE responsible for it! You may not be the reason for it, but that doesn't mean that you are not responsible in truth.

You need to know that unless you take responsibility, you are neither going to improve the situation, nor you are going to expand your inner space.

- *A person who does not feel responsible even for his own actions is an animal.* He lives in a very low-level consciousness! Duryodhana along with the Kaurava army represents this low-level consciousness.

- *A person who feels responsible for his own actions is a human being.* He lives in a middle-level consciousness! There were many warriors who felt responsible for their actions, their duties and even supported Duryodhana, they represent this middle-level consciousness.

- *A person who takes responsibility even for others' actions is Divine.* He lives in leadership consciousness, *Īśvaratva.* Śrī Kṛṣṇa is the

Īśvara, the leader of the Universe, responsible for the whole Cosmos, with the ability to do anything with the Cosmos.

We always feel that responsibility is a burden. NO! It is a power! Responsibility makes you powerful. Responsibility directly leads you to leadership consciousness, *Īśvaratva.* As long as you feel responsible only for your family, you remain as the head of just your family. When you feel responsible for the community, you become a leader of the community. As your feeling of responsibility expands in you, your leadership quality also expands as a power.

The decision to feel responsible for the whole Cosmos is Enlightenment! Feeling responsible for the Whole and declaring to live by your feeling is responsible declaration, known in Hindu spiritual practice as *nididyāsana.* Responsible declaration unlocks the power of feeling or *prema śakti* in you.

Listen. Cosmos functions on 'responsibilism.' The law of Cosmos, the natural law of Existence, *dharma* is responsibilism. The law of nature is responsibilism. Kṛṣṇa leads the whole war with this one truth, *satya* of 'responsibilism.'

The whole Mahābhārat war is Kṛṣṇa's expression of the power of His responsibilism, Īśvaratva. Even though Kṛṣṇa or His actions are not responsible for the war, even though He is not the reason for the war, He takes the responsibility even for others' inauthenticity and others' irresponsibility and reestablishes *dharma,* the cosmic law of responsibilism. This is the job of an Incarnation.

The rest of the Pāṇḍava army, including Arjuna, follow Kṛṣṇa's lead by blowing their divine conches.

Arjuna Falters

1.19 *This tumultuous sounding of the conches reverberated in the sky and the earth, and shattered the hearts of the sons of Dhṛtarāṣtra.*

1.20 *Then, seated in his chariot, which bore the flag of Hanumān, Arjuna lifted his bow, fixed his arrows and looking at the sons of Dhṛtarāṣṭra spoke to Kṛṣṇa.*

1.21, 1.22 *Arjuna said:*
O Acyuta (Infallible One), please position my chariot between the two armies and let me see the warmongers gathered here with whom I must wage this battle.

When Bhīṣma sounded his conch, it invited back the resounding response of the conches of the Pāṇḍava warriors. There is no mention by Sañjaya that Bhīṣma's conch or the accompanying sounds of drums and trumpets from the Kaurava army caused any concern amongst the Pāṇḍava army.

What he says now is different. With the roar of the conches of the Pāṇḍava warriors, led by Kṛṣṇa and Arjuna, Sañjaya says that the hearts of the sons of Dhṛitarāṣṭra were shattered.

The words used here are significant. He says that the blowing of the conches created vibrations in the sky and upon the earth. The conches of the Pāṇḍava princes and other great warriors were not mere musical instruments; they were filled with great spiritual power and divine presence. They were in fact *mantra* or sacred sounds, which created powerful vibrations affecting the environment. That is the uproar Sañjaya was talking about.

In the Hindu Purāṇas, epics, one finds references to weapons called *astra*. An *astra* is not a physical weapon. It is a thought, a word that was given enormous power by its creator to destroy, even to the extent of a nuclear device. Later in the Mahābhārat war, power nuclear weapons like *Brahmāstra*, deadliest of all the *astras*, capable of delivering destruction were attempted to be used. Just by the power of thought and words, the nuclear energy was invoked in the warrior's mounted arrow. Kṛṣṇa received the *Brahmāstra* on Him before it could do any damage.

The conches that the Pāṇḍava warriors used were not meant to destroy physically, but they were clearly successful in destroying the fantasies of the Kaurava princes. The purpose of sounding conches was to set the stage for the battle and to define its boundaries. The Pāṇḍava princes and warriors had the comfort of knowing that they were doing what was right, both in their own hearts and in the eyes of God, since they had the association and support of Kṛṣṇa Himself. The Kaurava princes were afraid. All that motivated them was greed and envy. They did not have divine purpose as their motivation.

Sañjaya, with his powerful *ājña*, third eye vision, was able to see far beyond the superficial responses on the battlefield. He was able to unravel the unconscious, deep rooted patterns, emotions and responses of the warriors. Whatever may have been the perceived reaction of the Kaurava army to the response from the Pāṇḍava warriors, Sañjaya concludes that the Kaurava princes were demoralized, imbalanced. The armies went face-to-face in military formation. The conches had sounded in anticipation. The warriors on both sides were waiting for their commanders to signal the first move in offense.

Arjuna was at the forefront of the Pāṇḍava army. He had blown his conch, Devadatta, at the same time as Kṛṣṇa sounded His Pañcajanya. Arjuna had taken up his divine bow Gāṇḍīva, and had fixed the arrow to the bow. However, instead of releasing the arrow, Arjuna looked at the Kaurava army amassed in front of him, with all the Kaurava princes, his cousins, facing him. He then addressed Kṛṣṇa, his friend, mentor, divine guide and charioteer.

For the first time in this scripture, Arjuna speaks. Arjuna is not the mere hero of Mahābhārat in this *Gītā* scripture. He is the embodiment of all humanity. He is *Nara*, the human aspect of Nārāyaṇa, Lord Viṣṇu, who in turn is Kṛṣṇa. Kṛṣṇa and Arjuna, as *Nārāyaṇa* and *Nara*, as the Divine and human, is the theme that runs throughout *Bhagavad Gītā* and also much of the epic Mahābhārat.

'*Achyuta*, O Infallible One,' said Arjuna to his friend and mentor, 'Please take me to a vantage point between the two armies so that I can see for myself who I am fighting with. Let me see who is assembled here on this battlefield,' he says. 'Kṛṣṇa, please show me who I must vanquish.'

Arjuna already knew to the last man, each one who was on that Kurukṣetra battlefield. He had no confusion about whom he was fighting. All these decisions, negotiations, changing of loyalties, dropouts, all these happened in the days before the war. The lines had been drawn very clearly, even if unwillingly in some cases.

It made no sense at all for Arjuna to ask Kṛṣṇa at this last minute to show him clearly who he was fighting against. It was as if he was hoping that at the last minute something would occur to change the course of events. If that were to happen, he knew that it could only take place through the grace of his charioteer, friend and guide, Mādhava.

It is as if Arjuna was making a desperate plea to Kṛṣṇa, 'Please show me something that I do not know. Show me something that You alone know, Oh *Achyuta (*Infallible Divine). Take me there, where You will, and show me.'

Intelligence Questions

1.23 *Let me see these well wishers in this war of the evil-minded Duryodhana, who have come together here to fight.*

1.24 *Sañjaya said:*
O descendant of Bhārata, being thus addressed by Guḍākeśa (Arjuna), Hṛṣikeśa Kṛṣṇa then drew up the fine chariot in the midst of both armies.

Arjuna starts out on a challenging note. He says he would like to see all those who had assembled to fight him, in support of the evil minded Duryodhana. Accordingly, Kṛṣṇa drew up the chariot between the two armies so that Arjuna could have a good look at all those who had gathered.

Arjuna is being called *Guḍakeśa* in this verse—*Guḍakeśana Bhārata*, the one who has transcended sleep or the need to sleep. Sleep, here, also refers to the unconscious mind, the incomplete inner space. Please listen. Sleep is nothing but the rest we need to give to our tired inner chatter. Sleep is related to the incompletions of the mind. All our incompletions, that drive our actions, reside in our unconscious space as root thought patterns. Only thing we need to go beyond sleep is a complete inner space. Integrity brings deep sleep to us, makes us conquer tiredness and ultimately conquer sleep.

Arjuna's Integrity, the power of words

Let me define Integrity, the first spiritual principle. Integrity is the key which unlocks the power of words, or *vākśakti*.

Integrity is you fulfilling the word or thought you give to yourself and to others, and experiencing a state of completion, *pūrṇatva* with

yourself and with life.

Integrity has two dimensions—honoring the words you give to yourself and honoring the words you give to others. Integrity means not just fulfilling, but honoring the word you give to you and others as your very life, is Integrity. Listen. Honoring the word you give to you—that is the key point.

Who is the first person to hear the words you utter? YOU! When you honor the words you give to yourself, your confidence in yourself grows and your self-doubt melts away. YOU become powerful! When you honor the words you give to others, others' confidence in you grows. Your relationship with that person becomes powerful!

The words you utter are YOU! You become the words you speak to yourself and others. If you go on saying, '*I am sick, I am sick*', you simply will become sick. In the same way, if you constantly tell yourself, '*I am healthy*', your energy will wake up. You will be very healthy! Cosmic energy awakens in your system and makes your declarations a reality. It is important to choose the right words, because you can create your reality with the power of your words!

A small story about the power of words, vāk śakti.

> Once, a small town was visited by a saint. As the saint passed by a small hut, a woman came to him and begged him to pray for her dying child. Since the saint was new to the town, a crowd gathered around him, curious to see if he could do anything. The woman brought the sick child out to him and he said a prayer over her.
>
> Do you really think your prayer will help the child, when even medicine has failed? After all, they are just some words!', yelled a man from the crowd.
>
> The saint turned and started shouting at the man, 'You idiot, you don't know what I am doing! Just shut up!'
>
> The man was furious! His face grew red and hot. 'How dare you insult me,!' he shouted at the saint.

> The saint smiled at him calmly and said, 'If one word has the power to make you so angry, may not another word have the power to heal this child?'

That is the power of words!

Listen: every thought we complete is the word we give to us. We have to honor it. The first step of integrity is completing all the negative words we created within us about us and life, and completing all of them. With integrity, our inner chatter disappears, it never becomes tired.

By bringing integrity to his thinking and words, Arjuna had conquered his tiredness, his boredom, his powerlessness and conflicts. When we have integrity and authenticity, when we give our life to fulfill our words, Cosmos intervenes to fulfill our words and makes them into reality. Arjuna is being referred to here as one who has conquered sleep, as a result of tirelessly doing *pūrṇatva*, completion with all the negative words he carried. Because of Arjuna's integrity, the power of words or *vākśakti* became available to him. To fulfill the words of Arjuna, Śrī Kṛṣṇa, the Cosmos Himself becomes his charioteer, leading him to his total surrender to Divine.

Kṛṣṇa has been called *Hṛṣīkeśa*, one who controls the senses from His powerful space of completion.

A person who does not have even one moment of powerlessness or incompletion in his life is an Enlightened Being. A person who never had any patterns, any incompletions in his life, right from his birth, is an Incarnation. Physically, mentally, and spiritually, Śrī Kṛṣṇa is the space of eternal completion. His senses are complete as He knows what He experienced through them is not the source of happiness. The relationship between Kṛṣṇa and Arjuna is the highest form of interaction between the Divine and the human.

You see, for one who is caught in the sleep of unconscious patterns, this world of illusion, *māyā*, appears utterly real. But the enlightened Master has awakened to the level of pure consciousness and knows that this world is just another type of dream. When the disciple is able to completely trust the Master's senses that this world is illusion, and not his own senses that give the incomplete pseudo-idea that this world is real and is the source of his happiness, then the surrender is total.

When approaching the Divine or one's Master, the ultimate step is one of complete surrender.

Stages of Surrender

This surrender happens in three stages. At the first level it is an intellectual surrender, the intellectual acceptance of what the Master represents and what he means to you. A true seeker reaches this stage when he encounters the real Master, Sadguru destined for him. The seeker sees in the Master, qualities he has been searching for. His questions start dying down and answers come even before questions happen.

Intellectual surrender to the Master replaces inadequate questions with adequate doubts. Doubts are not violent like questions as they do not arise from the root patterns or ego. They arise from a genuine, authentic need to know, to create adequate, complete cognition. Despite his high level of surrender, one does see Arjuna initially in this state of questioning, perhaps as a lesson to us.

At the next level, one reaches the state of emotional surrender. From *śāstras* one moves to *stotras*, from the head to the heart. It is like coming home when the heart surrenders. One feels a deep connection with the Guru and constantly remembers Him. It is impossible to forget Him. His memory brings tears to one's eyes, tears of gratitude that are impossible to hide.

> Śrī Rāmakṛṣṇa says so beautifully, 'When thinking of the Divine or your Guru, Master, if you have tears streaming down your cheeks, be very sure that this is your last birth.' Emotional surrender leads one close to liberation.

At the final level, is surrender of the senses. One truly realizes Hṛṣīkeśa, Master of senses, and gives up one's distorted, incomplete sense of reality and embraces the Truth of the absolute reality of *Advaita*, non-duality that the Master and every Incarnation have expressed. Ultimately, we must move beyond both doubt and faith to completion that creates a deep trust in the Master, recognizing that everything the Master expresses is for our liberation. As Arjuna progresses through the *Gītā*, layers of his incompletions peel off, and he travels into deeper stages of surrender.

Arjuna calls Duryodhana evil minded. This was to paint a contrast of his own state of mind to that of Duryodhana and rest of Kauravas. When one's mind is filled with patterns of greed, lust, envy and fear, there is a single-minded focus on the potential material benefits. Duryodhana was like an animal, operating out of instinct from his low-level consciousness. Unlike Arjuna, he was not an intelligent man and did not suffer from doubts and guilt. Animals suffer no guilt. They do not consider hunting their prey as something that needs discussion. So it is with Duryodhana. He needs power and his objectives were to do away with the Pāṇḍava princes and usurp the entire kingdom, that's all. When a human behaves the way Duryodhana does, he is in an unconscious space, blindly driven by self-denial patterns.

Please understand, when we are driven by root patterns, we don't even know what we do, why we do—why we are making money, why we have married, why we are living. Nothing! The Kaurava warriors blindly driven by Duryodhana, did not know—why they are fighting, why they want power and exactly what is going to happen? With such an unconscious, incomplete space, Duryodhana and his allies did not suffer from any doubts. When our root patterns are driving our life, we may believe that we are winning, but we will never be driven to victory. If your enemy is driving you, will he be driving you towards victory? Mired totally in self-denial patterns, these Kaurava warriors followed Duryodhana blindly, unaware that the person they followed was blind himself.

Arjuna, on the other hand, is in turmoil. He is driven by Hṛṣīkeśa, the Master of senses, who can control and complete any root pattern. Arjuna's charioteer is Kṛṣṇa Himself, whose very life is a living science of completion. As Kṛṣṇa brings the chariot to a stop between the two armies, in a metaphoric sense, He brings Arjuna's inner space to a steady state to drive him to completion.

With Duryodhana's self-denial root pattern of saying 'no' to life, cloning itself into the manifold Kaurava army of conflicting patterns, even if Duryodhana won any war out of that pattern, he would never achieve satisfaction or completion. Because the reason he is fighting for power is to feel secure from his fear. He will feel secured only when he breaks that pattern, not by winning the war! It is the wrong strategy, for the wrong reason!

Arjuna, unlike Duryodhana, has become aware of his root patterns, he is exposed to his inauthenticies, and is working to free himself from their bondage. However, he is not in the zone of light yet. The conflict between Arjuna and Duryodhana is the conflict that all humans face within themselves—a conflict between their possibility and patterns, their deep unconscious desires, the incompletions driven by their root patterns, and the possibility of completion, consciousness. Completion is consciousness! Which part wins depends on one's ability to complete and surrender to the superconscious Divine or the Master, Śrī Kṛṣṇa.

As long as one is in darkness, one does not miss light. But, Arjuna is in the state of a person who has had sight and has now lost it, who was in the light of completion, but fell into the darkness of incompletion. Yet, only in its own light, can a moon even see its dark patches. And so is Arjuna now seeing his incompletions face-to-face and is blessed to have the source of light, Jagadguru Kṛṣṇa to enlighten him. He is an intelligent man, but suddenly wondered whether what he was doing might be wrong and evil. So he is disturbed.

Duryodhana, on the other hand, has a mind that is always in darkness, He has never experienced true intelligence or completion. Therefore, words like 'immoral' or 'non-integrity' or 'inauthenticity,' '*dharma*' or '*adharma*' would make no sense to him.

Arjuna's Dilemma

1.25 to 1.30

In the presence of Bhīṣma, Droṇa and other rulers of the world,
Hṛṣīkeśa said, Pārtha, behold all the Kurus who are assembled here.
There, Arjuna could see within the armies of both parties,
His elders, grandfathers, teachers, maternal uncles, cousins, sons, grandsons
And friends, as well as his fathers-in-law and well wishers.
When Arjuna, the son of Kuntī, saw all these friends and relatives present there,
He was overwhelmed with deep pity and said:
Kṛṣṇa, seeing my friends and relatives present before me, eager to wage war,
I feel my limbs trembling, my mouth drying, and my hair standing on end.
My bow, Gāṇḍīva, slips from my hands, and my skin burns.
I am unable to stand here any longer.
I am forgetting myself, and my mind reels.
I foresee only evil omens, O killer of the Keśī demon.

Kṛṣṇa parked the chariot between the two armies and said to Arjuna, 'Here are the people you wished to see.' Arjuna wanted to see those who were about to fight him and die, and Kṛṣṇa, with no mercy at all, showed him that these were Arjuna's near and dear ones.

Kṛṣṇa Himself was related to Arjuna. Kuntī, Arjuna's mother, also known as Prithā, was Kṛṣṇa's aunt, sister of Kṛṣṇa's father Vāsudeva; so He addresses Arjuna here as Pārtha, the son of Prithā, emphasizing their relationship. Kṛṣṇa is also referred to in *Gītā* as Pārthasārathi, the charioteer of Pārtha, Arjuna.

Assembled in front of Arjuna were compatriots of his father Pāṇḍu, grandfathers and great grandfathers such as Bhīṣma, his own teachers such as Droṇa and Kṛpa, uncles such as Śakuni, brothers and cousins as all the Kaurava princes were, friends and well wishers. At one time or another, each of them had been an object of affection and respect to Arjuna. Now, they were part of this enemy army.

Arjunaviśāda, Root pattern of a thinking man

The expression of Arjuna's dilemma starts here.

The theme of *Gītā* is the story of Arjuna's dilemma, his incompletion and its completion by Kṛṣṇa.

As a warrior, as a *kṣatriya*, Arjuna was used to killing in battle. He was no stranger to death and violence. As long as those who faced him were his enemies Arjuna had no difficulty in carrying out the execution. However, those in front of him now were his *svajanam*—his relatives, people who actually were like his father, grandfathers, uncles, brothers, sons and grandsons, tied to him with bonds of blood. Many others were his friends with whom he had previously enjoyed bonds of loyalty.

Arjuna's dilemma was not one of nonviolence, *ahiṁsā*. As a *kṣatriya*, this word had no place in his dictionary. His dilemma was one of violence, violence born out of his ego, his identity. He could kill people he did not identify with, but he could not bear to kill those whom he could relate with himself in one way or another. The bonds of family were far stronger than Arjuna had imagined. These bonds were rooted in his ego, and to cut these bonds was to destroy himself. This was Arjuna's dilemma.

What follows now is a bunch of fantasies, inauthenticies that Arjuna's mind weaves in an attempt to justify his dilemma. It is what the human mind conjures up time and again as its projection of the unconscious root thought patterns, trying to justify as authentic action.

Sañjaya says that Arjuna was overwhelmed with pity. Some translate this as compassion. Compassion, true compassion, which is the hallmark of an Enlightened Being, is non-discriminatory; it does not differentiate.

Please listen. When responsibility expresses through your heart, it is compassion. To the truly compassionate person, the whole world, of both living and nonliving beings, is an extension of his own self. Anything that hurts any object around such a person would hurt him, and he too would feel the pain.

However, Arjuna's emotion was discriminatory, inauthentic. He felt pity only because they were his kinsmen, only because he identified with them, not because of his authenticity and responsibility to enrich them, not because he felt that all of them were his own extensions, and so by not fighting them he would in turn not fight himself.

This was not compassion born out of *ahiṁsā*, nonviolence, but pity born out of *hiṁsā*, violence. Arjuna's emotions arose from his root pattern, his ego.True compassion arises from a state of integrity and authenticity, the absence of ego where one's inner and outer identities are aligned, and one expresses peak of one's positivity and possibility. It arises from a state of responsibility, out of no-mind and no-thought, where the feelings of 'I' and 'mine' have disappeared and one realizes that one is the Source of everything and so one is responsible for everything. True compassion is a state of completion and bliss, one of true surrender to the Universe.

Our Four Great Inner Powers

Please understand, the four spiritual principles of integrity, authenticity, responsibility and enriching are the four *Vedas*, *caturveda* to experience surrender to the Cosmos and to have the power to simply manifest the reality of your choice!

Listen! Whether you know it or not, whether you believe it not, you have four giant powers sitting inside you. Though you use these powers everyday in your life, you don't use them consciously, with a clear intention. Please understand, all these powers are great energies, just like electricity or wind power. If you handle them properly, they can shower you with everything you want. But if you don't handle them properly, they will continue to impact your life in negative ways.

These powers are related to the four major dimensions of your life—

your words, your thinking, your emotions, and your living. When you awaken your peak possibility in each of these dimensions, it becomes a great power and support in your life.

Each of the four powers is guided by a spiritual principle known as *tattva*. The *tattva* is the key to unlock the corresponding power in you.

> *First spiritual principle is Integrity. When you practice integrity, the power of words or vāk śakti will be available to you.*
>
> *Second tattva is Authenticity. When you practice authenticity, the power of thinking or mano śakti will be open to you.*
>
> *Third tattva is Responsibility. The power of feeling or prema śakti will be possible when you practice responsibility.*
>
> *And the fourth tattva is Enriching. You will have access to the power of living or ātma śakti the moment you decide to enrich others.*
>
> *The foundation for these tattvas is pūrṇatva—completion of all the patterns we carry.*

When we live these spiritual principles and express these four great powers, the individual self merges with the universal Self, and true compassion happens out of the space of completion with the Cosmic Consciousness; from the experience that one is part of that Brahman.

Listen. Arjuna's pity arose out of fear of losing his identity, his fear of expansion, his root pattern or ego. Arjuna was mortally afraid. He claimed that his throat was parched, his hair was standing on edge and his divine bow was slipping from his sweaty hands. If one did not know Arjuna better, one would have considered him a coward.

Arjuna was no coward. He had no fear for his own physical safety. He was not concerned that he might be injured or that he might die. As a warrior of warriors, these feelings were beneath him. But, Arjuna was afraid of breaking social and ethical laws. His values and beliefs, his bio-memories, his root thought patterns, told him that what he was doing was wrong and unacceptable. So powerful was this feeling that he was reeling, quivering, dazed and unable to think or function.

Can something like this really happen? Can a hero lose his composure and exhibit the physical symptoms of a frightened coward? A true hero to whom death is play, who is trained from childhood by the greatest of Masters not only in the control of his body, his sleep, but of his mind as well? Arjuna's situation shows how the mind can play games with the best of us, how the root patterns can take over the mind in so powerful a manner as to make us powerless, without our awareness.

Arjuna was frightened that he would be held responsible for the death of his kinsmen, people who were father, grandfather and other such important figures to him. He was afraid that even if others did not blame him, he would suffer the guilt and regret for his actions for the rest of his life. So great was this fear root pattern of potential guilt, that it drove Arjuna into behaving inauthentically like a coward. All he could foresee was disaster and evil all around him. At another, far deeper level, Arjuna was terrified of his own destruction. The moment one starts identifying with *svajanam*, kinsmen, family, friends and relatives, it is a material identification, born out of possession arising from one's ego, the feeling of 'I' and 'mine.'

Possession is born of attachment, and leads to attachment as well. There can be no feeling of possessing something unless one is attached to it. People speak of attachment, liking and love. All these are valid only as long as a sense of possession exists. The moment the object of love turns around and displays independence and unwillingness to be possessed, the liking and the love disappears.

Possession arises out of our survival need, from our *mūlādhāra cakra*, an energy center located at the base of the spine. It is a primal feeling that yokes us to mother Earth. Out of the need for possession, feelings of lust, greed and anger arise. Often what one cannot possess, one wants to destroy.

'What I cannot have, let no one have,' we often feel, out of our incompletion. Possession leads to violence. It is also the deep-rooted desire for possessions, the feeling of 'mine,' that gives rise to your identity 'I.' The need to possess does not stem from your identity. It is the other way around. 'Mine' leads to 'I,' not 'I' to 'mine.' This is why you cannot eliminate your identity till you renounce your attachment to all your desires and possessions. You need to get rid of the 'mine' first. Only then the 'I' disappears.

Understand, incompletions will make you feel the whole world should be yours. Incompletions will continue to make you feel you can own, possess the whole world. Incompletions continuously make you exploit others.

Arjuna is in this mood and frame of mind. It strikes him at the moment of waging war, that what he is about to destroy are his own possessions, his own identity. If he were to destroy them he will be destroying a part of his own self, his own mind-body system. It is true that when someone dear to us dies, a part of our mind-body system dies with them. Arjuna knew that the destruction of so many of his near and dear ones, his kinsmen, would take a massive toll on him, akin to committing suicide.

Arjuna's dilemma was an existential one. What is the point of eliminating others, if it results in one's own elimination? It is a dilemma born out of partial understanding, an incomplete cognition, a peek into the truth of collective consciousness. If Arjuna were to be as unaware as Duryodhana, this doubt would have never entered his mind. Were he enlightened as Kṛṣṇa was, the answer would have been obvious. Arjuna was in between, hence his dilemma.

Why should I destroy myself? What for? These are the questions that naturally follow this line of reasoning. Arjuna was far wiser than many modern philosophers in posing this as a doubt, without venturing into any answers himself.

Many philosophers have concluded that there is no meaning to life when they encountered similar doubts. They would not even want to enter their doubt, their dilemma. They would not want to take any logical arguments arising in them to the logical conclusion. Since they did not have the integrity of Arjuna to face the conflicting thoughts arising in them, or the guidance of Kṛṣṇa to take them to their logical conclusion, they provided their own answers created out of non-integrated reasoning lacking any experiential backing.

Here, Arjuna is undergoing a process of transformation; he is going to rewrite his future! He started off in this war with the basic assumptions of the *kṣatriya* codes of conduct, on which his outer image, *ahaṁkāra* was formed. When challenged, a *kṣatriya* must fight; that is his code of honor. Arjuna had no self-doubt in doing this as he was brought up in this belief system, this default societal pattern.

However, the problem was that Arjuna was a thinking man. Unlike Duryodhana, or his own brother Bhīma, he was not a thoughtless man. This ability to think, to be aware, to be integrated was what had got him into trouble now. When he brought deep integrity into his thinking, doubts assailed him. 'Am I really doing the right thing? Am I not destroying myself and all that I stand for when I wage this war against my own people?' He finally landed up in utter confusion.

Listen. Utter confusion, dilemma is the first thing any person has to face in his life for Enlightenment. If we have not yet faced the dilemma, the possibility for transformation has not yet opened. When we are in dilemma, be very clear, the seeking has started in us.

Arjuna has become a seeker of Truth. He was no longer satisfied with what he had imbibed all these years—*śāstras, stotras* and *sūtras*. He wished to go beyond. He questioned them, as he had doubts. He was in a dilemma.

Arjuna-viśāda-yogaḥ is the name given to this first chapter of *Gītā*. *Viśāda* can mean many things in Saṃskṛit—grief, sorrow, despondency, despair, depression, powerlessness, dilemma and such. Here what we see is the dilemma that Arjuna was in, not knowing whether what he had been taught all his life, and what he had believed to be true, was really true after all.

> Understand, sometimes people ask me, '*Swamiji*, after becoming your disciple, I see a lot of struggle inside my mind.'

> I tell them, 'I am doing it! I will not let you rest till you become completely authentic. Even one point inauthenticity cannot be tolerated. Understand, you have to do the job when you are in the body. You have to achieve It. Whether you feel the urgency or not, if you feel the urge, it is urgent for me. Whether you getting enlightened is urgent for you or not, *you* getting enlightened is urgent for me.'

When you look into my eyes, why are you afraid? Because I expose your *mamakāra*, your whole inner image to you. I will expose your inauthenticity to you. I will expose your actual inner image, that which is hidden from you.

Arjuna's actual inner image, his whole *mamakāra* that was hidden from him, his root pattern of attachment, his deep fear of expansion, and his inauthenticities are now being exposed by Kṛṣṇa. The transformation that Kṛṣṇa leads him to over the eighteen chapters is the revelation of truth to Arjuna, and to all humanity.

Kṛṣṇa is referred to by many names thus far. The word 'Kṛṣṇa' itself refers to His dark blue color, the color of the sky, and as infinite as the sky. It also means *Sat-Cit-Ānanda*—Truth-Consciousness-Bliss, and 'who graces liberation to those who surrender to Him.'

He is called *Keṣava* as He destroyed the demon Keṣin. Keṣava also refers to His beautiful hair. The embodiment in Him of the trimūrti, holy trinity of Hindu tradition (the Saṃskṛit words K referring to Brahma, A to Viṣṇu, Īśā to Śiva) is another meaning of this name. Govinda is a combination of '*go*' referring to all living beings and '*vinda*' which means knower, Kṛṣṇa being the ultimate knower of the mind, body and being of all living creatures.

Rigors Of Incompletions

1.31 *I foresee only evil omens, O Kṛṣṇa, I do not see any good coming out of killing one's own kinsmen [svajanam] in this battle.*
I do not covet my dear Kṛṣṇa, victory or kingdom or pleasures.

1.32 *What use is kingdom, pleasures or even life, Kṛṣṇa?*

1.33 *Those for whose sake we seek kingdoms, enjoyment and happiness*
Now are arrayed in this battlefield ready to lose their lives and wealth.

1.34, 1.35 *Even if I am about to be slain by my teachers, fathers, sons, grandfathers, maternal uncles, fathers-in-law, grandsons, brothers-in-law and all relatives,*
I would not like to slay them even to gain control of all three worlds.
Why then, Madhusūdana, would I wish to kill them for control of this earth?

Arjuna now started developing his theme in detail. He started expressing his doubts with clarity. One may ask, 'How can such doubts be clear?' Doubts need to be clear if they are to be resolved. Thoughts need to be integrated if they need to be complete.

Listen. A clearly expressed word is fulfillment. The word which constantly keeps you in completion and expands you is Integrity. Everything starts with the word. Unclear doubts lead only to more confusion. Thoughts and words lacking integrity lead to incompletions. Unintelligent beings that lack integrity have unclear doubts.

Integrated Listening to yourself

Arjuna's doubts were precise. Arjuna started listening to himself. Listening to you is the first step to spirituality. Constantly listening to your inner space is the beginning of integrity.

Listening brings integrity into our words. We never ever really listen, either to ourselves or to others. When you really start listening to yourself, you will naturally become more aware of the words you give to yourself and others. You will also have the ability to listen to others' words with integrity.

Listening is directly connected to your ability to handle reality as it IS, without creating your own unconscious ideas and conclusions. When you don't have listening, you always come to a conclusion even before the information is cognized in you. **That is why the very first step of Hindu spiritual practice is *Śravana*, Integrated Listening.**

Because Arjuna was listening to himself, he started thinking with integrity. When we bring integrity in our thinking, the first thing is that we will know what is happening inside us. Arjuna has clarity about the doubts arising inside him, and is now exposed to his own inauthenticies. How could he seek happiness through destruction of his kinsmen, he asked. How could any good come out of this action? How could he desire power, possessions and pleasures through such action? And if he did gain those things as a result of killing his family, of what use would such a life be to him?

Though Arjuna was in a dilemma, it was a dilemma born out of intelligence, not out of ignorance. Arjuna had been taught all his life to seek power, possessions and pleasures, and he had done it. Up to this point, he had not come across a single situation where the cost of acquiring these had seemed to be greater than the accruing profit, the resulting enjoyment. Perhaps he had never bothered to evaluate the cost and benefits.

For the first time in his life, he has faced a situation that forces him to evaluate his options. 'Do I forge ahead and destroy what is dear to me so that I get more power and possibly more pleasure?' he asks. What a fundamental question, one that each one of us should ask ourselves. How often do we lack integrity and go behind activities that promise us more material benefits, even though we know that these may in some way damage our life or the lives of those we care about?

The problem is that life is not so predictable, yet we try to control it as if it is. The bigger problem is that we are deeply conditioned by our root thought patterns, our unconscious space, which ensures that in spite of all precautions, we keep making the same mistakes, living our past memories even in our present.

Please listen! The ideas we carry about our old failures, every idea we carry about the past, is wrong. Before changing our future, by avoiding or replicating our past, we need change our past. Unless we change our past, we cannot change our future. We will immediately think, '*How can I change my past? It has already happened.*' No! The idea we carry about our past is completely wrong. We are not carrying it as it happened. We are carrying the edited version, with all the sound effects, volume effects and music effects, etc!

People usually say, 'Don't bother about the past, change your future!' I tell you, don't bother about the future; change your past. Because your future lies in the past! Change your past. The hangover you carry about the past is the disease you carry. Unless you complete with the past, your past cannot be transformed.

I tell you, not having the hangover with the words you committed with you and with others, is Integrity. Not having the load of the past negativity is Integrity.

Positivity means absence of the load of the past negativity. Integrity starts only when we are in a state of completion, when we complete with the root thought pattern .

Very few of us stop and bring integrity to our thinking and question the purpose and value of our actions. With few exceptions, we are taught how to live and what to do with our lives, first by our families and later by society. We do our best to seek fulfillment. Most often, we are taught the wrong mediocre ideas about life, and try to keep up with our personal and professional commitments, and it never occurs to us to ask ourselves—are we truly fulfilled and successful? Never do we doubt, 'Why am I doing, what I am doing?' Instead, our lives become a constant series of—'what next, what next?'

For example, as youngsters we think, 'As soon as I get out of my parents' house and into college, I will be happy.' When that is accomplished, our minds immediately rush to the next goal, 'As soon as I graduate and get a good job or career I will be happy.' Once that is done, it is marriage, home, children, and vacation. On and on it goes, until we have all the things that we want but not the completion for which we worked. Invariably we realize only in our old age that something is wrong in the way we worked and we don't know why. If we look into our lives, exactly this madness is going on. The '*why*' is not kept alive in us consistently. We do not discover the '*why*,' '*for what*' we are doing things!

'What is the Why of my Life?' cries Arjuna

It takes a lot of courage of authenticity to bring integrated listening to our thinking, to stop and question our lives, our actions and society's plan for us. Understand, the attitude of asking 'WHY' needs awareness, but we forget to ask the '*why*'. We don't take our thoughts, words and deeds to the logical conclusion. It takes authenticity, the power of thinking, the inner strength to say to the world, 'Stop, I want to get off; I want to know why am I doing, what I am doing? I want to seek true inner bliss!'

It takes tremendous courage of authenticity to recognize the transitory nature of life and its limited offer of happiness, to say—'I want something more.' It takes enormous courage to complete with the materialism of the world to seek one's true purpose in life.

I tell you, if just the '*why*' is kept alive, '*why* am I feeling powerless?', '*why* am I feeling tired', '*why* am I feeling sick?', '*why* am I depressed?'; just if the '*why*' is strong enough to take you to the logical conclusion, our problems will be solved. If we just keep this one question alive, '*Why am I doing what I am doing?*' and are able to take this one question to the logical conclusion in our life, I tell you, we will be enlightened. You will radiate enriching!

'What is the purpose of my life, Kṛṣṇa?' wailed Arjuna.

Arjuna is now thinking with integrity and questioning himself, his training and his purpose when faced with the task of fighting against his kinsmen. The scene from his chariot has taken him off balance! In his heart he knows that what he is about to do is correct. All of his training as a *kṣatriya* confirms this as well. But when faced with the reality of actually killing those who have been near and dear to him, he loses his will. He is feeling completely powerless. Why?

Arjuna is a courageous man. Only a courageous person will have the confidence to open himself up so transparently and expose his innermost fear patterns, his lack of integrity and inauthenticities and seek help. Arjuna was not depressed, he was confused. He could certainly differentiate between right and wrong. His sudden confusion grew out of his awareness of his parental and societal patterns that what he had been taught throughout his life, might be wrong! Fortunately for Arjuna, his charioteer is none other than Kṛṣṇa Himself, Lord of all beings and knower of all! Only He can see what is at the heart of Arjuna's grief. Only He could provide answers to Arjuna's doubts and completion to his dilemma.

Arjuna argues that the reason one would fight to gain power and wealth was for the sake of one's near and dear ones. However, his near and dear ones were the people with whom Arjuna should fight! Even if they killed him, he would not consider killing them at any cost, 'If I would not kill them for all the riches of the three worlds, why would I destroy them for the sake of earth, this one world, alone? Arjuna questioned Kṛṣṇa. When asking, Arjuna calls Kṛṣṇa as *Madhusūdana*, which means the slayer of the demon Madhu. Arjuna implies that Kṛṣṇa may be a destroyer, but Arjuna himself would not like to be one like Him.

Arjuna's dilemma had now become deeper and more complicated. He had now got into justifications as to why he should not kill; he began to justify his lack of integrity and authenticity. To any observer, his dilemma had validity. This is a common cunning, safe game we all play with ourselves. When the stakes are high in any competitive environment, when we don't want to expand to our peak capability, we play this inauthentic game. We fantasize about rewards far greater than what could possibly materialize. The more unrealistic and unlikely the reward, the easier it is to refuse it.

Arjuna is playing this same safe, inauthentic game. Understand, when we are authentic, we will commit words which express our maximum peak capacity, as per our understanding, and as per others' understanding of our peak capacity. When we unlock the power of thinking, we will be able to spontaneously focus our thoughts to achieve our highest potential.

Constantly functioning at your peak possibility is Authenticity. Authenticity is the key that unlocks the power of thinking, mano śakti.

Arjuna said he would not kill even if he were to be killed. This is just a spontaneous lie. I tell you, spontaneous lying means you feel powerless. You are inauthentic to yourself. It is Arjuna's own loss of identity that is bothering him, the loss of identity that would result from the destruction of his lineage. Arjuna then says that he would not consider killing his kinsmen and teachers, even if he were offered all the three worlds of Universe in return. Why then, he queries, would the reward of just this planet Earth, be attractive to him?

Who was offering Arjuna the three worlds anyway? The notion was a figment of his overexcited imagination born out of his powerlessness. If Kṛṣṇa had turned around and offered Arjuna the control of the Universe, Arjuna's dilemma would have actually become far worse! However, posing it as a symbolic question as Arjuna did, made him look noble.

Arjuna is consoling himself with the idea that the rewards of winning this battle are too small and that even if he were to be offered control of the Universe, he would not be tempted. It is a safe position he is taking, since the chances of his being offered the control of the Universe are infinitely small. What matters is that it calms his bruised, powerless mind and keeps the focus off the real source of his fear.

Time and again, people play this safe game with themselves and others. It starts when we cannot face the truth with integrity and authenticity and therefore cannot tell the truth. We just give up on ourselves and go out-of-integrity with our words and become inauthentic with our thinking. For the majority of us, our identity lies in the roles we play, the responsibilities we have, the worrying we do and the acceptance that we receive from others. Without these possessions and relationships to form the foundation of our personalities, without the foundation of 'mine,' we feel lost and have no 'I.' Like us, Arjuna found it better to invent a host of other inauthentic reasons to avoid facing the truth.

We create illusions in our mind about the situations we face, about how critical they are to our existence. Then we create fantasies in our minds about what is going to happen to us, be it an imagined good or difficulty. We do everything except being in integrity and authenticity with our space of positivity and possibility, and facing the present moment with completion.

As we will see later, facing the present moment with the space of completion, *pūrṇatva*; living the four spiritual principles of life—*integrity, authenticity, responsibility and enriching,* and awakening the four great inner powers is precisely what Kṛṣṇa forces Arjuna to do.

When Arjuna is able to surrender to Kṛṣṇa's teachings and brings completion to his root patterns, then his self-doubts and illusions dissolve. Arjuna then realizes the truth, *satya* of these sacred *tattva*s and reaches his highest possibility—living enlightenment, *jīvan mukti.* He understands what he needs to do and becomes a spiritual warrior, a pure instrument of Kṛṣṇa and goes about powerfully radiating responsibility, enriching himself and the world with Divine purpose.

Good Men Do Not Kill

1.36 *What pleasure will we get by destroying the sons of Dhṛtarāṣṭra, Janārdana? Only sin will overcome us if we slay these wrongdoers.*

1.37 *It is not proper for us to kill the sons of Dhṛtarāṣṭra and our friends. How could we be happy by killing our own kinsmen, Mādhava?*

1.38, 1.39 *O Janārdana, although these men are consumed by greed and they see no fault in killing one's family or quarreling with friends, Why should we, who understand the evil of the destruction of a dynasty, not turn away from these acts?*

Here is Arjuna's dilemma spoken plainly. He had two options and is looking to be convinced of one or the other. The first was that going to battle was wrong, especially against his kinsmen. Therefore he should cease and resist, walk away from the war before it starts. All his arguments up to this point were in this line of thinking. At the same time, Arjuna was open to the possibility that what he had set out to do was indeed correct, in which case he would go back into battle mode, as a true kṣatriya would do.

To begin with had Arjuna been totally convinced that war against his kinsmen was wrong, he would not have come to the battlefield. It was his lack of integrity that raised within him the question of retreat from his duty. To Arjuna's credit, he listened to himself, to what his mind had to say and turned to the Master for guidance. He allowed Kṛṣṇa to speak into his listening. Understand, the whole spiritual life starts with authentic listening.

Arjuna's mind now brings up one more argument. Arjuna agreed that Duryodhana and his allies were the aggressors and wrongdoers. Whatever they had done to him, his brothers and his wife was not pardonable, and they needed to be punished by the laws of the land. By all rights Arjuna was quite justified in killing those wrongdoers. 'But,' Arjuna asked, 'Would one wrong be corrected by another wrong? How can I be happy killing my kinsmen, however justified I might be in doing that? Their misdeeds cannot be remedied by my misdeed and that would only make me miserable.'

Arjuna's Violence Erupts

There are two incompletions central to Arjuna's dilemma.

The first incompletion is that of relationship. The problem that Arjuna faced is one that we all face when asked to do unpleasant things to people we know. It is always easier to criticize and punish people one does not know. To be faceless is to be fearless. With people one knows, there is a danger of breaking the relationship through perceived negative behavior, even when it may be fully justified. To face this incompletion in one's relationships, one must first develop detachment that allows action without worrying about the consequences. This detachment only comes from completion with every relationship with oneself and with others in one's life. One follows the path of completion and leaves the result to the process. As long as the path is right, whatever destination the path takes one to, will also be right.

Listen. Vedic civilization is established on completion. You realize your potentiality, you establish yourself in the space of completion, you are God! Understand, only if we start living completion, we will understand the quality of life. I tell you, when there is incompletion, your life is stolen away from you.

Let me define Completion.

Completion is removing the delusion of incompletion, which makes you cognize that the other is separate from you. Understand, incompletion has no existence; it is only a delusive cognition. Incompletion is the delusive cognition that stands between you and the

Whole. Complete with everything.

To overcome this isolation, this incompletion we need to realize that no man is an island. We are all connected at the spiritual level.

When we complete with everything, animate and inanimate, we will experience the space of non-duality, *advaita*, where there is no one, no two but infinite, everything is infinitely powerful. See, relationships are nothing but our own extensions. Relationships are not outside; they are just our own extensions. The '*you*' extended outside you is our relationships. Completing with all our extensions,we will learn to complete the incomplete 'you,' if present in other.

When we arrive on planet Earth, we are complete, integrated beings. We are open to all possibilities. Over time, we build walls believing that these walls will keep us safe and that the connections that we have established inside the walls are ours to keep. We create a delusory cognition that we possess everything within the wall. Slowly, the open space we started with becomes a maze and we are lost inside! The islands need to be bridged. We need to complete with everyone, with everything instead of isolating them and competing. Competition does not ensure survival; completion does. Understand, with competition you may have survival success, but you will never expand. Success in crisis moments is only survival success, not life success. Success in life happens only with completion.

The other incompletion that Arjuna faces is the problem of directness of action. In a war of this type, Arjuna faced transparent consequences of his action. If he shot an arrow and killed a kinsman, death was a direct result of his action. Arjuna did not have the luxury of remote destruction. He had to look the victim in the eye before releasing his arrow. He was aware of whom he was killing and why. He felt the destruction within himself when he killed someone else.

Please listen! Life is continuously happening in front of us. Arjuna is frightened in front of the eyes of life; from his disowned self, his relationships which are his forgotten extensions. This anxiety, fear, shivering is nothing but the expression of the incompletions Arjuna was carrying.

Arjuna was affected by the combination of these two delusory incompletions: that of being connected by kinship to his enemies and the fact that he had to kill them directly and personally. It affected him because he was not a Duryodhana, who was in self-denial about the consequences of his actions. It affected Arjuna because he was not a Kṛṣṇa who would have taken responsibility for his and everyone's good or bad actions, being in the powerful space of completion at all times. Arjuna was neither Kṛṣṇa nor Duryodhana. His mind was doubting that he might be doing wrong, but his mind had not yet ascended to be able to complete with his kinship bonds. This was Arjuna's dilemma. This was Arjuna's incompletion.

Earlier Arjuna said that even if his kinsmen had made big mistakes, he should not repeat the same mistakes; even if offered the entire Universe. He said that his kinsmen blinded by greed for power, were in darkness that saw nothing wrong in destroying one another and their own kinsmen. He asked Kṛṣṇa, 'Shouldn't we be distancing ourselves from these people and their attitudes, we who are not ignorant, not in darkness and not blinded?'

Now, he condemned the same kinsmen, his *svajanam* that he had referred to so passionately a few moments earlier; the same people who he claimed to hold in great respect and affection and therefore did not wish to kill. He shifted gears now and moved from the position of not killing them because they were his flesh and blood to a greater moral position of not wishing to kill them because it was morally reprehensible.

Arjuna said that destruction of the lineage, the dynasty, is evil, and that he recoiled from such a deed even though his opponents had no such compunction, blinded as they were by greed. Arjuna's dilemma now jumps to a larger arena. It was now a matter of tradition and respect for the lineage that could be traced back to the moon and divine beings, and an old, established tradition that would be a sin to dismantle and destroy. It's no longer about individuals; it is about the destruction of a race that had existed for thousands of years. How could he be expected to carry out such a horrible act, he pleaded.

In Arjuna's mind this was a big self-doubt. Killing a few individuals, even if kinsmen, was a mistake. Killing a whole generation was a far bigger sin, and now he was expected to destroy a whole race, the foundations of a proud and legendary dynasty. How could the future generations forgive him? This was how the argument of Arjuna's dilemma shifted. His incompletions led to greater delusory incompletions, from individual to racial destruction. When Arjuna talks about the threat to his dynasty, it arises out of a fear of his own mortality.

He has asked, 'Even if I am to die, as I must, should I not ensure the continuance of my dynasty that bears my signature, my identity, my DNA?'

Arjuna is pleading with Kṛṣṇa, 'Please tell me, am I right? Please tell me, should I withdraw from this battle?' Arjuna is now violently asking for a single instruction to escape the fear of losing his identity on which his *mamakāra*, inner image is built. Understand, Arjuna's identity is based on his *kṣatriya* up-bringing, the mentality of a warrior. Asking for one single instruction comes from his mentality of fighting, of violence that always excludes. In a fight who is the winner? Only one. In survival instinct, who is the winner? Only one.

As we will see, Kṛṣṇa never gives him a single instruction but gives him inspiration. He gives him the whole inspiration based science of *Gītā śāstra*, so he can find his own answers and he raises himself by himself!

The Breakdown Into Powerlessness

1.40 *With the destruction of dynasty, the eternal family tradition is destroyed too, and the rest of the family becomes involved in immoral practices.*

1.41 *When immoral practices become common in the family, O Kṛṣṇa, the women of the family become corrupted,*
And from the degradation of womanhood, O descendant of Vṛṣṇi, arise social problems.

1.42 *As these social problems increase, the family and those who destroy the family tradition are cast in hell,*
As there is no offering of food and water to their ancestors.

1.43 *Due to the evil deeds of the destroyers of family tradition,*
All kinds of rituals and practices of caste and family are devastated.

1.44 *O Janārdana, I have heard that those who destroy family traditions dwell always in hell.*

1.45 *Alas, we are preparing to commit greatly sinful acts by killing our kinsmen, driven by the desire to enjoy royal happiness.*

1.46 *I would consider it better for the Kauravas to kill me unarmed and unresisting, rather than for me to fight them.*

1.47 *Sañjaya said: Having said this on the battlefield, Arjuna cast aside his bow and arrows and sat down on the chariot, his mind overwhelmed with grief.*

By now, Arjuna had become desperate. His arguments seemed weak, even to him. They include the tragic impact this war would have on future generations and the entire Kuru race. Arjuna starts quoting the scriptures of social laws to explain to Kṛṣṇa the evil his destructive actions would bring to the noble lineage, which would lead to the decline in commitment to the rites and rituals that make society civilized and moral. He then elaborated upon these immoral and unrighteous acts.

He said that women in the family would become unchaste and result in children of mixed castes, which would be undesirable. Those who destroy family traditions would ruin all sacred practices and such people had no place to go but hell. To understand what Arjuna said, it is important to understand the origin of the caste tradition in Hindu religion.

At the age of five, a child was given to the care of a spiritual Master by the parents in the ancient Indian education system called *gurukul*. The Master became mother, father and teacher to the child. In the *gurukul* itself, the science of completion was taught to the child. The child grows up as a complete being. The child's natural aptitudes formed the basis for the caste classification, *varṇāśrama*. *Brāhmaṇas* (priests/teachers), *kṣatriyas* (kings/warriors), *vaiśyas* (tradesmen) and *śūdras* (service) are these four classes.

The Vedic *gurukul* system was not concerned with whether the child's parents were *brāhmaṇa* or *vaiśya*. Irrespective of parentage, children were taught the *Gāyatri* mantra at age seven, which allowed their natural intelligence to blossom. If the Guru found that the child had the natural aptitude to learn the scriptures, he would be trained as a *brāhmaṇa*. Others were trained to enrich through materially relevant arts and sciences to re-enter the world with a mature and complete personality.

Over time, this caste system was corrupted through human greed. Those who believed that they were doing more responsible work, and therefore were more respected, such as the *brāhmaṇas* and *kṣatriyas*, decided to pass on their caste qualification to their children as if it was their birthright. Such a practice had no scriptural sanction.

Arjuna's doubts about caste pollution had no scriptural base or merit. What he referred to became the societal norm because of human greed, the collective root patterns of society. There were many instances of caste mixture even in the great *Kuru* lineage that Arjuna claimed would be destroyed. Satyavati, his great grandmother, was a fisherman's daughter. Arjuna himself had wives who were not of *kṣatriya* lineage by birth. He talked as if mired in total confusion when he linked practice of rites and rituals with morality and chastity. His logic was distorted.

Rites and rituals, as prescribed in the scriptures, are an expression of one's inner completion. Completion is not created by blind practice of rites and rituals. Arjuna voiced the sentiments of organized religion and priesthood, which derive their power and monetary base from such rites and rituals. This is how, in each culture and religion, the power of the priestly class was established, as if they were the sole mediators to God.

Arjuna talked about ancestral worship and implied that the offspring of mixed caste have no right to make offerings to their ancestors, leaving them lost in the realms beyond death. It is the confusion that has prevailed over the ages that Arjuna captured and presented. He raises doubts on behalf of mankind and seeks clarification. There are no ancestral spirits waiting to be pacified by us. If the spirit is enlightened it merges with the infinite energy. If not, it gets reborn within three *kṣanas*, three moments.

Hell and heaven are in our minds. They are psychological spaces, not geographical places. We are in hell when we are depressed, guilty, and in suffering and incompletion. We are in heaven when we are in completion and feel and express love, joy and gratitude.

Arjuna is not a fool; he understands all this perfectly. Yet, he voices his doubts as if ignorant, as if confused. He acts out of compassion for humanity when he articulates these self-doubts so that the Divine, Kṛṣṇa can answer and destroy the root of the self-doubt. A thoughtful man of integrity like Arjuna cannot talk about the lack of chastity of women without blaming the men who are equally responsible. He reflects here the superior attitude of men over the ages, those who have treated women with undue superiority. The doubts he voices are those of the society he lives in, and those doubts have not changed in thousands of years.

Please listen! The truths expounded in the *Gītā* are about personal transformation. Each verse of the *Gītā* is a *sūtra*, a technique that can work on your being and transform you. That is how Kṛṣna brings Arjuna into the space of completion.

Completion is the space and state where you will be totally connected with life and with people in your life in the present moment without any limiting, restraining influence of the past happening in your life.

The essence of the *Gītā* is living in the space of completion in the present moment. Rāmakṛṣṇa Paramahamsa used to say that the *Gītā* is '*tāgi*', a corruption of the word 'tyāga' that means renunciation or surrender. *Gītā* is about surrendering the past and the future incompletions to the present and experiencing completion.

Now, Arjuna was ready to give up on himself. He had collapsed both psychologically and physiologically. His cognition was totally imbalanced and he was now completely powerless. He was all set to run away from the battlefield and escape from the reality of his responsibility. He had convinced himself through his own illusory arguments that what he had embarked upon was evil, nothing but evil, and therefore he wanted no part of it. He said, 'I am ready to lay down arms and be defenseless. Let Duryodhana and his men kill me.'

For a *kṣatriya* to say this means one of two things: His act is one of total surrender, or powerlessness of extreme confusion. A kṣatriya warrior, a supreme warrior such as Arjuna knows no fear. It is neither fear of death nor fear of injury that compels him to say what he did.

Arjuna was not in a space of total surrender yet. Nor was he in the space of *ahimsā*, nonviolence. He was not in tune with the Cosmic Consciousness—the space of non-duality, *advaita*, the experiential expression of infinity to say that—'*Killing others is killing myself, as I feel they are one with me*.' His arguments about not killing his kinsmen being like killing himself were born out of his incompletions,and not out of self-realization or completion.

Arjuna's desperation was becoming extreme. He was an intelligent, thoughtful man, who was torn between his responsibilities as a *kṣatriya* prince, and the scriptural codes of morality. His distress, his delusion, his powerlessness was now complete. He sat down, unable to bear the weight of his emotions. He put down his bow and arrows, which signified that he was out of the battle. He was as far away from reality as he could possibly get.

Arjuna, the greatest of warriors and men of his time, *Bharatarṣabha*, was in the depths of despair due to the conflict between his inner and outer identities, his upbringing and value systems, his root patterns. Arjuna, at this point, was no example of a true *kṣatriya*. Arjuna, now being human, was a true example of mankind. He was torn between darkness and light, between patterns and possibility. He was experiencing deep conflict between the unconscious patterns that were driving him and the possibility, the reality of what he ought to do. The clarity that would come about with the grace of the greatest Master, would be his Enlightenment, his complete Completion.

The darkness that surrounded Arjuna at this stage was *māyā*, the illusion that prevents us from perceiving the Truth of Reality that pervades all our experiences. *Yā mā iti māyā*—that which is not real but appears as absolute is *māyā*. *Māyā* is not unreal in the sense that it does not exist. *Māyā* truly exists as reality. It veils, it covers reality, the ultimate Truth—the truth of our inner divinity, our infinite powerfulness; and therefore it is unreal, an illusion.

Had Arjuna been enlightened as Kṛṣṇa, he would not have been tormented by the play of his *māyā*. Had Arjuna been a Duryodhana, or even a Bhīma, whose individual consciousness was not awakened, he would have accepted the *māyā* without question. But, Arjuna is *Nara*, he is intelligent, partially awakened, he is a seeker. He is in the presence of the greatest of all Masters. He is struggling to rid himself of his *māyā* and seek clarity.

It is Arjuna's root pattern that created the *māyā* of powerlessness in him. His own unaligned identities and his own identification with who he was, along with his conviction that he should preserve his lineage—all these delusory incompletions created the illusion in him that he was something other than who he was. These gaps between his identities created the self-doubt in him that he should do something other than what he was there to do.

All of us come into this world with no identity. As we grow we collect labels describing ourselves as mother, father, brother, employer, enemy and so on. We become so associated with the labels and their accessories that we forget *who we really are*! We forget to associate ourselves with our true space of completion and instead associate with our incompletions. Our life is then about seeking completion and happiness in the wrong places.

Listen. Eternal happiness that constantly flows as bliss is always within. You cannot find it outside. You cannot reach it through material possessions, through relationships, through selfish philanthropy. Just as we learned how to stop feeling blissful, we can relearn how to connect with our blissful nature again. That is the process of relearning that Arjuna was going through. The process of *Inner Awakening* at the hands of the Master was about to begin. If we become integrated and authentic to that process, and follow it carefully over the eighteen chapters that the Master takes His disciple through, we too can become awakened, complete and blissful.

Ādī Śaṅkara says beautifully: If you imbibe even a little of *Bhagavad Gītā*, if you drink even a drop of Gaṅgā water, if you think even once about that great Master Śrī Kṛṣṇa, you will never have to face death.

Thus ends the first chapter named ***Arjunaviṣāda Yogaḥ****, 'The Yoga of Arjuna's Dilemma,' of* ***Bhagavad Gītā Upaniṣad, Brahmavidyā Yogaśāstra****, the scripture of yoga dealing with the science of the Absolute in the form of* ***Śrī Kṛṣṇārjuna-saṁvād****, dialogue between* ***Śrī Kṛṣṇa, Arjuna.***

CHAPTER

2

Sāṅkhya Yogaḥ

YOU ARE GOD

MAKE NO MISTAKE, YOU ARE DIVINE!

WHATEVER STATE YOU ARE IN NOW, YOU ARE STILL DIVINE WITHIN! LET KRSNA TELL YOU HOW TO LIVE AND RADIATE YOUR DIVINE POTENTIAL.

You Are God

It is here that we enter into the real *Gītā*. It is from here that Bhagavān or God, Nārāyaṇa starts speaking and singing the *Gītopaniṣad* into the listening of Nara Arjuna, and through Arjuna into the listening of the whole of humanity.

Until now Kṛṣṇa was speaking as a man, as *Vāsudeva* Kṛṣṇa, in His human form, but it is only from here that Kṛṣṇa sings as *Parabrahma* Kṛṣṇa, in His divine state as Bhagavān, the universal Kṛṣṇa.

Understand, only an intelligent man will allow the other person to speak. Only a man of completion will provide integrated listening to himself and others. We all speak continuously to each other, but a conversation does not really happen. When the other person speaks we do not listen; we are busy preparing our own reply. We never speak into the listening of others, we just speak into the non-listening of others! We need intelligence; we need integrity to allow the other person to speak into our listening.

Listen...

> A person was telling his friend that he had not spoken to his wife for a whole week. His friend asked him whether he was angry with her or if he had fought with her.
>
> The man replied, 'No, I am afraid of interrupting her!'

Not speaking does not mean we listen! Same way, just speaking continuously does not mean others listen!

There are no extraordinary speakers; there are only extraordinary listeners! It is extraordinary listeners who are extraordinary speakers. Because Kṛṣṇa is an extraordinary listener, He allows Arjuna to speak into His listening!

We may either speak verbally or mentally, but in any case; we are speaking continuously without giving integrated listening to ourselves and others. We are not speaking into the listening of others. Even when we keep quiet, we are not listening.

But Kṛṣṇa does listen! He is the embodiment of completion. He listens completely to Arjuna's dilemma from His pure space of listening and only then does He speak into the listening of Arjuna and answers compassionately to enrich him. Of the original 745 verses in the *Gītā*, as part of the *Bhīṣma Purāna* of Mahābhārat, He responds in depth to Arjuna's 57 questions through 620 verses.

In the first chapter, Kṛṣṇa does not say a word to interrupt Arjuna. He allows Arjuna to speak fully into His listening for one whole chapter of *Arjunaviśāda Yogaḥ*. He keeps quiet, even on seeing the depth of Arjuna's confusion and depression. He consciously analyzes the root of Arjuna's thoughts, his root thoughts patterns to determine the platform of powerlessness upon which Arjuna is standing.

Look in! When was the last time you really listened to your own words? We never ever really listen, either to ourselves or to others. When you really start listening to yourself, you will naturally become more aware of the words you give to yourself and others. You will also have the ability to listen to others' words with integrity.

Listening is directly connected to your ability to handle reality as it is, without creating your own unconscious ideas and conclusions.

Please listen, the moment you start talking to somebody, when you don't have listening, you start coming to your own conclusion even before the information is cognized in you, either by rejecting that person or taking that person as a big threat. Both will lead you to suffering.

That is why the very first step of Hindu spiritual practice is *Śravana*, Integrated Listening. It is possible to become a successful businessman just by studying the first few chapters of *Gītā*. You can reach the peak possibility of your profession and of your life just by learning the art of integrated listening from Śrī Kṛṣṇa. Once you provide your integrated listening to yourself and others, you will automatically be able to speak into the listening of others and thus communicate to enrich yourself and commune to enrich others as well.

When you experience the words you utter to you and to others as the extension of your life, they directly affect you. When the words uttered by you are not listened to, the completion is disturbed. I tell you, if the person to whom you are talking to is not in the space of listening, the ideas you want to express will never be delivered. It may lead to an argument, but it may never lead to intelligence transfer.

Listen! Information transfer is argument. Intelligence transfer is Listening. In arguments, information can be transferred, but never intelligence. Only in integrated listening can intelligence be transferred.

A devotee once asked me, '*Swamiji*, how is it that you are able to answer so many questions?' There is only one secret to this. I know how to give my integrated listening to the question, that's all. If you know the technique of right listening, the reply is immediately ready in your being, ready for the intelligence transfer to others.

Listening makes you God

Listen! Please come to the space of listening. Many teachers tell you, 'However much you listen, unless you practice, it won't help you.' I tell you now, 'However much you try to practice, unless you listen, it won't help you!'

The problem is that we do not trust ourselves and our innate intelligence to respond to a question without preparation. That is why we start preparing the reply even before listening. Whenever we allow our incompletions to wake up and interfere into our thinking or cognition process, listening stops. Hearing is not listening.

Integrity, the power of words starts with listening, continues with listening. Human beings miss life when they miss listening. For a person who wants to begin the life, the first thing he needs to learn is listening. Listening is God. Just by listening you experience God!

In *Vedānta*, the first principle is *Śṛavana*—Integrated Listening; the second principle is *Manana*—Intranalyzing, meaning analyzing the truth for the sake of internalizing it not for rejecting it; and the third principle is *Nididhyāsana*—Living and radiating the truth!

Any transmission of knowledge, energy or experience happens between a Master and disciple only when the disciple gives his or her listening! Even *Vedic Ṛṣis* start with this chant: *śrunvantu viśve amṛtasya putrāḥ—Oh! Sons of Immortality, please listen to me!*

Here, Kṛṣṇa is giving His integrated listening to Arjuna! He is interested in the real problem and not in expressing what He knows. He wants Arjuna to learn the ability to give integrated listening to himself, to have the clarity of mind. He is interested in enriching him to find a solution to his own problem. He allows Arjuna to speak so that He can listen and transmit the ultimate knowledge and experience of completion to him.

One needs intelligence, or I may say enlightenment, the space of completion to listen. Unless you start living completion, you will not even be able to maintain listening. Even listening is achieved with completion. Completion brings listening to you. Only an Enlightened Master, an Incarnation like Kṛṣṇa can listen, only He can speak into the listening of others. In the first chapter He listens fully and completely. Even in this second chapter named *Sāṅkhya Yogaḥ*, He allows Arjuna to speak into His listening in many verses.

Please understand the definition of Listening. Let me define what Right Listening is, *śravana*.

Right listening means allowing the words to enter your inner space automatically; letting them cognize, without you constantly interfering with your incompletions, is Listening.

> People come to me and say, '*Swamiji*, you know our problems; please give us the answer.' I ask them to speak out and state their problems clearly.
>
> They say, 'You are enlightened, you already know our problems, please give us the answer.' I say, 'Yes, I know your

problem even if you don't speak, but you will not know your own problem if you do not speak into my listening!'

Listen! When we know how to speak into the listening of the listener, we also know how to speak into our listening. Listen! The power of thinking or *mano śakti* is open to us when we practice authenticity. Our mind should be open to the space of possibilities.

When you listen, you understand, you become God. Listening makes you God! Only God can make you God. Nothing else can make you God. Only diamond can cut the diamond! Listen. Any listening is God. If you are listening to the sparrow's sound now without giving any meaning to it—just pure listening—that is God. Only if you learn pure listening, you will also be able to learn and give the right meaning.

On the Kurukṣetra battlefield Kṛṣṇa delivers the *Gītā* to Arjuna. People who have the rationality to compute time may wonder, 'Arjuna spoke for so long. Now Kṛṣṇa speaks for so long. How is it possible for these two to hold such a long conversation in the middle of a battlefield? Wasn't Duryodhana fed up or didn't he think that this was a good opportunity to get rid of Arjuna and Kṛṣṇa?'

That's how the logical, unaware mind thinks. Such a mind cannot conceive the possibility that a conversation can indeed take place in silence, in the space of pure listening. Understand, pure listening happens only when you start listening into your listening. At the higher level of communication, in the pure space of listening your mind needs to be still to allow the grace to move in. Only with completion inside, you can even listen at this moment. Understand, in the state of incompletion, you don't listen! You act like you're listening, but you don't listen! You act like you're seeing, but you don't see! It is very important.

Understand, sitting in completion with listening is *Upaniṣad*. This is the subtlest and most powerful of all communications. At this level, communication becomes communion. So, please move to the space of *Upaniṣad*. Listen! Sit in *Upaniṣad*, in the space of listening. When you are in completion, you can sit even facing the wall for twelve years that

Bodhidharma did. He was facing the wall of the cave sitting for twelve years, because he was in completion. When you are in incompletion, even watching a movie facing the television, you can't sit more than ten minutes; you go on changing channels.

The essence of all the *Vedic* scriptures is called *Upaniṣad* or 'just sitting.' It is the ultimate technique. When you sit with the Master, the *Upaniṣad*, the sitting happens; some strange process starts happening in you, which can neither be called a technique nor a no-technique. It is literally like cooking or boiling.

In my *satsangs*, which are *Upaniṣad*, I give gaps in between my words. These gaps are the moments when I actually listen to you. Because in the gaps, based on your body language, I know whether you are restless or restful! Are you listening? Or are you just arguing inside you?

Listen. I am not a professional speaker; I am a professional listener. Before I start speaking, in the silence I listen to you. Every time I give a break between words, I listen to you. I speak what will make you listen. I speak into your listening. That is why my listening ends up as your listening! As I am a listener, I make you listen! I end up making you listen!

Just by listening, you will reach the depth of you; you will experience the depth of you. Even now, look inside you. Find out, are there any incompletions? Is there any restlessness inside you? Then you will not be able to listen.

Whenever you listen to you, you listen to others. When you don't listen to others, you don't listen to you also. Get it? Listen to you and listen to others. Only when you listen to you first and see that you are in completion, you can listen to others. If there are incompletions inside—**I have not done this, I have not done that, this has not happened, I am restless**—if you have such incompletions inside, be very clear, you will not be listening to me. You may be sitting here out of compulsion, or some other reason, but you will not be listening to me. When you don't listen, more and more incompletions happen.

When they talk of great Masters like Ramaṇa Maharṣi

communicating in silence, it was indeed true. To communicate, you need not open your mouth. You only need to bring completion and give your right listening, *śravana.* In the presence of the Master, answers will appear even before your questions are asked.

Intellectual seekers, with years of questioning behind them, come to me and ask, '*Swamiji,* why is it that when I come to you with hundreds of questions, when I am in front of you, there is no need to ask you about them? I feel as if the answers are already there!'

This is not imagination; this is the truth. Questions are a reflection of your inner ego, your root pattern, which is violence. When you are in front of the Master, with *śravana*, integrated listening, the first thing that happens is the melting of your root pattern like snow melting in the sun. Therefore, questions also disappear. You start feeling that miraculously, the answers appear in front of the Master. The truth is that the answers were all already there. The Master's presence dissolved the root pattern and let the answers out.

You can open up to the Master at three levels. You can converse and convey through words and the Master will listen. At the next level you can communicate from the heart in silence; you can visualize instead of verbalizing in speech. Finally, you can commune in silence through *Upaniṣad* and the Master will grasp this even more powerfully.

Here Kṛṣṇa allows Arjuna to verbalize, He allows him to speak into His pure listening, so that to begin with, Arjuna himself will develop the ability to have integrated listening and understand his problem. Once Arjuna cognizes and expresses his confusion, he can relapse into silence and commune with the Master of completion in the space of *Upaniṣad.*

Drop The Powerlessness And Stand Up

2.1 *Sañjaya said:*
As Arjuna's eyes overflowed with tears of pity and despair,
Madhusudana (Kṛṣṇa) spoke to him thus.

2.2 *Bhagavān Kṛṣṇa says:*
Where from have these impurities descended on you
at this critical time, Arjuna!
You behave unlike a nobleman and
this will keep you away from realization.

2.3 *Do not yield to fear, Pārtha! It does not befit you.*
Drop this powerlessness of heart and stand up,
O Parantapa, destroyer of enemy.

Arjuna was distraught with pity and despair. His pity was for his opposition that consisted of his *svajanam*, kinsmen, elders, teachers, relatives and friends. He despaired at the thought of what would happen if he did have to kill them. He had collapsed in his chariot and his bow and arrow had slipped from his hands.

Kṛṣṇa allowed Arjuna to exhaust himself, physically, emotionally and spiritually. He listened to him carefully, completely. Kṛṣṇa wanted to give Arjuna time to open his mind, heart and being to Him, Arjuna's friend, guide and master, so that His answers would penetrate Arjuna's very being.

Then He spoke for the first time, as if opening His being directly. Bhagavān Kṛṣṇa says, 'My dear Arjuna, how have you acquired these impurities? They do not at all befit a man who knows the value of life. They lead not to higher planes but to infamy, *akīrti karam arjuna*.'

śrī bhagavān uvāca
kutas tvā kaśmalam idaṁ viṣame samupasthitam |
anārya juṣṭam asvargyam akīrti karam arjuna || 2.2

This verse is connected to the next one.

'O Pārtha! Do not yield to this degrading impotence. It does not befit you. Give up such petty powerlessness of heart and arise, O Parantapa, destroyer of enemy.'

klaibyaṁ mā sma gamaḥ pārtha naitat tvayy upapadyate |
kṣudraṁ hṛdaya daurbalyaṁ tyaktvottiṣṭha parantapa || 2.3

Kṛṣṇa gives the direction to the whole *Gītā* with this one truth to awaken Arjuna from his delusory incompletions. Kṛṣṇa is the true Master and does not beat around the bush. Understand that Kṛṣṇa is not a philosopher; He addresses the dilemma of Arjuna straightaway.

Kṛṣṇa asks Arjuna directly, 'How did such impurities, such incompletions come upon you? They are not for a man like you. They will not lead you to higher planes but only defame you.' In the next verse He asks Arjuna to give up this powerlessness and asks him to arise, addressing him as '*Parantapa*, destroyer of the enemy.'

Kṛṣṇa knows Arjuna's root thought pattern. Please understand that Arjuna is not depressed because of a spiritual search. It is just that he does not want a solution; he wants only support.

Understand, asking for solutions and asking for support are two different things. What Arjuna needs is support, not a solution. This is why Kṛṣṇa does not speak of spirituality in these two verses. Arjuna's root thought pattern originates from fear and worry. His *maṇipūraka cakra* (navel center) and *svādiṣṭhāna cakra* (being center), energy centers that get locked due to worry and fear, are now completely locked! Because of his fear pattern, he has deep seated incompletions, stress and worry.

Kṛṣṇa addresses Arjuna's deep fear and powerlessness straightaway without any philosophy, and asks him to give up his foolish weakness and get up and fight—*tyaktvottiṣṭha parantapa*. He does not offer any consolation, just a straightforward scolding, and a slap to awaken him!

KṚṢṆA HITS ARJUNA'S ROOT PATTERN

If Arjuna had been in a mood of *stotra,* meaning devotional surrender that he reaches only later on, these two verses would have served as *sūtra* or techniques for him. Had he been without fear and expressed full faith and devotion in Kṛṣṇa, these two verses would have been enough to wake him up and stand powerfully.

At this point, Arjuna is in the state to be intellectually convinced and Kṛṣṇa employs *śāstra* as the right approach. Since he was not in the mood of *stotra,* not yet ready with devotion and faith, Kṛṣṇa had to create the *śāstra* or method, to bring him to the *stotra* state. The whole issue was due to his root pattern of fear plus worry and powerlessness because of this fear.

All our depression, worry patterns are nothing but root pattern of a deep fear of life, a deep self-doubt, fear of expansion and fear of losing something. You need to stand up and complete with your root thought patterns to be rid of them. Please understand, even your ignorance is nothing but your fear of expansion. Many times, you continue to pretend to be in ignorance, because of your fear of failure.

There are many levels of fear: fear of losing our wealth and status, fear of losing a limb or our health, fear of losing our near and dear ones and fear of the unknown or death. That is why Kṛṣṇa says that Arjuna is not behaving as an *ārya*, a word that can be interpreted as a nobleman; an integrated human, not a particular race or caste. Vedic literatures say that an *ārya* is one who is evolved, cultured, integrated and authentic, a prince amongst men.

Arjuna is confronted with all the four fears: fear that he may lose whatever he possesses, that he may be maimed in the war, that he may lose his near and dear ones, and fourth, that he may lose his very life. These fears have in turn led to his powerlessness of heart. Understand, all your fears, all your anxieties, all your patterns are directed only in one line—fear of your possibilities!

Listen!

Your bigness frightens you. You always believe that you are suffocated by your smallness. NO! You are suffocated by your bigness! Whenever bigness is demanded of you, whenever you feel you are being 'forced' to expand, you shrink even further into your comfort zone. Arjuna's tiredness, his weakness, his powerlessness all these are nothing but the resistance he has to seeing his own bigness!

That is why, when someone tells you that you are weak, poor and a sinner, it is so easy to accept it. But if someone tells you that you are Divine, you are powerful, you are complete, your whole identity starts trembling with fear! Arjuna trembles and collapses totally fearing his bigness, shrinking into his weak-heartedness!

But life always demands your expansion, because expansion is the natural law of life. Here, Kṛṣṇa, the source of life, demands Arjuna to stand up and expand into his powerfulness, and give up his degrading powerlessness unbefitting an *ārya* prince, who is also famous as *parantapa*, conqueror of enemies.

But Arjuna is carrying such a deep fear of life, especially fear of life in the form of other people—because people are the most living expression of Life! The whole Kaurava army and his dear ones are the people who now represent his deepest fears of life.

Listen! The more you engage with life, the greater the expansion that will be demanded of you. Whenever you are feeling weak, tired, and powerless, the first thing you should do is this: immediately take on ten responsibilities and commit to fulfill them within an impossibly short time! Shake your inner space so powerfully with that commitment that there will be no way for weakness and tiredness to grow inside you.

Kṛṣṇa directly addresses this weakness, powerlessness in Arjuna and the fear of life in the form of his kinsmen with the *śāstra*, the explanation of wisdom that is directed to the head, the intellect. He shakes Arjuna's inner space demanding of him to take up the responsibility to stand up and commit to powerfully uproot all his impossibilities, and fight—

tyaktvottiṣṭha parantapa!

Later on in the *Gītā*, in the eleventh chapter, after beholding Kṛṣṇa's cosmic vision, Arjuna realizes who Kṛṣṇa truly is; that He is beyond everything and beyond his imagination, his comprehension. He is not surprised any longer that all the deities worship Him and surrender to Him. Kṛṣṇa then repeats the same words that He says now, after which the *Gītā* ends and Arjuna engages in the war.

These same words uttered by Kṛṣṇa later on, when Arjuna is in the state of *stotra*, a state of pure devotion and faith, become the *sūtra*, the technique of enlightenment for Arjuna. Listen! When you are in devotion, you will just live life. You will not have any fear. Fear is always out of powerlessness. When you are in love, you will not know anything called fear or worry. That stage is yet to happen. Since Arjuna is not yet in the devotional state now, these words are only plain wisdom.

Kṛṣṇa is not a philosopher; He is a personification of enlightenment, of infinite powerfulness. All philosophy is an attempt to convince the other to do what the philosopher wants of him. Philosophers are the most dangerous people who invent logical reasons that encage, enslave or engage you to follow their words. Here Kṛṣṇa straightaway enriches by giving the conclusion directly to Arjuna. However, as Arjuna is not in the complete space to receive it because he is not mature enough to assimilate it, Kṛṣṇa needs to give Arjuna the experience.

Please listen! When you started having a root pattern, when you first had powerlessness, after that you never grow. Arjuna's age is sealed mentally. Physically he may be a grown-up, as a warrior among warriors, but mentally his age is sealed. Only when Kṛṣṇa gives the experience of His own space of completion to Arjuna, he expands; he becomes powerful, he matures into a ripened enlightened soul.

There is a beautiful story in the *Upaniṣads*:

> A disciple goes to the Master and asks, 'O master! Teach me *atmajñāna*, knowledge of inner Self.'
>
> The Master says, 'Thou art that! *Tattvamasi*. You are God.'

> The disciple, unable to believe this, thinks to himself, 'How can I be God? I am still afraid of my wife. I have all these problems and a thousand questions!'

Only when the Master proves to him that the Master himself is God, the disciple trusts the Master's words.

The Master needs to first prove that he is God in order to make you understand that you are God. Here Kṛṣṇa does the same thing by repeating that He is all of this. Kṛṣṇa later explains His glory and that all the deities, *Vedas*, the scriptural wisdom, are worshipping at His feet; the whole world is in Him. He makes these incredible statements that would appear egoistic to a normal person. And yet Kṛṣṇa says all this, even at the risk of being misunderstood. He repeats that *He is God* to make you realize that *you are God.*

With authority He states, '*I am God*' to make you realize that *you are God.*

Continuously human beings resist expansion. **Incarnations happen on the planet to remind human beings about their possibilities, to expand human consciousness.** That is why again and again they are doubted. Arjuna is *Nara*, human being who resists his expansion, and Śrī Kṛṣṇa is *Nārāyaṇa*, Divine Incarnate who reminds him of his highest possibility of expansion—that he is God, that *Nara* is the reflection of *Nārāyaṇa*, who is mirroring the infinite inner space of God!

You would not believe the words of ordinary people. You need to listen to the words from a source of authority that has the right to say them. Here Kṛṣṇa says the same words that He repeats throughout the entire *Gītā.* But as of now Arjuna is not able to take it all in. It is too much for him to grasp in his present condition.

Once Kṛṣṇa proves His divinity, Arjuna believes His words and is ready to follow them. Similarly, when masters prove their divinity and express great powers or miracles of their energies, they do not do so for their ego satisfaction. They do them to prove that they are God, so that you believe their words and experience that you are God.

Understand: when I am expressing the *aṣṭa-mahā-siddhis*, extraordinary eight yogic powers, it is not to show that I am extraordinary; it is just to show that it is possible for you! Nothing more is required than carrying the space of possibility, with the understanding—'When *Swamiji* can do it, I can do it!' That's all!

It is the authority with which Kṛṣṇa is seen transmitting the *Gītā* that makes it a scripture. **'I am the Divine,' says Kṛṣṇa. 'If you believe in Me, you too shall realize your inner divinity.'** It is this profound and yet simple message that has resounded so deeply in the hearts, minds and beings of generations of Hindus, in turn establishing the scriptural sanctity of the *Gītā*.

Possibility of Sudden Enlightenment

Here all the verses of the *Gītā* are reduced to just two verses by Kṛṣṇa.

He straightaway addresses and completes the root pattern where Arjuna is stuck, that is in his need for name and fame or *rajas*. A man who is centered on *satva*, goodness, who has neither greed nor lethargy but a neutral attitude, will work out of compassion. A man who is centered on *rajas* will work only for name and fame. A man who is centered on *tamas*, lethargy, will work only for sensual pleasures.

Duryodhana works only through *tamas*, which explains his cruel and gross behavior. *Dharmarāja Yudhiṣṭira* works on *satva*, out of compassion. Here Arjuna is centered on *rajas*, therefore he is working only for name and fame. This is why Kṛṣṇa asks him not to work in this way as it would ultimately bring Arjuna a bad name, *akīrti karam arjuna*. This is how He straightaway puts His hand on the tumor, the tumor that is the subtle root pattern working within Arjuna.

Fortunately for us, Arjuna is not intelligent enough. Or rather, he acts as if he is not intelligent enough to understand these words. He has lived with Kṛṣṇa for more than thirty years in close friendship and must have intelligence. He puts his questions and doubts not for himself but for enriching the future generations and for the whole of humankind.

Most of the time our problems are very simple. It is we who

complicate them. Our patterns are not as big as we think they are. When we verbalize, analyze, label and associate with them as impossibilities, we have created a whole new problem that had not existed earlier in our being.

You have only one mind. You can either use it to enrich yourself in solving the problem, or it will naturally enslave you in creating more problems. Understand that if you are not solving your existing problems, you will be creating more problems. At the level of the mind, there is no position of simply standing, no status quo—you either climb or fall, you are either in space of possible or impossible!

Here Kṛṣṇa straightaway addresses Arjuna's root pattern. Kṛṣṇa is not creating any philosophy but gives the answer straightaway in just one line. However, as Arjuna is not mature enough because of his root pattern, he has to be given an intellectual explanation of his possibility.

All Western philosophies begin with logical analysis and end with the conclusion. All Eastern processes begin with the conclusion and then give the analysis. Eastern masters are compassionate. They first give us the option of grasping the solution, if we have the intelligence. They expect us to transform with just the trust in them. If we don't have this qualification of grasping and trusting, they have no other option but to go into detailed explanation, they start the regular process.

Here Kṛṣṇa tries the first method of sudden enlightenment, the immediate liberation, the ultimate possibility but Arjuna is not mature enough to receive it or comprehend it. So Kṛṣṇa now starts the process of explaining it to him step- by-step.

Kṛṣṇa is God and So are You!

There are two ways in which people react to the sanctity and divinity of Kṛṣṇa in *Bhagavad Gītā*. To one set of people, Kṛṣṇa has no special qualification to be called divine and these people may not even believe in anything such as the Divine. As atheists or agnostics, the only way such people can be convinced is initially through the rationale of the dialogue in the *Gītā*. The dialogue surpasses anything written in any language at any point in time in its clarity and wisdom. The message of Kṛṣṇa is universal and timeless. Those who do not accept and understand, it just means that as of now, it is not their time to understand and transform.

The laws of nature do not change just because we do not accept and understand them. The earth was always round and never flat and it always revolved around the sun, even when the societal leaders denied these truths and killed people for expounding these truths.

There is another class of people who say that there is only Kṛṣṇa, who is divine and all other divine manifestations have no relevance. One such group of people came to me after I had spoken on the *Gītā*, very perturbed.

They said, 'From what you say, we see that you accept the divinity of Kṛṣṇa.'

I said, 'Yes, I very much do. He is the *Pūrṇāvatār*, the complete incarnation.'

They complained, 'Then how can you worship Śiva in your *ashram*? We believe you have a Dakśināmūrti (Śiva) temple in your Bidadi ashram in India. How can you do this?'

I asked them, 'Have you read *Anu Gītā* which is also another part of Mahābhārat?' They said, 'No.'

I then explained to them about *Anu Gītā*: After the war, Arjuna and Kṛṣṇa are together and Arjuna says, 'Dear Kṛṣṇa, I do not remember all of what you taught me at the battlefield, when you delivered the *Gītā* to me. Can you please enlighten me again?'

Kṛṣṇa says, 'Oh, you have forgotten? I too have forgotten what I then said!' Arjuna exclaims, 'Kṛṣṇa, how is that possible?'

Kṛṣṇa says, 'At that point I was *Parabrahma* Kṛṣṇa, the universal Kṛṣṇa. I was Bhagavān, Superconsciousness. I was the Divine. Now, I am *Vāsudeva* Kṛṣṇa, son of Vāsudeva. So, I do not remember what I spoke to you as

Parabrahma Kṛṣṇa. I shall try and remember.'

What he remembered and recounted was *Anu Gītā*. Kṛṣṇa, as *Parabrahma* Kṛṣṇa, is the Divine energy, the formless *Brahman*, the same as Śiva, Viṣṇu or Devī. He is the ultimate Truth, the *Puruṣottama*, as are these other manifestations of the same Brahman.

It is only the ignorant cows of Kṛṣṇa who fight with the equally ignorant monkeys of Rāma, forgetting that Rāma and Kṛṣṇa are both the same energy.

The constant, repetitive reference to *Bhagavān* in the *Gītā* is to emphasize this point that Kṛṣṇa is not just the mere charioteer of Arjuna, *Pārthasārathi*, or *Keśava*, destroyer of the demon Keśin or *Madhusūdana*, destroyer of the demon Madhu, but that He is *Parabrahma* Kṛṣṇa, the Supreme Energy, who is formless and nameless. This is also to reinforce the satya, truth that you too, like Arjuna, are God and no less.

Understanding the divinity of Kṛṣṇa is a step to intranalysing and living one's own divinity. That possibility of divinity is what completes and liberates. That is why Ādī Śankaracārya, the great Incarnation sings in Bhaja Govindaṁ, 'Even a little reading of the *Bhagavad Gītā* will liberate you from death.'

Surrender Is Not Based On Powerlessness

2.4 *Arjuna says:*
O Madhusūdana (killer of demon, Madhu), how can I oppose in battle, Bhīśma and Droṇa, who are worthy of my worship?

2.5 *I would rather beg for my food in this world*
than kill the most noble of teachers.
If I kill them, all my enjoyment of wealth and
desires will be stained with blood.

2.6 *I cannot say which is better; their defeating us or us defeating them.*
We do not wish to live after slaying the sons of Dhṛtaṛāṣṭra who stand before us.

2.7 *My heart is overwhelmed with pity and my mind is confused about what my duty is. I beg of You, please tell me what is best for me.*
I am your disciple. Instruct me, as I seek refuge in You.

2.8 *Even if I were to attain unrivalled dominion and*
prosperity on Earth or even lordship over the Gods,
How would that remove this sorrow that burns my senses?

Despite what Kṛṣṇa had said with total clarity, that Arjuna should get up and fight, Arjuna now recounts all his previous arguments. It is as if he had not listened to Kṛṣṇa at all.

He once again implores Kṛṣṇa, 'You, as the Lord of the Universe, have the right to destroy what you please. As the Lord, You destroyed the demons Madhu and Keśin and many other enemies. How can I, a mere mortal, be bold enough to wage war against my grandfather and my teacher, with the intent to kill them? They are ones I should worship, not destroy. I shall be condemned if I fight them.'

Take Decisions out of Completion

Arjuna is now pleading Kṛṣṇa, 'Oh Lord, leave me now! I will beg and eat becoming a *Sannyāsi*.' He continues, 'It is better for me to seek alms as an ascetic or even a beggar than kill these elders—*śreyo bhoktuṁ bhaikṣyam apīha loke* (2.5). Once my hands are stained with their blood, how can I enjoy worldly pleasures? I am confused as to which would be better, for them to slay me or for me to slay them, *yadvā jayema yadivā no jayeyuḥ* (2.6). How can we live after slaying our kinsmen and elders?—*yān eva hatvā na jijīviṣāmas*.'

Understand, Bhagavān is not against Arjuna's *Sannyāsa*. He does not want Arjuna to take *Sannyās* out of powerlessness.

Arjuna says, 'Oh Lord, leave me. I will beg and eat—*bhoktuṁ bhaikṣyam*.' No! I tell you, Arjuna would not have become a sannyāsī. He would have gone and asked for food in a royal way, 'Hey, give me food.' If somebody doesn't give, he would have picked up his *gāṇḍiva* bow and arrow to shoot the person for his food.

To become a *Sannyāsi*, Śrī Kṛṣṇa says, 'Go to *Sannyāsa* out of completion.' Bhagavān is only saying one thing, 'Out of completion, take any decision. Out of completion, take any decision!'

Listen. Bhagavān denies Arjuna even his decision to take *Sannyāsa* because Arjuna takes that decision out of powerless pattern. He accepts Arjuna's decision to fight, because he took the decision out of powerfulness, completion! Whether it is *Sannyās* or fight, powerlessness never leads your life to any next steps.

Arjuna says further, 'Now I am confused about my duty and have lost all composure because of misery and weakness—*kārpaṇya doṣhopahata svabhāvaḥ* (2.7). I can see no solution to my dilemma. Even if I slay these people and gain control over the earth, or even control over the heavens, what good will it do me? In this condition, I ask you to tell me, for certain, what is best for me, *yat śreyaḥ syān niścitaṁ brūhi tanme*. Now I am your disciple and the soul is surrendered unto you. Please instruct me—*śiṣyas te'haṁ sādhi māṁ tvāṁ prapannam* (2.7).'

I must now tell you an important truth.

Here Arjuna says, 'My soul is surrendered unto you—*māṁ tvāṁ prapannam*.' This is a lie. Had his soul been truly surrendered to Kṛṣṇa, he would simply have followed what Kṛṣṇa said and would not have waited for an intellectual explanation.

Arjuna says his soul is surrendered to Kṛṣṇa but when Kṛṣṇa asks him to do His bidding, he is not ready to do so and is confused! Surrender out of confusion is not surrender, as you do not even know if you are doing the right thing.

Understand that surrender after clarity, intelligence of *śāstras*, out of completion, is true surrender.

Here Arjuna surrenders only verbally as he says that he is confused, that his mind is bewildered, *sammūḍha cetāh*. You must either do what you think is right or do as the Master instructs. Here Arjuna wants the Master to say what he wants to hear, not what the Master wants to say. So, although Arjuna says he has surrendered, he has not done so.

Time and again, people come to me for advice and ask, '*Swamiji*, I have this problem. Please advise me what to do. Whatever you tell me I shall do.' Then, if I ask them to come to the ashram for a few days or attend a meditation course, they give me a dozen reasons why it cannot be done. Some even say, '*Swamiji*, the time has to be right before we do that. Perhaps the time is not right.' Nonsense..simply nonsense! Understand, you are not controlled by some unknown destiny that you can conveniently blame just because you cannot do something right. Your destiny is in *your* own hands. Each one of you has the power to decide what you want to do, what you want to create. So does Arjuna!

Arjuna is asking Kṛṣṇa to tell him what he needs to do in the same way that I just described how people come and ask me. Kṛṣṇa knows this only too well. However, only out of compassion, Kṛṣṇa continues to enrich, express and teach him the Truth.

Here begins the *śāstras*. The two verses that Kṛṣṇa speaks bidding Arjuna to give up his powerlessness and stand up and fight are *sūtra*, techniques. But as Arjuna is not ready to receive them, he has to commence the *śāstra*, the background knowledge.

Kṛṣṇa, fully aware of Arjuna's dilemma, moves forward in his mission to destroy Arjuna's identity, the root pattern. The Guru, Master is a surgeon who removes the cancer of ego, the root thought pattern. This is what Kṛṣṇa does throughout the *Gītā* dialogue. To give Arjuna credit, he stays through this surgery. Many weaker men would have run away from the operation theatre, this battlefield, with no desire to let go of their identities. Arjuna's greatness lies in his integrity, his powerful determination, his decision to listen to his Master and be guided by Him.

Arjuna Decides to Surrender Powerlessness

So, Arjuna implores his Master, 'Kṛṣṇa, please tell me what to do. I am your disciple. You are my refuge.'

Arjuna's integrity lies also in not making any decision when he is feeling powerless. When you are in the space of powerlessness, the only one decision you have to make is to come out of powerlessness. No other decision should be made. When you are in powerlessness, any decision made leads to more and more powerlessness, more and more suffering.

In his deepest powerless moments, the only decision Arjuna takes is to come out of his powerlessness. He declares to Kṛṣṇa that he is His disciple and exposes his inauthenticies to Kṛṣṇa. It is this readiness to surrender to the Master that brings completion to Arjuna and enriches him to take the responsibility to win the war, which in reality is the war within himself. This is the war that each one of us is fighting each day with our powerlessness, if we are truly aware. This is the war that we need to fight to drop our root pattern, our mind, and the identity that binds us to all the bondages upon this earth.

Listen! Whatever you think is yours and whatever you think is you, is different from the truth. It is the Master who can lead you through the path of self-completion, as Kṛṣṇa is now leading Arjuna. To be led, you need the attitude of surrender, the decision to surrender your powerlessness.

We Never Cease To Exist

2.9 *Sañjaya said:*
Guḍākeśa (Arjuna) then said to Hṛṣīkeśa (Kṛṣṇa),
'Govinda, I shall not fight,' and fell silent.

2.10 *Then, Hṛṣīkeśa, Kṛṣṇa smilingly spoke the following words to*
the grief-stricken Arjuna, as they were placed
in the midst of both armies.

2.11 *Bhagavān said:*
You grieve for those who should not be grieved for and yet,
you speak words of wisdom.
The wise grieve neither for the living nor for the dead.

2.12 *Never was there a time when I did not exist;*
nor did you, nor all these rulers,
And nor shall any of us ever cease to be hereafter.

2.13 *Just as the spirit in this body passes through childhood,*
youth and old age, so does it pass into another body;
the man centered within himself does not fear this,
or deluded by this .

Even though it is written here in the past tense, I feel Kṛṣṇa should always be addressed in the present tense. He is still relevant, present to each of us today. We cannot say, 'Kṛṣṇa was' but 'Kṛṣṇa *is*', not 'Kṛṣṇa said' but 'Kṛṣṇa *says.*'

Once again, having lamented about what he is being forced to do, and not wishing to do what he is expected to do, Arjuna, like a petulant child sits down saying, 'Govinda, I am not going to fight, *na yotsya iti govindam* (2.9).' It is as if Arjuna is waiting to be persuaded. He is seeking an explanation.

Kṛṣṇa says to him gently and smilingly, 'While speaking learned words, you are mourning for what is not worthy of grief—*aśocyān anvāśocas tvaṁ prajñā-vādāṁś ca bhāṣase*. Those who are wise lament neither for the living nor for the dead—*gatāsūn agatāsūṁś ca nānuśocanti paṇḍitāḥ* (2.11).'

Again, Kṛṣṇa addresses Arjuna's incompletion directly, 'O Arjuna! You speak as if you are intelligent, enlightened, *prajñā-vādāṁś*.' You speak the words without having experienced them. Therefore, your words do not carry conviction. Your emotion, your being, shows that you are not enlightened, that you have not understood. A truly enlightened person will never worry for the living or the dead.' If you worry for somebody living or dead, you cannot be an intelligent person. What is death and life after all? There are thousands, rather millions, who have lived and gone.

Kṛṣṇa's first enriching words are Sāṅkhya

See the brilliance of Śrī Kṛṣṇa! He is so soaked in the space of completion. The moment Kṛṣṇa opens His mouth, the first truth that comes out from Him is *Sāṅkhya Yogaḥ*. I can be sure that Kṛṣṇa is filled with Kapila.

Kṛṣṇa is the greatest follower of *Sāṅkhya Yogaḥ*. Please understand, when you are in a crisis, the first few words you utter are the words with which you solve your own problem. When somebody asks you for advice, what comes up first? The words that you use to enrich yourself, will only come out to enrich others. Understand, if suddenly, if I am forced to solve a problem, the first solution that will come out of my mind will be the solution or philosophy with which I am solving my own problems.

So, Śrī Kṛṣṇa Himself is not a *bhakti yogi*. *Bhakti yoga* comes only from His archives. From His table, only *Sāṅkhya Yoga* comes. You may be a master of the books that you have in the archives, but the books you have on your table have mastered you! That is why they are occupying your table. They are master for you.

Please listen! I can be sure that Kṛṣṇa is more shocked than Arjuna because He has never seen this dimension of Arjuna—shivering, shaking! It was a shock even for Kṛṣṇa when Arjuna drops his *Gāṇḍiva* bow and says, 'I am not interested in fighting!' Kṛṣṇa has never seen this powerless, weak side of Arjuna. See, trusting Arjuna, He went all the way as a peace ambassador to the assembly of Kauravas. The great war of Mahābhārat was the first World War because at that time, the whole of humanity, fifty-four deśas (countries) were divided into two parts. The whole world was participating. Either you are on the side of Duryodhana, the Kaurava clan or on the side of Arjuna, the Pāṇḍava clan.

And suddenly, Arjuna is saying, 'I am not waging the war!' How will you handle this? How Kṛṣṇa feels! Everyone knows Kṛṣṇa may not be in the front, but He is running the whole show, the whole war play! So, Kṛṣṇa is completely cornered now. He has to solve Arjuna's problem.

The first idea with which Kṛṣṇa is sorting out Arjuna's problem is Sāṅkhya Yoga. This means Kṛṣṇa Himself was practicing Sāṅkhya Yoga. He is a person established in the knowledge of completion!

It is important to understand the rules of Existence, of the Divine. Only the ignorant worry about people who are living or dead. A truly intelligent person does not bother about death.

Often people ask me, 'How was the Universe created? Was it by Brahma, as Hindu scriptures say? From my personal experience, I say to them what Buddha said thousands of years ago based on His personal perception. 'The Universe,' Buddha said, 'has neither been created nor will it ever be destroyed. It always has been.' The Universe created itself. It is the creation that embodies the creator and results in what has been created. Our questions regarding the 'right' and 'wrong' of what happens around us arise only when they threaten us. These questions, these issues about the morality of the Universe, spring forth only when our ego, our identity is threatened, when our life is threatened.

The creator is also the destroyer. What is created will be destroyed. We have no agreement with God that when we are born we will be assured of so many years of life along with the knowledge of the timing and nature of our death.

You are Responsible for Everything

When you truly realize your Self, when you are complete, enlightened, you will be aware of when you will die and how you will die. It will then make no difference to you whether your body is alive or dead. Living and dying are no longer issues in which you feel you need to play a part. They are progressions of nature and being enlightened and complete, you flow with Nature.

We are just playing with words when we talk about *karma* and destiny, saying that they are responsible for everything that happens to us. Let me tell you this: We are responsible for everything that happens in and around us. We are responsible for what we do. It is a misrepresentation of Nature's law of responsibilism to blame nature for what happens to us.

When you take responsibility for how you think and feel, instead of leaving the responsibility to destiny, society, media and others, if you take the responsibility, you can awaken your inner power of leadership, you can make your non-mechanical parts of the brain to function. Listen! When you don't take responsibility, others take it on their own and make you a follower. Society and all other power-hungry people who are interested in controlling you, take the responsibility for your body, mind and brain if you don't take the responsibility.

Some people question, 'Is it fair that we are held responsible for what we did in another lifetime and are not even aware of now?' What do we know of fairness except what we determine to be fair out of our own selfishness?

It is possible to be conscious of previous births; it is even possible to have a conscious birth, coming into this world fully conscious and aware. For that to happen, we need to drop our root thought pattern and merge with Nature. We need to responsibly surrender our existence to Nature. When we do so, Nature responds and opens up. Listen, when you take responsibility for all the happenings in and around you, a new energy and a new possibility opens up in you. The first step to realize the divine in you is to take responsibility. Decide whether you are reason or not, you are taking responsibility for all happenings in and around you, because it is affecting you!

YOU EXIST IN PAST, PRESENT AND FUTURE

Sañjaya says Kṛṣṇa was smiling as He uttered these words. Kṛṣṇa must have been laughing at Arjuna. 'You fool; you pretend to be wise and quote the scriptures. Who do you think you are quoting the scriptures to? What can you understand of what I Myself have said?'

Kṛṣṇa continues: 'Never was there a time when I did not exist, nor you and all these kings, and never in the future shall any of us cease to be.'

na tv evāhaṁ jātu nāsaṁ na tvaṁ neme janādhipāḥ |
na caiva na bhaviṣyāmaḥ sarve vayam ataḥ paraṁ || 2.12

With this verse begins the essence of the whole *Gītā*. This is *ātmajñāna*, Self-Realization, the knowledge of completion. If you can understand this one verse, you can become enlightened straightaway and enter into eternal bliss.

If you think our souls will also die with our bodies, you are wrong. We were there before our birth and will remain after death. It is not true that any of us will not be in the future.

Listen. You existed in the past, exist in the present and will exist in the future. Your face and body may change but you continue to exist. Then why do we think we will die and why do we fear death? If what Kṛṣṇa says is true, why are we worried about this life and about death? You need to first understand the concept of the past, present and future to enable you to understand what Kṛṣṇa says.

Let me explain this concept of time first.

Time is like a shaft continuously moving from the future on the right into the past on the left (see diagram). The future is on your right and the past is on your left. The future is continuously moving into the past; every moment and every second it is turning into the past. The present is the point where the future and the past meet. Your mind as such is nothing

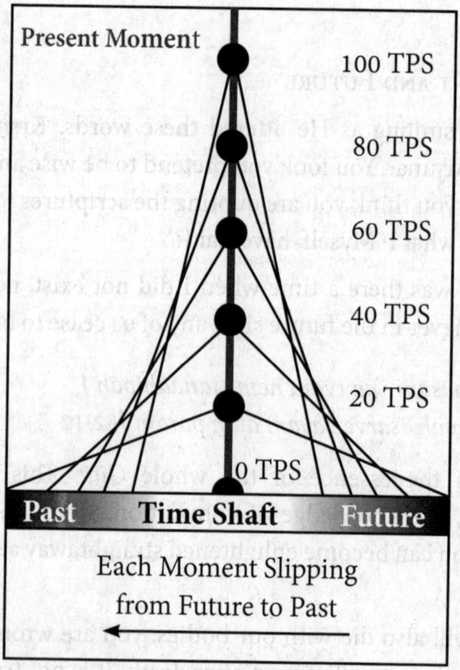

but movements between the past and the future.

You cannot have any thoughts if you stop thinking about the past and the future. Your thoughts consist of nothing but the constant movements between the past and the future. The more your thoughts shift from past to future or future to past, the higher the frequency of thoughts. The less you shift from past to future or future to past, the lesser the number of thoughts. Try to think of something in the present, you will find that you cannot. You can think of it only by taking it into the past or future. You are either worrying about the future or remembering the past.

The higher the frequency of thoughts, the more you are caught in the physical and material world. For example, if you have 100 Thoughts Per Second (TPS,) it means you have jumped 100 times back and forth between the past and future in one second! If you have 80 TPS, it means you have jumped 80 times between these two dimensions. The higher the frequency, the more you will be away from the present and more problems you have. If the number of thoughts reduces, you fall into the present moment.

The past, present and future, all the three put together are eternal, *Nitya* or *Ātman*. Only when you come to the present moment do you experience *Ātman*—your true Self, but as of now you are constantly shuttling between the past and future. When the number of thoughts reduces, you will not even be aware of the passage of time. For example, when you are with someone you love, even two or three hours will seem like a short while. But, when you are with someone whose company is boring, even a short time seems very long.

Time is more psychological than chronological. That is why, in our scriptures or *Vedas*, we have the word *kṣaṇa* to describe the unit of time. *Kṣaṇa* does not denote one second, but is defined as the gap or time interval between two thoughts. The larger the *kṣaṇa* or the gap between two thoughts, the more in the present we are. Each person's *kṣaṇa* will be different depending on how busy his mind is! When our TPS is lower, we will naturally be in completion, in ecstasy, in bliss. When the number of our thoughts is high, we are in hell. Hell and heaven are nothing but the number of thoughts that we entertain, that's all. That is why I say heaven and hell are not geographical places, but psychological spaces.

With a higher frequency of thoughts, you think you are the body. When the frequency of thoughts reduces, you think you are the mind and just emotion. When the thoughts become zero, you realize you are *Ātman*, Self; you exist in the past, present and future. Only a man who's TPS is zero can realize what Kṛṣṇa says—You will be there forever. But now, as the frequency of thoughts is very high, you do not have the patience or energy to undestand who you are and your nature.

Kṛṣṇa says beautifully, 'You were there in the past, you are in the present and you will be in the future; you do not die. You existed before birth and will remain after death. Whatever dies, can never live. Whatever lives can never die.' When Kṛṣṇa says, 'You are the eternal soul,' He means that as a being, you are beyond time.

Here, your deep consciousness says that something is living in you. This quality you wrongly attribute to your body and mind. You are not the body or the mind. As long as you are caught in the past and the future incompletions, you think that you are the body-mind. The moment you come down to the present moment, you are in the eternal space of completion, you experience that you are beyond the body, beyond the mind.

COMPLETION, THE ETERNAL SPACE IN THE PRESENT

Please listen! Anything which does not allow, anything which stands in between you and the present moment, acting as a barrier; which does not allow you to connectcompletely with life and with other people in your life in the present moment, is what I call incompletion.

So, the first thing you need to do in life is bring completion. Kṛṣṇa does not mean that we existed in the form that we are here now, or that He was present always as Kṛṣṇa in the form we imagine Him to be, with a flute and a peacock feather. He means that our spirits which are eternal, always existed and will always exist. In our spiritual state, that of our soul, we are divine, one with the universal energy, Brahman.

The gist of the second chapter, *Sāṅkhya Yogaḥ* is that you are the soul, that you are complete, that you are divine and that you are God.

Completion is the only methodology where you can complete with your past and future incompletions. You need to know that when you do completion now, don't think that only your future will be in completion and complete. No! Even your past gets altered. Even your past becomes complete! The moment you create the space of completion, what Kṛṣṇa declares, 'you are the eternal soul, beyond your body and mind,' becomes reality in your life.

Kṛṣṇa is established in the space of *Sāṅkhya* knowledge. Kapila Muni, the founder of *Sāṅkhya*, does not elaborately talk about God, but he talks about the methodology to reach God. *Sāṅkhya* does not speak about God, because completion itself is given the place of God. Please understand, *Sāṅkhya* does not have the system of God because the methodology to reach God is made as God. It is a lifestyle. The methodology of completion is God. Completion is God!

Even as the spirit resides in this body, the body passes through its seasons of childhood, youth, middle age and old age as the seasons of Nature do in each year. Finally, it passes through death, and then reappears, just as trees shed leaves in autumn and produce new leaves in spring.

Transition of the spirit through the body as it ages is no different from the transition of time through the seasons. One does not grieve as one enjoys the pleasures of childhood, youth and middle age. Why then should one grieve the onset of old age and then death? At death, the spirit passes from one body into another body. It has three *kṣaṇa* to achieve this, each *kṣaṇa* being the time period between thoughts. A person who is in a high thought frequency, a high TPS state, has a much shorter time to shift from one body to another. A person in a no-mind, no-thought state has infinite time, as the time between thoughts is infinite. His spirit is at liberty to stay free without taking another body as long as he chooses, or more correctly, as the universe chooses. All Enlightened Masters are in this category. When the spirit leaves the mind-body system, it becomes one with the Universal Energy.

Imagine a number of circles drawn on a whiteboard. Think of the whiteboard space as the universal energy. Individual body-mind systems are represented by the circles drawn on the whiteboard. The white space enclosed in the circles is the spirit and this is the same energy as the white space outside the circles. The space within or inner space is the individual soul, *Ātman* and the outer space is *Brahman*.

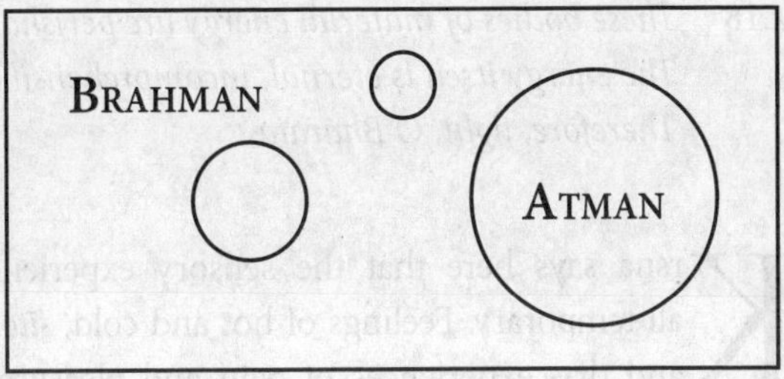

When a body-mind dies, when an individual dies, all that happens is that these perimeter lines get erased, that is all. The space within the circle merges with the space outside the circle. White merges with white. Energy merges with energy.

When the spirit, the energy, is ready to move into another mind-body system, it enters another circle. It is a continuous, ongoing process and a natural process. One who cognizes this process and accepts it is an integrated and authentic person living in the space of completion. Kṛṣṇa refers to him as '*dhīraḥ*', one who is firm, centered, aware, and complete.

The Only Reality Is Impermanence

2.14 *O Kaunteya (son of Kuntī), contact with sense objects causes heat and cold, pleasure and pain, and these have a beginning and an end. O Bhārata, these are not permanent; endure them bravely.*

2.15 *O Purṣurṣabha, chief among men, these surely do not afflict*
the brave person who is centered and complete,
Pleasure and pain are the same to him and
he is certainly ready for immortality, amṛtatvā.

2.16 *The non-existent (asat) has no being;*
that which exists (sat) never ceases to exist;
This truth about both is perceived and concluded
by the Seers of Truth.

2.17 *Know It to be indestructible, by which all this body is pervaded.*
Nothing can destroy It, the Imperishable.

2.18 *These bodies of material energy are perishable.*
The energy itself is eternal, incomprehensible and indestructible.
Therefore, fight, O Bhārata.

Kṛṣṇa says here that the sensory experiences, *mātrā-sparśhaḥ* are all temporary. Feelings of hot and cold, *śītoṣṇa*, sweet and sour, wet and dry, experiences of pain and pleasure, *sukha-duḥkha*, as well as other experiences of like and dislike are all temporary, *anityāḥ*. These experiences do not affect the centered person who is qualified to be enlightened, *so amṛtatvāya kalpate*.

These sensory experiences are *anitya* or impermanent and unreal. Moreover, they are relative. What may be considered hot by one person may not be perceived as hot by another.

There are many *sādhus* or ascetics, who stay in the higher reaches of the Himalayan mountains with least clothing; in temperatures everyone would consider bitter cold. There are those who carry out the *parikramā*, circumambulation, of Mount Kailaśa and Lake Mansarovar. Studies conducted on Tibetan Lamas in their high altitude snow-covered monasteries showhow the Lamas can bear extreme cold without any discomfort. Renowned scientists from reputed institutions such as the Harvard Medical School have conducted such studies. When Nature is accepted totally, heat, cold, rain, dryness and all these changes do not affect the body-mind system

If we walk around without footwear, the earth that we walk upon becomes our friend. As long as we wear footwear to protect ourselves from Nature, we are treating Nature as an outsider, as an enemy. One who is firmly grounded in himself is grounded in Nature. Kṛṣṇa says that such a person is qualified and ready for enlightenment. Such persons have brought their senses under control, and as a result have their mind too under control.

What Kṛṣṇa says here, and what has been experienced by the wise sages of the East for thousands of years, is only now being grasped by scientists and researchers. It is now accepted by medical science that the body-mind dies many deaths before its final exit. Cells within our body die in thousands every day and get reborn. Over a period of a few years, every single cell in the body-mind system is replaced and renewed. What you were two or three years ago is not what you are today. Every single cell in your body-mind system, and therefore, every single bone, muscle, tissue, artery, vein, limb and body part is new, completely different from what it was two or three years ago.

The body-mind continually ceases to exist and gets recreated. It is not permanent. Separate from the body-mind system is our spirit that lives on eternally. The spirit remains the same throughout our life with no change, despite all the changes in the body-mind system. It continues to be, to exist, even after our death. The spirit does not die with the body. It lives on. It is permanent and true.

When one understands this difference between what is eternal, *nitya*, and what is ephemeral, *anitya*, one becomes a seer and knower of Truth.

Make Your Perception Pure and Patternless

Nitya and *anithya* do not translate into real and unreal. In the same way *māyā* , loosely translated as illusion, is not unreal. *Māyā* and *anitya* are real and perceived by our senses but they refer to things that are not true, that are not lasting. They are factually real but truthfully unreal! That which is true will always be true; it cannot cease to exist. Truth here refers to the state of permanence, of being eternal.

I say a living master is not present as you feel, and a dead master is not absent as you think. The presence of a dead master, an enlightened dead master, is permanent and always real. A living Master's form is not His only presence. He is present in His absence as well.

Our perceptions through our senses may be real but not necessarily true. A dream is very real when it happens. You may get angry, frightened, excited, lustful, and such when you dream. Your body responds to these emotions and your senses react to what you observe in the dream. Yet the moment you start witnessing the dream, you awaken. You cannot dream when you become aware. The dream is not true, though it seemed real.

The same happens when you are awake and daydreaming, which is most of the time! You are awake but you fantasize. Even when you think you are fully awake, what you perceive through your senses may not be what you interpret it to mean. Your mind always filters through its own lens of the root pattern or ego. You judge whatever you perceive through your conditioned memories and then selectively put together pieces of what you perceive, to support your judgment.

Please listen!

> A blind man was sitting in front of a huge fire with a burning stick in his hand. Somebody came and asked him, 'What is this? Such a huge fire! Don't you see? What are you

going to do about it?'

The blind man said, 'Yes, yes! That is why I took this burning stick and put it on my eyes. Now I am not seeing the fire!'

Can that be the solution? You may laugh now, but all your solutions are usually of this type. And you even accept as your master, the fool who tells 'Take the stick and put it on your eyes!' Will not seeing the fire, solve the problem? Burning your eyes is not going to give you liberation from the scenes you are seeing. Look in! Shrinking from life is nothing but putting the burning stick in your eyes!

Just because your eyes are burnt, it does not mean that the fire will not impact you or the world will not impact you. Perception of fire is still burning from inside you, as per your experience. The innermost perception has to change. You need to realize that it is not the outside scene, but the innermost perception you carry for the outside scene, which is impacting you and giving you the experience of your reality.

I tell you, if there is fire burning and you sit at a distance and just go on gazing at the fire, you will feel the heat in your body! If you just turn your eyes away while maintaining the same distance—you will not see the burning and no more experience the burning in your body! How? The seeing has reduced the distance between you and the fire! That is perception and reality!

This is what Śrī Kṛṣṇa means when He says, 'O son of Kuntī, contact with sense objects causes heat and cold, pleasure and pain, and these have a beginning and an end.'

Understand, a pattern is any action that is unfulfilled as per your fantasy, either because of an outside hindrance or an inside hindrance, and is in incompletion!

Please listen! Now, I am defining perception.

The way your patterns react and respond to the facts is perception. Perception is nothing but processed facts. There are three levels of perception:

- No pattern, no perception—that is the worst.
- Pattern with perception—that is okay.
- Perception but with no pattern—that is the best.

I am giving you the essence of philosophy, which is a combination of your patterns and facts. If only facts are playing a hundred percent role, you don't have any pattern. These are the non-responders who are soaked in dullness. They neither have patterns nor have consciousness. The vast eleven *lakh* (one hundred and ten million) army of Kauravas signifies this dull unconscious space of '**no pattern, no perception**.' They lived in stupid materialism with their life philosophy as stupid atheism. That is why Duryodhana is never attacked by any pattern or dilemma that overpowers Arjuna.

Then, there are responders who have '**patterns with perceptions**.' The moment Arjuna sees the vast Kaurava army, his whole body and being shivers with the fear pattern. His patterns do not let him see the army as *army* and just fight as per his natural perception of himself as a warrior. No! He sees relatives, friends and teachers and wants to escape the war; he wants to shrink from life!

Ultimately, we have the Lord of all perceptions, the one with complete consciousness, Bhagavān Kṛṣṇa Himself! His very existence is the pure space of perception. He is the destroyer of all patterns, who enriches Arjuna in destroying and completing with the army of root patterns by transforming Arjuna's own perception!

Sāṅkhya, Best Enriching Philosophy of Completion

Please listen! The best enriching philosophy on the planet Earth is Kapila's *Sāṅkhya*! Do you know why? Because He has no patterns.

Kapila is established in completion—the space of pure perception! No patterns are involved in the processing of information through the senses. The fire is seen as the fire. Not even an iota of the idea of heat or cold is superimposed on it! Superimposing any idea on life takes away the joy of life.

The great news for human beings is that *māyā* (illusion) can be transformed. Perception can be transformed. You can become enlightened! O humanity! I am here to give you the great news! Perception can reach completion! When you bring completion into the perception, a moment of perception can literally bring enlightenment!

Let me give you an example. Recently I visited the cremation grounds in Vārāṇasi with a group of disciples. When we were watching the dead bodies burning in front of us for some hours, some people were just sleeping, some were affected and were feeling nauseated, and some were not at all affected by the same scene of the body burning part by part in front of our eyes. What is the difference? It is just the processing of information with patterns. The possibility of perception!

That is the reason why the great Masters have always urged their disciples to wake up. *Jāgrat* is the word used to awaken them. This is not the call to wake up from sleep but the call to wake up into completion! It is the call to emerge from the non-existent reality of processed facts or patterns into the truly existent Truth of self-experience.

Most of the time we exist in our past or future. We are constantly caught in the experiences of the past, under the excuse of learning from them. But in actuality, we are caught in guilt, regret or pleasure from remembering the past memories. The future is just as unreal as the past. Yet, we build castles, we plan, we dream, and we fantasize about the future without the capacity to execute any of it. We are not even sure we will take our next breath. How can we control events of the future when we cannot control our next breath? The futility of our constant movement between past and future and back again is the greatest wonder of all.

Now, I am giving you the best possibility of perception. Listen! Bring integrity in your thinking. Your eyes, your senses will not forget the reality even at that moment, and will not cognize heat or cold, pain or pleasure. Many times, due to lack of integrity our mind and body cognize their own facts, their own concepts.

The only truth, the only true reality, is the truth of this very moment.

As long as we are in this present moment, we have a pure perception without any patterns, only then we are truly complete and integrated. The present moment never ceases to exist. In fact, that is all that does exist. The present moment alone is *sat*, truth, everything else is *asat*, untruth.

One who realizes this truth and acts out of completion, says Kṛṣṇa, is enlightened. We are all made of body, mind and spirit. The body is tangible; we can feel its boundaries. When a part of the body is sick, we can feel the discomfort. As long as we feel the body working smoothly, we say we are in good health.

Our mind is subtle. We do not feel the mind in the same way as we feel the body. We do not feel its boundaries. Yet, we feel the effects of the mind: thoughts, desires, emotions etc. Modern scientific studies have shown that what we term as mind is spread all over the body. Mind and its intelligence are inbuilt into our cellular structure. Recent studies have shown that it is our root thought patterns not genetics, which in turn arise from our earliest experiences of powerlessness, which define the birth and development of our mind, and in turn influence the cellular structure. Earlier it was believed that genetic modifications to the cellular structure influenced the way we cognized.

The process where we perceive or receive information through five senses, internalize it with our root thought patterns, and respond based on our patterns is Cognition. Now it is proven that it is our root thought pattern that leads to our cognition and thereafter determines our genetics.

Even subtler is the spirit. In fact, many people question this entity called spirit. What it is, they ask. What is this thing called spirit or soul? We cannot see it and we cannot touch it. Becoming aware of this subtle spirit or soul is just what Self- realization is all about.

In these verses, Kṛṣṇa says first that the spirit pervades the body—*avināśi tu tad viddhi yena sarvam idaṁ tatam*. His definition of body is the body-mind system. Secondly, He states that the body and mind are destroyed at death—*antavanta ime dehā nityasyoktāḥ śārīriṇaḥ*. Thirdly,

He declares that the spirit does not die at death—*vināśam avyayasyāsya na kascit kartum arhati*. Fourthly, He explains that the spirit is beyond our mental comprehension—*anāśino 'prameyasya*.

When death happens, bodily functions stop and the senses, which are a function of the mind, stop working. The entire body-mind system is then left by itself and it degenerates. This part is clear to all of us who have seen death. What is unclear or unknown to us is that there is something within us that does not perish at death. Kṛṣṇa clarifies here that this is the Self, *Ātman*, the energy that never dies.

What is death? Is it the spirit leaving the body that causes death, or is it that death forces the spirit into leaving the body? The body-mind system is perishable, that it has a definite shelf life and comes with an expiry date. However, beyond this expiry date, there is something that lives on and that is the spirit. This spirit is energy; it is the energy of life.

Kṛṣṇa urges Arjuna to fight saying, 'Therefore, fight, O Bhārata, *tāsmad yudhyasva bharāta*', with the full understanding that what he thinks of as real is unreal, that what he thinks of as permanent, *Nitya* is impermanent, *Anitya* and what he thinks he is about to destroy can, in truth, never be destroyed.

Kṛṣṇa tells him to open his eyes and see with pure pattern less perception; that what he is about to do will only destroy that which is going to perish anyway. Even if he wants to, Arjuna cannot destroy the imperishable, *avināśi* spirit that lives on.

Arjuna's concern about the death of his kinsmen and elders arises out of his root pattern of fear and insecurity about his own death. He does not realize his true imperishable nature and therefore he is afraid of dying. By extension of this fear, he is afraid of others' deaths as well, especially at his own hands. Kṛṣṇa tells him that there is no such thing as death and that death is unreal, *anāśinaḥ*.

All our lives we see people around us dying. Death is the only certainty in this otherwise uncertain world. Everyone, whether a beggar or a prince, must die. When we wake up from a dream, we don't mourn our dream lives, as real as they felt at the time. Do we? No. In the same way, when we awaken into the highest state of consciousness, we have the same experience that this 'real' life was only a dream. There is nothing to mourn or fret over. The lineage of all enlightened masters has again and again supported Kṛṣṇa's declarations with their own direct experience. The body is just the shell that houses your spirit. Even when the body perishes, you do not. It is impossible because you are eternal, *Nitya*; you are bliss, *Ānanda*.

Kṛṣṇa is firmly stating this reality that there is no such thing as death, *nābhāvo vidyate sataḥ*. He says what dies or seems to perish is unreal, *nāsato vidyate bhāvo*; it had no permanent existence anyway. What does have existence, what is truly real, exists now, has always existed and will exist forever!

Look in! When you drill with integrity and authenticity, normal perception itself is nothing but perception of God! Because any perception will directly lead you to the space of the root of all actions, including perception! You will see that the ultimate perception, what Kṛṣṇa declares as your true nature of eternal existence and indestructible energy becomes your reality!

Sāṅkhya is reality. What exists as reality is perceived by you without the interference, perversions created by your powerless patterns. *Sāṅkhya* is the philosophy of reality—ultimate existentialism. Completion will lead you to experience that *Sāṅkhya*, the reality, existential reality—*Tattva Satya, Satya Tattva*!

You Are Immortal

2.19 *Neither understands, he who takes the Self to be slayer*
nor he who thinks he is slain.
He who knows the Truth understands that
the Self does not slay, nor is It slain.

2.20 *The Self is neither born nor does It ever die.*
After having been, It never ceases not to be.
It is Unborn, Eternal, Changeless and Ancient.
It is not killed when the body is killed.

2.21 *O Pārtha, how can man slay or cause others to be slain,*
When he knows It to be indestructible, eternal, unborn,
and unchangeable?

2.22 *Just as man casts off his worn-out clothes and puts on new ones,*
The Self casts off worn-out bodies and enters newer ones.

2.23 *Weapons do not cleave the Self, fire does not burn It,*
water does not moisten It. And wind does not dry It.

2.24 *The Self can neither be broken, nor burnt,*
nor dissolved, nor dried up.
It is Eternal, All-pervading, Stable, Immovable and Ancient.

2.25 *The Self is said to be unmanifest, unthinkable and unchangeable*
and able. Knowing this to be such, you should not grieve.

Then Kṛṣṇa is slapped with shock by Arjuna—this is the right description I will give, Kṛṣṇa wakes up! The first thing that comes out from Kṛṣṇa is *sāṅkhya yogaḥ*. In *Sāṅkhya*, you are recognized as a soul. The idea taught to you about *you* is—you cannot be cut by weapons, you cannot be burnt by fire, you cannot be made wet by water, and you cannot be blown away by air. Nothing can do 'nothing' to you. Nothing can be done to you by anything.

Understand, the moment Bhagavān is opening His mouth, you are given an amazing introduction about you!

Kṛṣṇa is one of the greatest followers of Kapila, the celebrated Incarnation of Mahādev and Viṣṇu in *Śrimad Bhāgavatam.* Kapila is the first thinking man on the planet who experienced completion, the founding father of this great *Sāṇkhya* philosophy, the founder of Mahānirvaṇi Pīṭha. That is why even when Bhagavān addresses His own glory later, when He introduces Himself, He says, '*siddhānāṁ kapilo muniḥ* (10.26)—Among the great perfect beings, the complete beings, I am Kapila.' 'I am Kapila among the *siddhas*, the great incarnations!'

Siddha means a complete being. This means that in Śrī Kṛṣṇa's time, Kapila was the star of the spiritual world. That is why He remembers Kapila. That is why I say that Bhagavān Śrī Kṛṣṇa is also the Mahāmandaleśvar (spiritual head) of Mahānirvaṇi Pīṭha. Śrī Kṛṣṇa also studied *Sāṅkhya*; He is a follower of *Sāṅkhya* philosophy.

THERE IS NO DEATH IN REALITY

Kṛṣṇa directly addresses some of Arjuna's earlier doubts in these verses. Arjuna has claimed that destroying his people, *svajanam* will bring him untold grief, not only in this world but in future births as well. Kṛṣṇa explains to Arjuna that all his fears are misplaced. There is no death in reality. What is seen as death is the destruction of the impermanent body. No one therefore can kill another person or be killed by another person. Both are illusions.

The spirit that occupies the body lives on forever. It occupies the body temporarily, but by itself the Self is eternal, indestructible, and has no births and deaths. It is the body, the sheath that covers it, that dies and is reborn. The spirit or the Self lives on forever.

What Kṛṣṇa says here is radically different from what any other scripture has said. Kṛṣṇa denies the concept of death here. He says there is no such thing as death. He is not saying: be good, and you will be taken care of when you die and if you are bad, you will suffer. He says there is no death, that's all.

Here Kṛṣṇa is talking to someone who has witnessed death. So, He has to explain to him that death does not exist. It is the individual's attachment to the body that creates the illusion that the individual also perishes with the body. Attachment to the body is the most intense of all attachments. We also get attached to material possessions as well as our relationships. The potential loss of these leads to fears similar to that of losing one's body. One who understands that all these attachments are temporary and are the cause of all our suffering, understands the truth. Understanding this truth removes all fears.

In some cultures, people are bred on the pattern that one's life ends at death. This pattern leads to desperate inadequate cognition, as if there is no further time to seek happiness. Once a person understands that death, like birth, is merely a passage, and sees the continuity of being, the fear of losing one's identity disappears along with fears of sin and hell.

This is why religions that accept the continuance of life after death, as Hinduism and Buddhism do; breed a culture of tolerance amongst their followers. There is no rush to live and extract the maximum juice out of one's life in a single birth. They propound that we all come from a common energy source and we go back to this source, and the cycle continues. Those who understand this spiritual truth teach completion, inclusion and compassion, and they have no desire to convert others to their beliefs.

It is easy to misinterpret these verses and propose that if there is no one really killing or being killed, then what stops us from mindless killing? Listen. That is not what Kṛṣṇa intends. One who truly understands that death is not the end of the path, but only a milestone in the journey, is not perturbed by death when it happens naturally or when it is caused for a purpose.

Here Kṛṣṇa reveals to him a more subtle level of truth that he hasn't yet grasped. Arjuna shies away from killing, not because of his conviction of *ahimsā*, non-violence, but because of his root thought pattern that he identifies with the people he has to destroy. His hesitation is from his delusory incompletions, ignorance, attachment and fantasy, not from the wisdom of non-violent compassion.

Kṛṣṇa's message to Arjuna is as it would be to someone who has to uphold *dharma* at all costs. However, it would not be a blind acceptance of orders, it would not be a powerless action driven by fear and greed. It would not be killing for gain and or killing out of fear that one would be killed. It would be an ultimate powerful action from the space of completion; born out of the knowledge that such destruction is needed for universal good and that such destruction would lead to creation.

You may ask, 'If nothing is destroyed and nothing can be destroyed, is there no sin in killing at all? So Kṛṣṇa is indifferent to mass violence? No, He is not. For one thing, Kṛṣṇa speaks as an enlightened Master from an existentialist perspective and declares that, even when the body perishes, the spirit lives on, and therefore, there is no death.

COMPLETION WITH VIOLENCE

Violence and killing are not merely physical acts. They are psychological compulsions acted out of incompletion in the physical realm. The ruler of a country who orders warfare against others is the violent one, even if he hides behind his throne. Violence of the mind carries on as the *vāsana* or desires; the essence of the spirit, that incarnates from birth to birth. That is the horror that does not end with death. The spirit is violated, degraded, and degenerated by this attitude of violence.

A violent man is always a coward, an inauthentic person who does not have the courage to face the truth. He does not have the sensitivity to treat others as he expects to be treated. He goes out-of-integrity, losing his power of words, isolating himself in a cocoon of lies, using the excuse of defending himself, and commits violence against others.

When we become aware and conscious that the person next to us is actually an expression of the energy of God, how can we possibly respond with violence? It has nothing to do with whether someone is family, part of our culture, religion or nation; or part of our history, habits or beliefs. The other person may oppose all that we believe in. Yet he is as much a part of this Universe as we are.

That is why Kṛṣṇa says, 'O Pārtha, how can that man slay or cause others to be slain, who knows him to be indestructible, eternal, unborn, unchangeable?'

ya enaṁ vetti hantāraṁ yaś cainaṁ manyate hatam |
ubhau tau na vijānito nāyaṁ hanti na hanyate || 2.19

How can we? How can violence develop in us when we recognize ourselves to be God, which automatically enables us to be aware that every other living being, animate and inanimate too is God's image?

If this message of Kṛṣṇa is truly understood, there can be no violence in this world, no self-hatred and no killing at all. You will not even kill an insect. You will not kill even in self-defense because once you are in completion, your space of completion is transmitted to the other being and that being will not even attack you.

Understand what Kṛṣṇa says and you will never have fear, either for yourself or for others. You are imperishable, you are complete; everyone around you is imperishable, complete. Shed your fear and violence and be complete. Let enriching others; let love for others fill your being.

Please listen from the space of listening!

One of the important secrets I want to share with you.

Any root pattern you carry can be destroyed if you just have love for people. Decide to go on enriching everyone who is happening in your life. When you enrich others, be very clear, you are constantly getting enriched. Decide life is for others. Life is for enriching. Enriching is life!

I tell you from my own experience, when I decided any wealth that comes around me is for others, the Cosmos showered me with wealth more than what I needed even for doing the work I am doing. In the same way, my knowledge is for others. I am not going to keep anything secret to me. Because I decided that whatever knowledge I have is for others, Cosmos is going on showering!

Listen to the definition of Enriching. Enriching is the power that unlocks the power of Living, *ātma śakti* in you.

Enriching is you taking the responsibility with integrity and authenticity that you are continuously committed to enriching, which is expanding yourself and life in and around you.

Listen! The purpose for which you are born is enriching yourself and others. When you operate out of this understanding, you are most alive, at your peak and living enlightenment!

When Ādī Śaṅkara decided to bless a poor lady, immediately the golden *amalaki* (gooseberry) showered. If it happens in your life, you will have a bag to collect everything and you will tell the lady, 'You gave one *amalaki*. You take one *amalaki*!' The old lady gave only one *amalaki* to Śankara. That is why Cosmos doesn't shower when you ask.

Just decide that life is for others! All the best things will be showered on you. You will get back to the space you were in when you were born—the purest space of life, the imperishable space! This is the jumpstart technique for enlightenment. Decide from this moment, 'Life is for Others! Life is for Enriching!' All your insecurity, fear, anger, greed, all your root patterns will become rootless patterns. Kṛṣṇa is giving this jump-start technique of enlightenment to Arjuna so that he enriches himself and others and fights to destroy the very root of his root pattern of fear and violence .

Do not Fear Death, You Are Imperishable

Kṛṣṇa continues with *Sāṅkhya*, the knowledge of completion:

Just as man casts off his worn-out clothes and puts on new ones, the Self casts off worn-out bodies and enters newer ones, *anyāni saṁyāti navāni dehī* (2.22).Weapons do not cleave the Self, fire does not burn It, water does not moisten It, and wind does not dry It. The Self can neither be broken, nor burnt, nor dissolved, nor dried up. It is eternal, all pervading, stable, immovable and ancient.

nainaṁ chindanti saśtrāṇi nainaṁ dahāti pāvakaḥ |
na cainaṁ kledayanty āpo na śoṣayati mārutaḥ || 2.23

These verses are amongst the most quoted verses of *Bhagavad Gītā*. Here, in very few words, Kṛṣṇa expounds upon the entire truth of life and death, mind, body and spirit. He clarifies why we should accept death gladly, as a matter of fact and course, instead of grieving over it. He says this so simply that even an innocent child can understand this truth.

Do we grieve over a dirty shirt that we have cast away when we know we will have a new one? Do we say, 'Oh, I am so attached to this shirt. I cannot let it go. Let me keep wearing it. I shall be heartbroken if I have to take off this shirt?' If only we understand that a body needs to be changed when it grows old, in just the same way as the shirt does when it is dirty, there would be no grief, no attachment.

Kṛṣṇa goes on to explain further what that unchanging continuity is. What is the nature of that spirit? How is it that it is everlasting?

Kṛṣṇa says, 'O Arjuna, the Soul is not destroyed at all. No *astra*, no *brahmāstra*, no nuclear weapon can destroy the energy within the body. Fire cannot burn It, water cannot wet It, and air cannot dry It. It is not made of the elements and cannot be destroyed by the elements. It is the energy behind the elements that creates the elements. How can It then die?'

'It cannot be disintegrated in any manner, by breaking, dissolving, burning or drying, *acchedyo 'yam adāhyo 'yam akledyo 'soṣya eva ca*. It is eternal. It transcends all the elemental powers. It pervades the Universe, *nityaḥ sarva gataḥ sthānuṛ* (2.24). It has been there always, *sanātanaḥ*. Therefore, It never can be destroyed.'

An understanding of the truth that Kṛṣṇa unveils here is the key to immortality. It is the key to liberation from the bondage of life and death. It is the doorway to enlightenment.

'Do not fear death, *nānuśocitum arhasi* (2.25).' Kṛṣṇa says, 'neither yours nor that of others. It is just a passage. It is the disappearance of this material body. However, you are beyond this material body. Even if the body perishes, you live on, so you do not have to worry or fear.'

What survives death is the sacred spirit in you that can never be destroyed. This spirit is not matter; it is pure energy. How can you destroy energy? Science states that energy can only appear in another form; it cannot be destroyed. As I said before, it is the energy behind the elements; it is that source which creates the elements. It is the energy that has always been and will be, never created, never destroyed. It is unchanging, eternal and all pervading. The experience of every enlightened being verifies the truth that Kṛṣṇa is uttering.

'When you are that spirit, that energy,' asks Kṛṣṇa, 'what is there to grieve about? When you are the Divine yourself, what can you fear? What more can you ask for?'

Listen. At the heart of all torture and killing is fear and greed. When we sincerely contemplate on these teachings, we complete with our fear and greed patterns, and we live peacefully in completion. From this space of completion, comes enriching. Enriching brings the space of Enlightenment in you. The whole cosmos will simply be pouring its energy into you, through you, because you are sharing it with the whole Cosmos!

It is when we are driven by our root patterns that we get fixed in obsessive beliefs and become intolerant of other beliefs, that we become afraid to lose our identity. That insecurity and fear of loss of identity is greater than the fear of death. So we respond violently. To avoid being killed, we kill.

Once we understand what Kṛṣṇa says, that death is like changing a worn-out garment, our fears will disappear. Why do we need that garment at all? We will feel freer, fully liberated when we do not have that garment. Going beyond the garment is going beyond the pattern of body-mind. It is going beyond the root of the root pattern, the cycle of life and death, *saṁsāra*. It is going to the ultimate liberation, in this life itself. It is the ultimate relaxation.

Death Is But A Passage

2.26 *O Mahābāho (mighty-armed), even if you should think of the Soul as being constantly born and constantly dying, Even then, you should not lament.*

2.27 *Indeed, death is certain for the born and birth is certain for the dead. Therefore, you should not grieve over the inevitable.*

2.28 *O Bhārata, all beings are unmanifest in their beginning, seemingly manifest in their middle, and unmanifest again in their end. So, what need then for grieving?*

2.29 *One sees It as a wonder, another speaks of It as a wonder, another hears of It as a wonder. Yet, having heard, none understands It at all!*

2.30 *O Bhārata, This that dwells in the body of everyone can never be slain; Therefore, do not grieve for any living being.*

When you understand what Kṛṣṇa is saying in these verses you get over any fear of death. In fact you will celebrate death.

Sometime ago, when I was delivering a discourse in India, news arrived that my father had died. I continued with the discourse. Later that night, many of our disciples traveled with me to Tiruvannamalai where the body lay. If you see the videos of this event, you will find that my mother never once cried. She is a very traditional person, brought up in a rural environment that sets great importance on social behavior. When one's husband dies one is naturally heartbroken; especially as in the case of my mother and father, who were very close to each other. His departure would have been a great loss to her. She understood the meaning of these verses of Kṛṣṇa without my ever having to explain them to her.

When I told her my father, her husband, is now in the energy form that is eternal, she trusted my words implicitly and joined me in celebrating his release. We are not talking about philosophers and saints here. We are talking about ordinary people whose lifestyle was all about fear of death and grief at death. They understood very easily what Kṛṣṇa is saying. They understood that the spirit lives on after the body perishes and death is indeed an event to celebrate and not to grieve. It is only the scholars who have a mere intellectual understanding of what *Gītā* says with no trust in Kṛṣṇa, and still suffer from the fear of death. Kṛṣṇa's words are not about logic; they are about trust in the Master.

Death is inevitable for the born, *jātasya hi dhruvo mṛtyur*; and birth is certain for the dead, *dhruvaṁ janma mṛtasya ca*. Whether the spirit lives on after the body perishes and locates itself in another body may be a debatable point to some. Kṛṣṇa says that this is not a reason to lament death, *na tvaṁ śocitum arhasi* (2.27). In either case, death can be a passage that one can look forward to. We all know death is inevitable. Yet for many It is a wonder.

Kṛṣṇa says, 'One sees It as a wonder—*āścarya-vat paśyati*, another speaks of It as a wonder—*āścarya-vad vadati*, another hears of It as a wonder. Yet, having heard, none understands It at all—*śrutvāpy enaṁ veda na caiva kaścit* (2.29)!

Listen. Bringing the dead back to life is not a wonder or miracle. The real wonder and mystery though, is the transformation of individuals instilling in them the truth of completion to live integrity, authenticity, responsibility and enriching, and causing these four powers of words, thinking, feeling and living as reality. This indeed is the miracle that only a true Master can perform.

I tell you, mystery school is nothing but the Master's inner space with his vast responsibility—whoever comes inside, in whatever form is processed, transformed and released! Integrity, authenticity, responsibility, enriching—these are the real wonders of transformation.

Many of us do believe that life is a wonder; truly so. Life is wondrous! We do not understand how life is created. We may have a biological explanation as to how a new life is created.

Even today there is no absolute proof as to how the Universe was created. All one has are theories such as Big Bang etc. What was there before the Big Bang? No one knows, how the first life form originated. Again, there are only theories. From time immemorial what happens after life, or more correctly, after death has been the human quest. The cycle of life and death is a mystery and a wonder. While Quantum Physics and Molecular Biology are making rapid advances in this area, yet there is no 'scientific' proof, as the logical mind would demand.

Those who are authentic enough to accept and be complete with the truth of the eternal nature of the spirit are the fortunate, the blessed. Those who fight and grieve are the wretched, the miserable, the incomplete. You cannot fight life or death. They are both beyond you, out of your control. You can marvel at them and be happy and joyous. Or you can keep questioning and doubting them, and be miserable. This is the choice and free will you have.

FEAR OF UNFULFILLED DESIRES

The illustrious King Yayāti lived for hundreds of years.

Bhāgavatam, the great Hindu epic, says that when Yama, the god of death, came to Yayāti at his appointed time of death, Yayāti begged to be allowed to live on. Due to his deep incompletions with life, he said he had not lived life enough and he needed more time. Yama relented and said that if one of his sons would give Yayāti the rest of his life, then he could live that long. Using the life span of his son, Yayāti lived many more years but with more and more incompletions.

Finally the realization dawned on him that no matter how long he lived, his incomplete desires would never cease and that his completion would never happen through material enjoyment. Yayāti completed with his root pattern and gave himself up to Yama once he realized this truth.

It is not death that frightens us. It is leaving our incomplete desires and unlived life that frightens us. The problem is that we do not know how to live a fulfilled life in the space of completion. All our desires are partially fulfilled or incomplete because, before they are fulfilled, we move on to other desires. The hangover of that past incomplete desire continues to chase us as a pattern in the present. The simple fact is that we do not know how to be complete, joyful.

Please listen. Every thought, every desire you have is a commitment you have given to yourself. Every thought you complete is a word you have given to you. You have to honor it. You cannot entertain any thought of fear or greed, doubt or denial because you are literally sitting under a kalpataṛu, a wish-fulfilling tree, all the time!

There is a beautiful story.

> Once a traveler was resting under a tree in a forest, without knowing that the tree was a Kalpataṛu.
>
> Suddenly he had a desire, 'If somebody brings me some food now, how nice it will be! I am so hungry.'
>
> Immediately the food appeared before him! The man was overjoyed and happily ate the food.
>
> Then he thought, 'If somebody gives me a cot, it will be so nice. I could lie down and sleep peacefully.' Immediately a cot with a soft bed appeared!
>
> The man lay down happily on the cot to rest.
>
> Suddenly he had the thought, 'Oh, God! Whatever I am thinking is happening! But it is getting dark now. What if a tiger suddenly appears and attacks me? What will happen?'
>
> You know the rest of the story!

Understand, it was not only that man who was sitting under a *Kalpataṛu tree*, all of us are always under the *Kalpataṛu*, the wish-fulfilling tree. Every thought we give to ourselves will be honored if we don't complete with it. Now I know, everyone has a fear—Oh God! I have had so many negative thoughts. What to do?

Listen: there is nobody alive who has not entertained the thought of suicide at least once! All of us have fear. What do we do if all the words which we gave to ourselves now start getting fulfilled? You don't have to worry; you just have to complete them. Sit and declare to yourself consciously that you are not going to honor all the negative words you gave to yourself, and you are dropping them, completing them.

So listen. You cannot entertain any desire in you leaving it incomplete. It will continue to chase you as the tiger and will not let you be complete with anything you do and experience. Only when you complete, integrity, the power of words starts expressing through you.

Start creating the right inner software, the right inner space, by bringing integrity as the principle of life. Integrity means not just fulfilling, but honoring the words you give to others. The first step to integrity is completing with all the negative words you created within you about you and life, and completing all of them.

Listen. Completion means feeling empowered, feeling powerful, without any hangover, without feeling powerless, during and after every situation in your life! If you are powerful, you won't be violent. You will not be in guilt, fear or carry incomplete desires.

Kṛṣṇa reveals that to be truly complete, joyful, to be eternally blissful, is to cognize the truth that you are indestructible, that your spirit lives on, and that life and death are but a mere passage. When you cognize this truth and start living it with integrity and authenticity, you will be living death. If not, you will be dead living. I have seen people who are dead living and I have seen people who lived death.

Death is not an end; it is a passage of sorts. The truth is that the spirit is not satisfied with mere material pleasures. However much you please your senses, you cannot achieve satisfaction, you cannot achieve completion. The more you enjoy through your senses, the more the need for enjoyment. It never stops. Discontentment with material pleasures alone is hardwired into the human psyche.

Spirituality is the total understanding and cognition of completion with life—materially, physically, emotionally, relationally and in all senses without any incompletion and responding to life with the four *tattvas*, spiritual principles of integrity, authenticity, responsibility and enriching. These *tattvas* arise out of the space of completion.

Completion makes you integrated; completion makes you authentic; completion makes you responsible; completion makes you enrich yourself and others. This completion arises out of our ability to be complete with the present moment. The present moment is the only moment when we are truly alive, awake.

Whether one believes in God or not, and accepts the inner divinity within oneself or not, is irrelevant to how one understands life after death. If, instead of believing in God, we choose to believe in science, we still need to accept that there are no answers to what we were before we were born and what we will be once we are dead. It is still unmanifest at both ends; it is still a mystery before and after, with no answers.

This understanding can only come with the understanding that we live on in spirit.

Kṛṣṇa declares to Arjuna, 'O Bhārata, whatever is permanent and real was unmanifest before it became manifest in the middle—*avyaktādīnī bhūtani vyakta-madhyāni bharāta* and again it will become unmanifest—*avyakta-nidhanāny eva*. Therefore, what is the need to lament, *tatra kā paridevanā* (2.28).'

Everything is in a state of becoming something else. At every moment we die and are reborn; millions of cells in our body-mind system die every day and are reborn. Yet, through all this change there is continuity. There is a continuity that we cannot see, touch or feel. What we see as manifested, as this body and mind, hides from us the process of constant change that happens within us, as well as the continuous thread that holds the whole process together.

Responsibility Of The Kṣatriya

2.31 *You should look at your own responsibility [svadharma}*
as a kṣatriya. There is nothing higher for a kṣatriya
than a righteous war. You ought not to hestitate.

2.32 *O Pārtha, happy indeed are the kṣatriya who are called*
to fight in such a battle without seeking;
This opens for them the door to heaven.

2.33 *If you will not fight this righteous war, then you will incur*
the sin of having abandoned your own responsibility [svadharma],
and you will lose your reputation.

2.34 *People, too, will remember your everlasting dishonor, and*
to one who has been honored, dishonor is worse than death.

2.35 *The great generals will think that you have withdrawn*
from the battle because you are a coward.
You will be looked down upon by those who
had thought much of you and your heroism in the past.

2.36 *Many unspeakable words would be spoken by your enemies*
reviling your power. Can there be anything more painful than this?

2.37 *Slain, you will achieve heaven; victorious, you will enjoy the earth.*
Therefore, O Kaunteya (son of Kuntī), stand up determined to fight.

2.38 *Pleasure and pain, gain and loss, victory and defeat—treat them*
all the same. Do battle for the sake of battle. You shall incur no sin.

Kṛṣṇa works on Arjuna at two levels. At one level He talks to Arjuna at the super conscious plane educating him on what the ultimate Truth is.

He talks to Arjuna about how the undying and indestructible spirit lives on. Here, Kṛṣṇa addresses Arjuna's fears about killing his *svajanam*, his relatives, elders and teaches him that what he considers to be the end of life for these people is just one step in their journey.

Kṛṣṇa then descends to the practical level at which Arjuna exists and begins addressing his *svadharma*, Arjuna's own *dharma*, the natural path of his responsibility. Kṛṣṇa explains to Arjuna why, from a societal point of view, he should not run away from the battlefield, but instead, stay on and fight as behaves a warrior. Kṛṣṇa here addresses Arjuna as *kṣatriya*, the warrior.

In each society there are groups of people who are the designated protectors of that society. They are the warriors, the soldiers, who defend their country and countrymen. In the same manner, there are others who are designated as clerics and priests, as teachers, as businessmen and as workers.

To Fight is Your Responsibility, O Arjuna

When Kṛṣṇa refers to Arjuna as a *kṣatriya*, he is referring to the entire personality of Arjuna, the great warrior, which has been decided only partly by birth and mostly by training based on his aptitude. Arjuna is the quintessential warrior who knows no fear, and yet is now disturbed by issues of whether he is doing right or wrong by fighting against his kinsmen.

Kṛṣṇa says, 'Fight! You are a *kṣatriya*. By fighting as your own responsibility demands, *svadharmam api cāvekṣya* (2.31), you earn merits and go to heaven. If you run away from this war, you commit a sin for being out-of-integrity with your responsibility, *hitvā pāpam avāpsyasi* (2.33). You will also be termed a coward and people who know you will laugh at you, *akīrtiṁ cāpi bhūtani kathayiṣyanti te 'vyayām* (2.3). You will be dishonored, and for a *kṣatriya*, dishonor is far worse than death, *sambhāvitasya cākīrtir maraṇād atiricyate* (2.34).

'Do not worry about victory or defeat. If you are defeated and slain you will ascend to heaven. If you are victorious, you will enjoy material benefits in this world itself. Therefore, O Kaunteya, fight as it is your responsibility as a *kṣatriya*.'

hato vā prāpsyasi svargaṁ jitvā vā bhokṣyase mahīm |
tasmād uttiṣṭha kaunteya yuddhāya kṛta-niścayaḥ || 2.37

Kṛṣṇa says to treat pain and pleasure, gain and loss, victory and defeat all the same. He says to fight without worrying about the outcome. To fight is your responsibility. You shall incur no sin.

sukha-dukḥe same kṛtvā lābhālābhau jayājayau |
tato yuddhāya yujyasya naivaṁ pāpam avāpsyasi || 2.38

When the *Paramātma*—supreme Soul says this, it means that Arjuna does not have to worry about right and wrong, about sin or merit. Isn't fighting, isn't killing people a sin, you may ask. Then why is it that Kṛṣṇa encourages Arjuna, not merely encourages, but actually forces Arjuna to fight and kill? What is the operative logic here, you may ask.

There is no logic. Kṛṣṇa's exhortation is beyond human rationale. It is *not what you do* that matters; it is *who you are being* that matters. It is your space that matters. Whether you are being complete or incomplete matters. An Enlightened Master can do no wrong even if he kills, because when he kills, it would be with completion, not with compulsion for personal benefit. On the other hand, any average person with incompletions, even while doing an act of kindness, he may be doing something wrong.

Kṛṣṇa is not worried about *what you do*, He is concerned only about *who you are being*. If your actions are from completion, if they are innocent of motives, whatever you do is right. If what you do is motivated by patterns of fear and greed, pain and pleasure, victory and defeat, you can do nothing right. Whatever you do for gain is sinful.

Understand, if the gap between *who you are* and *who you want to be* is without responsibility, it is greed. If it is with responsibility, it is possibility! When there is no responsibility-bridge, it is greed. When you are building the responsibility-bridge to achieve what you want to be, then it becomes a possibility; it is no more greed!

I tell you, Kṛṣṇa is enriching Arjuna with the bridge of responsibility to expand Arjuna's shrinking identity as a *kṣatriya*. Even Śrī Rāma had to build the bridge to reach Sītā! When you add responsibility to greed, the gap suddenly reduces. The gap reduces drastically! Responsibility infused into thinking removes the agitation and disconnection with you.

We always feel that responsibility is a burden. NO! It is a power!

Responsibility directly leads you to leadership consciousness. As long as you feel responsible only for your family, you remain as the head of your family. When you feel responsible for the community, you become a leader of the community. As your feeling of responsibility expands, your leadership quality also expands.

The decision to feel responsible for the whole Cosmos is Enlightenment! Feeling responsible for the Whole and declaring to live by your feeling is responsible declaration, known in Hindu spiritual practice as *nididhyāsana*.

Responsible declaration unlocks the power of feeling, prema śakti in you. But the moment you hear that you are responsible for everything happening around you, you think, 'If I feel responsible for all the garbage on the streets, I will be stuck cleaning it up the whole day! I will not be able to do anything else!'

Please listen!

I am not saying that if you feel responsible for the streets, you will need to clean them yourself. I am also not saying that you will NOT clean them yourself. Anything may happen, but don't be afraid to dive into the feeling of responsibility just because of your imaginary complications. Don't stop yourself from feeling it at all.

Understand the science of feeling. You can feel anything as joy or anything as pain—it is your freedom! Even the greatest achievement can bring pain to you, and even the worst experience can be a joyful learning. You have the ability to decide how you want to feel!

Listen: whenever you feel empowered, you are joyful. Whenever you feel powerless, you experience suffering. All your suffering pain, anger, guilt, fear, jealousy, frustration is nothing but powerlessness expressing in different ways! When you feel responsible for everything that happens in your life, you will feel that everything is joyful—because nothing can make you powerless. So, empower yourself with responsibility and unlock the *power of feeling.*

By unlocking the power of feeling, you will always act from a space of power and completion and start focusing on the solution, not the problem; without worrying about its outcome. As Kṛṣṇa says, you will begin holding success and failure, pain and pleasure the same and just fulfill your responsible declaration. With responsibility, your inner space expands and opens up new possibilities and you gain higher control of your life. Ultimately, you raise yourself to the next level of success and evolve into a new being.

Please listen. When you take responsibility to fulfill what others expect from you, the whole Cosmos expresses through you! You will have extraordinary powers, because it is directly *seva*, enriching others. Whenever you enrich others with a feeling of responsibility, without having any other motive, the Cosmos celebrates your Existence. It just celebrates your Existence!

What happens when the fear of loss of reputation and loss of identity disappears? Will your greed still last? Fear and greed are strong motivators because we are not sure about ourselves; we are caught in self-doubting pattern. We do not know who we are and we do not take responsibility for who we want to be. Here Kṛṣṇa is breaking that mould. Act without fear and greed, He says. Do not worry about consequences. Do not doubt yourself and your actions. This is against all societal and religious conditioning.

Kṛṣṇa, as the transcendental *Parabrahman*, is not concerned about the practical and societal consequences of Arjuna walking out of the battlefield. He is only concerned about what that would do to

Arjuna's inner self. He wants Arjuna to reclaim his inner space, which is occupied by his self-doubt. If Arjuna had truly been steeped in *ahiṁsa*, non-violence, Kṛṣṇa would have never attempted to persuade Arjuna into violence. Arjuna however, was trying to avoid fighting, not because of any moral and conscientious objection, but out of his root thought pattern of emotional attachment to his kinsmen and others arising out of his own identification with them.

In these verses, Kṛṣṇa is trying to bring Arjuna out of his root pattern, his dilemma, which has obscured his normally clear vision. Kṛṣṇa is trying to get Arjuna to transcend his conditioned actions based on fear and greed relating to the killing of his kinsmen, his *svajanam*. He is getting him to act out of completion, out of his *svadharmam*, without worrying about the outcome.

Experience Matters Not Knowledge

2.39 *Thus far, what has been taught to you concerns the wisdom of Sāṅkhya. Now, listen to the wisdom of yoga [buddiyoga]. Having known this, O Pārtha, you shall cast off the bonds of action.*

2.40 *There is no wasted effort or dangerous effect in this path of yoga. Even a little knowledge of this, even a little practice of this dharma, protects and releases one from very great fear.*

2.41 *O Joy of Kuru, on this path (of yoga), the intelligence is resolute with a single-pointed determination. The thoughts of the irresolute are many, branched and endless.*

2.42, 43 *Men of little knowledge, who are very much attached to eulogizing the flowery words of the Vedas, O Pārtha, argue that, 'there is nothing else'; these advocates of Vedas (vādīna) look upon and recommend various fruitful actions for elevation to heavenly planets, resulting in high birth, power, and so forth. Thus being desirous of sense gratification and opulent life, they say that there is nothing more than this to living.*

2.44 *Those whose minds are attached to sense pleasures and lordship, who are diverted by such teachings, for them, the determination for steady meditation and samādhi, fixed intelligence does not happen.*

2.45 *O Arjuna! Be you above the three guṇas (attributes) that the Vedas deal in: free yourself from the pairs-of-opposites and be always in satva (goodness), free from all thoughts of acquisition (yoga) or preservation (kṣema), and be established in the Self.*

2.46 *The Brāhmaṇa (sage), who has known the Self, has little use for the vedic scriptures, as these are like a pool of water in a place that is already in flood, overflowing with a great water reservoir.*

Kṛṣṇa begins His teachings of *karma yoga* to Arjuna in these verses. These verses should be read carefully by those who believe solely in scriptural authority, based on their superficial understanding of what has been said.

Kṛṣṇa unequivocally says here, 'Forget the *Vedas*.'

He says, 'All the knowledge contained in the *Vedas* is of as much use as water in a flood to one who has realized himself. The *Vedas* are limiting; they concern the three attributes, *satva*, *rajas* and *tamas*, the attributes of calmness, aggressive action and lazy inaction. The time has come now to move beyond these attributes; at least move from *rajas* into the state of *satva*, calmness.'

'Do not quote to Me what the scriptures say,' Kṛṣṇa says. He continues, 'Do not tell me about what you should do and should not do through rituals and practices that will please the deities and ancestors so that you will benefit materially in this life, and spiritually in some after-life. All this is for people with limited understanding of their own Self, who have not experienced the Truth, who still hanker for sensual pleasures and name and fame.'

'Move beyond them to the single-pointed determination of yoga that I shall teach you,' Kṛṣṇa says, 'and be established in a state where you are no longer concerned about creation, preservation and destruction. You will be beyond these and reach the state of *Parabrahman*.'

Only the Master of the Universe, can say such things and get away with it! Kṛṣṇa's authority as He speaks these words is compelling. He is casting away the divinely transmitted scriptures, the *Vedas*, to instill truth in the inner space of Arjuna. It is the truth as spoken by the Divine who Himself has all the knowledge contained in the *Vedas*.

The *Vedas*, the collection of knowledge as directly experienced by the great sages, the *Ṛṣis*, was conveyed for generations by word of mouth and was referred to as *Śruti* meaning, 'that which was heard internally, not as an external expression.' The moment an experience is expressed, it is no longer the truth of that experience.

All the great scriptures, *Vedas*, *Upaniṣads* and *Gītā*, exist at different levels of understanding, seven levels, to be precise, depending on the energy level that one dwells in. At the highest level one understands that all that there is, is INFINITE, each one infinitely powerful. There is no experiencer, experienced or experience as separate entities at the highest energy level; ALL is INFINITE.

Kṛṣṇa refers to that truth here in these verses, the truth of the highest energy. 'Do not be carried away by the apparent ritualistic approach of the *Vedas* as propounded by half learned scholars,' the Master says, 'go beyond; go beyond duality, *nirdvando*. All these seem to bring joy but are transient; that joy is the brief intermission between periods of sorrow. Go beyond the three attributes, *nistrai-guṇyo bhavārjuna* and seek the firm truth of the Infinite, the Union, that is Yoga,' He says to Arjuna.

'There is something beyond the superficial understanding,' Kṛṣṇa says, 'that will take you beyond the three human attributes of *satva* (calmness), *rajas* (active action) and *tamas* (passive inaction) and into liberation arising out of true understanding. At that stage you will be beyond creation, preservation and destruction, as these would have no meaning in the understanding of the permanence of the Ultimate energy—*nirdvando nitya-sattva-stho niryoga-kṣema ātmavān* (2.45).'

Kṛṣṇa finally says, 'Once you understand and realize Brahman, all the knowledge of the *Vedas* that you quote so passionately, will be of as much relevance to you as a lake in the midst of an ocean.'

Kṛṣṇa is leading Arjuna step by step as if teaching a baby to walk. One by one the Master demolishes Arjuna's conflicting patterns, arguments and fears, dispelling his dilemma. These first baby steps address Arjuna's intellect, for that's all Arjuna has been using till now. Kṛṣṇa shows Arjuna how meaningless his intellectual knowledge is. It is all borrowed, with no experiential backing. He now leads him into experiential knowledge.

Act Without Worry About Results

2.47 *You have a right only to work,*
but never to the fruits (outcome) of action.
Never let the fruit of action be your motive;
and never let your attachment be to inaction.

2.48 *O Dhanañjaya!*
Do your actions dropping all attachment to the outcome,
being centered and complete in Yoga.
Be balanced in success and failure. Such evenness of mind is Yoga.

The entire teaching of *Bhagavad Gītā* can be summarized in the above two verses. The sheer brilliance of the wisdom of the Universal Master is reflected in these verses. Whenever I get a chance I refer to these verses to explain how one should lead one's life.

Kṛṣṇa says many, many things in these few words. He says, 'You have the right and responsibility to work. You have no responsibility or right to the results of that work. Do not focus on the result and make it either a pattern of greed to chase or fear to stay away from. Do what you have to do with a centered mind, a complete inner space without worrying about whether you will succeed or fail.'

karmaṇy evādhikāras te mā phaleṣu kadācana |
mā karmaphala hetur bhur mā te saṅgo'stv akarmaṇi || 2.47

Nothing more can be said or ever needs to be said about why and how one should perform.

Many people wrongly communicate and misunderstand these verses. There are people who stay away from work that they fear may end in adverse negative results. As long as the results can be positive either to themselves or others, they will carry out and complete what they are assigned sincerely. But when they think that something bad may happen, that they may fail, they will stop doing whatever they are doing.

One of the biggest problems human beings have is this—you love to be successful, but you deeply believe that you are a failure. This is one of the biggest paradoxes. This shows the lack of integrity in your thinking. Understand, some of your actions may be a failure, some of your decisions or dimensions may be a failure, but YOU are never failure, because you are still breathing!

There are others who feel that doing nothing and disengaging from all action or *akarma* is the best solution, since all actions result in reactions and they accumulate *karma*. Of course, almost all of us go on blindly doing whatever we are told to do when we see money or material rewards in front of us.

Do My Work with Integrity and Authenticity

Kṛṣṇa says, 'Stop! Who do you think you are? You are here to do My work. You have no right to take the results that are Mine.'

His position is similar to that of a landowner who has sharecroppers working on the land. The sharecroppers have no right to anything but their sustenance wages. They need not worry about whether the land will yield well or not. All that they need to do is honor the work they have committed to and fulfill their own responsibilities to their peak capability in caring for the land. They just need to be in integrity and authenticity to their work. That's all! The landlord is the owner and ultimate beneficiary.

Listen. Awareness of what Kṛṣṇa says here is the solution to all our day-to-day problems. Do what you have to do as your right and responsibility, without worrying about the results. Do not act with hopes of a certain reward. Do not stop doing what you need to do because you are afraid of what may lie ahead.

Constantly bring integrity to your thinking, authenticity to your feeling, responsibility to your actions, enriching to your lifestyle! You will see, you will realize an extraordinary space in your life, what Kṛṣṇa calls as being balanced in success and failure and being complete in yoga, *siddhy-asiddhyoḥ samo bhūtvā samatvaṁ yoga ucyate* (2.48).

With integrity, you will literally clean your inner space of the constant unwanted beliefs that you carry, like the strong belief that you will be a failure. This continuous belief holds you from taking responsibility for your actions, makes you worry about the results, and leads you towards failure! When you start thinking with integrity, you will diagnose those self-fulfilling negative prophecies that you constantly give to yourself.

When even a small thing happens, you immediately declare failure. We go on doing this. The first thing to do is to declare your integrity, not your failure. When you start thinking with integrity, you will diagnose your own self-fulfilling negative prophecies.

If you have a strong idea or self-doubt what you are doing is going to be a failure, the moment you think that it is a failure, it is a commitment and word you are giving to you. Do you understand? So if you give that word, you naturally have to fulfill it. Do you want to fulfill that word? No. Then tell yourself that I am not going to fulfill it. It means that whenever you have a thought, 'I am a failure,' you should know—this is a commitment I am making to me, and I have to honor it. You may say that it comes on its own. Then complete it! Consciously disown and complete with it.

Listen! Not fulfilling your everyday commitments will only make the weeds hide behind your unconscious patterns. Swami Vivekananda is very clear, yoga can happen in you, only along with responsible actions. *Karma yoga* does not happen without responsible actions.

Sometimes, you execute actions the whole day, but there is no feeling of responsibility for it! When you have *not* lost the inspiration to take responsibility, nothing is lost. I tell you, if you take responsibility, even death cannot come near you. Death waits for you to complete your responsibility. So for anybody who wants to live long, just practice authentic responsibility for your actions. Do not worry about the outcome of your work—*mā karmaphala hetur bhur* (2.47)!

Listen. When you take responsibility with authenticity, consciousness starts growing more intensely in the body! Shrinking does not happen. Consciousness growing in your body is enlightenment!

Many of you in corporate life are focused on results. You will do something only if we think that it will be effective. You get caught in the result even before you start. So how do you define what is effective? Ninety percent of the time effectiveness is interpreted as something that benefits our self-interest. Even if it benefits the organization, we do it because our performance will be recognized and we will be rewarded. We learn this lesson early in life. Our elders teach us this rule from infancy. 'Do this and we shall reward you; do that and we will punish you.' We are all brought up with the deep root pattern of what is good for us and what is bad for us, what will be successful or what will be a failure. Both success and failure, *siddhya-asiddhyoḥ* are based on anticipated rewards or punishments.

Sometimes, you take up failure as a self-sympathy creating mechanism. Or you think that you have to work for success, but failure is natural. No! Success is natural; you have to work for failure. Bring integrity; you will understand that success is the natural flow of your life just like Nature.

INTEGRITY TEACHES RESPONSIBILITY IN ACTION

Society operates on this principle of greed and fear to prevent us from doing actions that it does not want us to do. Religions do the same. Society threatens you with legal punishment here and now; religion threatens you with punishment in the hereafter, in hell. What is hell or heaven? Do they exist? No, they do not.

When you clean your inner space with the power of integrity, you will realize that all the contradictions, conflicts and confusions you carry are responsible for your whole life, for all reactions you attract from others and society. You are responsible for all your actions, the reactions you attract from others and the happenings of life. Integrity will automatically teach you responsibility. You will understand that for everything happening in and around you, you are responsible.

You are not in integrity with yourself, when you say one thing and do another. You do not walk your talk. But, when you do walk your talk and your talk is in integrity and authenticity, then your words will become reality. You will have *vāk siddhi*—the power to manifest your word as reality! But if the talk itself is lacking integrity, then your walk and your actions will also be out-of-integrity and you lose self-confidence. Ultimately it is all about the truth of integrity, authenticity, responsibility and enriching from your space of completion.

Integrity is the first lesson of spiritual life. Integrity is not just a simple vow, a simple word. Integrity is all about ironing out your thinking, aligning your thinking. If you bring integrity to your inner space, you will realize that even accidents are attracted by you. You are attracting everything in your life, whether it is wealth or poverty, right or wrong. You are responsible for your life.

You need to know a beautiful story about the child devotee, Prahlād's life.

> When Prahlād's angry father asked Prahlād—'Is your *Narāyaṇa*, your God, in this pillar? Is He inside that pillar? Is He in this stone?'
>
> Prahlād was about to raise his small finger and show his father that his God was really there in the pillar. When Prahlād was about to point-out the pillar, Narāyaṇa started running from his heavenly abode in Vaikuṅṭa!
>
> His consort Lakṣmī asked, 'What happened? Why are you running so fast? What is there to be in such a hurry about?'
>
> Narāyaṇa said, 'No, you don't know! Wherever my devotee Prahlād points his finger, I have to enter into that pillar! Wherever he points, I have to occupy that place and emerge from it!'

Listen! When a child is established in integrity, just for his hand movement or the direction he shows, God lands! Listen! The whole world moves as you want when you are established in Integrity.

When you are in completion, with integrity, without internal conflict or contradictions, whatever you project on the cosmos is a project for the cosmos! Simply cosmos does it. When you are integrated, the outer world obeys you just like that. That is the power of integrity! Please listen: nothing is political or accidental on the planet Earth. Everything runs on the natural law of life, *dharma* of these four principles.

Be Complete In Yoga, Drop All Attachments

What Kṛṣṇa says here is the law of Nature. Nature just is. Nature just acts as per these four cosmic principles. Nature does not think about end results, successes or failures, rewards or punishments.

People ask me, '*Swamiji,* why is nature so cruel? Why are there natural disasters? Why do young children die?' The answer is what Kṛṣṇa gives here. Nature goes about its job without any thought about what the end result will be. What happens will happen. It is bound to happen. Nature follows its *dharma*, its path of righteousness. The problem is that we do not understand the laws of nature; we measure natural actions by our yardstick of logic.

You will then ask me, 'How do we know what to do? How do we know what is *svadharma*, our path of righteousness? Do we decide we are a *kṣatriya,* therefore we should fight and kill and not worry about who dies, or, we decide we are a *vaiśya*, a businessman, in which case our *svadharma* is to make money without worrying about how we make money?' No, Kṛṣṇa is not talking about acting in selfishness; the Universal Master is talking about acting from the space of completion. He says, 'Be centered and complete in yoga, and drop all attachment to results; do what you have to do.'

yoga-sthaḥ kuru karmāṇi saṅgaṁ tvaktvā dhanañjaya |
siddhy-asiddhyoḥ samo bhūtvā samatvaṁ yoga ucyate || 2.48

What beautiful wisdom!

Yoga is union, union of man and Divine. Yoga is completion with the Divine.

Yoga is your realization of your own Self, your realization that you are divine. It is the state of completion, the state of truth, the state of the present, when all that you do will be in righteous consciousness, *dharma*. When you perform with this completion, and with no expectations, you will do what is right and just.

Suffering Happens When We Link Thoughts

Our thoughts are unconnected, illogical and unpredictable. It is only when we link thoughts together that problems start and suffering happens. We remember a few out of hundreds of events and try to create a link between these few. Ninety percent of what we cognize and experience is never recorded by our conscious memory; it just slips into our unconscious. Within the ten percent of what we retain, what stays in our memory is always that which falls outside the pattern. If it is part of a normal pattern we will almost always ignore and forget the event.

So, do not link thoughts and create a shaft of thoughts. Unclutch from your thoughts by bringing integrity and weed out all your negative self-fulfilling patterns, and automatically the mind will drop. This is the way to stay in the present. Some of you misunderstand the word '*Unclutched*' as 'not to do anything.' You think that to drop the mind is to be passive, inactive, doing nothing. No, not at all! You can be doing nothing and yet occupy your mind fully. That is what they mean by saying that an idle mind is the devil's workshop. When you have nothing to do, what you end up doing is creating fantasies.

Listen! Constantly listening to your own inner space is the beginning of integrity. If your inner space says that there is nothing more to listen, if only silence is there, then that is the end of integrity. You have achieved integrity. As long as you are hearing something from your inner space, it is lack of integrity. Go on listening. Even while you are in action, *karma*—sitting, driving, talking or walking, listen to you.

Inaction, *akarma* is not what is advised. Understand: When you experience integrity and your mind drops, when thoughts cease, and your energy level is high, you cannot be inactive. You will act spontaneously out of sheer necessity. Physical and mental idleness are never produced by a no-thought mind or inner space. One must not link idleness with calmness. One with a no-thought mind, one who is complete in *yoga*, dwells in peace, calmness and harmony—the space of restful awareness, but is always aware and alert to act spontaneously in the way that would best suit each situation in every moment.

With a no-thought mind comes great awareness and energy; idleness or lethargy is far from it. An incomplete, confused, restless and overworked mind is constantly occupied with chatter and fantasies that can result in apathy and idleness.

Integrity is the basic requirement for Unclutching. When you are in a state of an unclutched inner space, you are in completion and you are in the present moment, where regrets of your past and expectations of the future are absent from your mind. Whatever you do in such a state of completion would be the right thing to do. You are not influenced either by fear or greed regarding the outcome. You do what you have to do, naturally.

That is why Kṛṣṇa says that you must act with responsibility in the present moment of completion. He says, 'Do not get attached to the results of your action, nor get attached to inaction, thinking that it could be an easy way out of this problem.'

Be Steady With Authenticity In Action

2.49 *O Dhanañjaya, beyond the action with selfish motive is Yoga*
(of action) in wisdom [buddhiyoga].
Wretched are those whose motive is the fruit (outcome);
Surrender yourself fully to the wisdom of completion.

2.50 *Endowed with the wisdom of evenness of mind,*
move away from both good and evil deeds in this life;
Therefore, devote yourself to Yoga.
Authenticity in action is Yoga.

2.51 *The wise, having abandoned the outcome of their actions and*
possessed of knowledge of completion,
are freed from the cycle of birth and death.
They go to the state that is beyond all sorrow.

2.52 *When your wisdom takes you beyond the delusion,*
You shall be indifferent to all what has been heard
and what is yet to be heard.

2.53 *When you are not confused by what you have heard*
and your wisdom stands steady and unmoving in the Self,
You shall attain Yoga, Self-realization.

Kṛṣṇa emphasizes what He has said before and ends with a punchline. He says, 'Act without attachment. Do not worry about success or failure in results. Center yourself in wisdom of completion that takes you beyond action and the desire for fruits of action. Once you are centered in wisdom of completion you will act wisely. Once you give up attachment to results, you will be freed from the cycle of birth and death and you will be beyond sorrow.'

In the next verse, Kṛṣṇa begins initiating Arjuna into yoga with the second *tattva* of authenticity or *śraddha*. Kṛṣṇa is the greatest strategist of life.

Here, He begins revealing the truth of authenticity, the strategy of life, the strategy that will make Arjuna succeed and expand!

Kṛṣṇa declares, '*yogaḥ karmasu kauśalam*.' Please understand, I first want you to understand these words: '*yogaḥ karmasu kauśalam*—yoga is authenticity in action.' Not just 'perfection in action' but I am translating it as 'authenticity in action.'

buddhi yukto jahātīha ubhe sukṛta-duṣkṛte |
tasmād yogāya yujyasva yogaḥ karmasu kauśalaṁ || 2.50

Let me define Authenticity.

Authenticity is you being established in the peak of your energy, the peak of your capability, and responding to life from who you perceive yourself to be for you and who you project yourself to be for others, and what others expect you to be for them.

Authenticity in your thinking means raising you to the peak. Raising you, again and again, higher and higher, expanding you more and more.

Listen, the moment I say 'expanding you more and more, continuously,' do you feel, 'Oh, God! Then it is unending process? I will never be able to rest at all!' If you cherish this idea in you, then you are death-oriented; you are entertaining death in your heart. The idea you entertain in your life invites different happenings of life. So, don't blame, if you get any killer diseases in your life, because you invited them. Understand, first thing you need to do is break that pattern.

Kṛṣṇa gives the ultimate winning strategy of life to Arjuna—to stand up with the courage of authenticity in all his actions, *yogaḥ karmasu kauśalam*. He urges Arjuna to devote himself to yoga, *buddhau yogād dhanañjaya buddhau śaraṇaṁ anviccha* (2.49)—to bring authenticity in his action, to expand himself to the peak of his energy. Arjuna can complete his root pattern of fear, only when he raises and expands himself fighting as a *kṣatriya* warrior. Only then Arjuna will be authentic. The state of fear can be born in you only when you are inauthentic.

Listen! Every time inauthenticity is allowed in you, it leaves a powerful fear in you. Arjuna's inauthenticity in not raising himself to his responsibility and to others' expectation of him as a warrior, led him to be death-oriented and collapse with fear.

Listen. Life is expansion. Life is expansion. When you feel, 'Wow, I am going to expand, expand, expand! Authenticity is the best principle,' then understand, you are entering into *akśardhām*—eternal life!

Break the pattern of—'am I never going to rest or what?' Why do you need rest? Increasing the speed of running is rest. Make it into flying! That is rest. You see, when you drive or run on the road, there is friction. If you want bliss, joy, peace, don't reduce the speed of life; reduce the friction. Just take off! Your body, mind, inner space, consciousness, whatever you feel about you, go on expanding, expanding, expanding! That is the only way life can continue to ooze in you, overflow in you.

If you say, 'No, I can expand. Now I do two hours of work, which I will make into four hours; not more than that. Then I will rest.' No! Make it into twenty-four hours and few more minutes, and penetrate into time. Whenever you need more time to do more work, stop the time, complete the work, and allow time to move. You can do! Listen. Something has to grow in your body—either life or death. Life has no pause button. Either life has to grow in your body or death has to grow in your body. The inauthenticity, which you entertain, is death for you.

Power of authenticity! I tell you, my strategy for life is—everything should only be from authenticity. Authenticity is my strategy plan. Pick up authenticity as your strategy plan in every moment of your life. Whether it is to do with health, creativity, solving relationship problems, creating wealth or achieving inner fulfillment, have authenticity as your strategy plan.

Kṛṣṇa then adds, 'When you are centered in wisdom of completion you will no longer be deluded by what you hear. When you are no longer deluded by what you have heard, you are liberated.' Kṛṣṇa's immediate reference here is to the scriptures, the *Vedas*. He chides Arjuna and says, 'Don't be confused by what you hear, even if it is supposed to be divine knowledge, the *Vedas*. Remember: If you are really centered in wisdom, you can never be deluded; you will be in completion.'

Vedic scriptures are not dead knowledge that is a burden upon us to abide by. The *Vedic* scriptures, the *śrūti*, divine in origin, and the *smṛti*, rules and regulations laid down later by Manu and other sages, make no such claims. They are the living guidelines that lead us into wisdom and liberation. In fact, Hindu scriptures have both the humility and the power to challenge us to transform ourselves according to the needs of the day, but stipulate that we first experience what is said.

'So,' Kṛṣṇa says, 'let the *Vedas* say what they want, but put what you hear, see, and read to the test of wisdom to go beyond delusion.' Kṛṣṇa is the *Vedas*, the source of all knowledge. He himself declares this in *Gītā* and yet He asks Arjuna to experiment and be guided by his inner wisdom, not by what he merely hears.

What courage, what authority! Only one who is so sure about the truth can say, 'Do not listen to what I say and how I act, but listen to your inner voice of truth born out of your own experience.'

Kṛṣṇa says, 'Don't be inactive, do what you need to do. Do it with no expectations and no attachment to results. Do it with a centered mind, and in wisdom of your own inner calling, and not because of something you have heard. You will then go beyond all suffering and be liberated.' These steps are so simple that everyone can practice them; in fact everyone should practice them. Stay fully in the space of completion, and based on the truth of integrity and authenticity, act. You can never go wrong. I promise you that.

When you feel integrity is your responsibility, you are in the zone of practice; you are a seeker. When you understand integrity is your right, you are in the zone of enlightenment! Kṛṣṇa is taking Arjuna on the path of Enlightenment through simple steps initiating him into the *tattva* of integrity and authenticity.

Listen. With integrity you experience the space of positivity. With authenticity you experience the space of possibility. Only a man who lives authenticity is a liberated one, a yogi, the one devoted to authenticity in action. Only when you surrender yourself to practice integrity in thinking and authenticity in action—*yogaḥ karmasu kauśalam*, you will realize that you are responsible for success and failure, for good or bad, for everything you experience. You drop your attachments and your fear patterns, and experience self-realization—*tadā yogam avāpsyasi* (2.53).

Follow That Complete Man

2.54 *O Keśava. What is the description of Sthitaprajña,*
one who stays fixed in completion and is merged in the restful awareness of truth and wisdom? How does one of steady wisdom speak, how does he sit, how does he walk?

2.55 *Śrī Bhagavān says:*
O Pārtha, a man who casts off completely all desires
of the mind and is satisfied in the Self by the Self,
He is said to be Sthitaprajña, one of steady wisdom in completion.

2.56 *He whose mind is not disturbed by adversity, and who,*
in prosperity does not go after other pleasures,
He who is free from attachment, fear or anger
is called a sage of steady wisdom.

2.57 *His wisdom is fixed on one*
who is everywhere without attachment,
Meeting with anything good or bad,
and who neither rejoices nor hates.

2.58 *As the tortoise withdraws its limbs from all sides,*
when a person withdraws his senses from the sense-objects,
His wisdom becomes steady in completion.

2.59 *Though for the embodied, the sense enjoyments may be restricted,*
the taste or desire for sense objects remain; but, such tastes or desires also leave him on seeing, experiencing the Supreme.

Arjuna is now curious and wants to know more. He asks Kṛṣṇa, 'You are telling me all this, that is wonderful. You tell me that I must perform without expectations and attachment and that I must be complete in wisdom. I would like to live that way and move on the path of wisdom. Pray, tell me what kind of a person is this, the one who always stays in the steady space of completion—*sthita prajñasya kā bhāṣā samādhi-sthasya keśava* (2.54).

How does he behave, walk and talk? Let me model myself on him.'

For the fifth time Arjuna expresses authentic interest in what Kṛṣṇa is saying. Arjuna has realized that whatever he said earlier had arisen from his confusion, his patterns. Arjuna is intelligent enough to know that he does not know.

When Kṛṣṇa tells him to behave in a manner befitting the code of the warriors, this piece of advice certainly makes good sense to Arjuna. However, what Kṛṣṇa says further confuses Arjuna. Kṛṣṇa says to do what you have to do without being concerned about the outcome. This is a strange idea to Arjuna. He has rarely done anything in his life without thinking about the result of his action.

Arjuna, the greatest of marksmen, is conditioned with the pattern to first define his target and then act. Kṛṣṇa has confused him totally now. Kṛṣṇa says, 'Release your arrow; where it lands is my business.' At least, this is how Arjuna understands what Kṛṣṇa says. Arjuna has enough trust in Kṛṣṇa not to ignore this instruction from the Divine.

So he asks, 'Tell me who is it who acts without any interest in the outcome? Who is it who is not concerned about the result, whether it is good or bad, painful or joyful, and how do I identify such a person?'

Kṛṣṇa responds, 'This man is free from desires and emotions. He has neither greed nor fear. He has no patterns. He is always complete in himself. Pleasures through the senses do not interest him. He has withdrawn his senses from the external or outer world and has integrated them inwards into his inner space, directed them towards that Supreme Truth that is beyond all pleasures, attachments, emotions and sense objects.' Kṛṣṇa thus describes the Realized Yogi, the *Sthitaprajña* to Arjuna so that he too may emulate him and realize himself.

Seek the Unattached

'*Nirmohatve niścalatatvaṁ*,' says Ādī Śaṅkarācārya, taking a cue from the Master. It means: Absence of desires leads to a clear and still mind and inner space, steeped in the wisdom of completion. When there are no desires, there are no emotions such as joy, depression, sadness, anger, disappointment, jealousy that normally arise from the fulfillment or non-fulfillment of such desires. When the mind is without fear and anger, without expectations of success and failure, the unattached mind seeks that which is unattached. First the objects drop, then the desire for the objects disappears as truth dawns. This may sound complicated, but is as simple as counting '1, 2, 3.'

This Universe is responsible for all of us. We exist not because of ourselves and our actions but in spite of it. The Universe functions on the science of responsibility, *upāyanaṁ*. Responsibility is the science of life.

Listen. The whole Universe is a holographic structure. For example, if there is a ten-by-ten meter hologram or a picture, on cutting it into several ten-by-ten millimeter ones, the same picture will be there inside it. That is a hologram. It means that whatever is in the macrocosm—the whole Universe, is also there inside your body—the microcosm! If you dissect, dissect, and go into a small atom, the *brahmāṅda* (macrocosm) will be there in *piṇḍāṅda* (microcosm). Whatever is there in the *piṇḍāṅda* is there in the *brahmāṅda*. The cosmos functions with the principle of a hologram. Responsibility is the DNA, which awakens the cosmic hologram in you. If you want to experience the macrocosm hologram in the microcosm, awaken responsibility.

Listen. The macrocosm and microcosm are just mirroring each other's possibility. When we feel the responsibility for existence, we become existence and existence feels responsible for us. When we let go of our patterns, when we listen to the Universe and feel responsible, the Universe feels responsible for us and gives us all that we need to live with abundance.

But the problem is that we don't listen and we don't take responsibility and destroy our own possibility! We do not stop with our needs but get greedy with our wants as well. There is no way all our wants can be fulfilled without taking away the needs of other beings in this Universe.

Feel responsible! You are the microcosmic hologram of the macrocosmic diagram. Once we choose to live based on responsibility, we know our real present needs and not futuristic wants. We rise into the present moment of completion. Desires based on past and future dissolve. We then realize that we too are the *brahmāṅda*, Universe and that we can have all that we need as all that belongs to the Universe belongs to us also.

Be Steady in Wisdom of Completion

Kṛṣṇa aptly provides the analogy of the tortoise, *kurma* to illustrate how to withdraw one's senses inwards and how to be centered and steady in wisdom of completion in the Self, *tasya prajñā pratiṣthitā* (2.58). Its entire cycle of life is tuned to the wisdom of nature. An animal, when it indulges in any act, whether of mating, caring, killing or saving its own life, does all and any of these with tremendous focus. The animal always lives in its present moment. Not so the human. For the human, where his body is his mind never is.

Corporate people ask me how to make right decisions. It is simple. When you take responsibility for the job at hand and make a decision to act out of your peak possibility based on the information available at that moment, without the influence of past or future incompletions, your decisions will always be right. The Universal energy guides you in your decision when you take responsibility, when you settle into yourself, focus inwards and withdraw your senses as the tortoise does.

You are responsible for everything. If you feel that you are poor, take responsibility for it. If you feel that you are sick, take responsibility for it. Responsibility makes everything, from an ordinary desire to have a good meal tomorrow to your desire to be in desirelessness become a reality. Everything is realized when you take responsibility.

What do you all do instead? Half the time you do not take the responsibility and postpone decisions because you are afraid of the consequences of the decision. So things happen without your control and which do not favor you. The other half of the time you are led by greed and prejudices based on past experiences and future fantasies and you decide with no relevance to issues of that moment.

When have you last done anything whatsoever with complete integrity? When were you integrated only to the food that you ate, instead of chatting, reading, and watching? You may say that we are only human, we wish to enjoy life and we wish to enjoy sensual pleasures. Please do! However, when you enjoy, enjoy fully. Be fully in integrity with that object of enjoyment and with all your senses integrated only on that activity. When you do whatever you do with one hundred percent integrity, authenticity and responsibility, you are in the space of completion. You become God!

Monkeys In The Mind

2.60 *O Kaunteya (son of Kuntī), the turbulent senses*
carry away the mind of a wise man,
Though he is striving to be in control.

2.61 *Having restrained them all, he should sit steadfast, intent on Me.*
Whose senses are under control, his mind is steady in the present.

2.62 *When a man thinks of objects, it gives rise to attachment for them.*
From attachment, desire arises; from desire, anger is born.

2.63 *From anger arises delusion, from delusion, loss of memory,*
from loss of memory, the loss of discrimination,
from loss of discrimination, he perishes.

2.64 *The self-controlled man, moving among objects*
with his senses under control,
free from both attraction and repulsion, attains peace.

2.65 *All pains are destroyed in that peace, for the intellect of the*
tranquil-minded soon becomes steady.

2.66 *A person not in self-awareness cannot be wise or happy or peaceful.*
How can there be happiness to one without peace?

2.67 *He loses his awareness of the present moment when his mind follows the wandering senses,*
Just as the wind carries away a boat on the waters.

Kṛṣṇa continues to explain to Arjuna how difficult it is to control the senses and what happens when one loses control of the senses.

Kṛṣṇa says that our senses are turbulent, and however much we try to control them, they stay out of control. He says that the only way is to integrate and fix one's mind on Him once the senses are under control and the mind is steady. The mind cannot be stopped. Thoughts cannot be stopped as long as the body exists. You can bring integrity to your thinking by doing completion with your root patterns. Thus integrating your mind on something that transcends sensory pleasures, it will become quiet by itself. Once the mind discovers the bliss of this completion, it will never want to stray again.

A small story:

> A man, intent on spiritual progress, went to a master and begged him to teach him how to control his mind. The master tried to explain that the mind couldn't be controlled in the way he was seeking, by stopping his thoughts, but he wouldn't listen. Fed up, the master gave him a bottle of a liquid and told him to drink three drops three times a day.
>
> The man asked, 'That's it? It will control my mind?'
>
> The master said, 'Just one thing, make sure you don't think of a monkey when you drink the medicine.'
>
> 'Oh, sure, quite simple!' said the man as he walked out. At the door he turned and asked, 'By the way, in case I do think of a monkey, what should I do?'
>
> 'Take a shower,' said the master, 'and try again.'
>
> As soon as the man went home, he took out the medicine and opened his mouth to drink it. Just then he remembered the master's warning—and remembered the monkey!
>
> 'Oh, my God!' he said to himself, 'Now I have to take a shower. What else to do!'
>
> You can guess the rest of the story. Each time he opened his bottle of medicine, monkeys invaded his mind and all he did was keep taking showers. It got to a point where as soon as he got out of the shower, thoughts of monkeys arose in his mind.

He ran to the master and pleaded, 'Forget the medicine. Just get rid of the monkeys, please!'

You can never destroy thoughts or suppress them. Suppression does not work on the mind, only completion does. Suppressed emotions solidify as a volcano of root patterns and explode when they get the chance. You can only complete with thoughts by doing self-completion with them, and gradually the mind will settle down. Lack of integrity is nothing but suppressing your thoughts and putting all your problems under the carpet.

Please understand, however much you try to push the incomplete conversations with you under the carpet, they do not die. They run around under the carpet like Tom and Jerry cartoon! In the same way, the incompletions pushed under your inner space, say, 'No, no, no! Why are you asking too many questions? Somehow I will win. Keep quiet!' Without completing, if you push your own questions under the carpet, they will not die or keep quiet. Today or tomorrow, you have to face those questions. You have to face that part of you.

When you do completion and settle into the present moment, with no expectations and no attachments, you will find that your inner space becomes quiet and your senses slow down.

Be Complete in the Present Moment

Kṛṣṇa says that from attachment springs desire, from desire arises anger, from anger arises delusion, from delusion comes loss of memory, and from loss of memory develops loss of discrimination which then leads to one's destruction. The only way to stop this, the Lord says, is to control one's senses, complete with oneself and surrender to Him, the Universal energy, and achieve everlasting peace.

The map has been so clearly laid down by the greatest Master, not because He wants you to follow it, but because in His infinite grace and compassion He is making you aware of what is in store for you if you do. He teaches that if you do not control your senses, you will be destroyed.

Go through each of these stages laid down by the Master. The path will be crystal clear. Each one of us develops attachment, liking, hatred and dislike for many things through our experiences. These likes and dislikes stay in our unconscious memory as root thought patterns and even without any conscious awareness on our part, drive us into actions through desires or into inaction through fears. When the desires are fulfilled, there is temporary satisfaction; then the desires grow. When the desires do not get fulfilled we are disappointed, we get angry.

We should be angry with our own selves for having had the desires or for not having worked with authenticity, wholeheartedly at the peak of our capability towards fulfilling the desire, but we actually get angry with other people who we think are responsible for our failures. We do not realize that blaming others will make us feel more and more powerless!

Kṛṣṇa reveals two very important truths here in the last two verses. One is that you can never be peaceful unless you are complete, conscious. The other is that you cannot be complete if you are led by your senses. Therefore, as long as your senses lead you into what you think is a pleasurable journey; you cannot really be happy or peaceful. It is just another trick your mind is playing on you. Your happiness is not real happiness. It is just a gap between two periods of sorrow. What you hear, what you think you hear, what you see, what you think you see, and so on, all these sense inputs are unreliable, incomplete cognitions.

I tell you, with anybody who succeeded, till that success happened, he only failed! But if he had held on to his past record, success should not have happened in his life. This journey never stops all through your life unless you make a serious attempt to complete with it. Your mind, on its own, would never want to stay in the present moment, which is the only moment of truth. Self-completion, *svapūrṇatva* is the only direct method to reclaim your space of completion. This is your basic right. Reclaim it!

Understand, you can make whatever you can visualize as reality. With integrity and authenticity, visualize yourself in the space of non-falling, moving only from completion to completion, fulfillment to fulfillment.

Your past is history. Your past record is the dumping ground of all your regrets and guilt. There is no greater sin that you can commit than carrying past records of these regrets and guilt.

Or your mind dwells in the future, a future that does not exist. You speculate, and dream creating stories and arguments, building a case for your future. If you are questioned, you would say, 'I need to plan.' How much of what you plan is based on present reality? There is nothing wrong at all if you are grounded in reality and plan to progress in that reality. That is what I call chronological planning which is necessary if you live in the world. I do it too. For example, it is planning the day ahead, with what time you will wake up, what time you will have the meeting and then return home etc. But most of the time what you do has nothing to do with reality. You either worry about things that you have no control over and plan how to escape such worries, or desire things not in your reach out of sheer greed. Just think with integrity, feel with authenticity and act with responsibility.

Drop the past records. The past track never gives you the confidence, the possibility. Unless you see the possibility, life does not flow in you! Excitement does not happen in you. The past records always bring deep sorrow, because by nature, past records are death. Possibility, by nature, is Life! The past record is neither as bad as you remember, nor worthy of being remembered. Possibility is life. Life is possibility, not past record.

Our senses aid us very ably to see only the past records and project them as worries and desires. They make us believe that all this is real and make us react to situations as if they are real. It is the same way that we get up from a nightmare sweating profusely out of fear. Although just a dream, it makes us sweat. In the same manner, these projections of our mind, even when we are fully awake, appear real to us.

Kṛṣṇa says, 'Get away from your senses; escape from their control; ground yourself in the completion of the present. Only then can you be at peace. How can there be happiness for one without peace, *aśāntasya kutaḥ sukham*? (2.66).'

What is this present moment? What is this completion? When we do the self-completion process, our mind and inner space becomes integrated and authentic and stops moving back and forth between the past and future, it will by itself land in the present moment. The present moment is what we are doing now. If you are reading this book, don't half read this book and half listen to music; don't half read this book and half talk with someone. Either be complete and focus completely on what you are reading or don't read at all.

The next time you do anything, bring completion and be integrated to what you are doing at that moment. If you are brushing your teeth, just focus on how the brush moves and how the paste tastes. Stop thinking about the meetings later at your office or getting your children ready for school, or whatever it is that you need to do a few minutes or hours later.

When you settle into the space of completion, you are out of the clutches of your senses and mind. You will still see and hear, but none of what you see and hear will divert you from what you are integrated to doing. You will be aware of only what you are doing in that present moment. This is what we call meditation. Meditation is nothing but being integrated completely to what you are doing at a particular moment.

When you plan for the unimaginable, when your nervous system is loaded with things that you are not able to even comprehend, the excitement that oozes in your nervous system is bliss! Understand, bliss does not come to lazy bums! Bliss does not happen to people caught in the past records. This is what Kṛṣṇa says will lead you into peace and very soon to being steady—*prasanna-cetaso hy āśu buddhiḥ paryasvatiṣṭhate* (2.65). When you are complete, your senses are in your control instead of you being under their control. You become peaceful, you are in bliss.

Wake Up

2.68 *O Mahābāho (mighty-armed one), his knowledge is therefore steady whose senses are completely detached from sense objects.*

2.69 *The self-controlled man is awake in that which is night to all beings. Where all beings are awake, it is night for the sage who sees.*

2.70 *Just as all waters enter the ocean, which, though always being filled from all sides, remains unmoved; likewise, he, into whom all desires enter themselves, remains unmoved, undisturbed, can alone attain peace; not the one who desires to fulfill desires.*

2.71 *The man who moves about abandoning all desires, without longing, without the sense of ego—'I' and 'mine', attains peace.*

2.72 *O Pārtha, this is the state of Brahman, Brāhmī-sthiti; none is deluded after attaining this. Even at the end of life, one attains Brahmanirvāṇa, oneness with Brahman, when established in this state.*

In His concluding words in this chapter, Kṛṣṇa clarifies to Arjuna once again, how to reach liberation, how to become one with Brahman which is one's true and natural state. We have seen that a person not centered in self-completion cannot be peaceful or happy or wise. A person who is led by his senses cannot be complete. A person who is in control of his senses is firmly in control of his mind and emotions. Only such a person is truly awake.

We all think we are awake; are we really? We live in daydreams even if we are awake. The only occasion when we are truly awake is when we are in the space of completion. A person in such a space of completion is whom Kṛṣṇa calls a '*Muni*,' a realized being living in the present. Such a person is always awake, having experienced his inner awakening, whether physically awake or asleep.

Kṛṣṇa says that such a person is in sleep when others are awake, *yasyāṁ jāgrati bhūtāni sā niśā paśyato muneḥ* (2.69). The realized person, although he may appear to be living and actively participating in the activities of the same world that we live in, is in reality, in a state of passive alertness or restful awareness.

This means that his senses are not immersed in worldliness and he is centered and complete in his Self. He is dead and asleep to this world because he has moved beyond his senses. A truly realized person is also awake when others are asleep, *yā niśā sarva-bhūtānāṁ tasyāṁ jāgrati saṁyamī* (2.69). Even in his sleep he is aware, in what is called the state of *supta chittam*.

A person who is in the space of completion is still as the waters in the bed of the ocean. Though there are waves in the surface, they do not disturb the bed of the ocean. Even when desires assail him, they are mere waves in the periphery of his consciousness, and do not disturb him at all. He has abandoned all attachment to 'I' and 'mine.' He is without thoughts and desires and when thoughts and desires come to him, they merge into him without disturbing him.

How this is possible? The '*Muni*,' one who is still, in silence, is one who is in total control of his senses. When the senses are controlled, when the ego is out of action, all thoughts and desires are just witnessed. The '*Muni*' does not get involved in these thoughts and desires. He does not even try to stop or suppress them, as he knows it is impossible. He just lets them be watching them go past, just like the ocean watches impassively as other waters merge into it.

We are all enlightened because we are all a hologramic part of the reality of the Universe, Brahman. All that we lack is the awareness of the truth of our Enlightenment. What prevents you from realizing that you are enlightened is your root pattern, ego. This ego is not necessarily about any arrogance. It is the perception of who you think you are, your inner-image; what you project yourself to be for others, your outer-image; and what others expect you to be for them, others' image. It is the collection of thoughts, experiences and emotions that go to make up that 'I' and 'mine.' This identity is that of the body and mind, not of your spirit. Therefore, it perishes with your body and is transient.

A person who is in control of his senses, his mind and thoughts, lives in the present moment, in full awareness of his true nature and is one with Brahman. For such a *Muni*, the knowledge of *Advaita*, the space of oneness with Brahman, becomes a living reality. He conquers all the wrong self-identification with his inner and outer identities. Such a person who is self-aware is fully awake even when he is asleep.

People with a strong consciousness of 'I' live out of their blocked *mūlādhāra cakra*, the root energy center. They are at the very beginning of their spiritual evolution. Their main concerns will be about their own survival, and they are caught in lust, anger and greed. The person with a strong attachment to 'mine,' the possessions belonging to the 'I,' constantly lives in fear of losing these possessions. Such people live out of their blocked *svādiṣṭhāna* or spleen *cakra*—the energy center that gets locked due to fear. They live in insecurity of losing possessions, of losing identity, and finally, of death.

Energization of the *mūlādhāra* and *svādiṣṭhāna cakra* and moving the energy up through the *anāhata* or heart *cakra* to the *ājña* or third-eye *cakra* (energy center between eyebrows) opens us to completion, the reality of looking at others, at Universe as our own self and finally dropping the root pattern—one's identification with 'I' and 'mine.'

Listen! Completion can make you experience *Advaita* (non-duality), the ultimate space of Consciousness, immediately. Then, true surrender to the Universe and identification with one's true nature occurs, and Enlightenment happens. You then become God!

Kṛṣṇa completes His description of the person established in yoga whose profile Arjuna has asked for. Kṛṣṇa concludes by saying that a person steeped in yoga is complete in reality and is one with Brahman—*eṣā brāhmī sthitiḥ pārtha*. He says that this person is liberated even if he were to reach that state at the end of his life—*brahma-nirvānaṁ ṛcchati* (2.72).

Kṛṣṇa is in the process of enriching Arjuna what he truly is and how he can realize that truth. Control over the senses, being in the state of restful awareness instead of letting the senses control you, surrendering to the Universe instead of fighting the Universe, dropping one's mind and identity; staying in the space of completion are the surest ways to realize the truth, the truth that you indeed are God.

I tell my disciples time and again, 'I am not here to prove my Divinity. I am here to prove your Divinity.' This is the timeless message of Kṛṣṇa, the message of *Bhagavad Gītā*.

Arjuna's confusion is slowly reducing. Actually, it is good to be confused. It is much better to accept that one is confused than to live in the delusion that one knows everything. Arjuna had the courage of authenticity to come out and tell Kṛṣṇa his fears and doubts. This is the first step towards clarity. How long it takes for that clarity to emerge doesn't matter. One is on the path of completion and that is what matters.

Listen to the Truth.

The science of completion is the essence of *Sāṅkhya Yoga*. Completion makes you experience the Sāṅkhya of life. In this second chapter of *Gītā* on *Sāṅkhya Yogaḥ* or Transcendental Knowledge of Completion, Śrī Kṛṣṇa who is the space of completion Himself, sets Arjuna on the path of completion. May all of you travel that path too!

Let us pray to the ultimate Existence, *Parabrahma* Kṛṣṇa, to give us all the experience of eternal bliss, *Nityānanda*. Thank you!

Thus ends the second chapter named ***Sāṅkhya Yogaḥ****, 'The Yoga of Knowledge of Completion,' of the* ***Bhagavad Gītā Upaniṣad, Brahmavidyā Yogaśāstra****, the scripture of yoga dealing with the science of the Absolute in the form of* ***Śrī Kṛṣṇārjuna-saṁvād****, dialogue between* ***Śrī Kṛṣṇa, Arjuna.***

CHAPTER

3

Karma Yogaḥ

Beauty Of Purposelessness

Life is to enjoy living in completion and acting with authenticity in action; not to chase goals. There is no real purpose to life; life in fact is purposeless. Once we create goals to reach, we create sorrow to follow. Coming to terms with the reality of life is Completion.

Beauty Of Purposelessness

The whole of Existence, the whole Universe, is purposeless. Of course, it would be very shocking to hear this. At a very young age, we are taught and socially conditioned to believe that life has some purpose. We are always made to run towards some goal, towards some purpose.

'What is life without purpose?' you may ask. We feel that any activity, let alone one's entire life, has to have a purpose, a definition, and an end point. Only then does it become meaningful. That purpose is what drives us, motivates us.

You will say I am confusing you. 'All our life we have been brought up to believe that we are here for a purpose. As children we are expected to do well at school, and later at college. Once we grow up, we are supposed to get married and bring up our children. In each phase of our life, we have specific templates that society has set up for us. How can we let them down? How can we believe that all these expectations are wrong, and that there is no purpose to life?'

The more you run towards a goal, the more you are considered a successful person. The greater the speed, the more you are respected. From birth, again and again, you are taught that life has a purpose and a goal. Life without purpose seems meaningless to us. Understand that this is only what you have been brought up to believe. This is not the truth of Existence. Life does not need a defined goal to make living worthwhile, meaningful and happy. The absence of purpose makes our life meaningful. The absence of goals in life makes living worthwhile.

The Universe, Nature has no purpose. It just is. It exists. A river runs downhill towards the ocean because it is its nature to run downhill. It is not because it has a purpose, to meet the ocean. Our life too, has no purpose. We were not born for a purpose. We were born to live, to enjoy life and to be happy. Instead, we set ourselves up for unhappiness; we set goals for ourselves, and almost always these goals are based on fantasies and not on realities. In the process, we stop enjoying life.

The more you run towards the goal, the more you miss Life itself! A person who is continuously bothered about goals will never be able to enjoy and enrich his life. He lives in the future and ignores the present. When we are complete in the present moment, the here and now, we do not need a goal to guide us.

Just the space of completion in the present moment will help us decide what needs to be done at each point in time. When the present moment is taken care of with completion, the future gets resolved on its own. As long as the path is right, whatever destination we reach will be right. We do not need to define the destination; the right path defines its own destination.

However, we constantly worry about the future, relating it with the past. We continuously postpone our happiness without enjoying the present. For example, when you are studying you think, 'When I get a job, I will be happy.' When you have your job you think, 'After marriage my life will be happy.' After marriage, you think, 'When I have kids and my own house, I will be happy.' After achieving that you think, 'When the kids grow up and all my responsibilities are over, I will be happy.' By the time your responsibilities are over, when you want to relax, your being is so conditioned to running that you can't relax!

With this default cognition, we are constantly running to stay in the same spot. Happiness is *where we are*, not where we think *we should be.* We do not understand what it is to relax.

When I tell people to relax during meditation, they say, 'Swamiji, please give us detailed guidelines on how to relax!' We feel we need to lose our happiness before we can start searching for it. The tension of running after something out of compulsion has become a part of our being. Resting is no longer relaxation. When we run behind goals, all that seems to matter is the achievement of that goal. Any sacrifice seems to be worth it, including those we claim we love and care for.

ONLY A COMPLETE BEING CAN RELAX

The more you run, the more titles you receive. You are called a 'multi-dimensional personality.' This is just another name for schizophrenics. Only a person who has deeply experienced himself, who is complete in himself, who rests in himself, who experiences inaction in action can be a multidimensional personality. Only such a person understands himself and his many personalities, and is comfortable and complete with all of them.

Only a Kṛṣṇa, a complete being can be a multidimensional personality. Only a man who completely rests in himself, who knows how to relax within himself, can be a multidimensional personality.

A person who runs to satisfy society, who is compelled to run by society, can never experience peace. Society doesn't want you as you are. It wants you as it thinks you should be. If you are a doctor, a lawyer, or an accountant, if you are useful to society in some way, then you are rewarded; otherwise you are made to feel inadequate and incomplete. You are respected just for your title, not for what you are. The more titles you have, the more respect you get.

Life is purposeless. Look into your life. Whatever you think of as the goal of your life, even if it were fulfilled, do you think you will be able to rest and feel complete? You will only look for the next goal. There is no resting point. There is no time to appreciate or celebrate what you have achieved. You are driven from one goal to another, from one desire to another. There is always a feeling of discontentment, a deep incompletion. You run not because your being wants to, but because society drives you to.

With Completion starts Life. Otherwise you are running out of compulsion. Either you run life in compulsion or in completion. With compulsion, not only don't you have any Life, you also constantly reduce the level of your life.

A person came to me and said, 'Earlier I used to smoke and drink. My wife used to fight with me all the time, always blaming me. She would connect everything to my smoking and drinking. If the kids did not study well, she would say, 'You are a drunkard. You don't care for your kids. That is why they are not studying well.'

So finally, somehow, I gave up smoking and drinking.'

I asked, 'Oh! Is she happy now?'

He said, 'No! Now she is unhappy that she is not able to complain about anything anymore!'

When you are inauthentic, you can have something or someone to blame, you can always put the responsibility on them and feel comfortable. When you can't put the responsibility on someone else, you suffer. It is easy to escape the reality by putting the responsibility on someone else. Here, Arjuna is doing the same thing by asking Kṛṣṇa this question in the third chapter called *Karma Yogaḥ*.

Coming to terms with reality is Completion. Reality should not make you powerless. Arjuna is being inauthentic by shifting responsibility away from him, not facing his own reality. Kṛṣṇa initiates him into the science of authentic action to powerfully take responsibility for his highest reality and be a complete, blissful being.

To Act Or Not To Act

3.1 *Arjuna says:*
O Janārdana, Why do You urge me engage in this terrible war,
If You think that knowledge is superior to action, O Keśava?

3.2 *My intelligence is confused by Your conflicting words.*
Therefore, please tell me certainly what is most beneficial for me.

3.3 *Bhagavān says,*
O sinless Arjuna, as I said before, in this world there are two paths of firm faith; jñānayoga, the path of Self-knowledge for the intellectual and karmayoga, the path of action of the knowing.

3.4 *A person does not attain freedom from action by abstaining from work, nor does he attain fulfillment by giving up action.*

In the previous chapter on *Sāṅkhya Yogaḥ*, Kṛṣṇa tells Arjuna that knowledge of the Self is the supreme path to Enlightenment. He explains the nature of the indestructible Self. Kṛṣṇa tells Arjuna to shed all root patterns of fear, abandon his desires and go beyond success and failure; to practice authenticity in action, to be unattached and steady in completion of the Self, the state of Brahman.

Arjuna is still in the space of inauthenticity. He is confused as to what he should do. At one level, he understands what Kṛṣṇa says to him. However, the explanation about the spirit living on while the body dies, and the idea that all those he is about to fight and destroy have already been destroyed in the cosmic sense, does not appeal to him. Arjuna is a warrior. To him, what is seen in front of him is what exists. He sees all his elders and relatives arrayed against him in battle and he has to make a choice to kill or be killed. This is the physical reality that he faces.

Kṛṣṇa tells him not to take this reality seriously. He says all the living people in front of him are already dead, and therefore he is committing no sin by killing them again. In fact, if he does not fight them, he is being out of integrity; by running away from the battle as an inauthentic coward. He also tells Arjuna that he has the right to do his duty but no right to its results.

'Let not the fruit of action be your motive and let not your attachment be to inaction either,' Kṛṣṇa warns him.

Violence Asks for Single Instruction

Arjuna is totally confused. He tells Kṛṣṇa, 'I do not understand what you are saying. First, you tell me to fight. Then you tell me to shed anger. You say I must kill my enemies, who are my elders and relatives, but then you say I should not worry about the end result.' Arjuna says, 'All I need to know is whether I should act or not. You say knowledge is superior to action and yet you say I must act. What should I do?' he asks.

Arjuna is clearly in violence. Asking, expecting or thinking only one act can be important IS violence. Only violence asks for instruction without inspiration. A violent person cannot be inspired. He can only be instructed.

Arjuna is asking for a single instruction from Kṛṣṇa, he says, 'Tell me clearly what is best for me?' Arjuna's pattern of asking for only a single best instruction is the pattern of violence. By asking for a clear instruction, he can hold Kṛṣṇa responsible for his own inauthenticity and escape the responsibility for his actions.

I want you to understand that asking for a single instruction itself is from the violence. And if the single instruction is given, that is encouraging your violence., only inspiration should be given. Before you take up any philosophy the first quality you should check for in that philosophy is this—how does it introduce **yourself** to you?

If any religion gives you a manual, that religion is born from violence and will continue to flourish in violence. In the *Bhagavad Gītā*, you will rarely see Kṛṣṇa giving Arjuna instructions. All seven hundred verses are literally nectars of inspiration uttered out of Bhagavān Kṛṣṇa's love and compassion. They are all inspiring, empowering and enriching. Nowhere will you see instructions!

You see, in the beginning of *Gītā* when Arjuna says, 'Leave me, I am going and becoming *Sannyāsi*.' Bhagavān Kṛṣṇa says, 'No!' He asks him to fight. Later, when Arjuna is asking, 'Why should I act? How can I fight?' Bhagavān tells him about *Sannyāsa*, how to become a *Sannyāsi*.

Arjuna is supposed to fight, but he is being taught the knowledge of completion with *Sāṅkhya Yoga*! He is being taught to meditate with one full chapter for *dhyāna yoga* and he is being taught the different great aspects of *Sannyāsa yoga*! *Karma-Sannyāsa Yoga*! *Jñānakarma-Sannyāsa Yoga*!

This is the beauty of Hinduism! No single instruction can work because the root pattern of asking for a single instruction is violence. Why? Because we feel either we should be alive or the other person should be alive. The mentality of fighting and violence always excludes. The root of the problem should be solved. Anything that talks about one and only one solution is born out of survival instinct, never out of inspiration.

What Arjuna leaves unsaid is, 'What use is knowledge if it cannot be used in action?' Arjuna is a *kṣatriya*, a warrior, not a brāhmin, a scholar or a philosopher. Philosophers can keep arguing for both sides of an issue, without bothering about any logic. They are only interested in advertising their so-called knowledge. But warriors are men of action. They have no time to waste in idle talk. So Arjuna says, 'Cut out all this superficiality; tell me the truth as it is. Tell me what I should do.' True to his conditioning, Arjuna is uncomfortable when he is not in action; when he has no clearly defined purpose and motivated instructions before him.

FULFILLMENT IN PURPOSE, AN ILLUSION!

Your whole life is purposeless, but again and again, you are conditioned to run towards something—whether it is in material life or spiritual life. Some goal is always put in front of you. The so-called goals in material life or spiritual life continuously make you feel you are not good enough.

Just understand, whatever you think of as your purpose in life, whether it is money or relationships or name and fame, even if you have fulfillment in that dimension, you will not rest, you will not be complete!

Someone told me this, I believe a management consultant said it, 'If you place a ladder somewhere and climb as fast as you can, you will quickly reach the top of the ladder. But unless the ladder is placed where you want, where you reach will be of no consequence!' Climbing as fast as you can is efficiency. We all think we are very efficient. Placing the ladder where you want is effectiveness. Not all of us know where to place the ladder. So, the consultant says to focus on where to place the ladder.

But I say even he is mistaken. It does not matter where you place the ladder as long as you enjoy the climb! As long as your 'why' is with the right context, with completion as your root cognition, 'what' and 'where' does not matter. More than your actions, it is the space from which the actions are done, and the context and reason from which the actions are done that matter!

The trouble is that we spend the entire climb obsessed with where we will reach and what we will do there. If we spend that time enjoying and being enriched by the journey, any destination we reach will be the right destination. The destination is not important; the journey is. The goal is not important; the process, the path is.

We are always greedy for more. We continuously pursue material goals. As a result, we never relax within ourselves. That is why even when we become old we are unable to relax. Have you seen a single man above seventy relaxing? People can never sit with themselves! If they have company, they will start talking about their golden past. If they don't have company, they will watch television or read the same old newspaper, from the first line to the last with a big magnifying glass! They just can't sit with themselves.

A man who can't sit with himself misses one of the major dimensions of his being. Continuously running, thinking there is some purpose to life, his whole being will be in a state of tension, conditioned to running out of compulsion, never out of completion.

Root thought pattern is nothing but this first social conditioning, this strong cognition which imbalances you from your purposeless space and gives birth to the mind, the idea that there is some purpose to life. Life has no purpose. Even if you achieve whatever you want, you can't take it with you. You can't carry even a single dollar when you leave. Nothing will come with you.

There is no exchange offer. If you give fifty rupees in India, you will get one dollar in USA. But no matter how much money you give in this world, you cannot get a single rupee in heaven or anywhere else. No cheque will be useful. None of your money can be carried over to the next world.

The only currency that works everywhere in existence is completion. As of now, this material world appears four-dimensional and multi-colored as you enjoy it with all your senses. The moment you leave the body, the same world will appear black and white, one dimensional. When you are dreaming, your dream looks and feels very real. When you are awake, this world around you looks like reality and the dream looks dull. But there is no scale to determine the reality and the dream.

People tell me, 'But everyday when we enter a dream, we are not entering the same dream, *Swamiji.* Yet, everyday when we return to reality we are entering the same reality. So with this scale we can tell the reality apart from the dream.'

Listen, in one night's dream you can live even 20 years of life, am I right? Don't you sometimes have such dreams where in one night's dream you live 20 years of life? Then why can't your dream be reality, because of its consistency? This whole life time span, which you think is reality, may be part of the dream! There is no scale to prove reality and the dream. When you leave the body, all you see now as multi-colour will become black and white.

Nothing can be carried with you at the time of leaving the body. You can't cash your cheques! You can't talk to your relatives. If you speak, they will run away! Your car will not be useful to you anymore. When you are not able to take anything with you, what is the purpose of life then?

The moment you accept the beauty of purposelessness, you will realize the meaning of living.

LIFE HAS NO PURPOSE, ONLY MEANING

Life has no purpose, but it has meaning. Purpose means goal orientation. You always think about the goal; you keep running and one day you just drop dead! The more goal-oriented you are, the more you will miss life and the more you will be incomplete.

Purpose is different from meaning. When I say 'meaning', living itself becomes meaningful. Come to this present moment of completion and the path itself is life; the path itself is meaningful.

There is no such thing as, 'in the end you will be happy.' You always postpone joy and so you always postpone living. Life is lived in a very superficial way because you think life has a purpose.

For the man who works just for his salary, only payday will be a beautiful day. He will be happy only on that day. He sells 29 days every month for that one day of happiness. I don't say, 'Don't take your salary.' But let it not be the only goal in your life. Let it not play a major role in your consciousness. That is what Kṛṣṇa means by these words: *karmaṇy evādhikāras te mā phaleṣu kadācana* (2.47)—you can do only your duty, you have no right to its fruit. If you think of the fruit, you will lose the joy of doing, living, enriching! The meaning of living is experienced only when you understand the beauty of purposelessness. This is a beautiful verse! It is the essence of the *Gītā*!

YOUR INNER SPACE IS THE SPACE OF COMPLETION

Two things you need to understand from this: One, He says, let your inner space not be contaminated by the purpose of life. When I say inner space, I mean your mind and how you feel about yourself, about things and life inside you. When you close your eyes, what comes into your mind is your inner space. If your inner space is filled with the purposes of life, be very clear you are running behind something which will never give you completion. He says, 'Let your inner space not be disturbed or filled with purposes or incompletions.'

By nature, your inner space is the space of completion, it is filled with energy; your inner space, what you refer to as *ātman*, spirit or soul, is filled with blissful energy. The more you empty yourself of goals or incompletions, the more the space for completion and bliss.

For example, this room is filled with space. The more furniture you put in it, the more space will leave this room. This room is not empty; no place is empty. It is filled with space. This room is filled with the energy of ether. The more furniture you bring in, the more ether will be pushed out; the lesser will be the ether energy. In the outer space, if you furnish your home, it will look very nice. But if you furnish your inner space, it will look very ugly.

Completion straightaway gives you whatever you want and takes away whatever is not. The whole problem of humanity is what you want outside is not with you and what you don't need inside in your inner space is with you. You need to empty your inside, which is filled with unnecessary furniture. You need to have all the necessary things outside.

Creating the inner space of completion with integrity and authenticity will immediately do that job. Completion will clear out all unnecessary things from your inner space. It will get you all that you need in the outer world. Don't furnish your inner space. Let your inner space be empty. Of course then, it will never be empty. It will be filled with completion, *pūrṇatva*. It will be filled with bliss! The more complete inner space you create, the more blissful your life will be. That is what Kṛṣṇa means by saying, 'Don't be attached to results.'

If you continuously think about the result, you will never be able to perform your action with completion. You will always be goal-oriented and you will never enjoy and enrich the path of completion. Not enjoying and enriching the path is the worst hell you can be trapped in.

Again and again Kṛṣṇa says, '*paritrāṇāya sādhūnāṁ vināśāya ca duṣkṛtām dharma saṁsthāpanārthāya saṁbhavāmi yuge-yuge* (4.8).' It means: I come down again and again to save the integrated and authentic, the complete and innocent people, and to destroy the evil-minded incomplete people.

People ask me, 'You say *dharma* (responsibility to enrich) is the only thing to be practiced with integrity and authenticity, but in our lives we see people who are not living according to *dharma*, yet they are living more happily; they have more property, more wealth. Why is that?' Understand, they may have more property, they may have more things in the outer space, but never think they are happy in their inner space; never think they are blissful.

When does someone not follow *dharma*? When he follows his ambition! Ambition causes you to go out of integrity and authenticity. Don't think we go to hell because we commit sins. We commit sins because we are in hell. The very ambition is hell; there is no need for a separate hell. Don't think we will reach a separate place called 'hell' at the end of our life.

If you are complete and blissful, you will never disturb others. If you are unhappy, naturally you will vomit that violence on others. The very ambition is punishment enough. Just because of their ambition, they miss authenticity in action, their whole life's possibility.

You can easily miss life's possibility by having a purpose to Life. Unless your thinking itself becomes integrated to your positivity, unless your working itself becomes authentic to the peak of your possibility, unless your life itself becomes the responsibility to enrich yourself and others, unless that itself becomes completion and bliss, you cannot experience what Kṛṣṇa says in this verse: *karmaṇy evādhikāras te mā phaleṣu kadācana* (2.47).

Purpose can be fulfilled, but through purpose, your life can never be fulfilled. When you carry purposes in your life, you are not living; purposes are living through you, that's all. In your childhood somebody gives you some purpose like, 'You should become a lawyer or a doctor.'

You are given a purpose and that purpose is fulfilled through your life, but you will never feel fulfilled or complete.

Never make the mistake of thinking that you will be fulfilled when your purpose is fulfilled. Your fulfillment is completely different from the fulfillment of your purpose. If you want to experience fulfillment, the space of completion, you have to work in a totally different dimension of your life. If you want completion of your being, listen to what Kṛṣṇa says here.

Kṛṣṇa's Technique for Success in Inner-Outer Worlds

Kṛṣṇa is the first and the last Master who declared the truth as it is.

There are two things to understand: Always, people who are active in the outer world know the techniques to achieve success in the outer world. People who are active in the inner world know the techniques to achieve success in the inner world.

But Kṛṣṇa knows both! He is the only Master who is an enlightened man and a king as well. He knows how to achieve total success in the outer world and in the inner world. He shows you how to furnish your outer space with enriching, and how to keep your inner space empty with completion. That is life in totality.

The entire Gītā is only about this one idea: how to furnish your outer space with the ultimate luxuries and how to keep your inner space in the ultimate bliss.

Kṛṣṇa is the only one who has produced a formula for inner space and outer space together. He teaches you how to keep your inner space in eternal bliss and keep your outer space in ultimate luxury at the same time. You can't expect this from a Buddha because Buddha gave up the outer space. He lived with just three pieces of clothing and he lived the life of a monk. So he taught us how to remain simple and blissful.

But Kṛṣṇa lived as a king. He wasn't just like a king, he was a king. Only Kṛṣṇa can give a complete solution for practical spiritual living. Kṛṣṇa gives immediate solutions, permanent solutions, not long-term solutions. Only Kṛṣṇa's solution is useful for people who are living a regular lifestyle.

Here He says, 'Not merely by abstaining from work can one achieve freedom from action. Nor can fulfillment come by giving up action.' You can't achieve freedom from action by moving away from work.

na karmanāṅ anārambhān naiṣkarmyaṁ puruṣo 'śnute |
na ca sannyasanād eva siddhiṁ samadhigacchati || 3.4

Every step in your life, anything you try to protect by hiding only becomes more and more powerlessness and more and more suffering. You move out of your life more and more. Moving away from your spouse, business partner, family or any of the forces that exist in your life is not an intelligent decision. We always think moving away from people or actions to protect our habits and patterns is freedom. That is the biggest bondage! People who move away from life, work and people to save their pattern are in the worst bondage!

Abstaining from work or moving away from work cannot give you freedom from action. It puts you in the biggest bondage. To have freedom from action, your inner space needs to be purified. Your inner space should become empty to allow the natural space of completion in you. You need to remove the furniture of incompletions from your complete inner space. Renouncing furniture in the outer world is not going to help you. Only removing furniture from the inner world is going to enrich you.

Please understand, whether you are hiding something inside you from life or trying to hide something outside you from life, your own incompletions will destroy you. You don't need a separate punishment.

Life is too powerful to cheat it with your logic. It functions with a simple, natural law of Existence, a natural *dharma*. The power of the natural law of Existence is such that nobody needs to teach you. By your very birth, if you start growing, you will get it!

The inauthentic idea that life has a purpose should be renounced. Life is a possibility, not purpose. That is why Kṛṣṇa says, 'Just by renouncing, just by outer renunciation, authenticity in action, *karma yoga* can never be achieved.'

What is authenticity? Building your own identity to the peak possibility and renouncing the identity built on purpose. What do you want to become? Every one of you, deep down, has a fantasy about becoming all-powerful, all-knowing, *sarvajña*. So now build that peak inner image, project the peak outer image, and take the responsibility to fulfill others' image of you.

I tell you, authenticity in action is the strategy plan for your life. The quality of cunningness may be useful for a short time—a few days, a few years, a few lives, but not for all lives! If you learn and develop the quality of authenticity in action, it is the strategy planning for life after life. Authenticity will help you identify your real enemy. Your real enemy is not the powerlessness you experience in moving away or running after a purpose; it is ignorance of your purposelessness! One more thing, if you renounce the outer world, you will think about the outer world even more.

A small story:

> An Enlightened Master and his disciple were walking near a river. They were supposed to cross the river to go to their monastery (ashram). On the way, a young lady was standing near a river. She wanted to cross the river but was afraid to do so.
>
> She asked the Master, 'Master, can you help me cross this river?' He said, 'Why not? Please come.'
>
> He just lifted her, crossed the river, left her on the other bank, and continued walking towards the ashram. The disciple was observing the whole scene. He was not able to digest what he saw. He was angry. Maybe he was jealous!
>
> After reaching the ashram he was not able to control himself and asked his master, 'Master, you are a Sannyāsi

(monk). How can you touch a woman, that too a young woman, and carry her through the river?'

The Master turned, smiled at him and said, 'I left her long ago. Why are you still carrying her?'

Please understand, renouncing your identity in the inner space, or emptying your inner space and creating the space of completion and creation is the real thing to be achieved. That is *yogaḥ karmasu kauśalam*, authenticity in action! That is what Kṛṣṇa says here. Once you have renounced in the inner space, it doesn't matter what you do in the outer world. Nothing will touch you.

To Act Is Human Nature

3.5 *Surely, not even for a moment can anyone stand without doing something. He is always in action, despite himself, as this is his very nature.*

3.6 *He who restrains the sense organs, but who still thinks of the objects of the senses, is deluded and is called a hypocrite.*

3.7 *He who begins controlling the senses with the mind and performs selfless work through the organs of action is superior, O Arjuna.*

3.8 *Do your prescribed work, as doing work is better than being idle. Even your own body cannot be maintained without work.*

Usually people ask, '*Swamiji*, you say that life is purposeless. Then I may as well just lie down and relax. Who will give me food? Who will pay my bills?'

Let me tell you, you can never lie down forever. You may lie down for the next four or five days or for a week at the most, because you always go to the extreme, like a pendulum. After that, you will not be able to lie down. By your very nature you will start doing some work. When I say life is purposeless, I am not asking you to just lie down and relax in your house. All I am saying is, 'Let your body and mind work without disturbing your inner space of completion. You don't have to sell your inner space to enjoy the outer place. You don't have to sell your inner bliss to have outer comforts.'

Here, Kṛṣṇa assures you, 'By your very nature, your body and mind will work. If you just keep quiet, it is enough.' Somebody asked me, '*Swamiji*, how should I train my mind to do the right thing?' I told him, 'Just keep quiet. Automatically your body and mind will do the right thing. If you just get out of your system, it is enough, the Divine will get in.' All we need to do is just get out for the Divine to enter.

'By nature,' He says, '*sarvaḥ prakṛti-jair-guṇaiḥ*—by their very nature your body and mind know the right thing to do.' The problem is that you never trust your body and mind. You always trust your ego and it finally dumps you! Yet you never trust your body and mind. Be very clear, your body and mind will do their work. All you need to do is keep quiet and relax from your ego. Don't think your inner space is needed for outer work. The person who understands what *nitya* (eternal) is, and what *anitya* (ephemeral) is relaxes into Existence and is always in eternal consciousness. He always resides in *nitya ānanda*—eternal bliss!

Karma Yogi Works with Courage of Authenticity

Śrī Kṛṣṇa says, 'A *karma yogi*, one who lives the path of authenticity in action, is a man who relaxes into *nitya ānanda* and does his work from the space of completion.'

Just relax into your inner space and be complete, you will automatically be guided. You always think, 'If I relax mentally thinking life is purposeless, how will I know what is right and what is wrong? How will I finish my work on time?'

When you worry about what is right and what is wrong, you will not make small mistakes, you will commit big blunders. The person who doesn't worry may make small mistakes. But the person who continuously worries will never make small mistakes; he will commit big blunders. And to take this leap of faith needs the courage of authenticity. Even if you make one or two mistakes, what is wrong?

Taking the risk and jumping into the space of completion, and living without worry and self-doubt is what I call courage of authenticity, the courage to enter spiritual life.

When you take the jump, you will naturally make some small mistakes. Don't worry about them. Putting up with that mistake is what I call penance, tapas. Penance is nothing but accepting and completing with the small mistakes you make and restoring your integrity and authenticity when the conscious transition happens in your being.

When you move from worry to bliss, when you move from falsehood to truth, when you move from incompletion to completion, you will make a few mistakes. You will fall and rise just like a baby learning to walk. When babies learn to walk, they always fall the first few times. But just because of that, can you say they should never walk? Even if they make one or two small mistakes, they have to stand up and start walking. Those small mistakes of falling and trying to stand up are the penance done to learn how to walk.

In the same way, when you start trying to live with integrity and authenticity without the root patterns, initially you may commit mistakes. But don't worry about that. That is penance. Have courage of authenticity and just enter the space of completion. Enter the space of eternal consciousness.

Decide consciously, 'From today onwards, I will live without worry and incompletions. I complete with all my worries and incompletions.' Life is too short to be spent worrying about your incompletions. Don't bother about the goals—just drop them. The moment you understand the beauty of purposelessness, all the wounds you have created in your inner space will be healed. You will fall into the comfort of Eternal Bliss.

A man who keeps his senses under control but who is not able to keep his inner space under control by completing with his patterns related to senses is called a hypocrite, *indriyārthān vimūḍhātmā mithyācāraḥ sa ucyate* (3.6), says Kṛṣṇa.

Please listen, the quality of your life will be judged only based on the quality of your inner space, not the quality of your outer space. When you leave your body and enter your next life, nobody is going to keep a count of the car you drove, of the house you lived in or your bank balance. These details will not come with you. How you lived and the quality of your inner space is what will carry forward with you. That is why the scriptures state, 'You are going to carry with you only the *saṃskāra* (root thought patterns), the *karma* (unfulfilled desires) and the *vāsana* (mindset) of your inner space—not the outer space.'

A beautiful story from Śrī Rāmakṛṣṇa Paramahamsa.

A monk was living in a temple, preaching the glory of the Lord. Opposite to his dwelling lived a prostitute who was busy all day long. She was deeply devoted to the Lord. No matter what her business was, she was immersed in the silent contemplation of His glory.

Everyday, this monk would notice everyone who entered the prostitute's house. He maintained a complete diary of who came and who left because he had no other work.

But the prostitute lived in a different way. She thought, 'My life, my natural duty is this. This has been given to me in this life. I don't know any other profession. But please save me, O Lord! Let my mind and heart always be at Your feet.' She was deeply devoted to Kṛṣṇa. Her inner space was filled with Divine love and His name.

Life went on. After many years, suddenly, both the monk and the prostitute died on the same day.

Both of them reached Yama Dharma's (Lord of death) court for judgment. First, the prostitute came in. Yama Dharma saw her list of sins and merits and said, 'Alright! Don't worry. You lived all your life thinking of the Divine, so you can go to heaven.' She was sent to heaven.

It was then the turn of the monk. The moment the monk arrived, Yama Dharma said, 'This is your list of sins and merits. Throughout your life you thought about the wrong things, so you must go to hell.'

The monk started shouting, 'How dare you send me to hell!' He was a professional preacher, so he knew how to shout! He started shouting, 'I will sue you.'

Yama Dharma said, 'Please relax. Up here in heaven we

don't bother about what you do in life; we bother about how you live. Through your body you lived a pure life. Look at planet Earth and see how your body is being honored.'

There the monk saw that his body was being honored like that of a celebrity; people were falling at the feet of his body. Big garlands and grand worship was being offered.

Yama continued, 'Through your body you lived a pure life and your body is now getting the rewards. But through your mind you lived an impure life so you have to go to hell.'

Yama continued, 'Similarly, she lived an impure life through the body. Look at her body.' Because she was a prostitute, there was no one to do the last rites. The scavengers came and dragged the body and dumped it somewhere.

Yama concludes, 'See! Through the body she lived an impure life. Her body is suffering. But through the mind she lived a pure life, a divine life. She is therefore going to the Divine.'

It is important how you live in your inner space; whether your inner space is established in completion or incompletion, only that matters.

Master Your Senses

Please be very clear, again and again Kṛṣṇa declares:

karmendriyāṇi saṁyamya ya āste manasā smaran |
indriyārthān vimūḍhātmā mithyācāraḥ sa ucyate || 3.6

If you can't create completion in your inner space, even if you control your body or your senses, you are just a hypocrite. Your life will not be a complete, blissful life. Not only will it not be a spiritual life, it will not even be life! The meaning of living is bliss, but there is no purpose. The more you think about purposes, the more worries you will create; the more will you try to squeeze the most out of life. But life is much more intelligent than you. When you try to squeeze the maximum out of life, it just slips through your fingers.

Life is like a river. If you place your hands in the river and keep them open, the river will always be there in your hands. But if you try to hold it, you will have only empty hands! If you just allow it to happen it will continuously flow through you. The moment you try to possess it, you will have only empty hands. You will not be able to have life itself.

The moment you experience, in your inner space, that nothing is going to be with you permanently, a deep healing, a breeze enters your consciousness. Your whole inner space is healed. You have so many wounds of incompletions in your inner space. Wounds created by your incomplete desires, by your failures, and by your near and dear ones. All these wounds will be healed with this one medicine. This one understanding that life is purposeless, that whatever you achieve is just nothing, and that nothing is going to be with you, is enough.

A small story:

> Alexander, who committed so many murders, can never be called 'the Great.' Please be very clear: never teach your kids that Alexander is great. You are inspiring them to commit murders! Unconsciously, you are putting all these ideas into their heads. Of course, fortunately or unfortunately, he met an enlightened Master in India. Somehow, his teacher in Greece gave him the idea, 'Bring one Enlightened Master and the Vedas from India, and I will change the whole society.'
>
> So, Alexander decided he would take at least one enlightened person from India. He invited him to his country. The Master just laughed and said, 'No, no! I don't want to come anywhere. I am happy here.'
>
> Alexander said, 'No! Please come with me. I will give you a big palace and all the comforts. Here you are living like

a beggar without clothes or food.' The Master just laughed and said, 'No. I am quite happy here, I don't want to come.'

You know the next step a king will take. First, he tried to entice him. When it did not work out, the next step, he tried the fear factor. He simply took out his sword, pointed it at the Master and said, 'If you are not ready to come, you will be killed.'

Faced with the naked sword, the master just laughed. Laughing now is very easy, but laughing when faced with a naked sword is very difficult, especially when the person who is holding the sword is a king— if he kills nobody will even question him.

But in front of the naked sword, the Master laughed and said, 'Fool! You are a liar.' He straightaway looked into the eyes of Alexander and said, 'Fool! You are a liar.'

For the first time Alexander was shaken. He asked the Master, 'Are you not afraid?'

The Master replied, 'Afraid of what? You can never kill me. You may destroy this body, but you cannot kill me.'

That is the courage of authenticity and the confidence of integrity gained by the spiritual experience of completion as we study in *Sāṅkhya Yogaḥ*:

nai 'naṁ chindanti śastrāṇi nai 'naṁ dahati pāvakaḥ |
na cai 'naṁ kledayantyāpo na śoṣayati mārutaḥ || 2.23

It means: *ātman* or the soul cannot be killed or destroyed; it cannot be burned. This had become an experience for the Master. That is why he had such courage and confidence. He just laughed.

Slowly, Alexander started thinking, 'If he can laugh in front of my naked sword, how courageous he must be!' For the first time he was shaken, because he had never seen anybody who could laugh in front of a naked sword, in the face of death. Even he was afraid.

Listen. All the so-called great warriors are cowards. They kill others before they are killed, that's all. They live in constant fear of death. Alexander was totally shaken and shocked to see the courage of this Master.

He asked him, 'Please tell me something. How are you so courageous, so bold?'

The Master asked him in return, 'Tell me, why did you come to India?'

Alexander replied, 'To conquer India.' The Master continued, 'After that, what are you going to do?' Alexander replied confidently, 'I will conquer the next country.'

The Master again asked, 'After that, what are you going to do?' Alexander continued, 'I will conquer the next country.' The Master persisted, 'And after that?'

Alexander replied as if the answer was obvious, 'I will conquer the whole world.' The Master questioned further, 'After that?' Alexander replied, 'I will relax and enjoy.'

The Master said, 'Fool! Don't you see, that is what I am doing now in front of your eyes? Why do you need to go around and conquer the whole world to relax and enjoy?'

Only a man who has understood the impermanence of life can relax and surrender totally even in the face of death. The Master gave a glimpse of the Truth to Alexander. That is why Alexander said to his ministers, 'After my death, during the funeral procession, please let both my hands hang out of the coffin, visible to all. Let people know that even the great Alexander could not carry anything with him.'

A beautiful story! You need to understand three things. The first thing is the courage of authenticity, the space of possibility and confidence of integrity, the space of positivity radiated by an enlightened person, the one established in space of completion. The next thing is the purposelessness of our running. Why was Alexander running? To relax and enjoy, to be complete in the Self. This Master was already doing the same thing! The third thing is that we are not going to carry anything with us when we leave. Even if the whole world worships you as a king, you cannot carry that with you! You have to go empty handed.

Never think that having comforts in the outer world will give you inner completion. All developed countries are filled with depression. They have the best roads, the best infrastructure, but their people are depressed. Never think outer space will give you inner space. If you want inner space, you need to work towards creating it. You need to understand the science of completion and the creation of inner space.

SCIENCE OF CREATING THE RIGHT INNER SPACE

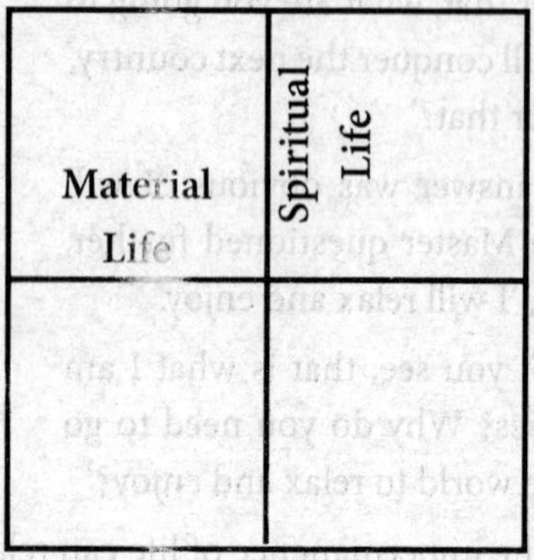

Here, Kṛṣṇa is giving you the science of creating the right inner space. Let us see how we work, or how our mind moves. This graph represents your being. Material life is the horizontal line and spiritual life is the vertical line. You continuously worry about whether to choose the horizontal line or the vertical line; whether to go on this (horizontal) path, or that (vertical) path.

You are always stuck somewhere on the horizontal line or somewhere on the vertical line. You try to move but you are always caught in the dilemma of whether to go this way or that way.

Mind is nothing but dilemma. Whaever you choose, whether material life or spiritual life, you will always feel you are missing the other part. You will continously feel you are missing something. As long as you think you are the mind, as long as you live with the mind, you will have this problem of material life verses spiritual life.

Just like people have goals in material life, they have goals in spiritual life too. There are so many people who say, 'I should meditate for seven hours daily. I should become enlightened. I should become that, I should do this.'

Please listen, goals in material life and in spiritual life; both drive you mad. If you want to become mad, continuously think of some goal. But if you can just withdraw into your being, you will just forget about the goal. And you can still work. By withdrawing into your being, you stop trying to locate a purpose somewhere all the time and running towards it.

The man who runs behind the material goals, will always feel he is missing the spiritual goal. That is why all rich communities invariably follow spiritual masters. They carry a deep guilt and fear that they are missing spirituality. The person who travels along the horizontal line feels he is missing the spiritual life and the person who travels along the vertical line feels he is missing the material life. Both are trying to fulfill each other cerebrally. The materialist fulfills the spiritualist's ideal and the spiritualist fulfills the materialist's ideal.

The man who realizes the purposelessness of both these goals, the purposelessness of the running, just falls back into his being. When you realize that whatever you consider the purpose or goal of your life is ultimately meaningless, the very moment you realize this and the glamour is gone, that very moment the need for perspiration is also gone; you stop running.

Mind you, it is not inspiration; it is just perspiration that you give up! The moment all respect for the purpose is gone from your life, you will simply fall into your being. One important thing: The moment you fall into your being, you explode! Not only do you start flowing in the direction of both horizontal and vertical lines, but you also explode in 360 degrees in all dimensions. Whatever you can imagine and whatever you can't even imagine will start happening. Only then do you become a truly multi-dimensional being.

A man who has fallen into his being, one who has dropped goals, who has tasted the beauty of purposelessness of Existence, who has realized the space of completion, who has fallen into his being, explodes in 360 degrees, in all dimensions. He simply radiates completion in all directions!

The space of completion or incompletion, purposelessness or purposefulness does not work horizontally, logically. It works vertically and explodes in all dimensions. A man who is in the space of incompletion can fall vertically down. A man in the space of completion flies vertically up. He starts experiencing the ultimate bliss of spiritual life and the ultimate happiness of material life and something more! Only he enters into eternal bliss or Kṛṣṇa consciousness. Travel with completion or incompletion is not horizontal, it is vertical. Whether you fall vertically down or fly vertically up, your idea of horizontal or linear traveling is wrong!

As long as you are caught up with material goals or spiritual goals, you travel only in one horizontal direction of incompletion, because you think you are body or mind. Sometimes people tell me, 'I don't want spiritual life. I don't want these four *tattvas*, life principles.' It is like saying, 'I don't want to breathe. I don't want blood circulation.' You need to understand that there is no such thing as spiritual life and normal life. Life has no purpose. Life is Life!

The more you are caught up with purposes, the more you think you are the body or the mind. When you realize the purposelessness of it all, you will straightaway fall into the depths of your being. Actually, to become complete and enlightened, you don't need the whole *Gītā*. This single verse is enough to make an individual enlightened. Then why am I talking about all the verses? It is only because there are so many different kinds of individuals.

BRING COMPLETION AND BECOME ONE

If you can, just look into yourself and understand this one verse for your self. Whenever I speak, understand that I am speaking to you. Don't prepare notes in your mind to go and repeat it to somebody else. When you do this, you are sure to miss the experience yourself!

Just allow this one idea to work on you: the truth of the purposelessness of life. You can just close your eyes and think, contemplate for two or three minutes: 'What is really the purpose of my life? Why am I doing what I am doing? Where am I going? What is happening?' Many times you do not even know what you want to achieve in life; what the purpose of life is. It is just because of incompletions.

See, it is like each part of your incompletion claims, 'I am you!' For example, if your name is Sundar, each part of the broken you claims, 'I am Sundar!' 'I am Sundar!' and who screams loudly, he thinks he is Sundar. And one of the worst things is one part of you spends so much of energy to disprove that the other part is not you. So finally, whoever wins, whoever loses, who is the loser? You! One part of you winning is not you winning. Even if one part of you wins, you are the loser! Unless your whole wins, you are a loser!

Understand, each part of you screaming that that part is you finally lands you in deep confusion. Unless you heal yourself and bring yourself to purposelessness, unless you align yourself as one being, life doesn't start for you! Only with deep completion you even become one being. The purpose of all great spiritual practices is for you to become ONE; for you to be complete, integrated!

If your inner eye opens, if your inner space experiences the beauty of purposelessness, that is enough to experience the space of completion. You will fall into your being. As of now, you can experience neither material life nor spiritual life because when you are here, you are looking there and when you are there, you are looking here. When you don't have integrity, the life you want to have around you will change hour by hour. In the morning you will have one idea of a certain kind of life, at noon you will have a different idea and the next morning you will have some other idea.

With lack of integrity, there is such a huge confusion. Your mind is not where your body is. You are not living inside your boundary. The grass on the other side of the river always looks greener. Something else is always calling you. Only when you align yourself to integrity, you will experience the beauty of purposelessness, only then will you be able to understand what Kṛṣṇa says throughout *Karma Yoga*.

When you bring integrity into your thinking, you become aware of every anxiety you go through, every fear you go through; you see how you are responsible for creating negativity in your life, and you also see how you can align yourself with yourself, and the world can just align itself with you. When you are one being, the reality you want, the reality you need and the highest Reality, all three become one and the same.

Relax! This one idea can transform your whole way of thinking with integrity, working with authenticity, and living with responsibility. When you understand there is no purpose of life, you will start enriching and enjoying every single moment; you will start living intensely in every single inch of your body. Every moment will become meaningful.

When you think that life as a whole has a purpose, the individual moment will lose its meaning. If you think one month of your working time is worth 50 thousand dollars, you will judge the value of that one month as being only 50 thousand dollars. Suddenly, if someone says, 'I will give you 50 million dollars, give me your life,' will you be able to give him your life? No! But, this is the way you are calculating and working! We are ready to sell our mind, our moments, our inner space by calculating the value of our lives. You forget the work itself or living itself.

If you think the whole has a purpose, then the part loses its meaning. When you realize that the whole has no purpose, the part will become meaningful. Your very living, every day itself, will become very beautiful. Your life every day, your living, your sitting, your walking, your standing, everything will become a joyful, complete experience. That is why they say *Sat-Cit-Ānanda*, which means 'the bliss of the very Existence.' Your very existence is blissful. You don't have to think that at the end of your life you will have bliss. Your very Existence is blissful. The meaning of existence is bliss, eternal bliss, *Nityānanda*. But you need to take steps towards that bliss.

DO WORK WITH DEVOTION, DROP EXPECTATION

By nature, man has to work. The senses have to be engaged in some action. Even if you try and control them and do nothing externally, the very act of restraint is an action in itself.

Kṛṣṇa says very beautifully, 'By nature, the senses are tuned to be extrovert.' 'Extrovert' is not something negative. Extrovert senses will always be alive, creative, active and contributing. All great creative persons took the responsibility for their extrovert senses. If you want to be wealthy, have the company of wealthy people, or make the people in your company wealthy! If you want to be spiritual, have the company of spiritual people, or make the people in your company spiritual. There is no other way. Intranalyze what I am saying. To experience the reality of your choice in your life, you should first work to transform and enrich the reality of others around you.

Kṛṣṇa says, your senses, by nature are programmed to go out! You are programmed to work, to go out. Going out can happen only in two ways: either to enrich or to swindle! Surely, swindling others is not going to transform you. Only enriching others is going to transform you.

The choice is really about how to work. Here, Kṛṣṇa gives the answer to that. He says that we should perform work with devotion with authenticity in our actions, only to enrich, and without attachment to the results, *karmendriyaiḥ karma-yogam asaktaḥ sa viśiṣyate* (3.7). Work without unnecessarily being bothered about whether or not it will fetch the results that you expect.

When we work, our thoughts are on the future, we are not in the present moment. Am I right? Then how can we perform to our fullest potential? How can I say that I am doing my work with full devotion if my mind is not totally merged with the task at hand? It's not possible. When do you get worried or afraid? It is when you have an expected result, when there is an unwritten expectation, an unconscious desire to achieve something as the result of an action.

Kṛṣṇa says, 'Drop the very desire and drop the very expectation.' We wonder, 'How can we function if we drop expectations?' I am not saying you should not plan and or you should do something without thinking. I am saying, 'Plan, but plan chronologically, not psychologically.'

You see, there are two things: chronological planning and psychological planning. Chronological planning is planning on a times-cale. You decide you to get up at a particular time, finish the list of tasks you planned at the office by a certain time, and so on. This is a practical way to organize your work in a way that it can give the best results. This is fine.

But what do we do? We don't stop at this. We review the plan in our head over and over again, thinking in different ways, internally preparing for eventualities, expecting results from our plan even before the action. We keep supposing, 'What if this happens? What if that happens?' Psychological planning boosts your ego, your root pattern. It makes you feel great and worthy. It makes you stay serious and feel that you are handling great things.

It is very unfortunate, but we carry a strong pattern that we should be ready to accept failure, because failure is a part of life. Then you are constantly giving a commitment to you that there is going to be failure. You always internally prepare yourself for failure. When you prepare, you usually remind yourself of the worst possibilities and then prepare tools and weapons to handle it. In the name of contingency planning, we just worry and give a commitment to failure. Instead, if we apply our awareness to the problem with integrity in thinking and authenticity in action, the solution will be visible. But we complicate the whole process. We get worked up about contingency situations and introduce a complex negativity in the whole thinking process.

It is the power of completion that empowers you to face the worst eventualities. Preparation for the worst eventualities mentally strengthens your belief in failure. Are you successful in handling any eventualities by preparation? So, from today, decide, you will not mentally prepare yourself for the worst eventualities. You will spend all your energy removing the weed of the worst eventuality from your inner space.

Now have awareness inside. You have never handled the worst possibilities because of preparation. You always handled the worst possibilities because of your completion! If you are in the space of completion, you face the worst possibilities in completion and win!

Kṛṣṇa says, 'One who does devotional work with authenticity, without attachment, and controlling the senses—*yas tv indriyāṇi manasā niyamyārabhate arjuna*, is superior to one who merely pretends to be in control of his senses and acts in renunciation, *karmendriyaiḥ karma-yogam asaktaḥ sa viśiṣyate* (3.7).'

There are intellectual type of people, the philosophers, well versed in the scriptures, who look down upon the devotional and emotional practitioners! Intellec uals believe that their dry understanding of the non-duality of the Self is superior to that of those who fall at the feet of the Divine. Kṛṣṇa firmly says, 'No, it is not so!' Kṛṣṇa says that what makes the difference is your space of completion that brings lack of expectations of either failure or success, the sense of purposelessness that defines your state.

Listen, listen! The senses are extrovert, flowing naturally. By nature, they function towards achieving, purposelessly. It means that you are programmed by nature to be successful. The natural programming is for you to be successful. Lack of integrity allows the poison of preparing for failure, for the worst eventualities to grow in your system. The first thing a human being needs to do is weed out all worst possibilities.

Sannyāsa, renunciation, is a state, not a label. The state of renunciation is not a state of doing nothing. You can never sit without doing anything. Even if you sit still in one place, you are sitting, you are breathing, is it not? The internal functions in your body are happening. Maintaining this very body requires that work be done. The breath that you take in carries prāna, the life energy that sustains you. So, you cannot say you are not doing anything.

You may think it is better not to do any work rather than to analyze what work you should do, how to do it, whether it will suit you etc. You can take this as an excuse for laziness, for your tamas. *Tamas* means laziness, lethargy. When Kṛṣṇa says, 'I am not the doer, it is just the senses performing the actions according to their nature,' you say, 'Why should I even bother to do anything? '

Be very clear, by your very nature, you will act. Your body and mind are by nature, forced and programmed to do something. Just try to sit with a completely blank mind, with no mental activity. Just relax and try this simple exercise. You will initially try not to think about anything and try to be aware if any thought comes to your mind. But, after a few moments, you will find yourself having some random thoughts, about something from the past or the future. By nature, your mind will think about something or the other. If you try to force silence upon your mind, you will be forcing a dead silence, the silence of suppression. How long can you sustain that? The moment you drop your guard, your mind will express its nature and start wandering.

So, neither expression nor suppression is the solution. Only completion is the solution. It is better to—complete with yourself to bring integrity to the nature of the senses and the mind, and be engaged with authenticity in action, with a sense of devotion to enrich others and yourself. Be aware that when you are in action, it is the senses acting. Then you will not get attached to the action or its result. Then you are free; you are liberated from the bondage of action. Action binds you only when you consider yourself 'the doer' and have expectations about things being a certain way.

Selfless Enriching Liberates

3.9 *Work has to be performed selflessly; otherwise, work binds one to this world. O son of Kuntī, perform your work for Me and you will do it authentically, liberated and without attachment.*

3.10 *Brahma, the lord of creation, before creating humankind as a selfless sacrifice said, 'By this selfless enriching, be more and more prosperous and let it bestow all desired gifts.'*

3.11 *The celestial beings, pleased by this sacrifice, will also nourish you; with this mutual nourishing of one another, you will achieve supreme prosperity.*

3.12 *Satisfied with the selfless enriching, the celestial beings certainly bestow upon you the desired enjoyments of life.*
He who enjoys the things given by them without offering anything to the celestial beings is certainly a thief.

3.13 *Those who eat food after selfless enriching service are free of all sins.*
Those who prepare food for sense enjoyment do grievous sin.

There are two techniques by which one can liberate oneself from attachment to work.

One is by telling oneself, 'I am not the doer.' By continuously reminding yourself that it is the senses and not you who is doing something, you distance yourself from the action. This is what Kṛṣṇa explains in the previous verses. The other way is by surrendering the fruits of one's work to the Divine to the ultimate life force that is conducting this Universe. This is the technique that Kṛṣṇa talks about here.

Bhagavān says, 'O Kaunteya, perform your work for Me and you will do it with authenticity, liberated and without attachment, *tad-arthaṁ karma kaunteya mukta-saṅgaḥ samācara* (3.9).'

When you do work as a sincere, humble offering to the Divine, the very attitude of this surrender will make you do the job authentically to your peak capability and you will be liberated. When you are excessively bothered about the results, you actually think you are the doer of the action! That is why you get attached to the work and its results. This is when you start getting stressed and tensed about results. Naturally, when you are tensed, you are not performing at your maximum efficiency because so much of your valuable energy is getting wasted in being tense. How will you then be able to get your job properly done?

I always tell people, 'When you are afraid to make small mistakes and are over- cautious, you end up making big blunders.' You waste your entire life trying to avoid making mistakes and attempting to be perfect, and your life becomes a blunder.

This doesn't mean you can be careless about your work. I am only saying that you should have the courage of authenticity to make mistakes and learn to not give up on yourself. Only when you make mistakes can you learn from them and complete with your unconscious inauthenticies. Only then have you been exposed to your inauthenticity and seen both sides of the coin. Then, with experience, when you have learnt from the mistake and stood up powerfully with completion, you will have the cognition of both sides. Otherwise, just at the crucial time, your inauthenticities that have been hiding from you will make you commit mistakes and you will powerlessly give up on yourself. You can have this courage of authenticity only when you are not attached to the ownership of tasks and results.

When you see that Existence is purposeless and you are living in the loving, caring arms of Existence, you will relax and surrender to that very Existence. When you are in this relaxed mood, you can function at your best and enjoy every moment of life without feeling like the doer and therefore not worrying about making small mistakes. Real surrender happens when this understanding becomes your experience.

SURRENDER—THE ULTIMATE RELAXATION

Utmost integrity and authenticity is enough for surrender. Nothing else is needed. Surrender has a tremendous power, a tremendous energy. Whether you surrender to an idol or to a person or to your Guru, or even a rock, is not important. What is important is surrender itself.

Vivekananda says beautifully: 'When you pray to God, your prayers actually awaken your own inner potential and it showers blessings on you.' Even if you see logically, surrender helps you to simply relax. When you are relaxed, you can work beautifully, with intelligence, rather than with your pre-programmed intellect.

A small story:

> There was once a bank cashier who used to take all the cash home everyday and bring it back with him the next morning. He had done this for a month and could not do it anymore.
>
> He found himself trembling all the way while driving back home and was not able to sleep at home with all the money in his custody. He finally asked his boss to relieve him of the job since he could not bear the stress any longer.
>
> His boss told him that even if the money were to be lost, he would not be blamed and he could continue with his job. The cashier slept peacefully from that day onwards.

What was the difference in him? He was doing the same job, but why was the fear and tension not there anymore? It was because the responsibility had been shifted to a higher authority, that's all. This is surrender! Do your work with authenticity and responsibility to enrich others and yourself, surrendering the responsibility of the results to Existence.

Understand, Existence loves you and understands you better than you understand yourself. See the example of Arjuna; Kṛṣṇa knew Arjuna better than Arjuna knew himself. The very trust, the very connection enabled Arjuna to relate with Kṛṣṇa, who took him to the Ultimate Consciousness.

Have simple trust in Existence, in the intelligence of the life force. This is the very life force, the energy that is keeping you alive. This is the energy behind the marvelous functioning of your brain, of your digestive system, of your nervous system. This is the energy that runs our solar system, all the galaxies and the entire Universe so smoothly. Imagine, is it possible for so many billions of stars and planets to move in such beautiful order even if you had the most modern traffic control system in place? Such a beautiful order, in what appears to be chaos when seen superficially!

Enrich Others Because They Are Part Of You

A very beautiful story from the great Indian epic history, Mahābhārat:

> King Yudhiṣṭra, the eldest of the Pāṇḍavas, performed a great sacrifice after the battle of Kurukṣetra was over. He gave very rich offerings to the priests and the poor. They were all impressed by the grandeur of this sacrifice. They praised him saying, 'We have never seen such a great sacrifice in our lifetime.'
>
> Just then, a small mongoose appeared. Half of his body was golden and the other half was brown. He rolled on the ground where the sacrifice was performed. He then exclaimed with sorrow, 'This is no sacrifice at all. Why do you praise this sacrifice?'
>
> The priests were aghast and angry, 'What! You silly mongoose! Did you not see the sacrifice? Thousands of poor people have become very rich. Millions of people have been sumptuously fed. So many jewels and clothes have been distributed!'
>
> The mongoose replied, 'That may be a big sacrifice for you. But to me the sacrifice offered by the poor *brāhmin* was much bigger.'

'What *brāhmin* and what sacrifice are you talking about? We never heard of this!' said the priests.

The mongoose continued, 'There was a poor *brāhmin* in a village. He lived in a small hut with his wife, son and daughter-in-law. Once, there was a great famine. The whole family starved for days on end. One day, the poor man brought some food home. When they were ready to eat, they heard a voice at their door. The *brāhmin* opened the door and found a guest at the doorstep. In India, we say, *atithi devo bhava*, which means 'the guest is God Himself'.

The *brāhmin* said, 'O Sir! Please come inside. Please have a seat and have some food.' He gave his portion of the food to the guest.

The guest said, 'Sir, I am still hungry. I have been starving for the last fifteen days.'

The wife gave her share also to the guest. The guest ate this portion also, but he was still hungry. The son said, 'Father, please give him my share also.'

The guest ate this and yet he remained dissatisfied.

The wife of the son said, 'O Sir, please have my portion too.' The guest ate this portion also and was fully satisfied. He then blessed the poor *brāhmin* and his family and departed in great joy.

I entered the hut that day and found that four persons had died of starvation. A few grains of rice were found on the ground where the guest had eaten. I rolled myself on those grains. Half of my body became golden. Since then I have been traveling all over the world to find another sacrifice like that.

Nowhere have I found one. Nowhere have I been able to convert the other half of my body into gold. This sacrifice of Yudhiṣṭra has not turned the other half of my body into gold; That is why I say that this is no sacrifice at all.'

The sacrifice that Kṛṣṇa refers to comes from a true sense of surrender to the Universe. When we enrich others what we can afford to give, it is no sacrifice. When we enrich others by denying ourselves, then it is a sacrifice. That is why most of the charitable work done by people, even with good intentions, does not fit into the essence of what Kṛṣṇa says here. Of course, it is better to enrich others rather than foolishly stuff yourself.

Enrich others for the sake of enriching. When you enrich others at your own expense, by denying yourself, you function at the level of the Universal energy; you function as part of the principle of *Vasudaiva kuṭuṁbakaṁ* meaning 'The whole world is my family' as said by Kṛṣṇa; you operate out of compassion. Then there is no compulsion or no moral injunction to give. There is no expectation that you will go to heaven if you give and to hell if you don't.

That's why, time and again, I tell people, 'Do not donate anything to the mission in the belief that I will help you pass through the gates of heaven. First of all, there is no heaven, and second, I am not its gatekeeper!'

Many times even your enriching others has a selfish motive. You think, 'If I enrich, I may get this, this, and this back!' Do not enrich with purpose. Let enriching be a purposeless happening. Now, I am giving the right and complete reason for enriching. Because everyone is part of you, enriching every being is nothing but enriching some part of you. Only then are you practicing the *tattva* of enriching *Vasudaiva kuṭuṁbakaṁ*, the whole world as your family.

Enrich others. Anything you see, anything you experience is extension of you. Anybody whom you experience in your life is extension of you. Your wife is the extension of your unbending logic. Your husband is the extension of your confusion. So, when you enrich them, the parts of you are enriched. When they feel completion, part of you will become complete.

Somehow, even in enriching you continuously have your own small understandings, small goals and small purposes. If you do the same work with a small reason, you will have small result. If you do it with higher reason, you will have higher result. That is why it is said, 'You serving and an enlightened being serving, brings totally different result, even if both do the same action.' Everyone, whether you accept or not, realize or not, everyone is part of you.

When people come and ask me, '*Swamiji,* my spouse is torturing me. Please somehow stop it.' I tell them, 'actually *you* torturing yourself is ten times more than your spouse torturing you. Please stop torturing yourself first.'

Kṛṣṇa says that enriching should be practiced because everyone is part of us. Nobody is separate from us. Only then does enriching become a selfless sacrifice, *yajña bhāvitaḥ*. There is a joy, a bliss that enters your being when you act out of sacrifice, selflessly to enrich others. The bliss is always there, but when you are free from the filtering root pattern and mind, you start experiencing that bliss. The garbage of expectations disappears and bliss is experienced.

This was the principle on which various sacrificial rituals came into existence in the vedic culture. These were instruments of mass meditation. The energy of the cosmic space (*ākāśa*) was captured by the vibrations of the air created by chanting *mantras*. This energized air fueled the sacred fire in the sacrificial fire pit (*homa kuṇḍa)*. This energy was transferred to pots of water by physically linking the pots to the fire pit through many threads. This energized holy water was then sprinkled on bodies, deities and the earth to complete the energy cycle. All five energy points: space, air, fire, water and earth were connected through such a ritual to benefit humanity!

It was only a metaphoric offering of all that was sacrificed to the fire. During these rituals, great kings and nobles who performed the rituals gave away to those who lacked material wealth. These rituals helped to maintain material balance.

But, as the mongoose said, even the *rājasūya yāga* of Yudhiṣṭra, performed to celebrate his victory, lacked the spirit of enriching as the sacrifice of the poor *brāhmin* family. So enrich to give away what you need, not what you do not need!

We very conveniently forget an important fact, and take life happening for us with others for granted. Anything you receive without enriching, is stolen!

Kṛṣṇa explains enriching beautifully to Arjuna,

iṣṭān bhogān hi vo devā dāsyante yajña bhāvitaḥ I
tair dattān apardāyaibhyo yo bhuṅkte stena eva saḥ II 3.12

'Satisfied with the selfless enriching, the celestial beings certainly bestow upon you the desired enjoyments of life. He who enjoys the things given by them without offering anything to the celestial beings is certainly a thief, *yo bhuṅkte stena eva saḥ*' Bhagavān Kṛṣṇa says, 'If you don't do *yajña* and give back to the divine energy, you are certainly a thief!' Kṛṣṇa does not mean just pouring some offerings into a fire; He also means doing the proper authentic action. For example, if you are cutting a tree, you have to plant at least five trees. If you are taking water from the river, you should make sure that the recycled water is purified and added to the river.

Constantly enriching the source and keeping it alive for the next generation is *yajña*. Do not touch anything which you can't replace, like sources which can be exhausted but not replenished. Do not use nonrenewable energy sources. Use only renewable energy sources. That is part of enriching *yajña*.

Kṛṣṇa is very clear. Listen! If you are not enriching, but only taking and enjoying, you are a thief. *Asteya* (non-stealing), one of the important vows of *Sannyāsa*, can be maintained only by enriching. Only when you continuously enrich others will non-stealing be maintained.

Enriching is where life happens to you. I can say that enriching means infusing all the three *tattvas* of integrity, authenticity, responsibility into *satya*, truth.

Life happens to us with others. Whether it is *Sannyāsa* or *Saṃsāra*, the joys of spirituality or the joys of the world, everything happens with company, with *sanga*! Understand, whether it is *satsanga* or *dussanga*, good or bad association, you need a *sanga*. Whether it is basic food or the ultimate luxury, everything happens to you with others. If you don't enrich others, it is stealing and life does not happen to you. I tell you, decide to enrich everyone you see with these *tattvas*; in just a few months you will see that you are surrounded by gods and you are living in heaven. Go on enriching people.

Enriching Sacrifice Or Sin

3.14 *All beings grow from food grains,*
from rains the food grains become possible,
the rains become possible from selfless sacrifice of enriching.

3.15 *Know that work is born of the Creator and*
He is born of the Supreme. The all-pervading Supreme
is eternally situated in sacrifice of enriching.

3.16 *O Pārtha, he who does not adopt the prescribed,*
established cycle lives a life full of sins.
Rejoicing in sense gratification, he lives a useless life.

This metaphorical explanation in a few verses actually has a deep meaning about life, about how we connect with life, how we depend on the Universe, and how we affect the whole Universe. Just this concept that Kṛṣṇa explains in a few verses here is explained in detail in the *Chāndogyopaniṣad.* Our relationship with the activity of Nature is a very deep one. Our actions are like oblations offered in a fire sacrifice. Our activities are not just movements of the limbs. When we perform a yajña, a fire sacrifice of enriching the Source, the Cosmic Energy we pour various offerings into the fire. We do so to tap the Cosmic Energy and to flow in tune with Existence, with Nature.

The subtlest, most powerful and all-pervasive Cosmic Energy is invoked through the slightly less subtle air element when we chant the mantra and we connect and enrich the still, less subtle fire energy through the fire ritual. Energy is then transferred to water, a grosser energy, and then the water in the pots is poured over plants, idols and humans as well as the earth, which is the grossest form of energy.

When we chant the *mantra,* it is a very powerful way to enrich the world, through our integrity and authenticity. You take the responsibility for the words, and for making the mantra into reality. When you take the responsibility for the words you utter and start working, you enrich the world mystically and physically, metaphysically and physically.

A physical action is a gross expressed action, something that can be seen on the physical plane. Thoughts, mental actions, are subtler unexpressed actions, and they cannot be seen on the physical plane.

Enrich to Relate with Expressed and Unexpressed God

Enriching is the way in which you relate with the expressed component of God, the expressed part of God. Integrity and Authenticity are the ways in which you relate with the unexpressed, *avyakta* part of God. Responsibility and Enriching are the ways in which you relate with *vyakta*, the expressed part of God.

When we perform a sacrifice, we perform certain invocations to the higher energies. So, we attract corresponding effects for our actions. Our actions are like offerings in a sacrifice. When the actions are in tune with *tattvas* of integrity, authenticity, responsibility and enriching, which is the flow of Existence, it is like offering *ghee* (clarified butter) into the fire. When we do not flow in tune with Existence, it is like offering mud into the fire. You know the kind of smoke comes out of the fire when you offer *ghee* and the kind of smoke that comes out when you offer mud. Just like you can determine the quality of the offering you gave to the fire from the quality of the smoke, the result of your actions can be determined from the quality of your actions. The quality of the end result is based on our input, our offerings, our enriching.

Integrity and Authenticity are the right ways to relate with the unexpressed part of God, *avyakta*. Responsibility and Enriching are the right ways to relate with the expressed part of God, the world, *vyakta*. If you do not enrich, you actively create a selfish pattern and your offerings bring that same result. Be very clear, either you give or you swindle. There is no middle.

Kṛṣṇa says that rains become possible from the enriching sacrifice, *yajñād bhavati parjanyo* and the enriching sacrifice is born of actions, *yajñaḥ karma-samudbhavaḥ* (3.14).

Rain is a grosser form of energy that is activated by the subtler unexpressed energies which are influenced by our authenticity in actions and integrity in words, thoughts and vibrations.

Rain is the cause, the source which is responsible for the growth of food grains. Food is the enrichment needed to sustain our bodies and minds, which give rise to further authentic action and integrated thinking. So, you see this cycle now, of how the subtle energy, *avyakta*, the unexpressed part of God manifests itself in the grosser world as *vyakta*, the expressed part of God, and how the actions in the grosser world affect the subtler elements.

If we just understand this, we will realize that everything that we do and experience is caused by our **own** actions. We realize that we are the source of everything, and therefore responsible for everything that is happening. We invite our destiny. As we sow, so shall we reap.

Enriching is sowing the seed for the fruit to happen. Integrity is the root, authenticity is the tree, responsibility is the fruit, enriching is sharing the fruit to create more fruits. Every person who eats the fruit is responsible for sowing the seed for more fruits to happen.

Understand, this is what Kṛṣṇa says, 'O Pārtha, he who does not adopt the prescribed, established cycle lives a life full of sins, *aghāyur idriyārāmo*. Rejoicing in sense gratification, he lives a useless life, *mogham̐ pārtha sa jīvati* (3.16).'

When you do not enrich every person with the fruit of enriching after constantly being enriched by the sacrifice of the Existence, the Supreme, your life becomes full of sins and you live a useless, incomplete life. That in turn brings the cycle of more and more incompletions!

If you are rich, be the ground on which the seed can be sown. If not, at least pour water for the seed to become a tree. If not, at least be a gardener to weed out the unnecessary things for the seed to become fruit again. Either offer your time, talent, or treasure. If you have eaten the fruit, it is your responsibility to make the seed again into a fruit. After eating the fruit, be responsible to sow the seed and make sure the seed again brings more fruits for more people to enjoy.

Our body-mind is highly influenced by our thoughts and words. The words you constantly repeat to yourself, have to be enriching you, inspiring you, exciting you and enlightening you. The words you give to you are *āhara* (food), what you consume to create life in you.

Power of Creating the Space of Enriching

Bliss attracts fortune. You may wonder, 'Fortune can bring us bliss but how can bliss bring us fortune?' In India, when any new activity is started, be it a business or construction or education, the first thing that we do is sit down and create the space for a few moments; we close our eyes and remain in a meditative mood. We try to bring about some kind of an energy play or transformation inside us.

Of course, over the years, this has become a prayer and a ritual. That is a different issue. But the first thing that we do is sit down and try to kindle the energy flow, the space of completion in us.

You need to know an important lesson, when you decide to become responsible, the whole Cosmos simply listens to you; it simply follows you! With responsibility, even if you sit in one corner, your very space changes the way the world responds to you!

> Swami Vivekananda says beautifully, 'In India, even if we want wealth, we sit under a tree and create the space. It happens around us!' He said these words in America, the country which teaches you that you have to work hard to accumulate wealth.

If you sit with yourself, you may accumulate peace but not even a piece of bread! Yet, He says, 'In India, even to accumulate wealth, we just sit and create the space, and it happens!'So, when you take responsibility, sit by creating the space and be ready to sacrifice. The world will simply move based on your word! The world will move as you want!

When the energy flow, the space in us becomes complete, it has the property of influencing and causing external incidents as we want. Whether you believe it or not, accept it or not, like it or not, want it or not, you are deeply connected to Existence. You are an integral part of Existence, not an independent island as you think.

Every subtle movement or subtle thought in one part of the Universe causes a counter-effect at that same moment elsewhere in the Universe. Our thoughts and energy flow have the capacity to create and attract incidents and people of the same nature. What I have said here is one of the age-old truths expounded by our *ṛṣis*, sages in *Upaniṣad*, the Vedic experience. It is interesting that modern science is coming up with some startling evidence that reveals some of these truths now.

Dr. Masaru Emoto, a Japanese doctor and research scientist is renowned for his book, The Hidden Messages in Water. He conducted extensive experiments on water samples taken from all over the world. He took similar samples of water and exposed the water to different influences. To one set of samples, he spoke positive words such as 'love' and 'gratitude,' to some he recited Buddhist chants. To another set, he spoke words such as 'anger' and 'war'. Then he froze the different water samples so that he could photograph their crystal form. In the samples that had been exposed to positive energy, beautiful clear crystals were formed, like diamonds! The water exposed to negative energies did not form into crystals; they looked like a tumor: dark, cloudy and without any distinct geometrical pattern.

Several hundred experiments were conducted to prove the effects of the vibrations created by our words and thoughts on matter. Water being the most common molecule in our bodies, we can now see the obvious and dramatic effect our thoughts have on ourselves and others! It doesn't stop there. Our thoughts have the capacity to affect the oceans and the seas.

Recent research by Russian scientists throws an entirely new light on how our DNA can be influenced and reprogrammed by words and frequencies. They did experiments where they superimposed certain frequencies onto a laser ray and with it influenced the DNA frequency and thus the genetic information itself!

Science is beginning to touch what our Vedic Seers have declared thousands of years ago about collective consciousness. What we do in any plane, physical or mental, expressed or unexpressed affects our consciousness. And since we are all a part of the common fabric called Existence, our consciousness is a part of the collective consciousness, which also gets affected by our thoughts and actions.

Weather is strongly influenced by earth resonance frequencies, and the same frequencies are also produced in our brains. When many people take the responsibility to bring integrity and authenticity to their thinking and actions, the individual consciousness aligns and expands to affect the collective consciousness. So we can actually even influence the weather by our thoughts. This is what Kṛṣṇa means when He says that rains are caused by sacrifice—*yajñād bhavati parjanyo* and enriching sacrifice is born of actions—*yajñaḥ karma-samudbhavaḥ* (3.14). It is an ultimate statement that proves the power of enriching, the power of living.

When a large number of people collectively integrate their thoughts and align their actions to enrich others with no expectations and with full faith in the abundance of the Universe, the Universe responds. Rain falls, grains grow, and abundance results.

It has actually been revealed by various studies that when a number of people integrate their thoughts with something similar, like during celebrations or a football world championship, then certain random number generators in computers start to deliver ordered numbers instead of random ones! Also understand, all so-called natural calamities are nothing but the effects of global collective negative thoughts.

At a young age, we were trained in 'mathematical logic' but never in 'Existential logic'. Mathematical logic is very straightforward and should be applied only where it is appropriate. In matters concerning life and relationships, mathematical logic will only cause chaos. With it, we will always look to conclude with a 'good' or 'bad' judgment. There is something deeper than this—and that is Existential logic. This comes with a mature understanding and flowering from within.

Your integrity, the thoughts and energy directly affect your body, your cell structure, your decisions, your capacity to fulfill your decisions, the outer world incidents, and even accidents.

Integrity is the mathematics of Life. It is simple, straightforward mathematics. If you add one thing and another, this is the result. You can simply practice it like mathematics. If you add two negative statements, two negative commitments to your thinking, you will have two negative happenings. If you repeat a negative commitment hundreds of times, it will be strong, equivalent to a hundred times! So, you have to complete until your negative commitments are dropped. But even if you have millions of negativities, if you just multiply it by zero, the whole thing will become zero! Master's initiation is like multiplying by zero!

Currently, you are always centered in either greed or fear. Every action is performed either out of desire or out of fear. It becomes very easy for others to exploit you because of this. You become very vulnerable. Some people have become so selfish that they care only about their personal pleasure or pain. Only when life hits at them there, they understand the constitution of Life, not otherwise. They create a powerless space that attracts similar incidents into their life. They also corrupt the energy flow of their inner space this way.

If you are sensitive enough to understand life and the facts, and the truth, the Cosmos does not teach you in a very hard way; it teaches you in a mild way. If you can change your inner space from this incomplete space to the space of completion, the space of bliss, *Ānanda*, then the energy flow in your inner space will start brimming and your thoughts will become declarations of integrity, which is like multiplying all your past negativity by zero. Then you will be complete in the present moment.

When you do this, you have power to control external incidents because you and Existence have a very deep connection at the energy level. This is the thread you need to catch in order to understand that bliss attracts fortune. When you are blissful, when your inner space is not one of worry, fear and greed patterns but one that is in the space of completion in the present, you will automatically attract the best of things.

If you divide it by zero, then even if your negative commitments land into infinity, they become positive, because there is no infinity in negativity. Darkness can never be infinite. Light can be infinite, negativity can never be infinite; only positivity can be infinite because infinity needs to exist. Negativity does not exist.

When you throw a pebble into a lake, ripples start from that point to the edge of the lake. Similarly, your thoughts have a permanent effect on the Universe. Imagine if the lake were infinite light. Ripples with a continuous effect would be created, even though the magnitude of each ripple would be different.

The Universe is a huge wave of '*Tathāstu*!—so be it!' So everything is as you create, as you organize, as you arrange! Put a little intelligence, time and energy into creating the right space in you. If you carry the space of many births, you will have many births! If you carry the space of a soul, you will have a soul! If you carry the space of no-soul, you will NOT have a soul!

That is why I say this—decide to create the space for the best possibility. You have a soul, and it can do anything you want! This is the best space. Create it! That will be your reality! I don't want to say it will become your reality; it will be your reality!

Every action has a cause and an effect. Using the same principle, I can say that you can actually create the desired effect by just causing its visualization in your inner space. For example, when you meditate, if you visualize you are bliss, bliss is bound to happen in and around you as an effect. It would seem that the cause has created the effect. But in life, cause and effect are actually a cycle, each generating and being generated by the other.

Understand, anything that has not made its effect completely in you is cause. Anything caused which has made its completion in you is effect.

Anything which has not caused its complete effect in you is cause. This is the endless cycle Kṛṣṇa refers to when He says that work originates with the Creator, who in turn originates from the Supreme Existence, and therefore all sacrifices are from the Supreme to the Supreme.

Live the *tattvas* intensely! Bring them into your life layer by layer. Your body will listen to you. Your mind will listen to you. The world will listen to you. The Universe will listen to you. Humanity will listen to you. You will enrich the Universe and the Universe will enrich you.

When we are in the mood and space of surrender to these *tattvas*, we no longer retain our identity. We are one with Existence. Whatever we do, we do by Existence and for Existence. There is no separation.

Act Without Attachment

3.17 *One who takes pleasure in the Self, who is satisfied in the Self and who is content in his own Self, for him certainly, no work exists.*

3.18 *Certainly, he never has any reason for doing*
his duty or not doing his duty in this world.
He does not depend on any living being.

3.19 *Therefore, one should work always without attachment.*
Performing work without attachment, certainly,
man achieves the Supreme.

3.20 *King Janaka and others attained perfection by selfless enriching.*
To guide others, you too must act selflessly.

Our Eastern Masters have declared again and again, 'You are bliss. You are love. You are eternal bliss itself.' When you are bliss itself, what more can you ask for? When you understand and experience this truth, you are enough unto yourself; you are completely satisfied. Nothing exists for you to achieve because you are already the ultimate you can achieve!

As of now, you are running behind something out of greed, thinking you will have bliss when you possess it. Either you are running behind something out of greed or you are running away from something out of fear. You are afraid something will take away your joy, your life. Both running towards something and running away from something become irrelevant when you understand you are a part of this loving Existence, taking care of you every moment.

Existence is Taking Care of You Every Moment

Existence is taking care of you every moment. Do you think you can be alive even for one moment if Existence does not want you to be alive? The very fact that you are alive proves that Existence wants you here, now, in this form, in this place. This is the ultimate cause for celebration! What more do you want?

Existence has provided, is providing and will provide for each and every one of your needs. Your suffering, your struggle, your incompletion is only because you don't trust that you are being provided all that you need; because you carry a deep self-doubt and consider yourself separate from Existence, who you think is your enemy.

People often look at my feet and tell me that I have such smooth and soft feet. They do not know I have wandered thousands of miles barefoot in all types of terrain. When you walk upon Mother Earth with great respect, trust and love, She will simply cherish you. I never wore footwear in the early years of my life. Even now when I enter Tiruvannamalai, my birth town, I don't wear footwear.

I was once on an elephant safari on a jungle path. The guide showed me a path which was used by humans, alongside the one on which the elephant was walking. The guide's path had no grass on it. The guide said where man walks, no grass grows, but where the elephant walks, the grass does not die!

As humans we have lost touch with Nature, with Existence. We have fallen out of tune with ourselves and with Nature. That is why we experience Nature unpleasantly. Even in our prayers there is no gratitude, there is only asking. We have become beggars. Also, you are not satisfied with how Existence chooses to take care of your needs. You look at others and have a big list of wants based on what others have. You fail to understand that each of us is unique and each of us has been provided with exactly what we need. Instead, you start looking at what others have and want that also. Greed sets in.

This is how you waste your entire life running behind desires and running away from reality. We are focused only on the outer world. As long as the outer world is responsible for your happiness, there can be no permanent happiness. The person centered in completion does not depend on external causes or people to feel joyful, blissful. Constantly, the fountain of bliss is happening within him. He is enjoyment itself!

SELFLESS, UNATTACHED ENRICHING

Here Kṛṣṇa says a beautiful thing:

King Janaka was a beautiful example of a true *karma yogi*, a man of selfless authenticity in action with a continuous commitment to enriching life in and around him. He was a king. He ruled a kingdom and yet was unattached, liberated. Just like Kṛṣṇa who ruled a kingdom and yet was a *Sannyāsi* in the truest sense of the word, Janaka was a model king who was complete unto himself, untouched by the external world.

> Once, an ascetic went to the court of King Janaka and saw how Janaka was neck-deep in the activities of his kingdom, living like a king. He then thought to himself, 'Janaka seems to be a materialistic person. He is entrapped in so many worldly matters.'
>
> Janaka understood what the ascetic was thinking.
>
> Janaka called him and asked him, 'What kind of an ascetic are you? Instead of being happy and content within yourself you are trying to find fault with others? This is a grave sin especially for an ascetic, a person who is supposed to know about these things. For this, I have to give you the most severe punishment. You will be hanged to death next week.' Now, the ascetic was terrified. He could not sit in peace. He spent sleepless nights thinking of the gallows. He dreamt daily that his neck was being tied to a rope. He became very thin and pale.
>
> Janaka sent a servant to call him on the day of the execution. The ascetic was unable to stand before the king. He trembled and fell on the ground. Janaka offered him some fruits and a cup of milk. He ate the food, but his mind

was on the gallows.

Janaka asked him, 'How do you like the taste of the milk now? Is it good? Did you relish your food these past seven days?'

The ascetic replied, 'Oh king! I could not taste the food or milk that you offered me just now. My mind is only on the gallows all the time.'

Janaka said, 'Just like your mind is always on the gallows, my mind is always fixed on the Divine, even though I am involved in worldly activities. Though I am in this world, I am out of the world. Work for the world, unattached like myself.'

Janaka, though neck-deep in the administration of his kingdom, was completely unattached, liberated.

Once, Janaka was brought news that there was a fire in the city. Ordinarily, a king would have been agitated that a part of his kingdom was in danger.

But Janaka said, 'My wealth is unlimited and yet I have nothing. Even if the whole of my capital Mithilā is burnt, nothing is lost to me.' It is not that Janaka was not bothered that there was a fire in his kingdom.

He was completely involved in what he had to do, but at the same time was completely detached from the incident. He was complete in his being, not attached to the world.

Only when you are completely detached can you be completely involved. Otherwise, your very sense of ownership and emotional attachment will be a hindrance to plunging headlong into the task. Only when you work without any incompletion, can you perform the task authentically to your peak possibility, without expectation and without being concerned about the results.

Responsibility, The Space Of Leadership

3.21 *Whatever action is performed by a great person, others follow. They follow the example set by him.*

3.22 *O Pārtha, there is nothing that I must do in the three worlds. Neither am I in want of anything nor do I have to gain anything. Yet, I am always in action.*

3.23 *If I did not engage in work with care, O Pārtha, certainly, people would follow My path in all respects.*

3.24 *If I do not work, then these worlds would be ruined. I would be the cause of creating confusion and destruction.*

3.25 *Even the ignorant do their work with attachment to the results, O Bhārata, the wise do so without attachment, for the enrichment of the people.*

Here, Kṛṣṇa talks about the practical aspects of why a leader needs to act in a responsible manner. With responsibility, you experience the space of leadership consciousness, *Īśvaratva*.

There is a difference between the state of a leader and the status of a leader. Most of us want to attain the status of a leader but not the state. When you achieve the status of the leader, it is ego-fulfilling and you feel great. Some politicians are good examples for this. They exert the power of their position on others without even feeling responsible. They were a little more dominating and convincing than the people whom they were trying to dominate, that's all. It is not that they were more intelligent or more capable.

The state of the leader is something totally different. It is the state of the leader born from the principle of responsibility that enriches people to become responsible. Problems of all kinds, ranging from stress to discontentment and violence, result because the leader has achieved the status and not the state.

LEADER CREATES MORE RESPONSIBLE LEADERS

A leader with the status remains only as a slave. A leader with the state takes the responsibility to create more and more responsible leaders.

Only when you express all the possibilities out of liberation cognition, are you living your life. Life is lived when *jīvanmukta saṁbhāvana*, the space of possibility, the space of leadership becomes your lifestyle. Nothing else is required for you to be a leader; just leadership consciousness is enough. When Vivekananda walked the length and breadth of India, he did not have anything other than leadership consciousness in his life. But wherever he went, kings washed his feet, gave their own thrones for him to sit on, received his blessings and guidance, and requested his spiritual support.

Responsibility is thinking, feeling, acting, responding and cognizing from the truth that you are the Source of everything!

It is responsibility that makes you realize all possibilities. It is leadership consciousness that brings not just success, but fulfillment in you. I have seen thousands of politicians who have power without having the state of leadership consciousness. Sometimes, people sit on the throne or get the power and become power centers, without having the state of a leader. I have seen them dying in depression or suffering in suffocation, due to the power! They never enjoy the power.

Unless you achieve the state, the status is a liability! If you have not achieved the state, the status binds you and also brings suffering to others. The state of responsibility, the state of leadership consciousness, *Īśvaratva* has to be achieved first. When you do not carry the consciousness of a leader, even if you get the powers of the leader, you are bound by it and you also bind the people who accept you as leader and follow you.

Leadership consciousness is an independent intelligence; it cannot be hidden from others. Once you have it, the whole world will know that you have it; the world simply listens to you! You do not need any power, political strength or infrastructure for the world to know that you are a leader. Even if you walk on the street, you will stand tall—as a man among men; what Kṛṣṇa names Arjuna as *puruṣarṣabha*, the best among men. And the world will respect you!

Listen! I am not talking to you about some corporate values and principles, or on something that *Ṛṣis, Vedic* Seers have uttered in the *Upaniṣads*. I am talking to you about what I have directly experienced, which you have to experience. I am talking from the context of being responsible for making you responsible.

Be very clear, the person who talks has only one reason—making you responsible. I am responsible to make you experience responsibility as I have experienced it. A person with wealth is responsible to guide a poor man to wealth. A person with knowledge is responsible to make ignorant people knowledgeable! When you own, you become responsible to make everyone own. Because I own responsibility, I own the responsibility of making everyone own responsibility.

Kṛṣṇa, who owns responsibility, the space of leadership consciousness, *Īśvaratva*, is making Arjuna own responsibility. Kṛṣṇa says, 'Whatever action is performed by a great person, others follow. O Pārtha, there is nothing that I must do in the three worlds. Neither am I in want of anything. Yet, I am always in action.'

yad yad ācarati śreṣṭhas tad tad evetaro janaḥ |
sa yat pramāṇaṁ kurute lokas tad anuvartate || 3.21

na me pārthāsti kartavyaṁ triṣu lokeṣu kiñcana |
nānavāptam avāptavyaṁ varta eva ca karmaṇi || 3.22

There are only two types of human beings on planet Earth—those who feel responsible for everything and those who don't feel responsible for anything. People who feel responsible become leaders. People who don't feel responsible continue to be slaves. There are some people who don't feel responsible even for their own actions because they forget their action is going to bring its result. Many times, even when they plan out a business, they only plan out the people they will hold responsible if it fails! They don't plan to make it successful.

Plan for success! Don't plan for failure. Right when you start planning, if you wonder 'If this fails what do I do?', you immediately think, '*I will hold him responsible!*' But holding the other responsible is not going to bring you success. Even as the thought—'I will hold him responsible' arises, cut it.

I always tell my disciples, 'Take responsibility for practicing what I teach you by bringing authenticity into every action. Don't just preach what I teach. Only by example can you cause others' reality and radiate the teachings powerfully.' Deep understanding and experiential expression of the truth happens only with taking responsibility for all your actions. Only when the space of leadership becomes your own experience does the responsibility become complete. Otherwise, if the understanding is just based on someone else's words and experience, then there is always the possibility that anyone can come and shake your belief and you will either hold the situation or others responsible. The roots of responsibility, in this case, are not deep and strong enough to withstand all kinds of questions. Others' questions are nothing but your own unanswered questions that you chose to suppress within you!

That is what happens to Arjuna as *kurusattama*, the leader of all Kuru warriors, as *bharatarṣabha*, the best of Bhārata. Even though he takes the responsibility to fight and avenge the collective irresponsibility of the Kauravas, he falls from his space of leadership and gives reasons to escape his responsibility. Arjuna, the one of taintless, pure fame, becomes a slave to his incompletions. Only when he allows the Master to enrich him does he surrender to the Master of all masters, *Jagadguru* Kṛṣṇa as His disciple!

Unless we enrich ourselves and allow ourselves to be enriched by the Master, nothing good can happen to us. Allowing the Master to enrich you is the best way of enriching yourself. If you don't enrich yourself, no one can save you. If you enrich yourself, whatever you touch will be successful. If you are in the space of completion, anything you touch will be successful. Powerfulness always showers success, it never brings failure. It is a law of life!

There are three types of people: the disciples (or the followers), the Masters, and the leaders (or guides).

The disciple is one who has not yet experienced and enriched himself with the teachings of the Masters, but who is authentically interested and has responsibly embarked upon the path. He needs some guidance on the path. He does not yet know how to practice what is being taught.

The Master is one who is in the eternal space of *Īśvaratva*, leadership consciousness and is in the ultimate experience of Enlightenment. Out of compassion, He enriches by showing the path of responsibility to reach His state to all those who would like to be in that state. It is not necessary for the Master to practice what He preaches because he is beyond the common rules of conduct. Masters need not follow what they tell you to do to reach their state. They understand the illusion of the physical plane that their body-mind system operates in. Whatever they may do physically is in a state of complete awareness.

I always tell people that they need to be aware and completely present when they eat. But if you have been around me, you will see that I never concentrate on my food when I eat. When I eat, I am reading or talking to someone. It is like this: For you, you have to meditate to be aware of the food you are consuming so that you eat only as much as is needed. But for me, if I am aware, I will not be able to eat the amount of food my body needs. I have to distract myself and remove the awareness, the self-remembrance, and only then will the food go inside! An enlightened being's system is totally different from an ordinary person's system.

A leader or guide is someone who is a spiritual activist, he is between the Master and the follower. He has not yet reached the ultimate state of the Master but he has had glimpses of that state. He is not as inexperienced as the follower. He is the bridge of responsibility to lead the follower to the Master.

One more thing: It is not that you need to practice the *tattvas* just so that others get inspired and enriched. Understand that the very practice will give deep understanding and completion to you. Automatically you cause what you want to cause in your life. That is the first effect, the actual result. Being an inspiration and causing the reality for others will be just a by-product. It will automatically result from the confidence of authenticity you radiate in your body language and the power of integrity you express in your words, when you enrich people out of the intelligence and strength of your own responsibility as a leader.

Nothing Binds Me, Yet I Engage in Responsible Work

In these verses, Kṛṣṇa beautifully explains what walking the talk means through His own example. He says there is nothing in the three worldsthe nether world, earth or heaven, for Him to achieve. There is no duty that binds Him. Even though He has nothing to gain, lose or even to do, He is constantly engaged in action and enriching the three worlds. Why?

Because people look up to Him as God, they would obviously follow the path He sets. People's *anyakāra*, the expectation that world has from Kṛṣṇa is that He is God, He is *Bhagavān*. They would simply follow what He does. He is now responsible to fulfill even others' image about Him for leading them on the correct path. That is Bhagavān Kṛṣṇa's authenticity and responsibility!

I tell you, the one who takes responsibility for the whole world's *anyakāra* is God. God takes responsibility for the *anyakāra* of even atheists. That is why when they say God never helps, He never helps them, and makes sure that He fulfills even their *anyakāra*! So, even though Kṛṣṇa Himself has no reason to engage in work, He does so for the sake of enriching the people who will follow Him. If He did not engage in action and did not take the responsibility to make others' responsible, people would follow His example and fall into irresponsibility, inaction or *tamas*.

Listen! By taking responsibility to enrich Arjuna with the science and direct experience of Enlightenment, Kṛṣṇa fulfills the *anyakāra* of not just Arjuna but of the whole humanity embodied by him; relieving the planet Earth from *bhūbhāra*, the burden of the collective unconscious, incomplete beings.

Understand, others' *anyakāra* about you has two dimensions—how they perceive you and how they want you to be in their life! For example, they may perceive you as a fool and a cheat, but they may want you to be intelligent and authentic! When you take responsibility for both parts of others' *anyakāra*, life just oozes out of your *ānanda gandha*, your blissful inner space.

Listen. Taking responsibility for what others perceive and what others want just makes life ooze, explode and express through you. If you want your skin to shine, your eyes lit and your body radiating grace and joy, take responsibility for others' *anyakāra* in both directions. If others perceive you as a cheat and fool, don't be angry. It means that you have not raised yourself in some way.

Every year, I guide people on spiritual *yātras*. It is a lifetime experience to be in the lap of nature. In the Himalayas, the living energy field, we do various types of rituals at the *cārdhām* (four sacred pilgrimages). Of what use are the rituals to me? But I do them for you so that you understand their significance, get enriched to do them, and take the responsibility to enrich others with them. After Enlightenment, I came from the Himalayas to be amidst the people to enrich them with Enlightenment. I could have just stayed there happily and blissfully. But I have come here because of my responsibility to guide people with the right path of living Enlightenment. That is why Masters come to planet Earth out of their deep responsibility, their love and compassion to enrich people with Enlightenment.

Listen! When responsibility expresses through your head, it is leadership. When responsibility expresses through your heart, it is compassion. When responsibility expresses through your being, it is Enlightenment, *Sātori*.

Seeing me work constantly, being intensely involved in work, whether it is administration or giving satsanghs or planning activities or healing people, whatever the action may be, people are inspired and enriched to be engaged in authentic work and responsible leadership constantly, blissfully enjoying every moment. I don't have to give you my words. You can see me, learn and be enriched from my body language much more than from my words.

Stretching to Others' Expectations is Authenticity

Please understand, what you feel as *you*, the idea you believe as *you*, is *mamakāra*. For example, I can very authentically say I feel that I am a pure empty space.

There is something in front of the pure empty space which operates to create the *Sangha*. I believe myself as a pure space, I project myself as an Incarnation who wants to give this pure space to you. My belief as me, my cognizance of me as a pure space is my *mamakāra*. My decision to project myself as an incarnation who shares this space to be experienced by others is my *ahaṁkāra*.

What others believe and perceive as me, is *anyakāra*. When somebody looks at me as Śiva, I need to take the responsibility of Śiva and do for him whatever Śiva will do for him by stretching my ability. He may expect some boons from Śiva. So now it is my responsibility to stretch my super-consciousness to give him those boons. That is authenticity.

I go on stretching. Then people ask me, 'What will happen, *Swamiji*? Then you will almost become like a slave to other people!' You will be a slave only if you are forced. If you are a Master, you will take it on willingly. I decide to fulfill whatever people project on me. Even if it is a negative *anyakāra*, stand up, face it and take responsibility even for that. Don't give up on people! Only when you take responsibility, you will feel powerful enough to solve the problem.

As Kṛṣṇa says, I need to be responsible for what I do for the sake of enriching those who follow. The problem is, what I do is an expression of my experience, my pure empty inner space. Unless you experience it yourself, it cannot become your truth. The same action will have a completely different meaning and effect when done by a disciple than when done by a Master. But if you follow the Master's teachings and watch his body language, you will imbibe and be enriched with Enlightenment itself.

It is the energy behind the action, the energy of the being that decides the quality and hence, the effect of the action. It is not the action itself that decides the quality.

Masters act out of pure compassion in whatever they do. That is why so often, even when I scold people, the person does not carry vengeance towards me. Scolding is also for your good, for your ego to be removed. It will seem painful because the ego, which you have been thinking is you, is being pulled out. But your being understands that what is not you is being removed. That is why in the very next moment after scolding, I can be completely different, showering love. It was just complete truth at that moment, pure compassionate energy.

But what happens when you get angry with someone and scold him, say your child? Instead of you controlling the anger, it controls you and you misuse it because you are not conscious during the action. Be very clear, the other person's vengeance is the result of your very own vengeance, which you did not realize was there in your own action because you were not in the space of completion when you were scolding.

Please listen. Your own suppressed part, which is yet to be realized, goes and sits in the other's heart. When you fulfill the expectation of others, only then you realize that it is your own expectations that are fulfilled. Others' expectations are a wake-up call based on the time you fixed the alarm! The alarm is not your enemy, you fixed it. The alarm is only helping you to wake up, because you requested it.

Others' expectation about you is only your friend helping you to wake up. So when others have expectations towards you, bow down to them as the embodiment of Mahādeva; the *Antaryāmi* who is inside you, waking you up!

I always tell people, 'When I am compassionate, I cheat you. When I scold you, I teach you. Either way, you grow.' When I scold you, you are jolted into the present moment. Suddenly, in a flash, you get the awareness that you have been missing your natural space of completion. The energy behind my words is purely for your transformation. There is only pure compassion.

Role Of The Wise

3.26 *Let not the wise disturb the minds of the ignorant*
who are attached to the results of work.
They should encourage them to act without attachment.

3.27 *People, confused by ego, think they are the doers of all kinds of work while it is being done by the energy of nature.*

3.28 *One who knows the Truth, O mighty-armed one, knows the divisions existing in the attributes of nature and work.*
Knowing well about the attributes and sense gratification,
he never becomes attached.

3.29 *Fooled by the attributes of nature, those people with less wisdom or who are lazy become engaged in actions driven by these attributes. But, the wise should not unsettle them.*

An ignorant man says to himself, 'I shall do this action and thereby enjoy its result.' A wise man should not unsettle this belief. Instead, he himself should set an example by performing his responsibilities diligently from the space of leadership, but without attachment. If the wise man condemns the actions performed with attachment, the ignorant person may simply decide to neglect his responsibilities.

It is like this. Can you explain to a child that his toys are not precious? No! The child will never be able to understand that. It has to grow and automatically its attachment to toys will drop when maturity happens. Similarly, the ignorant person can first do the action only with attachment. But upon seeing the wise person being unaffected by his own actions and being always blissful, naturally, the ignorant one will get curious to know the secret behind happiness. The example of the wise man will automatically pull him towards work with detachment.

Take the example of relating to God. Most of us pray to God to get something. All our prayers to God are asking Him to fulfill some desire or to protect us from something. It is perfectly all right to start a relationship with God like this. When you get what you asked for, your trust towards Him grows. This is important. If you ask a person who has not eaten food for three days to meditate, will he be able to? You will be foolish to tell this person to meditate. What he needs now is some means to get food and then he can be told about meditation.

When a person is doing work and expecting certain results, the wise person should not disturb him, even though he knows that work should not be done with attachment. At least the person is working and not sitting idle! He is in *rajas* (aggressive activity), which is better than *tamas* (laziness). Of course, he needs to be guided from *rajas* to *satva*, a state of calmness, a space of detached action, action without expectations. That is the job of a Master.

We are all governed by our basic nature, attributes, or *guṇa*. The mental set-up, patterns from previous births, called *vāsana* determines what we are, what we do in this birth, and also what happens to us in our future births. The desires born out of *vāsana* carry their own energy for fulfillment. If you are conscious, you will be able to fulfill them. Once fulfilled, these *vāsana* and *karma* get dissolved. One who reaches this state of completion with desires also realizes that he is not the doer.

The potter's wheel goes on turning around even after the potter has ceased to turn it. The *vāsana* or desires with which you took this body and mind will make the body-mind go through whatever activities it was made for. But the wise person goes through all these activities without the inadequate cognition that he is the *doer* of them. Actually, your desire to lead life in a particular way is what creates the corresponding mental set-up or pattern. Once you choose to live life in a particular way, your body supports this decision and acts accordingly. You create a *vāsana* or seed of karma to aid you in living life the way you desire.

Karma is nothing but the unfulfilled or incomplete patterns and desires, which are inside your being, that constantly make you travel in the same path again and again, trying to give the experience of completion in your inner space.

You are the one who chooses and acts, but any choice comes with effects and side effects. On seeing the side effects, you feel powerless and blame your fate or destiny. Actually, you are the one who chose it in the first place. You are responsible for the cause and effect, as you are source of everything!

A small story:

> Once a man went to a restaurant and ordered various items: pasta, drinks, sweets, and so on. He had a hearty meal and relaxed. The waiter brought the bill. The man took a look at the long bill and exclaimed, 'But I didn't order this bill!'

When you eat, you don't think about the bill, but the bill comes only as a result of all that you ate. Similarly, in life, all that you undergo are the effects of your own incomplete actions. Due to lack of integrity and authenticity, you are not aware of what those effects can be and therefore you perform the actions unconsciously.

Then when you do not take responsibility for these actions, the very actions and their effects bind you into further incomplete actions or desires. Please listen! Any *karma* left incomplete, any action done out of incompletion is *pravritti*—incompletion leading to more incompletion. It is more and more dangerous, and makes you more and more powerless.

YOU ARE NOT THE DOER

To understand, 'I am not the doer,' this concept of 'I' and 'mine' needs to be understood. Śiva says that the concept of 'I' itself comes from the concept of 'mine.' We think, when the sense of 'I' happens, the sense of 'mine' happens. But if you look deeply, our idea of what we think of as 'ours' is what defines what we think of as ourselves. Just imagine, if your possessions, your status, your wealth, your relations all are taken away from you, what will you think of as you? How will you define yourself? Your idea of 'I' is also relative, is it not?

Many devotees feel they are touching a soft pillow or even feel nothing when I initiate them during energy *darśan* (transfer of bliss energy). Basically, enlightened beings are just energy. In this plane, in these dimensions of space-time, you see them in this six-foot form and say '*Nithyananda*,' but in truth, this '*Nithyananda*' does not exist. It is just energy. There is no 'I.'

When you get attached to anything, you start creating suffering for yourself. When you understand that it is the mind and the senses doing what is in their nature, you become detached from your body-mind and do things with the clear understanding that just the mind, body and senses are doing their job. When you don't understand this, you get caught in what you are doing, you get emotionally attached to incidents and people, and you start living without awareness.

Do As I Teach With Authenticity

3.30 *Dedicating all actions to Me, with consciousness filled with spiritual knowledge of Self, without desire for gain and without sense of ownership, without being lazy or agitated, fight.*

3.31 *Those persons who execute their duties according to My teachings and who follow these teachings faithfully with authenticity without envy, become free from the bondage of fruitive actions.*

3.32 *But those, out of envy, who do not regularly perform their duties according to My teaching, are considered all-ignorant, senseless and ruined.*

Next Kṛṣṇa makes an important point. Kṛṣṇa says: Those persons who execute their duties according to My injunctions and who follow this teaching faithfully with authenticity, without envy, become free from the bondage of actions.

ye me matam idaṁ nityam anutiṣṭhanti mānavāḥ |
śraddhāvanto 'nasūyanto mucyante 'pi karmabhiḥ || 3.31

Here you need to understand two things. He says, 'according to My instructions, My words, *ye me matam idaṁ nityam*'. It means when you enter into your being, whatever your being says is Kṛṣṇa's words. When he says My instructions, He means the instructions from the *ātman*, the being.

When you complete and drop the goals and fall into your being, the Divine will guide you and you will become an instrument in His hands. If you become a hollow bamboo without any blockages inside, you will become a flute in the hands of Kṛṣṇa. Dropping your purposes or dropping your root pattern is what I call becoming a hollow bamboo. If you are a solid bamboo, you will be used only to carry dead bodies. But if you drop the root pattern and fall into the being, you will become an instrument in the hands of the Divine; a divine flute. When you become a flute, the air that enters into you comes out as music. Your words become *mantra*, sacred words that enrich people, your actions become *tantra*, sacred techniques to realize the Divine, and your form becomes *yantra*, sacred form, you become Divine.

Here, He says, 'Those persons who execute their responsibilities according to My injunctions, according to your inner consciousness...' Understand, as long as you follow the goals set by society, you will be carrying a social conscience. The moment you drop social conditioning, the purposes taught to you by society, you will drop conscience and start living with consciousness. Please listen, conscience will become consciousness the moment you bring responsibility to it. Conscience means struggling with do's and don'ts, guilt and desires. Consciousness means the pure flow of life. As long as you do not take the responsibility, you will be struggling with goals, with do's and don'ts. If you live with goals, you will carry a social conscience in your life. If you realize the beauty of purposelessness you will carry spiritual consciousness in your life.

Śraddha, Your Peak Possibility

'The man who lives according to his consciousness, believing in and having *śraddhā* towards these teachings...' Why does Kṛṣṇa ask for *śraddha* here? This is the first time Kṛṣṇa says '*śraddha*. Why? *Śraddhā* cannot really be translated as faith. It means faith plus the courage of authenticity to execute the highest level of possibility. In English, there is no equivalent for *śraddha*. I will describe *śraddha* as authenticity, but authenticity is not all-encompassing translation of *śraddha*.

The courage of being established in the peak of your capability, and responding to life from who you perceive to be for yourself, who you project yourself to be for others, what others expect you to be for them and what you expect them to be for you is what is called *śraddhā*, Authenticity.

Here Kṛṣṇa says, *'śraddhāvanto 'nasūyanto,'* the man who executes the teachings with *śraddhā*, with the courage of authenticity to the peak of his capability. Why do we need courage of authenticity?

A small story:

> A man born blind goes to the doctor and asks, 'Doctor, will you help me gain my eyesight?' The doctor says, 'Don't worry, I will perform an operation. You will get your vision and after that you can walk without your stick.'
>
> Blind people always carry a stick to feel their way around. The doctor tells him that he will be able to walk without the stick.
>
> The blind man asks, 'Doctor, I understand you will do an operation. I understand I will have my eyesight restored. But I don't understand how I can walk without the stick?'

By and by, the blind man had forgotten that his stick was just an aid. In the same way, just live without the mind. Just live without purpose and goals, you will be able to walk without the stick. The stick is nothing but your planning and worrying. By and by, worrying has become a part of you, an incomplete default cognition for you. When I say you can live without worrying, you will say 'No! How can it be possible? If I don't worry what will happen to my children, my house? What will happen to my property, my lawsuits?' Your life is going smoothly in spite of you, not because of you!

Courage is the fragrance of authenticity. When you have the courage of authenticity, *śraddha* towards living these teachings and start living without purpose, only then will you realize that you don't need the stick to walk. That is when you become authentic to your peak possibility. Once you enter into the depths of your being, you will enter into a totally different dimension. Whatever you think now as spiritual life or material life both lose their meaning and you will enter a new dimension of life. You will be established in authenticity, in the space of possibility.

For example, can you explain life to a four-year-old child? He can understand only toys. Once he becomes older, naturally he will be able to understand what life is. Automatically toys and dolls will leave him. Do you miss your toys? Do you feel you have renounced your toys? When you grow, you start experiencing a different dimension of your life and the toys simply fade away. Similarly, dropping smoking is not important, smoking dropping you is important.

When you enter into your being, when you experience the purposelessness of life, the so-called material life and spiritual life both drop you and you enter what I call 'Quantum spirituality' or Eternal Consciousness. You are then in eternal bliss. Only then you will understand you don't need worries to live. You don't need your mind. Until you reach the being, you need to have *śraddha*. Until you gain your vision, you must have *śraddha* and lie on the operating table. You need to allow the doctor to work on you as per his expectation from you. That is the reason Kṛṣṇa says, '*śraddhāvanto anasūyanto*'.

The next word is a beautiful word: '*anasūyanto*,' which means 'without envy.' This is important. We all think, 'My brother has purchased two houses. My sister is getting a big new car. How can I live like this?' The moment you get such thoughts, 'He has that, she has this,' what happens? All your spirituality, all your authenticity, all your purposelessness, everything just disappears. You are again in the same rat race. If your neighbor buys a new air-conditioner, the temperature in your house shoots up.

Kṛṣṇa says, '*anasūyanto*, without envy.' Envy is the parasite pattern that puts you back in the same rut of inauthenticity. The problem with the rat race is this—even if you win, you are still a rat!

Any pattern you create before the age of seven is the root pattern. Any pattern created after the age of seven is a parasite pattern. First you will have to work on completing with the parasite patterns and then completing with all the root patterns. The moment the parasite pattern of envy or jealousy enters your being, authenticity disappears, purposelessness disappears. Again, you fall into social conditioning and you start running behind goals like a rat.

Kṛṣṇa is asking Arjuna to bring *śraddha* or authenticity in action to the peak possibility of what he perceives as himself and what he projects as himself, without the parasite pattern of envy, *anasūyanto*.

When you bring yourself to your peak, there is no wastage of inner power, there are no parasite patterns that can attack you. When you waste your love, it becomes lust. When you waste your responsibility, it becomes jealouly. The lower dimensions of you are nothing but rejected parts of your higher dimensions. When your higher dimension is not materialized, your lower dimension is empowered!

THE POWER OF ILLUSION

There is a beautiful idea from *tantra* about *māyā śakti* (the power of illusion). Illusion makes us all dance with this one stick, jealousy. Have you seen guys who make money using monkeys in India? On the road-side, they perform a small show with monkeys. With a small stick they make the monkey dance and do whatever they want it to.

In the same way, the power of illusion is making you run as it wants with just one stick called jealousy. The moment you compare, you just jump into your lower dimensions, the same rut which I call the purposeful life. Then you become a *karmi*, not *karma yogi*.

The man who lives in eternal consciousness, *Nityānanda*, and allows his body and mind to work according to their nature is centered in eternal consciousness. He is called a *karma yogi,* one who has espoused authenticity in action without attachment as the ultimate renunciation. But the man who acts out of jealousy, enters his lower dimensions of social conditioning. He is caught in the rat race, and is called a *karmi*, one who is focused on inauthentic action arising from patterns of greed.

A *karmi* is an inauthentic person who rejects his highest possibility. A *karma yogi* is one established in authenticity in action, empowered to live his highest possibility. The difference between a *karmi* and a *karma yogi* is this: The man who is driven by inauthenticity, his lowest possibility, jealousy is a *karmi*, and the man who allows authentic action, his highest possibility, the eternal consciousness to drive him is a *karma yogi*.

One more thing: When we do things out of comparison, we do only foolish things. Our intelligence stops working and our performance falls short of our peak potential, because we now use someone else's productivity as our measuring stick. If you do things out of the parasite patterns of jealousy, you will end up being inauthentic in your actions.

Comparison or jealousy is the root from which inauthenticity justifies itself and continues to exist in you! Do not allow it. Tell yourself very clearly, 'Whatever others do is their responsibility and my life is my responsibility. At the end of the day, even if he is not responsible, I am responsible for his irresponsibility!'

Each one of us is unique. There is no need to compare with any other person. You are unique. The main problem is that you compare only with the nearest person, five inches above you and five inches below you. You don't compare yourselves with Bill Gates or Buddha, do you? Why?

The problem is not failure, the problem is your worry about failure. That is why you don't aim for unreachable goals. You aim only for reachable goals. All your joy, the very bliss of living is swallowed by this one illusion called comparison. Just like the Earth is destroyed by the ocean at the time of the final deluge, *pralaya*, your whole life is destroyed by comparison.

Jealousy and comparison have no absolute existence, they are delusory patterns. There are two levels of reality: comparative reality and existential reality. If you build your life based on existential reality, you will never suffer. If you build your life based on comparative reality, you will continuously suffer till death. Not only at the time of death, even after death.

LIFE IS FOR REALIZING YOUR HIGHEST POSSIBILITY

When you are in conflict, you will naturally suffer. People constantly say, 'I am in suffering because of his or her inauthenticity!' Wherever you are in conflict, be very clear you are in conflict, even though you point at others' inauthenticity.

If life is not continuing to happen in the seed, it is dead! If authenticity is not continuously happening in you, you are not a possibility, you are dead! Constantly make authenticity happen in you, in your work, in your thinking, in your health! Constantly expand your thinking, constantly expand your perception!

Constantly practicing authenticity brings you to the space of possibility. *Śraddha* or Authenticity continuously connects you with yourself and your highest possibility. Life is for realizing that possibility. Life is for realizing the Self. Life is for realizing itself.

Authenticity is Life! Life is continuous expansion! Add authenticity to your thinking in every step. Constantly go on expanding! Don't settle down with the lower perception. What you know about humans, what you know about the world, what you know about *you* is all imperfect perception, comparative reality. When you settle down with comparative reality, you make the most horrible mistake of your life. Don't build your inner space on comparative reality. Let your inner space be built on existential reality which is the space of highest possibility. If you build your life on existential reality, you will live your life blissfully in eternal consciousness, as a *karma yogi*.

By nature, a person with a body and mind has to act in one way or the other. If you follow your nature with authenticity, you can be comfortable and flow in tune with Existence. When you are relaxed, when you are blissful, you express yourself beautifully.

When you become possessed by the root pattern of greed or fear and try to be what you are not and project yourself to be what you are not, you suppress yourself and become inauthentic. What can suppression do? You cannot suppress energy. You can only transform energy. It can never be destroyed or suppressed.

Neither expression nor suppression is the solution, only completion with your inauthentic identities is the solution. The solution is to infuse *śraddha*, the courage of authenticity into this process. For example: your reaction of irritation has nothing to do with what the person has done. If you look a little deeper, you can see it is how you choose to react based on your root and parasite patterns that decides what you feel about the person. You choose to get irritated by what he is doing. Why should you allow yourself to get worked up about the other person's actions? Also, factually the person may have a completely different intention. Yet you are already biased by your own past perception about him.

Authenticity is the key. If you bring authenticity to what you perceive as you, to what is happening within you and what you project yourself outside you, you will not be controlled by your unconscious patterns. You will be able to see clearly when lower emotions arise or unconscious reactions arise. The awareness of your inauthenticity will itself bring you to your peak capability. Then, you will naturally drop all your lower level emotions and live what Kṛṣṇa calls as *śraddhāvanto anasūyanto*, authenticity without envy, the space of possibility.

Do Your Responsibility

3.33 *Even the wise person tries to acts according to the modes of his own nature, for all living beings go through their nature. What can restraint of the senses do?*

3.34 *Attachment and repulsion of the senses for sense objects should be put under control. One should never come under their control as they certainly are the stumbling blocks on the path of self-realization.*

3.35 *Better it is to do one's own responsibility, even if done faultily, than to do someone else's responsibility perfectly. Death in the course of performing one's own responsibility is better than doing another's responsibility, as this can be dangerous.*

3.36 *Arjuna says, 'O descendant of Vṛṣṇi, then, by what is man forced to commit sinful acts, even without desiring, as if impelled by force?'*

3.37 *Bhagavān says,*
'It is lust and anger born of the attribute of passion, all-devouring and sinful, which is one's greatest enemies in this world.'

Here, it is important to understand what duty means. If I have to do my duty, I need to know how to identify my duty.

The idea of duty is different for different people, different countries, different cultures, and different religions. Hence the term 'duty' is impossible to clearly define. We have always been trained by society to consider certain acts as duty; some as good and others as bad. Duty and responsibility are totally different.

For example, it is our duty to help elderly people, to follow principles of truth, non-violence, non-stealing and such tenets. We are brought up with these concepts of morality, but have we experienced the beauty of implementing them?

Then there are certain principles that get handed down depending on the religion we follow. For example, a starving person who finds a piece of meat has no problem eating it if he is a non-vegetarian. On the other hand, a vegetarian would feel it is his duty not to touch meat even if it means losing his life. These are all socially defined duties. Never judge the customs of other people by your standards. There is no common standard for the Universe.

What Kṛṣṇa talks about here is not socially defined duty or conscience. He is talking about responsibility, the leadership consciousness, the law of the cosmos. The Cosmos functions on responsibilism. The Cosmos does not believe in socialism, communism, capitalism, corporatism or any other 'ism.' The law of Cosmos and the natural law of Existence—*dharma* is not comparison based philosophy of communism, socialism, capitalism or corporatism. The law of the Cosmos is responsibilism.

You always measure the result of your responsibility based on the little money and the name and fame you get. That is where you fail. When you take responsibility, the higher energies start expressing through you. That is why I am asking you to not measure the results with your small logic. When you actually take responsibility, Indra enters your hand; it becomes *vajrāyudha*. Yama enters your lungs; it means 'not-stopping'. Lakṣmi enters your heart; it means 'continuously sharing'. Kubera enters your liver and kidney, keeping the whole thing alive; Mārut, Agnī, Mārīci, all of them enter your intestine, burning anything that is offered and keeping the whole system active and alive!

When you take responsibility, when you start expressing authenticity, you get a thousand times more benefit than what you calculate through your small logic. When you start living with responsibility, not only will your monthly earnings move from two *lakh* to twenty *lakh* but you also build a space where you live in deathlessness. Your body gets built as you want. Your consciousness gets built beyond your body; you build a space of deathlessness.

UNATTACHED WORK LIBERATES YOU

Vivekananda talks about a sage, a yogi in India. He was a peculiar man. If you asked him a question, he would not answer. However, if you asked him a question and waited for some days, in the course of a conversation, he would bring up the subject and throw wonderful light on it.

He once told Vivekananda the secret of work. 'Let the end and the means be joined as one.' When you are doing any work, do not think of anything beyond that. Do it as worship, as the highest worship, and devote all your energy to it for that time. The right performance of duty at any point in life, without attachment to the results, leads us to the highest realization.

The worker who is attached to results is the one who grumbles about the nature of the duty. To the unattached worker, all duties are equally good. He takes responsibility and welcomes what he has to do, irrespective of the external nature of the job. He approaches every act with the same enthusiasm and liveliness and becomes completely involved in the task at hand. He is authentic to his authenticity and does the action to his peak capability.

In the great epic Mahābharat, there are actually three versions of the Gītā: *Bhagavad Gītā* and *Anugīta*, both delivered by Śrī Kṛṣṇa; the third and equally important one is called *Vyādha Gītā*, the song of a butcher.

A butcher delivered this *Vyādha Gītā*; a man who is considered as a low caste or a cāndāla delivered this great scripture.

> There lived a great yogi who had special powers but was not yet enlightened. He was a highly egoistic person. He was meditating under a tree in a forest. A bird sitting on the tree relieved itself and the droppings fell on him. He lost his temper and he opened his eyes, staring at the bird. The bird was killed by the power of his gaze. The yogi was very proud of what he had done.

He then went on his daily round of begging for alms. He came to a house and begged for food. The lady of the house called out from inside the house and asked him to wait as she was serving her husband. The yogi was upset. He thought to himself, 'Foolish woman! She is serving her husband, an ordinary man, and she is making a great yogi like me wait!'

Suddenly he heard the lady's voice again as if in answer, 'I am not like the bird in the forest to be killed so easily. Your powers may be used against birds but not against me, so relax!'

The yogi was shocked! The lady actually knew not only what he was thinking, but even what had happened in the forest! The yogi apologized to the lady when she came out to give him food.

He asked her, 'Mother, how did you know what I was thinking? And how did you know what happened in the forest? Please teach me how I can achieve this.'

She replied, 'You have attained śakti (power) but not buddhi (intelligence). Go to the butcher who is down the road and he will teach you.' Now the yogi was even more surprised. He thought, 'How can ordinary butchers teach me anything about buddhi?'

But what the lady had done was too much for him. So he quietly took the lady's counsel and went down the road to the butcher's shop.

When he reached the butcher's shop, he saw that the butcher was busy cutting up the meat of the animal he had just slaughtered. He could not imagine learning from a butcher. But he wanted intelligence, so he approached the butcher and asked, 'I was told by a lady living nearby to ask you about intelligence. Can you explain to me how to attain intelligence?'

The butcher explained how he himself had achieved intelligence, the ultimate experience. All he did to achieve it was do his job with complete awareness and total authenticity. He did his job with complete integrity and used the money that he earned to take care of his aged parents, which he did with equal devotion. Just the very doing of his responsibility had liberated him. The nature of his work, the act of slaughtering animals, was not important. The attitude, space from which he did it was what mattered. You may be doing the greatest acts of social service. But if the attitude, the energy behind the act is not out of completion, the action is just hypocritical and inauthentic.

Causing Responsibility Out of Completion

In the Mahābhārat, Karṇa is a great warrior and close friend of Duryodhana; his acts of charity and generosity are much admired. He is the immaculate son of Surya, the Sun energy and the eldest son of Kuntī, the mother of Pāṇḍavas. Being born before Kuntī's marriage to King Pāṇḍu, the unwed Kuntī abandoned him at birth. Karṇa lived as the adopted son of the royal charioteer of the Kurus, and struggled with misfortune throughout his life.

Karṇa's famous charity was out of a deep incompletion and a feeling that he is not respected. What was Karṇa's inner image, *mamakāra*? 'I am a failure; I am not respected anywhere I go.' This is because he did not know his parents' names, his origins. So, his inner image, *mamakāra* at a young age was 'I am not respected!' So he was exploding with the outer image, *ahaṁkāra*—'I have to be respected, I am respectable!' And the best way to be respected was to do charity work. Even his charity came from incompletion. That is why his death itself was because of his charity.

See, at every level, he is destroyed by his acts of charity. First, Indra, the king of gods, comes and takes away his invincible protective shield and earrings, *kavaca* and *kuṇḍala* that he embodied from his birth as the son of Sun. At the end of Karṇa's life, all his accumulated good karmas out of his charity stand as a shield and protect him. So Lord Kṛṣṇa, in order to liberate Karṇa, comes in the disguise of a poor *brāhmaṇa* and asks in alms all the good effects of his charity. You see, Karṇa might have done the charity work out of incompletion, but the people who received it were complete. So their blessings were protecting him. Foolishly, knowing that Kṛṣṇa Himself is asking him for alms, Karṇa thought, 'I am giving even to Kṛṣṇa!'

Even the great acts like charity, when done out of incompletion, only lead to the wrong effect. Finally, because Karṇa no longer has the protection of his good karma, Arjuna is able to kill him. If you cause anything out of completion, what you get back will be miraculous. If you cause even a great charitable act out of incompletion, what you get back will be hell. Even the so-called moral, good deeds will only have bad effects.

THE NATURAL DHARMA

Each of us is unique in our capabilities and interests. Accordingly, our responsibilities are different. If you try to imitate others, thinking their responsibility appears more attractive, you will be making the mistake of following somebody else's path. Comparison literally rules our lives. When we use our energies with authenticity for our peak growth without comparing ourselves with others, we do our responsibility according to our nature.

These verses on *karma yoga* by Kṛṣṇa have been misused by some to defend the caste or *varṇa* system in the Hindu tradition. They say what Kṛṣṇa means is that one should not swerve from one's *varṇa dharma*, the duty of one's caste. They do not understand the origin of the caste system.

In the vedic culture, a child was taken to a *Gurukul*, the ancient system of living, learning at the feet of Master, before the age of seven. The Guru taught the child based on his or her abilities. If the child had the aptitude to become a scholar he was trained in scriptures, and became a *brāhmaṇa*. If the child was aggressive and courageous, he was trained in martial arts, and became a *kṣatriya*, meaning warrior, and so on. *Varṇa* or caste classification was based on one's natural abilities, not on birth. Over time, this practice degenerated into a classification based on heredity. One needs to understand Kṛṣṇa's injunction in the vedic educational context.

Arjuna then asks Kṛṣṇa why even a centered person is led to commit sinful acts, as if forced by unknown powers. Arjuna's question is the eternal dilemma of expression or suppression.

For example, if you see a beautiful woman and you feel attracted to her, you feel this is not right according to what society has taught you and you try to suppress your feelings. Can this inauthenticity work? If you try to suppress something, it will surface with more intensity. We are always conditioned to believe that anyone with passion or lust is a lower human. There is no lower or higher person. Only a transformation of energy needs to happen. People who pretend to be moralists are either afraid or guilty of their lust. They are completely inauthentic. The moment you think you are a lower human, you start fighting that feeling. Then it becomes very difficult to get out of it and to transform. Anything you resist persists. What you need is to bring completion and allow the transformation, the ultimate reality to happen.

The Alchemy Of Possibility Into Reality

These four principles of integrity, authenticity, responsibility and enriching exist in our very DNA. A seed becomes a tree or man realizes his potential only when these four principles are lived. A human has everything needed in him to become the ultimate reality, the divine reality. The DNA, the very structure with which the human consciousness is built, in Saṃskṛit we call it *dharma*—are these four principles!

As of now, man is only a possibility. Only when these four principles become reality do you experience your actuality. Then the base energy of lust can be transformed into the higher energy of love. It is an alchemic process of changing any base metal to a higher metal. Similarly, changing our base emotion, lust, to the highest emotion we are capable of, love, is alchemy.

First, the impurity, an animalistic emotion, should be removed from lust. Your lust is contaminated by all kinds of fantasies, feelings of guilt and desire we have picked up from the society and media. In earlier times, people were able to drop their lust by the age of forty. Lust simply dropped from them. In Indian marriages, there is a beautiful verse which couples recite. The meaning of the verse is, 'In the eleventh year of marriage, let the wife become the mother, and the husband the son.' This may sound strange. What it means is, let the relationship reach ultimate completion. The ultimate completion for a woman is when she expresses the motherliness in her. The ultimate completion for the man is when he comes back to the innocence of the child. So, by the eleventh year, let the relationship mature so that both the husband and wife attain ultimate completion.

First, the impurity in lust needs to be removed so that a deep friendship at the being level and not just at the physical or mental level can be added. When you feel deeply connected to a person, there will be no need for physical proximity to that person. You will feel happy and satisfied with just the feeling connection. For the final transformation of lust into love, the relationship needs to go through the process of patience and perseverance. You need to be patient for the other person to accept your transformation. Then he or she will automatically be transformed as well.

Here Kṛṣṇa refers to lust and anger, both born out of passion. Anger is also an emotion born out of lust. When the other person rejects your lust, it turns into anger towards that person. Anger is a tremendous energy we misuse because we do not understand and respect it. Greed, anger and lust are all *rajasic* qualities that arise from passion and aggression from the blocked *mūlādhāra cakra*, the root center. These are instinctive emotions that we inherit from our animal ancestors. Indulging in these base emotions keeps one in bondage to his instinctive nature. This is the reason Kṛṣṇa classifies these as the root causes of sin.

A human being is endowed with Consciousness that rises above these instincts. The meaning of a human life is not mere survival; it is the realization of one's Superconscious nature, one's highest reality. Anything that stands in the way of Self-realization is a sin.

Control Your Senses

3.38 *As fire is covered by smoke, as a mirror is covered by dust,*
or as the embryo is covered by the womb,
So also, the living being is covered by lust.

3.39 *The knowledge of the knower is veiled by this*
eternal enemy in the form of lust,
Which is never satisfied and burns like fire, O Kaunteya.

3.40 *The senses, the mind and the intelligence are the locations of this*
lust, which confuses the embodied being and veils the knowledge.

3.41 *Therefore, O Bharatarṣabha, chief amongst descendants of Bhārata,*
in the very beginning, control the senses and curb the symbol of sin,
Which is certainly the destroyer of knowledge and consciousness.

3.42 *It is said that the senses are superior to the body.*
The mind is superior to the senses.
The intelligence is still higher than the mind and
the consciousness is even higher than intelligence.

3.43 *Knowing the Self to be superior to mind and intelligence,*
by steadying the mind by intelligence,
Conquer the insatiable enemy in the form of lust, O Mahābāho
(mighty-armed one).

Just like smoke veils the fire, just as the dust on the mirror masks your reflection, and just as you cannot see the embryo when it is covered by the placenta in the womb, we are not able to see our true nature of bliss because we are caught in base emotions like lust.

Lust is linked intimately to the survival of the species. Without lust, there can be no mutual attraction between genders, no reproduction, and no continuity of the human race. This basic survival instinct is lodged in our primal root energy center, the *mūlādhāra cakra*. When this *cakra* is blocked we behave out of instinct, like animals. When this *cakra* is energized, we learn to live in intelligence as we are truly meant to.

Once a person reaches physical or sexual maturity at adolescence, it is very difficult to control the effects of lust arising out of the *mūlādhāra*. One needs to be spiritually awakened before sexual maturity so that the energy can flow upwards towards the *sahasṛāra* or the crown *cakra*. The *mūlādhāra cakra* is the seat of all fantasies, primarily sexual fantasies. These fantasies are the ones Kṛṣṇa says are like dust on the mirror, completely clouding our judgment.

We live by templates that we carve out in our mind based on these fantasies, and live towards fulfilling these fantasies.

Completion in the present moment is the key to unlocking the *mūlādhāra* and dissolving lust. It is only completion that brings you in touch with reality as it is and dissolves your fantasies.

Kṛṣṇa closes his dialogue with Arjuna in this chapter with these words, 'Be aware that you have a higher intelligence. Use that intelligence to control your senses and curb your lust, which is your most dangerous enemy on the path to completion.' Please note that Kṛṣṇa does not say, 'Arjuna, come here, I shall help you dissolve the lust in your body and mind. You can then be at peace.'

Arjuna started the dialogue saying he was confused by Kṛṣṇa's words about action and inaction. Kṛṣṇa then told him to carry out his own responsibility with authenticity and without worrying about the result of his actions. He guides Arjuna to lead a purposeless life, free from obsession with the final goal and to be detached from the result of action. 'Authentic action is our nature,' He says, 'not inaction. Act, work, but surrender the result of action to Me.'

Now, Kṛṣṇa says clearly, 'Control your senses, be aware, be complete living in the present moment and give up lust.' Lust, here, not only refers to sexual desire but also to all desires related to the outer world. It is our sense of identity, the sense of possession that drives us to acquire and enjoy. The truth, however, is that acquisition only leads to the desire for more acquisition, not to enjoyment and fulfillment.

To be blissful we need to keep our inner space clean and empty. Only then can bliss fill that space. The outer space can be filled, that is not a contradiction. As long as the outer material space is filled without attachment, the inner space remains empty.

To make this happen, the senses have to be in control, not suppressed. Anything suppressed waits for an opportunity to explode. However, creating the space of completion can transform the mind and senses. When we realize that life has no purpose, that the meaning of life is to enrich others and ourselves and to enjoy the path, we learn to give up attachment to end results. We drop expectations. We move into the present moment and live in the space of completion.

This is the whole essence of *Karma Yogaḥ*. Be complete and drop your attachment to the goal and the fruit of your actions, and live an enriching life with integrity in words, with authenticity in thinking and action, and with responsibility in feeling. Live life blissfully. You will achieve the Supreme. You will achieve the space of Enlightenment.

Kṛṣṇa says, 'You will achieve the Supreme.' You will achieve the eternal consciousness, *Nityānanda*, eternal bliss.

So let us pray to the ultimate Divine, *Parabrahma* Kṛṣṇa, to help us understand His message, to help us imbibe Him in our being. May He guide us. May He enrich us to experience the eternal consciousness, the eternal bliss, *Nityānanda*!

Thus ends the third chapter named ***Karma Yogaḥ***, *'The Yoga of Action,' of the* ***Bhagavad Gītā Upaniṣad, Brahmavidyā Yogaśāstra****, the scripture of yoga dealing with the science of the Absolute in the form of* ***Śrī Kṛṣṇārjuna saṃvād****, dialogue between Śrī Kṛṣṇa and Arjuna.*

CHAPTER

4

Jñānakarmasannyāsa Yogaḥ

The Path Of Knowledge

Logic can never lead you to Self-Realization. The ultimate Truth is beyond logic. The qualification to receive the Truth is Devotion. Kṛṣṇa begins revealing the mysterious supreme science of Enlightenment to His devotee and friend, Arjuna.

The Path Of Knowledge

The human psyche longs for continuance. Continuation and perpetuation of one's identity is of utmost importance to us. We trace our lineage back as far as we can go in memory and records. We keep looking for something noteworthy there. We are anxious to provide for the weak ones in the family. This is a general anxiety on the account of our own lineage.

Arjuna has been driven by the same dilemma. To defend the fears he has about his own identity, he cites historical moral codes that discuss how one's ancestors and descendants are affected by one's deeds in this life. It is a simple transference of his present uncertainty to the past and future.

People ask me, 'When was this Universe created? How and why?' I tell them that the next time God calls for a conference, if I am invited, I shall ask this question and find out the answer! As far back as I can see this Universe has existed. As far into the future as I can see this Universe will continue to exist. There is no beginning and no end. It has been there forever and will be there forever.

The form and identity that we are familiar with is perishable. It is matter subject to creation, destruction and re-creation. But the Universe is formless energy. As it sees fit, it transforms into matter and again back to energy. That energy is imperishable. This is what Kṛṣṇa explains earlier to Arjuna. This energy of the Universe is the same energy that is within us.

All religions may not accept this principle of energy in man and the Universe as eternal. Views of religions change and have to change as new knowledge arises. Scientists now agree that matter and energy are inter-convertible in time and space. Advances in Quantum Physics have shown that sub-atomic particles can appear in different forms and shapes depending on when they are viewed, how they are viewed and who views them. For example, people think materialization of objects is magic or trickery. It isn't! It is simple science. It is converting matter into energy, moving the energy and converting it back to matter. We can demonstrate this scientifically with the help of modern technology such as Kirlian photography.

I showed the ashramites (*ashram* residents) how this can be done. I made them count the number of *rudrākṣa* necklaces in a cupboard. I produced one from the air as if by magic and showed it to them. Then, I sent them back to count the number of necklaces in the cupboard. They found there was one less in the cupboard! Anyone can do this. All that they need is to know how.

No matter can be produced from nowhere. It can only be produced out of energy. Fortunately this energy source is infinite in the Universe. This Universe is known to be constantly growing.

The very first verse of the first Hindu scripture, *Īśa Vāsya Upaniṣad*, says that 'out of energy arises all matter—*īśā vāsyaṁ idaṁ sarvaṁ*.' Upon reading this verse, Albert Einstein, the famous physicist said, 'It is only now that I could establish that energy arises from matter. Thousands of years ago, *Vedic* sages knew more. They knew that matter arises from energy. Science has yet to establish this. The last frontier of science is the threshold of spirituality.'

Understand that the constant factor in us as well as in the Universe is this energy that is eternal. Once we understand that there is no separation between the Universe and us, all our confusion will be at rest. There will no longer be any fear of death, and there will no longer be the greed to acquire and hoard.

After all, the energy that is who we are is forever. Once we understand, cognize and accept this, we are in eternal bliss, *Nityānandam*!

I Taught This Science To Sun

4.1 *Bhagavān says:*
I taught the Sun god, Vivasvān, the imperishable science of yoga
and Vivasvān taught Manu, the father of mankind and
Manu in turn taught Ikṣvāku.

4.2 *The supreme science was thus received through*
the chain of master-disciple succession and the saintly kings
understood it in that way.
In the course of time, the succession was broken and
therefore the science as it was appears to have been lost.

4.3 *That ancient science of Enlightenment, is today taught by Me to you*
because you are My devotee as well as My friend.
You will certainly understand the supreme mystery of this science.

You need to understand that Kṛṣṇa is just thirty-two years old when He makes this statement! Physically His body is only thirty-two years old. But He says, 'I gave this imperishable knowledge to Sūrya, the Sun god—*imaṁ vivasvate yogaṁ proktavān aham avyayam* (4.1).'

Of course, this is very difficult to understand! With logic, you cannot understand this statement. With ordinary logic, which you use in your daily life, you cannot make any meaning out of this statement. In the next statement He says: *The supreme science, this yoga as it was, appears to have been lost in course of time.*

These two verses should be understood clearly. The first thing is that the truth is not new. It is eternal; neither new nor old. Eternal means it is there forever. It never becomes old. It was never new. Eternal means that which is beyond time and space. When you are in completion, anything you create stands for eternity. It is immortal and eternal. Otherwise there is no reason why Hinduism should be still alive. The invaders and fanatics brutally attacked and assaulted anything in front of their eyes, killing millions of people and destroying temples of Bhārat (India). They invaded and ruled India, not for one generation but for hundreds of years, yet how is it that Hinduism is still left alive, flourishing and expanding? Because it was created out of the eternal space of completion.

See, for a religion or any civilization to be alive, three things are important. First, the knowledge and the science of lifestyle, *Upaniṣad*—what is birth, what is death, why life, what is the purpose of life—the answer to all questions of living and leaving. Second, the buildings—architecture and arts. And third, the language. All these three are made out of the magnetic field of completion in *sanātana-dharma*. That is why these three things can never be destroyed, no matter how much anyone tries.

The architectural wonders and monuments created out of completion, and the linguistic monument and wonder, *Saṃskṛitaṁ* born out of completion—these can never be destroyed. Just like the wonders of the world, if you analyse the linguistic wonders of the world, *Saṃskṛitaṁ*, the *devabhāśā*—language of Divine, will be the first and only linguistic wonder of the world. Understand, the word *Samskrit* means well done, refined, perfect. The *vedic* tradition is such a powerful, refined system that no matter how much anyone tries to manipulate, morph or misrepresent it, it gets backfired! The system is so foolproof, so evolved to perfection; that is why we say *Saṃskṛitaṁ* means refined.

And the great science of lifestyle is the *Upaniṣads*. All three are created out of the magnetic field of completion. That is why nothing could destroy or kill it.

This *yoga* is imperishable as Kṛṣṇa declares, *avyayam*. **Anything created out of the space of completion stands forever, stands eternally. Completion is eternal, *Nitya*.** Only the things described and created based on time can be said to be new or old. Anything new will become old one day. Anything old was new at one time. Eternal means it is beyond the new and the old. It has been there from time immemorial. Here, this *yoga*, the science of Enlightenment is eternal or *Nitya*.

The science of *Karma Yogaḥ* that we learned in chapter three, the same *yoga* is going to be explained further in chapter four, *Jñana-karma-sannyāsa Yogaḥ*. I gave the first glimpse of this in the previous chapter. The first thing that needs to be understood is the first glimpse. If you allow those words to penetrate you, then straightaway those words can give you the first glimpse of Enlightenment. They can lead you to the first step of ultimate liberation.

Understanding the purposelessness of life will wash away all its incompletions, stresses, pressures and burdens from your being, whether they are physical or mental. You are liberated in that same moment. You are in the space of completion that very moment. Kṛṣṇa doesn't give you any technique that works over lengthy periods of time. Some techniques work over long periods of time, which you will have to practice forever. Your son or your daughter may get the result!

Kṛṣṇa says, 'Now, here or nowhere!' Either have the result now and here, or nowhere. All His techniques straightaway give you the experience. If you can allow that one idea of purposelessness, the beauty of purposelessness, into your inner space, that very moment the breeze of Enlightenment enters your heart. That very moment, the healing of your being starts. Healing of *bhāva roga*, emotional diseases and healing of *saṁsāra roga*, the disease of birth and death, start.

Five thousand years ago, Kṛṣṇa said, 'I gave this science to Sūrya, the Sun god and the Sun god instructed Manu. The Sun god is Vivasvān. Vivasvān instructed Manu, the father of mankind. Manu passed this wisdom on to Ikṣvāku.

Here, Kṛṣṇa gives the succession, the lineage through disciples, the Master-disciple lineage. 'In course of time, the science of yoga was lost, *sa kāleneha mahatāyogo naṣṭaḥ parantapa*', He says.

LEARN ONLY FROM A LIVING ENLIGHTENED MASTER

Understand why this yoga of completion was lost. When a disciple is not in the space of completion, if he is not completely ready to listen, naturally the technique becomes a ritual. Understand, there is only one difference between technique and ritual. When it is done with integrity and authenticity, even an ordinary ritual becomes a great meditation technique that leads you to Enlightenment. When it is done without any integrity, as a routine, then even a meditation technique becomes a ritual.

'In course of time, the science was lost.' Kṛṣṇa uses a beautiful phrase, 'the supreme science was taught by Me, *imaṁ vivasvate yogaṁ* and the supreme science was received through lineage, *evam paramparā prāptam*.' You don't lose that supreme science in just one generation. In course of time, even a single unenlightened disciple is enough to destroy the whole science.

The problem is, your Master creates a big movement and you succeed him without the necessary qualifications. People who simply ascend the throne only because they are the successor are the most dangerous people. They have everything except Enlightenment. One who creates a spiritual movement, creates it only out of the energy of *Enriching with Enlightenment*, from his love and compassion. For the person who succeeds the founder, the whole movement is a gift.

When you get somebody's throne as a successor without the energy of responsibility, you will be filled with ego. You will create damage. You carry just the book and not the knowledge. Responsibility is the energy in which your life flowers and blooms. First learn to think with these four *tattvas* as reality. That is why our *Vedic* Masters always transmitted and mirrored the truths through the oral tradition of disciple succession from the enlightened Master to the disciple. The disciple sits in *Upaniṣad* at the feet of the Master.

***Upaniṣad* means sitting with the Master.** *Upaniṣad* is nothing but—a Master who gets into a space and lets the disciples sit around and mirror his neuron activity in their brains. *Upaniṣad* is the best way to transmit the experiential expression of the great *tattvas*. This is how Bhagavān Kṛṣṇa transmits the science of *Bhagavad Gītā* to the Sun god, Vivasvān and now to Arjuna.

Understand: If you are not enlightened, you can easily get carried away by anything that you see! The truth or the spirit of anything can be easily lost. If you want to destroy any law, all you need to do is just follow it to the letter and miss the spirit. That is why time and again our *Upaniṣads* insist upon going to a living enlightened Master. All our books are only manuals. *Vedas* are the only books that are courageous enough to declare that they cannot give you Enlightenment. If you want the ultimate experience, you have to go to a living enlightened Master. What do all medical books say in the end? Consult your family doctor! All these things are only manuals. You can't take medicines just by reading a medical book or from a person who is not a doctor.

In India, compounders, the doctors' assistants, are the ones who prepare the medicines. In course of time these compounders learn that for a headache you are meant to take a yellow tablet, for stomach pain, the green tablet, and so on. It is very dangerous. Taking medicines from compounders and learning from unenlightened masters are one and the same. A compounder, at the most, harms your physical body. But an unenlightened master can misguide, destroy you life after life. This is because the whole context is lost if you have missed even a single crucial point.

Spirituality, the Ultimate Luxury!

Here Kṛṣṇa says,

evam paramparā prāptam imaṁ rājarṣayo viduḥ |
sa kāleneha mahatā yogo naṣṭaḥ parantapa || 4.2

One important thing, He says, '*rājarṣayo viduḥ*,' meaning, this science is given to kingly saints, not to just any saint.

If you have listened to the previous chapter, *Karma Yogaḥ* you would know that the science He taught is Quantum Spirituality, which gives you both the material and spiritual world. That is why He says, 'the science is given to kingly saints.' Had it been only for ordinary saints, he would have emphasized only on the inner world, the inner space. Had it been only for kings, he would have emphasized on the outer world and wealth. The science is delivered to the kings, enlightened masters; enlightened masters who are kings. Only they can preserve the science as it is. Be very clear, only an enlightened person who is a king or a king who is an enlightened person can know the totality of spirituality.

Only a rich man who has enjoyed material wealth can understand the meaning and relevance of spirituality. Poor men who have not seen the outer world wealth can only go and beg in front of God. They can never understand the ultimate spirituality.

I have a story for you:

> At the entrance of a temple, a beggar was always stretching out one hand asking for alms, begging. One day, people saw that his both hands were stretched out for begging!
>
> They asked him, 'What happened? Today, you have suddenly stretched both your hands! Until now you were stretching only one hand! Why?'
>
> He said, 'I have started one more branch!'

You may have any number of branches. It may look like easy money. But you will never become a millionaire by begging! If you work with the 'beggar mentality' you will never be successful until the end, you will never be complete!

Only a person who has seen the outer world thoroughly realizes its emptiness. Only he can enterthe inner world. If you still have hope in the outer world, you cannot experience the ultimate spirituality. Only a king can be utterly frustrated. Only a king can enter into enlightenment, because he knows there is nothing in the outer space that can fulfill him. He has seen everything; all possible comforts, enjoyments and pleasures.

If somebody who has not experienced depression of success enters spirituality, he will stand in front of God and beg, 'God give me this, give me that.' He may be a religious person, but never a spiritual person. There is a huge difference between a religious person and a spiritual person. When you know God has got the *śakti* (power) to give whatever you want, your religion starts. When you understand he also has the *buddhi* (intelligence) as to when to give you what, then you enter into spirituality!

We all believe God has the *power* to give us what we want, but we don't trust that he has also got the *intelligence* to give it at the right time! That is why we beg and beg! Only a person who trusts that God has the *power* and the *intelligence*, can enter spirituality, trusting implicitly that He knows when to give and what to give.

Listen. I am not here to judge that one is lower and the other is higher. No! If you can't pray to God, where else will you go? You have to pray to Him only. But the teaching of religion has to start with the science of restful awareness, by helping human beings create the right space inside. The concept of prayer should come next.

Spirituality is the ultimate luxury. I always say that only a person who carries the space of completion, who understands the purposelessness of life can heal himself and others. Only he can be a real spiritual being. Here, Kṛṣṇa uses the words '*rājarṣi*, kingly saint. Only a person who has authentically lived aligning the inner space and the outer space, can experience the truth of the totality. Of course, when a person who is not authentic enough to realize this truth enters into the system, he corrupts it. Inauthenticity is the corruption that can happen in your soul. Don't allow this corruption to happen to consciousness.

BECAUSE YOU ARE MY DEVOTEE AND FRIEND

So, Kṛṣṇa says, 'In course of time, the science was lost.' In the next verse, Kṛṣṇa says:

sa evāyaṁ mayā te 'dya yogaḥ proktaḥ purātanaḥ |
bhakto 'si me sakhā ceti rahasyaṁ hy etad uttamam || 4.3

He says, 'I am telling you about this very ancient science of the ultimate Enlightenment or entering eternal bliss, and being My devotee and my friend, you will understand the supreme mystery of this science.'

This has to be understood very deeply. One cannot tell this ultimate truth to a person who is not ready. I repeat, this truth cannot be delivered to a person who is not ready to listen. And truth told to a person who is not ready creates danger for everyone.

People ask me in my meditation programs, '*Swamiji*, please talk about your Enlightenment.' I never speak about my spiritual experiences unless I know them well. I wait. If intimate experiences are shared when you are not ready to listen, you always create a self-doubt and spoil things for yourself. If you have courage, you will straightaway question the experience. If you don't have that much courage, you will just think, 'Alright, this is one more story! I have heard thousands of stories. Leave it!'

The spiritual experiences cannot be shared just for nothing. If it is shared it should become a source of inspiration that transforms your life. By sharing the spiritual experience, if it gives you the courage to take the same jump, if you also feel, 'I think I should also experience the same joy, the same bliss, I should not postpone it,' if it becomes an inspiration for you, then it is worth sharing. Otherwise it is not worth sharing.

Listen. There was a great Master in South India. He sang a set of poems on Śiva. He did not even write, he just sang the verses. Close disciples who lived around him requested him to put it in writing so that it could be useful to society. He said, 'No, they are my intimate love letters to my Lord. It is my personal relationship. How can I publish it?'

If, for example, you see somebody for the first time and he straightaway starts asking you personal questions, how would it be? It is too rude! You can't share your personal experiences straightaway with anybody. In the same way, the Master says, 'If somebody comes and asks you about your personal life, you can't share it. Only if you become intimate with him, it is possible to open up.' For a conversation to happen, you need a certain intimacy. If both sides are filled with their own ideas and arguments, a conversation can never happen.

I always tell people, in the first year of marriage, the man speaks and the woman listens. In the second year, the woman speaks and the man listens. The third year onwards, both of them speak and the neighbors listen! The conversation never happens! Only arguments happen. As long as the other person is in a mood for arguments, the *satya* (truth) cannot be expressed.

The Master says, 'It is my intimate relationship with God. How can I share that with the public?' Then one disciple, who considers himself intelligent asks, 'Why? When you can share it with us, why can't you share it with the world?'

Then, the Master says, 'By becoming a disciple, *you* have become a part of *me*. Only with a person who has become a part of me can I share these poems. Physically you may be another body, but mentally, you have fallen in tune with me. You have become like a womb, completely ready to receive the divine energy. This is the reason I share my experience with you.' Unless you enter into a deep receptive mood, unless you become a simple, innocent being, you cannot receive the ultimate truth.

The ultimate truth is beyond logic. Initially when you start to teach the truth, it always starts with logic. Words go logically. But after some time, you have to leave logic behind. Otherwise, you can't reach the Divine. You can't talk to God through logic. You cannot relate with him in prose. Only in poetry you can relate with God. That is why, be it Eastern or Western cultures, whenever it comes to prayer it is only through songs and poems.

If you want the divine relationship to happen, you need love. You need the language of poetry. Here, only a person who understands, who has become a part of the Master can receive the Master's experiences. Unless you become part of the Master, it is very difficult to understand his message. When you speak the ultimate truth to a person who is not ready, it leads to many troubles. With the right person, even a lie told by him will be good for society. In the wrong hands even truth will do harm to society. To whom it is delivered is important, rather than whether it is the truth or a lie. With the wrong person, even a great truth like *advaita* (non-duality) —'*I am God*,' may make him think he is God and make him do all nonsensical things.

A wrong person can never understand the truth told by Kṛṣṇa. For example, Kṛṣṇa says, 'I am God. I am everything. Surrender unto me.' If the person is not completely devoted to Kṛṣṇa, if he has not understood Kṛṣṇa, what will he think? 'What an egoistic person he is! How dare he tell me to surrender to him?' Naturally the person, instead of understanding Kṛṣṇa, will create more trouble for Kṛṣṇa.

Beyond Logic Lies Devotion

Here, the qualification to receive the truth is devotion. If you have heard all the things I have said in the other three chapters of the *Gītā*, it is expressed logically. Until this point, I am able to bring both logic and spirituality together. Now, the time has come when I have to give you the pure truth as Truth. Understand, great truths can never be expressed by logic, because logic is not sharp enough!

Somebody asked me, '*Swamiji*, why don't you prove God logically?' I told him, 'If I can prove God logically, then logic would become God!' Logic will become greater than God. God is great because He cannot be proved by logic. He is beyond your logic.

Here, Kṛṣṇa is going to talk about something that is beyond logic. This is where you leave your logic behind, become completely open, sit in a totally passive mood, and be ready to receive. With logic, either you will understand everything or you will not understand anything. There is no other danger. When it comes to the deeper level teachings, either you understand, or you misunderstand. The teachings which Kṛṣṇa is going to deliver now are much deeper, much subtler than the teachings delivered earlier.

That is why He says, 'Now I am telling you these secrets just because you are my devotee and friend, just because you are near and dear to me.

You are my own, *bhakto'si me sakhā ceti rahasyaṁ hy etad uttamam* (4.3).' That is the reason He uses the word *bhaktosi*. He says, 'You are my devotee and you are my friend.' *Sakhā* means friend. The person who does not have a connection with Kṛṣṇa, cannot receive the message.

Now Kṛṣṇa enters deeper level truths where you need to come down from your head to your heart, where you need to sit with your whole being and listen to the truths. Here, Kṛṣṇa gives a warning, *rahasyaṁ hyetad uttamam*. 'I am giving you these secrets, the mysterious science of realizing the Ultimate, my dear friend and devotee, Arjuna.'

So, now let us enter into the science that is taught by Kṛṣṇa. Let us come to the space of listening. Let us begin with a small prayer to Kṛṣṇa:

vasudeva sutaṁ devaṁ kamsa cāṇūra mardanaṁ |
devakī paramānandaṁ kṛṣṇam vande jagad guruṁ ||

Understand, *Vedānta* always emphasizes on three things: *śravana, manana* and *nididhyāsana*. Śravana means integrated listening. *Manana* means meditating, contemplating on it with deep active thinking. *Nididhyāsana* means expressing and radiating it powerfully in your life, or experiencing it in your life. Here, these truths do not need these three steps. Just listening is enough for it to become an experience. *Śravana* is enough; authentic *śravana* becomes *nididhyāsana*. Nothing more needs to be done. All you need to do is to sit with a complete open being in the space of listening, with a complete relaxed feeling.

These words are uttered for *your* sake, not for the sake of the Master. So, we will just take a few minutes to meditate on Śrī Kṛṣṇa, the greatest Enlightened Master, *JagadGuru*. Let us pray to Him to allow His words to penetrate our being. Let Him reside in our consciousness. Let Him lead us to eternal bliss.

Just take a few minutes, close your eyes and intensely pray to Him: Master, lead us to the experience. Give us the understanding. Let Him raise our inner space by His presence. Let Him be in our inner space and enlighten our consciousness.

I Myself Appear Age After Age

4.4 *Arjuna says:*
'O Kṛṣṇa, you are younger to the Sun god Vivasvān by birth.
How am I to understand that in the beginning
You instructed this science to him?'

4.5 *Bhagavān says:*
Very many births both you and I have passed.
I can remember all of them, but you cannot, O Parantapa!

4.6 *Although I am unborn, imperishable and*
the Lord of all living entities,
By ruling My nature I reappear by My own māyā.

4.7 *Whenever positive consciousness declines,*
when collective negativity rises, O Bhārat,
again and again, at these times, I appear Myself.

4.8 *To protect the pious and to annihilate the wicked,*
to re-establish dharma (righteousness),
I Myself appear, age after age.

Kṛṣṇa starts His message as a response to Arjuna's question. This shows that Arjuna still needs to have the maturity. He asks, 'The Sun god is elder to you by birth; he is so much your senior. How am I to understand that in the beginning you instructed this science to him?'

Arjuna and Kṛṣṇa are almost of the same age. Suddenly, Kṛṣṇa says He gave this science to the Sun god thousands of years ago! Moreover, Arjuna lived with Kṛṣṇa for a long time. He knows and has seen the human side of Kṛṣṇa, all of Kṛṣṇa's *līlā* (plays), all of Kṛṣṇa's moods. So now, it is very difficult for Arjuna to believe Kṛṣṇa's words.

This is what all disciples who live around Enlightened Masters undergo. They find it difficult to understand the Divine descending and walking on the planet Earth in human form. Arjuna struggles to understand. How can the Divine descend? Arjuna is shocked when Kṛṣṇa says, 'Thousands of years ago, I taught this science of Enlightenment to the Sun God, Vivaṣvān.'

For example, suddenly if I tell you, 'A hundred years ago, I was the person who taught all these sciences to some enlightened Master!' How will you feel? Naturally questions will arise. Here the same thing happens. Arjuna thinks, 'How can I understand?' He has become a little polite and intelligent. In the second chapter, when Kṛṣṇa says, 'Arjuna, go and fight,' Arjuna asks, 'How can you say this? How can you tell me to sin?' Now he says, 'How can I understand? Please tell me.' He does not say, 'How can you say this?" He is now ready to believe, but he wants a little explanation.

Kṛṣṇa Declares His Divinity

Whenever enlightened Masters descend on the planet Earth, they face this trouble, again and again. When Rāmakṛṣṇa declared that the same being who came as Rāma and Kṛṣṇa had now come down in the form of Rāmakṛṣṇa, he was called mad! People did not receive or respect him. But a few qualified people received his words and transformed their lives.

See, all movements can be started in two ways. One is the political movement which starts with huge numbers of followers. The bigger the crowd, the more powerful he feels. He makes all kinds of claims. These movements, over a period of time, slowly dwindle in quality and quantity. Once the founder dies, the movement dies. The second type of movement is the spiritual mission. When the Masters declare the truth, the quantity may not be there, but the quality will be there. When Rāmakṛṣṇa made this declaration, hardly sixteen disciples were ready to trust Him. These few transformed their lives. It started as a very slow, small movement but expanded into an international mission. Today, millions worship him as

God. These spiritual missions start in a very small way but expand and explode.

For a political person, the inspiration is in numbers. How well is it covered in media? It matters to him how many newspaper cuttings he can collect. But for a spiritual person what matters is how many ego-cuttings he can do and liberate? For a political person it is the paper cutting, for a spiritual person, it is the ego- cutting. I always tell people, my best discourses are always given to small, close devotees. Because when you speak the truth to an intimate group, it will be straight. It will shake your whole being and transform your whole life. Those who are not yet ready cannot receive it. For a spiritual discourse, what matters is the quality of the people present.

This very *Gītā* is delivered to *only* one person. When Kṛṣṇa delivered *Gītā*, only one person listened to it. But today, millions and millions, not even millions, billions read and practice it. For a billion Hindus, this is the basic scripture. Only one person listened to Kṛṣṇa. Today the whole world uses it. To express the truth, the quality of the person who listens is important, not the quantity of persons.

Now Kṛṣṇa starts to answer this question. Let me repeat this beautiful verse:

śrī bhagavān uvāca
bahūni me vyatītāni janmāni tava cārjuna |
tāny ahaṁ veda sarvaṅi na tvaṁ vettha parantapa || 4.5

Bhagavān says, 'O Arjuna, many, many births both you and I have passed. I can remember all of them but you can't.' Then He says, 'Although I am unborn, imperishable and the Lord of all living entities, I reappear by my original *māyā*, by controlling my nature.'

ajo'pi sann avyayātmā bhūtānām īṣvaro'pi san |
prakṛtiṁ svām adhiṣṭhāya sambhavāmy ātma-māyayā || 4.6

I think this is the first time He declares His divinity! All this while, Kṛṣṇa was only playing the role of *ācārya* (teacher,) intellectually enriching Arjuna of the truth and giving him knowledge. For the first time, He opens up. He declares the truth about His nature. He shows the divinity of His nature. I think this is the point where Kṛṣṇa starts to speak the ultimate truth as it is. Till then, I think He was a little shy to open up to Arjuna!

When a disciple is not ready, you can't open up, you can't tell the truth. Now, the disciple is ready. So Kṛṣṇa opens up. He says, although I am unborn and my transcendental body never deteriorates and although I am the Lord of all living entities, I still appear in every millennium in my original transcendental form.

Three things we need to understand here. First He says, 'I am unborn, *ajopi*. I never take birth. I am the ultimate *Parabrahma*. I am the ultimate energy.' I don't think anyone else has declared it so clearly. Here, Kṛṣṇa straightaway declares the truth. 'I am God, *bhūtānām īsvaro'pi san*,' He says.

Please listen, when the disciple is mature, the Master is understood. Here, straightaway Kṛṣṇa declares, 'I am unborn, *ajopi*, I am unborn, eternal consciousness, and my transcendental body never deteriorates, *avyayātmā*. You can always relate with me. I am unborn and I never die.'

Understand, that which never takes birth can never die; only that which takes birth can die. Here Kṛṣṇa declares, I never take birth and I never die. I am the Lord of all living entities—*ajo'pi sann avyayātmā bhūtānām īsvaro'pi san*.

Somebody asked me, '*Swamiji*, can dead Masters teach us like Paramahamsa Yogananda, Mahavatar Babaji etc.? If I pray to them, can they show me the path?' I told him: dead masters are not dead as you think. When they are alive, their presence had a body. When they are dead, their presence has no body, that's all. Having a body or not having a body is in no way going to affect their presence. They are eternally alive and available to you. All you need to do is just turn towards them. When normal human beings die, the soul leaves the body. In the case of masters, they leave the body! The very wording is different. So having a body or not having a body is in no way connected to their presence. They are available to the planet always, to the whole of humanity.

It is very difficult to understand Masters. With integrity and authenticity, if you reach out, even if they don't have the body, you will be able to relate, connect, and talk to them. When you don't have integrity and authenticity, even with a living Master you will miss him. Understand, He says, 'I am the Lord of all the entities. But I still happen in every millennium in my original transcendental form; using my own *māyā* (Illusion). Because of my māya, I assume the body and and incarnate Myself, *sambhavāmy ātma-māyayā*.'

Kṛṣṇa means that He happens on the planet Earth again and again in so many forms to guide and enrich the people. Ordinary human beings are in the clutches of māyā or illusion due to which they take birth. But Kṛṣṇa has *māyā* itself under His control and takes birth due to His own wish! But again and again we miss Him. We are all conquerors of Buddha, conquerors of Kṛṣṇa. Conquerors of Rāmakṛṣṇa. We conquer Ramaṇa Maharṣi. That is why we are here again and again! Please listen, we conquer them. Again and again we miss them. That is why again and again He has to happen on planet Earth to lift us, to show us the way, to enrich us with Enlightenment.

Kṛṣṇa Promises to Happen Again and Again

The next two verses, if they are understood, then not only the whole *Gītā* but all the spiritual scriptures can be realized. Here He declares:

yadā yadā hi dharmasya glānir bhavati bhārata |
abhyutthānam adharmasya tadātmānaṁ sṛjāmyaham || 4.7

paritrāṇāya sadhūnāṁ vināśāya ca duṣkṛtām |
dharma saṁsthāpanārthāya sambhavāmi yuge yuge || 4.8

Whenever there is a decline in individual consciousness, whenever the collective unconsciousness increases, to establish the righteousness of the eternal consciousness, the science of eternal bliss, *dharma saṁsthāpanārthāya*, I Myself appear, millennium after millennium—*sambhavāmi yuge yuge*.

Only a Master like Kṛṣṇa can declare the truth so clearly. **Here Kṛṣṇa declares, 'I come down again and again, to set right the wrong.'**

He keeps the generation of enlightened Masters open for the future, the possibility of enlightenment open for the future generations on planet Earth. He keeps the whole science open for the future. Only a courageous being like Kṛṣṇa can declare this truth; *sambhavāmi yuge yuge*.

People often ask me, '*Swamiji,* are there more Enlightened Masters on the planet?' I tell them, 'Surely. There are hundreds of Enlightened Masters. Don't think I am the only one.' If you own any business, you would not give out the address of similar businesses in the city. Only if you are authentic, you can declare—yes, there are so many other things available. People ask me, '*Swamiji,* if I take initiation from you, can I go to another master?' I tell them: 'Not only can you go, I also encourage that you should go. Pluck flowers from all the beautiful gardens and make a beautiful bouquet for yourself!' The human ego is such that it needs to be beaten by more than one person for it to die! So go and learn the best things.

This verse is a promise; it is deliverance to all of humanity. This one single idea, if understood, can straightaway make you enlightened. In science, the principle of entropy states that the energy level of every system, including the Universe, degrades with time. So it is with consciousness. Over time individuals start losing their positive consciousness and collective negativity builds up. Of course, this does not imply that every single person becomes evil intentioned, but on an average, spirituality, awareness, righteousness and consciousness of individuals deteriorate at certain periods of time.

Understand that the consciousness is always individual. When one is conscious and complete, one accepts all of humanity as an extension of oneself; yet, each individual needs to be aware of his own consciousness. On the other hand, negativity or unconsciousness can be collective. A whole nation can become collectively unconscious as Germany did under Hitler and Lankāpurī under Rāvaṇa. In history, over many thousands of years, each time such collective unconsciousness built up, there has been deliverance. It is as though there is a cycle of positivity and negativity, up and down, over time. Dharma, righteousness is restored eventually. This is Kṛṣṇa's promise.

To Know Me Is To Be Liberated

4.9 *One who knows or experiences the reality of My Divine appearance*
and activities does not, upon leaving the body,
take birth again in this material world,
but attains Me, O Arjuna.

4.10 *Being freed from attachment, fear and anger,*
being fully absorbed in Me and taking refuge in Me,
many beings in the past have become purified
by the knowledge of Me, and thus they have realized My being.

4.11 *I reward everyone, I show Myself to all people, according to the*
manner in which they surrender unto Me,
in the manner that they are devoted to Me, O Pārtha!

4.12 *Men in this world desire success through activities and*
therefore they worship the gods.
Men get instant results from active work in this world.

This is a very strange statement. He says, 'One who understands the nature of My appearance and activities will be liberated from this birth and death cycle.' How can it be? He says, 'Understand my transcendental nature of birthlessness and deathlessness.' Just now He said he is birthless and deathless. *Ajopi*—I am birth less. Just now He says, *ajo'pi sann avyayātmā bhūtānām īsvaro'pi san*. He says, 'I am birth less and deathless.'

Now He says, 'If you understand the truth of the transcendental nature of My appearance and activities, once you leave the body you will not take birth and death like ordinary humans do. If you understand My transcendental nature, you will also achieve the same transcendental nature.'

'If you understand that I don't take the body, you will not take the body either. If you understand I am liberated, you will realize that you are also liberated.' How can it be?

We will start with an incident from Bhagavān Ramaṇa Maharṣi's life, an enlightened saint from India. In the presence of Ramaṇa Maharṣi, devotees used to sing some songs. There is a song called *'Ramaṇa SatGuru,'* which means 'Praising Ramaṇa Maharṣi, an enlightened Master.' When the song is sung, Ramaṇa himself used to sing along with the devotees! Somebody asked him, 'What is this?

You are an enlightened person, you yourself are singing your own name. What do you mean by this?' Bhagavān says, 'Fool! Why are you reducing Ramaṇa to this six-foot body?' This is a deep, very subtle thing. He says, 'I see my body just as you all see it. I don't associate myself with this name and form. That is the reason why, just like you, I enjoy singing this name.'

An egoistic person, at least in public, will not show that he enjoys praise, because if he does, people will see that he is egoistic. He will never be open. Here, Ramaṇa Maharṣi is totally open and straight. He says, 'Just like you, I enjoy this name and form, because I don't feel this is me. The name is just getting repeated.'

Another incident: One of Ramaṇa's disciples, Muruganar wrote 'Ramaṇa Puranam'. It is the stotra (verses in praise) of Ramaṇa Maharṣi. He wrote a few lines and somehow he was not able to write further. So he just brought the paper and put it at the feet of the Master and said, 'Bhagavān, I am not able to write.' Ramaṇa Maharṣi says, 'Alright, you go, let us look into it tomorrow.' The next day when the disciple came back, he saw that the poem was completed.

Ramaṇa Maharṣi himself wrote the whole poem and completed it! The disciple was surprised. Bhagavān himself had written his own praises! Later, when the disciple published it, Bhagavān saw that he had put a small footnote: 'From this line onwards it was written by Bhagavān himself', just so that the devotees would know that those particular verses were Bhagavān's own words.

On seeing the first copy of the book, Ramaṇa Mahaṛṣi turned to the disciple and asked, 'Oh! Were the other lines written by you then?' Understand, He asks, 'Oh! Does it mean that the other lines are all written by you?' When you wrote all those verses, it was 'I' who wrote through you. As such, you cannot think about me or write about Me. What do you know about Me? Unless I express Myself through you, you cannot know anything about Me.' Only a man who has disappeared into the Divine consciousness can write his poem.

LORD OF ALL LIVING BEINGS!

In the *Bhāgavatam* (life history of Lord Kṛṣṇa,) Kṛṣṇa Himself sings, '*I am the Lord,*' just like how He now says —*bhūtānām īsvaro'pi.* This words are so beautiful: *bhūtānām īsvaro'pi*—I am the Lord of all living beings!

A mere cowherd boy from Briṇdavan says this! You should not look at Kṛṣṇa from today's perspective. You should understand the whole scene as it happened, on the battlefield at Kurukṣetra. Now, because of time, we have accepted Kṛṣṇa as God. But this was said when He was alive, when people could not accept him as God. When Rāma was walking on planet Earth, only the Saptaṛṣis (the energy of seven sages that controls the world) knew He is an Incarnation. Similarly, when Kṛṣṇa was alive in his body, very few people recognized who He is. At least Rāma lived a controlled life; he is easy for people to accept. But Kṛṣṇa lived such an ecstatic and spontaneous life, it is very difficult to realize who He is!

For a so-called religious person, it is very difficult to realize and understand Kṛṣṇa. But He says, *bhūtānām īsvaro'pi*—I am the Lord of all living entities. Somebody asks Ramaṇa, 'Why are you expressing your own glory?' Bhagavān says, 'If I don't speak about myself, you can never understand me. Unless I reveal, you can never realize me. Just out of my compassion, I express the truth, I express myself.'

It is like this: You are caught in a traffic jam on the road. You ring up and ask your friend who is traveling ahead of you on the same road, 'How is it there? Is there a traffic jam? Can I come by the same road or should I take some other road?'

Will he not have the simple courtesy to guide you?

With the same basic courtesy, Kṛṣṇa is revealing His truth to all of us. Here, when He says, 'I am God, I am the Ultimate,' He says there is a possibility, 'When I can achieve, why can't you?' He shows the space of possibility, He gives us the courage of authenticity, He encourages us. Here He says, 'When I can achieve, why can't you?'

It is like a seed is always afraid of rupturing to become a tree. The seed always feels, 'If I break and the tree doesn't happen, then what will happen? I will die.' But the tree tells the seed, 'Unless you open, I cannot happen.' The seed says, 'No, let the tree happen, then I will open.' But the tree says, 'No, no, first you have to open, only then I can happen.' The problem between the tree and the seed continues endlessly.

It is necessary for somebody to give a little courage to the seed. A tree that was a seed once can say, 'Be courageous. Be authentic to your highest possibility. Don't worry. You will never perish. Open. Just like me you will become a tree.' In the same way, Kṛṣṇa gives courage of authenticity to us, 'You can also become God, like Me. You can also experience the truth like Me.'

Please listen! Inside the seed, if life is not happening, the tree won't come out. Inside the seed, life has to happen, the tree has to come out! Inside your body, authenticity has to happen, enlightenment has to come out! Inside your body, if authenticity is not happening, the completion, fulfillment, enlightenment, won't come out. Add authenticity to your thinking in every step. If life is not continuing to happen in the seed, it is not a seed, it is dead! If authenticity is not continuously happening in you, you are not a possibility, you are dead! Constantly make authenticity happen in you, in your work, in your thinking, in your health!

Defining yourself to you should be done with life, with authenticity. If the seed defines itself saying, 'I am a seed. I cannot do anything. Ah, my life is over!', it is dead! If the seed decides to be authentic and say, 'No, today I will at least just break my shell, I will sprout one small leaf. Now, let me make my second leaf!' Then life is happening! Our huge banyan tree seed also would have had this dilemma when it was breaking! Because it decided to break and become a tree, today it is standing as a *kalpavṛkṣa*, a wish-fulfilling tree!

When Kṛṣṇa says, 'I am the Ultimate,' He expresses the space of possibility. He reminds us of our potentiality. He enriches us to define ourselves with authenticity as He defines Himself. He inspires us to enter the same consciousness, to experience the same bliss. When Kṛṣṇa reveals this truth, be very clear, Kṛṣṇa is not egoistic. He is expressing His true nature out of basic courtesy to His fellow travelers. The senior tree encourages the junior seed to open up and become a tree. The tree assures the seed. It says, 'Don't worry, I have become a tree. You can also become like me. You don't have to feel you will disappear.' It is an assurance.

A small banyan tree seed is a huge tree in the form of possibility. In the same way, you are God in the form of possibility! You are the seed for God in the form of possibility! Just as how the banyan seed is a possibility for banyan tree; you are a possibility for God Himself! That is why again and again I tell you, when Kṛṣṇa tells us '*I am God*', He means, '*You too are God.*' He gives you the courage of authenticity.

Understand, when Enlightened Masters say 'I', they don't have any meaning behind that 'I'. Only divinity speaks. For you, the word 'God' is just a word with no solid meaning. But when you say 'I,' you attribute a solid meaning, a solid identity to it, which is supported by solid experience. You know it. You feel it. If somebody asks, 'Are you mad?' you shout at them and prove it! But when you say 'God', your understanding is not supported by any experience. With enlightened people, when they say 'God', it is based on solid experience and when they say 'I,' it has no meaning.

Somebody went to a great Enlightened Master, Nisargadatta Maharaj in India and asked him, 'Master, you say enlightened people don't have *karma*. But how can you speak? How can you do all your activities if you don't have *karma*?'

He said, 'I am not doing anything!' The disciple asked, 'No, you are speaking to me. How can you speak to me if you don't have *karma*?' Nisargadatta Maharaj said straightaway, 'I am not speaking to you!' He was speaking and yet he said, 'I am not speaking to you.' It is very difficult to understand!

He continues, 'Because you wanted me to speak, the speaking is happening through this body. There is nobody inside.' He was just like a hollow bamboo. When a breeze enters a hollow bamboo, it comes out as music. There is nobody inside. That is why whatever goes in comes out as music. When you become a hollow bamboo, whatever words come out of your mouth become *mantra*, sacred syllables. Your form becomes *yantra*, the tool of liberation, and your whole life becomes *tantra*, a technique for liberation.

Your words are *śāstras,* scriptures. Your form is the center for *stotras,* devotional prayers. And your very life is the *sūtra*, the technique.

Here, when Kṛṣṇa says, 'I,' there is just the Divine that is speaking. There is nobody inside. It is pure emptiness. Just the Divine, the pure Existence speaks through Him. He has become a hollow bamboo. That is why He can courageously declare in a battlefield, *bhūtānām īsvaro'pi*—I am the Lord of all beings. Sitting comfortably at home where you have all the security and protection and declaring 'I am God' is very easy, because there is nothing to risk. You don't need to prove anything. But Kṛṣṇa is making this statement in a place where He needs to prove it. He is making this statement in a battlefield, where His life itself is at risk. One arrow is enough to finish His body. Yet He boldly declares, 'I am God.' What courage and energy behind His words! It can come only from a solid experience, a deep conscious experience.

UNDERSTAND DEATH FIRST

One of the great disciples of Vivekananda, Sister Nivedita asks him, '*Swamiji,* if I come with you what will you teach me? What will you give me?' Vivekananda says, 'I will teach you how to face death.' That is the ultimate teaching. Here, Kṛṣṇa is giving that ultimate teaching. In these verses, He is saying something very strange:

janma karma ca me divyam evaṁ yo vetti tattvataḥ I
tvaktvā dehaṁ punar janma naiti mām eti so 'rjuna II 4.9

It means: if you understand the secret of My birth and death, you will be liberated from birth and death, Arjuna. How? Let us see the secret of the birth and death of Kṛṣṇa, how we all go through the birth and death cycle. Now, just as Kṛṣṇa made the statement, 'I tell you this because you are my devotee and friend', now I have to make the same statement to you all again. Here I am going to speak on something, which is beyond logic. It is pure experience. Before speaking, I take an oath: *With integrity and authenticity, whatever I speak is the truth.*

Whenever the ultimate truth is uttered, whenever something beyond our logic is uttered, we never receive it completely. If we are courageous, we fight, we question, we argue. If we don't have that much courage, we don't allow that word to enter into us. Listen! We never believe anybody. It is always an argument, sometimes open, and at other times, in the mind. If we can't express it openly, we continuously repeat the same words in the mind.

That is why, before entering the truths, I tell you what I speak is the truth. If you can, receive it. There is a possibility of transformation, because here I speak the truth that is realized only by experience, which cannot be logically true.

Different religions describe the process of death in different ways. Some say if you have done *puṇya* or merits, you will reach a place called heaven and if you have committed sins, you will be taken to eternal hell. Each one has his or her own faith. Some say there will be a special *pushpak vimānam* (aircraft) sent from Śiva's abode and you will be directly taken to Śiva's place. The Kaṭhopaniṣad says you will pass through a tunnel and see '*Anguṣṭha mātra puruṣa antarātma*—meaning the thumb sized light, which is your soul when it leaves the body.

There are so many explanations, so many versions as to how death happens and how your spirit enters into the next body. Here, Kṛṣṇa beautifully explains that people belong to different religions only when they are alive. When they are dead, they follow only one path, which is described in the Kaṭhopaniṣad.

See, when you leave the body, the moment the physical body dies and relaxes, that very moment the soul leaves the body. At that time, what you perceived as the highest pleasure in your life surfaces. If you thought eating was the highest pleasure in your life, naturally while leaving the body, you will think, 'I should take a body which will continuously help me to eat. You go through all the choices and you decide to take a pig's body. Whatever you think is the greatest experience in your life, whichever experience occupies your maximum inner space, you decide your next birth based on that desire. Please listen, nobody else decides your birth. It is simply *you* who chooses. It is clearly the conscious decision of your soul.

Here Kṛṣṇa says beautifully, 'I am telling you the secret of things.' Kṛṣṇa says, '*rahasyaṁ hy etad uttamam.*' 'I am telling you the mysterious ultimate science, Oh, my dear devotee and friend, *bhakto'si me sakhā ceti*.'

I made a few statements: 'You take birth based on your desires, based on how you lived in the previous birth. Birth and death are your conscious decisions.' We will now analyze these statements. Only then will we be able to intranalyze and powerfully live them.

Listen. We will analyze to internalize this whole concept, the secret of birth and death, the mysterious science that Kṛṣṇa delivers.

The moment this truth is understood, you will immediately see that Life is a blessing. This life is your decision, please be very clear about it. Including poverty, everything is your decision. Don't think poverty has been forced upon you. Even that is your decision. When we take birth, we take birth based on our fear and greed. On one side, greed pushes us, 'Let me become the son of a king, let me become the son of a rich man.' On the other side, our own fears say, 'No no, I can't take on so much responsibility.'

Along with money comes the responsibility of protecting it. That is why goddess Lakṣmī, the goddess of wealth, is handed over to Lord Viṣṇu, the Protector! Lakṣmī, the goddess of wealth, is neither with the Creator, Brahma nor with the Destroyer, Śiva. She is with the Protector, with Viṣṇu. Along with Lakṣmī who represents wealth, the responsibility to protect Her also comes. Most of the time, we only want the enjoyment, we don't want the responsibility. A person who is ready to take on the responsibility as well as the enjoyment will never be deprived.

If you understand this secret clearly, this very moment you will feel your life is a blessing and not a curse. Usually we always blame life. We do not realize we are responsible for everything happening in and around us. We say, 'If I am given a chance, I would make the world much better than what it is now!' We always think we can develop on existing creation.

Surely God is much more intelligent than us! Whether it is to do with your life or to do with the whole of Existence, He has done the peak of enriching from His vast responsibility. The one who achieves the peak of responsibility becomes a powerful enlightened being. The one who achieves the peak of enriching is God, an Incarnation. Because we don't understand the mystery behind our decisions, we continuously blame life and the person who gave this life to us.

INCARNATION HAPPENS OUT OF LOVE AND COMPASSION

The greatness of God is that He gives you the freedom to be in bondage. Even if it is the ultimate freedom He offers you, He never forces it on you. He gives you the freedom to be in bondage if that is your choice. Your whole birth is based on your fear and greed. But the Incarnation, the enlightened Master's birth is based on love and compassion. The whole secret is this. Ordinary man takes birth based on fear and greed. That is why his whole life is driven by fear and greed. Enlightened Masters assume the body out of love and compassion.

That is why Kṛṣṇa beautifully says, '*ātma māyayā*, because of My own energy, I take birth. With my own energy, just out of My love and compassion, I land on this planet Earth.' The next question that follows is this: How can we be liberated by knowing this truth? How will it help us?

Understand, when I say the words birth or death, I don't mean just dying at the end of life. I mean, every night's sleep is your birth and death. Every night when you go to sleep, you die! When you come back in the morning, you take birth one more time. Every day, you assume the body. Every day, you leave the body. When you go to the causal body in deep sleep, you actually die and come back. When you come back, every day you are new. As of now, every morning, how do we come back to life? How do we take this body? Just look deeply. What happens when you wake up?

Usually, the moment you become aware that you are awake, either a thought based on greed or fear hits you. Maybe you want to meet somebody or meet some deadline. Immediately you jump out of bed. If you have analyzed your waking up, how you assume this body every morning, that moment is actually your taking birth. That moment when you take the body matters. These are the basic, very subtle, mysterious secrets of altering the whole consciousness. Whichever thought you enter your body with every morning, will play a major role in your consciousness for that entire day.

But an Incarnation, an Enlightened Master assumes the body out of love and compassion. He comes back just to pour His compassion out, just to share Himself with the whole world. When I say He comes back, I mean His coming back every day, every morning. If you understand this once and alter your thoughts at the time of waking up, you will alter your whole consciousness; the very quality of your consciousness can be changed. It is just like how a camera works. The first moment the lens is opened, whatever scene is there in front of the camera eye, is recorded on the film. That will remain forever. In the same way, during the first moment of consciousness, the thought that you have while entering into the body, plays a major role on your consciousness for the whole day.

When you get up, let the first thought be of love and compassion.

Get up only to express your life in bliss. The moment you become aware of yourself, express, 'Oh Lord, it is so beautiful! You have given me one more day! I am blessed that You have given me one more day's extension to see Your Existence!' Please understand, you have no right to any extension. Don't think Life is your birthright. I have seen many people taking things for granted. Before they get the job, they say, 'If I get that $10,000 per month salary, I will be really safe. I will feel blessed.' The moment they get the job, in one month, they think it is their birthright.

Birth itself is not your right. Then how can you say something else is your birthright? The word birthright is completely wrong. You have no right even to your own birth. It is a pure gift. You can't inhale or exhale for even one single moment unless the Divine allows you, unless the Universal Energy gives the extension. So every day is a blessing. When you get up from bed, assume the body with this gratitude to the Divine. The quality of your whole consciousness will change and you will become an Incarnation.

You too can Happen as Divine

Here I am giving you the straight technique to become Kṛṣṇa, how to enter Kṛṣṇa consciousness, how to become an Incarnation. The man who assumes the body out of love and compassion is an Incarnation. If you assume the body out of greed or fear, you are a man. If you assume the body out of love and compassion, you are an Incarnation and you are divine. Your whole life will become pure eternal bliss. Your whole life will be a happening with a different consciousness.

Here Kṛṣṇa gives us a technique to attain Him, to experience *janma karma ca me divyam*. If we are able to live in such a way as to be free from the attachments born out of anger and fear, then we can be absorbed in Him, we can attain Him. All actions create their own reactions. When we sow a seed, the action, though it may appear to be complete, is in reality not so. We have set into motion a cycle, a chain of events. The seed sprouts and becomes a plant or tree. Thus it is in the order of Existence that every action or cause has its own reaction or effect. It is therefore quite difficult to escape from the clutches of the cause-effect cycle.

Here Kṛṣṇa gives a technique to cut these kārmic bonds, to be complete and realize the reality. Actions that are complete and free from fear and anger do not create bonds, *vītā-rāga bhaya krodhā*. They lead us towards elevated consciousness. Fear and anger that arise out of greed pattern are two of the most provocative emotions, the root patterns that create incomplete action, and lead to bondage.

Attachments are our bondage to the future based on experiences of the past. We have unfulfilled desires that we hope to fulfill. We look for results. When the results happen the way we wish them to, there is temporary satisfaction. More wishes arise. More attachments are formed. When things do not happen the way we want them to, we feel sorrow, we are depressed. We strive again. Either way it is a never-ending cycle that brings sorrow in the end. When we let go of attachments and perform complete actions with no expectations, we enjoy the path of action. There is no stress regarding what must happen, since there is no attachment.

Please listen. Completion is stopping the effect immediately and rewinding the effect towards the cause, and merging the effect into the cause! Stopping the effect immediately and rewinding it back to the cause, and the effect merging into the cause is Completion.

Kṛṣṇa offers a way to be in His space of completion. He says, 'Be drowned in Me, *man-mayā mām upāśritaḥ*; you will have no anger, no fear. All actions will thus be without bondage. In this manner, you can be purified and realize Me, *pūtā mad-bhavām āgatāḥ* (4.10).' He gives the assurance that having followed this path, many people in the past have achieved Realization.

He is not saying, 'if you do this, maybe something good will happen.' He straightaway gives us positive assurance. 'Do it, you will achieve! Many people have done so and have realized Me, *bahavo jñāna tapasā* (4.10).' Completion directly liberates you from the *karmas;* completion directly leads you to experience the truth; completion directly makes you experience the reality of life!

Masters are like mirrors reflecting us. If the devotee is praying for wealth, he gets it. If he wants healing for body or mind, he is granted it. To a devotee who says, 'Oh God, I want nothing except knowledge of Your true reality,' the God grants him that. He shows him the way to the ultimate reality. If you visit our ashram, you will see that there is something for everyone. We have healing prayers, fire rituals, yoga and meditation-Nithya Dhyana Yoga, Nithya Kriyas, enriching temple etc. for people from all walks of life. For the ones who connect with worship, we have temples. For the ones who wish to attain their reality through yoga, there are various Nithya Yoga programs. For those on the path of experiential knowledge, there are meditation programs. For those who want to rewrite their future as they want and live enlightenment, we have the Inner Awakening program. Only in this manner can we raise the consciousness of society.

We cannot hope to transform society through any mass movement. It can happen only through individual transformation. When such people act together, it will have the same power as a laser beam. Each devotee and each disciple is unique. The way I treat each one is unique. What I tell one person is not applicable to another. I warn my disciples, time and again, please do not advise someone else based on the advice I have given you. It will only cause more confusion.

Here, Kṛṣṇa promises and reaffirms what He has said earlier, that—*He will take care of the need of every one of His devotee.* Only the most compassionate being who cares for all, will make this statement. Now it is left to the devotee to have some intelligence as to what to approach the Master for.

Kṛṣṇa explains here why non-attachment is so difficult. It is in our nature to look for success in whatever we do. It is impossible to embark on an activity expecting it to fail. There is nothing wrong in looking for success at the end of an activity. What creates problems is the illogical attachment to that expectation of success.

What Kṛṣṇa says here shows that our mindset, human nature, has not changed in over five thousand years. Even then they were looking for material success. They were looking for instant results. When they prayed to God they were praying to fulfill their expectations of material success.

Kṛṣṇa is the greatest psychologist who ever lived and lives. He has measured human nature accurately. What we want is tangible and instant results. In Kṛṣṇa's days, when *saṁskāras*, root patterns were relatively fewer, people had a different concept of time. There was much less rush and much less aggression. Yet the Master uses a term '*kṣipra*', instant. The master is talking about humanity; past, present and future. He says you normally pray to God not as an expression of gratitude, but to seek unfulfilled material desires and all that you think will bring you happiness.

All your actions, Kṛṣṇa says, are based on material success, and He says such activities bear instant results in this world, *kṣipraṁ hi mānuṣe loke* (4.12).Whether you understand it or not, all these prayers and actions do produce instant results. This does not mean whatever you pray for is instantly granted by the God you prayed to. God, fortunately, has far more wisdom than we have. God uses His *buddhi*, wisdom, to grant what He deems appropriate. However, the result of your actions is instant. The *karmaphala* is immediate. When religions talk of *karma* (action) and *karmaphala* (the fruits or outcome of action,) they speak in terms of merits and sins, *pāpa* and *puṇya*. They tell you that you will go to hell if you accumulate sins, and you will go to heaven if you gain merits. They try to control you through fear and greed of heaven. There is no hell or heaven.

When you think good thoughts, do good deeds, you feel good, you are in heaven. When you think evil, you act evil, you feel evil and you are in hell. That is all there is to *karma*. This is the cosmic cause-effect principle. You are what your intent is; you become what your intent is. *Karma* acts instantly, here and now. Do not blame others for your actions. *Karma* is in your hands. You are a free spirit; you have the power of thought, the power of words, the power of action, and the power of living. It is not merely guaranteed by your national constitution, but by God's own constitution. What you sow, you shall certainly reap.

Understand And Be Unaffected By Action

4.13 *Depending upon the distribution of the three attributes or guṇas and actions, I have created the four castes.*
Yet, I am to be known as the non-doer, the unchangeable.

4.14 *I am not affected by any work; nor do I long for the outcome of such work. One who understands this truth about Me* also does not get caught in the bondage of work.

4.15 *All the wise and liberated souls of ancient times have acted with this understanding and thus attained liberation.*
Just as the ancients did, perform your duty with this understanding.

4.16 *What is action and what is inaction, even the wise are confused.*
Let Me explain to you what action is, knowing which you shall be liberated from all ills.

Now we come to the controversial topic of the caste system. Kṛṣṇa says, 'I have created the four castes depending upon the distribution of the three *guṇas* or attributes.' *Guṇa* means 'attribute' or 'quality' that we are born with. It is a reflection of the *prārabdha karma*, the *vāsana,* and the mindset with which we are born. There are three basic *guṇas: satva* or purity, *rajas* or activity and *tamas* or inactivity. People quote this verse whenever they want the support of religion for making the caste system more solid.

They say, 'Kṛṣṇa Himself has sanctioned it' or, 'This system has been given by the Incarnation Himself.' Listen, Kṛṣṇa uses the words, 'depending upon the distribution of the three *guṇas.*' He does not say, 'depending upon birth.'

No two persons on this planet can be the same. Every person is unique and possesses a unique ratio of the three *guṇas*. There are basically four kinds of people; based on the more dominant guṇa in them. He says, 'Based on the *guṇa* one is born with, I decide his *varṇa*, his caste.' The varṇa system was four-fold. Brāhmaṇas were the scholars and priests, intellectually inclined. Kṣatriyas were the soldiers and kings, ambitious and physically strong. Vaiṣyas were the business community with strong commercial acumen. Śudras were the workers, physically able and skillful. Based on their *guṇas*, their skill sets and not birth, the children in ancient *Gurukul* were trained into their vocations, their *varṇa* or caste.

Over time, this system was manipulated. Those who believed that they had a better varṇa, caste, decided to make it a hereditary right. Earlier, the son of a brāhmaṇa could not to be a priest, if he was unsuitable or the son of a *kṣatriya* to be a warrior if he was inadequate. Kṛṣṇa states very clearly that only the one who transcends these three *guṇas* can reach His state, can reach the higher levels of consciousness. To reach Kṛṣṇa one has to be a *triguṇa rahita*, beyond the three *guṇas*. Then, one becomes a non-doer, a no-caste, no-attribute person.

When a desire is fulfilled, it no longer creates ripples in the mind. Desires that get fulfilled are the basic needs one is born with, which are the result of the carry-over *vāsanā*, the *prārabdha karma*. We acquire all other desires by comparing ourselves with others. These are wants, not needs. Existence has no way of fulfilling such wants. When one works out of basic need, he acquires no karma. These possessions born out of our wants can never be fulfilled or enjoyed. Once acquired, we seek the next acquisition. The cycle goes on. Have you ever seen a rich man enjoying his meal in the same manner as a hard working laborer eating his simple home cooked meal? The rich man is more worried about his illnesses than the quality of the food.

Only a person who has taken a conscious birth is aware of his *prārabdha karma*. Only he can extinguish his *karma* by fulfilling this list of needs. These needs carry an energy of their own that gets them fulfilled. Once fulfilled, they leave no *karma* trace.

Kṛṣṇa, the ultimate Master, is always conscious and complete. He has no *karma*, no unfulfilled desires, no incompletion, and no attachment. So it is with every enlightened Master. His so-called desires get fulfilled as they arise. When I desire food, it appears. When I feel the need to sleep, I rest. There is no gap between my desire and its fulfillment. There is no trace of that desire after it is fulfilled. The fulfillment is complete. The attachment is zero. Therefore, there is no *karma*. This is the lesson every Master teaches his disciples. Work from your *needs*, not from your wants. Act without attachment. You shall attract no *karma* and you will be liberated.

Action In Inaction And Inaction In Action

4.17 *The complexities of action are very difficult to understand. Understand fully the nature of proper action by understanding the nature of wrong action and inaction.*

4.18 *He who sees inaction in action and action in inaction is wise and a yogi, even if engaged in all activities.*

4.19 *He who is determined and devoid of all desires for sense gratification, he is of perfect knowledge. The sages declare such a person wise whose actions are burnt by the fire of knowledge.*

4.20 *Having given up all attachment to the results of his action, always satisfied and independent, the wise man does not act, though he is engaged in all kinds of action.*

Here, Kṛṣṇa says that the person who sees inaction in action and action in inaction has attained completion.

karmaṇy akarma yaḥ paśyed akarmaṇi ca karma yaḥ |
sa buddhimān manuṇyeṣu sa yuktaḥ kṛtsna karma kṛt || 4.18

When you see that it is not the 'I' in you that is doing the activities, but it is the senses following their nature; when you see that it is the mind that is creating the false sense of identification of you with the action, then you have realized; you have attained completion because you are now no longer in the clutches of the mind.

It is the mind that makes you attached to something and repulsed by something else. When you are not in the clutches of the mind, you are free. You do actions because the senses by nature have to perform their functions. For example, the eyes see, the ears hear, and the nose smells. Yet, you are free from the bondage of action because you do not have any identification or any emotional attachment to anything. So naturally, you are liberated and you can do actions most beautifully without expecting any particular result. This is what it means to be '*Unclutched*.'

BY YOUR VERY NATURE, YOU ARE UNCLUTCHED

Being 'Unclutched' is the state where you are free and liberated. Let me expand on the word 'Unclutching.' If you observe your mind keenly, you will see that you are constantly connecting all your thoughts and creating links in your mind.

For example, the headache that happened ten years ago, five years ago and yesterday are all independent experiences. For easy reference, you categorize all these into 'headache,' just like you file documents in your office. By and by, you start believing all these experiences are connected. When you start believing they are connected you create a shaft.

You connect all painful memories, create a pain shaft and conclude, 'My life is suffering, my life is pain.' Now when you start believing your whole life is suffering, you have created a pain shaft and you are waiting only for painful incidents in your life so that you can elongate that shaft. First understand, whatever you believe is what you create within you and outside you. You will see that manifesting in your life over and over again. That is why vedic ṛṣis, sages, say that you create what you want. By seeing, you create. You will wait unconsciously for painful incidents to strengthen that belief, that life judgment.

Second thing, whenever you add the painful incidents unconsciously, you will be elongating that shaft, even though you may want to consciously end the pain by breaking it. If you believe your whole life is a shaft of joyful experiences, which we do very rarely, constantly you are in fear about whether the joy will continue. If you believe life is a shaft of painful incidents, you do two things: Unconsciously you gather more and more incidents and strengthen your faith about how your life is painful, and consciously you try to break the pain shaft! If you believe life is a chain of joyful incidents, unconsciously you will be in fear that it will end, and consciously you will try to prolong it. Understand these are two big dramas we are continuously enacting with ourselves.

You forget that you can neither break the shaft nor elongate it because the shaft itself does not exist! The shaft itself is your own imagination. Just try this experiment:

Sit down for ten minutes with a pen and paper. Now, just start jotting down whatever thoughts come to your mind. Please do not edit your thoughts; write them down as they are. Do not judge yourself and do not try to control what comes to your mind. If you try to judge, you are playing a hypocritical game with yourself. Now, read whatever you have written. You can see for yourself how unconnected and illogical your thoughts are! One moment you would think, 'I think I should go to my office tomorrow,' then the next minute, 'No I should just wake up and decide then,' then, 'What should I do about dinner tonight?'

Have you seen how the bubbles rise up in a fish tank? There is a gap between one bubble and the next. But the gap is so small that it looks like a continuous stream. Similarly, there is a gap between one thought and the next thought in your mind. Your thoughts are independent like the bubbles. By their very nature, your thoughts are independent.

For example, if you see a dog in the street, suddenly you remember the pet you used to play with as a child. Then you will remember the teacher, then the place where your teacher used to stay, and so on! The dog and the teacher are not connected in any way, but your mind simply flows. Look a little deeply, you will understand that your thoughts are illogical, independent and unconnected.

When you believe that your mind is logical, you have created the first 'original sin' for yourself. Understand, by your very nature you are unclutched. Every moment you are renouncing the thoughts by your very nature. A new thought can appear only when the old thought has been renounced. But even after renouncing them you try to pick up the thoughts from the dustbin and try to create a shaft with them.

Listen, first understand consciously that you are creating a shaft of pain or a shaft of joy and trying to fight with it, by either trying to elongate it or break it. Second, you don't even have to unclutch yourself from the shaft because the shaft is imaginary. By your very nature, if you stop creating a shaft, *you are Unclutched.*

Then we will start asking, '*If I unclutch, how will I do my job? How will I take care of my things? Will I not just lie in bed and waste my life?*' I ask you, why should you not go to work? The moment you say you will not go to work, it means you have a little hatred towards your job. The moment you get an excuse you want to escape from your job! By saying all these things, you are expressing your anger, your violence against your routine.

That is what Kṛṣṇa means by action, *karmaṇi* and inaction, *akarmaṇi*. You cannot be inactive by nature. You will daydream, clinging on to fantasies. You will try to escape from reality by deluding yourself, because your mind is clutching onto a soft and easy dream shaft.

When you truly Unclutch, without any attachment to the past and future, you will realize that you are full of energy. You will have to do something. That 'something' will be dictated by your present moment completion, not by fantasies. What you think of as 'you' is not necessary to run your day-to-day life. This is the basic truth. If you just observe yourself, if somebody is happily independent of us, we can't tolerate it, it is too much. Constantly we need to feel we are needed. That is why we expect people to project their sufferings on us and we too project our sufferings on them, so that we feel important.

What you think of as 'you' is not necessary to run your day-to-day life. People ask me, 'Constantly I repeat positive affirmations, 'I should stop smoking, I should stop smoking,' but it is not working. Why, *Swamiji*?' All these creative visualizations create more and more trouble. Because in the very words, 'I should stop smoking', the word 'smoking' is contradicting the words 'I should stop.'

You end up empowering the word 'smoking' as much as you are empowering the words 'I should stop'! Instead you should create the space of health and say, 'Let me have only healthy habits' or something totally positive without even the word 'smoking' in it. Similarly, if you have a headache, instead of empowering the thought of the headache, just decide to have a glass of water. The moment you decide to have a glass of water, it becomes a fresh thought and the old thought of the headache has to disappear. Once you keep replacing the thoughts, you break free from the headache-based thought patterns and eventually expel the headache from your system itself.

You may ask me, 'How can it be so simple, *Swamiji*?' It is simple. You are constantly taught that it is not so simple. But soon after doing this, if the thought of the headache comes back, then what do you do? Understand: You are so faithful to the thought of the headache that you forcefully drag it back into your system; you bring back a trashed file. Think of it this way: If it comes back, it can go back again. Why don't you celebrate those moments it left you? Why do you constantly remember the moments it came back?

People ask me again and again, 'I fail when I try to unclutch, *Swamiji*.' I ask them, 'Why are you connecting your past failure with your present failure?' When you connect all the past failures, you create one more shaft—'failure'. Just relax and stop connecting and suddenly you will see a deep inner healing, a deep peace happening in you. Suddenly you will see that you have dropped out of the war, the constant running. Just relax. When you drop out of this whole game, suddenly you will realize the whole thing is just a psychodrama.

Unclutch From Your Thoughts

Try this simple meditation:

Just close your eyes and sit. Whatever words are rising in you, just let them rise. Just do not connect them with any other thought, that's all. Just don't create a shaft; *simply Unclutch*. If you feel bored, or if your mind asks you what to do, just unclutch from that thought as well. Do not even connect with that thought. Just sit, be Unclutched. If your mind connects with a thought, just unclutch. Do not create, maintain or destroy any thought. Try this for a few minutes and you will see the effect for yourself.

Kṛṣṇa says to understand what action is, you need to understand what inaction is. In my programs, I tell people, 'To understand what meditation is, you need to understand what meditation is *not*.' I spend a day and a half explaining what meditation is *not* and less than half a day explaining what meditation *is*.

When you unclutch, you are seemingly in inaction or *akarma*. However, the removal of the various shafts of pain, pleasure, fantasies etc., releases so much energy within you that you are now actively passive. You are at the height of potential energy, ready to release that energy for whatever purpose you decide in that moment. If instead, you are actively daydreaming, caught in pain and pleasures shafts, then you are seemingly active and busy, but totally useless. In fact, you are counterproductively busy, pushing yourself deeper into more suffering.

In the process of Unclutching, you transcend both action and inaction, *karmaṇi* and *akarmaṇi*. You successfully destroy the false cognition of the connection between the thoughts and rest in the present moment, the space of completion, the state of no-mind, the state of dropping thoughts. In this unclutched space, you are active and yet not attached to any activity. You are truly in Kṛṣṇa consciousness.

All suffering and pain arises when we associate ourselves with the senses and the mind. The real Self in you is eternal, timeless, never changing. It is like this: When you see the clouds drifting in the clear sky, is the sky actually changing? The sky is like the canvas over which clouds of different forms and shapes drift across, sometimes completely covering the sky behind them, and sometimes drifting apart to reveal the sky behind. Just like this, due to māyā, delusion, it appears as if the Self is being affected by the emotions and the perceptions of the senses.

If you see yourself in a clear lake or a mirror, what you see is a reflection of what is being projected, right? Just like that, in the lake of the Self, of the being, whatever quality is projected is what you will see reflected in the lake. Does it mean that the lake has become dirty? The reflection has no reality, no solid existence.

Actually, the Self is permanent. The Self in you, in me, in the person next to you is all the same. When everything is *you*, what is there to fear? Where is the question of conflict, jealousy, fear or greed? Everything is you. Enjoy this world in its many forms and manifestations. However, enjoy without getting caught in attachment. Our senses are treacherous. They create incompletions, addictions that overwhelm us. The more we have, the less we enjoy, and yet we cannot do without them. True wisdom is to step back from what the senses tell you.

Have you seen a person sell something, say a painting? You can see the seller busy trying to convince people to get the best bargain. But see someone standing, witnessing this whole scene, someone who is neither interested in buying the painting nor in selling it. Only he can completely enjoy the painting!

See, if you have the right ideals, you will reach the truth much faster. We are taught that we are powerless, that we are sinners. But time and again, the vedic sages have declared, 'We are the children of immortality—*amṛtasya putraḥ*.' Let us bring integrity to our thinking with life affirmative thoughts rather than continuously repeating negative and self-doubting thoughts to ourselves. The positive thoughts are not mere statements. These are great truths that our sages have experienced, and encourage us to experiment and experience as well. With them come the energy of possibility and power of the experience to make it our reality.

When we are blissful and complete within ourselves, we would never see anything disturbing outside. That is what Kṛṣṇa says here: Be involved completely in the action yet be detached, independent and satisfied within. Then you can function spontaneously, flowing in tune with Existence. Life then becomes a celebration. Every single thing you do is an act of joy and an expression of the loving energy in you. Your joy is no longer dependent on what society says or thinks about you, because you are complete in yourself.

Equanimity In Success And Failure

4.21 *The person who acts without desire for the result;*
with his consciousness controlling the mind,
giving up all sense of ownership over his possessions and
body and only working, incurs no sin.

4.22 *He who is satisfied with profit which comes of its own accord and*
who has gone beyond duality, who is free from envy,
Who is in equanimity both in success and failure, such a person
though doing action, is never affected.

4.23 *The work of a liberated man who is unattached*
to the modes of material nature and who is fully centered in the
ultimate knowledge, who works totally for the sake of sacrifice,
merges entirely into the knowledge.

4.24 *The offering, the butter offered to the Supreme in the fire of the*
Supreme is offered by the Supreme.
Certainly, the Supreme can be reached by him who is absorbed
completely in action.

4.25 *Some yogis worship the gods by offering various sacrifices to them,*
While others worship by offering sacrifices in the
fire of the Supreme.

A sense of ownership over possessions or your body is the same thing. What are your possessions? You came with nothing at all. Can you claim that you were born with anything that is your own property? In the same way, you are going to leave this world empty-handed. Can you say that all your possessions will go with you when you leave this body? No!

This very prāṇa, the life breath going inside your body is not your property. It is the property of Existence. Your very life is a sheer gift to you from Existence. When you realize this, you will immediately see that all your fears and worries and greed are so baseless. You are running behind something, thinking it is yours, but of what relevance is it really? When your very life is a gift to you, how can you claim that anything else is your possession?

Please listen! Real knowledge comes with experience, not through words. The moment you internalize any single dimension of truth and internalize it authentically, truthfully, it can do wonders for you. Vivekananda says beautifully, 'Even if you memorize all the books in all the libraries of this world, it will not help you in any way other than increasing your ego. Instead of having a whole library in your head, just realize five concepts in your heart.'

I tell you, enrich yourself with only one idea and try to internalize it in your being, experience it in your life. Your life will be transformed by just a single idea. In Tamil Nadu, South India, they describe beautifully the lives of 63 enlightened Masters in *Periapurāṇam*, a Tamil literary work. If you study the lives of these masters, you will find some masters did not really do anything. They just plucked flowers and offered them to God. Yet they achieved enlightenment! Understand, it is not what you do that is important, it is the space from which you do that matters. How integrated and authentic you are with the act is what really matters. When they performed the act of offering flowers, they were in the space of completion; integrated and authentic to the action.

You may ask, 'We also offer flowers everyday. The only thing we get is the extra expense of maintaining the garden!' The problem is that we don't take responsibility for our space and we are not in integrity and authenticity with thoughts, words, and actions. When these Masters plucked flowers to offer to God, they were thinking of Him. They were complete, totally devoted to the thought of the Lord. I have seen these people who do rituals regularly. Whenever they are doing any rituals, they will be thinking of something else, either their office or their home.

There are some who regularly chant the 1000 names of the gods as in the *Viṣṇu Sahasranāma*. Even while chanting, they start looking at the verse count they have reached.

FOUR GREAT POWERS OF YOUR SPACE

Create the space of completion. Complete with your patterns! Bring integrity into every step! Nothing else is going to help you. There is no shortcut; this is the shortest cut! Complete and create the space of integrity and authenticity; they have no replacement. Whether you live a spiritual life or a regular life, integrity and authenticity form the basis for life!

The space you carry, the attitude, the intention, and the thoughts behind the action actually decide the energy behind the action. The power of space and thought is immense. In fact, some of the latest research shows how our DNA can be influenced and reprogrammed by words and frequencies. When a group of people focus their thoughts on something similar, like chanting peaceful, healing Vedic mantras every morning, just listening to these words coming out of completion, you will suddenly see that those very words change your inner space. The collective declarations to bless the world—*lokāsamastā sukhinobhavantū*, let the whole world be prosperous, *can* change your entire inner space. That is the power of completion!

I tell you, all the so-called natural calamities are nothing but the effects of global negative thoughts born out of collective incompletions. Your space, your thoughts and energy directly affect your body, your cell structure, your decisions, your capacity to fulfill your decisions and outer world incidents, even accidents. You create a pattern that creates and attracts similar incidents to you.

If you can complete with your greed and fear patterns, which is what we have normally, and create the space of bliss or Ānanda, then your energy flow will start brimming and your thoughts will be authentic, your words will be integrated and you will be more in the space of completion. When you do this, you have every power to control outer world incidents because you and Existence have a very deep connection at the energy level. When you are blissful, when the space you carry is not one of worry, fear and greed but one that is in the present, always complete and joyful, you will automatically attract all good things to yourself.

When you practice Integrity with integrity, Authenticity with authenticity, Responsibility with responsibility, and Enriching with enriching, you will simply have the four great powers—the power of words—*vāk siddhi*, the power of thinking—*mano siddhi*, the power of feeling—*prema siddhi*, and the power of living—*ātma siddhi*.

When you unlock the *power of words*, you will have the spontaneous intelligence to use the right and most effective words towards yourself and others. Next, what is Authenticity? The decision of authenticity has to come from your very soul. Your soul has to awaken. Till then, you may be practicing a little authenticity in your yoga, or in your waking hours. But that is not completely authentic. When your soul wakes up, only then do you become a completely authentic soul. When you start practicing authenticity, your soul wakes up. Your being wakes up. When you discover *the power of thinking*, you will be able to focus on your thoughts to achieve success in your job, relationships, education, finances and life itself!

See, when you are so integrated with your words, your words just move the world. When you are completely authentic, your soul can simply express anything because energy and matter both listen to your soul. Matter listens to energy.

Authenticity is nothing but remembering that all powers are at your disposal. You can just possess and express any power you want. With responsibility, *the power of feeling*, you will learn to express these powers. The power of feeling teaches how to launch yourself to the next level of life through empowered responsibility. And with enriching, you will truly be enjoying *the power of living* when you realize that the greatest rewards come when you live your life for others.

YOUR INNER SPACE IS CONNECTED TO THE UNIVERSE

All our minds are not individually separated pieces of the Universe. They are all one and the same. Not only interlinked, our minds directly affect each other. This is what I call the 'collective consciousness.' Though each one is independent in his consciousness, when one is conscious of one's true nature, one feels that one is part of the whole Universe. Each one's thoughts straightaway affect the others around. Not only are those staying around you touched by your thoughts, everyone who is living on the planet is touched by your thoughts.

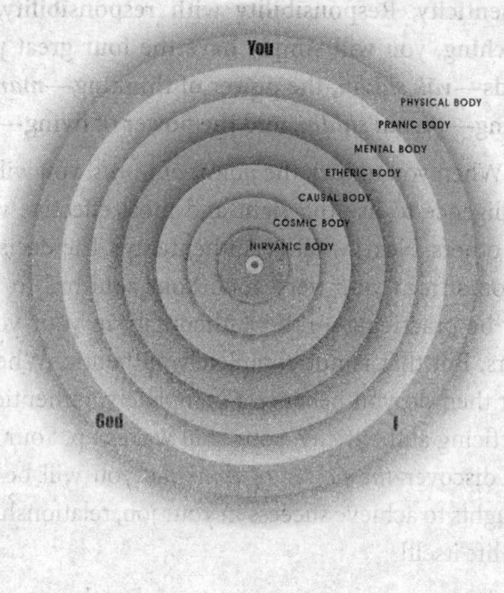

Understand, the inner space you carry is such a powerful space! It is *hiranyagarbha*, the space where the planets get created! Your inner space is so powerful; worlds can be created or destroyed by it. You may be an individual, but your inner space is not individual; it is well-connected with the whole Universe. So, anything you decide in your inner space becomes a reality in the Cosmos, reality in life.

The next truth: Not only at the mental level are you connected; even at the deeper conscious level you are connected to every other being. Your body is not just *one* body. Actually, there are seven layers or bodies. The first layer is the physical body.

The second is the pranic body. There are seven such energy layers or bodies. These energy layers can be represented as concentric circles, with the physical layer as the outermost circle and the seventh layer and the nirvanic body as the innermost layer.

At the physical layer, *you, God* and *I* can be represented as three different points in the outermost concentric circle. At the physical level, the distance between these three is more. At the pranic level, the distance is reduced. If you come down deeper, to the mental level, the distance between *you* and *I* is still reduced and so is the distance between *you, God* and *I.* When you go deeper and deeper, these three entities finally merge into one at the innermost nirvanic layer, the ultimate consciousness. At the deepest point of all these layers—*God, you* and *I* are one. There is no distance between the three.

Once you become aware and realize that you are a part of the collective consciousness, that you don't have an individual identity; you realize that you do not have a separate ego. You think you own your individual identity. In Existence, there is no such thing as a separate individual identity. Once you know this truth, you go beyond pain, suffering, depression and diseases. As long as you are individually conscious, you will be continuously suffering. Why do you think you are continuously resisting Nature? Whatever Nature offers, you resist.

You think you are different from Existence. I have seen *Sannyāsis* and monks living in the Himalayas, almost nude in the cold. I myself have lived in such conditions, but the body was never disturbed. I never had the feeling of separation from Nature. When you think you are different from the atmosphere, you start resisting it.

When you are in tune and become a part of the collective consciousness, Nature is your friend and it will protect you. As long as you think you are an individual consciousness different from Nature, it will protest. There's one very simple thing you can practice now. If you are feeling cold, just relax and witness the area where you are feeling cold. In that area, don't resist the atmosphere, don't resist Nature. Just say to yourself, 'I am not going to resist Nature. Let me relax and be complete.' Consciously decide this.

With this you will see the body relaxing and the idea of cold disappearing from that part. You become completely comfortable.

Wherever you want to achieve success, in a social or in an economic context, only when you feel complete with the whole group and fall in tune with the collective consciousness will you be able to achieve what you want. As long as you feel you are an individual, be very clear that you will be resisted and you will be resisting. Whether it is at home or at work, this will happen. If you disappear into the collective consciousness, you will be protected and taken care of. Not only will you attain social and economic success, but you will also experience a deep feeling of completion.

Even in the physical layer if you think you are separate, you will invite diseases. If you think you are separate in the mantal layer, you will be sowing seeds of violence. With collective consciousness you unify, but with individual consciousness you cut things into pieces. If you think you are an individual at the soul level, there is no possibility for any spiritual growth. Even at the physical level, you are not an individual. Your body and the body of the sun are directly connected. Any small change in the body of the sun can make changes in your body. Any small change in your body can change the body of the moon. Even if you are not able to relate to this logically, it is true. Even in the mental layer, you are not alone. Any thought put in anyone else's head comes and touches you and any thought created in your mind goes and touches someone else. It is like ripples created in a lake. If you are creating a strong wave, you will be creating an impression with your thought. You will be leading and inspiring others with your thought. If your thoughts are not solid enough, other waves will impress you. When you bring complete integrity into your thinking, the words you utter to yourself and to others will be experienced as your very life. That is the power of words!

Even though your child is out of your body after you deliver it, it is not like you are disconnected from your child. His good or bad experiences continue to affect you as long as you exist. In the same way, the words that come out of you continue to have power over you, whether they are fulfilled or unfulfilled, respected or not respected, listened to or not listened to. Understanding that the word you utter continues to have power over you even years after it is uttered makes you utter the words with responsibility.

Either you live like a leader or you will be a follower. There is no in between. You always think, 'I will not be a leader, I cannot do that much; I will not be a follower either; I shall maintain my own stand.' This is simply impractical. There is no such thing as 'my own stand.' Either you lead or you follow.

At the spiritual level, the moment you understand you are deeply connected to the whole Universe, not only do you start experiencing bliss, but you also start really living in the space of oneness and opening many dimensions of your being. See, just with this body you can think so much, you can enrich and enjoy yourself and others so much. If you disappear into the collective consciousness, you will experience so many dimensions, so many possibilities, you cannot imagine it!

During the Indian festival of Holi (festival of colors)—*Rās Pūrnima*, Radhā and the gopīs, experienced the collective consciousness of Kṛṣṇa. This is referred to as *rās līlā*, when Kṛṣṇa gave them the experience of collective consciousness. Some people have the wrong idea of this *rās līlā* and think it signifies Kṛṣṇa having relationships with women. Kṛṣṇa was just ten years old then! What actually happened is that He gave the experience of collective consciousness to the whole group of gopikās and Radhā. This collective consciousness is what I call God.

Throughout our *Inner Awakening* program, you will realize you are a part of the collective consciousness. Not only are you a part, you *are* the collective consciousness. When we go deeper layer by layer, you will realize that you are one with everything. So automatically the diseases disappear. You start feeling the well being in the mental layer, the pranic layer, and all the other layers. You think you are an individual consciousness but if you peel the individual layers, you will experience that you are nothing but the collective consciousness!

In *Inner Awakening*, that is what we do—the opening of your minds and inner space. You are taught the science of completion with yourself, with others, and with life. You are initiated into the completion process to complete with your pains, desires, guilt and pleasures. You intensely write down and relive your own incompletions to relieve them permanently. People ask me why I ask them to write and relive all this when they already know it. Listen, by writing them down, they are opening their inner space in my presence, so that I can heal their space and initiate them into creating the right space.

First of all you should understand that I do not heal; my presence heals. When the sun rises, the lotus blooms by itself. The sun need not go and open the petals of the lotus. Similarly, in the presence of the Master, healing happens. Healing is not done, it simply happens. I can heal your body while it is in my presence. In the same way, if you open your mind and inner space and expose your incompletions, it can be healed. If you open it, the sun can heal it; the energy heals all the wounds. Inner Awakening is about opening up your energy layers one by one. When they open up, you experience completion with them and you experience God. Not only do you search for God, but you experience God as well. Completion is God! A pure mind is God itself and not something separate from it.

The Essence of Life is 'Enriching'

We are all taught from childhood that there is a purpose to life. We are guided to work towards goals in life, which are almost always material goals. We are expected to live up to the expectations of our parents, later our teachers, much later our spouses and finally our children.

There is no purpose to life, except to live in completion and to enrich others and yourself with completion. The purpose of life is to enrich life with completion. Life is for Enriching. Enriching is Life! How can we enrich and enjoy life if we get saddled with a bagful of goals that bind us down to duties and obligations? We are so deluded by incompletion and stressed out by all that is expected of us that we have no time to enrich ourselves and enjoy what we are doing we have no energy to enrich others for their expansion.

Life is not about purpose or goals. Life is not lifestyle. Life is not about impressing people with how rich, clever, beautiful or skilled you are. Life is about enjoying the journey. It is not about the stressful incompletion of looking for the destination. When the path is right, when you enjoy the path, the destination is always right; it will always enrich you and others.

Please listen from the space of listening! I am giving you the essence of all my teachings and satsangs. **Listen! Satsang means infusing the Truth again and again into you, helping you wake up and realize the decisive component of life. This is the essence of life itself!**

Please listen: Life is all about increasing your capability to infuse the Truth in you and others. That is all is the essence of life on planet Earth. The essence of life in the Universe is neither money nor infrastructure development, nor just some social power or relationships. The essence of human life is expanding your ability to infuse the great spiritual truths in you; the ability to enrich yourself and enrich others! Only the person who realizes the purposelessness of life can have the strength to enrich himself and others, only he can go beyond duality and surpass envy, only he can be satisfied in any action with whatever profit comes from that action of its own accord, what Kṛṣṇa calls—*yadṛcchā lābha santuṣṭo dvandvātīto vimatsaraḥ* (4.22).

Understand: Life has no purpose but it has a meaning. Living in completion and enriching others with completion is the meaning of life. You need to know this truth: if you are enriching with a vested interest, you will give up on people. Don't have any vested interest. All the time, we are taught that life has a goal, a purpose, and we run behind various goals hoping to achieve satisfaction in life. But life has no goal; the very life, the very path itself is the goal. When you realize this, you relax into the space of completion, you expand in your ability to infuse the great spiritual truths, enriching yourself and others with them, and you are unaffected by success or failure, although doing actions, as Kṛṣṇa says beautifully, '*samaḥ siddhāv asiddhau ca kṛtvāpi na nibadhyate* (4.22).'

Kṛṣṇa says here, 'One who works for the sake of enriching sacrifice, merges into the knowledge—*yajñāyācarataḥ karma samagraṁ pravilīyate* (4.23).' Enrich just for the sake of enriching. All these parasite patterns of jealousy and envy come when you think life has a goal and somebody else has been given something more than you to reach the goal. When you understand that you are unique and Existence has equipped you with all that you need to fulfill all your desires, you will actually be able to live life in completion and work sincerely for the sake of enriching. Otherwise, you will only be running behind some goal or the other. You will envy others who you think are closer to that goal towards which you are running. You will be caught in this roller coaster of success and failure.

Understand that the goal of life is like a mirage. It does not exist in reality, but it continuously creates illusions of its existence. Live life every moment in bliss and you can see the tremendous difference it makes to the very quality of your life.

A small history:

> This has happened as per the history at my native place, Tiruvannamalai, a cosmic spiritual 'nerve center' in India.
>
> The history goes that once Lord Śiva appeared as *jyotistaṁbha*, an infinite column of light to settle a conflict between Brahma, the Creator, and Viṣṇu, the Sustainer as to who was greater. As per Lord Śiva's orders, Lord Brahma had to find Lord Śiva's head and Lord Viṣṇu, the Sustainer, was asked to find Śiva's feet. Whoever found their part first would be declared the greater one. The story has a beautiful meaning. Brahma is the consort of Sarasvatī, the goddess of knowledge. Viṣṇu is the consort of Lakṣmi, the goddess of wealth.
>
> The history says that Brahma started searching for the

head. Viṣṇu started searching for the feet. Viṣṇu came back after some time and accepted, 'I am not able to find Your feet; please forgive me. I only now realised that it is an impossible task!' Brahma also realized he would not be able to find Śiva's head. But instead of accepting the fact, he decided to cheat. He took a flower as a false witness to testify that he had touched and brought it from Śiva's head.

Understand the truth of this happening, *Purāna*—Viṣṇu is the embodiment of wealth. Brahma is the embodiment of intellect. Neither by wealth nor by intellect can you achieve enlightenment. If you travel in the line of wealth, you will get frustrated, you will understand your incompletions, you will face depression of success and you will become really humble. You will fall, you will understand and complete with yourself to rise. This is symbolized by Lord Viṣṇu surrendering first to Lord Śiva, the embodiment of completion. Mahādev is completion! But if you travel in the line of intellect, you will never accept your inauthenticity that you are defeated. This is symbolized by Brahma bringing a false witness in order to escape defeat.

If you travel in the line of external ego, *ahaṁkarā* or the path of material success in the outer world, at least at one point you will understand the futility of your pursuit and reclaim your space of completion. You will experience depression of success. But the person who travels in the line of internal ego, *mamakāra* or the line of intellect, not only does he never achieve, he will not even be able to understand that he cannot achieve. The intellect, the ego becomes so sharp, so subtle; it will bring false claims and false techniques to say that he has achieved it. Those false claims are only these false flowers, the false witnesses.

The ultimate knowledge can be reached only by surrendering to completion, to the four tattvas of integrity, authenticity, responsibility and enriching, not through intellect or wealth. The being which has surrendered to the four *tattvas* is *brahmaṇyam bahuputratām*—the favorite inheritor of the Cosmos. Then you are not caught in running behind the senses, behind the inner world or the outer world.

Know Sacrifice And Be Purified

4.26 *Some sacrifice the hearing process and other senses in the fire of equanimity. And others offer as sacrifice the objects of the senses, such as sound, in the fire of the sacrifice.*

4.27 *One who is interested in knowledge offers all the actions due to the senses, including the action of taking in the life breath into the fire of Yoga, and is engaged in the yoga of equanimity of the mind.*

4.28 *There is the sacrifice of material wealth, sacrifice through penance, sacrifice through yoga and other sacrifices, while there is sacrifice through self-study and through strict vows.*

4.29 *There are others who sacrifice the life energy in the form of incoming breath and outgoing breath, thus checking the movement of the incoming and outgoing breaths and controlling the breath.*

4.30 *There are others who sacrifice through controlled eating and offering the outgoing breath, life energy. All these people know the meaning of sacrifice and are purified of sin or karma.*

4.31 *Having tasted the nectar of the results of such sacrifices,*
they go to the supreme eternal consciousness.
This world is not for those who have not sacrificed.
How can the other be, Arjuna?

4.32 *Thus, there are many kinds of sacrifices born of work*
mentioned in the Vedas.
Knowing these, one will be liberated.

In all these verses, Kṛṣṇa talks about various types of sacrifices. 'Sacrifice', it is not just the *act* of giving, but the *attitude* of giving. Otherwise, you may do everything, following all rituals according to the scriptures, but you will miss out on the real intent for which the act had to be done.

A beautiful story from the Bhāgavatam, the ancient Hindu epic:

> Once, Kṛṣṇa was playing with his friends. After playing, his friends were tired and they asked Kṛṣṇa for food.
>
> Kṛṣṇa replied, 'Go to the nearby hall where the learned brāhmaṇas (priests) are performing a great ritual to attain heaven. Tell them that you have been sent by Me and request them to give you some cooked rice.'
>
> Kṛṣṇa's friends went as directed and asked the brāhmaṇas, 'Kṛṣṇa sent us here. We are hungry and Kṛṣṇa asked us to seek food from you.'
>
> The brāhmaṇas were all caught up in the rituals and sacrifices, not knowing the intent of the sacrifice. The very divine energy for which the sacrifice was being made was asking for an offering, but the brāhmaṇas could not realise that and did not give the boys any food. Kṛṣṇa's friends returned disappointed.
>
> Kṛṣṇa, on hearing about the foolish brāhmaṇas, just laughed and said, 'Now, go to the innocent wives of these brāhmaṇas and ask them the same thing.'
>
> The friends now went to the wives told them, 'O ladies, we have been sent here by Kṛṣṇa who was playing with us nearby. We are hungry and have come to you for food.' The ladies, on hearing that they had been given such a wonderful opportunity to enrich by serving, gathered all the food from their houses and rushed to feed Kṛṣṇa and his friends.

Listen. The very act of enriching, the welcoming attitude is what is important.

A beautiful verse in the Mahābharat that says, 'A guest comes with all the gods. If the guest is honored, so are the gods; if he goes away disappointed, the gods are disappointed too.' That is why in Saṃskṛit, we say, '*atithi devo bhava*', the guest is God. '*Tithi*' means date and prefix 'a' negates it. Therefore, one who arrives unexpectedly without a prior appointment is *atithi* or guest. When somebody comes unexpectedly also, serving him is the real welcoming attitude. The word used for ritual giving in Saṃskṛit is '*dāna*', which means sharing, imparting.

The true meaning of sacrifice lies in the meaning with which it is done. Look at the trees. They live for the welfare of others, themselves facing the winds, heat and snow, all the while protecting us from them. All their parts, leaves, flowers, fruits, roots, bark, etc. are useful to enrich others.

When you give away something you cannot afford to give, it is a true enriching sacrifice. When you give away something you can afford to give, then it is not a true enriching sacrifice. A wealthy man giving away alms is not sacrificing anything. He may be doing a good deed but not more than that.

Kṛṣṇa mentions many forms of sacrifice here. He talks of sacrifices of material wealth, yoga and penance—a combination of material, physical, mental and spiritual sacrifices. When a person does these at some cost and pain to himself, they would be genuine sacrifices. Otherwise they would merely be meaningless rituals. However, even that which is given away by someone who can afford what he is giving, if done with good intentions of enriching, would result in gains to that person. His very intention to enrich will alter his mindset and liberate him. A person who does not believe in sharing his wealth will not only suffer in future births as a result of his mental makeup, but he will also be unable to enjoy his own wealth in his present birth.

When one sacrifices whatever is dear and whatever is difficult to give away, he enters a completely different plane of sacrifice, one that liberates the person. Such a person enters a plane of true non-attachment, leading to liberation.

You Are No Sinner

4.33 *O Parantapa (conqueror of foes), the sacrifice of wisdom*
is superior to the sacrifice of material wealth.
After all, all activities totally end in wisdom.

4.34 *Understand these truths by approaching a spiritual Master,*
by asking him your questions, by offering service.
The enlightened person can initiate you into wisdom
because he has seen the truth.

4.35 *O Pāṇḍava, knowing this you will never suffer*
from desire or illusion,
You will know that all living beings are in the Supreme, in Me.

4.36 *Even if you are the most sinful of all sinners,*
You will certainly cross completely the ocean of miseries
with the boat of knowledge.

We spoke about the history of Brahma and Viṣṇu trying to reach Śiva's crown. Viṣṇu was able to accept that he failed and completed with Śiva, whereas Brahma could not. A person of knowledge becomes arrogant and refuses to acknowledge the limitations of knowledge. Sacrificing knowledge is far more difficult than sacrificing wealth. For a scholar to admit that he does not know is to commit suicide. He is losing his identity.

Kṛṣṇa advises the seeker to sacrifice one's knowledge and one's intellect at His feet, at the feet of the Master, to experience the ultimate Truth. Beautifully He says, '*tad viddhi praṇipātena paripraśnena sevayā* (4.34).' A Master is one who has experienced the truth and who can simply transfer his experience of truth to you. He communes with you. A teacher, on the other hand, is one who imparts knowledge through communication.

In Saṃskṛit, there are three beautiful words to describe this. You are born in the *bhū garbha*, the womb of the mother; this signifies your physical birth. The teacher with his love and teachings gives birth to you in the hrid garbha, the womb of the heart. The master gives birth to a completely new you, a transformed being in the *jñāna garbha*, the womb of knowledge. You then become re-born, *dvijā*!

Surrender Transforms

Understand, Masters have no vested interest for themselves; they have no karma to exhaust. They descend on this planet Earth out of sheer love and compassion for humanity. Just like a low-pressure region attracts winds, a depression created in the world attracts the formless energy of Existence. This energy is what is known in different forms like Kṛṣṇa, Rāma, Buddha etc.

Actually, the Master lives in three dimensions of energies: the body, His teachings and His mission. Masters come to dispel the ignorance of seekers, to show them the path. Only one third of the Master's energy is in the physical body. The other third is in the teachings and another third is in the mission.

Nithyananda is *nitya-dhyāna-ānanda*, all in one. *Nithya*, the Master in the body as *Nithyananda, dhyāna*, my teaching and message of meditation and *ānanda*, my mission of bringing forth the fountain of bliss that is lying latent in you, all the three together constitute the energy called *Nithyananda*. Understand that.

It is easy to do the first step, which is to follow the Master in his physical form because Masters are so attractive by nature and they do not expect anything in return. The next level is to follow the *dharma*, teachings of the Master. This is slightly more difficult because you have to not only listen to his teachings but you also have to do something; you have to live his teachings, practice them. Though it is only for your own growth, your laziness (*tamas*) causes you to not do this. The final level is where you infuse your life with the truth that life is for others. Life is for Enriching! You give your life to the *sanga*, mission and become the cause of spreading the Master's teachings. This is the most difficult, since it requires from you the ultimate commitment for life.

When you surrender to the Master, you surrender to his mission, *sanga* and to his teachings, *dharma* as well. When you surrender at the physical level, you surrender your comforts to the Master like desires for luxury, wealth, food or sleep to imbibe and spread his teachings and mission. I cannot call it sacrifice because you will feel from your very being that this is what you really want to do. I tell you, when you take up the responsibility of the mission, you will realize that what seemed to you as a load is actually a blissful experience. How can the mission of the Master give anything other than pure bliss? The moment you surrender to the Master and his mission and you stand up taking responsibility, you will find that the divine energy simply flows through you and you just flow effortlessly and express yourself most gracefully and powerfully.

All you need to do is to be stable and available, and the divine energy will make you able! On the mental level, you surrender your intellect, your mental pursuits, your incompletions to serve the Master and the mission. You become like a liquid, flowing into the shapes and moulds created by the Master. The Master knows the best way in which you can grow. He creates the moulds for each of you according to your needs and abilities. Trust him, drop your solid ego and become fluid so you can fill in the spaces he creates for you.

At the being level, when your very being surrenders to the Master, your being clearly recognizes the call of the Master. You become a part of the Master. You no longer carry any separate identity. This process of transformation automatically happens when you surrender to the Master, his teachings and his mission. The water is converted into formless steam. Like steam, you now explode in all directions. There are no limitations because all limitations exist only in the mind. You now transcend the mind and express your peak potential. The Master tirelessly and compassionately pushes you in different ways so you can also experience and be in the same state of eternal bliss as he is. The only emotion that a Master knows is love. I always tell people, 'When I show compassion to you, I cheat you. When I fire you, I teach you. Either way, you grow.'

The Vedas also clearly declare that a living Master is needed. You may have access to all the books, the recorded teachings of all the great masters. But, you have only the words; where is the body language? For example, yoga as it is taught now has been reduced to just a form of physical exercise. But physical health is just one of its benefits. Yoga as taught by Patañjali is a means to enlightenment. But the body language of Patañjali no longer exists; only his words exist. You need a living Master who is in the same consciousness as Patañjali, to transmit the essence and experience of the words.

A beautiful verse in the *Guru Gītā* says, 'The Guru just wipes off with the big toe of his left foot your fate which Brahma has written on your forehead.' The Master can change your very destiny and take you to a new dimension. An astrologer may be able to predict your future, but a Master can simply recreate your future. He is one with Existence, which is operating this whole Universe. Can the energy which runs the planets and stars not have the power to handle your life?

It is very difficult to relate with a living Master. You see, it is very easy to relate with dead masters. You can project all your imaginations about God on him. When Kṛṣṇa promises that He descends again and again—*sambhavāmi yuge yuge*—what He means is the Kṛṣṇa energy will descend. People think Kṛṣṇa will come down in the same form with the yellow clothes, the flute and the two peacock feathers. Again and again, Kṛṣṇa happens on planet Earth, but our incompletions are so cunning, they manage in making us miss Him in any form. We miss all the living Masters. It is easy to fool yourself, escaping from a living Master and just worshipping a Master who has left the body. You escape all the possibilities of transformation.

You can just say, '*Amayaṁ anahaṁkāraṁ arāgaṁ amadaṁ tathā*...' 'I offer my non-attachment to you', 'I offer my ego to you.'

You can say that to an idol and that idol will be just standing. But, if you tell me that, I will simply catch your neck and say, 'Hey! Where is your non-attachment? Give it. Where is your ego? Surrender it!' With the living Master, he will be constantly working on you, to cut your ego and to show you your true Self. But the ego is afraid to die at the Master's hands, so you try to escape. Just being open to his energy can get rid of the biggest cancer in you, your ego.

When you realize the truth that you too are one with the Universe, there is nothing more to desire; nothing to be attached to. There is no longer any differentiation between who you are and what the Universe is. Māyā, the illusion of that separation, disappears. That is why the Master is called *Guru*, one who leads you from '*gu*', which is darkness, to '*ru*', that is light; one who leads you from ignorance to bliss.

A Master does not differentiate between good and bad. He is not care if what you do is considered meritorious by society or sinful. Here, Kṛṣṇa says beautifully, 'Even if you are the most sinful of all sinners—*sarvebhyaḥ pāpa-krt-tamaḥ,* you will certainly completely cross the ocean of miseries with the boat of knowledge—*sarvam jñāna-plavenaiva vṛjinaṁ santariṣyasi* (4.36).'

At the spiritual level, the concept of sin does not exist. It is a creation of man-made institutions, of societal and political organizations to control others through fear. When you have the true knowledge, the intelligence of why you are doing what you are doing, the very knowledge will make the action divine, the act will no longer be just a ritual but a means to reach the Ultimate. Automatically, you will cross the ocean of miseries because misery itself is a result of ignorance of your true self. When 'spirit' is added to a 'ritual', it becomes 'spi-rituality'.

Self-doubt Destroys

4.37 *Just as a blazing fire turns firewood to ashes, O Arjuna,*
So does the fire of wisdom burn to ashes all actions, all your karma.

4.38 *Truly, in this world, there is nothing as pure as wisdom.*
One who has matured to know this enjoys in himself
in due course of time.

4.39 *A person with śraddha (courageous authenticity) achieves wisdom and has control over the senses. Achieving wisdom, without delay, he attains supreme peace.*

4.40 *Those who have no wisdom and authenticity,*
who always have doubts, are destroyed.
There is no happiness for the ones who doubt the self,
either in this world or the next.

4.41 *O Dhanañjaya (winner of riches), he who has renounced the fruits of his actions, whose doubts are destroyed, who is well established in the Self, is not bound by his actions.*

4.42 *O descendant of Bhārata, therefore, stand up, be established in yoga. Armed with the sword of knowledge, cut the doubt born of ignorance that exists in your heart.*

A small story:

Once, a blind man went to a doctor to see if he had any hope of getting back his eyesight. The doctor checked him and said, 'Yes, I can do a surgery and you can get back your eyesight. Then, you can drop your stick and start walking.'

The man replied, 'Doctor, I understand I will get back my

eyesight, but how can I walk without the stick?'

The blind man could not understand that he can walk without a stick! He does not even know what it means to be able to see. The doctor has to do the surgery to give him back his eyesight, then automatically he will drop the stick.

When I tell people to declare completion and drop their mind, they look at me as if I am a mad man. They ask me, 'How can we drop the mind? It is easy for you, you have renounced everything, you have no wife, no responsibilities, and on top of it you are enlightened. So, you can talk. How can we, living in this ocean of bondage, the *saṁsāra sāgara*, be in no-mind and yet survive?'

It is only when you drop the mind, drop your self-doubts, it is only when you stop connecting your thoughts to form a shaft, that you really start 'seeing'. Your ego stops interfering with the truth of what you see. It stops filtering and adding tones to what your senses experience. Your baggage of embedded memories, your *saṁskāras*, dissolve, and the new 'you' is born. All your actions then arise out of intuition, from the super conscious state, the state of truth, where no mind can exist.

Śraddha Enriches you with Knowledge

In the next verse, Kṛṣṇa uses the word 'śraddha' again. What a beautiful verse, '*śraddhāvān labhate jñānaṁ*—the one established in authenticity is enriched with knowledge.'

Actually, *śraddha* means faith plus the courage of authenticity to live to your highest possibility; the courage to be established in the peak of your capability. Understand, continuously committing with words that express your maximum peak capacity, as per your understanding and as per others' understanding is what is referred to as *śraddha*, authenticity.

Understand, authenticity means stretching, stretching, and stretching. Go on stretching, that is Life! Go on stretching without fear, and without giving up on yourself. Do anything to honor and fulfill your words. Stretch yourself. Let all the powers inside you be unleased!

Kṛṣṇa declares the power of authenticity here, '*śraddhāvān labhate jñānaṁ* (4.39).' Only the authentic one is enriched with knowledge. When you have the knowledge and the courage of authenticity to follow and live the teachings, then you can achieve the ultimate knowledge, the knowledge of enlightenment.

Many people do not have the courage of authenticity to see their research through. The eastern *vedic* sages did so much inner world research. Millions of them have stretched themselves fearlessly doing full-time research for thousands of years, using their bodies and minds as laboratories. Why? Just to enrich others! This knowledge of the inner world is the result of their authenticity, their space of possibility to do courageous experiments and studies just for enriching others. They were true inner scientists, true *śraddhavān* who had not only the curiosity, 'the great why' and the perseverance to know, but also the courage of authenticity to follow, live and express their findings.

Look at Patañjali, the father of yoga—He boldly declares that all that he says in the *Yoga Sutras* is completely open to experimentation and verification. He says, 'You are free to try this, and if you find anything more to be added or edited, you are free to do so.' He has presented his research report. He invites you to try out these in your life and if you learn something more from that, his work is open to editing. That is the beauty of our system; it is a living system open to being updated.

Of all religious and spiritual doctrines, it is only the scriptures of the *sanātana-dharma*, the eternal path of righteousness, as the Hindu philosophy is called, that allow themselves to be updated. The *Vedas* and the *Upaniṣads*, which we believe are the voices of Nature, are not rules and regulations. They are truths to be understood and followed only in awareness. There are no punishments if one does not follow them, nor is one condemned as a sinner if one doesn't follow them.

This is the greatness and pristine beauty of *sanātana-dharma*, the eternal path of living. We are the most powerful, most sophisticated, most intelligent, most cutting-edge presentation of the Truth left with the possibility to evolve more and more, open for the possibility of being updated! Nothing was sacred just because it was uttered. All that we follow blindly today as traditions came through societal interpretation. It is for us to sift through these truths with conscious awareness.

Once tested, proven, accepted and intranalysed, we need to have the courage of authenticity to practice these truths. Mere knowledge is insufficient. That is what *śraddha* is about. With *śraddha*, faith combined with courage of authenticity, you make the effort to constantly stretch and align yourself to the peak capability of what you feel as you, what you project as you, and what others' perceive as you. This dawns the ultimate knowledge in you.

With authenticity you conquer your senses, and direct your mind towards the truth, instead of your mind and senses leading you wherever they wish to. The state of fear can be born in you only when you are inauthentic. Only a man in authenticity, living authenticity, is a liberated one enriched with the ultimate knowledge, *śraddhāvān labhate jñānaṁ* (4.39).

Completing Self-doubt in any field is Education

In the next few verses, Kṛṣṇa says that there is no happiness for those who always have self-doubts and who have no knowledge and authenticity. He uses the word 'always.' He does not say that from the beginning itself you should not have any doubts. Having doubts is natural; as long as you have the mind, you will have doubts. But you can go beyond it by completing with your self-doubts.

Kṛṣṇa warns, 'The one without the wisdom and without authenticity, who always has doubts, is destroyed. There is no happiness for the one who doubts the self, either in this world or the next.' Self-doubt destroys you—*saṁśayātmā vinaśyati* and the one who has the self-doubt is never happy anywhere—*na sukhaṁ śaṁsayātmanaḥ* (4.40).

First, we need to understand what self-doubt is! What is the root of this self-doubt? In your life, when the first root incident happens, you make your inner image, you project the outer image, and you create the life image to protect yourself for survival reason. For example, at the age of three or four, you run around and play in the rain. Your mother sees you and strongly pulls you into the house and gives you a slap saying, 'Don't go out in the rain! You will catch a cold! Your health will be spoiled!' She screams at you. For a child, getting slapped, being pulled inside the house and locked up is too much. The child will not understand that it is only a slap. The child will literally feel he is going to die!

At that moment, the child will create the inner mage, *mamakāra*: 'I am helpless.' He will create the outer image, *ahaṁkāra:* 'I am powerful,' because he cannot survive with the idea, 'I am helpless in the society. I am helpless in life.' So, naturally, he will create a compensating outer image, 'I am powerful,' and he will create the life's image or *svānyakāra*, the image about his mother and life, that life is cruel.

So, when this root pattern is formed, you start living and you naturally project your pseudo outer image: 'I am powerful.' If you are not able to convince others with the pseudo outer image, it is good for you. But if you convince them with the pseudo outer image, when you come back to your private space like your bedroom, you will start thinking, 'Oh God! I made every one believe my outer image as the truth, but my inner image is different from my outer image!' So, this clash is self-doubt. This clash is what Kṛṣṇa calls as *saṁśayātmā*.

Please listen! I am giving you the example of a tree. If root pattern is the root of a tree, lust patterns are the parasites of the tree, every day suffering and powerlessness are the leaves of the tree, self-doubt is the fragrance of the tree.

So, please understand, when you convince others with your strong outer image, and your inner image starts questioning you; your inner image questioning you is self-doubt. That is where the self-doubt starts. This is where your root of unhappiness grows—*na sukhaṁ śaṁsayātmanaḥ* (4.40).

In any field if you carry self-doubt, you will continue to be powerless. In any field if you complete with your self-doubt, you are educated. For example, look into the first time you started doubting your ability to memorize poetry or mathematics tables. Complete with that incident and pattern. Suddenly, you will awaken your ability to memorize in an unimaginable way. That component in your brain, which is now non-mechanical, will be awakened. Similarly, if you complete with self-doubt in any field, suddenly that non-mechanical part of the brain will immediately be awakened.

Awakening all the non-mechanical parts of the brain is what I call Inner Awakening. In any field in your life if you complete with your self-doubt, you become educated in that field. Please understand, education is nothing but completing with self-doubt. If you complete with all your self-doubts in the field of dentistry, you are a dentist now. If you complete with all your self-doubts in the field of law, you are educated as a lawyer. If you complete with all your self-doubts in the field of transformation, you are a master of transformation.

Listen!

Education is nothing but completing with self-doubts. Education is nothing but completing with self-doubts. I can keep repeating just this one line.

I tell you, this is the precise, concise definition I have ever given about education: Completing with your self-doubt in any field is education. In any field, whether it is self-transformation, cooking, medicine, law, or construction, in any field, complete with your self-doubt. Your kuṇḍalini energy, your innate potential energy will flow in that direction and you will excel in that field.

MASTER-DISCIPLE RELATIONSHIP

> In the *Śiva Sutra*, Devi asks, 'O Śiva, what is your reality?
> What is this wonder- filled universe? What constitutes the
> seed? Who centers the universal wheel? What is this life
> beyond form pervading form? How may we enter it fully,
> beyond space and time, names and descriptions? Let my
> doubts be cleared.'

> Beautifully, She expresses Her whole state of mind through these few words. The last words are, 'Let my doubts be cleared. Let my doubts be complete.'
>
> She never says, 'Please answer my questions.' If She had made that mistake by asking, 'Answer my question', She would have produced one more *Gītā* through Śiva.

See, in the *Gītā,* Arjuna is not ready to surrender to Kṛṣṇa completely. That is why in the beginning Kṛṣṇa has to give him all the intellectual answers. Arjuna thinks he can solve his confusion through these answers; he doesn't know these are much deeper doubts that need to be cleared through the experience of the Truth.

That is why Kṛṣṇa has to give more than 700 verses to first convince Arjuna that he does not know. When Arjuna finally gives up saying '*I don't know*' then Kṛṣṇa reveals Himself! He reveals the truth and makes Arjuna experience it because that is the only way he will realize the Truth.

If you say, 'Let my questions be answered,' you want only intellectual answers. But Devi says, 'Let my doubts be cleared, whether you give words or energy or techniques, I am not bothered, but let me be free and complete from doubts.' When questions become a quest, you start speaking in this language. When the urge becomes urgent, you start speaking in this language. This shows the deep surrender of Devi.

A deep passive waiting without knowing what is going to happen is passive surrender. That is what I call total surrender.

Actually, the moment you decide 'I will wait forever,' things will simply start happening for you! As long as you are in a hurry and agitated, you stop things from happening in you. It is like trying your best to make the lotus bloom. You open out the petals by hand. Will it be a flower?

A lotus can be called a lotus only when it blossoms by itself. Give it a little space and time. The moment you decide to wait, things will simply start happening and you don't have to wait anymore. You only have to wait till you decide to wait! Just allow the Master to do the surgery and give you back your true Self, and automatically you will drop what you are not.

Here, Kṛṣṇa refers to the stages in the Master-disciple relationship. There are many levels.

> The first level is purely intellectual, doubt-based. 'Doubt-based' refers to the negative self-doubts, which are purely intellectual. It is like you are telling yourself on seeing the Master, 'What is he going to do? Let us see. How is he able to mobilize such a big crowd at such a young age? He seems hardly thirty. What is going on here?'
>
> The next step is intelligence; from intellect to intelligence. You tell yourself, 'Why not attend this program and see what he is really doing?' By this time, it has changed from, 'What is he doing!' to 'Oh, I think He means something. But I neither believe nor disbelieve Him. Ok, let us check it out.' The intellect is becoming intelligence. You are giving a little space for the Master.
>
> Then, if you continue to start looking in, first from intellect to intelligence, then from intelligence to intelligence with emotion, like 60% intelligence, 40% emotion, that is the time you will feel like a friend towards the Master. After that, it becomes 60% emotion and 40% intelligence. That is the time you will feel like the Master is like an elder, like a father or mother or lord or teacher. You feel respectful towards him. And then, the relationship becomes pure emotion. You will feel a deep connection like a mother and son.
>
> Then, after that, it is neither emotion nor intellect nor intelligence. It is a being-level relationship. It is the deep connection of a beloved, the *madhura bhāva*.
>
> And suddenly, you will see, he is not even the beloved, he is beyond the beloved. You start experiencing the *mahā bhāva,* what I call the Guru-disciple experience,

> experiencing yourself as the Master. That is what I call—'*Tat Tvam Asi.*' *Tat Tvam Asi* means *That art thou*. It means you are the Master.

First it is just intellect, where you have self-doubts. But you have to go beyond that. If you are stuck in this level of self-doubts, naturally you will suffer with misery, with self-hatred and self-denial. Then, the next level is intelligence, then emotion, then pure emotion, then emotional and being level feeling connection, then pure being level connection, and then all these and something more. When you go beyond doubts and faith, into the realization of the formless energy that is you, then you find yourself.

So, let the divine *Parabrahma* Kṛṣṇa guide us all to the right energy, to the right path of knowledge and the right experience. Let Him shower eternal bliss.

Let Him make us experience and radiate eternal bliss, *Nityānanda*.

Thank you.

Thus ends the fourth chapter named ***Jñānakarma-sannyāsa Yogaḥ****, 'The Yoga of Action In Knowledge And Renunciation,' of the* ***Bhagavad Gītā Upaniṣad, Brahmavidyā Yogaśāstra****, the scripture of yoga dealing with the science of the Absolute in the form of* ***Śrī Kṛṣṇārjuna saṃvād****, dialogue between Śrī Kṛṣṇa and Arjuna.*

CHAPTER

5

Sannyāsa Yogaḥ

Live All Your Possibilities

Seeking more and more does not lead to happiness. It leads to depression. Then what leads to happiness that is eternal?.

Live All Your Possibilities

If we look closely at our lifestyle, what we accept as normal is actually chaotic and crazy. But we have been conditioned with it since childhood so we are not even aware of this. From an early age we are taught certain beliefs and habits that cut deep grooves in our mind. For the rest of our lives we follow these patterns of thinking.

In Indian villages, even today, they grind oil seeds in a traditional expeller, powered by bullocks. These bullocks are tied in such a way that they walk in circles to crush the seeds inside the expeller. If we analyze the way we live, we are very much like these bullocks! We get caught in a root pattern and we go around driven by our senses and memories. Just as the bullocks chew the cud as they walk around, we too chew the cud of our memories and perceptions as we unconsciously follow the same routine day after day, year after year.

Even when we think we are breaking the routine and doing things creatively and rationally, it is just an illusion of our mind. We are still driven by our unconscious mind. These engraved memories or root thought patterns stored in the deep unconscious mind make decisions on our behalf, even though we are completely unaware of it. What we may think of as an intuitive decision is actually an instinctive decision that arises from our unconscious.

Understand the difference between intuition and instinct. Instinct is the unconscious. It is what drives animals. It is the deeply grooved root patterns that are encoded as bio-memories in the genes and DNA. Since the unconscious brain acts much faster than the conscious brain, the instinctive action of the unconscious is of crucial value to our survival.

Intuition is a super conscious state of the mind. In any field when you allow your peak possibility without self-doubt, when you complete with your self-doubt, your logic gets so refined that it becomes intuition. Understand, in any field if your logic is refined, it becomes intuition. In any field if you allow your Kuṇḍalini (potential energy) to express itself to its peak possibility without self-doubt, in that field you become a leader. Take the example of self-transformation. Understand, you can allow your potential energy to flow in the direction of enlightening you if you complete with the self-doubt, 'Will I ever be enlightened? Can I ever be enlightened?' If you are young, you think, 'I am too young for enlightenment.' If you are old, you think, 'I am too old for enlightenment.'

Listen. *Prākṛitaṁ* is logic. *Saṃskṛitaṁ* is intuition. Refined logic is intuition. It is where we reach when we move inwards through our senses. It is a state of living and being in the present moment of completion, the space of enlightenment. Intuition transcends time and space. Intuition allows us to explode in all directions while instinct restricts us to the logical path of our unconscious memories, our incompletions.

BY NATURE YOU ARE MULTI-DIMENSIONAL

Time and again people tell me, '*Swamiji*, it is easy for you to do what you do. You have no family ties. You have renounced wealth. We are bonded to relationships and material possessions. How can we become spiritual?'

Let me tell you clearly that this is your instinct speaking. You are caught in the inadequate cognition of your unconscious mind, in your root patterns, believing that you can do only one thing at a time. You have sold yourself into the bondage of believing you are one dimensional. By nature we are multi-dimensional. By nature we are intuitive. By nature we are enlightened.

Listen! By nature, God built you with the power of words, power of thinking, power of feeling and power of living. Your inbuilt innate nature is expressing these great inner powers. That is why you feel so fulfilled whenever you are in integrity. That is why you feel so complete when you enrich others. That is why you feel so blissful when you cause others' reality. We can live a beautiful life! All that we lack is the awareness of our potential and all possibilities of our life.

See, the possibility of human life is what we call Kuṇḍalini energy. There are multiple possibilities in you. You are multi-dimensional. It is like a set-top box where you have the possibility of 170 channels, but the channel you watch is up to you. Kuṇḍalini is your possibility. Letting your possibility happen in you, trusting your possibility without self-doubt, responding to your possibility without self-doubt is Kuṇḍalini energy.

Please understand, each human being allows himself to be expressed without self-doubt in at least one dimension. Even if you think you are a useless fellow, to be useless in that dimension, you allow your possibility without self-doubt.

Somebody allows their possibility, without self-doubt, in the field of cooking. He may be useless in all other fields but in cooking, he has no self-doubt. He knows that he will be able to cook any dish he sees. Every person allows and expresses his peak possibility in at least one field without self-doubt. It is not that you don't express your possibility in any field at all. If that were true, you wouldn't be alive. Even to be alive, you have to allow the Kuṇḍalini, the potential energy to breathe through you at least in one field.

I have seen some people who are so cunning that in their cunningness, they allow their peak possibility to express itself. A great lawyer may have a lot of doubt about his character but in his legal field, he will not have any doubt. So understand, when you express your peak possibility without any self-doubt in any field, you allow your Kuṇḍalini to be awakened in that field. In that field your logic gets so refined, it becomes intuition.

Helping you realize your possibility and supporting you to complete with your self-doubt is Kuṇḍalini Awakening.

Many recent neurological researches are proving what I am saying. I am giving it as a formula. Either you are multi-dimensional or non-dimensional! There is no such thing as 'persons in single dimension.' You are multi-dimensional, meaning you can think for everyone, or you are non-dimensional, it means you cannot think even for yourself and somebody else thinks for you! When you start thinking for everyone, you develop a beautiful faculty. It is actually through thinking that you reach the thoughtless space, not the other way!

In the verses that follow and in the rest of the Gītā, Śrī Kṛṣṇa, the Master of all possibilities enriches us on how to break away from our bondages and become multi-dimensional to realize our peak possibility, and to express the powers of our possibilities.

Constantly turning many impossibilities into possibilities by playing that within human laws, rules and regulations is the job of an Incarnation. Bhagavān Kṛṣṇa, who is the possibility of all Incarnations, teaches us how to reach our true state. This is what the word *samādhi* means—to go back to our true nature.

Kṛṣṇa constantly turns what Arjuna thinks as 'impossible' into 'possible' by demonstrating His peak possibilities to express themselves through Arjuna within the laws of human realm, within the laws of Kurukṣetra warfield. Kṛṣṇa Himself does not use a single weapon throughout the Mahābhārat war, but becomes the cause for Arjuna to live and express his own peak possibilities. It is through the multi-dimensional space awakened by Śrī Kṛṣṇa in the Pāṇḍavas that they stand victorious.

Throughout the Gītā, Kṛṣṇa talks about yoga. Each chapter refers to one type of yoga or another. Yoga is the same as samādhi. Yoga means 'uniting'. It means uniting with our true nature. When we unite with our true Self, we become multi-dimensional, we become the space of possibilities. We can be material and spiritual. There are no constraints and no limitations. We are free. We had wealthy kings like Janaka, who were realized souls. Material wealth does not limit anyone from being spiritual. It is only the attachment to wealth through greed and the fear of losing wealth that stops one from being free.

Further, for the first time, Kṛṣṇa gives a meditation technique in this chapter. Until the fifth chapter, He was giving only intellectual advice, *śāstra*. Kṛṣṇa now thinks that Arjuna has become mature, or Kṛṣṇa realizes that without some technique, it is now impossible to relate to Arjuna. Kṛṣṇa realizes, 'If I don't give him a technique, I cannot escape from him!' Masters give meditation techniques in two situations, either when they see the person is mature enough, or when the person is constantly questioning them without transforming.

So I don't know whether Kṛṣṇa thought Arjuna was now mature or He thought 'let him at least sit quietly for a few minutes with closed eyes!' Either way, He gives him a technique.

Action Or Renunciation

5.1 *Arjuna says:*
Oh Kṛṣṇa, you asked me to renounce work first
and then you asked me to work with devotion.
Will you now please tell me, definetely,
which of the two will be more beneficial to me?

5.2 *Bhagavān says:*
The renunciation of work [sannyāsa] and
work in devotion [karmayoga] are both good for liberation.
But, of the two, work in devotional service is better than
renunciation of work.

5.3 *He who neither hates nor desires the fruits of his activities*
has renounced. Such a person, free from all dualities,
easily overcomes material bondage and is completely liberated,
Oh Mahābaho (Arjuna)!

5.4 *Only the ignorant, not the wise, speaks of the path of action*
[karma-yoga] to be different from the path of renunciation
[sāṅkhya yoga]. Those who are actually learned say that one who is
firmly established in either of the paths, achieves the fruit of both.

In all the previous chapters, Kṛṣṇa talks with such clarity and authority that it would dissolve the doubts of anybody listening to Him. And yet Arjuna has come back to the same point. It seems like Arjuna was playing a game so that the *Gītā* could be delivered to the world. A person who was a great king could never have been so ignorant. There is no other book that is so clear, so direct. There is no other Master who is so straight in giving the Truth and the experiential expression of the Truth.

After all the explanations given by Kṛṣṇa, Arjuna continues to ask, 'Oh Kṛṣṇa, first of all, you asked me to renounce work and then again you recommend work with devotion. Now, will you kindly tell me clearly, which one of the two is more beneficial?—*yac chreya etayor ekaṁ tanme brūhi su-niścitam* (5.1).'

We will never get an answer or solve a problem if we start thinking about which would be more beneficial. Before we evaluate the benefits of something, we should be clear about the scale we want to use to measure the benefits. What is beneficial for one person may be completely useless for another. The scale that we use for measuring success is a very important thing. Unless we know the scale, it does not make sense to conclude anything. Even jumping to a conclusion should be done with clear intelligence and completion. Jumping to a conclusion without intelligence is like falling out of an airplane without a parachute! We just wouldn't know where we will land.

Before measuring life in terms of success or failure, one should know how this success is to be measured in the first place. If we are going to measure our life on a scale of dollars, then we have to work only for dollars. So, from morning to evening, we need to work only for that goal. Based on this, we can conclude whether we are succeeding or failing in our life. But you see, by the time we reach the end of the day, the very scale changes! We start our life using a certain scale and after a few years we measure it again using a totally different scale.

It is fortunate that the scale changes with maturity. If we grow with every mistake in life and complete with it, then the scale with which we measure success in life should also change. If it does not change, we will start our next life from ground zero. It is an endless game unless we learn lessons and move on. If the scale with which we measure our success changes in the right way, it shows we are becoming mature. If the scale stays in the same level of dollars and wealth, not only will we be unable to measure our life clearly but we will also attract unhappiness and incompletions. This is because there is no end to accumulating money or any material wealth. First of all, we set high standards for ourselves. Even if we achieve these, we are not successful in our own eyes because we would have extended our target by comparing ourselves with others. Out of greed we keep saying 'What next, what next'. There is no end to this.

At the end of our lives, we feel we have not done enough. Again we start a whole new game of birth and life with the same incompletions, same limited maturity. Listen! If money and worldly comfort alone is our scale, again and again we will feel we did not do enough and that we missed out in life. There is no absolute scale that defines success, especially in monetary terms. For any amount of money that we have, we would be happier with a dollar more.

YAKṢA'S JAR AND BRAHMA'S HEAD

Let me tell you a small story:

> A king's barber used to live a very happy life. Every morning he would go to the palace, do his work and the king would give him ten gold coins. He led a happy and peaceful life without any worries. One day when he was returning from the king's palace, suddenly, he heard a booming voice, 'Dear son, do you want forty gold coins?'
>
> The barber said, 'Forty gold coins? What am I going to do with them? My expense is ten gold coins and that is enough. I don't need anything more.'
>
> The booming voice said, 'I will give you twenty-four hours to think. You can go home, think about it, come back tomorrow and tell me. If you decide that you want them, I shall give you a magical jar full of gold coins.'
>
> This poor barber went and said this to his wife! She started to scream, 'You fool! Don't you have any sense? You should have brought that jar. She raved and ranted, 'All my life, I am wearing the same clothes and jewelry. You have never taken me on a vacation. What have I enjoyed after marrying you?'

When she started shouting at him, the barber said, 'Alright, fine. Don't worry. The booming voice has given me time till tomorrow morning. Tomorrow, I will talk to him and get the jar.'

The next day morning, he told the voice, 'Please give me that jar.' Immediately, a yakṣa (an astral being) appeared before him and said, 'Have this jar. This jar has got 990 gold coins, just 10 gold coins less than 1000.'

The guy brought the gold jar back to the house. He was very happy that he could spend it for at least 99 days if he spent ten coins per day. But the moment his wife got the jar, she said, 'What is this? The jar is not overflowing. There is something missing.'

He said, 'I don't know. This is the way I got the jar. The yakṣa told me that it is a little less.'

She started worrying, 'Had it been full, how nice it would have been!' The next day, when the barber came back, she hurriedly grabbed all the ten gold coins for that day and put them in the jar. She wanted the jar to overflow. But to her surprise, again the level in the jar was not full.

The barber's wife now waited anxiously for the next day's wages to fill the jar. The next evening, again, she took the money from the barber and put them into the jar. Again, it was almost full but not completely full. This went on continuously for a week. She stopped giving the barber food and cut all expenses. She took away all the gold coins from him and desperately waited to see the jar overflow. In one week's time the barber had become tired and dull.

The king started enquiring, 'What happened? You used to look so fresh. You have started worrying. What happened to you? Did you accept the yakṣa's jar?'

The barber was shocked at hearing this. He said, 'Oh king,

how do you know?'

The king said, 'Whoever is suffering in this country, all of them have one thing in common. They accepted the yakṣa's jar at some point in time. When you go back home, get rid of the yakṣa's jar if you wish to be happy again.'

The man did so and lived in completion, happily and blissfully again from that day on.

What the king said applies to all of us. Go back home and see if you have yakṣa's jar or not, and if you do, complete with it. If you are worrying, if you are suffering with incompletions, there is every chance that you have the yakṣa's jar of incompletions in your house. The yakṣa's jar never gets filled, it is always incomplete!

Of course, when I say yakṣa's jar, I mean it may not literally be there in your house. But it will surely be there in your head as incompletions. Sometimes yakṣa hands over the jar in the form of a bank balance. Sometimes he hands it out as knowledge. Sometimes he hands it out as name and fame! It may be in your mind, in your inner space sitting as complicated patterns, as incompletions claiming over your own power.

Listen! Yakṣa's jar is made out of the Brahmakapāla—meaning one of Lord Brahma's heads that Lord Śiva, in the form of Māhākāla, destroys. Mahādeva assumes the form of Kālabhairava to destroy the incompletions of Brahma. Brahma once got into the hypocritical incompletion of thinking he is Sadāśiva. Sadāśiva had five heads, Brahma also had five heads. But Brahma forgot that Sadāśiva had one more space in Him, which is called *Adho Mukha*—the Superconscious, Enlightenment, *avyakta*—the unmanifested. Brahma had not realized his unmanifested side. So he suddenly started behaving like Mahādeva, saying, 'So what? I have five faces. He also has five faces.'

Mahādeva then took the form of Māhākālabhairava and removed one of Brahma's heads. Once Mahādeva removed the head, Brahma automatically settled into the space of completion. But all the incompletions of Brahma were stuck in Mahādeva's hand in the form of that Brahmakapāla or skull, which simply swallows anything that is put into it and asks for more. Then, Devi offered food to that skull and completed it. Viśveshvara, Viśvanātha became Kālabhairava to complete Brahma. Mahādevi became Annapūrni (mother who bestows completion with food) to complete the Brahmakapāla.

Understand the truth from this powerful happening! The yakṣa's jar is the head of Brahma that makes us feel that we are not enough, that we are not complete, that we are not powerful and joyful. Our head makes us continuously feel powerless, insecure that we are not enough unto ourselves and we are not complete.

On one side, no matter how much we have, in ten days, we feel it is not sufficient. In ten days, Brahma's head, our incomplete mind, will take everything for granted. On other side, it makes us cunningly believe that we know, when we *don't* know.

Yakṣa refers to an incomplete, powerless person with complicated patterns, who has wealth and the power of completion but neither does he enjoy his powerful space nor does he enrich to share it with the world. In India, they keep a few dogs in many agricultural fields. The dogs will neither eat the grains nor will they allow other animals to come and eat. In the same way, if we have the power of completion and enriching, and we neither enjoy nor share it with others, we are called a yakṣa.

One of the biggest problems is, in spite of reminding you again and again, you put all your energy to support your incompletions saying 'If I don't support my incompletions, people will exploit me because others are in incompletion.' If you feel insecurity, be very clear, you have already become Brahma. Now you need Kālabhairava to happen in you. Any form of insecurity is Brahma. Remove that insecurity and incompletion from your life. Be like Kālabhairava when you have to complete with all your incompletions, because your incompletion always behaves like Brahma. Even though it does not know, it acts as if it knows.

When accumulation of wealth or knowledge is done greedily, there is never an end, like the yakṣa's jar, because there is always scope for more. And secondly, when one is so preoccupied about accumulating, completion and joy never happens. The greed of wanting more and more power and the fear of losing the power hinders the true power and joy of the wealth. Why are we accumulating possessions if we do not stop and enjoy them?

I tell you, Kālabhairava is power and joy. These two qualities complete all your incompletions. All your incompletions will be complete. Your very DNA should be programmed with the space of Kālabhairava, power and joy! Mahākālabhairava is embodiment of power and joy! Only power and joy brings completion and keeps you alive, awake, aware.

I always tell people, 'Either you do *dāna* (charity) or you achieve *mahādāna* (the final and grand sacrifice or death). If you do *dāna*, you share some of your completion while also enjoying and enriching yourself. You will be enriched and so will others. If you don't do some *dāna*, you will achieve *mahādāna*. This means you will leave everything and go away carrying the mahādāna of your incompletions once and for all when you die.

Ramaṇa Maharṣi says beautifully, 'Before achieving it, even a mustard seed will look like a mountain.' It will seem like your life will not move without it. It will seem like it is the basic and most important thing for your life. 'Once you achieve it, even a mountain will look like a mustard seed.' This is because something else looks like a mountain now. We get caught in the trap of achieving, and lose the ability to relax and enjoy what we have achieved.

KARMA OR SANNYĀSA, WHAT IS MY PATH?

Here, Arjuna asks: 'Kṛṣṇa! Now, will you please tell me surely, which of the two: *karma*, action or *Sannyāsa*, renunciation is more beneficial—*sannyāsaṁ karmaṇāṁ kṛṣṇa punar yogaṁ ca saṁsasi* (5.1)?'

Again and again, all of us ask ourselves this question. The mind is in dilemma! The mind asks for a single instruction! Our mind will be alive as long as we are caught between any two extremes. The moment we come to any single conclusion we will be liberated. We will be ignorant as long as we are moving from one extreme to the other. Don't say 'Ignorance is bliss.' If ignorance is bliss why are so many people suffering on this planet? Ignorance is not bliss. Innocence is bliss.

Innocence means we will not carry a scale with which we are continuously measuring our life. Ignorance means we will have a scale but we will not be able to fulfill our life according to that scale.

We have made our mind itself a disease, a dilemma. Dilemma is the disease of incompletions with which man starts his life and ends his life too. Even 'ends' is not the right word to use because he is in a dilemma about whether or not to end it! But death comes and his life is just taken away from him. Here, Arjuna is in a dilemma as to which of the two is *more* beneficial for him. If we look into life as a utility, as some means to a benefit, then we are creating our own hell. If we reduce life to this, we will be in hell.

Listen! Life has no separate benefit. Life itself is a benefit. There are people who have achieved all that they wanted in life. But they feel a deep void, a deep incompletion in them. This is what I mean by the term 'depression of success.' They feel something is deeply lacking and are unable to comprehend what it could possibly be.

This is because they ran the rat race of life without carrying the space of completion, without stopping to complete with their root patterns of desires, of fear and greed, without any self-inquiry. They ran foolishly because everyone else was running. They never stopped for a minute to question—'why am I doing what I am doing', 'what do I really want', 'why do I feel the way I feel'. So, without finding the root patterns that drive them in the rat race, when they stop running or when they can't run anymore, they fall back into their incompletions.

They suddenly find themselves diseased with their own being. This is what becomes depression or disease. So, if you constantly look for some benefit from life, if you don't achieve, you will feel life is a failure and if you achieve, you are bound to face the depression of success. Either way it is trouble.

Life itself is a benefit. If we constantly try to see which of two things is *more* beneficial, it means we have a pure business mind. We can't do business with life. At some point we need to relax from the business mind. I always tell people, 'For at least half an hour per day, do some enriching which will not get dollars for you—some painting, some writing.' When you start painting, don't think of a big gallery with your paintings! Do some creative work without bothering about how to show off your artwork to people. Even before starting to paint, we will think, 'My friend will come home. I will show him how I developed this concept.' You will decide how to bore your friend with your plans.

Do something enriching just for the sake of enriching, not for any purpose. Enrich just for the sake of enriching. You will see that during that half hour, you will fall into your very being; which is the space of completion!

You can also enrich at some place of worship by cleaning it without expecting anything in return. Engage yourself in any form of selfless enriching activity. Serve food to people. Even while volunteering, we do it so that we can tell others about it and get applauded for it. So now at least for 30 minutes, authentically enrich with responsibility, without the cognition of getting yourself any benefit. No money or name and fame should come to you from that half an hour. If you can just do this, you will start tasting the real power of life. Enriching is the power of living, *ātma śakti.*

Listen! With enriching, you will achieve the ultimate result of establishing your existence into everything. You establishing your existence into everything is what I call 'serving.' In any form of serving or enriching, you expand and become part of it.

As long as you are in your own head, continuously calculating, you will only be bargaining with life, 'What is *more* beneficial? What am I going to achieve by this?' You will see the power of living—a different dimension of your being, if you practice this technique of enriching. I promise you that this enriching will lead you to Kṛṣṇa consciousness, the consciousness of completion.

When you stop calculating for getting benefits, you will start tasting the fruit of life. Listen! Enriching is enjoying and sharing the fruit of life! When you enrich others you will come alive. A mango does not achieve its ultimate, if you just eat the fruit and destroy the seed. The fruit realizes itself only when the seed is able to give more fruits.

Life is not and can never be business. Here, again and again, Arjuna is stuck because he thinks that life is business. Of course, Kṛṣṇa is very compassionate. He is the embodiment of kindness! Literally, inch by inch, He brings Arjuna up without giving up on him. He does not lose His patience. He does not say, '*I told you earlier...*'

I can say that Kṛṣṇa uses at least 100 verses to explain this one concept of *Karma-Sannyāsa yoga*, the paths of responsibility and renunciation. But He does this without losing His patience at any point. Not once does He shout at Arjuna. He is an embodiment of compassion. He comes down to the plane of Arjuna and gradually transforms him by enriching him with the same teachings in different ways.

The question concerning *Karma* and *Sannyāsa*—responsibility and renunciation—has been asked from time immemorial, and each time it has been answered. Yet this question remains.

Somebody asked me, 'Why is the *Gītā* still relevant today?'

I said, 'Because we never learned it.' Although *Gītā* was uttered at least 5,000 years ago it is still relevant today. Why? It is simply because man has not listened and he has not learnt his lesson yet! History repeats itself.

The unconscious process never comes to the conscious energy. Man as such is governed to a large extent by the unconscious. He is not even aware of what he is going after. He thinks he wants something and runs after it. But by the time he gets his hands on it, he wants something else. So there is a constant restlessness, powerlessness within. This puts man in constant incompletion, dissatisfaction and depression.

Listen! By merely flooding completion into this depression you can get out of it. I always tell people, if you just allow a single instance of depression, powerlessness to work on you and you face it consciously with the process of completion, in the process you will become enlightened. Nothing else is necessary. A single instance of depression is enough. It will completely burn you and you will become enlightened. But we never allow anything to work on us completely. We are scared to confront our own selves. We just allow the unconscious space of powerlessness to overpower us instead of boldly facing it with power and joy, and seeing it through its completion. Look into every moment you feel powerless in your life even now. Don't try to escape from those moments! You can never escape!

Life is the greatest Master, it continuously teaches us. But we never learn from it. We never mark the spot where we stopped our journey in this birth. That spot where we stopped life's journey is the root pattern. When we stop our journey, if we at least mark the spot in this life saying, 'I covered this distance, I learnt all these things. In the next birth I will continue from where I left last,' it is enough.

Please listen. The moment your root pattern is born, your life is destroyed! Your growth is stopped! Only when you find your root pattern and complete with it, you come back to life again. When I say birth, I do not mean just the totality of our life. I am referring to each day and night. Each day and night is a birth. It is a life cycle. We die and are reborn every day.

Do Self-completion, Svapūrṇatva

Everyday at least for forty-two minutes, consciously decide to do the self- completion process, *svapūrṇatva kriya*. Decide consciously to be complete: 'Let me sit and face my powerlessness and complete with my patterns. Let me restore my space of completion today.'

Tell yourself, 'I will allow the cognition of completion to enter into my consciousness this week. I will solve all my problems only with this complete cognition. I create the space of completion.' If you had completed with all your patterns before sleeping every night and allowed the cognition of completion to enter your consciousness every week, you would have been enlightened by now. Your life would have been blissful. But the problem is we do not take the responsibility for our possibility. Instead, we always mark the spots of our life's journey in the wrong places—in our patterns.

We mark our patterns, not our possibilities. We never mark where we should in the bigger picture of our lives. We are so caught up with marking our small desires and goals fueled by our incompletions. We never mark the spot of our peak possibilities. These markings of desires and worldly goals continuously get washed away and new markings are made. They update themselves based on inputs from the world around us, based on what society has to say. We forget that these markings are temporary and do not reflect *the space of possibility* within, which comes only from completion.

What truly matters is inner transformation, which we never bother to think about. We never allow any understanding of completion to work on us. If we are consciously aware of our root patterns, why we are doing what we are doing and what our pitfalls are, we can start to complete with them and grow to be powerful, complete individuals. But again and again we make the same mistakes. The scale may differ but the mistakes are the same!

A leader is one who commits mistakes on a large scale and hides them, whereas a follower is one who commits the same mistakes on a smaller scale and justifies them. That is the difference between a leader and a follower. To be honest, we are not intelligent enough to create new patterns. We are not creative and innovative enough to make new mistakes. Even if you merely decide not to make the same mistake out of the same pattern once more, your life will be transformed. But again and again, we make the same kind of mistakes because our mind works in the same route. That route is only called *saṁskāra*: a recorded route, an engraved bio-memory or a root pattern. If we take up the life of either *karma* or *sannyāsa* based on an incomplete recorded bio-memory, we will never achieve completion, bliss.

SURRENDER TO EXPERIENCE KARMA-SANNYĀSA AS ONE

Let us deeply analyze these paths of *Karma* and *Sannyāsa.* Karma is normally out of greed and desires. Sannyāsa is always invariably out of fear, *bhaya.* There is a fear of life. When you are not ready to take the risk, you renounce everything. The fear of getting hurt is the first reason for *Sannyāsa*. *Sannyāsa* is a way of escapism, turning away from the responsibilities that life presents. When a person is bogged down by responsibilities of life, he takes *Sannyāsa* as an easy escape route. In the name of renunciation, he covers his deep fears. This is not true *Sannyāsa.*

Then we have people running after material wealth in the name of *karma.* On one side are the people who are running away from fear. On the other side are those who are running towards their greed. Both categories of people are not going to achieve eternal bliss or consciousness. Both are not on the right track of completion.

In the entire world, only three types of human beings exist: One who has surrendered to greed, one who has surrendered to fear and the one who has surrendered to the supreme intelligence, divine consciousness. The person who has surrendered to greed gets lost. Such a person runs after many things in life to possess them, which in turn leads to more greed. He literally becomes a slave to greed.

There is a beautiful story in *Muṇḍaka Upaniṣad*:

> There are two birds on the same tree.
>
> One bird, a completely satisfied and fulfilled being, is sitting calmly, enjoying the silence of its own inner space.
>
> Another bird is sitting a little below, busily pecking at the fruits. It keeps flitting from place to place, trying to eat the fruits. When the fruit is tasty, it enjoys. When the fruit is not tasty, it suffers. It continuously oscillates between enjoyment and suffering.
>
> Suddenly, this bird looks up and sees the bird that is

> sitting silently and thinks, 'How is this bird so calm and beautiful? Let me go closer and see. Let me talk to this bird.' Slowly, the small bird moves towards the peaceful bird.
>
> As it goes closer to the other bird, it continues to taste more fruits and suffers because the fruits are sour. Suddenly, when it is close enough to the other bird, it realizes that the other bird is nothing but its own *self*, which is sitting silently and beautifully watching the small bird getting distracted in its path, suffering with sour fruits! The small bird simply becomes one with the other bird.

This is a beautiful story!

In the same way, as long as you are a *jīvātman*, an ordinary soul, you struggle between fear and greed. You go from one extreme to another. The moment you realize there is something inside your being that is untouched by your greed and fear, you start traveling towards it. When you get closer to it, you realize you are that Consciousness.

Here, Kṛṣṇa explains the same thing, we are caught between fear and greed. Either we constantly surrender ourselves to fear or we surrender ourselves to greed. Very rare individuals surrender to intelligence, to Divine Consciousness.

Arjuna asks here, 'Which is more beneficial for me?' Keeping track of accounts is good in business but not in life. People come and ask me, 'Why should I surrender to the Divine? If I surrender, what will I get?'

If you don't surrender to the Divine, you will be surrendering to your fear or greed. I am not asking you to surrender to the Divine just to get something out of it. When it comes to life, profit and loss doesn't work. Life is beyond calculation. The moment we ask, 'What will I get by surrendering to the Divine?', we miss the whole idea of surrender.

Venkaṭeśvara (incarnation of Lord Viṣṇu) holds the cakra (discus) in one hand, and this represents fear. In the other hand, He has the śankha (conch), which represents success. The conch is blown when you achieve success or victory. This represents greed because man is constantly seeking success in everything and is never satisfied.

If you don't surrender to Venkaṭeśvara's pāda (feet) and His pāduka (sandals), you will surrender to His conch and discus. In other words, you will surrender to fear or greed. Those who constantly approach God for fulfillment of their desires or for refuge for their problems are actually surrendering to greed and fear. Only very few surrender to the feet of Venkaṭeśvara, which is the ultimate surrender.

Our whole life is spent running behind greed or fear. The path of *Karma Yoga*, seeking liberation through action or responsibility, happens because of greed. The path of *sannyāsa yoga*, seeking liberation through renunciation, happens because of fear. Neither the path of *karma* (action) nor the path of *sannyāsa* (renunciation) will enrich us unless we complete with our greed and fear and transform our very space into the space of completion. If we change the incomplete space to that of completion, *karma or sannyāsa* or anything can enrich us. All we need to know is this—it doesn't matter if we are a *karma yogi* or a *sannyāsa yogi*. It is the attitude, the space from which we approach and live life that is most important. Let your inner space be the space of completion.

Listen! When you are in incompletion, you constantly feel powerless and anything you do comes out of powerlessness. Anything done out of incompletion, be it *Karma Yoga* or *Sannyāsa yoga*, leads you to more and more incompletion. Anything done out of completion, leads you to more and more completion.

I am defining Sannyāsa.

Sannyāsa is you living in the space of completion and constantly enriching everyone to be in the space of completion.

Again and again, Kṛṣṇa is placing the emphasis on the space of completion, on the being. If we don't know the root cause of our actions, why we are living with *karma* or why we pick up *Sannyāsa*, we will not be able to solve our problems. Our suffering is neither because of *karma* nor because of *Sannyāsa*. Suffering is because of our wrong attitude of incompletion. And with this wrong attitude of incompletion, be it *karma* or *sannyāsa*, the path will feel only like a punishment. With the right space of completion, any path will feel like a true blessing for you and for others.

With the wrong space of incompletion, if you take the path of *karma* or *sannyāsa*, you will struggle and suffer, and make others suffer as well. If you decide to enter *karma*, drop the goal. Just enjoy doing the *karma* and don't worry about the goal. Living itself is beautiful. Realize that life itself is beautiful. On the other hand, if we decide to take up *Sannyāsa*, again drop the goal. The goal of a *Sannyāsi* (monk), which is renunciation, is also a goal and it must be dropped. The karma yogi runs towards the goal, the *Sannyāsi* runs away from the goal.

Kṛṣṇa says—*sāṅkhya yogou pṛthagbālāḥ pravadanti na paṇḍitaḥ* (5.4). Indirectly He tells Arjuna that he has yet to learn, that he is still ignorant. Only the ignorant man says that *karma yoga* is different from *sāṅkhya yoga*, the *Sannyāsa*. Here, the words *karma* and *sannyāsa* are equated to *Karma Yoga* and *Sāṅkhya Yoga*.

The experienced say that both *karma* and *sannyāsa* lead to the same truth. Through both these paths, one achieves the results of both. If we complete with the pattern of greed in *karma yoga* and complete with the pattern of fear in *Sannyāsa Yoga*, we will drop into eternal consciousness. Through both, we will achieve when we create the right space—the space of completion.

So Kṛṣṇa says here, 'Only the ignorant person says that one is superior to the other or that they are two different paths. Both the paths are one and the same.' A person who can travel alone, who is courageous enough to live in the space of completion and decides to enrich others with completion takes the life of *Sannyāsa*. A person who decides to live in the space of completion and who wants to enrich others by sharing his life takes the life of *karma*. It is up to us. Both the paths are one and the same.

What is important is having the right reason and the right space, not what we are doing. What we are *doing* is not important, who we are *being* is important. These three words should be understood: *being, doing and having*. If we are continuously *doing* only for *having*, we will never *have* it. Even when we are *having*, we will be *doing*. The man who is doing just for having will never be able to experience or enjoy life because even when he is having, he will be doing. The man who is established in his *being* will enjoy both *doing* and *having* at the same time. By just *being*, he will enjoy *doing* and *having*. All we need is a simple technique. The whole idea is now reduced to a one-line message.

Let all our feelings, let all our mental thoughts, let all our physical deeds be directed towards gratitude to the Divine.

Don't work out of fear or greed, because no matter how much we achieve out of greed, we will not be fulfilled. It is like pouring ghee (clarified butter) into the fire. Can we quench fire by pouring ghee into it? Never! All our actions that are done out of greed will only create more desire and make our senses weak, tired and incomplete. In the same way, all our laziness born out of fear will only make our mind restless and incomplete. We may not be doing things physically, but our mind will be worrying.

If we have become a *karma yogi* out of greed, our senses will be weakened. How much can we run? If we become a *Sannyāsi* out of fear, again, we may not do anything physically but the whole day we will be worrying.

A simple truth:

When a man doesn't have money, the problem is money. When he gets money, the problem is sex. When he gets sex, the problem is comforts. When he gets comforts and everything is going well, he starts worrying about death. Some incompletion or the other will always make his mind powerless.

Don't think that all the *Sannyasis* sitting in the Himalayas are in bliss. No! Unless they create the space of completion, they cannot experience power and joy. Unless the very space changes, they cannot experience bliss. Bliss is directly related to our inner space. Our whole life will be spent in doing and having if we are caught in fear and greed. If we surrender ourselves to being, doing and having both will happen to us with tremendous ecstasy.

Never work out of greed because whatever we achieve is going to be taken away at the time of death. Never become silent and inactive out of fear because there is really nothing to lose. Whether we are afraid or not, everything is going to be taken away at the time of death. So why be afraid? In either case, why not be blissful?

One important thing: Working without motivation is completely unheard of today. All psychologists, psychiatrists and scientists always emphasize that we cannot work without motivation. That is why there are so many motivational Gurus today. These people have come to the conclusion that 'work without motivation is not possible' after analysis on diseased patients, not on enlightened beings. They never had a specimen of a Buddha! They never encountered an enlightened person. That is why they say that work without motivation is impossible.

I tell you, work without motivation is the only real work. It will never make us tired! Every moment we will be working out of bliss.

Devotion Above Action

5.5 *He who knows, knows that the state reached by renunciation*
[sāṅkhya] and action [karma] are one and the same.
State reached by renunciation can also be achieved by action,
know them to be at the same level and see them as they are.

5.6 *Renunciation without devotion afflicts one with misery, Oh mighty-armed one. The wise person engaged in devotional service attains the Supreme without delay.*

5.7 *The person working in devotion, who is a pure being, self-controlled and having conquered the senses, identifies his Self with the Self of all beings. Though engaged in work, he is never entangled.*

5.8, 5.9 *One who knows the truth, though engaged in seeing, hearing,*
touching, smelling, eating, going, dreaming, and breathing, always
knows within himself that—'I never do anything at all.'
While talking, letting go, receiving, opening, closing,
he considers that the senses are engaged with their sense objects.

yat sāṅkhyaiḥ prāpyate sthanaṁ tad yogair api gamyate I
ekaṁ sāṅkhyaṁ ca yogaṁ ca yaḥ paśyati sa paśyati II 5.5

One who knows that the state reached through *sāṅkhya yoga* and *karma yoga* are both one and the same, and that the state reached by *sāṅkhya yoga* can also be achieved by *karma yoga*, sees both of them in the same level and sees things as they are.

Beautiful verse! Not all of us are *karma yogi* or doers and not all of us are Sannyāsis or monks. No Sannyāsi is a Sannyāsi for 24 hours. When he surrenders himself to the greed, he is a doer. No *karma yogi* is a doer for 24 hours. When he surrenders to fear, he is a Sannyāsi. So, whenever we make an optimistic decision, we are a *karma yogi.* Whenever we make a pessimistic decision, we are Sannyāsi. It is we who play both the roles.

Who is an optimist and who is a pessimist? An optimist is a man who created the airplane. A pessimist is a man who created the seat-belt. In life you always play both the roles. Sometimes you are an optimist and sometimes you are a pessimist. Here, both can lead to the same goal if the inner space is pure and complete. Anything created out of greed will create more greed. Anything created out of fear will create more fear. Anything created out of incompletion will create more incompletion.

Please listen: Whenever we move our body while feeling a particular emotion, that emotion gets settled inside our system. That emotion will become part of us and get created again and again in our system. Jiḍḍu Kṛṣṇamurti, an Enlightened Master from India, made a wonderful statement about emotions. He says, 'If you can, try to remain centered, silent, without moving your body when a particular emotion rises in you, without co-operating with it. Within eleven times, or I can say within eleven emotional upsets, if you have managed to be this way, you will be liberated from that emotion.'

For example, if you are caught in an emotion, say lust or fear, then for eleven cycles, whenever that emotion rises in your being, don't allow your body to co-operate. Don't allow your body to flow or move with that emotion. Within eleven cycles, I assure you, you will be liberated from that emotion. You may think, 'What is this, *Swamiji?* Just eleven times! Is it so easy?' It is easy. All great things are easy. Only we complicate them because we don't believe that anything is easy.

A small story:

> A person goes to the doctor and asks, 'Doctor, how much will you charge to pull this tooth out?' The doctor says, 'Ninety dollars.' This person asks, 'Ninety dollars just for a two minute job?'
>
> The doctor says, 'I can do it more slowly if you like!'

We don't believe in simplicity. We want to complicate things.

I can tell you with integrity and authenticity, eleven times is too much. When that emotion rises in you, don't cooperate. Let your body not go after that emotion. Don't be taken away by that emotion, whether it is anger, irritation, depression, lust, fear or anything else. Just decide, 'I am not going to be taken away by this emotion. I am completing with it.'

I tell you, within three or four times, you will be liberated from that emotion because you will learn the technique of completion. You will have the key now in your hand: How not to be taken away by that emotion, how to be complete, rooted in your Self, in your being. Whether it is anger or fear or greed, it gets more power and strength if your body cooperates with it. With whatever emotion your body moves, that emotion gets recorded inside your system. And that emotion will happen again and again, and much more intensely. Both frequency and intensity of that emotion will increase.

There is a movie, 'What the Bleep Do We Know?' In this movie, they show this idea beautifully. It is a truth from *Vedānta*. They say that whenever an emotion happens within your system, it is like a shower of rain. The emotion pours like rain. It happens inside your system, in your being. There are particular cells that catch these emotions. For example, if you think with anger, there are particular cells that catch anger as an emotion. Not only do they catch the emotion, they start reproducing as well. Each cell will create at least four or five more cells that can catch this emotion.

Listen. An important truth is that the basic quality of life is reproduction and expansion. This is the survival instinct governed by the *svādiṣṭhāna cakra*, the fear energy center within our body. Reproduction is governed by the *mūlādhāra cakra*, the sex energy center in our body. These cells that catch the anger emotion start reproducing and each cell creates five or six more cells. Next time, when the anger shower happens, all these cells will also catch the same emotion. They grow to the same original size. Now these cells also start reproducing. The third time, when the shower happens, all these cells catch the emotion and start storing it. That is why, every time we experience the same emotion, it becomes stronger and stronger. We are addicted to that emotion. If we are affected by anger for ten minutes the first time, then the next time, it becomes twenty minutes, then half an hour. This is how the emotion becomes stronger and stronger.

In our being, again and again, when we cooperate with these negative emotions, we create the same type of mood, the same type of pattern and lifestyle in us. Not only will this emotion get recorded in us, but we will express the same thing to others also. What we have within us is what we will vomit on others also.

Drop Greed and Fear, Live Power and Joy

If we are working to strengthen our greed, we will be caught by the emotion of greed and we will radiate that emotion. Next, if we strengthen our fear, again, we will be caught by that emotion of fear and express that emotion, torturing others with it. Be very clear: Warriors are caught in fear. That is why they torture others. They give fear to others. Warriors are the most cowardly people. A real warrior is a person who has conquered his being; who has won his being. Only he can be the only real warrior. If we do anything out of fear, we will reproduce the same fear in others.

Now, take a few minutes to sit and analyze, 'Throughout this life, all these years I was driven by greed and fear. What have I achieved? What have I got? Where am I standing? What has really happened?' Consciously and actively think about it. Consciously allow this idea to work on you. Decide, 'From today, I will not do anything out of greed or out of fear.' Immediately the fear will rise in you, 'What will happen to my bills? What will happen to my house? Who will repay the mortgages? What will happen to my car? My kids, who will feed them? What will happen to my social prestige and name and fame?'

Understand, you have enough energy and strength to maintain yourself without fear and greed. All you need is trust that you don't need energy from fear or greed to run your life. That is the first thing you need to understand. You have enough potential energy to live your life and to achieve what you want.

When you come down to this planet, you bring enough energy to live all your desires or to achieve whatever you want to achieve in this life; to create your reality as you want. You have already brought enough fuel. You don't need fuel from fear or greed. You always think, 'If I stop fueling myself with fear or greed, I may stop working.' No. There is enough reserve fuel in you. But psychologists can never believe that unmotivated action is possible because they have never seen a Buddha. They conclude, 'Only with motivation can a man work.' What motivation have birds got to sing? But modern day psychologists are so focused on sex that even for that, they have started giving a meaning! They say that the bird is calling out to its partner. They can't see anything as it is.

That is why here, Kṛṣṇa beautifully says—'*yaḥ paśyati sa paśyati*'. The man who is beyond the pull of fear and greed is the only one who can see things as they are. If you are caught in fear or greed, you will see things only as you *want*, never as they *are*. For example, on seeing a beautiful, tall building, a man who is caught in greed will think 'If I have at least one building like this, how nice it will be!' The man caught in fear will think, 'I should not see these things. They stress me out. I should go and live in the forest.' But only a person who is liberated from these two emotions will see it as it is.. His seeing will be a pure perception of *seeing*, beyond any patterns.

Now, decide strongly, 'Throughout my life, I have been either pushed by fear or pulled by greed. Do I want to continue that?' For someone trained and conditioned by society, it will be very difficult to believe that you don't need energy from greed or fear to live. I know you are thinking, 'He is talking, so let us listen. What can be done?' I know thousands of questions are rising in your mind. But let me tell you: Your whole past, whatever your age may be, you lived only fueled by fear and greed.

Just decide, 'For the next ten days I will trust the words of Kṛṣṇa. I will practice this truth with integrity and authenticity. I don't need fuel from fear or greed because I have brought enough energy.' When the Divine sends you to earth, He sends you with whatever you need. In *Vedānta*, that is what we call *prārabdha karma*. When you come down you bring enough of energy for your senses and body to acquire whatever it needs to live life blissfully. The only problem is you don't trust that you have brought everything. And after coming down, you accumulate more and more desires from others and then you try to fulfill all those desires too.

Work only for your desires. Don't waste your life working for others' desires. Decide clearly, 'For the next ten days, I will work only out of my power, my joy and bliss. I will do everything out of my completion.' I can assure you, it will transform your life. Anyway, I am going to be here even after ten days. If it does not work out, come and catch me! I tell you, just living ten days out of joy and bliss rather than fear and greed will transform your whole life. This one idea can liberate you straightaway from all bondages.

When you start practicing this, for the first few days you will feel a little unsettled because a new inner space is created. Say 'No' to any desire or any fear that comes up. Initially, you will feel some emptiness, a vacuum, but don't worry. In a few days you will beautifully settle with the new space. Don't worry when you fail a few times. Starting this way is much better than staying in fear of failure. So start! At least you will know the technique. If you don't even start, you will not even know where you are failing. I tell you with integrity, it will transform your whole life. It will give you such great strength and courage that invariably you will be liberated. Don't be bothered about the initial feeling of emptiness. It is like this: If we don't have anybody to nag us we will feel we are missing something! So, when you practice this, you will feel you are missing that constant nagging. Don't worry. You will settle into that new consciousness. Your whole being will become new.

It is important that you trust that you have enough energy to run without fear and greed. Only children need candy to make them work. For you, trust in power and joy of completion should be enough. Now, you are all grown-up. If you still need fear or greed, then you have grown only physically and not mentally.

One more thing: In just ten days, you will not lose your wealth. Is there anybody who thinks, 'If I practice for ten days, I may lose all my wealth?' If that is the case, that wealth is not worth having. It is better to lose it. In ten days if you can lose it, do you think it is worth having it? The earlier it is lost, the better it is for your being.

Remove the tremendous stress and load from your inner space. Decide, 'For ten days, I will do all my actions out of deep bliss, out of a settled mood of powerfulness and joy.' If you practice this, the constant irritation that remains in you will disappear. Knowingly or unknowingly, you carry constant irritation in you. That is why all of us are just waiting to burst and explode even for small things.

Look into yourself: How many of you can authentically cognize, agree that you carry that constant irritation in you? Raise your hand (A few raise). Others are not authentic! Everyone carries it. This irritation we carry in our inner space is because of fear and greed. There is uneasiness between you and your being. That uneasiness expresses itself continuously to others. That uneasiness is what I call dis-ease.

Let you be liberated from it from today. So, decide that just for ten days, you will not fuel yourself with fear and greed. You will suddenly feel a new energy coming up from your being—pure enthusiasm and causeless auspicious energy. Causeless auspicious energy is what we call Śiva.

In Saṃskṛit, 'Śiva' means causeless auspiciousness, reasonless energy. It is possible to live with that reasonless, unmotivated energy. Only two things are needed for that. The first thing is trust that you have that energy. The next thing is starting to live it. Only these two things are needed to reach the Divine Consciousness. When we start working with the causeless auspicious energy, we become Śiva. Otherwise, we are Śava (dead body).

Here, Kṛṣṇa does not refer to renunciation the way we traditionally understand it. Normally we think renunciation is giving up everything, especially responsibility. Just by so-called renunciation without completion, if we just go to the Himalayas and try to meditate, we will not become a Sannyāsi. When we use the word 'renounce' the way we understand it, we exclude something. Exclusion can never be the solution. When we say 'I should give up or avoid something', we exclude some creation of Existence. When we try to renounce the world, we are renouncing the creation of Existence. We are trying to prove that we are more intelligent than Existence. Our renunciation then becomes a show of our ego, even though this may not seem very obvious to us.

Actually, we try to renounce because we want to escape from the situation. The outer world, situations or people are never the cause of trouble in us. How can they control us? It is our patterns of fear and greed and the projections of our mind that are really the cause of all the trouble. Ever minute, our mind continuously creates subtle expectations of how things should be, how people should be, how life should be. The thought pattern needs to change from running away from something due to fear of it to facing the reality. Running away from material pleasures due to fear of facing reality or guilt imposed by society cannot be called renunciation.

Just sit down for five minutes and be aware of how you perceive situations. With completion and awareness, look at everything you think and do, and you can understand what I mean. When we come to an understanding of our own self and are able to live as a witness to everything that goes on around us, unaffected by situations and people around us, we become a realized soul, living enlightenment. If we do things fueled by fear and greed, we become hypocrites.

Brahmacarya literally means living with reality. It does not mean celibacy, as you understand it. When we are complete and ecstatic, flowing spontaneously in tune with the wonderful symphony of Existence, we are true brahmacāris.

When we are completely in the present space of completion, totally involved in what we are doing, we become the action itself, we no longer exist as the doer. That is when we have truly renounced the sense of 'I am doing', or the ego. Then we are true *Sannyāsis*. All we need is to experience that behind the shallow emotions that exist in the periphery, at the very core of our being is a complete, solid, silent center that is absolutely unaffected by external incidents. It is a pure witness to everything and is eternally pure. Don't try to go to the Himalayas to escape from the world. Create the Himalayas within you. Realize the silent, complete center in you. Create the space of completion in you! Look at the cause and address the root pattern in *your world* rather than addressing the symptoms of *the world*.

You see, renunciation, *Sannyāsa* is going beyond desires, including 'desirelessness.' Apart from material desires, the desire to be spiritual and attain God is also a desire. The mind always hankers after something in the future. Only when we drop all desires, when we are completely at ease and ecstatic in the present moment of completion, we have gone beyond the clutches of the mind. Only then do we see reality as It exists here and now.

Seeing this reality *as It exists* is what Kṛṣna beautifully calls—*yah paśyati sa paśyati*. Otherwise, we always live in our world of illusion, *māya*, because the future is unreal; it is an illusion. The real, the present, can never be perceived by the mind because it is beyond logic. That is why Existence can never be understood and experienced by the mind. The truth can only be experienced. How can the limited mind even come close to understanding the vastness and the splendor of Existence? How can we desire God or Enlightenment, which we have never known? We can always desire Enlightenment in a way that fits our limited, inadequate cognition, but that is still our imagination.

EXPERIENCE YOUR TRUE NATURE

You can never possess or achieve Enlightenment. It is only Enlightenment that can possess you. It happens to you when you drop all desires. Actually, our true nature is neither pure nor impure. Whether we accept it or not, believe it or not, we are bliss. Our very nature is bliss. Our true nature itself is self-control. When we realize and experience that our being is pure bliss, the other emotions automatically drop.

When we allow ourselves to be our true nature, to be bliss, we live spontaneously and respond with intelligence instead of programmed unconscious reactions. Then there is no need to control the senses because they are under the control of the ultimate Existence. There is no question of having to control them.

In the Mahābhārat war, Kṛṣṇa drives Arjuna's chariot. The horses represent the senses held beautifully in control by the divine charioteer. He drives the being represented by the warrior, in the body represented by the chariot towards victory, towards bliss. When the individual consciousness surrenders control to the Divine, the Divine controls the body-mind-spirit and steers one towards one's true nature, bliss.

We have programmed reactions, default cognitions about everything. We see a situation and we react based on others' expectation from us, *anyakāra* and our expectation from others, *svānyakāra*. We can only react by looking up our database of the past records, referring to the reaction of people then. If what we did was appreciated, we will react the same way. If we are not appreciated and there is a gap between others' expectation from us and our expectation from others, we create a self-doubt and feel uncomfortable and restless. And to remove the discomfort, we now react in a different manner, one that we think will be acceptable to others.

We have forgotten what it is to respond with intelligence. No situation can be exactly the same as before. How can it be? Can a river flow in exactly the same way at two different points? The very water would have changed from the time it flows from one point to the other. Life is like a river. It is continuously changing.

Existence is energy. It can never repeat itself. Every moment is unique. We see it from the limited perception of our mind, and organize life into different categories. We say, 'These are pleasant situations, those are unpleasant situations, this is good, that is bad, this is right, that is wrong, this should happen, that should not.' It is not Existence that makes these distinctions but us. If we can allow this new cognition to penetrate us, we can simply relax. We will then allow our consciousness to respond.

Have the courage to live life with intelligence, with consciousness and completion, with spontaneity. Just this small shift in your space can do wonders for you; every moment will then be a celebration! When the intelligence happens, the compassion also descends. Compassion for the whole world automatically happens in you because you see yourself in every one. How can you feel anything but compassion then? That is why Masters can only feel compassion and responsibility towards the whole world.

When we flow in tune with Existence, we become a channel for the divine energy to flow through us. If the bamboo can remain hollow, it will become a beautiful flute and simply the air from the lips of the Divine will come out of the flute as heavenly music. Instead, if the bamboo is blocked with dirt in the form of ego, it will remain dead and can only be used for carrying a dead body!

These verses of Kṛṣṇa are very powerful, but often misinterpreted.

'One who knows the truth, though engaged in seeing, hearing, touching, smelling, eating, going, dreaming, and breathing knows that he never does anything.' It is like you commit a murder and then claim you didn't do it but your hands did it! Be very clear: Not being the doer does not mean we give up responsibility for our actions. It means exactly the opposite. When we are so involved in the action, when we are completely relaxed, we are overflowing with compassion and love, and we just do out of the blissful energy in us.

Listen. When we are complete and total in what we do, our whole intelligence, our whole energy will be behind the act; we become the action. The action and we are no longer separate. Energy is intelligence. So, when our energy is not total, our intelligence is not completely behind the action. When the energy behind the action is total, whatever we do will always radiate the blissful energy that is behind the action.

Another important understanding from this verse: Every moment, every action, whether it is talking or breathing or seeing, should be done with awareness and completion. That is true meditation. Many people claim that they have been meditating for thirty or forty years. Even after so many years, the person inside remains exactly the same. Absolutely zero transformation has happened. Meditation is actually a quality that needs to be added to our life. It should permeate the very way in which we view life, the space from which we perceive everything. When we infuse the space of completion into every action, we are in meditation.

So how to be in completion? We can be complete only when we can distance and disidentify ourselves from what is happening now and what we think happened in the past. When we can witness the past happening without identifying and getting involved in it ourselves, only then can we watch the scene as It Is. Otherwise we assume some role in the scene. When that happens, we create some incomplete cognitions, some vested interest in it. We have some expectation that things should happen in a certain way. The moment we get involved and identify ourselves with the happening, the distance between the scene and us has dropped and we can no longer be the witness to see things as they are.

It is just like when we are in a dream, we don't realize it is a dream. We think everything that is happening is reality. The moment we wake up from the dream we realize in a flash that it was just a dream. The way we are living life now is exactly the same. We are living life in the dream of the future and the past. And we think that the dream is reality.

The reality is actually in the present, which is the space of completion. When we realize this, we simply wake up to the true reality from the dream of illusion. Then, we understand that the senses, body and mind are not us. We are something much beyond these. With this awareness we become complete and blissful.

Controlling The Mind

5.10 *He who acts without attachment, giving up and surrendering to the eternal consciousness,*
he is never affected by sin, in the same way
that the lotus leaf is never affected by water.

5.11 *The Yogis, giving up attachment,*
act with the body, mind, intelligence,
even with the senses for the purpose of self-purification.

5.12 *One who is engaged in devotion, gives up attachment*
to the outcome of one's actions and is centered, is at peace.
One who is not engaged in devotion, attached to the outcome of one's action, becomes entangled.

5.13 *One who is controlled, giving up all the activities of the mind,*
surely remains in happiness in the city of nine gates (body),
Neither doing anything, nor causing anything to be done.

Time and again Kṛṣṇa talks about detachment. This is the whole essence of the *Gītā.* This detachment is renunciation. Renunciation of attachment is true renunciation. You can give up all material possessions and move into a forest or an ashram, but if the mind still hankers for those possessions, renunciation has not happened.

One can still be very much in the material world, busy with wheeling and dealing, and yet be totally detached about the outcome.

Kṛṣṇa says here, '*saṅgaṁ tyaktvā karoti yaḥ* (5.10)—Action without attachment is renunciation.' It is only this renunciation that leads to liberation.

If you see the lotus flower, it grows in a dirty pond; its stalk is completely inside the dirty water. The flower is so beautifully above the water and the dirt around it is hardly noticed! Similarly, when you are neck-deep in the activities of the world and yet unaffected by what goes on, when your core is undisturbed, you have reached the goal of renunciation.

A small story:

> A Master was walking with his disciple when they came to a river.
>
> The disciple asked, 'Master, are we going to cross this river now?'
>
> The Master calmly replied, 'Yes, we are. And be careful not to wet your feet.'

The Master was trying to tell him that spirituality is all about crossing the ocean of life without getting your feet wet. Spirituality is *not* about running away from worldly things. Be very clear about this.

A beautiful history about Swāmi Brahmānanda, a direct disciple of Śrī Rāmakṛṣṇa Paramahamsa:

> One day Swāmi Brahmānanda was meditating in Brindāvan.
>
> A devotee came and placed a costly blanket before him as an offering. Swāmi said nothing. He just silently observed what was going on. A couple of hours later, a thief came by, spotted the blanket, and took away the blanket. Still, the Swami watched in the same way, silently, with no reaction. Some of the junior disciples were very perturbed that a costly blanket had been stolen.
>
> However, it made no difference to Brahmānanda.

These realized souls were so centered in themselves that the outer world incidents happening in the periphery did not affect their core in any way. When we can become like this, we won't identify with outer world incidents. We will not get caught in the sway of emotions.

The basic truth behind creating this space of centeredness and completion is really this: Existence is a loving Mother caring for us every moment, providing all that we need. When this understanding happens, we surrender to Existence. The wave drops into the ocean, blissfully aware that it is a part of the ocean. It no longer feels it is a separate entity trying to fight Existence, thinking that the ocean, the Whole, is its enemy.

Surrender needs to happen out of a deep understanding, not out of a superficial acceptance of the inevitable. If it happens out of acceptance, it will be just a compromise out of fear. There is no point in saying, 'Oh, it is destiny. It is written on my forehead and it is foretold by the stars.' This is not true. We have free will and we can do what we want. We neither have to accept nor reject, but surrender to the flow of life with the true understanding that we are being taken care of. When this completion happens out of deep understanding, it is beautiful, total and it is true.

Listen. One more important truth. To whom or to what we surrender is not important. What is important is the surrender itself. Swāmi Vivekānanda says that all our prayers to God do only one thing: they awaken our own inner potential energy. When we pray intensely, our own inner potential energy is awakened and it showers its blessings on us in the form that we believe as God, irrespective of what form we worship. Having the wisdom or *buddhi* to understand that Existence cares for us, and surrendering to Existence is the ultimate intelligence. Realizing that Existence is not just a brute force or power but that it is intelligent energy is the key to a life of bliss.

WITNESS AND BE COMPLETE

Again and again, Kṛṣṇa is repeating a single point in various ways: action without attachment—*saṅgaṁ tyaktvā karoti yaḥ* (5.10). He emphasizes that life happens only when we live as a witness to everything that happens, when we do not identify and attach with external incidents. We just have to watch what is happening in and around us without letting what happens outside affect our inner space.

The moment we catch this thread and start living life in the space of completion, we will find that all our incompletions simply disappear. It is not that anything outside has changed. It is just that what we wish to see has changed.

Of course, the way in which we live automatically creates an effect, a transformation in others as well. We attract incidents that fall in tune with our desires and thoughts. When we are blissful inside, whatever happens outside will also be blissful. This is because what we see outside is just a projection of what is inside us. It has been scientifically proven that the results of experiments conducted by different researchers under identical conditions vary depending on the mood of the scientists. In one study of elementary particles such as quarks, scientists were amazed that the behavior of these particles varies with different observers. What we see is our reality. If we see without wishing to change anything, we are in completion with reality.

Even the same situation will be seen in a completely different way when we witness it with completion. Automatically, no emotion can sway us because now we are just witnessing, we no longer have any vested interest or incompletion in the situation. Our state is in no way affected by what others say or do. Then, we are Masters unto ourselves.

We are never totally involved in anything that we do. The person who is aware, who is complete, who is in the present, is completely involved every moment. He feels the hunger completely through every cell of the body when hunger happens. He lives the hunger totally. When the food is before him, he enjoys every morsel of the food completely. Just like having the sense of taste is very natural when we eat with awareness, so it is with all the senses.

Just being totally involved in whatever we do is meditation. Just living in the space of completion, enjoying the present moment is meditation. You must have experienced in your own life, when you are intensely involved in something, you forget yourself. It can be as simple as painting or reading or anything. When you go deep into it, you forget yourself. When we go deeply into any emotion, only that emotion remains and we cease to exist. This is what we mean by 'totality.' This moment of 'you' disappearing, you may experience for just a few seconds in your current lifestyle. But if you work on being intense and total in everything, this experience of 'you' disappearing will happen more often to you and for longer periods. Soon, you master the art of doing work intensely, and just being absent. We become independent of the work that goes on outside.

Here, Kṛṣṇa gives us a technique to realize who we are. By giving up attachment to the sense objects, by dropping all false identifications with the body, senses and mind, we can live life with intelligence and this leads us to self-purification, self-completion.

Kṛṣṇa tells us that our job is only to do the work, not to be concerned about the results. He beautifully says, '*brahmaṇy ādhāya karmāṇi* (5.10)—do the work surrendering to the eternal consciousness.' We need to keep doing things because we have so much loving energy inside us. We can just exude energy without any reason or any expectation. When we are like this, we are not bothered about the results. When I say we are not bothered about the results, I don't mean that out of a frustrated or cynical conclusion. What I mean is that we don't even know to expect results because we are continuously moving and expressing our blissful inner energy, that's all.

We are just living in the space of completion and doing whatever that comes in our way to do. We are just flowing joyfully, that's all. We flow with the Universal energy. This flowing energy is real love.

When we identify ourselves with our body, mind and ego, we alienate ourselves from the rest of Existence. Instead of playing our role in the divine drama as an actor, we start thinking that we are the actor and we actually go through all the emotional turmoil that we were just supposed to enact. When we become entangle and we miss the whole joy of the divine drama, and feel that life is a big trauma!

In the same way, when we just do what we have at hand, without being bothered about the result, we are always happy. Once we start thinking about the result of our actions, we lose the joy of doing what we are doing at this moment. When we are established in ourselves, we are automatically in peace irrespective of anything that exists or does not exist around us. We are not bothered about the result because we have given our best, to our peak possibility.

> Once a man went to Ramaṇa Maharṣi, and said, 'Bhagavān, I want peace!'
>
> Ramaṇa replied, 'From your own statement, just remove the word 'I,' remove the word 'want' and what remains is *peace*!'

All our want for peace is all a want. We don't know how to be satisfied as we are. Just think, how can we want something like peace, that by its very nature has the absence of want as the criterion to be able to exist? When we start to want peace, we create desires in us. That desire drives us to do various things for getting peace and we once again start to worry about the results of those actions. These worries take us away from peace and then again we want peace. So this becomes a vicious circle. We wanted peace in the first place; so we do something to fulfill that want. Doing something creates worry and then once again we want to be free from these worries and be peaceful. This is a vicious circle because we want peace. When we drop the idea of wanting peace, when we can just be and let Existence take care, peace automatically happens. So, absence of want is the criterion to be peaceful.

Some people say that they want to be left peaceful without worries. The peace they are talking about is not a living peace; it is a dead peace because life is too much for them to handle. Real peace is something that is in us all the time irrespective of what is going on outside. Our peace is in no way related to or dependent on the people and situations around us. Real peace is nothing but the bliss that we feel inside ourselves. When peace is born out of bliss, it keeps us as well as others in a peaceful state. When we are satisfied and complete with ourselves, we do not depend on anything external to be peaceful.

We don't understand that every tomorrow comes only as today. When the tomorrow comes as today, we simply miss it because we are now looking at tomorrow once again! When we work without unnecessarily thinking about the result, all our energies will be used towards realizing the goal. The energy will not be dissipated in imagining the results. The power of desire, *icchā śakti*, will be converted to the power of action, *kriya śakti*. The desire may initially be a goal, but what is important is the path and not the end result. The goal is merely a byproduct.

Suppose a child is playing with some small toy and you bring him a new big toy. If you take away the small toy from its hands, what will the child do? It will start yelling and crying. Even if you explain you have a much better, bigger toy, will it listen? No! Just give it the new toy and suddenly, it will forget the old one and start enjoying the new one.

In the same way, Existence also tries to give us a big toy. Just imagine the kind of toy that Existence has given us—the whole of Itself! Enjoy it to the fullest. Celebrate it and express your gratitude! Your mind will always tell you that the small toy, your little dreams, your ego, is the most important thing and you need it to survive. For a few days, decide to drop your expectations, your fears, and your protection of the ego.

Just live life in a simple way. Be complete every moment, enjoying the splendor of nature. Enjoy every thing that Existence has created. Start witnessing simple yet wonderful things like the sunrise in the morning; listen to the chirping of the birds. Look deeply into a flower and you will find God. Just these few moments will show us a whole new dimension of our Being. They will show us what it is to enjoy life without a reason, without running behind or away from something. They will teach us how to relax into the welcoming, embracing arms of Existence.

THE CITY OF NINE GATES

In these verses, Kṛṣṇa refers to the body, which has nine gates to the external world: the two eyes, two nostrils, two ears, mouth and the two organs of evacuation. It may seem strange and absurd that we can just be neither doing nor causing anything to be done.

Here, Kṛṣṇa does not refer to not doing anything out of laziness and indulgence. Actually, if we can become intensely lazy, we can be in meditation! Here, the laziness is a deep mental laziness where the mind has been stilled. It has stopped all activity but the body moves according to the will of the divine. We are in the midst of intense activity and yet are not doing anything. The mind separates the doer from the action. It is the mind that defines who the doer is and what the action is. In the conventional sense, when we say lazy, we are referring to the body. The body is lazing around but the mind is completely active. It is carrying on its work of creating and linking unrelated thoughts. When the mind becomes lazy, instead of the body, we drop the mind also. That is when we stop identifying the action as being separate from ourselves.

Kṛṣṇa is talking of being so completely involved in something that we become the very action itself. First, we become the witness to the action, only then we can become completely involved in it. When we start distancing ourselves and become a witness, only then we can be completely involved in the action and then the doer and the action merge into each other. It is not the action that gives us the joy but the conscious experience of the bliss within us through the action that actually gives us happiness and bliss.

A small story:

> A dog found a piece of bone and was very happy. It started chewing on the bone but the piece was very dry. It chewed and chewed and after some time, its own gums started bleeding from rubbing against the dry, hard bone.
>
> The dog was very happy to finally taste blood. It licked the bone even more, making more blood ooze from its own mouth. Little did the dog realize that the blood it was enjoying was its very own! The bone had nothing to do with the taste of the blood!

When we realize through experience or understanding that the bliss in life is completely within us, we will get over our wrong cognition that external pleasures are what give us joy. When we really cognize that we are already all that we can imagine we want to be and much more than that, we have reached the ultimate goal.

We will relax into the loving arms of Existence and just flow with it beautifully. Until then it will be a struggle to achieve what we already are.

You see, when we leave the ownership to someone else, we are free. The burden is not on us. That is when we can be peaceful and blissful. As long as we think we are the owners, we always have to face the worry that comes with ownership. Why do you want to carry that worry? Let the Universe take care and you carry on with your work!

Cleansing Ignorance With Knowledge

5.14 *The Master does not create activities or make people do*
or connect with the outcome of the actions.
All this is enacted by the material nature.

5.15 *The Lord, surely, neither accepts anyone's sins nor good deeds.*
Living beings are confused by the ignorance
that covers the knowledge.

5.16 *But, whose ignorance is destroyed by the knowledge,*
their knowledge, like the rising sun lights up everything,
throws light on the Supreme Consciousness [tat param].

5.17 *One whose intelligence, mind and faith are in the Supreme and*
one who has surrendered to the Supreme,
his misunderstandings are cleansed through knowledge
and he goes towards liberation.

Kṛṣṇa gives a very deep understanding here. He says, 'I do not create activities or make people do or connect with the fruits of the actions. All this is done by the material nature of humans.'

na kartṛtvaṁ na karmāṇi lokasya sṛjati prabhuḥ |
na karma phala saṁyogaṁ svabhāvas tu pravartate || 5.14

Kṛṣṇa is talking about the creation of the Universe itself here, not just about individuals. Understand, nothing in this Universe can be created or destroyed. When I say, nothing, I mean nothing. Everything that exists has always existed in some form or the other. It will continue to exist in some form or the other.

Science also says the same thing that matter and energy are

inter-convertible and energy can never be destroyed. The beauty of the *Vedas* is that they say what science is now understanding. What is the last line of science was the first line of the *Upaniṣads.*

THE END OR THE BEGINNING?

The *Īśāvāsya Upaniṣad* opens with the words—*Īśā vāsyaṁ idaṁ sarvaṁ*—meaning, 'all that exists arises from energy.' Now after so much scientific research, quantum physics has concluded that matter and energy are one and the same. But thousands of years ago, this was the first statement in the *Īśāvāsya Upaniṣad,* which says everything is energy.

People ask me, 'Who created this Universe?' I tell you, the Universe itself is the creator, the created and the creation. If the creator and the creation were different, it means that the Creator is more intelligent than the creation. But the creation and the Creator are one and the same; they are both divine. That is what is meant by *līla*, the divine play. The unmanifest, *avyakta,* the formless Energy made itself manifest, *vyakta* in the creation. The Universe created itself.

Why? We cannot answer the question 'why' for this in the logical plane. If we get caught in the 'why' in the beginning, we will be stuck with it forever. Understand, these questions cannot be answered by the mind since we cannot answer these questions logically. God created man in His own mould so that He could experience Divinity. You see, God as God, as the *avyakta or* unmanifest, as pure energy cannot see the Divinity outside of Himself. When He is everything, how can He see Himself separate? Everything exists as a part of Him; so He cannot look to see the Divine outside.

It is like this: Can you say how you experience, how you feel your hand from inside your body? No! On the other hand, can you describe how you feel when you touch your own hand with the other hand? You will have some feeling, do you not? You can feel it because from outside, your two hands are separate; you can perceive them as different parts of your body. Similarly, God can experience and express Himself through man. Man is a part of God just like both the hands are a part of the same body and can be felt separately.

Now, just like one hand in itself cannot understand that the hand it is touching is a part of the same body man cannot understand that he is a part of God. What does it take for the hand to understand that the other hand is actually a part of the bigger whole called the body? It takes the cognition that the entire body is a single entity with the different parts of the body being integrated in it. Similarly, it takes the understanding of our consciousness to see that we, the individual consciousness, are a part of the Whole and are an integral and connected part of the collective consciousness. The individual ego can never understand the truth that it exists as a part of the Whole. The ego has to dissolve for the truth to be revealed and understood.

It is as if we want to see our own beauty, we can do that when we see our own reflection in a mirror. The mirror in which God sees Himself is man. Can the reflection be a separate entity from what it is reflecting? No! Man can experience and express the divine in him.

The game of life is all about man trying to realize the Divine in him and the Divine trying to express itself through man.

What Kṛṣṇa teaches here is actually a *sūtra*, a technique. Understand, when you are disturbed or angered by anything, the disturbance cannot disappear suddenly because it is a physiological happening. Your hormones have been released into your system; the body has been poisoned. But when you remain in the space of completion as a witness, even though the anger cannot go away immediately, there is the awareness in you that will dissipate the effect of the anger that remains in the periphery. The center, the core is untouched. You are now aware of these two points, the core and the periphery as two distinct identities co-existing.

This one glimpse will enrich you and become the strong support for you. The next time you see that you are being swayed by incompletions, you will remember this and such awareness will make you conscious and complete. Only when you are unconscious and ignorant you come under the sway of emotions or incompletions. This is what is meant by the term '*being centered in completion.*' You are no longer a slave to your emotions, or to others. Otherwise, anybody can shake you. They can push and pull you in different directions and you won't be integrated and whole.

Kṛṣṇa separates morality from spirituality in these verses. Heaven and hell are purely psychological. They exist only in our heads. You don't commit sin and then go to hell. You commit sin because you *are* in hell. When you are not aware, when you are disturbed and not at peace with yourself, you are in hell. The quality of your inner space is what decides whether you are in heaven or hell.

Please listen: live with the consciousness of completion and you can never make a mistake. Morality is just skin-deep. Understand, there is no such thing as virtue or sin. Everything is energy. What exists is energy. Energy cannot be categorized as good and bad. Emotions such as lust and anger are also energy. These so-called base emotions arise due to our own ignorance. When our awareness and understanding transform the base emotions, they become higher emotions. For instance, lust becomes love when the understanding happens. Just live every moment in bliss. Consciously decide that you will face every moment with deep completion, with deep ecstasy. The very decision will transform your life. Not only will you feel total and complete, you will radiate the bliss to others as well.

As long as the mind comes into play, liberation and bondage cannot exist independently. They depend on each other. Anything can be felt by the mind only in contrast, in opposites. We are in ignorance when we think that liberation is some state that we need to achieve. The moment we want to achieve or possess something, it will simply slip from our hands, like sand or water from our hands the moment we close our fist tightly.

The light of knowledge dispels the ignorance and we realize the state in which we have always been. We cannot remove the darkness directly. This is what I mean by something having a negative existence. Ignorance also can be removed by just shining the light of knowledge on it! Just like the rising sun removes the darkness of the night, the light of knowledge dispels the darkness of ignorance. What is that ignorance that we need to remove by bringing in the light of knowledge?

Whatever we do, we want to be happy, right? But the strange truth is, we are already pure bliss. I am not saying we have achieved bliss. I am saying we are bliss. Each one of us is pure bliss. The problem is we are not ready to accept this ultimate truth and relax, because the moment we accept this, we no longer have a separate personality; the ego has no basis to exist. It is our ego that makes us feel incomplete. The ego needs us to be a solid entity for it to exist. The mind always yearns to be occupied, running behind something. Only then can it survive. When we are pure bliss, we have nothing to run after because we are complete unto ourselves. If we look deeply, we can see clearly that it is us who choose to stay in suffering. We think that we want bliss and that we want to drop our ego. But deep down, we choose to stay with our ego.

Surrender Leads to Liberation

Kṛṣṇa gives us another technique to liberate ourselves. He says surrender leads to liberation, and happens when one's intelligence is focused on Him.

When we believe and cognize that there is a life force that is conducting this Universe and is taking care of us, we relax. When we relax, we can live and function at our peak potential. We can express our creativity and live spontaneously. We experience great freedom and liberation. This is surrender. This is true knowledge too. This is the knowledge that cannot be taught or picked up. The Master can simply transmit it when our being is ready to receive it.

All we need is the faith, the courage of authenticity to allow the supreme intelligence to guide us, to surrender our mind that oscillates between the extremes. The knowledge removes the ignorance. All our problems are due to lack of knowledge, due to ignorance. Whether it is fear or greed or worry or anger, all these emotions are able to control us because we are not aware. We allow them to unconsciously control us. When we bring a deep completion into anything, the solution simply stands out. When we go deeply into any emotion with deep awareness and complete with it, we can flower out of it. This is true knowledge, the knowledge of completion.

In times of extreme self-doubt, doubt your ego. Never doubt the Master. The Master is the only truth you can cling to when all else gives way. The Master is the only one who can guide you when everything seems to be confusing. So, first of all, you need to complete with this self-doubting pattern of constantly doubting yourself. Because you constantly doubt yourself, you doubt the truths of completion, the four *tattvas* (principles), you doubt everything. You doubt you. Because you doubt you, you doubt me.

Please listen, if you doubt you, you will doubt *me* also because I am inside you more than you exist in you! If you are occupying twenty to thirty percent of you, I am occupying sixty to seventy percent of you. So, naturally if you doubt *you*, you will doubt *me*. And, if you have anger towards *you*, you will have anger towards *me*!

Surrender can happen at different levels. Understand that the Master lives in all three energies—the body, his teachings and mission. The Master has no vested interests, no desires to fulfill in life. Masters come out of sheer compassion for the whole of mankind, to dispel the ignorance of seekers, to show them the light.

The Dog And The Dog-eater

5.18 *One who is full of knowledge and compassion sees with equal vision [samadarśinaḥ] , the learned brāhmaṇa, the cow, the elephant, the dog and the dog-eater.*

5.19 *In this life, surely, those whose minds are situated in equanimity have conquered birth and death.*
They are flawless like the Supreme [Brahma]
and therefore, are situated in the Supreme.

5.20 *One who does not rejoice at achieving something pleasent*
nor gets agitated on getting something unpleasent,
who is of steady intelligence, who is not deluded, one who knows
the Supreme [brahmavid], is situated in the Supreme.

5.21 *One who is not attached to the outer world sense pleasures,*
who enjoys in the Self, in that happiness,
he, having identified with his Self by engaging in the Supreme
[brahma-yoga], enjoys unlimited happiness.

Kṛṣṇa succinctly explains the neutrality and equanimity of Existence. Existence has no favorites. All comparative and hierarchical definitions are manmade.

Kṛṣṇa says there is no difference between a human and an animal, and that there is no difference between those we consider to be saints and those we consider to be sinners. A learned scholar, the priest and the brāhmaṇa should be seen as equal to an animal or a person who eats dogs. Even more dramatically, He says that one in full knowledge sees the dog and the dog-eater as the same—*śuni caiva śva-pāke ca paṇḍitāḥ sama-darśinaḥ* (5.18).

This is what Ādī Śaṅkara means when he sings the six verses of his Ātma Śatakam. 'I am not the enjoyer. I am not the enjoyed. I am not the enjoying. I am beyond all that; I am just the embodiment of Śiva.' This is one of the most beautiful messages from Śaṅkara. 'I am not the doer, I am not the deed, I am not the doing,' he says. 'I am just the witness, beyond all these.'

When we go beyond all three, the subject, object and verb, all connotations disappear. The eater and the eaten merge. We reach the source. There are no thoughts and there is no mind. There is just you, your being. That is the true you, the Supreme.

Existence continuously showers bliss upon each of us. Only we are not open to receive it. Existence sees everyone as equal. It does not discriminate. Everyone is a part of the same Existence. Similarly, Masters see the whole world as one with their own selves. That is why only they can show compassion to anyone and everyone.

EVERY ATOM IS DIVINE

External appearances are ephemeral. When we see the eternal, blissful being as the core of each and every one of us, we will realize the inherent divine nature of each of us. This knowledge, gained through the experience of the Self, results automatically in deep compassion towards the whole of Existence.

Classifications of lower species and higher species, good and bad are all made by society and by our minds, not by Existence. Only human beings think they are more intelligent than the rest of Nature!

A small story:

> One night, a thief knocked on the door of a monastery located in the middle of a forest. The master opened the door and allowed the man to spend the night in the monastery.
>
> The next morning, the thief thanked his host and asked for his permission to leave. He also confessed to the master

that he was a thief and had burgled the palace the previous night. The master was aghast.

He started weeping loudly, 'What a great sin I have committed by allowing a thief to spend a night in my monastery! I gave him food too. What can I do to make up for my sin?'

At that time, he heard a voice from the sky, weeping even louder than him, 'You are upset and weeping because you have looked after him for one night. What about me? I have been looking after him everyday for all these years!'

The master had actually become egoistic. He started feeling holier than others because of which he looked down upon the thief as a less holy person. God never differentiates between a sinner and a saint. These are all societal.

Every atom on Earth is divine. When we just realize this very life is a divine gift to us, our attitude changes from taking life for granted to one of gratitude to Existence for everything! Have you worked hard to earn this life? With every breath that you take every moment, the life energy flows into you and keeps you alive. We take for granted the life energy that converts bread into blood. The mind continuously runs behind 'more and more.'

If we make two lists: one list of what we have, what Existence has showered upon us and a second list of what we really want to have to feel happier, we will quickly realize how much longer the first list is. Have we ever strongly considered what our life would be like if we did not have even a small limb? Can you imagine the limitations we would have without a toe or thumb, not to speak of our eyes or ears? We take so much for granted. We assume that what we have been given is our rightful due and so we only crave for more. We are here as gifts of Nature. Instead of being grateful to Existence for what we have been showered with, we complain about what we do not have.

Remember that when God does not grant us what we seek, He is doing it out of deep compassion and wisdom. He does not grant many of our prayers because He knows that far better than us. We have no wisdom when it comes to asking.

The Divine is far wiser and knows what we really need. There is a huge difference between what we want and what we need. For the next couple of days, just try living with the attitude of gratitude, with love for everyone and everything around you, with a deep completion. Automatically, you will begin to experience every person and every happening as a unique creation of Existence, as a reflection of the Divine. Just decide consciously that you will respond with love, whatever may be the situation. Just the very attitude change will bring tremendous peace and relaxation into you.

Kṛṣṇa says, when you look every single thing without differentiation, without fear or favoritism, without attachment, then you are a true renunciate, a true *Sannyāsi*.

Death, Only A Passage

Can you look at death and birth in the same manner? We celebrate birth, we condole death. Why? Both are passages. Neither is a beginning nor an end. The cycle of life is continuous. We move seamlessly from birth through living into death and again into birth. It is just that in this life, we do not remember what happened in the period between our death in our previous birth and our birth this time. That loss of memory is for our own safety. We are perturbed by that loss of memory.

What we do not know frightens us. If we understand that death is no different from birth and that life after death may be no different from our current life, there will be no fear. This can happen when we have the experience of death while we are still alive. This is what we teach in our programs. An important thing: How we look at death reflects a lot of the way we look at life. I can say our perception of death changes our way of life.

Death is feared by most of us because it is considered a discontinuity. When we realize that death is just a continuation in some other form, we will not fear death. Then the joy of birth and the sadness at death will both be seen as the same. Our idea of birth and death is direct evidence of how we look at various situations in life. That is why understanding about birth and death is actually fundamental to leading a life of realization.

Understand, one who knows that what he sees is illusion, just a play of mind, he will not fear death. As long as we hold on to this illusion created by the mind that we call reality, we have a feeling of losing it when we think of death. When we see pain and pleasure as the same and are not affected by either of them, we will be free from the fear of death. Because then we realize that nothing is taken away from us when death comes.

Enlightened Masters' experience about death teaches us a lot. Bhagavān Ramaṇa Maharṣi got his enlightenment through a conscious experience of death. When Bhagavān was a young boy, one day he was just lying on his bed at his Uncle's house in Madurai, South India. Suddenly he got the feeling that he was going to die! He had two choices: to resist the feeling or to go through it. He chose the second, to go through death as it is, consciously. He became enlightened after he experienced the process of death.

Usually people resist, so they pass into a coma and leave the body in a state of unconsciousness. In our second level program, the *Nithya Kriya Yoga* or Life Bliss Program Level 2, we go into the complete understanding of death, what happens exactly when we die. We enrich you to experience the process of death and to understand how and what happens, so that there is no mystery and, therefore, there is no fear. At least once if we go through death with deep consciousness, we will lose our fear for death automatically.

Bhagavān was courageous enough to choose the second path. He allowed death to happen without any resistance. He saw clearly one by one, the parts of his body dying. Slowly, his whole body was dead, turning into ashes. Suddenly, he realized that something remained even after that, which cannot be destroyed. At that moment, it hit him that he was pure consciousness, beyond the body and mind! He was simply a witness to the whole thing! That knowledge was tremendous and it never left him. When he came back into his body, he was *Bhagavān Ramaṇa Maharṣi*, the Enlightened Master! When we conquer the fear of death, we conquer death itself, because death is just one more imagination! When we get over the cycle of greed and fear, we can be in equanimity in all situations in life; then we are situated in the supreme consciousness. It is then we have touched our core, our real Being.

STEADY YOUR INTELLIGENCE, GO BEYOND OPPOSITES

Kṛṣṇa goes on to explain the characteristics of one who is Supreme. He says that one who is of steady intelligence, *sthira buddhir asam-mūḍho;* one who does not get caught in the play of opposing emotions or patterns like pleasure and pain, happiness and misery, is truly not deluded and is established in the truth, and in the Supreme, *brahma-vid brahmaṇi sthitaḥ* (5.20). He is Supreme himself.

What do we need to know to get out of the whirlpool of emotions? If we look deeply, we will see that all our emotional incompletions like fear, greed or worry, at the root, are born of an expectation for a certain situation to happen in a certain way. We live in a virtual world of fantasy and when there is a gap between reality and imagination, the trouble starts. The greater the gap, the more tension and disappointment we experience. We start to like or dislike something based on this gap. The likes and dislikes are a product of the mind, not of the being which is just bliss.

Beautifully, Kṛṣṇa says, 'An object of enjoyment that comes of itself is neither painful nor pleasurable for someone who has eliminated attachment and who is free from the dualism of self and the other and therefore, from desire.'

This is actually a *sūtra,* a technique that Kṛṣṇa gives. If we put our attention neither on pleasure nor on pain, but between the two, we actually go beyond both and transcend the play of the mind. What do we normally do? If we are in pain, we try to run away from it. If we are in pleasure, we try to cling onto it. Understand that both pleasure and pain are of the mind. They are based on our saṁskāras, root thought patterns from our past. They are not of the being. Instead of trying to hold onto pleasure or running away from pain, just be with it, just witness it. The nature of the mind is to move to the opposites. Using this technique, we can transcend this nature of the mind.

For example, if we have a headache, don't try to resist it. Just witness it. As the tree is there, as the night is there, so also the headache is there. On the other hand, if we are very happy, don't try to cling onto it. Whether it is happiness or pain, just be a witness to it. It is like standing in front of the sun and watching it, with no attachment to the sun rising or setting.

Be involved but be aware without resistance to life, neither rejecting nor accepting anything. When we are aware and do not resist anything, we can never be unconsciously pulled into it. Then desire cannot overcome us. We are always the Master. When we are not conscious, then we either start resisting or accepting and we get caught in the cycle of guilt and desires. After the desire gets fulfilled, we go through guilt for having succumbed to the desire. But we did not live the desire fully with completion, so we can't get out of it either. Next time, the desire happens and again we go through it incompletely and then feel guilty. The only way to get out of this vicious cycle of desire and guilt is to go through the desire with completion without any resistance to it.

Normally we either suppress or express our desires. Suppression does not lead to elimination of that desire. It temporarily blocks access, but that desire will rise with renewed vigor again. Expression also does not mean completion. Again and again, the desire will rise even after repeated expression because we rarely experience anything with completion. In expression of a desire, once we experience a desire with full awareness and declare completion with it, whether related to food, sex or material desires, we will find that the desire is fulfilled and we will not be bothered by it anymore. We will transcend the desire. It is actually that simple.

Listen. This is what I term karma.

Karma is nothing but unfulfilled desire that makes us repeat the same experience again and again, simply because we do not have the intelligence to enter into that experience with complete awareness.

Once we experience the situation with awareness and complete with it, we will experience what Śaṅkara experienced. We will not be the doer, the deed or the doing. We will transcend all three. We will transcend our *karma*. We will be supreme.

TUNE IN TO ETERNAL BLISS

Kṛṣṇa advises us to turn inwards. Move away from your senses, move into your Source, He says. By nature, by our very being we are tuned inwards. By conditioning, we lose the capability to turn inwards. We will see that most children are blissful, just curious and happy to be what they are. Then unfortunately, they grow up to be adults! They lose that bliss and that natural response to turn inwards. Society teaches them to trust their senses. One who indulges in sense pleasures is just caught in the push and pull of desires and guilt. He is just under hormonal torture. Again and again, we look outside for solutions that keep us happy.

Everything that happens around us gives us sensory pleasures. If we see our list of desires, most of them are not even ours, they are borrowed from others. We will be totally happy with our car until our neighbor gets a new car. We will be totally happy with our job until our colleague gets promoted to a higher post. We constantly update our list of desires by looking at what is going on outside, and we start believing that fulfilling these desires will give us what we define as happiness or pleasure. So to fulfill these desires, we keep on running the rat race, not knowing what exactly we want.

We look for fulfillment and solutions outside. However, the real solution lies inside. We need to be able to connect to our true self. We should realize that our being is blissful by nature. If we realize this, we will always be centered and complete in ourselves. He who is free from being and non-being, who is content, complete, desire-less, and wise, even if in the eyes of the world he does act, does nothing.

We must have seen, on the surface, a mad man with tremendous laziness will look very similar to a mystic in deep bliss. They may seem very similar but inside, they are the complete opposites. A madman is lazy and is lying around with many things occupying his mind. A mystic, however, is sitting completely relaxed because he is centered and complete in his being with no-mind. To us he may seem the same as a madman. But the mind of the mystic is not doing anything. He is complete unto himself.

When we are situated in the core of our being, when we are one with the Self, we are not shaken by the emotions that happen on the periphery. It is like a rock that is standing in the ocean. The waves of the emotions are continuously lashing against the rock, but the rock still stands unperturbed, established in completion. The happiness arises from our very being, from our Self. It is unlimited eternal bliss because it cannot be stopped by any external agent, thus says Kṛṣṇa—*sukham akṣayam aśnute* (5.21).

The Path To Self-Realization

5.22 *The intelligent person surely does not enjoy the sense pleasures,*
enjoyments, which are sources of misery and which are subject to
beginning and end.

5.23 *Before leaving this present body, if one is able to tolerate the urges*
of material senses and check the force of desire and anger,
he is well-situated and he is happy in this world.

5.24 *One who is happy from within, active within as well as illumined*
within, surely, is a Yogi and he is liberated in the Supreme
[brahma-nirvāṇa], is Self-realized and attains the Supreme.

5.25 *Those, whose sins have been destroyed, who have dispelled the*
dualities arising from doubts, whose minds are engaged within,
and who are working for the welfare of other beings,
attain the eternal liberation in the Supreme [brahma-nirvāṇa].

5.26 *They who are free from lust and anger, who have subdued the mind*
and senses, and who have known the Self,
easily attain liberation [brahma-nirvāṇa].

Kṛṣṇa says that sensory pleasures are bound to end; they do not last forever.

Generally, we are controlled by what happens outside us. Our happiness is an emotion that is created by something outside of us—a pleasant situation, the presence of someone we like, and so on. When we experience happiness due to some event outside us, be very sure, sadness is around the corner. When we experience the joy in us because of an external source, we will experience sadness once that external source is taken away from us. We always attach our happiness to something that is external to us. If these things are taken away from us, we are left with sadness. It is like a pendulum swaying from one extreme of happiness to the other extreme of sadness.

The event and the person do not cause happiness and sorrow. It is caused by our sensory perception and by the judgment based on this perception. That is why the same event that may be joyful to one is sorrowful for another, and would leave a third one undisturbed. It is our attachment to that person or event and our judgment based on our patterns that creates the sorrow or happiness. The incident by itself is neutral.

There is a beginning and an end to these states of sorrow and happiness. But bliss is something that continuously happens in us for no reason. Bliss does not depend on external sources. It is inside us. Once we are centered in us, we are always in bliss. When we are constantly experiencing the inner joy or bliss, whatever happens outside us does not affect our space of bliss.

Happiness or sadness happens because of our sensory pleasures that are again a result of our mind and ego. Our ego, our false association of ourselves with various emotions is actually the cause of our misery. At the core of our beings is pure bliss. But we are functioning at our periphery and are not able to see this core. The ego is what is really meant by *māyā* or illusion. *Yā mā iti māyā*—that which does not exist but which troubles as if it exists is *māyā*. We don't see reality as it is because we are all the time looking at life through glasses tinted with our biased perceptions, through our limited view of life.

When we start watching these sources with awareness and complete with our root patterns, we break the chords of attachment of our state of joy with these external sources and desires. When we are aware of what we really want, this dependency on sensory pleasures breaks. When we are centered and complete in ourselves, we start taking things as and when they come.

I am not saying you should not enrich yourself with the joy that you get from external sources or fulfillment of our desires. No. All I am saying is, be aware of it when it happens, that's all. Do not attach your internal state of joy to these sense pleasures. If they happen, let them happen. Let them not dictate your state of happiness.

Kṛṣṇa gives us now a beautiful technique to reach that ultimate Kṛṣṇa consciousness, to reach the beautiful space of bliss. He is saying exactly what I said earlier. If we can, at least once, settle inside our being, into our space of completion, when we are attacked by this incomplete emotion of desire and anger, without moving our body, without cooperating, without being taken away by that emotion, we are well-situated. This means that we achieved what has to be achieved; we are blissful in this world.

GĪTĀ—OWNER'S MANUAL FOR BODY-MIND

People ask me again and again, '*Swamiji,* what is the purpose of this body and mind?' The purpose of body and mind is only one thing: to achieve, to learn how to experience joy without body and mind. If we can learn to have happiness and bliss, without the body and mind, we have achieved the purpose of the body and mind; over! After that, we can throw away the body and mind; we can live without the body and mind.

The person who is able to live without the body and mind is called a *jīvan mukta*—a person living enlightenment. Even if the body and mind are with him, he will not be touched by them. If we don't have any need, will you go to Los Angeles? Unless you have some reason, you will not go there.

In the same way, unless you have some reason, you will not assume this body. If you had a single glimpse of bliss without this body and mind, the bliss that is beyond this body and mind, you will never be disturbed by this body and mind. Even if it is there, it will be following you; you will not be following it.

It is like this: If you don't know how to put the brakes on when you are driving the car, it means you are not driving the car, the car is driving you! Without reading the owner's manual and learning to drive, if you sit in the car, you will only be in trouble. Without the manual, if you directly drive the car, you will make all sorts of mistakes. Only when you know how to start or to stop or apply the brakes properly, you are driving the car. Otherwise, the car is driving you.

So read the owner's manual before getting into the vehicle. The *Bhagavad Gītā* is the owner's manual for your body and mind. If you read the owner's manual before getting into the body and mind, you will be able to stop when you want to stop. You will not get into the accident of repeating the life and death cycle.

Here Kṛṣṇa says: The man who is not moved, who can tolerate the urges of material senses, check the force of desire and anger, is well-situated and he is happy in this world. He knows where he is. He knows his place.

In this world, many of us don't know our place. That is why we feel uprooted. We don't feel we belong to this life. We don't feel we are at home because we don't know our place. Only a person who has gone beyond greed and fear can relax into his being. He will know what his place is in this planet Earth.

If we don't fuel our being with fear and greed, suddenly, we will see a new clarity. We will start working out of intelligence, out of Divine Consciousness, out of Eternal Bliss. Just decide, 'Whatever I do out of greed will only result in more greed. I have been getting nowhere. Enough!' In the same way, if we are escaping from something out of fear, decide, 'Alright, how long can I escape? This fear will come and attack me in some other form. If I am afraid of this now, I will be afraid of something else later. So let me face it now.'

It is just the fear, not the object about which you are afraid of. You may escape anywhere but you are carrying the canopy of fear and greed with you. Wherever you go for a picnic, you open your own little canopy. There are so many places for great escapes today! These places show how much of depression people are carrying inside them. If so much entertainment is necessary, it means they are carrying so much depression inside. By his very nature, man doesn't need so much entertainment. If we need so many things to make us happy, there is something seriously wrong with the whole system. We need to look into the system and repair it.

Again and again, Kṛṣṇa declares, 'Let you live in the space of completion. Let you work out of bliss.' And I tell you, if you are complete and work out of bliss, you will create bliss for yourself and for others; you will never know what tiredness is.

Let me tell you honestly that I still can't understand the meaning of the word 'tiredness.' How can you have tiredness? Tiredness is the inner contradiction between the *icchā śakti* (power of desire) and *kriya śakti* (power of action), between your being and your action. Inside, there is a deep problem. Your greed and fear are attacking each other. If we are feeling tired, it means there is a big war going on inside you. The Mahābhārat war between fear and greed is happening within you.

Man whose consciousness is complete can never experience tiredness. When I was in college, I used to sit and meditate for four hours every morning and evening. My roommates would ask me, 'How are you able to sit for so many hours?' And I used to tell them, 'Why not? It is my body, my mind. If you want, can't you sit? If you can't even sit with your body and mind, what are you going to achieve?'

Why do we feel tired? We feel tired when we are not integrated within ourselves. One half of our being that wants to express itself but we have suppressed it for various societal reasons. The other half of our being is what is expressing itself in the manner that we are forcing it to. Because we constantly have to put in an inauthentic effort to be what we naturally are not, we become tired at some point. When we become tired, the suppressed, unconscious half of us becomes more powerful than the conscious, pretentious half, and it starts dominating.

Just integrate yourself. Be with completion rather than suppressing yourself, and there will be no unconscious half to fight with. Then where is the question of feeling tired? We feel tired only when we are not completely involved in what we are doing. Become complete, integrated, and whole. Then you can never feel tired, whatever you may do.

See how is it that you don't feel tired aftrer sitting with me for so many hours? It is because when I speak, I speak from my being, with a totality. When I speak with totality, you automatically receive me and my energy. This is the state from which enlightened Masters operate. That is why there is no sense of tiredness in them even though they are intensely involved in what they do.

We feel tired only when there is a gap between what we are doing and what we want to do. When we are driven by greed for something, we are caught up in the goal and the goal is something we want to achieve. What we are doing is not yet the goal and hence, we feel we are running towards the goal. Or we are driven by fear of something; we want to escape from the object of fear and hence we are not completely involved in what we are doing.

Honestly, I can't understand how a man cannot sit with himself. It is our body, our mind after all. Just sit! You are not able to sit because you continuously pour the wrong fuel into your system.

We are continuously chasing power. The hunger for power is so high in us that we are always running behind something to get control over it. First, let us get our body and mind under our control. As of now, it is under the control of fear or greed. Let that be controlled by us. Then, automatically, we can get anything under our control. If our body and mind are not under our control, whatever we wish to bring under our control will never come under our control.

One thought from greed is enough: our body just runs. One thought from fear is enough: our body just runs. Let it be completely under you. May you be complete with your body and mind!

JUST BE HAPPY FROM WITHIN

Here is a beautiful *sūtra,* a beautiful technique from Kṛṣṇa to enter into the supreme consciousness: 'Just be happy, restful and complete from within', says Kṛṣṇa, '*yo'ntaḥ sukho antar-ārāmas tathāntar-jyotir eva yaḥ* (5.24).'

Just be happy from within. Let your smile be a deep expression of the love in your being. All of us are so used to living an artificial life that we have forgotten our being. Every moment, we are continuously either in greed by running after our desires or in fear by continuously running away from something. Our happiness in every moment is measured only by greed or fear. This means we are not actually experiencing the moment of completion. We can enjoy something totally only when we are completely in it and we can be complete only when we are totally in the present moment, enjoying what we are doing here and now.

When you are in the space of completion in the present moment with full enthusiasm, you are in a state of bliss. Bliss is the state of joy that has no reason and which is not affected by the past or future. Naturally, the present blissful moment will give birth to future moments of bliss. We enter a virtuous circle rather than being caught up in the vicious cycle of fear and greed that we are now caught in.

Why do we run behind our desires or why are we afraid of something? It is because we think life has some goal to be achieved and we continuously run towards the goals. Understand, life in itself has no goal. The very life itself is the goal. The path itself is the goal. If we think the goal and the path are different, we will run towards the goal; we will run towards the horizon. Can we ever touch the horizon? The more we run towards it, we will find it receding from us, because the horizon is imaginary, it is an illusion.

If we are running behind a goal in life, we will be disappointed at the end of life. But when we see life itself as a goal, we make the path itself as the goal. So every moment is blissful! The goal is achieved every moment of our life. So every moment when we live with full completion, with full enthusiasm, with powerfulness, we actually enjoy that moment. When we are completely immersed in the present moment, we enjoy the path. When the path itself becomes the goal, we enjoy the goal also every moment.

The self-realized one is complete, powerful, active and happy because he is completely in the present moment, living in reality. The Divine energy blissfully flows through him and he no longer needs to derive energy for his activities from desire or fear.

Here, Kṛṣṇa refers to the state in which we are in the peak of activity yet in the ultimate relaxation. Such a state is indeed possible and is the only state in which we can really be involved in what we are doing, and completely satisfied, complete and blissful in what we are doing.

Why To Feel Responsible?

This is what Kṛṣṇa says: When we are tuned fully inwards, we no longer have any attachment to what happens outside; we are one with the All, the Existence, and we have transcended all *karma*. We are then in *brahma nirvāṇa*—the ultimate liberation, one with Existence, and we are in *nityānanda*, eternal bliss. When we feel genuine love for others, we feel responsible for everyone, and we take up more and more responsibility. We want to enrich others and share that love with as many as people as possible.

When we are tuned inwards, we live in the present; the past and future do not exist for us. When we are in the present, we are one with Existence. I call this All-one-ness. We are All-in-One. We are in the space of Advaita, non-duality. We encompass everything. In this state, we are at the height of spontaneity; we are at the peak of our possibility. Spontaneity does not mean creativity. Creativity is a byproduct. Spontaneity is being in the present, being responsible for everything. Nothing is excluded. We flow out, we expand and cover.

The more responsibility we take up, the more we expand. Responsibility is something that can be easily shrugged. But if we don't shrug it and keep on shouldering it with the right reason, we will expand and the divine energy will automatically flow in us. And we can take up more and more responsibility only when we feel overflowing energy in us.

With responsibility, we harness the power of feeling. When we feel the space of responsibility, we take it up without any doubts.

Usually whenever we are asked to do something, the mind comes in between and the responsibility feels like a load. Without the right context of responsibility, our mind creates dilemma. We start analyzing intellectually and logically. So at the end of it, we act out of greed or fear. As long as we intellectually weigh the situation for good and bad, the mind exists. We have to cross this barrier by completing with our greed and fear patterns. We have to cut across the wall of incompletions and enter the space of feeling the responsibility. The dilemma of wanting or not wanting to do something should not come at all. Many times when people come to me and I ask them to do something, just by the way they say, 'Yes, I will do it,' I can tell whether they really want to do it or not!

Our response to take up a responsibility is shaky and inauthentic when we are in a dilemma, when our mind operates. We should take up responsibility spontaneously. Then the mind will not have its say. We just know, that's all. We operate from an extreme relaxation and spontaneity. The ability to respond spontaneously out of the space of completion is what I call responsibility.

Please listen! Responsibility can happen to you only after completion. If you take responsibility because you have to be a performer, or a leader, or be productive, you will feel responsibility as a weight on you! If responsibility is taken out of wrong reason, you are not going to feel responsible!

Listen! Understand, only when you complete, you will know the right reason for taking responsibility. Only then, you taking responsibility will be really useful to you. So understand, responsibility can happen in you only after completion!

I'll now tell you *why* you need to feel responsibility, why you should **take responsibility. Listen. Whatever happens in and around you—you ARE the source!** That is why you need to take responsibility for whatever is happening in and around you. You need to take responsibility because you are responsible, and not for any other reason.

Whether you believe it or not, you ARE the source. With this clarity, out of this context, if you take responsibility, every action, whether it is taking your children to the school, attending to your calls or your business meeting, everything will become a spiritual practice leading you to *jīvan mukti,* living enlightenment.

When you learn responsibility, you may naturally perform well in your office, in your business, in your family. You will become responsible, no doubt. I am not against it. I am not against you performing in your office or you taking responsibility for your family. But all that should be the side effect! The main effect of you feeling responsibility should be—you becoming *jīvan mukta*, living enlightenment!

Live this principle of responsibility. Then you will understand that all your decisions will be out of the experience—'I am the Source.' Listen! If you function with this truth, '*I am the source, so I am responsible*'; everything you do will become a spiritual practice for you to become a *jīvan mukta.*

Only when we go beyond the incompletions of the mind, beyond duality, we see the absolute oneness and synchronicity of the entire Existence and we start living in the state of Advaita. When we reach this state, there is no mind that is acting. We are in a state of deep relaxation, completion and bliss. And this awakens the power of feeling in us to spontaneously respond to everything with responsibility.

When we feel genuine love for others, we will take up responsibility because we want to share that blissful love with others around us. Only when we work out of bliss, we will do things to enrich others and ourselves. Taking responsibility and enriching makes life happen to you! When we take up responsibility spontaneously, we do not act out of fear or greed. We will always be giving.

Know Me And Be In Bliss

5.27, 5.28 *Shutting out all external sense objects, keeping the eyes and vision concentrated between the two eyebrows,*
Suspending the inward and outward breaths within the nostrils and thus controlling the mind, senses and intelligence,
The transcendental who is aiming at liberation, becomes free from desire, fear and the byproduct of desire, fear and anger, all three.
One who is always in this state is certainly liberated.

5.29 *One who knowing Me as the purpose of sacrifice and penance,*
As the Lord of all the worlds and the benefactor of all the living beings, achieves peace.

Here, 'Me' refers to the supreme witnessing consciousness, the Kṛṣṇa consciousness; it is not the six-feet Kṛṣṇa frame.

I always tell people, the outer Guru, the Master is needed only to awaken the inner Guru. Once the inner Guru, the consciousness is awakened, the outer Guru needs to be dropped. Just like after burning the dead body, the very stick that is used to stoke the wood is dropped into the same pyre, so also the outer Guru needs to be dropped.

For the first time, Kṛṣṇa gives a beautiful technique to move your energy from fear and greed to divine consciousness, eternal consciousness. Your fear is rooted in the *svādiṣṭhāna cakra*, the energy center situated two inches below the navel. Your greed is rooted in the *mūlādhāra cakra*, the energy center that is in the root of your spinal cord.

Kṛṣṇa gives us the technique to elevate ourselves from these two cakras to the eternal consciousness, the *ājñā cakra* at the brow center, where the eternal consciousness resides. When we have elevated our self to *ājñā*, we go beyond our ego or mind. We are all caught in the *mūlādhāra* and *svādiṣṭhāna*, fear and greed.

That is why, continuously, we can watch and see that we have a sort of a tensed feeling. We will be continuously holding our *mūlādhāra* and *svādiṣṭhāna* tightly. Now, just feel yourself in your *mūlādhāra* area. You will see that you are tightly holding yourself in tension.

Kṛṣṇa explains how to relax that area, how to stop the fuel coming from greed and fear, and get the *amṛta-dhāra* (flow of nectar) from the eternal consciousness. Shutting out all external sense objects, keeping the eyes and vision concentrated between the two eyebrows, suspending the inward and outward breaths within the nostrils and thus controlling the mind, senses and intelligence, the transcendental who is aiming at liberation, becomes free from desire, fear, and the byproduct of desire, fear and anger—all three. One who is always in this state is certainly liberated.

First, He gives the technique to enter that state. Then He says if you can stay in that state, you are liberated. Now, at least let us try to have a glimpse of this state that Kṛṣṇa explains in this verse. I will guide you step by step through this meditation. Please try to enter that state.

MEDITATION

Please sit straight and close your eyes. Let your head, neck and backbone be in a straight line. Intensely pray to that ultimate energy, *Parabrahma* Kṛṣṇa, to give us the experience of this meditation.

First, visualize all your senses completely shut; your eyes are completely closed. Don't allow any visualization to happen inside your being. You should close the eyes too, because we continue to see things from behind our eyelids even though we shut our eyelids. Visualize that your eyeballs have become completely dark. You are seeing only darkness in front of you.

Visualize your ears are shut. Visualize your sense of touch is shut. Visualize your smelling capacity is shut. Visualize your face to be shut. Feel deeply that all the five senses have been shut down.

Inhale and exhale as slowly as possible. Slowly, let your nostrils blow the air. Let your consciousness reside between the two eyebrows. In a very relaxed way, be aware of the space between your two eyebrows. Don't concentrate; don't tense yourself. Just be very relaxed, have a deeply relaxed awareness.

Let your *mūlādhāra cakra,* located at the base of your spine, be relaxed. Let your *svādiṣṭhāna cakra*, located just below the navel center, be relaxed. Let your whole consciousness come up to the *ājñā cakra,* which is between the eyebrows.

Concentrate on the space between the eyebrows.

Visualize cool, soothing light in the *ājñā cakra*, in the space between the eyebrows. Relax in the *ājñā cakra*. Forget all other parts of your body. Forget about the body, mind and the world; remember only the *ājñā cakra*, the space between the two eyebrows.

Go deeply into the *ājñā cakra*, in the space between the two eyebrows. Visualize a beautiful, cooling, soothing light in the *ājñā cakra*. Let you experience beautiful, blissful light in the *ājñā cakra.* Don't tense yourself; let your awareness be in the *ājñā cakra* in a very relaxed way; let your consciousness rest in the space between the two eyebrows.

Relax in the same space of eternal consciousness. Let you be beyond the body and mind. May your intelligence be awakened. Let you work from your eternal consciousness. Let you have the pleasant awareness of the *ājñā cakra*. Let you all have the grace of the divine consciousness. Let you be established in the eternal consciousness. Let you all be in, with and radiate eternal bliss, *nityānanda.*

Om śānti, śānti, śāntihi...

Om tat sat.

Relax. Slowly, very slowly, you can open your eyes.

Try to remain in this mood at least for the next ten days.

Understand: Don't concentrate by force. Have a pleasant awareness. When you keep the pleasant awareness around your *ājñā cakra*, your whole energy will be directed towards the Eternal Consciousness. You will receive energy from Eternal Consciousness, from immortality, *amṛtatva*. You will be driven from above by the Eternal Consciousness. If you are driven from below by fear or greed, you are man. If you are driven from above, you are God.

Let you learn the science of how to connect yourself with the Divine energy, how to be driven by the Divine Consciousness. Let you live all your possibilities. Let you function through the Eternal Consciousness.

Thus ends the fifth chapter named ***Sannyāsa Yogaḥ****, 'The Yoga of Renunciation,' of the* ***Bhagavad Gītā Upaniṣad, Brahmavidyā Yogaśāstra,*** *the scripture of yoga dealing with the science of the Absolute in the form of* ***Śrī Kṛṣṇārjuna saṃvād****, dialogue between Śrī Kṛṣṇa and Arjuna.*

CHAPTER

6

Dhyāna Yogaḥ

Look In, Be Complete Before Any Conclusion

You are your best friend and you are your worst enemy. Whether you wish to degrade yourself or raise yourself by yourself is in your hands. Kṛṣṇa gives the technique to unite with Him in yoga, the Supreme Consciousness by becoming a Yogi.

Look In, Be Complete Before Any Conclusion

We will start with a beautiful history from Mahābhārat:

Once the elders of Kuru royal family wanted to test the intelligence of their new generation of princes, the Kauravas and the Pāṇḍavas as to—who is more intelligent and wise—Kaurava kids, the hundred sons of King Dhritarāṣṭra or Pāṇḍava kids, the five sons of King Pāṇḍu. So, they devised a competition.

They said to all the Kaurava and Pāṇḍava young princes, 'You will be given one gold coin. With that one gold coin, you will have to fill your palace house!' This was the test laid out for them.

The Kauravas took the gold coin and sat together. Naturally, hundred brains will mess-up any plan, any program. See, you can have hundred hands but not hundred brains. Be very clear, all great things are done by hundred hands and hundred legs, but not by hundred brains. Brain should be only one. In life, unfortunately, we have thousands of brains, but not a single hand!

So, these hundred Kaurava brains all sit together, intensely discuss, argue, and even fight among themselves, 'How can we fill the whole house with one gold coin?' they speculated. Each brain came up with its own strategy, just to be pulled down by the other. Then, finally after enough squabble and confusion, they came to the conclusion, 'The elders are all cheats, they are abusing us, trying to exploit us, and making us feel we are failures!'

After this whole drama of blaming others, of feeling deprived and cheated, finally they decided that for one gold coin they could get only hay grass, which is the left over chaff of grains and paddy after crop harvesting.

Here, the Pāṇḍavas sat together into the listening of *dharma*. Even though each Pāṇḍava is a peerless specialist with unmatched expertise in some field, they all were always aligned under Dharmarāja, *dharma*! Understand, Yudhiṣṭra, the eldest of the Pāṇḍava brothers is Dharmarāja, the king and embodiment of *dharma*!

Listen! All the five Pāṇḍavas are sons of Nature born as immaculate conceptions of Divine powers. Yudhiṣṭra is *dharma* incarnate, who along with the four Pāṇḍava brothers, embodies all the four *tattvas* of integrity, authenticity, responsibility and enriching, empowered with the powers of words, thinking, feeling and living.

Bhīma, the son of Vāyu (wind god), represents the physical valor, the strength of integrity and authenticity. Arjuna, the son of Indra (the king of gods), is Nara incarnate, the highest evolved human energy of Nārāyaṇa, Lord Kṛṣṇa. Arjuna is physiological power, the power of feeling awakened by responsibility! Both Bhīma and Arjuna are totally different expressions of unique divine powers. The ability to thrash is different, the ability to aim is different! Arjuna, the embodiment of physiological power, has the ability to aim and shoot, which needs mastery over the body, mind and senses. Nakula embodies the sense of intelligence and the space of possibility that is awakened by authenticity, the power of thinking. Nakula is one of the most intelligent strategy planners, who plans all the war strategies. Sahadeva is the aligner of time, he is a great astrologer expressing integrity, the power of words. All of them are always aligned under *Dharmarāja* Yudhiṣṭra. Because they are aligned to *dharma,* Pāṇḍavas are like one brain having ten hands, all together united to express enriching, the power of living.

Listen! I am defining Dharma. The power of your words, the power of your thinking, the power of your feeling, and the power of your living, this is Dharma. Dharma is aligning yourself to the flow of the Cosmos.

So, they all sit together aligning to Dharmarāja and discuss, 'What will fill the whole house with one gold coin? When our elders say then *it is possible*.'

Please understand, you can look at this test of intelligence from two possibilities. One group *looks out* and wails, 'I think these elders are all fools. They don't know what they are asking us to do. They are just trying to prove we are all small fellows.' This is the thought trend of Kauravas. Then come the sons of immortality, Pāṇḍavas, who *look in* and wonder, 'When elders say, then there must be way. They are trying to teach us, educate us, and enrich us through this. When elders say, *it is possible*.' So finally, Pāṇḍavas also decide to fill the house with one gold coin! How they did it, let us see!

At the time of supervision, all the Kuru elders—Grandsire Bhīśma, Droṇa, Vidura, and Dhritarāṣṭra assembled; they first went to Duryodhana's palace house. On reaching, they saw the whole house full of hay and all these Kauravas were standing outside! They could not even get into the house!

Bhīśma asks them, 'What happened? Why are all of you standing outside?' Kauravas reply, 'What can be done? You only told us that we have to fill the whole house with one gold coin; what else can we get with just one gold coin? So we filled it with hay grass. Here you see! We won the competition!'And all these Kauravas are now standing outside! Neither these hundred brains nor the Kuru elders are able to get into the house.

Dhṛitarāṣṭra, the father of Kauravas becomes very happy! He hurriedly concludes, 'See my sons and their intelligence! They filled the whole palace house. They should be declared victorious!' Droṇa, the teacher of Kurus and Pāṇḍava princes, once a poor Brāhmaṇa, was supported by King Dhritarāṣṭra. So, whatever Dhṛitaraṣṭra says becomes the *conclusion* for Droṇa; and so, he simply agrees to the blind king's conclusion. But, Bhīṣma stops Droṇa, saying, 'Wait! Let us go to the other house also to see, and then decide who won the game.'

On entering the Pāṇḍava palace home, they see the whole house is filled with light and perfumed with fragrant incense. Understand, for that one gold coin, they bought earthen lamps and lighted them up along with pleasing, special perfumed incense. The moment the elders entered, the Pāṇḍavas washed their feet, gave them seat and fruits. Enriching them thus, Pāṇḍavas tell them humbly, 'Please see, the whole house is filled! Filled with light and perfume, pleasant smell!'

Of course, the blind King Dhṛitarāṣṭra is not ready to accept this! So, he goes to every corner, puts his sharp nose and smells to investigate if every corner is filled with pleasant perfume. He finds that all corners have the pleasant fragrance. Finally, the Kuru elders come to the right conclusion and declare that Pāṇḍavas won the game. Pāṇḍavas stand victorious!

Please understand, listen!

Completion is creating a space which is full where you can Live! As the space of Pāṇḍavas is full with light and filled with pleasant fragrance, so is the inner space of completion full with power and filled with the fragrance of bliss—*ānanda gandha,* where you can live.

Both palace houses are full. You also always keep yourself full; but the question is do you keep the house full like Kauravas or Pāṇḍavas? Find out that! Is your inner space like Kauravas or Pāṇḍavas? That's all! Have you brought the hay and filled it all around your house, or have you brought the pleasant smell and the light within?

Please understand, completion keeps you full and gives you the fulfilled space to live! Incompletion keeps you full but never fulfilled; you will never be able to live there. Because of their deep incompletions, Kaurava brains fight violently. Finally when they get tired of fighting with their incompletions, they get utterly confused, and jump to the wrong conclusion of filling their house with hay! The Pāṇḍavas who are full with the space of completion and filled with the power of living, beautifully enrich the elders and enrich themselves, enjoying the light and fragrance!

Please understand, the modern day CEOs, leaders are filled with stress. What is stress actually? It is nothing but filling yourself with hay! You are filled not fulfilled. You are occupied but not useful. Before making one decision, when you think about it two hundred times, you are tired just like the Kaurava brains! Usually, when there are so many incompletions fighting in your brain, either your projects die down, or they take a totally opposite turn!

Reduce the incompletions you infuse on yourself; reduce the abusal you do to yourself. Reduce the mental setup of Duryodhanas' on you. Duryodhanas' are nothing but bunch of incompletions, no power! Actually, they took the decision of buying the hay and filling the house because they were not able to handle the whole confusion and fight among themselves. So, they just jumped to the wrong conclusion, '*let's do something*!' Listen! Any decision made out of incompletion in the mood of '*let's do something*' is suicide! So understand, '*let's do something*' out of incompletion, restlessness generated by incompletion, is the pesticide! If you do it just for yourself, it is suicide; if you do it for the family, it is homicide; if you do it for many people, it is genocide.

What Pāṇḍavas did is out of the pure space of completion. I tell you, when you create the space of completion, every moment you create a new way of thinking, new way of feeling, new way of knowledge, new way of being, and a new way of making yourself available to society and to humanity.

Look in, create the space of completion before coming to any conclusion! This is the message of this chapter.

The sixth chapter of the *Bhagavad Gītā, Dhyāna Yogaḥ* starts with Kṛṣṇa's words. In this chapter Arjuna is not asking any questions to Kṛṣṇa. Kṛṣṇa continues His answers from the previous chapter.

Attain The State Of Yoga

6.1 *Bhagavān says:*
One who performs his actions without being attached to their fruit (outcome) of his work is a Sannyāsi, and he is truly an ascetic; a Yogi also.; not the one who renounces to light the fire and performs no action.

6.2 *O Pāṇḍava, what is called renunciation, or sannyāsa, you must know to be the same as yoga, or uniting oneself with the Supreme., for never can anyone become a yogī, until he renounces the desire for self-gratification [saṅkalpa].*

6.3 *A one desirious of achieving the state of yoga or no-mind state, action is said to be the means and for the one who is already elevated in yoga, cessation from all actions is said to be the means.*

6.4 *Any one is said to have attained the state of yoga when, having renounced all material desires, he neither acts for sense gratification nor engages in result-focused activities.*

Kṛṣṇa continues with what He said earlier in a little more detailed way. He says, the person who is not attached to the fruits of his action is an ascetic and a *karma yogi*, one who continuously does authentic work without being attached to the results.

Please understand, *karma*—the state of action, or *sannyāsa*—the state of renunciation, is not related to your doing. It is directly related to your being. Being a sannyāsi, a renunciate monk, is not a status, it is a state of mind. Whether you are doing *karma yoga* or you remain a *Sannyāsi* is in no way going to affect you. If one is a *karma yogī*, one goes about doing the work that is allotted to him without attachment and without expectations. This is done even in the middle of one's life as a householder, a businessperson or an employee. The status is not of any consequence.

In the same manner, it is immaterial whether one dons saffron robes to be a renunciate or an ascetic. One can wear all the outer trappings of a monk and still be fully attached to the *saṁsāra māyā*, the illusion of life. In the verses of *Bhaja Govindam*, Ādī Śaṅkarācārya, the Enlightened Master of ancient India, says this beautifully about the ascetic who cheats the world and himself. He says, the ascetic has his hair knotted, or he shaves his head bald, or he pulls out his hair one by one in penance, he wears saffron robes, but he does not see, even though he has eyes. He does all this only to fill his belly!

One's attitude, one's inner space, one's *being* alone matters. Here Kṛṣṇa gives the gist of the previous chapter.

People repeatedly ask me, '*Swamiji,* should we renounce everything to achieve Enlightenment? How can we lead our day-to-day life and yet hope to achieve spiritual progress?'

I tell them, 'No! Just renounce what you don't have. That is enough. You don't have to renounce what you have.' I tell them to live with completion with whatever they have, and to just renounce what they don't have. We fantasize about all that we do not have, that is the problem. There are thousands of things that we don't have, but we live with all those things mentally. The problem is not what we have, we have got used to those things anyway. That is our reality. It is what we don't have that creates problems. Just renounce what you don't have. That is enough to solve all the problems. Then you will start living intensely with what you have.

One of the major problems we bring upon ourselves is that we chase desires and possessions. And once we have achieved what we want, we don't enjoy it. It is as if the enjoyment is only in the chase and not in the possession itself. The present has no meaning to many of us. Because of this, we miss reality, we miss true enjoyment. It is the illusion of the speculative future that draws our interest and causes misery to us.

Live with Reality, Live like God

There is a beautiful word in Saṃskrit: *brahmacarya*. Just like many other Saṃskrit words, this word has no equivalent word in English. The word has often been wrongly translated as celibacy. *Brahma* means Existence, reality, divinity. *Carya* means 'living like'. Brahmacarya refers to a person who lives like the gods, who lives with Existence, who lives with reality. Brahmacarya does not mean one who is unmarried. Brahmacarya refers to one who lives with reality, one who lives unattached. One of the four stages of life as defined by the scriptures is brahmacarya. This period of brahmacarya at Gurukul, under the Master's guidance in one's early years, provides the background to shed fantasies and live life in reality.

In today's world most of us live with fantasy. We don't live with the reality of our existence. From our childhood, we are exposed to so many different forms of media that flood us with fantasies. On physical maturity, everyone searches for an ideal person who can match their fantasy with great vigour and determination! Even if you find someone who matches your so-called ideal, when you start living with the person, life will slowly reveal that the ideal image so carefully built over many years is different from the person with whom you are living. There is always a screen of fantasy between your spouse and you, just like between life and you. You are continuously developing on life but you are not ready to look into life as it is.

A person who is mature enough to live with reality in the space of completion has achieved the state of brahmacarya. He is living with the real person or situation. He is complete in the present moment for what it is; he does not dream of how it should be. So just drop your fantasies. Live with reality. That is what I call brahmacarya. Brahmacarya is nothing but high energy, that's all.

I am defining brahmacarya. It is nothing but being authentic with high energy happening in you. Only when you have low energy, you need other person's presence in your life. Brahmacarya is nothing but being authentic with your high energy.

Here, Kṛṣṇa says, 'Just renouncing the sacred fire and not performing one's duty does not mean one is an ascetic or *sannyāsi.*' In those days, fire was the basis for everything, whether it was cooking or spiritual practice. For everything one needed fire. I can replace the word 'fire' with 'cell phone' for today's world! In this age, we can say, 'Don't think that by sacrificing the cell phone and laptop you become a *sannyāsi* or a great *karma yogi.*' Just like how the cell phone and laptop have become a basic necessity today, in those days *agnī* (fire) was a basic need in life. Just like how we are able to relate with people through the cell phone, our ancient *ṛṣis* (mystics) knew the techniques of relating with the higher energy through fire.

Understand, the Vedic Masters knew how to use fire to communicate with the higher energy, just like how we use the cell phone to communicate. All of science is based on using light particles, whether it is electricity, atomic energy, or other forms of energy, but with different formulae. Whether it is our fan or a microscope or a laptop or atomic bomb, everything can be reduced to that one single thing, the technique of handling light or electro-magnetic particles. Scientists worked on light energy and created all these objects. Our eastern sages worked with sound energy and created all these products. We really had the *pushpak vimāna* (flying chariot) and we did really have the *brahmāstra* (nuclear weapon). Everything is true.

But in the course of time we lost the technology, that's all. As the technology for handling sound waves was lost, the existence of these things is being questioned today. People now believe that all these things are just mythology, just epic stories. No! I tell you, Purāṇās are histories not stories; they are 'His-stories'. Just because we have lost the key and are not able to open the lock, don't think that there is no treasure.

The entire collection of scriptures, the *Vedas* is nothing but learning the techniques of tuning oneself to work with sound particles. Just as scientists work with light particles, the sages have worked with sound particles. They were able to relate with higher energies and were able to communicate just with the vibrations through fire. Whether it was Sañjaya, the minister of the Kaurava king Dhritarāṣṭra, who saw the Mahābhārat war through telepathy with his third eye, or the *puśpak vimāna*, the flying chariot, or *brahmāstra*, the ultimate fire weapon, these were all true. When the cultural invasion of India happened, these techniques were lost.

I have seen a *Sannyāsi* create fire by just uttering a few words. Even now, if we go to the *Kumbha Melā* (the holy river Gangā festival, planet's largest spiritual gathering in India), we can see hundreds of people like this. I have seen many Sannyāsis—some bury their heads inside the Earth for more than twenty-four hours; many can play with sound energy. I have seen a sannyāsi floating in the air and another sitting on a board full of sharp nails, with people watching them in awe.

Be Complete and Renounce your Thoughts

So here, Kṛṣṇa says that just by renouncing fire, a person cannot become a Sannyāsi. Similarly, here I can say that just by renouncing our cell phone in life, we cannot become a sannyāsi. The space needs to be transformed. To truly renounce, the mind has to renounce thoughts. Usually, wherever our body is, our mind is not. When we are at home, our thoughts are at the office. When we are at the office, we worry about what is happening elsewhere. When we are on vacation, we worry about work. To bring the mind to where the body is to renounce the inner chatter by completing with thoughts patterns. This is the starting point of renunciation.

Thoughts cannot be suppressed. The more we suppress them the more they erupt. We need to let go. We need to constantly bring ourselves back to where our body is, to the present space of completion, to the here and now, away from the dead past and the unborn future.

Renunciation of the past and the future, by bringing our mind to focus on the present space of completion, is true renunciation.

This renunciation does not happen by giving up objects of material welfare such as the fire and the cell phone. It also does not happen by giving up what we think is superficial to spiritual progress, such as rituals. Giving these up without bringing in the true completion of consciousness is not renunciation.

In the first verse Kṛṣṇa gives the essence of the previous chapter. Now He continues. Kṛṣṇa has already said that renunciation for the sake of renunciation, renunciation of material things without renouncing desires, is of no value.

Please listen. You have to renounce fantasies. These fantasies are the creation of the ego, mind, identity, root patterns—whatever name you wish to call it. This self creates up all these unreal fantasy visions, to keep you occupied and under control.

We may think that we are in control of our mind. But actually, our mind controls us. This is what Kṛṣṇa means by *saṅkalpa*, self-interest, because the mind wishes to satisfy the senses that it operates and controls. By visualizing, by hearing, by smelling, by tasting, by touching, through the sense organs, our mind wants us to experience pleasures that will keep us under its hold. Only when we renounce the mind's control by going beyond the senses can we become a true renunciate. 'Control your senses and still your mind so that you can reach Me,' Kṛṣṇa says in earlier chapters.

When Kṛṣṇa talks about 'self', it is the small 'self', the external identity that we confuse with our Self, the real inner core, the Truth. Only when we do renounce this so-called identity, which is not the true Self, then we will perceive our self as the supreme Self that is our true identity. An ordinary person sees his own self as being the body, mind, memories, senses and the identities that he creates for himself. These are the channels through which we can project ourselves onto the outer world. Normally we create two identities. One identity called *ahaṁkāra*, the identity that we project to the outer world. This identity is usually based on our achievements in society, our profession, our possessions, etc. The second identity is called mamākara, the identity we project to our inner self. This identity is usually based on our ideas about our attitudes, our beliefs, and our self-esteem. Through a combination of these two identities we create an image about ourselves that we hold on to with deep conviction and belief. Our true Self is beyond all these inner and outer images.

Please listen. If we don't want to be controlled by the mind, any activity that we perform to satisfy this false identity or ego should be renounced. As long as we allow our senses to feed us, we will be nurtured and controlled by sensory pleasures that satisfy our ego. Our mind will then keep us in its control.

Listen. I am defining Yoga.

Renunciation of these fantasies that we feel we need for self-satisfaction is Yoga. Yoga is the state when our desires, expressed through sensual pleasures, dissolve. We unite with our true Self in this state. In this state, there is no gap between the Divine and us.

Whether we believe it or not, accept it or not, want it or not, we are God. We are divine. All we can do is accept it, experience it, live and powerfully express it or we can just continue to struggle and fight with it. This is the truth.

A small story:

> A man was informed that his wife had just fallen into the river. He ran to the river to save her. To everyone's surprise, he jumped into the river and started swimming in the opposite direction, against the current.
>
> People who watched the scene shouted to him and called him a fool. They asked him, 'Why are you swimming against the current? Your wife has been carried with the current, downstream.'
>
> The man said, 'You don't know my wife. Even in the river, she would go only against the current!'

We can be like a rock in the water, forever resisting the flow of the water. The river pounds the rock, eventually reducing it to sand that settles at the bottom. Or we can be like the reed that bends and flows in whichever direction the water flows. By giving in to the water flow, the reed rests in the water.

In Saṃskṛit there are two terms, '*dṛṣti sṛṣti*' and '*sṛṣti dṛṣti*'. *Dṛṣti sṛṣti* means to look at the world as it is and take life as it comes. *Sṛṣti dṛṣti* is just the opposite, when we want to create the world as we would like it to be, as we want to see it. We want the world running according to our fantasies, instead of coming to terms with the reality of the world. This is a sure recipe for disaster, much like the woman swimming against the current and meeting with disaster.

We have a choice. We can either move against the current, believing that we control our destiny, and struggle all the time. Or we can flow with the current, surrender to the Divine of which we are an integral part, and be in bliss. Whether we go against the current or go with it, we are in the water. Whether we realize it or not, we are Divine. When our desires for external sensual pleasures are controlled, we experience the divinity within.

YOGA—UNITING THE BODY AND MIND

This is the state of yoga that Kṛṣṇa talks about—*yogārūḍhasya tasyaiva śamaḥ kāraṇam ucyate* (6.3), the state of true renunciation where there is no suppression. Instead, there is transformation into completion. The path is no longer towards self or sensory satisfaction. In fact, there is no 'towards' or 'goal.' The goal is the path itself. When we lead our life with no expectations, the mind cannot speculate or control us.

Kṛṣṇa says next, 'A person who initially wants to start practicing a yoga system laid down by the sages should carry out all activities in line with that system. Activities for all other reasons will then cease.'

This is such a beautiful instruction for anyone doing yoga. Today, the true meaning of yoga is completely lost. Yoga is not about physical exercise or sweating in high temperatures. Its purpose is not bodily fitness.

Yoga integrates body, mind and spirit. It is a journey into the inner Self, towards the Self.

Patañjali, the great sage and the father of Yoga, who authored Yoga Sūtras, laid down an eight-limbed system called *Aṣṭāṅga Yoga*. Today this is being misinterpreted as 'eight steps of yoga'. Patañjali laid down eight limbs or parts that needed to be practiced simultaneously, not separately or sequentially. There is no meaning in practicing yoga through only two of the eight parts: *āsana*, physical postures, and *prāṇāyāma*, breath control. But these are the only two parts taught by most yoga teachers today. What is the point? Nothing of real value will come out of it.

In Patañjali's Aṣṭāṅga Yoga, bliss is the goal, the path, and the end result. Have you seen even one yoga practitioner enjoying what he or she is doing? They are grimacing all the time, forcing their body, controlling their breath, torturing themselves. What for? Patañjali never asked them to torture themselves or their students. Yoga as it is practiced now only breeds ego. They have added many components to yoga: Deluxe yoga, Super deluxe kuṇḍalini yoga! Yoga should be done as *bhoga*, not as *roga*. Yoga should be done as an enjoyment, excitement, bhoga and not as a roga, disease. The excitement you radiate in your body, the whole bio-memory should be alive. Whole intelligence should be alive, up!

Patañjali's system of yoga is a way of life. Starting with inner and outer regulation, *yama* and *niyama*, his system cleanses our body, mind and spirit. Just *yama*, which is one of the eight limbs, has five parts, one of which is *satya* or truth. If we practice this with integrity and authenticity, it will lead us into enlightenment. Another part is *brahmacarya*, which is living enlightenment or walking in completion with reality. Actually, we need to be in the eighth state of *samādhi* to truly be able to practice even one of the yama principles with awareness.

Discovering your root pattern and completing it is the first step towards yoga. Please understand, yoga is not just moving your body or blowing your nose. No! Yoga starts when you discover your root thought pattern and complete with it. The yoga system is a parallel system, not a sequential system. When each of its parts is acted upon with awareness, every single thing that we do will be in completion with Nature. We will automatically surrender to Nature and attain the true yogic state of *samādhi*.

Ahiṁsā, non-violence, is another part of the first limb, *yama*. Religion teaches non-violence as a moral injunction. But I tell you, no morality can be practiced. Even if we are successful, then we will be schizophrenic. If we can understand and practice, it will never be a discipline. It will be just falling in tune with Existence. *Ahiṁsa* should be practiced out of deep understanding and then we will start radiating it in our very walk and talk. Even animals will be attracted to us. Our very being will be a blessing to planet Earth.

One of the other rules in *yama* is *satya*, truthfulness. Truthfulness can happen in us only after we have experienced *samādhi*, the eighth limb. Until we attain enlightenment, whatever we think of as the truth is only a perception of our five senses, not reality. The rules of *yama* and *niyama* (discipline) will only be established firmly after we have experienced *samādhi*.

More than what actions you do, the space from which the actions are done and the context and reason from which the actions are done, that matter. Whether we believe it or not, accept it or not, we are divine. To realize our divine nature, ancient mystics have created this wonderful eight-fold formula of the yoga system. Yoga in modern days is practiced just for health reasons.

Listen! You can do yoga with a smaller reason and smaller context like just to have flexibility or to get out of back pain. Or you can do the same yoga with the right context of becoming in tune with Cosmos, *Brahmāṅda*. In what context you do yoga, that result you reap. When you practice the right reason, right results come. When you practice the same yoga with the smaller reasons, only the smaller results come. At the most, you will have good health. Good health is just a by-product of practicing yoga, not the end.

The actual reason, the right reason that our wonderful Sages created this formula, was to create the divine experience within anyone who used the formula. Yoga is a straight technique to achieve the Divine experience. This formula cannot be modified or altered or practiced in parts and pieces. This formula has to be practiced with this right reason as prescribed for one to realize the divine nature of one's Self, asserts Kṛṣṇa. Yoga is a formula in which there are techniques that can be practiced to reach the Divine.

Learning yoga means bringing integrity to your body. Once we become intensely tuned to the eight-fold formula, it will become such an integral part of our being that it will become difficult to forget it even for a minute. When we practice yoga to meet with the Divine we will not treat yoga as an activity to be performed at a particular time of the day. We will live and breathe yoga. These eight limbs of yoga will influence any activity that we perform. For example, if you are speaking to someone you will constantly be aware of the need to speak the truth. You will constantly bring integrity into the words you utter to others and to yourself.

'*Yogasya prathamaṁ dvāram vānga nirodhaḥ.* The first step in yoga is reduction in the words inside and outside of you.' Why will the words you create be reduced when you step into yoga? Because you bring integrity and awareness into your system! Now you become responsible for the words you utter to you and to others. What will happen? Naturally, reduction in words will happen.

When you bring integrity, the words inside and outside you automatically drop, drastically. When we bring authenticity, the words will increase, and our capacity to fulfill it will also increase.

'*Yogaḥ karmasu kauśalam*—yoga is authenticity in action!' When authenticity is in action, it is yoga. If you are performing an activity, your awareness will be completely on that activity. You will bring authenticity in every level—the way you do business, the way you maintain relationships, the way you take responsibility, the way you think, cognize, and respond to the world, the way you behave with you, with your body; with everything bring authenticity.

I was taught *Aṣṭāṅga Yoga* by a great yogic Master, Yogirāj Yogānanda Puri (lovingly called Raghupati Yogi). He started training me when I was barely three and he was then already nearing one hundred years of age. I truly believe that he was a descendent of Patañjali; he was so much in tune with the *Yoga Sūtras* of Patañjali. I hated a lot of what he made me do then. He made me climb pillars in the Arunachala temple in Tiruvannamalai with one hand behind my back! But it was this training that allowed my body to withstand the rigors of my spiritual wandering through the country and the Himalayan mountains, in search of Enlightenment.

Now, I teach Aṣṭāṅga Yoga, as it was taught to me, with the additional experiential insight of Patañjali's vision that I have gained since then. I call it *Nithya Yoga.* The path and purpose of *Nithya Yoga* is bliss. It is bliss arising out of the merging of body, mind and spirit, when the glimpse of what we truly are is experienced by us.

The word 'yoga' in Saṃskṛit means to unite or to become one with. Actually, yoga refers to the process of uniting. What is important in yoga is the journey, the path, and the process. For whatever purpose, with whatever intention we move our body or bend our body, that idea, that intention, is completely inserted or recorded into our body and mind, our bio-memory. This may appear startling to us but it is the truth from my experience.

Whatever thought pattern and intention, the *saṁskāra*, you hold when you move your body, that *saṁskāra* will get inserted into you and will start expressing itself in your body. For example, if you move your body with the intention and the strong belief that you will have health, in whichever way you move your body, health will simply happen. With any physical movement, including just sitting, if you strongly believe that you will have health, health will simply happen in you.

This leads us to an important conclusion: the method in which we do postures in yoga is not important. It is the thought, the idea with which we move our body in the posture that matters. Understand that the body itself is made out of bio-memories and muscle-memories. Whether we believe it or not, we are an expression of our own self-hypnosis. Here is a simple technique to experience this truth: For just ten minutes in the morning, visualize your whole body as a bliss bag filled with bliss. Then move the body in whatever way you want. The body will start working, experiencing and expressing the bliss.

When we reach the state of yoga, we are in a meditative state of bliss. In this state, all desires for sense gratification and activities cease. Our existence becomes an outpouring of bliss. There will be so much bliss bubbling up from inside that there will be no need to look for an outer object, person or location to influence this bliss. The desire to run after goals will automatically drop. This bliss is beyond the body and the mind. This state of bliss can radiate and flow out to touch outer objects, but the outer objects cannot influence this inner bliss!

Are You Your Friend Or Your Enemy?

6.5 *You are your own friend; you are your own enemy.*
Evolve yourself through the Self and do not degrade yourself.

6.6 *For him who has conquered the Self, the Self is the best of friends. For one who has failed to do so, his Self will remain the greatest enemy.*

6.7 *For one who has conquered the Self, who has attained tranquility, the Supreme is already reached. Such a person remains in this state, in happiness or distress, heat or cold, honor or dishonor.*

6.8 *A person whose mind is contented, because of spiritual knowledge, who has subdued his senses and to whom stone and gold are the same, and who is satisfied with what he has, He is said to be established in self-realization and is called an enlightened being.*

6.9 *A person is considered truly advanced when he regards honest well-wishers, affectionate benefactors, the neutral, the mediators, the envious, both friends and enemies, the pious and the sinners with equality of mind.*

You are your own friend; you are your own enemy. Evolve yourself through the Self and do not degrade yourself.

uddhared ātmanātmānaṁ nātmānaṁ avasāyadet |
ātmaiva hy ātmano bandhur ātmaiva ripur ātmanaḥ || 6.5

In my discourses, if I have quoted any Gītā verse more than twice, it is this one. I can say this single verse provides the essence of the whole Gītā.

In the last session, we saw how to move from 'doing' and 'having' to 'being'. Usually we are stuck in 'having'. We are constantly focused on our possessions, our status. It is always 'I' and 'mine'. Loss of possessions affects our ego and identity deeply.

A slightly more intelligent person moves from 'having' to 'doing', from passivity to activity. Then, from doing we are supposed to move to 'being', from activity to active-passivity. This shift to 'satva', active passivity, helps us evolve spiritually as we move deeper into completion. In the last chapter we learned the technique from Kṛṣṇa for moving from fear and greed into Divine consciousness and bliss.

In this verse, Kṛṣṇa says:

'One must raise himself with the help of his own being and not degrade himself. The being is the friend of the conditioned soul and his enemy as well.' You are your own friend and you are your own enemy. If you know the technique of how to lift yourself by yourself, you will become a friend of your Self. If you let yourself down, you will become an enemy of yourself.

A small story:

> There was a big spiritual organization. A monk was sent to a remote tribal area to perform service. Suddenly the headquarters received a lot of complaint letters about that monk.
>
> After reading the complaint letters, the president said, 'We have posted the right person. Don't worry.'
>
> The secretary was puzzled and asked him why he thought this despite all the complaints received.
>
> The president replied, 'If we are getting complaints, it means that he has already started working. At least something is happening.'

When we start anything new, we will always have three phases. The first is resistance. The second is avoidance. We just avoid, neither caring nor resisting. The third is acceptance. This is the way anything starts. Similarly, when we start doing anything inside our system, we start growing in the same way.

First, resistance: we will repeatedly fall. We will forget. Our system will resist. We will try to create complications and complaints and all possible arguments. Sometimes, if we can't follow the teachings of Kṛṣṇa, we start blaming Kṛṣṇa. I have seen many people, when they are unable to follow the teachings of Kṛṣṇa, they will go ahead and start blaming Kṛṣṇa saying, 'What Kṛṣṇa are you talking about? He was always flirting. What type of a person was He?' We can easily escape Kṛṣṇa by criticizing Kṛṣṇa.

When we can't practice these teachings, we start justifying ourselves. Since we are unable to follow, we start criticizing Kṛṣṇa. This is the best way to escape and avoid the teachings of Kṛṣṇa. When our being resists, if we allow the resistance to grow, we are our worst enemy. This is what Kṛṣṇa means by saying, 'May you lift yourself by yourself. May you raise yourself by yourself' If we don't, we will be our worst enemy. It is up to us to enrich ourselves as best friend or to hurt ourselves as our worst enemy.

Please listen: Nobody can hurt you unless you allow him or her to. Nobody can help you unless you allow him or her to.

May you lift yourself by yourself. May you lift yourself to your Self. Again and again, these Masters stress the same point. If you have fallen, if you have failed while practicing these words, the teachings or the meditation techniques, if you have forgotten, don't worry. Again and again, lift yourself. Don't give up on you. Don't feel depressed and don't have guilt. Don't get dejected thinking you will not be able to do it. Don't doubt your self. Again and again, lift yourself.

Here Kṛṣṇa says, 'May you lift yourself by yourself. Nobody can do anything unless you lift yourself—*uddhared ātmanātmānaṁ nātmānaṁ avasāyadet.*'

Don't give up on you and people! Internalize this important truth—do not give up on yourself and people! Even if people fail a hundred times, continue to work with them. When you are frustrated at other people's failure, understand that it is nothing but your frustration towards your own failure. If we turn our back on people, we are not living *dharma*, because when we give up on others, we have also given up on ourselves! So never give up on you and people!

Listen. Nobody really wants Enlightenment! And even if we do, we want it as one more item in our showcase. We are not ready to risk anything for Enlightenment.

Whenever people come to our houses, we can say, 'This is from Delhi, this is from New York, this statue is from Japan.' Just like that, we can say, 'Oh... this enlightenment... do you know that Master, Nithyānanda? He gave it to me. He was giving a Bhagavad Gītā discourse that I attended and he just gave it to us. How does it look?' Just as one more showpiece, we are ready to accept it, but we are not ready to commit or risk anything for it. We are not ready to take up the responsibility for it.

Here, Kṛṣṇa says, 'May you liberate yourself by yourself. Unless you liberate yourself, nobody else can liberate you; uddhared ātmanātmānaṁ nātmānaṁ avasāyadet. If you help yourself, you will be the greatest friend for yourself. If you don't, you will be your worst enemy—*ātmaiva hy ātmano bandhur ātmaiva ripur ātmanaḥ*'

This is an important verse. This has to be understood well. Let us see the next two verses to get the complete context and then we will enter into the meaning of the verses.

Conquer Your Senses, The Self is Already Achieved

A small story:

> There was a great enlightened Master. He was always in ecstasy, always in joy.
>
> One of his disciples asked him, 'Master, how are you so blissful? I have never seen you suffering. You are always joyful. How is this possible?'
>
> Master replied, 'Every morning when I get up from bed I ask myself, what do you want today? Do you want to be blissful or do you want suffering today?

Naturally what will the mind choose? It will choose to be blissful. Then, immediately, I tell the mind: alright, be blissful. That's all!'

We may think, 'How can it be so simple?' Be very clear, we know our twenty-four hour routine. Just try this tomorrow morning. Just decide whether you want to face your normal routine with bliss or with suffering, with joy or with the usual long face. Decide for yourself. You have the choice. And whether you go with a long face or with a smiling face, the routine is going to be the same.

I always tell people, 'Pain is inevitable; suffering is a choice.' We have one thing that we can choose—and that is our inner space. Do we want our inner space to be incomplete like the Kauravas filled with hay or do we want our inner space to be fulfilled with completion like the Pāṇḍavas, radiating the light and fragrance of bliss? We have complete freedom to create our inner space. That is purely our own decision with no one to blame. Pain is independent of suffering. Pain is an external thing, suffering is an internal choice.

Hell or heaven is our conscious choice. People always have another question, 'What do I do if my mind says, I want to suffer?' Then suffer, that's all. What is there in it? When our mind wants to enjoy suffering, then even suffering becomes an enjoyment for us.

So when you get up every morning, ask your mind, 'What do you want today?' If your mind chooses bliss, just tell your mind, 'Be blissful. That's all!' This single conscious decision can change the quality of your life. But don't make a commitment to do this for three days or one week. You will forget. Decide every day for just that 24 hours. People will immediately think, 'Let me decide for my whole life today itself.' No! You will forget. You will be back with the same face again tomorrow. No, don't decide for your whole life. Decide only for one day. Only then will you be able to maintain it.

A small story about this natural face:

> The head of a monastery, was teaching the young novices to preach. He was giving them tips on how to speak in public.
>
> He said, 'When we speak, our whole body should express what we are saying. Our face should express the idea that we are talking about. When we speak about heaven our eyes should sparkle and our whole body should show the bliss, we should express the joys of heaven clearly. Our face should shine.'
>
> He continued, 'When we speak about hell, we can just remain as we are. People will understand!' At least in our life, let us not maintain the long face as our natural face.

When we conquer the mind, happiness and distress are both one and the same and we are not touched by it. Now, Kṛṣṇa has an important point here. He says, 'For one who has conquered his Self, has already attained the supreme bliss, *jitātmanaḥ praśāntasya paramātmā samāhitaḥ*, for him happiness and distress, heat and cold, honor and dishonor are all the same, *śītoṣṇa-sukha-duḥkheṣu tathā mānāpamānayoḥ* (6.7).'

Throughout this chapter Kṛṣṇa emphasizes this one idea—senses. Kṛṣṇa speaks about the senses. How can happiness and distress, heat and cold, honor and dishonor be the same for a man? How is it possible?

The first thing is that when our senses do the work, we decide '*yes*' or '*no*' only based on our past experiences, the experiences with which we have grown or the words with which we have conditioned our mind and memory. Our intelligence decides based on our root thought patterns which are the incompletions of our mind and memory. Please be very clear: something that is tasty for us may be like poison to our neighbour. Why even go as far as our neighbour... Take your spouses for instance. You might like something, but she or he might hate it.

Whenever our mind is caught in dualities, again and again we fall back to our dilemma, to our nature, to our suffering, to our instinct level.

Here Kṛṣṇa says the person who has achieved bliss is not affected by heat or cold and joy or sorrow—*śītoṣṇa-sukha-duḥkheṣu*. How do we reach that state? First, understand that when I say conquering the senses, I don't mean controlling the senses or destroying the senses. If we try to control or destroy the senses, we will only struggle and suffer more and more. If we try to control our body, that is not going to work either.

Kṛṣṇa says beautifully, 'For one who has conquered the self, *jitātmanaḥ*.' When He says self, He means the whole cognition where the decision-making happens. Mind-Intelligence-Ego is the spot where the decision-making is happening. When we just try to conquer the senses, we will fail again and again. If we fail two or three times we will lose the confidence to try again. If we fail in a fight with our senses, we will automatically start thinking that it is impossible, and we will lose confidence. We need intelligence to progress in this path.

We need to learn the science of creating the space of completion to conquer the senses. If we try to work from the wrong side out of incompletion, from the side of the senses, we will never be able to succeed. If we try to create more pressure on the cooker we will not be able to open the cooker lid. First, we need to put out the fire, the energy supply. Putting out the fire is doing completion with our root patterns. The ego or root patterns or the intelligence, the place from where we make decisions, is continuously supplying energy to our senses. So all we need to do is to work at the level of the mind and not at the level of the senses to become *jitātmanaḥ*. If we try to work at the level of the senses, we will create only more and more perverted desires, leading to more and more incompletions.

For example, normally, if we fast for one day, that night in our dreams we will be feasting! Our body has got its own balance, its own intelligence. If we avoid something, it has to supply and rejuvenate itself. If we are hungry, we can't sleep. In order to sleep, our bio-memory itself should be made to believe that we are not hungry. For this, we need to do completion with our patterns of food not suppression of the desire of food. So, the unconscious energy creates a dream as if we are feasting.

Whenever we deprive ourselves, our unconscious energy will satisfy itself in the dream state. This is because in the dream state, there is noone to control us; all our incompletions simply come out in the dream. We just project our world and enjoy it.

See, I initiate thousands of people into a powerful spiritual process called *Nirāhara Saṁyama*, liberating them from their food patterns. Listen. It is awakening, rekindling the power of your bio-memory to produce energy and food directly from air, water and space. It is not fasting. An important rule in this process is the moment one feels hungry or tired, one has to start eating. One cannot use his or her willpower. Understand, if you fast, in the dream you will be dreaming as if you are feasting, eating! But, not a single one of my *Nirāhara Saṁyama* participants has a dream of eating food and feasting! Why? Because they are initiated into the most practical method of completing with all the root patterns. They don't suppress their hunger, they just go beyond it, they go beyond their senses!

Understand, if we suppress something, it will automatically express itself in our dreams. Dreams are nothing but expressions of our suppressed desires and fears. Not only that, it expresses itself in a perverted way. If we do completion with our root patterns and out of completion when we enjoy with the senses, we will never become tired. But when we suppress our senses, our being suffers in our dreams.

Now there is a new concept called 'fear stroke'. These are imaginary fears, such as imagining ghosts lurking in dark corners, or the sudden ringing of the telephone, etc. We also get these fear strokes in dreams. Please listen. If we are suffering with incompletions at the dream level, there is something seriously wrong at the mind-intelligence level. We are trying to control the senses instead of conquering the mind. Instead of removing the fire, we are trying to create more pressure in the cooker. All we need to do is to work on the mind, do completion to remove the fire, to stop the supply of fuel to the senses.

Completion! Again and again complete! Understand, if you have dreams, whatever type of dreams they may be, whether they are good or bad, you are not worthy of *sannyās yoga* or *karma yoga*. Sannyāsi is a person who should be in that level of completion where no dreams happen in him. The day you start sleeping without dreams, you have become a real sannyāsi, a real *karma yogi.*

Dreams are nothing but the incompletions expressing in your inner space when you are unconscious. Understand, I am defining what is dreaming and thinking.

Incompletions expressing when you are unconscious are dreams. Incompletions expressing when you are conscious is thinking. Incompletions expressing when you are unconscious is dreaming.

Arjuna is called *Gudākeśa* by Kṛṣṇa, the one who has not just conquered dreams but who has conquered sleep itself. While addressing Arjuna as *Gudākeśa*, one who is in the light, having conquered sleep, Kṛṣṇa readies Arjuna for liberation.

Here Kṛṣṇa says, 'For one who has conquered the mind, *jitātmanaḥ*.' He means that this applies to one whose mind has learned the right cognition of completion. If our intelligence and memory are filled with past incomplete memories, we cannot make correct decisions. Don't think the mind makes decisions in a logical manner. For example: when you see me, if you have had any problems with any other person who was wearing this same color robe in the past, suddenly that memory will be awakened. Then, the intelligence is not even ready to sit and listen. Immediately, our ego gives the order to leave. This is what we call prejudice.

A man whose senses are complete, meaning one who is not driven by his senses, has the ability to make decisions with clarity from the pure space of completion. Such a being is *jitātmanaḥ*—the conqueror of the mind and the self.

Fountain of Bliss is within you

We can never achieve bliss by controlling the senses. We can only achieve bliss by controlling the mind by completing with our root thought patterns, which give birth to the mind. By changing the servants, we can't change the leader. But by changing the leader we can change the servants. The mind is the leader or the master who is making decisions and leading the senses. So all we need to do is work on completing with the mind, not the senses.

Kṛṣna says, 'One who has conquered the mind achieves the *Paramātman* (divine Self), *jitātmanaḥ praśāntasya paramātmā samāhitaḥ* (6.7).' We don't need to achieve bliss. It is always there within us. If it has to be achieved, there is every possibility it can be lost. If it can be lost, what is the guarantee it will be there forever? Anything, if it has to be specially achieved, is not worth achieving. But if it is our very nature, then it becomes easy. Kṛṣna says that all we need to do is conquer our mind. We don't need to achieve anything.

The fountain of bliss is continuously happening in us. Our very life energy is bliss. Unless we have the bliss energy in us, we cannot inhale and exhale. But we are stopping the bliss fountain again and again. All we need to do is stop the stopping process. That's all. We don't even need to create anything or achieve anything. Kṛṣna says that we just have to conquer the mind because the Self has been already achieved and we are with it. All we need is completion with our Self.

Here is a small story to explain how happiness and sorrow are in no way related to the outer world but to the inner world.

> An old man went to a nearby city for some work. When he was coming back to his village, from a distance he suddenly noticed that his house was on fire. He started shouting, screaming and rolling on the ground and weeping.
>
> His son came to him and said, 'Dad, don't worry. Don't you remember, we sold that house just yesterday?'
>
> Immediately, the old man sat up and wiped his tears. The sorrow just disappeared. In ten minutes, his other son came

to him and said, 'Dad, yes, we have sold it, but we are yet to get the money.'

Again the man started rolling on the ground and weeping, 'Oh, I don't know what I will do now. I don't know how to save myself.'

Some ten minutes later, his wife came on the scene and said, 'Don't worry, just this morning I saw that the money was deposited in our bank account.'

Again the man got up and wiped his tears and became perfectly normal!

If you notice, it is the same situation and the same person. But when he thinks the house is his, he is suffering, and when he thinks it is not his, he is liberated. So what gives us suffering? It is just this single thing: thinking that something is 'mine'. The habit of thinking, 'mine', 'mine'.

In the same way, there are people who can't enjoy something unless it is theirs.

One day I was going for a walk on the beach.

One of our devotees started saying, '*Swamiji*, I think we should have a cottage here. It would be very nice. We can come out and enjoy the breeze.'

I asked him, 'Are we not enjoying ourselves now? Why do you need a cottage here to enjoy? Just enjoy yourself now!'

But the mind never enjoys unless we are sure it is ours. Unless we possess something, we don't enjoy it. By the time we own the cottage we start worrying, 'I think I should have this kind of furniture, that type of arrangement.' Or we have already started thinking about another cottage in some other place.

Ramaṇa Maharṣi was a great devotee of Arunachala, the sacred hillock in Tiruvannamalai, Śiva's own form, my birthplace. Someone who visited Him for the first time said, '*Master*, what a beautiful place this is! The Arunachala hill is so beautiful!'

Ramaṇa Maharṣi said, 'Just be here for three days, all these ideas will disappear!' In three days, we take things for granted.

Something will be beautiful only for three days. The person who enjoys only by possessing will never enjoy. The person who enjoys will not bother about possessing. It is just our mind. Sometimes, the mind will not allow us to enjoy something unless we know for sure that it is ours. And at other times when we know it is ours it creates suffering. Suffering or joy is created only by that one link, the mind. There is no other difference between an enlightened person and us other than this mind, which continuously thinks, 'What is in it for me? In what way am I connected?'

We always complain about the senses. No, we are corrupting them. Don't put the responsibility on the senses. Just look into your life. It might be late at night, even two a.m., but we will still watch our baseball or cricket game on television. Our eyes are begging for some rest, but we continue to watch the game. We abuse our eyes, our senses because we want to enjoy ourselves. Please listen, it is this pattern: 'What is there for me?' This 'I', 'I', 'I' is where we start abusing the senses. All we need to do is control the mind, not the senses.

Understand, our thoughts create our senses. Don't think we are living with what we have. We create what we want to have. Our thoughts are so powerful that they can just change the whole body. For example, just think of one thought that creates disturbance inside you. Or think of a person who took money from you and has not returned it. Immediately, we experience the change happening in our system. Our blood boils, our blood pressure rises, our heart rate and pulse rate rise. A single thought can change the whole body chemistry.

Our body is created only by our thoughts. In India there is a great science called *sāmudrikā lakṣaṇa.* Just by seeing the body-language—the face, the body, the way of standing, sitting and walking, the trained sage can tell everything about the person's mind. This is because he knows the secret that the mind creates the body. The body is the outer expression of the mind. The mind is the inner experience of the body. If our mind changes, our body can be changed and our whole system can be changed.

A man whose mind is clearly reprogrammed according to spiritual ideas can completely change his senses. As of now, our mind is programmed for misery. It is looking outward. If we can reprogram our mind to look inward, towards bliss, our entire sense experience can be changed. All we need to do is to reprogram our mind to look-in and be complete. This is the gist of this whole chapter.

Kṛṣṇa says one more important thing about heat and cold. Let me tell you very clearly: I lived in the Himalayas and I used to sleep on the snow with this same cotton dress. It may be very difficult to believe but it is the truth. All we need to do is stop resisting. Just try this experiment: the moment you feel the cool breeze, don't create the idea, 'It is cold, I may catch a cold, I may have wheezing or sinus problem.' Just don't create such words.

The words you give to yourself can be nectar or poison. The words you constantly repeat to yourself, have to be enriching you, exciting you and enlightening you. The words you give to you are āhara (food), what you consume to create life in you. The words you give to yourself are more important than the words you give to others. Because the flow of your life–the level of contentment that you feel in your life and the experience of fulfillment that you feel in your life, everything depends on the words that you have given to you. Whenever we repeat something, we create that quality in us.

Here is a simple experiment you can do: Close your eyes and repeat ten times: 'Śānti, Śānti, Śānti,' you will have peace inside (Śānti means peace in Saṃskrit). Just by repeating the word 'Śānti', the quality of peace will start happening in you. In the same way, if you repeat the names of diseases, you will start creating those diseases in you.

Whatever we think, we express. We need to do only one thing: Work to bring completion to the mind. Do completion with your thought patterns. Just liberate the mind with completion. Then our whole system will be purified. Our senses will be reconstructed. Kṛṣṇa gives us a beautiful technique to work on the mind.

He says one more important truth, 'Honor and dishonor will be the same—*māna-apamānayoḥ*.' This is very difficult to believe. Cold and heat or hot and sweet can be the same. We can even accept that. But honor and dishonor, how can the two be the same? A single word thrown at us is enough to anger us and hurt our honor.

Please listen!

A thought pattern is a pre-defined way of responding to any situation based on a powerful past experience like failure, rejection, being punished, being subjected to abuse or witnessing the death of a loved one. During such moments of crisis, you create an idea about yourself and life—like 'I am weak' or 'I am a failure' or 'Nobody loves me' or 'Life is dangerous, so I have to be very careful.' Almost all root thought patterns are negative, even the ones which may lead to success in your life, because they are born out of your feeling of powerlessness. You have many thought patterns, but a root thought pattern is one of the few defining thought patterns that are continuously running your life without your knowledge!

Align Your Images and Go Beyond Duality

Someone asked me, '*Swamiji,* why do we bother so much about others' opinions?' We bother about others' opinions because we don't have an opinion about ourselves. We know about ourselves only through others' words and their opinions. Our identity is built based on others' opinions. We understand and identify ourselves through others. If everybody says, 'You are beautiful,' we get that certificate. If everybody says, 'You are intelligent,' we get that certificate. We collect all these certificates and we build our personality with them.

Even the conflicts among your identities are nothing but the result of your root thought patterns. If you have a certain idea about yourself inside, but you project a different personality outside, that is inauthenticity. If you look deep, all your problems arise from conflicts among your dentities. When any of your dimensions is out of alignment with the others, it causes disease, suffering and incompletion in your life.

In the Inner Awakening Program, the first session is about the understanding of root thought patterns. It is about why we get depressed, why we are in conflict, why we repeatedly fall into a powerless state. It is because our energy source is others' certificates. We don't have any self-respect and self-completion. We constantly live in self-doubt, self-hatred and self-denial. If others' opinions about us are good, we think we are great. If others' opinions about us are not good, we immediately lose self-completion and fall into self-denial. If our idea about ourselves is 'nobody loves me', then we project the outer personality of 'I am very loving person' or 'I am very friendly person.' This is inauthenticity.

But our root pattern is—we don't even love ourselves. That is why there is so much of self-hatred. We don't have any self-respect, only self-hatred, self-denial. That is the reason for the wars within and around us.

Living is a power. If we want to live, we must learn how to stand on our own two feet, learn how to be complete with ourselves, how to raise ourself by ourself without giving up on us and others. This is the science of completion that is taught and transmitted experientially in the Inner Awakening program.

As of now, our source of energy is others' opinions or others' image about us. If somebody tells us, 'You are really great,' we may project an outer image of acting humble and try our best to say, 'No, no, I am not,' but what happens inside us? Our life image, the expectation from others' and life says, 'Please tell me a little more!' And our inner image may feel, 'I am a failure' or 'I am not good enough.' Outside we feel shy but inside our mind we feel powerless, and that powerlessness makes us want them to go on praising us to fill our incompletion within.

Please understand, all these identities you carry are actually thought patterns that you carry about you. Even others' image about you is an idea that you have created in them. So you are the creator of all your identities. Understand?

Now, when one identity is fighting with another identity, how can your thinking be focused? All your energy is going to be used in reconciling your fighting identities. When all your identities or 'images' are in tune, all your thinking will be aligned in one direction. Your thinking becomes clear and sharp, like a laser beam. You will awaken the power of thinking. With authenticity, there is no more space for unconscious thinking and living, because you will always be aware of the causes and effects that are playing in your life.

Winner of Senses is the Self-realized One

Kṛṣṇa says, 'A person whose mind is content because of spiritual knowledge, who has subdued his senses and to whom stone and gold are the same, and who is satisfied with what he has, is said to be established in Self-realization and is called an enlightened being'

jñāna-vijñāna tṛptātmā kūṭa-stho vijitendriyaḥ |
yukta ity ucyate yogī sama-loṣṭrāśma-kāñcanaḥ || 6.8

First we should understand why Kṛṣṇa is speaking of all these qualities of a Master. These qualities are techniques. If we practice them we will reach the same enlightened state.

There are three things we need to understand here: First, experience comes out as expression. Second, the quality of experience and the quality of expression, are very closely associated with one another. And third, a very important thing, is that if you concentrate on the expression, you will reach the experience. Here, again and again, Kṛṣṇa speaks about how an enlightened person lives and the qualities that an enlightened person expresses, so that we can meditate on it. When we begin internalizing these ideas in our lives, we can reach the consciousness of an enlightened being. When we contemplate upon these ideas, we start expressing them naturally and they sink into our being.

Kṛṣṇa says repeatedly, '*Vijitendriyaḥ*'—one who has subdued and won his senses. This whole chapter is just about the senses, indriya. Kṛṣṇa gives us a beautiful technique to heal the problem. He gives us a method to complete with the root thought pattern and go beyond. All we have to do is understand the root thought patterns; understand where we are caught and where our incompletions lie.

Beyond the ego or root patterns we have the *ātman,* the Self. Just the presence of the *ātman* or the light of the ātman radiates and makes our ego work. The whole trouble is when we doubt, judge for ourselves and start thinking, 'What is there for me? How am I going to gain or to lose from this?' Here is where the root problem starts. If the ego and the intelligence are removed from the system, the self starts radiating its energy directly through the senses.

That is why enlightened people have sharp senses. Their senses are not contaminated. Whether it is their vision or their listening, it will be sharp and deep because it is not corrupted by the root patterns. Only a person whose being is clear and complete will have pure senses. A man who continuously uses his senses abuses them. He will not have energy or *tejas* in his senses.

The first thing that happens to a man who has used and abused his senses is the loss of his sense of smell. Then you need to be immediately admitted into the ICU of spirituality. You need Inner Awakening immediately. When our mind is under our control and complete we develop equanimity. We look at everyone the same way. This really happens when we reach enlightenment. When we become enlightened there is nothing to be achieved. Our being will start respecting, loving and enriching everyone automatically.

Here the word 'equal' is used, but the exact translation of the word 'sama' should be 'unique'. When we understand that everyone is unique, we respect him or her. Sometimes when we say we treat everyone equally, we start disrespecting everybody equally! We are not all the same. We are all unique. God is an artist not an engineer. That is why He painted each one of us so differently, so uniquely. If He was an engineer, He would have just ordered ten thousand pieces of Mr. India or one million pieces of Miss Universe so all of us would look the same. When we understand that each one of us is unique, we will start enriching every being. Understand, even our enemy is necessary for our life. Just like our friends, our enemies also may be playing a role in our life. When we understand that each and every being is unique, we will see everybody with the same mind or in the same way.

One more thing that Kṛṣṇa says here is about 'the pious and the sinners, *sādhṣv api ca pāpeṣu*'. Be very clear, there is no such thing as sin, except calling human beings 'sinners'. Kṛṣṇa rightly states that the enlightened being sees only Divine Consciousness in everyone and so can never label anyone as being pious or a sinner.

Understand: God accepts each one of us as we are. The society created the idea of sin and merit. Immediately, the next question will be, 'Then can we do whatever we want?' A man who understands this spiritual science will never disturb others. Our sin and merit should not be based on fear or greed. If it is just based on heaven or hell, I don't think we can claim to be matured beings.

Let discipline happen to you as an understanding out of the space of completion, a natural flowering. Let our morality not be based on fear and greed. That is why in Patañjali's *Yoga Sūtras*, there is a beautiful word '*yama*', which means discipline. It also means death. If we understand that our life is going to end in death, if our consciousness internalizes this truth, we start thinking and meditating upon death. We will automatically be disciplined and will completely restructure our whole thinking and our life. If we start thinking about *yama* (death), then *yama* (discipline) will happen in our life. In Saṃskrit, for both discipline and death, we use the same word. Let our discipline happen only out of the complete cognition of death and not out of incomplete cognitions of fear or greed.

Bring Integrity To Control The Senses

6.10 *A Yogī should always try to concentrate his mind on the Supreme Self; situated in a secluded place, he should carefully control his mind without being attracted by anything and should be free from the feeling of possessiveness.*

6.11 *In a clean and pure place, one should establish his seat by laying kuṣa grass, a deerskin and a cloth one over another, neither too high nor too low.*

6.12 *Sitting firmly on that pure seat, the yogi should practice the purification of the self by controlling the activities of the mind and the senses.*

6.13 *Holding the body, head and neck steady, looking at the tip of his nose without looking in any other direction.*

6.14 *Let him sit with an unagitated mind, free from fear and in tune with Existence, controlling the mind, focusing it on Me and making Me the Supreme goal.*

In these verses Kṛṣṇa gives directions for the practitioner of Yoga, the Yogī. There are instructions about both the state of the mind and the state of the body.

These verses are often quoted and misused with a literal understanding and without grasping the inner meaning and significance. We can sit with closed or half closed eyes, with spine erect, in a sound-proofed dark room, and still be far away from enlightenment. Understand, these are general and practical guidelines given to help us with how we should sit and meditate. These are not essential qualifications for Enlightenment.

Kṛṣṇa repeats the importance of controlling our senses again and again. Why?

Senses are our doors to the external world. As long as they are open and uncontrolled, we are immersed only in the external world. It is impossible to understand our true reality when we are studying the external world. We may become a great scientist or a wealthy businessman by observing the outer world, but never an enlightened person. For this path, looking inwards is the only way.

Unclutch and Become Liberated

Controlling the senses requires controlling the mind. Controlling the mind requires control of thoughts. Controlling the thoughts requires integrity. When we continuously live integrity, we will become aware of the thoughts and processes happening in our inner space.

And constantly listening to our own inner space is the beginning of integrity. If our inner space says that there is nothing more to listen, if only silence is there, then that is the end of integrity. We have achieved integrity. When we start listening to our inner space, we start integrity and when we listen to only silence from our inner space, we have achieved integrity. As long as we are hearing something from our inner space, it is lack of integrity.

Go on listening. Even while you are sitting, driving, talking or walking, listen to you. Also listen to you, when you are talking! It is listening to you that is going to bring integrity to you! Listen! Listen! Untiringly listen! Intensely bring integrity to your life. If we sit for a few minutes and intensely listen and analyze our thoughts, we will find that there is no connection between one thought and another. There is no logic in our thinking process. By their very nature our thoughts are illogical, unconnected and irrational. Thoughts keep swinging from past to future and back to the past.

We need to do two things to control our thoughts. First, we need to stay in the present moment by refusing to move to the past and future and second, we need to disconnect thoughts. I call this Unclutching. We need to be aware that thoughts are not inherently connected. We connect them into a shaft of joy or sorrow. These shafts do not exist at all. So I say to you, unclutch and become liberated. I am not saying to stay without thoughts. That is not possible; just witness thoughts. Understand that thoughts are unconnected. Detach yourself from the emotional baggage of the thoughts. If we detach ourselves from the regrets of the past and the speculations about the future we will automatically rise into the present.

People again and again ask me, 'The moment I sit for meditation or Unclutching, I have more thoughts! I have more confusion, I have more problems. Next time, I don't want to sit for meditation or Unclutching. *Swamiji,* what should I do?'

How will you not have thoughts or confusion? Unclutching is not like switching off the electricity to your house. It is like cleaning, sweeping and wiping your house. It is not like electricity that you will just switch off and be unclutched. No! It is like cleaning, sweeping and wiping. First, listen to your inner space! That is the first step to meditation, to life. Listen!!

We cannot live without desires. If anyone tells us that we can reach Enlightenment through elimination of desires, it is incorrect. First of all, we are already enlightened. Our inner Self knows it is connected to the Divine. We are just not aware of it, that's all. If we are already there, how can we achieve it? Second, desires are energy. We cannot inhale and exhale without the desire to live. Simply dying will not give us the experience!

That is what Kṛṣṇa talks about here—dropping the attachment and possessiveness to desires, not the desire itself. It is the feeling of 'mine,' the desire to possess, that creates the feeling of 'I,' not the other way around. Our identity is made up of all the things that we want, that we desire, that we are attached to. These constitute our mental make-up. The seeds of desire and embedded memories are the stuff our package of 'I' is made of. Once the feeling of possession, the feeling of 'mine' disappears, it is possible to shed our identity as well. When we are free of the feeling of 'mine' and 'I', when we are not attached or attracted to external objects, when we are not led by our senses, we have steadied the mind and senses. To facilitate this, Kṛṣṇa stipulates the conditions.

We should go to a secluded place. Why? Whatever said and done, in the house, the phone may ring, somebody may knock or some salesperson may call. A secluded place is really just a means to move us away from these disturbances. Śrī Rāmakṛṣṇa continuously recommends in his books that every person should retire from the regular activities at least for two or three days a month, or at least once in six months, and re-align himself towards the higher ideals. I also recommend this for all my followers and disciples, at least once in six months, take three or four days off. Come and spend your time in the Bidadi ashram campus, realigning yourself to integrity. Here, you will see and hear the miracles happening just by integrity and authenticity. Only when you see all these miracles with your eyes, you will understand the power of integrity, the power of authenticity. Whatever is happening is the power of *dharma.*

Buddha means a person who has aligned with *dharma.* Sangha means a group of people who are aligning with dharma. But *dharma* is the center. It is the power of *dharma*. Once in a while, you have to retreat from the regular activities and align yourself to integrity, authenticity, responsibility and enriching.

The *kuṣa* (a grass ideal to sit on and meditate), deerskin and all those things are like insulation, so that the earth will not absorb the energy we create. But now we don't have to bother about that, since we usually sit in a chair, raised a little from the ground. The seat should neither be too high nor too low and it should be comfortable. That's all. The most important thing to be aware of in any meditation is to be relaxed. We cannot meditate in discomfort. *Sthira* (stable) and *sukha* (pleasurable) are the basic essentials of any meditation posture.

Here Kṛṣṇa updates the technique that He gave earlier. Here He gives three more instructions:

1. Head, spine and neck should be in a straight line.

2. We should fix our eyes on the tip of the nose. If we look at the tip of the nose, naturally, our awareness will settle on the third eye. Our concentration will settle on the *ājña cakra* (the brow energy center).

3. We should meditate on 'Me' as the supreme goal.

These are simple, commonsense instructions. Keeping the head, neck and spine, all in one line, helps in two ways. Firstly, it prevents us from dropping off to sleep. If we doze, our neck will drop, and we will no longer be steady. Secondly, as long as the head, neck and spine remain steady and vertical, the flow of pranic energy, the life-giving energy, through the energy pathways will be unblocked and smooth.

Whether we close our eyes fully or half close them, it is important that we disconnect from the external world. When the eyes are focused on the tip of the nose, they are not looking at external objects and ninety percent of sensory inputs are cut off. In addition, the focus is on the third eye between the brows, which, when energized, dissolves the ego block.

Finally, Kṛṣṇa says, 'Focus on Me—*manaḥ saṁyamya mac-chitto*. Make Me the Supreme goal—*yukta āsīta mat-paraḥ* (6.14).' He means our true Self. If we like, we can meditate on the form of Kṛṣṇa, with a flute and peacock feather. But I always prescribe going beyond the form. Go into your being. Of course, when we enter into our third eye, automatically we will go beyond the form. We will start meditating on the formless energy that is beyond the form.

Neither Too Much Nor Too Little

6.15 *Always practicing control over the mind and established in the Self, the yogi attains peace, the supreme liberation and My kingdom.*

6.16 *Yoga is neither eating too much nor eating too little;*
It is neither sleeping too much nor sleeping too little, O Arjuna.

6.17 *One who is regulated in food, rest, recreation and work, sleep and wakefulness can reduce misery.*

6.18 *When the mind is disciplined and one is established in the Self, free from all desires, then one is said to be established in yoga.*

6.19 *As a lamp in a place without wind does not waver,*
so also the yogi whose mind is controlled remains steady, engaged in yoga, in the Self.

Kṛṣṇa talks here about control of the mind and being established in the Self. He talks about the path and the goal of yoga. The first line of *Yoga Sūtras* starts with '*yogaḥ citta vṛtti nirodaḥ.*' It means: Yoga is cessation of the mind. The very first line gives the path and the goal of yoga. The word yoga means uniting with the Divine. To reach the Ultimate, the goal and the path is the practice of Yoga.

We have two lives in us. One is the life we want to live–the dream. The other is the life in reality–the life we are living. The meeting of these two lives is what I call Yoga.

You can unite the two either by reducing the depth of fantasies or by increasing the expression of your energy so that reality can come closer to the dream. If you reduce the depth of the fantasy, your expectation, the dream plane and the reality plane will come closer together. On the other hand, if you increase the energy expressed through reality, the reality plane will come closer to the dream plane. The meeting and merging of these two planes is what I call Yoga.

The goal is uniting with the Ultimate or experiencing the ultimate spiritual energy, or the Divine and realizing our inherent nature. The path is dropping the mind, which means going beyond thoughts. We are spiritual beings having a human experience; we are not human beings having a spiritual experience. This is the truth. Bliss is our very nature. All that we need to do is go back to the source and realize our true nature.

The mind pulls us towards the temporary happiness that we experienced by pursuing sense pleasures. For example, we may like a particular sweet. We are attracted to its taste. When we sit down to eat it, for a few minutes our mind seems to stop thinking about it. There is a sense of peace when we are eating the sweet. Actually, we are at peace because the number of thoughts has come down for those few minutes. But we think the peace we experience is due to the sweet itself.

Understand that there is nothing wrong with liking the taste of the sweet. But if we think that the sweet is the cause of our fulfillment, then the problem starts, because the next time the same sweet may not give us the same experience of fulfillment. The experience of fulfillment has nothing to do with the object of experience.

In the same way, if we hold on to an object that we think gives us bliss, we will create an attachment to that object. But the experience of bliss is different from the object. Bliss is beyond attachment to any object, material or spiritual. Bliss is beyond the pairs of opposites. When we are happy due to some pleasurable event or person, the momentary joy comes because the number of our thoughts comes down when we meet the person. When the number of our thoughts comes down, bliss happens in us. But the bliss itself comes only from our own being, not from the person who we met. In fact, it continuously happens within us, irrespective of anything that goes on outside. Then why do we not feel the bliss continuously? It is because we are under the control of the mind, which needs the pairs of opposites to survive. We can go beyond the mind.

When we are completely in reality, in the present, we are complete with Existence and we are in bliss. This is eternal bliss. '*Nitya*' or 'eternal' means the past, present and future all put together, because it is beyond time. Being in the present is what eternity is. The present blissful moment gives birth to the next moment, which will be blissful. But if we try to look for bliss in the future, thinking that we can do various things to create a blissful future, it will never happen. When we are not in reality now, we are creating the blissful future from our fantasies. So come to terms with reality here and now and be blissful; automatically the future will also be blissful.

Bliss is like the water in a river. We can keep our hands open in it and enjoy it. But if we try to hold the water with closed hands, it will simply flow away from us leaving our hands empty. If we want to be in eternal bliss, we need to be blissful this very moment. We should not bother about whether we had bliss in the past or whether we will have it in the future. Just be blissful now.

When Kṛṣṇa talks about the mind and the senses being controlled, He is not talking about suppressing the mind and the senses. That is impossible to do. People who claim to renounce the world and its material aspects still cling to desires. Their efforts result in misery. Instead of directing our senses towards external objects and the pleasure derived from these objects, it is possible to turn our focus inwards and experience inner joy. Once the senses and the mind discover this inner joy, they will give up their attachment to external pleasures. Suppression never works; what works is completion.

To be balanced in whatever we do and to act without attachment is the path of a Yogī. Whether it is eating or sleeping or working, we should be sensitive to our body's intelligence. Understand, when we are complete, we will be sensitive in all our actions. Only when we are not complete or conscious will we be caught in confusion.

Yoga manuals will not tell us what Kṛṣṇa tells Arjuna here. Guidelines on sleeping too much or too little or eating too much or too little is in no way a prescribed method for yoga. Controlling or regulating the senses does not mean we should suppress the senses. Eating too much will only make us lethargic—*tāmasic*. Eating too little will make us crave more food. If we sleep too much, it will lead to laziness and lethargy, *tamas*. If we sleep too little, we will end up feeling tired because the body-mind is not rejuvenated enough.

How do we know what is too much or too little? Here, Kṛṣṇa actually refers to our body intelligence. We do not trust our inherent body intelligence. We run our body according to the mind or according to our desires and senses. Otherwise, why would we stay up in the night watching television when our body is begging for some sleep? Why would we overeat? Has anyone seen any animal ever overeat? They eat according to their body intelligence. When the body signals that it needs food, they eat. When the body signals that it needs sleep, they sleep. We have forgotten how to relate with our own body intelligence.

After eating, we should feel energetic. But do we feel energetic after lunch? Why do we feel lazy and sleepy after lunch? It is because we do not eat the right type and amount of food. Most often, we don't need to eat the amount we do, for our body to run. Just try this for a few days: When you eat, eat just enough until you are about full but not completely full. Try this for a few days and you will see a difference.

Similarly, we do not need to sleep for as long as eight hours as most of us do. Even science has established that there are periods in our sleep—the dream and deep sleep states that determine our holistic health. Actually, it is in the deep sleep state that we access the causal body, the *kāraṇa śarīra*, where we touch the source of our energy. Touching this layer is what gives us energy and rejuvenates us. This state can be achieved through meditation as well. In the course of an eight-hour sleep cycle, we are in the deep sleep state only for a couple of hours. That is why even a few minutes of meditation can actually refresh us as much as a few hours of sleep, because we access the same energy of the causal body through meditation. We should trust our body intelligence and just try to live by becoming sensitive to the body, rather than be driven by the mind, the senses.

Kṛṣṇa talks about *āhāra* in these verses. *Āhāra* in Saṃskṛit means food. It is the food that is taken in through our five senses, not just the mouth. Pratyāhāra, one of the eight parts of yoga, is the control of sensory inputs. It means going beyond these āhāra, beyond the sense objects, so that the higher level of consciousness can be awakened. When we move away from the senses and experience bliss, we will automatically realize that what we experience through external sense objects is not bliss. What we experience through the senses can be called pleasure or joy. That is why, the opposite of joy that is pain, is bound to follow this temporary pleasure. Bliss is beyond the pairs of opposites like pleasure and pain; it is not related to external incidents or people. It is an internal happening.

The main aim of all our yoga and meditation techniques is to reach the level of our being. When we reach the being, we are in '*nitya ānanda*' or 'eternal bliss'. We are in union with the Divine. Bliss is actually what we are running after but we think it can be achieved through money, comforts, relations and what not. We do not realize that all these objects only give us temporary states of pleasure and happiness. Our inherent nature is bliss and that is the reason why we are constantly searching for this state of bliss. When we realize that bliss is happening inside us all the time, the desires will drop automatically. You cannot drop desires or suppress them because they will surface again with greater intensity.

When we are aware of our actions, we can never be addicted to anything. Be very clear, all addictions, whether smoking or drinking, drugs or anything else, cannot exist if we are conscious and aware when we are engaged in the action. We try to suppress the desire instead of doing completion with it, and that is where the problem starts. An addiction has power over us because of a feeling of guilt or regret, or unfulfillment.

When we drop the guilt pattern by doing completion, many of our repetitive negative behavior patterns drop automatically. Moreover, we cannot consciously send something harmful into our system. We cannot consciously inhale harmful smoke into our system. To those who come to me for help with addictions, I say, 'Smoke as much as you want. Drink as much as you want. But do it with awareness. Do it with enjoyment out of completion.' In a few days, they come back and say they cannot smoke or drink anymore. That is because the innate body intelligence refuses to cooperate with the disastrous activity.

Completion is the key to bring the mind under control, because then we become the master of our mind, instead of the mind being our master. Normally, our mind oscillates between the past and the future just like the flame of a lamp that's wavering in the wind. When the same lamp is placed in a windless place, it stops flickering. By nature, the mind is in dilemma. We cannot suppress it or control it just by allowing it to wander either. All we can do to still the mind is to stop bothering about it, just witness it and complete with it. So just relax.

Be in the Present to be Complete

All our patterns, desires, and fears arise because, at the root, we feel that life has some goal, some purpose. Understand that life has no purpose. It has only meaning. The path itself is the goal; enjoy the path. We think life is as we are living now. Understand that the way we are living life in our world of fantasies is actually like living in our dream world. When we realize the purposelessness of life, we can drop our desires and fears, we can plunge into reality, into the present.

The moment we decide to stay in the present space of completion, the mind stops flickering. When the mind does not flicker and stands still in the present, then we reach the state of 'no-mind'. In this state of 'no-mind,' we don't creates, sustain, or destroy any thought. We relax from all these three things into the space of no-mind.

Our mind is like a lake. When we throw a stone in a lake, many ripples will be created. If we want to stop these ripples, we cannot put our hand in the lake to try to smoothen out the ripples. This is what we end up doing when we try to still our minds. Instead if we just watch the lake, and ensure no more stones are thrown in, the ripples will disappear and the lake will become still. If we just relax and watch our mind with complete awareness, then no new thoughts will be created.

In Bhārat (India), we say that God has three roles—creator, sustainer and destroyer. Brahma is called the Creator or god of creation. Viṣṇu is known as the Sustainer or the God of maintenance. Śiva is called the Destroyer or the God of rejuvenation. Listen, when our thoughts stop performing these three roles of creation, sustenance and rejuvenation, when we transcend all these three, we become *Parabrahma,* supreme Self. When there are no new thoughts being created, sustained or destroyed, then the mind is absolutely still.

There is a beautiful story described in Śrīmad Bhāgavatam, the history of the various Incarnations of Lord Viṣṇu:

> Devatā, the demigods were oppressed by the demons and appealed to Lord Viṣṇu for help. According to His directions, the demigods were to churn the ocean of milk using the Mahā Meru mountain as the staff and Vāsuki, the serpent, as the rope.
>
> During the churning, many products emerged out of the ocean of milk including an elephant, a horse, a divine chariot and many other divine things. Then, *hālahāla,* a deadly poison emerged, that threatened to take the lives of everyone. Lord Śiva came to their rescue by consuming the poison Himself. He drank the poison but did not completely take it in. He just held it in His throat. That is why He is referred to as Nīlakanṭha, the one with a blue throat who has swallowed the poison and holds it in His throat.

Listen. When the churning of the milky ocean started, everyone was waiting only for the nectar. That is why, when the poison emerged, it was a suffering for them. But Mahādeva was waiting for the poison also, that is why it could not bring suffering to Him. Śiva is never surprised by the poison brought to Him. That is why He is Mahādeva, Śiva!

This is actually a metaphysical representation. Nīlakaṇṭha is embodiment of responsibility. Nīlakaṇṭha is the symbol that Mahādeva is complete with both desires and fears. Life is like the churning of the ocean of milk where we are churned, pulled towards the desires and pushed away from the fears. There are various products that emerge out of the churning, out of the decisions and choices we make in life. Some of these products appear pleasing while others appear dangerous like poison.

When we exist with responsibility without taking in the poison or throwing it out, meaning without running towards the desires or running away from the fears, we become Śiva and live life blissfully as Nityānanda, irrespective of what comes our way.

Self Is Satisfied In the Self By The Self

6.20 *In yoga, the mind becomes quiet and the Self is satisfied by the Self in the Self.*

6.21 *Supreme bliss is grasped by intelligence transcending the senses. The person who knows this is based in reality.*

6.22 *By attaining that Supreme, one does not consider any other gain as being greater. By being established in the Supreme, one is not shaken by the greatest of misery.*

6.23 *When yoga is practiced with determination without deviating, the misery by contact with the senses is removed.*

6.24 *Giving up completely all the fantasies born of the mind, one can regulate all the senses from all the sides by the mind.*

Kṛṣṇa talks about two important things: practice with determination and practice without deviating from the prescribed way. Both are key elements to experience yoga. After a few days of practice it is easy to fall into inertia, tamas, and give up on ourselves. Our mind has been programmed with our old routine for years and will will draw us back to the old ways. This is where determination is needed. Determination driven by the curiosity and the quest to see and experience the truth is what will give us the energy to practice yoga.

The other important element is practice without deviating from the prescribed way. We are re-introducing, re-presenting yoga in the form of *Nithya Yoga*—the yoga of eternity. I can say re-presenting because it is a new expression. The method has evolved but the system, the truth itself is the same as the original system offered by the great master, Patañjali.

His system is so complete that we can't add even a single word to the techniques. It is the experience of Truth and Truth cannot be developed. Only lies can be developed. All we can do is help evolve the teaching of Truth to suit the current minds.

Kṛṣṇa emphasizes here that yoga should be practiced in the prescribed way. All eight parts of yoga need to be practiced, simultaneously. Even one part of Patañjali's *Aṣṭāṇga Yoga* will take many lifetimes to achieve, given the modern man's mindset.

Please understand, Patañjali's *Aṣṭāṇga Yoga*, eight organs of yoga or *aṇga* has unfortunately been wrongly translated by the English yogis as 'eight steps of yoga'. Because of this, it has become just a small few techniques or methods to make your body flexible and a little healthy. That is a disgrace done to yoga. When you get a diamond and you use that diamond just as a vegetable cutter, it is a disgrace to the diamond. In the same way, when you use such a great power, the powerful science of yoga just as technique to bring a little health, it is so unfortunate!

Satya, truth, is a part of *yama*, the first of the eight steps of Aṣṭāṇga Yoga. If we consistently practice truthfulness alone, we will reach samādhi, the state of liberation. Our thoughts, words and actions become pure and truthful only when we are enlightened; only when we bring integrity in our words, authenticity in our thinking and actions, responsibility in our feeling, and enriching in our living.

Please listen! Yama is Integrity. Niyama is Authenticity. Āsana, Prānāyama, Prayāhara, Dhārana are Responsibility. Dhāyana and Samādhi are Enriching.

This is what Kṛṣṇa means when He says, 'Self is satisfied by the Self in the Self, *yatra caiva ātmanātmanaṁ paśyann ātmani tuṣyati* (6.20).' All of this has to happen together, not part by part. When one aspect is complete, all others also become complete. This is the state of pūrṇa, complete completion. Nothing can be taken away from it. Nothing can be added to it that would make any difference to its state of completeness. No joy can make it more blissful, no sorrow can make it less blissful. One becomes centered in bliss. When centered in bliss, it is forever!

Kṛṣṇa talks about moving into reality, transcending the senses and the mind. The way yoga is taught and practiced in many places, one is moved away from reality into a fantasy world, to fulfill one's imagined needs. The senses and the mind wander aimlessly. We cannot suppress desires, because anything suppressed will surface with more intensity. We might have experienced in our own lives that a desire may be satisfied momentarily, but soon afterwards, it arises again. Instead we need to understand what is happening and how it is happening. The way out of the mind is also through the mind and not by avoiding it. Completion process is the key through which all our emotions can be handled. They basically originate from the root patterns of greed and fear. As we witness and do completion with our root patterns, the fear and greed lose their grasp on the mind.

Take fear for example. What do we do when we feel afraid of something, whether it is fear of insects or fear of heights? The moment we are faced with the object of fear, we try to escape. Have we tried facing the fear? The next time you are afraid, try this. Instead of running away, just try looking at the fear consciously, go through it fully and declare completion with it. Do not identify with it by trying to suppress it or run away from it. I tell you, when you look at fear with completion, you will see that the fear does not exist as you thought it existed. It simply does not exist because fear is born out of ignorance, when something is unknown to you.

When we bring the light of knowledge upon fear, ignorance is removed and we get the courage to see the object as it is. Because now there is nothing hidden, our mind cannot fantasize about the unknown.

So understand, our fears are nothing but negative fantasies and we can complete with them. The same also applies to greed. Why do we always feel that we need more? We start running after the next desire before one desire is even fulfilled. We are so tuned to running after things.

'What next? What next?' becomes our chant. Have we ever stopped to think what we are running for? After fulfilling a desire, have we stopped to think whether we have achieved what we wanted? Have we stopped to enjoy what we just fulfilled? If we sit and contemplate sincerely over one desire after fulfilling it, by now, we would have gotten out of the vicious cycle of desires.

Can we ever drink water from a mirage? Running after the fantasies created by the mind is just like running after a mirage or running after the horizon. We can never achieve bliss by running behind these fantasies because these fantasies have no existence in reality.

Be In The Self And See The Supreme

6.25 *Gradually, step-by-step, one should become established in the Self,*
held by the conviction of intelligence, with the mind
not thinking of anything else.

6.26 *From wherever the mind becomes agitated due to its wandering*
and unsteady nature, from there,
one must certainly bring it under the control of the Self.

6.27 *The yogi whose mind is peaceful attains the highest happiness;*
His passion is pacified and he is free from sins
as he is liberated by the Supreme.

6.28 *The yogi always engaged in the Self and*
free from material contamination
is in touch with the Supreme and attains the highest happiness.

6.29 *The yogi sees the Supreme established in all beings and also all*
beings situated in the Supreme.
One established in the Self sees the Supreme everywhere.

Here Kṛṣṇa says that we need conviction and intelligence to be established in the Self. Why does He talk about conviction? Understand that intelligence cannot happen without a strong conviction, a strong intellectual base

Our Vedic seers, Rsis have created *śāstras,* the foundations of knowledge that give the intellectual understanding, conviction and commitment to this process. Logically, we will be clear about the questions that naturally arise. 'What is the path? What is the goal? Why do we need spirituality?' All these questions are answered logically in the *śāstras.* The conclusions are given to us. *Śāstras* are the scriptures that take away all our doubts completely.

Saṁśaya rākśasa nāshana astraṁ—it means saṁśaya is a rākśasa—'doubt is a devil'. Once a doubt enters our mind, until we clear it, we can't rest. The śāstras help us get rid of these doubts intellectually. Unless we have complete intellectual clarity, even if we believe, our belief will be a pseudo belief.

There are different ways to learn and develop clarity and conviction. We can learn from our experiences as well as from others' experiences. For example, when we touch the flame of a candle, we learn that it burns. When we touch a burning gas stove, we learn again that fire burns. One by one, we can experience and learn that all fires burn. Or, when we touch the first form of fire, immediately we can learn that all fires will burn! Coming to a conclusion and a clear understanding that all fires burn, after just one experience, is intelligence!

We need a strong conviction for spirituality to flower in our lives. Only then can we stay on the path without faltering. If we do anything with knowledge about the science of the whole action, then the activity becomes a meditation. When the science is lost and only the activity remains, it becomes a ritual. When the juice of wisdom is not in the activity, it becomes a ritual, and we become religious nuts. When we add the juice of wisdom, we become spiritual fruits! We need to add 'spirit' to the 'ritual'. Then it becomes 'spirituality'!

We can start with simple things. We can try to infuse completion into simple actions in our everyday life like eating, having a bath, driving. Gradually, when the completion extends to more actions of our life, we can see that such awareness of completion results in bliss. Completion is bliss. We need to bring the light of awareness and completion into everything we do. It is a conviction arising out of our innate intelligence and understanding that we must return to our true nature, that is Divinity.

Persevere and See Me In Everything

Now, Kṛṣṇa is emphasizing an important spiritual quality—

perseverance. In the previous verse, He spoke about conviction. Now, he talks about persevering with that conviction. What happens most of the time to most of us is that when we realize we need to transform, we try a few times and then we give up on ourselves thinking we cannot do it. We expect the mental setup that we have created and solidified, to be broken and restructured in a few attempts, almost instantly. How is this possible? We need to be more patient and persevere in our efforts for the real change to happen.

So what if we fail sometimes? Why don't we look at the positive side and see that we succeeded a few times? Why do we want to count the failures and feel depressed? We can also look at the successes and feel inspired. Once the conviction is there, nothing can stop us except our own mind. The mind is like a faithful servant. It reproduces whatever it has been fed. All along, we have been feeding the mind negative memories of failure and we have been storing all the past memories related to failure. What will the mind reproduce? It will recollect and present the same instances of only failure. When we want to measure the strength of a chain, we measure the strength of the weakest link in that chain. But we cannot apply the same logic to measure ourselves.

When we measure our lives based on our weakest moments, our failures and our incompletions, we take a wrong reading of ourselves. We cannot do with our lives what we do with the chain. Why can't we give credit to ourselves for the strong, successful moments of our lives? We have been conditioned by society to consider ourselves weak beings, that we are not powerful. We have been taught to feel guilty. Does that help us in any way? No! It only creates low energy and powerlessness.

Listen. Strength is Life. We should just decide that we will not be trapped in this cycle of guilt and desire. We need to measure ourselves by our strongest moments, our greatest moments of powerfulness, when we have displayed extraordinary awareness, courage, compassion, love and such other divine qualities. A human being is the sum of his greatest moments of completion. He is not a mechanical device that fails based on its faults. He is a spiritual being who thrives on his strengths.

Understand that you attract 'like' incidents in your life. 'Like attracts like.' The energy of one frequency attracts the similar frequency. When we are angry, the low energy attracts similar low energy. Pain attracts pain. Joy attracts joy. Bliss attracts fortune. If we are joyful, we will create a beautiful community of joyful people around us. It is for us to decide what we want to attract.

We must persevere in our efforts to change our space and we will see the results in front of our very eyes. Failures are merely tests to verify our mettle. Irrespective of how many times we may fail, with complete faith, with integrity and authenticity, we can trust in that inner strength that we all possess. Then we shall succeed. This is what is meant when Kṛṣṇa says the true yogi reaches the state of ultimate happiness, the state of eternal bliss and divine consciousness by his identification with the Absolute.

In the next verse, Kṛṣṇa talks about passion and sins.

Passion is nothing but a deep attachment to something for the pleasure that it gives. Usually we associate passion, sin and such terms with deeds that we classify as right or wrong. But here, Kṛṣṇa does not talk about sin in the way society teaches us. It is not morality that He is talking about. I tell you, there is no sin except the sin of connecting thoughts and thinking that we are logical beings.

So, the key is to be in the space of completion every moment. The solution is not to condemn ourselves as sinners and expect some external force to bring completion to us. It is we who choose everything in our lives and how we want to live. But since we do not participate in this process consciously, we call it 'fate'. We are the ones who do the actions, but we don't want to accept that fact when we get the results. Somehow we choose to do whatever we want to do and then blame everyone else for the consequences! When we infuse completion into our actions, automatically the very completion will ensure that we have the integrity to do the right things. Listen! When you are integrated, so many resources which are present in you as a potential, suddenly becomes a reality in you! When we are integrated, we don't need to depend on society and morality to teach us the right things to do.

I tell you, live according to your intelligence and awareness. If you depend on others, even after becoming an adult, it means you are not mature. Anything done out of conscience does not have the conviction of experience to back it. That is why it is never done whole-heartedly, because your energy, your intelligence is not behind the action. Have you seen a child doing anything, like looking at a flower? A child will look at a flower not just with its eyes, but also with its entire body. A child does anything and everything completely. We should try to look at life in a similar way. Many of us have not experienced the joy of enriching someone whole-heartedly. On the other hand, if we are smokers, do we need somebody to convince us to smoke? No! Smoking has become our experience.

When we are in bliss or the highest happiness, we can never commit any sin because we are aware and conscious and we cannot be caught in passion or lethargy. When we are in a 'no-mind' state, we are in bliss and we are not caught in the passion or sin that are products of the mind. When the mind drops, the Divine hand that is orchestrating every single event will guide every one of our actions.

What does it mean to be freed from all past sinful reactions? Our past reactions are nothing but our root patterns, the past memories along with the associated emotions, deeply inscribed in our unconscious space. Whenever we hold on to any past incidents or emotions as root patterns, our actions are bound to be impacted by them. But, if our action is not based on the past but arises from a spontaneous decision based on the present situation, then we are 'responding' to the event or incident or person. When we are in bliss, our actions will be only a response not a reaction, which is based on these past memories that Kṛṣṇa calls past sinful reactions.

Have the courage to complete with your root patterns, to make decisions without referring to these past incidents, because every single incident and moment is a brand new one. How can we compare what is happening now with what happened before? The situation is different, the person is different and so are we. Every moment, each one of us is dying and being born again; we are changing. Our intelligence is being constantly updated. Then how can we analyze the present situation through the lens of the past? We must complete with all regrets and guilt that we might have about the past, and immerse ourselves in the present moment. We don't need the past to live beautifully in present space of completion. In fact, we can't live blissfully in the present if we continue to use the past as a reference point for how to manage our lives.

Realized One Sees the Supreme Everywhere

Kṛṣṇa says that the realized person, *yoga-yuktātmā*, sees the Supreme in everyone and everything. He sees everything situated in the Supreme and all beings situated in the Supreme. The yogi is in touch with the higher Self and is in bliss.

sarva-bhūta-stham ātmānaṁ sarva-bhūtāni cātmani |
īkṣate yoga-yuktātmā sarvatra sama-darśarsanaḥ || 6.29

When we experience the Truth, we see everything in ourselves and ourselves in everything. In fact, in my first spiritual experience at the age of twelve, this is what I clearly saw.

> When I was twelve, I was playing with this technique of just watching where thoughts came from, the source of my thoughts. At that age, I didn't even realize it was meditation. One day, at the foothills of Arunachala, in my hometown of Tiruvannamalai in South India, I was sitting on a rock, just playing with this technique that I had been practicing for two years.
>
> Suddenly, something happened; something opened within me. I felt as if I was being pulled inside. Suddenly, I could see 360 degrees in all directions. My eyes were closed but I could see everything in front of me and behind me.

Not just that, I felt that whatever I was seeing, was all me. I could see myself in everything—in the trees, in the rocks, in the ground, in the hills, everything!

An Enlightened person sees no difference between Himself and the rest of the Universe. He is one with the Universe. His boundary does not end where his physical body ends. In fact, now with Kirlian photography, we can even check the auric body. For ordinary people, the aura just surrounds the physical body but when you are one with the universe, the aura extends infinitely. The *Viśvarūpa Darśan*, vision of the cosmic form, that Kṛṣṇa gives Arjuna is the glimpse of the same Truth, where Arjuna sees that Kṛṣṇa is one with the Universe.

In the ultimate sense, the moment we understand that we are deeply, totally and intensely connected to the whole Universe, not only do we start experiencing bliss, we really start living in the space of completion. Many dimensions of our being start opening. Right now we are stressed out and disturbed continuously because we think of ourselves as individual egos. If we disappear into this collective consciousness, we will experience so many dimensions and so many possibilities that we simply cannot imagine right now!

When we see an Enlightened Master, we understand how all-encompassing he is. He never excludes anything or anyone. He is just pure love, that's all. And pure love sees no imperfections. When we see every human being as a part of God, then that is real worship. It is easy to worship god in the temple. Real worship is seeing everything as God. Existence is pure love.

Deep inside, society is actually against Existence or god. It is against pure love. The best way not to follow anything is to start worshipping it. Society escapes in the name of worship. Society will never approve of us if we were to let go and love every plant and animal with endless love. It will tell us that we are mad. But I tell you, we must keep on loving with all our hearts, and expand to see Existence in everything.

The root of God is love. The root of God lies in seeing Him in

everything. People are afraid to go to the roots and so they delude themselves in superficial layers. Have the courage to go deep inside and love. We will start feeling the common thread of Existence in all that we see. We will understand that all that we see are illusory happenings held together by the real thread that is Existence. Automatically we will start loving everything in the same way without any trouble because we will see only Existence in everyone and everything. Each and every atom in this Earth is unique, is divine, and is an expression of Existence.

Controlling the Wavering Mind

6.30 *For one who sees Me everywhere and who sees everything in Me, for him I am never lost nor is he lost to Me.*

6.31 *He who is in oneness with Me in all respects, worships Me situated in all beings and remains present in Me.*

6.32 *One who, by comparision to his own Self, sees the true oneness of all beings, in both their happiness or misery, is Supreme Yogi in My opinion, Arjuna.*

6.33 *Arjuna says: O Madhusūdana, this system of Yoga as described by You, appears unendurable to me, for the mind being restless and unsteady.*

6.34 *O Kṛṣṇa, the wavering mind is agitated, strong and firm. I think it is difficult to control the mind like it is difficult to control the wind.*

6.35 *Bhagavān says:*
O mighty-armed Kaunteya, it is undoubtedly difficult to control the wavering mind but by practice and detachment, it can be controlled.

Here, Kṛṣṇa gives a promise. He says that for anyone who sees Him in everything and who sees everything in Him, He is always available. Neither Kṛṣṇa is lost to him nor he is ever lost to Kṛṣṇa.

yo māṁ paśyati sarvatra sarvam ca mayi paśyati ||
tasyāhaṁ na praṇaśyāmi sa ca me na praṇaśyati || 6.30

What He means is not that we should see the form of Kṛṣṇa in everyone, with the flute and two peacock feathers. Of course, that form is beautiful but do not get caught in the form. The form is there one day and not there the next; it is ephemeral. It is like this: if my finger is pointing in the direction of the moon, look in the direction of the moon and enjoy its beauty. Instead, if you watch my finger, you will miss the moon!

What Kṛṣṇa means by 'Me' is the Kṛṣṇa energy, the Divine consciousness. See the Divine in everybody and everything and automatically, you will relax. You will no longer fight because you will see everything around you as a part of the Divine, including yourself. What is there to fight with and what should you fight for? You will simply relax.

Existence is waiting with open arms to engulf us, to dissolve us into Itself, but only if we are ready to let go. If we just have the courage to let go with an open heart, we will meet and merge with it. When we are ready to feel the embrace of Existence, we rise into a higher plane, a plane of higher consciousness. We enter into a space we never even knew existed. With Existence we always fall in to rise.

All Are Infinite

People ask me, 'How can we tell that you are the right Master for us?'

I tell them simply, 'Forget about any analysis or intellectual reasoning. If I am truly your Master, you can never forget me. I will be there even in your dreams!' The relationship between the Master and disciple is one of pure love. When we are truly in love, we see the object of love in everything around us. We are consumed by that feeling. The Master fills every pore of our being. We never need to ask, 'Are you my Master?' We just know! He has filled our being, touched us at our core, because to him, there is no separation. Here, Kṛṣṇa is describing the state of the enlightened person. An enlightened person can empathize with everyone because he experiences himself as everyone.

An incident from the life of Swami Vivekananda:

> One night, Vivekananda woke up at two a.m. and woke up his disciples. His disciples became anxious. Vivekananda said that he was feeling a lot of pain and that

> in some part of the world there was a natural calamity happening that was causing him the pain. The next morning, the newspapers carried the news of a terrible earthquake in Fiji Islands that consumed many lives. Vivekananda was sensitive to a calamity that happened in some corner of the world thousands of miles away!

What happened in Vivekananda is what we call empathy. It is not sympathy. Sympathy is a very superficial word. We are all capable of sympathy. When someone tells us that they are suffering, we make some noises and just confirm their suffering for them. That is sympathy. When we sympathize, we affirm to them that their worries are big, so we actually give them a subtle ego boost.

What an Enlightened person or a Master feels is never sympathy. It is empathy. Empathy is when we feel another's suffering in our own being. It is when a person does not have to tell us he is suffering, but we simply know because the Existential energy in us feels it. Masters are one with us because they are one with Existence and we are a part of Existence. It is only that we see them as separate. In reality that is not the case.

When we realize the sense of non-duality and infinity with the entire Universe, we experience a tremendous overflowing of love and compassion for every being without discrimination, because we realize that everyone is a part of the same Whole. That is why we can see that Masters are such an ocean of infinite love and know only how to give. They are Existence itself. They shower love without asking questions because they feel a constant devotion towards the entire Universe or life force or *Parabrahma* Kṛṣṇa. They cannot see anyone as a separate entity because there is no separateness.

It is only our senses, mind and logic that perceives information and categorizes it and analyzes it to create the separateness. As long as we use our logic, our collected information, words and our little dictionaries to analyze the information received through our senses, we will be excluding and judging. Existence or the Universe is a living energy with infinite potential, which is simply beyond our logic. Only when we drop our logic, mind and ego can we merge with Existence and become whole, and start seeing that everyone and everything is an extension of the same life force with just different expressions.

Just as the fingers on the hand and the toes on the feet belong to the same body, we will be able to see that everyone is a part of the same Universal Energy. This is when true compassion, empathy and sincere service towards enriching everyone can happen. Until then we will only be using our logic, mind, ego and conditioning, to enslave others.

When we realize the infinity of everyone, we will express our unconditional love and compassion towards everyone without discrimination, because we know that all discrimination is baseless and false. Our very walk and talk will start radiating so much bliss that our very presence will start healing others. We will become a blessing for planet Earth and the people who experience our presence.

There are a few disciples who have internalized me so much, that they express me in everything that they do. People who come to the āśram are amazed to see these people who walk and talk like me. Some people think that these disciples are doing it to show off. No, they are so much in tune with me that they reflect my body language, my presence is in them.

Kṛṣṇa goes further to explain the state of an enlightened person or a person who is one with the Divine Consciousness. He says that the enlightened person will feel equally the happiness and pain of another person as he feels his own. Such a person feels one with the whole world. For him, everything is a part of him, so there is nothing else other than his own self. His boundary does not end with the boundary of his own physical body. What does Kṛṣṇa mean when He says that the enlightened person feels happiness and distress equally in himself and in others?

First, He said that the Enlightened person is beyond the opposites, the dualities, beyond the opposing emotions of happiness and distress.

It is like this, say there are two trees in a forest. Now, if one tree falls on the other, we can say that the tree on which the other tree has fallen feels the impact or the pain of a falling tree. Now, say the tree actually feels the entire forest as a part of its own self. Can we say that it will feel 'another' tree falling on it? When everything is a part of its own self, where is the idea of 'other'? When the idea of 'other' disappears, then where is the pain? The idea of pain is relative. The enlightened person is just immersed in enjoying Existence. No separate identities or judgments about right or wrong, happiness or misery exist.

A Yogī in the state of super-consciousness will just watch everything in Existence without judging or labeling it. He will be in a state of complete celebration of life. Existence is love and nothing else. Yet, the compassion of the yogi, the Master, is such that he feels the experiences that others undergo and he empathizes with them. The Master's state of equanimity is not disturbed and yet he feels the pain and joy of others.

This expression of collective consciousness is what Kṛṣṇa has described elsewhere as *Vasudaiva Kuṭuṁbakaṁ*. It means that the world is our family and we should feel the rest of the world as we would for our immediate family. When we exist in this state of consciousness, we are true Yogīs.

Arjuna introduces the word 'difficult or *su-duṣkaraṁ*' here. Be very clear, the moment we categorize something as easy or difficult, we have made it that way. Understand that the ego can be fulfilled only through difficult things. Simple things cannot satisfy the ego.

After listening to Kṛṣṇa about controlling the mind, Arjuna expresses his doubts about being able to still the mind. Arjuna is actually asking about problems that will be faced by future generations also. His question is not just an individual's question. The questions are the fundamental quest of the individual and the answers are the eternal Truth. We now have become more complex than our forefathers because of this cerebral layer that has formed with all the fantasies bombarding us from all directions. Arjuna cannot understand how to practice yoga, given the unsteady and wavering nature of the mind. Five thousand years ago, even though there was no infiltration by television and media on the scale that we have now, Arjuna expressed his doubt about how to handle the mind.

Here, Arjuna addresses to Kṛṣṇa his concerns about the mind being so strong that it sometimes overcomes the intelligence. The first and foremost thing is to accept that we have a problem, we have a root pattern. The next thing is to understand how the root pattern is created. That is what Arjuna does here. It is only then that we can overcome the root pattern. If we ignore or run away from the pattern we can never resolve and complete with the pattern. So, the first thing to accept is that our mind does oscillate, then to understand how it oscillates. For this we need to watch the mind and do completion with the thought patterns. This is meditation. The very act of watching, being aware of the mind, and completing with it will take us beyond the mind.

Here, Kṛṣṇa has to answer from the same plane that Arjuna asks the question. Arjuna says that the mind is wavering and difficult to control like the wind, *vāyor iva sa su-duṣkaram* (6.34). Just as one thorn is used to remove another thorn, Kṛṣṇa has to give Arjuna a technique. He has to support the idea that it is difficult to control the mind. So, Kṛṣṇa has to give some technique at this point—practice and detachment. Now, if He tells Arjuna that this problem is not a problem at all but a creation of his mind, Arjuna will not understand. Kṛṣṇa has to give a technique for the mind to play with.

THE PATH TO SELF-REALIZATION

Masters give meditation techniques so that we try all these and ultimately realize we are bliss, and that meditation is our natural state, and that there is nothing to be achieved. But, if I tell you that right away, you will not believe me. The mind cannot believe something so simple. It will create all kinds of contradictions and self-doubts as to why it cannot be so simple. Kṛṣṇa also has to give a solution for the doubting mind. He emphasizes perseverance and penance. Don't think penance means leaving home, going to the Himalayas and sitting in meditation while fasting. Penance is persevering with authenticity until we experience the Truth.

Kṛṣṇa also reveals the root of the problem of controlling the mind and gives the technique to complete with it, which is detachment. Here we need to understand the word 'detachment'.

Whether we say ego or mind, it is just the collection of thoughts. Thoughts can exist only in relationship to our identity and the past or the future. In the present, we cannot have thoughts because the very moment we think, the present has slipped into the past. The mind moves only because it is attached to the identities that we carry. Either we fear losing the carefully constructed inner image or we are greedy to develop a better outer image of ourselves in our own eyes and in the eyes of society.

The mind becomes so attached to these identities that it is constantly reviewing the past incidents or it is constantly planning the future to either protect or develop these identities. This constant pre-occupation of the mind with the past and future is the root cause of the oscillation of the mind. If we look deeply, staying in the present moment of completion means total insecurity. It requires us to be ready to embrace the present without planning for the future or reviewing the past. This seems like a great danger for our ego.

Listen. I tell you, any identity that we create about ourselves that is less than the idea of our being God, is a false identity. If we consider ourselves to be anything less than God, we suffer from an inferiority complex. If we have the courage to detach ourselves from the certificates of society, if we have the courage to drop these false identities, then we can embrace the Divine.

Detachment is the direct technique that Kṛṣṇa is suggesting here. Detachment at the root level will lead to detachment from everything else. Detachment from the ego or the identities will lead to detachment from desires. This is detachment from the past and future. This is being 'Unclutched'.

Where Do I Go Without Yoga

6.36 *For one whose mind is uncontrolled, it is difficult to attain yoga in My opinion. But, it is practical to achieve control over the mind by appropriate means.*

6.37 *Arjuna says: O Kṛṣṇa, if a person is engaged in yoga with faith but does not attain completion in yoga, because of the wavering mind, what destination does he achieve?*

6.38 *O mighty-armed Kṛṣṇa, does not such a person, who is deviated from the path of Absolute Consciousness [Brahman], perish like a scattered cloud without any position?*

6.39 *This is my doubt, O Kṛṣṇa and I request You to dispel it completely. Certainly, there is no one to be found other than You who can remove this doubt.*

6.40 *Bhagavān says:*
O Pārtha, the person engaged in auspicious activities for good, does not meet with destruction either in this world or the next life; he never faces degradation.

Kṛṣṇa continues to declare in this verse that it is possible to achieve Self-realization by stilling the mind if one intensely practices the appropriate techniques. Here, Kṛṣṇa explains that it is possible to achieve control over the mind. and to also stay in that state where we are in control of the mind.

Actually, having an experience of Sātori or the first glimpse of bliss is not a big thing. It is easy to get a taste of enlightenment. But to stay in that same state, the same consciousness, needs preparation of the body and mind. To express that high energy through the body and to radiate that experience of bliss requires that our body and mind be prepared. Preparing the body and mind for enlightenment is what yoga is all about. This is what sage Patañjali created yoga for. The problem is that only the verbal language of Patañjali remains, but the body language is absent. That is why so much confusion and mutated forms of yoga are around today. How much can words convey?

Only a person in the same space, in the same consciousness as Patañjali can convey what He wanted to convey. This is what Nithya Yoga is all about. Nithya Yoga is my offering to the world. It is the science, the formula, that will give others the same experience of Enlightenment which happened in me. It is yoga taught by an Enlightened being who can convey the body language and experience of Patañjali, because he is in the same consciousness as Patañjali. The whole purpose of Nithya Yoga is to prepare the body to experience, to stay in and radiate eternal bliss. Its purpose is to 'Unclutch' and enlighten. I can say it is a direct means to Enlightenment.

Here, Arjuna again asks the questions we all will have in our minds. What happens if we start with faith but somewhere, we fail in controlling the mind? Be very clear, this situation will happen. When we start off, we will face failure in our attempts to control and complete with the mind. If we don't experience this, we should check ourselves because we may be fooling ourselves with whatever we are doing!

Enlightenment is Possible for All

Arjuna wants Kṛṣṇa to give an assurance that Enlightenment is possible for all kinds of people; that even if a person starts practicing intensely but fails due to the wavering mind, it is still possible to attain the Divine Consciousness, Brahman. Actually, at the very root of Arjuna's question is the mind that is generating the fear and making him believe that it is hard to find the no-mind state.

The mind does not want to lose its existence. The mind always looks for a reason to convince us that we cannot carry on our lives without it. In our day-to-day life we face the situation that Arjuna faces here. Even with activities that we have carried out successfully many times in the past, we feel nervous when we start again. Will we succeed? What will happen if we fail? Even before we begin, we start imagining the worst.

Actually, it is okay to imagine the worst. I tell people that to overcome fear and face fear, it is good to imagine the worst-case scenario. Visualize it fully, relive such an experience consciously, taking it to its logical conclusion, and the fear will disappear. However, if all we can do is to think and brood over the worst things and continue with our fear unconsciously, we will be in the same situation as Arjuna—totally confused!

The future is not ours to see. The goal as we imagine it does not exist. There is no purpose to life. The meaning of life is to live. That is all. If only Arjuna was comfortable with just practicing the techniques that Kṛṣṇa has already outlined for him, trusting Kṛṣṇa and enjoying the path shown to him, he would not be asking such questions. Arjuna still does not believe Kṛṣṇa. He has heard and intellectually understood the meaning of what has been said, that is all. He has not fully listened and internalized the Master and His words. Arjuna has yet to learn.

Kṛṣṇa assures Arjuna by saying that there is no destruction either in this life or the next life for one who is on the right path, the path of yoga. He provides the assurance that Arjuna is looking for, since he knows how frail Arjuna's state of mind is. Kṛṣṇa is giving a wonderful assurance for all of us that even a small amount of practice of this yoga will save us from the cycle of birth and death. Any yoga practiced will give us tremendous benefit. The very intent to practice yoga itself means that we have gained knowledge about the problem of the mind.

Listen, any movement of the body with a strong intention will cause that intention to get deeply inscribed into our bodies and muscles. If the intention is wanting to become one with our true identity and wanting to drop our false identity, it will get deeply inscribed or recorded in our body and will remain there and automatically the body will start moving towards that one goal. If we move our body with the thought of bliss, the bliss emotion gets ingrained in our system. If it is anger that moves our body, the anger emotion gets ingrained. This is such an important and beautiful truth. Don't miss it!

Understand, the basic quality of life is reproduction and expansion. Therefore, it is possible for us to replicate happiness, joy and bliss as well. It is up to us to choose what type of emotion we want to allow in our bodies, what emotion we want to be ingrained in our system. All that we need to do is to intend to be joyful and joyful cells will keep reproducing. This process cannot stop. We will be full of joy.

We can try this when we meet people we do not like. Just smile at them. Not the plastic smile that only covers the lips, but a smile from our heart with warmth, so that the smile spreads to our eyes. See what happens. All our negativity will disappear. In addition, any negativity that we create in others also will disappear and they will respond with the same smile. Spread that love around and you will find that the negative emotions of people who approach us with anger, fear or jealousy will be consumed by the energy of love that we unleash.

Rare Birth Of A Yogi

6.41 *The person who has fallen from yoga {yogabṛasṭa}*
after many years of living in the planets of the pious and
doing virtuous deeds, takes birth in the house of the virtuous
and prosperous.

6.42 *Or the Yogī certainly takes birth in a family of wise people.*
Certainly, such a birth is rare in this world.

6.43 *O son of Kuru, on taking such a birth, he revives the*
intelligence, consciousness of the previous body,
and tries again to attain complete success [yoga].

Kṛṣṇa talks about how we choose everything in our lives, including our birth, when and where we are born and whom we choose as our parents. This truth may seem difficult for most of us to believe. Our birth is not just an accident. It is an incident and we are the ones who choose all the details about this incident. We must understand that it is only we who program and design everything and everybody in our life, including our parents and environment. Our choice of the next body is based on the way we have lived our life in this body.

For example, if we live to eat rather than eat to live, at the time of death, we will still have the desire to continue eating. So, we will design our next body to fulfill this desire. We might choose the body of a pig. Or, if we have lived our life only for sleeping and doing no creative work, we might choose the body of a buffalo. So, based on the attitude we have lived with, we choose the next body. This is the basic idea on which our *janma-maraṇa cakra* (cycle of life and death) revolves.

We go into a birth-death cycle. We go and come back again, taking a new body. This phenomenon happens again and again.

Whatever we choose at the moment of death will become reality in the next birth. You will be that. Some people think that they can manage if they remind themselves to think of the Divine, at the last second of their lives. But that will never happen unless we make that a habit throughout our life. If we keep chanting 'Coca-Cola' our whole life, we cannot and will not think of Rāma or Kṛṣṇa during our last moments! How we live our life will decide the quality of our death as well.

Here, Kṛṣṇa gives the assurance to Arjuna and to the whole of humanity that a person who has performed virtuous activities takes birth in a family of wise people or in a prosperous family. His pious activities will earn him a place among the higher worlds. After dwelling there for a while he will take birth in the family of righteous people to once again enable his spiritual seeking.

We can choose our body and the time that we wish to be born. When we live our life running behind our greed and desires, running after 'what next? what next....?,' naturally, at the time of our death also, we will not be ready to leave the body. The body will be tired of running behind desires continuously, but the mind will not be ready to leave. So we will leave the body in the pain and suffering of this push and pull of desires and fear. If we can just relax into the present and take life moment by moment, we will leave the body in a relaxed way, peacefully.

Once we leave the body, in three kṣaṇa, three moments, we get into a new body and we are reborn. *Kṣaṇa* in Saṃskṛit does not mean 'seconds'. It means the gap between two thoughts. If we have been constantly running behind desires, the gap between two thoughts will be really small for us. When we learn to relax into the present, the gap between two thoughts increases and the three kṣaṇas can be a long time. In three *kṣaṇas*, we take on the new body to fulfill whatever desires were unfulfilled when we left the previous body. Here, Kṛṣṇa says that on taking birth, we gain the intelligence of the previous body and continue the journey where we left off.

One thing we should understand here is that when we say death, it is not just the death that happens at the end of our life. It is what happens every day and night. Every night, we go from the physical body to the dream body and causal body. In the morning, we enter the physical body again. We die and take birth again.

People tell me, 'No, no, *Swamiji*. Everyday when we enter into the dream we are not entering into the same dream, but everyday when we wake up to the reality we are entering into the same reality. So with this scale we can say this is reality and that is dream.'

Please listen, in one night's dream we live even twenty years of life, am I right? In one night's dream, don't we live even twenty years of life? In that twenty-year span, we are in the same dream. But is that reality? No! So be very clear, this whole life which you think as reality, may very well be part of one dream! This whole span that we are thinking of as real can be part of one dream.

Every day we leave the body. We go to the causal body when we fall asleep. Every day we die. When we wake up, we come back. Every day we come back to life. As of now, every morning, how do we come back to life? How do we take this body again in the morning? Just look deeply. What happens at the time when we get up from bed?

First thing, usually, the moment we gain awareness, either a thought based on greed or fear will hit us. There will be thoughts based on greed such as, 'I need to get this today,' or thoughts based on fear such as, 'I have to finish this work today in office. Will I be able to?' Some thought based on fear or greed will hit us. Immediately, we will jump out of our bed. The moment we assume our body, that moment is a moment of taking birth. Please be very clear, that is the moment we take the body.

Early morning, the thought with which we enter into the body, which makes us assume the body, is going to play a major role in our consciousness. The first thought is going to play a major role in our consciousness throughout the day. Just as the thought with which we leave the body on dying decides the kind of body we will assume in our next birth, in exactly the same way, every day the thought with which we get up in the morning and assume this body decides the quality of that day, that life. If we understand this once and alter our thoughts at the time of waking up, we will alter the whole consciousness.

When we get up from bed, let the first thought be related to love and compassion. Wake up only to express life in bliss. Wake up just out of joy. When we get up from bed, let us assume the body with gratitude to the Divine. With this, the whole quality of our consciousness will change. We will become a Divine Incarnation!

Kṛṣṇa is actually giving a technique on how to become Kṛṣṇa, how to enter into Kṛṣṇa Consciousness, to become an Incarnation. The man who assumes the body out of love and compassion is an Incarnation.

If we assume the body out of greed or fear, we are human. Early morning, let the first thought be gratitude. Let it be out of love and compassion. Our whole life will become pure eternal bliss, Nithyānanda.

Become A Yogi

6.44 *Due to the practice in his previous life, he certainly gets attracted automatically to Yoga and he is inquisitive about Yoga and transcends the scriptures.*

6.45 *And when the Yogī engages himself with sincere endevour in progressing fruther, being cleansed of all incompletions, then ultimately, achieving perfection [saṁsiddhi] after many births of practice, he attains the highest state [parām-gati].*

6.46 *A Yogī is greater than the ascetic [tapasvi], greater than the wise [jñāni] and greater than the fruitive worker. Therefore, Arjuna, do become a Yogī.*

6.47 *Of all Yogīs, one who always lives in Me, thinking of Me within himself, who worships Me in full faith, he is the most intimately united with Me in Yoga and is the highest of all Yogīs; that is My opinion.*

Kṛṣṇa is describing the process of the human experience. Why do we assume the body? We think that we can experience bliss through the body and mind; that is why we assume the body. When we realize that bliss cannot be experienced through the body or mind, we know that going beyond the body is the only way to experience it. Then we will not assume the body. Assuming the human body is simply our choice.

People ask me, 'Why do we choose to have the human experience?' That we should find out for ourselves. Why did we assume this body? I asked the question and I got the answer. I know why I chose the human experience. Ask the question yourself and pursue it as a quest and you will get the answer. You will be enlightened.

We claim that we want to experience the ultimate and that we want to be enlightened. But I tell you, if we really want to be enlightened, there is nothing that can stop us. There is no hindrance to our being enlightened except our own self. As of now, actually, Enlightenment is last on our laundry list of items that we want to do in life! When the urge becomes urgent, when the question becomes a burning quest, then we get the answer. There is no other way.

In these verses, Kṛṣṇa promises a few things. He says that whatever we have learned in one life does not get wasted. We do not start from ground zero in the next birth. We start from where we left off. Our *vāsanas*, our mindset in one birth, continues into another. He also promises that if we keep practicing, if we keep trying, we will be cleansed of all sins and reach the highest state. Such a person, Kṛṣṇa promises, will reach Him.

At the end of the day, what Kṛṣṇa implies is this: We need to do our bit. We need to practice yoga, the path that leads to self-awareness, to self-completion, the path that leads to Kṛṣṇa, with dedication, perseverance, with integrity and authenticity. There is no other way. There is no short cut. Once you do your bit, the Master promises deliverance. He promises that you will be one with Him. We will enter into a technique given by Śrī Kṛṣṇa to go beyond the mind, to awaken our senses, to *look in.*

MEDITATION

Now it is time to look in. Now it is time to tune ourselves to that highest teaching given by Śrī Kṛṣṇa in this *Dhyāna Yoga*. Now we will enter into the meditation. If we are ready to sit for the next ten minutes, we will start the meditation.

Please sit straight and close your eyes. Keep your head, neck and spine, all three in a straight line. Inhale and exhale as slowly as possible and as deeply as possible.

Slowly, in a relaxed way, bring your awareness to your *ājña cakra*. Concentrate between the two eyebrows. Bring your awareness between the two eyebrows.

Remember and pray to that Energy that came as Kṛṣṇa, that is guiding us and helping us in our life. Pray to that Energy that gave us the *Bhagavad Gītā.*

Meditate on the pure light energy. If your mind wanders here and there, don't worry. When you remember, bring it back again and relax in your *ājña cakra*, between your eyebrows. Don't concentrate. In a very relaxed way, be aware of the *ājña cakra*, the space in between the two eyebrows.

(a few minutes pass)

Slowly, very slowly bring your mind to your heart and meditate on your heart center. If you want, you can touch your heart center with the hand and feel it. Try to bring your awareness to the heart center. Try to remember the heart center. Forget all other parts of your body; forget your mind. Just become the heart center. Just be in the heart center. Inhale and exhale as slowly as possible.

May you experience your pure inner space. May you experience the eternal bliss, *Nityānanda.*

(a few minutes pass)

Om śānti, śānti, śāntihi...

Relax. Slowly, very slowly, open your eyes.

We may wonder how a simple technique like this one can lead us into our Self.

Please understand that we always live in the head. Start living from the heart. We will then start acting from intelligence. We will start acting, not from our head but from our heart. When we start acting from the heart, we don't calculate. The very calculation disappears, the 'I, I, I' disappears. And naturally our senses become sensitive. We don't abuse our senses. We don't destroy our senses. Too much of the energy that is supplied to the heart is taken away by the mind. The fuel supply to the mind will be reduced and the fuel supply to the heart will be increased.

So try to continuously remember this heart region, *anāhata cakra.*

Naturally, we will have awareness in the *ājña* also. In the last session, Kṛṣṇa gave the technique to be in the *ājña*. Today, He says start with the *ājña* and come down to *anāhata*. This is because in the heart, there is a possibility of much more happening. The possibility of reaching is easier and greater in the heart. **Kṛṣṇa says, 'Let you be in the heart.'**

Look in! You will realize 'You are That.' Just look in, you will experience the eternal bliss, *Nitya-ānanda*. Let us pray to that Ultimate Energy, *Parabrahma* Kṛṣṇa to give us all the Eternal Bliss, *Nityānanda*.

Thus ends the sixth chapter named ***Dhyāna Yogaḥ****, 'The Yoga of Path of Meditation,' of the* ***Bhagavad Gītā Upaniṣad, Brahmavidyā Yogaśāstra****, the scripture of yoga dealing with the science of the Absolute in the form of* ***Śrī Kṛṣṇārjuna saṃvād****, dialogue between Śrī Kṛṣṇa and Arjuna.*

CHAPTER

7

Jñānavijñāna Yogaḥ

Listen, Cognize And Radiate

All living beings are caught in the duality of attachment and aversion. The greatest Master, Kṛṣṇa explains how to move out of this bondage. He reveals the knowledge of associating with the Divine to radiate the Divine.

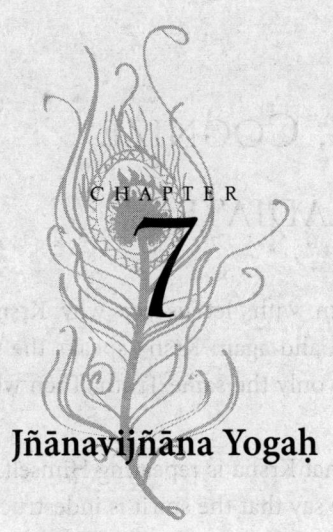

Listen, Cognize And Radiate

Listen! To begin with, let us see why Kṛṣṇa has given us this chapter. Again and again Kṛṣṇa speaks the same Truth. Nothing else is spoken, only the same Truth. Then what is the need for so many chapters?

People can say that Kṛṣṇa is repeating Himself. They may ask, 'How many times must He say that the spirit is indestructible, or that all work must be done with authenticity without expecting returns or that one must surrender to Him to reach completion?'

Understand, if you have already listened even once, Kṛṣṇa will not repeat it again. Anything you listen from Kṛṣṇa, understand you are listening *now*, for the first time! If you had already listened, I will make sure the words do not fall in your ears the second time, because I won't waste your time or my time. I am Kāla (time)!

For a person who wants to begin the life, the first thing he needs to learn is listening! Understand, by 'hearing' you won't understand the Master. Only by 'listening to yourself' you can understand the Master. I tell you, people who listen to themselves can understand what I am saying, even without any introduction to any spiritual philosophy. People who don't listen to themselves, they do not understand. Listening! Listening to yourself and speaking into the listening of yourself and others, makes our inner space cognize the right declarations.

Many times people come and tell me, 'I am not able to convince myself to drop my incompletions.' This means that they are not able to speak into their listening!

Speak into your listening! There is no shortcut, there is no cross cut. The shortest distance between two points is a straight line. So, the shortest route for anything is a straight line, a straight path.

Listen! Please understand, I am defining Completion.

Ability to speak into the listening of yourself is Completion. Ability to speak into the listening of yourself is ability to complete. That is the ability to complete.

It is all about developing your ability to speak into your listening, developing your ability to speak into others' listening, developing your ability to give authentic listening to yourself, and developing the ability to provide authentic listening to others, that's all!

How many ever new words Kṛṣṇa may use, how many ever new words Arjuna may use, it is all about the ability to provide authentic listening to yourself and to to others, the ability to speak into your listening and the ability to speak into the listening of others, that's all!

Kṛṣṇa shows the power of authentic listening and teaches Arjuna the ability to provide authentic listening to himself and to others, and to speak into the listening of himself and others! In the first chapter of Gītā—*Arjunaviṣāda Yogaḥ*, Kṛṣṇa provides authentic listening to Arjuna's dilemma. So complete is Kṛṣṇa's listening that Arjuna is able to listen to himself, his dilemmas and is able to pour out the depth of his root patterns into Kṛṣṇa's listening. Just by His pure, authentic listening, Kṛṣṇa transforms Arjuna's questions into quest, incompletions into completion, and his patterns into possibilities.

Please listen from the space of listening!

If you have authentically listened, if you have done *śravana*—listening authentically and *manana*—intranalyzing authentically, you *will* be radiating authentically. Nothing can be done about it! Intranalyzing and radiating! Please listen, your life needs to be constantly powerful. You should be living to do what you want. You should be talking to get the result of what you want. You should be talking to move the other person the way you want. And you should not be talking by fighting with the patterns of the listener. You should be talking into the listening of the listener! When will that happen? If you are established into your listening, you will talk into the other person's listening.

Listen! When Arjuna listens to himself, he becomes a *disciple*; when Kṛṣṇa speaks into the listening of Arjuna, Arjuna becomes enlightened—*Radiating Enlightenment*!

If I have to simply translate the word *'radiating'* or *nididhyāsana* in a very colloquial way, it means: Minding your business! Not wasting your life! Laziness, boredom, diversion, and postponing do not have a place in your life when you are radiating. Radiating means RADIATING! It is straightforward! Live your life authentically. Live your life with strength. Live your life intensely with clarity and powerfulness.

First thing you need to learn to *radiate*, the first thing for *nididhyāsana* is: Learn to think and speak with the same cognition you arrive at by intranalyzing.

Please understand, I am explaining step-by-step:

First, you authentically listen to the great Truths. Whenever you authentically listen, whatever you listen will be converted as great Truths by your inner space. Your inner space has the capability; it has the power to separate the right from wrong.

There is a very beautiful example of Paramahamsa in *Vedic t*radition! Paramahamsa is the supreme swan. If you mix milk and water and leave it, this great bird Hamsa (swan) will separate the milk from the water and suck only the milk and leave the water! The Hamsa bird has that power. The Hamsa bird is said to be the only creature that has the rare capability of separating milk from water.

In the same way, a person who takes the right things inside and leaves the unnecessary things outside is *'Paramahamsa'*. If you bring authentic listening in you, you will become *Paramahamsa*! Anything you listen, you know what to internalize and what to reject. Paramahamsas are actually enlightened Masters who take the bird body. Soaring high in the skies, they express their freedom and enjoy their bliss! They are metaphysical birds, seen only through enlightened eyes or by people who live in the higher consciousness. If you see the emblem of *Nithyananda Dhyanapeetam*, you will see this Paramahamsa bird is our emblem. I had a beautiful vision or experience, from which I created this emblem.

Authentic listening brings tremendous clarity. See, this clarity is really lacking in the seeker's life. Especially when somebody is interested to be enlightened, to live the life of a *jīvan mukta (*one who lives enlightenment), clarity is a very predominantly important quality. Please listen! Clarity is *Viveka*. Ādī Śaṅkara has written a separate book on clarity called *Viveka Chūḍāmaṇi*.

Authentic listening, *śravana* leads to clarity. And intranalyzing, *manana* leads to cognitive shift. If you don't live that cognitive shift powerfully, you will lose it. Please listen! Powerfully living the cognitive shift is what I call radiating, *nididhyāsana*.

I will tell you, how to find out whether you are radiating or not? Simply life around you will constantly be getting enriched, that is the signal! If the constant enriching is happening, then you are radiating! Around me, whether you are six or sixty, eight or eighty, you cannot go without getting enriched!

Radiating, *nididhyāsana* means such powerful body language, such powerful words, such powerful thinking that you go on enriching, constantly winning the game of life!

Śrī Kṛṣṇa is the personification of all these three—*śravana, manana, nididhyāsana,* powerfully enriching Arjuna to learn authentic listening, authentic intranalyzing and radiating. First, Arjuna learns *śravana* to give his authentic listening to himself and to Kṛṣṇa; getting to the root of his root patterns in the chapters of *Arjunaviṣāda Yogaḥ, Sāṅkhya Yogaḥ, Karma Yogaḥ* and *Jñāna-karma-sannyāsa Yogaḥ*. Once he gets the tremendous clarity through authentic listening, he learns to do *manana,* intranalyzing the great truths in chapters such as *Sannyāsa Yogaḥ, Dhyāna Yogaḥ* and *Jñānavijñāna Yogaḥ*.

Understand, because Śrī Kṛṣṇa is the complete Incarnation, He directly transmits the space of radiating, *nididhyāsana* to Arjuna without the need for *manana,* intranalyzing. When you are in the space of authentic listening to an Incarnation, who is also your Master, He can directly transmit the energy and experience of Enlightenment into you. *Parabrahma* Kṛṣṇa does this transmission in *Vibhūti Yogaḥ* and *Viśvarūpa Darśana Yogaḥ* to Arjuna. It is only for enriching the humanity that He continues to take Arjuna step-by-step into deeper levels of completion through the eighteen chapters.

Ultimately, when the cognitive shift happens in Arjuna, he experiences *nididhyāsana*, radiating the same cognition he arrives at by intranalyzing. When Kṛṣṇa enriches him to powerfully live and radiate His very body language and experience Enlightenment, dropping everything and surrendering to Him in *Mokṣa Sannyāsa Yogaḥ*, Arjuna wins the game of life called Mahābhārat war!

People ask me, '*Swamiji*, how many days will it take for us to learn meditation?'

I tell them, 'To learn meditation, two minutes are enough. To learn what meditation is not, you need ten days!' Kṛṣṇa knows that Arjuna is just like us. He represents the sum total of humanity. To explain to a man or woman what needs to be done, and why it is right is not enough. The human mind will find a hundred reasons why ninety-nine other things are just as good. So the Master must also tell why the other ninety-nine things are not the straight path, and why we must stick to what the Master prescribes.

That is exactly what Śrī Kṛṣṇa does. Again and again, the great Master explains patiently why the ninety-nine other options are not really options at all. He does this to prove that the *one* option He outlines sinks deeply into Arjuna's consciousness. As a result, this truth also sinks into the consciousness of every individual who reads the *Bhagavad Gītā*.

When we express the truth logically, our mind always goes to the other end of the logic. So, we need to understand and cognize the truth from both ends. There is a beautiful philosophy in India, *Nyāya Śāstra*, or the scripture of logic. According to this, any statement has two lines of logic. The first line of logic is regular logic; *nyāya* means regular. For example, if I make the statements, 'All men have one head. Sundar is a man,' we can easily conclude that the third statement will be: Sundar has one head. This is simple logic.

There is another kind of logic, a higher-level logic. For example, the first statement says, 'There are two doors.' The second statement says, 'One door is open.' An average person immediately jumps to the conclusion that the other door is closed. However, in this kind of logic we cannot jump to this conclusion. The second door may also be open.

In order that the listener, reader and disciple do not make mistakes in the understanding, the Master ensures that we know which door is open and which door is closed. It is not left to assumption on the basis of the disciple's intelligence. But the Master does not explain for this reason alone. When the truth sinks into us, it should sink in without a trace or resistance. However, when something is not fully explained, our mind moves away from what is being explained. When this happens, instead of being integrated to what is said, the mind gets constantly distracted and becomes tired. A tired mind makes mistakes and falls from integrity.

Usually, in life, we go out of integrity and make mistakes when we jump to incomplete conclusions using the first kind of logic when we should have made those decisions using the second kind of logic. The moment somebody makes a statement, 'You don't have compassion,' we immediately become defensive and say, 'Do you mean to say I am cruel? You mean I am violent?'

We don't have to jump to such an inauthentic conclusion. When we jump to conclusions, we create trouble not only for ourselves but also for others. Many times we make this mistake of lacking integrity in our listening. Don't be in a hurry to cognize what is spoken, because your cognition is so much filled with judgments, opinions, attitudes, personal beliefs, and attributes.

Listening is life. Non-listening is death. When we handle our mind without integrity and authenticity, we make this mistake. The totality of words that we repeat inside our system creates our whole life. If our mind jumps to illogical conclusions like this, naturally we create trouble for ourselves and others.

Ordinary Masters express their philosophy or their experience with the second kind of logic, which is why there is so much misunderstanding. There is a possibility of missing listening to their message and concluding with the wrong cognition. However, Kṛṣṇa is a *Jagat Guru*. He is not an ordinary Master. He is the Master of the whole Universe and He knows the minds of all possible types of human beings. He knows the problems of non-listening, non-integrity, and inadequate logic.

Kṛṣṇa is delivering this message in such a way that we cannot miss giving our authentic listening to Him and jump to any inauthentic conclusions, or wrongly cognize any statement in the flow of incomplete logic. He makes all the three statements. He is clear and complete. He says, 'There are two doors, the first door is open, the second door is closed.' He allows no space for us to lack listening because He speaks into our listening. He protects us from ourselves.

That is why He repeats the same truth in each chapter from a different level of logic each time to take us to higher and deeper levels of completion. He takes the complete responsibility for all three—*śravana, manana,* and *nididhyāsana.*

In this whole chapter of *Jñānavijñāna Yogaḥ*, Kṛṣṇa speaks about the same message from a different view so that we now learn to listen from the space of authentic listening—*śravana*, we understand and intranalyze to have the cognitive shift—*manana*, and we powerfully radiate the space of completion—*nididhyāsana.*

One In A Billion Reaches Me

7.1 *Bhagavān Kṛṣṇa says,*
Pārtha (Arjuna), now listen to Me, you can know Me completely,
without doubt, by practicing yoga in true consciousness of Me,
With your mind attached to Me.

7.2 *Let Me explain to you in full this phenomenal knowledge [jñāna]*
of the Absolute along with its conscious realization [vijñāna];
by knowing which, there shall remain nothing further to be known.

7.3 *Out of many thousands of men, hardly one endeavors to achieve the*
perfection of self-realization; of those so endeavoring, hardly one
achieves the perfection of self-realization, and of those, hardly one
knows Me in truth or reaches that state of oneness with Me.

7.4 *Earth, water, fire, air, ether, mind, intelligence and false ego,*
all together these constitute My external eightfold energies.

7.5 *Besides these external energies, which are inferior or material in*
nature, O mighty-armed Arjuna, there is a superior energy of Mine.
This comprises all the embodied souls of all the living entities
[jīvabhūta] by which this material world is being utilized.

Again and again people ask me, '*Swamiji*, why did you choose to speak on the Bhagavad Gītā? Why didn't you choose books like *Aṣṭavakra Gītā, Patañjali's Yoga Sūtra, Brahmasutra* or the *Upaniṣads*?' I tell them that the *Gītā* expresses the truth in totality. Kṛṣṇa has created keys for all kinds of human beings. Kṛṣṇa fulfills every need of every human being.

He says, '*Listen,* Arjuna, by practicing yoga in full consciousness of Me, with mind attached to Me, you can know Me in full, without doubt.'

In this statement, Kṛṣṇa uses the word '*Me*' three times. Having read that, a psychologist will conclude that Kṛṣṇa is egoistic. According to psychology, if we use the word 'I' or 'Me' three or more times in a statement, we are egoistic. A person might hate Kṛṣṇa because he feels Kṛṣṇa is egoistic. Again and again, He declares, 'Surrender to Me. I am everything.'

We should understand here that He is expressing His glory. The person who hates Kṛṣṇa thinking He is egoistic, misses the truth or spirit expressed by the *Gītā*. In the same way, a person who loves Kṛṣṇa gets caught in His form and misses the juice of the *Gītā*! Whenever people are caught in the form, when they worship the form, they slowly start saying, '*Gītā* is great. Kṛṣṇa is God. He can express all these things, but surely it is not for us. It is not practical.' In this way, they slowly create a distance between themselves and Kṛṣṇa. They worship the *Gītā* instead of practicing it. If we have a pot full of milk and we worship it but never drink it, will we get the benefit of the milk? Understand, unless we drink the milk, we will never get the benefit of the milk. Unless we imbibe Kṛṣṇa, we cannot get the benefit of the *Gītā*. When we don't imbibe Kṛṣṇa's teachings in our lives, when we don't work towards experiencing Kṛṣṇa, worshipping Kṛṣṇa is nothing but inauthenticity. It's a cunning method of escaping from the truth. Worshipping without intranalyzing and living is the worst form of inauthenticity.

People who hate Kṛṣṇa think He is egoistic. And people who love Kṛṣṇa are caught in His form and think they should surrender to the personality called Kṛṣṇa who came down in human form. Only a person who experiences Kṛṣṇa realizes the *Gītā*.

Approach Divine the Right Way

This chapter is about how human beings approach the Divine, why they approach the Divine, and at what level they approach the Divine. We approach the Divine in the way we want It. According to our maturity, we approach the Divine.

At what level do we approach the Divine? What do we receive in return? How do we grow in maturity? Kṛṣṇa gives the answers to these questions in this chapter. Here He says, 'Out of many thousands among men, *one* may endeavor for perfection, and out of those who have achieved perfection, hardly *one* knows Me in truth.'

Beautiful! Here He says, 'out of thousands'. In those days, the population must have been less, which is why He makes the statement 'out of thousands'. Now we should say, 'Out of billions, one may endeavor for perfection.'

manuṣyāṇāṁ sahasreṣu kaścid yatati siddhaye |
yatatām api siddhānāṁ kaścin māṁ vetti tattvataḥ || 7.3

'Among millions of men, *one* man may endeavor for perfection, and out of those who achieve perfection, hardly *one* knows Me in truth.'

There are millions of people out there, but only a few hundred are present today to listen to this *Gītā* discourse. And out of these few hundred, only a few will listen authentically, as it is expressed. We may sit here. We may even hear, but never think that we really listen.

I request people to never repeat what I have said to others. If you do repeat it, then please don't say, '*Swamiji* told me these things.' Be very clear, you heard those things. Tell them, 'I heard these things.' Never say, '*Swamiji* said'. Many times we miss much of what is said. Modern scientists say that we observe hardly two percent of the things that happen around us. If a hundred things happen around us, we observe and intranalyze only two!

It is as if you have a hundred-page storybook, and somehow you lose the whole book except for two random pages. If you try to reconstruct the whole novel with only those two pages, how true will it be to the original? In the same way, you remember hardly two percent of what I say. With that two percent, if you try to reconstruct this whole discourse, naturally it will be your discourse, not mine. If you want to tell people what I spoke, please always say, 'I heard *Nithyananda* say this.' Never say, '*Nithyananda* said…' Because you jump to conclusions, and because of your inner chatter, you miss authentic listening.

The Master is always ready to share and enrich with his experiences. That is his mission in life. The infinite compassion that fills an enlightened being is forever bursting to be let out to share, to teach, to guide, and to enrich. He is available continuously to the whole humanity, enriching with Enlightenment. That is why Kṛṣṇa says that He is now ready to explain.

Listen! You will see miraculous transformations happening in your body and mind. Listening is God! Just by listening, you experience God! The question is whether or not Arjuna is ready to listen. Even if Arjuna was ready to listen and he became enlightened, are we ready to listen today, now?

Why does Kṛṣṇa say that a few even try, and of those who try, very few succeed? Remember that He is talking about Self-realization, about understanding who we are. Why is it so difficult even to try?

We do not want to try because we are afraid. We are restless in any form of silence. If I am silent for a few minutes after I sit down before an audience, the entire audience becomes restless; they start fidgeting. Why do we find it difficult to meditate? After all, all we do in meditation is close our eyes and remain silent. Why is it difficult? We give appointments to everyone else every day of our lives, willingly and unwillingly. Why is it so difficult to give half an hour a day to ourselves?

Why would we rather watch television, knowing fully well that nothing of value will come from it? Why would we rather read the same old newspaper or social media pages again and again? Understand, all these are because we are afraid of being with ourselves. Why are we afraid of being with ourselves? We must ask and answer these questions ourselves. If Self-realization means going back to where we came from, and where we came from is a state of bliss and divinity, then why are we afraid to be with ourselves?

The truth is that we have forgotten where we came from. Nothing in the way we are brought up and 'educated' tells us that we come from Bliss and we can regain that bliss. If we realize how easy it is to be blissful and return to our original state, no one can control us. That is what liberation means. But society, religion, and political and family structures operates on the principle of control.

The moment we realize who we are and we are liberated, these institutions cannot make us do what they want us to do. From childhood we are conditioned to avoid looking too deeply into ourselves because if we do, we may find the truth and be liberated. Most of society doesn't know these deeper truths. This is how society puts generation after generation of people in deep illusion.

The only true love is that of the Divine and that of the Master. Such love comes out of infinite compassion. It expects nothing in return. What can we offer God and our Master? So, if we need to follow the Truth, we must enrich ourselves to enrich others. We must be selfish; selfish to enter into this path of Self-realization. However it is not a selfishness born out of the usual material nature. It is selfishness born out of the desperate need to be *selfless*. When we reach our center or our core, we become *one* with humanity. Then there are no differences among us. That is why even our spouses will be unhappy if we realize ourselves, because they cannot possess us anymore. At that point they must share us with humanity. But they won't understand that the love of Self-realization is infinite, that there is no reduction in sharing, there is only growth in sharing.

The path to Self-realization is the path of aloneness. It is not a lonely path; it is an 'alone' path. When we are alone, we are not lonely. We are all-in-one; that is what being alone means. From being fragmented, we become whole. From being islands, we become the Universe.

This is the knowledge that Kṛṣṇa offers humanity. Out of His deep compassion He says, 'Please listen to Me and realize your Self and be liberated.' One in a million may heed His words and start on this path. He then says that only one in a million who starts on this path will eventually find his own Self, and thus find Me.

Is the path so difficult? No, it is not. Why then does it seem so difficult? We find the external world so attractive that we rarely stay on course in our internal voyage of self-discovery. It is always easier to blame other people or life and remain where we are than to step on the path of transformation.

Throughout the *Gītā*, Kṛṣṇa talks about how to control the mind. He gives specific science of what to do and what not to do. All we need to do is to follow the guidance of this Universal Master. Without any doubt, surely we can then become that one in a thousand or one in a million. But to follow Him, to allow Him to enrich us, we need to understand Him.

In these verses Kṛṣṇa explains who He is. Kṛṣṇa explicitly separates Himself from His manifested energies in these verses. What we perceive as manifested energies—the five natural elements that are earth, water, fire, air and ether, and the three inner elements of mind, intelligence and ego—are His energies no doubt, yet they are not Him.

The Manifest and The Unmanifest

Puruṣa and *prakṛti* are considered the operative principles of the Universe in the Hindu philosophical systems of *Sāṅkhya* and *Vedānta. Puruṣa* and *prakṛti* are unmanifest energy sources, *puruṣa* being inactive and *prakṛti* capable of being active. Everything else arises from these two elements when they operate together.

Prakṛti gives rise to the Cosmic and individual intelligence and the five natural elements. The *Taittreya Upaniṣad* explains that the Cosmic energy gave rise to etheric energy or the energy of space, *ākāṣa*, which pervades the Universe. This is the largest and subtlest quantum of energy that pervades the Universe. From etheric energy the energy of air arises. It is this energy of air, or *vāyu*, that sustains us in our body-mind system as the carrier of pranic or life energy.

From the energy of air arises the energy of fire, *agni*. Many salutations in the *Ṛg Veda*, the first of the Hindu scriptures, are addressed to the fire. Almost all Vedic rituals are performed for the fire god. *Āpas*, the energy of water, arose from the energy of fire. *Pṛthvī,* the energy of earth arose from the energy of water. The *Taittreya Upaniṣad* goes on to say that it is from the earth energy that plants, herbs, food were created, from which came humans. Within the human is the intelligence that is a hologram of the Cosmic intelligence. The energy cycle is now complete.

This energy tree, from its subtlest beginning to the grossest manifestation, is also the story of creation. Ten thousand years ago, sages of our ancient *Vedic* culture propounded these truths with no external devices to aid them. They intuited them, as they looked inward rather than outward. Our *Vedic* rituals were full of meaning. Today they are condemned as old fashioned and meaningless activities because we lost the link to their meaning. Spirituality is nothing but spirit infused into rituals.

The fire rituals are methods to transfer the energy from the ether to earth, from the Cosmos to the individual. Through the power of chants, sound energy, that activates the etheric energy, the energy is transferred through air to the fire in the sacrificial pit. The water stored in pots around the fire pit collects this energy. The energized water is then poured onto the earth, a deity or individuals to transfer this energy to them. Of the energies in the five natural elements, we can directly access the energies of earth, water, fire and air. We eat, drink, warm ourselves and breathe with these energies. However, we cannot directly access the etheric energy. Our ego, our mind, becomes a barrier to our absorption of this energy.

Meditation is the key to imbibe the etheric energy of the Cosmos, the largest. subtlest energy source. *Vedic* fire rituals are mass meditation processes—meditation for dummies! We just need to be there to absorb the energy, even if we do not have the capacity to meditate.

The Cosmic intelligence is reflected in the human as the mind. The mind in turn uses the senses to access the external world. Each of the senses, sight, hearing, smell, taste and touch are related to the natural elements. Ether is linked to sound or the ears; air is linked to touch and the skin; fire is linked to color and form, and hence to sight and the eyes; water is linked to taste and the tongue; earth is linked to smell or the nose.

The mind receives information through the senses of perception, and executes decisions through the senses of action. When the senses are denied access to the external world, which is their sustenance, the mind shuts down. Thoughts cease! Ego is a creation of the mind. It is an illusion because it is not permanent; it is not the truth. True realization of the Self is achieved when the ego is shed and when the mind stops. Then, inner intelligence awakens to the Cosmic intelligence.

Here, Kṛṣṇa refers to ego as *ahaṁkāra.* It is our identity that we project outwards, which is always in excess of what we think of as ourselves. There is another side to our ego, called *mamakāra*, which we project inwards; what we think of as us inside us. This *mamakāra* is always lower than what we think ourselves to be. The perpetual gap between this outer projection and inner projection creates self-doubt, stress, suffering and dis-ease within us.

When we realize our Self, we realize that *we are Divine* and nothing less. Anything we think about ourselves which is lower than this, is low self-esteem, is self-doubt. What Kṛṣṇa says is true for all of us. We are above the energies that constitute us. We too are the energy that constitutes our body-mind system. All that we lack is the awareness of this Truth.

Our natural state is to know ourselves. Once we realize the Truth that *we are God,* there is no difference between Kṛṣṇa and us. We are enlightened. That is what Kṛṣṇa came to prove. He has no need to prove that He is God. He doesn't care if we know it or not. His mission was to enlighten Arjuna, and through Arjuna, the rest of humanity. His mission is to prove to us that *we too are God!*

I Am The Thread

7.6 *Know for certain that everything living is manifested by these two energies of Mine. I am the Creator, the Sustainer and the Destroyer of them.*

7.7 *O Dhanañjaya, there is no Truth superior to Me.*
Everything rests upon Me, as pearls are strung on a thread.

7.8 *O Kaunteya (son of Kuntī), I am the taste of water, the radiance of the sun and the moon, the sacred syllable Oṁ in the Vedic mantras. I am the sound in ether and ability in man.*

7.9 *I am the original fragrance of the earth, and I am the heat in fire.*
I am the life of all living beings, and I am the penance of all ascetics.

'I am the thread,' He says. 'I am the thread, the *sūtra*, the technique on which all Existence is strung.'

mattaḥ parataraṁ nānyat kiñcid asti dhanañjaya |
mayi sarvam idaṁ protaṁ sūtre maṇi gaṇā iva || 7.7

'O Dhanañjaya, conqueror of wealth, there is no truth superior to Me. Everything rests upon Me, as pearls are strung on a thread.' He declares powerfully—'*mayi sarvam idaṁ protaṁ*—In Me is strung everything! *sūtre maṇi gaṇā iva*—Everything rests on Me as pearls strung on a thread.' He declares with complete clarity that He is the thread of everything.

What a beautiful analogy! That is why He is the *sūtradhāra*, the controller and director of the Cosmic play! Nothing moves, nothing can move without Him. Nothing can be created, sustained or destroyed in the absence of His energy.

People often ask me why I call myself 'Swami'. They question me as to why I dress up in these ways and allow myself to be photographed. I tell them that I do not even identify with this body. This skin itself is alien to me. There is no difference between this skin and other coverings? So how does it matter? I look at myself the way you look at me, as a witness! Or the way you and I look at an idol. If this body is dressed well, I feel good—the same way you feel good seeing it dressed up, that's all. I am just a witness.

God—An Idea?

For you, God is a mere concept; He is just an idea. It is another play of your mind. You think of God and attribute various concepts to Him. You talk about Him in the same manner in which you would talk about a friend or relative, perhaps more glowingly or less glowingly depending on your inclination at that point in time.

To you, your identity and your identification with your body-mind is real. Without this identity you are lost. If someone does not recognize you, you suffer. The moment someone praises you, you are in the seventh heaven. Your identity is your reality. 'I' is what makes you alive.

To me, God is reality. I live with God every moment. The body, mind and the body-mind identification does not exist for me. It is only a concept! Therefore, when I refer to myself, I refer to that body-mind the same way that you refer to it. I too call it Swami or whatever! I cannot move a finger without permission from Existence, from that *Parabrahma* Kṛṣṇa, that cosmic Kṛṣṇa. You may think, 'This sounds nonsensical. He says he is enlightened and then he says there is nothing that he can do; he can do only as Existence dictates.'

Nonsense or not, this is the truth. Whether you understand it or not, whether you accept it or not, this is the truth. What makes me move, talk, see and do all that you do is only what the Universe dictates.

My disciples know that when someone with deep faith in me comes with a problem, I say, '*I'll take care.*' If it is someone who is yet to develop that deep faith, I say that I shall meditate or pray to Nityānandeśvara (Lord Śiva gracing as chief deity at Nithyānanda ashrams) for them! They go away happy to hear that. When I say, 'I shall take care,' there is nothing special that I do. I just pass it on to Existence. It is for Her to take care. Because I have that immense faith in Her, She always obliges! Things happen.

People know that the energy beads that they wear, the string of *rudrākṣa* beads or sandalwood beads, is not a mere rosary. It is their hotline to connect to Existence. There have been so many people who share their experiences with the *rudrākṣa*. When someone is desperately in need of help of some sort, they simply hold onto the *rudrākṣa* beads and pray. The results are always instantaneous.

All this has nothing to do with me although they hold onto the rudrākṣa thinking of me. It has to do with Existence. The moment I feel that it is a result of my penance, it will stop happening! There is nothing that 'I' can do. There is nothing that this energy can do.

That is what Kṛṣṇa talks about here. The great Master says, I am not what you see. I am not the energy that is manifested. It is not this six-foot Kṛṣṇa with a flute and peacock feather that makes things happen. It is the formless energy beyond Vāsudeva Kṛṣṇa (Kṛṣṇa, the being in body, son of Vāsudeva). It is Parabrahma Kṛṣṇa (the Cosmic energy).

When we see a necklace or garland, do we notice the thread, the sūtra? If it is a pearl or diamond necklace we may get it threaded in gold, but still we rarely notice the thread. We delight over the pearls or diamonds, yet never think about the thread that holds them together, unless it snaps and all the pearls and diamonds spill on the floor. Then, we blame the thread!

Kṛṣṇa says, He is the unseen thread—*sūtre maṇi gaṇā*, without which no *rudrākṣa* can exist. He says He is the unseen essence—*mayi sarvam idaṁ protaṁ*, without which there can be no substance. He says He is the unseen ultimate energy without which there can be no Universe—*mattaḥ parataraṁ nānyat kiñcid asti dhanañjaya.*

Have you ever wondered how this Universe operates? There are billions of planets like ours, millions of solar systems, thousands of galaxies and many Universes. There is nothing that anyone can see that is controlling this Universe. We need traffic lights and policemen to control traffic on our roads. In the Milky Way there are no policemen to control the movements of planets and stars. Yet they move unerringly!

Can you imagine the intelligence that controls multiple Universes? How is there such discipline and order in that seeming chaos that no one is in charge of? No one is responsible, or is someone? On the other hand, within this small body of ours we try to control everything. We control the food we eat, how much we exercise, how much we play, etc. Yet we can predict nothing about it. Despite all the order that we impose, there is chaos sometimes! Control does not bring about order; it never can. Freedom brings about order. Chaos is freedom. Chaos is choice. The ultimate chaos is the cosmic Kṛṣṇa; He is also the Ultimate order too.

Kṛṣṇa illustrates what He said earlier with specific examples. The beauty of Kṛṣṇa's teaching in the *Bhagavad Gītā* is the depth to which He goes to make everything crystal clear to Arjuna. He makes no assumptions, takes nothing for granted. It is as if Arjuna is a child and He is the parent or teacher. For the Lord of the Universe to take the trouble to ensure complete understanding shows the depth of His compassion.

I explained earlier that in the five natural elements, the essence of ether is sound, of air is touch, of fire is form and heat, of water is taste and of earth is smell. Kṛṣṇa explains that He is the essential quality in each of these elements; also that He is the *praṇava mantra*—primordial sound—'Oṁ' and the radiance of the Sun and Moon.

Life, any form of life in this and any other planet, cannot exist without this energy of cosmic Kṛṣṇa. But living within this energy field we lose sight of this energy. We become energy-unconscious. Kabir, the mystic poet said hauntingly, we are like fish that are immersed in life-giving water yet cry out saying, 'We are thirsty.' Kabir advises: Fool, become aware! You cannot be a fish in water and be thirsty!

This is an incident from Śrī Rāmakṛṣṇa's life.

> Rāmakṛṣṇa asks his disciple Vivekananda, 'Narendra (his pre-monasteral name), what would you do if you were a fly and you sat on the edge of a pool of divine nectar, amṛta?'

Without hesitation Vivekananda responds, 'I shall sip from it, of course.'

Rāmakṛṣṇa says, 'Fool, you should fall into that pool and drown! How can you fear drowning in life-giving nectar?'

We are afraid, always afraid. We have no trust in ourselves and therefore no trust in Existence.

If God were to come in front of us in any form other than what we recognize as Him, we would ask for His identification card! Our intelligence is limited to visualizing Kṛṣṇa in His yellow dress with His flute and a peacock feather stuck in His hair. If Kṛṣṇa comes covered in ash, with a snake around His neck, the Kṛṣṇa follower will throw stones at Him saying, 'That is Śiva. I do not worship Śiva.' There are people who claim to have imbibed the *Gītā,* understood every word the Lord says, and yet have questioned me as to how I can worship Śiva in the āśram when I say Kṛṣṇa is the ultimate!

It is for these people that Kṛṣṇa goes into such depths to explain that He is everything and above everything. He is the Creator—Brahma, the Sustainer—Viṣṇu and the Rejuvenator—Śiva. He is not either or; He is all and above all.

I Am Eternal

7.10 *O Pārtha (son of Prithā), know Me to be the eternal seed of all beings, the intelligence of the intelligent, and the brilliance of all those who are brilliant.*

7.11 *I am the strength of the strong, and I am the procreative energy in living beings, devoid of lust and in accordance with dharma, the religious principles, O Bharatarṣabha (lord of Bhārata).*

7.12 *All states of being—be they of goodness (sāttvika), passion (rajas) or ignorance (tamas)—emanate from Me. I am independent of them but they are dependent on Me.*

7.13 *The whole of this creation is deluded by the three modes or guṇas (goodness, passion and ignorance), and thus does not know Me. I am above the modes and inexhaustible.*

7.14 *My Divine energy, consisting of the three modes of material nature, is difficult to overcome. But those who surrender unto Me can cross beyond it with ease.*

7.15 *Those miscreants who are foolish, lowest among mankind, whose knowledge is stolen by māyā, illusion, and who have taken shelter in demonic nature, do not surrender unto Me.*

'I am the procreative energy,' says the Lord. 'I am the seed of all living beings.' He makes no excuses, no apologies.

He says, 'I am that procreative energy but without the fantasies of lust, *kāma-rāga vivarjitam dharmāviruddho bhūteṣu* (7.11).' How can one be a Creator, if one cannot procreate?

Many of our great sages in the past, the ṛṣi and maharṣis, such as Vaśiṣṭa and Vyāsa were gṛhastas (householders), who were family men with wives and children. Yet they were realized souls, enlightened. Other than Hanumān and Gaṇeśa all our deities are married! Kṛṣṇa is reputed to have had 16,008 wives!

How can the life form continue without procreation, without the sex act? TFor celibacy to happen naturally, the first spiritual experience must happen before adolescence, so that the life-giving sex energy moves upwards as transcendental spiritual energy rather than descend as procreative energy. People who have this spiritual awakening because of their prārabdha karma (desires one is born with) are the Paramahamsas. That is their nature. Celibacy happens to them naturally. To force celibacy after adolescence is difficult. It can be done but must be done with great caution and under supervision. Otherwise the so-called renunciate monk, the Sannyāsi, will pretend to follow brahmacarya, celibacy. Inside he will be filled with fantasies, ready to explode. The word brahmacarya means 'moving in reality'.

> It is said that once Kṛṣṇa was crossing the river Yamuna with a group of gopīs, women devotees. The river was in spate. Kṛṣṇa said to Yamuna, 'If it is true that I am a *brahmacāri*, part and let me walk across.' The river parted and Kṛṣṇa walked to the other bank.
>
> A *Sannyāsi* who watched this was dumbstruck. 'Kṛṣṇa, a *brahmacāri*? He walks with these women who are His lovers, and He says He is a *brahmacāri* and the river parts for Him! How can this be?'
>
> That is what Kṛṣṇa explains here, 'I am the procreative energy, but without lust, without attachment and without fantasy. I am the ultimate reality!'

Fantasies are the root cause of our problems. With each fantasy coming true, more fantasies arise. We can never be in reality. To be in reality one must be in the present moment. When you are in the present moment you are Kṛṣṇa.

When we hanker after the past and speculate about the future, we slip into fantasies. We are no longer within the boundaries of our body. This way of living will lead only to suffering. All you need to do to be blissful is, renounce your fantasies. You do not need to renounce what material things you have with you.

Enjoy your wealth, enjoy your work, enjoy your spouse and children. You have earned what you have. Enjoy what is your due. Just stop fantasizing about what you *do not* have. Stop running after more acquisitions; stop and take time to enjoy what you have acquired. Move into the present, here and now, into reality, and you will be a *brahmacāri*!

BEYOND THE GUṆAS

Kṛṣṇa talks about the *guṇas*, the natural attributes in these verses.

Prakṛti, the energy that manifests in the Universe, has three elements called *guṇas*. When *prakṛti* is in equilibrium, it is pure potential energy. When it is disturbed, the *guṇas* come into operation. Like building blocks, they combine in many ways and create, sustain and destroy.

Rarely is only a single element or *guṇa* present in a person. The three *guṇas* that Kṛṣṇa refers to are *satva*, *raja*s and *tamas*, commonly translated as goodness or calmness, passion or aggression and ignorance or inaction. The interplay of these *guṇas* creates the functioning of the mind and through the operation of the mind, activity. *Guṇa* does not refer to the state a person is in. *Guṇa* causes that state to happen. *Satva* by itself is not goodness or calmness. It is the building block that leads to calmness.

No living being influenced by the mind is beyond the influence of the *guṇas*. When one transcends the *guṇas*, as Kṛṣṇa says about Himself, one becomes a *triguṇa rahita*, one who has transcended the three *guṇas*. Such a person is no longer influenced by the mind and its actions.

Listen. Even an incarnation, an enlightened energy being reborn into this planet on a mission, needs to initially be born with some *guṇa* infused into that being. It is like this: We cannot make jewelry out of pure gold. We must alloy it with copper. In the same way, even an energy source that has transcended the three *guṇas* needs to have some *satva guṇa* infused in it to be born into this planet. The same is true of Kṛṣṇa. As Vāsudeva Kṛṣṇa, the son of Vāsudeva, He has some *guṇa* at play in Him.

Remember that *Bhagavad Gītā* is rendered by *Parabrahma* Kṛṣṇa, the cosmic Kṛṣṇa, and not by Vāsudeva Kṛṣṇa. So He boldly says, I am beyond the *guṇas*. He says, I am the *Param Puruṣa*, the supreme being, who sets *prakṛti* into play, and I am beyond its influence. Kṛṣṇa is the creator of Nature, which is even beyond prakṛti, and is therefore beyond the plays of Nature.

We can see the interplay of the guṇas in people as they move through this material world. People are generally more in a state of *rajas*—aggressiveness with passion, with various proportions of *satva* and *tamas*. *Rajas* is needed to create, to make things happen, and is the predominant *guṇa* of action.

Especially when you move into an environment, committed to a life of renunciation and detachment, many fall into deep state of *tamas*, inaction. It is not a state of ignorance, but one of inaction where all your suppressed opposition to your earlier life of meaningless activity surfaces and forces you into sheer inactivity.

You may sleep long hours, far more than normal, disinclined to do anything. However, this is a passing phase. All these suppressions surface and dissolve. Let them. You then move into *satva*. To many, it is surprising that one falls into *tamas* before moving into *satva*, yet it happens and it is a reaction to one's earlier lifestyle.

On the other hand, a person steeped in *tamas* is the person Kṛṣṇa refers to as one who does not surrender to Him. Such a person is in deep darkness and ignorance. He is unaware of his potential. He is no better than an animal. In fact, an animal is better because it knows how to live in Nature, with Nature. Besides, an animal has no fantasies.

Unfortunately, a human being can distort his perceptions to such a point that he can deny his rightful nature. *Māyā*, illusion, is also the interplay of the guṇas.It is a collection of our fantasies. Just as darkness needs light to destroy it, we need awareness to destroy *māyā*. Otherwise *māyā* destroys us.

In Bhagāvatam (Hindu epic that describes Lord Viṣṇu's incarnations, especially His incarnation as Kṛṣṇa), there is this history.

> Nārada is the greatest devotee of Viṣṇu. He forever sings His praise and has nothing else on his mind. Over time Nārada became conceited about being the most celebrated devotee. This happens to all devotees at some point in time.
>
> As a true master, Viṣṇu took action. He called Nārada and asked him to fetch a pot of water. Nārada rushed out. Suddenly he was in front of a house asking for water. A beautiful maiden came out with water and Nārada fell instantaneously in love with her. He married this girl and they raised children together.
>
> One day there was a great storm. The house and the entire surroundings were flooded. The rushing water carried Narada and his family away. Soon they were separated and his family died. Nārada wailed and screamed for help.
>
> Suddenly he heard a voice, 'Nārada, where is my water? What happened to you?'
>
> Nārada awoke, as if from a great sleep, and saw Viṣṇu smiling at him. He said, 'Even my greatest devotee is not immune to māyā!'

As long as the mind is active, no one is immune to māyā.

Four Pious Men

7.16 *O Bharatarṣabha, best among Bhārata, four kinds of pious men*
begin to render devotional service unto Me.
They are: the distressed, the desirer of wealth, the inquisitive seeker of knowledge, and the wise knower of the Absolute.

7.17 *Of these, the wise one who is in full knowledge and ever united with Me through single-minded devotion is the best.*
I am very dear to him, and he is dear to Me.

7.18 *All these devotees are indeed noble; but the wise one who knows Me, dwells in Me is My very Self, this is My opinion.*
Being merged in My Consciousness and engaged in My mission, he is surely established in Me, the highest destination.

7.19 *After many births and deaths, he who knows Me surrenders to Me, knowing Me to be the cause of all causes and all that is.*
Such a great soul is very rare.

Kṛṣṇa now goes deeper. He talks about the Indian community system.

Before entering into this subject, I bow down to the system that has been created by the *ṛṣis* (sages), which has made the whole spiritual science a reality. I bow down to the community system, which kept our scriptures alive, the spiritual science alive.

In these modern times, abusing our social system created by the *Ṛṣis* has become a fashion! Especially in Southern India, abusing the Vedic system and abusing Swāmis has become the trend. If you want to show you are educated or an important person, abuse our Vedic system. You can immediately gain popularity. Not only have we not understood our vedic system, we have also started disrespecting this great system created by our ancient masters. Please understand, only because of our *Ṛṣis* and because of the system that they created, Bhārata (India) itself is still alive today, which is the greatest miracle of God.

No other culture has survived or lived for such a long time. All other cultures that came into existence after the Indian culture—Babylonian, Roman, Greek, etc.—knew how to fight, how to build empires and big cities in a professional way. They knew how to protect themselves. They were great warriors! Yet they were unable to survive. Today we see only their relics. These cultures are not alive today. Of the Indian culture, the Indian system, we have at least 10,000 years of recorded history.

There's a beautiful book written by Swami Prakashananda Sarasvati. The book is a comprehensive encyclopedia of the authentic history of religion in Indian culture. According to him, *sanātana dharma*, the Indian culture is trillions of years old. And we have at least 10,000 years of recorded history of the Indian culture.

No other country has been invaded as much as India. India has been invaded again and again by practically every culture, every country. Yet, no country has been invaded by India. India has never invaded any country. Out of the forty-eight civilizations, which were over 5000 years old on the planet, the Hindu civilization, the *vedic* culture is the only one civilization that is still alive and flourishing! All the other forty-seven did not survive. Only because of this community system is the Indian culture alive today.

Another important thing to understand when we read these things is—'Man cannot live without creating a community.' Man is a social animal. He creates some form of community or other. You cannot say that the United States does not have some form of community system. In other countries also the community system is there. However, these community systems are based upon money.

When I went to Brazil, I gave a discourse to a large company called Petrobras. One man asked, 'How do you justify the community system in

India? The high caste people look at the low caste people in a disrespectful way. How do you justify this?'

Of course, there are a few issues in Indian culture also. Indians made mistakes in the sense they missed the spirit with which the community system was developed, and started following the letter. Some mistakes happened. That's true. However, the whole community system cannot be labeled wrong because of a few mistakes. For example, if someone has a tumor in his body, the tumor must be operated on and removed. You cannot straightaway kill the person! We can't abandon the whole person because of the tumour.

And it is we who committed mistakes, and now we are abusing the whole system. I told him, 'Yes, one or two mistakes happened. But look at the developed countries or so-called cultured countries. If you enter an airplane and walk to the economy class past the first class, watch the way the first class passengers look at you! Have you observed how passengers in first class look at you? Just by observing, you can see how disrespectfully they look at you.' Don't think there is no community or class system in other countries. In every country, there is a community and class system.

The Indian community system

The *Vedic Ṛṣis* at least created the community and caste system based upon intelligence and wisdom. In other cultures, the community system was created based upon money and power. The countries where the rulers are *kṣatriyas* (warrior class), are the ones who create the community system based upon power. The more powerful a person is, the more respected he is. In other countries, people who do business, the business class people, control the whole system. There the the wealthy people are respected more.

India is the only country where people who respected intelligence and wisdom created the whole system. The system was created based upon intelligence, based upon wisdom. So that is why, in India, the more wisdom a person carries, the more spiritual he is, he more he is respected.

The whole social system was created based upon sharing from an enriching consciousness. Understand, you can create anything only when you see it and experience it from the state of enriching consciousness. Man must contribute something to enrich the community by doing actions in the enriching state.

Let me describe the spirit with which the whole system was created, and how we abused it. First, the whole system is not based upon our birth. It is based upon our character.

Kṛṣṇa says again and again that it is based upon our *guṇas* (nature), based upon our attitude towards life. A person who works driven by fear, one who works out of fear, belongs to the working class called *śūdra.* A person who works out of greed, belongs to the merchant or business class called *vaiśya*. A person who works to get attention or to prove that he is superior, belongs to the *kṣatriya* community. A person who works out of gratitude from the enriching consciousness, expressing his bliss, is a *brāhmaṇa*. This was how people were categorized in those days.

Everybody must contribute something to enrich the society. A person may enrich by sharing his time if he has nothing else. A person who shares his time is a worker, a *śūdra*. He belongs to the working class. A person who enriches by sharing products, has time and a little bit of intelligence to create products, is a *vaiśya*, a merchant. A person who enriches by sharing confidence, who gives courage to the whole community, is a *kṣatriya*, a warrior! He unites the whole group as a community in a solid way by giving confidence, by sharing his confidence. A person who enriches by sharing his knowledge, bliss or spiritual wisdom, is a *brāhmaṇa*.

This type of division is completely based upon our role, the role we play in the community, which is based upon our character. In no way is it related to our birth. This is the spirit with which the whole system was created by the *Ṛṣis*. Here nobody is higher and nobody is lower. In the course of time, one or two mistakes happened. But because of that we can't say that the whole system is wrong.

caturvidhā bhajante māṁ janāḥ sukṛtino'rjuna |
ārto jijñasurartharthī jñānī ca bharatarṣabha || 7.16

'O best among the Bhārata, four kinds of pious men begin to render devotional service unto Me: the distressed, the desirer of wealth, the inquisitive, and he who searches for knowledge of the Absolute.'

Here Kṛṣṇa talks about those who approach the Divine and the ways in which they approach the Divine. Man is centered on seven basic emotions. Basically we live and work based on these seven emotions: greed, fear, worry, attention-need (name and fame), comparison and jealousy, ego and the last one, the seventh emotion, deep discontentment.

These are the qualities with which man lives and he works. Man is centered on these seven different emotions. These seven emotions are seven energy centers that supply energy to us, fuel for us. Everything that we do in life is rooted in one of these seven emotions.

If we are centered on greed, we approach God in the same way. Goddess Lakṣmi (goddess of wealth) appeals to us. Or we continuously run behind Kubera (Lord of wealth) and perform Kubera pūjā (worship of Kubera); we continuously repeat the concept of Kubera. When we feel we are missing something, we try to get fulfillment by creating our own God and approaching Him in that mold. We approach the Divine with the same emotion, the same feeling that we miss in our being.

One more thing: When we become mature, we approach the same Lakṣmi as *Jñāna Lakṣmi* (goddess of wisdom as wealth)! We pray to the same goddess to give us wisdom, to give us knowledge. According to our maturity we project and see the Divine. Understand, there's nothing wrong in approaching the Lord from greed. There's nothing wrong in starting our life with prayers for boons. However, we should not end our life also with prayers. Then there is something wrong. It's a good start, but a bad end!

Vivekananda beautifully says, 'It's good to be born in the church, but not to die there.' Before we die, we should grow out of it. We must become mature; we must realize the other dimensions of the Divine within us.

In prayer, we pray to God; in meditation, we become God! Prayers give us immediate results. Praying to that higher principle or to the Divine is not wrong, yet it is not enough. Whereas in meditation, we become that higher principle or the Divine to which we constantly pour out our prayers. This is permanent.

The Divine is nothing but a mirror; we see our own reflection. And whatever we do to the Divine comes back to us. The more we understand, the more we grow and relate with the Divine in a more mature way. Otherwise we are confused and caught like a drunkard.

A small story:

> A man returns home very late, completely drunk. Unable to walk, he somehow makes his way into the house, stumbles over a table and breaks a piece of glass. Not only does he break a piece of glass, the glass cuts him badly. He goes to the bathroom and tries to bandage himself, looking in the mirror. Then slowly, without making a sound, he enters the bedroom and falls asleep.
>
> The next morning, his wife starts her enquiry, 'What happened? What did you do last night?'
>
> He replies, 'I didn't do anything. I am ok.' The wife says, 'No, tell me why you were late.'
>
> He says, 'I went and had a few drinks.' She says, 'That's ok, but did you hurt yourself?'
>
> He replies, 'No, I did not hurt myself.' She asks, 'Then why did you put so many bandages on the mirror?'
>
> Instead of putting the bandages on himself, he put the bandages on the mirror!

If we are drunk, if we are unaware, we land up doing the same thing! We would do everything to the mirror. Catching the mirror and catching the form is one and the same. If we put the bandage on the mirror, we can never be healed. The mirror should be used to find out where to put the bandage on us. In the same way, we should use God or the Divine like a mirror to find out where we have a problem. Don't miss and try to do the healing work on the mirror. If we do that we will miss the whole thing. So be very clear: Starting life with prayers is a good start, but it is not the right place to end.

WE CHOOSE GOD BASED ON OUR EMOTIONS

At the next level, the person is centered on fear and so he worships gods who will protect him. He does the *Sudarśana homa* (homa refers to making offerings into a consecrated fire; Sudarśana homa refers to the fire ritual done for general protection), or he continuously does *Mṛtyuñjaya homa* (fire ritual done to avoid untimely death, improve longevity) for protection. He continuously goes about worshipping some planet or god. That's why tribal gods have big swords. In many Indian villages also, you see gods with swords and big weapons. People who are fear-centered worship gods with weapons. All this is ok, nothing wrong, but it is not the place to stop.

The third level is, approaching the Divine because of worry. Again, worry is nothing but mixture of fear and greed. With worry, we approach the Divine in the same way. We pray to the Divine, 'Please help me stop worrying. Please help me come out of these worries.' At this point, we may do yoga or meditation for the sake of peace—not for spiritual Enlightenment, but to calm our mind, to get a little peace.

The next level is based on attention-need. We approach the Divine for the sake of name and fame, for the sake of capturing the attention of people. Not only do we pray to the Divine, we gradually start representing the Divine also. If you go to India, you will see that the people who run temples behave almost like God. It's a big problem.

I tell people: Unless you are mature, never take up the task of running a temple. One person asked me, 'I don't believe in spirituality. But, I want to run a temple as a social service. Shall I do it?' I told him, 'Never make that mistake! If you are not spiritually mature and you enter this work, surely you will trouble yourself and others. By and by, it will become a pure name-and-fame game! And naturally you will not only hurt yourself, you will hurt others too.'

There's a beautiful ritual performed during the installation of a deity in a temple, called *prāṇa pratiṣṭha*. The scriptural instruction is that the person who installs the deity must be enlightened. Otherwise, the person who installs the deity receives the collective negativity of the people who pray in that temple. It may be a frightening idea, but don't think it's a lie. It has meaning. The person who takes up this job without spiritual maturity will naturally end up with name and fame problems. He creates problems for himself and others. He starts representing the Divine and acts on behalf of the Divine.

The people who stand and pray in front of God, the deity, are gullible because they are caught in fear and greed. You can easily exploit them. They are waiting for a solution. That is the reason why repeatedly, it is emphasized that only an enlightened person should run a spiritual organization.

If we give a spiritual project to a person who has only the attitude of a businessman, he turns the whole thing into a business. The Divine cannot be brought under accounts and mathematical calculations! The whole thing loses its spirit. That is why Masters emphasize that we need spiritual maturity before we enter into these activities.

The next is comparison and jealousy. This is an extreme step. People always compare with others, and they feel jealous of the others' position, their status or their wealth. A person who compares and feels jealous can never rest. Look into what makes us run in our lives. Why are we in a hurry? Listen, don't be in a hurry! We don't need to run. If we are centered on jealousy and comparison, again we approach the Divine from that angle and only for that purpose.

EXPRESSING THE DIVINE

It is hard to imagine the extent of foolishness people go to if they are caught in jealousy and comparison. One is constantly caught in: this is *mine*; that is *mine*; this is the way I do it, etc. We need to realize that each of us is unique. God is not an engineer; He is an artist. He sculpts each of us with His hands, lovingly and uniquely. Therefore, each one of us is different.

When we approach the Divine with the mentality of jealousy and comparison, we are caught again. People ask me, '*Swamiji,* in our epics, we read about gods and goddesses fighting out of jealousy, greed, and anger. What do you say about that?' Listen, those epics were written for people caught in jealousy, so that they could relate with them. Don't think that the Divine makes those mistakes! But if people think so, it means that they are relating with Him in their own mold!

Even rituals are done only so that people feel comfortable with God and they start coming closer to Him. When people witness the ceremony of Gods getting married, they feel comfortable and safe. To make people feel relaxed, these stories are told and expressed. You see, unless the Divine is expressed in our language, we will not be able to relate with It. That is why these stories are written.

Next is the person who is centered on ego. This is slightly more difficult to deal with! The person who is centered on ego tries to get name and fame for himself. He starts claiming that he is divine without expressing the qualities of the Divine. That is why there's a beautiful Upaniṣad verse that says: If you are divine, express it by your quality. Let people recognize it by your quality, not by your words.

What you do speaks for you; what you speak will not do anything for you. What you do, the way in which you work, speaks for you. Your words will not work for you. There's a short, beautiful *Upaniṣad* called *Paramahamsa Upaniṣad.* It says, a Paramahamsa should not wear the saffron robe. Actually, technically speaking, I am not supposed to wear this saffron robe. They say we are not respected the way we have to be if we wear this saffron robe. By our very quality, because of our Divinity, we should be respected. The divine qualities expressed in our life, that alone should be respected, and not this robe or tradition. It should come because of the enlightened qualities expressed through us.

Yesterday there was a question: How do we know if a person is egoistic or he is a real spiritual Master? Please listen. A person who is egoistic can only play with words. Only a person who has achieved Enlightenment can radiate the energy to reproduce the same experience in you. If you get the experience, then be very clear your Master is enlightened. He is divine. He is the embodiment of spiritual experience and knowledge. If you get the words but not the experience, be very clear, the person or the path you are following is not the Ultimate.

Words are like the menu card. Experience is like the food. If you go to a restaurant and they give you a menu card and say, 'Here is the menu card, but the food is not available here,' can you call that a restaurant? No! The menu card is not enough to satisfy your hunger. In spiritual life we cannot stop with just the menu card.

The person who has approached the Divine with ego always tries to represent the Divine without having the solid experience himself. That is why the *Upaniṣads* again and again emphasize experience. If we don't experience, there's something seriously wrong with the person whom we are following.

I always tell people, if you have not experienced anything with me, please follow some other person. It is easy to put the responsibility on the disciples and continuously blame them by saying: 'You are not qualified, you are not practicing perfectly, you have not tried, and that is why you have not had any experience.'

This is a cunning way of cheating the disciple and evading the truth. The disciple comes to a Guru because the disciple has not yet experienced. And the Guru says, 'You are imperfect and that is why you do not have spiritual experiences.' To learn this, one doesn't need a Guru: a spouse is sufficient! Anyway, this is what the spouses tell each other continuously.

A true Master will reproduce in you the same experience that happened in him, no matter what your condition is. I am enlightened only if you can experience my enlightenment, not otherwise. Aim directly at the Divine.

The person who approaches the Divine with ego gets everything and boosts his own ego. He never surrenders to the Divine. His ego becomes stronger by getting all the knowledge. Be very clear, these are the most dangerous people. Instead of surrendering their ego to the Divine, they strengthen their ego with their knowledge. Listen. Knowledge can be used in two ways. With this knowledge, you can surrender to the Divine; or with this knowledge, you can make others surrender to you! It is up to you how you use it. When we approach the Divine with ego, instead of surrendering our ego, we strengthen our ego with knowledge.

Approach Me with Gratitude

The next level is the ultimate level. In this level, we go to the Divine with the attitude of gratitude, with the ultimate gratitude. Here, the whole relationship takes a different turn. We feel so grateful, so deeply connected to the Divine, that our whole life changes.

We move from the first level of greed, where we pray to boon-giving gods, to the next level of fear where the gods who can protect us appeal to us. The next is worry. Buddha appeals to us if we are centered on worry because he appears to be so peaceful and calm. To the person who is centered on name and fame, gods who give name and fame appeal the most. In the same way as with gods, people also approach Masters from all these various levels.

I have seven kinds of people who approach me: *One*, people who approach me out of greed; *two*, people who approach me out of fear; *three*, people who approach me out of worry; *four*, people who approach me for name and fame; *five*, people who approach me out of jealousy and comparison; *six*, people who approach me out of ego, to strengthen their ego by saying, 'I am a disciple of Paramahamsa Nithyananda. I am close to him. He knows my name.' Just to have ego satisfaction they come to me; finally, *seven*—there are a few, very few who approach me out of gratitude.

There's one more problem with people who approach me out of greed. Not only do they have greed, they also have their own ideas and fantasies about a Master. They come with a frame and see whether I fit into that frame or not. Also, I face a big problem because of my young age. Let me narrate to you an incident that happened in our India ashram:

> One day I was sitting alone at outdoors in the ashram, without my turban. I was sitting there on a small rock, enjoying the cool breeze. One well-read, elderly scholar came to me and asked, 'I want to meet Swamiji. Where is he?' I told him, 'Please go and sit in the Ananda Sabha (meditation hall). He will come in half an hour's time.' He went and sat in the meditation hall.
>
> He went and sat in the hall. After half an hour, I wore my turban and went there and was about to take my seat. This man said, 'No! I want to meet the big *Swamiji*. I want to meet Guruji (master).'
>
> I said, 'Please forgive me. In this ashram I am the Swami. Whom do you want to meet?'
>
> He said, 'I have heard about Paramahamsa Nithyananda. He healed my cousin. I want to see him.' Then I told him his cousin's name and the disease he had and that I had healed him. I told him, 'I am Paramahamsa Nithyananda.' You will be surprised; he was not ready to believe me. He just stared at me.
>
> Then I said, 'Usually, Swamis don't carry any identity card in India. Still, if you don't believe me, look at that photograph (on ashram signboard). See the name, and see that face. I am that Swami!'
>
> You will be surprised! I tell you, this is the truth. He said, 'I am not ready to learn from you.' He did not speak to me, and also went away. Because of his strong fantasies and imagination about what a Guru should be like, he was not able to even relate with me!

When we have such strong fantasy or imagination about things, we will not be able to relate with reality. It is the same with fear; people who come with fear will never be able to get rid of that fear. They will be stuck with that because fear itself is a fantasy.

At different levels, people approach the Master or God. The more mature we are, the more we will feel connected to that person who will give us fulfillment. When we become mature, when we are above fear and greed, we will approach the same Master, the same God, with more maturity, with more intimacy. We will feel deeply connected to him.

In Bhāgavatam (Hindu epic glorifying devotion onto incarnations), we learn about five different attitudes with which we normally relate with a Master or God:

1) *Dāsa Bhāva*—seeing God as a lord or master and oneself as a servant, as with Hanumān who saw Rāma as his master and served Him as a path for liberation.

2) *Vātsalya Bhāva*—seeing God as a divine child, as with Yaśodā who saw Kṛṣṇa as her son.

3) *Sakha Bhāva*—seeing God or the master as a friend, the way Arjuna related with Kṛṣṇa.

4) *Mātṛ Bhāva*—seeing God or the master as a father or mother, the way Śrī Rāmakṛṣna related with goddess Kāli (representation of the divine mother).

5) Finally, the fifth attitude is *madhura bhāva*—seeing God as a beloved, the way Radhā saw Kṛṣṇa. This attitude needs a tremendous amount of maturity. Only if we experience the consciousness which is beyond the body, can we relate with the Divine with the attitude of a beloved, *madhura bhāva*.

These are the five different *bhāvas* (attitudes or feeling connection) with which people relate with the Divine. With different maturity levels, different attitudes suit our minds. The more mature we are, the more the gratitude happens. The less the maturity, the more we fill our life with prayers. Prayer is greed; confession is fear!

That is why I say, 'Gratitude is the greatest prayer, and thank you, the greatest mantra.' When we go beyond prayer and confession, we experience gratitude. We experience the Divine. Kṛṣṇa explains how we can grow step-by-step, how we can reach the ultimate maturity, how we can create and experience the Divine at the ultimate level.

Let us see how Kṛṣṇa explains the process step-by-step. What is the technique Kṛṣṇa offers us to grow in maturity and experience eternal consciousness?

Based on how we approach the Divine, only based on how mature we are, the whole community system has been created. How much we enrich and share with society depends on how mature we are. With the same maturity, we approach God also.

If we feel money is missing in our lives, we go to the God who gives money. If we miss knowledge, we go to Sarasvatī (the goddess of knowledge), who gives knowledge. If we feel insecure, we go to the god who protects us; we go to Mother Durgā or Kāli. If we miss spiritual experience, the ultimate experience, then we go to the divine incarnations, the ultimate expressions of the Divine.

Kṛṣṇa says, 'Four types of people come to Me—*caturvidhā bhajante māṁ* ' He explains the four types as four communities. The first are the people who are distressed, i.e., the working class or *śūdra*. The second are the people who desire wealth, i.e., the business people or *vaiśya*. The third are inquisitive people who continuously enquire, continuously ask, '*Tataḥ kim? Tataḥ kim? Tataḥ kim?*' (What next?) A *kṣatriya*, for example, never rests because he constantly asks, 'What next? What next? What next?' The fourth is the person who searches for knowledge of the Absolute: He is a *brāhmaṇa*.

'All four come to Me, all four reach Me, but from different levels.' From different levels all four go to the same God, but they will not experience Him in the same way. They experience Him in different ways, according to their maturity. As long as you are caught in fear or greed, you will be attracted and go only to those types of gods. It is easy to go to a temple and pray, but difficult to go to a living Master and meditate.

It is for mature people, not for everyone In the temple we see thousands; but in spiritual places, we see a few hundred. It is not for all; it's a luxury!

SPIRITUALITY IS A LUXURY

Spirituality is a luxury; only a few intelligent people can afford it! The price of spirituality is the limit of our suffering! Only if we have had enough suffering can we afford to get into spirituality. It is only for people who have understood that they have suffered. There are two things: It is not only the suffering, but the understanding that we suffer. This understanding is what I call intelligence. This intelligence happens even beyond age and experience. Just a glimpse of life is enough if this intelligence is there; we will understand how suffering happens and we will not get caught in it! Both—the suffering and the understanding—are needed to enter into spiritual life.

'The person who approaches Me out of love and gratitude, is the best person, for I am dear to him and he is dear to Me.' By this one verse, Kṛṣṇa ends the whole conversation, the whole concept.

teṣāṁ jñānī nitya yukta eka-bhaktir viśiṣyate |
priyo hi jñānino 'tyartham ahaṁ sa ca mama priyaḥ || 7.17

Kṛṣṇa says, 'Starting at different levels is ok, but don't stop there.' We can start or take off from any level. However we should not stop and stagnate there. It is like failing to proceed to the second standard from the first. It is as if we want to stay in the same cozy, familiar level. It takes many lifetimes to understand and achieve this maturity. When I say it takes many lives, some think, 'Let me take some more lives and become mature.' Now, that's a big problem. Whenever we speak, we must make things very clear, otherwise you can't imagine how many different ways people will interpret it!

A small story:

Once, a great scholar recounted the story of Hariścandra. Most people in India know the story of Hariścandra, a king who lived to uphold the truth with integrity and authenticity, and sold his wife for the sake of the truth. Just to keep his promise, he sold his wife. Such was his greatness.

The scholar narrated the whole story. After narrating the story, he asked one person, 'What did you understand from this story?'

The person said, 'Master, I understood that truth is the most important thing in life. We should give up everything for the sake of the truth. Truth is the ultimate.'

The scholar was pleased. He asked the next person, 'What did you understand?' The man said, 'Master, I understood that in an emergency, it is ok to sell your wife.'

From the same story, two people have two different understandings! So be very clear, don't miss the understanding. A common saying is, 'As many Masters, so many paths.' However I say, 'As many disciples, so many paths!' The Master may utter the same truth to his disciples, yet each understands and interprets in his or her own way. They all approach the Divine, but from different planes. Hence the attitude, the context with which one approaches matters how one experiences the Divine.

Here Kṛṣṇa says, 'Out of these, the wise is always devoted to Me. He is the best person.' To start with, you can start at any level, yet you must strive to reach the Ultimate. And please don't think, 'Oh! Kṛṣṇa says it will take many lives; let me take some more lives and become mature.'

No! If you can enter into the knowledge this moment, the experience can happen to you this very moment. You don't need to postpone. Every moment is a new birth for you and every moment is death. The outgoing breath is death, and the incoming breath is birth. So be very clear, every moment you die and take birth. This moment can be a new birth for you. The person who understands this truth takes a new birth. He is called *dvijā*. A person who is initiated is called *dvijā* in Saṃskrit, which means twice-born or reborn. All *Sannyāsis* are twice-born or *dvijā*. 'Reborn' does not refer to being reborn physically, but at the being level. They give birth to themselves. So understand that in this moment, a new birth can happen to you.

HE IS VERY DEAR TO ME

Kṛṣṇa says: *ahaṁ sa ca mama priyaḥ*—He is dear to Me, and I am dear to him. He is in Me and I am in him. Kṛṣṇa says beautifully that He is in you and you are in Him. The moment you understand this ultimate Truth, the moment you approach the Divine with the right attitude, you become the Divine. All you need to do is change your attitude. Over! Change your inner space and the whole thing is done.

Please listen, one important thing. The Master or the Divine is in you only when you engage yourself in enriching service to Him. Sitting in front of the Master or the Divine, just enjoying the form, is not the enriching service Kṛṣṇa talks about. Then you are only chasing Him from a purely selfish motive.

When you devote yourself to the divine mission, you become a devotee. That is when you become dear to Him. Your worship is no longer selfish. It is towards the mission of the Divine, in whatever form. I tell my followers: Stop sitting in front of me, gazing and waiting for words to drop. Work for my mission. Enrich yourself and others by helping me to transform people. As long as you sit and gaze, you chase me. When you work for my mission, I chase you. I shall always be with you.

Here Kṛṣṇa says clearly, 'one who knows Me, dwells in Me. Being engaged in My mission, he attains Me, *āsthitaḥ sa hi yuktātmā mām evānuttamāṁ gatim* (7.18).'

When the scriptures say, 'Follow the Master,' they do not mean to follow the form. They advise you to follow the teachings of the Master, so that you can be the master too. They tell you to follow the institution of the Master, his community, his *sanga*. When we follow these three, the Master, his teachings and his mission, we are on the path to liberation. Only after many births and deaths can we relate to an enlightened person. We will not be able to relate to an Enlightened Master unless we undergo many births and deaths.

I told you about the seven steps in spiritual progress—1) go around many temples, perform many rituals, pilgrimages, etc. 2) do rituals by yourself 3) concentrate and pray to one God 4) instead of rituals, chant verses in praise of God 5) instead of chanting, visualize His form and meditate upon it 6) instead of meditating on any form, fall into that same consciousness, realize that the form and your soul are one and the same, that God and the soul are one and the same 7) experience reality! Don't think these seven steps will be done in one lifetime. People take hundreds of lives to achieve this maturity. It is rare to achieve this maturity.

Kṛṣṇa says: *sa mahātmā sūdurlabhaḥ* (7.19)—indeed, very rare is it to see such great souls who have achieved that maturity. It is easy to relate with gods in the temple because they don't demand discipline or purity from us. We can pray to Him, do whatever we want, and think He has blessed us and go away. However, relating with a living enlightened Master is difficult. People ask me, 'Why do Masters become popular after their death?' This is because it is easy to cheat ourselves with a photograph. We can do whatever we want and project everything as His blessings. And most importantly, we don't have to give up our ego with dead Masters. Connecting with dead Masters is easy because they don't demand our ego. We don't need to surrender. That is why there will be large crowds with dead Masters and temples. Sometimes we sit beneath that photograph and represent the Master. But this whole game is nothing but an ego fulfilling game.

But with a living enlightened Master, we need to transform our life. We need to experience the truth. He will not let us sleep or rest. He will haunt us until we realize the truth. He will not let us do what we want. He will not fulfill our ego.

I always tell people, 'Dead masters are dead. The living Master is death!' The living Master will be death for us, death for our ego. We cannot play our games with him. We must grow and become mature beings. We cannot play the same old game and put his name in front. He shakes us. He awakens us.

LIVING MASTER IS A NIGHTMARE, SIṂHA SVAPNA!

Living Masters are nightmares. That is why people are afraid to come near a living Master. We can't play the same game with him. The game will be his! He is the director. Only a person who has understood, after many, many births and deaths, who has matured, who has enough knowledge, surrenders to Me, surrenders to the living Master, says Kṛṣṇa.

In India, especially in Tamil Nadu, kids play with wooden dolls. For one doll, they will drape a *sāri* and say, 'This is mother.' They will dress another in a *dhoti* and call it father, then brother, and so on. They say, 'Mother is cooking. Father is going to office,' and place the father doll in a small car. And then, they will say, 'Sister is going to school.' They will make cry sounds as though the sister cries not wanting to go to school.

This seems like a game for kids. But please understand, you play the same game too in your life. You catch somebody and say, 'You are my mother, you are my father, you are my wife, you are my husband, you are my son, and you are my brother.' And if that doll doesn't behave according to your frame or your image, you say, 'It's not a good doll,' and you throw it away and cry. In the same way, when somebody doesn't behave according to your frame, you feel they hurt you. You want all the people in your life to play their role the way *you* want them to play. When that doesn't happen, you feel hurt. Then, suddenly, you die. You leave the body.

When you go to another place, in your next birth, you again catch one more set of dolls and start the same game. Sometimes you bring dolls into the game, sometimes you throw dolls out of the game, sometimes you fire and sometimes you pamper them. If you don't have enough dolls, you get some cats or dogs to play with. Again and again, you play the same game. Only a person who is a little mature thinks, 'What am I doing? How many times will I do this same psychodrama?'

Please listen! The whole thing is a psychodrama! Whether it is a relationship, or whether it is life itself, it is nothing but a psychodrama. You have an agenda. Society has taught you that, as a father, as a husband, or as a son, you should behave in a certain pre-defined manner. The person who understands that he is playing the same drama again and again, has achieved knowledge, the real intelligence about what is happening. Then naturally you surrender. You surrender unto Me, asserts Kṛṣṇa.

Kṛṣṇa says, 'One who understands that the cause of all causes is Me, realizes the ultimate divine. He realizes thus, 'How many times will I play the same drama? How many times will I make the same mistakes?' Until this realization, the whole thing is repeated again and again without end, without the experience.'

'The person who has understood, who has knowledge of this truth, surrenders unto Me, surrenders to the Master, an enlightened being—*jñānavān māṁ prapadyate*, knowing Me to be the cause of all causes and all there is. Such a great soul is rare—*vāsudevaḥ sarvam iti sa mahātmā sūdurlabhaḥ* (7.19).'

Only a person who has achieved this knowledge sees and relates with the Master in the real sense. There's a beautiful verse that says, 'Even if you have seen an enlightened Master *once*, you will become enlightened.' Some people ask me, 'Why haven't I become enlightened yet, *Swamiji?*' Be very clear, 'Never think that you are seeing *me*; never think that by seeing through your eyes, you can see the Divine. You can see *my form*, but not *me*. Even if you have seen many Enlightened Masters, never think that you have seen them.' The attitude or the space from which you have seen them plays a major role. If you went to them with fear or greed, you went to a demigod and not to an enlightened Master.

Only if you go with an attitude of love and gratitude, with maturity, only then do you *see* a living enlightened Master. The moment you see an enlightened being *as He is*, you *will* become enlightened. There's no doubt about it.

I Am In Your Heart

7.20 *Those whose discrimination has been distorted by various desires, surrender unto deities. They follow specific rules and regulations of worship according to their own nature.*

7.21 *I am in everyone's heart as the Super Soul.*
As soon as one desires to worship some deity, I make his faith steady so that he can devote himself to that particular deity.

7.22 *Endowed with such a faith, he endeavors to worship a particular demigod and obtains his desires;*
In reality, these benefits are granted by Me alone.

7.23 *Men of limited intelligence worship the demigods and their fruits are limited and temporary. Those who worship the demigods go only to the planets of the demigods, but My devotees reach My supreme planet.*

He says: I am in everyone's heart as the *Paramātman* (super soul). As soon as one desires to worship a particular deity, I make his faith steady so that he can devote himself to that particular deity.

Please understand that when He says 'deity' or 'demigod', He doesn't mean the Supreme. Even if you approach Kṛṣṇa out of fear or greed, you approach only a demigod. When He says the word demigod, He means the attitude with which we approach the Divine; how we approach the Divine. With the right approach, even if you approach a demigod, he will be supreme! He will give you enlightenment. With the wrong approach, even if you approach Kṛṣṇa, you will have only material benefits.

There is a beautiful *Līlā*, happening of a divine play from Bhagavān Kṛṣṇa's life.

A rich man prayed to Kṛṣṇa to become a king. Twice a day, morning and evening he repeated, 'Kṛṣṇa, Kṛṣṇa.' He always asked Kṛṣṇa thus, 'Kṛṣṇa, please give me a kingdom. Kṛṣṇa, I want to become a king.'

There was another poor lady, who had only one cow. With that milk she made a little butter and some sweets and offered it to Kṛṣṇa. The whole day she sat and chanted Kṛṣṇa's name.

Suddenly one day Kṛṣṇa appeared and responded to both of them. This man, who had asked for a kingdom, became a king. And in the case of this lady who prayed everyday toKṛṣṇa, her cow died.

Nārada asked Kṛṣṇa, 'What is this, Kṛṣṇa? That man who repeats your name only twice a day has been made a king by you. This lady who remembers you 24 hours a day, got deprived of her only cow. What is this? Is it fair?'

Kṛṣṇa says, 'That man only wants the kingdom. He came to Me only for that. I am a utility to him. So I blessed him with what he wants. But for her, I was her whole life. There was only one small hindrance, only one thing that stood between her and Me, and that was the cow! I took that away. I removed that hindrance also. Now she has come to Me and completely become Me!'

Whatever our approach to the Divine is, it plays an important role in our spiritual progress. If we approach Kṛṣṇa out of fear or greed, we worship a demigod. But Kṛṣṇa says we are not wrong, but just that it is not enough. Kṛṣṇa is not here to discourage us. Understand, nothing is wrong, but it is not enough, it is not complete. That is not the place to stop. It is a good place to have a visa, but not to have a green card or citizenship. Here, the planets or palaces of demigods are good places to visit, but not the right place to stay.

Kṛṣṇa says, 'Because I am in everyone's heart as the super soul, the moment you desire to worship some demigod, I shall make your faith steady, so you can devote yourself to that particular deity.'

STAGES OF SEEKING

Let me describe how a seeker usually travels through all these paths and eventually reaches. When you start as a normal seeker, you hear about all kinds of rituals. You hear that a particular *pūjā* (worship), a particular *homa* (fire ritual) will give some specific benefit, and you starts doing these things. On Friday, you fast for Devi (the divine mother), on Saturday, you fast for Bālāji (another name for Lord Viṣṇu), on Sunday you fast for some other god, on Monday you fast for Śiva, on Tuesday for Skanda (Lord Subrahmanya), on Thursday for the Guru (the master), and so on.

This is the way it starts. Then slowly, you not only go to all these *pūjās* and *homas*, you also go to many different temples. After some time, you understand that these rituals and trips to the temples are too much. Then you think, 'Why let somebody else do these things for me? Let me directly do it and relate with the Divine.' You start your own temple in your own home. You engage in worship. This happens when you become a little mature. You think that you should feel directly connected to the Divine. 'Let me do it by myself,' you think.

The first level in spirituality is going around visiting all the temples, watching all the types of offerings. The second level is doing it yourself. The third level is realizing, 'The Divine is there in all the gods, in all the forms. But I think I feel more attracted towards this one god, this particular god. So let me concentrate on worshipping the Divine in this form.' Having one form and offering only to that form is *iśṭa niṣṭa*. This is the third level. The fourth level happens when you think, 'More than these types of offerings, sounds imbued with energy is more powerful. Let me chant the sacred verses.'

Understand: surrendering through the body is *pūjā*; surrendering through words is *japa*, chanting verses in praise of the Lord; surrendering through the mind is *jñāna*, wisdom or knowledge of

the Self. So here you think, 'Why not chant the name of God?' You start repeating the name of your favorite deity.

At every level of completion, different gods appeal to you; at every level, different Gurus or masters appeal to you, and you grow in your feeling connection or devotion with them. When you are at the level of going to pilgrimage places, people who guide you to these pilgrimage centers appeal to you. When you come to the level of *pūjā* and *homā*, other people who also do these rituals appeal to you! The person who teaches you *pūjā* appeals and connects to you. Even the people who teach you any skills like dancing, acting, martial arts, or even those who educate you in your studies and profession, they connect to you. The *pūjā ācarya* or anyone who teaches and inspires you becomes your guru.

Next, when you come to the level of completion where you begin focusing and offering to only one deity, the deity becomes your guru. This is *iśṭa niṣṭa*. ***Iśṭa niṣṭa*** **means bowing down, revering only your** ***iśṭa*****, your chosen deity.** Wherever you bow down, even if you bow down to your father or mother, you should know that I bow down to my *iśṭa* who is in your heart—your *ānanda gandha*.

Next, after some time you think, 'Why only repeat this verse? Why not do some meditation?' Now the person who teaches you meditation appeals to you. Meditation is again *saguṇa brahman*, which means meditating on a form. This is *Līlā dhyāna*, the next level of completion or next space of *iśṭa niṣṭa*.

Līlā dhyāna **means strongly feeling connected to your own version of your chosen ideal.** You are free to choose your ideal in Hindu tradition. You can choose your own Guru. You need to understand, living with your chosen ideal is called *iśṭa niṣṭa*. *Līlā dhyāna* means constantly remembering the actions and the life of your chosen ideal and being immersed in the qualities, words, actions, body language and life of the Master; whatever you may be doing, being totally immersed in Him.

Understand, you may accept all divine beings. It is not that you will not go to Viṣṇu temple or Devi temple, but if you are connected to Śiva, if you have chosen Śiva as your ideal, you will know only He is your ideal.

Śrī Rāmakṛṣṇa Paramahamsa gives a very beautiful example of *iśṭa niṣṭa.* A woman in the house will serve everybody. She will serve the brother-in-law, sister-in-law, father-in-law, mother-in-law, husband's elder brother, younger brother, sister's husband; she will serve everyone, give them food and take care of them. But she knows her personal space is only for her husband! Same way, you may bow down in front of any god, any deity, any guru, but you know you are bowing down only to your Guru in these forms.

LIVING WITH GOD—LEVELS OF COMPLETION

Listen, I am defining *Līlā Dhyāna.*

***Līlā dhyāna* means being lost in the pastimes of the guru or god.** With god, one thing is that you may not be directly involved in the whole līlā. So you have to remember, remember and try to practice. With a living Guru, you are directly part of the divine play. So, you don't need to try to remember, remember; He will be remembering you! He will be remembering you! This is called *līlā dhyāna*. Even if you are afraid that he is going to shout at you, it is *līlā dhyāna*.

Listen! Practicing the presence of God is constantly feeling you are with Him, He is with you. Practicing the presence of God is the greatest, most powerful technique to put you in *bhāva samādhi* immediately. Bhagavān Śrī Rāmakṛṣṇa did it; Bhagavān Ramaṇa Mahaṛṣi also practiced it.

You know you are bowing down only to your chosen ideal, *Iśṭa niṣṭa*. Same way, if your chosen ideal is Śiva, or Devi, or Kṛṣṇa, even if you bow down to me, you should bow down to me as an embodiment of your chosen ideal. And, if your chosen ideal is me, then even if you bow down to anybody else, you should bow down to them only as an embodiment of me. That is *iśṭa niṣṭa*. Practicing the presence of God, *Līlā dhyāna*, and *Iśṭa niṣṭa*, all the three boil down to the same space, space of *bhāva samādhi.*

I tell my disciples to practice *Iśṭa niṣṭa*, with the whole

Existence cognizing—'I bow down to Nithyananda who is in your *ānanda gandha*; whether he is awakened or not, whether you experience or not, He is there in your *ānanda gandha*. If you are initiated into *ānanda gandha*, you will also experience him. If not, you may not experience, but I can experience. I bow down to Nithyananda who is in your *ānanda gandha*.'

Understand, *ānanda gandha* is a nādi, a subtle cosmic energy center just below *anāhata cakra* (heart center) and above *maṅipūraka cakra* (stomach center), which is awakened only by an Incarnation. The Inner Awakening program participants are initiated into *ānanda gandha* and they become Nithya Spiritual healers as the channels of Cosmic energy transmitting healing to the world. Listen! What you are carrying in the *ānanda gandha* will become reality. Please understand, your *ānanda gandha* is the source of your life. Just like any slide kept in front of projector light becomes reality, any truth kept in front of your inner space, your *ānanda gandha* becomes a reality.

I have seen so many people, ordinary village men and women in India, living with their chosen ideal and living the highest enlightened life without even knowing the words integrity, authenticity, and all that! Without knowing any of these words, they are radiating Enlightenment! I tell you, just this one truth of *Iśṭa niṣṭa* and *Līlā dhyāna* has made millions of village Indians, Indian villagers enlightened! Millions of Indian villagers practice the presence of God.

Practicing the presence of God makes you more and more authentic. That is the beauty of the Hindu tradition! Beauty of the *Vedic* spiritual tradition! *Iśṭa niṣṭa* makes you do lot of self-completion with you.

So, the *first level of completion* is attending rituals and visiting temples, *pūjā* and *yātrā*. The second level is doing the rituals yourself, *pūjā*. The third level is having the feeling connection and concentrating on one deity, and offering only to that deity, *iśṭa niṣṭa*. The fourth level of completion is realizing that the verses are more powerful than rituals, and you start chanting the name of your *iśṭa*. The fifth level is visualizing a form and meditating on His pastimes and being immersed in His qualities, words, actions, body language and life; instead of chanting, you enter the space of feeling and living with His presence. Then, when you sincerely meditate, He Himself appears. He gives you His *darśan* (vision) and guides you to the higher level of practice. He guides you to the right living Master. Sometimes He gives you *darśan* and guides you; sometimes He automatically makes you feel connected to your Master.

Only a person who has come to this level of completion can feel directly connected to a living Enlightened Master. Till you reach this level of completion, till this maturity happens, you cannot straightaway feel completely connected to an enlightened person.

You need to go through all five levels of completion, only then will you feel completely connected to a living Master. When you come to the stage where you meditate on a single form, the Master happens in your life and guides you to the highest level of completion, enriching you with Enlightenment.

The form upon which you meditate and your own form are expressions of the same divine energy. So the Master puts you into real meditation. This means turning towards yourself, turning towards your own consciousness, turning towards your own being or soul. He gives you the technique to realize your being. This is the *sixth level of completion*.

The *seventh level of completion*, the ultimate completion, the complete completion is when you experience that *you are That*. You achieve Enlightenment!

This is the usual route of completion that seekers travel on, starting from the first level of completion, moving to the second level, and ending with the ultimate and complete completion of experiencing the Self. Completion is Self! Now find out in which level of completion you are in and try to go to the next level. That's all. That is all you need to do. Just go on completing, completing, completing with everything, with Guru, with God, with Sadguru, with life!

Here Kṛṣṇa says, 'Because I reside in everyone's heart as the super soul, when somebody desires to worship a demigod, I make his faith steady, so that he can devote himself to that particular deity.' When you approach the Divine even from the first level of completion, He helps you. He enriches you without doubt. He never gives up on you. You may give up on yourself, but He never gives up on you. One of the biggest qualities of an Incarnation is that He never gives up on you!

When you start, you are like 18 carat gold. There's nothing wrong with 18 carat gold, but you need to be put into the fire a little bit, and slowly, you become 22 carat gold. Then you reach the Master, a living enlightened Master. Then slowly you become 24 carat gold, and you become enlightened. If you throw away the first step, giving up on the 18 carat gold, you never reach the second step. Unless you have gone through the earlier steps of completion, it will be difficult to relate and have feeling connection to a living Master.

One morning, a man came to visit me and started speaking to me. He expressed his confusion. This happened after he had read many books. He said, 'I am now more confused than before.' In the *Gītā,* Arjuna says the same thing. After a few chapters, he says, 'Oh Kṛṣṇa, I am now more confused than before hearing the *Gītā*!'

Understand, this clearly means that you have done your spiritual practice well! You really did your practice. Understanding that a particular practice is not helping you is the right enriching derived from the practice!

Buddha teaches meditation to one of his disciples. The disciple tries his best to meditate and comes back and says, 'Buddha, I am unable to meditate!' Then Buddha says, 'Don't worry. You have understood properly. That is the purpose of this meditation. Understanding that you are not able to meditate is the purpose of this meditation. You have done it. Now forget about it and come to the next step.'

Sometimes these techniques make us mature by giving us the understanding that we are unable to do the technique. That understanding is a big maturity. There's nothing wrong in it.

Approaching the Divine in some form is the first step, or the first level. There's nothing wrong in that, but don't stop there. Here Kṛṣṇa says, 'I make his faith steady, so that he can devote himself to that particular deity,' which means that he can grow in that particular space of completion. There is the possibility of growth. He says, 'I don't discourage him; I make his faith steady, so that he will slowly come up to higher levels of completion.'

Kṛṣṇa says, 'Even if you approach Me with an attitude of fear or greed, I fulfill your needs. It is My own energy which fulfills them, so that you grow, and you come up to the next level of completion.'

If you receive boons through demigods, do not think that those deities are responsible for it. Do not think that the idols that you pray to are the ones who granted your prayers. All these are granted by the ultimate energy, the Existential energy. But you are not expected to stop with these boons. You are expected to grow further levels of completion.

I always tell people, when you approach the Divine, first all your dreams will become reality. The divine will bless you. All your desires will be realized. Later on, the Divine will give you the understanding that the reality you perceive is itself a dream! First God gives the *śakti* (energy) to turn your dreams into reality. Then He gives the *buddhi* (intelligence) to realize that reality itself is a dream!

That is what He says here: When I bless you, according to your maturity, as per your level of completion and based on the way in which you approach the Divine, I give everything.

There are many educated individuals who question me about the wisdom of idol worship and rituals. A small happening from Swami Vivekananda's life.

> A disciple was massaging Vivekananda's feet. A follower, a young student, came to Vivekananda, prostrated at his feet and said, 'I adore you. I adore you because you despise all these superstitions about idol worship and bathing in the Ganges. You are truly educated.'

> Vivekananda roared at him, 'You fool, what do you know about my beliefs. I pray everyday to Ma Kāli and bathe in the Ganges. Shed all your notions that worshipping idols is foolish and learn how to pray.'
>
> Soon after, an elderly scholar came to Vivekananda and said, 'Master, you are the greatest. Whatever you have said about learning the scriptures and going to temples is so powerful. I wish everyone would talk like you do.'
>
> Vivekananda said to him, 'What do you know about the scriptures? Is there any point in reading all this outdated material? It only makes your ego stronger. Stop this nonsense and meditate.'
>
> After the scholar left, the shocked disciple asked Vivekananda, 'Master, I am confused. You have just reversed your position with these two people. What should I do?'
>
> Vivekananda said, 'Just keep your mouth shut and massage my feet. That is good for you.'

When you go to a temple and worship an idol, when you are in the first level of completion, you might feel that you are praying to a stone or metal idol. As your completion grows, you will realize that the idol is not just stone or metal; it is living energy. Even without much effort, you will start feeling the energy inside the temple.

Why do you think millions of people, visit holy shrines in Tirupati or Varanasi or Tiruvannamalai? A few hundred people can be misled, but not millions, and that too without any enticement. They go because they feel relieved, they feel deeply enriched; not all of them go merely out of greed and fear. There are thousands who go because unknowingly they feel the hand of God, as it were. They feel the touch and they feel the 'energy connection'.

Hindus worship *through* the idols, not the idols themselves; our rituals address the energy behind these idols. Logic cannot make us understand this. Only faith can, the *śraddha* that comes from authenticity. We need to go through this stage of worshipping the form before we realize the formless. Otherwise we will all be intellectual monsters. Religions that condemn idol worship without understanding the philosophy behind worship breed confusion that leads to destruction.

In every form of learning we need to advance step-by-step. Only if we are an exception can we be promoted to university education without attending high school. Such exceptions are rare, and prove the rule. When we consider idol worship foolish and meaningless, it only means that we are foolish and ignorant. The minute science advances and when a scientist measures the energy vibration of our temples and proves that these are centers of cosmic energy, *kṣetras,* the same people will be queuing up at the temples.

When thousands and millions of people congregate to celebrate the Divine and offer gratitude, any place becomes a temple, a place of worship. Every twelve years, tens of millions of people gather by the sacred river Gaṅgā in India to celebrate Kumbh Melā. In certain years 100 million people have gathered on this occasion, in what is certainly the largest gathering in the world. No invitations or promotions are done, just the dates of Kumbh Melā mark the vedic calendar or Pañcānga on a Hindu's home wall, that's all! Simply millions and millions gather.

As these people bathe in the sacred river with deep *śraddha* (authenticity), gratitude and prayers, the river gets purified and in turn purifies them. It is a deep bio-spiritual interaction that raises the energy of the planet and the Universe.

When Kṛṣṇa says, 'He goes to the planets of the demigods,' don't think there is some planet out there! He talks about inner space and experience. If we worship some god out of greed, we never come out of that greed. We will be continuously caught in greed. If we worship some god out of fear, we will be always in that fear. If we worship the Divine out of love and gratitude, we experience a totally different inner space, the space of completion, the space of Enlightenment.

Hell and heaven are not geographical; they are psychological. Now all we need to know is how to create heaven, how to create the space of completion. There's nothing that needs to be learnt about the art of creating hell. Now, it is time to learn how to create heaven.

Kṛṣṇa says: Men of small intelligence—people caught in greed or fear, attention-need or worry—worship the demigods. Of course, sometimes we worship the demigods; sometimes we approach Bhagāvan Kṛṣṇa or the ultimate God with the same incomplete attitude—the attitude of asking and begging.

If we carry the incomplete cognition of greed, whether we worship Kubera, the god who gives money, or Kṛṣṇa, in effect we worship only a *devata* (demigod). Even if we worship Kṛṣṇa with that same incomplete cognition out of our space of incompletion, we worship only a demigod. It is the cognition of completion or incompletion that makes Kṛṣṇa either the ultimate God, *Bhagavān* or a demigod, *Deva*. It is we who create the cognition, the space. It is we who create the energy. By worshipping *Devatas*, we attain *Devatas*.

This is an important *sūtra*, a technique. It says:

antavattu phalaṁ teṣāṁ tad bhavaty alpamedhasāṁ |
devān devayajo yānti madbhaktā yānti mām api || 7.23

It says that when we get boons from demigods, they are temporary. God will bless us with wealth when we ask Him. But we need intelligence to preserve and to protect wealth. So be very clear, when we receive anything out of energy, without having the maturity to receive and sustain it, it is only temporary. If we have enough intelligence and maturity to have wealth, then naturally, we would have created it. Because we don't have *buddhi*, wisdom, we ask God to give us *śakti*, energy. If we get *śakti* without *buddhi*, it will only be temporary.

That is what Kṛṣṇa says: If we get *śakti* without *buddhi*, it is temporary. It will not remain with us. That is why He says that boons derived from demigods are temporary, not permanent. And if we continue to worship them, we are stuck with them. We create that kind of energy in our inner space. We live with that kind of energy in our being.

GRATITUDE—THE GREATEST ATTITUDE

He makes one more statement: *madbhaktā yānti mām api*—My devotees attain Me. Then He says these words: If you approach Me with the ultimate attitude, with the attitude of love and gratitude, you achieve Me. The greatest attitude is gratitude. If you approach Me with gratitude, you experience Me.

Again and again people ask me, '*Swamiji*, when I have so many problems, how can I be grateful?' Listen, we continuously pray, 'Oh God, please give me a diamond ring.' Do we feel grateful that He gave us the finger to wear the ring? We don't feel grateful that He gave us the finger. Be very clear, the finger is not our birthright. There are thousands of people who don't have hands. There are thousands who don't have a finger. It's not our birthright.

We continuously pray intensely, in all possible ways, 'Oh God, give me this. Oh God, give me that.' But we never feel grateful for the things that are showered on us.

This very life is a blessing! Can we say that our life has been given to us as payment for some job that we did in Vaikuṇṭha (abode of Lord Viṣṇu) or Kailāśa (abode of Lord Śiva)? No! It's not as if we worked for 100 years in Kailāśa, and earned a check that says, 'Alright, have 70 years of life.' If we work in the army, they give us money to study. It's not like that; we did not get life as a salary. It's a pure blessing showered on us.

Every breath is a blessing! The breath that we inhale and exhale is a boon given to us. This very life is a blessing. Continuously we miss things that are not part of our possession. But we never experience the things that are showered on us by the Divine. Each of us has a big list of things that God has not given us and we also have a big list of things that God has given us. If you take a paper and pen and start writing these lists, both lists will be endless. Every moment of our life is a gift from the Divine. We are alive, we are still conscious; that by itself is a gift from the Divine.

Now it's up to us whether to look at the list of things not given to us and constantly feel miserable and live in hell, or look at the list of things showered on us and be in heaven. The second way makes us feel deeply grateful. It makes us say, 'Oh God! You have showered so much on me, and given me the blessing of life.' We feel grateful and create our abode, Vaikuṇṭa or Kailāśa. It's purely our choice.

Kṛṣṇa says, 'These men of small intelligence worship demigods. Their results are temporary.' We continue to live that way. When we feel life is a blessing and we approach the Divine with deep love and gratitude, not only do we experience divine consciousness, Kṛṣṇa says: They achieve ME. They attain ME—*madbhaktā yānti mām api.*

There's another verse where Kṛṣṇa beautifully says: 'If you ask for something, I will give you that. If you don't ask for anything, I will give you Me.' People say, 'Who wants Him? We want Him only as a utility, not Him. As long as He serves our purpose, things are ok. So we don't want Him.' People want only solutions. They don't want the Divine.

No One Knows Me

7.24 *Unintelligent men, who do not know My Supreme Nature,*
think that I, the Supreme Divinity, the Bhagavān, who was
unmanifest before, and have assumed an embodied form now.
They do not know that I am imperishable and Ultimate,
even when I assume the body.

7.25 *I am never revealed to the foolish and unintelligent,*
covered as I am by My divine power [yogamāyā].
The ignorant do not know Me, the unborn and eternal.

7.26 *O Arjuna, as the Supreme Divinity, I know all that has*
happened in the past, all that is happening in the present,
and all that is to happen in the future.
I also know all living entities; but no one knows Me.

7.27 *O scion of Bhārata [Arjuna], all living entities are born*
into delusion, overcome by the dualities of attachment
and aversion, Parantapa, conqueror of foes.

Unintelligent men, who do not know my supreme, illimitable and immortal form, assume my illimitable form as manifested.

Here is another important verse. When He says earlier—My devotees achieve Me, attain Me—naturally Arjuna would have had the doubt: are you one more *devata* (demigod)?

So Kṛṣṇa gives the explanation: 'Unintelligent men, who are not mature, think I am just this form. Only an intelligent man understands that I am immortal. Even when I assume this form, I am that same consciousness. I have not become an ordinary human being by assuming a human form.' He declares His divinity openly. He declares, 'I am the same even when I assume a human form. Don't think I am one more demigod.'

He says, 'I am unborn, immortal, illimitable, even when I assume this form. Even when I assume this form, I am that same ultimate divine. I am not an ordinary man.' This is an important statement. This statement is made to declare His enlightenment and to express clearly and explicitly, 'I am enlightened. I am the embodiment of the ultimate consciousness.' The problem is that the person who is receiving this is not mature enough to recognize it as such.

People ask me again and again, 'Why is Kṛṣṇa repeatedly declaring that He is enlightened?' That's a big problem. If you talk about something again and again, people tend to think that something is wrong with that.

There is a proverb in Tamil: If you wear a new ring, you always gesture with that hand because you continuously show it off. If you wear a new earring, what will you do? You shake your head to show it off! If you speak about something again and again, there's something wrong with that thing. If you are clear about it, why should you speak about it again and again? This is how a spiritually immature person will misunderstand what is said.

Arjuna is approaching Kṛṣṇa out of fear and greed. When the Gītā started, Arjuna approached Kṛṣṇa out of fear and depression, and also out of greed, with the 'What is beneficial for me?' attitude. He asked Kṛṣṇa what would give maximum benefit, which is an expression of the attitude of greed.

Next he experiences fear. He is afraid of what will happen in the war. Fear and greed—that is the way he approaches Kṛṣṇa. So initially even Arjuna sees Kṛṣṇa as a demigod. At the initial level, Arjuna's approach is also as though it is towards a demigod. That is the reason why Kṛṣṇa now declares His glory, or His true form.

He says, 'All types of people come to Me. I fulfill them at different levels, to encourage their faith and to enrich them to grow. But only intelligent people understand, that even if I assume this body, I am the ultimate,

I am enlightened. Unintelligent people think by seeing my body, by seeing my form, that I am not the Divine. So please be very clear: I am THAT.' He makes a clear statement again and again, so that Arjuna understands.

We need to understand two important issues here. First, the formless energy of Kṛṣṇa defines His supremacy, His divinity, His Kṛṣṇa consciousness. Second, in whatever form the formless is expressed, it is divine. It is the awareness of that divinity in Him that makes Kṛṣṇa divine, the supreme Master. If that awareness happens in you, you will be in Kṛṣṇa consciousness, immersed in Him; and you will be divine too. The intelligence Kṛṣṇa talks about is the intelligent awareness of one's own divinity, not merely that of Kṛṣṇa. They are both one and the same. It is only when we are aware of our divinity that we appreciate the Divine.

I say to my disciples, 'Till you become enlightened, you will have no clear awareness of who I am. Till then you try to reach me only out of fear or greed, however slight it may be. It is only when you are enlightened and are in the same awareness as me, only when it is no longer necessary for you to fear me or desire through me, that you open up to me in sheer gratitude.'

That is the intelligence that Kṛṣṇa speaks about. When that intelligence exhibits itself, when that awareness surfaces, then and only then true recognition of the Divine happens. That true recognition happens when you recognize the Divine within you.

How To Recognize Divinity?

Kṛṣṇa asks: How can you recognize divinity when you are covered in ignorance? How can you recognize Me when you are not aware?

Out of the thousands who come to me, tens of thousands, the vast majority seeks favors of one kind or another. They come for the healing of the body and mind, or they come for repairing relationships, and for material benefits. Even those who do not look for material benefits may aspire to that intangible peace and bliss.

It is the rare person who comes without asking anything. It is not even seeking a benefit, tangible or intangible, that leads such people. It is an awareness of what they need to be and where they need to be. They are attracted like iron filings to a magnet. It is a call from their being which leads them to me.

In Mahābhārat, the Pāṇḍava princes could recognize the reality of Kṛṣṇa. No one needed to coach them for it. On the other hand, their cousins the Kaurava for the most part denied Kṛṣṇa. They rejected and ridiculed Him. Duryodhana, who was offered the first choice by Kṛṣṇa to choose either Him unarmed or His Yadava army, chose the utilitarian army! That was all Duryodhana could see. That was his level of awareness, steeped as he was in ignorance.

Arjuna jumped at Kṛṣṇa's offer. All Arjuna wanted was Kṛṣṇa, His presence, not His army, not His divine powers, nothing else. It is a choice that all of us need to make, whether we wish to be Duryodhana or Arjuna. It is not a difficult choice, as it will be determined by our being and our awareness. It will not be a choice at all. It will be a happening.

'No one knows Me, *māṁ tu veda na kaścana* (7.26)', says the Master. How true! 'Don't take me for granted,' says Kṛṣṇa. 'Do not put me in a frame for I shall not stay there,' He says.

Can you know Nature? Can you predict Nature? Each time you think you can, Nature does things differently. Then you say Nature is cruel, and ask why Nature is so cruel. Nature is Nature, not cruel, not kind, it just is.

So is Kṛṣṇa. His compassion is not pity as we imagine. The compassion of the Master is beyond our frames of time and space. So we cannot fathom what that means. When a tsunami kills a thousand people, we weep. When we pray and then win a lottery, we make a donation to the temple, since we are very pleased. Divine compassion is not related to these. It is the truth that is beyond time and space.

Those who stay around me have experienced that whatever I say is the truth and it happens. They don't question me, not because they are afraid. What control can I have over them? They are free to leave any time they want. In fact, I tell them the only thing that causes me to pause is when a disciple leaves me, because then I have lost the chance to enrich him. They know the way enlightened beings flow. They recognize that and they simply follow. They know that when I tell them something, it is not just a fact but the truth: truth that is not constrained by time and space.

Over two years ago when I went to the Himalayas with a group of disciples to the *cār-dhām* pilgrimage centers, I had asked them to tell the local religious authorities that I am a Mahāmanḍaleśvar. This title is given to the leader of a very large Hindu religious organization. It is more than a title; it confers spiritual leadership, like being canonized as a saint leader. Without questioning, they announced that a Mahāmanḍaleśvar had arrived. They accepted the statement and gave the due respect when I visited the temples.

Back in 2007, I was at the Ardh Kumbh Melā at Prayāg in Northern India, which normally happens every 4 years. However this time the sacred river Gangā reversed Her direction, and this happens once in every 144 years. So it was more significant and 90 million people gathered for a dip in the holy river. I went with a large group of disciples. In every Kumbh Melā, the first right to dip on the day of the royal bath is given to the *nāgā sādhus*, who are a special sect of naked monks, and among them the Mahānirvanī Akhāḍa, the oldest apex body of Hinduism.

During part of my wandering days before my self-realization, I had been with a group of these monks and they had accepted me as their own. Now at the Kumbh Melā they conferred upon me the title of Mahāmanḍaleśvar of their akhāḍā (religious sect), just a few days prior to the day of the royal bath, and also gave the first right to enter the Gangā on that special day.

Amongst the disciples was one who was present two years earlier during the Himalayan trip. He couldn't

> believe how the words he had heard from me were manifesting themselves now! I explained to him, it had nothing to do with what I had said. It is just the way Existence wants things to happen. What is spoken through enlightened beings is what Existence directs, and there can never be a contradiction in that.

The Truth is unpredictable because it is not bound by time and space as we know it. Truth cannot be known unless we are in truth ourselves. We cannot know Kṛṣṇa unless we are in Kṛṣṇa consciousness.

Kṛṣṇa consciousness is not just about going around chanting Hare Kṛṣṇa, Hare Kṛṣṇa. Such chanting, unless done with awareness from the space of completion, is of no real consequence; True Kṛṣṇa consciousness needs no words. In fact, it has no words because the experience is beyond expression. One who experiences it does not express it.

Fear and greed are what drive us, says Kṛṣṇa. That is our delusion that leads us away from Him. Attachment and aversion, *rāga* and *dveṣa*, form the duality, the polarity of human life. Even at the fundamental cellular level, biologists have shown that this tendency is exhibited. If you place a single cell in a petridish and place a drop of nutrient, it is attracted to it and moves towards it. If you place a drop of toxin in the same dish, the cell moves away from it. If on either side, you place drops of nutrient and toxin, the cell remains immobile.

At the cellular level, attraction aids in growth and aversion in surviv-al. A cell can either grow or protect itself. At the multi-cellular level with higher intelligence, human beings act in the same way as the primary cell. They get attached to what they think is good for them and flee from what they think is not good.

Unfortunately, what works well at the cellular level does not work so well at the human level simply because humans have greater intelligence. Cells obey Nature and are directed by Nature to recognize instinctively what is good and what is bad. They also automatically accept the conse-quence.

Humans are different. They bypass signals from their body, refuse to accept what Nature tries to tell them and indulge in or avoid activities or objects based on their logic. Logic overriding Nature always leads to suffering.

Shedding attachment and aversion is the first step to awareness. Attachment and aversion are born out of our past; based on experiences and memories that form the root thought patterns, what we call *saṁskāra* in Saṁskrit. Based on these *saṁskāras*, we try to define our future. The problem is that these *saṁskāras* operate at an unconscious level and drive us from unawareness to unawareness, from incompletion to incompletion. Therefore, we end up acting instinctively, but unlike our cellular brethren, without listening to Nature.

Human beings are given intelligence so that they can rise above instinct and logic and operate out of intuition. This intuition is born from awareness. It comes through meditation. With awareness, we understand that there is truly nothing that we can be attached to, since everything is impermanent. As I said earlier, every moment of our life is a psychodrama.

The same is true of aversion. It arises from insecurity and fears. What is there to be afraid of in life? Every occasion that we are afraid, we actually die inside us. If we shed our fear of death, we lose all our fears.

When we move into awareness, through meditation, we settle within the boundary of our body-mind and we enter the present moment. When we are in the present moment there is no duality of like and dislike, attachment and aversion. We respond to each event as it unfolds with clarity, with intuitive intelligence, with completion and we are always right.

No Sin, No Virtue

7.28 *Persons who have acted virtuously, whose sinful actions*
are completely eradicated and
who are freed from the duality of reality and unreality,
engage themselves in My worship with firm resolve.

7.29 *Persons, who are striving for liberation from the cycle of birth, old age and death, take refuge in Me. They are actually Brahman, Consciousness, because they entirely know everything about conscious activities that transcend these.*

7.30 *Those who know Me as the Supreme Lord, as the governing principle of the material manifestation [adhibhūtam],*
who know Me as the one essence of all the gods [adhidaivam],
and as the one sustaining all enriching sacrifices [adhiyajñam],
can, with mind engaged in Me, understand and know Me,
even at the time of death.

Kṛṣṇa talks here about *pāpa* and *puṇya*, sinful and meritorious acts. The concept of sin and merit itself is a delusion, one of duality. At the level of Kṛṣṇa consciousness there is no *pāpa* or *puṇya*, no sin and no act of merit. All are the same.

Your immediate question will be, 'Can I do anything I want? Can I kill, maim, annihilate, and be a Hitler?' When you reach *Kṛṣṇa* consciousness you will not be a Hitler. It is impossible. At the level where you are now, it is necessary to follow some regulations because you still operate in duality. You operate from attachment and aversion. You act out of fear and greed.

Unfortunately, instead of these statements being guidelines for self-awareness as they were intended to be, they have become tools in the hands of institutions, whether religious, political or societal, to control us.

Thousands of years ago, great masters like Patañjali outlined prescriptions for Self-realization. In his *Aṣṭāṅga yoga*, Patañjali established practices of *yama* and *niyama*. These are internal and external regulations for your guidance, not for others to manipulate you with. These are milestones to guide your way. Once you reach the destination, you don't need the milestones; you don't need any regulations.

Every year, I take a group of disciples to the Himalayan mountains on a pilgrimage, and the first stop is Rishikesha, where the river Gangā is about to enter the plains. Here I make them take the sannyās vows prescribed in *yama*. It is for their protection and guidance. It is not to instill notions of sin and virtue.

These five vows are *satya, ahiṁsā, asteya, aparigṛha* and *brahmacarya*. *Satya* is truth in thoughts, word and action; *ahiṁsā* is not harming anyone in thought, word and action; *asteya* is not coveting, not stealing what belongs to another; *aparigṛha* is living with minimal needs; *brahmacarya* is living without fantasies. They take these vows after a dip in the sacred river Ganga and participate in a *vṛaja homa*, a fire ritual of purification. For the next two weeks they wear the saffron cloth that I give them.

These vows are for self-discipline and they lead one to awareness and completion. No one needs to control us. Understand, as long as we need to look over our shoulder to see if someone is watching us, we are still living in hypocrisy.

Kṛṣṇa addresses mortal beings here, in the form of Arjuna. So He talks about doing virtuous acts and avoiding sinful acts. What follows is more important. He says to go beyond duality, the duality of sin and virtue. This is only possible when we become aware. It is only when we become aware that we can reach Him.

In the verses of the famous Bhaja Govindaṁ, Ādī Śankarācārya says hauntingly, *punarapi jananaṁ punarapi maraṇaṁ* ... Birth and death again and again; lying in a mother's womb again and again. This [ocean of] repeated birth and death is so difficult to cross. Please save me, O

Murāre Kṛṣṇa!'

The greatest philosopher that Hinduism has known, prays to the greatest Master that the Universe has known, 'Save me from this endless cycle of *saṁsāra*, the cycle of birth and death.' To know that one needs to be saved from this cycle needs great wisdom. To seek the feet of the Master who can lead you to that liberation needs great wisdom and awareness.

You can be born again and again and still think that you are being born for the first time, and that this is the only life that you have. This knowledge requires no wisdom. With this knowledge, you focus on this life and want to extract the maximum juice out of it. You run after everything possible, as if there is no tomorrow. You live in a fantasy world. You enact a psychodrama.

Please understand, this is not your only life. This body is not who you are. All this is temporary. What you chase is a dream. One day you will wake up and discover that this life is nothing but a dream. You are more than this body and mind; you are above this body-mind. What you are endures after death. When you understand this Cosmic Truth, you are liberated. At some time, you do not wish to be part of this psychodrama anymore. You are bored. You ask, 'What for?' just as Śankara plaintively asks Kṛṣṇa, 'Again and again, without end, I come and I go. Please save me from this useless journey; let me be with You.'

Buddha calls this cycle of birth and death a bondage. It is sorrow because it is not real. It is not the real *you* that dies and is reborn. The real *you* changes bodies as you change clothes.

It Is Never Too Late To Reach Me

Kṛṣṇa ends this chapter with the prescription for how to know and understand Him and reach Him.

Even at the time of death, He says, even if all your life you lived a dissolute life, if at the point of departure you realize your folly, the futility of the psychodrama that you have enacted, that is enough to redeem you. The mere recognition of that can save you. His compassion is unlimited.

He promises: Knowing me at the time of death, even at the time of death, will lead you to Me.

Please understand, this is not easy, not so easy as it seems. If you have been ruled by greed, greed for power, wealth, possessions and all such material objects throughout your life, nothing can change suddenly at the time of death. You will be full of the same fantasies that you were obsessed with throughout your life. Your last thoughts will be on those very same things.

We cannot change our nature at the last minute. If we want to die with the thought of the Divine uppermost in our mind, we must cultivate the habit of remembering Him now. We should start knowing and understanding Him today. Then and only then will we know and understand Him at the time of death.

Some may ask, 'What is the need to understand and know Kṛṣṇa, whether at the point of death or before? If I do the right things in the right manner, why should it make any difference whether or not I understand and know Kṛṣṇa?'

Please understand that Kṛṣṇa is not talking about the physical Kṛṣṇa, or even about the Cosmic Consciousness that He is. He speaks about our understanding, about knowing ourselves, *who we are.*

The ultimate Master resides within us, not anywhere else. The external Master, be He Kṛṣṇa or Nithyānanda, is a guide to make us understand, know and accept the Master within us. Yes, it may be possible in rare cases for that wisdom to dawn on us at the point of death, but it is not common. Someone who constantly seeks that truth will continuously search for that Master within, and has a better chance of making that connection earlier rather than later in life.

Kṛṣṇa in His deep compassion says, 'Even if that happens at the point of death, I shall redeem you.' He does not want us to miss that chance, even if we have not thought about Him all our lives. He does not rule out the possibility, even if we have not been seeking all our lives. He wants us to discover the master within. Even if we do that at the point of our last breath, it is okay with Him.

Many read *Gītā* and claim that they understand what Kṛṣṇa says. What they mean is that they understand that language into which the *Gītā* they are reading has been translated, that's all.

How can we even intellectually understand that Kṛṣṇa is supreme? Forget the demigods, how can we even accept that He is greater than us? We are so full of our identity and root patterns, that even if a thousand Kṛṣṇas were to descend in front of us, we would ask them for their identification cards! We will recognize Kṛṣṇa only if He comes in front of us in the mold and image of Him that we have stored in our minds!

Kṛṣṇa must come to us in our image of Him. Then we will accept Him as the Supreme and hang His picture on the wall. Everyday, Kṛṣṇa comes to us in many forms. He comes to us in the form of every person we meet. We decide whom we will accept and whom we will reject. We cannot accept Kṛṣṇa in parts and reject Him in parts. Either we accept Him totally or reject Him. We have to surrender to Him. We have to surrender our identity, our root patterns to Him. We have to surrender to Him that foolish image that we have in our minds of Him.

Meditation is a technique for surrendering one's identity. Completion is the process of surrendering one's root patterns. Throughout the *Gītā*, Kṛṣṇa suggests to Arjuna techniques, *sūtras* that leads to liberation. Combined with the cognition at the intellectual level, *śāstra*, with the higher devotional acceptance of His glories through verses, *stotra*, the *Gītā* leads you through the path of surrender into liberation.

Dropping one's identity requires a deep cognition, acceptance, intranalization, and completion which brings the merger of the Self, World and God. Simply put, we accept our Divinity and become one with the Divine. We become complete, whole! This is what Enlightenment is about.

At the Inner Awakening program, you are initiated into the science of completion with everything—with yourself, others and life and into the creation of the space to cause the reality for yourself and others. You are empowered with the four great powers of words, thinking, feeling and living to rewrite your future as you want.

You can choose to be initiated into a meditation process that enriches you to reach your innermost core. This meditation process, called the *ānanda gandha* meditation or 'fragrance of bliss' meditation, enriches you to constantly be in the space of completion and complete with any patterns as they surface. It anchors you to the present moment of completion where no root patterns or the branches of parasite patterns can form in you. In this state, you don't create further *karma* (unfulfilled actions) and your mindset of unfulfilled desires is extinguished. You are liberated. You are in the space of perpetual completion!

The simple truth is that the present moment of completion is Kṛṣṇa consciousness. When we reach this state of being in the present moment, we reach Him and we are complete. So it is not the mere intellectual understanding of what we read in the verses, but the authentic listening, *śravana*, authentic intranalying, *manana* and powerfully living and radiating, *nididhyāsana* of what Kṛṣṇa speaks into our listening, that can complete us.

So, let us pray to the Ultimate Kṛṣṇa to give us the intelligence and awareness to realize the truth about ourselves, to give us this experience of eternal bliss, *Nityānanda*

May you reach Kṛṣṇa consciousness and realize eternal bliss, *Nityānanda*!

*Thus ends the seventh chapter named **Jñānavijñāna Yogaḥ**, 'The Yoga Of Knowledge and Conscious Realization of Absolute', of the **Bhagavad Gītā Upaniṣad, Brahmavidyā Yogaśāstra**, the scripture of yoga dealing with the science of the Absolute in the form of **Śrī Kṛṣṇārjuna saṃvād**, dialogue between Śrī Kṛṣṇa and Arjuna.*

CHAPTER

8

Akṣarabrahma Yogaḥ

THE ART OF LEAVING

DEATH IS OUR ULTIMATE FEAR. ANYONE WHO CLAIMS NOT TO BE DISTURBED BY THE THOUGHT OF DEATH IS ONLY LYING. THE MOMENT WE UNDERSTAND DEATH, OUR LIFE BECOMES A CELEBRATION. KṚṢṆA REVEALS THE SECRET OF DEATH, UNDERSTANDING WHICH, WE CAN LIVE EVEN OUR DEATH.

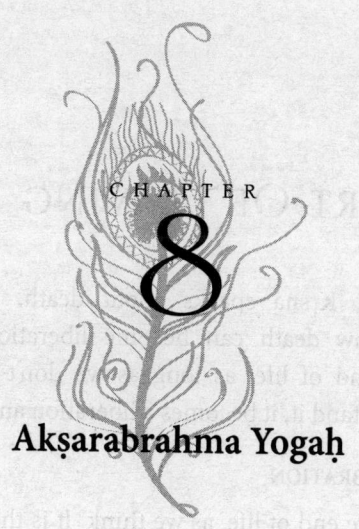

The Art Of Leaving

In this chapter, Kṛṣṇa speaks about death. He gives us deep insight into how death can become liberation and celebration. Death is the end of life, as long as we don't understand it! The moment we understand it, it becomes a liberation and celebration.

Death Is A Celebration

Death is not the end of life, as we think. It is the climax of life. End is different from climax. The moment we think that death is the end, we wonder about it, trying to figure out what happens next. We create more trouble for ourselves. We worry about death the moment we think it is the end. Our lives become dull because of such worries. The shadow of death happens even when we live.

A man who is unable to understand death is like the living dead. A person who understands death will live even his death. A person who does not understand death dies even when he is alive. A person who understands death lives even when he dies. Death or life are not incidental, they depend on our intelligence. When we have clear intelligence, we live our death. When we don't know, when we do not have the clarity about death, we die even when we live.

The fear of death haunts everyone from birth. All religions sprang up from this one fear, this one question: Why do we die? What happens after we die? How can we escape death?

Each religion answers this question in its own way. Most religions answer in such a way that they can control us through the fear of death and the greed of escaping death. They talk about sins and merits and threaten us with hell and entice us with the promise of heaven. None of these really exists. There is no heaven or hell that any religion can threaten or entice us with. These are not physical locations or even metaphysical locations; they are merely states of our mind.

Death is not an end; it is a passage. It is a passage in a journey that continues. It is not a one-time event, as some religions seem to believe. We do not live and die once; we live again and again. As Kṛṣṇa says, the undying spirit casts off bodies as one casts off garments and puts on new ones. The spirit within is immortal. The spirit within us is part of the Cosmic energy and lives on, whereas the bodies that it assumes perish.

Enlightened Masters of the Vedic tradition experienced the state beyond life and death and have provided us with guidelines about how to achieve the same state. However, they expressed this to a select audience of disciples in a language coded for the understanding of those mature enough to work with that knowledge.

Here Kṛṣṇa, the greatest of all enlightened Masters, out of His infinite compassion, provides this knowledge in a form that anyone can understand. All one requires to imbibe this knowledge, is an open mind and the willingness to work sincerely with integrity, authenticity and with dedication.

When we understand the art of living, the process of leaving becomes a celebration. When we understand that this life and the departure from this life is a single journey in a continuous cycle of birth and death, there is no urgency in living this life and there is no fear in leaving this life also. When we understand that what we do in this life and how we do it determines how we are reborn, we will have a far greater understanding of how to lead this life.

Arjuna starts here with questions.

Knowing Him At the Time Of Death

8.1 *Arjuna says:*
O my Lord, O Supreme Person, what is Brahman?
What is the Self? What are result-based actions?
What is this material manifestation? And what are the demigods?
Please explain all this to me.

8.2 *How does this Lord of sacrifice live in the body,*
and in which part does He live, O Madhusūdana?
How can those engaged in devotional service know You
at the time of their death?

These are two beautiful questions! Of course, when I translate them into English, much of the taste is lost! No English words can convey the meaning of so many beautiful words expressed by Arjuna. A single word has many meanings in Saṃskṛit. The moment I translate, I give only one dimension, a single dimension of the verse.

Understand, the Saṃskṛit language is that it is not only linguistic, but also has importance at the phonetic level. Just the vibration of the words can transform our whole inner space. The sound changes the energy of the place and the inner space of those who hear it or are chanting it.

We should understand the concepts called *padā* and *padārtha*. For example, when I say the word 'cow,' immediately a figure appears in our mind—an animal with four legs, a tail, head and two horns. The word is called *padā*, the figure is *padārtha*. What happens in our mind when we hear the word is *padārtha*. In all languages the distance or gap between *padā* and *padārtha* is significant.

In Saṃskṛit the connection is immediate; the result is instantaneous. That is why I tell people to listen to Saṃskṛit devotional verses for at least 10 minutes a day. It does not matter whether you understand it or not. Just listen to any Saṃskṛit verse—whether it is *Viṣṇu Sahasṛanāma, Bhagavad Gītā, Śiva Sahasṛanāma* or something else. Even if you don't understand the meaning of the verses, the very energy of the vibrations will purify your body.

There is something called *śabda tattva*, the principle of sound. When air travels from our navel area to the throat, the *śabda tattva* changes the air into words. If this element is not there, only air comes out; no words come out. In other languages the more we use *śabda tattva*, the more tired we become. However in Saṃskṛit, the *śabda tattva* strengthens us. The more we chant, the more energetic we become! It is like the generator automatically re-charging the battery and the battery running the generator. It is completely interconnected.

The Saṃskṛit language strengthens the *śabda tattva* that converts air into sound or words. This is why it does not matter whether or not we understand it. Listening to the sound, the very vibration, has an effect on our being. Modern day research proves that the vibrations of the verses can straightaway remove impurities. This is why masters ask us to offer different types of worship as a means to chant Saṃskṛit verses. We simply heal ourselves.

Here, Arjuna asks beautifully, 'O Lord! What is Brahman? What is Self? What are result-based actions? What is this material manifestation? What are demi-gods? O Madhusūdana! How do You live in the body, and how can those engaged in devotion, those who are practicing the eternal consciousness, know You at the time of death?'

arjuna uvāca
kiṁ tad brahma kim adhyātmaṁ kiṁ karma puruṣottama |
adhibhūtaṁ ca kiṁ proktam adhidaivaṁ kim ucyate || 8.1

I had seriously wondered how Arjuna, a great *kṣatriya* (warrior) who ruled a kingdom, could ask the same questions again and again in different ways! I read a version of Mahābhārat which says that Arjuna is also an embodiment of Kṛṣṇa: the Incarnation of *nara* and *Nārāyaṇa.*

These are two different energies of Lord Viṣṇu; one manifested as Arjuna and the other as Kṛṣṇa. The whole drama happened so that the Gītā took shape to enrich humanity! Otherwise, even the disciple with the least consciousness would not have asked so many questions, again and again.

Understand one thing, when we have so many questions, we are not ready to wait for answers. We are simply expressing our confusion. It is almost a catharsis. Here Arjuna asks so many questions.

However, the main question to Kṛṣṇa is: *How does a person who is engaged in practicing Your teachings know You at the time of death?* Here starts the whole teaching of Kṛṣṇa. He reveals the secrets of death.

One thing I want to tell you: The West has spent all its energy to understand life. The East has spent all its energy to understand death. Nobody has gone so deeply into, or achieved such deep experiences of death, as our *ṛṣis*, sages have. These masters have done a great service by bringing the knowledge of death to the people who are living.

People ask me, '*Swamiji*, why should I know about death? Knowing about life is enough; after all I am still young.' The word 'death' creates fear in people. When it comes to death, they are not ready to listen. They think, 'Why should we know about death? If we know about life, it is enough.'

Please be very clear, our understanding about death impacts our understanding about life. Life and death are two sides of the same coin. Understand one thing: In the East, all religions, Hinduism, Buddhism, Jainism, talk about many births or reincarnation. Most Western religions talk about a single birth.

This concept of reincarnation has influenced Indian society so deeply that nobody bothers about time! In India, people do not bother about time. They are so relaxed. Till 10 o'clock in the morning, people sit in teashops! If we ask for anything, they say, 'Not today, tomorrow; if not tomorrow, next birth!' They have eternity in front of them because somewhere they know they will come again. They are in no hurry and therefore do not run behind anything. Indian people are utterly and completely relaxed.

In the West, whatever they desire to achieve, they must finish achieving within 75 to 80 years. They do not have time. They either live now or never because there is only birth according to them. That is the reason why people run and run!

Please be very clear: Our understanding about death influences our whole social structure. Our whole thinking system, our whole mentality can be transformed with the right understanding about death. I gave a single example about how the idea of reincarnation influences Eastern society and how the idea of one birth influences Western society. Thousands of such examples can be given.

The idea and understanding of death is much more important than the understanding of life. Whether we understand life or not, it remains the same. But the moment we understand death, the whole quality of life changes and our consciousness changes.

The moment we realize the truth of death, if we experience even an intellectual understanding of death, it is enough to transform our whole way of thinking. That is why the moment we think of *Yama*, god of death, our whole life has *yama*, or discipline. The Saṃskṛit word '*yama*' means both 'death' and 'discipline'. For your convenience, I pronounce it a little differently; yet the spelling is the same.

Understanding of Death, Instills Discipline

The first technique of sage Patañjali in his work—*Yoga Sūtra*, is *yama*. Death is also *yama*. If we understand death, our whole life will be automatically disciplined. A strange but authentic discipline will happen in our life.

Why do I say 'strange but authentic?' It is because discipline as we know it is hypocrisy. But the discipline that is *yama* is a new kind of discipline, which is strange yet totally authentic. Why do I say 'strange'?

A person well read in Bhāgavatam, the Hindu epic that describes the Incarnations of Śrī Viṣṇu, asked me, '*Swamiji*, Kṛṣṇa is enlightened and He was a *brahmacāri*, celibate. How is that possible?'

We need to understand that *brahmacarya* does not mean celibacy. I have not said that Kṛṣṇa is celibate. I said Kṛṣṇa is in the consciousness of Brahman. Here we translate the word '*brahmacarya*' to mean celibate. The moment we translate it, the meaning is lost. Kṛṣṇa's inner space was totally pure, untouched.

Let me tell you a small history, Purāṇa:

> Once Vyāsa, the ancient sage of India attended a function. After having a feast at the function, on his way back, he came to a river, which he had to cross in order to reach his ashram, his monastery. He stood before the river and said, 'If I am sincere in my *ekādasi* fasting, let this river give way so that I may cross over.' Ekādasi refers to the eleventh day of the moon's cycle when normally people fast.
>
> The moment Vyāsa uttered those words, the river gave way. Vyāsa crossed it followed by his devotees and they reached the ashram.
>
> The devotees were astonished and asked, 'What is this? You enjoyed a feast just a few hours back. Yet, when you asked the river to give way on the condition that you have been sincere in your *ekādasi* fast, the river gave way! How can this be?'
>
> Vyāsa replied, 'When you eat with the consciousness that you are not the body, you never feel that you are touched by food. You never feel that you are eating, digesting and living. The body ate; I do not know anything about it.'

Of course, it is difficult to understand this concept. We can easily cheat ourselves with this idea. The problem with all great truths is, there is the danger of our misusing and abusing them. Take atomic energy; we can use it for good purposes, to serve the whole of humanity. Or we can destroy, we can abuse humanity with that same energy.

People ask me, 'How can I find out whether I am living in the out-of-body-consciousness or not; how can I live like Vyāsa?' Listen, when we reach the state of Vyāsa, we will not have this question. Vyāsa says he is fasting after having eaten a feast because he does not feel connected to his body. He does not feel that his body is related to him. He is untouched. His inner space is so pure and filled with bliss, nothing touches him.

Going back to the question, 'How can you say that Kṛṣṇa is a *brahmacāri*?' Please understand that His inner space was so pure that He was never touched by body consciousness. He never experienced that He had a body and He never came down to body consciousness.

Let me tell you one more thing: It is not easy to live with so many women as Kṛṣṇa did, and yet survive! If we start living, then we will understand. When I say women, I mean men also. When a single man or woman enters our life, we understand how difficult it is to adjust and live. When the other person enters our life, by their very quality hell seems to be created. Here we see somebody living with many persons, and yet remaining blissful. This shows that Kṛṣṇa's inner space was never touched. His inner space was pure and radiating bliss.

The person whose inner space is filled with bliss will never be touched by any impurity. Of course, it is a difficult concept to understand. However, the moment we understand the depth of it, we will understand this concept.

A small story:

> A Sannyāsi (monk) goes to the Indian king Janaka who is an Enlightened king and one who enjoyed both the material world and spiritual enlightenment. The Sannyāsi questions him, 'How can you say you are enlightened when you enjoy the benefits of worldly life?'
>
> Sannyāsis are jealous of people who enjoy life! If you are complete with the world and experience bliss within you and consciously leave the world to enter monastic life, you will never feel jealous. Then you are a real Sannyāsi. If you have escaped from the outer world thinking that you will find something worthwhile in the inner world, and there

too the experience has not been solid, you start wondering what to do. You have neither the inner space of bliss nor the outer possessions.

Such people console themselves by abusing and disrespecting householders! They say to them, 'You people are not doing things properly. You are too attached to everything...'

So this Sannyāsi asked Janaka, 'How can you say you are enlightened and have both material and spiritual enjoyments?'

Janaka said, 'Please stay in my palace for a few days. I will talk to you after that. Right now I am busy, a party is going on, so I cannot talk about philosophical things now!'

Accordingly, arrangements were made for the Sannyāsi's food and stay. However, above his bed a sharp knife hung, suspended on a thin thread.

The Sannyāsi asked, 'Why do you hang this knife exactly over my head?' The palace workers said, 'We do not know, but these are our king's orders. You must sleep here.'

Throughout the night the Sannyāsi sat up, awake, thinking when the knife might fall on him.

The next morning Janaka asked, 'O Swami! How are you today? Did you sleep well?'

The Sannyāsi said, 'You know what you have done! Why do you then ask? How can I sleep when a knife hangs over my head?'

Janaka laughs and says, 'When death is in front of you, you cannot do anything; your whole life changes. However, although I know death is in front of me, I am unaffected. I know that the knife hangs over me, yet my whole consciousness lives in an unaffected way in this palace.

> That is the difference. Just because of one knife you are unable to enjoy the beautiful bed and all these luxuries. Yet even though all these things are there externally, my inner Self is not touched. It is pure because I know clearly that at any moment death can happen; death is hanging in front of me. Because I live with this moment-to-moment awareness of death, I enjoy the material world fully without getting caught in it.'

That is why I said, 'Yama can make a strange, yet authentic *yama* in your life. Death can instill a strange but authentic discipline in your life.'

Understand death, intellectually. Your whole thinking will change. Your whole way of living, your very being will be transformed. You need not leave this place as the same person. Your core can be touched.

Kṛṣṇa starts with the secrets. He explains the secrets of death.

Your Last Memory Follows You In Next Birth

8.3 *Bhagavān says:*
The indestructible, transcendental living entity is called Brahman and His eternal nature is called the Self.
Actions pertaining to the development of the material bodies is called karma, or result based activities.

8.4 *Physical nature is known to be endlessly changing.*
The Universe is the cosmic form of the Supreme Lord, and I am that Lord represented as the Super Soul, dwelling in the heart of every being that dwells in a body.

8.5 *Whoever, at the time of death, quits his body remembering Me alone, attains My nature immediately.*
Of this there is no doubt.

8.6 *Whatever state of being one remembers when he quits his body, It is that state one will attain without fail.*

Before going into what happens at the time of death, let us understand how we assume the body, how we live through it and how we leave it. Please understand that we create our whole body out of our fear, greed, guilt and our engraved memories, called the root thought patterns (*saṁskāras*). Whatever *saṁskāras* we have, we create the body to work them out, experience them and enjoy them. Once we have created the body and live our life, we do not live out only the root thought patterns (*saṁskāras*) that created this body, we also acquire more *saṁskāras*, more patterns.

For example, we take $10,000 and go downtown to buy things that we need. On the way, we meet a friend. He says, 'Let us go to Disneyland' and we go and blow up all the money. Finally, when we go downtown to buy what we need, we are broke. Now, with the credit card we buy what we want and live our life just to pay credit card bills, feeling we do not have sufficient things. We have fulfilled our friend's desires not ours, through our body, our time, money and energy. But we never got what we desired, what we needed.

In the same way, when we came down to planet Earth, we came with enough energy to work out and complete our root thought patterns, *saṁskāras*. Listen! God never sends us empty handed. He sends us with everything. He sends us with our inner powers, but we have forgotten that we even have these great powers. Whatever *saṁskāras* or desires we bring, we bring enough energy to live them out and enough power of enjoy them also.

Listen: you can fulfill your desires that you bring and live an enriching life of completion! You actually have the power to simply manifest the reality of your choice! You have the potential for self-transformation that will enrich every aspect of your life, bringing you everything from health to wealth to meaningful relationships to lasting happiness.

Inside each of you is an enormous potential energy known as *Kuṇḍalinī*. *Kuṇḍalinī* is nothing but your own latent inner energy which you have never used, and which you may not even know about! *Kuṇḍalinī* expresses through you in four different streams, known as the four inner powers. All these inner powers are the different expressions of *Kuṇḍalinī* energy in your life. The key to health, success and lasting happiness lies in unlocking the four inner powers that are continuously available to you.

Though you use these powers everyday in your life, you don't use them consciously, with a clear intention. Please understand, all these powers are great energies, just like electricity or wind-power. If you handle them properly, they can shower you with everything you want. But if you don't handle them properly, they will continue to impact your life in negative ways.

The key is to create the right space inside you to express your greatest and highest possibility. When you create the right space inside you, all the events of your choice will simply flow into your life without any effort! Everything you do will be successful. When you learn to use these powers in the right way, you will immediately transform not only your own life, but the lives of all those living around you.

To be able to unlock these great powers inside you, you must first understand a little more about yourself—the way you *live* and the way you *leave*! As I told in earlier chapters, your four inner powers are: the power of words or *vāk śakti;* the power of thoughts or *mano śakti*; the power of feeling or *prema śakti;* and the power of living or *ātma śakti.*

Please listen! *Karma* refers to the unfulfilled desires that we create over many births, which pull us back again to take birth and fulfill them. We have three types of *karma—sañcita, prārabdha* and *āgāmya.*

Sañcita karma is our complete bank of unfulfilled *karmas* like our safety deposit or the files archived in our office vault. *Prārabdha karma* are those *karmas* that we have brought and come in this life, like files in filing cabinets which we access and work on regularly. *Āgāmya karma* are like the new files on our table that we keep creating—new *karma* that we create in every life.

We must exhaust all three types of *karmas* to experience enlightenment. *Sañcita karma* is all that we have accumulated over many births. *Prārabdha karma* is *karma* that we brought with us to work out in this life. *Āgāmya karma* is what we acquire newly in this birth.

Prārabdha karma is like our opening bank balance in this life. We have enough energy to exhaust this *prārabdha karma*. Then why do we feel that this life is not sufficient? Why do we feel unfulfilled?

The problem is that after coming down, we forget what we came down for, the *saṁskāras* and desires that we brought to live out and complete. Instead we accumulate more and more desires from family, friends and society. We accumulate desires from others in society and work out their desires in our life.

For example, if our neighbor wears a new *sari*... I mean in India... in America, we do not even know who our neighbor is! A devotee in Oklahoma told me that his neighbor passed away and he came to know of it only six months later! The Indian lifestyle is different. Anyway, when our neighbor gets a new *sari,* we think, 'I should also get one.' We try to work out her desire. Naturally we run short of money, energy, and time; we run short of everything.

When we live out others' desires in our life, we feel deeply discontented, deeply incomplete because the energy that we brought with us will become insufficient. If we go downtown with a plan and a particular amount of money and suddenly our plan changes, naturally we run short. After coming down to planet Earth, we forget what root patterns or *saṁskāras* we brought and we collect more and more desires from society.

So much social conditioning happens through advertisements. All advertisements make us poor. The advertisers become rich, no doubt, but we become poor. Advertisement agencies know that whatever touches the *mūlādhāra* is automatically recorded in our system. That is why whether it is soap or shampoo or clothes or cars, it is promoted with the undertones of sex appeal. We forget one thing: when we pay $2, we get only the soap and not the model who is using the soap in the advertisement! But both the soap and the model are recorded together in our system.

Whatever root patterns get recorded in the *mūlādhāra* energy center are so deep that we unconsciously act in accordance with them. As long as we fulfill our own desires, it is fine. However, when we live out others' desires, the problem starts. In the next verse, Kṛṣṇa goes slightly deeper into this.

Kṛṣṇa says here, 'O best of embodied beings! The physical nature that is constantly changing is called *adhibhūta* or the universal form of the Lord, which includes all the demi-gods. For example, the nature of the Sun and Moon is *adhidaiva*. As the supreme Lord represented as the

Super Soul in the heart of every embodied being, I am called *adhiyajña.*'

adhibhūtaṁ kṣaro bhāvaḥ puruṣaś cādhidaivatam |
adhiyajño 'ham evātra dehe deha-bhṛtāṁ vara || 8.4

We have seen how we are ruled by our desires at every step. Please understand: This gives us a background against which to understand the secret of death. When we understand why we take birth, it is easier to understand what happens when we leave the body. We will see the secrets of death in the next verse. Here Kṛṣṇa throws light on the physical matter in front of us. If we understand this deeply, our desire to 'possess' automatically drops.

Let us take this chair you are sitting on. To our knowledge, there is some solid object placed at this location. However, if we go one level deeper, we see that this solid plastic can be broken down into many particles that make up this plastic. Now if we go one step further, we see that there are atoms and molecules. We can keep dividing into smaller and smaller particles and there is no end to it. And more than ninety percent of the volume within each particle is empty space.

Modern science has proven that matter and energy are mutually convertible. You see, this solid object that our eye sees is not solid. It is pure energy. This physical matter is energy and it constantly changes because of the fluid nature of energy. That is what Kṛṣṇa says: *adhibhūtaḥ kṣaro bhāvaḥ.*

This physical or material nature constantly changes. Understand, because of the fluid nature of energy, it constantly moves; it changes. Change is the only certain thing. That is why everything around is temporary. We think something is permanent and hence we try to possess it.

Everything that we call matter is energy and it constantly changes. This truth was given by inner scientists or *ṛṣis* thousands of years ago. Kṛṣṇa clearly says it. And we find this truth declared not just in *Gītā.* We find similar statements in the *Upaniṣads* also. All physical matter is energy and it keeps changing.

In the last verse, we talked about our desires. Why do we run behind materialistic desires? Why do we constantly operate from the *mūlādhāra cakra*? It is because we do not have a good understanding about the physical world, about the matter. If we understand this verse, we will understand the futility of running after the fulfillment of material desires.

When we look at something, we think of it as only matter, as a physical object. We think we can possess it. We think we can keep it with us. We take ownership of that physical object. This is where the problem lies. Our ego sees the material world as only matter, and it asks for more and more of it to keep under its control.

We fail to understand one important thing—it is all energy and energy cannot be kept in one place. Listen, energy cannot be kept in one place. It is Universal. The physical object that we see is a manifestation of the Universal energy. Please understand this clearly. There are energy waves and these waves manifest as physical matter. When we understand this, we can understand the futility of holding onto something or running after something.

One more thing, this root pattern of possessing is not only with inanimate objects, but with people as well. We are continuously looking for a partner, friend, wife, husband or child to possess. When we have someone, we hold onto that person. If that person leaves, we feel terrible. When a close family member passes away, we feel depressed. Why?

It is because we hold onto them as if they are physical matter like any other possession, like jewelry, laptop, car and house. If our car meets with an accident, we feel sad. We feel that we have lost something. In exactly the same way, when someone passes away, we feel that part of us is lost. We feel depressed.

I do not say that we should be insensitive to relationships. I mean we should stop being possessive. Understand that everything and everyone is created out of the same underlying energy.

Kṛṣṇa says clearly in this verse: Everything, whether living or non-living, is an embodiment of the Supreme Soul—*adhiyajño 'ham evātra dehe deha-bhṛtāṁ vara* (8.4). The same Supreme Soul lives in everything. When we understand this, we see the truth that we are a part of everything around us and we complete with everything. There is no difference between *you* and *me*. There is no difference between this *chair* and *me* or this *tree* and *me*. We see ourselves in everything.

When we understand this great truth, a new dimension of ourselves is revealed to us. When we see ourselves in everything around us, our compassion towards everything grows a thousandfold. By being compassionate to others, we are being compassionate to ourselves because everything is *one*.

Please listen! This is what I mean when I say, 'Enriching others enriches you.' Enrich yourself and enrich everyone. Then, experientially you understand that you are one with others, others are one with you. Please understand this great truth of enriching, the space of Enlightenment, the power of living. This changes the way we look at life and everything around us. This completely changes the way we perceive our desires, our fantasies. Kṛṣṇa answers all the questions with a single *sūtra,* a single technique.

The Secret of Death

Now we enter the main subject. Here, Kṛṣṇa reveals the secrets of death.

He says, 'Whoever dies remembering Me alone at the time of death will attain Me at once.' What does He mean when He says, 'remembering Me alone?' He says, 'Whoever, at the end of his life, quits his body remembering Me alone, at once attains My nature. Of this there is no doubt.'

anta-kāle ca mām eva smaran muktvā kalevaram |
yah prayāti sa mad-bhāvaṁ yāti nāsty atra saṁśayaḥ || 8.5

Why should He say the words *nāsty atra saṁśayaḥ* ? Why should He say, 'there is no doubt?' He emphasizes, 'this is the truth.' He takes an oath.

We have a meditation program lasing two days on this *sūtra,* called *Nithya Kriya Yoga* Program (LBP level 2). The whole program is based on this single verse. Before starting the session on death, I always take the oath, '*I hereby state that whatever I say is the truth*,' because there are some truths that cannot be logically expressed. They cannot be explained using logic that you understand. You need a little patience to listen.

The big problem with our mind is that we question, refute or straight-away don't want to listen to anything not presented in a logical form. Otherwise, we hear it as one more story. We think, 'Anyhow, I have come all the way, let me sit and hear what he has to say.' We allow the speaker to speak; however, we do not listen.

That is why, before I talk about death, I say, 'Hereby I promise that whatever I am going to say is pure truth. If you are interested, take it, digest it and transform your life. If you are not, it is ok; it is up to you; it is your choice.'

Kṛṣṇa says: *nāsty atra saṃśayaḥ*, because He is going to speak something that is beyond logic. When we want to understand the outer world, we need logic. When we want to know about the inner world, we need a Master who takes us beyond logic. Logic gives us the outer world; it cannot give us the inner world.

Here Kṛṣṇa says: *nāsty atra saṃśayaḥ*: Have no doubt, what I am speaking is the truth. Please wait. Let Me finish the calculation, then you will understand. For now assume that X equals 2.' At the end of the calculation, you agree that X should be substituted with 2, but at the start, you need to believe the Master's word and patiently wait until he works it out and shows you.

Until you realize it, till it becomes an experience for you, for a few minutes you need to accept the Master's word as it is. When you finish the calculation, naturally it becomes your understanding. It starts as *my* understanding. In the end, it becomes *your* understanding. When it becomes your understanding, you naturally see the truth behind the words.

So Kṛṣṇa says:

'Whoever, at the end of his life, quits his body remembering Me alone, at once attains My nature. Of this there is no doubt.' Why? Why does He say, 'remembering Me, *mām eva smaran*?' and that too 'alone?'

In Mahābhārat there are at least 100,000 stories. One story goes like this:

> There was a king who lived for a hundred years. Then Yama, the god of death comes and tells him, 'Your life is over, O King, come now, it is time, let us go.'
>
> The king says, 'What is this? You gave me such a beautiful kingdom, such a beautiful life, such wonderful wives, kids; you have given me everything. 100 years is too short to enjoy this life. Please bless me with 100 more years.'
>
> Yama explains that no extension is possible. The king continues to plead, 'No, please bless me with another 100 years.'
>
> Yama says, 'Alright, if one of your sons gives his life, I will extend yours as an exchange offer.' Somehow one son agrees to give his life for his father and the king gets 100 more years.
>
> After 100 years when Yama appears again, the king does not realize that his time is up and says, 'What is this? I asked for 100 years and you have come so soon.' Yama tells him that 100 years are over.
>
> The king pleads again, 'Please help me somehow; I did not realize that 100 years are gone. Please give one more extension.' Yama tells him it is too much and that a second extension is not possible. However the king begs Yama

to let him live a few more years. Finally he gets one more extension.

The next time when Yama comes, again the king is in the same mood. Now Yama gives a beautiful teaching. He says, 'By pouring oil on it, you can never put out the fire. Now it is time, you must come.' The king understands and follows Yama.

In the same way, by chasing our desires, we can never feel fulfilled. Only more desires will come up. By fulfilling our desires, we can never hope to have contentment. When we acquire more and more desires from the outer world, we naturally feel that life is not sufficient, that we had not been given time or resources to fulfill these desires.

Understand that if we have lived 70 years, at the end of our life, when we leave our body, the whole scene, the whole 70 years appear before us as a flash, as a fast-forward movement. The whole thing appears in our consciousness again so that we can make the decision about our next birth. Now, we have *karma* that we brought with us but have not enjoyed or experienced, as well as *karma* that we accumulated from society in this birth, but have not exhausted. Both are there.

I want to give you one more understanding: *karma* or *saṁskāra* means any desire that is not completely experienced by you. By nature you are a fulfilled complete being. But whenever you do not fulfill any action completely, with totality, you create a hangover. You create a recorded memory of that action, a *saṁskāra*. A *saṁskāra* is not merely a dead memory stored in your unconscious mind; it has the power to make you repeat that action again and again till the desire is fulfilled.

Please be very clear, *saṁskāra* is living energy because it has the power to make you repeat the same action again and again as a pattern. It can make you travel the same path over and over again. That is why *saṁskāras* are called engraved memories, the root thought patterns. The more you travel on a path, the more it will be strengthened. But if you have completed with that pattern by living a single *saṁskāra* totally, completely, that *saṁskāra* leaves you! It drops from your being; you are liberated from it. Completion directly liberates you from *karma*. Completion directly leads you to experience the Truth. Whatever you have not lived completely remains as a *saṁskāra* in you, as a *karma* in you.

Here you have brought some *karma* that you have not yet experienced and completed, as well as newly accumulated *karma*. The whole thing appears in front of you at the time of leaving the body, so that you can decide your next birth.

Please listen! Every birth is your declaration of completion and you start the whole thing anew. You decide, 'Come on! I declare completion. I will now work from the space of completion!' But during your birth, when you fail in your declaration and fall from the space of completion, you bring some of your past incompletions back. That is what is *prārabdha karma*.

***Karma* which you bring back from the past incompletions is *prārabdha*. If you don't fall at all and continue to be in the space of completion, you don't become incomplete at all, then, I can tell you, you are an Incarnation!**

If you need to make an important decision, don't you call for all the files, all the old files from the archives before you make the decision? Now you are going to decide a few important things: where to take birth, what type of parents and family to choose, what type of family to choose, whether to choose a male body or female body.

All these decisions *you* are going to make. Understand, all these decisions are taken by your consciousness, not by anybody else. However, your consciousness is influenced by incomplete, inadequate data, *karma* collected when you lived on planet Earth.

Understand one important thing! Even sense enjoyments look like enjoyment because from a young age you are taught that it is enjoyment. An important research report I read spoke about the lifestyle of a group of African tribal people. It said that they do not know anything called joy or sense pleasures. It is not that they do not eat. They eat good food: not food, good human beings! Yet, because they have not been taught the idea of pleasure, they do not run after it.

Let me share another example of how the patterns created out of social conditioning work. During my days of wandering, I lived near Omkareshwar in Madhya Pradesh with a small group of tribal people for months. I was really surprised about the way they lived. Nobody, not a single person there was depressed. What I say is the truth, the honest truth. Human beings *can* live on planet Earth without getting depressed!

I was surprised that not a single person in that village was depressed, and nobody ran behind sense pleasures. I thought to myself, 'How come these people lived without running behind sense pleasures?' It was because they had not been taught that there is something called sense pleasure. The basic corruption had not happened.

When I was with these tribal people in Madhya Pradesh, I lived in a small temple in the center of the village. While wandering about one day I came upon a small hut. A pregnant lady entered it. Half an hour later, she came out with a newborn baby! There was no pain, no attendant, no doctor, no medicine, no screaming. Within half an hour she walked out with a baby.

I was shocked! Of course, I could not ask her anything because I did not know their language. After one month, another pregnant lady did the same thing. Within half an hour she came out with a baby. Now it was too much!

I asked the local priest who came to the temple, 'How does this happen? Don't they have pain?' He asked in surprise, 'Pain? Why pain?' I was surprised! They do not have pain at the time of delivery. The idea that women should have pain during delivery does not exist in their society. Not only that, nobody suffers from menopause problems or gynecological disorders.

I enquired about their lifestyle. Then I understood that they respect women a lot in their culture. Women are never disrespected. They are never told that they become impure during their monthly periods. Women are never taught that they are lower than men. The moment a girl comes of age, she is honored and told, 'Now you are qualified to become a mother.' She is respected. People fall at her feet and she touches and heals them. They believe that if a woman touches and blesses them during her menstrual period, they will be healed. Because the conditioning is totally different, nobody suffers any pain there.

In the so-called civilized society today, women are disrespected. Again and again, they are taught, 'This is impurity; you are not pure now; don't stand here, don't sit there.' Especially in India, it is real torture. Because of the wrong conditioning, women suffer pain. If they are not conditioned in this way, they will never feel pain.

Social conditioning divides everything into pleasure and pain. Even this decision—'What kind of life will I choose in my next birth? What kind of body will I take?'– is based upon your social conditioning. You decide to achieve whatever you think is the highest thing in life. You automatically run behind whatever is kept as an ideal in front of your eyes. Whatever you consider the highest ideal of your whole life, only that comes to your mind when you leave the body.

What you remember at Death, So you attain

Kṛṣṇa says, 'Whatever state of being one remembers when he quits his body, O Kaunteya, that state he will attain without fail.'

yaṁ yaṁ vāpi smaran bhāvaṁ tyajaty ante kalevaram |
taṁ tam evaiti kaunteya sadā tad-bhāva bhāvitaḥ || 8.6

What exactly happens at the time of leaving the body? We should understand that. When a person leaves the body, he goes through seven layers of his being. The first and the outermost layer is the physical layer. When a person leaves the body, it creates tremendous pain in his whole system, what the *Upaniṣads* liken to 'thousands of scorpions stinging at a time.'

Please don't think I am frightening you. I must state a few truths and facts as they are. Even though it may hurt, it is better to tell them now. At least we will be better prepared for the journey that we are going to take or that will be forced upon us. Whether we will take it or it will be forced upon us we don't know, but we must make this journey. Let us at least understand what happens then.

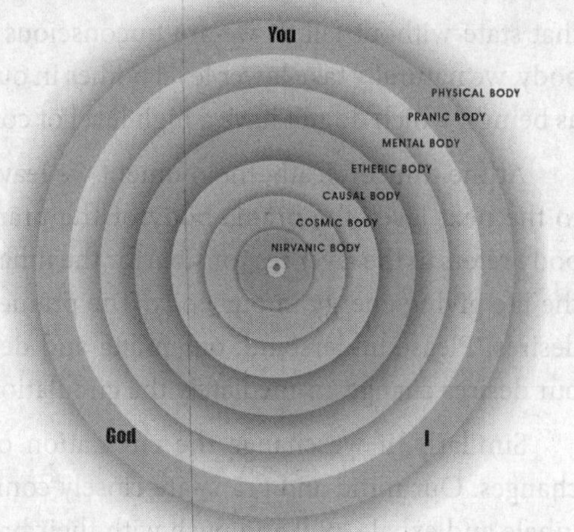

There will be tremendous pain at first. We may ask, 'Why pain?' It is because our being wants to stay in the body, but the body cannot host the being anymore. There is no need for our being to leave unless the body is completely tired or exhausted. If death starts happening, this means the body is completely exhausted, or damaged. In natural death, the body is exhausted, so we leave the body. In an accident, the body is damaged.

Understand: You know what pain we experience if we cut our finger half an inch wide while cutting vegetables. What would the pain be like if we extend the same thing to our six-foot body? It will be simply torn, is it not? Naturally there will be tremendous pain. But one thing: there is an automatic mechanism in our being, an automatic painkiller mechanism. What happens is, the moment the pain becomes unbearable, we fall into coma. If we fall into coma, we will not experience pain. But the big problem is that we die in unconsciousness when we die in coma. That is the worst thing, because we remain unaware of why we took this birth, and we will not be able to make the decision about the next birth consciously.

That is the reason Kṛṣṇa says: *yaṁ yaṁ vāpi smaran bhāvaṁ*—in whatever state you are at the time of leaving the body, you will achieve that state without fail. If we are unconscious at the time of leaving the body, we naturally take lower level bodies in our next birth; we come back as beings, which do not have a high level of consciousness.

At the time of death, the moment we leave the physical body, we go to the next level, the prāṇic body or the prāṇic layer in us. The prāṇic body refers to the layer responsible for the inhaling and exhaling of prāṇa, the life giving energy in our body. The prāṇic body is filled with all our desires. Please understand, our prāṇa and desires are closely related. If our desires change, immediately the circulation of our praṇa changes.

Similarly, if we change the circulation of *prāṇa*, our whole mind changes. Our mind and prāṇa are closely connected. That is why people inhale and exhale, pull and push with their breath at the time of leaving; they suffer. The body says, 'I can't host you anymore; relax, go out.' But the being says, 'But I have so many desires. I must live in this body. I must enjoy this body.' The tug of war happens between body and being.

Next we move to the mental layer, *mana śarīra*. All the guilt that we harbored throughout our lives, stays in this layer. Desire is expectation about the future. Guilt is regret about the past. Guilt is: *I have not lived in this way*—thoughts about the past. Desire is: *I should live like this*—a thought about the future. Understand, guilt is nothing but the emotion created in our being when we review our past decisions with updated intelligence.

Let me give you a small example. At the age of seven we are playing with our toys. Our mother comes and calls us for dinner, 'Come and eat.' We say, 'No, I don't want to eat; I want to play.' By force our mother takes away the toys and pulls us to come and eat. Immediately we say, 'You go and die; give me my toys, I want to play.'

At that moment, we feel that toys are more important in life than our mother. But as we mature, we understand that this isn't true. Once we mature, if we think, 'O what a grave mistake I made. I shouldn't have said those words to my mother. How important the mother is! But I never thought of it at that time!'... If we create guilt in this way, there is no point or utility in it. At that moment as a young child, we had only that much intelligence. Now, our intelligence has been updated. If we review our past decisions with updated intelligence, we create only one thing: guilt.

If God gives us one more life, we will make the same mistakes that we made when we reach seven years of age because we will have only that much intelligence at the age of seven. Now our intelligence has been updated to an adequate cognition. Just because our intelligence has been updated now, we can't review our actions and create guilt in ourselves about what we did earlier. We should see what data was available to us to make decisions with at that time.

We had such and such inadequate data and only that much intelligence to process the data at that time. Based on that, we made the decision. Now the intelligence to process the data has been updated; our software has been updated with an adequate empowering cognition. Because our software has been updated, we now say, 'O! I made the wrong decision at that time; I am suffering from guilt.' This does not make sense.

One more thing: Guilt is a wedge inserted in our being. It creates uneasiness between you and your being. Be very clear, the worst sin is guilt. Guilt is the only sin; nothing else is a sin on planet Earth. We can never become pure through guilt. We can never become a better person, an integrated and authentic person or a pure person through guilt. Instead, guilt becomes such a load on us that again and again we make the same mistake. If we have deep guilt about smoking, we can never quit smoking because the habit is strengthened when the guilty thoughts are continuously repeated in our system. Whatever is continuously repeated in our consciousness becomes strong; we never grow out of it.

> In Rāmāyaṇa, there is a strong character called Vāli. He had obtained a boon from Lord Śiva that whosoever comes in front of him to fight him, half of that person's power

> would go to Vāli. If we stand in front of Vāli, half of our power goes to Vāli! Naturally who will win? Only he will win!
>
> Understand, our guilt is Vāli. The moment we fight the smoking habit, we give half our power to the habit. We struggle with the habit. Then how can we come out of it?

Listen. If we complete with guilt, at least our personality will be integrated and authentic. When our personality is integrated, we will naturally become pure and energetic. All immoral, inauthentic behavior is because we don't have enough energy. The person with plenty of energy is always pure. The person without energy is immoral and inauthentic. In society we have a wrong idea that people who are full of energy do nonsensical things. Never think so.

Doing immoral things means a person wants energy through that action. Understand, even our sense enjoyments, running behind our senses, are in the same league. We feel that we will get energy and we will feel blissful through that action. Running behind the senses is nothing but running behind energy.

When we review past decisions with updated intelligence, we create guilt. Never make that mistake. If we create guilt, the whole thing sits in the mental body and when we leave the body it becomes a big obstruction.

Listen! If you complete now with your guilt pattern, the disempowering cognition about yourself will melt down. Completion melts down all the obstructions. The obstructions for your realizations are like heap of mountains. The process of completion can melt down even the mountains of incompletions. So complete, complete, complete!

The next layer we cross in the process of death is the etheric body. Here, all the painful experiences that we had in life are stored.

These four layers are hell. When the energy crosses these four layers: physical body, prāṇic body, mental body and etheric body, the being undergoes hell. Understand that hell is not situated in a place above our heads, but in these four layers, comprising all our desires, guilt and painful experiences.

During our life in the body, if we have kept these four layers clean and complete, we never enter hell. That is, if we can technically clean these layers; when I say 'technically', I mean through meditation, through the process of completion. If we keep these layers clean with the proper meditation techniques, we will never have a problem at the time of leaving the body. We will have a clear highway. Straightaway we will travel!

That is what Kṛṣṇa says: This is the path on which a man can easily leave and liberate himself, and also the path on which he can suffer and destroy himself. Both ways are now shown by Kṛṣṇa. These are the major obstructions when we leave the body.

After these first four layers, the three inner layers where all our blissful memories are stored are called heaven. Even if we are stuck there, we need to move on. Please be very clear, even our *puṇya*, merits, are *karma*. Even that will not allow us to become enlightened. We may feel good, ecstatic, for a few days. After that our mind takes that also for granted. In the case of heaven also, we will take it for granted after a few days. When you take it for granted, you have to come back to take another body, another birth.

Be Sure To Reach Me

8.7 *Arjuna, think of Me in the form of Kṛṣṇa always,*
while continuing with your prescribed duty of fighting.
With your activities dedicated to Me and your mind
and intelligence fixed on Me, you will attain Me without doubt.

8.8 *He who meditates on the Supreme Person, his mind constantly*
engaged in remembering Me, not deviating from the path,
O Pārtha, is sure to reach Me.

8.9 *One should meditate on the Supreme as the one who knows*
everything, as He is the most ancient, who is the controller,
who is smaller than the smallest, who is the maintainer of
everything, who is beyond all material conception,
who is inconceivable, and who is always a person.
He is luminous like the sun and, being transcendental,
is beyond this material nature.

8.10 *One, who at the time of death, fixes his mind and life breath*
between the eyebrows without being distracted, who by the power
of yoga and in full devotion engages himself in dwelling on Me,
He will certainly attain Me.

In the first two of these verses Kṛṣṇa says, 'Arjuna, you should always think of Me. You should always be in My state of consciousness even when you are doing your regular duty, even in your activities. Let your mind and intelligence be fixed in My consciousness. You will attain Me without doubt.'

tasmāt sarveṣu kāleṣu   mām anusmara yudhya ca |
mayy arpita-mano-buddhir   mām evaiṣyasy asaṁśayaḥ || 8.7

Again He uses the words, 'without doubt, *asaṁśyaḥ*.' 'Without doubt, you will achieve Me, *mām evaiṣyasy asaṁśayaḥ*.'

One important question we may ask, 'Anyhow, I have to think of Him only at the time of leaving the body, so why bother doing that now? Right now, let me lead my life. At the time of death, I will think about Him.' Please be very clear, these verses answer that question.

We cannot think about Him then unless we think about Him now. Don't think that when we live our whole life chanting the words, 'Coca-cola, Coca-cola', suddenly at the end of our lives we will be able to say, 'Rāma, Kṛṣṇa.' No!

Whatever we think during our whole life, the same thought will come to us in the end also. But we think, 'Now I can say 'Coca-cola, Coca-cola'; at the end, I can always say, 'Rāma, Kṛṣṇa.' No! At the time of death, we will not be able to remember what we want to remember. Our Consciousness will *not* be under our control at that time!

At the time of our death, automatically the totality of our whole life will come up. The whole file will come up. Whatever we spent the maximum energy on, that file will automatically come up first. That's all. We can't do anything in that moment. Don't think that we can forget about it now and tackle the issue of our last thought at the time we leave the body. It does not work that way! Only the thought that we lived with intensely throughout our life will come up at that moment. That is why He says, 'Even when you do your duty, may you be absorbed in Me.' This means that when we live, we should try to continuously be in thoughtless awareness, the witnessing consciousness, the Kṛṣṇa consciousness.

THE SUPREME WITNESS

The next question: 'How can I be in the witnessing mode when I live my regular life?' Start in a simple way. When you drive, when you sit, when you talk, see what is happening inside and outside you. You don't need to close your eyes. At least while driving, please don't close your eyes! Just move away from your body. See what is going on in your mind and what is going on outside your being.

When you talk to someone, witness and listen to how he talks and how you respond. Even before he finishes his statement, notice how you come to conclusions and how you are ready to jump on him with your own opinions! See and listen how you prepare your speech before he finishes his statement. Witness, continuously try to witness. Continuously listen. You will see the influence of desires, guilt and pain on your being automatically disappear.

The moment you create a gap between you and your body-mind, immediately the suffering disappears. Suffering is due to attachment to your body and mind. All your sufferings disappear the moment you witness, that very moment. Actually, you may fail the first few times. After you face failure, you think, 'It is difficult, I cannot do it,' and you create an idea that it is difficult.

Somebody goes to Ramaṇa Maharṣi, the enlightened saint from India, and asks, 'Master, is *ātma vidya* (knowledge of the self) difficult?' He says, 'The word difficult is the only difficulty.' He sings beautifully in Tamil, '*Aiyye ati sulabham atma viddai, aiyye ati sulabham*'—Oh! So easy! The knowledge of the Self is so easy! He sings beautifully, 'To achieve money you must work, to achieve name and fame you must work, to achieve anything else you must work. To achieve the knowledge of the Self, you need to just keep quiet. Nothing else needs to be done.' Such a simple thing; a few moments of witnessing consciousness is enough.

Now don't start calculating, 'From tomorrow onwards, 24 hours a day I will be in the witnessing consciousness.' Then you will become frustrated if you are unable to be that way. So don't bother. Even if you stay in that consciousness for five minutes, it is a big blessing. When you experience the relief that happens when you remain as the witness, even once or twice, when you experience the relief, you can see how the stress disappears from your being. Then you will automatically stay in that same state, because now you have tasted it. Once you know the taste, you will automatically come back to the same state, the same mood again and again.

> Śrī Rāmakṛṣṇa says, 'If you give a little bit of abhin (an opium variant) to a peacock one evening at four o'clock, the next day exactly at four o'clock, it will be in front of your house!' In North India they give abhin to peacocks to make them dance. Rāmakṛṣṇa says that once you supply abhin, they will automatically be there in search of abhin the next day at the same time.

Similarly, if we just experience the relaxation that happens once, when we witness the body and mind, we will automatically come back for that experience, for that peace, again and again. If we feel witnessing is difficult, witness that thought also; be aware and authentically listen to that thought also. Go into the consciousness of your being. Experience samādhi so that all hindrances disappear. You will experience the ultimate, eternal consciousness.

In the next verse Kṛṣṇa says, 'At the time of death, fix your mind between the eyebrows.' He adds, 'without being distracted and with devotion.' See, all this is not in our control at the time when the life force is about to leave the body. We cannot decide at that time, 'Ok, let me focus between the eyebrows, let me think of devotion, let me not be distracted.' But if we have led a life in such higher consciousness, this automatically happens at that time! When Kṛṣṇa talks about the space between the eyebrows, He speaks of the higher *cakra* or energy center in the body, related to higher consciousness.

Our mind is nothing but a bunch of conditionings. All these conditionings influence us at the time of death. How do we condition our mind? If we think that eating is the best thing in life, when we leave the body, what comes in front of us? All kinds of food and the Macdonald arches!

If we are taught that eating is the greatest pleasure in life, we see only all kinds of food when we leave this body. Then the last thought will be, 'Let me take birth in a family where I will be given food and nothing but food, where I will not have any other responsibility.'

We call for the archived files. The essence, the research report, is in front of us. From all the experiences of our past, we choose what we think is best and what we have worked for all our life. Based on that, we make a decision, 'Alright, if I want to eat, this is the right country.' There we will spend our next life, in *tamas*, in dullness, not doing anything, in just pure laziness.

A small story:

> A man goes to a doctor and says, 'Doctor, please examine me. I don't feel like doing anything. I feel dull.'
>
> The doctor thoroughly examines him. The man says, 'Doctor, please tell me in plain English, what is my problem?'
>
> The doctor says, 'If you ask me, in plain English, you are 'lazy'. Nothing else is the problem.'
>
> The man says, 'Ok, now tell me the medical term for it; I will go and tell my wife!'

If we have lived that kind of a life, a lethargic, dead, dull and lazy life, that same laziness will make the choice for us when we take the next body. I have seen amazing laziness amongst people. If you want to see the ultimate laziness, come to the Himālayas. That is why Vivekananda says openly in his lectures, 'The people who eat and sleep in the name of *sannyās*... make them stand up, and simply beat them!' Pure laziness!

If we live our life spending our energy in laziness, we just get lazier. We actually spend energy when we are lazy. Don't think we are not spending energy. Have you heard the phrase, 'tired of sleeping?' Many people are tired of taking rest. To be tired of taking rest is *tamas*. If we have lived life completely in ***tamas***, we naturally decide, 'Anyhow, the ultimate thing in life is sleep. Now which country is the right country to allow lots of sleep? What type of body is the right body—whether pig or buffalo or human being? What type of family should I take birth in?' We make a decision. Please be very clear, the whole calculation happens based on our own data, the data that we have collected.

As I said, at the time of leaving the body, the whole data appears before us in a single flash: the gist of the whole data, the gist of all three files—*āgāmya* (acquired) file, *sañcita* (bank balance) file and *prārabdha* (current) file. Based on the files, we decide, 'What am I supposed to do? What should be my next birth?' The moment we decide, we enter that kind of body. One more important thing: Because we are so attached to the body and mind, we cannot live without a body for more than three *kṣaṇas.* The Saṃskrit word '*kṣaṇa*' does not mean 'seconds' or 'moments'. It does not measure chronological time. It is the gap between one thought and the next thought. For most of us, *kṣaṇa* will be a few microseconds because of our endless stream of thoughts.

While still in the body, if we have experienced 'thoughtlessness' at least once, (thoughtlessness means being alive without a sense of body and mind), if we have experienced thoughtless awareness, if we have been in Universal consciousness for a single moment without the body and mind, that is what I call *Samādhi*.

FOUR STATES OF CONSCIOUSNESS

Here is a small diagram to explain what exactly I mean by the word 'thoughtlessness'.

FOUR STATES OF CONSCIOUSNESS

	with thoughts	**without thoughts**
with 'I' consciousness	**Jāgrat** Wakeful State *Thinking*	**Turiya** Blissful State *State of Full Awareness*
without 'I' consciousness	**Svapna** Dream State *Dreaming*	**Suṣupti** Unconscious State *Deep Sleep*

In our life, we experience two states of being and two levels of mind. For example, now, while we are awake, we have thoughts. In deep sleep, do we have thoughts? No! So the two possibilities for the mind are with thought and without thought.

In the same way, in the being, there can be 'I' consciousness and no 'I' consciousness. As of now, while we are awake and talking and moving, we have the idea of 'I' all the time, that of 'I' consciousness. In deep sleep, do we have this consciousness? No. The 'I' consciousness does not exist at that time. So the two levels of the being are: with 'I' consciousness and without 'I' consciousness. These two levels of consciousness and the two levels of mind and thought overlap each other and create four states of being in us.

The state with thoughts and with 'I' consciousness is the waking state, *jāgrat,* in which most of us are now (not all, some of us are in the dream state—sleeping already!)

The next state is when we have thoughts, but 'I' consciousness is absent. This is the dream state—*svapna*. You may ask, 'How?' It is like this: In the dream state, the frequency of thoughts will be more than the frequency of 'I' consciousness. That is why we are not able to control our dreams. When we are awake, the frequency of 'I' is more, that is why we can control our thoughts; we can suppress them, divert them, create them; we can do anything we want because the frequency of 'I' is more than the frequency of thoughts. In the dream state, the frequency of thoughts is more than the frequency of 'I'. That is why we cannot control our dreams. If we can have the dreams of our choice, we know what kind of dreams we will have! Dreams are not in our control. We cannot influence them. We cannot have choices because the frequency of thoughts is more than the frequency of consciousness. So we have thoughts but no 'I' consciousness. The flow of thoughts happening in our being is the dream state.

In the next state, neither 'I' consciousness nor the flow of thoughts exists. This is deep sleep. This is called *suṣupti*. The three states are *jāgrat, svapna, suṣupti*—conscious, sub-conscious, unconscious.

There is a fourth state that we have not experienced in our life, where we have no flow of thoughts yet we have 'I' consciousness, pure 'I' consciousness. This is *samādhi*, thoughtless awareness—*turīya avastha, ātma jñāna, brahma jñāna*, Self-realization, *nirvāna, ātma bhūti*, state of the Divine, *nityānanda* consciousness, eternal bliss!

All these words refer to the state where we have pure awareness but no thoughts, where we exist without body and mind. *Jāgrat, svapna, suṣupti,* in these three states, we live with the body and mind. In *jāgrat*, we live with the body that we have now—the *sthūla śarīra* or gross body. In *svapna*, we live with the *sūkṣma śarīra* or subtle body; please understand in the dream state also we assume a body. That is why we are able to travel in our dreams. For example, we fall asleep in Los Angeles but suddenly dream we are in India! It means we travel with a body, a subtle body called *sūkṣma śarīra*. In deep sleep, we assume a body called the causal body, *kāraṇa śarīra*.

In turīya state, we experience boundarilessness, bodylessness. There we have pure 'I' consciousness, with 'I' but without thoughts. Vivekananda says, 'If you experience even a single glimpse of this consciousness when you are alive, the same thing automatically repeats when you leave the body. You leave the body in *samādhi*.'

All spiritual practices directly or indirectly aim at achieving this state where we exist with the awareness of 'I', but without the consciousness of body and mind. That is why Kṛṣṇa says that if we experience at least one moment of consciousness beyond the body and mind, we can choose our next life in a relaxed way.

If we have not lived a single moment of our life without the feeling of being the body and mind, we cannot be without the body and mind once we die. So once we die, we immediately try to catch hold of another body. Because we have never lived a single moment without body and mind, the moment we die, we will not bother about which body we are getting into. We rush as fast as possible. It's like we are late for a train, so we run and jump onto the first train that we see, not thinking about where it's headed. We say, 'Let me just get into some train!' We rush and get into some body or the other and come down to planet Earth yet another time.

After coming down, we again forget the supreme purpose of assuming the body; this is the biggest problem. If we have experienced a single moment of complete rest and thoughtless awareness, the state of *restful awareness*, then naturally at the moment when we leave the body, we will be in the same state. This state is also called 'bodyless' awareness because when we are in *turīya* state, all the three bodies do not touch us; neither the gross body nor the subtle body nor the causal body touches us.

We experience awareness that is beyond the three bodies. If we have experienced this thoughtless restful awareness for even a single moment earlier, we will have the required clarity in the end. If we have experienced that we can exist without the body and mind, we will have the patience to work with our data files before assuming the next body. We will go through the data line carefully and decide, 'Should I take birth at all? What is the need?' Sometimes, if we decide to take birth, we can even take a conscious birth, like the great Masters!

Kṛṣṇa says *yogabraṣṭha*. We take birth in a family that will be conducive to our spiritual growth, which will not create obstacles to our spiritual practices. Kṛṣṇa says that only very rarely do souls take birth in this type of family. I have rarely seen parents who do not object when the son does spiritual practices. If your family does not object, if they do not disturb you, please be very clear, there is every chance of your being a *yogabraṣṭha*!

Otherwise, I have seen even religious parents creating obstacles if their son wants to enter *sannyās* or spiritual life. They say, 'Go to temples but not to ashrams!' But if you grow beyond the maturity of the parents, it is something that they cannot digest. Very rarely do souls take birth in families where they will not be disturbed.

When I left home for my *parivrājaka* (wandering Sannyāsa life), I was young; just 17 years old. I told

> my mother that I was going, that I wanted to live the *parivrājaka* life, I wanted to taste Sannyāsa life.
>
> She started weeping. So I asked her, 'Do you mean that I should not go?'
>
> She said beautifully, 'No, I don't want to stop you. But I am not able to digest the idea of your leaving, so I am weeping.' Even today I am grateful to my parents because they did not stop me. Not only that, from a very young age I did all sorts of things that you can't even imagine. Sometimes I used to spend the night meditating in the graveyard in the outskirts of my village! I don't think other parents would have tolerated it. Yet somehow the atmosphere was such that I was able to continue my spiritual practice.

If your family and surroundings do not disturb you but help you instead, please be very clear that you have taken a conscious birth—you are a *yogabraṣtha*.

But if you have not experienced a single glimpse, a single moment of thoughtless awareness, you cannot live without the body and mind once you die. So within three *kṣaṇas*, you take birth in some way or the other.

Even a glimpse of consciousness, a moment of realization, a single moment of thoughtless awareness, when you live with the body and mind is enough. Inner Awakening and *Nithya Kriya Yoga* Program, or LBP 2, are directly focused on this concept. All I try to do is give you a single glimpse of consciousness, thoughtless restful awareness.

Actually, if you achieve one glimpse of thoughtless awareness, you achieve whatever has to be achieved in life. If you have not achieved one glimpse of *samādhi* or thoughtless awareness, whatever else you achieve is not ultimately useful. In the next step, Kṛṣṇa explains how to achieve thoughtless awareness and gives a deeper understanding about death and the art of leaving.

Remember Me Constantly

8.11 *Persons who are learned in the Veda and who are great sages in the orders of renunciation, enter into the Brahman. Desiring such perfection, one practices brahmacarya. I shall now explain to you the process by which one may attain liberation.*

8.12 *Closing all the doors of the senses and fixing the mind in the heart and the life breath at the top of the head, one establishes oneself in yoga.*

8.13 *Centered in this yoga practice and uttering the sacred syllable Oṁ, the supreme combination of letters, if one dwells in the Supreme and quits his body, he certainly achieves the supreme destination.*

8.14 *I am always available to anyone who remembers Me constantly Pārtha, because of his constant engagement in devotional service.*

Kṛṣṇa gives different ways to attain *Brahman* or God or Ultimate consciousness. He says that people learned in the Vedas attain Brahman. This does not mean that we need to just read the vedas and then forget about them. Kṛṣṇa speaks at a far deeper level.

Remember what Kṛṣṇa says in the last verse. He says that whatever we think of at the time of death is directly related to our next birth. If someone is completely immersed in the scriptures, his thoughts will continuously be along those lines. That is what Kṛṣṇa means by His words 'Immerse yourself in the scriptures'. Keep reading some scripture or the other and imbibe its truth. It will have a tremendous impact on you.

Even if we do not understand the deeper meanings of these scriptures, it is ok. These scriptures are energy hubs. When we read them, the sound that is generated is enough to cleanse our inner being. That is the power of those verses. They will transform you. If you listen to *vedic* chants, you will find that they are chanted in a specific tone and pitch. When they are chanted, they completely cleanse our system, our inner being.

If we visit the ancient temples in India, we will see that the sanctum sanctorum has a beautiful peace inside it. When we enter that place, automatically our being becomes peaceful. Why do you think we feel a moment of bliss as soon as we enter the sanctum sanctorum? When the priest chants, that place gets energized. The sound of the chants carries tremendous energy and energizes everything in the place.

One more thing, these scriptures talk about realizing the *Self*. They are guides to Enlightenment. So when we read them, we will get into that mood of Enlightenment! Our mind will be tuned to that frequency. It is like this: After watching a movie, our mind keeps processing the scenes of the movie, is it not? For one or two days, we experience a hangover. In the same way, when we read these scriptures, even if we don't completely cognize them, we will experience a hangover. We will continue to think about what they say; what Enlightenment is, how to realize our *Self*, how enlightened Masters live… these thoughts will fill our mind again and again.

This is what Kṛṣṇa wants! When our thoughts are always directed towards Self-realization, our thoughts will be of Enlightenment at the time of death also.

Kṛṣṇa says, when we read the scriptures, when we practice this lifestyle, we practice *brahmacarya*. The literal meaning of *brahmacarya* is one who follows the path to attain the Self. '*Brahman*' means the Self and '*carya*' means to walk the path. Anyone who is on the path to attain Brahman is a *brahmacāri*.

Suppression does not lead to transformation. It only creates depression. Suppression of desires is very dangerous; it is like a volcano ready to erupt anytime and we won't even know it. Only completion leads to transformation. *Brahmacarya* is not about leaving everything and becoming a celibate. Our inner space must be cleansed with the power of integrity and authenticity. Our inner space must be the space of completion, free from fantasies and we should strive to merge with the Brahman. That is *brahmacarya.*

Here Kṛṣṇa talks about deep concepts of *yoga.* All great truths were told by different masters in different ways, yet the truths remain the same. If somebody who does not know the actual meaning of yoga reads this verse, he will be totally confused. Nowadays when people hear about yoga, they think of physical exercise, about how to become slim doing yoga! Yoga has a much deeper meaning and Kṛṣṇa talks about it.

Yoga means the continuous process of uniting our mind, body and soul. This truth is revealed by great enlightened Masters in different ways. Patañjali, the father of yoga, talks about this verse in his *Aṣṭāṅga Yoga*, in the two limbs of yoga—*pratyāhāra* and *dhārana.* These two parts talk about what Kṛṣṇa mentions.

Let us understand this verse. How do we bring about that continuous process of uniting body, mind and soul? You see, our body-mind system reacts to different external situations. These external situations are like food, *āhāra* to our system and our five sense organs are the points through which we take in this food.

Our mind functions because we give food to our mind through our senses. We react to situations and our mind is continuously occupied because of this. Our mind exists because we have thousands of thoughts, constantly jumping from past to future and back to past. Our five sense organs act as gateways through which this food goes in to our mind.

Pratyāhāra means getting ourselves out of the clutches of these senses. This does not mean that we physically shut down our senses. Listen, *pratyāhāra* does not mean we shut our senses physically. Even if we close our eyes, an internal television runs in our system, does it not? Even if our ears and mouth are closed, there is inner chatter, is it not? We don't really shut down our senses. Even if we shut them physically, our mind functions. When I say, 'Close the doors of your senses,' I mean, 'Do not process the data.' What I mean is, continue to hear everything going on outside, continue to smell everything around, but do not process anything. Whatever comes, just witness, that's all. That is the only way we can close the doors of our senses. We should neither suppress thoughts nor create thoughts. We should just watch them.

We cut the continuous flow of inputs from our senses when we increase our awareness. The number of thoughts slowly drops as awareness rises. As we increase awareness, our thoughts per second, TPS, drops.

This is what Kṛṣṇa means by closing all the senses. When we do this, our awareness becomes more and more concentrated on the present moment. When we shut our senses and remain in pure awareness, we focus on our divinity. We keep a single-minded focus on the divinity resonating in us. We automatically fall into the present moment. Awareness of our breath becomes more acute. We feel life energy or *prāṇa* filling our system. This is called *dhārana,* single-minded focus. We can focus on the life force energizing our system when we increase our awareness and close all the inputs from our senses. We automatically unite mind, body and spirit. This is *yoga*.

Kṛṣṇa continuously tells Arjuna the importance of the last thought before death. We saw in the previous verses how much importance He gives to this truth. You see, it is a powerful technique. These are not mere words to be read and not put into practice.

People have used these words and left their bodies gracefully, understand that! They merged with the Ultimate consciousness by practicing these techniques. Thousands of enlightened beings have constantly thought about God. They have expressed their undaunted devotion in so many carefree ways. People laughed when they danced and sang the glory of God. People realized the power of that devotion only after these Enlightened beings left their bodies, completely merging with the Cosmos.

Kṛṣṇa says the people who reach Him are those who remain continuously on the path of yoga, continuously fixed upon the Divine without deviation. Kṛṣṇa asks us to be in that state all the time. He asks us to be in Kṛṣṇa consciousness all the time. The problem is when an Enlightened Master says, 'Think of Me all the time,' we question, 'What kind of an egoistic person is He? Why should we think of Him?'

Actually, our ego plays the game. We think Kṛṣṇa is exploiting us when He advises us to be in Kṛṣṇa consciousness. Many people think I am exploiting them when I make such statements. They think I profit from all of this.

Please listen! Kṛṣṇa, or any Enlightened Master or Incarnation, only asks us to keep our inner space completely free of desires. Our thoughts are generally related to greed and fear. We keep piling up desires because our root thought patterns are of greed and fear. When we die, our soul re-experiences these desires. Attachment to these desires makes our death painful. An Enlightened Master has seen this process and speaks from experience. He is pure compassion and He wants everyone to know the secret of mastering the art of leaving.

That is why Kṛṣṇa says again and again: When we direct our thoughts to the Divine, greed and fear are completely wiped out. Our whole being is filled with gratitude to the Divine. One more thing, many people think of God because they want to go to heaven. Some people are afraid of death so they think of God. Both are only because of greed or fear.

When we think of the Divine, we should do so out of gratitude, and not out of greed or fear. Our thoughts about God, our devotion to the Divine should be out of pure gratitude to Existence.

Brahma's Day And Night

8.15 *After attaining Me, the great souls who are devoted to Me in yoga are never reborn in this world.*
This world is temporary and full of miseries and they have attained the highest perfection.

8.16 *From the highest planet in the material world [brahmaloka] down to the lowest, all are places of misery wherein repeated birth and death take place.*
One who reaches My abode, O Kaunteya, is never reborn.

8.17 *By human calculation, a thousand ages taken together is the duration of Brahma's one day. His night is just as long.*

8.18 *From the unmanifest all living entities come into being at the beginning of Brahma's day. With the coming of Brahma's night, they dissolve into the same unmanifest.*

Now He says, 'After attaining Me the great souls who are steeped in yoga never return to this temporary world, which is full of miseries, because they have attained the highest perfection.'

mām upetya punar janma duḥkhālayam aśāśvatam |
nāpnuvanti mahātmānaḥ saṁsiddhiṁ paramāṁ gatāḥ || 8.15

The understanding of this science, the very intellectual understanding, gives the inspiration to experience truth and naturally leads us to the ultimate Truth.

Here Kṛṣṇa says, 'If you achieve this state, you never come back.' He inspires us; He persuades us to enter that state, to enter thoughtless awareness.

The only job of an Enlightened Master is to make everyone realize the truth that he himself has experienced. That is the only aim. There is no ulterior motive or vested interest.

People again and again look at an Enlightened Master with suspicion. They suspect foul play. Understand one thing: A person who remains at the inner source of bliss never cares for anything external. Please understand that he does not need external sources of happiness because he has something more powerful. The inner guide is so powerful that the being is always blissful.

That is the reason he does not see the world as a collection of miseries. You see, an enlightened Master may not get food for days, yet he is always blissful. Even in such situations, the only things that he experiences are gratitude and compassion.

He is neither attached to sorrow nor to happiness. He is detached from both to the same degree. He is always in a state of gratitude to the Universe. Worldly things do not affect him. Happiness and sorrow are not in his dictionary. An enlightened Master looks at misery and happiness with total gratitude and surrender to the Universe. Enlightened beings are beyond happiness as you understand it. They are not attached to anything. They are pure compassion.

One more thing, an enlightened being surrenders everything that he has and gets, to Existence. When he gets food, he surrenders that; when he is hungry for days, he surrenders that to Existence. Whether he has money or is in poverty, he is rich inside because he surrenders everything.

He says, 'Let Existence take care.' All his responsibilities are handed over to Existence. There is a great relief inside when that state of surrender happens. We suddenly light up in joy. We consider something as misery because we think we are responsible for that something. We think we control it. That is why, when something does not happen according to our expectations, we see it as misery.

But an Enlightened being is not like that. He simply flows. Whatever comes, he accepts it and surrenders it to Existence.

BEYOND KARMA

In the next verse, Kṛṣṇa talks about the misery-filled world and we see how good deeds cannot get us out of the cycle of birth and death.

Kṛṣṇa says here:

ā-brahma-bhuvanāl lokāḥ punar āvartino 'rjuna |
mām upetya tu kaunteya punar janma na vidyate || 8.16

'From the highest planet of Brahmaloka in the material world down to the lowest, all are places of misery wherein repeated birth and death takes place. But one who attains Me, one who attains My being, one who attains My consciousness, never takes birth again.'

I told you earlier about the different energy layers. Even if we reach the cosmic layer of Brahmaloka, the land of the Divine, we must come back and take birth again. It means that even if we are full of good intentions and good deeds, even if we are attached to good things, we must come back into a body.

Please be very clear, even if we are caught in doing good deeds, we return. Our good deeds, *puṇya*, cannot give us enlightenment. I tell people, 'Even if you give money for my ashram, I cannot give you a speed pass to enlightenment!' I cannot give you any speed pass. Be very clear, unless you have the conscious glimpse, unless you achieve at least one moment of thoughtless awareness, nobody can save you from the cycle of birth and death.

Some people believe that when they give money to institutions, they receive a receipt and a pass to heaven when they die. They are buried with the receipt so that they can show the receipt to the gatekeeper of heaven and he will let them in!

I tell you honestly that at least I don't have such a system with this institution. Let me be very clear! I never tell people, 'Do charity and good acts and I can get you into heaven.' Do things out of love and gratitude with no attachment, and you will be in heaven as a result of your mental setup. Do it out of gratitude, just for the sake of doing it, not expecting that tomorrow you will be given a special place in heaven.

I tell people, 'Even if you give money to my ashram, I cannot give you any speed pass; nothing can be done. This is the honest truth.' People ask, 'Then why do you build ashrams and temples?' I build them because they are laboratories where the spiritual sciences can be practiced. All over the world I build vedic temples and ashrams as inner science laboratories where these truths can be practiced and intranalyzed, and where people will radiate the science of living enlightenment with integrity, authenticity, responsibility and enriching.

Listen! Do charity and good acts with the consciousness that you are engaged in research in the inner sciences in these laboratories, just as the *ṛṣis* of the great vedic tradition did. Don't do it for some special ticket to heaven.

Don't expect that if we do these things for Lord Viṣṇu, He will send a special flight with a *garuḍa* (eagle, Lord Viṣṇu's vehicle) when we leave the body, and the airhostesses, Rambhā, Menaka and Urvaśi (celestial beauties), will take us there. Nothing of that sort happens! If we expect these things to happen, we will sit, sit, sit and wait. Nobody will come and no such thing will happen! Be very clear, whether we acquire sin or merit, we suffer when we leave the body. Whether it is sin or merit, both are *karma*.

Then what is to be done? When we live in the body, at least once, in one way or another, by meditating or by surrender, experience one glimpse of thoughtless, restful awareness.

Work intensely for it, for at least one glimpse of thoughtless awareness, the witnessing consciousness, the space of completion. If we achieve one glimpse, it's over. That one glimpse acts like a conscious torch, and guides us through these seven layers when we leave the body. We will walk beautifully; we will slide through all seven layers. The enlightened Master's initiation is the torch of consciousness that guides us through this path, through our living and leaving.

If we achieve that one glimpse of consciousness, we achieve what has to be achieved. If we have not had that, whatever we achieve is a pure waste. All merits and sins—nothing comes with us. We will not be judged by anything except this glimpse of *samādhi*, the ultimate truth.

Samādhi in Saṃskṛit means: being in our original state. Once we realize this state, we have arrived.

Vivekananda says, 'If you achieve even a single glimpse, you leave your body in that experience.' It is because this intense experience of Self-realization will come up at the time when we leave the body. At the time of death, our whole life is played back to us in a fast-forward mode in a few seconds. And only the important scenes appear in multicolor again and again; all other scenes appear in black and white. They become the background. If we have had thoughtless awareness, the *samādhi* experience when we were alive, that alone will appear in multicolor; all other things will fade away in the background.

And naturally, we stay in that state and leave the body. One more thing—if there is a scratch on a videotape, the tape gets stuck in that place when it runs in fast-forward mode, is it not? So when the fast-forward happens, the remainder of the tape is erased. Similarly, thoughtless awareness is the stuck point in our life because in that space we never had a thought. We will be stuck there and whatever fast-forward happens beyond that, all the *karma* associated with it will be erased, washed away!

It is like a virus entering our software; the more we try to operate the software, the more the virus destroys the software. Similarly, thoughtless awareness is the divine virus for our *saṁsāra sāgara*—ocean of worldly life, for our desires, for the software that is our mind. Our mind is the software. Our mind is just a pre-programmed software.

Please listen! Don't think that the mind is intelligence. The mind is just a programmed software. For example, let us say we experience anxiety every morning because of office-related worries. Gradually, every morning at 10 am, we experience a low mood. The funny thing is, eventually we start experiencing the same depression even on the weekend when there is no office to attend!

If we are a little aware and sensitive, if we observe ourselves, we will see that this is true. How many of you have experienced this? If we have observed ourselves, we would have experienced this at least a few times. Then we tell our mind, 'No, this is the weekend. I don't need to go to the office. I don't need to worry about those things.' But every weekend, our mind goes back to the same mood because our mind is a pre-programmed software.

Thoughtless awareness is a benign virus, if such a thing exists! The more we work with the software after the virus has entered, the more the software and programs will be destroyed. Similarly, if we have one glimpse of Consciousness in our lifetime, this glimpse takes over our being at the time of leaving the body, and the whole software is completely erased.

We do not have to take another birth. We assume the body and mind only if we believe there is something to be enjoyed or achieved through the body and mind. Unless we believe there is some work or enjoyment to be found downtown, will we go downtown? We will not. Similarly, unless we believe there is something to be achieved or enjoyed through this body and mind, we do not come down to planet Earth.

When we are in this body, if we work on our root thought patterns, *saṁskāras*, and complete with them, we will liberate ourselves from their influence, and hence from the cycle of re-birth. Kṛṣṇa speaks in a detailed manner on these truths later.

Actually, you do not normally become aware of these root thought patterns, *saṁskāras*. In our *Inner Awakening* program, we take you through root pattern analysis techniques to uncover them first and complete with them. You write down, analyze and relive all that has happened in your life and all that you have stored in the various energy layers that the spirit will pass through when it leaves the body-mind system. You analyze: What is the root of your desires? Which of these are superficial incomplete desires? Which desires have been imposed on you by others? What are your own desires, for fulfilling which, you carry your own energy?

For instance, guilt is initially imposed on us by society. Later we master the art of creating guilt and continue to create it for ourselves! First society teaches us; then we master the art. Next, pain and suffering. Society creates a scale deciding what pain is and what suffering is. Then, we actually turn our whole life into suffering by measuring it with that scale. In the Inner Awakening meditation retreat, we initiate participants into the science of completion and work deeply on every emotion related to root thought patterns or *saṁskāras*.

Understand, this science is not only for dying but also for living! If we are stuck with guilt, we can never enjoy our desires. When we don't enjoy our desires, we create more guilt, that's all. When we are stuck in guilt, we will not leave the desires and they cannot leave us. When we don't leave our desires, we create more guilt. This becomes a vicious circle of incomplete emotions. So not only for dying, even for living we need to learn this whole science of completion, the space of thoughtless awareness.

Experience His Līlā, Cosmic Play

As of now, understand this one thing: Throughout this chapter Kṛṣṇa conveys the single message:

Experience His consciousness, the thoughtless awareness or the witnessing consciousness in which Kṛṣṇa stays and plays the whole game of life, how He lives through the whole of life. That is why Kṛṣṇa's life is called *līlā*—cosmic play, *Kṛṣṇa līlā*. It is not history. It is *līlā*; it is a Cosmic play.

For ordinary human beings, after they die, their life will be written as history. For incarnations, their life itself is a script that has already been written; they just come down and enact it, that's all! For them it is a script; for us it is history. For us, after we die, somebody may write about us if we have achieved something! For the great Masters, it is a script. They come with the script and enact the whole thing. They play the whole game. That is why their life is called *līlā.* If we achieve the witnessing consciousness, our whole life becomes līlā. We know the script and we are ready. When we know the script our whole life is a līlā. When we don't know the script, it becomes history.

***Līlā Dhyāna* is a such a powerful space creator.** Please understand, your pastime always leads you to incompletion. An Incarnation's pastime or *līlā* always leads you to completion. Your past always leads you to incompletion. An Incarnation's pastimes, always lead you to completion. If you constantly remember what you did when you were a child, you will be in more and more incompletion. If you constantly remember what Kṛṣṇa does when He is a child, you will be more and more in the space of completion. Understand, remembering your pastimes, creates more and more incompletions. Remembering the Incarnation's pastimes creates more and more completion and the higher space.

Whether it is Kṛṣṇa or Buddha, Mahādeva or Mīnākśi, even remembering their *līlās*, their cosmic play creates so much of completion in you, it heals your *mamakāra*, your inner image.

Actually, because of this *Līlā Dhyāna* practice you become more complete with you. And if you observe deeply, you will find out if you have incompletion with you, that day you will feel that the Divine is angry with you! Understand, the completion you need to do with you and with others is responsible for how you feel connected to your Guru or God, outside and inside.

Kṛṣṇa conveys one thing: All we need to do is work to achieve a glimpse of thoughtless awareness, the space of completion. In the next few chapters, He speaks deeply, intensely about how to open every layer, how to progress, how to clean and complete with every layer and how to achieve the conscious glimpse or thoughtless awareness. He says further:

'By human calculation, the thousand ages taken together form the duration of Brahma's one day and such also is the duration of his night.'

As I told you, one year for us is one day for the devatas, demigods. For Brahma, a thousand ages are taken as one day. Only when we achieve the consciousness of *nirvāṇa*—thoughtless awareness, will we not take rebirth. Here He says a beautiful thing about *kṣaṇa*.

At the time of death, our soul has three *kṣaṇa* to take another body. Three *kṣaṇas* can be three microseconds, three seconds or three minutes or three hundred years according to the person's frequency of thoughts. It depends on his state of mind. If we have lived a restless life, our *kṣaṇas* will be in microseconds. If we have lived a peaceful, blissful life and achieved at least one glimpse of thoughtless awareness, our *kṣaṇa* can be even two or three hundred years. If we can stop the next thought from happening within our inner space, our *kṣaṇas* can be increased to any extent. It can extend to eternity. So, *kṣaṇas* is relative and not absolute.

Time is actually not chronological, but psychological. If we sit with a friend with whom we are comfortable and joyful, after three or four hours, we suddenly notice the time and say, 'Oh! I don't know how the time has passed by so quickly!' At the same time, if we sit with somebody with whom we don't feel comfortable, we will look at the watch and think, 'Why is the watch not moving? Is there a problem with it? The time is simply dragging on.'

The number of thoughts that happen in our mind decides the time consciousness. If thoughts are less, even after ten hours, we will not feel that ten hours have passed. If the number of thoughts is more, two or three minutes will seem like years.

A small story:

> A lady goes to the doctor for a check-up. After a thorough examination, the doctor says, 'I'm sorry. I have bad news. You may live only six months more at the most.'
>
> She says, 'What is this? What should I do now?'
>
> The doctor says, 'I have one suggestion. Marry an accountant.'
>
> She asks, 'Will that cure me?'

He replies, 'No, no. But then the six months will seem very long.'

You see, at the most, we can extend time psychologically. And when it happens, it is what we call 'eternal hell'. The word 'eternal' is not chronological. Even if we make all possible mistakes in a hundred years, how can we be punished in eternal hell? It actually means that those hundred years seems eternal because of the crowd of thoughts, time will not seem to move.

One year of human life equals one day of the *devatas*, demigods, because their thoughts per second (TPS) is very less. That is why the deity Natarāja in the temple at Chidambaraṁ in South India, has only six prayer offerings throughout the year. In one year, they worship the deity only six times! Normally, the worship is carried out six times a day in other temples. But this temple is supposed to be where the *devatas* worship the Divine, so the worship is carried out according to their time!

The six offerings of worship required for the deity are conducted in our one year because our one year is one day for the deities or *devatas*. *Devatas* refers to those whose TPS has come down, who have had a glimpse of *samādhi*. If our TPS is low, we too are in heaven. If our TPS is high, we are in hell. Heaven always looks brief; hell always looks eternal, because of the number of thoughts.

When we are in the body, if we have had a single glimpse of thoughtless awareness—the experience of meditation, then automatically this consciousness comes up at the time of leaving the body and we will have two benefits. We can choose to become enlightened and not take another birth, or we can choose the right place to express and work out our *karma*, to live as we want. We have both choices if we experience thoughtless awareness while living.

My Supreme Abode

8.19 *Again and again the day comes, and this host of beings is active;*
And again the night falls, O Pārtha, and they are automatically annihilated.

8.20 *Yet there is another nature, which is eternal and*
is beyond this manifested and unmanifest matter.
It is supreme and is never annihilated.
When all in this world is annihilated, that remains the same.

8.21 *That Supreme abode is said to be unmanifest and indestructible and is the Supreme destination. When one gains this state one never comes back. That is My supreme abode.*

8.22 *O Pārtha (son of Prithā), the supreme person, who is greater than all, is attainable by undeviating devotion.*
Although He is present in His abode, He is all-pervading,
and everything is situated within Him.

Kṛṣṇa explains how transient this material world is. During a single 'blink of Brahma'—the Lord of creation, so many things change. In our concept of time, we see things as permanent, but when we operate in a different zone of space and time, all this becomes temporary.

Our ignorance makes us think that all that we see is real and permanent. Once we understand that this entire life and the world around us is impermanent, we see everything from a completely different space. Why do we run behind material things? Why do we again and again want to possess things?

In our concept of time and space, we see material things as

permanent. We think we can control them. We want to have ownership over everything that is available. And the problem is everyone wants the same thing! Everyone fights to take charge of the same thing. We are like cats fighting over a piece of bread.

Please listen, we fight to catch hold of this body. We want to hold onto this body for as long as we can. Even at sixty or seventy, many people go in for plastic surgery. They do things to look young. Why? They do not want to accept the truth that the body is impermanent.

When you look around, you see that the Earth is stationary. It is not moving. When you look from the moon, you see the earth moving. When you go beyond the moon, you see that the moon also moves.

Once we raise ourselves to higher dimensions, we see the actual truth. As long as we limit ourselves to this space, we think the earth is stationary. When we change our concept of space and time, when we change our reference point in space and time, we realize that all we think of as permanent, all that we think is ours is not permanent. It is continuously being created and destroyed.

This is what Kṛṣṇa says. We believe in a concept of finite time and limited space and we cling to that without realizing what is beyond this dimension. We are greedy to accumulate more and more material pleasures because we see them as real and permanent. We think they will stay with us forever. That is one side. On the other side we fear that they will be taken away from us. We are always in a state of fear.

Both these—greed and fear—are the main sources of our misery. When we live in bondage to fear and greed, we continuously build *saṁskāras*. We create more and more desires. First of all, we are not trying to fulfill our true desires or *prārabdha karma*. Then on top of that, we build a whole new set of desires. In our concept of time and space, we think things are permanent. We think we own them and we should take care of them and control them.

When we understand that at higher dimensions, all that we see is destroyed and created continuously, we realize the futility of holding onto things, even our own body.

Kṛṣṇa says that in all this creation and destruction, only one thing is neither created nor destroyed and that is the 'Ultimate Consciousness'! What we think of as an age is a fraction of a second to Brahma and everything we see as permanent is being made and destroyed every time Brahma blinks. Do not analyze the literal meaning of this. Do not analyze how it is possible. Do not worry about how many hours, how many seconds make one day of Brahma? Do not worry about what is Brahma's time or what is Śiva's time or Kṛṣṇa's time. Kṛṣṇa refers to the concept of time and space as it exists in the Ultimate consciousness and as an Enlightened Master experiences it.

Appreciate and intranalyze the deeper meaning. Understand that whatever we see is transient. Nothing is permanent. It is like putting our hand in a river and trying to hold the water in our hand. What happens? The river flows past, and our hand is empty. Once we realize this truth, our whole idea about time and space will change. We will see everything around us in a different way and understand the futility of the rat race.

I mentioned the seven layers that the spirit travels through at the time of death. The first four layers are related to the physical body-mind system. They store emotionally laden memories: patterns related to desires, guilt and pain experienced during that lifetime. The fifth layer is experienced during deep sleep and when leaving the body. The sixth layer is associated with happy memories and the seventh layer is beyond sorrow and happiness; it is the Ultimate consciousness.

Please understand, even attachment to happy memories brings us back into the cycle of birth and death. It is not enough if we transcend pains and sufferings alone. Understand that happy incidents are also temporary and try to move beyond them.

THE ABODE OF NO RETURN

The secret to liberation is what Kṛṣṇa gives here—'One who attains My abode will never return, *yaṁ prāpya na nivartante tad dhāma paramaṁ mama* (8.21).'

The abode where one will not return to refers to the state of the *being* when it transcends joys and sorrow. Kṛṣṇa again and again talks about focusing one's thoughts on the Divine. The only way to think of the Divine at the time of our death is by thinking about Him all the time. At that time, we suddenly cannot think of God. In such pain and suffering, we suddenly can't think of God if we have always been thinking about money and food in our life. It is impossible.

That is why Kṛṣṇa insists upon continuous devotion to the Supreme—*bhaktyā labhyas tv ananyayā* (8.22). When we live in a state of continuous devotion, our last thought will be of the Divine. Please be very clear: Our last thought determines our next birth. There is no doubt about it.

When we continuously think about God, we understand the truth that everything around us is Him. When we are continuously in that meditation, we see Kṛṣṇa in everything around us. You see, thousands of thoughts come to us every minute. Let as many thoughts as possible be of God. We do not need to reduce the number of thoughts. Let the thoughts be of God. Let us immerse ourselves in thinking about the supreme soul. This purifies our inner space.

Throughout the day, how many times do we think of God? Maybe before a meal, or before going to bed. Otherwise, it is only when we face some problem, that we think of God! But how many times do we think of some film actress or actor? Everything in the newspapers, on television or on the internet is about something with which we are not really connected.

Out of thousands of thoughts, less than one percent is probably related to God. Everything else is related to something external. Please listen, every thought is energy and we waste more than ninety nine percent of our energy on something that is not really needed for us. If we can channel this energy to look inward, to see the source of our existence, we explore a new dimension of our *Self*.

We are ready to do anything other than think about God or our *Self*. Why? We think it is a waste of time. We always make business plans.

We do something only if we feel we will get something from it. But if we analyze our thoughts carefully, we are not thinking of anything productive. Our thoughts are simply completely illogical. Most of the time, we justify ourselves when someone asks us to think of God. We say, 'Why think of God? What will we get? I have better things to think about like work and my studies.' However these are mere justifications. If we sit and write down our thoughts, we will see that we are not thinking about work or anything productive. Our thoughts are completely illogical and random.

So why not think about God? We feel thinking about God does not give us any immediate results. But be very clear, when we are completely immersed in thoughts of God, our inner space is purified and transforms into the space of completion. Completion is God! We are preparing our *Self*. At the time of death, these thoughts will liberate us. Constantly thinking about God enriches us when our soul passes through the energy layers at the time of death.

Passing In Light

8.23 *O best of the Bhārata, I shall now explain to you the different times*
When passing away from this world, one returns or does not return.

8.24 *Those who pass away from the world during the influence of the fire god, during light,*
at an auspicious moment, during the fortnight of the waxing moon and the six months when the sun travels in the north,
And those who have realized the supreme Brahman do not return.

8.25 *The mystic who passes away from this world during the smoke, the night, the fortnight of the waning moon, or the six months when the sun travels in the south,*
Having done good deeds, goes to the cosmic layer and returns.

8.26 *According to the Vedas, there are two ways of passing from this world—one in light and one in darkness.*
When one passes in light, he does not return; but when one passes in darkness, he returns.

In these few verses, Kṛṣṇa describes at what time one can achieve Enlightenment, how one can achieve enlightenment and how to reach that state. He also talks about how people come back into this cycle of birth and death.

He says:

agnir jyotir ahaḥ śuklaḥ ṣaṇ-māsā uttarāyaṇam |
tatra prayātā gacchanti brahma brahmavido janāḥ || 8.24

Those who know the supreme Divine attain that Supreme by passing away from the world during the influence of *Agni*, the fire-god, during light or at an auspicious moment of the day, also during the fortnight of the waxing moon or during the six months that the sun travels in the north, referred to as *uttarāyaṇaṁ*.

Understand, these are not chronological calendars. If it were a chronological calendar, then at *uttarāyaṇaṁ* time, all of us can commit suicide and be done with it, that's all! But that is not what is meant here. All these things have metaphorical meanings. When He says *uttarāyaṇaṁ*, Kṛṣṇa means when our mind is totally balanced and when we are not agitated.

In the Mahābhārat war it is said that Bhīśma Pitāmaḥ waits for *uttarāyaṇaṁ* to leave the body. Don't think he waited for January. He waited until his mind settled down from the agitations and incompletions, and he establishes himself in the space of completion.

He had fallen in battle and was lying down on a bed made of arrows. He must have felt agitated. He must have felt, 'My grandson, whom I taught everything, for whom I did everything, did this to me.' He would have been disturbed. So he waited until the agitation settled down. That is what is meant by the words, 'he was waiting for *uttarāyaṇaṁ*.'

Don't think these are chronological concepts. They are psychological. If it were chronological, then do you think that the millions of people who die in those six months become enlightened? Enlightenment is not an accident! It is a pure conscious choice.

So be very clear, when He says *agnir jyotir ahaḥ śuklaḥ*, He means if we are conscious...*agnir jyotir...* means when your being is conscious... when your being is fully alive, awakened, naturally you go up. (*śuklaḥ* means going above, *kṛṣṇa* means going down).

Listen. If we live throughout life centered on the eyes, our energy leaves through the eyes. At the last moment, we open the eyes and the soul leaves. If we live throughout life centered on the tongue, eating, our mouth opens and the soul leaves through it. So if we live throughout life centered on higher consciousness, our energy leaves through the *sahasrāra*, the crown cakra, the energy center on the top of our head.

Kṛṣṇa says *brahma brahmavido janāḥ*. He means that if we have always lived with our attention focused towards higher consciousness, we will travel in that path and disappear into *Brahman*. We will become enlightened.

So be very clear, these conditions are not chronological. They are psychological. Bhīśma waited until his mind settled, until he felt completely peaceful, till he was able to forgive and complete with everybody and himself, and till he was able to reach conscious awareness. Then he entered enlightenment.

Next, Kṛṣṇa says that the person who passes away from this world during smoke, the night, the fortnight of the waning moon or those six months when the Sun travels in the south, referred to as *Dakṣināyaṇaṁ*, reaches the Moon but comes back again.

Again, this is psychological. They can't say that in these six months nobody can become enlightened. They can't say, 'During the six months of *dakṣināyaṇaṁ*, the Enlightenment gates are locked, no entry. Only at *uttarāyaṇaṁ* time, the gates are open. Come at that time.' No! They can't say, '*Dakṣināyaṇaṁ* time is non-working hours and only *uttarāyaṇaṁ* time is working hours.' There are no working hours for enlightenment. It is purely because of the conscious choice of one's being.

Kṛṣṇa says that according to the *Vedas*, there are two ways to pass from this world: one in light and one in darkness—*śukla-kṛṣṇa gatī hy ete jagataḥ śāśvate mate*. When one passes in light, he does not return, but when one passes in darkness, he comes back again—*ekayā yāty anāvṛttim ananyāvartate punaḥ* (8.26).

What does Kṛṣṇa mean by light and darkness, *śukla-kṛṣṇa*? They refer to the levels of consciousness one has reached. If a person leaves the body without knowing what drove him all along—his *saṁskāras*, his desires, fears, guilt, etc., which we call root thought patterns—then this ignorance is what He refers to as darkness.

If you look inside, the reason for your low inner space, powerless inner space will be some root thought pattern. Break that! Reclaim your freedom! Declare your freedom! Raise your inner space to the peak joy, fulfillment, and excitement.

Please understand, when Śwetaketu, a young seeker mentioned in *Upaniṣads*, was initiated by his Guru, his Guru said only nine times—'*Tat Tvam Asi! Tat Tvam Asi! Tat Tvam Asi*!' (thou are that), and Śwetaketu became enlightened. Why then, even if you listen to '*Tat Tvam Asi*' nine-thousand times, you don't become enlightened?

Carry the right inner space! On the rock, seed cannot sprout as a tree. In the right fertile ground only, the seed can become tree. In the right inner space only, the teachings can become reality. Right inner space means where all the root thought patterns of suffering are destroyed. Listen! All root thought patterns are destroyed where your inner space is fertile for experiencing the higher ideals and ideas.

When we become aware of these root thought patterns and are free from them, we leave the body and become liberated. This is what He means by light. He says that when this happens, the being does not return to the body.

Be Fixed In Devotion

8.27 *O Pārtha (son of Pritha), the devotees who know*
these different paths are never bewildered.
O Arjuna, be always fixed in devotion.

8.28 *A Yogī, realizing the path of devotional service,*
transcends the results derived from studying the Vedas,
performing austerities and sacrifices, giving charity or pursuing
pious and result-based activities.
At the end he reaches the Supreme and Primal Abode.

In the last few verses Kṛṣṇa summarizes the essence of the whole chapter. He says, 'O Pārtha, the devotees who know these different paths are never bewildered. Therefore O Arjuna, be always fixed in devotion.'

naite sṛtī pārtha jānan yogi muhyati kaścana |
tasmāt sarveṣu kāleṣu yoga-yukto bhavārjuna || 8.27

He means that a person who understands the different paths that a spirit can take while leaving the body will always be prepared for death. He immerses himself in devotion throughout his life so that he becomes liberated. Kṛṣṇa first gives Arjuna an intellectual understanding of the whole death process. He clearly tells him that the last thought while leaving the body governs the path that the spirit chooses when entering the next body.

Again and again He emphasizes that this thought cannot be divine unless we spend our entire lives in devotional service. When I say devotional service, devotion is more important than service. I tell people, never give money in charity because some priest told you that it is a good thing. Never follow these rules blindly. I do not say, 'Don't do charity work.' I am only saying, 'Let it just be a natural expression of yourself, not with any expectation.'

We have a head to think with and a heart to feel with. We do not need to refer to society every time to decide what to do and what not to do. Another thing, do not work in the name of 'devotional service' to please someone else or society. If you expect something in return, then be very clear, it is not devotional service. If it springs purely out of devotion, the act itself should be the reward.

I tell people, every day for half an hour, just for half an hour, work without expecting anything in return. It could be anything. Without any calculations, immerse yourself in some work for half an hour. You will suddenly see a new space open up inside you. When you work without expecting anything in return, just for the joy of doing it, you will see how liberating it is. Gradually, when this becomes ingrained in you, you will be enriched and enjoy whatever you do much more. You will no more bother about who thinks what about you.

Kṛṣṇa says, 'Performing austerities and sacrifices, giving charity or pursuing pious result-based activities will take a person to the Supreme abode.'

While doing each of these activities, it is the attitude that matters most, not the action itself. I have seen people give money to temple priests out of fear and greed. They are told that if they don't give money, the gods will be angry. Or if they give money, their family will be protected. The attitude behind these actions is what counts. Kṛṣṇa says, if one engages in activities with devotion, then He will be there at the time of one's death.

He has given intellectual knowledge until now. In the following chapters, He gives deeper level techniques to experience this truth, to experience completion by removing root thought patterns, by removing bio-memories.

Let us pray to that Ultimate Energy, *Parabrahma* Kṛṣṇa, to give us intelligence and the experience of thoughtless awareness, witnessing consciousness, *ātma jñāna*, the eternal bliss, *Nityānanda*.

Thank you.

*Thus ends the eighth chapter named **Akṣarabrahma Yogaḥ**, 'The Yoga Of Imperishable Brahma' of the **Bhagavad Gītā Upaniṣad, Brahmavidyā Yogaśātra**, the scripture of yoga dealing with the science of the Absolute in the form of **Śrī Kṛṣṇārjuna saṃvād**, dialogue between Śrī Kṛṣṇa and Arjuna.*

CHAPTER

9

Rājavidyā Rājaguhya Yogaḥ

Secret Of All Secrets

The whole universe is intelligence. It responds to our thoughts. KṚṢṆA transmits the king of all knowledge and all secrets, which is eternal, easy, and joyfully done. To the one who is non-envious and trusts Him, KṚṢṆA promises yoga (success) and kṣema (protection).

Secret Of All Secrets

We are now at the halfway mark of the Bhagavad Gītā. Arjuna started in total confusion and dilemma. His questions were varied and repetitive. It was as if he did not listen to what Kṛṣṇa told him. As I said, questions arise from inner violence. They arise from the ego to prove one's correctness.

These questions gradually transform into doubts. Doubts are essential for any seeker. Doubt and faith are two sides of the same coin. Without doubt, we cannot develop faith. Blind faith will not help the seeker. It is just based upon root thought patterns and will collapse under pressure. Real faith develops in the seeker when he sincerely questions spiritual truths. Raising sincere doubts before an Enlightened Master actually does a lot to integrate a person and strengthen his faith.

Kṛṣṇa sees the change that is happening within Arjuna. He feels Arjuna's inner violence and conflict is clearing up and that his individual consciousness is opening to the space of completion. The Master is ready to change gears now and take the dialogue to the next level that is needed to address this change in inner space.

In previous chapters Kṛṣṇa explains to Arjuna how to act without attachment by renouncing the outcome of his actions to Existence. In the last chapter He enriches Arjuna with an understanding of the process of death and liberation.

Now Kṛṣṇa reveals to Arjuna the greatest of all secrets—*Rājavidyā Rājaguhya Yogaḥ*, the secret about Himself.

Eternal, Easy And Joyfully Done

9.1 *Bhagavān Kṛṣṇa says:*
Dear Arjuna, because you trust Me and you are not envious of Me;
I shall therefore impart to you this profound and
secret wisdom and experience;
This will free you of all miseries of material existence.

9.2 *This knowledge is king of all knowledge and*
the greatest secret of all secrets.
It is the purest knowledge, sacred, and
because it gives direct perception of the Self
by Self-realization, it is the perfection of religion, dharma.
It is eternal, easy, and it is very joyfully performed.

9.3 *Those who have no faith in this knowledge cannot attain Me,*
O Parantapa, conqueror of foes;
They will return to the path of birth and death
in this material world.

Kṛṣṇa assures Arjuna with these verses. He says, 'My dear Arjuna, because you are never envious of Me, I shall impart to you this most confidential knowledge and realization, knowing which, you shall be relieved of the miseries of material existence.'

śri bhagavān uvāca
idaṁ tu te guhyatamaṁ pravakṣyāmy anasūyave |
jñanaṁ vijñāna-sahitaṁ yaj jñātvā mokṣyase 'śubhāt || 9.1

Beautiful lines!

He says, 'Because you are never envious of Me.' Depending on the context, this verse can be taken to mean 'Because you are not envious of

Me' or 'Because you have trust in Me.'

We may wonder how Arjuna could be envious of Kṛṣṇa. Please listen, you don't know the ways in which the human mind works, especially since in our generation, we always think of Arjuna as being human and Kṛṣṇa as Divine. We accept Kṛṣṇa as God. However, when Kṛṣṇa was alive, when He was in the body, people did not always accept that He is Divine. In addition, Arjuna and Kṛṣṇa were friends. They were close friends, so Arjuna treated Kṛṣṇa as a human and related to Him with human emotions.

We should first understand the atmosphere, the background. Only then will we intensely understand this whole chapter as it is expressed.

The Ultimate Secret

The very idea that Arjuna might be envious of Kṛṣṇa may surprise us.

Understand, whenever the Masters were in the body, people never respected them. This problem always existed. Only after they left the body did people accept and worship them. Actually, it is easy to worship a photograph. There is no sacrifice or transformation required. However, it is never easy to worship a living being. The living person will always be questioned and envied.

There is a beautiful one-liner: During his life, the grandfather is forced to live in the family outhouse. After his death, he is brought into the house and respected as a photograph!

As long as he is alive, he lives in the outhouse. Especially in India, every village home has a front porch. When he is dead, his photo is kept inside the prayer room. When he is alive, he has no place inside the house! However, once he dies, his photograph has a respected place inside the home.

It is the same way with the enlightened Master. When a Master is alive he is never understood. He is never respected and he is never received. When he has left the body, when he is no more in physical form, it is easy to worship him.

A beautiful incident:

> A group of devotees from Śrī Caitanya Mahāprabhu's (an enlightened Master, Incarnation from East India) birthplace, Māyāpur, came to Śrī Rāmakṛṣṇa. They told him, 'Oh Master, we missed Caitanya Mahāprabhu. We could not see him. If we had that fortune, we would have become enlightened. We would have experienced devotion to Kṛṣṇa.'
>
> Rāmakṛṣṇa laughed and said, 'When Caitanya was alive, many people went to him and complained, 'Oh Caitanya! We missed Kṛṣṇa. We could not see Kṛṣṇa. If we had seen Kṛṣṇa, we could have enjoyed the devotion, the energy!'
>
> Rāmakṛṣṇa says, 'Open your eyes and see. Caitanya is here. Just as people went to Caitanya and talked about Kṛṣṇa, you come here and complain that you have missed Caitanya.'

Whenever Masters are alive, it is difficult for people to accept their divinity. However, once they leave the body, people say, 'We missed Rāmakṛṣṇa,' 'We missed Ramaṇa Maharṣi,' and so on. We complain about what we missed. We never realize what we have.

Here Kṛṣṇa says, 'Because you are never envious of Me—*pravakṣyāmy anasūyave*, I will give you the ultimate secret—*idaṁ tu te guhyatamaṁ* (9.1).'

Here, please understand, Kṛṣṇa is giving the ultimate secret, *guhyatamaṁ*. Once we know this secret, then there is no difference between the Divine and us. Here He gives us the straight, ultimate secret.

In the business world, the leader usually never gives secrets to anyone, whatever they may do, however close they may be. Corporate people maintain secrets.

Here Kṛṣṇa says, 'I am not going to maintain any secrets. I am going to open the whole thing.' He says that knowledge is free. It is up to us to use it. Now, modern day IT companies declare that knowledge is free. Yet five thousand years ago, Kṛṣṇa declared that knowledge is free.

He says, 'I am opening all the secrets—*idaṁ tu te guhyatamaṁ*.' He decides, 'I am giving you this secret because you are never envious of Me—*pravakṣyāmy anasūyave*.'

There is an important thing that people who go near the Master should know, especially people who live around the Master. By and by, these disciples, instead of trying to achieve the *state* of the Master, they try to achieve the *status* of the Master. State is different from status. The enlightened *state* of the Master should be achieved, not the *status* that His Enlightenment confers. When we work for status, we are in trouble.

> Once I went to a college for a public lecture. It was a meditation program in Tamil Nadu.
>
> One young boy questioned me, 'Why should you be respected so much? After all, you are my age.' Of course, it is true. I am barely a few years older than him. He asked, 'Why do they shower so many roses at your feet when you come?' In India, spiritual masters are usually received with flowers wherever they go.
>
> The first thing I told him was this: 'I tried my best to avoid these arrangements. However, they have done it out of devotion. Next thing, you only see the flowers that are showered now. You don't know how many austerities this body has endured. You don't know how many thorns these feet had to cross to come to these flowers.
>
> So don't be envious for the *status.* Be envious of the *state.* Try to achieve the same state in which I live. Then, not only will you be showered with flowers, you will be showered with everything. Achieve the *state*, not the *status*.'

When you see the status, you will always be caught in jealousy. If you see the state in which I live, I will become a source of inspiration for you to achieve the same state. I will be a role model. You will think, 'When he can achieve this, why not me?' I become an inspirational source for you!

I tell people that the one and only difference between an ordinary person and an enlightened being is that an ordinary man is sleeping while an Enlightened person is awakened; that's all. The Consciousness is the same.

Again and again I repeat, 'Whether you believe it or not, accept it or not, realize it or not, you are God. You are Divine. You have two choices. You can either sleep as long as you want without experiencing this truth, or you can make the conscious choice to experience your Enlightenment, your Completion. But the truth is, '*You are That.*'

Here, Kṛṣṇa says, 'Because you never try to achieve My status, I am trying to give you My state.' The person who never tries to achieve the *status* of the Master achieves the *state* of the Master. First, *state* comes; then *status* follows. If we try to create the *status*, the *state* will never be achieved.

Rāmakṛṣṇa says, 'First God, then the world.' The world is like a shadow. Status is like a shadow. Try your best to run after the shadow. Can you catch it? No. If we run after it, we can never grab it no matter how much we chase it. However, if we walk on the path, it simply follows. The outer world is like a shadow. Go towards the state, status will follow you.

Here Kṛṣṇa says, 'Because you are never jealous, never envious of My status and Me, I give you the ultimate secret of this state.' And I tell you, this *is* the ultimate secret. Really, this is the ultimate secret. And He says, 'Knowing which, you shall be relieved of the miseries of material existence—*yaj jñātvā mokṣyase aśubhāt* (9.1).'

What are the miseries of material existence? Whether we have something or not, it is misery. If we don't have, then the misery is, 'I don't have.' If we have, then we have the misery, 'I must protect it.'

Rājavidyā, King of All Knowledge

Yoga means achieving. *Kṣema* means protecting. Both are miseries.

Whether we have or not, it is misery.

Kṛṣṇa says that the miseries of having wealth and not having wealth, both miseries that are caused by material existence disappear by knowing this secret. And I tell you honestly this is the ultimate secret that needs to be understood. Knowledge of this secret liberates you.

He says, 'This knowledge is the king of all knowledge. The greatest secret of all secrets, it is the purest knowledge and because it gives direct perception of the Self by realization, it is the perfection of religion. It is everlasting and it is joyfully performed.'

rājavidyā rājaguhyaṁ pavitram idam uttamam |
pratyakṣāvagamaṁ dharmyaṁ su-sukhaṁ kartum avyayam || 9.2

See, religion or a spiritual path should have three characteristics. First, it should clearly describe the goal of life. Next, it should clearly give you the path to achieve the goal. Third, it should make you happy to travel in that path. The path itself should be joyful, blissful.

A small story:

> One herbal doctor's billboard said he could cure all diseases that we know the names of, as well as all diseases that we don't know the names of. He put up a billboard with all these claims. One person came with a disease.
>
> The doctor asked, 'What is your disease?'
>
> This person said, 'I don't know the name. Please diagnose it yourself.'
>
> The doctor tried his best to diagnose. However, he was unable to determine the disease. But he had put up the big advertisement, so he had to cure. There was no other way. So he gave some medicine. The medicine was: 'Swallow a crowbar without it touching your teeth and drink three liters of water. You will be cured!'

What kind of medicine is this? The medicine clearly shows that the person will not be cured! In the same way, our solution or the path we are shown should not be impractical. If it is impractical, naturally, we cannot practice.

There was once a yogi in the Himalayas. When disciples came to him, he gave a technique: 'Hold your nose for two hours and sit.' Can anybody sit like that? He said, 'If you do that, you will become Enlightened.' Who can travel that path? Nobody can travel it. The path must not be complicated. It must be simple.

So here, Kṛṣṇa says, 'It is eternal—*avyayam*', meaning that the result that we achieve is everlasting. He uses all the advertising terms! And it is joyfully performed—*su-sukhaṁ kartum*. It is easy. We don't need to struggle or suffer for it. It is the deepest secret. All we need to do is to realize the secret. Understand the secret.

Why is it a secret? If it is going to enrich so much then why is it a secret? Why not let the whole world use it?

Please listen! The ultimate secret, the ultimate knowledge is not for the masses. Masses always get stuck with small things and shallow entertainment. That is why, if we run a cinema theatre, you can see how such a big crowd gathers! Only a few hundred people are here today because we built only a temple. Temples are for the chosen few, not for all. We need intelligence to come to a temple. We need intelligence to enter spirituality. It is not for everyone.

Yesterday one lady asked, '*Swamiji*, my husband does not accept or understand the path I am traveling. Coming to this program is important to me. But, it is difficult for my husband to come to terms with it. Do you have a suggestion to help bridge this gap?'

Honestly, the answer is that it cannot be done. It only has to happen on its own from within the person.' I can say one thing: Don't give up on people! Listen. If you have to learn just one thing from me, learn this one thing. I never give up on people. Whether you give up on me or not, I don't care. I will not give up on you! Understand, I am a person who has no individual family. But thousands see me as their family member! Even on

Facebook, I get so many family requests!

Don't give up on people based on their past record. Earlier your spouse may not have listened to you, because you yourself may not have been integrated and authentic to your spiritual path. Now, bring that integrity and authenticity. And don't give up on people! Enrich people, enrich people and enrich people. If you give up on people, you will give up on yourself. You will lose your confidence.

Not giving up on people is life! People are life. If you give up on them, you are giving up on life. Whenever you give up on people, you commit partial suicide. Enrich him with some intelligence about life. You cannot directly give spirituality. Please don't ask him to meditate or come to the temple. Listen, authentically listen to him and don't give up on him. That's all. Nothing else can be done.

Only by intelligence can a man come to spirituality. That is why this is preserved as a secret. If this spiritual intelligence is given to all, without bothering about the qualifications of the receiver, the person who receives will harm himself and others also.

First, he harms himself if he has not completely understood it. For example, what will a criminal do if he is told, 'You are God?' He will think, 'I am God. So let me do whatever I want. I don't have to bother.' He misuses the knowledge. He abuses it. That is why I say he harms himself.

A person who experiences God radiates compassion. He radiates simplicity. He radiates innocence. Divine qualities express through him. He never hurts anybody. We see a beautiful innocent shine in him and such simplicity. He never hurts anybody. He never harms anybody.

If we are relaxed, blissful, in a good mood, and our employee or co-worker makes a mistake, do we shout at him? No. We will say, 'Alright, leave it. What can be done?' However, if we are in a bad mood, an irritable mood, nobody needs to make any mistake. We shout at everyone for no reason. We are waiting to rant and rave. We are waiting to shout.

Our mood, our inner space decides our action. If we are in the space of completion and blissful, we never do anything wrong. If we are in incompletion with a hellish mood, we always make mistakes. Please don't think people go to hell after making mistakes. No! We make mistakes because we are in hell. We do the right action because we are blissful. Someone who experiences that he is God never makes a mistake and never harms anybody. If this knowledge is given to all, including those who don't have the maturity, naturally they harm themselves and they harm others. They say, 'I am God. Come here. I will do whatever I want.' That is why this knowledge is kept as a secret.

That is why He says, 'this king of secrets is the king of knowledge—*rājavidyā rājaguhyaṁ*.' Kṛṣṇa reveals the secret only to qualified people.

In this chapter Kṛṣṇa says, 'I am not even God; I am something more than God. Whatever you think of as God rests in Me. All created beings rest in Me.' He declares, 'I am God.'

We need to see whether a person is mature enough or not to receive the truth before we share it. Here, Kṛṣṇa says it is a secret, because it can be delivered only to a person qualified to receive it. You see, in the first two to three chapters, He speaks about *śāstra*, intellectual knowledge that can be given to anybody. However, these chapters are intimate secrets, delivered only from a Master to a disciple, only to a disciple who is qualified, who is really interested to receive the knowledge and who really wants the knowledge.

> One person asked me, '*Swamiji*, please teach me about God. Give me Enlightenment.'
>
> I told him, 'See, it is time for prasād (food offered to God and eaten by devotees with His blessings). Please go and take prasād in the ashram. I will talk to you in the evening session.'
>
> He immediately said, 'No *Swamiji!* I must leave by the next bus. I have half an hour left. In this half an hour please tell me about God.'

In half an hour what can I tell him? What can a person understand in half an hour? Naturally, God cannot be given out like instant coffee!

Coffee can be instant, but not God! We cannot have God instantly. We need to realize God; we need a little patience and intensity. The more we hurry, the more we will delay. Please understand that speed is not the technique of the inner world. In the inner world, the more we hurry, the more we delay. The hurrying, the tension, the stress, postpones the process, postpones the experience. It will not let us relax.

That is why Kṛṣṇa says that these secrets can be told only to a person who is really integrated and interested, who is really intimate, and who really desires to know.

Beautiful words!

All our scriptures are called Upaniṣad. Even Gītā is called Upaniṣad—*Śrimad Bhagavad Gītāsu Upaniṣatsu...*' The word *Upaniṣad* literally means 'sitting down near someone'. It refers to the teaching style of a traditional Vedic school or gurukul of ancient India where students sat by their Master to learn. Knowledge was transmitted in close groups in a trusted environment. It was knowledge not merely through intellect as verbal communication. It was a communion of beings wherein the experience of one was experienced by the other.

JÑĀNA YAGÑA-PATH TO SELF-REALIZATION

In our home we keep everything prepared for our outwardly life. Whatever we need is there: a bed for sleeping, the kitchen for cooking, a dining table for sitting and eating. Then we also collect luxurious things like jewelry. Our jewelry changes according to the color of our sari (traditional clothing of Indian women). Sometimes, the shoes also change! We have everything to match each other. Whatever we need for the outwardly life and comforts, we collect and store.

However, we forget an important fact. In the same way that we collect things for outward Existence, for the outer space, we need to collect knowledge for our inner space: life solutions, solutions for our inner space. If we feel depressed or low, if we face some adverse situation, how are we to react? How are we to handle it? We need this knowledge to handle our inner space.

Like collecting things for the outwardly life, we need to collect life solutions for a happy, blissful life. Collecting life solutions is what Kṛṣṇa calls *jñāna yajña*. What is *nitya* (eternal) and what is *anitya* (temporary)? What is *satya* (truth) and what is *asatya* (falsehood)? Acquiring all this understanding is *jñāna yajña*.

If I literally translate this word *jñāna*, it refers to higher knowledge or wisdom and *yajña* refers to the purification process that leads to this higher knowledge. What Kṛṣṇa means through *jñāna yajña* is the spiritual path that leads one to Self-realization. It is the path that creates awareness in us about our Divinity. This realization of the deepest truths about oneself happens in many cases through a combination of two things: understanding about similar spiritual experiences by observing others and our own efforts to contemplate upon these experiences so that they are reproduced within.

Please focus on the life solutions offered by great Enlightened Masters while gathering knowledge. I request that people to read books that enrich you with life solutions as experienced by Enlightened beings, for at least for half an hour every day: books of Śrī Rāmakṛṣṇa, Vivekananda, etc. We have the books like 'Guaranteed Solutions', 'Living Enlightenment', based on my teachings in my meditation programs and daily morning satsangs, and over ten-thousand hours of life solutions available on my YouTube channel. Spend at least half an hour every day reading, watching truths based on the teachings of Enlightened Masters.

If we can't spend half an hour reading, then listen to audio CDs in the car. In the USA and even in Indian cities, we spend at least one hour a day driving. Don't waste that hour. Always listen to some audio that gives life solutions in the car.

It is not that it must be my *satsangs* (discourses). Read, watch or listen to anything that enriches you into leading a better, complete life. However, let it come from an Enlightened Source, which experientially gives solutions for your life. Let that hour become your *jñana yajña*, your spiritual journey. Add more and more life solutions into your inner space.

I tell you one thing: A life solution may suddenly come up from your inner consciousness at the time of need and can reduce the depth of depression you experience. That is why I am telling you to make driving your *jñana yajña*. Whether you understand everything or not, listen, listen and listen! Let listening become your habit. Automatically those life solutions, those powerful words, uttered directly from the enlightened consciousness, stay in your inner space. You will be surprised how they will come as knowledge weapons to your aid when you need them!

If we don't do that, when we drive we will think about our worries. If we don't spend time finding life solutions, we spend time finding problems. Even if we don't have problems, we will create problems! Whether we have problems or not, we worry. Better not to allow the mind to worry and create incompletions. Listen to something that enriches with life solutions. Let that hour become *jñana yajña* in our lives.

Kṛṣṇa says that doing *jñana yajña* is one step. Understanding that the whole Cosmos is energy is one step. If we understand that whatever exists *is* energy, automatically, fear will be taken away from our being.

The next question is, 'How can we say that whatever exists is energy, *Swamiji*? How can we say whatever exists is God? That is impossible. All these things are good to listen to, but are not practical to practice!' Our mind never accepts that these things can be practiced and experienced.

So Kṛṣṇa continues; He goes on and comes out with the basic secrets.

WHO CAN KNOW THE ULTIMATE SECRET

Here Kṛṣṇa gives the qualification of people who can attain Him. He clearly describes the people who can reach Him. When I say *'Him'*, it is not the form named Kṛṣṇa that I speak about. When I say Nithyānanda, I do not mean this six-foot Nithyānanda. I mean the Universal energy, the cosmic energy called *Nityānanda*—eternal bliss.

In the first two verses He says, 'It is a great truth that I am going to tell and it is a secret that I am revealing to you.' Now He lets Arjuna know what kind of people can know the secret. He says people who do not have *śraddha*, faith in *dharma* or His teachings go back to the path of rebirth without Enlightenment, without attaining Him. He says the qualification required is to have faith in His teachings. Only those people can come out of the vicious cycle of birth and death.

You see, having authentic faith, *śraddha* is one of the most important things, especially in the spiritual path. Whenever an Enlightened Master speaks, every word he utters is the Absolute Truth. That is why I always add the words, '*Whether you believe it or not, accept it or not, understand it or not*', whenever I talk about some Truth. When I say we are part of the same Consciousness, when I say that we are all *one*, and *each one is infinitely powerful*, our mind cannot accept it because it tries to find a logical solution, an intellectual answer to everything. So you must have *śraddha*, faith in me to understand what I speak.

Śraddha, Authentic Faith in Master

There are three possible levels in which you can put faith in what a Master says.

With the first level or group, you can have doubt. That is obvious. You doubt what I say, what an enlightened Master says, because you can't comprehend what I say. See, you can have doubts. In fact, you *should* have doubts, only then you question what I say. However, you should look-in to find out if those doubts are genuine. If they arise out of ego, then it is your mind playing a game. Your mind creates a wall between *you* and *Me*. As long as your doubts are genuine, as long as you question to know the Truth out of curiosity, it is fine. In my discourses, I encourage people to ask questions and to raise doubts. Only then can you fully internalize.

The second group or level is when you believe whatever I say. This is dangerous. Believing whatever I say without intranalyzing, cognizing, and experiencing it for yourself is dangerous. When I say that '*you are God*', if you just straightaway believe me it is dangerous, because you have not experienced it. If someone questions you on your belief, you will be unable to stand by it. You will stammer and stumble and do yourself harm.

I know lots of people who call themselves my devotees. When I ask whether they watch the daily satsang, meditate, do completion and enrich, they stammer, 'No *Swamiji.* There is so much work. There is no time.' Then they say, 'But I pray to you everyday, *Swamiji.* I offer fresh flowers and incense sticks.' They talk as if they do me a big favor. They are believers. Their foundation is weak. Only when they meditate and do completions, with integrity and authenticity, will they experience what I speak.

The third approach is trust. When you trust me, you accept what I say. You still have doubts. However, you are willing to break that wall and try to see and experience what I am saying. You build your foundation and you make it strong because you trust me. This is the way authentic faith, *śraddha* should develop. Faith should arise from a strong foundation of integrity and authenticity. First you trust me, then you try exploring the truths I share and when you have a glimpse of the truth, you believe me with a stronger foundation. Now nobody can shake you because you have developed a strong base. You have done the work yourself.

Here, Kṛṣṇa talks about faith in *dharma*, His teaching. You see, we are different from animals because we can have faith in *dharma*, meaning the higher levels of consciousness. Without *dharma*, we are the same as any animal. It is completely controlled by instincts. It does not make a decision consciously, based on right or wrong. However, a human being has one extra power. He has free will to follow *dharma,* to live with integrity, authenticity, responsibility, and enriching. He has free will to do or not do, to accept or not accept.

When Kṛṣṇa says *dharma,* He means anything that leads us to a higher level of Consciousness. Man without consciousness is an animal, a *dānava.* In Hindu epics there are two types of people, *mānava* and *dānava*, humans and non-humans. The first category has faith in *dharma* and a higher level of consciousness. *Dānava* are nothing but animals. They do not have faith in any *dharma*, so their level of consciousness is low.

Listen. The only difference between man and an animal is the seed of Consciousness implanted in us. We must water this seed and allow it to germinate. We must nurture this sapling to flower into a fully-grown tree. We need authentic faith, *śraddha* in *dharma* for this tree of Consciousness to happen in us.

Kṛṣṇa clearly says that if we do not have faith in *dharma*, we go back to the cycle of birth and death. He gives it straight.

aśraddadhānāḥ puruṣā dharmasyāsya parantapa /
aprāpya māṁ nivartante mṛtyu-saṁsāra-vartmani // 9.3

He says we must allow consciousness to flower in us and in order to do that we must have faith in *dharma*. When our faith is complete, when we have internalized His *dharma*, with integrity and authenticity, in everything that we do, our consciousness automatically blossoms. When we reach that state of consciousness, we merge with Universal consciousness and then we are free from the cycle of birth and death.

So, Kṛṣṇa gives a technique. He says, 'Have *śraddha*, faith in *dharma* and it will lead you to the Ultimate.'

All Rest In Me

9.4 *By Me, the entire Universe is pervaded in My formless form. All beings are based in Me, but I am not in them.*

9.5 *And yet everything that is created does not rest in Me. Look at My mystic powers! Although, I am the Creator and Sustainer of all living entities, I do not depend the Cosmic manifestation; for My Self is the very source of all creation.*

9.6 *As the mighty wind, blowing everywhere, always rests in eternal space, All beings rest in Me.*

9.7 *O Kaunteya (son of Kuntī), at the end of every age all beings merge into Me, At the beginning of every new Age I create them again.*

9.8 *The whole Cosmic order is under Me and My material nature creates the beings again and again, and it is controlled by My material nature.*

It is time to reveal the secrets.

Śrī Kṛṣṇa starts:

mayā tatam idaṁ sarvaṁ jagad avyaktamūrtinā |
matsthāni sarva bhūtāni na cāhaṁ teṣvavasthitaḥ || 9.4

'By Me, in my formless form, this entire Universe is pervaded. All beings are in Me, but I am not in them.'

Before entering further into this verse, the meaning of the verse should be understood.

I want to tell you about my meeting with Charles Townes, a Nobel Laureate and a great scientist. He discovered some secrets related to Laser and Maser.

I asked him, 'How did you discover? How did this truth happen in your being?'

He answered, '*Swamiji*, to tell you honestly, I was relaxing in a park in Washington. It was early morning about six a.m. I was supposed to give a lecture on this subject to a group that day at nine a.m. I tried my best to recollect everything. I was completely frustrated because I could not achieve much. Suddenly like a revelation, as an intuition, the conclusion was revealed to me! The whole truth came into my consciousness. I discovered it! I immediately penned down what I got.'

And he says, 'I then realized I had a difficulty: I knew the conclusion. I knew the truth, however, I didn't know the logical steps to arrive at that conclusion! I would not be able to present it unless I knew the steps. So after that, I needed to think and develop the logical steps. Only then could I present it to others. Like an intuition, suddenly, it had been revealed to me.'

Actually, even this experience is not a big thing. The truth, the important thing is this: I asked Charles Townes, 'How did you feel when it happened to you, when the revelation happened to you?' Because what he experienced was intuition just as our sages experienced.

He said, '*Swamiji*, I don't know how to exactly express; however one thing is certain: from that moment onwards, I know for sure that the whole Universe is intelligence!'

This is the truth! The whole Universe is pure intelligence. The whole Universe is not dead matter. The Universe is not an accident. It can respond to our thoughts. Please understand, the whole Universe, planet Earth, air, oceans, rivers, earth, fire, or the space, sun, moon, this whole Universe, is intelligence. It can reciprocate. It can respond. It can react to our thoughts.

This is an important, basic understanding. The moment we understand that we are this energy that is intelligence, the moment we are aware that we are inside the energy that is intelligence, at that moment, we immediately settle into a deep relaxation. The moment we experience, we understand: we are under the guidance of an intelligent energy. We are taken care of by an intelligent energy, we are part of the Cosmic intelligence and we don't need to struggle or stress ourselves. We don't need to torture ourselves with insecurity problems, unnecessary worries.

Actually, all our problems, tensions and stresses arise because we think we do everything. We think the Universe runs because of us. Understand that the Universe runs in spite of us! We should understand that the Universe is intelligent and it responds to our thoughts. If we trust the Universe, we experience how light we are. We can unload all our troubles including the extra responsibility of thinking that we do everything.

This does not mean that we just sit and relax and say, 'Okay, the Universe is intelligence. It will take care of everything.' This is laziness and escapism. We must still work; however we can enjoy the process. You see, we think of the result all the time. Our thoughts arise out of fear or greed: fear of whether we will get the results or greed of wanting more and more. However, we never enjoy the process of doing that work. When we enjoy the process and trust the Universal intelligence, thoughts arising out of fear and greed will disappear. We will enjoy the process of doing and we will let the Universe take care of the results. Kṛṣṇa says elsewhere, 'You do what you have to. Do it, but surrender the results to Me.' When He says 'Me', He refers to the Universal consciousness or intelligence.

This is what Kṛṣṇa means in the next verse when He says that the beings do not depend on Him, nor does He depend on them. Of course, it is clear that the Universe does not depend upon us; yet how can He say that we, the beings created and sustained by the Universe, do not depend upon it? What He means is this: it is not a passive and lazy dependence of letting everything happen while we sit idle. It is an active understanding. One does what one must do as part of his life process but without attachment and ownership.

One way or the other, we are in this Universe. Because the Universe is intelligence, it responds to our thoughts. It makes things happen. Since we are part of this Universe, just flow with the energy of the Universe. Do not resist it. If this understanding penetrates our life, it is enough!

If we know the Universe is intelligence, we never question how life unfolds. We don't say, 'I am moral. But I see people who don't live morally living luxuriously, happily. Yet I always suffer!' We never have these frustrations, these incompletions with others and with life, because we know the Cosmic intelligence will take care ultimately. Whoever is immoral or whoever goes around and disturbs others will naturally face the consequences, because intelligence takes care. In the same way, if we are integrated and authentic, living a spiritual life, we will live a beautiful life. We are rewarded because the whole Universe is run by an intelligence that responds to this.

Don't think the Cosmos is just matter. If we think the Cosmos is matter, we are materialistic. If we understand that the Cosmos is intelligence, we are spiritual, that's all. The only difference between the materialistic and spiritual person is that the materialist thinks the whole thing is material: 'Let me acquire more and more material things.' The spiritual person understands that the whole thing is spirit, energy. If we understand that the whole thing is spirit, energy, intelligence, then a tremendous relaxation and bliss consciousness happens to us.

Please understand, bliss is not just a mood. Bliss is our very Consciousness. If it comes and goes as a mood, we are only having one or two experiences. One devotee asked, 'Bliss comes and goes, what to do?' I explained, 'You are having initial glimpses of bliss. Through your mind, you are trying to touch the bliss. Nothing needs to be done; just relax, that's all.' Once we understand this secret, a deep relaxation happens to us. In such a deep relaxation, we straighaway experience bliss consciousness. Once we experience Bliss Consciousness, it is everlasting. The bliss mood comes and stays. Bliss Consciousness is everlasting.

Kṛṣṇa declares, 'By My formless form, this entire Universe is pervaded. All beings are in Me—*mayā tatam idaṁ sarvaṁ jagad avyaktamūrtinā.'* He speaks of Cosmic intelligence.

Be very clear, such a big Universe is moving and happening. All the planets move around the sun. Each planet has its own moons. There are so many suns, moons and planets. Yet, each one travels in its route properly. No traffic police! Accidents are rare. Unless intelligence runs the whole thing, do you think things can happen so beautifully? And even on this planet Earth, see how the whole thing is beautiful! The whole thing happens in an order, in a complete way. Only wherever human beings live, there is chaos! Except human beings, nobody creates chaos. Even in chaos, the Divine creates order.

Understand, the whole Universe is intelligence and it operates out of intelligence. This intelligence responds to our thoughts and we can relate with this intelligence. When we internalize this truth, then we naturally experience a deep peace. Rest, a real, ultimate rest and confidence to live, happens within us.

As long as we think the world is matter or material, there is no use living. Nothing matters. Even if we become the president of one country, other countries will not be under our control. So naturally, we can never achieve the whole matter. As long as we believe the world is material, we create more and more violence because we live materially. Materially means that we must snatch from others. One way or another; violence will exist. Only a person who experiences, who understands that the whole thing is energy, intelligence, only he can relax.

Let me repeat the next verse.

yathākāśasthito nityaṁ vāyuḥ sarvatrago mahān /
tathā sarvāṇi bhūtāni matsthānīty upadhāraya // 9.6

He says, 'Understand that as the mighty wind blowing everywhere rests in the sky, all created beings rest in Me.'

Please understand this principle: He says, 'Just as the wind rests in the sky energy.' Please understand how the Earth is energy. We know earth is Energy. Take a stone. If a stone is thrown at us or if we throw a stone, we know the energy behind that stone. Next, consider water. We know the energy of water. Whoever knows about the waters that devastated New Orleans knows the energy of water! Or, if it floods, we know what water does; water is energy, we can understand that. Next is *agni*, fire. All of us know the power of fire. Next, air: storms, hurricanes, and tornados. We know the power of air.

In the same way, *ākāśa* (space or ether) is also energy. We do not know the power of *ākāśa* because it does not directly create impacts and effects in our lives. *Ākāśa* is disturbed by our collective negative thoughts, collective poison. The collective energy of the Universe is *ākāśa*.

When the earth element is disturbed or poisoned, only one person suffers. For example, if our food is poisoned, we alone suffer, that's all. If water is poisoned, the whole region suffers. Whoever uses the water supply, suffer. If whatever creates fire in us is corrupted, a big group suffers. We can use medicines as an example for fire because medicines keep the fire inside us alive. If medicines are corrupted, people who take the medicines suffer. If chemicals pollute the air, the whole country suffers. If air is corrupted, if the air is polluted, the whole society suffers. But if space, *ākāśa*, is polluted, the whole world suffers.

Corruption at higher levels of energy creates suffering for more and more people. The higher the level of energy that is corrupted, the number of people suffering is more. Our thoughts corrupt space. Space is energy.

Because ether or space is so subtle and so sensitive, we cannot feel the happenings in the space of ether. We feel the happenings in the other four spaces: earth, water, fire and air, so because of that we can understand the happenings in them. However, we fail to understand that space, ether, is also energy, a power. It is more subtle and more powerful because the subtler it becomes, the more powerful and energetic it becomes.

Levels of Space, Ākāśa

There are three levels of space.

The first level is when we are limited to what is inside this skin. *This is Ghaṭākāśa,* what is contained within our body. We limit our whole understanding of everything around us to this body. We become conscious of how this body should look, how it should be maintained. We think we are only this body and nothing else. This is the lowest level.

The next level is *Cidākāśa*. This space refers to what our mind perceives as the world. Let's say we are sitting here but our mind is in Los Angeles. Then that (Los Angeles) becomes our *cidākāśa*, the space perceived by our mind. The next moment our mind shifts to Bangalore. Then that becomes our *cidākāśa*. The space that our mind operates in is *cidākāśa*.

The third and final level is *Mahākāśa*. The whole Cosmos, everything that is outside and that is inside forms *mahākāśa*. This is the ultimate level. This is the level where everything that we see as different becomes *One*.

Please clearly understand these three spaces. Our body, everything that is inside this skin is *ghaṭākāśa*. Next, the space governed by our mind, by our thoughts, is *cidākāśa*. Finally, the whole Universe, the whole cosmos, forms *mahākāśa*.

Now, if something happens inside our body, we immediately feel it. If we are hurt, we clearly see the blood flow. We see a rash or a cut. We clearly see and feel any disturbance or event in *ghaṭākāśa* at a gross level.

When we go to the next level, *cidākāśa,* events that disturb or change this space are subtle. Our thoughts affect *cidākāśa*. Listen! Whether we believe it or not, our thoughts have a huge effect on the external world. Whatever thought comes, don't think that it simply comes and goes. Every thought is energy. It manifests as something in the external world. The problem is that we are unaware of the effect. The effect is subtle so our mind cannot see that what happens is because of those thoughts we entertained.

Our mind thinks something. It affects this *cidākāśa,* our inner space. These changes are projected into the external world, yet our mind is unable to recognize that all it sees is because of *itself.*

So, as we advance one level higher, the changes become more subtle but the effect is more powerful. In *ghaṭākāśa,* the effect is limited to our body. In *cidākāśa,* our thoughts affect the space around us. The effect is seen in a bigger space. The effect is more widespread.

Now the highest level is *mahākāśa.* This level is subtler than *cidākāśa.* Any change here affects the whole Universe. When something happens in this space, the whole Universe responds. When we enter this space, we realize the ultimate Truth. We merge with everything, with the whole Cosmos.

The fifth element, *ether,* is like *mahākāśa.* Actually they are the same. Ether is everywhere. Mahākāśa pervades everything. We are just not aware of it. This space takes any shape and any form. Even in vaccum, it is there. Understand this: If water is compressed by a compressor, it becomes energy. If air is compressed by a compressor, it can even move a train; it becomes energy. In the same way, if ether is compressed in a particular space, in a particular shape, again that becomes energy.

An iron piece; if it is a square piece, it is different. If it is an 'I' shape, it is totally different and can be used for a different purpose. The same iron, one kilogram of iron, if it is a rectangular bar, the effect or power is totally different. Do you understand? It is a subtle concept, but if we understand, we realize the great gift of the great research that our *Vedic* Masters accomplished. They did a great enriching sacrifice by doing all this research and enriching us selflessly with all this wisdom.

Like earth, ether, *ākāśa* can be used to create the space we want. It can be used in different forms and shapes. Certain techniques allow us to use the ether energy at its best, to its maximum level. When ether is put in one particular size – inside that room or inside that space—whoever lives there will be controlled by that ether and the ether is in turn controlled by them. Their thoughts affect the ether and the ether affects their thoughts.

This science of using the energy of space or ether is the basis of *Vāstu Śastra*, an ancient Vedic science related to the science of architecture. We can live in harmony with the Universal energy by constructing dwellings in a manner that fits in with the spatial energy of the Universe. *Vāstu Śastra* lays down details for where various activity spaces should be located in a dwelling, as well as the direction. It tells where the kitchen should be located in a house, where fire resides, and so on.

Kṛṣṇa says, 'How the wind rests in the space, in the same way the Universe rests in Me, *tathā sarvāṇi bhūtāni matsthānīty upadhāraya.'* Don't think space is emptiness. It is energy. Just because we are not able to see, we can't say it is emptiness. It is energy. Just as the air rests in the space, our being, the whole Universe including our being, we all rest in the Divine. Kṛṣṇa says, 'All beings rest in Me, *mat-sthānī*.'

Can you see why Kṛṣṇa calls all that He is speaking of a secret? He is being very careful as to whom He is telling this secret knowledge. He wants to tell all this to a qualified person, Arjuna, who is both a friend and a disciple. He knows now that Arjuna is ready to take in this secret.

Actually, till this point Kṛṣṇa has slowly prepared Arjuna. Now He knows Arjuna is ready to take in some truths, some secrets of this Universe. If Kṛṣṇa had told these strong truths in the beginning of the Gītā, Arjuna would not have understood.

In these two verses, Kṛṣṇa talks about the creation and destruction of the Universe. He makes bold statements. Only an Incarnation can make such bold statements because he speaks from experience. Some people do not agree with what I say. They think their own understandings are correct. When they tell me, '*Swamiji*, how can you say that? In so-and-so book, it is written like this,' I laugh and let it pass. First of all, they did not understand what exactly was written in those scriptures and then they tell me I am wrong. What can be done? Even if I argue, they won't listen. All the old people are dangerous!

In the first verse Kṛṣṇa says, 'The whole material manifestation enters into Him when the Universe is destroyed and He projects it again to create the Universe.' Understand that when Kṛṣṇa says, 'The Universe enters Me,' He refers to the Cosmic Kṛṣṇa, the Cosmic consciousness, and not the Kṛṣṇa we see in human form. Let us understand this very deeply.

For a long time, the Big Bang theory was used to explain the creation of the Universe. It said that there was a big ball of fire and an explosion. After the explosion some smaller parts cooled down to become planets, meteors and asteroids. Bigger parts stayed on as stars and suns. In the theory of evolution on planet Earth, Darwin talks about how life originated. However, modern science disproves these theories. Modern scientific findings go towards what ancient Indian scriptures, the *Upaniṣads* said thousands of years ago. According to the *Taittirīya Upaniṣad*, first there was ether. From ether, came air. From air came fire. Then water appeared and finally earth appeared. From earth, other living beings appeared.

Actually, this order shows the process of evolution from a subtle form of energy that is ether, to a gross form that is Earth. We feel gross forms through the senses; however as it goes to subtler forms of energy, we must experience it. Can we hold water like we can hold earth in our hands? Can we feel fire the way we feel water? Can we see air like we see fire? No. As the energy goes from gross to subtle, the way we experience it changes. Earth is tangible matter; ether is intangible energy. The subtlest form of energy is ether, *ākāśa* and we can only experience this through meditation.

Kṛṣṇa says at the end of each age, called a *kalpa* in Saṁskṛit, the materially manifested Universe with all its creations merges back into Him. If we analyze the Big Bang theory, the first question we ask is, 'Where did the ball of fire come from?' The Big Bang theory does not answer this fundamental question. You see, the so-called scientists have no answer to this question yet. Here Kṛṣṇa, the inner scientist, answers this question in these verses. Science has now proven that the vacuum has something in it. The subtlest form of energy, ether, is present in the vacuum. See how science is tending towards spirituality.

This whole Universe was created from *ākāśa*, ether and it goes back into ether again. All that we see outside as the material world is the manifestation of this subtle form of energy. The material world is the gross form of energy that we can see.

When Kṛṣṇa says, 'All material manifestation enters Me,' He means, it enters the Universal Consciousness. Everything we see and feel using our senses is part of the Universal Consciousness. The problem is that we see it only as matter. If we see things as matter, we are in the gross level and we run after them. Our mind says, 'These things will make you happy; go and get them.' When we get this thought, the rat race starts, and our suffering starts. When we understand that whatever we see and feel are only material manifestations of the subtle energy, we operate in a different plane. We see the futility of the race we are running. We realize that all material things are a projection, a manifestation of our own inner self. Our desires and thoughts are projected as the materials that we see. In actual fact, there is no such thing as material, separate and independent. Everything is one; everything is energy.

Kṛṣṇa says that only He can create and destroy this Universe at His will. This whole Universe is a manifestation or a projection of our own self. Please listen: We make our own world. We create the reality what we want. We create our world through our needs or desires. We don't see what IS! We are only seeing what we want. Only an Enlightened being sees the real truth, as it IS. Once we understand everything is a mirror image of our own self, we become enlightened. Once we realize that we, along with everything else around us, are part of the same energy or Consciousness, we become enlightened.

In these two verses, Kṛṣṇa says this truth clearly. Every material manifestation is created by Him and goes back into Him. He says only He can create and destroy it at His will, which means the world that we see, the Universe that we perceive, is a projection of our own Self.

How To Be Unattached

9.9 *O Dhanañjaya, all this work does not bind Me.*
I am ever unattached from these activities, seated as though neutral.

9.10 *The material nature or prakṛti works under My direction,*
O Kaunteya, and creates all moving and unmoving beings
through My energies. By its cause, this manifestation
is created and annihilated again and again.

9.11 *Fools deride Me when I descend in the human form.*
They do not know My transcendental nature as
the Supreme Lord [maheśavara] of the entire creation.

9.12 *Those who are thus deluded are demonic and atheistic.*
In their deluded condition, their hopes for liberation,
their result-oriented actions and their culture of knowledge
become false and useless.

Being attached or bound to what we do or what we have is a major hurdle in realizing our Self. Kṛṣṇa says He is not bound to this Universe. This is the reason, He says, that keeps Him unaffected when the Universe is created and when it is destroyed.

The whole Universe is being born out of Him and it is getting destroyed. Even then He is not affected because He is not bound to the Universe. It is because He is a mere spectator.

Let us understand this in the context of daily life. When we start to internalize these great truths in small things that we do, a great change happens in us. Kṛṣṇa speaks of a divine play. He talks in terms of the Universe being created and destroyed from Universal consciousness. If we understand His words, we can apply them to day-to-day activities.

That is why *Bhagavad Gītā* is a beautiful scripture, which can be easily internalized and applicable for any age or generation.

When we understand this truth, we feel a great sense of liberation. You see, we become attached or bound to what we have. We think that all we have is ours. When we create that attachment, we create a strong bond. Be very clear, now the problem has started.

Drop Your Attachments, Be Unclutched

Our material possessions create greed and fear in us. We are either in fear of losing them or we want to get more and more of them. We attach so much importance to them that getting more and more of them becomes our only goal. Naturally when we have so much, we create a fear of losing them. The problem is we associate ourselves with material possessions. Again and again, we run after them and forget who we are. So many people are in the rat race. They spend their lives accumulating money, bungalows and cars. And at the end of their life, they regret; they wonder what they have done in their lives. We are in a state of continuous fear.

This is one kind of attachment. There is another kind of attachment. We are attached to people. We create strong bonds in relationships. These are also attachments. We start possessing people. The possessiveness grows so strong that we suffer when someone leaves us or dies. We become so dependent on persons that our whole life seems to lose meaning when they die.

Actually, in this kind of bondage we define ourselves based on the opinions of other people. So we constantly hold on to that relationship because it gives us energy; that relationship helps us define ourselves. So when a person dies, we feel depressed because whatever we were holding to very tightly was the source of energy for us. That was defining us till now and now it is no longer there. It has disappeared. So our whole system is shaken.

Now there is the third kind of bondage or attachment. It is related to our thoughts and emotions. Whenever something happens, we start linking it with our past and start fantasizing about the future. Be very clear, a thought arises because our mind jumps from the past to the future. When a thought arises, we link up that thought with other thoughts and create thought patterns.

None of the thoughts are linked to each other. We create a shaft binding all these thoughts. Each thought is like a bubble in a fish tank. If you see bubbles rising in a fish tank, they are unrelated, unconnected and disjointed. However we create an illusory shaft and link them up. We attach ourselves with that shaft and start experiencing them. We let the thoughts control us.

In the same way, we deal with our emotions also. We create a shaft of all our pains and all our joys and associate with it. If we see that our pain shaft is longer than the joy shaft, we conclude that we had a painful life; we had a miserable life. Otherwise, we say we have a happy life. Yet if we look deeply, each of the pains is completely unconnected, disassociated, and disjointed.

For example, the headache that you experience today is not associated to the headache that you had one week ago. The headache that you had one week ago is not associated to the headache that you felt one month ago. But what do we do? We associate and connect all these and say we have always had headaches or migraines. We fail to see that all the events were independent events. We create a shaft through all these pains and come to a conclusion.

In the same way, if we have a joful experience, we want to hold onto it. We want to experience that joy again. We look for that source of joy and continuously run after it. This again leads us into the rat race.

Please understand, don't associate yourself with your incompletion. One of the great things my yoga guru, Yogirāj Yogānandapuri (lovingly called Raghupati Yogi) did is—he broke my laziness pattern. When I was a boy, he made me do *surya namaskār* from morning sunrise to sunset! Please understand, these happenings are all literally true. I am talking with integrity and authenticity. Then, when I would almost be dead and lie down, he will tell me, 'Eh! Don't associate yourself with your body! Don't associate yourself with your incompletions! Don't associate yourself with your laziness!'

I tell you, it really, really, really worked on me. When you don't associate yourself with your incompletions and the tortures you need to go through because of your incompletions, moving towards completion and getting enlightened becomes such an easy job. Don't associate yourself with your incompletions. Tell yourself, 'Yes, I had this incompletion. This is the way my system was functioning. Now it is time. Let me say 'bye' to my incompletions!'

Understand, your incompletions get more and more powerful as long as you associate yourself with them. Don't associate yourself with your incompletion. Don't even own up! Just disown!

Disowning incompletions is complete Completion! If you are convinced you have disowned these incompletions, you are complete!

Here Kṛṣṇa says He is neutral. Kṛṣṇa is in the space of complete completion, the eternal completion! How do we get ourselves unconnected from these attachments? Please understand that being unconnected from material possessions does not mean you leave everything and go away. Being unconnected from relationships does not mean breaking your relationships, forgetting your children, parents and others.

Please understand this very deeply. Being neutral or unconnected has a deep meaning. Being neutral means being a spectator. It is like this: When you watch a movie, you watch something on the screen. Do you become an actor in that movie? No. You watch it and let it go.

In the same way, we need to watch attachments. When we watch them as a spectator, we get detached from them and complete with them. What do I mean by that? When we watch our materialistic wealth, we will not run after it. We do our job because we love it, not because we want to accumulate wealth. A scientist should do research because he likes to do it, not because he wants something out of it. When that is the attitude, the Universe starts showering. The results happen of their own accord. The materialistic wealth comes on its own.

In relationships also, we must be a spectator. When we stop seeing someone as a possession and when we become a spectator to the relationship, our dependency on that person and expectations from that person drop. When dependencies and expectations drop, there is no give and take in the relationship. There is only giving, only enriching. The relationship becomes stronger and completion with other happens.

When we become a spectator to our thoughts and emotions, we feel a great sense of liberation. All we have to do is break the shaft that we create between different unconnected thoughts and emotions. We have to '*unclutch.*' When we see thoughts like passing clouds in the sky, we stop associating ourselves with them. We are no longer controlled by them.

Listen, being a spectator to thoughts does not mean that we suppress or destroy thoughts. We are not Brahma, the Creator, or Viṣṇu, the Sustainer, or Śiva, the Rejuvenator. When we become a spectator, we go beyond these three states. We transcend the trinity. By being a spectator, we remain unaffected and unattached to what happens in and around us. This is the truth. If we can internalize this completely, we will be enlightened this very minute!

Kṛṣṇa says that although He is a mere spectator, everything happens under His supervision. Here He shows His authority. He says the material world is created and annihilated according to His will through the power of *prakṛti*, Nature and the energy of *māyā*, Illusion. Actually, Kṛṣṇa is repeating what He said in the previous verse. Kṛṣṇa wants to clearly get this idea across to Arjuna.

The whole material manifestation is a projection of the energy of Universal Consciousness. This is what is reflected within us in our individual Consciousness. We create and project the reality what we see and what we wish to see. It is like this. You stand in front of a mirror and see yourself. Now all that you see outside you is a projection of what you have inside you.

Power of Our Inner Self

Kṛṣṇa says, 'I am the supreme power. The material nature of *prakṛti* works under My direction—*mayā adhyakṣena prakṛtiḥ sūyate sa-carācaram* (9.10).' Everything happens under His supervision. What He says is simple. Whatever happens is a drama of creation and annihilation through Nature and Illusion. Kṛṣṇa, the director and producer of this cosmic drama, stands unmoved as a spectator.

This truth is reflected within us, too. We create and destroy ourselves. Everything, our happiness, our pains, our fantasies, our sorrows, our relationships are created by us. If we see from a higher level, we influence the whole Universe. Kṛṣṇa shows how powerful we are, how powerful our inner Self is. Whether we believe it or not, it is the truth. We create everything that we see, feel and hear. That is the power of our inner Self. Yet we do not stay detached the way Kṛṣṇa does.

Our thoughts and words have a tremendous impact. The Cosmic consciousness responds to our thoughts. All the Enlightened Masters have talked about the power of thinking and words. What we think and how we think affects what happens around us.

You have seen people who always shout and yell at others. Some people keep shaking their legs. All this happens because of inner restlessness. Instead of looking inside, we blame others. We see negativity around us because there are negativities inside us. Because of such thoughts inside us, we project them outside. You see, this is how we create our own world.

Understand the power of thoughts. A person is blissful not because of what happens outside him; it is because of what is inside him. There is a difference between being happy and being blissful. Happiness happens inside because of external factors. If we feel joy inside because of something happening outside us, that joy is happiness. The problem with happiness is the source. If suddenly the external source disappears, our happiness also disappears. The outer world is affecting our inner world.

However, bliss is not like that. Being blissful does not depend on external sources. If we are at peace internally, we express that bliss. No external event or happening affects this state. Bliss is eternal; however happiness is temporary. When we are powerful and blissful inside, we project the same power and bliss outside. We enjoy the external material manifestation because we are blissful inside as spectator. However, when we try to possess that bliss, that bliss is gone. Be very clear, when we think and enjoy something from our mind, it is not bliss.

So in this verse Kṛṣṇa tells us clearly that we create our own world. The material manifestation is solely because of our inner Self and nothing external is responsible for it.

FOOLS DERIDE AN INCARNATION

In the next verse Kṛṣṇa says, 'Fools deride Me when I descend in the human form. They do not know My ultimate nature, eternal nature, as the supreme Lord of all that is.'

avajānanti māṁ mūḍhā mānuṣiṁ tanum āśritam |
paraṁ bhāvam ajānanto mama bhūta maheśvaram || 9.11

Here Kṛṣṇa uses a strong word: 'Fools, *mūḍhā*'. Incarnations, Enlightened Masters don't edit their words. They speak the truth as it is. Usually, normal people edit because they fear others' opinions. See, normally in all your minds, three processes happen: first, words are created, then edited and then finally presented. In Masters, these three processes don't happen. Straightaway what is created is presented. That is why, whatever words they utter become reality.

Listen. The *world* does not create words in them. Their *words* create the world around them. They express integrity, the power of words, *vāk śakti.* The words you utter towards you and towards others can do so much to your life. If you want to harness the power of words, the practice you need to do is integrity. Bring Integrity. Align all your words more and more towards completion.

Please understand, I am defining integrity.

Integrity means aligning your words, internal and external, more and more towards completion; that is integrity. Aligning the words you utter inside and outside you towards completion is integrity.

One American University professor who attended many of my discourses, said, '*Swamiji*, you are speaking continuously for hours without notes?' Listen, here also in front of me, only the Gītā verses are there, no other notes. I see these verses so that the original pronunciation is not lost. I can say that the *Vedas* is the purest and most unadulterated scripture. Even the *chhandas* (vedic meter), the tune in which they are chanted, cannot be changed. Just to preserve the purity, I read the Saṁskṛit verses from the original.

He asked me, 'How are you able to continuously speak?' I told him, 'Because the process is easy and integrated in me. I don't edit. My internal and external words are aligned. I don't have the three mechanisms: creating words, editing and presenting. Usually, for all people, these three mechanisms have to happen.'

Then he put one more question, '*Swamiji,* speaking for hours is different. For me, I must prepare three hours before even for a one-hour lecture!'

In my meditation camps, sometimes the program is eighteen hours long per day; people listen to my talks and meditate. I told him, 'You prepare because it has not become your authentic experience.' Then I asked him, 'If somebody asks your name, do you prepare? Your name has become your experience, your being. So you immediately respond. Similarly, whatever I speak is from my experience. So I don't need to prepare, I spontaneously express it.

One more thing, why do people fear public speaking? Why do they again and again prepare and rehearse? They fear that they may speak what they really think inside! They do not want to express what is going on inside them. They want to express polished words.

Only for an integrated person whose inner chatter has become pure, not only his words, his thinking becomes pure. That person can talk in a relaxed way for hours in public. To speak in public, that too in a relaxed and casual way, we need our inner being to be in pure integrity with our words and pure authenticity with our thinking. Only then can we talk whatever comes and be relaxed and complete. Otherwise, continuously we must edit. If we edit and speak, within half an hour or one hour, we are tired and drained. We do not radiate the same energy.

Understand this truth! When we practice integrity, we will experience the power of words. But the power of thinking is deeper than the power of words. The power of thinking will be available to us when we practice authenticity. Masters don't edit; they express whatever they think. With authenticity, their thinking has become so pure, they simply harness the power of thinking and words, and so they don't need to edit. Even if they use sharp words, they are spoken to awaken you.

Here Kṛṣṇa uses the word, '*mūḍhaḥ*', meaning 'fool'. 'Fools deride Me.' He gives a jolt to the ego. 'Fools deride Me when I descend in the human form. They do not know My eternal nature as the supreme Lord of all that is, *mama bhūta maheśvaram*.' He says, 'When I land in the world in the human form as a Master, people, fools, deride me. They don't understand.'

Why Masters Descend?

He again and again tells this to Arjuna, 'Don't think that just because I am in the body, I am your friend. Don't think that I am the person who was sitting in Briṇḍāvan (the forest place where Kṛṣṇa spent his infant years), who is your own friend. I am the energy that takes care of the whole world. I have come down in this form to liberate all of you. So only fools deride Me, fools miss Me. Don't miss, Arjuna, understand the Ultimate nature of Me and liberate yourself.'

In these verses, Kṛṣṇa tells some interesting truths. These were true during His time and they are true today. When an enlightened Master lives in his body, people do not accept him, people ignore him, and some even abuse him. In fact, people do not even want to accept that he can be an Enlightened Master.

People stay away from the living Master. However, when the Master is no longer in the body, people visit his final resting place, offer flowers, and do all kinds of things. This has happened to all enlightened Masters. Rāmakṛṣṇa was considered a mad priest. When Rāmakṛṣṇa entered into an ecstatic mood, people said that he was acting. However now, if you go to Kolkata, Dakśineśvar has become a pilgrimage center. People worship Rāmakṛṣṇa; they keep his photo in their home, in their wallets. They call him an Incarnation, God.

You see, over time nothing has changed. When I am in the ashram in Bidadi, many people come with speculation. They have questions about what I say, what I wear and everything I do. They say, 'You are so young. How can you be enlightened?' Some say, 'If you are enlightened, why do you wear a golden *rudrākṣa* necklace? Why do you charge money for courses?' These same people will come to my final resting place after one hundred years and offer flowers on it. They will accept me as their guru when I am not in human form.

Kṛṣṇa says, 'Fools lose Me when I come in human form—*avajānanti māṁ mūḍhā mānuṣiṁ tanum āśritam* (9.11).' He calls them fools. This is the truth. When an enlightened Master is in human form, we do not accept him as a Master. Only after the Master leaves the body do we pay our respects to the Master. Why do people again and again do this?

You see, when the Master is in his body, in human form, our mind sees him as another human being. Then our ego comes between him and us. It reasons, 'He is another human like me. Why should I listen to him?' All these questions come. We decide we don't have to follow another human being and go back.

A simple act of ego makes us miss a living enlightened Master. Our being wants it; however our mind and ego create a strong wall of questions between the Master and us. We miss the opportunity. And one more thing, some people know that a person is a Master and what he says is good for them, yet they escape. This is because they know that the Enlightened Master can see through them. They do not want anybody to know what a mess they have created in themselves.

We should understand why an Enlightened Master, an Incarnation happens on planet Earth. If we know this, we will not be fools. We will not miss or run away. If we understand, then we can break the wall between the Master and us and let our being experience the Master's energy.

A small story from Rāmakṛṣṇa:

> Three men walk near a village. They see an orchard. One of them jumps into the orchard to see what is happening. He sees a big party going on inside. He sees so much joy and bliss inside the orchard. This man also starts enjoying. He forgets about the two men outside the orchard.
>
> After some time, the two men who stand outside get impatient. The second man says, 'Let me go and see what happened.'
>
> He enters the orchard. He sees people dancing, singing, enjoying. However, before he joins the party, this man thinks he should tell the third man standing outside the orchard about what he has seen. He has concern for the third man. So he tells the third man what is going on inside the orchard and runs back into the orchard and joins the party.
>
> Now this third man goes in. He sees the bliss everyone is in. He thinks, 'I should tell everyone in the village about this; everyone should enjoy.' So he goes out, tells everyone in the village and brings them into the orchard.

Enlightened Masters are like the third man. They have experienced the truth, the bliss. They are the embodiments of compassion. Be very clear, the only mission of an enlightened Master is to get everyone to *Live Enlightenment*. There is no ulterior motive of the Master. People ask me lots of questions. Why this? Why that? People look at me with suspicion.

They think by telling them something, I make some profit. If I suggest to them to attend some meditation course, they think I will make money. They run away thinking I want to make them a *Sannyāsi*. They do not understand that an Enlightened Master is beyond all that. They miss the opportunity of being with a Master because of their own ignorance.

Whenever Enlightened Masters save mankind, people try to make their life hell, due to their ignorance and self-doubts. Understand that an Enlightened Master does not have desires. So He does not have any vested interests. All He wants is everyone should experience the bliss that He has experienced.

In the case of a normal man, when he takes birth, he carries over desires from his previous birth. These are called *vāsanas.* However, an enlightened Master does not have desires or *vāsanas*; he is in a no-mind state. His spirit can merge directly into the Universal energy. Whenever there is a need on planet Earth, the energy of the Enlightened Master is sent down to Earth with a mission to fulfill.

Be very clear, nobody can help when we create a wall of doubt between the Master and us. The Master can help only if we break the wall, only if we allow the Master to take charge. As long as we hold onto our ego, we remain a fool. **If we meet an Enlightened Master, that is the best happening that can happen to us. Now it is up to us to enrich ourselves with Enlightenment or miss it. Kṛṣṇa tells everyone: if you miss an Enlightened Master, you are a fool.**

Kṛṣṇa does not ask us to follow His form. He asks us to follow His energy. He wants us to internalize Him and follow Him. Follow Kṛṣṇa by understanding Kṛṣṇa Consciousness, not by following what you imagine to be your understanding of the form of Kṛṣṇa. Kṛṣṇa Consciousness is the same as Śiva Cosciousness or Buddha Consciousness or Nithyānanda Consciousness. There is no difference.

That is why Kṛṣṇa says, 'These fools mock at Me when I come in human form. Don't mock the form, follow the Consciousness. You will no longer be a fool. You will be in eternal bliss!'

Worship Me In Any Form But With Devotion

9.13 *O Pārtha (son of Prithā), the great souls, who are not deluded,*
are under the protection of My Divine nature.
They are fully devoted to Me with a single-pointed mind
as they know Me as the origin of all creation, the unchangeable.

9.14 *Always chanting My names and glories, fully striving with great*
determination, bowing down onto Me, these great devotees
of firm resolve, perpetually worship Me with devotion.

9.15 *Some worship Me by acquiring and spreading wisdom of the Self*
[jñāna-yajña]. Others worship Me in My non-dual form in
oneness, in My infinite form as many, and in My Universal form.

Kṛṣṇa speaks about *bhakti* or devotion in these verses.

You see, devotion can be one of the most powerful ways to reach God. Many saints showed the world the path of devotion. Caitanya Mahāprabhu was devoted to Kṛṣṇa. He sang songs and danced in ecstasy while singing Kṛṣṇa's glory. Mīrā was another devotee of Kṛṣṇa who loved with Him. Mīrā's devotional songs, Mīrā bhajans, are sung even today to show her devotion towards Kṛṣṇa.

Devotion is one of the most powerful ways to reach God; however it depends on how we express devotion. Many people have a habit of going to a particular temple every week. If somebody asks, they say, 'Oh, every Saturday I pray to Lord Venkaṭeśvara. Every Tuesday I go to the Hanumān temple.' Going to temples becomes a fashion statement.

Making mechanical visits to the temple is not devotion. It is just a sort of ego. We mostly go to temples to ask for something. Our devotion is dependent on how much Venkaṭeśvara answers our prayers. If we ask for something and He gives it, then Venkaṭeśvara is great; otherwise we switch Gods!

This is our devotion! We make business deals. We pray to God, but not with devotion. As long as God gives what we want, he is our God; otherwise He is no longer God. Prayer should express our devotion, gratitude, and love to God. All great devotees of Kṛṣṇa and Rāma showed complete gratitude and love. When devotion reaches that state, they reach the Ultimate Consciousness.

Devotion or Knowledge?

Prayers are powerful; however, we should not get stuck at prayers. Prayers are powerful in the initial stages when we pray as we go towards God. Let the prayers express devotion rather than asking for boons. We should go beyond words. When we pray, we are stuck in words. Our devotion should enrich us to see the ultimate energy behind the idol of Kṛṣṇa, Rāma, or Śiva.

Actually, complete devotion puts us in a completely different plane. When we show our devotion to someone, we surrender ourselves to him or her. Have you heard the story of the great child devotee, Prahlād?

> He was a young boy less than ten years old. His father Hiraṇyakaśipu, a great devotee of Brahma (the creator), does intense penance and asks Brahma for a boon to be made immortal; however Brahma says that is impossible. Hiraṇyakaśipu then comes up with lots of conditions such as: he should not be killed by an animal, a bird, a human, or anything living or non-living, either during the day or the night. Brahma grants him that boon.
>
> Hiraṇyakaśipu thinks his boon covers all the ways in which he might be killed. So he declares himself to be God. He asks all the people in his kingdom to worship him as God. So people worship his idol. However his son, Prahlād, turns out to be a great devotee of Lord Viṣṇu.

Obviously his father is not happy about this. He tries to persuade Prahlād; but it is of no use. The more he talks to his son, the more intense Prahlad's devotion becomes. He then tries to get Prahlād killed through various ways.

Prahlād worships Viṣṇu with such great devotion that Viṣṇu saves Prahlād every time. Prahlād prays to Viṣṇu every second, with every breath. His devotion is deep. Even when he is about to be executed, he prays to Viṣṇu with gratitude and love. His devotion is that of surrender rather than a prayer asking Viṣṇu to save his life.

This is the story of Narasiṃha avatār, the Incarnation of Viṣṇu in which He is half-lion and half-human.

Kṛṣṇa continues to explain to Arjuna the ways in which people worship Him. Here he talks about the path of *jñāna*, knowledge: Those following the path of knowledge try to worship Me by acquiring and propagating knowledge.

Understand that mere accumulation of knowledge only increases ego. It does not give enlightenment. Internalize the knowledge by authentic listening, by meditation, and contemplation, and by enriching others and yourself with the experiential wisdom. Then the breeze of joy will flow into your life.

How can we internalize knowledge? Do meditation. When you are alone, think and contemplate upon great truths. Deeply immersing ourselves in contemplation is a meditation. Question those truths and try to find answers within yourself.

Swami Vivekananda beautifully says, 'Even if we sit day in and day out, and memorize all the books in all the libraries, nothing happens, except that our head becomes a little big, that is all! Just know one single dimension of the truth and imbibe that completely, that is more than enough. It can do wonders. Take any one teaching and internalize it fully.'

Meditation helps us internalize our experience and process it into wisdom. It is an alchemy that happens internally, an alchemy that transforms our lives. Meditation helps us experience the truths.

Please understand, acquiring knowledge can be done in another way. Many people read many books and scriptures. They have shelves filled with books. These people take great pride in showing off their knowledge. Many people discuss spiritality and have debates over this subject. Debates are not wrong; however the motive with which they discuss should be correct. If they discuss to show others how much they know, then they are debating purely out of ego. Please be very clear, if we use our knowledge just to show how much we know, there is no use of that knowledge.

The only way knowledge in the scriptures enriches us is through experience. Instead of debating and showing off knowledge, apply it in day-to-day activities. See the results on yourself first. Experience completion in your own life. Only when we experience it, we have the right to speak about it to others. Till then, they are mere words.

Meditation enriches us here, especially in the path of *jñana* or knowledge. You see, the path of knowledge is not an easy path. In the path of devotion, all we have to do is pray to some form: either Kṛṣṇa or Rāma or someone, have complete devotion to that chosen God. We must completely surrender. Actually, total surrender is difficult; however, in the path of devotion, at least we have someone to talk to, pray to and look up to.

However in the path of knowledge, there is no reference point. No one is in front of us. In this path, there is nothing called you and He. In the path of devotion, there is a clear separation between Kṛṣṇa and us. In the path of knowledge, Kṛṣṇa says that everything is Kṛṣṇa. There is no duality.

When we meditate, we experience the great truths. Through meditation we connect to our inner space and learn to create the space of completion. All the knowledge in the scriptures, the *Upaniṣad*, talks about microcosm and macrocosm. If we talk about this knowledge without experience, all our knowledge is bookish knowledge, nothing else. The difference happens when we experience that truth. During meditation, we merge with the cosmic energy. Meditation helps us enter that space where our inner space merges with the outer space: microcosm merges with macrocosm.

Actually, all paths are one and the same. Even if we meditate on the form, after a point we will see that there is nothing like a form. Everything is the same. So even in the path of devotion, we experience the same thing as in the path of knowledge. Be very clear, nothing is better than the other. Everything is the same. The greatest enlightened master Śaṅkara who spoke the greatest truths on non-duality, *advaita* wrote poems on devotion also. Swāmi Vivekānanda was an intellectual being, yet he bowed down to the devotion of Rāmakṛṣṇa's disciple, Gopale Ma, a devotee of Kṛṣṇa.

This is what Kṛṣṇa says in this verse. In the previous verse, He talked about the path of devotion. Here He talks about the path of knowledge. He says, 'Some worship the form, some worship the formless. There are many ways to worship Me.'

There are many different ways people worship the Divine. We have customized paths for our personal growth. So naturally wherever one is, one can grow and reach the level we are supposed to reach. There are all sizes of ladders, all kinds of steps. We are continuously given choices, options. So, naturally one tends to take up something or the other.

He gives options among the different paths; *satatam kīrtayanto mām* (9.14)—worshipping through singing the glories of the Lord or *jñāna-yajñena cāpy anye yajanto mām upāsate* (9.15)—cultivation of knowledge and offering everything at the feet of God.

I Am Immortality And Death!

9.16, 17, 18, 19

I am the ritual, I am the sacrifice, I am the offering, I am the herb,
I am the mantra, I am the clarified butter, I am the fire,
and I am the oblation.

I am the supporter of the Universe, the father, the mother,
and the grandfather.
I am the object of knowledge, the sacred syllable "OM",
and also the Ṛg, the Yajur, and the Sāma Vedas.

I am the goal, the supporter, the Lord, the witness, the abode,
the refuge, the friend, the origin, the dissolution,
the foundation, the substratum, and the immutable seed.
I give heat. I send, as well as withhold the rain.

I am immortality as well as death. I am also both the Eternal
and the temporal, O Arjuna.

Kṛṣṇa says in specific terms what He is. He is the creation of the act, the actor and the action. He is the fire to which the sacrifices are made, He is also the offering and He is the sacrifice as well. He is the seer, the seen and the seeing, all in one.

He tells Arjuna that everything we do, everything we see, everything we feel, everything we know is because of Him. He says everything has come from Him. He is the seed of everything. Everything that we see is Parāśakti or universal energy. This is Kṛṣṇa's message here.

ahaṁ kratur ahaṁ yajñaḥ svadhānam aham auṣadham |
mantro 'ham aham evājyam aham agnir ahaṁ hutam || 9.16

Great Masters lived in this realization. Ramaṇa, Rāmakṛṣṇa, Sadāśiva Brahmendra, Raghavendra and many masters lived in this consciousness of being one with the Universal Consciousness. Many people could not relate to the experience or the expression of their experience; so they considered these Masters mad.

All Are Brahman

A small story:

> A disciple returns to his ashram. From a distance he sees a huge crowd. Getting curious, he pushes his way through the crowd and he is shocked. A dog is trying to eat food kept in his Master's vessel and his Master is sitting on the dog!
>
> The disciple does not understand. 'What nonsense is going on here? Oh Master, what are you doing?' he asked, utterly confused. The Master calmly replied, 'Don't you see? Some *Brahman* has kept some *Brahman* on a *Brahman*. One four legged *Brahman* tries to eat it. Another *Brahman* rides on it. Many *Brahmans* stand and watch this event. That's all.'
>
> On hearing this, the crowd disperses saying, 'What is this madness?' However the disciple feels that nothing his Master utters can be untrue.
>
> He sits under the nearby tree and contemplates. The potent words 'plate, food, dog, master, people are *all Brahman* rings again and again in his ears. As the power of his Master's words sinks in, the disciple realizes that all things surrounding him are the same Existence, Brahman.
>
> He realizes and understands that divine energy blissfully moves about in each and every thing. In a moment everything changes for the disciple. The thought of 'I' drops; instead, the feeling of 'Self' dawns. The fulfilling

feeling of completion that 'All is Brahman, everywhere is Brahman, Brahman is within me too' is born. He has the first experience of enlightenment.

We are all Brahman; we are all divine. God is everywhere. Divine energy fills and overflows in all the places. This is what Kṛṣṇa says in these verses.

This is the basic truth. Whether we believe it or not, accept it or not, understand it or not, this is the truth. We can call 'It' God—Kṛṣṇa, Śiva, Universal Energy, Cosmic Energy, Parāśakti or Brahman. Whatever we may call It, It is present everywhere. When we worship some idol or form, we actually worship the formless energy behind that idol. People ask me, 'Why do we keep your photo in front of us and pray to it? Why can't we meditate on the formless?'

I tell them, 'First start meditating on the form, then you can go to the formless.' Our mind is continuously jumping everywhere. In such a state, we first need a form to bring our mind to the present. A form is necessary in the initial stages for the mind to calm down. Once we Master this, meditating on the formless becomes easier. We should understand that we are worshipping *through* that idol and not the idol itself.

The basic truth in spirituality is that God is in the form of energy and He is formless. God cannot be an individual. He must be energy. Religions give shapes and forms to this divine energy. It is a good beginning, but not the end. You can start with idol worship and move into worshipping the formless energy.

Thousands of years ago, our sages clearly said in the *Upaniṣad* that everything is energy and everything arose from energy. The formless God is nothing but space, ether, or energy. Now it has been proven scientifically that there is ether even in vacuum. This energy is all-pervading. It is there everywhere. We now know with the help of powerful tools that 99.99% of an atom is empty space. Continuous vibrations go on in that empty space. Only these vibrations exhibit themselves as energy. Each and every body is filled with energy. Today science says, 'Everything is filled with energy.'

Our Enlightened Masters expressed it this way, 'God is energy and He fills all space and is omnipresent.' Kṛṣṇa says this clearly in these verses. This energy cannot be destroyed. It can only change form. You see, when we switch on a light, electrical energy is converted into light energy. Electrical energy is not being destroyed. It has only changed form.

In the same way, Universal Energy is everywhere. It is in everything around us and I tell you, it is within us also. Once we realize this great truth, we see that everything around us is the same as us. Only the form in which everything exists is different. Kṛṣṇa tries to explain this great truth through these verses.

When I say everything, I mean everything is Kṛṣṇa, everything is Brahman.

Reside In Me, I Give And Preserve

9.20 *Those who practice the vedic rituals and drink the soma juice,*
worship Me indirectly seeking the heavenly pleasures.
They go to heaven and enjoy sensual delights.

9.21 *Once they have thus enjoyed heavenly sense pleasures,*
they are reborn on this planet again.
By practicing vedic rituals as result-oriented actions,
they are bound by the cycle of birth and death.

9.22 *When you reside in My consciousness,*
always fixed in undivided remembrance,
whatever you lack I give [yoga].
And whatever you have, I preserve [kṣema].

9.23 *Even those who worship other deities with faith, they actually*
worship Me, O Kaunteya, but without the true understanding.

9.24 *I am the only enjoyer [bhokta] and the only Lord [prabhu] of all*
sacrifices. Those who do not recognize My true transcendental
nature are born again and again.

Kṛṣṇa says that people who read scriptures, the Vedas, and who perform pious ritualistic activities based on scriptural injunctions with the aim of acquiring merits, enjoy heavenly pleasures; however they fall back into the cycle of life and death after they finish enjoying these pleasures.

You see, many people do lots of rituals and read scriptures. Kṛṣṇa says this surely helps elevate them to a higher plane of consciousness; however they are still caught in the cycle of *saṁsāra*, birth and death. He says we should go beyond momentary pleasures that we get by reading and practicing *Vedic* injunctions.

Understand these verses. By reading scriptures and performing different rituals, we will enjoy the pleasures of *Indra loka*, the heavenly pleasures; yet when the rituals are performed with that objective, we will again enter the vicious circle of birth and death.

Kṛṣṇa speaks about the attitude or the context from which we read *Vedas* and *Upaniṣads* or how we perform rituals. Scriptures have immense knowledge. Rituals have immense power. They are meditations; however they are useless if done with the wrong context of fear and greed.

Many people fear that if they do not perform certain rituals, they will go to hell and miss their place in heaven. In India, after a person dies, certain rituals are performed. People perform these rituals fearing that without these rituals the dead person will not gain a place in heaven and the living will not live in peace. Another class of people operates with greed. They donate large sums of money thinking that the gates of heaven will be eternally open for them. Their names get carved on temple walls. They donate electric bulbs to light up temples, but half the bulb will have their name written on it. What is the use?

Please understand, even when performing rituals and sacrifices, if you feel powerful, excited, energetic and blissful, and you think the external happening is the reason for that joy and powerfulness, then for that bliss, you are having joy out of the wrong context. It will not stay in you. It is not going to become lifestyle in you! When we do pious activities with the wrong context of fear or greed, though we see improvement, some transformation, we will go back to where we started.

That is what Kṛṣṇa means by *Indra loka*, the momentary transformation or elevation of our state. Understand, not only the right experience, but also the right context is needed. So, whether you feel powerful or powerless, excited or depressed, rich or poor, healthy or sick, nothing comes from the external happening. If you think that the external happenings contribute for you feeling powerful or powerless, that is what

I call wrong context, it is an incompletion.

When we perform certain rituals, be it *pūjā* or prayer or reading scriptures, it should become a meditation. It is the experience of *you* that you are having about *you*. Our ego, our fear and our greed should not come in the way. It is like this: when we perform rituals, do them with integrity and authenicity, out of the right context of completion.

What You Lack I Give, What You Have I Preserve

Now, please come to the space of listening.

The next verse is the main core that reveals the secret of secrets. Kṛṣṇa tells Arjuna and all of us:

'Those who always worship Me, those who always reside in Me, those who have *ananyāś cintayanto*—means the non-dual mood, the space of *Advaita*, means those who have become Me, people who have experienced eternal consciousness, those who reside in eternal consciousness—to them, I carry what they lack and I preserve what they have. I personally take care of them.'

ananyāś cintayanto mām ye janāḥ paryupāsate I
teṣāṁ nityābhiyuktānāṁ yogakṣemaṁ vahāmyahaṁ II *9.22*

Please be very clear, no other Incarnation has revealed this truth so clearly. He says, 'If you reside in eternal consciousness, divine energy, bliss consciousness, I take care of you in all ways.'

***Yoga and kṣema:* I give them whatever they want spiritually and materially and I take care that it stays with them. I take care that nobody takes it away from them. This is a beautiful statement and assurance.**

Please understand, it is not only an assurance; it is a promise. Kṛṣṇa gives a promise, 'If you reside in My consciousness, if you reside in eternal consciousness, whatever you lack will be given and whatever you have will be preserved.'

The strange thing is that He says we will have everything and nothing will be lost. It is difficult to believe! At least for people trained in so-called present day education, it is difficult to believe! 'How can I have what I want by meditating?' This will be the immediate question.

Now in the modern day, especially after the breakthrough with the principles of quantum physics, science clearly proves our thoughts create the whole Universe. If we reside in Eternal Consciousness, we create our own Universe. Not only that, the Universe responds to our thoughts.

A small but important experiment report that I read:

> A professor did an experiment using three rose bushes kept in different rooms. They were the same height, same kind.
>
> He entered the first room and used beautiful words, 'You are beautiful. You are nice. You are great. Don't worry, I'll protect you. Why do you need thorns?' He gave assuring and caring words. He created a loving mood. Next, he went to the second plant. He did not do much; he looked and came back: neither negative nor positive. To the third plant, he cursed, 'What nonsense are you doing? You are ugly.' He created negative energy with his words. He continued this experiment for twenty-one days studying how plants respond to thoughts as a research.
>
> The report, the end result, is shocking. The first plant that received positive words doubled in size and had no thorns! I saw photographs of that plant. There were no thorns on that rose plant just because he gave the assurance, 'I'll protect you. Why should you protect yourself? Don't bother. There is no need for thorns.' Can you imagine a rose plant without thorns!
>
> The second plant to which he spoke neither positive nor negative words grew just as a normal rose plant. It experienced normal growth, that's all. The third plant, to which he spoke negative words, died. Not once, but several times he repeated the same experiment in different places

and in different ways. He says the third plant, that received negative thoughts, died at all times.

Sir Jagdish Chandra Bose, an Indian Nobel Laureate, proved that plants are alive with 'feelings'. They are capable of responding to our thoughts and emotions. This experiment proves that Existence, the outer world, responds to our thoughts.

I tell you, many times my *gurukul* kids give me the confidence on this truth, when I see them playing with the Nature, bringing rain or stopping rain without failing even once! Please understand, it is not that they can play with rain only in the rainy season. They practice a unique process of completion of healing themselves and healing others. Each child has this own rose plant. The child talks to that plant and gives security to that rose plant. Automatically, the rose plant drops all the thorns!

Once, from a distance I stood at the Nithyananda Gurukul, to see exactly what is happening. Please understand, if a hundred priests, *Śivācāryas* sit and do *ādī rudra yajña* (enriching sacrifice offered to Lord Śiva) with integrity, what amount of positive energy will be released, I saw so much of energy being released just by these few Gurukul kids! Of course, nowadays you don't need to believe all these ideas of energy. Unique photography methods have come like kirlian photography, where you can photograph all the energy released and the energy expansion.

Please listen. Existence responds to our thoughts. Each of us is not an island. We are not isolated. Don't think we can think whatever we want in our inner space and that our outer life will be different. Our outer life and inner life are deeply connected. If we live a spiritual life, we automatically attract only spiritual friends. Our outer world also becomes spiritual. All other relationships drop by themselves. We do not even feel like relating.

Many devotees tell me, '*Swamiji,* nowadays I am unable to go to a party. Even if I go, what is there to talk about at a party? Same stock market or who ran away with whom, who is going with whom. Nothing useful.'

Understand, Existence responds to our thoughts. It does not need this network. People who enter spiritual life can't indulge in the same old talks. Only based on our thoughts, we create relationships, friends, society, our circle and naturally, our whole world.

Again and again, Vedānta says, *dṛṣti-sṛṣti*, we create what we see. We create the Universe from the angle of our vision. When our *dṛṣti* (vision) changes, the *sṛṣti* (world around us) changes too. We project our world and see. It is the truth.

See, whatever we place in front of a projector, whatever slide we position there, that will appear on the screen. If we place the slide of God, the picture of God appears on screen. If we place an actress, that actress appears on the screen. The screen represents the physical planet Earth. Whatever we keep in front of our consciousness, we project that in our life, our world and our experience. A small change in our inner space changes our whole world. The backdrop screen remains the same; however the scene changes. Similarly, if the words, thoughts and feeling in our inner space change, the whole Universe changes. The whole of Existence responds to our inner space.

Don't think that each of us is a separate island. We are part of this whole Existence. We are not alone here. If we think we are alone, we will continuously fight with Existence, with the whole Universe. We will see the rest of the Universe as an enemy. The part can never see the whole as enemy. We are a part. This is the Whole. If we see this as an enemy, we can never rest. Only a person who understands that the Whole is his own being, that he is part of the Whole, realizes tremendous relaxation and bliss.

Kṛṣṇa says beautifully:

'When you reside in My consciousness, whatever you lack, I give and whatever you have, I preserve.'

ananyāś cintayanto mām ye janāḥ paryupāsate /
teṣāṁ nityābhiyuktānāṁ yogakṣemaṁ vahāmyahaṁ // 9.22

You may think, 'Yes *Swamiji*, we understand when you say the Universe responds to our thoughts. However, how can we get what we want?'

Please understand, the moment we bring integrity into our thinking and complete with all our incomplete thoughts and all our negative commitments, the moment our inner space changes into the space of completion, automatically we attract good things. It is like: if we tune our television to BBC, we see the BBC channel. If we tune it to Nithyananda TV, we see the Nithyananda channel. Similarly, if we tune our consciousness to completion and bliss, continuously even material wealth will shower on us.

All I am telling you is, when you create the space of completion in you, so much of unimaginable, auspicious, and good things happen in your system which are incomprehensible. Please listen! If I say: I am making a statement that if you acquire the space of completion in you, all your problems, externally and internally, melt away; all the moments of powerlessness, externally and internally, disappear from your life, you may think that it is too big a promise, too good to be true. I tell you, it is too small promise! Because, when you create the space of completion, whatever I promise like your external and internal problems will melt away, will be only a small benefit you will be having.

We may think, 'How can this be possible? How can this happen? What kind of words is *Swamiji* giving?' But I tell you, it may feel it is difficult to understand. But start experimenting with creating the space of completion. I tell you with integrity and authenticity, I declare from my own authority, this verse is the solid truth.

I can say this with authority because I experienced this truth for nine years. I tell you, this is a promise by the Divine. Nine years I lived in utter insecurity. I know Kṛṣṇa still proves His words. His words are guaranteed—*yogakṣemaṁ vahaṁyahaṁ*, He does!

I can quote thousands of incidents from devotees' lives. From so many devotees' lives, Tukarām, Tulsidās and so many masters' lives I can quote to support these words. I can quote numerous incidents from my own life, from the life of people I have met.

Let me tell you a small incident that happened in my own life during my days of spiritual wandering before the happening of enlightenment.

I was staying in Hardiwar at a place called Kankhal. I was doing spiritual practice. Every day morning, I went for alms to places where they feed monks. In so many ashrams, they give alms to monks. I used to get my food, eat two or three rotis (Indian bread) and then start meditating.

Suddenly, one day, I fell sick. I had a high temperature and diarrhea. I was unable to walk. I thought, 'What can be done? Alright! Let it be.'

Suddenly, a young Sannyāsi came from nowhere and gave me food. Not only for one day but continuously for three to four days, he came; he brought food for me. Not only food, he brought medicine also. I asked him, 'Who are you? Where have you come from?' He said, 'Oh, my name is Śaṅkar. They call me Śaṅkar Mahārāj. I stay at a nearby ashram called Sādhana Sadan.' He pointed towards a distant place and said that is where he stayed.

Everyday he brought me food and medicine till I recovered. He came for at least four days. Because he came everyday, I talked with him. We became acquainted.

I saw that he wore a beautiful pen with a diamond in it. I was surprised at how a monk got a diamond pen. I asked, 'What is this, *Swami*?'

He said, 'This is a diamond pen. Some devotee gave it to me. It looks nice, so I wear it.' Anyhow, I did not bother about it.

After several days, when I returned to normal, he stopped coming. By then, I was okay. Then I thought, 'I must go and see him. Now I can walk and move, so I should go and see him.' I felt a little connected to him because he served me. I felt I must thank him. After a week, when I became completely alright, I started walking.

I went to this ashram and asked an elderly person sitting there, '*Swamiji,* I want to see Śaṅkar Mahārāj.' The Swami said, 'Śaṅkar? Who are you talking about?' I said, 'I want to see Śaṅkar, a young swami. I met him two to three days ago. He came everyday and brought me food. Is this Sādhana Sadan?'

This Swami replied, 'Yes, this is Sādhana Sadan. In our ashram, there is only one Śaṅkar. Go to the temple and see. He is the only Śankar Mahāraj we have!' He pointed towards their temple.

I tell you, what I am telling is the truth. When I entered the temple, I saw a Śiva deity as a white marble statue with a cloth draped on His upper body, and wearing the same diamond pen on Him!

Of course, tears rolled down from my eyes. So much gratitude overflowed. Later, I asked the temple priest, 'How did this pen come to Śiva? Who put a pen on Śiva's statue?' He said, 'One week ago, a devotee came and offered the pen. It looked nice and he said it was a diamond pen. We just wanted to decorate Śiva with diamond jewelry. So we put the pen on Him.' It was the same pen! The very same diamond pen!

I asked, 'Who gave a pen to Śiva?' Other jewelry, we can understand, but a pen?

He replied, 'I don't know. A devotee came and offered this pen.

I asked, *Why should a Sannyāsi have a diamond pen*? *I will give it to God instead.* So I put it on Śiva. I just inserted it into Śiva's clothes.'

He then continued, 'For the last few days all the food offering, prasād that we place in front of Him, disappears. I suspect that rats have been eating the food. So now I am careful. I sit for a while after placing the food for Śaṅkar Mahārāj.'

I did not want to tell him that I was the rat who ate Śaṅkar Mahārāj's food!

During the 2006 Himalayan trip I searched for this ashram and Śankar Mahārāj's temple with my devotees. After many years, it was still the same, the same temple and the same Śankar Mahārāj; but no diamond pen now!

Of course, I do not ask you to believe the whole thing because of this one incident. But you can experiment in your life. You may say, 'This is your experience. How can this be truth for us, *Swamiji*?' An ordinary mind doubts.

Let me tell you that your consciousness, your inner space has the quality to create miracles in your lives. Miracles can happen in your life. What you need, you will receive. Continuously, miracles are happening.

Let me try to show you how miracles might have happened in your lives. You might have noticed, when the telephone rings, you suddenly remember a friend's name. When you pick up the phone, that same friend is on the line. Or at times, you remember a person and when you open the door, that very same person stands there. This is what I call the power of coincidence! These are miracles in their own way. In each one of us, the power to create the space, exists. All we need to do is create that space. Understand that we have the power to create the space and cause our reality.

Trust that your Consciousness is connected to the Universe. Continuously, the Universe cares for you. The Divine waits for you. It responds to your thoughts. We create what we want. Just as we create the whole world in our dream, we have the power to create the world when we are conscious, when we are in the waking state. When we can create a world in the dream state, can't we create that in the waking state? We can do it.

Even now, we create our world. Next question, 'If we are creating our world, why do we create so many miseries, *Swamiji*?' The answer is simple. We do so because we have vested interests in our sufferings. Please be very clear. We have vested interests in our sufferings. Somewhere we feel comfortable when we suffer. So we create the whole thing.

Bliss Attracts Fortune

When our inner consciousness changes, when we reside in eternal consciousness, we automatically attract the power of coincidence. We attract the power of creating the space and causing our reality.

The moment we understand, that the whole Universe is pervaded by the Existential energy of Viṣṇu, we attract Lakṣmi, Viṣṇu's Consort who represents wealth! When we understand that the whole Universe is Divine, when we experience Viṣṇu, meaning when we experience eternal bliss, we attract Lakṣmi, wealth!

There is a beautiful mantra in *tantra śāstras*: *'ānanda kamaprānaḥ'* that means 'bliss attracts fortune.' When we create a blissful inner space, automatically we attract external wealth.

Tell me, what creates wealth? We need three things: clear integrated thinking, a creative authentic mind that aligns our thoughts and words, and the ability to make spontaneous decisions. The ability to respond spontaneously to any situation with the truth, that we are responsible for everything happening inside and outside us, is responsibility.

Just let your inner space be completely integrated with the words you utter. If we are able to respond spontaneously to any situation standing with the strength of integrity and authenticity, we take that responsibility. We need integrity, *the power of words* that brings the experience of completion with ourselves and with life. We need authenticity, *the power of thinking* that expresses as the peak of our creativity and the *power of feeling* to take responsibility. Only these three create wealth and preserve wealth.

If we enter the bliss space, if we keep our inner space blissful, if we enter into bliss consciousness, all three automatically happen to us. Automatically, these three powers: integrity, authenticity and responsibility happen to us. Then wealth will be created around us and it will also stay with us to enrich us and others. It is not that we should be showered only by a lottery. Wealth can come simply by creating a blissful inner space and such wealth stays with us, it is everlasting.

Please listen, whomsoever wins through a lottery never preserves it! Without knowing the value of it, they simply blow it away. Wealth comes by intelligence. When it comes by intelligence, it stays with you. When we take care of our inner space, automatically, the outer space showers on us. We become a blessing for planet Earth and it blesses us by showering on us.

Existence responds to our inner bliss and blesses us. Never think that Existence is not alive. Never think that the Universe is mere matter. It is live intelligence. People ask me, '*Swamiji,* I am searching for a Guru. I feel inspired to do spiritual practice. But I need a Guru.'

I tell them, 'If your search is intense, God sends you the Guru. He never misses His responsibility. If you do not have the right Guru, the right Master, it means, something is seriously wrong with your seeking.' If our seeking is authentic, straightaway the Master happens in our life. He never delays. He has a much faster system than UPS or any other overnight delivery service. He can deliver in seconds. He never delays. The Divine never delays.

Please listen! All we need to do is transform our inner space to the space of completion, the space of eternal bliss. The first thing is to understand this secret. Whether we believe it or not, it is the truth: a basic secret. Once we enter spiritual life, once we decide we want to lead a spiritual life, all our worldly things are taken care of by the Divine. It responds to whatever we need and it takes care of whatever we have.

We may ask funny questions, '*Swamiji*, from today onwards if I stop working, will I have everything?' If we enter the spiritual mood, if we enter the meditative life, we will never think of dropping our work. Why would we think of dropping our work? We will only drop our worries about work. Then we will work in a much better way to our peak capability. Automatically we will work out of completion. We will have tremendous confidence, 'The whole of Existence protects me. The whole of Existence is my friend. I am not an enemy of this Whole. I am a friend of this Whole.'

When we understand that we are a friend of the whole of Existence, even after death we will not disappear because we know we will be there in the Universe in some form; that there is nothing to worry about.

I tell you this from experience: It is practical. From experience I tell you, we never perish. We continue to exist, in some form, somewhere. Even if we become enlightened, we become a pure conscious energy. We will be there, everywhere. We never die when we understand that Existence is intelligence.

Life After Life

9.25 *Those who worship the deities will take birth among the deities;*
those who worship ghosts and spirits will take birth among such
beings; those who worship ancestors go to the ancestors
Those who worship Me will live with Me.

9.26 *Whoever offers Me with love and devotion a leaf, a flower,*
fruit or water, I will accept and consume what is offered
by the pure-hearted.

9.27 *O Kaunteya (son of Kuntī), all that you do, all that you eat,*
all that you offer and give away, as well as all austerities
that you may perform, give them as an offering to Me.

9.28 *You will be freed from the bondage of work and its auspicious and*
inauspicious results. With your mind fixed on Me in this state of
renunciation, you will be liberated and come to Me.

We should study and understand these verses very deeply. Kṛṣṇa talks about the life that we lead now. He talks about the birth that we will take next. Understand that our present life is a result of our previous life. Whether we believe it or not, accept it or not, this is the truth. There is life after death as long as we are not enlightened.

Once we are enlightened, we merge into Universal Consciousness. Until then we take birth and go through the process of life and death.

Kṛṣṇa talks about the kind of life that we lead now. The last thought that we have at the time of death determines our next birth, next life. Please listen, our next life is completely dependent upon our last thought at the time of our death. If we think of money, we will be reborn as a rich man or as a dissatisfied man who always thinks about money. If we think of food, we will be reborn as a glutton or a pig. If we think of lazily elaxing, we will be reborn as a buffalo.

This is the truth. Our last thought determines our first thought in our next life. Actually we need not go to the extent of life and death. We see this in daily life itself. Our last thought affects our first thought. Every night we die and every morning we take birth. During the day, when we are in the waking state, we use our gross physical body or *sthūla śarīra* to carry on with our activities. When we sleep, if we have dreams, we use the subtle body or *sūkṣma śarīra* to travel to the places that we see in our dreams. When we are in deep sleep, when we have no dreams, then we are in our causal body or *kāraṇa śarīra*.

When we sleep at night, we actually change bodies. We are not aware that this happens. When we dream, we see ourselves doing various things in the dream. We run, talk, eat, and do everything in the dream. In our dream, we have created a world in which we live. If our body is on the bed, then who is this body in the dream? Our gross body is on the bed, while our subtle body is active in the dream. In the same way, the causal body is active during the deep sleep state.

Now, when we sleep, we actually die and are reborn in the gross body in the morning. We see that our last thought before sleeping affects our first thought upon waking. If we come back from the office with a frustrated mood about our boss, we wake up with the same mood in the morning. If we sleep with a blissful smile on our face, we will be happy the next morning.

This is the reason I tell anyone who think that they are following me or want to follow me: do completion for forty-two minutes before you sleep every night. Always sleep in the space of completion. If you have a dreamless sleep, I guarantee, you will have birthless life! If you have dream-free sleep, you will have birth-free, death-free life! That's all!

Because, even to have a dream, you need incompletions! If you don't have incompletions even to have dreams, how will you have incompletions to have one more body? So, whether you are going to have a body or not, is going to be decided only based on whether you are going to have dreams at night or not! While you sleep if you have a dream, you are going to have a body after death, unless the Master interferes and liberates you. If you don't have dreams, be assured, you are already liberated, and you are going to be liberated once you leave the body, completely!

When we do completions every night with full awareness, we enter a meditative state. In the meditative state, we can only be blissful. When we sleep in a blissful state, we wake up in the same state. Whatever feeling we wake up with in the morning, that same feeling stays with us throughout the day. Listen, the first thought we have in the morning stays with us throughout the day. How many have felt this? If you wake up dull in the morning, you will be dull throughout the day. If you wake up energized, you will be active and energetic throughout the day.

I tell people, 'When you wake up, dance your way to the bathroom! Feel the toothpaste on your teeth, feel the water on your body when you bathe. Bring in full awareness to every action. I am telling you, start the day every morning with heavy yoga, heavy weight-lifting, like your whole body should really sweat! That kind of heavy yoga and weight-lifting! Start the day with a blissful thought. For that we must sleep in the space of completion, in a blissful mood.

Every night do completion and every morning do heavy weight-lifting and yoga! I tell you, just these two will make you enlightened. Because, every night completion will lead to *vedic mind* and every morning heavy yoga will lead to *yogic body*. And these two will take care the whole day that you will have *enlightened living*. That's all! You don't need any other spiritual practice.

Exactly what happens everyday during sleep is exactly the same thing that happens during the time of death. Be very clear, the process of sleep and the process of death are not different. During the process of death, the soul passes through seven energy layers. The next body it enters depends on the *vāsana*, or the carried-over desires, the root patters that it comes with, from the previous life. It takes up a body that can help shed that *vāsana* in the next life. Our soul always tries to merge with the colorless and formless universal consciousness. However, the *vāsana* creates a slight tinge on the soul and it cannot completely merge with the Universal consciousness. So the soul takes up another body that can help remove this tinge and help it merge.

Now it is up to us how we make use of this lifetime. We can either fulfill our unfulfilled desires of the previous life by completing with our root patterns or we can build new desires in this life and stay in the cycle of birth and death. The kind of life that the soul chooses in the next life depends entirely on the *vāsana* and the last thought at the time of death.

People ask me, '*Swamiji*, I was not inclined towards spirituality at all. I was not into meditation; however, when I did the meditation I felt like I had been doing this for a long time. Why is it like that?'

Understand that you see only this life. You may not have done any meditation in this life. But you see a deep connection with meditation because you might have meditated in your previous life. You might have been a seeker in your previous life.You see, our next life depends on our last thought in this life. That does not mean that throughout our life we can think about money and food and suddenly at the time of death, we can say, 'Rāma, Kṛṣṇa or Śiva.' If we think about money, name and fame throughout our entire life, how can we expect to think about God when we leave our body? Naturally we will only think about money.

This is what Kṛṣṇa says in the first verse. When we are continuously aware of the Existential energy, when we continuously meditate on It, when our thoughts are on it all the time, whatever we may call it: Kṛṣṇa, Rama, Buddha, Universe, Parāśakti or anything, we will have *only* the same thought when we leave the body also. That is enough. We will start living with this energy. And It will ensure that our next birth takes us closer to this energy and liberates us from the cycle of birth and death.

IN SIMPLICITY LIES GREATNESS

He says next: 'If one offers Me with love and devotion, a leaf, flower, fruit or water, I will accept it,' He says, 'The Existence, the Divine is so alive that It responds to even simple things.'

Listen, He doesn't say, I accept only big things. He says, even simple things, I accept.

patraṁ puṣpaṁ phalaṁ toyaṁ yo me bhaktyā prayacchati I
tadahaṁ bhaktyupahṛtam aśnāmi prayatātmanaḥ II 9.26

'If one offers Me a leaf, flower, fruit or water with love and devotion, I will accept it.' This is the greatness of the Divine. The greatness of the Lord is that He is simple. Simplicity is the greatness of the Lord. Listen, simplicity is the real greatness. To be big, you don't need intelligence. Any one can show himself as big.

Simplicity is the great quality of the Divine. He says, 'Just a leaf, a flower, a fruit, a little water... simple things are enough. I accept it. I am pleased. I respond to it.'

He says in the fourth verse of this chapter:
mayā tatam idam sarvaṁ jagadvyaktamūrtinā
I am all-pervading, great, ultimate, divine.

Now, He says even though He is all-pervading, even though He is big, He accepts any small thing given with love and devotion. One major problem: Even if we know somebody is big or great, we can't relate with him unless he relates with us, unless he comes down to our level. Real greatness is not only being great. He must be able to relate with everybody. Otherwise, even if he is great, what can be done about it?

Many people in India know that great Masters are there. Again and again, they tell me, 'Yes, I know they are there, *Swamiji*. But how can I relate with them? They are somewhere. They are great, no doubt. Yet I have no way to relate with them. I have no way to establish communication with them.'

Here, Kṛṣṇa creates a way, even for ordinary people to relate with Him. On the one side, He shows His greatness. He declares with authority His greatness. On the other side, He shows us how to relate with Him. He says, 'Even if you offer a leaf, flower, fruit or water with love, I accept it. I relate with it.'

That is why, from time immemorial, enlightened masters are requested to live by begging, so that people can relate with them. In India, *Sannyāsis* live by begging. Even Buddha lived by begging. See, Buddha didn't beg because He wanted food. He can sit in His place and kings will bring food for Him! He comes down to beg so that we can relate with Him. We will feel He is a human being. When we give food, we talk to Him, we relate with Him, we feel that He is like us.

To make us feel comfortable, He comes down to our level. Modern day psychology has a beautiful term, 'zeroing down the distance'. To zero down the distance, Buddha begs. Here Kṛṣṇa zeroes down the distance completely. The distance between the Divine and us is zeroed down. That is the next important truth Kṛṣṇa reveals.

First thing Kṛṣṇa reveals is: He proves that the whole Cosmic energy, the whole Universe is intelligence. Next, the moment we understand it is intelligence, we relax from all tension, worry, fear and insecurity. He makes us understand that He is next to us and we can relate with Him easily.

See, as long as we think the world is material, matter, we feel like protecting ourselves from it. We feel that is the Whole and we are part. We fight with the Whole. That is why we feel deeply uprooted. We don't feel connected and relaxed. We don't feel homely because we fight with the Whole. The moment we understand we are part of the Whole, the Whole is the intelligence that responds to our thoughts, to our being, which responds to our consciousness, we relax into enlightenment!

I tell people, this verse is the lazy man's guide to enlightenment! If we are lazy, if we want enlightenment, this verse is the right way! The only way! Understand that the Universe is intelligence. It responds to our thoughts, words, actions and consciousness. When we understand this, we immediately relax and rest and enter divine consciousness, eternal consciousness.

Next, He says, 'When you drop yourself into the Eternal Consciousness, I take care of your *yoga* and *kṣema*. I take care of whatever you lack. I will supply what you lack and preserve what you have.'

Next He says, 'Even a simple leaf, water or a fruit or flower when you offer with love and devotion, I accept it.' Please be very clear, He is not asking because He doesn't have these things.

When you give a pack of cookies to your child and he opens it, you say, 'Give one to mummy!' It is not that we don't have a cookie or we want it. But if the child opens the pack, picks up a cookie and gives it to us, how happy we feel! We brought the cookies. However, when the child gives it back to us, we feel beautiful. We feel connected. And we know he wants to connect and relate with us.

Similarly, when we offer something to the Divine, don't think that He does not have and so you are offering. He is the one who gives everything to us in the first place! But when we offer, we show to the Divine: I want to connect to you. We show the Master, 'Oh Lord, I want to connect to you.' And the Master feels, 'When he wants to connect to Me, let Me connect to him.' We show a green signal for the Divine to enter into our space.

I tell people, 'Don't go to the temple empty-handed. Take at least two or three fruits. At least, take a few dollars. Take whatever you have. Always offer something to the Divine. Never think that the Divine doesn't have and so I am asking you to take these things. By giving to the Divine, you express a willing attitude to relate with Him. When you offer it to the Divine, He accepts it and He relates.'

Again and again, out of His compassion Kṛṣṇa reveals truths and techniques to Arjuna to liberate him. That is the job of an Incarnation. He comes down to the Earth to liberate as many as He can. Enlightened Masters are compassionate. They want everyone to become enlightened, liberated.

In these verses, Kṛṣṇa asks Arjuna to surrender everything to Him.

I tell you, surrendering to an Enlightened Master, an Incarnation is the easiest way to become enlightened. Be very clear, if we can surrender completely to the Universal energy or an Enlightened Master, we become enlightened. If we can surrender every action to the supreme Self, we experience a great sense of liberation.

We constantly worry. We are always tense. Again and again we think of the future or past. Why do we do that? Why do we always have a long face? We take too much on our shoulders. We think *we do* everything. We boost our ego when we do things successfully. When they do not go according to our plan, our ego is hurt. We think, 'How can I go wrong? How can my plan go wrong?'

Our ego is working continuously. It is either getting excited or getting hurt. In this process, what do we do? We think, 'How can I keep the ego continuously excited or how can I stop the ego from getting hurt?' We again and again think of ways to keep our ego in the excited state or look for ways to stop our ego from getting hurt.

We do not understand that by *letting go*, by surrendering to the Existential energy, we will be free, completely free. All our burdens will be gone. We do not realize this. All Enlightened Masters have spoken about surrender. It is the easiest way; however we make it the most difficult due to our ego.

Levels of Surrender

There are three levels in which we can surrender to the Existential energy.

The first level or basic level of surrender, is that of our actions. Whatever we do, whatever our actions are, surrender them to the Universal energy. All our actions, whether good or bad, when we surrender, will be taken care of. This is the basic level. Kṛṣṇa clearly says this in these verses, 'All your reactions to good and evil will be taken care of, if you offer all your actions, all your austerities to me.'

So many people offer worship every day in the temple. If they do that with the ego that they are doing it, then all they do is chant some verses mechanically and throw some flowers on the deity, that's all. When worship is done, when you chant verses, do it with full surrender to the Divine. Do it as if it were your last prayer. Feel the prayer. Put in your complete awareness and surrender it to the Divine. That should be the feeling when you do anything.

Not just prayers, everything that we do should be done with that level of surrender. When we surrender, we feel light. You see, when we surrender, our efficiency goes up. This is true! When we surrender our actions, we are not bothered about what will happen in the future. We know that now the ball is in His court; He will take care of whatever is going to happen; He knows best. When we surrender our actions, we put our entire burden on His shoulders. Whatever good or bad happens, He is now responsible and we also know that He can never do anything wrong.

The second level of surrender is that of intellect and mind. The first level is easier compared to this. When I say surrender our actions, we can say, 'Okay, I have done it.' But surrendering our mind is more difficult because it is not in our hands. You see, we can see our actions. We can say, 'O God, I have surrendered my actions to you.' But now will our mind keep quiet? No. It will keep saying, 'No, no, no. How can you do that? How can you not think about your future?' Our mind continuously analyzes!

One more thing, when I speak great truths, your mind analyzes them using its limited intellect. It thinks, 'What is He saying? Maybe it is possible for Him; but it is not for me. I can't think of completely surrendering myself to the Divine.' Your mind always looks for opportunities to hold you back. It logically analyzes using the intelligence it has.

When I say there are eleven dimensions in our system, you think, 'What are you saying, *Swamiji*? How is it possible?' This is what I mean by surrender of mind and intellect. When you surrender your mind and intellect to the universal energy, you experience great truths. When you do not surrender, your intellect continuously stops you from moving forward. Once you surrender, you experiment and you see quantum progress. You go beyond words. You start to experience.

The third and the most difficult level of surrender is that of the senses.

A history from Mahābhārat illustrates this:

> Once, Kṛṣṇa and Arjuna were walking outdoors. While they walked, Kṛṣṇa suddenly pointed at a crow on the tree and told Arjuna, 'Hey Arjuna, can you see that green crow?' Arjuna replied, 'Yes Kṛṣṇa, I see it. I see the green crow.'
>
> After some time, Kṛṣṇa pointed to another crow and said, 'Arjuna, can you see that black crow?' Arjuna immediately replied, 'Yes Kṛṣṇa, I see the black crow.'
>
> Kṛṣṇa asked Arjuna, 'Are you a fool? Earlier when I showed a green crow, you said you can see a green crow. Now when I showed a black crow, you say you can see a black crow. Are you a fool? How can a crow be green?'
>
> Arjuna replied, 'O Kṛṣṇa, I don't know all that. When you asked me to see a green crow, I saw a green crow. Now when you asked me to see a black crow, I saw a black crow.'

This is surrender of the senses! Arjuna had surrendered completely to Kṛṣṇa. He had surrendered even his senses to Kṛṣṇa. If the Master says something, the disciple takes it *as it is*. That is the level of surrender. When we reach this level of surrender, we are *one* with the Divine. The Divine takes cares of us.

Kṛṣṇa says this clearly. Every Enlightened Master makes this promise. When we surrender ourselves to the Master, to the Divine, to the Universal energy, it takes care of us. When we offer all our actions to the Universal energy, It takes care of us. The entire burden on our shoulders is offloaded. This is the promise of every Enlightened Master.

Anyone Can Reach Me

9.29 *I am equal to all beings. No one to Me is hateful or dear.*
But, whoever worships, offers enriching service onto Me in devotion, is in Me and I am also indeed in him.

9.30 *Even if the most sinful person engages himself*
in devotional service, he is to be considered saintly
because he is properly situated in his determination.

9.31 *He quickly becomes a righteous being [dharmātma]*
and attains lasting peace.
O Kaunteya (son of Kuntī), declare it boldly that
My devotee never perishes.

9.32 *O Pārtha, anyone who takes shelter in Me, women, traders,*
workers or even sinners can approach the supreme destination.

9.33 *How much easier then it is for the learned, the righteous,*
the devotees and saintly kings, who in this temporary miserable
world engage in loving service unto Me.

9.34 *Fix your mind on Me, be devoted to Me, worship Me, and bow*
down to Me. Thus, uniting yourself with Me by setting Me as the
supreme goal and the sole refuge, you shall certainly come to Me.

An Enlightened Master wants nothing from this world. After realizing the supreme knowledge, he is beyond material pursuits, what can he want from anybody? He is here out of his compassion to awaken mankind into this reality.

A true Master is never envious of anybody. Envy enters us when we think that somebody else has something we do not have and something that we want. There is nothing wrong with desiring something because we need it. See, each one of us is born with a certain set of desires and we bring with us the energy to fulfill them also.

Ramaṇa Mahaṛṣi says beautifully, 'The Universe has enough to satisfy each man's *needs*; however it does not have enough to satisfy a single man's *wants*.' Our *needs* become *wants* when we look at others and accumulate their desires into our own list. If you notice in life, most of our actions are governed by comparing our lives with others. Buddha says, 'Nothing exists but in relationship.' See, all adjectives of good, bad, tall, thin, ugly or beautiful, come when you compare with others, right? Something is good because something else is bad in comparison to that. So, our lives are run by constant comparison with those around us. When we have a clear context about what we really want, then we will spend all our energies in fulfilling those needs, without worrying about what others want or think.

In this verse, Kṛṣṇa says that he does not dislike anybody. He also says that He is not partial to anyone. Normally, in our lives we are partial to those who are helpful to us. From childhood, we are taught to love those who are potentially useful in our lives, based on what we get back in return.

Everything has been reduced to a business transaction. If someone is nice to us, we are nice to them. If someone says something that hurts us, they become our enemies. We are vulnerable to the outside world, to what others say and do. As long as we are beggars, we differentiate a rich man from a poor man. A beggar is constantly seeking, begging. A beggar is on the road begging money; we are in temples begging God for something or the other. There is no real difference! This is what we do all the time, with or without our knowledge.

My Devotee Never Perishes

An Enlightened Master wants nothing. He gives constantly. He radiates love because that is his true nature. He does not care who receives it; he simply gives. A river flows happily from one region to the other all the way from the hills to the ocean. It meets various kinds of stones and grass along the way. All kinds of people bathe in it; even buffaloes bathe in it.

Does the river differentiate? Does the river say, 'No, I will give water only to such and such a person?' No! A river flows continuously, happily without bothering about who comes in contact with it. The same is the case with an Enlightened Master.

Now Kṛṣṇa says, 'If one is engaged in devotional service, then even if he commits the most abominable actions, he is considered saintly. He quickly becomes eternal and attains Eternal consciousness. O Kaunteya (son of Kuntī), declare it boldly, that My devotee never perishes.'

He goes on to say that His devotee never perishes. He says, 'Not only I am declaring to you, you declare to the whole world, My devotee never perishes.'

He says in the verse:

kṣipraṁ bhavati dharmātmā śaśvac-chāntiṁ nigacchati I
kaunteya pratijānīhi na me bhaktaḥ praṇaśyati II 9.31

'He who quickly becomes righteous and understands this truth, enters into eternal bliss, eternal consciousness, O Kaunteya; declare it boldly, *pratijānīhi* means 'declare it boldly', that my devotee never perishes, *na me bhaktaḥ praṇaśyati*.'

Understand that Existence is intelligence. You will never perish, you will never die because you will be in Existence somewhere in some form. This body may move; however you will be there forever. When we understand the whole Cosmic energy is intelligence, our whole life will be blessed with what we want. Whatever we lack will be supplied and whatever we have will be preserved.

And I tell you a practical thing. Consciously decide, 'From today I will live in the space of completion and bliss, in a blissful mood, in a blissful way, in utterly relaxed consciousness.' I promise you will attract Lakṣmī (goddess of wealth). You will attract wealth. You will create much more than a goldsmith.

When we really, intensely understand this truth—the whole Universe is energy, the whole Existence is energy—please listen, *yoga* (success) and *kṣema* (protection) happen in our life.

> Let me tell you from my personal experience.
>
> I can quote so many great devotees' lives, where the Divine came down and served them, where the Divine took care of them. When Mirābāi was poisoned, Sri Kṛṣṇa came and protected her. So many millions of stories I can narrate!
>
> But let me tell you about my own life. Since I left home, when I was seventeen, I have lived without touching money. With one water pot, with this two-piece robe, walking the length and breadth of India, living under trees, begging and eating, I have lived. I tell you, whether you want it or not, accept it or not, believe it or not, the Divine always protects. This is the solid truth.

When we understand this truth, not only in this world, wherever we go, we are protected. We relax into the consciousness that Existence continuously protects us, takes care of us.

When we think that the Whole is our enemy, we will be continuously antagonizing it. When we understand that the Whole is our friend, we will relax and enjoy the whole of Existence. Making our life into hell or heaven is dependent upon understanding this single verse, understanding Existence and trusting it.

Understanding Rituals

The whole chapter reveals this single secret, that is—the Cosmic energy, the whole Universe is intelligence. It responds to our thoughts, again and again. It answers our dreams, our thoughts and our very consciousness.

Again and again Kṛṣṇa talks about the correct understanding and context of rituals and sacrifices to God. We see many people going to the temple. They take one hundred and one coconuts and break them in front of the deity. In the Tirupati temple of Lord Venkaṭeśvara (incarnation of Śrī Viṣṇu), people offer their hair as a sacrifice. If we offer hair and pray and come back home, nothing is going to happen.

When we offer something, it represents the surrender of our ego. When we sacrifice our hair in Tirupati, we surrender our ego to Lord Venkaṭeśvara. When we break a coconut, the shell of the ego is broken into pieces. But what generally happens? When we do some sacrifice, we think we did something great. All the sacrifices that we make are only to boost our ego. Listen, if a sacrifice is made with complete gratitude and surrender, it is an enriching sacrifice.

Sacrificing in temples has become a two-way business. People who act out of ego make a business deal with God, 'I will donate so much money for the temple; leave one spot for me in heaven.' Another class of people sit outside the temple and make money from sacrifices. People ask me, 'Are sacrifices wrong? Is worship and sacrifice for a particular deity wrong?' No, it is not wrong; but understand that we are not worshipping or sacrificing to that one particular deity. We must go beyond that. When we make a sacrifice from our being, we merge with the Existential energy. Every deity will then appear the same.

Everything is Kṛṣṇa or Rama, Śiva or Buddha. This is what Kṛṣṇa says here. He is the only enjoyer of all sacrifices. When we understand His transcendental nature in everything around us, any small thing that we give from our whole being to even a rock becomes a sacrifice. That rock need not be carved into a statue of Kṛṣṇa or Śiva. We need not name it because we see the energy behind that rock.

These two verses must be carefully understood. If not, they can be conveniently used as a justification to do whatever one wants. See, Kṛṣṇa does not give a license to do whatever we want here.

If we are classifying an action as good, bad, saintly or sinful based on guidelines laid down by society or someone else, then be very clear we operate at the conscience level. No action is good or bad in itself. The entire situation, the whole context should be considered. The act may remain the same; however, the situation and the context might have completely changed.

A small story:

There was a snake that lived in a village. It bit the villagers even if they didn't disturb it. Nobody dared to go close to it. The entire area where it used to stay was feared. Nobody entered that area.

One day a monk passed by that village and saw that the villagers did not approach that area. On enquiring, he understood the situation. He asked the snake, 'Why do you bite everyone? What do you gain from being so violent? Everyone fears you!'

On listening to the monk's words, the snake promised he would mend his ways from that day onwards. Days passed by. Slowly, there was a change in the scene in the village. The snake stopped bothering everyone. It lay quietly in one place. People started to test it by poking it with a stick to confirm that the snake had really softened up. The snake never reacted.

They now started torturing the snake. Kids from the near-by village threw stones at it. They ill-treated the snake and played with it. The snake quietly allowed all of this without uttering a word. Soon, the snake was reduced to almost a pulp and lost all life and vigor.

After a few months, the monk once again passed by that village. He was shocked to see the condition of the snake. He enquired what happened and the snake told him all that had happened.

The monk asked, 'I told you only not to bite; did I tell you not to hiss?'

You see, this is what happens when we operate from our conscience, from the wrong context. Because somebody said something, if we apply it blindly without considering the present situation and context. We invite trouble for ourselves. In this case, the monk's advice was taken literally and the snake ended up suffering.

There is a deeper layer of operation called Consciousness. In Consciousness, we become spontaneous. When consciousness flowers, we know what is the context, what needs to be done at that point in time. When this happens, whatever is done is for the good of everyone. Even if an action seems to violate the norms of society, it is always for the good of humanity. Kṛṣṇa killing demons may appear like the act of a criminal. Yet He established truthfulness and justice by doing it.

Please listen. When devotion matures, consciousness flowers. Devotion may seem different from knowledge when it is not ripe. Kṛṣṇa says that His devotee never perishes. Devotion is not simply offering worship daily to Kṛṣṇa's photo, lighting camphor, lamps and offering garlands. When one is a true devotee of Kṛṣṇa, he becomes Kṛṣṇa. He experiences Kṛṣṇa consciousness. The ultimate consciousness is where no good, bad, evil or virtue exists.

Devotion, knowledge and wisdom appear to be different when they are not ripe. When they mature, they become the same. One experiences true wisdom at the peak of devotion or peak of knowledge.

Let me tell you about Triveni Sangam, what is called Prayag in India. It is a confluence of three sacred rivers—Gaṇgā, Yamunā and Sarasvatī, near the city of Allahabad. While Gaṇgā and Yamunā are visible, the third, Sarasvatī flows underground and becomes visible only at the point of merging. Gaṇgā is the river of Lord Śiva and stands for knowledge or *jñāna*. All Śiva temples are on the banks of river Gaṇgā. Yamunā is the river of Lord Kṛṣṇa and stands for devotion or *bhakti*. All Kṛṣṇa temples are on the banks of river Yamunā. When Gaṇgā and Yamuna merge, when knowledge and devotion merge, Sarasvatī or wisdom automatically happens! Unless this merging happens, we cannot see or experience wisdom. That is why Sarasvatī remains hidden until the point of merging!

The last two verses can be misunderstood if misinterpreted. Kṛṣṇa says, 'Anyone can reach Me through devotion, whether they are women, traders or workers, or even sinners.' He makes a point that there is no pre-qualification. Even in the age of Kṛṣṇa, there was a distinction between various trades as well as between men and women.

Kṛṣṇa is pragmatic in acknowledging this fact and is not trying to justify the distinction. Someone asked Ramaṇa Mahaṛṣi whether he was qualified to enter a spiritual path. Ramaṇa asked him, 'Are you still breathing?' Taken aback the man said, 'Yes.' Ramaṇa said that was qualification enough; if he was alive, he was qualified. Kṛṣṇa's message is the same. All one needs is devotion to attain Kṛṣṇa consciousness. Nothing else is needed.

In the Vedic system, the caste system was a scientific practice to enable each one's potential to radiate. The *varṇa* or caste system practiced by Hindus from time immemorial had its roots in the *gurukul* education. Actually *varṇa* meant vocation, which was determined by the Master for each child. It was not based upon birth as birthright, rather it was based upon aptitude. Unfortunately, over time this practice became a birthright. This corruption of such a scientific practice has led to many social inequalities and injustices. The son of a *brāhmaṇa* has no right to call himself a *brāhmaṇa*, unless he has the aptitude. In our ashram, we have brahmacāri priests, who are of faiths other than Hindu. In no way are these young priests inferior to any *brāhmaṇa*.

The point Kṛṣṇa makes here is that irrespective of caste, a person who has faith and devotion to Him can attain Him. Even if a person does not lead the life of a *brāhmaṇa*, he can reach and experience the ultimate consciousness. A person may follow any profession; however, if his inner space is cleansed, he can attain and experience Kṛṣṇa consciousness.

Now, a *brāhmaṇa* is exposed to the scriptures and is trained to attain the knowledge of the ultimate Truth. He is exposed to the atmosphere that is conducive for meditation and other spiritual practices in the ashram. How much easier it is for a *brāhmaṇa*! See, if Kṛṣṇa is so accessible for anybody, then imagine how much more accessible He is for a person constantly engaged in His thoughts!

All practices, like meditation and rituals, cleanse the inner space and allow the space of completion to flower. When this space is cleansed, transformation automatically happens. Many times people tell me, '*Swamiji*, I have been meditating for twenty five years.' They tell me this proudly. I tell them, 'What a shame, if even after twenty five years of meditation, this remains your state!'

Always Think Of Me

In the last verse of this chapter Kṛṣṇa says, 'Engage your mind, always thinking of Me.' Please understand that the whole Universe, the whole Cosmos is intelligence and it responds to our thoughts, it responds to our consciousness, to our very being.

man-manā bhava mad-bhakto mad-yājī māṁ namaskuru |
mām evaiṣyasi yuktvaivam ātmānaṁ mat-parāyaṇaḥ || 9.34

Let me narrate an incident from my life:

> Some time after Enlightenment, I was sitting in a forest in Tamil Nadu. There was a big snake lying just next to me. I had my eyes open but was resting in the universal consciousness, in a meditative mood of restful awareness. Several hours must have passed before I came out of my meditative state and the first thought that came to my mind was, 'Oh, it is a snake.' As long as I was in the meditative state, I did not think of the snake. You will be surprised that as soon as the thought of the snake came to my mind, the snake began to realize that I was a man! It looked up, put down its hood and moved away. The fear in me triggered the fear in the snake.

The entire Universe responds to each and every thought that we have. It is pure intelligence. So we must be careful and integrated to what we think. When you start listening to you, integrity happens in you.

We are careful when we talk to others to make sure nobody is hurt. However when it comes to ourselves, we treat our inside worse than a garbage can. Almost all the time, you use very loose words inside you and outside you. A continuous stream of random thoughts, worries, fantasy, etc. goes on all the time. It is like a continuous television going on inside and we have misplaced the remote control to stop it!

Please listen! Integrity does not mean only fulfilling the word you utter in front of people. Integrity is honoring the words and thoughts that happen inside you, even when you are in your bedroom or bathroom. For example, suppose you utter a word, 'I commit with me that I will do morning yoga properly.' Then, you should give your life to fulfill it. Listen, the commitment you make to others is *word*, the commitment you make to yourself is *thought*.

Whenever some people come and tell me, 'I surrender to you,' I laugh at them. We use loose words; we speak so casually. Each word you utter and honor integrates you, strengthens you. Each time you don't respect or honor your word, you are weakened. Understand, each time you honor the words you give to others, *their* confidence in you grows. Each time you honor the word you give to yourself, *your* confidence in you grows. Success is nothing but *you* having confidence in you and *others* having confidence in you. That is all. Life is complete.

See, our inner space reflects the outer incidents. The entire Universe responds beautifully to each and every thought. That is why it is so important to keep our inner space cleansed and complete. The thought patterns that happen inside can be cleansed with integrity and kept in the space of positivity. When the thought patterns are positive, only positive incidents are attracted.

Listen! Take the words you utter in your inner space very seriously. The most powerful being in your life is telling you, '*tathāstu! tathāstu (so be it)!*' to whatever words you utter. Who is that being? YOU! He is sitting inside you as the *antaryāmi* (inner being) and saying '*tathāstu! tathāstu! tathāstu!*' to whatever you utter.

If you utter the words, 'I am the most healthiest person, I am going to live until Swamiji lives in the body,' the inner most being says, '*tathāstu!*

tathāstu!' If you think, 'I am sick, I have back pain. I cannot do this, I cannot do that. I am broke. I am really having tiredness. And if I can do the work, they will exploit me.' Then, your being inside says, '*tathāstu! tathāstu!*'

See, it is like this. If we are constantly worried and fear that we will fall ill, we attract incidents that make us fall ill again and again. Similarly, if we are constantly happy and blissful, we attract blissful events and happy people in our lives.

When Kṛṣṇa says, 'Engage your mind in always thinking of Me,' He speaks about cleansing the inner space. When our mind is engaged in thinking of the Divine, we become Divine. The moment we understand this, we relax into eternal bliss.

The moment we relax into eternal bliss, the Divine takes care of us. Whatever we lack is brought to us and whatever we have is preserved for us. Naturally, we will experience, enjoy and enrich both the inner space and the outer space. This is the ultimate secret that Kṛṣṇa reveals to Arjuna.

Let us pray to the *Parabrahma* Kṛṣṇa, the Divine consciousness, the Cosmic intelligence to make us understand this secret of all secrets and experience the outer space and the inner space with eternal bliss, *Nityānanda*.

Thank you!

Thus ends the ninth chapter named ***Rājavidyā Rājaguhya Yogaḥ****, 'The Yoga of Supreme Knowledge and Supreme Secret,' of the* ***Bhagavad Gītā Upaniṣad, Brahmavidyā Yogaśāstra****, the scripture of yoga dealing with the science of the Absolute in the form of* ***Śrī Kṛṣṇārjuna saṃvād****, dialogue between Śrī Kṛṣṇa and Arjuna.*

CHAPTER

10

Vibhūti Yogaḥ

You Are The Ultimate

I am the Creator, the Created and the Creation. I am the beginning, the middle and the end. All else is illusion. He who knows this glory and power of mine, is fully united in Me. Know Me and be liberated.

YOU ARE THE ULTIMATE

This chapter, the tenth chapter of the *Bhagavad Gītā*, is called *Vibhūti Yogaḥ*, the yoga of Divine manifestations. In this chapter, Kṛṣṇa explains His glories.

In the last chapter, Kṛṣṇa gave the technique or the understanding of feeling deeply connected with the Whole, with Existence. He told Arjuna that He is revealing the greatest of all secrets to him because Arjuna is His dear friend. Now He explains the next step. He goes on at length and in great detail explaining how He is the ultimate and how He expresses Himself.

People often see me observing and appreciating my own photographs. They see me listening to songs in my praise and enjoying them. They see me dressed in finery at times and think I am admiring myself. To me, this body, 'I,' is not reality. My skin is foreign to me, leave alone what I wear on top of my skin.

An enlightened being has no identity. His only identity is the merged identity with the Universe. When Kṛṣṇa, the ultimate Master, talks about Himself in this chapter, He talks from the perspective of *Parabrahma* Kṛṣṇa, the cosmic Kṛṣṇa and not Vāsudeva Kṛṣṇa, son of Vāsudeva, the embodied Kṛṣṇa. The entire *Gītā* is delivered from Kṛṣṇa's Cosmic consciousness. In this chapter especially, He is at the peak of His Cosmic consciousness, before He reveals Himself as that consciousness to Arjuna in the next chapter.

Every word that the great *Jagadguru*, the universal Master utters here, is a gift to Arjuna and to humanity. The verses in this chapter are the authority on which the *Bhagavad Gītā* rests. It is these verses that make the *Gītā*, a sacred scripture.

Because You Are My Dear Friend

10.1 *Bhagavān Kṛṣṇa says:*
Listen carefully again, Oh mighty-armed Arjuna!
Because you are My dear friend, I shall speak further
on the Supreme knowledge for your welfare.

śri bhagavān uvāca
bhūya eva mahā-bāho śṛṇu me paramaṁ vacaḥ I
yat te 'haṁ prīyamāṇāya vakṣyami hita-kāmayā II 10.1

A Master's relationship with his disciple is in many forms. Usually it is described in five forms.

The most basic relationship between a Master and disciple is that of a Master and a servant, *dāsa bhāva.* The relationship of Hanumān with Rāma represents this type. Another is the relationship of a mother with her child, *vātsalya bhāva,* as in the case of Yaśodā to infant Kṛṣṇa. The third is the relationship of a child with the mother, *mātru bhāva,* like the relation of Rāmakṛṣṇa to Ma Kālī.

The fourth relationship is that of friendship, *sakha bhāva,* feeling that the Master is the closest friend. The fifth is that of the beloved, *madhura bhāva,* like the relationship of Radhā to Kṛṣṇa.

Here, Kṛṣṇa refers to the fourth relationship, *sakha bhāva,* as exemplified by His friendship with Arjuna. He is the Master to His disciple Arjuna as well as Arjuna's friend.

Usually, as an individual ego, we see the Whole as our enemy. We are like small waves in a big ocean. However, suddenly, the wave starts thinking that the ocean is its enemy. When it is created, while it exists or when it drops, the wave is connected to the ocean. However, the wave thinks that it is in some way different from the ocean. Not only that, the wave starts fighting with the ocean. For the wave to realize that it is fully connected to the ocean, it must be consumed by the ocean. The ego must dissolve. The individual identity of the wave must disappear. This is the first step to Enlightenment.

We live in the illusion of our self-created identities. Each wave relates to another wave but not to the ocean. It adopts another wave as its father, mother, wife or child and relates with them. However, ultimately, each one of these related waves disappears into the ocean just like the wave itself.

If we look at the human body, we can see this *oneness* so beautifully exemplified. The human body consists of trillions of cells living in total harmony. The individual cell, though it has intelligence by itself, can survive even if its center, the nucleus, which is considered the central intelligence of the cell, is removed. However, when it is a part of the whole body, it is not the intelligence of the individual cell alone that is at work, but the collective intelligence of the body-mind system that governs. This collective intelligence ensures that this remarkable system of the human body-mind works smoothly.

Listen. Enlightened people think they are ordinary. And unenlightened people think they are extraordinary! When we feel that we have undergone maximum suffering, our ego feels good; we feel we are extraordinary. Only when our enemy is big, we feel big. When our enemy is small, we feel small. For the same reason, if our suffering is big, we feel good and our ego is satisfied. We measure life by the amount of our suffering. That is why we constantly torture others as well as ourselves.

Because of our ego, we think that we are extraordinary and that a lot of things happen in this world because of us. We are all unique creations of Existence but we are not responsible for the world. The wave cannot attribute to itself the power of the ocean. It must realize that it is a part of the ocean. Instead, if it tries to separate itself from the ocean, it is a futile effort. Please be very clear that the world does not run because of us. It runs in spite of us! Fifty years before our birth, don't you think the world was running as it is now? Fifty years hence, do you think the world will stop because you are not here?

A proverb says that if the cat closes its eyes, it thinks the whole world has become dark! It thinks because it can't see the world for those few moments, no one can see it either!

Rāmaṇa Maharṣi describes a beautiful story:

> A man was traveling on a train carrying his luggage on his head. A fellow passenger asked, 'Why are you carrying your luggage on your head? You can put it down and sit peacefully.'
>
> The man replied, 'It would be too heavy for the train!'
>
> Little did he realize that the train was even now not only carrying him, but his luggage as well! In the same way, the Divine not only takes care of *you*, it also takes care of *your mind*. But you always think you are taking care of yourself. That is the foolishness of the mind.

We are waves of the Divine. We are part of this Whole. We cannot be an isolated existence. We exist in the cosmic Whole just as the wave exists in the vast expanse of the ocean. The ego gives us the feeling that we are individual, separate and isolated whereas the reality is that we are a part of this Existence, in It and supported by It.

Existence Is Your Friend!

There are two ways in which we can live. First, we can embrace and welcome reality, in which case our ego or root pattern must dissolve because only then can we face reality. Please understand that *this* reality is God. God is not some entity hidden in some remote corner of the Universe or in the sky. He is the reality around us.

God is not remote, He is immediate. It is unfortunate that this word *God* is destroyed by the remote meaning of some old man with a long beard sitting in some remote heaven or hell. If He is sitting in a remote heaven, it is useless hell. God is immediate! Divine is immediate!

The second way of living is how most of us live: We create a shell, a dream world around ourselves to defend a false ego which has no substance in reality. This is what is meant by *māyā*—illusion. Since we are hidden in this capsule of our unreal world with our ego as the center, we cannot feel the immediate presence of God, who is actually the closest to us.

The *prāṇa* (vital energy), the air that we breathe, which is going inside our body and coming out, is not our property. It is the property of Existence. We do not need air to survive. We need *prāṇa* to survive. Constantly, we take *prāṇa* through the air from the Cosmos. If the incoming breath carries more *prānā* than the outgoing breath, we are going towards life. Then, we expand, we strengthen our body, our energy. If the outgoing breath carries more *prānā* than the incoming breath, be very clear, we are going towards death. Understand that whatever we think of as our being cannot function, if *prāṇa* doesn't go in and come out.

Again and again, we think that we end where the physical boundary of our body ends and anything outside that boundary constitutes the external world. This physical boundary is not our boundary. We think that whatever is outside the physical boundary of our body constitutes Existence and that it is our enemy.

Imagine that the sun disappears one day. Do you think we could live without the rays of the sun? If the air were to disappear, will we be able to survive? If we are dependent for our survival on the sun that is billions of miles away, how can our boundary end where the physical boundary of our body ends? Understand, we are deeply related to Existence. We are not completely separate, self-sufficient entities. When we lose sight of the Whole, we become unaware of our links to one another.

Since you consider Existence to be your enemy, you continuously try to protect yourself from others. Look at yourself carefully and you will notice that you always look at people with the attitude, 'Why has he come? What is he going to take from me? How will he exploit me?'

Continuously, you are in a protective mood, trying to protect yourself from others. This is because you feel threatened by the Existence of the other. The moment you think Existence or the Whole is your enemy, you become defensive. Defending is a polite word for offending. All over the world, the military forces of all countries are called defensive armies. Then who is offending? Every country claims that its army is an army for defending itself. Then who is really offending? When you feel the Whole is your enemy, that everybody except *you* is your enemy, you spy continuously and fight constantly. The fighting mood creates an increasingly violent feeling in you, with more and more restlessness

Listen! The first thing Kṛṣṇa teaches as *rājavidya rājaguhyaṁ* (secret of all secrets), is that Existence is *not* your enemy. It responds to your thoughts. It continuously cares for you. It is intelligence.

Please listen!

If you live with the attitude of enmity with the Whole, even when you live, you will constantly be tortured. When you live with the feeling of friendliness or *sakha bhāva*, with the attitude that Existence is your friend, that Existence is your own, you feel a deep easiness.

We need to realize that we are part of the same energy system as the Universe. Hindu scriptures describe the five energy elements that comprise Nature: earth, water, fire, air and ether. The human system is a combination of the same elements as the Universe, so are all beings, inanimate and animate.

Above all, more than the easiness, you will feel deeply connected to Existence. Even if the wave thinks that it is different from the ocean and starts defending itself from the ocean, ultimately it will fall into the ocean, however much it tries to defend itself! By its very nature, the wave starts in the ocean, exists in the ocean and falls into the ocean. If it understands that it is a part of the ocean, it will be utterly relaxed. It will live a blissful life. If it fights the fact, it will fight with the ocean. But eventually it has to fall into the ocean.

The ultimate secret that Kṛṣṇa wants to reveal is that Existence, Parāśakti, Brahman, is your friend, not your enemy. It is intelligence and it responds to your thoughts. This is the first understanding.

Next, in this chapter, Kṛṣṇa says, 'I am That.' He says, 'I am the whole of Existence.' In the next chapter, He gives the experience of the Cosmic consciousness to Arjuna. These chapters lead Arjuna step-by-step to an elevated consciousness.

In the previous chapter, *rājavidya rājaguhyaṁ yogaḥ* Kṛṣṇa says, 'Drop your enmity with Existence, against the Universal energy, Brahman and Ātman.' In this chapter, *Vibhūti Yogaḥ*, He says, 'I am the same energy. Not only you don't need to have enmity, you can have *deep love*.' Now, He explains how to feel connected to Existence. In the next chapter, *Viśvarūpa Darśana Yoga*, He gives the Cosmic experience to Arjuna that He is in the whole Cosmic consciousness.

First, He removes enmity, then, He creates the feeling of connectedness, deep friendliness. Finally, He gives the *advaitic* (non-dual) experience. These three chapters lead Arjuna step-by-step. They elevate Arjuna from a low level to a higher level.

Let us study this scripture, Yogaśāstra, with intense devotion and deep sincerity. Along with Arjuna, we will grow into completion. We will not miss it.

Kṛṣṇa says, 'For your benefit, because you are My dear friend, I shall speak to you further, giving knowledge that is better than what I have already explained.' Kṛṣṇa explains His glory not for His own sake but for Arjuna's sake. Kṛṣṇa does not explain His glory to show His ego.

Understand an important thing:

The ego of the king is based upon how many people accept him as king. Suddenly, if all his citizens are taken away from him, what will happen to his kingdom? He will lose the base, he will lose the very idea of kinghood. His ego will be totally shaken.

GLORY OF ĀTMAJÑĀNA (KNOWLEDGE OF THE SELF)

A beautiful happening:

A great saint called Dakṣiṇāmūrti Swamigal lived in Tamil Nadu. He lived the life of a *Paramahamsa* (enlightened one). The sky was all that covered his body. He never wore clothing. He lived like a child, in bliss.

One day a king came to meet him. Swami was sitting under a big tree meditating blissfully. The king expected Swami to stand up and receive him with respect. Swami however did not bother. The king egoistically said, 'What! You are an ordinary beggar. I am a king. Don't you know how to respect me?'

The Swami laughed and said, 'Actually, you are the beggar. You are begging respect from me. You feel respected only when somebody gives you respect. However, I don't feel respected when somebody gives me respect nor do I feel disrespected when somebody doesn't give me respect. Whether somebody respects me or not, it is not in any way related to my consciousness. I do not ask you why you are not respecting me.'

Then he continued, 'Your personality or ego could be shaken if your army and all your ministers leave you. Oh king, your being is dependent upon somebody else.'

That is why it is said that when Buddha begged for alms, He looked like a king and the kings looked like beggars! Outward possessions cannot make us regal. The inner bliss that radiates makes us regal.

Dakṣiṇāmūrti Swamigal says, 'You are a king as long as your citizens accept you. So naturally, directly or indirectly, you will be begging your citizens to accept you because your consciousness is dependent upon them. In my case, whether somebody accepts or not, I am blissful! I am a

> *Paramahamsa.* My Paramahamsa-hood can never be taken away from me. But your kinghood can be taken away from you. So, be sure that the moment you ask for respect, you are a beggar. I am not.'

A clear truth is that the person whose ego is fed by more and more citizens is a politician. He is an egoistic person. But an enlightened man reveals himself for the sake of the disciple's understanding. Here, Kṛṣṇa does not speak about Himself out of ego. Whether Arjuna accepts it or not, Kṛṣṇa *is* Kṛṣṇa.

Kṛṣṇa was in a blissful state even before Arjuna became His disciple. Kṛṣṇa will be in a blissful state even after Arjuna becomes His disciple. Irrespective of whether Arjuna is His disciple or not, Kṛṣṇa is in the same blissful consciousness.

One important thing: In the next chapter, Arjuna says, 'Oh Kṛṣṇa! Forgive me. I called You by Your community name: 'Hey Kṛṣṇa, Hey Yādava, Hey Saketi! I called You by Your first name.' In India, if you are a very close friend to a person, only then you call him by his community name: Yādava (Kṛṣṇa's community). Arjuna wails, 'I called You Kṛṣṇa, Yādava and I called You my friend! I called You by these names thinking that You are my friend, a normal human being like me. But now, I understand. You are the God of gods. You are Mahādev (supreme God). Forgive me please, I beg of You! Please accept me as Your disciple. Forgive me for my ignorance. I did not know Your greatness, please forgive me!'

Because of this statement, Kṛṣṇa's ego does not become big. Please understand: Kṛṣṇa has all the glory from day one until the very end. Even with all His glory, He allowed Arjuna to call Him by His first names. He never said, 'Don't you know who I am? How dare you call me by my first name?' He never carried a business card!

Even when Arjuna was talking to Kṛṣṇa in a friendly way, He was humble. Kṛṣṇa responded to Arjuna in the same way that Arjuna spoke to Him. Kṛṣṇa is simple and humble. Before the *Gītā* started, at the time of the *Gītā* and after the *Gītā*, Kṛṣṇa is the same, eternally. Only Arjuna undergoes a tremendous change.

Here, Kṛṣṇa does not explain His glories out of ego. He explains so that Arjuna will understand, intranalyze and experience Him. When Kṛṣṇa says, '*I am*,' He means the cosmic consciousness, the egoless being and the enlightened energy. Again and again, He expresses the glory of enlightenment, the glory of *ātmajñāna* (knowledge of the Self). That is why He is so complete and confident. With such clarity, with such integrity and authenticity, He explains, 'I am Everything.' Even to utter these words, you need courage. No normal man can say, '*I am God*' to somebody else. If he does, the next day he will be in a mental asylum with a special seat reserved for him!

Here, Kṛṣṇa is courageous enough to declare and the person who is listening experiences it. What is the science? What does it take for an enlightened man to declare himself as enlightened, as Incarnation and as God, *Bhagavān*? What do we need as a disciple to experience that as the truth?

Many hundreds of enlightened Masters declare this truth again and again. Sometimes the people who listen to them become enlightened like Arjuna or Vivekananda. Sometimes the disciple is hurt and disturbed by the statement and abuses the Master.

Śrī Rāmakṛṣṇa said, 'The one who came as Rāma, who came as Kṛṣṇa, is residing in this body as Rāmakṛṣṇa.' He boldly declared this, not when he was healthy, but when he was suffering from throat cancer. These words did something in Vivekananda. It was then that Narendra became Vivekananda.

When Kṛṣṇa declared, 'I am God,' Arjuna became enlightened. How? What do you need to create this experience?

TRUST GOD HAS INTELLIGENCE, AND SURRENDER

See, be very clear that the experiences of Kṛṣṇa, Śiva, Buddha and Mahāvīra, are all one and the same. As the enlightenment experience, it is the same. When they express the enlightenment, why are there different reactions? When they express their enlightenment and declare their divinity, some people become enlightened and some run away.

How can we also become enlightened when we listen to Kṛṣṇa's words? How can we listen? How can we have that benefit? With what mood are we supposed to receive the words?

When people who hear this declaration of truth, *vibhūti,* the glory, are egoistic and aggressive, they abuse the Master. If they are egoistic but not aggressive, they run away.

Next, Arjuna, Kṛṣṇa's disciple, is totally in love with Kṛṣṇa. He has totally surrendered to Kṛṣṇa. He is not ready to suspect anything. By now, he is clear. His head has stopped working. His logic has stopped analyzing.

This truth should be declared only to a person who is totally, intimately related and feeling connected to the Divine. Arjuna has completely surrendered to Kṛṣṇa. What is surrender? When we hear the word 'surrender', we think that it is the easiest thing to do since we don't need to do anything. For example, if we meditate, we need to do something. But if we need to surrender, we think we don't need to do anything. Hence, we think it is easy.

This is because we think about surrender in a totally different way compared to what the Masters mean by the word 'surrender'. When we use the word 'surrender', we only *say* that we have surrendered. We do not really surrender.

Our faith and surrender are mere words. We delude ourselves thinking we have surrendered. In fact, we have not. Our faith, our surrender is never total surrender. There are three levels of surrender: Surrendering the 'I,' surrendering the mind, and finally, surrendering both the 'I' and the mind. Surrendering the 'I' is surrendering the individual ego. Surrendering the mind is surrendering the mental setup, the root thought patterns.

When you truly surrender to the Divine, surrender can work miracles on you. When you offer yourself at the feet of the Master, your ego disintegrates. The mind is just your collection of all thoughts and habit that you have formed. For example, if you get up in the morning, your mind instinctively tells you that you need your morning coffee since that is a habit. Similarly, if you are constantly worried, it becomes a habit and you worry in every situation without realizing it. When someone praises you, you choose to get flattered. If someone criticizes you, you choose to get disturbed. The mental pattern has been etched so deeply that you don't realize that it is *you*, who is making the choice of how to react. When you surrender, you cannot choose.

A small story:

> One day, Lord Viṣṇu and goddess Lakṣmī were chatting in a relaxed mood in their abode, Vaikunṭa. Suddenly, Viṣṇu jumped up from His seat and ran a few yards. Then he made a U-turn and returned to His seat.
>
> Lakṣmī was perplexed and asked, 'Lord, why did You run in the first place? Then, why did You return immediately after running only a few yards?'
>
> Viṣṇu replied, 'I saw a man in the process of stoning one of My devotees. I ran to help. Then I saw him pick up stones to retaliate. Seeing that, I decided that he did not need My help.'

When you surrender, you cannot choose to react. When you surrender, the egocentric 'I' totally disintegrates. Please understand: The egocentric 'I' is eccentric.

When you surrender, you will be bubbling with joy and bliss. You will be like a kid. Have you seen an ugly child? Even in the poorest country, the kids are beautiful. On the same count, have you seen a single adult who is beautiful? Enlightened people are like children, bubbling with bliss. They are called *dvijā* (born again). After the death of the ego, it is a new birth. The father and mother give us our first birth. The second birth is given by God and the Guru.

If you understand that Existence is your friend and it deeply cares for you, you will not feel the need to live according to a script for life. Instead, you will have tremendous courage and trust in yourself to live life spontaneously. Then, instead of re-living life and reacting to life based upon past memories and experiences, you live life with spontaneous responses to situations. If you live in a simple way, you don't need a script.

Please understand, Existence constantly cares for you. Trust the intelligence in you. Be complete and welcome life as it flows.

Kṛṣṇa says, 'If you continuously merge in Me, I will take care of all your needs and necessities. You will be My responsibility.' In the last chapter Kṛṣṇa promises: *yogakṣemaṁ vahāṁyahaṁ:* My responsibility is *Yoga*—to get the things that you need and *kṣema*—to take care that they remain with you. *Yogakṣemaṁ*: He makes this promise. He says, 'I will take care of you spiritually and materially. You shall not lack anything. You will always be in bliss.' You may wonder how this is possible. When you surrender to the Divine, your higher consciousness will be activated and you will have the intelligence and courage to live everything.

The ultimate intelligence is first understanding that Existence cares for us, and secondly, surrendering to that Existence. Realizing that Existence is not a brute force or power but an intelligent energy, is the key to a life of bliss.

When we surrender the mind, we go from 'mind' to 'no-mind' state. The mind actually arises from possessiveness. Tantra says that the ego is based upon possessions. Look deeply and we will see that the origin of our mind lies in whatever we think of as ours. Our idea of 'mine' creates the sense of 'I'. Most of us think that from 'I,' the 'mine' arises. No! It is from the sense of 'mine' that 'I' arises. The root of the tree of 'I' is 'mine'.

We think that if we have more possessions, we have more freedom. Yes, we will have more freedom, but only the freedom to choose between one suffering and another suffering. We can never choose between suffering and joy through possessiveness. How can we enjoy something with the feeling of possessiveness? We will be in constant fear of losing our possessions. The feeling of 'mine' never lets us enjoy anything.

Just understand. When we surrender ourselves to Existence, it carries us in its very arms. We won't feel the pain of life. But if we try to calculate things after saying that we have surrendered, we project our mind onto the idea of what will happen after surrender. When we say that we have surrendered, how can we say that nothing has happened in spite of our surrender? If we have truly surrendered, we have no right to expect something to happen after we have surrendered.

A Master was asked, 'How do I know that I have really surrendered?' The Master replied, 'If you have really surrendered, this question itself will disappear. There will be a feeling of utter bliss and relaxation.'

Just surrender everything, not only your pain and suffering but also your responsibility. This does not mean that you stop doing household work or going to office. You continue to do so but with the mood of utter relaxation. Surrendering yourself is a clear, conscious decision.

Listen! Total surrender with total responsibility is Living Enlightenment. If we look into our lives, we see that our relating with God is never true surrender. Most of the time, we beg God to give us what we want. The next stage is when we bargain: If you give me this, I will give you that. The third stage is blaming God: I went to this temple so many times; yet, God has not listened to me. Understand, we don't have the intelligence to know what we want. If God were to listen to our requests and desires, this world would have perished a long time ago! This game of begging, bargaining and blaming in the name of praying has nothing to do with true devotion.

There is a beautiful story in the Mahābhārat:

> Before the war started, Duryodhana and Arjuna went to Kṛṣṇa's palace to seek help from Kṛṣṇa for the war. Both of them were relatives of Kṛṣṇa and wanted Kṛṣṇa's help. Kṛṣṇa was sleeping. Arjuna, the Pāṇḍavas' representative, sat at the feet of Kṛṣṇa. Duryodhana, the Kauravas' representative, sat near the head of Kṛṣṇa.

The moment Kṛṣṇa opened His eyes, He saw Arjuna sitting at His feet. He asked him, 'How are you, Arjuna? When did you come?

Arjuna said, 'I have come to seek your help.'

Kṛṣṇa smiled and assured him, 'Surely I will help, don't worry.'

Duryodhana, who was sitting at the head of the bed, demanded from Kṛṣṇa, 'I came before Arjuna. You should help me first.'

Kṛṣṇa turned and saw Duryodhana.

Kṛṣṇa replied, 'Surely I will help, don't worry.' He added, 'I will be on one side and My powers will be on the other side. And I will not raise weapons in this war. As Arjuna first came in front of Me, he gets to choose, first. Which one do you want, Arjuna?'

Arjuna thought, 'Let us have *buddhi* (intelligence).' He was happy to have just Kṛṣṇa, *Nārāyaṇa* on his side.

Duryodhana thought, 'Let us have *śakti* (power).' He replied, 'I will have your powers and weapons, *Nārāyaṇi senā*.'

Obviously, the Pāṇḍavas were the ones who won the war.

If you have a Master like Kṛṣṇa with you, you can conquer even Duryodhana's *sena* (army)! You can win any number of warriors. All the warriors of the Kauravas' side are your sufferings, your root thought patterns, your 'mine' and 'I'. Kṛṣṇa alone is enough! He will finish them off. But, when you don't have Kṛṣṇa on your side, any struggle you try to do, any plan you try to do, it will be failure.

There are only two possibilities: either you choose *Nārāyaṇa* or you choose *Nārāyaṇi senā*, either you are in peace or in piece-piece. You can bring peace to you or piece-piece to you.

The man who chose intelligence, the man who trusted God, had intelligence, had peace and won the war. Arjuna won the game of life.

He had Nārāyaṇa, God Himself who is the source of all the powers, the source of *Nārāyaṇi senā*. The man who chose just the power was in piece-piece. Duryodhana neither remained with power nor with God.

If we look deeply into what kind of a relationship we have with God, we will see that when we pray, we think that God has the power, *śakti* to give but He does not have the intelligence or wisdom, *buddhi* to know what to give. This is what we believe when we insist that He gives us what we want right now.

If we trust God has only power, *śakti*, we never win in life. When we trust He also has intelligence, *buddhi*, we surrender. Only then things can start happening. When we surrender, we believe that God has power and intelligence. When we believe God has only power, religion starts. When we believe He has wisdom, spirituality starts.

When we believe He has only power, we do rituals and pamper Him. We start doing all possible things to continuously bribe Him to give us what we want. We go to the temple and tell the priest not only our name but our father's name, our forefathers' names, and so on. Do we think God doesn't know where we are from and who we are?

Understand, your whole life is nothing but Mahābhārat.

In your life of Mahābhārat, victory or failure, who is going to win or lose is going to be decided only based on which side you are going to side; whether you are going to side your Consciousness or your unconsciousness, your Completion or incompletion. Listen, whichever side Kṛṣṇa sided would have won the game. Kṛṣṇa is Consciousness! Kṛṣṇa is Completion!

Please listen. Decide consciously that from this moment, you will surrender everything at the feet of God, to the energy that runs this whole world. We don't need to believe in any name or form. Trust the energy pervading the Universe and trust it to run your life.

Now, even after we surrender, at some time, a doubt will naturally arise in us whether we have totally, actually surrendered. Understand that the divine intelligence gave us the intelligence to surrender in the first place and that same divine intelligence has given us this doubt to doubt our surrender. Surrender the doubt also at the feet of the divine energy. So, do not wait to change and become perfect before surrendering. No! Surrender yourself as you are, consciously, totally. Surrender deeply and your whole being will be flooded with new bliss.

TRUE LOVE IS DIVINITY

Kṛṣṇa says, Because you are My dear friend, you are deeply connected to Me, I am revealing this truth to you.

bhūya eva mahā-bāho śṛṇu me paramaṁ vacaḥ /
yat te 'haṁ prīyamāṇāya vakṣyami hita-kāmayā // 10.1

Let me explain a few basic things. Actually, when we feel deeply connected to some person, the person will almost look like God. Whether it is our spouse, kids, parents or our Master, he will look like God. Whatever he does, we will feel that he is divine.

When we feel deeply connected, when we are in love with another being, that other being will look almost like God. Look at the great Mīrābāi. She was so much in love with Kṛṣṇa who was not even physically in front of her. Yet, she felt so deeply connected to Him. She talked to Him, sang His praises and became totally immersed in Him. When Mirābāi was given poison, she even drank that, totally surrendering herself to Kṛṣṇa. The power of her love and devotion was such that even a deadly poison had no effect on her!

We have forgotten how to connect through the heart. All our relationships have become superficial. Now, the wife is no more a wife. In the modern day society, the husband is no more a husband. He is just a boyfriend.

Be very clear: In Saṃskṛit, we don't have an equivalent word for divorce. The idea never existed! In Hindu marriage, no divorce is allowed. Both take an oath in front of *agni* (fire), 'As long as you are alive, as long as I am alive, I will support and enrich you.' With the cultural invasion of the so-called developed cultures, the materialistic cultures, changing the wife, house and car has now become a fashion. Once in three months, the house, car and wife become outdated.

The outer world is a projection of the inner world and the eye projects it. Whatever is visible as the outer world is a mere projection. We try without success to change things in the outer world. Our frustration and depression are due to our attempt to manipulate the screen rather than the projector.

We fantasize about a holiday on a beautiful beach in Hawaii as ultimate bliss. However, when it happens, our thoughts are not of the beach but of our office and deadlines! I tell people that if we sit in the house and worry, it is homework. If we sit in the office and worry, it is work and if we sit on the beach and worry, it is vacation! The mind is the same incomplete mind, only the location is different. How can we change the incomplete mental state by changing the place?

In Saṃskṛit, we have two beautiful words: *pravṛitti* and *nivṛitti*.

Pravṛitti means the incompletions that you carry, leading you to more and more incompletions. The incompletion you carry makes you do many actions, which lead you to do more and more incompletions. That is pravṛitti.

Nivṛitti means the completion that you carry, leading you to more and more completion. Your actions should be nivṛitti based not pravṛitti based.

You need to change the state of incompletion to completion. When you begin to change the state, you work directly with the projector and make progress from completion to more completion, *nivṛitti.* Working with the projector is the process of completion.

But changing your status is like working with the screen and associating with your incompletions that lead to more incompletions, *pravṛitti.* Changing your wife, your house or car is like working with the screen and it does not enrich you. Changing your mind by completing with your patterns, your relationships and therefore your fantasies is the only way.

Your actions should be *nivṛitti* based not *pravṛitti* based.

When we don't pass judgment on life, on others and on us, we reach the state of non-resistance, the state of completion, the state of compassion. When intelligence happens, we reach the stage of non-resistance leading to completion. When we welcome people and situations from the space of completion, compassion happens. Beloved means being loved, not 'body love.'

What is the difference between intellect and intelligence? Intellect is always prejudiced. Intelligence is always fresh. When we pass judgment and collect evidence to substantiate our decision, it is intellect. When we first collect evidence and pass judgment without bias or prejudice, it is intelligence.

Look into your life and see how your mind works out of incompletions and creates conflicting images about you, about others, and about life! How do you act in your daily life? The vast majority of the time, your judgment is ready. For example, after living with your wife for a few months, you create a concept, an inadequate *life image* or *svānyakāra* about her. Then, whatever she does, you pick only those arguments that are necessary for your already formed judgment.

Whenever we think too much of ourselves, we believe only in our judgments and lay the blame on others. When we start completing with ourselves and others, we create a new *inner image* about ourselves, a new *mamakāra*. We understand that we are simple, complete beings, we start seeing the arguments clearly before passing judgment and restore our integrity and authenticity.

Actually, we have forgotten how to relate through the heart, the intense way of relating. Our relationships have become superficial. We don't really know the meaning of the term, 'falling in love.'

Whenever Rāmakṛṣṇa worshipped, did *pūjā*, he felt that Devi was present. He never felt that the statue was a stone. He spoke to Kāli Devi directly. When we deeply fall in love, even a stone can become God and guide us. When we don't feel connected, even if God comes down, we will ask for His business card!

Let me tell you a beautiful happening from Śrī Rāmakṛṣṇa's life:

> Śrī Rāmakṛṣṇa was the priest in the Devi temple. He used to taste the food before offering it to Devi. All the temple authorities told him, 'No! You cannot do this. That is sacrilegious.'
>
> Rāmakṛṣṇa said, 'I don't know all these things. I feel that She is my Mother. How can I offer the food unless I know that it tastes good? And if you don't want me to offer, I will stand outside and offer. But, I will offer.'
>
> They agreed, 'Alright, do whatever you want.' Not only that, when he decorated the idol of Devi, he placed a small thread near Her nose to see whether She was breathing or not, alive or not. And the history says, the thread moved due to Devi's breath. He felt Devi everywhere.

When we feel deeply connected, when we know how to surrender, then even a stone can become God and guide us.

Feel Deeply Connected to Kṛṣṇa

Now, all we need is the mood of being deeply in love with Kṛṣna, deeply connected to Kṛṣṇa, deeply related to Kṛṣṇa. If we can open ourselves to Kṛṣṇa when He describes His glories, His *vibhūti*, it will not be words. We will feel it.

First, Kṛṣṇa removed the enmity between *jivātma* (Self) and *paramātma* (supreme Self). Arjuna is the *jivātma.* Kṛṣṇa is the *paramātma.*

We may not be aware but we continuously maintain enmity with *paramātma*, Existence. That is why we suspect life. We have fear about what will happen in the next moment. We are afraid of life because we don't believe what is going to happen the next moment will enrich us. We don't trust Existence.

All life insurance policies are only because we don't trust Existence. Understand that life insurance is not *life* insurance. It is death insurance. Real life insurance is devotion to the Ultimate. Understanding that Existence is taking care of us is the only real life insurance. All other things are death insurance that goes to our families who are waiting for it!

A small story:

> A young child was playing on the beach. He wanted to wade into the ocean. His mother ran after him and said, 'Don't go into the ocean. Play in the sand. Don't go into the water.'
>
> The boy asked, 'Why? Daddy is going into the water. Why are you not stopping him? You are stopping me.'
>
> The mother said, 'He is insured!'

So please be very clear: All our insurance is death insurance. It is not life insurance. Understanding that Existence is taking care of us and that it is not our enemy is the only life insurance we need.

One more thing: When we have the deep love—the connection with Existence, even when we die, we know that He knows where to keep us. We will be utterly relaxed as we know He will protect and guide us. So now itself, our mind should be prepared to fall in tune with this energy; to obey, to surrender to the ultimate will. Now itself, our body and mind should be prepared.

If we live life fighting with Existence, our life will be hell. Nothing else can be done. All we need to do is know how to feel connected.

First, Kṛṣṇa removes the enmity between the individual Self and Existence. Now, He explains the glory of Existence. Next, He gives the experience that the individual Self and the supreme Self are the same.

Step-by-step, He leads Arjuna from *viśiṣṭādvaita* (a school of thought which says that the individual self is a *part* of Existence, with its own attributes) to *dvaita* (duality, a school of thought which says that the individual self is separate from Existence), to *advaita* (non-duality, truth that the individual self is Existence), to beyond *advaita* into *anubhūti*, experience. He leads Arjuna to a spiritual experience step-by-step. I spoke earlier about the three essential identities in our lives. These are:

jīva—individual Self; *jagat*—the world in which this self lives, and *Iśvara*—creator of *jīva* and *jagat*, or in other words God.

Initially, we see these three as separate entities, just as the water drop sees itself as separate from the ocean. There are different approaches in Hindu philosophy as to how the individual Self can reach the Creator, the Divine. The concepts of *viśiṣiṭādvaita* and *dvaita* are based on a separation between the Self and the Creator, with deep devotion connecting the two. Devotion leads the Self to the Divine and an understanding of the Divine. Yet they remain separate. It is like the water drop realizing it is part of the ocean and yet separate.

Advaita philosophy integrates the Self and the Creator into one non-dual entity, of which *jagat*, the world, forms a part. So the three seemingly separate entities merge into oneness. *Advaita* says that separation is an illusion, *māyā*, and that true realization of the non-dual aspect of the Self and the Divine leads to liberation and Enlightenment. These are different ways of looking at the same truth. None of them is wrong.

Kṛṣṇa leads Arjuna from the concept of separation into the understanding of integration. Kṛṣṇa makes Arjuna understand that nothing stands between him and Kṛṣṇa, except his level of understanding of the space of completion.

Please be very clear: These are not contradictory. Many people ask me, '*Swamiji*, is *dvaita* or *advaita* right? Is *viśiṣiṭādvaita* or *dvaita* right?' They are not contradictory. They complement each other. They lead us step-by-step to more and more understanding of completion. They lead us step-by-step to the ultimate spiritual experience.

Listen! Completion makes us understand that we are connected with the whole Universe – this is the essence of *viśiṣṭādvaita*. Completion makes us understand that we are deeply connected to the *paramātma* (supreme Self)—this is the essence of *dvaita*. Completion makes us understand that we are not one, but we are the ultimate *infinity* with each one infinitely powerful, which is the essence of *advaita*.

In India, this clash between *advaita* and *dvaita* is a big fight. Is the

Śankara bhāṣya (Śankara's commentary) big or is Rāmanuja bhāṣya big? Śankara was the founder of *advaita* philosophy and Rāmanuja founded the *dvaita* philosophy.

All Enlightened Masters speak the same thing in different ways. If we surrender, we will have the same experience of *advaita-anubhav*, non-duality experience. If we achieve the non-duality experience, we will have deep surrender. The man who has achieved *advaita-anubhava* has tremendous devotion. For example, the verse of Śankara says:

bhaja govindaṁ bhaja govindaṁ govindaṁ bhaja mūḍhamate
samprāpte sannihite kāle nahi nahi rakṣati ḍukṛñkaraṇe

Śankara says, 'Oh Fool! May you start meditating on Govinda (Kṛṣṇa's name) now. May you start remembering Govinda now. *Nahi nahi rakṣati ḍukṛñkaraṇe* means: When Yamadharma, the Lord of death comes, intellectual knowledge will not help you or protect you.

A great *advaita-jñāni*, sage of non-duality experience, will be a great devotee. And a great devotee will be an *advaita-jñāni*! Both are one and the same. Only those who have not realized the experience argue.

If you go inside *dvaita* and *advaita* philosophies, both show the same knowledge, wisdom and experience. All we need to know is how to open ourselves and surrender to this Existence. Then we will experience at the level of our being that Existence is taking care of us. Please be very clear: If Existence doesn't want us here, we cannot be here even for a single moment. There is no reason for Existence to keep us alive. If it is keeping us alive, we are wanted in this form, in this way, in this place. That is why we are still alive.

God continuously cleans all the garbage. He never waits. Everyday He clears away all the old things. He is the perfect energy that maintains cleanliness. They say that cleanliness is next to Godliness. I say that cleanliness is Godliness. It is not next to Godliness.

Trust Existence and Radiate Divine Grace

Unless we are needed, we will not be kept alive. Just by being alive, He proves that we are needed. We are wanted. We are not an accident; we are an incident. Don't think that we are alive as an accident. We are an incident. When we understand that we are an incident, we feel deeply connected. We open ourselves to Existence.

I tell people: Trust, even if you are exploited. You may say, 'What is this, *Swamiji?* What kind of teaching are you giving? You are asking us to trust even if we are exploited.'

Be very clear: There are two kinds of lives. One is living completely with trust and the other is living completely with an insecure feeling. The person who lives in insecurity may have more wealth. He may have two or three more beds, a little bigger house, yet he can never rest. The person who lives with the insecure consciousness may have more comfort but he will never be blissful.

On the other hand, the person who lives with deep trust in Existence may have less comfort but he never misses that comfort. People who trust Existence are always showered with blessings. They will live like God on planet earth. They will be a blessing for the whole planet. The Earth is alive because of a few people who live radiating this trust, who live radiating the divine grace.

We should trust, even if we are exploited. After all, we are going to live on this earth for a maximum of seventy to eighty years. In those years, why should we continuously suffer? If we defend ourselves because of our insecurity, we will not only offend others but we will also miss the joy of living on planet Earth.

According to the Hindu purāṇic histories, Śrī Veda Vyāsa lived longer than any other man. Someone asked why he didn't build a house. Vyāsa replied, 'After all, I am only going to live for a few years. Why should I build a house? Why waste my time?'

If we can, let us live with the completely relaxed mood of deep trust. Our presence will be a blessing. Our existence will save planet Earth. No matter what crosses our path, we will just be living, enjoying, and enriching everything. It is a blessing.

What have we brought here to lose? Our insecure consciousness is nothing but ignorance of the truth. What are we going to carry with us after death? Nothing! A simple truth: Neither have we brought anything nor are we going to take back anything.

While we are here we can relax and trust that Existence will provide for us. If the energy moving inside our body can convert bread into blood, can't it bring bread to us? The big problem is that we don't trust our energy. We don't trust the cosmic energy. When it can convert bread into blood, can't it help us with our small things? Can't it give us the intelligence to bring bread, sustenance into our lives? It *can* guide us. It *can* give us enough intelligence to bring bread for our life. When the energy can move planets and run the whole Universe, can't it take care of us?

Let me narrate to you a real incident:

> Śāradā Devi, the consort of Rāmakṛṣṇa, opened a charitable hospital in Calcutta. There were two counters: one counter where medicines were given free for the poor and another for people who could afford to buy medicines.
>
> One employee of the hospital complained to Śāradā Devi, 'Mother, even rich people stand in the counter for the poor and take advantage of the free medicines. What should we do about this?'
>
> Śāradā Devi replied, 'Don't be concerned. When a rich man stands in the line for the poor, be assured that he is also poor, and give him medicines. Even if he has money, he is a poor man. He has come here as a beggar.'
>
> She makes a beautiful statement, 'Outer wealth doesn't make one rich or poor. It is the inner space that matters. If you live with trust, even if you are exploited, even if you

lose your comforts of the outer world, you will live like God on this planet Earth. You will simply float. You will become a divine person.'

I am asking you to trust Existence, not based upon my intellectual knowledge but from my personal experience. If you trust my words, when you trust Existence and relax from your tensions, headaches, worries and problems, be sure that you will be taken care of. Miracles will happen in your life. When you put your energy totally on trust, an alchemy takes place in you.

Understand, when you surrender, there is utter relaxation in you and your responsibilities are shifted to a higher authority. This is surrender. Do your duty and leave all of the responsibility to Existence. She will take care!

So we have two choices: We can live offending and defending continuously. Even if we have comfort, our being will carry a wound. Or we can lead a totally relaxed life with utter freedom and complete trust in Existence. We can have physical, mental, emotional and psychological freedom. We can have liberation *here* and *now*.

The moment we live with trust, we are liberated. Nothing hurts us anymore. If we live with the truth, we beautifully live even our death because we trust that Existence will take care of us even then. If we live without trust, we will be killed by the fear of death. Every moment, we will be dying. With trust, even in our death, we will be living, celebrating!

Here, if we can relax and feel deeply connected to what Kṛṣṇa says, we will experience the state that Kṛṣṇa is now going to express about His glories in Yoga of His Divine Manifestations, *Vibhūti Yogaḥ*.

I Am The Source

10.2 *Neither the hosts of deities nor the great sages*
know My origin, My opulence.
I am the source of the deities and the sages.

10.3 *He who knows Me as the unborn,*
without beginning, and Supreme Lord of all the worlds,
Only he, who has this clarity, is wise and freed from all bondage

Kṛṣṇa says, 'Neither the *devatās* (gods) nor the *ṛṣis* know Me.' He means that neither people who work in the line of comforts and luxury nor the people who work in the line of religion and tapas (penance) know Him. 'But, I am their origin, *aham ādiḥ.*'

na me viduḥ sura-gaṇāḥ prabhavaṁ na maharṣayaḥ |
aham ādir hi devānāṁ maharṣīṇāṁ ca sarvaśaḥ || 10.2

Whether we live a spiritual or a materialistic life, our root is our consciousness. We should understand an important thing: Whenever Kṛṣṇa says, 'Me, Me, Me, *aham, aham, aham.*' He is referring to the enlightened consciousness.

Let me narrate a real incident from my life:

> I was invited to a conference by a group of Kṛṣṇa *bhaktas* (devotees). I can't say devotees as the word devotee is a beautiful word. They were more like fanatics. I went humbly, in a friendly way.
>
> Suddenly, they confronted me and started arguing. They asked me, 'Do you believe in the Gītā?'

I said, 'Yes, Gītā is the ultimate book. I respect it and I worship it.'

They questioned me, 'Then why do you worship Śiva?' I was shocked. They asked me, 'You should worship only Kṛṣṇa. Why are you worshipping Śiva? Why do you put *vibhūti* (holy ash) on your forehead? Why you wear rudrākṣa (fruits of rudrākṣa tree)?'

I asked them, 'How does respecting Śiva and wearing rudrākṣa contradict respecting and following the Gītā?'

They said, 'No. Kṛṣṇa says in the Gītā, 'I am everything,' so how can you worship Śiva?' I was surprised.

I said, 'When Kṛṣṇa says 'I,' He means the *Parabrahma svarūpa* (universal Self) of Him. He means the formless consciousness of His being. He represents the Universal energy. He doesn't mean the six-foot form with the flute and peacock feather. The form is beautiful as long as it leads you to the formless.'

If He means the six-foot form, how could He say that He taught this knowledge to Vivasvān?

He says, 'I gave this knowledge to Ikśvāku. I gave this wisdom to Surya.' He says again and again, it is He who gave this knowledge to these great people who lived thousands of years before Him!

When the Gītā was delivered, Kṛṣṇa was thirty-two years old. If He was speaking about His form, how could He say, 'I gave this knowledge to Surya. I gave this knowledge to Manu?'

When Kṛṣṇa says 'I', He means the cosmic consciousness.

Immediately, the people who were arguing asked, 'How can you say the form and energy are different? When He says 'I,' He means the form also.'

I explained, 'I do not want to disrespect Kṛṣṇa's form. When the form represents the energy, the form is also energy, no doubt. But it is not that you cannot worship another form. You don't have to become a fanatic.'

One person started arguing, 'How can you say that when Kṛṣṇa says 'I', He doesn't mean the form but He means the energy?' Then, I had to refer to another important scripture, the *Anu Gītā* that was delivered in the Mahābhārat after the *Bhagavad Gītā*.

After the war is over, Arjuna asks, 'Kṛṣṇa, please tell me whatever You taught to me earlier. I remember the essence but I forgot the words because You taught me the whole thing during the war. Please repeat them once more. I want to listen to those great teachings.'

You will be surprised but Kṛṣṇa says, 'Arjuna, not only you, I have also forgotten.' He says:

na cākhyaṁ tanmayā bhūyastataḥ
bhaktom aśeṣataḥ param hi
brahma rati yoga yuktena tanmayaḥ

This is in the Mahābhārat in Aśvamedhika Parva. Kṛṣṇa says, 'Arjuna, I can't give the teachings again because they were said in that high spiritual, Eternal Consciousness. At that time, I was in that high, Eternal Consciousness. I was radiating My enlightenment. That very Enlightenment spoke through Me. The Universal consciousness spoke through Me. That is why all those teachings came out. I represented the Universal energy, the Universal consciousness at that moment. Now I cannot give you the same teachings again.'

He says that these things are expressed in that high, Eternal consciousness. Please understand that when Kṛṣṇa says 'I', He means the Enlightened energy, the Universal consciousness. However Kṛṣṇa recollected a few things from what He told and delivered what is called the *Anu Gītā*, to Arjuna.

When I quoted this verse, the senior religious pundits (scholars) arguing with me said, 'You look young, but you seem to be well read. We cannot argue with you!'

The greatness of *Sanātana Dharma*—the religion of eternal righteousness later called Hinduism—is that it doesn't propagate the religion or produce fanaticism.

Whether you worship Kṛṣṇa, Śiva, Devi or Buddha, it does not make a difference. Please continue to worship whomever you believe in and whomever you connect with, that's enough. Be intense in your path. Nothing else needs to be done. There is no need for fanaticism because all forms are representations of the same divine energy.

There is a question here from the audience: 'I am a worshipper of formlessness, the formless energy. Can I become your disciple and follow *dhyāna* (meditation)?'

Only *then* can you become my disciple!

Only if you are the worshipper of the formless, you can become my disciple. There is a strict instruction for my disciples that they should not meditate on my form. If you have done any of our meditation camps, you know. There is a strict instruction: You cannot meditate on my form. And be aware, if any guru tells you to meditate on his form, escape from him. You are falling into the net of indirect slavery. You will slowly get exploited. Spiritual slavery is the worst slavery. Never, never be caught in that.

The basis of spirituality is that it should lead us to liberation. In spirituality, if we are caught in slavery, then even God cannot save us. Never meditate on my form. In our spiritual healing initiation, in the Inner Awakening program, there is a clear instruction: You cannot meditate on my form. The form will be here today and gone tomorrow. It will disappear tomorrow. How long will forms be here?

Form is a representation. Understand: It is like the finger pointing to the moon. I am telling you, 'There is the sun. There is the moon!' Instead of looking at the sun or moon, if you catch hold of my finger, you miss what I am showing you! You miss what I represent. When the finger points to the moon, if you catch the finger, you miss the moon.

In the same way, the Master represents the Divine consciousness. If you catch His form, you miss the Divine. Never be caught in the form. All I want you to understand is that when Kṛṣṇa says 'I', He means the Universal consciousness.

In the next verse, He uses the word *mūḍhaḥ*, fool. Again He uses the word 'fool'. He says only someone who is free from all the sins understands Him. Again and again, what does He want to convey? what does He expect as a qualification from us in order to experience Him?

WHERE EXACTLY ARE YOU MISSING IT?

There is one more question: '*Swamiji*, again and again, you say all we need is *one* simple understanding. Exactly what am I missing? I think I have that understanding. I almost feel I am around the corner. Yet, I am unable to experience what Kṛṣṇa says. Where am I missing? Please tell me.'

The person who asked this question is totally frustrated. He says, 'Everyday at the end of the discourse, you bring everything to the one point that the inner being should be transformed. Exactly what am I lacking? Please tell me.'

Everyday I stop at that subject so that you will ask this question. Now, I can tell exactly where you are lacking. First, the thirst should be created. The quest should be created. Then, the quest should be answered. When the question becomes a quest, you speak in this language. When the urge becomes urgent, you speak in this language.

Listen. Many seekers are just like window shoppers. They go from master to master. Going from master to master is not wrong. It is perfectly alright. However, not learning from anybody is wrong. I tell people,

'Go to all the gardens, but pick flowers and make a beautiful bouquet.' But, we don't pick flowers from any garden. That is where the problem starts. A lot of people are just window shoppers. They go around doing nothing. They act as if they are seekers. Above all, they want to satisfy themselves that they are seekers. This is hypocrisy. Listen, either put your whole effort into seeking, or forget it and carry on with life.

Rāmakṛṣna says beautifully, 'If somebody's hair is burning, will he keep quiet? Will he say, 'I have no time now. I still have many more years. Later on, I can take care?' The moment there is fire on a person's head, he tries to put out the fire. He runs towards water.

Exactly where are we lacking? Because we feel too much ego in our being. When Kṛṣṇa says He is God, we feel He is egoistic. For example, if I suddenly say, 'I am God,' what will you naturally think? 'This guy has gone crazy and he has too much ego.'

Please understand: When you say the word 'I', the meaning is different from when a Master says it. When you say the word 'God', the word is empty for you. It is just a superficial understanding for you. It has no solid truth behind it. Whereas when you say the word 'I' or your name, there is a solid meaning and experience behind that word for you. When it comes to enlightened Masters, the word 'I' has no solid meaning. It is vague, superficial. However, the word 'divine' or 'enlightened' or 'God' has a solid meaning. It is their very experience.

Just because you have ego, you think Masters have ego and you miss the meaning of their expression, their declaration. Just push your ego a little aside, *let go* off it, be complete and authentically listen to the words of the Masters.

I Am Everything

I know, I can see how this whole scene of the **Gītā** between Arjuna and Kṛṣṇa would have happened. After Kṛṣṇa's teachings Arjuna completely and totally melted in front of Kṛṣṇa.

Kṛṣṇa explains, 'Oh my dear! Understand, I am everything—*vetti loka maheśvaram* (10.3). I have come down. I have happened in this body to liberate you.'

Immediately, the man who is centered on fear, says, 'If you are everything, do all these things for me. Alter this world.' If he is centered on greed, he says, 'If you are everything, give me all these boons.'

The moment the Master says he is God, the moment Kṛṣṇa says He is God, if you are centered on greed, you catch him and ask him to give you all the boons. You start begging, 'Give me this, give me that.' If you are centered on fear, again, you catch him and say, 'Please protect me from this or that.'

The moment we demand, divinity disappears because we have brought in the business mind. The attitude which exists between the Master and us plays a major role in our experiencing Him as divine and our experiencing ourselves as divine.

Many people say, '*Swamiji*, if my son is healed, I will give you so much money. If my daughter is healed, I will give you this property.' I start laughing! First of all, I never asked them for anything. Second, the moment we start bargaining, the whole beauty of the relationship is gone. For healing to happen, a special bridge is necessary. The bridge or deeply feeling connected is required. A deep love is necessary.

The moment we bring in the business mood, it is over! As soon as we start bargaining, neither can I heal nor can the person being healed receive the energy. The bridge is disconnected. If that bridge is there, even without seeing me, you can be healed. You don't need to be in my physical presence.

Continuously, I receive emails from all over the world, '*Swamiji*, you gave me darśan (vision) and removed my sufferings. *Swamiji*, you appeared in front of me and answered my question.' Then they ask, '*Swamiji*, are you aware of the times when you appear and give darśan to us?'

Now, let me tell you clearly, honestly: I do not know when the darśan is happening. Let me break the business secret. Let me tell the whole truth as it is. Just because of your trust, deep love and devotion, the cosmic energy guides you by giving darśan using this form, that's all. I rent this body to the Divine. Because I disappeared, because my ego disappeared, the Divine uses this form to guide you. Over! Otherwise, it is totally between *you* and the cosmic energy. I cannot involve myself. I have no say. I cannot appear for any specific person and say, 'He is my favorite!' No! I cannot show favoritism. It is not under my control.

It is between your inner space and the Divine. It is your ability, your attitude to receive, that creates the bridge. Again and again, I tell people: All I can do is, go back and download the information regarding the darśan that you had, and tell you what exactly happened and what instruction was given to you. That's all.

With all enlightened people, this is what happens. The moment I claim that I gave darśan, the whole thing is over. Then, the Divine will stop using this form. As long as I am clear that this is *not* me and it is Parāśakti, Existence, using this form, She continues to use this flute to play Her songs. She continues to use this form to carry on with Her mission. She continues to use this form to bless Her devotees.

When I say Parāśakti, I mean the cosmic energy. Don't think there is a lady with four hands! It is the cosmic energy. She does Her job using the forms of people who have surrendered their form to Her. Because I vacated, She is lives in my body.

All you need to do is—just get out of your system. The Divine will get in. If you get out of your system, the Divine will get in.

Surrender, A Deep Passive Waiting

Listen. When you feel connected, you are open. You don't need to see the Master. The cosmic energy will guide you. There is no need for His nearness. But when you spoil the relationship, when you bring business into the relationship, nothing can be done because the bridge is broken. The very bridge does not happen between you and the Master when business enters.

For the bridge to happen, we need the space of complete surrender or feeling deeply connected. Here, by now, Arjuna is almost feeling connected. He has just dropped his fear and greed. The big problem with the spiritual process is that you will have what you want when you drop the idea of having that.

A deep, passive waiting without knowing what is going to happen is passive surrender. That is total surrender. The moment you decide, 'I will wait forever,' things happen.

As long as you are in a hurry, you are agitated. You stop things from happening in you. It is like trying to get the lotus to blossom. You open the petals by hand. Will it be a flower? It will never be a lotus flower. The lotus flower blooms by itself when the sun's rays pierce it. Give a little space to yourself so that your being blossoms.

Listen. The moment you decide to wait, things start happening. You don't need to wait anymore. You must wait until you decide to wait. The moment you decide to wait, you don't need to wait anymore.

A beautiful story:

> Nārada, a devotee of Viṣṇu, was going to Vaikuṇṭa (abode of Lord Viṣṇu). On the way, he saw a yogi sitting in meditation. The yogi asked Nārada, 'Oh Nārada, please ask Viṣṇu how long I must wait before I become enlightened?' Nārada said, 'Surely I will ask,' and he went on his way.
>
> Next, Nārada encountered a man who was jumping and dancing under a tree.
>
> He asked Nārada, 'Oh Nārada, please ask Viṣṇu when I will have his darśan.' Please listen, he never asked when he would become enlightened. He asked Nārada when he would have Viṣṇu's darśan, His vision.
>
> He said, 'Ask Him to grace me. How long should I wait for His grace?' Nārada said, 'Surely I will ask, don't worry.'
>
> Nārada went to Vaikuṇṭa and came back with the replies.

Nārada said to the first yogi, 'Viṣṇu said you must wait four more janma (lives) to become enlightened.' The yogi fell into depression, 'Oh, four janmas! What will I do?'

The person who was dancing around asked Nārada, 'What did Viṣṇu say?' Nārada said, 'He said you must wait for as many janmas as there are leaves on this tree. Then you will have His darśan. Only then His grace will fall upon you.'

As soon as he heard this, the man said, 'Oh! He gave me the assurance that He will grace me! That is enough.' He started jumping and dancing again.

The moment he uttered this, there was a stroke of lightning and the Divine descended. The man became enlightened.

So understand, deep patience and the decision to wait is surrender.

Take the life of Buddha as an example. With utmost sincerity he tried to get enlightened with all meditation techniques and spiritual practices. When nothing worked, He relaxed and let go of everything, trusting Existence. That very moment, He became enlightened.

In my life, as long as I was doing meditation, I never became enlightened. As long as I was doing all the practices, penance, I was so agitated. Nothing happened. Actually after my enlightenment, I came to know that because of the penance, I had postponed my enlightenment. To tell you honestly, at the age of twelve, I had become enlightened. I did not know that I had become enlightened. I tried to hold on to the experience. I tried to possess *nitya ānanda*, eternal bliss. The moment I tried to possess it, it started slipping away, like wet soap. The day I decided ultimately that I would do no more catching, no more searching, no more seeking, when I decided to relax and wait, it simply happened.

The day you decide to wait, things happen.

Usually, when somebody is blessed and if he is healed, he tells someone else about it. If the second person comes with the attitude of getting healed, he naturally misses the whole game. If he comes with a fresh mind, healing automatically happens as a by-product. When we want it as the main product, we miss the whole bridge. Especially when we bring the business approach, like a deal between friends, the whole attitude, the relationship is no more that between Guru and disciple. Energy cannot be transmitted in a business relationship.

Understand, we need courage to stake everything on trust. It is like that moment when a seed must let go of its fears and break to open and become a tree. This is why we call *Nirvāṇa* as the last nightmare.

If a dream is too wild, we will wake up! Similarly, when we get a jolt or shock in life, we wake up to enlightenment! Enlightenment happens when there is a sudden shock to our dream state. The wonder with Masters, Incarnations is that there is no failure, ever. Their's is a foolproof system!

A small story:

> A *nāgā* (Hindu sannyāsi who is usually unclothed) was so fond of his Master that he would stand behind the master and constantly imitate his hand and body movements. The master did not mind this on account of his sincerity. Once when a discourse was on, the master raised his hand and so did this disciple.
>
> The master turned to the disciple and cut off his hand with a sword. So great was the disciple's devotion that along with his severed hand, his ego fell and he became enlightened! The other disciples asked the master if this was not too high a price to pay for enlightenment.
>
> The Master replied, 'Compared to the number of lives people must take to achieve this state, this is a small price indeed!'

We need the energy to let go, to allow the transformation to happen. Like the seed that lets go of its fear in becoming a tree, we too must have the energy to let go, to allow the transformation to happen. In that moment, when our ego is dying, we must be willing to let go of the past.

Enlightenment never happens as a continuity of something. It happens in a flash, as a new birth. In Saṃskṛit we call it *viṣāda*. The first chapter of the Gītā is *Arjuna Viṣāda Yogaḥ*. Arjuna's dilemma was so great, yet he was willing to trust Kṛṣṇa and let go. In such a powerless situation, no mental decision taken is correct and when the Master guides you, you must be ready to let go and follow what he says completely, implicitly.

Arjuna had the courage to believe totally in Kṛṣṇa and let go, which was why he had the *Viśvarūpa Darśan*, the cosmic vision of Kṛṣṇa. We must have the energy to let go, to allow the dark night to happen to us. Only if we have trust in the Master can the ultimate gain happen to us.

We need to trust in order to experience the unknown space. At that moment, we have only the Master to hold onto. We must accept the new experience happening to us, and deeply trust that the energy to transcend our old personality is entering us.

Kṛṣṇa emphasizes the feeling of connectedness. Feeling deeply connected to the Master is the basic need to understand this Truth. That is why the East gave so much importance to the Guru, the Master.

I Create You

10.4,5 *Intelligence, knowledge, freedom from doubt and delusion, forgiveness, truthfulness, control of the senses, control of the mind, happiness, distress, birth, death, fear, fearlessness, non-violence, equanimity, satisfaction, austerity, charity, fame and infamy, all these qualities of living beings are created by Me alone.*

10.6 *The seven great sages and before them, the four great Manus, come from Me, they arose from My mind and all the living beings populating the planet descend from them.*

10.7 *He who knows all this glory and powers of Mine, truly, he is fully united in Me; of that there is no doubt.*

If you understand this first verse, you can immediately relax. Kṛṣṇa says, 'Whatever you have, whether you have a good name or a bad name, it is created by Me.' Then be certain that whatever you have is a gift from the Divine.

Kṛṣṇa asks us to complete with life as it is. Only when we accept ourselves as we are, can we accept others. Only then we will feel deep friendliness with others. Deep friendliness with others is spirituality. Understand that spirituality is honest and deep friendliness with others.

I Am Everything, Complete With Everything

Love is the flowering of our consciousness. Whenever our consciousness expresses itself through the heart, compassion happens, lust becomes love. The touch will become so vibrant, so soothing. I firmly believe that love is the greatest healing power on planet Earth. I tell my healers, 'If you can't spread love, you can never heal.'

When people meet me, I stretch out my hands as soon as I see them. Many feel strange. They feel that spirituality means seriousness and being reserved. Here I am reaching out to people with my stretched hands. It doesn't match the picture of spirituality or the spiritual person that they carry in their heads! According to them spirituality is never associated with sharing or loving.

People from various backgrounds visit our ashram for healing: young and old people, cancer and HIV patients, and people with various other disabilities. If a person has pain in the leg, naturally I get up from my seat and touch their leg to heal. After all the foot is just another part of the body.

An elderly, traditional and conservative Swami gave me friendly advice about this practice. He remarked, 'You are a Swami. It is unbecoming of a Swami to come down from his seat and touch someone's feet. It is against the tradition.' I replied politely, 'The very seat and the cloth which I wear (saffron robes) mean compassion. I acquired this seat because of my compassion. I am not here *for* the seat.'

Spirituality means flowing. Spirituality means radiating, spreading love and compassion. Whenever we enrich out of compassion, we never feel that we have served. We feel that we have been given an opportunity to serve, to enrich.

Whether we believe it or not, as of now, we have a deep enmity or hostility towards others and ourselves. We live in constant self-doubt, self-hatred and self-denial. We may smile at others like models posing for the camera. We may smile, but we never feel friendly. We keep a safe distance and play a safe game because we never feel any real friendliness with others.

To correct this, the first thing you need to do is completion with yourself and accept yourself as you are. Some people tell me, 'I am unable to accept myself as I am, *Swamiji.* What can I do?' I tell them, 'At least accept that you are unable to accept yourself, that is enough.' If we accept that we are unable to accept ourselves, it is enough. We will drop from the mind. That very acceptance will bring completion in us and open a new consciousness in us.

Forgiving others and forgiving yourself are one and the same. When we torture others with our judgment and prejudices, we torture ourselves, too.

Please listen. If your inner image aligns itself to life image, it is destruction. When your inner image stands up to life image, it is destruction. Because your inner image, what you feel as you, is always lower than life's image, the idea you carry about life and others. If the inner image, *mamakāra* tries to make the life image, *svānyakāra* you carry as reality, it will be destruction. We use the same sword to kill others and to commit suicide ourselves. The same mind deals with others as well as with us.

When we try to poison others, there will be a deep sense of guilt in us because the same mind is working in our inner space. We use strong words when we are angry. And once the anger dies down, the sharpness that had been emitted outward turns inward to create a deep guilt. The height of the anger and the depth of the guilt are equal. If the height increases, the depth increases as well.

When Kṛṣṇa says, 'Happiness and distress, birth and death, fear and fearlessness, non-violence and equanimity, satisfaction, austerity, charity, name and fame, fame and infamy, all these various qualities of living beings are created by Me alone,' He means be complete with life as it is, be authentic to all aspects of your life: your inner image, outer image, others' image and life's image. If all the four images reach their peak possibility, it is Enlightenment.

The moment we create the space of completion and complete with life as it is, we experience divinity in everything. We don't exclude anything. The moment we complete, a cognitive shift happens in us. As of now, the cognitive process happening inside our mind, is centered on enmity. The moment we declare completion with ourselves and with life, we complete with the whole world. Then, the complete cognition happens inside our system, which will be centered on bliss.

Kṛṣṇa explains His glory. He says, 'I am everything.' He declares, 'I am the Universal Consciousness. The person who truly knows My glories and powers, engages in yoga, the union of individual consciousness with the divine consciousness, and undoubtedly attains liberation.'

etāṁ vibhūtiṁ yogaṁ ca mama yo vetti tattvataḥ **/**
so 'vikalpena yogena yujyate nātra saṁśayaḥ **//** *10.7*

Listen! When you are complete with you, the Universe will be complete with you. When you are incomplete with you, the Universe will be incomplete with you. Completion with you is *sātori*. Completion with the Cosmos is *samādhi*.

The *Saptarṣis*, the seven sages that Kṛṣṇa talks about, are not seven old men with flowing beards sitting in meditation and penance, waiting for something to happen. From my experience, this is the energy field that drives this Universe. This energy field referred to as the *Saptarṣis* has the intelligent power to make decisions that determine the course of the Universe.

During my *parivrājaka*, wandering days before enlightenment, I lived for several months in Tapovan, beyond Gaṅgotri and Gomukh, in the Himalayan mountain range at a 17,000 feet altitude. Even now, no roads lead to Tapovan and there are no permanent structures to stay in. I lived like many other Sannyāsis, staying in caves, covering myself with jute cloth and newspaper in the winter and eating whatever fruits were available. Tapovan is referred to as Śambāla, heaven on earth. It is the point from which one can move from the material earthly plane up to the spiritual plane.

Kṛṣṇa refers to the *Saptarṣis* as the Universal consciousness that was born from His mind, from Him, the Primal Source and Primal Creator. He is the Saptarṣis. His energy decides what enlightened beings should do and directs their actions. Every movement that I make is governed and decided by this energy.

In Hindu tradition, Manus are the children of Brahma, the Creator. There is a lineage of Manus, fourteen Manus, who populated the earth. Each Manu ruled for a period. The collective period of all fourteen Manus equals one *kalpa*, one day in the life of Brahma. In Saṃskṛit, all humans are termed *Mānava*, meaning those descended from Manu.

As the Universal consciousness, Kṛṣṇa is *all in one*. He is the Creator, Sustainer and Rejuvenator. He is Brahma, Viṣṇu and Śiva. He also transcends all three as the *Parabrahman*, the Supreme Superconsciousness.

One needs to do nothing except understand and accept what Kṛṣṇa is. The Master says that understanding and completing alone liberates us. Nothing more is needed.

Experience The Light Of Knowledge

10.8 *I am the source of all the spiritual and material worlds.*
Everything arises from Me.
The wise, who know this, are devoted to Me and
surrender their heart to Me.

10.9 *With mind and lives absorbed on Me, always enlightening one*
another and talking about My glories,
the wise are content and blissful.

10.10 *To those who are always engaged in Me with love,*
I give them enlightenment by which they come to Me.

10.11 *Out of compassion to them, I destroy the darkness born out of*
their ignorance by the shining lamp of knowledge.

Now, instead of understanding these statements of Kṛṣṇa intellectually, we should try experiencing them. In the deep meditative mood, let us feel connected to the *Parabrahma* Kṛṣṇa, to our very life source, to our very life energy.

Let us enter into meditation, because all the following verses in this chapter must be experienced. They cannot be understood. There is nothing much to understand.

Later Kṛṣṇa says, 'Amongst the *Ṛṣi*, I am Nārada. Among the months, I am Margazhi. Among the rivers, I am Gangā. Among the fish, I am Makara.' He explains His glories at length.

We may think, 'Why does He explain these things in a detailed way?' He makes us understand, wherever we see the glory, wherever we see the Divine radiating, there lies the greatness. We realize this is true when we start experiencing, when we deeply understand these basic truths of completing with ourselves and connecting with the Universe.

We experience life as divine and a blessing when we understand these things. It happens when we connect with the Divine, when we trust, when we completely open up, when we don't have other vested interests and when we do not beg for anything from life.

As long as we are begging for things in the hope that, 'with this, I will feel blissful,' or 'with that, I will feel blissful', we will ask only for this or that. Only when we understand, 'I want just Him, nothing else. I want the pure experience of the Divine, nothing else,' we experience the whole of Existence in a totally different way. The cognitive shift starts happening in us.

I can imagine how Arjuna felt when Kṛṣṇa revealed these things for the first time, inch by inch. 'Oh Arjuna, I am that. I am this. I am everything.' Arjuna may not have said anything, but he surely must have felt that he was expanding.

Understand this example: You and your husband were ordinary people when you were first married. Slowly, your husband entered politics and became a mayor. After five years, he became governor, a well-known person. Already, you feel connected to him since he is your husband. Now, he becomes a famous person or you understand him as a big person. You deeply feel the gratefulness or the gratitude to him because his expansion has helped bring about yours.

In the same way, Arjuna already felt deeply connected to Kṛṣṇa as his friend. Now, he understands the glories of Kṛṣṇa. When Kṛṣṇa reveals His glories and expands, Arjuna also expands. He says, 'Oh God! I am a friend of such a great person. Oh Kṛṣṇa, You are a great person. I am your friend. I am deeply connected to You.'

When we deeply feel connected to the Master and He expresses His glory, we expand. Here, Arjuna is enjoying the same mood that Kṛṣṇa enjoys. Inch by inch, Arjuna is enjoying the joy and bliss.

Arjuna asks, 'Oh Lord! It is so beautiful. I never feel bored. Please tell me again and again, all of your glories.'

Always Engage In Me

Kṛṣṇa explains inch by inch. He reveals who He is and how He is shining. He talks about *Līlā dhyāna*, meditating on the divine play of the Lord. What the eyes see intensely gets registered in the mind. What gets registered in the mind, the eyes see intensely. When the mind is engaged in the Divine, when the heart is captivated by the Divine, we automatically live every moment remembering the Divine. We enjoy talking to each other about the Divine glories because all around us, we see these glories. We are so full of Divine ecstasy and bliss, so fully complete and not wanting anything, because we see life overflowing with Divine bliss and glory.

This was the state of the gopīs, the blessed girls who tended cattle in Kṛṣṇa's home Briṇḍāvan. They constantly played with Kṛṣṇa from the time of His infancy. Their entire world revolved around Him. Their minds and hearts were filled with Kṛṣṇa, with no intellect filtering their emotions.

> Viṣṇu, whose incarnation Kṛṣṇa is, wanted to teach a lesson to his disciple, Nārada. Nārada considered himself to be Viṣṇu's greatest devotee. Kṛṣṇa played His *līlā* (divine play) and pretended he had a headache. His devotees brought him all kinds of medicines, which he tried and pronounced useless.
>
> He told them, 'The only substance that will cure my malaise is the dust from the feet of a true devotee.'
>
> Nārada and the great sages were shocked. How could they allow the dust of their feet to fall on their Master's head? 'It will be a sacrilege,' they argued.
>
> One day Viṣṇu pretended to become annoyed. He told Nārada, 'Get out of My sight. Go to the gopīs in Briṇḍāvan and tell them what I said and seek a solution.'
>
> When Nārada reached Briṇḍāvan, the gopīs were so busy

with their chores that they would not talk to him. Nārada explained, 'I have come from Vaikunṭa.' They were not impressed. He told them, 'Vaikunṭa is the home of Viṣṇu.' 'Who is Viṣṇu?' they asked. Nārada said, 'Viṣṇu is Kṛṣṇa.'

As soon as he uttered the word Kṛṣṇa, they gathered around Nārada and asked him in one voice, 'How is our Kṛṣṇa, our darling?' Nārada said, 'He is suffering from a headache.' They asked, 'What can we do? We cannot let our Kṛṣṇa suffer.' Nārada told them that Viṣṇu had asked for the dust from the feet of one of his true devotees.

One gopī immediately removed her upper cloth. She placed it on the ground and all the gopīs danced upon this cloth to collect the dust from their feet. Folding the cloth, not worried that she had nothing covering her breasts, the gopī said, 'Here take this to our Kṛṣṇa. We do not know which of us is his true devotee. So this has all the dust from all our feet. Go now and give it to Him.'

Nārada asked, 'Aren't you worried that you are giving Kṛṣṇa the dust from your feet to put on His head?'

In one voice, the gopīs answered, 'Are you crazy? He, our Lord and Lover, is suffering and has asked for the dust from our feet. If it would cure Him, we are ready to dance on His head! We shall give our lives for Him.'

Nārada, humbled, returned to Vaikunṭa with the gopī's upper cloth filled with dust from their feet. Viṣṇu took the cloth in His hands, smelled the dust and pronounced Himself fully cured. The sages, devas and Nārada watched in amazement.

'What did they tell you, Nārada?' He asked. 'Did they give useless reasons and advance futile arguments as to why they could not apply the dust from their feet on their Lord and Master, as you all did?'

Nārada hung his head in shame.

Even to this day all main entrance steps to Viṣṇu temples have the imprint of feet carved upon them. These imprints represent the feet of devotees whose feet dust Viṣṇu covets more than all the crowns He is adorned with!

Kṛṣṇa says, 'With mind and lives absorbed on Me, always enlightening one another and talking about My glories, the wise are content and blissful. To those who are always engaged in Me with love, I give them enlightenment for which they come to Me.'

teṣāṁ satata yuktānāṁ bhajatāṁ prīti pūrvakam |
dadāmi buddhi yogaṁ taṁ yena mām upayānti te || 10.10

Kṛṣṇa here talks about satsang, the collection of people whose hearts, minds and bodies are immersed in Him. They are the ones who can talk about nothing except Him, who are filled with bliss and love for their Lord and Master. He promises He will provide them the intelligence to enlighten them and bring them to Him.

I keep telling my devotees about the importance of satsangs. These are regular get togethers where people listen to the Master's words, dance to the kīrtans and go home with refreshed and reinforced memories of their Master. Everyone who attends satsangs regularly can tell you that the Master is present with them, wherever they may be, at that particular moment.

Master Destroys Ignorance

An ashram is an intensified satsang that is forever, twenty-four by seven. That is why I motivate groups of people to form ashrams, spiritual communities, where they can follow their spiritual quest with one-pointed minds.

We are eligible to be part of an ashram community when we are deeply in love with our Master. The motivation to live in an ashram is neither fear that he will hurt us if we leave, nor greed that he will take us to a non-existent heaven if we stay. Rather, it is love born out of this present moment of completion. We must have shed our entire ego and surrender ourselves to the One who has already surrendered Himself. Only then the process works. Otherwise, it is just the blind leading the blind, which is a cult.

Here Kṛṣna talks about such an energy field, an ashram. An ashram is not a serious center of penance with old people meditating in painfully distorted postures. Come to one of our ashrams and see for yourself. No one will be serious. They will be laughing all the time. They are not like Nārada and the sages engaged in intellectual arrogance. They are the gopīs who are in love with their Master; with their entire being filled with love for Him. Their being carries the space of *brahmaṇyam bahuputratām*, the feeling that they are the favorite inheritor of the cosmos.

At the ashram, each one does what he can, noone forces them to do anything. But the energy of the Master provides them with intelligence to live for others, to enrich others to the peak of their possibility. It does not allow them to waste themselves in frivolous activities. They live and radiate the truth that life is for enriching! One does not work out of fear, greed, motivation or necessity. An ashramite (ashram resident) works out of gratitude. Once we start to measure what people do and start comparing, we create a political organization, not a spiritual organization.

Listen. A man who works out of fear and greed is a *śūdra*. The man who works out of attention need is a *vaiśya*. The man who works out of jealousy or comparison to prove that he is superior to others is a *kṣatriya*. The man who works out of gratitude is a *brāhmaṇa*.

These differentiations do not come by birth. They are a result of our *guṇas*, our attributes, our mental make-up, our root patterns. They come into our being when we earn and develop them.

A man cooked for a certain monastery for thirty years. He never bothered to be around the Master, nor did he attend the Master's discourses regularly. When it was time for the Master to leave his body, he called everyone to announce the heir to the monastery. Everyone expected someone who was always very close to the Master to take that seat. Instead the Master said, 'You have all listened to my discourses all these years. However, this cook lived my teachings. He is my successor.' By saying that, he gave the cook the experience of his enlightenment.

People are not equal. Each one comes with his own *karma* (unfulfilled actions) and a particular root pattern. As long as the Master is there, He takes care of everything. When the Master is not there in body, the whole thing becomes *dharma*, righteousness. When the Master is there, everything becomes *mokṣa*, liberation. That is the difference between *dharma* and *mokṣa*. Work for *mokṣa*. That is the difference between an ashram and a monastery.

My mission is for people to live together focused on spiritual evolution; to enrich with science of living enlightenment, towards transformation of oneself through meditation. Soon people will find out how much better this system works compared to their normal lifestyle.

I say to all of them, as Kṛṣṇa said: *those who are always engaged in Me with love, I give them Enlightenment by which they come to Me.*

The Master defines Himself in the last verse:

'I destroy the darkness of ignorance within them, with the shining lamp of wisdom, through my compassion.'

teṣāṁ evānukampārtham aham ajñāna-jaṁ tamaḥ |
nāśayāmy ātma-bhāva-stho jñāna-dīpena bhāsvata || 10.11

The Saṃskṛit word 'Guru', meaning Master, has two syllables: *gu* refers to darkness and *ru* to light. The Master leads the disciple from darkness into light with compassion. This darkness of ignorance is the identification that one has with one's self, one's material attachments and material possessions. This identification surely leads to sorrow since this attachment is for things that are fleeting and not for something long lasting.

Wealth gets created overnight and disappears just as quickly. Relationships, however sound, last only as long as the body lasts, most often far less, since the mind is even more incomplete in holding onto relationships. Nothing that exists in this world, nothing that is of material creation, can last eternally. Our impression that material possessions and attachments last, comes from ignorance. This ignorance is born of self-identity, ego.

The Master is the only person who can dispel that darkness. Only He can light up that wisdom within you in order for you to realize that you are already one with Existence and therefore need nothing from this material world. Your Master gains nothing from teaching you. He gains nothing from enlightening you. He does it out of sheer compassion, so that others may experience the same bliss that He constantly experiences.

10.12 *You are the supreme Truth, supreme sustenance,*

Know Yourself By Yourself

supreme Purifier, the Primal, Eternal and Glorious Lord.

10.13 *All the sages like Nārada, Asita, Devala, and Vyāsa*
have explained this.
Now you are personally explaining to me.

10.14 *Oh Keśava, I accept all these truths that You have told me.*
Oh Lord, neither the gods nor the demons know You.

10.15 *Surely, You alone know Yourself by Yourself,*
Oh Perfect One, the origin of beings, Oh Lord of beings,
Oh God of gods, Oh Lord of the world.

10.16 *Only You can describe in detail Your divine glories*
by which You pervade this Universe.

10.17 *How may I know You by contemplation?*
In which forms should I contemplate on You, Oh Lord?

10.18 *Tell me in detail of Your powers and glories, Oh Janārdana.*
Again, please tell for my satisfaction as
I do not tire of listening to Your sweet words.

Arjuna becomes the perfect disciple. He has no doubts about whatever Kṛṣṇa has said to him so far. It only corroborates what the great sages have said. All that Arjuna seeks is that his Lord and Master tells him more about Himself, His glories, 'I just need to know how I should approach You, how I should see You. Tell me more, I can never tire of listening to Your words.'

Arjuna is in love with His Master. When you are in such deep love as Arjuna is now, and as the gopīs were with Kṛṣṇa in Briṇḍāvan, there is nothing to be said. There is nothing even to be heard. Whatever Arjuna says is merely to keep his end of the dialogue going. Arjuna knows that there is no need for Kṛṣṇa to say anything now. Yes, he would be delighted if Kṛṣṇa were to speak of His glories, His *līlā*. However, Arjuna is in such a state of meditation, ready for his ultimate experience, that whatever his Master says or does would not matter to him.

Therefore, when Arjuna asks the Lord to talk about His glories that no one else understands, Arjuna is not requesting on his behalf, He is requesting on behalf of humanity. Arjuna would have been perfectly happy to sit in silence, in deep meditation upon Kṛṣṇa. And in His compassion, Kṛṣṇa would have eventually revealed Himself to his chosen disciple. However, the rest of humanity would not have been enriched from a revelation that came to Arjuna alone. Hence Arjuna requested that Kṛṣṇa speak about His glory.

Arjuna wants to know about *Parabrahma* Kṛṣṇa, the Ultimate Superconscious being. He does not want to know about his friend and charioteer, *Vāsudeva* Kṛṣṇa, the son of Vāsudeva. Arjuna is in the mood of the perfect devotee and disciple. Anything that he can listen about his Master is nectar to his ears. He is in a state of complete immersion.

> Rāmakṛṣṇa asked Vivekananda, 'If you were a fly and you were on the rim of the cup of nectar, what would you do?'
>
> Vivekananda said, 'Sip from the cup, of course, what else?'
>
> 'You fool!' said the Master, 'You should fall into the nectar and submerge yourself! When would you ever get this opportunity again?

Arjuna is on that verge of immersion. His intellect has almost disappeared. He needs the last nudge, so to speak.

You too, as the reader, make your plea to *Parabrahma* Kṛṣṇa, the *Jagatguru*, so that He may tell you about His glory, and so that you may meditate upon His glory with single pointed focus of the mind. As He promised, He will provide the light of wisdom for you to be enlightened.

10.19 Kṛṣṇa said, 'Yes, Oh Kurusreśta, I will talk to you surely

I Am The Beginning, Middle And End

of My divine glories;
But only of the main ones as there is no end
to the details of My glories.

10.20 *I am the Spirit, Oh Guḍākeśa, situated in all living beings.*
I am surely the beginning, middle and end of all beings.

10.21 *Of the Āditya, I am Viṣṇu. Of the luminaries, I am the bright sun.*
Of the Mārut, I am Māricī. Of the Nakṣatras, I am the Moon.

10.22 *Of the Veda, I am the Sāma Veda. Of the gods, I am Indra.*
Of the senses, I am the mind and in living beings,
I am the consciousness.

10.23 *Of the Rudra, I am Śaṇkara and of the Yakṣa and Rākṣasa,*
I am Kubera, god of wealth.
Of the Vasu, I am fire and of the peaks, I am Meru.

10.24 *Of the priests, understand, Oh Pārtha, that I am the chief*
Bṛhaspati. Of the warriors, I am Skanda.
Of the water bodies, I am the ocean.

10.25 *Of the great sages, I am Bhṛgu. Of the vibrations, I am the OṀ.*
Of the sacrifices, I am the chanting of holy names.
Of the immovable objects, I am the Himālayas.

There is no way to describe the Divine fully because the Divine pervades every bit of this entire Universe. When it exists in every atom, when it is the essence of all that exists, how can we describe or comprehend it in its entirety?

So Kṛṣṇa explains the main manifestations that give a glimpse of the unfathomable Divine.

Kṛṣṇa refers to Arjuna as Guḍākeśa, meaning one who has conquered sleep! He implies that Arjuna has overcome sleep, signifying darkness or ignorance. Therefore Arjuna is ready to receive what Kṛṣṇa is about to deliver. Throughout the Gītā, Kṛṣṇa refers to Arjuna by different names. Each one is appropriate within a particular context. Sometimes He calls Arjuna—*Kaunteya* or *Pārtha*, meaning that he is the son of Kuntī. Kuntī in Mahābhārat is the epitome of patience and forbearance. No one suffers like she does. When Kṛṣṇa addresses Arjuna as the son of Kuntī, it is in the context of advising Arjuna to be patient and listen carefully. While addressing Arjuna here as *Guḍākeṣa,* one who is in the light, having conquered sleep, Kṛṣṇa readies Arjuna for liberation.

Kṛṣṇa declares that He is everything that really matters. Kṛṣṇa says that He is the ultimate consciousness in all beings and He is the beginning, middle and end of all beings. He declares that He pervades the entire space and time and beyond.

aham ātmā guḍākeśa sarva-bhūtāśaya sthitaḥ /
aham ādiś ca madhyaṁ ca bhūtānām anta eva ca // 10.20

Kṛṣṇa is both the macrocosm and the microcosm: the *Brahmāṇḍa*, Cosmos and the *pindāṇda*, individual being. His energy permeates all living and non-living entities and He decides upon their nature.

Young Prahlād was subjected to an inquisition by his demonic father Hiraṇyakaśipu. His father asked, 'You speak about Nārāyaṇa all the time and refuse to give up even when I command you to do so. Where does your Nārāyaṇa live? Where is he now?'

Prahlad replied, 'He may be in this twig lying on the floor. He may be in this pillar next to you. He is everywhere.'

Hiraṇyakaśipu kicked the pillar in fury daring Nārāyaṇa to appear. Nārāyaṇa appeared in the form of Naṛsimha, half-man half-lion!

> Prahlād trusted fully that Nārāyaṇa was everywhere. He did not have one iota of self-doubt about it.
>
> When Prahlād was being challenged by Hiraṇyakaśipu to show Nārāyaṇa anywhere, it is said that Lord Viṣṇu (Nārāyaṇa) suddenly started preparing to leave Vaikunṭa, His abode, when Lakṣmī, His consort asked, 'Lord, where are you going?' Viṣṇu smiled and said, 'I have no idea where this devotee of mine, this young boy Prahlād, is planning to call me from. Wherever he calls from, I need to appear from there!'

Not only does the Lord reside everywhere, He will also go to any length to ensure that His true devotee's words don't go futile!

In this Universe, there are twelve planes of existence. These are a combination of the factors of length, breadth, depth, time, space and consciousness. At best we are aware of the first five and only partially that too. It is difficult for those in the human plane to comprehend even time and space fully. We can only exist in one aspect of time and space in relationship with the three dimensions of length, breadth and depth.

Quantum Physics now recognizes that fundamental particles can exist simultaneously in different locations at the same time. Matter can transcend time and space. Matter and energy can exist beyond the bounds of time and space.

A Master is one who can transcend time and space and reach consciousness. Kṛṣṇa, the great Master, is in the twelfth plane, that of pure consciousness. He is beyond all dimensions, beyond time, and beyond space. He is the beginning and He has no beginning. He is the end and He has no end.

He is the Creator. He is the Created. He is also the Creation. In this huge canvas of the Universe, He is the canvas. He is the paint. He is also the strokes and He is the painting. There is nothing that He is not. The only way to understand even a part of Him is to become immersed in Him.

In the *Chandogya Upaniṣad*, Āditya is a name of Śrī Viṣṇu in His Vāmana avatār. In the ten incarnations of Śrī Viṣṇu, Vāmana is the fifth incarnation as a small brāhmin boy.

> When King Bāli of the demon race was performing a series of fire rituals to attain supremacy over the Universe, the demigods requested Viṣṇu to prevent Bali from conquering the Universe. On King Bāli's last fire ritual, Viṣṇu appeared as a small brāhmin boy. The king, as per the custom, respectfully welcomed the brāhmin boy and offered to give anything that he wished for.
>
> Vāmana asked king Bāli to give him three steps of his land as his property. Once Bāli consented, Vāmana grew from the size of a small boy to a huge figure. He stepped over the entire earth in a single footstep. In the next step, he stepped over the heavenly worlds.
>
> Having thus conquered the worlds, Vāmana asked Bāli where he could place his third step. Having nothing else to offer, Bali offered Vāmana his own head. Vāmana placed his foot on Bali's head.

The history symbolizes how arrogance and pride leads to one's downfall since all possessions are temporary and of no inherent value.. Surrendering only to the Divine, to the Ultimate consciousness, leads us to liberation.

Kṛṣṇa says that among the Māruts, He is Māricī. The Māruts are the thought-gods associated with power and knowledge. Māricī is the father of sage Kaśyapa who is the father of the Māruts. Many Ṛgveda hymns are dedicated to the Māruts. The Māruts aid the activities of Indra, the representation of the mind. This is a metaphysical representation of the power of thoughts that originate from the mind. A common representation of the Maruts in the Ṛg Veda, is a flock of birds. This symbolizes the power of thoughts that influence the recipient. When a person is established in integrity, and radiates positive thoughts, he is receptive to similar thoughts and attracts similar incidents in his life. If we are blissful, people with a similar attitude will be attracted towards us. If we are dull, lethargic and depressed, the same type of people will be attracted towards us.

Thoughts and desires are energy. They contribute towards shaping our actions and lives. Everyday we create our bodies, minds, actions and our reality by our thoughts. We are what our thoughts are.

Next, Kṛṣṇa says that He is the sun amongst all the shining objects, and among the stars He is the moon. We may say that the moon is not a star. We would be factually correct. Kṛṣṇa refers to the influence that the moon wields upon earth and humans. It is scientifically established that out of all celestial bodies around planet earth, the two most important influences are the sun and the moon. No one doubts that the sun is a star and that it is the brightest object that can be seen.

The moon influences the tides of the ocean as well as the tides of the human minds. Of all planetary, non-planetary and solar bodies that surround us, with the exception of the sun, the moon exerts the greatest influence on us both in a broader planetary sense and in an individual sense. People have mood variations depending on the phases of the moon. New moon and full moon days dramatically influence our emotional well-being, for good and for bad. Being the physical mass closest to the earth, the gravitational force of the moon affects each of us deeply.

This is why the Hindu astrological and astronomical systems consider the moon to be a planet. This belief is not based on whether the moon revolves around the earth as a satellite instead of around the sun as a planet. It is based on the effect that the moon has on human beings and upon planet Earth.

In *Vedic* astrology, the stars, are the different positions in the sky that the moon passes through in a cycle of 27 to 28 days. These stars are referred to as the wives of the moon. This is why Kṛṣṇa refers to Himself as the moon amongst the stars, that He is the pride of the stars.

I Am Viṣṇu. I Am Śankara. I Am Oṁ

Kṛṣṇa declares that amongst the Vedas, He is the *Sāma Veda.* The Vedas are the timeless truths expounded by the *ṛṣis* (sages) as the expressions of truth experienced by them. These are the revelations of the truth experienced through intuition by the seers. There are four Vedas: *Ṛg Veda, Yajur Veda, Sāma Veda and Atharva Veda.*

Each *Veda* consists of four parts: *mantra-saṁhita* or hymns, *brāhmaṇa* or explanations of *mantras* (or rituals), *āranyaka*, forest books which give the philosophical meaning of rituals, and the *Upaniṣads*, essence of the *Vedas.*

The Sāma Veda is a collection of hymns in praise of *agni* (fire), Indra (king of the gods) and *soma* (drink of the gods). While the Ṛg Veda is the oldest *Veda*, Sāma Veda is the basis for all musical systems of India. The basic notes of all music, not just of Indian music, originated with Sāma Veda. The seven notes, which are the fundamentals of all music all over the world, were derived from Sāma Veda, which even today is sung, and not recited.

The Ṛg Veda and other Vedas may be recited only by a few scholars today, but Sāma Veda is heard everywhere. It is the essence of Carnatic and Hindustani music forms, the two major classical music forms of India. As the essence of music, Sāma Veda is also the essence of dance forms. One does not need to understand music and dance. It is enough to indulge and experience. So it is with Kṛṣṇa. All we need to do is experience Him.

Among the gods, Kṛṣṇa says He is Vasava (Indra), the king of gods.The five senses, *jñānendriya*, namely sight, hearing, smell, taste and touch, originate from the mind and are of the mind. Without the mind, the senses cannot function. He says He is the subtlest and most powerful, the mind. In living beings, He is the life force, the consciousness, not merely body and mind.

Rudras are the elemental powers worshipped by the *Ṛg Veda*. The word *Rudra* means to cry. Metaphorically the *Rudras* were worshipped to obtain some gain. When in deep anguish, if one prays to one of the

Rudras in awareness, it was believed to bring results. There are eleven Rudras: Aja, Ekapāda, Ahirbudhnya, Vīrabhadra, Girīśa, Śaṅkara, Aparājita, Hara, Anakaraka, Pināki, Bhaga and Śambhu. Śankara is the doer of good. Śankara is also the precursor to Śiva in the evolution of the Hindu constellation of divinity.

Śiva means causeless auspiciousness; auspiciousness born without a reason. Wherever Śiva is, good happens for no reason. Of the Rudras, Kṛṣṇa says He is Śankara, *rudrāṇāṁ śankaraś cāsmi* (10.20).

Yakṣas are celestial beings considered to be the creators of wealth. The king of the Yakṣas is Kubera, the god of wealth. Rākṣasas too are celestial beings of a negative nature of hoarding power and wealth. Yakṣas and Rākṣasas are keepers of wealth. They do not enjoy wealth. Of the Yakṣas and Rākṣasas, Kṛṣṇa says He is the god of wealth, the king Kubera.

The Vasus are the attendants of Viṣṇu. They represent various aspects of Nature. The ***Brihadāraṇyaka Upaniṣad*** mentions eight Vasus: agni (fire), pṛthvī (earth), vāyu (wind), antarikṣa (space), āditya (light), dyaus (sky), candramas (moon) and nakṣatrāṇi (stars). Kṛṣna says among the Vasus, He is the formless fire.

Meru is the golden peak, the metaphoric abode of gods, and its foothills are the Himalayas. It also represents the human spine. Amongst the peaks, Kṛṣṇa says He is the majestic Meru.

Bṛhaspati is the priest of the gods. He dispels darkness and ignorance and destroys the enemies of the gods. Among the warriors, Kṛṣṇa says He is Skanda, the supreme General of the forces of gods. Skanda is the son of Śiva and Pārvati, who destroyed Tārakāsura, the demon who, along with his hordes of demons, tormented the devas. This is a metaphysical representation of the Divine as the Supreme General of the being, vanquishing the senses, desires and ego.

Of the water bodies, Kṛṣṇa says He is the mighty ocean, infinite in expanse and essential to all life forms. In fact, it is the origin of all life forms.

Of the great sages, Kṛṣṇa says He is Bhṛgu, one of the *Saptarṣis* (seven sages who form the cosmic energy). Bhṛgu is believed to have been created by Brahma to aid him in the creation of the Universe.

Of the vibrations, Kṛṣṇa says He is the transcendental OṀ—*girām asmy ekam akṣaram* (10.25). OṀ is the primal sound from which the Universe manifested itself. It is the *praṇava*, the mystic symbol.

The symbol of OṀ—ॐ contains three curves, a semi-circle and a dot. Out of the three curves, the upper curve symbolizes the waking state, the lower curve denotes deep sleep and the right curve denotes the dream state. It thus represents the three states of individual consciousness. The dot represents the fourth state of consciousness, *turīya,* complete awareness. The semicircle represents *māyā,* illusion, and separates the dot from the three curves. But the open semicircle represents the Absolute which is unaffected by *māyā.*

Of the different types of sacrifices, Kṛṣṇa says He is the *japa* or chanting of holy names—*yajñānāṁ japa-yajño 'smi* (10.25).

Of the immovable objects in the world, He says He is the mighty and majestic Himalayas. The Himalayas, literally meaning 'the abode of snow', is home to hundreds of peaks, including the highest peak in the world. Some great rivers originate in it and flow through it, including Gangā, Yamunā, Brahmaputra and Indus.

The Himalayas have a great unique spiritual significance as well. Kailasa, abode of Śiva, is the earthly representation of the metaphorical Meru. The Himalayan mountains are the spiritual incubator of the world. The Himalayas are truly a powerful energy field.

For thousands of years, millions of *Sādhus* (sages) have lived there and left their bodies from there. When Enlightened Masters leave their bodies, the result of their penance, the energy of their spiritual penance, is not carried by the spirit. They leave behind this energy in their bodies. Imagine how much energy is in the Himalayas, where so many Enlightened beings have left their bodies! We should be thankful to the Himalayas since their positive energy balances the collective negativity in the world.

> The Himalayan Mountains are home to me. I never believed, when I left home to travel to the Himalayas, that I would return to South India. It was in the Himalayas that I met **Mahāvatār Bābā,** the great Master who has been living in these mountains for thousands of years. You may believe it or not believe it, but that is the Truth.
>
> On the way to Kedarnath, Mahāvatār Bābā called me by the name I am now called. He walked into me after calling me **'Paramahamsa Nithyananda'.** I thought he was asking me to look for a master named *Nithyananda*!
>
> So I went searching for this master. More than a year later, at Calcutta, on the banks of the river Hooghly, a tributary of the river Gangā, an old Sannyāsi insisted on giving me Sannyāsa before he died. I was not keen to take Sannyāsa. I was looking for Enlightenment. But he insisted. So I agreed.
>
> **To my utter surprise he gave me the name—*Paramahamsa Nithyananda.***
>
> I asked this Sannyāsi, 'Why?' He said, 'I do not know. This is what I was asked to do.' He did not explain who asked him to give me the name and initiation. So, I tell my disciples that Mahāvatār Bābā is our *Kulaguru*, Master of our lineage, and Kedar is our *kṣetra*, our spiritual location.

When Kṛṣṇa says, 'I am the Himalayan Mountain out of all unmoving things, *sthāvarāṇāṁ himālayaḥ (*10.25).' I can feel the energy of Kṛṣṇa in these mountains. Everyone who has been with me on these trips have felt it at some point. They are blessed. They have been in Kṛṣṇa consciousness!

10.26 Of all the trees, I am the Banyan tree and

I Am Banyan Tree, I Am Time

of all the sages of the gods, I am Nārada.
Of the Gandharvas, I am Citraratha.
Of the realized souls, I am the sage Kapila.

10.27 *Of the horses, know me to be Ucchaiśravas born of the nectar generated from the churning of the ocean.*
Of the elephants, Airāvata and of men, the king.

10.28 *Of the weapons, I am the thunderbolt.*
Of the cows, I am Kāmadhenu;
For begetting children, I am the god of love.
Of the snakes, I am Vāsuki.

10.29 *Of the serpents, I am Ananta. Of the water deities, I am Varuṇa.*
Of the ancestors, I am Aryamā and
of the ones who ensure discipline, I am Yama.

10.30 *Of the Daitya (demons), I am Prahlād and*
of the reckoners, I am Time.
Of the animals, I am the king of animals (Lion)
and of the birds, I am Garuḍa.

Kṛṣṇa says among the trees He is the banyan tree, *aśvatthaḥ sarva vṛkṣānāṁ* (10.26). The banyan tree develops its root-like structures from the branches. These grow into the earth as secondary roots. The metaphysical meaning of the banyan tree is that just as the banyan tree grows its roots upside down unlike other trees, the spiritual person shuns the illusory outer world, the world that most people run after. Instead, he goes inwards towards the Absolute.

In a later chapter Kṛṣṇa says that the leaves of the banyan tree are the

Vedas. He who knows this tree is the knower of the Vedas.

Of all the spiritually enlightened Masters, the *Ṛṣis,* Kṛṣṇa says He is Nārada. Nārada is considered the greatest of all devotees. His mind is immersed in remembering Viṣṇu, forever chanting '*Nārāyaṇa, Nārāyaṇa*'. Kṛṣṇa identifies Himself with His greatest devotee.

Of the Gandharvas, the celestial beings, Kṛṣṇa says He is Citraratha. Gandharvas are celestial beings skilled in music and they are guardians of the soma juice—the nectar of the divine beings. Citraratha is the king of the Gandharvas.

I AM THE COMPLETE BEING

Among the Siddhas, the complete beings, the Self-realized persons, Kṛṣṇa says He is Kapila, the complete sage. Kapila is the author of the *Sāṅkhya Yoga* system of philosophy, which deals with the elements of the physical Universe and the spiritual world. He is also the founding father of *Mahānirvāṇi Pīṭha—Kapila Sarvajña Pīṭha.* Kapila is considered an incarnation of Viṣṇu and Mahādev.

Listen. Śrī Kṛṣṇa is the greatest follower of *Sāṅkhya Yoga* of *Mahānirvāṇi Pīṭha,* the oldest apex body of *sanātana-dharma.* Understand, after the first chapter, *Arjuna Viṣāda Yogaḥ*, the first words that come out of Bhagavān's mouth are *Sāṅkhya Yoga—nai'naṁ chindanti śastrāṇi nai 'naṁ dahati pāvakaḥ* (2.23).

I can be sure that Kṛṣṇa was filled with Kapila. So, here Bhagavān introduces Himself saying, 'Among the perfect complete beings, I am Kapila—*siddhānāṁ kapilo muniḥ* (10.26).' This means that in Kṛṣṇa's time, Kapila was the star of the spiritual world. That is why He mentions Kapila. I can see the whole compassion of Kapila. I know for sure that he was the first man who started thinking. Till then, thinking was not part of humanity. The first human being on planet Earth who started thinking and experienced completion was Kapila.

Kapila Muni is one of the great Incarnations celebrated in Śrīmad Bhāgavatam. There is a beautiful book called *Kapila Gītā*, Kapila's teachings to his mother, Devāhuti recorded in Śrīmad Bhāgavatam and other books Kapila's *Sāṅkhya Sūtra* and *Sāṅkhya Kārika* based on his philosophy. When I was studying them, I found such beautiful expressions! If you read Kapila, you won't find a single moral lesson or even a definition of morality or immorality. But, the followers of Kapila will be the most beautiful moral beings on planet Earth, because He just puts you into the natural flow of your being. You don't hide anything from others and yourself. You are not afraid of anything that is within or outside you.

What pristine purity! Kapila is the definition of the natural law of Existence, the innate intelligence. I tell you, Kapila is as beautiful as the gopikās of Bhāgavatam, as intelligent as Kṛṣṇa's Gītā, and as natural as Dharmarāja (name of Yudhiṣtra, the righteous king). Only with certain completion, can you understand the intelligence, beauty, and naturalness, all that can flow together in one space, that is Kapila.

Next, Ucchaiśravas is the legendary snow-white horse that emerged during the churning of the ocean of milk described in the Bhāgavatam.

According to the history, the *devas*, the good, oppressed by the *asuras*, the evil, appealed to Lord Viṣṇu for help. Viṣṇu directed *devas* to churn the ocean of milk upon which Viṣṇu rests, using Meru, the mountain, as the staff and Vāsuki, the serpent, as the rope. Viṣṇu became the base as a tortoise upon which Meru rested. Since the *devas* did not have the strength to do the job alone, they took the help of the *asuras* promising them a share in whatever materialized.

During the churning, various divine entities emerged. Among these were the divine horse, Ucchaiśravas, and the four-tusked king of the elephants, Airāvata, whom Indra took as his mount.

As part of the churning process, a deadly poison *hālahāla* also emerged that threatened to take the lives of the *devas* and *asuras*. Śiva came to their rescue and drank the poison. Finally, the nectar of immortality emerged. Viṣṇu, in the form of a beautiful damsel Mohini kept the *asuras* occupied, while He allowed the *devas* to drink the *amṛta*, nectar of immortality, and become invincible.

This is a metaphysical representation signifying how we are pushed and pulled by desires in our lives. From this churning in our life, various products emerge. The nectar of immortality emerges when we offer our entire being to the Divine, as we go beyond the push and pull of desires, beyond life and death. Then we dwell in ultimate bliss. There may be obstacles in the path. Yet, the Master supports and protects us during our churning, as we endeavor to realize the ultimate state. Just as Śiva drank the poison that came out as a result of churning the ocean, the Master holds the disciple steady as the unconscious root patterns, *saṁskāras* rise to the surface during our spiritual maturing.

Kṛṣṇa says, among the weapons, He is *vajra*, the thunderbolt. This is the weapon of Indra, king of the demigods. Viṣṇu is considered to be present in the *vajra*. Indra was specifically given this weapon—the thunderbolt, for a purpose. Kṛṣṇa does not choose His own weapon, the *cakra*, the mighty discus. Instead he used Indra's vajra that was made from the bones of the great sage Dadhici, who gave up his life to destroy the evil Vṛtāsura.

Among the cows, He says He is the sacred cow, Kāmadhuk or Kāmadhenu, which also emerged during the churning of the ocean. In the Hindu way of life, the cow is worshipped for her essential utility. Kāmadhuka is considered to be the cow that grants all wishes and is the mother of all cows.

Kṛṣṇa says, for begetting children, He is the god of love, the basis for procreation. He says He is the Vāsuki of serpents. Vāsuki is the king of snakes. Vāsuki was used as the rope and he wound himself around Meru, the staff, for churning the ocean of milk.

Kṛṣṇa says, among the *nāgas*, non-poisonous snakes or creatures of the nether world, He is Ananta, the many-hooded serpent who forms the bed of Lord Viṣṇu. He is said to support all the planets on his various hoods, including the Earth.

Among the water beings, Kṛṣṇa says He is Varuṇa, the god of the mightiest water body, the ocean.

Among the ancestors, Kṛṣṇa says He is Aryamā, one of the Ādityas, who presides over a planet occupied by the energy bodies of our ancestors.

Of the ones who ensure discipline, Kṛṣṇa says He is Yama, the Lord of death. Death is the perfect equalizer of all beings. Death is the only certain thing in the life of all beings and it treats everyone exactly the same whether they are big or small, rich or poor. So the Lord of death, Yama, ensures perfect discipline. The Saṃskṛit word *yama* means both discipline and death. Yama is the first of the eight limbs of Patañjali's *Aṣṭāṅga Yoga*.

Of the Daityas, Kṛṣṇa says He is Prahlād—*prahlādaś cāsmi daityanāṁ* (10.30). The Daityas are considered to be a race of beings that warred against the demigods. Prahlād was the son of a powerful Daitya King, Hiraṇyakaśipu. Prahlād was a pious child, an embodiment of integrity. The young Prahlād is a supreme example of devotion. His life is the example that total surrender to the Divine is possible and that such surrender leads the Divine to completely care for His devotees, in all situations and at all times.

Of the reckoners, Kṛṣṇa says He is Kāla, Time itself—*kālaḥ kalayatām aham* (10.30). Time is the ultimate reckoner. No being exists who can beat Time. Irrespective of who it is, Time always moves on. It cannot be stopped by anyone.

Of the animals, Kṛṣṇa says He is the Lion, king of the jungle. Among birds, He says He is Garuḍa, king of birds, the eagle who is the mount of Lord Viṣṇu.

10.31 *Of the purifiers, I am the Wind.*

I Am Rāma

Of the wielders of weapons, I am Rāma.
Of the water beings, I am the Shark and
of the flowing rivers, I am Jāhnavi (Gaṅgā).

10.32 *Of all creations, I am surely the Beginning and end and the middle, Oh Arjuna. Of all knowledge, I am the Spiritual knowledge of the Self. Of all arguments, I am the Logic.*

10.33 *Of the letters, I am the 'A'. Of the dual words, I am the Compounds and surely I am the never-ending time. I am the Omniscient who sees everything.*

10.34 *I am the all-devouring Death and I am the Creator of all things of the future. Of the feminine, I am Fame, Fortune, Beautiful speech, Memory, intelligence, Faithfulness and Patience.*

10.35 *Of the Sāma Veda hymns, I am the Bṛhat Sāma and of all poetry, I am the Gāyatrī. Of the months, I am Mārgaśīrṣa and of the seasons, I am Spring.*

10.36 *Of all the cheating, I am Gambling. Of the effulgent things, I am the Effulgence. I am Victory, I am Effort, I am the Goodness of the good.*

10.37 *Of the descendants of Vṛṣṇi, I am Vāsudeva Kṛṣna. Of the Pāṇḍava, I am Arjuna. Of the Sages, I am also Vyāsa and of the thinkers, I am Uśāna.*

10.38 *Of rulers, I am their Scepter. Of the victorious, I am Statesmanship. Of all secrets, I am also Silence. Of the wise, I am Wisdom.*

Of the purifying elements, Kṛṣṇa says He is the formless and pure wind—*pavanaḥ pavatām asmi* (10.31). The wind pervades the other elements such as earth, water and fire and removes impurities.

Of the wielders of weapons, He says He is Rāma, the seventh incarnation of Viṣṇu—*rāmaḥ śastra-bhṛtām aham* (10.31). Śrī Rāma defeated Rāvaṇa, the demonic ruler of Lankā who abducted his wife, Sīta. Rāma was a righteous ruler and chosen heir to his father's throne. Yet, Rāma went into exile to uphold his father's vow. Rāma is considered the greatest archer ever known. Of the ten incarnations of Viṣṇu, Rāma is the incarnation just prior to Kṛṣṇa. Of the aquatic beings, the fish, He says He is the Shark, the most powerful and feared.

Of the rivers, He says He is Gangā. The river Gangā is worshipped in India as goddess Gangā. Millions of people pray in the waters of the Gangā everyday. On its banks, millions of people gather everyday to offer *pūjā* to Gangā and to take a holy dip in the waters. The sage Jahnu swallowed Gangā as She rushed down the Himalayas into his ashram. Bhagīratha begged the *ṛṣis* to release Gangā. That is why Gangā is known as the daughter of Jahnu and has the name 'Jāhnavi'.

As Gangā descends from the Himalayas to the plains, there are multiple places of pilgrimage where people revere the river and offer daily prayers. Gangā is considered the sacred river that descended from the heavens, blessing the planet with the Ganges based civilization. Millions of people standing and praying in the waters have energized the whole river and this explains why Gangā has the inexplicable ability of cleansing Herself.

Let me share a factual observation recorded in the reminiscences of the British who ruled India. When the British traveled by ship from England to India, their water became spoilt during the long journey. However, on the return trip from India to England, the water from the Gangā remained pure even after reaching England. The research showed that the Gangā water had the miraculous power of cleansing Herself.

Of all the creations, Kṛṣṇa says He is the beginning, the middle and the end, thus establishing that He is *all* that existed, exists and will exist. He is the creator, created and creation—*sargāṇāṁ ādir antaś ca madhyaṁ caivaham arjuna* (10.32).

Of the various branches of knowledge, He is the ultimate spiritual knowledge, Self-realization—*adhyātma vidyā vidyānāṁ* (10.32). Other branches of knowledge result from intelligence. Only Self-realization requires intuition and something beyond.

Of all arguments, He says He is the logic that binds everything together. Of the letters, Kṛṣṇa says He is the first letter, '*aksarānāṁ a-kāro 'smi*', the origin of all that is spoken and written. Of the dual words, a class of words in Saṃskṛit, He is the compound word.

He affirms He is never-ending time and the Creator of this Universe, Brahma. Kṛṣṇa says He is the Creator and Destroyer.

Of the feminine qualities, He says He is the seven *Devīs*, goddesses, who impart fame, fortune, beautiful speech, memory, intelligence, faithfulness and patience. In Saṃskṛit all these qualities have feminine nouns to represent them. He says these attributes in women come from Him.

Kṛṣṇa said in an earlier verse that among the *Vedas*, He is the *Sāma Veda* that contains beautiful songs and hymns. Now, He says, among these hymns, He is the *Bṛhat Sāma,* a unique melody.

I AM GĀYATRĪ

Of all poetic meters, He says He is Gāyatrī—*gāyatrī chandasām aham* (10.35). Various invocations and prayers in the *Vedic* literature are set to Gāyatrī meter, including Devi Gāyatrī, Rudra Gāyatrī, etc. This *chanda*, meter is 24 syllables, usually in 3 or 4 lines.

This verse can also be translated to mean that Kṛṣṇa says, 'I am Gāyatrī amongst the *mantras*.' *Mantras* are the sacred syllables that create awareness of the divinity within our inner space. The very vibrations created while chanting the Saṃskṛit *mantras* purify the mind-body system and raise the energetic frequency. Here, Kṛṣṇa states that Gāyatrī is the greatest of the *mantras.* Its popularity has been evident from the earliest *Vedic* times. This was the first *mantras* taught when the child entered a *gurukul*, the traditional Cedic schools of Enlightened Masters.

Gāyatrī literally translated means 'the song that liberates'. Gāyatrī is an invocation to the ultimate intelligence. This prayer creates self-awareness, self-completion:

Om bhūr bhuva suvaḥ
tat savitur vareṇyam
bhargo devasya dhīmahi
dhiyo yonaḥ prachodayāt

Freely translated, this means:

> We bow to You, that Ruler of physical, mental and spiritual planes, That which is beyond all, the supreme Brilliance, May You kindle our inner awareness! It is a prayer to the supreme intelligence to awaken our inner intelligence.

Gāyatrī is not merely a prayer or a *mantra.* It is far more than that. It is a *tantra,* a technique that can create tremendous awareness and intelligence in our being. *Mantra* means the syllable that shows the way to go beyond joys and sufferings of the world. Mantra makes us more centered and complete. *Tantra* is more than that. It is an instant delivery system.

Generally, religions condition us from childhood by installing in us value systems and beliefs, our *saṁskāras*—root patterns or past bio-memories. Gāyatrī is a technique that completely liberates us from our *saṁskāras.* It is like a torch to guide one on one's path. Children were taught this *mantra* from early childhood in ancient times so that they could be free from their *saṁskāras.*

Gāyatrī is not about giving someone a belief or prayer to be chanted to any gods or during any form of worship. It is a pure technique that can lead to pure intelligence. Continuous meditation on this *mantra,* just continuous recitation of this *mantra* with awareness, directly leads one to the ultimate intelligence.

Gāyatrī mantra says, *'Let us meditate on the energy which awakens the intelligence in our Being. Let that intelligence help us meditate on It.'*

Contemplating on the meaning of Gāyatrī *mantra,* creates a beautiful vibration inside our being. Repeating the *mantra* mentally and letting the *mantra* sink into our being is like planting a seed in our being that will lead to thousands of fruits in the outer world as well as inner world. It gives us what we want along with giving us the inner space, in which we don't want anything.

Among the months, Kṛṣṇa says, He is the month of Mārgaśīrṣa, November and December in the Gregorian calendar. In India, these months bring joy to people as they are the time when grains are collected from the fields. Also, the month has a lot of spiritual significance because the auspicious days of *Vaikunṭa Ekādasi* fall in this month. This month in the divine calendar is the early morning time, the *brahma muhūrtaṁ*, the most auspicious part of the day. This is the time recommended to focus on worship.

Among the seasons, Kṛṣṇa says, He is spring. Nature is at the pinnacle of Her creation in spring with new blossoms on trees and pleasant weather, which is neither too hot nor too cold. Spring thus signifies life, growth and the beginning of the cycle of life.

Kṛṣṇa declares that of all vices, He is gambling. Even in the vices He says He is present! Anybody who deludes himself by thinking that He is not present in 'unvirtuous' activities should realize that the Divine exists everywhere and in all activities and things. By this, Kṛṣṇa also refers to the fact that Yudhiṣṭra's vice of gambling brought about this Great War. Known as the wisest of all men, the most righteous being, Yudhiṣṭra, the Pāṇḍava prince, had one vice that brought him down. That was his weakness for gambling.

Kṛṣṇa says, He is the effulgence that is the essence of all radiant things. He declares He is the Victory of the victorious, the effort needed to succeed, and *satva*, Goodness, amongst the attributes.

Kṛṣṇa's father, Vāsudeva, was a member of the Vṛṣṇi or Yādav race. Amongst the Vṛṣṇis, Kṛṣṇa says He is the ultimate, *Vāsudeva* Kṛṣṇa.

Amongst the Pāṇḍavas, He says He is the arch bowman, Arjuna.

Of the sages, He says He is Vyāsa, author of the great epic Mahābhārat that includes the *Bhagavad Gītā.* Vyāsa is also referred to as Veda Vyāsa, the compiler of the Vedas who split one Veda into four Vedas so that the common person could understand the knowledge in the Vedas.

Of the thinkers, Kṛṣṇa says, He is Uśāna, also known as Śukra, guru of the *asuras,* celestials with a negative bent of mind.

Kṛṣṇa says, 'I am the scepter, the *daṇḍa*, the rod of punishment of the King.' As a Master, Kṛṣṇa wields the *yoga daṇḍa*, the divine staff of wisdom. A ruler is not merely a refuge for his subjects, but also the rule giver, the disciplinarian. So is the Master.

There Is No End To My Glories

10.39 *Also, of whatever beings exist, I am the Seed, Oh Arjuna. There is nothing that exists without Me in all creations, moving and unmoving.*

10.40 *There is no end to My Divine glories, Oh Parantapa. What has been said by Me are examples of My detailed glories.*

10.41 *You should know that whatever glories exist or anything beautiful and glorious that exists, all that surely is born of just a portion of My splendor.*

10.42 *Of what use is it to know about the many manifestations of this kind, Oh Arjuna? I pervade this entire world with just a part of Myself.*

Kṛṣṇa says to Arjuna, 'Enough has been said. You can take no more. Whatever I have said, whatever more I can say, will only be a drop in the ocean, a small fragment of what I am. There is nothing that is not Me, nothing that can exist outside of Me, and nothing that has not been created from and by Me.'

yac cāpi sarva bhūtānāṁ bījaṁ tad aham arjuna ||
na tad asti vinā yat syān mayā bhūtaṁ carācaram || 10.39

nānto 'sti mama divyānāṁ vibhūtīnāṁ parantapa |
eṣa tūddeśataḥ prokto vibhūter vistaro mayā || 10.40

He has given the background to Arjuna, so that Arjuna is prepared to see His formless form. Arjuna is now in a mode of total surrender and in deep gratitude.

Now, let us also experience these words of Kṛṣṇa in a mood of absolute surrender and total gratitude.

Close your eyes, and meditate on the divine glory of Kṛṣṇa.

Express deep gratitude for whatever way your life has been elevated. Express deep gratitude to whoever has helped you achieve health, wealth and education. Each and every one of these are expressions of the Divine.

Remember every one of them for the reasons they were in your life. Remember all of them who helped you to flower in your life. Remember all of them with love and respect, with love and gratitude.

Remember your mother who gave you this body. She is the embodiment of the Divine, *Parabrahma* Kṛṣṇa. Give her your gratitude. Remember your father who gave you life. Feel him and give your gratitude to him.

Remember all the teachers and professors who gave you education. They are embodiments of the Divine. Feel deeply grateful to all of them for enriching your life and to your being.

Whoever has helped you to grow economically, whoever contributed to your economical growth, directly or indirectly, remember all of them and give your gratitude to them. Feel deeply connected to all of them.

Whoever gave you mental strength and understanding about life when you needed it, whenever you were depressed whoever gave you courage, remember all of them. They are embodiments of the Divine, representatives of the Universal Consciousness. Remember all of them and give them your gratitude.

Whoever helped you grow spiritually, whoever helped you grow in spiritual understanding, remember all of them. Give them your gratitude. They are representatives of the Divine.

Whoever helped you with understanding on the level of material wealth or spiritual growth, remember all of them and offer them your gratitude.

Ultimately, give gratitude to the divine energy, *Parabrahma* Kṛṣṇa, who gave this intelligence and understanding to us in our life.

Just drop yourself and become one with the Cosmic energy. May you become part of the whole Universe, part of the energy that is moving the sun, moon and planet Earth.

Oṁ śānti, śānti, śāntihi...

Relax. Now open your eyes. Continue to spend at least the next few hours in this mood of surrender. Drop yourself. You will see this experience works miracles in your being. It can transform you.

Forget about yourself. Drop yourself and let the Divine, let this Cosmic energy prevail. Let Him be. Let the Divine be. This surrender mood can transform your whole consciousness. It can make you experience the ultimate truth that Kṛṣṇa explains here: His glories, His *vibhūti*, His Divine glory.

When you are blissful, whatever you see looks divine and glorious. May you reach that bliss.

Let us pray to *Parabrahma* Kṛṣṇa, the Universal energy, Existence, to guide us all and to give us all the experience of eternal bliss, *Nityānanda*.

Thank you!

Thus ends the tenth chapter named ***Vibhūti Yogaḥ***, 'The Yoga of Divine Manifestations,' of the ***Bhagavad Gītā Upaniṣad, Brahmavidyā Yogaśāstra***, the scripture of yoga dealing with the science of the Absolute in the form of ***Śrī Kṛṣṇārjuna saṃvād***, dialogue between Śrī Kṛṣṇa and Arjuna.

CHAPTER

11

Viśvarūpa Darśan Yogaḥ

Kṛṣṇa: The Cosmic Window

How does one experience Universal consciousness? What exactly happens? What basic qualification does one need for this experience? Kṛṣṇa explains and gives the direct, pure experience with His very Cosmic Presence!

Kṛṣṇa: The Cosmic Window

In this chapter, Kṛṣṇa shows His Cosmic and Divine form to Arjuna. Kṛṣṇa gives Arjuna the experience of Universal consciousness. For the first time, Arjuna is about to experience Kṛṣṇa's Divine form. Of all the chapters in *Bhagavad Gītā*, this chapter, *Viśvarūpa Darśan Yogaḥ—Vision of the Cosmic form*, has a very special significance. It is in this chapter that Kṛṣṇa reveals His Divine Self, that of *Parabrahma* Kṛṣṇa. Elsewhere He speaks with the authority of *Parabrahma* Kṛṣṇa, but He is still present as the mortal human Kṛṣṇa form. Now, at Arjuna's request, He reveals His true Cosmic Self to Arjuna.

In this sense, this is the most important of all the chapters in *Bhagavad Gītā*, not for its philosophical or spiritual importance, but because of the direct revelation of the Divine. When the Cosmic form is revealed to Arjuna, if one is immersed in this chapter's content as he was, nothing more needs to be said to be experienced.

In the previous chapter, along with Arjuna, we too listened to the glories of Kṛṣṇa, the complete expression of the Divine. Kṛṣṇa declares, 'Amongst the trees, I am the Banyan tree, amongst the wielders of weapons, I am Rāma, amongst the *siddhas*, I am Kapila; whatever is best, I shine in that.'

Kṛṣṇa is not boasting that He is the best. All that He conveys is that whatever there is, is manifest in Himself. He is the very essence of Existence. Now, Kṛṣṇa goes beyond all verbal expressions of His glories. Enough words have been said. It is now time to demonstrate. Kṛṣṇa proves who He is by giving a solid experience to Arjuna.

The difference between an enlightened person and an egoistic person is that an egoistic person also declares what he perceives to be a fact, but only the enlightened person can give the experience itself. A mortal can talk, that is all he can do. He has no experience to back it up with.

Our entire existence as we know it, is unreal. So therefore, what can be true about it? How can we boast and take credit for a life that we don't have any control over? We have no control over the next breath we take. We have no control over how long our loved ones will live. We have no control over what will happen during the course of our lives. Yet, we believe we are in control of the whole of our lives.

DIVINE OR DELUSION?

Hiraṇyakaśipu, the demon king, thought he was God and he made his subjects chant his name, '*Hiraṇyāya namaḥ*'. Kṛṣṇa also stated that He was God. The difference between the two was that Hiraṇyakaśipu could not give the experience to his subjects. He told them, 'Either believe that I am God or I will kill you!' He threatened his subjects into this behavior, whether or not they actually believed he was God. Please understand that conversion by blood or bread does not help. While both of them declared they were gods, Kṛṣṇa could actually prove it. He could give the experience of Universal consciousness to people!

No great Master believed in spreading his words through fear and greed. All great Masters spread their words through unconditional love and compassion. That is the only way truth can spread. Unfortunately, the disciples who followed these spiritual Masters were not always masters themselves. They were there to establish business practices in the form of religions. They were organizers, not leaders. Fear and greed became handy tools of organization and propagation, since these followers did not have the experience of truth within themselves.

How to find out whether a person is an Enlightened Master, an Incarnation? How to establish whether a person is enlightened or just egoistic? Listen! This is the scale: If he can give the experience, then whatever comes from him is the truth. Here Kṛṣṇa shows clearly that *He Is Everything*. He demonstrates His Divinity to Arjuna. Kṛṣṇa walks His talk in this chapter.

In the Bhāgavatam, there is a beautiful verse that the gopī (cowherdess of Briṇdāvan), sings to Kṛṣṇa, who is everything to her clan:

tava kathāmṛtaṁ tapta jīvanaṁ
kavibhirīritam kalmaṣāpahaṁ
śravaṇamaṇgalam śrīmadātatam
bhuvi gṛhṇanti te bhūritā janāḥ

'O Kṛṣṇa, *tava kathāmṛtaṁ tapta jīvanaṁ*...Your words and the words uttered about You are *kathāmṛtaṁ*, words of immortality, words of nectar, words both *on* You and *by* You. Just by listening to these words, You create auspiciousness in us.

'These words are worshipped and expressed as the highest truth by the great *Ṛṣis.* We who have experienced You, feel the joy again and again by speaking about You. You rejuvenate our whole being. Just by listening to these words about You and by You, we are transported to a different plane.'

If you have fallen in love with Kṛṣṇa, this is the chapter to know Him and enjoy Him. Here in this chapter He does not give any teachings. All intellectual teachings are over. He gives the experience directly: '*I am Everything.*' He gives the experience of the ultimate Universal consciousness and the realization that He is present in everything. Arjuna experiences the Universal consciousness. This whole chapter is pure experience.

The first thing we need to understand is whether it is possible to have the experience of the Universal consciousness. Secondly, what is the basic qualification to experience it? Thirdly, what really happens inside our being during such an experience? These three things we shall understand from this chapter and explore the wonderful possibility of experiencing Kṛṣṇa as the Cosmic window.

LOVE KṚṢṆA TO EXPERIENCE KṚṢṆA

In the previous chapter, Kṛṣṇa gave the intellectual explanation that He is the Ultimate. More than an intellectual expression, I may say that this is an expression given to a person who is deeply in love. Kṛṣṇa can be God only when a person achieves the maturity of Arjuna. The truth should be declared only when a person is qualified and mature. Only when you reach the maturity of Arjuna can you experience the divinity of Kṛṣṇa. When you feel deeply connected to a person, he looks divine even though he may be quite ordinary in reality.

Śiva says in Tantra that when one drops one's fantasies, he becomes Śiva and his wife becomes Uma. He reaches the state of *Śivatva*, the state of Śiva, and she reaches the state of Devi. Truth can only be expressed when the listener is ready.

Kṛṣṇa rules by love. Though He was the king of the Yādava clan, He ruled not by authority and power, but by personal example of love and compassion. Those who lived with Kṛṣṇa identified with Him and loved Him beyond their own selves.

How does one attain Enlightenment living a normal life? In the *Śiva Sutra*, Śiva says there is nothing wrong with a husband and wife living a normal conjugal life, but they need to drop their fantasies about one another. When we live without fantasies, the other person looks like God. Only then the other person is real.

Please understand, everybody is God, including *you*. But each of us carries our own idea of God and tries to put everyone else into that frame. When they do not fit into the frame, we throw the person out instead of throwing the frame.

Just understand. When you are deeply connected with the other person as they are, when you can be complete and accept anybody as he or she is, you establish a divine relationship. However, to do so, you must first learn to do self-completion and accept your own self as *you* are. Listen, when you try to chisel each other constantly, you will only cause unhappiness and incompletions in your life. But when you do completion with yourself and completion with others, and accept everyone as they are, the whole world appears as God.

This can be achieved in two ways. Firstly, by your own *tapas*, your spiritual penance, you acquire maturity by undergoing this experience repeatedly. You need to keep dropping your fantasies about other people. Secondly, a Master can also give you this experience by infusing tremendous energy in you, by bringing you to his own frequency. But even to retain the energy of the Master, you need a certain level of maturity. This is what happens here in this chapter. The frequency of Kṛṣṇa's Cosmic form is too much for Arjuna to bear and he cries out to Kṛṣna to resume his normal form.

A small example: Once I was watching the disaster of Hurricane Katrina in the USA on television when an ashramite asked me why such calamities were taking place. I tried to explain to them that it is something like driving your car or SUV and incidentally it goes over a small anthill. As far as the ants are concerned this is a natural calamity for them. They may call it 'Hurricane SUV!' But as far as you are concerned you are not even aware of this disaster. You are just driving the SUV. Can you relate with the ants in this incident or say that driving over their anthill was pre-destined? Their logic and yours are completely different. Neither can they question you nor can you answer them.

We can only conclude, 'This is all God's will.' The kind of explanation any organized religion gives is also this! No logical answer or explanation can ever be given for these experiences. The frequency, logic, perception and concepts of the ants are completely different from ours, just as ours is again completely different from the Cosmic consciousness. The frequency of this consciousness is in a completely different dimension. From the Cosmic level, it is something like a mug of water spilling onto an anthill, washing away the ants.

It is not possible to comprehend what that level or frequency is. What is possible is for us to raise the frequency of our will or consciousness to be one with It, to learn to live with It and experience It. Neither God nor your wife can be understood; just learn to live with them!

If the person is charismatic, has a way with words, he will have created a new philosophy and cheated a group of people. This is probably why great philosophers convince others, but they themselves are not convinced. I know a great atheist who chanted God's name when he lay dying! The very act of trying to convince and convert others testified to the fact that he was not convinced himself.

Please be aware that conversion is an intellectual and psychological crime. And preachers who convert others without any deep, personal experience of the divine, always fall into the worst kind of depression. They punish themselves by their own acts.

One person from Oklahoma who was associated with us was a reverend of the clergy. He enjoyed our programs and eventually went on to become a teacher of our meditation programs. I had never asked him to convert himself to our religion. To begin with, I myself do not have any religion! There is no need because what I teach is pure *satya*, the truth.

It is like this: The truth of the inner light given by Kṛṣṇa belongs to humanity and not to any particular religion. It is not necessary to convert to any religion. It is enough if you understand the truth and live your life happily and intensely in the space of completion.

Please understand, each one of you is divine! You are all cast in the mold of the Divine. All you need is this awareness that you too are divine and just start powerfully living and radiating the Divine.

That is the difference between Kṛṣṇa, the Incarnation, and Hiraṇya, demon. Hiraṇya is just trying to play the game when he himself does not have the experience. Kṛṣṇa gives the experience directly. When He declares that He is God, it is not for Him to satisfy His ego but for us to experience the truth. He tells Arjuna that He is uttering these words for Arjuna's sake.

Let us now go into the verses and examine three questions:

Can Universal consciousness be experienced? What is the basic qualification for this experience? What happens when one experiences it? These three questions are explained beautifully by Śrī Kṛṣṇa in this chapter.

I Wish To See Your Divine Form

11.1 *Arjuna says: O Lord! By listening to Your wisdom*
on the supreme secret of Existence and Your glory,
I feel that my delusion has disappeared.

11.2 *O Lotus-eyed Kṛṣṇa! I have listened from You in detail*
about the creation and destruction of all living beings,
also Your inexhaustible greatness.

11.3 *O Parameśvara, Lord Supreme, though You are here before Me*
as You have declared Yourself, I wish to see the Divine Cosmic
Form of Yours, Puruṣottama, Supreme Being.

11.4 *O Prabhu, my Lord, if You think it is possible for me to see*
Your Cosmic Form, then please, O Yogeśvara, Lord of Yoga and
all mystic power, kindly show me that Imperishable Universal Self.

In the minds of many, Kṛṣṇa is considered an Incarnation. It is in this chapter that Kṛṣṇa reveals Himself as not just an Incarnation but as also the very source from which everything flows. He is the Source of all sources, the Cause of all causes, the source of all the worlds and Universes.

Arjuna has already listened from Kṛṣṇa about everything that he needs to do. Arjuna's questions have all disappeared; his doubts, his incompletions and delusions have dissolved. In the previous chapter, Kṛṣṇa explains to Arjuna who *He really is*.

It is not that Arjuna is not aware of the greatness of Kṛṣṇa and His Divinity. It is based on his deep faith in Kṛṣṇa that Arjuna chose to have the Master assist him unarmed as his charioteer, while Duryodhana chose Kṛṣṇa's vast Yādava army.

Despite the faith that Arjuna has in Kṛṣṇa, he has self-doubts too. Doubts and faith are two sides of the same coin. You cannot have one without the other. At the intellectual level, Arjuna had shed his doubts. At the emotional level he had shed his doubts. But at the being level, at the very core of his being, Arjuna had self-doubts. He was still troubled by what he was about to do.

Arjuna has no one else to ask but Kṛṣṇa. Intuitively Arjuna sees his own Self in Kṛṣṇa. *Nara*, the man, meets *Nārāyaṇa,* the Divine. Arjuna knows at the depths of his being that Kṛṣṇa and Kṛṣṇa alone can provide the answers to the self-doubts that have risen within him.

Can Universal Consciousness Be Experienced?

Step by step, Kṛṣṇa clears Arjuna's self-doubts. First, Kṛṣṇa addresses Arjuna's doubts of the intellect. Kṛṣṇa explains to him the misconceptions that Arjuna has from the literal reading of the scriptures and what he has understood to be right and wrong. 'All the people in front of you are already dead,' says the Lord, 'I eliminated them long ago; why are you then worried? Do what you need to do.'

Kṛṣṇa then clears any lingering emotional doubts that Arjuna may have by explaining to him what He, the master of the Universe, is all about. He tells Arjuna who *He really is*. After detailing all His glories, Kṛṣṇa says that there is no end to His divine manifestations, His *vibhūti*. Wherever there is something glorious, powerful and prosperous, Kṛṣṇa is in existence. Kṛṣṇa concludes, saying that there is no need for detailed knowledge, as He supports all of Existence within just a fragment of His divine Self.

And now, finally, the time has come for Arjuna to see Kṛṣṇa as *He truly is*. Arjuna is standing on the last step. He beseeches, 'My delusion has been dispelled and I am now aware of Your divinity. Please show me now who You really are.'

mad anugrahāya paramaṁ guhyam adhyātma saṁjñitam /
yat tvayokaṁ vacas tena moho 'yam vigato mam // 11.1

And yet, Arjuna still hesitates. He wants to know, but he is not sure if he can bear to experience the truth. He says one phrase clearly, 'If you think I can behold Your form,' which indicates that there is already some fear in him. He also has self-doubts. Yes, Kṛṣṇa said that He had already destroyed all of Arjuna's enemies. But physically they are in front of Arjuna. He believes what Kṛṣṇa says. But his senses tell him a different story.

It is not important what others think; what is important is what *we* think. We should be ready to take the responsibility and face whatever comes. Even simple truths or experiences cannot be given so easily, since the receiver must have the maturity to hold what he has received.

> In 2005, during the pilgrimage to the *cār dhām* (four sacred sites of Hindus) in the Himalayas, a devotee from the USA kept asking me for a darśan of Mahāvatār Bābā. Mahāvatār Bābā, the *Paramaguru* of Paramahamsa Yogānanda, lives eternally in these parts of the Himālayas. He blessed me with my name before my Self Realization, so He is, in fact, the *Paramaguru* of my lineage. I said to her that there was nothing I could do but if she had faith, He would appear. When she was riding a pony on the way from Gaurikund to Kedār, she saw Bābā passing by. When she told me about this, I found that she indeed had an experience. I told her that she would be experiencing the effects of that energy for quite some time. For six months her body was adjusting to that intense energy experience.

Here Arjuna says, 'If you think I can behold your Cosmic form, My Lord, show me Your unmasked, manifested Universal Self.' Please understand, before entering into the experience you must have the courage to take whatever comes.

There are people I know, who after meditating for about a year, start experiencing the state of boundarilessness. They get frightened and shaken and afraid of losing themselves. I tell them that the meditation itself was to give them the experience of boundarilessness. It is like taking all the trouble to invite a guest to your house and when he does arrive, you are surprised at his arrival! Invariably when people have the experience for the first time, they are shaken and try to escape.

In many instances, during the darkness meditations in Inner Awakening program, people come to the point of losing their body consciousness. They get scared and refuse to go along with the experience. After the meditation session is over, they tell me what happened. By then it is too late, they have missed the opportunity!

This is also the case with people who practice chanting intensely. When the Divine starts giving them the experience, they are shaken by fear and stop. When you are meditating on the Divine, a chant or God, do not try to escape when you get the vision or darśan. Please understand that the Divine will never disturb you, only your fear disturbs you. When you have the experience, have the courage to go with it. With the Divine, nothing is too much. Therefore, don't worry about overdoing anything in spirituality. There is nothing called too much in spiritual energy and spiritual experience. There can never be too much of *bhakti* or devotion, too much of the Divine, too much of bliss.

Here, Arjuna says, 'If you think I can behold your Cosmic form…' Arjuna wants the experience but puts the responsibility on Kṛṣṇa. He wants the sweet but not diabetes! Of course, the divine sweet can never make you a diabetic.

> I had occasion to visit Melkote, the place where Rāmānujacārya, the Indian saint had lived.
>
> The *prasād* (food offered to the Lord and distributed to people) was so tasty and intensely sweet. I wondered if the devotees would have become diabetic , but was surprised when I was told there was no diabetic in the entire village, although everyone consumed the prasād daily! Understand, food offered to God gets energized and becomes *amṛta* or nectar. What we chant while offering the prasād cleanses and energizes it.

When food is put before the deity in a temple where *mantras* are chanted constantly, the food absorbs the pure, spiritual energy. It starts radiating the energy of the divine positive qualities. One cannot fall sick by eating prasād.

With divine energy, the effect is always positive, never negative. You cannot die in the *amṛtasāgara*, the ocean of nectar. When it comes to the Divine, all you need to do is jump into It with your whole being. All you need to do is to relax into It for transformation.

Arjuna says:

manyase yadi tacchakhyaṁ   mayā draṣṭum iti prabho |
yogeśvara tato me tvaṁ   darśayātmānam avyayam || 11.4

'If You think I am able to behold, O My Lord, Yogeśvara, Master of all mystic power, please show me Your Cosmic form.'

Many of you are like Arjuna. In fact, all of you are like Arjuna. You do not wish to take any risks. The Master has to calculate all the risks for you. You want the Master to make the experience risk-free, safe and pleasant. Unfortunately, it does not work that way. Yes, the experience is bliss, it is liberating, but that blissful experience destroys your identity, kills the ego and recreates the Divine in you.

If you wish to be as you were, do not ask for the experience. The Master's job is to transform. The Master is a surgeon, the surgeon of egos. Once you come to Him, it is a point of no return. I tell people that once they enter the gates of the ashram, they have made a life-long, no-return commitment. Even if they go out, they cannot get me out!

There is no such thing as partial surrender to a Master. There is no such thing as, 'Please give me what I can take. Let me take a sip and see if I like it. If I do, I shall ask You for more. If not, I shall not take anymore.'

Of course, the Master knows your readiness far better than you do. That is why I work on you in stages. As long as you are not ready, what I give you is brain and eye candy, that's all. You can gaze in happiness and go away. The form is all that you can take. It is only when your seriousness of purpose is established that I can start working on you without fear that you will run away from the operating table. Till then you only behave under the delusion that you have surrendered. It is one more fantasy, that is all.

The brahmacāris who train at the ashram understand the power of the Master's words. They listen and listen completely, without applying logic and reason. Logic and reason come with ego. To be egoless, you need to be mindless and shed logic.

Arjuna is an evolved disciple. What he says only seems to reflect what an ordinary person would have said. In fact, what Arjuna implies here is far more. 'Please give me Your Cosmic vision,' Arjuna pleads, 'if it may please You. I am keen to have it, but the decision is Yours. Let what happens be decided by You,' he says to Kṛṣṇa. What he implies is this: 'I have listened all that You have said. My questions have disappeared and my delusions have evaporated. I truly understand Your greatness. May I see You in Your true form?

'I have no right to ask all this of You. It is not any penance I may have done that makes me deserve this. It is not that I have reached a level of intellectual understanding of You that makes me deserve this. It is not that I have reached the peak of devotion that makes me deserve Your vision. I have no right to demand. However, in all humility, as Your devotee, as one who surrenders to You, I ask of You to show me who You really are. Please show me Your entire splendor, Your valor, Your wisdom, Your truth and all that You really are!'

Let Me Give You The Divine Eye

11.5 *Bhagavān says:*
O My dear Pārtha, behold now My hundreds and thousands of forms, of infinite divine sorts, of infinite colors and shapes.

11.6 *O Bhārata, see here the different manifestations of the Āditya, the Vasus, the Rudras, the Aśvins, the Māruts and all other gods. Behold the many wonderful forms which noone has ever seen before.*

11.7 *O Arjuna, see at once now in this body of Mine, the whole Universe completely in this one place, all the moving and the unmoving, and see everything else you desire to see also.*

11.8 *But you cannot see Me with your own physical eyes.*
Let Me give you the Divine eye;
Behold My Divine power and opulence!

In this verse, Kṛṣṇa summarizes the entire chapter as He explains the whole darśan (Vision). It needs to be read and understood as one verse.

Kṛṣṇa says, 'O Pārtha, behold the hundreds and thousands of my Divine forms. These are infinite Divine forms, of diverse colors, shapes and sizes. O Bhārata, see the different manifestations of Āditya, Vasu, Rudra, Aśvini Kumār, Mārut and many wonderful beings whom no one has ever seen before.'

But before He gives *darśan* of the Universal form, He makes an important and beautiful statement, 'O Arjuna! You cannot see my form with ordinary eyes. To behold this form, you would need *divya netra*, the third eye or the divine eye.

na tu māṁ śakyase draṣṭum anenaiva sva-cakṣuṣā |
divyaṁ dadāmi te cakṣuḥ paśya me yogam aiśvaram || 11.8

'*divyaṁ dadāmi te cakṣuḥ...*' Let me give you the divine eye to enable you to see and experience Me.' From this verse He starts giving the *Viśvarūpa darśan*—Vision of His Cosmic Form.

Kṛṣṇa says, 'O Arjuna, may you start seeing whatever exists, the *sthāvara* and the *jaṅgama* (immovable and movable), the Universe that no ordinary man can see. Even the great sages have not seen this sight and are not aware of it.'

Arjuna was an intimate friend of Kṛṣṇa and their attachment to each other as friends was deep. They had known each other from their early years and even though Kṛṣṇa was close to all the Pāṇḍava brothers and also the Kaurava, His bond with Arjuna was special. Over and above their friendship, Arjuna was a very intelligent and learned man in his own right.

But neither the deep friendship nor his intelligence or wisdom could give Arjuna any idea of the real nature, the true nature of Kṛṣṇa, and about His many facets. There are so many forms and manifestations of the different energies that humans have not even heard of. Kṛṣṇa, in His infinite compassion and love for Arjuna, shows him all these wonderful forms.

Here is a wonderful phenomenon. Now Kṛṣṇa gives Arjuna the power to see what is happening in the whole Universe, not only in the present, but in the past and the future also!

DARŚAN, SEEING THE DIVINE FORM IS POSSIBLE

Here again are the three questions that are the essence of the whole chapter.

> ***Can the Divine form be seen?***
>
> ***What is the qualification to see the Divine form?***
>
> ***What really happens when you see the Divine form?***

I tell you categorically—it is possible to see the divine form. There are many enlightened Masters who have experienced this consciousness.

Let me give you an instance from *my* life.

> After nine long years of penance, I was completely frustrated at one point. I wondered if I was wasting my whole life reading books, following what the earlier Masters said and applying them in my life. I wondered, was there really something called enlightenment or was it a waste of my whole life?
>
> At one point I began to fear that I had wasted the very essence of my life, my youth, by pouring all of it into *tapas* or penance. Was it really worth the sacrifice?
>
> All of a sudden at one point in time, I felt myself going into deep depression. Actually, I later realized that this was not depression. It was a desperate situation, a deep personal quest, and an urge to do or die. Now I know that one needs to reach this stage before one can realize the truth.
>
> Whatever had to be done as spiritual penance, I had done and had not left even an inch untried. For example, at one point in time, I created a wall of fire six feet in diameter, sat inside it and chanted continuously so that I would not fall asleep. In this way, I had tried hundreds of techniques to the best of my ability. Since nothing was still happening to me, I concluded that there was either no such thing as enlightenment or it was something I could not achieve.
>
> I strongly began to think that Enlightenment was simply something that some people were cheating humanity with, for their own ego-fulfillment. I began to doubt and lose faith in the whole system. The photo of Rāmakṛṣṇa, who had all along been my inspiration, the photo I used to worship everyday, I threw away in disgust,

depression and anger and with such force that the glass frame broke.

At that time I was staying in Omkareshwar, in a forest in Madhya Pradesh, on the banks of the holy river Narmada. I had my rosary, with which I used to say my prayers and do my penance for hours together. It was my constant companion and was something to which I had given utmost respect, almost like my life-line.

In my anger and depression, I threw the *rudrākṣa* (sacred energy beads) into the river Narmada and cast the *mantra* out of my mind.

I decided, 'No more meditation, no more spirituality. Enough!' I had had enough of the game being played by the so-called Enlightened Masters. I simply threw everything away, dropped everything.

I then walked into the river Narmada with my eyes closed. The river was at least sixty feet deep at that point. I just kept walking with my eyes closed. Fear gripped me but I continued. When I opened my eyes, I was on the opposite bank of the river! Till date I have no idea what happened. I have no idea whether there were rocks all along the path I walked on the river, or whether I floated or whether the river parted. But I did not have the resolve to walk back through the river again, that much I know! To return to the point I started from, I had to walk to the nearest bridge, many miles away!

The seventh day after this incident, I joined the Masters in their game! The experience of Enlightenment and Cosmic consciousness simply happened to me. It never left me thereafter.

So to answer this question, 'Can this be experienced?', the definitive answer is *Yes*. As a person who was just like you—I tell you out of courtesy the simple truth, *'Yes, honestly, it can be experienced.'*

This is the solid truth; a promise that this can be experienced. Please understand, I have no vested interest in convincing you of this ideology. All I have is simple courtesy, like informing a friend of the traffic situation in a particular place and guiding him through a different route.

It is definitely possible to experience this truth, this Cosmic form, in our lives. Never think, 'This is not for me.' It is for everybody! However, unless you are sure of the possibility of having this beautiful, intense experience, listening to all this is a waste of time. If you think this is one more story, do not waste your time here.

The first thing that you need to know is that it is possible. Only then what Kṛṣṇa says will work on our being. I will be really happy if you go out after experiencing this Cosmic form. At least go out with a glimpse of it. If these words of Kṛṣṇa are to work on you, you must first be convinced of the possibility of it happening to you and know that these are not just words. Let me tell you openly and directly, from my experience, *'It is possible.'*

These words of Kṛṣṇa are not mere words; they are not mere scriptural words. These words are techniques that go deep inside you and work on you with amazing results. All that you need is complete trust in the Master that what He says *will* happen. I promise you it will.

Who Can See The Divine Form?

Next, what is the qualification?

Basically, by giving this experience to Arjuna, Kṛṣṇa proves that there is no need for any qualification because Arjuna himself has no qualification. Arjuna neither took the responsibility nor understood fully the teachings of Kṛṣṇa. He was simply fortunate to be in the presence of Kṛṣṇa, that's all. Likewise, you too are fortunate to be here and not caught in some traffic jam! There were thousands of possibilities for you to be elsewhere; so many options were available to you. But out of all of them, you chose to be here. This is the only qualification required.

In fact, you are the Arjuna who missed Kṛṣṇa in an earlier form. You are here now, listening or reading, not by any mere accident or Divine coincidence. You are here now for a reason. That is qualification enough. Make sure that you do not miss Kṛṣṇa again this time!

By coming here every day, your unconscious mind has already accepted whatever is being said here. If this had not happened, you would not return here the following day. You would not be listening to or reading this chapter.

A person told me that when he woke up every day for these few days, he found himself waiting for 5:30 in the evening so that he could attend the Gītā discourse! If you a e waiting, it means that all these words have already entered your being. So have the trust that you are ready for this experience.

One of the problems is that even if you are qualified, you do not have the trust or belief that you are qualified! This is because society and religious preachers have blamed you continuously for many things and created a kind of guilt and self-doubt in you.

Because of this you have lost faith and confidence in yourself. Now, after having listened for all these days, your still being here is proof that your unconscious mind has accepted and enriched by these ideas. Your conscious mind may struggle with the question of why you are here, but the fact that you are here shows that unconsciously you have allowed enriching yourself and begun enjoying these ideas. Understand, allowing the Master to enrich you is the best way of enriching yourself.

You are fortunate to fall in tune with the great thought of Śrī Kṛṣṇa. After understanding the verse, we will enter into a meditation to have at least a glimpse of what the Cosmic Kṛṣṇa gave Arjuna. Arjuna had no qualification to receive what he got from Kṛṣṇa. When He could give it to Arjuna, why not to us?

First, we acknowledge the possibility of having the experience. We have all understood that it is possible to have it. Next, the qualification: we have all understood that simply by being here we are qualified for the experience.

Somebody once asked Bhagavān Rāmaṇa Maharṣi, Enlightened Master from India, what was the qualification for enlightenment. Bhagavān replied that merely being alive, simply existing, was the only qualification required!

At the most, the only qualification can be said to be openness. If you did not have it, you would not come here every day. We never allow the belief that we have the qualification to enter into our being. I tell you, drop everything! You are qualified by your very presence here!

THE DIVINE EYE, DIVYA CAKṢU

Next, what happens when you have the experience?

Kṛṣṇa's words:

na tu māṁ śakyase draṣṭum anenaiva sva-cakṣuṣā /
divyaṁ dadāmi te cakṣuḥ paśya me yogam aiśvaram // 11.8

'Arjuna, you cannot see Me with these ordinary eyes. You need the divine eye, the third eye, *divyacakṣu*. To see My Cosmic form, I give you the divine eye.'

What is this divine eye?

Let me tell you *my* experience that happened when I was twelve years old.

> During that age, I used to do a particular meditation, or rather I used to play with a technique given to me by a master. When I was about ten years old the great Master Annāmalai Swamigal, disciple of Rāmaṇa Maharṣi, first taught me the technique of exploring to see where thoughts originated.
>
> Once when I visited him with my parents, he was addressing a group of seekers and was saying, 'We are not the body, we are *ātman*, the spirit. No pain or suffering touches us.'

I wondered how this could be, for if my mother beat me, I could feel the pain! (In India, if kids were mischievous, they would be roundly beaten, you could not call 911!) To experiment, I went home and cut my thigh with a knife to see if I had pain or not. I bled profusely.

Naturally, it not only hurt me, but I had to be taken to the hospital for the wound to be stitched, with more scolding from my mother! I had both pain and suffering. I wondered why this Swami had taught us such a thing as 'no suffering or pain'!

Experimenting on others was easy. Arjuna was intelligent. After understanding everything, he started killing others; he never experimented on himself!

I approached the Swami and related what had happened to me.

First he asked me, 'Did I ask you to go and cut yourself?'

He then made a profound statement that transformed my life.

He said, 'You may have pain and suffering now, but do not worry. Your attitude of analyzing and searching for the truth, your courage to experiment with truth, will liberate you from all pains, so go ahead!'

He then advised me to start searching for the source of my thoughts. Of course, at that age I was only irritated by his comments and my attention was on the fruits and sweets that devotees had brought him. I was hoping he would give me some in consolation! Honestly, I neither understood nor was convinced of what he said.

However, after a few days I began to playfully and casually try out the technique of trying to see the origin of my thoughts. I did not do this with any expectation or idea. All I knew was what the Swami had told me—that I would go beyond pain or suffering if I did this technique. I had no concept of God, Brahman, *ātman* or *jñāna*.

One evening, at the foothills of the sacred Arunachala hill, I was sitting on a rock known locally as *pavala kundru*, the Coral Rock, trying out the same technique with eyes closed. I had fallen into deep meditation.

After some time, suddenly something opened, something seemed to happen inside my being, a feeling of being pulled or sucked inside.

The next moment it was as if a door had opened inside me, and I had complete 360-degree vision, both laterally and vertically. I could see on all four sides – the temple that was behind me, the hill that was in front of me, and the city that was on my left and right. I could see vertically too—the sky, the rock on which I was sitting, again the temple behind me.

For normal people who have only a maximum of 120-degree vision, I know this is very difficult to comprehend. All I can do is promise solemnly that it *did* happen! No other intellectual explanation is possible. Not only was I able to see all around, I was also able to feel that whatever I was seeing was Me. Whether they were plants or rocks or the city or the hill, whatever I could see, I felt they were all just Me. The experience was so intense and ecstatic that it was more than three or four hours before I opened My eyes. I felt feverish with bliss and this mood continued for three days.

But after this I was overtaken by a fear that there was something wrong with me. I thought a ghost had possessed me and I decided never to go to that rock again. I even began to avoid that route, which I normally took.

I related my experience to an elderly Sannyāsi, Mata

> Vibhudānanda Devi (Kuppammal), who was my mentor. She held my hand and seeing the energy, exclaimed, '*You are not possessed by any ghost. You are possessed by God!*' She encouraged me to continue with meditation but I never dared to do so for the next six months and was even afraid to close my eyes!

I also related my experience to a close friend of mine. I told him about my 360-degree vision and my not knowing what was happening to me, etc. He did not believe me until I proved it to him by telling him about an ant climbing up the tree behind me, and correctly telling which side of the coin that he hid in his hand was exposed. He ran away from me in terror!

He came to the the ashram and said to one of the ashramites, 'I was the first person to receive *energy darśan* from him, but I missed it!'

But despite the fear I experienced, the whole body was bubbling with joy and ecstasy.

So welcome was the feeling, that I had a small temptation to go to the rock again. I never really understood what had happened. A year later another enlightened person gave me the explanation; the seeking, however, started after this experience. Nine years of penance followed. All this penance was in order to have this experience again. When it did come the next time, both body and mind were ready and the experience stayed within my being.

The vision of 360 degrees is what Kṛṣṇa means by *divyacakṣu*, *trinetra*, divine eye or third eye, also called *ājñā cakra*. When this eye opens you will see 360 degrees not only in the horizontal but in the vertical dimension too. You will see the whole Existence as You and experience it as You. This experience is what Kṛṣṇa calls Cosmic consciousness.

I felt that everything I saw around me was living, just as how we feel our living bodies, expanding the body consciousness to the Universal consciousness. **When you feel the whole Universe as you would your own body, it can be called a cosmic experience.** Unfortunately, we do not feel alive even within our own bodies!

Just as I was frightened when I had my first experience, Arjuna too was frightened when he started seeing Kṛṣṇa's cosmic form. In such instances, a living Master is required for help and guidance.

I am often asked this question, 'Who was your Master?,' to which I reply, 'Arunachala.' Arunachala, the sacred hill of Tiruvannamalai, my birthplace, is a living Master. For a premature baby to survive, it must be put into the incubator. Similarly, Arunachala is the incubator for the Enlightened person-to-be. The energy of Arunachala takes care just by your being near it.

'Let me give you the third eye, to enable you to experience the Universal consciousness.'

You need to understand that after this verse, neither Kṛṣṇa nor Arjuna speaks. Suddenly, it is Sañjaya who is speaking. After the first chapter in *Bhagavad Gītā* until now, there is no word from Sañjaya. But here it is he who is speaking. This is a symbolic representation.

Arjuna is unable to speak because he is in the ecstatic experience. Kṛṣṇa does not speak because his voice is beyond audibility. His voice is in the Cosmic frequency, which is not audible to us. So Sañjaya interprets.

A Thousand Blazing Suns

11.9 *Sañjaya said:*
O King, having spoken thus, the great Lord of Yoga,
Mahā Yogeśvara Hari (Kṛṣṇa), showed to Arjuna
His supreme Cosmic form.

11.10 *Infinite mouths and eyes, with infinite wonderful sights, infinite divine ornaments, with numerous divine weapons uplifted.*

11.11 *Arjuna saw this Universal form wearing Divine garlands and clothing, anointed all over with celestial fragrances. All wonderful, brilliantly resplendent, endless, with all-pervading faces on all sides.*

11.12 *If the splendor of a thousand suns were to blaze all together in the sky, it would be like the splendor effulgence of that Great Supreme Lord.*

11.13 *There, in the body or Universal Form of the God of gods, the Pāṇḍava then saw the whole Universe resting in One place, while all its infinite expansions divided into many, many thousands.*

11.14 *Then, Dhanañjaya, filled with wonder and astonishment, his hair standing on end, then bowed his head to the Supreme Lord and began to pray with joined palms.*

These verses show the unlimited, never-ending, wonderful, all-pervading nature of the Lord.

Rāmakṛṣṇa says that when he experienced the form, the Cosmic consciousness, he could not pluck a single flower from a plant because he felt that all the plants were garlands offered to God.

Anyone who has had this experience is reborn. At one level this experience is one of boundarilessness. The body expands to fill everything. The entire Universe is part of the body. There is no separation of the individual and the whole. The whole is part and the part is whole. At another level the whole Universe exists within you. You are everything that you see around you. The grass outside the hut, the dog in the distance, the tree beyond, every single entity, animate and inanimate, resonates within you, as a part of you.

In that mood, plucking a flower hurts. A wild animal responds peacefully to your presence. There is no violence in Cosmic consciousness. There is only completion and inclusion.

This is what Arjuna saw in the Universal form, an unlimited number of mouths, eyes and wonderful visions. The form was decorated with many celestial ornaments and bore many divine upraised weapons. He wore celestial garlands and garments. Many divine scents were smeared all over His body. All was wondrous, brilliant, unlimited, all-expanding.

Here he sees an unlimited number of mouths and eyes in Kṛṣṇa. Now Arjuna sees 360 degrees in both horizontal and vertical dimensions. He sees the whole universe, all the people on the battlefield; all of them inside Kṛṣṇa, as the Universal consciousness. He sees the Whole as his own being.

There is no boundary to Kṛṣṇa's universal form. The word Viṣṇu, which is his real form, means one who expands infinitely. The splendor that Sañjaya talks about is beyond anything the mind can comprehend, because it is the source of all splendor.

Notice, it is Sañjaya speaking these words, not Arjuna. Sañjaya is far from the battlefield and has been given the power to see what happens on the battlefield so that he can describe the events to his king Dhṛitarāṣtra. Though Kṛṣṇa says that this form is being shown only to Arjuna, by default Sañjaya has the great fortune to witness and participate in this vision.

Arjuna is awestruck and is in silence. He is yet to speak. What he has witnessed is beyond anything that he could have imagined or asked for. But the silence is a very active silence. It is a silence in which he experiences the truth of Kṛṣṇa. It is a silence in which he is actively participating in the process and is being immersed. Those who experience do not talk. Those who talk have not experienced.

Sañjaya then summarizes Arjuna's reaction to the divine form of Kṛṣṇa in the last few verses. Arjuna is still silent and it is Sañjaya who describes what happens.

What Arjuna saw was beyond his understanding. Wherever he looked was Kṛṣṇa; Kṛṣṇa in many forms, many shapes, many non-forms and non-shapes. There are no words to describe what Arjuna saw. How does one describe what is beyond the mind, beyond logic, beyond words, beyond all comprehension?

In the body of the supreme Lord, Arjuna saw the whole Universe divided in different ways and at the same time united in one form. The Universe is divided into many parts such as the sun, moon, earth, planets and other bodies in space. Here he sees all of them as one form. You need to understand this description, which is so beautiful. Later we shall enter into a meditation and pray to the *Parabrahma* Kṛṣṇa to give us all a glimpse of what Arjuna received.

Arjuna is able to see the whole and at the same time all the parts. Even the word hologram that we now so commonly use to describe the totality of something preserved in a fragment does no justice to Arjuna's vision. In a hologram, one needs to make the effort to see the whole in the fragment. In this divine vision granted to Arjuna, the whole existed with the part, with no separation, no discontinuity. The whole was part and the part was whole.

Of all the people on the battlefield of Kurukṣetra, only Arjuna had this great fortune to behold the Cosmic Vision of Kṛṣṇa. Only he was granted the boon of divine vision to see the entire Universe within Kṛṣṇa. The vision that Arjuna beheld enveloped him completely. He was, in fact, part of that Vision. In addition, he was the experience of that vision as well.

Arjuna and Kṛṣṇa grew up together from childhood. Kṛṣṇa's sister Subhadra was Arjuna's wife. They had a deep relationship as friends. In this one moment, that relationship was redefined.

In most cases, the relationships are not absolute in time and space. They become mixed. In this particular instant, when Arjuna beheld the Cosmic form of Kṛṣṇa, all thoughts of friendship disappeared. He became the typical *dāsa*, servant.

Hands trembling, hair on end, tears in his eyes, unable to comprehend what he was witnessing, Arjuna bowed down deep in front of his erstwhile friend and started speaking in deep ecstasy.

Arjuna was not afraid of Kṛṣṇa. What he now felt towards Kṛṣṇa did not arise from his mind. It was involuntary. It was intuitive. You cannot make your hair stand on end even if you try the whole night and day. Ecstasy cannot be willed. Arjuna is in adoration. He is in awe. He realizes that he is in the presence of an energy that has no equal. Nothing he has ever experienced before comes close to this. His being opens while his mind rests.

In fact, Arjuna at this moment is beyond the five defined *bhāvas*. He is in the state of *mahā bhāva*—the state beyond the five *bhāvas*.

Worlds Tremble With Fear

11.15 *Arjuna says:*
O dear God, I see all the gods assembled in Your body and various other living beings too. I see Brahma, the Lord of creation, seated on the lotus, as well as Īśam (Śiva), and all the sages and celestial serpents.

11.16 *I see Your infinite form on every side, with many arms, stomachs, mouths and eyes; Neither the end, nor the middle nor the beginning do I see, O Viśveśvara, O Lord of the Universe, O Viśvarūpa, Cosmic Form.*

11.17 *I see You with crown, club and discus; a mass of radiance shining everywhere, difficult to look at, blazing all round like the burning fire and Sun in infinite brilliance.*

11.18 *You are the imperishable; the Supreme Being worthy to be known.*
You are the great treasure house of this Universe.
You are the imperishable Protector of the eternal order.
I believe You are the eternal being.

11.19 *I see You without a beginning, middle or end, infinite in power and with many arms, the sun and the moon being Your eyes, the blazing fire your mouth, the whole Universe scorched by Your radiance.*

11.20 *This space between earth and the heavens and everything is filled by You alone. O Great being, having seen Your wonderful and terrible form, the three worlds tremble with fear.*

11.21 *Many celestials enter into You; some praise You in fear with folded hands; Many great masters and sages hail and adore You.*

11.22 *The Rudra, Āditya, Vasu, Sadhya, Viśvadeva, Ashvin, Marut, Uśmapa and a host of Gandharva, Yakṣa, Asura and Siddha are all looking at You in amazement.*

11.23 *Having seen Your immeasurable form with many mouths and eyes, with many arms, thighs and feet, with many stomachs and frightening tusks, O Mahābāho, Mighty-armed, the worlds are terrified and so am I.*

11.24 *Seeing You, Your form touching the sky, flaming in many colors, mouths wide open, large fiery eyes, O Viṣṇu,*
I find neither courage nor peace; I am frightened.

As Arjuna is in the same consciousness as the Lord, this verse should actually start with '*Bhagavān uvāca*' meaning '*the Lord says!*' These statements are said to come from Him for us to record.

These are such beautiful ways that he describes the form. You may wonder why he does so. Please understand, he does so to inspire us to work to achieve this form and this experience, to move in this path. Arjuna is showing us the way.

He says, 'O Lord! I can see all the gods and deities in Your body. I can see the special union of living entities. I can see Brahma seated on the lotus flower. I can see all the sages and divine serpents. O Viśveśvara, Lord of the Universe, I see many arms, stomachs, faces, eyes and your limitless form. O Viśvarūpa, Universal form, I cannot see your beginning, middle or end.'

aneka-bahūdara vaktra netraṁ
paśyāmi tvāṁ sarvato 'nanta-rūpaṁ |
nāntaṁ na madhyam na punas tavādiṁ
paśyāṃi visveśvara viśvarūpa || 11.16

As a matter of fact, when you begin to see 360 degrees in both horizontal and vertical dimensions, there really is no beginning, middle or end to see. It is a continuum. It is like seeing one of these special movies on a circular screen. It is an infinite circle. The Divine is an infinite circle, with no beginning, no end and therefore no middle. Without a beginning and an end, to talk about the middle makes no sense.

The form is difficult to see in its sheer glowing radiance, spreading on all sides like blazing fire or the immeasurable brightness of the sun. Yet Arjuna sees this glowing form everywhere adorned with various crowns and discs. He sees Kṛṣṇa wearing the diadem, holding the mace and discus.

Arjuna says, 'Your magnificence is shining everywhere, from all sides, difficult to see. You are blazing from all sides with the luster of the sun, limitless.'

Part of what Arjuna sees here is the traditional representation of Lord Viṣṇu. Viṣṇu is always depicted with His weapons of mace and discus, the *gada* and *cakra,* and wearing the jewel-studded crown. Viṣṇu is also depicted resting on the ocean of milk upon the giant serpent Adiseśa, with Brahma rising from Viṣṇu's navel upon a lotus flower.

Some of what he sees is formless energy. He perceives radiance more powerful than a thousand suns, blazing and dazzling, impossible to look at even with his newly endowed divine eye. What Arjuna sees is beyond any sensory perception, something that could be experienced in that moment in time, impossible to express.

Suddenly the scene changes in these verses. Arjuna is terrified. What he is seeing now is quite different from what he expected when he asked to see Kṛṣṇa's divine form.

Arjuna is now incoherent. What he keeps saying is neither logical nor well thought out. What he sees he reproduces to the best of his mental abilities. Arjuna is convinced, seeing the Universal form of Kṛṣṇa, that what he sees is the supreme being, the *puruṣa*, the imperishable, the very origin of all, the Eternal.

He says, 'You are without origin, middle or end with unlimited power. You spread throughout the heavens and through all other directions. O supreme soul, *Paramātman*, after having seen your wonderful form, all the worlds and the whole universe is trembling with fear. All the celestial beings are shuddering before this form and entering into this formless form, some of them afraid, offering prayers with folded hands, along with hosts of realized sages praising this form in silent acceptance and wonderment.'

There is no other record so clear about the Cosmic frequency of the Universal form as in the Gītā. What Arjuna perceives is what is always present, but which he normally has no capability to see. Now he sees Kṛṣṇa in all His manifestations, from the highest to the lowest frequency levels of energy with nothing filtered.

But suddenly the form seems to change from the magnificent, comforting and expanded form, to one that is now disturbing. It is still not clear to Arjuna what is happening, but he can anticipate that something he is about to see is not going to be as pleasant as what he had seen so far.

What Arjuna sees disturbs him.

'O All pervading Viṣṇu! I see You with your many radiating colors, burning fire in your gaping mouth, heating up the entire Universe with radiance, touching the sky, and Your form unnerves me. My heart trembles in fear and I have no courage or peace to behold You.'

Until now Arjuna was saying there was no beginning, middle or end. Now he says the form is touching the sky; an indication that he is settling, coming down from the experience. 'Seeing your gaping mouth, your great glowing eyes, overcome by fear, I can no longer maintain my mental steadiness or equilibrium.'

Please understand, as long as you want to maintain the equilibrium of your mind, you will be in this mad world. There is no such thing as equilibrium. What we think of as equilibrium is not so.

Arjuna says he wants equilibrium, meaning that he wants his mind to be under his intellectual control. He wants to know the cause and effect and feel that they are in his control. As long as these are under your control, you feel as if you are a leader; your ego is strong. But the moment these are taken away from you, you feel at a loss and no more a leader. You are just a drop in the ocean. He is afraid of that and is not able to stay in that same state.

The wave in the ocean is part of the ocean. As long as it feels itself to be part of the ocean, there is no separation. However, when the wave experiences its own identity, creates its own identity, it no longer feels itself a part of the ocean. It feels itself to be a separate entity. When it is time to merge back into that ocean, it is afraid. When it looks back at the ocean with a feeling of separation, it feels afraid.

When Arjuna had his first glimpse of the Cosmic Vision of Kṛṣṇa, he identified with the Vision. There was no separation. Now, suddenly there is separation. Along with separation there is fear!

Tell Me Who You Are

11.25 *Having seen your fearsome mouths with blazing tusks*
like the fire of the end of the Universe,
I know not the four directions nor do I find peace.
O Lord of the Deva, O Refuge of the Universe, be gracious.

11.26 *All the sons of Dhṛitarāṣṭra with many kings of the earth,*
Bhīṣma, Droṇa, the son of the charioteer, Karṇa,
with our warrior chieftains

11.27 *Into Your mouths with terrible tusks, fearful to behold, they enter.*
Some are seen caught in the gaps between the tusks and their heads crushed.

11.28 *Even as many torrents of rivers flow towards the ocean, so too these warriors in the world of men enter Your flaming mouths.*

11.29 *Just as moths hurriedly rush into the fire for their own destruction, so too these creatures rush hastily into Your mouths of destruction.*

11.30 *Swallowing all worlds on every side with Your flaming mouths, You lick in enjoyment. O Viṣṇu, Your fierce rays are burning, filling the whole world with radiance.*

11.31 *Tell me who You are, so fierce in form; salutations to You,*
O Supreme; have mercy. Indeed I know not Your purpose,
but I desire to know You, the Original being.

In these verses Arjuna expresses his discomfort.

Arjuna says earlier:

'I see O Lord! All the manifestations of Śiva, Āditya, Vāsu and

Viśvadeva, Aśvin, Mārut, Gandharva, the forefathers, Yakṣa, Asura and all the celestial beings and demi-gods, all rolled in You in wonder, all part of Your Cosmic consciousness. Whatever You are is divine energy. O Mighty Armed One, all the planets with all the demi-gods are disturbed, shaken by Your form with many faces, eyes, arms, legs, thighs and bellies and Your many terrible teeth. As they are disturbed, so am I.'

Now he slowly comes down. From this verse we should say, '*Arjuna uvāca!*' meaning Arjuna says... It is no longer the divine state that Arjuna talks from. The moment he started feeling fear, he descended to his normal state. You should understand that it is only your fear that separates you from Cosmic consciousness.

When Arjuna says, 'So am I, *pravyathitās tathāham* (11.23)', that he is frightened, he becomes Arjuna, the man.

FEAR, THE DESTROYER OF ECSTASY

There are two things that make you a human—the instinct to possess and the instinct to survive. The instinct to survive arises out of fear, from the *svādiṣṭhāna cakra* (fear energy center in your body), and the instinct to possess comes out of greed, from the *mūlādhāra cakra* (greed energy center in your body). This sums it up. Here the instinct to survive has appeared and he has become Arjuna, the man. We do not understand that when we drop the instinct to survive, we become Kṛṣṇa; we exist forever. We become Bhagavān, the Universal consciousness. But most often, we hold onto the instinct to survive. Now Arjuna slowly comes down and becomes Arjuna, the man.

Arjuna exclaims, 'I see all the sons of Dhṛitarāṣṭra, along with their allied kings, Bhīṣma, Droṇa, Karṇa and other chief soldiers rushing into Your fearful mouths. I see some trapped with their heads smashed between Your teeth, ground into nothing.'

He describes the whole scene. He sees the heavy losses on both sides; his own side, his warriors and generals, but even heavier losses on the other side, including Bhīṣma who is invincible, Droṇa and Karṇa who are unconquerable. By inference he sees his own victory in the end.

In the beginning Arjuna sees what he wished to see. He sees what he believes to be the Cosmic form of the great Viṣṇu in His traditional attire and weapons, surrounded by Gods and sages. The form changed suddenly into a terrifying one of death, all-consuming and terror-inspiring, to which the entire Universe bowed down in fear.

From this macro perspective, Arjuna comes down to see the same destruction being played out at the level of the battlefield at Kurukṣetra. His enemies, the great warriors arrayed against him in battle, fly into the gaping mouth of destruction like moths into fire. Arjuna sees with convincing reality, the destruction of all the great warriors who would have been expected to give him trouble.

However, this scene does not fill him with peace and comfort. Arjuna is terrified at this vision of destruction. The destruction of those whom he perceives as his mortal enemies leaves him with no comfort.

The truth is that Arjuna is not in control. He has no clue about what is happening to him and around him. He is in the presence of a primal force before which all that is obvious is his own insignificance. Victory and defeat seem to make no difference. The vision of destruction implies that he too is mortal. Arjuna is terrified.

'Who are You?', asks Arjuna plaintively. 'What are You here for? What are You doing? You are so fierce. You are not the form I asked for. There seems to be some mistake!'

'I see men disappearing into You as rivers rush into the mighty oceans. Like moths rushing into fire, I see creatures speed into destruction within You.'

'You are not the compassionate Lord whose glories I heard from You. You are not who I thought You were. I needed You to comfort me. Instead, You terrify me.'

'Have mercy upon me.'

ākhyāhi me ko bhāvan ugra-rūpo
namo 'stu te deva-vara prasādi |

vijñātum icchāmi bhavantam ādyaṁ
na hi prajānāmi tava pravṛttim // 11.31

Death is the ultimate fear. Even the great warrior Arjuna trembles when faced with death. It is not that Arjuna is not aware of the inevitability of death or the nature of death. For a long time now Kṛṣṇa has been educating Arjuna on the perishability of the body-mind and the imperishability of the spirit. Arjuna has fully understood. Yet, Arjuna is petrified. What is Arjuna so afraid of?

One thing, Arjuna does not expect the Cosmic form of Kṛṣṇa to be anything but loving and compassionate. Kṛṣṇa can be the friend, the master, the beloved, the child, the mother and all combined. In every one of these moods, in each *bhāva,* Kṛṣṇa is still lovable, still reachable. However, in the form that Kṛṣṇa has presented now, the all-devouring monster as it were, Arjuna is unable to comprehend any aspect of Kṛṣṇa that he has known.

For the first time, Arjuna realizes that the Master cannot be predicted! He now knows that the Master cannot be put in a frame. The primal energy that the Master is has to be experienced in whatever manner it is presented, without expectations and fears.

Nature and Existence are neither cruel nor kind. The very term 'compassion' has a different meaning in the Cosmic dictionary. It is not the sympathy offered by each of us to another with or without any real feeling. It is not kindness. It is not the desire to be doing 'good,' whatever that looks like to us. True compassion is the result of experiencing that we are *one* with all of Existence. There is no 'other'.

It is so easy to fall in love with a handsome Master. Kṛṣṇa is the most beautiful of all the gods. He is so easy to fall in love with! To fall in love with a terrifying Kāli or an impassive Śiva is far more difficult. When you do, you expect the form to be different too. You need to be a Rāmakṛṣṇa to accept and love Mother Kāli who dances on dead bodies. You need to be a Śaṅkara to fall in tune with Śiva who is forever in silent contemplation.

But anyone can love Kṛṣṇa, and everyone does. No one expects Kṛṣṇa to be terrifying. So when Kṛṣṇa presents another form to Arjuna, the ground literally slips from under Arjuna's feet. *He has no support. He does not know where to turn for help.*

So Arjuna pleads, 'Please have mercy upon me. Tell me who You are—*vijñātum icchāmi bhavantam ādyaṁ*. Tell me why You are here. I would like to know. I bow down to You—*namo 'stu te deva-vara prasādi.*'

Get Up And Gain Glory, Be Not Afraid

11.32 *Śrī Bhagavān says:*
I am the mighty world-destroying time.
I am now destroying the worlds.
Even without you, none of the warriors
standing in the hostile armies shall live.

11.33 *Get up and gain glory. Conquer the enemies*
and enjoy the prosperous kingdom.
I have slain all these warriors;
you are a mere instrument, O Savyasācī (Arjuna).

11.34 *Droṇa, Bhīṣma, Jayādṛta, Karṇa, and other brave warriors*
have already been slain by Me; destroy them.
Do not be afraid; fight and you shall conquer
your enemies in battle.

Kṛṣṇa explains in these verses what He really is.

'I am time, *kālo asmi*' says Kṛṣṇa. 'I devour and destroy the world, *loka-kṣaya-kṛt*.'

kālo 'smi loka-kṣaya-kṛt pravṛddho
lokān samāhartum iha pravṛttaḥ |
ṛte 'pi tvāṁ na bhaviṣyanti sarve
ye' vasthitaḥ pratyanīkeṣu yodhāḥ || 11.32

This is one of the most potent truths uttered by Kṛṣṇa in Gītā. He has earlier talked to Arjuna about *Ātman*, about rebirth, about the nature of *karma*, about doing work without getting attached to the result of work and about His glories.

For the first time, He takes off His mask and says matter-of-factly, 'I am the Destroyer.' He pulls no punches in responding to Arjuna's query, 'Who are you, and what is your purpose?'

'I am *kāla,* time,' says the Lord, 'and I destroy.'

Time never stands still. It moves on. Nothing can stop the flow of time. Nothing can bring back time. Nothing can move time forward. Time destroys.

The future constantly moves into the present, and then into the past. At the frequency of our life, we can only see the present, and remember what we can of the past. The sad part is that though we can only experience the present, we constantly try to escape the present. We are forever caught in the fantasies of a future we know nothing about and the regrets of a past we never really lived when it was our present.

Our entire story is one of missed time. We destroy time. We allow time to destroy us. We miss and kill the present, which is the only facet of time that is available to us. Instead of being where the present is and shaping our future, we fantasize and let the present as well as the future be destroyed.

The only certainty in our life is that when time moves on, it is forever lost. However much we may regret and repent, nothing will change what has happened. But we do have the power at the moment of the present to rewrite our future. Every human being has the freedom and free-will to choose his action at the present moment. He can let go by default and claim that whatever happened was predestined. Predestination is simply the choice that we did not exercise.

Only when we are aware and complete in the present moment, can we rewrite our future. Not when it is still the future and not when it slips into the past. The first is impossible and the latter is too late. By being grounded in the present state of completion, one can become aware of the future and one can shape one's future. We need to use all our intelligence, energy and creativity to live blissfully in this moment, not in the incomplete thoughts about the future or regrets about the past.

Kṛṣṇa is stating a simple fact here. 'With or without you,' He says, 'all these warriors will be dead. As Time, I shall devour them. It is not you who are the cause. You can be the superficial reason. By being the instrument of their destruction, be the gainer of fame, wealth and power.'

tasmāt tvam uttiṣṭha yaśo labhasva
jitvā śatrūn bhuṅkṣva rājyaṁ samṛddham |
mayaivaite nihatāḥ pūrvam eva
nimitta-mātraṁ bhava savya-sācin || 11.33

It is easy to interpret these words of Kṛṣṇa to mean that the future is predestined, since He says all these enemies of Arjuna will be destroyed. From this we can even interpret that His role is to protect the good and destroy the evil.

As *Mahākāla*, time personified, Kṛṣṇa destroys all, the good and the bad. Time does not differentiate. Time does not keep accounts of whether you did good deeds or bad. Time moves on and destroys the present into past, future into present and past. As time, Kṛṣṇa is neutral. He just is. He knows what will happen in the future and yet He does not influence it. As time, He lets happen what happens. He is the supreme energy that just flows.

When one is in completion with Kṛṣṇa, when one surrenders to Him, to His Will, things happen as they should. There is no interference on our part. We do what we ought to, what we need to, without worrying about what ought to happen and how. We then are in the flow of time; we are in the flow of Kṛṣṇa's energy.

When we resist and try to have things the way we wish them to be, rather than the way they would be, we get in the way. Like the rock that gets pounded by the river and eventually gets reduced to fine dust, we too get reduced to nothing by time. By imitating the reed in the river that bends offering no resistance, we can flow with time.

Struggling to choose is not freedom. It is the bondage of the mind. There is no need to make a choice. Choice happens at the level of the mind, not at the level of the being. When we relax into our being, we are in bliss, choiceless awareness. We can let the choice happen by itself. Choicelessness can be the choice.

When Kṛṣṇa speaks of destroying and wiping out the world, He is talking about the destruction of the illusory physical and material world. He is the destroyer of fantasies, He is the destroyer of identities, He is the destroyer of egos and He is the destroyer of all that is unreal.

As He has said earlier on, what gets destroyed is the shell, the perishable body-mind, not the imperishable *ātman*. What the *Mahākāla*, time, destroys, is the psychodrama that is being played out on the battlefield.

It is important to understand what Kṛṣṇa means in these words. As the supreme consciousness, He too is the energy of Śiva, the Rejuvenator. Śiva is not the Destroyer as He is made out to be. He recreates by destroying. There can be no creation if there is no destruction. There can be no life without death. Śiva's aspect of Kālabhairava is the time that Kṛṣṇa refers to. He is the controller of past, present and future and all that happens in these time zones.

When one surrenders to this supreme consciousness, one loses all fear of time. One completes with time. One flows with time. Whatever one does is the right thing at the right time. When one loses fear of time, one also loses fear of death. All that dies is recreated.

Arjuna expressed his dilemma earlier as one of having to destroy his elders, his teachers and his relatives. He wondered whether he was causing the destruction of his entire lineage by doing this. In truth, Arjuna was fighting against the destruction of his own root thought patterns, his *saṁskāras*, past memories of parental, teacher related and other conditionings that were difficult to destroy. This great war is really the fight between Arjuna and his root thought patterns, *saṁskāras*.

Kṛṣṇa once again takes responsibility for this destruction. Earlier there were only words. Now Arjuna had seen the destruction for himself. He had seen the Kaurava warriors being consumed by the destructive destination that Kṛṣṇa had bcome. It was impossible for Arjuna to disbelieve what he had seen—Bhīṣma, Droṇa, Karṇa and others disappearing into the vast form of Kṛṣṇa.

Now Kṛṣṇa consoles Arjuna. 'You have seen the truth of what happens. They have been destroyed already. Do not lose heart. Do what you have to do. Fight and destroy what remains, which is just the illusion of your fears.'

You Are Everything And Everywhere

11.35 *Sañjaya said:*
Having heard this speech of Keśava, the crowned Arjuna with joined palms, trembling, prostrating himself,
Again addressed Kṛṣṇa, voice choking, bowing down, overwhelmed with fear.

11.36 *Arjuna says: O Hriṣikeśa (Kṛṣṇa), it is but right that the world delights and rejoices in Your praise. Rākṣasas fly in fear in all directions and all hosts of sages bow to You.*

11.37 *And why should they not bow to Thee, O Great Soul,*
greater than all else, the Creator of even Brahma the Creator?
O Lord of Lords, O Infinite being, O Abode of the Universe,
You are the imperishable, that which is beyond
both the seen and the unseen.

11.38 *You are the primal God, the ancient being,*
the Supreme Refuge of the Universe.
You are the Knower and the One to be known.
You are the Supreme Abode, O being of Infinite forms,
by You alone is the Universe pervaded.

11.39 *You are Vāyu, Yama, Agni, Varuṇa, the Moon,*
Prajāpati and the great-grandfather of all.
Salutations unto You a thousand times,
and again salutations unto You!

11.40 *Salutations to You, before and behind!*
Salutations to You on every side!
O All! Infinite in power and Infinite in prowess,
You are everything and everywhere.

Arjuna now reaches the third stage of his perception of Kṛṣṇa's Cosmic form.

In the first stage, Arjuna's expectations of the glorious Universal form of Kṛṣṇa were fulfilled. He saw Kṛṣṇa the way He expected: with His crown, discus and mace, with Brahma rising on a lotus flower from Viṣṇu's navel.

Even as he was getting used to the enormity of the vision that he beheld, Arjuna found this form replaced by a terrible, all-devouring form of Kṛṣṇa that filled Arjuna with fear. Arjuna cries out: 'Who are you? Why are you here?'

Kṛṣṇa explains who He is; that He is the all-devouring time. Still overcome with fear, but recovering from the primal fear that had overcome him a few moments ago, Arjuna now surrenders himself to Kṛṣṇa.

Arjuna is so overwhelmed by the fearsome sight of Kṛṣṇa as Mahākāla, devouring everything around Him, and is so relieved to still be alive and coherent, that all Arjuna can do is to sing Kṛṣṇa's praises. He no longer has any self-doubt in his mind about the Universal consciousness of Kṛṣṇa, who till a while ago was his friend and charioteer. Whatever names and descriptions he is aware of to address this Supreme being, he uses now.

namaḥ purustād atha pṛṣṭhastas te
namo'stu te sarvata eva sarva /
ananta-vīryāmita-vikramas tvaṁ
sarvaṁ samāpnoṣi tato 'si sarvaḥ // 11.40

At this stage, Arjuna understands who Kṛṣṇa is. He understands what Kṛṣṇa's purpose is. Arjuna's devotion is at its peak. He salutes Kṛṣṇa as the source of all beings, the creator of Brahma, who in turn created Prajāpati from whom all beings originated. He salutes Kṛṣṇa as the elements of Nature. Since Kṛṣṇa extends everywhere and there is no place where He is not present, Arjuna salutes Him in all directions. Arjuna now truly appreciates the unfathomable magnitude of Kṛṣṇa.

Kṛṣṇa, Yādava, My Friend

11.41 *Arjuna says: Whatever I have rashly said from carelessness or love, addressing You as Kṛṣṇa, Yādava, my friend regarding You merely as a friend, unaware of this greatness of Yours.*

11.42 *In whatever way I may have insulted You in fun, while at play, resting, sitting, or at meals, when alone with You or in company, O Achuta, O Immeasurable One, I implore You to forgive me.*

11.43 *You are the Father of this world, moving and unmoving.*
You are to be adored by this world.
You are the greatest Guru; there is none who exists equal to You.
O Being of unequalled power, how then can there be another, superior to You in the three worlds?

11.44 *Therefore, bowing down, I prostrate my body before You and crave Your forgiveness, adorable Lord.*
Even as a father forgives his son, a friend his friend,
a lover his beloved, You should, O Deva, forgive me.

Arjuna is afraid again. Having seen what he has seen and understanding the unlimitedness of Kṛṣṇa's form, he remembers that all this while he had treated Kṛṣṇa like a friend, so casually. Remorse fills his being.

Arjuna's worry is not fear of any reprisal, now that he knows who Kṛṣṇa is. It is guilt that bothers him.

'I called You by Your caste name, Yādava,' Arjuna cries out, 'I called You, 'Hey friend, Hey Kṛṣṇa'. I knew not Whom I was addressing, Whom I was dealing with. Please forgive me.'

'How could I have done this? Please forgive me for the love I had for You that made me careless in addressing You. Bear with me; forgive me as a father would a son, a lover his beloved and a friend, his mate.

A small story:

> With great sincerity and seriousness a devotee of Śiva offered prayers to Śiva's idol at his home altar every day for many years. He had no thought other than Śiva, and all he desired was to have Śiva's vision, His *darśan* one day or the other.
>
> Since nothing happened year after year and he was getting old, the devotee gave Śiva an ultimatum, 'Either you appear before me or I will seek an alternative. Before I die I need to have the Lord's *darśan* so that I may be liberated.'
>
> Śiva still made no appearance.
>
> After a few days the devotee bought and installed an idol of Viṣṇu at his altar, replacing Śiva. But he did not have the heart to throw Śiva away, and merely moved Him to one corner, telling Him, 'See, I waited all this while patiently; all this is Your fault.'
>
> The next morning, he lit incense as usual and placed it before the altar, this time in front of the idol of Viṣṇu. To his irritation he found that the incense smoke was drifting towards the corner where he had cast out Śiva. 'You need no incense!' he cried out, and covered the nose of the idol to prevent it from smelling the incense.
>
> The next moment he felt Śiva standing in front of him, smiling. The devotee was overcome with deep guilt and overwhelming emotion. 'Lord!' he cried, 'All these years I prayed to You without fail and You never appeared to me. Today, when I cast You out and covered Your nose You gave me darśan. Why?'
>
> Śiva said: 'It is only today that I became real to you, when

you covered My nose. That is why I came to you now.'

COMPLETION WITH MASTER IS ENLIGHTENMENT

As his friend, Kṛṣṇa was the reality to Arjuna. He took liberties with his friend because He was so real to him. But his updated intelligence of Kṛṣṇa's Cosmic form shook him up so badly that he was now consumed by guilt. It was because of the intense devotion that Arjuna had for Kṛṣṇa, that Kṛṣṇa gave him the invaluable gift of His divine form. Had Kṛṣṇa not considered him worthy, Arjuna would not have seen his Cosmic form.

All our life, guilt rules us from our past. Whatever we do, we do with the intelligence available to us at that point in time. Often, what we did before seems wrong to us and we feel guilty. We start doubting our *self* and doubting others. There is no greater sin than carrying such guilt and self-doubt. What we did was not sinful; to carry the guilt with us is sinful. When complete with the guilt pattern, we drop the guilt and self-doubt. With the power of completion, a deep imprint is made within our *self* which is far more powerful than carrying the guilt and doubt.

Arjuna is demonstrating to the rest of us the power of completion with the Master, the ultimate relationship; in this case his incompletion is the guilt that seems to arise from the deepest of love.

Please listen. One of the important complications you carry in your life is doubt about yourself and doubt about your Master. You will project that self-doubt on your Master. Listen! Complete with that self-doubt. Only then you will have complete relation with the Master.

In one sense, Arjuna does not wish to carry that self-doubt and guilt with Kṛṣṇa. With integrity and authenticity, he completes with his guilt, his self-doubt and drops it in front of his friend, Lord and Master saying, 'Forgive me.'

Fear concerns the future. We can never be afraid of the past; it is dead and gone. Guilt and remorse plague us from the past. We need not have done it or we could have done it differently are the incompletions that we carry in the present. One by one these negativities pour out of Arjuna and he is getting cleansed and complete in the presence of the Master.

I tell you, completion with Master is enlightenment! If you just have completion with the Master, nothing else is required! His space will just gush into you. His space will just raise your inner space.

From Friendship to Enlightened Relationship

Arjuna is one of the greatest examples of *sakha bhāva*, friendship relationship between master and disciple. It is the immediate effect of realizing the true nature of Kṛṣṇa, especially in His destructive form, that terrifies Arjuna, that makes him afraid.

Sakha bhāva is not a relationship of equals. A disciple cannot be equal to the Master. Even when a disciple becomes enlightened and in that sense at the same level as the Master, the mood of the disciple would be one of sheer gratitude. It is after Enlightenment that a disciple realizes the true nature of the Master and the real master-disciple relationship flowers. The disciple imbibes the nature of his Master, he communes with the Master and this is how the lineage of great Masters is sustained.

In true *sakha bhāva*, everyone is a friend, not just the Master. One turns non-judgmental and respects everyone around as an expression of divinity. In one sense this is the problem that Arjuna has in waging war with his clansmen, who are his enemies. As an extension of his *sakha bhāva* relationship with Kṛṣṇa, he finds it difficult to hate his clansmen enough to fight and kill them. He gives many reasons but these reasons are only excuses.

Arjuna is no coward. He is the greatest warrior. Killing is second nature to him. But destroying a friend is not. His innate devotion to Kṛṣṇa extends to the Kauravas and he finds it difficult to keep this friendship feeling aside on the battlefield. In these verses, Arjuna also expresses the fear that his space of friendship may have been tinged with dislike or enmity or anger at some time. Though he seeks forgiveness for having called Kṛṣṇa his friend or a Yādava, etc., these are not really good reasons for a good friend to apologize, even if the friend turns out to be God.

Arjuna doesn't know yet where he stands. Kṛṣṇa has revealed Himself as the Supreme God to him. Arjuna knows that he had not always had noble thoughts about Kṛṣṇa. This is how we all treat God as well. As long as God provides us with what we want, we worship him. The moment our requests don't get fulfilled, the Divine becomes a stone idol. It is the same with a Master.

Arjuna is in transition. He represents the person who is about to move from the intellectual seeker level to the devotee and disciple stage. In fact, he has already moved after the Vision. There is no longer any self-doubt in him about Kṛṣṇa's identity. Until Kṛṣṇa showed him His divine form, it was theory to Arjuna. Now after the Vision, it is completely real. He has moved from *sakha bhāva*, friendship, to *mahā bhāva*, an enlightened relationship. It is this transition that brings out the residual guilt in him.

Your Familiar Form

11.45 *After seeing this form which I have never seen before,*
I am filled with gladness but at the same time
I am disturbed by fear. Please bestow Your grace upon me and
show me Your form as the Supreme Personality,
O Lord of Lords, O Refuge of the Universe.

11.46 *O thousand armed Universal form! I wish to see Your form*
with crown, four-armed with mace and disc in Your hand.
I yearn to see You in that form.

Arjuna now makes his final plea in these verses.

'Show me Your form that I am familiar with,' he says, 'the One that I am comfortable with. I am grateful and overwhelmed by the Visions that You have shown me, but what I am comfortable with is Your four-handed form holding the discus and mace, as the Protector of the universe. I am not comfortable, I am indeed fearful of the terrifying form of You as the Destroyer, however real it may be.'

kirīṭinaṁ gadinaṁ cakrahastam icchāmi tvāṁ draṣṭumahaṁ tathaiva |
tenaiva rūpeṇa caturbhujena sahasrabāho bhava viśvamūrte || 11.46

All of us are in the same situation as Arjuna. We all have fixed ideas of what divinity is, what motherhood is, what love is and what friendship is. Divinity is benign, comforting, protecting, nurturing, forgiving and all that is sweet and nice. So are motherhood, love and friendship. Existence does not work that way. Existence does not differentiate between good and bad, between beautiful and ugly. It is we who make judgments and create emotions within us to promote those judgments.

In the *Viṣṇu Sahasṛanāma*, which is recited by Bhīṣma as he was awaiting his liberation, he describes Viṣṇu as *'śāntākāraṁ bhujaga śayanaṁ padmanābhaṁ sureśaṁ'*. 'Peaceful, emanating bliss...' is how Viṣṇu, whose incarnation Kṛṣṇa is, is described. Just the very words bring to us so much peace and calmness! If instead, Bhīṣma had used words to describe the fearsome attributes of Viṣṇu such as:

'Frightful destroyer, with burning mouths...' and so on, how many would recite the *Sahasranāma*? It is a different matter that most people who go through the motions of reading and reciting the thousand names of Viṣṇu do not understand a word of what they are saying! So they are safe, whatever Bhīṣma may have said.

But if you do understand what the words mean, and if you are not in equilibrium, you will be disturbed. These words, understood to be negative by your logical mind, will create severe emotional turbulence within you.

A Yogī is one who has passed beyond these turbulences. He understands that the Divine is without attributes, neither peaceful and comforting, nor fearful and terrifying. These manifestations are also illusions. Beyond and behind these apparent manifestations, Divinity just *is*. It is beyond the three *guṇas*.

Arjuna at this point in time is yet to reach this stage. He still seeks the safety and comfort of the four-handed divine Protector that he is used to, rather than the terrifying Mahākāla. When we realize that both are masks of the Divine, that neither is His true Self and that both are His true Self, then and only then are we rid of illusions, and are liberated.

Only You Have Seen This Form

11.47 *Bhagavān says:*
Dear Arjuna, I have favoured you with this Transcendental form within the material world of My internal power.
No one before you has seen this unlimited, brilliant form.

11.48 *O best among Kuru warriors, no one has ever before seen this Universal form of Mine,*
for neither by studying the Vedas nor by performing sacrifices or charities, can this form be seen. Only you have seen this form.

11.49 *Do not be disturbed any longer by seeing this terrible form of Mine. Dear devotee, be free from all disturbances.*
With a peaceful mind, you can now see the form you wish to see.

Kṛṣṇa consoles Arjuna in these verses. He is again His compassionate Self to His disturbed disciple.

He tells Arjuna that no one, but no one, has had this great privilege of seeing His Cosmic form that He had just displayed to Arjuna. No penances, no rituals, no amount of scriptural reading and no other charities would gain this Vision for any one. 'However, you are terrified. That is OK. See Me now in My normal form that you are used to worshipping.'

Kṛṣṇa is clear on this point. It is He who decides how He reveals Himself to His devotees and disciples. It is a gift from the Master, from the Divine. It is not earned through effort. Of course, effort prepares one for the receipt of this great gift, but it is not the only necessary condition for the gift to be showered.

Of course, in this chapter Arjuna seeks Kṛṣṇa's Vision and it happens. It could have also happened without his seeking. The favor is for the Divine to give, not because we ask. It does not matter to Kṛṣṇa that Arjuna seemingly spurns this gift and would like to see Him as He normally does. What Kṛṣṇa offered was an unconditional gift that required neither acceptance nor appreciation.

A Mother's love for her child does not happen as a result of any effort on the child's part. The presence of the child spontaneously evokes the deep unconditional love of the Mother for the child.

It is ultimately the surrender of the devotee to the Master, like the surrender of the infant to the mother that evokes this unconditional love. In the case of an infant, it is a reflex action. The nature of an infant is to be defenseless and in absolute surrender to the caregiver. In the case of a devotee, the root thought patterns of mental behavior need to be given up. This is far more difficult.

The devotee has to return to his original and natural state of surrender to experience unconditional love. To achieve this he has to drop his mind. He has to give up all the root thoughts patterns, both conscious and unconscious. When the mind is wiped clean of its templates of comparison, it makes no difference if the Divine appears to be loving or terrifying. In both aspects one accepts Divinity.

Kṛṣṇa leads His disciple in stages through this path of Self-Realization, which is no different from the realization of the Divine.

Only In This Way Can You Reach Me

11.51 *Arjuna says: Seeing this wonderful human form,*
My mind is now calm and I am restored to my original nature.

11.52 *Bhagavān says:*
The four-armed form that you have seen is rare to behold. Even the celestials are forever aspiring to see this form.

11.53 *The four-armed form that you have seen with your transcendental eyes cannot be understood simply by study of the Vedas,*
nor by undergoing penances or charity or worship;
One cannot see Me as I am by these means.

11.54 *My dear Arjuna, only by undivided devotional service can you understand Me as I am, standing before you, being seen directly.*
Only in this way can you reach Me.

11.55 *My dear Arjuna, one who is engaged entirely in My devotional service, who surrenders to Me as the supreme, free from attachment, full of love for every entity, surely comes to Me.*

This statement coming from the mouth of Kṛṣṇa may be taken as the simple, direct truth.

Kṛṣṇa now appears in front of Arjuna first in His four-handed beautiful divine form that Arjuna is comfortable with, and finally as *Vāsudeva* Kṛṣṇa, in His gentle human form that Arjuna is so familiar with. But the familiarity ends there. Having seen what Kṛṣṇa really is through His divine form of *Nārāyaṇa*, with four arms bearing the discus and mace, and also in His terrifying Cosmic form as Mahākāla, Arjuna now has an understanding of the unlimited magnitude of the personality in front of him.

In whatever form Kṛṣṇa now appears, this understanding would remain with Arjuna. It is said that when Kṛṣṇa was born to Devaki, He presented to her and Vāsudeva, His father, His form with four hands to comfort them in their captivity, and later changed it to the human form.

Arjuna has now seen Kṛṣṇa in all His forms. The true Universal form of *Virāṭa rūpa* or *Viśvarūpa*, that Arjuna found fearsome; the beautiful, much gentler, adorable form with four hands (bearing mace and discus in two hands, and the other two hands signifying protection and the giving of boons), and finally back to the human form that Arjuna has always known.

Kṛṣṇa says even the great sages, the enlightened Masters have not seen the sights that Arjuna has seen. That is very true. Enlightened Masters cannot see visions. When an enlightened being sees another Enlightened being, it is in the energy form. To be able to see the gross physical form, both need to readjust their frequencies. For other people, no amount of spiritual practices and knowledge can make this happen. This is the space of *bhakti,* pure devotion.

Śrī Rāmakṛṣṇa says about one's relationship to a Master: 'The love of a chaste wife for her husband, the attachment of a miser to his hoarded wealth, the craving of a pleasure seeker for sensual pleasures, all these rolled into one and directed towards the master is true *bhakti,* devotion.'

EXPERIENCE YOU AS UNIVERSE AND UNIVERSE AS YOU

Kṛṣṇa concludes this chapter with a clear direction of what a devotee should do to reach Him. It is as simple as 1, 2, 3.

'Work for Me,' He says, 'work for My mission, *mat karma kṛn.* Surrender to Me as the supreme with no reservations, *mat paramo mad bhaktaḥ.* Have no attachment to whatever you do, leave the results to Me, surrender the fruits of your action to Me, *sanga varjitaḥ.* Look upon everyone as your own Self, without dislike and hatred, *nirvairaḥ sarva bhūteṣu.*'

mat karma kṛn mat paramo
mad bhaktaḥ sanga varjitaḥ **/**
nirvairaḥ sarva bhūteṣu
yah sa mām eti pāṇḍava **//** 11.55

What Kṛṣṇa says here is very significant. 'Work for Me. Enrich for Me—*mat karma kṛn*,' He says. 'He who works for Me comes to Me—*yah sa mām eti pāṇḍavaḥ*' All disciples and devotees must understand this. Devotion is not about keeping a statue or a photo and praying to it. You can be a gazer all your life and nothing will come out of it. What is really needed is authenticity in action and your effort to enrich others and yourself, which is in tune with what the Master teaches.

Please listen. *Rūpa* means the parts of you which you remember and associate yourself with, and make others experience as you, is *rūpa*.

For example, when you associate yourself with this skin, bone and flesh, and you cognize this as you and make everyone experience this as you; then, when someone worships this, you are happy, and when they abuse this, you are unhappy. Usually, whatever you associate yourself with and show as you to others is *rūpa*. A normal man associates himself, cognizes himself as his body and makes everyone cognize that he is his body.

***Viśvarūpa* means cognizing the whole *viśva* (universe) as you and making the the whole *viśva* cognize you as *viśva*. Listen! Enriching is the direct process to cognize you as *viśva* or *viśva* (universe) as you.**

Enriching is directly successful in life because with more and more enriching, you will less and less cognize yourself as this six-feet body and you will more and more cognize yourself with the people who carry the completion space you are living.

See, when you enrich others with the space you are living, whoever starts carrying the same space, you will feel connected with all of them. You will feel the strength of all of them. They will feel your strength, you will feel their strength. This is the way enriching becomes of practical use.

Listen!

I tell my disciples:

'If you sit and gaze at me and feel joyful seeing my form, you are chasing me. At best you get eye candy and brain candy, sweet words and a sweet form that makes you feel happy. Then you think I will be leaving soon and feel unhappy. You miss the present moment of my being with you and speculate with regret on my absence that may follow.'

'If instead, you work for my mission, enriching others with my words and teachings, I shall chase you. I shall always be with you, wherever you are! You do not even need to come to me. I shall come to you.'

Understand, my cognition about my success or failure has nothing to do with my body, it is to do with my ideology, which I already established in many bodies through which I'll continue to live forever. Whoever has cognized inside their heart, in the space of completion—integrity, authenticity, responsibility and enriching, I live in all of them. I am radiating *me* through all of them. Whoever I initiated already into the truths that I am living, whoever has caught the fire, I am living, I am continuing to live, and I'll continue to live through all of them.

Please understand, bring enriching as your strength. You will win in any war! Hinduism has always survived in all wars by using enriching as the weapon. *Śāstra* is our śastra; the knowledge was our weapon. It is by *śāstra*, the right cognition and the strength of enriching that we won all the wars, all over the world.

I tell you, take up enriching yourself and others again and again as your cognition. Suddenly you will realize, not only you are *rūpa*, the center of your life, you are *Viśvarūpa*, the center of the Cosmic life.

Please listen, I am not giving you theories and stories. I am giving you the practical tips from *my* personal life. You are not just center of your life, you are centre of the whole Cosmic life. If you associate yourself with the six-feet body you are *rūpa*, just form. If you associate yourself with the ideology and cognize yourself as sacred truths, whoever practices that, you expand; and you cognize all of them as part of you, so you become

Viśvarūpa. Enriching is the direct process to transform you from *rūpa* to *Viśvarūpa*.

May the blessings of *Parabrahma* Kṛṣṇa, the Supreme Lord be upon you all!

MEDITATION

> I think it is now time for us to meditate to experience what Arjuna is seeing. Once again the two points:
>
> ***Is it possible to experience Kṛṣṇa consciousness? Yes, it is possible.***
>
> ***What is the qualification? Our being present here is enough.***
>
> Now all we need to do is put our whole consciousness intensely into the meditation.

The meditation will take at least 20 minutes. If you feel you cannot or do not want to sit for 20 minutes, you are free to leave. If you can do so, we shall enter into the meditation. Please don't leave in between. Please sit straight and close your eyes. I shall guide you step by step.

Pray intensely to the *Parabrahma* Kṛṣṇa, Universal consciousness, in whatever name you know, in whatever form you know. Pray to that energy to give a glimpse of His being to you, a glimpse of the experience that Arjuna received and which all the enlightened masters experienced.

Pray to the Universal energy. It responds to your thoughts. Don't think your prayers are dead words. They are living communication.

Inhale and exhale as slowly as possible and as deeply as possible. Concentrate and bring your attention between your eyebrows, on your *ājña cakra*. Slowly, but very deeply concentrate on your *ājña* cakra. Without forcing yourself, put your awareness naturally on your *ājña cakra*.

Slowly start visualizing the whole Universe moving inside your head. Feel this clearly inside your head.

The space that is in front of you, in your inner space, the whole Universe is moving. See the sun, moon and all the planets. Visualize this clearly, intensely. Slowly relax the body, be one with the Universal consciousness. Feel the experience of being one with the Universe.

You are seeing clearly the sun, moon, stars and planets. Just disappear into the Universal consciousness. Forget your name, your form, all the conditionings, your profession, your gender and your country, everything about yourself. Forget your identity and see the whole Universe intensely. Just see the moving Universe intensely, all the planets, the stars, all the suns, moons.

Disappear into the Universal consciousness. Lose the identity, the root cause of all the thoughts; let it disappear into the Universal consciousness. Experience the bliss, the fulfilling bliss of the whole Universe. Expand and disappear into that Universe.

Dissolve into the Universal consciousness. Be in *Nityānanda*, eternal bliss!

Thus ends the eleventh chapter named ***Viśvarūpa Darśan Yogaḥ****, 'The Yoga of Cosmic Vision,' of the* ***Bhagavad Gītā Upaniṣad, Brahmavidyā Yogaśāstra****, the scripture of yoga dealing with the science of the Absolute in the form of* ***Śrī Kṛṣṇārjuna saṃvād****, dialogue between Śrī Kṛṣṇa and Arjuna.*

CHAPTER

12

Bhakti Yogaḥ

Love Is Your Very Life

In love, life comes to its ultimate peak. It is only in love that we will find God. Kṛṣṇa declares the experience and expression of His devotee, who is very dear to Him and reaches Him without a doubt.

Love Is Your Very Life

In the previous chapter, Arjuna asks for and receives the *viśvarūpa darśan*, the vision of the Universal form of Kṛṣṇa. Kṛṣṇa very patiently resolves Arjuna's doubts and answers all his questions. Arjuna then wishes to see the true reality of Kṛṣṇa, the form behind the formless, the Imperishable, the Eternal. Kṛṣṇa obliges his friend and disciple, Arjuna, the true representative of the human being, *Nara*.

Seeing this cosmic form of Kṛṣṇa, and unable to withstand the energy, Arjuna begs Kṛṣṇa to show him the benevolent four-armed form of Viṣṇu that he is used to worshipping with devotion. Finally, Kṛṣṇa reverts to His normal human form as Arjuna's charioteer, and the King of Yadāvas. After showing His cosmic form and having given the experience of Cosmic consciousness to Arjuna, Kṛṣṇa now speaks about *bhakti*, devotional love.

Kṛṣṇa's Universal form, as displayed to Arjuna, is His Cosmic consciousness, which is our collective consciousness. Arjuna understands from Kṛṣṇa that he too is a part of this Cosmic consciousness, and at the same time he is aware that what he could see of Kṛṣṇa is a mere fraction of His eternal cosmic Self.

Arjuna's experience of the Divine form of Kṛṣṇa raises further questions in his mind. Is this form that he just witnessed the glorious reality of the Cosmos? Is this the true reality that he should focus on? Or is the formless Self that Kṛṣṇa had talked to him about earlier more important?

Understanding Bhakti and Love

Usually people think a spiritual experience happens only after *bhakti*, devotional love. However, *bhakti* happens only after a spiritual experience. Real *bhakti* cannot happen to you before a spiritual experience.

Only when a person experiences every being as part of the Cosmic consciousness can he radiate love. Only such a person knows what love is. Nobody else knows what love is. Others *think* that they love, or *act* as if they love. Be very clear, so many people act as if they love. Sometimes by acting, they think that they love. Never can we love by acting!

Love must flow from our being. Love happens when we experience cosmic consciousness, when we have a spiritual experience, when our ego disappears. Kṛṣṇa lays out the whole technique for us, step-by-step.

After a spiritual experience so much gratitude flows from our being, so much love overflows from our being that we start radiating it. We need not make an effort, it just flows. We cannot stop it. No one can show or experience love unless they have had a spiritual experience.

People ask me, '*Swamiji*, you tell your devotees to meditate, meditate, and meditate. What is the use? Isn't it a selfish practice? Why don't you tell them to do service? That will benefit a lot of people.'

There are many so-called spiritual organizations and organized charities that are caught in social service, just for name, fame and social prestige. The people running and involved in these organizations, are always preoccupied and busy being photographed for newspapers and magazines. Organized charity is a beautiful way of cheating yourself and others. Your ego is fed well when you do charity this way.

Charity can never be organized. It just has to flow. It is not an external expression. Understand, in the *Vedic* tradition, the concept of *dāna* is not charity. Charity is an ugly word. Our concept of *dāna* is totally different. *Dhana,* wealth becomes *dāna,* enriching with wealth. When we are filled with *dhana*, which means the wealth of completion, the overflowing *dhana* becomes *dāna,* the overflowing enriching expression of Love.

Listen. Dhana overflows as *dāna* when completion overflows as love. The greatest wealth is completion and the greatest enriching is love!

The moment we try to organize charity, the whole thing takes on a different quality, a different color, and a different purpose. Only when it flows after an experience of completion is it a solid expression of love.

Our inner transformation, our completion must happen before we enrich others to transform. Unless we feel that we are part of the Whole, unless we feel that every other person is irretrievably linked to us, it is impossible for us to contribute and enrich with true love. We will only be hypocrites.

We are part of the cosmic ocean. Each of us is a mere drop. As long as we remain droplets and do not understand the reality of being part of the same ocean, we remain separate; our feelings will be driven by 'I' and 'mine'. As long as this separation remains, there can be no true love. There can be no expression of complete love.

Whatever an enlightened being does, even if he kills someone, it will only do that person good. This is because an enlightened being is established in the space of completion driven by cosmic consciousness. Therefore it will always be good for everyone. However, whatever an unenlightened man does, even if he does great service, it may or may not do good to him and society. Good or bad is not decided by *doing*. It is decided by the *being*! When an enlightened man acts, even small things lead to great results in the world. When an unenlightened person acts, even great truths may lead to misery and destruction at times.

Think about the simple words uttered by Buddha, 'Watch your breath, witness your inhaling and exhaling.' Buddha discovered this simple truth through which thousands of people became enlightened. Yet, when an unenlightened person discovers a great truth, it leads to destruction. For example, the atomic theory is a great truth. Yet, when it comes from an unenlightened mind, it leads to destruction.

A statistical report in a magazine claims that the governments of all the countries in the world have enough atomic weapons to destroy the planet Earth over a thousand times. They have piled up enough atomic weapons to destroy the earth not once or twice but over a 1000 times! This is the result of one unenlightened mind.

Listen. Deeds or words by themselves don't do good or bad. They do good or bad based upon the consciousness from which they are expressed. This consciousness, this awareness is related to the *feeling* one has for others. The quality of our awareness decides whether the end result benefits or destroys humanity.

Only after a spiritual experience do we feel gratitude at the *being* level. If it is our solid experience that every living being is God, we radiate love and our being becomes love. *Bhakti* and love are expressions that flow from that spiritual experience.

Kṛṣṇa's discourse on *Bhakti Yogaḥ* starts after *Viśvarūpa Darśan Yogaḥ*. After the experience of completion, He talks about the expression of enriching, *Bhakti Yogaḥ*. He talks about the expression of devotional love.

Who Is Perfect?

12.1 Arjuna asks, 'Who are considered perfect, those who are always engaged sincerely in Your worship in form, or those who worship the imperishable, the unmanifest formless You?'

Arjuna now speaks in a totally different manner. His thought trend is different now. He asks, 'Which of these two types of people are considered to be better: those who are always engaged in your *bhakti*, devotional love towards you or those who merge in the *Brahman*, the unmanifest, formless, Cosmic consciousness?'

arjuna uvāca
evaṁ satata yuktā ye bhaktās tvāṁ paryupāsate |
ye cāpy akṣaram avyaktaṁ teṣāṁ ke yoga-vittamāḥ || 12.1

Please be clear, Arjuna is not asking for himself. From here, the discourse becomes a simple discussion. It is more like trying to record the truth for future generations.

The questions from here onward are neither doubts nor enquiries. Arjuna tries to put the whole thing down in the expression form, so that it will be a useful reference for future generations. A flow of Arjuna's love for humanity, an expression of his divine experience, prompts him to seek answers to these vexing questions and record the answers from the godhead Himself.

Arjuna asks, 'Who will be established in You totally? Will it be a devotee or a person who is enlightened?'

Religious people or so-called religious people, confuse others with this verse about Arjuna's question as to whether worshipping the form or worshipping the formless is right. These people are so confused that they do not know right from wrong. They use their intellectual arrogance and misunderstanding to confuse others. Let me tell you, this is not what Arjuna meant by asking this question. If we look at Kṛṣṇa's answers, we will understand.

EXPERIENCE OR EXPRESSION? COMPLETION OR ENRICHING?

Arjuna asks, 'Is it good to be established in the experience of the Divine consciousness, just to stay in it and enjoy the eternal bliss that flows from that experience? Or is it better to express that love and gratitude created by the conscious experience towards the whole world and every living being? Which is correct? Which one is preferred?'

See, when we have a spiritual experience, some people stay in that experience with closed eyes, that's all. Only with eyes closed can they see God. They do not seek to use their senses, since the bliss within is so great and beautiful that absolutely no sensory input remotely matches that bliss. However, there are others who are impelled to open their eyes, by the Universe to communicate that blissful experience through their expression to enrich others.

The so-called scholars enter into endless debates on *savikalpa samādhi* and *nirvikalpa samādhi*. *Savikalpa samādhi* is the state where the experience of *samādhi* continues. *Nirvikalpa samādhi* is when the expression of *samādhi* starts. *Savikalpa samādhi* is supposed to be a lower state, and one is supposed to work towards the second and higher state of *nirvikalpa samādhi*. But it is not an ironclad rule.

In my case, both happened together. I did not go through two stages. I went through just one and reached the state where the experience was allowed to be expressed. It was the will of the Divine, *Parāśakti*. Please understand that this is not a choice that people make. An option is not presented to those who have such experiences. Those who experience the Divine transcend that point of freewill. They are driven wholly, in each step that they take, by *Parāśakti*, the Universal energy; by Kṛṣṇa, the Super-conscious Divine.

Arjuna understands that he and others who have had an experience of the Divine, face the choicelessness. He knows that Kṛṣṇa decides what he should do. Yet, he asks because he wants everyone to understand. Arjuna asks, 'What type of a person is greater? Is it a person who closes his eyes and sees God within himself or a person who opens his eyes and sees God in every being? Who is greater?'

Please understand, he is not asking whether worshiping the form or worshiping the formless is greater. Yet so-called religious people have interpreted it that way, and created problems between the teachings of the great masters, Ādī Śaṅkarācārya and Rāmānuja.

Śaṅkara followed *jñāna*, the path of knowledge, and Rāmānuja followed *bhakti*, the path of devotion. *Jñāna*, focuses on the formless through intellectual queries. *Bhakti* focuses on the form, sheer devotion, as if the Divine were alive as It indeed is! However, those who have studied Śaṅkara and Rāmānuja in depth know that there was much devotion in Śaṅkara's approach and much knowledge in Rāmānuja's approach! Both approaches converge. One without the other never works.

Expressing the gratitude that happens because of the experience is devotion. Having that experience and rejoicing, staying in that experience is knowledge; that's all.

Kṛṣṇa's answer is that both paths are the same. The paths are intertwined. The first one leads to the second one and the second one leads back to first one. We have heard the term vicious circle. First one leads to the second and the second one leads back to the first one.

Now, I want to introduce another word, 'virtuous circle.' Vicious circle leads to low energy or lower level of consciousness. Virtuous circle leads to high energy, a higher level of consciousness! Bliss leading to devotion and gratitude, devotion and gratitude leading to bliss: these two form the virtuous circle that lead us to higher consciousness.

Bliss means the experience of completion that leads us to the expression of gratitude and enriching. Again, the expression, the gratitude of enriching, leads us to bliss, and bliss leads us to deeper completion. One leads to the other and therefore it is a virtuous circle.

Usually we are caught in the vicious circle. Fear leads to greed and greed leads to fear. More fear leads to more greed, and more greed leads to more fear. This is the vicious circle. Here Kṛṣṇa introduces the virtuous circle. Virtuous circle is what He calls *dharma*, righteousness, that which must be followed in the path of truth.

Dharma **means virtuous circle, that which leads us to live and express higher and higher levels of Consciousness.** That in turn leads us to higher and higher levels of blissful experience. Consciousness and bliss lead to expression of that consciousness and bliss, which in turn lead to higher level experiences.

Fix Your Mind On Me

12.2 *Bhagavān Kṛṣṇa says,*
Those who fix their mind on Me eternally and those who are steadfast in worshipping Me with supreme faith,
I consider them to be perfect in yoga, ready to be united with Me.

Bhagavān says, 'Those who are established in their consciousness that expresses devotional gratitude, *bhakti*, are always engaged in Me. Those who focus on the transcendental faith, meaning the experience that they undergo at the time of Cosmic experience, they are engaged in Me. Both are ultimate. Both are united in Me.

Saṃskṛit is a beautiful language. We can make any meaning out of any word. That is why thousands of commentaries on the Gītā are possible, yet the Gītā is still new. No book has been commented upon by so many masters, as much as the Gītā has been. Each master gives his own meaning. Again, I insist that if a person who has not had a spiritual experience starts expressing, lecturing, he will naturally be in trouble and create trouble for others as well. In the same way that the blind leads the blind, both end up in trouble. A person without any spiritual experience, when he translates or talks, he automatically does only 'text torturing.'

Real Completion Expresses as Enriching with Love

Understand this small example: Let us say I draw a diagram and explain the concept of an experience that I have had to you. Later, you present only an audio CD of this session to a friend who did not attend this lecture. You have not had the experience; you merely translate my experience. How much can you explain? He will not be able to grasp much. He will miss my body language completely. You cannot explain accurately either, because you are not the one who had the experience. A person who just has the audio recording or a book copy, cannot understand much. Like that, *Bhagavad Gītā* is a transcription of the audio recording. Even the voice modulation is not there. How much can you translate or interpret?

That is why Vivekananda emphasized, again and again, not to read or listen to anything expressed by a person who has not personally experienced the truth. Most importantly, he said, 'Bother about who is speaking, rather than what he is speaking.' He emphasized the personal experience. He added, 'All the books in the libraries in this world cannot lead you to the truth. Once you have realized the truth, you do not need books.' Spiritual experience transcends mind and ego. It is pure, uncolored and permanent. By expressing an understanding of someone's experience, one may express a fact or an opinion at best, but never the truth. Truth must be experienced to be expressed.

Here Bhagavān says,

mayyāveśya mano ye māṁ nitya yuktā upāsate |
śraddhayā parayopetās te me yuktatamā matāḥ || 12.2

Those who express their experience as devotion, see the world, *upāsate*. The word *upāssana* can be translated in many ways. When we see the Divine in everybody, when we express the truth of the spiritual experience, whatever we do is *upāssana*. Please be very clear, when we can't see the Divine in people around us, we can't see the Divine in any statue or any Master either. If we don't see the Divine in living beings, we cannot see the Divine in a God or a Guru.

If it were not for the great master Rāmānuja, South India would have completely lost its spirituality. Śankara settled in the north even though he was born and brought up in the south. He spent most of his time in North India. Because of Rāmānuja, devotion and spirituality thrived in South India. Until his end, Rāmānuja stayed in South India. Not only that, Śankara lived only until the age of thirty-two. Rāmānuja lived on planet

Earth for a long time and inspired thousands of people in the path of spirituality and meditation.

> One young man asked Rāmānuja, 'Master, please tell me how I can achieve *bhakti,* achieve God, achieve devotion?'
>
> Rāmānuja asked him, 'Have you ever loved anybody in your life?' This man was shaken. He said, 'I am a pure *brahmacāri,* a celibate. How can you ask me this question? I came to learn about God and you ask me this question?'
>
> Rāmānuja says, 'First go and love somebody. See how you feel when you love somebody. Then come back and I will teach you about God. I will teach you about *bhakti,* devotional love.'

This man was naturally taken aback. He could not understand Rāmānuja. Understand, unless we love the person whom we can see, how will we love an entity that we have never seen? If we can't love human beings whom we see everyday, how can we love the form of God whom we have never seen? What Rāmānuja says is true. We should also understand that unless we radiate love in the space where we stay, we can't love the whole world.

Again and again I tell people, loving the whole world is easy. Loving your wife is difficult. Loving the whole world is easy because we don't need to do anything to substantiate it! All we must do is to say, 'I love the whole world.' But when we love our wife, we must change our inner space to that of completion. We must change our mind, our words, our feeling and our very living. We must bring integrity to our words. We must bring authenticity to our thinking and our actions; responsibility in our feeling, and enriching in our living. There starts the problem!

Listen! You need to know that relationships are not something external. It is an expression of yourself, how *you* feel about you. The relationship you carry with *you* is projected as the relationship with the *world*! I tell you, when you bring integrity in your relationship with others, honoring the words you gave or completing the words you gave, the way others look at *you* will be transformed immediately.

To truly love and enrich someone whom we spend our life with, to prevent familiarity from breeding contempt, we need to complete with others and our self, and drop our 'I' and 'mine'. As long as we consider our spouse as a possession, what arises in our mind and heart is violence, not love. We will feel we must control the other being and we will feel we must prove that we are the owner. To even comprehend the meaning of true love, we need to drop the feeling that we possess.

Being established in that consciousness of completion or expressing it towards enriching the Universe is the same. When a person is merged, when a person is established, he automatically radiates. If the love is not happening, if the expression is not happening, the person has not experienced. When the real experience of completion happens, it automatically expresses as enriching. Experience is not something we can possess and keep in our cupboard. No! Experience will possess us and it will radiate as enriching through us.

This is because we cannot possess an experience. Only the experience can possess us. When experiences possess us, whatever we do will be a song. Any word that comes out will be a song. Our being will be so light. We will simply float. Our body language will radiate grace. All our expressions will be a great enriching service to humanity.

An Enlightened man never keeps quiet nor does he talk, he just sings. That is why the *Gītā* is given in the form of a song. The *Gītā* is not prose. It is poetry. Great truths can never be expressed in logic. They can only be expressed through poetry. Prose is logic. It is bound. It is rigid. But poetry is emotion. It is love and it flows.

Kṛṣṇa says that a person established in the consciousness of completion is great; however, the person who expresses, who shares, who automatically radiates the power of living by enriching is as great as the one who is established. The truth is that if a man is established in consciousness, he will radiate, he will enrich, and he will sing.

Let me tell a small story of a great devotee, a *bhakta,* who lived in Varanasi.

This man was a great devotee of Kṛṣṇa. He owned a small copy of the *Bhagavad Gītā*. That was his entire possession, his only wealth. Every morning he bathed in the sacred river Gaṅgā while reciting the *Bhagavad Gītā* with devotion. He spent the whole day sitting and meditating on Kṛṣṇa. He was continuously in the ecstasy of Kṛṣṇa. He radiated *Kṛṣṇa bhakti,* devotional love towards Kṛṣṇa.

Of course, we see these types of souls only in India. Society does not disturb people who just sit in ecstasy. Society takes care of them. In any other country such people would be called homeless, hounded by police and the public, put in a shelter and disrespected. Indian culture is beautiful. If we sit in ecstasy, we are respected and worshipped!

This person was in ecstasy, always singing Kṛṣṇa's name, in *Kṛṣṇa dhyāna*, in Kṛṣṇa meditation, in *Kṛṣṇa smaraṇa,* repeating Kṛṣṇa's name. He was lost in Kṛṣṇa consciousness.

One day a beggar came and asked, 'Oh Swami, please give me something. For the last three days I have not eaten.'

Now this posed a big problem to the *bhakta.* He himself was a beggar and had only one possession, the Gītā. He owned nothing else. If someone gave him food, he ate. Otherwise, he just sang Kṛṣṇa's name. His only property was the *Gītā.* He looked to see if there was something to give. There was only the *Bhagavad Gītā*, which he had preserved and worshipped for many years. That was his sole possession, akin to God for him. It was everything to him.

Suddenly, he gathered the courage of authenticity and

> took hold of the book and said, 'I have nothing. I have only this book. However, if you go to the city and tell people that this book was my possession, you will be able to auction it. Surely someone will buy it. Many people respect me. To some extent, they feel devoted to me. So Kṛṣṇa's blessing is there. Go to the market and auction this book. Take the money and eat and fulfill yourself, and be happy.'
>
> The beggar took the book and went away.
>
> The next morning, when he was about to chant the Gītā, the *bhakta* said, 'Oh Kṛṣṇa, I have given away your words to keep your words. What is your word? Your word is to radiate *bhakti,* to radiate devotion. I gave away your word to keep your word.'

This man was a true devotee. He had seen the truth. He had experienced it. So he was able to express it. He translated his devotion to Kṛṣṇa as love to enrich his fellow men. Keeping Kṛṣṇa's word was more important than keeping Kṛṣṇa's book. Actually, if we use His words properly with integrity and authenticity, we will have the experience of completion, of devotion. We will radiate His words, we will enrich with His love.

They Too Attain Me

12.3,4 *But those who worship the imperishable, the unmanifest,*
that which lies beyond the perception of senses, the all pervading,
inconceivable, unchanging, the non-moving and permanent;
those who worship by restraining their senses, and are working
with even mind for the enrichment of mankind,
they too attain Me.

Kṛṣṇa is *saguṅa brahman*, the physical Cosmos, who showed Himself in this form to Arjuna, in His *viśvarūpa,* Cosmic form. Kṛṣṇa is *nirguṇa brahman* as well, the formless consciousness. In both the form and the formless, He is Kṛṣṇa, the Divine consciousness who has all the attributes that He talks about here.

The Divine is imperishable. It is *akṣaram.* Everything else in this material Universe may come and go, appear and disappear, while the Divine remains forever. It is unique and incomparable and cannot be benchmarked against anything, as it is supreme. It is *avyaktam,* unmanifest and *acinytam,* inconceivable, and therefore cannot be comprehended by the senses. It cannot be grasped by thoughts and mind, which is why one's mind-body needs to be transcended to glimpse the Divine. The Divine resides everywhere and is omnipresent.

The true devotee sees his Lord everywhere. Rāmakṛṣṇa describes the love of a true devotee this way: 'It is the love of a chaste wife for her husband, the attachment of a miser towards his hoarded wealth, the craving of a worldly person for sensual pleasures, all rolled into one and directed towards the Lord, creating devotion.'

The true devotee, who follows either path with completion, with his senses focused on the Lord, experiences Him and also experiences the bliss of enriching humanity. The devotee sees the Lord in everyone he meets. His experience of His Lord becomes His expression of love to all.

> Kṛṣṇa's beloved Radhā tells the gopīkās (cowherdress who were around Kṛṣṇa), 'I don't know what has happened to me. I see Kṛṣṇa in everybody. I feel that everybody is Kṛṣṇa. I don't know what is happening.' One of the gopikās answers, 'You have devotion as the very black eyeliner in your eyes!'

It is like this: When you wear dark glasses everything appears dark; when you wear green-tinted glasses, everything appears green. In the same way, when you have devotion as your very eyeliner, whomsoever you see appears as Kṛṣṇa, appears divine! Here, Kṛṣṇa says, the person established in super consciousness space of completion and the person who radiates devotion and lives for enriching are the same. They are not two different groups.

FORMLESS OR FORM?

Kṛṣṇa does not create two groups. Arjuna presents two groups as the reality that he sees: those who are established and those who are radiating. Kṛṣṇa says both are the same. He does not divide them into two groups, those who are established and those who radiate, or those who are complete and those who enrich. Kṛṣṇa says, a person who is established always radiates and the person who radiates is always established. As I said earlier, it is a virtuous circle.

Rāmakṛṣṇa says, 'When a bell rings, each stroke has a sound form of its own. But even when the bell stops ringing, we continue to hear the sound. That's how God appears, both as form and as formless.'

Once again, Kṛṣṇa makes the point here. When one has realized the formless nature of the Divine, its imperishability and its unmanifest nature with controlled senses, one works for the enrichment of mankind. Once the experience of the formless divine happens, it is no different from the experience of the form. Both lead to the truth that one is a part of collective consciousness. The expression of this realization is one of deep humility and compassion. It is manifested as deep gratitude and surrender. One learns to flow with the energy of this Universe. One no longer struggles against the currents of life.

When we are full of ego we tend to control. We believe we can bring order to an otherwise chaotic world. It takes only a moment to realize that this entire Universe and planet Earth function not *because* of us, but *in spite* of us. Millions and millions of stars and planets in this Universe function in apparent chaos. But understand, the Universe is always in order.

We want to be in order but we are truly chaotic. Only when we surrender to the will of the Universe, we fall into the cosmic order. Things go well for us. When we give up wanting, we get what we want. When we get what we truly want, it enriches mankind. Because when we surrender, Kṛṣṇa takes care.

Kṛṣṇa is not the Kṛṣṇa whom you think He is. He is not the single form you are used to. He is the Super conscious energy, the Cosmic Energy, *Parāśakti*.

Formless Is Difficult

12.5 *For those whose minds are set on the unmanifest, the formless, it is more difficult to advance; attaining the formless unmanifest is difficult for the embodied.*

Kṛṣṇa says here what many of us know to be true. He says, intellectuals find it more difficult to comprehend the Divine.

Once, Brahma and Viṣṇu had a conflict as to who was greater. For any conflict, two egos are required. When anybody, who is in space, time and form, forgets to take responsibility for other's irresponsibility, there will be conflict.

Now, the Universe is at stake! So Śiva, the one who is responsible for everything, enters the realm of space and time as Aruṇācaleśvara, as *jyotisthambha*, an infinite shaft of light that spans the Universe.

Śiva said to them, 'The one who finds either of my two ends is greater.'

Viṣṇu assuming the form of a boar, dug through the earth searching for the lower end of the light shaft. Brahma flew up as a swan to reach the upper end. After a very long time, Viṣṇu realized the futility in trying to find Śiva's beginning and returned. He restored his authenticity by completing with Śiva, for attempting to look for His unmanifest beginning.

Brahma continued regardless. On his way up, he found a flower floating down, who said that it was falling from Śiva's head for many lifetimes of Brahma. Startled, Brah-

> ma realized there was no way he would reach the end of the shaft, and forced the flower to support his claim that he, Brahma, had picked the flower from Śiva's locks. Hearing Brahma's lie, his lack of integrity, Śiva became furious and taking the form of destruction, Rudra, cut off one of Brahma's heads and forbade him from being worshipped.

There is metaphoric meaning to this happening. Viṣṇu represents wealth or *sthiti* (sustenance) and Brahma represents intellect or *sṛiṣṭi* (creation). *Sṛiṣti* and *sthiti* think that they are the ultimate until *samhāra*, destruction enters their life. Only then, do they realize that they are not the ultimate! That is why Mahādeva has to happen in their life in the form of Rudra, destruction. Mahādeva appears to Brahma and Viṣṇu to expose their inauthenticity to them, and makes them responsible for their inauthenticity and others' inauthenticity.

In one's search for the truth, the Divine, the unmanifest, *avyakta*, which is what the intellectual seeker is focusing on, the intellect, the mind or ego will be the block that makes the path difficult to traverse. The individual carries not only the body but the mind as well. And with the mind, it carries the ego. As Kṛṣna points out—*avyaktā hi gatir duḥkhaṁ* (12.5). Unless the mind-body is transcended by the process of completion and surrender, spiritual advancement is difficult.

Shedding the ego and restoring completion is the most difficult thing for the mind-body system. Ego provides the mind-body with its identity, with its existence. Till then, Mahādeva, the embodiment of completion and responsibility, has to appear again and again in your life to remind you to take responsibility.

Whether now or in Kṛṣṇa's time, the world revolved around the power of thought, the power that seems to provide knowledge and skills. It was essential for one's recognition and status in life.

Dropping the ego and taking responsibility to restore authenticity is the most difficult thing for the body-mind, especially for one who is focused on the intellect.

Whenever you look at any destruction as a reminder of your inauthenticity and irresponsibility, it is no more a destruction in your life. You have learnt how to make anything negative into something positive, to strengthen your life. If you are able to make anything negative into positive, the moment it enters into your life, you are Śiva—Causeless Auspiciousness.

Liberation From Birth And Death

12.6,7 *But those who worship me with single-minded devotion, renouncing all activities unto Me, regarding Me as their Supreme goal, whose minds are set in Me, O Pārtha, I shall deliver them soon from the ocean of the birth and death cycle.*

Kṛṣṇa makes a promise here. Kṛṣṇa says unequivocally, 'I shall deliver them from their material existence, the ocean of *saṁsāra*, the cycle of life and death, *mṛtyu-saṁsāra-sāgarāt*. All that the Lord asks is that the devotee be devoted to Him.

ye tu sarvāṇi karmāṇi mayi sannyasya mat-parāḥ /
ananyenaiva yogena māṁ dhyāyanta upāsate // 12.6

Kṛṣṇa says, 'If you surrender to Me, surrender all your actions and the fruits of those actions to Me, do my service, meditate upon Me, remain single-minded upon My consciousness, I shall then liberate you. I shall make sure you never need to be born again.' It is the roar of a lion. It is the roar of the King of this Universe. 'Surrender to Me and I shall liberate you. Serve Me and I shall liberate you.'

To most of us, God is only a concept and we worship that concept. Most of the time, we beg of that concept. We pray, 'Give me this O Lord, give me that O Lord.' When we have one prayer answered, we begin the next. As long as God answers our prayers, as long as the Master provides us with what we ask for, our faith in Him lasts. The moment the prayer goes unanswered, our faith dissolves. We move on to another God or Master.

We do not realize that often God does not answer our prayers out of sheer compassion, out of sheer love for us. From time to time, God in His infinite wisdom turns down our requests such as wanting to become rich, wanting to be well, wanting to have children, and so on. We then move away from Him.

Listen. Surrendering to the Divine is not conditional. It must be total. There can be no 'ifs', 'ands', or 'buts'. It cannot be, 'If you grant my prayers, I shall be devoted to you.' That is business. Most of our relationship with God is business.

There are three kinds of surrender. First, there is surrender of one's intellect. For many, this is possible. Once we understand that there is a Universal energy far greater than us, most of us can accept and surrender intellectually to that supreme power. At least we can say, 'I surrender.' That's how many of us prostrate in a temple or before a master. The entire body touches the ground signifying our surrender. For that moment, our ego takes a vacation.

Surrender at the next level is emotional. One can melt at the thought of God or master. There is love, there is gratitude pouring out of our hearts and we feel tears streaming down. We become *bhaktas,* devotees. Rāmakṛṣṇa said, 'If you have tears in your eyes when you think of God or your Master, be very clear, this is your last birth! You are ready for liberation.' We are ready but not liberated until we reach the last and third step. This step of surrender is the surrender of one's senses. Our surrender is total at this stage: complete, spontaneous, instant and natural.

Kṛṣṇa says, 'When you surrender to Me, I shall liberate you.' To reach Him, we must surrender totally without deviation. Our senses must be surrendered to Him. Our entire consciousness, our complete awareness must *only* be of Him and nothing else. Nothing else needs to be done. The technique is so simple. 'Surrender and I shall save you,' says the Master. 'I shall save you without delay, immediately—*bhavāmi na cirāt pārtha mayy āveśita cetasām* (12.7).' The Lord has made it so simple. Yet, we find it so difficult to believe Him.

Live In Me Always

12.8 You fix your mind on Me alone, establish your mind in Me.
You will live in Me always. There is no doubt in it.

Just fix your mind upon Me, the supreme personality of the Divine and engage all your mind, body and senses in Me and you will thus live in Me always, without a doubt, assures Kṛṣṇa.

mayy eva mana ādhatsva mayi buddhiṁ niveśaya |
nivasiṣyasi mayy eva ata ūrdhvaṁ na saṁśayaḥ || 12.8

'*Na samśayaḥ*, without a doubt,' He says. Now He comes to the technique. At one point the virtuous circle must begin. First, He explains the virtuous circle of the ultimate experience and expression. Now He comes to the technique.

Please understand that love is not a mood. It is not a mere emotion. It is our very Existence. As long as it is our mood, it will come and go.

There are two kinds of love, horizontal love and vertical love. Let me explain. Horizontal love is like a horizontal line, flat. It is related to time: it starts and ends. Anything that starts must end. If it takes more time to end, don't think it is permanent. Anything that starts must end. It may take a few years or a few months, but it ends. It is impermanent and time bound. This is horizontal love. Horizontal love is related to time.

Vertical love is related to consciousness. Vertical love neither starts nor ends. It does not discriminate. It is our very quality. It flows. If we discriminate and love, it cannot be love. It is an infatuation. As long as the other person fits into our frame, our love grows. The moment the other person doesn't fit into our frame, our love disappears.

In our Inner Awakening meditation retreat, I ask people to make a list of at least one or two persons in their lives whom they really love. Usually, in the beginning, people come up with a big list: husband, wife, father, mother, brother, sister and so on. They include people whom they would like to please or need to please in order to be happy and be undisturbed themselves.

When I begin the process, people start crossing out names of people from their list, one by one. Understand, if you cross out something, then it was not love even in the first place. However, people get stuck when they come to the names of their sons or daughters. I say that all your love is for some reason. For economical benefit or psychological support, you hang onto these relationships.

The next reason we love is to receive good certificates, positive recognition. Sometimes we share love and show love. We may not do so for economical benefits or psychological support, but we may expect a good certificate or attention for being loving and kind. Some need for attention is always present. There is always some dependent need in us that motivates us to express love. It is never unconditional or complete love.

People say, 'No *Swamiji*. I don't love my son or daughter for any of these three reasons.'

I ask them, 'Alright, if suddenly your son starts to decide things on his own, if he doesn't fit into your frame, if he doesn't follow your guidance, will your love be the same? Enquire authentically.' Naturally people say, 'No, it will not be, the love will reduce a little.'

What does this mean? We love our next generation as long as they are extensions of our life. We fulfill our desires through them. Whatever we couldn't accomplish, we try to accomplish through them. As long as they act and live as an extension of our life, the relationship is beautiful. But the moment they start deciding on their own, the moment they feel we are suffocating them, the moment they stand up and say 'no,' the relationship takes a different turn.

This is horizontal love. That is why it ends with some reason. Vertical love never ends because it never starts. Suddenly, at some point we realize, we are living inside everybody just as we live inside our own body.

There is a beautiful example given in the *Upaniṣads.*

> A master asked a disciple, 'Do you enjoy all your five senses?'
>
> The disciple said, 'Yes.'
>
> The master enquired, 'What if one of your senses was missing, would you have the same amount of joy?'
>
> The disciple replied, 'No, it would be twenty percent less, and if two of my senses were missing, it would be forty percent less.'
>
> The master suddenly said, 'What if you had five more senses?'
>
> The disciple answered, 'Naturally my enjoyment would be a hundred percent extra. If I am given one more body, naturally I will enjoy everything twice as much. Or if I am given five bodies, naturally I will enjoy things five times as much.'

If we experience that we are living in all the bodies of this world, how much joy or ecstasy would we experience? It would be immeasurable, eternal and ultimate. That is what enlightened people experience all the time—living *Advaita*! When they experience themselves as the whole Universe, or as being in every body, they experience tremendous ecstasy, pleasure or bliss. That is why they don't need anything from the outer world.

An elderly person came to one of our programs. Afterward, he said to me with a lot of sympathy, 'You have become a master and an ascetic at such a young age. You have missed life.' He expressed his sympathy. He felt that I had missed out. I told him, 'Don't be sympathetic towards me. Actually I should feel sympathetic towards you. Even after sixty years, you are unable to liberate yourself. Even after sixty years, you are suffering in *saṁsāra,* the illusion of worldly life. I should be sympathetic towards you!'

REAL RENUNCIATION IS COMPLETION WITH THE WHOLE

When we experience ecstasy and bliss within, we don't feel we are missing anything from the outside world. Real renunciation is not about our renouncing the world. It is about the world renouncing us. When we have that completion, joy, ecstasy and bliss, we automatically radiate that bliss. We never feel that we miss anything or that we have lost something.

I tell people not to renounce the world unless they feel completion and ecstasy inside. Never renounce. Work towards completion and ecstasy. When that happens, renunciation automatically happens. If you renounce the outer world without having established the inner world with completion, you will fall into depression.

When you are complete with you, the world will be complete with you. When you are incomplete with you, the world will be incomplete with you! Completion with *you* is Inner Awakening. Completion with the *whole* Universe is Sannyāsa. Sannyāsa means completion with the Whole. You are clear with your accounts and there is no incompletion!

I have seen many Sannyāsis who have taken this path without achieving the inner experience of completion. They are caught in social service and then fall into depression. Around the age of forty to forty-five, they become depressed. They counsel the whole world while they are depressed. Never renounce the world unless you have had a solid experience of completion inside.

When you have had the experience, you don't need to renounce. Automatically renunciation happens. All these things will drop you. Instead of you dropping them, they will drop you! You dropping these things always creates problems. When *they* drop you, it is the right thing. When you start experiencing the joy in you, nothing needs to be renounced, automatically renunciation happens.

Establish Your Intelligence On Me

Here, Kṛṣṇa gives techniques to start the virtuous circle. 'Fix your mind on Me, *mayy eva mana ādhatsva.* Establish your intelligence in Me, *mayi buddhiṁ niveśaya.* In this way, after acquiring the boundary-less consciousness, you will live in Me always, *nivasiṣyasi mayy eva.*'

How should we establish our intelligence in Him? Continuously try to enrich yourself and others with these thoughts and ideas that Kṛṣṇa teaches. Rāmakṛṣṇa says that what we belch depends upon what we eat. For instance, if we eat some kind of vegetable or fruit, the smell of that comes out when we belch.

In the same way, if we add these ideas continuously to our mind and consciousness, we naturally radiate them. They start shining through our being. When He tells you to let your intelligence be established in Him, it means that when we are in trouble, the solution should automatically come to us based upon these ideas.

As of now we run and refer to a book, which means we have a Guru only in the outer world. If we digest and enrich ourselves with these ideas, even when we don't have problems, they will lodge themselves in us and take us to higher and higher levels of completion. When we have problems, they will guide and enrich us. If you read books only when you are in trouble or when you are seeking a solution, you will not digest the ideas because your mind will be confused. How will you receive them? How can you digest them when you are troubled and confused? It can't happen this way.

I tell you: *dharmo rakśati rakśitāḥ*

When you protect *dharma,* **it protects you.** When you excite *dharma*, it excites you. When you enrich *dharma*, it enriches you. When you are integrated to it, it is integrated into you. When you are authentic with it, it is authentic with you. When you take responsibility for it, it takes responsibility for you. Only when you enrich it, will it enrich you. **Dharma means the natural law of the Cosmos. It is an independent intelligence.**

When your mind is in the normal state, receive these ideas and enrich yourself and others constantly as a regular habit. Let it become your normal life style. Just as you eat and bathe everyday, in the same way, absorb these ideas regularly.

Understand, from my daily morning *satsangs* to Inner Awakening program, and even after that, I continue to speak on the four *tattvas* to enrich people with this *dharma.* Then, is it all the same? No! It is neither the same nor is it different! It means that you are being guided deeper and deeper, layer by layer, into the same tattvas!

In his commentary on the Chandogya Upaniṣad, Śankara has written beautifully about purification of food.

āhāra śuddho satva śiddho dhruvā smṛtiḥ

When our *āhāra,* food, is purified, our memory is purified.

Please understand that *āhāra* doesn't mean just the food that we eat. It refers to whatever we take in through the five senses. Television programs that we watch are *āhāra.* Music that we listen to is *āhāra.* The food that we eat is *āhāra.* The odours that we smell are *āhāra.* The touch that we enjoy is *āhāra.*

So, all that we take in through the five senses should be pure. Only then can we radiate purity, can we radiate bliss, can we radiate divine intelligence. Unless we purify the *āhāras* that is ingested through the other senses as well, we cannot expect purification of our memories. I feel blessed that when I was born and brought up, there was no television in my village.

People ask me, '*Swamiji,* how do you grasp things so easily?' Of course, I somehow pick up things easily, quickly. One small fact: Only a few years ago I started speaking English. I studied a little bit of English in school but that was through my native language Tamil in which I learned everything.

Look in! Look into your life. When you start taking responsibility, you can decide the way your heart beats; you can decide the way your lungs function; you can even control the automated organs of your body and you can decide the functioning of non-mechanical parts of your brain. Each one of us have mechanical parts and non mechanical parts of the brain.

Mechanical parts of the brain are responsible for the functioning of your body—like the heart, lungs, liver, kidney, intestine, the functioning of your nervous system, experiencing touch, taste, seeing etc. The non-mechanical parts of your brain are responsible for the extraordinary powers—like telepathy, teleporting, *vāk siddhi* (the power of words, wherein any blessing given becomes a reality).

Please listen. Extraordinary powers are not mythological stories or just some blind faith. I have already done enough scientific research to demonstrate the genuineness of the possibility of teleportation, telepathy and materialization.

Only when you take the responsibility, will you find the solution. I tell you, in every situation take the responsibility. You will have leadership consciousness happening in you, *īśvaratva.* Our brains are hardwired to experience higher possibilities and higher consciousness. It is this part that I call as non-mechanical parts of your brain.

Listen! Whether you accept it or not, understand it or not, your body carries at least seventy times more energy and power than what you use in your day-to-day life. Science has proved this through various methods and ways. Just one small alteration in your brain can make you live without food, for months! I am not giving you any fantasy theory. I am giving you the practical experience of hundreds of my disciples who are living this through *nirahara samyama*.

PURIFY YOUR SENSES, WITHOUT A DOUBT REACH ME

If you watch some horror movie continuously for three days, you will start seeing ghosts! Even a screen moving will look like a ghost. Whatever happens around you, you will connect it with the impression of ghosts that was left on your unconscious.

Another thing, ghosts as such don't have a physical body. As ordinary humans, you have three bodies—physical, subtle and causal. Even if spirit bodies exist, they don't have a physical body. Of course, first of all, they don't exist. But for argument's sake, if I collect all of your arguments and if I must argue and accept that they do exist, they exist only in the subtle body and causal body. No ghost comes to you with a physical body except your spouse!

Never allow these horrible things that cause suffering, into your consciousness. If you don't allow these things into your consciousness, your intelligence will automatically be established in the Divine. The thoughts that you take in, play a major role in the expression of your consciousness.

Just take in this one truth that Kṛṣṇa speaks of, 'Establishing your intelligence in Me.' Please understand that whatever you take in as your inputs, you establish your mind only on that. So let your inputs be purified. Let purification of your sensory inputs, happen to you. Your consciousness will automatically be established in the Divine.

Again and again, try to absorb these ideas. Let these ideas penetrate you. Don't go behind ideas that make you feel low and that put you into depression. For example, for the last eleven days you have been listening to these ideas. Now, when a problem arises, you will automatically remember, '*Swamiji* said this. I have heard this idea. I think this is what I must understand now.' This will start arising from your being. The truth will begin to enrich you from within yourself.

If it starts coming up, you have authentically listened to what I have said. Otherwise, you are just a silent listener, a silent listener who is sitting here and seriously thinking of something else or passing judgment on my oratorical skills! Whether you are a silent listener or somebody who really heard the discourse, can only be determined by how much these words get repeated in you.

I tell people that when the source of the words is enlightened consciousness, the words simply penetrate you and automatically come into your mind whenever you need their help.

People ask me, '*Swamiji*, how can we remember these ideas and practice them?' I tell them, 'Never bother remembering them. Just listen, that's enough. These words are from *my* experience. So naturally they will penetrate your being.'

Whenever it is necessary, you won't need to remember these words. The words will remember *you*. Without effort, these words will stay in you and surface. Automatically they will come up when needed. They will erupt into your consciousness, like a pop-up. Similar to the pop-up on your computer monitor, they come up in your consciousness and guide you. You don't need to do anything. All you need to do is authentically listen, as a means to put them into your being. Listen, listen to these words repeatedly. Naturally your consciousness will be established in the Divine.

Kṛṣṇa says, 'Immerse your mind completely in Me. Focus your entire attention upon Me. Without a doubt you will reach the blissful state.'

Practice To Perfection

12.9, 10 *If you are not able to fix your mind upon Me, then O Dhanañjaya (Arjuna), with the constant practice of yoga you try to attain Me. If you are not able to practice even this yoga, then performing your duties and surrendering all your actions to Me, you will attain perfection.*

Here Kṛṣṇa talks about Abhyāsa Yoga. What is Abhyāsa Yoga? Abhyāsa Yoga is the practice or method of yoga of holding the mind constantly in a state of union with Divinity. It is the state of complete immersion in the consciousness of Kṛṣṇa.

Why does Kṛṣṇa speak about Abhyāsa Yoga? In the last chapter, Kṛṣṇa gives Arjuna a glimpse of the universal consciousness, *Viśvarūpa darśan*. However, Arjuna is unable to stay in that state permanently. Arjuna comes out of the experience because of fear or old *saṁskāras*, root thought patterns of past desires. He slips from that state of consciousness. Therefore, Kṛṣṇa speaks about Abhyāsa Yoga, how to establish oneself in that consciousness. That's why He speaks about *abhyāsa,* which means practice.

A Path For Everyone

He gives a solid path, or a solid solution to take care of our whole life, to establish ourselves in that consciousness. Continuously, again and again, in our daily life, let us receive these ideas, intranalyze these ideas in our consciousness and let our inner space be filled with these ideas. Let us not waste a few moments. Let our whole inner space be filled with these great thoughts. That is the way to establish us in that super consciousness.

Kṛṣṇa continues to give more tips for establishing ourselves in that consciousness and radiating devotion. Kṛṣṇa instructs continuously over the next four verses. He gives various options, step-by-step. He says: If we can't do this, do that. If we can't do that, do this.

The first thing He says is, 'Oh Dhanañjaya (winner of wealth), fix your mind upon Me. With constant practice, try to attain Me. If you are not able to practice, then perform actions for Me. In this way, develop the desire to attain Me. '

atha cittaṁ samādhātuṁ na śaknoṣi mayi sthiram I
abhyāsa-yogena tato mām icchāptuṁ dhanañjaya II 12.9

Rāmakṛṣṇa Paramahamsa had advised a lady to meditate upon the form of goddess Kālī. She said that however much she tried she was unable to meditate on Kālī; she was always distracted. She came back to Rāmakṛṣṇa upset that she could make no spiritual progress. Rāmakṛṣṇa enquired whether the lady's attention was diverted to someone or something else. The lady confessed that she was thinking of a young nephew, a child, whom she was fond of. Immediately, Rāmakṛṣṇa advised her, 'Focus your attention on this child whom you love. Meditate upon him.' The lady came back after a few weeks satisfied. Having started her meditation upon the child whom she loved, she could meditate. And once she could meditate, she could transfer her focus to goddess Kālī!

The mind can be trained. What is important is concentration. Once we learn to focus our attention completely on something, single-pointedly, we can train the mind to be like a laser beam. That laser beam can then be transferred to any object with equal facility and success.

Vivekananda has said, 'Once you learn all that there is to be known about a handful of clay by focusing your complete attention on it, you will know about all the clay everywhere in the world.'

Kṛṣṇa refers to completing with the mind through constant practice of meditation, which is part of the yogic path. Meditation is not about sitting down with eyes closed for half an hour every day or every other day or when we get time. Meditation is incessant and obsessive focus upon the Divine. Meditation is a way of life.

Since He knows that we may not be able to lose ourselves in devotion to Him, He offers this as an alternative. 'If the mind cannot be focused on Me,' says the Lord, 'try this. Practice again and again uniting with Me through meditation.' When neither seems possible, Kṛṣṇa offers one more way. 'Do whatever you must. Do your duty as you need to and are able to. But then, surrender what you do to Me. Do what you do for My sake, *mat-karma-paramo bhava.*' By performing whatever we do with total faith in Him, and with a deep feeling of surrender to Him, we reach Him.

abhyāse 'pi asamartho 'si mat-karma-paramo bhava I
mad-artham api karmāṇi kurvan siddhim avāpsyasi II 12.10

Kṛṣṇa implies two things through His statement. First, the results of whatever is done with an attitude of surrender to Him, belong to Him. Our responsibility is to do, and do it well. We have the right to 'doer-ship' not 'owner-ship'. The Lord is the owner of the fruits of actions that we perform on His behalf.

When we learn to do this, we automatically imbibe the concept of non-attachment to the end result. What happens is in His hands, not ours. We then start focusing on the path, not the goal. We focus on the process, not the product. And when we do this, our performance gets better because we no longer are stressed by what the end result might be. We are no longer worried since the outcome is in safe hands. If we travel with this awareness, whatever path we take is the right path. Whatever destination we reach through this right path is the right destination.

When worship becomes a way of life, when spirituality becomes a part of daily life, there is an attitude of surrender to the Divine. One feels intuitively that whatever happens will be for common good and good for oneself. It does not matter if our neighbor has more than what we have. In fact, we rejoice that the neighbor has more than we have. We no longer have expectations of what we hope to get. When surrender happens, there is no end-point that one strives for. Wherever the path leads is the right destination. With focus only on the path and not on the goal, expectations of what may happen drop. Whatever happens is good.

This non-attachment and lack of expectations is the hallmark of a *karma yogi*, one who has surrendered his actions to the Divine.

Kṛṣṇa implies one more thing. He wants us to do His service. He wants us to work on and enrich His mission. He says, 'Engage yourself in activities on My behalf, and you will attain Me, *mad-artham api karmāṇi kurvan siddhim avāpsyasi*.'

I tell people, 'Do not worry about whether I am here physically with you or not. If you chase Me, you will never be one with Me. Work to enrich My mission. In whatever way you can, work on activities that enrich humanity. Work on My behalf. Then, instead of you chasing Me, I shall chase you. I shall always be with you.'

Working on the mission of the Divine is a sure guarantee to reach Divinity.

Work For Me

12.11 If you are not able to work even this way, surrendering unto Me, give up all the results of your actions to Me without ego.

Kṛṣṇa gives various possibilities to Arjuna, one after another. His compassion for Arjuna's spiritual evolution knows no limits. He never gives up on Arjuna. 'If you cannot do this, do that. And if you cannot do that, at least do this,' Kṛṣṇa continues. In the last four verses, He continuously gives options to Arjuna.

Kṛṣṇa says, 'Fix your mind upon Me alone. Live in Me.' Then He felt that He had to give Arjuna an option, in case Arjuna could not succeed. 'If you cannot fix your mind upon Me, steadily practice and practice again,' He advised. He relented further, 'If you cannot do this repetitive practice, if this is too much for you, then work on My mission. Whatever you do, do it for Me.'

Kṛṣṇa now says, 'If you are unable to do even this, which is work for My sake, then just abandon your ego and turn over the results of your actions to Me, *sarva-karma-phala tyāgaṁ tataḥ kuru yatātmavān* (12.11).' Kṛṣṇa relents from His standpoint that Arjuna should work only on those activities that are Kṛṣṇa's. He feels that there may be conditions that may prevent Arjuna from devoting all his time only to those activities that are Kṛṣṇa's.

See how relevant Kṛṣṇa's advice is, even by today's standards. None of us can hope to sit idle and be taken care of. We must do something to occupy ourselves. In our day-to-day reality of life, not all may be able to work on God's mission alone, all the time. We may be able to spend only some time on activities that are selfless activities that benefit humanity overall, and activities that are spiritual. We need to spend a lot of time on activities that are of material benefit to us and to others related to us. Nothing is lost, assures Kṛṣṇa, and He provides the bridge between material pursuits and spiritual pursuits.

Kṛṣṇa brings in the core concept of the Gītā, that of 'renunciation'. He says, 'Do what you must do with an attitude of surrender to Me and sacrifice the results of your actions to Me, with complete control over your self, your ego.'

We feel responsible for the results of our actions. Whether we succeed or fail in what we do, either proud and happy, or guilty and sad, our ego makes us feel responsible. We identify ourselves with what we do and the results of what we do.

Kṛṣṇa says, 'If you cannot do whatever else I have told you to do, do this. Drop your ego. Drop the fruits of your actions and renounce them to Me.'

The freedom that results from what Kṛṣṇa advises is true liberation. Once we realize that we no longer are the masters of our destiny, decision makers of the results of our actions, we feel a weight lifting off our shoulders. It is He who is now responsible for the results of our action. We still are the 'doers', but no longer the 'owners.'

One may wonder, how can I succeed in this rat race? Remember that even if you are the winner in this rat race, you are still only a rat! It is an illusion of our minds that we decide the results of our actions. It is pure fantasy to believe that we decide the result of our actions. We cannot even guarantee that we will survive our next breath. Our life is not in our hands. What arrogance, therefore, to imagine that activities in the outer world are subject to our control! There is a power higher than us that decides the results of our actions. Once we realize this and start believing in the wisdom of that higher power, strange and mystical things happen to us.

We just need to let the Universe, Kṛṣṇa, the Divine, decide what is best for the rest of humanity and us. Let us surrender the results of all that we do to this sacred power. Whatever then happens to us is for the good, for our good and the good of everyone in this Universe. We are surrendering to the cosmic power that surrounds us. Without Its grace we cannot live or take our next breath. Say, '*Do what you think is best for me*' with deep completion and see what happens. Not merely does the end goal materialize, but an immense spiritual relief will overtake you.

'Renounce unto Me,' says Kṛṣṇa, 'surrender yourself to Me, and I shall liberate you.'

Attain Peace

12.12 *Knowledge is better than mere practice. Meditation is superior to knowledge. Renouncing the fruit of actions is better than meditation. After renunciation of fruits of actions, one immediately attains peace.*

Kṛṣṇa gives so many possibilities. Step-by-step, He gives options. Actually, these are not only for Arjuna's mind. These are for all kinds of minds.

Let me tell a small story from Ramaṇa Mahaṛṣi's life:

Somebody goes to him and asks, 'Bhagavān, what spiritual technique should I use?'

He says, 'Do *ātma-vicāra*, Self-inquiry. Start questioning—*Who am I?*'

After a few days, the devotee comes back and says, 'It is difficult to do Self-inquiry, can I just meditate?' Bhagavān says, 'Alright, do meditation.'

After a week, the person returns and says, 'Meditation is also difficult. Can I do *japa*, repetition of *mantra* and recitation of verses?' Bhagavān says, 'Alright, do that.'

A few days pass and he is back again saying, '*Japa* is also difficult. Can I do *pūjā*, the ritual worship?' Bhagavān says, 'Alright. Do *pūjā*.'

Within a week the man is there asking, '*Pūjā* is also difficult. Can I start going only to the temple?' Bhagavān says, 'Alright, do what you want.'

Masters do not want to close the doors for anybody. They do not give up on anybody. Please understand, they give possibilities for everybody. Here, in these verses, Kṛṣṇa deeply enriches giving options to everyone.

We need to have tremendous spontaneity to understand this. Only with spontaneity will we be able to handle these instructions. For example, if you don't feel like meditating and are in a low mood, don't try sitting in a room with closed doors, forcing yourself to meditate. Just go out, go to the temple. Spend some time freely walking and moving around. It will relax you. Then you can enter into meditation. And if you are not able to do that also, do something else. Do something that helps to keep you in a relaxed mood that makes you feel relaxed. Then, you can enter into meditation.

DO SOMETHING ENRICHING

Here, Kṛṣṇa gives step-by-step instructions up to the ultimate and last step. The last step is being in the consciousness, being in bliss. But just because you can't do that, don't stop trying altogether. Don't give up on you. Do something enriching at least.

I have seen people speak about meditation, about *ātma-sādhana* and all sorts of complicated things. But when it comes to practice, just thinking of meditating makes them stop their rituals, everything. In the end they do not even meditate. They say, 'I don't have enough time, *Swamiji*. My mind won't concentrate and I cannot sit quietly.'

First they stop everything in the name of meditation. Then they drop meditation because of other reasons! Then they have neither this nor that. Kṛṣṇa doesn't want that to happen. We need spontaneity to decide what we need and what to do at each moment.

Actually spontaneity is a spiritual quality. Only a man who is not caught in his past, who is able to slip away from his past, can be spontaneous. We can only be spontaneous if we are complete with our past and we don't have a vested interest in our past decisions. If we have vested interests in the past, we may think, 'No, all these years I have lived believing this idea, and understanding things this way. Today just because something is said to me I will not change. I cannot! I am not going to change.' Then we can never be spontaneous and complete! We will miss life and miss it miserably.

The quality of life updates itself. It can be called intelligence only as long as it updates itself. When it stops updating itself, it is intellect. It can no longer be called intelligence. Intelligence is living energy.

The Saṃskṛit word *dhī* means 'that which is alive'. In Saṃskṛit, the word for intelligence is *dhī*. *Dhī* is energy that is alive, which continuously updates itself. In the *Gāyatrī mantra* (the sacred chant) that is central to Hindu worship, we seek to enhance this intelligence-energy when we pray to the Divine.

Only if we don't have a vested interest in our past, in the decisions of our past, or the way in which our past was lived, the way in which we lived our past life (not a different birth, but our life before this moment), will we be spontaneous. Spontaneity is a great spiritual quality.

An incident about spontaneity:

> Once I was giving a discourse on the *Īśāvāsya Upaniṣad*. An elderly person, who looked like a well-read scholar, walked into the hall. After the discourse, without any basic courtesy, he stood up and said, 'All these fools have not read anything, which is why you can make them listen to you. Can you make me listen to you?'
>
> I said, 'Please come nearer Sir. I cannot hear what you are saying.' When he came nearer I said, 'Please come to this side and repeat what you said Sir.' He moved to that side. Then I said, 'I think there is a table in the way, please move to the other side Sir.' He moved and came nearer. Then I said, 'You have already listened to me three times. Now sit and listen to what I have to say!'

You can never escape from spontaneity. After this incident, sometime later, I was reading a book about a similar incident that happened in a Zen master's life. I was surprised to see how history repeats itself! When you have spontaneity, nothing can stop you. Spontaneity is a great spiritual quality.

Here Kṛṣṇa gives four different instructions. Either you can establish yourself in *Bhakti Yoga* – Path of Devotion, or live a regular life of spiritual routine, or sacrifice all the fruits of action to God, or live in consciousness and act. You can do whatever you want.

He says, 'If not this, do this. If not these, then that…' Now all that we need to understand is that we should not limit ourselves at one of the lower levels of Kṛṣṇa's teachings. We should bring authenticity, the space of possibility and always try to move or expand to a higher level. When you can't reach a higher level of authenticity, at least stay at the lower level and keep trying without renouncing all efforts completely. Keep at it. You will be surprised at what happens when you put in your sincere authentic effort.

ULTIMATE FREEDOM

Somebody asked me, '*Swamiji,* why do we have so many gods in India or in the Eastern religions?' All Eastern religions have many gods, whether you consider Hinduism, Buddhism or Jainism. They all have many gods, so many saints and so many gurus, while Western religions have only one God. Why?'

Vivekananda puts it across beautifully in one discourse. Freedom is the basic condition for growth. In any field, if growth has to happen, freedom is the basic condition. In the East they have had inner freedom. No one disturbs your religion here. Spiritual practice is an option. That is why we have the concept of *iṣṭadevatā,* your favorite god. *Iṣṭadevatā* means you can worship whatever form suits your mind.

The scriptures mention 330 million *devatas,* demigods or gods. Actually I think that was probably the size of the population at that time! They wanted each person to have his own customized god. That is why they say 330 million gods! If the scriptures were to be written now, they would say six billion gods. Each one has the freedom to choose their path and one's own god. Each one has the freedom to consider himself as god as he realizes the divinity in himself.

People have inner freedom, which is why the East has grown so much spiritually. In the West, you can't have your own god. In India, anyone can declare himself to be a saint overnight. In the freedom of the East, many good things happen. Tremendous research happened in the inner world because of that freedom. Much research has been done in the inner world and many truths related to the inner world have been brought to light, brought to humanity, because so many people have entered into it. There will always be a few fakes. When so many millions of people take the path, and so many millions of things are expressed, one or two superstitions come about as well.

You may think superstitions exist only in relationship to spirituality. A lot more superstitions exist in science. At least in spirituality the masters do not have any vested interests in declaring something. Nothing significant will be added to their personal lives. They are still going to eat only that much and are going to wear only those few pieces of clothing.

But when it concerns scientists, whatever they declare is going to give them name and fame, money, and additional comfort in their lives. So naturally they have vested interests. With spiritual people, the more they renounce and the less they enjoy the outer world comforts, the more they are respected. So naturally, whatever truths they declare, whatever research they do will not add anything new to their personal lives. The respect they are given is based upon their lives, not their words. With scientists, it is based on their words. So in science, there is a greater possibility for superstitions than in spirituality. And when more and more people take to this spiritual life, there will always be one or two superstitions that result. Just because of this, we can't say that religious freedom or spiritual freedom is wrong. There is a lot of good in it also.

The West has social freedom. You can marry as many times as you want to. You can change your house to your taste. You can change your profession any number of times. You can dress as you wish. Nobody will mind. Even now, I know people in India who obey family traditions, who have not left their family homes. They don't change professions and they don't change lifestyles. In the East, they don't have social freedom. They have spiritual freedom. In the West, they have social freedom but not spiritual freedom. For any growth to happen freedom is a basic necessity.

Here, with these four options, Kṛṣṇa is expressing spiritual freedom for us. He says that there are so many paths, and tells us to choose whichever one suits our mentality, and to practice at least one option. It is not so important which option that we choose. It is essential only that we choose something!

Eastern traditions offer many choices. If you are an intellectual person, then Śiva could be your choice and you can continuously sit and meditate. If you are inclined towards devotion, then Viṣṇu could be your choice. The path includes singing and dancing like the great masters Caitanya. Just sing the glory of the Lord like the Alwars, devotional saints of Tamil Nadu, related with Viṣṇu. If you are inclined towards yoga, if you are a yogi, then Devi is the one for you. Meditate on Her, offer worship and tantric practices.

There are many different kinds of techniques, and the options are many. You have customized ways, customized paths for your personal growth. Thus, naturally wherever one is, one can grow and reach the level one is supposed to reach. You are continuously given choices, given options. Naturally, one tends to take up something or the other.

The East has explored and done much research on the inner space because of spiritual freedom. The West has achieved so much at a social level because of social freedom. Of course, India has struggled because of the lack of social freedom, but it has gained tremendously because of spiritual freedom. Here Kṛṣṇa gives many choices in spiritual freedom. One cannot expect any master, other than the Eastern masters to be so compassionate, concerned, caring, and generous as to give so many enriching possibilities. In the West, the law is compassionate as it gives a lot of options. In the East, the spiritual system is compassionate as it gives a lot of enriching options.

In India, spiritual freedom is given more importance. These four enriching options are representative of the spiritual freedom given to society. Here Kṛṣṇa gives Arjuna the spiritual freedom to choose and of course, not only to Arjuna, but through Arjuna, to all of us.

If you cannot practice the regulations of *Bhakti Yoga,* try to work for Me because by working for Me—*mat-karma paramo bhava*, you will enrich yourself and come to the perfect stage—*kurvan siddhiṁ avāpsyasi* (12.10).

SURRENDER, THE BEST ENRICHING OPTION

Then one by one He gives all enriching options and finally says,

śreyo hi jñānaṁ abhyāsāj jñānād dhyānaṁ viśiṣyate /
dhyānāt karma phala tyāgaḥ tyāgāc chāntir anantaram // 12.12

'If you can't follow these practices to enrich yourself, engage yourself in the cultivation of knowledge.'

He says, 'At least collect all these life solutions.' Cultivation of knowledge means collecting solutions to life's mysteries, such as how to avoid depression, how to be more courageous, how to be strong, how to avoid unwanted desires and how to prevent emotional blocks. This kind of knowledge that you can collect as life solutions can help and protect you.

In the USA, you are taught about earthquate kit, that water bottles and other vital safety things should be a part of the kit. Western society prepares people for these eventualities. But we also need to prepare people to face the earthquakes that happen within, the emotional imbalances that occur within. Just like preparing for an earthquake, one needs to be equipped with an inner earthquake kit. This inner earthquake kit is what I refer to as *'life solutions'* or knowledge.

Collect these things now so that when you face depression, you will be prepared. All of us will face some sort of inner earthquake at some point in time. As long as one is alive, naturally at some point, some friends will die, some relatives will die, or some near and dear ones will fall sick or die. All these things are inevitable.

The inevitability of each moment must be understood. Understanding the inevitability of life and collecting knowledge, collecting the tools, the ideas to support and balance us at those moments, is *jñāna,* knowledge. We need to prepare 'earthquake kits' for our lives. Otherwise we will be unable to recover. The aftermath will be terrible.

The Eastern system continuously prepares people for inner hurricanes and inner earthquakes. *Jñāna* or knowledge is the earthquake kit for the inner space. People are prepared. They do not have to choose between inner and outer spaces. Have an outer earthquake kit in your car, and an inner earthquake kit in your heart. Now, because of the internet, we can have both.

Someone asked me, '*Swamiji,* Buddha enlightened ten thousand people. What is your aim?' I replied, 'Without newspapers or telegrams, without the internet, without airplanes, if Buddha could enlighten ten thousand people, then with all these amenities, we should be able to enrich with enlightenment at least one million people. Only then is it worth having all these amenities.'

Now we can have everything in the inner world and the outer world. We can have an earthquake kit in our cars and an inner earthquake kit in our hearts or inner space. Never take inner earthquakes lightly. Taking inner earthquakes lightly means we are acting out of ignorance. When quakes come in the outer world, we can blame somebody and be rid of the responsibility. But when it comes to the inner world, we can't blame anybody. Each of us must take responsibility for everything happening in and around us.

As Kṛṣṇa says in an earlier chapter:

uddharet ātmanā ātmānaṁ ātmānaṁ avasādhayet **I**
ātmaiva hyātmano bandhuḥ atmaiva ripurātmanaḥ **II** *6.5*

You must help yourself ascend. You must raise yourself by yourself. If you can help yourself ascend, then you are your best friend. Otherwise you are your worst enemy. He gives enriching possibilities, among the different paths like practicing, cultivation of knowledge, meditation or renunciation of the fruits of actions, *karma phala tyāga*.

Among these paths, one is better than the other. First, He mentions that the path of meditation, *dhyāna* is better than knowledge, *jñana*—*jñānād dhyānaṁ viśiṣyate.* Better than meditation is offering everything at the feet of God—*dhyānāt karma phala tyāgaḥ.* He says that by renunciation of the fruits of action one can immediately achieve peace—*tyāgāc chāntir anantaram* (12.12). As long as we think that 'everything is mine,' we suffer. The moment we surrender, the moment we hand the whole thing over to the Divine, inner healing happens. Our inner space experiences the breeze of divine healing.

Often people think that surrender is some sort of loss of control. Giving up is an expression of weakness. Letting go is irresponsibility. Understand that control is an expression of ego. All control arises out of the need for 'I' and 'mine'. Control seeks power. Power corrupts.

Surrender is liberation. Surrender is the expression of choicelessness, of leaving the decision to the Divine after doing what one can do. Unless we let go of our expectations and our attachment to the results of our actions, we will continue to build unproductive stress and incompletions within us that will not raise us to our peak possibility.

When we learn to focus totally on what we need to do and work on the process, without worrying about the destination, whatever we do is done better, faster and more effectively. Kṛṣṇa's teaching is not merely spiritual. It is highly practical. It is not only after-life enhancing, but it is present-life enabling.

He says that for the person who renounces the fruits of action, eternal peace is the immediate result, *yāgāc chāntir anantaram* (12.12). When we renounce ownership to what we do and hand over the ownership to the Divine, peace and bliss descend upon us. There is true liberation in giving up attachment to the results of what we do. This liberation comes from not having expectations of any kind. We are detached from the results of our actions. That allows us to focus totally on what we have in hand, in the present moment of completion. Staying in the space of completion is peace, bliss, liberation, or *mokṣa*.

He Is Very Dear To Me

12.13,14 *One who has no dislike or envy for any being, who is friendly and compassionate to everyone, free from the sense of I and mine, the ego, maintains equanimity of mind both in joy and sorrow, forgiving, ever satisfied, united with Yoga, has a strong commitment to Me and has fixed his mind and intellect upon Me, such a devotee of Mine is very dear to Me.*

In all the previous verses, Kṛṣṇa tells Arjuna to do this or do that. Now, He is not saying do this or do that.

He says, 'Those who do all these things are very dear to Me. If you don't do these, that too is okay. However, if you *do* them, you will be very dear to Me—*yo mad-bhaktaḥ sa me priyaḥ.*' In other words, it is emotional black mail, not directly but indirectly, but all for a good cause!

'One who is not envious, but is a kind friend to all living entities, who does not think of himself as a proprietor, and who is free from false ego, who is equal in both happiness and distress, who is tolerant, always satisfied, self-controlled, and engaged in devotional service with determination, with intelligence fixed on Me, such a devotee of Mine is very dear to Me.'

adveṣṭā sarva bhūtānāṁ maitraḥ karuṇa eva ca I
nirmamo nirahaṅkāraḥ sama-duḥkha-sukhaḥ kṣamī II 12.13

santuṣṭaḥ satataṁ yogī yatātma dṛḍha-niścayaḥ I
mayy arpita mano-buddhir yo mad bhaktaḥ sa me priyaḥ II 12.14

Important Qualities Of Enriching

Understand here, He says, 'Who is not envious and a kind friend to every living entity.' These are important qualities. Let us analyze our minds. When we honestly analyze our mind, we realize that if somebody came to you and told you he loved you, you wouldn't believe it. The first thing you would do is figure out what he wants from you. You don't believe you are worthy of being loved. Next, you don't believe that somebody can honestly love you, because you don't love anybody honestly. Because you are calculative, you expect the other person also to be calculating. All our love is skin deep and you know how deep skin is!

Here, He says, 'A person who is a kind friend of everyone, who honestly serves, feels the friendliness in everybody and is free from false ego.'

Now we should understand the term 'false ego, *ahaṁkāra*'. Ego not only means showing what you don't have, but also hiding what you have.

There are two types of ego: active ego and passive ego. Active ego is showing what you have and passive ego is characterized by these kinds of thoughts, 'Oh, what can I do, I am a simple person, I cannot achieve anything, and I cannot do anything.' Hiding oneself is an outcome of the passive ego. An inferiority complex is a manifestation of the passive ego.

At least there is one positive point regarding the superiority complex. With a feeling of superiority, wherever one goes, one gets a big beating from society. But with inferiority complex, society does not attempt to correct you. It is a cunning way of hiding yourself from life. You will not even know that you have a problem. A person who looks for name and fame, and a person who doesn't want name and fame are both egoistic. If you ask for name, you are egoistic. And if you don't, it shows passive ego. Whereas a person who lets things happen and a person who allows things to flow, lives in reality.

Kṛṣṇa makes a comment, 'After all, who is going to know who you are? Why do you think you are a big person and your name is so great and that everybody knows your name? You think you are great, that is why you don't want name and fame. Nobody knows your name, relax.' Kṛṣṇa says clearly. Nobody knows our name. Asking for name and fame and saying, 'I don't want name and fame,' are different aspects of ego, different varieties of ego. The inferior ego is also ego, which is why he says 'false ego'. You are not only supposed to be free from ego, you are supposed to be free from false ego as well. You shouldn't hide yourself in inferiority complexes.

A small story:

> A master tells a disciple, 'Please press my feet.'
>
> The disciple says, 'Oh, I am a sinner, how can I touch Your feet?' He does not want to do it because he is lazy. So he says, 'I am a great sinner. I am impure. How can I touch Your feet; how can I do that?'
>
> Later, a devotee brought fruits and prasād, offerings. The master put a little in his mouth and left the rest. The next day, he saw nothing on the plate.
>
> He asked his disciple, 'What happened to the fruits and prasād?'
>
> The disciple answered, 'It was *guru prasād,* offering to the master. I could not let it go for a waste. I finished the whole thing because it was *guru prasād*.'

Look at the mind, how nicely it handles different situations! Wherever we want, we insert whatever is convenient.

The moment you understand the futility of your goal and wealth, that nothing is going to be with you forever, all of these divine qualities radiate through your being. You will be transformed into a person who is established in forgivingness, who maintains equanimity of mind, who is satisfied and united with yoga. Actually, when you are blissful inside, you radiate these qualities. A man who is totally blissful inside radiates pleasantness for absolutely no reason.

We continuously carry a sense of slight irritation in our being; we are waiting to pounce on people. We don't know what we are doing. We jump and bite people at the slightest provocation, because we carry some irritation pattern within us. We continuously vomit upon others the suffering and misery that we feel. This irritation pattern arises within us out of constant worry, inner chatter because of incompletions. We feel we may not get what we are planning for and what we want. Worry arises as a result of the gap between what we expect and what we think we are capable of getting.

Worry is futile because there are many factors other than our capability that determine the outcome of what we do. We cannot control even our own breath. We cannot say with certainty whether we will take the next breath. What arrogance it is then to think that we can determine our future or the outcome of our actions!

Worry and irritation are pointless and make you powerless. Worry, anxiety and irritation dissolve once we settle into the present, the space of completion. Only in the present are we in a position to influence our actions and the immediate outcome of those actions. When we settle into the present, thoughts cease and worry and irritation disappear. We realize how irrelevant, unproductive and inauthentic worry is. Only how consciously you live, with what consciousness you choose to live remains with you. Only the consciousness of completion remains with you. When you understand the importance of your state of being, you automatically start radiating pleasantness and joy.

Meditation For Devotion

I give people a simple meditation technique to experience *Bhakti Yoga*–the Path of Devotion. Just practice the technique of radiating pleasantness and friendliness. How does one do it? From morning till night whenever you remember, inhale, inhale, and inhale only the pleasant qualities of bliss. Visualize you are inhaling bliss and exhaling bliss. Your whole being will be filled with joy. In the beginning you will be visualizing, imagining. But in a few days you will realize it is your quality.

One more thing you should know is that imagination and visualization are two different things. Imagination translates into *kalpanā* in Saṃskṛit, while visualization translates into bhāvanā. Bhāvanā is different from kalpanā. Kalpanā means imagining things that are not there. For example, if you think of an elephant with ten trunks, that is imagination, *kalpanā,* that which is not there. But *bhāvanā* means visualizing that which is present but maybe eluding you.

If you sit during the day and visualize stars in the sky, that is not imagination. It is visualization. Because stars are in the sky even though you are unable to see them. So visualizing stars is not imagination. Perceiving what is there but what you are unable to see at this moment is visualization. Trying to perceive what can never exist is imagination.

So understand that meditating on gods and goddesses is not imagination. It is visualization. They are there. You cannot see them; that is all. You are supposed to fall in tune with them, like tuning your television. Similarly, visualization is tuning yourself. Just continuously visualize inhaling and exhaling bliss. Visualise *prāṇa* – the life giving energy—going inside and coming out. *Prāṇa* is energy and bliss. *Prāṇa* is not merely air. *Prāṇa* is the energy that goes through air. For example, a truck comes up to your house and unloads luggage and leaves. The truck is air and the luggage is *prāṇa.* Using air as a medium, *prāṇa* enters. *Prāṇa-śakti* is the subtle part of air. *Prāṇa-śakti* is bliss energy, *ānanda-śakti.*

So whenever you inhale, visualize yourself inhaling bliss. When you exhale, visualize yourself exhaling bliss. Inhale light and exhale light. Think that your whole body is a beanbag filled with light. Imagine your body is a beanbag filled with bliss and light. You will automatically start radiating bliss instead of irritation. Instead of vomiting the poison of anger and jealousy on others, you will radiate love and bliss.

'Such a devotee of mine is very dear to Me, *yo mad-bhaktaḥ sa me priyaḥ.*' Kṛṣṇa says that if somebody lives in this manner, that devotee is close to Him. He doesn't say 'Do or don't do.' He does not want to make more rules. He is tired of making rules. He has reached a point where his attitude is, 'If you can, do it, otherwise, what can be done?' He is in a relaxed mood.

I think this happens to all masters. After some time they say, 'Alright, do whatever you want, what can be done?' They can guide or show you only to a certain extent. Beyond that if masters persist, people start thinking that the masters have some vested interest in making people enlightened. Understand, they just share to enrich with what they have, out of completion, joy and bliss.

You are not ready to trust the Master. You keep resisting Him. When the Master says drop 'I and mine,' people are afraid that the Master may pick them up and take it with him! People are suspicious. That is why Masters sometimes say, 'This is the right way, but do as you want to do.'

'One who has fixed his mind and intellect upon me, *mayy arpita mano buddhir* (12.14),' says Kṛṣṇa. It is difficult for the devotee and disciple to have this attitude of surrender to the Master or the Universe. As long as things go the way the person wants, as long as the Master allows the devotee to do what he wishes, the Master is a great master and worthy of celebration. But once the Master turns serious and takes up his responsibility of spiritual surgery on the disciple, he wants to run away.

I tell people, 'Decide well in advance whether I am your right Master or not.' A Master takes his responsibilities seriously. His major responsibility is surgery; it is the surgery of the cancer of ego. Once the disciple makes a commitment, the Master makes his commitment too. It is dangerous to run away from the operating table. You lose your whole life by running away. You may have to wait many births before you get another chance.

Here, Kṛṣṇa is in the same mood and He says, 'Such a devotee of Mine is dear to Me,' that's all. He is talking about the commitment that the devotee makes to Him. He says, 'One who makes that commitment to Me and fixes his mind and intellect upon Me, he is dear to Me and will be liberated.' So says the great Master of the Universe.

Be Unaffected

12.15 *He, by whom the world is not affected adversely, and who in turn does not affect the world adversely, and he, who is free from joy, anger and anxiety, he is dear to Me.*

Kṛṣṇa says, 'He who is not affected adversely or agitated by the world and who in turn does not affect or cause agitation in this world, is dear to Him.'

yasmān nodvijate loko lokān nodvijate ca yaḥ |
harṣāmarṣa bhayodvegair mukto yaḥ sa ca me priyaḥ || 12.15

Only the person who is centered on his being, centered on the Ultimate consciousness, does not create havoc in the world. Just by being in the presence of an enlightened person, our minds calm down. We become steady. I can say that not only is the world not adversely affected by such persons, the world is blessed by their presence.

Once a person realizes that they are one with the Divine and all of Existence, how can there be any fight? How can there be any drama? There can't be! There is only the experience of intense love and compassion on its own and towards all beings. How can there be any small enjoyments or agitations when someone is continuously experiencing eternal bliss? It is impossible. For the enlightened one, it has all become a divine play, a *līlā*. And He sees that the play exists in Him and not that He exists in the play.

From Incompletions to Core of Completion

Here Kṛṣṇa is saying that the persons who are expressing from their core, unaffected by the happenings around them, are dear to Him because they are centered on Him—*mukto yaḥ sa ca me priyaḥ.*

For most of us, that isn't the case. We live on the periphery of our incomplete personalities and make a mess of things creating more and more incompletions wherever we go. To most of us, joy is a period between experiences of sorrow and unhappiness. It is like a period of quiet between two battles that we call peace, just as impermanent and just as unreal.

Joy and temporal pleasure from sensory experiences invariably lead to sorrow. Joy is the by-product of fulfillment, of an expectation. When the expectation is fulfilled the first time, we feel happy. Most likely, this may not happen the next time around. So instead of joy, sorrow follows.

Joy can only be experienced internally if it is to be long lasting. Such joy is more accurately called bliss. Bliss is eternal, unlike joy, which is transient. Bliss is eternal. It arises when we drop expectation, when we stay centered on our being, when we are in the space of completion, the mood and mode of non-attachment.

When Kṛṣṇa refers to a state of not being in joy, He refers to this temporary transient joy, which is a by-product of our desires, the joy that comes and goes. It is powered by our illusions and fantasies. Only when one goes beyond this joy with its peaks and valleys can one truly reach a blissful state. Both joy and sorrow must be transcended for us to experience bliss.

If we close our eyes and try to focus on an object or event, after a few seconds we see that we can't continue. No thought or idea can control our inner space eternally. Always there is another thought that comes along to replace the last thought. This is the inner chatter of our mind. Buddha refers to it as the 'monkey mind.'

This chatter is the constant jumping of our mind between past and future. It is the journey that our mind undertakes between what it has experienced and stored as incomplete memories and the unknown, which is full of expectations and speculations, also based upon the past. This jumping, this journey, is what we call thoughts.

Anxiety builds as our ego realizes that what it desires may not happen. This loss of something that has not even happened, the product of pure speculation, causes intense emotions within us. Anxiety lives and breeds in thoughts about the future. Its source is our ego. Ego creates expectations. Expectations related to 'I' and 'mine', 'identity' and 'possession' create the fear that what is expected may not happen. To move out of anxiety, we must move into the present moment of completion. That is the only point at which our inner chatter stops and anxiety disappears.

When Kṛṣṇa says, 'He who is without anxiety will reach Me,' He says that he who is in the present moment will reach Me. In the present moment our thoughts cease and we are in the space of completion, and we can see with clarity the truth of our Existence, Kṛṣṇa consciousness, and then we are one with Him.

'Let go of anger,' says Kṛṣṇa. 'He who is without anger shall reach Me.' By the literal understanding of this verse, none of us can reach Kṛṣṇa. All of us express anger at one time or another. Anger is a positive energy. Expressing anger can be positive, both for the person expressing the anger and the one receiving it. This may sound strange but it is true.

Anger is often the product of guilt. We move into a defensive position. We feel guilty when we realize we did wrong. But instead of completing with that action, we become angry. In a sense, this anger is also directed at ourselves. The guilt we feel is the result of the internal rage against our own weakness. Guilt is the biggest sin we commit. Whatever we do at a point in time, we do with the knowledge and awareness we possess at that time. Once we have done what we have done, there is nothing within our power to change it.

When we let go of guilt, then we can let go of our suppressed emotions of anger, regret, defensiveness and the internal fury. People who appear calm on the surface, controlling the anger that they feel without expressing it, are sitting on a time bomb. Either it can explode unexpectedly causing grave danger to themselves and others, or it can lead to self-destruction through cancer. It is perfectly possible.

We should learn to direct anger at issues and take responsibility for the issue rather than directing anger at people. When anger rises against people, divert it to issues instead of towards a person. The person is only the perceived cause as you see it. Anger breeds anger. It is a vicious cycle. If however, we express anger and express it fully against the incident, event, or issue, without personalizing it, we can let go of that anger without harm to others and us. It is possible. You need to practice, that's all. When the emotive memory of that anger is expressed, the memory dissolves and we experience completion with that emotion. Over a period of time, the anger disappears even before it rises. Kṛṣṇa says that one must reach this 'state beyond anger' in order to be able to reach Him.

Selfless In Action

12.15 *He, by whom the world is not affected adversely, and who in turn does not affect the world adversely, and he, who is free from joy, anger and anxiety, he is dear to Me.*

12.16 *He who is free from wants, who is pure and skilled, unconcerned, untroubled, who is selfless in whatever he does, he who is devoted to Me, he is dear to Me.*

Kṛṣṇa now moves into higher gear. Once you let go of joy, anxiety and anger, once you transcend these emotions, you reach a state of calmness that takes you close to Him. Now, He moves from '*nissaṇgatvaṁ*' to '*nirmohatvaṁ*,' from emotional non-attachment to non-attachment to desires.

We need to understand the difference between 'wants' and 'needs'. Needs are necessary for us to survive on planet Earth, like the basic needs of food, shelter, etc. The great Jain master Māhāvira says, 'The moment you are born on this planet, the Universe sends everything with you that you need.' We just need to trust the Universe and we shall get what we need to live. We shall not want anything else.

However, we end up seeking more. Basic needs are no longer enough. Everything we have is a match for what others have. It is a constant cycle of 'What next? What next?' Even before we start enjoying what we have got, we make a plan to get more. There is no joy in having, the joy is in chasing. There is no end point to this chase.

When you become the richest in your family, you need to become the richest on the street and then the richest in the town, then the richest in the country and then the richest in the world. There is no end. Wants are endless. Wants are suffering. Wants are born out of comparison with others. Needs, our basic needs, carry the energy within them for fulfillment. Wants only carry the seeds of our own suffering.

During our *Nithya Kriya Yoga* Program, or LBP Level 2, we take participants through the seven layers of the energy bodies that the spirit passes through when we die. In this process, the departing spirit remembers all that happened during its time in the body until the point of death. It is like a fast replay of all that has happened, every incident that is stored on the hard disk of our memory.

In one of the sessions, I ask people to make a list of their desires, their needs and wants. They fill pages with it. I ask them to review the list many times. Then they do a meditation process. At the end of the meditation, I ask them to recollect from memory their list of desires. What they can recollect is usually a fraction of what they have written. It is as if they started with a large tree full of leaves, their desires, and during this meditation the tree shed almost all its leaves, as if the leaves were dry and dead. What it retained glowed like golden leaves.

Whatever is left in their memories, those desires glow like gold. They are the ones that carry the energy for their fulfillment! These desires are the true desires that they carry. If the process is done with awareness, these desires are always selfless desires. They may enrich the individual, no doubt, but they always enrich humanity. Only such selfless desires carry the energy of the Universe with them for fulfillment.

When our desires are our own true desires, when they reflect our real needs, when they express themselves in our inner energy, we don't feel any desperation about trying to achieve them. The realization comes that, as a matter of the natural course of events, these desires will be fulfilled. We are not driven and we are not troubled. We accept that these will happen.

Therefore, Kṛṣṇa counsels Arjuna, 'Become free from wants, be selfless and you shall be untroubled, liberated and you will reach Me.'

Beyond Love And Hate

12.17 *He who does not rejoice or hate or who does not grieve or desire, and who renounces both good and evil and who is full of devotion, he is dear to Me.*

Kṛṣṇa now goes into another level of controlling the mind. He now refers to one who does not love or hate—*yo na harṣyati na dveṣṭi.* He is not talking about not loving anyone. When we love the way we do, with conditionality and expectations, it works well as long as these expectations are fulfilled. When something does not work the way we wish it to, the love disappears like a dewdrop in the sun. In its place, hate appears.

Hatred and love are opposite sides of the same coin as long as love is conditional. Love can flip into hatred in a moment, the moment we feel that our expectations are threatened. In love of this type, there is external rejoicing, sharing of joy and happiness and public expression of happiness as long as the emotion remains.

Often, love or what we believe is love is related to time and space. So long as the distance is large and the time of contact is minimal we see a few defects in those we profess to love. Once we get closer and spend more time, we see the real picture. It can also convert love into hatred. To transcend love and hatred which are two different expressions of the same perceived reality, we need to drop expectations. We need to develop a sense of non-attachment. We need to be complete in our love.

We all go through several stages of relationships in our lifetime. As children, we are totally dependent upon parents. Our parents influence us and our love for our parents is conditional. We love them only because there is no option. To survive, a child must depend upon its parents. As we grow into adolescence, we question many things we took for granted as an infant or a child; therefore, teenagers rebel. They wish to be independent. They break rules.

In adulthood, we learn that to survive and coexist, we need to follow societal rules and regulations. We develop skills to get along with others. We learn to work and relate with others. Otherwise, we may become misfits in society. The single most important lesson that people learn in adulthood is that it is important to relate with people meaningfully.

As we grow and mature, and the spirit and its development become important, we seek guidance. We look for a Master. With the Master, the relationship is the reverse of what we started with as a child. We are once again concerned about survival, but it is the survival of the spirit and not the mind or body. To help in this survival of the spirit, the relationship that we need with the Master is one of absolute dependence once again, but with a difference. For the relationship to work, it now needs to be totally unconditional and based upon deep trust.

The only relationship that will work with the Master is total and unconditional love out of completion. It is absolute surrender. Surrender transcends love and hate. When one is in a mood of total surrender to the Master or the Divine, both being one and the same, the concept of good and evil, sin and merit disappear.

In a spiritual sense, there is nothing that is a sin. No one is sitting up there with a notebook and pencil and deciding whether we should go to hell or heaven by measuring our sins. There is no hell or heaven. Hell and heaven are not geographical. They are psychological, within our mind. We commit sins because we are already in our own hell. We do well to others when we are in our space of heaven or bliss.

Kṛṣṇa breaks the mold. He tells us, 'Go beyond good and evil, *śubha-aśubha parītyāgī* (12.17).' He says this because there is no such thing as good and evil. It is all in our mind. When we understand this truth we are in His realm. That's His promise.

This Is Whom I Love

12.18,19 *One who treats friends and enemies the same, who faces in the same manner honor and dishonor, heat and cold, happiness and sorrow, fame and infamy;*
One who is always free from attachment, always silent and satisfied with anything, without a fixed home, who is fixed in mind and who is devoted to Me, such a person is very dear to Me.

12.20 *Those who truly follow this imperishable path of righteousness with great faith, making Me the supreme goal, are very dear to Me.*

Again Kṛṣṇa says, 'Such a person, full of devotion is dear to Me—*bhaktimān me priyo naraḥ* (12.19).'

He is not ready to put down any more rules, which means He is almost ending His instructions. He is almost saying, 'This is the way, if somebody is like this then I love him, that's all. I am not interested in anything else.'

He says, 'One who is neutral towards friends and enemies, who is the same in honor and dishonor, heat and cold, joy and pain, free from attachment to the fruits of action, who remains the same in criticism and praise; who is thoughtful, who is content with whatever he gets, who does not care for any house and is resolute in mind, such a man, full of devotion is very dear to Me.'

samaḥ śatrau ca mitre ca   tathā mānāpamānayoḥ /
śītoṣṇa-sukha-duḥkheṣu   samaḥ saṅga-vivarjitaḥ // 12.18

tulya nindā-stutir maunī santuṣṭo yena kenacit |
aniketah sthira matir bhaktimān me priyo naraḥ || 12.19

Here is a beautiful phrase, 'One who does not care for any house and who doesn't bother to build a house for himself, *aniketah sthira matir.*'

Let me tell you a story.

> Rāvaṇa lived for one *kalpa* (many thousands of years). Śrī Vyāsa lived for four *kalpas*. Rāvaṇa was building Lankāpuri, his capital in Śrī Lanka. He got Lankāpuri as a gift from Śiva and he was developing it.
>
> When Vyāsa came to the city, Rāvaṇa asked him, 'Oh Vyāsa, did you see my palace, and my country? How grand they look.'
>
> Vyāsa replied, 'Yes, I have seen them.'
>
> Rāvaṇa showed him everything with pride and asked, 'Why don't you build a house for yourself?'
>
> Vyāsa smiled and said, 'My life is just four *kalpas*. I have no time to waste building houses. After all, I am going to live here for only four *kalpas*, why should I waste time building houses?'

Rāvaṇa lived for only one *kalpa*, for which he built such a big house. Śrī Vyāsa whose life was four times as long, thought it was unnecessary to waste part of his life building houses!

'One who is not concerned about owning a house is full of devotion and he is near to Me, dear to Me.' Kṛṣṇa concludes this chapter on *Bhakti Yoga,* Union through Devotion, saying that one who lives in *dharma*, righteousness is devoted to Him.

ye tu dhamāmṛtam idaṁ yathoktaṁ paryupāsate |
śraddhadhānā mat-paramā bhaktās te 'tīva me priyāḥ || 12.20

Dharma is spiritual righteousness. It is not, and has nothing to do with rules and regulations laid down by society and religion. Human tendency is always to break rules. Societal rules seem to restrict one's freedom of expression and movement.

Understand that you are no sinner! Divinity resides within us. Our only sin, the original sin, is in not recognizing that we are divine. Therefore we don't need to strive to attain enlightenment. We just need to become aware of our inner divinity. In this modern age, the path of *dharma*, righteousness that Kṛṣṇa talks about leading to Him, is the path of meditation. When we follow meditation, one automatically gets into the virtuous circle of conscious awareness and completion that takes us to Kṛṣṇa consciousness.

Meditation is a process of shutting the mind down by completing with all root thought patterns of the mind. In this process of reaching the no-mind state, the ego drops. The barrier to the realization that our true nature is divine disappears. We become who we are. We realize we are complete. We realize we are one with the Divine.

Let us pray to the ultimate energy, *Parabrahma* Kṛṣṇa, to make us all experience the truths of *Bhakti Yoga*, that love is our very life. Let us pray to Him to give us the conscious experience of *bhakti,* devotional love, and make us experience and radiate eternal bliss, *Nityānanda*.

Thank You.

*Thus ends the twelfth chapter named **Bhakti Yogaḥ**, 'Union through Devotional Love,' of the **Bhagavad Gītā Upaniṣad, Brahmavidyā Yogaśāstra**, the scripture of yoga dealing with the science of the Absolute in the form of **Śrī Kṛṣṇārjuna saṃvād**, dialogue between Śrī Kṛṣna and Arjuna.*

CHAPTER

13

Kṣetra Kṣetrajña Vibhāga Yogaḥ

THE FIELD AND THE KNOWER OF THE FIELD

YOU ARE A WAVE IN THE OCEAN OF EXISTENCE. WHEN THE WAVE UNDERSTANDS THAT IT IS NOT SEPARATE FROM THE OCEAN, IT DROPS ITS RESISTANCE AND MERGES WITH THE OCEAN.

The Field And The Knower Of The Field

In this chapter, Kṛṣṇa speaks to enrich Arjuna about *kṣetra* (Field) and *kṣetrajña* (Knower of the Field). This chapter is known as the *Kṣetra Kṣetrajña Vibhāga Yoga,* or the yoga of discrimination of the *kṣetra*, the field, and *kṣetrajña,* the knower of the field.

Kṛṣṇa clearly talks about the physical matter in which we exist, as well as the consciousness that stays in the matter. In some way or other all of us are related to this whole universe, whether we understand it or not, whether we experience it or not. The consciousness is the root cause. It is not only the origin, but also the cause. It is the source from which we come and in which we stay. The whole Universe, the Universal consciousness, is the space in which we all happen.

Kṛṣṇa uses the wave and the ocean as an analogy. The ocean is the Universal consciousness or god, *ātma* or whatever we may call it. Buddhists use the word *Nirvāṇa*, Vedantis say *Brahman*. Kṛṣṇa reveals the secret that we are like the waves, and the whole is the ocean. He explains how we can experience completion and infinity with the ocean.

Our only problem in life is that somehow we have forgotten that we are a part of the ocean. We forgot that we belong to the *kṣetrajña*. The word *kṣetrajña* means consciousness, which is the cause for the field to function. *Kṣetra* means field and *kṣetrajña* means knower of the field. *Kṣetra* means body and *kṣetrajña* means the consciousness that knows it has a body. Our consciousness is *kṣetrajña* and our body or matter is *kṣetra*.

In this chapter, Kṛṣṇa reveals the secrets of *kṣetra* and *kṣetrajñya*. If we don't know the secrets of *kṣetrajña*, the *kṣetra* acts as if it is the owner.

Getting Into the Body and Mind

A small example: You buy a new car. You sit in the car and start driving. Suddenly, after ten minutes you realize that you do not know how to stop it. If you don't know how to stop the car, you are not driving the car, the car is driving you.

In the same way, we get into this mind and into this body and start living. Suddenly at one point, we find that we are unable to stop the body or mind. It goes on as it wants and it is uncontrollable.

Bring the body and mind under your conscious awareness. The body and mind are good servants but not good masters. As servants, they are great. Of course, without the body and mind you cannot live life, you cannot enjoy life. They are needed. But, unless they are under your control, they will become your masters.

Only two options are possible: Either you enjoy them or they enjoy you. In the beginning you may start smoking. After some time, you may not really be enjoying the smoke, but the smoke will be enjoying you. Similarly, in the beginning you may start drinking alcohol. After some time, the alcohol will be drinking you. In the beginning you start a habit and after some time that habit takes over your life. The habit will be enjoying *your* life. Then you are no longer a person with choices: You are a set of habits that is continuously repeated without your control.

When we start using a car without reading the owner's manual, suddenly we realize that we do not know where the hand brake is. We don't know how to turn left or right. When we enter into the body and mind without knowing how to handle them, we are in the same situation. Bring the body and mind under your control before you are brought under their control.

Whether it is a material life or a spiritual life, unless the body and mind are under our control, whatever we may think or whatever we want to do is of no use. Suppose we sit down in the morning and draw out a big plan for the day, analyzing all the data, 'I must do this,' 'I must do that,' but at the end of the day, beyond our control, we spontaneously indulge in a drink and sleep or do other things, what is the use of the whole day's plan? Nothing! We go on creating what we want to do in our mind, but at the end of the day, the body behaves the way it wants to. Even the mind behaves as it wants to. We get nowhere!

'Life,' the very word 'life,' can happen only when the body and mind are under your control. As long as the body and mind are not under your control, you will not even experience the word 'life.' Until the body and mind are under your control, you are not living. Only the root thought patterns or the engraved memories are living you. Unless you find your root thought patterns and complete, *life* does not start for you.

Until we experience the *kṣetrajña*, the knower of the field, the real life never begins. This is why the vedic system considers a person to be born only when his individual consciousness is awakened. Until then his physical birth is not accepted, nor is he considered a human being or a *manusya*. According to the *Vedas*, when someone's inner consciousness is awakened he is considered a human being or a person who has taken birth. Until then he is one among the animals.

The Saṃskṛit word *manuṣya* has two meanings. One is 'descendant of Manu,' and the other is 'the man who can handle the mind or one who has gone beyond the mind.' Manu is supposed to be our first forefather. Only when we can handle the mind, we become *manuṣya.* In Saṃskṛit they say, '*pratyagātma caitanya jāgrataṁ.*' It means that only when the individual consciousness is awakened is one considered to be a person.

In the Indian Vedic system, when a child turns seven he is initiated into the Gāyatrī, a sacred *mantra* or chant. You should understand one important thing here. The Vedic religion, or Hinduism, the integrated *sanātana-dharma,* is the only religion in which there is no enslaving or encaging or engaging philosophy. You are not given any faith, any concept and any philosophy; you are only enriched to awaken your highest possibility, your consciousness. You are not asked to believe in anything. You are just given a technique to do completion with your body and mind. That's all.

The first thing that our *Ṛṣis* or ancient Indian Enlightened Masters want us to do is to bring our body and mind under our control with the power of completion. They want us to learn how to live in completion with our body and mind. The *Gāyatrī mantra* is like an owner's manual for the body and mind. If we have a car, an owner's manual is a basic need. Without reading the owner's manual, if we start driving a car, then whose mistake is it?

Only at around the age of seven do we start to handle our body. After the age of seven the intellect starts working and we start making decisions. The moment we start making decisions, we should first know how to bring the body and mind under control. That is why the *Vedic* Masters teach the completion technique to awaken the inner intelligence and to master the consciousness. It is similar to reading the owner's manual before using the car.

What You Know Is Not You

13.1 *Arjuna says:*
O Keśava, I wish to know and understand
about prakṛti and puruṣa, passive and active energies.
The field [kṣetra] and the knower of the field [kṣetrajña],
and of knowledge [jñānaṁ] and of the end of knowledge [jñeyaṃ].

13.2 *Bhagavān Kṛṣṇa replies:*
This body, O Kaunteya, is called the field, kṣetra. Anyone who knows this body is called the knower of the field, kṣetrajña.

13.3 *O Bhārata, know that I am the Knower in all bodies [kṣetrajñā], the Creator. In my opinion, knowledge means the understanding of this body or the field of creation as well as the Creator, one who knows this field.*

Kṛṣṇa explains, 'O Kaunteya (son of Kuntī), O Arjuna, this body is called the field, *kṣetra*; the person who knows this body is called the knower of the field or *kṣetrajña*.'

śrī bhagavān uvāca
idaṁ śarīraṁ kaunteya kṣetram ity adhidhīyate |
etad yo vetti taṁ prāhuḥ kṣetrajña iti tad-vidaḥ || 13.1

Whatever you know is not you. If you know something, it is not you. For instance, you can read this book because it is separate and apart from you. Similarly, if you can know your body, then it is not you. If you can know your mind, then it is not you. If you can know your thoughts, then they are not you. Whatever you know is not you. You are separate from that or above that. That is why you are able to know it. Whether it is the body, thoughts or emotions, whatever you know is not you.

Now we need to separate these two, the field from the knower of the field. Once we separate these two, the body will be complete, blissful and joyful! Consciousness will be liberated. When these two join, that is where the problem starts.

A one-liner that I read somewhere said: A man tells his friend, 'My sign is earth and my wife's sign is water. Together we make mud!'

Water and earth are beautiful as they are. Only when they are mixed do we get mud!

Similarly, consciousness, as it is, is beautiful and so is the body. When the two meet, that is where the trouble of incompletions starts. All we need to do is understand and create the right cognition about the field and the knower, that is, what *we are* and what *we are not*. The problem in our lives is that when we identify ourselves with something, we believe we are that. Instead of understanding that we possess a mind, we believe we are the mind. The mind then becomes 'I'.

As long as I think this table is mine, there is no problem. If I start thinking that I am this table, the problem starts! As long as we think that our body and mind are ours, there is no problem. But the problem appears the moment we identify with them. Kṛṣṇa says, 'We must understand that whatever we know is not us.' Inch by inch He starts to explain the difference between *kṣetra* and *kṣetrajña*.

When we understand that something is separate from us, we never feel that we must renounce it. We simply need to renounce the inadequate cognition that we are that particular thing, that's all. We will simply know that there is nothing to renounce just by being aware of the way in which our body or mind works. Neither will we feel tortured by them, nor will we feel like torturing them. The people who are tortured by the body and mind are caught in this world and its troubles. Another group of people continuously torture the body and mind in the name of *tapas*, penance.

I have seen people in India practicing yoga by sitting or standing on nails for five years! There are people who torture the body by standing on one leg, rolling on the ground or walking on fire. There is no need to torture the body in such ways. Actually we torture the body because we think that it is torturing us. We take revenge. At one extreme, people are caught in pleasures of the senses and killing themselves. At the other extreme, people torture the body in the name of penance. Neither knows how to handle the body and mind.

A person who knows how to handle his body and mind enjoys the whole thing. He is totally at ease with himself. He feels completely relaxed with his body and mind. He intensely enjoys all pleasures and comforts and he never abuses the body.

Enjoying and abusing are two different things. Enjoying is when the mind and the body are in tune with each other. We feel ease, comfort, a deep sense of relaxation and a feeling of being at home with ourselves. Another category of people tortures the body for the sake of the mind, in the name of penance or *tapas*. These people are in search of peace and bliss. They go on disrespecting and torturing the body: going without food for months together, standing on one leg, or walking on fire. They continuously abuse the body or mind in one way or the other.

Torturing others happens when we torture ourselves. If we torture ourselves, naturally we will torture others. Please understand that we torture others when we do not feel comfortable and complete within ourselves. Torturing others is directly related to torturing ourselves. If we think that we are the mind, we torture our body; and if we think we are the body, we torture our mind. The person who knows the secrets of the body and mind neither tortures nor abuses them. He knows how to use and enrich them and live blissfully in completion with them. His inner space overflows with bliss, and his outer space enjoys comforts and real pleasures.

Kṛṣṇa reveals the sacred secrets of how to enrich the body and mind in beautiful and blissful energy, and how to create the inner space of completion, flowing in blissful consciousness.

Kṛṣṇa says further, 'O Bhārata, I am also the Knower in all bodies—*kṣetrajñaṁ cāpi māṁ*. To understand this body and the knower is called knowledge.'

Beautiful! Here, He makes two statements. He says, 'I am the Knower in all the bodies, and to understand the knower and the body is knowledge—*kṣetra kṣetrajñayor jñānaṁ yat taj jñānaṁ mataṁ mama*.' He says that understanding the field or the body-mind and the consciousness is knowledge. He says, 'I myself reside as the consciousness inside the beings—*sarva kṣetreṣu bhārata*.'

kṣetrajñaṁ cāpi māṁ viddhi sarva kṣetreṣu bhārata |
kṣetra kṣetrajñayor jñānaṁ yat taj jñānaṁ mataṁ mama || 13.3

Our consciousness is God and there is no separate thing as God. The problem arises when we start carrying an inadequate cognition thinking that we are the body and the mind. A person who carries the right cognition and understands that he is consciousness liberates himself. He is enlightened. He becomes the Buddha. Consciousness is God.

The Equation is: God + body mind = man
man – body mind = God!

YOU ARE CONSCIOUSNESS, KṢETRAJÑA

Whether we believe it or not, we *are* consciousness. Let us see how we miss it, how we miss and mess our life!

Here is a beautiful story about knowing the body and the mind and how we miss realizing that we are consciousness.

A pregnant lioness was hunting for food one day when she came across a flock of sheep. She tried to attack the flock but the effort was too much for her. She fell on the ground, giving birth to a cub and also died due to the pressure she exerted.

The flock of sheep saw the newborn lion cub. They started playing with him. They felt that they should take care of this cub, as one species often does for a newborn of another species. They just took pity on him and adopted him. The sheep started taking care of the cub in the same way they care for their young ones, feeding him with goat milk and grass!

The cub started behaving like a sheep and grew up along with the sheep. He lived happily amongst them, not knowing that they were different from him.

After some time the problem started slowly. It had to. The mother sheep started receiving complaints about the behavior of the cub, 'He is too arrogant,' 'He is too strong and rough,' 'He is not playing properly with us.' Naturally the cub was sidelined. Whenever any argument arose, they decided to punish him.

After a few days, the lion cub started to wonder, 'What is this? I don't feel that I am really living. Is this all a lie? Is this all that there is to life—eating grass, jumping around and bleating, just going around the grasslands? I don't feel I am leading a full life.' He felt that he was unlike the others, that somehow he was different. He did not feel that he was *being* himself.

Whenever he saw a forest, he was tempted to go and explore the forest. But his sheep mother had warned him that it was the one thing he should not do. She forbade him from straying away from the flock, obviously now considering him to be one of the sheep. She cautioned him that if he did so, the lions inside the forest would kill him.

This whole story is actually about the spiritual seeker! It is about how a person takes birth, starts seeking and how he achieves fulfillment. It's a wonderful story. I love this story. That is why I repeat this story whenever I can!

The mother sheep said, 'You cannot go there, there are lions out there.' The cub somehow managed to suppress his search or feeling of emptiness even though he felt drawn in and was tempted to go into the forest to explore. After some time he decided, 'I think this life is not for me.' But somehow the mother sheep managed to pressurize and control him. She played a big drama—weeping, crying, convincing, and finally she got this lion married! The lion cub got married and a few years passed by. After some years he again started thinking and analyzing, 'What is going on? I am leading the same old life, eating, bleating and jumping around! I feel something is seriously missing! I have found whatever best one can get—a good mother, good wife, nice life—but deep inside me, there is only emptiness. I don't feel fulfilled. What is happening to me?'

Again he started searching. The seeking started.

Then suddenly one day, a lion from the nearby forest attacked the flock of sheep. When this happened all the sheep ran away. This sheep-lion neither felt like running away, nor did he have the courage to stand and face the lion. He knew the lion was trying to attack, but he thought, 'He looks so graceful. Something about him is different.' He had never seen such a majestic beast before. So, slowly, somehow, unconsciously this sheep-lion felt attracted and drawn towards the lion. Because of the attraction, neither did he run away, nor did he have the courage to face the lion, because he thought he was a sheep under attack.

He started walking away slowly but kept his face and gaze fixed on the lion. The lion straightaway came near him and caught him.

The *sheep-lion* started bleating, 'Oh, please leave me alone and do not kill me!' The lion said, 'Fool, I have not come to kill you! You are a lion, why are you bleating and shouting for help? Why do you think I will kill you?'

'Lion?' the sheep-lion suspected that the lion was trying to cheat him and take him to the forest. He became frightened and cried, 'No, leave me.' The lion again said, 'Fool! You are a lion, why don't you understand that?' The sheep-lion refused to believe the lion. He escaped and ran away.

Even though he ran away, the sheep-lion was unable to forget the lion. For a week he was afraid. Fear is usually there after the first glimpse, after the first experience. He had had the first glimpse of the lion! This is how Arjuna felt after his first experience of the Divine, his first glimpse of Kṛṣṇa. It is an experience that evokes fear as well as a blissful attraction.

A week passed by and the fear slowly subsided. He felt drawn to the lion once again. The sheep-lion felt like meeting the lion. 'I think I should meet the lion once more,' he thought. One part of his mind was saying, 'No, no, no, I am afraid that he may kill me,' while another part was saying, 'No, it was such a blissful experience with him. He is so graceful and I want to meet him again!'

Please be very clear that unless you have Enlightenment within yourself, you will not feel attracted towards an Enlightened person. If we feel attached or connected to an Enlightened person and feel we are in tune with him in some way, understand that it is a sign that we have Enlightenment within us already. However, if we have not matured or grown to the level of feeling the Enlightenment within us, we may not feel even a slight connection with an Enlightened person.

There are millions of people living in this city. Why are only a few hundred sitting here for these discourses? Not only that, thousands came at least once and have not come back the second time. Why do only a few come regularly? The moment you feel attracted to an Enlightened Master's teachings, be very clear that the Enlightenment in *you* has started expressing or flowering!

That is the reason why the sheep-lion remembered the

lion and felt attracted to it. He felt the intense urge to see the lion again and finally decided to meet him. But how would he meet him? The lion never sent out flyers saying, 'In such and such a place, I am doing a program! You can meet me here.' The sheep-lion came to the edge of the meadow where the forest started, and waited expectantly every day for the lion to appear.

After a few months the lion appeared. The moment the sheep-lion saw him, his fear surfaced and he was caught in the dilemma once again despite having waited for months to see him.

This time the lion came towards him and asked, 'How are you doing?'

The sheep-lion started bleating again, 'I am, I am, I am….'

He was unable to answer, but did not run away, as he had done earlier. The lion said, 'Don't worry. If you are afraid, I will go away. I am not going to eat you because you are a lion. And because I can't eat you, I won't kill you. Also since I see no use in you, there is no reason for me to stay here if you are afraid.' Saying this, the lion started walking back towards the forest.

The sheep-lion immediately pleaded with the lion to stay and spend a few moments with him. He also added, 'Don't come too close. You can stand at a distance and talk. Please stand ten feet away and I will stand here. But please spend some time with me.' The sheep-lion was now neither able to forget the lion and escape, nor did he have the courage to go near him!

This is the next phase of growth for a seeker.

With around ten or fifteen feet between them they stood and talked. However, again and again the lion said, 'You are a lion. Fool! You think you are a sheep! You are not like the friends you live with. This is not the way you are supposed to live.'

The sheep-lion started to think about what the lion said. Slowly the doubt he had that the lion was going to take him to the forest and eat him disappeared. Now the sheep-lion was convinced that the lion did not have an ulterior motive. He thought, 'I have nothing to offer him and I am of no use to him.'

Only when this confidence comes into the mind of the disciple, he starts trusting the words of the Master!

That is why in the *Vedic* system spiritual knowledge is free. We start trusting the Master only when we realize that we cannot contribute to the Master in any way, that the Master has nothing to gain from us, that he is not missing us. The trust between the Master and disciple starts when the disciple understands that he has nothing to add to what the Master already has in his being. The Master has everything and he is sharing because he is overflowing. He is not giving in order to take something from us. His very being is overflowing. Only when you understand that, will you start trusting the Master's words.

The sheep-lion developed that much trust on the lion. He thought, 'The lion is not going to kill and eat me. If he wanted to do that, he would have done it long ago. One thing is certain. He is not going to gain anything from me. So why does he say I am a lion?'

Then, the sheep-lion thought about what the lion had said. When we understand that we have nothing to give the Master, that he is overflowing out of his ecstasy and he is only sharing the joy and bliss, we start experimenting with things more deeply. Until we understand that whatever the Master says is only for our own benefit, we never try to experiment with his words.

The sheep-lion thought about the lion, 'He looks so

courageous, so graceful, so bold, and he is radiating so much confidence. It doesn't look like he is lying.' We can clearly tell whether someone is lying or not by seeing the eyes of a person. We don't need a lie detector! All we need to do is look into his eyes. So the sheep-lion thought, 'He doesn't look like a liar. Then why is he again and again telling me that I am a lion? I know I am a sheep.'

The lion then said, 'I think you are not interested in believing me. Anyhow, I am not interested in wasting my time. I am going.' But the sheep-lion begged, 'No, no, no! Please, at least give me an appointment.'

The lion asked why he wanted the appointment. The sheep-lion replied, 'I will go home and think about whatever you have told me. Then I will come back and clear my doubts with you.' The lion agreed, saying he would meet him at the same place in one month's time.

The sheep-lion then started to contemplate, 'How can I be a lion? I know for sure I am a sheep. I eat grass. I bleat like a sheep and go around with sheep. So, how can I be a lion?' He thought and thought. He considered all the great philosophical questions, the very same questions that I have been answering all these days!

There must have been some books: 'sheep-philosophy,' 'sheep-Gītā.' The sheep-lion read all of them and thought of all the possible questions. He made a big list of questions that his mother and father never answered. One important thing though is that he never told his mother that he met the lion because if she knew, she would stop him! She would not have allowed him to go to the edge of the forest. She would have told him, 'Never go there! You must stay in the meadows. You cannot go to the other side into the forest.'

Parents are afraid for their young ones. They send their children to the temples but never to a Swami, never to a spiritual master! To them there is always a danger. See, Swami Vivekānanda is great as long as he takes birth in the neighbor's house, not in our house!

Anyhow, finally after one month, the appointment date arrived. The sheep-lion collected the best grass, whatever he thought was best, as an offering to the lion.

He gave it to the lion saying, 'Please have all these things. I preserved them carefully for you.'

Seeing the love of the sheep-lion, the lion also acted as if he was eating and enjoying the grass, just so that he could please the sheep-lion and make him feel more connected. He was zeroing down the distance. He wanted the sheep-lion to feel comfortable and connected in his presence. Only then could any transformation or transmission of knowledge happen. Just to make the sheep-lion comfortable, the lion acted like he was eating the grass.

Naturally, the sheep-lion asked, 'Is it good? Is it tasty?' The lion said, 'Yes, yes, it is tasty. I am happy. You cook well. You have done a great job.' Some compliment is given!

After accepting the grass offering, the lion started to slowly say the same things to the sheep-lion, 'I am telling you again and again, but you are not ready to listen. You are a lion, not a sheep.'

By now, the sheep-lion knew that what he was thinking was wrong. Still he was unable to accept what the lion was saying as right. How could he be a lion? He knew by now he was not a sheep.

He applied logic, 'My color is different. If I am a sheep, I should be like my friends. I think differently. I do not feel satisfied or comfortable with that life. This means I am something more. But I am unable to understand how

I could be a lion.' He was not able to comprehend what the lion said. At the same time he was not sure about what he had been thinking all along.

One day, the lion said to him, 'Come, let us go to a nearby lake for a picnic.' By now the sheep-lion was comfortable with the lion and agreed. When they reached the lake, the lion suddenly grabbed the neck of the sheep-lion, dragged him to the water, and told him to look at the reflection in the water.

The lion asked him, 'Do you see an image of a lion in the reflection?'

The sheep-lion replied, 'Yes, I see your reflection. You are standing.'

The lion asked, 'Do you see another reflection?'

The sheep-lion said, 'Yes, I see another small lion, your baby. Where is the baby? Your baby is not here but his reflection is here. Is he inside the water?'

The lion roared and said, 'Fool, it is you!'

The sheep-lion refused to believe and said, 'No, no, no, maybe your baby is hiding inside the water. Call him.'

The lion said, 'Fool, it is not my baby. It is you.'

The lion then told him, 'Look, I am now moving away. Only you are standing there. See what is happening!'

The sheep-lion then saw the reflection. Suddenly, the first shock happened to him, 'I think there is some truth in what the lion says.'

Again, he was frightened, 'If I am a lion, I must live in the forest. I cannot take that responsibility. If I am a sheep, I am so comfortable. Already, I know all my sheep friends and I get regular food. I know where food is available. I know where I cook. I know where I eat. I know where my house is. I know where my wife is. I know where my life is. I know all these things and I am completely accustomed to the life of a sheep. But if I understand that I am a lion, the whole thing must be dropped. I must renounce the whole thing. I must take a big jump. It's difficult.'

That fear pattern again came up and he simply ran away; he escaped one more time.

The First Experience

After a few months, the lion came in search of the sheep-lion. This time the sheep-lion did not have any grass offerings. Instead the lion brought an offering of meat for the sheep-lion! When he saw the sheep-lion, he didn't talk. There were no intellectual discourses, philosophical discussions or question-and-answer sessions. Straightaway, he caught hold of the sheep-lion, opened his mouth, and put the meat inside.

The moment the sheep-lion tasted the blood, the moment he tasted the meat, something reeled inside him. Something happened to his being. Something happened to his consciousness. Suddenly he swallowed the meat and roared!

The roaring is what we call Enlightenment! Most importantly, the sheep-lion realized that he had been a lion from the beginning, from day one!

The same thing happens in our lives. Again and again, we wrongly think we are sheep. At some point, we start suspecting, 'I am not feeling satisfied with this life. What is happening?' And after some time, suddenly we see a lion that teaches us, '*You are God. You are that energy. You are consciousness.*' We get scared and run away. At home we start thinking, 'I think he has some plans. He wants to build an ashram and he needs me for it. That is why he says these things.'

After a few days we realize that he already has an ashram; we don't need to build one for him or contribute to his ashram. We realize that he has everything and doesn't need anything. Then slowly we start analyzing, 'Why is he coming everyday and saying the same thing? Everyday he comes and for two or three hours he says the same thing in a loud voice. Why?' After a few days we think, 'One thing is certain, whatever I think about me is wrong. But I don't know whether whatever he says is right or not.'

During meditation, one glimpse of Consciousness happens. When that happens we again run away with the fear, 'No, no, no. This is not for me. If the same thing happens again, I may leave everything and go after him.' At this stage, the Master suddenly catches hold of us and puts the meat of solid spiritual experience into our mouth. Something happens in our system, in our consciousness. Suddenly we open our eyes and roar, declaring the experience that happened in our being. We realize that from day one, from the beginning, we have been That. The sheep-lion has always been a lion.

But it requires another lion to make a sheep-lion realize that he is indeed a lion.

From day one, we are the knower or the *kṣetrajña*, the Consciousness. But by mistake we start carrying the inadequate cognition thinking that we are the body-mind, in the same way that the sheep-lion thought that he was a sheep.

Suddenly a person who has already experienced that he is Consciousness guides and enriches us saying, 'This is Consciousness and that is body-mind. Understand that you are Consciousness.'

Here, the same story is happening between Kṛṣṇa and Arjuna. Kṛṣṇa explains *kṣetra* and *kṣetrajña*. He tells Arjuna that he is not a sheep but a lion; he is not merely the field; he is the knower of the field.

Consciousness And Conscience

13.4 *Understand my summary of this field of activity and*
how it is constituted; what its changes are, how it is produced,
Who that knower of the field of activities is, and
what his influences are.

13.5 *That knowledge of the field of activities and of the knower*
of activities is described by various sages in the scriptures.
It is presented with all reasoning as to cause and effect.

13.6,7 *The field of activities and its interactions are said to be:*
the five elements of nature, false ego, intelligence, the mind,
the formless, the ten senses of perception and action, as well as
The five objects of senses and desire, hatred, happiness, distress,
the aggregate, the life symptoms, and convictions.

Kṛṣṇa asks Arjuna to listen carefully to His explanation of what constitutes *kṣetra*—body-mind, and its activities, its changes, and how they are produced. These truths have been explained by many *Ṛṣis,* sages, from time to time. The Vedic scriptures, the *Brahma Sūtras* for example, express these truths with clarity, using sharp reasoning.

Thousands of years of research done by millions of inner scientists, *Ṛṣis*, in millions of inner science laboratories have led to the same truth: The true nature of man is pure consciousness, *kṣetrajña*, and man is the knower or witness of the field, *kṣetra*, the body-mind.

Throughout this chapter, Kṛṣṇa cautions Arjuna not to confuse the body with the knower of the body and not to confuse the mind with the knower of the mind. The whole problem arises when we mix the knower of the field with the field itself.

We have forgotten that we have taken this body and mind for a purpose and that is to live our desires, *saṁskāras*. We have forgotten that we have only rented this body-mind costume for this birth and we gradually associate ourselves with it! After a while, this costume becomes more important and dear to us than anything else. Once the costume begins to wear out, we start to worry.

This is what happens when we wrongly associate ourselves with the body and mind, instead of associating with the consciousness that runs it. We confuse *kṣetrajña* with *kṣetra*. Naturally, all the problems that arise at the body-mind level start to affect us. The activities that happen to the body-mind appear to be having a direct influence on our lives.

In the next few verses, Kṛṣṇa takes Arjuna step-by-step into what these activities are and how they interact with each other.

Kṛṣṇa talks about the five great elements, the false ego, the intelligence or the mind that makes decisions and all ten senses. Please understand, He says, 'ten senses, *indriyāṇi daśakaṁ ca*'. We think we have five senses. No. We have five *karmendriya* and five *jñānendriya. Karmendriya* are the senses or organs responsible for actions such as talking, walking etc and they are the mouth, hands and feet, organs of excretion and reproduction. *Jñānendriya* are our five senses that receive knowledge such as smell, taste, sight, touch, and hearing and they are the nose, tongue, eyes, skin and ear. So, all the ten senses, plus attachment, aversion, joy, sorrow, the body, mutual attraction and the consciousness contribute to the field of activities.

Actually the word 'consciousness' cannot be used. When our consciousness becomes rigid, it becomes conscience. There's a difference between conscience and consciousness.

For example, we do something based upon what we think is right or wrong according to our conscience. If we give these same teachings to the next generation, it will not work because something else may be right or wrong for them. When we force them to follow the same thing that we did, we are giving it as just a morality, as just a conscience. We are giving them a law without the spirit. On the other hand, when we give our next generation an understanding about life, we give them consciousness.

Conscience Is Suffering

Understand, a person with only conscience always suffers. He can never be happy, whether he enjoys or renounces. If he enjoys, he suffers from guilt. If he renounces, he feels the lack of it. He suffers either way. Never give conscience to the next generation. Always give them an understanding about life, what I call consciousness. Let them experience and explore.

I do not believe in morality. I believe in conscious experience. I do not believe in conscientiousness. I believe in consciousness.

Conscience is given to us by society. Consciousness is given to us by God. Conscience is social conditioning. Consciousness is our very nature.

Conscience naturally makes our whole life into a ritual. We should know why we are doing and what we are doing before doing anything. Only then will we do it intensely with integrity and authenticity. If we do not know the context and logic behind what we are doing, we will neither integrate ourselves completely into doing it nor take the responsibility to authentically dedicate ourselves to it.

Kṛṣṇa says that the rigid sense of conscience, all the rules that form the *kṣetra*, are also the field. They are matter. They are not energy. They are not your being. They are not you. Whatever is mentioned here is not you. Listen! We should understand we are liberated the moment we know what we are not. We are liberated even if we live with what is not us. Even if we live with our body-mind, if we know that we are not the body and the mind, then we are not their slaves!

Please understand that the word 'slavery' can be used as long as something goes against your will. With awareness and completion, even if you live with the body-mind, you are not their slave.

Nothing can enslave us once we understand and cognize that we are *not* body and mind. We can never become a slave to anything. Even slavery cannot enslave us. Slavery can enslave us as long as we are not ready to cooperate with slavery. This is a subtle point. So, please listen! When we cognize that we are beyond body and mind, we will feel no need to resist when somebody tries to enslave us. We know that we can never be slaves.

Only that which goes against our will can enslave us. Here we are in a totally different space, a totally different consciousness, the space of completion and nothing can go against our will. And we will never have a will that would make us feel like a slave. We will be flowing with the river, flowing with the current. We will disappear into the Divine. So slavery cannot happen to us. Our consciousness is beyond any form of slavery.

That is why Kṛṣṇa teaches the secret of understanding the body-mind and consciousness, *kṣetra* and *kṣetrajña*. In ancient times, man was only subjected to physical slavery. In the present day, man is subjected to psychological slavery. Understand, we are the psychological slaves of countless things.

When some product is advertised on television, straightaway it sits in our head. Within a few days, we somehow get money and buy that product. We live in a world of psychological slavery. Once we understand that we are not the body-mind, that we are beyond it, we will be totally free from physical and psychological slavery.

See, it is like this. When we badly want a particular object or event to happen, our happiness is in the hands of that object or event. That external object or event has the power to control our happiness. We feel depressed when things turn out other than the way we desired. We feel the world is unfair. Many people ask me, 'Why has God been so unfair to me? Why is it that only I face these difficulties?' Please understand, the moment you place your happiness in the hands of something or someone, you have become their slave. They can exploit you.

One more thing is that even the thought of wanting freedom can exploit us if we allow it. Many times we chase freedom in the name of spiritual seeking. Freedom happens only when we realize that there is no need to chase. We must drop the idea of wanting freedom and just trust the freedom. We will then experience it. Otherwise, craving for freedom can enslave us instead of enriching us. We realize the futility of this struggle and experience freedom only when we become aware that we are already free.

The minute we stop resisting whatever we have, we start flowing. We stop giving someone or something the power to control our happiness. Nothing will enslave us. Everything will enrich us. We will experience the consciousness of completion and freedom.

Inner Science Technology

13.8-12 *Humility, absence of pride, nonviolence, tolerance, simplicity,*
service to an enlightened spiritual master, cleanliness,
steadiness and self-control; renunciation of the objects of sense
gratification; absence of ego, the perception of the pain of the
cycle of birth and death, old age and disease;
Non-attachment to children, wife, home and the rest, and
even-mindedness amid pleasant and unpleasant events;
constant and unalloyed devotion to Me,
resorting to solitary places, detachment from the
general mass of people; accepting the importance of
self realization, and philosophical search for the absolute truth:
All these I thus declare to be knowledge and anything contrary
to these is ignorance.

In these five verses, Kṛṣṇa gives a beautiful technique. Until this point He gave us an intellectual understanding. Now He gives the technique and technology to realize and experience what He says. I call these five verses the inner science technology to liberate our inner space! It is a precise technique to liberate oneself from the *kṣetra.* It talks about how to be liberated from the body-mind and how to bring them under our control.

First, the moment we understand that we are more powerful than the body-mind, we are liberated from the body and the mind. Here, He beautifully gives the technique to liberate us from the body-mind and therefore, how to experience the consciousness.

Let me first give the translation of the verses:

Humility, non-violence, tolerance, simplicity, approaching the enlightened spiritual master, cleanliness, steadfastness, self-control, renunciation of the objects of sense gratification, absence of all egos, perception of all the evils of birth and death, old age and diseases, detachment, freedom from all entanglements, even-mindedness amidst pleasant and unpleasant events, constant devotion, aspiring to live in a spiritual way, giving importance to the ultimate truth, and detachment. All these I declare to be knowledge and besides these, whatever there may be, is ignorance.

Kṛṣṇa mentions a long list of things in these verses with many instructions. Let me be very clear that if we straightaway try to practice all the qualities He has given here, we will feel we are going mad! We cannot really practice these qualities. All we can do is help the consciousness to happen in us so that we start radiating these qualities. These qualities simply happen in us.

By way of comparison, let us say we want to remove the dirt from a muddy water tank. If we put our hands into the tank and try to take away the mud, what happens? We make it muddier, that's all. All the dirt that is settled below will come up to the surface. Instead, if we sprinkle a handful of lime powder inside the tank, it will absorb the dirt and we can have clean water in the tank.

Our mind is also like a muddy tank. If we try to suppress it and fight with it, we will create more incompletion. Instead just add a little meditation process of completion which is like the lime powder, and relax. Just put in your awareness to complete and relax. Automatically the impurities will settle down. The moment we become aware and complete, and the witnessing consciousness starts operating, the whole thing settles down. The witnessing consciousness is the lime powder that purifies our being.

Rāmakṛṣṇa says that if the straight line of integrity connects your mouth and mind, you will be liberated. We cheat ourselves if we engage in an activity because it is appreciated by society and not because we feel it from within. This constant mismatch of internal and external, of what we feel deep within and what we do is inauthenticity, it creates problems.

Instead of creating consciousness, we start creating the activity. Instead of working on our *being*, we work on our *doing*. Our doing is in no way going to help us. Only our being is going to help us. So work on the *being* and not on the *doing*. A person who works on his doing may continuously chisel, chisel and chisel his *doing*; however, his *being* will face the same old struggle, suppression, suffering, and fighting. Instead, if we work on our being, we will flower and automatically radiate the right energy, the right consciousness!

You Are Unique

If we practice these qualities just because Kṛṣṇa say that we should, the qualities will never really develop in us. They will remain skin deep. When true non-violence happens, our very being will radiate love, no matter what. Even if an enemy were to stand in front of us, no other emotion but love would remain in us, and that is what Kṛṣṇa really wants.

If we visit Sringeri, a temple in South India, we will see a stone statue of a snake protecting a frog with its hood. A beautiful sight! It depicts that emotion of divine love that is unconditional. Divine love does not consider whether a person is a friend or enemy. If we are centered in our being, qualities of love and non-violence happen. All the things that Kṛṣṇa has mentioned in these five verses are an outcome of the flowering of that consciousness, and not things to be practiced. If we practice them to please somebody else, we would become slaves to the people around us.

Normally we believe others' opinions about us. We accept their scale as a standard for measuring ourselves. Then we get into trouble. This is what I call 'guilt'. Guilt is reviewing our past decisions with updated intelligence. If we use our present intelligence to review our past decisions, we create guilt and suffering. Understand, we are updated every second. We are not the same as what we were a few hours ago. Our intelligence is continuously updated. So naturally when we look back and analyze what happened in the past we feel certain things could have been avoided. The problem is that we think we run the show. We take everything upon our shoulders and allow emotions like guilt and worry to come in. If we remember that the Universe is pure Intelligence that knows how to take care of our lives, we will simply relax. Also, when we allow the cosmic intelligence to operate, we spontaneously express the beautiful qualities that Kṛṣṇa enumerates. The same cannot be achieved by doing anything.

Kṛṣṇa first talks about humility or *amānitvaṁ*. Humility can never be achieved by effort. If it is attempted through effort, it looks ugly. Humility happens when we feel that every being is unique. It does not come by thinking that everyone is equal. There are no equals! If we deeply understand that every being is unique, we automatically respect everyone. Every being has something that he contributes to Existence, to life.

Listen. Even our enemy contributes to our growth! He may do it indirectly but nevertheless, he contributes to our growth. Never think that a person is useless. We are removed from planet Earth the moment we stop contributing to Existence in some way or other.

Normally we evaluate whether a person is worthy of our respect. We will see how well qualified he is, how much society respects him. Then we will decide, 'Okay, I think I can show him some respect.' It is as though our respect is so precious and the world continues to run because of that! When we understand that every being is a unique creation of the Universe, that the same divinity that is in us is in them also, we automatically radiate humility and the absence of pride. All these qualities that are supposed to be radiated by a seeker should simply happen from within. This is what Kṛṣṇa explains.

Another important thing: How should we approach an Enlightened spiritual Master or *ācāryopāsana*? He talks about this in another verse also—*tad viddhi praṇipātena paripraśnena sevayā* (4.34). It means that we should approach the Master with questions and request him to answer the questions. Why? Why does Kṛṣṇa say that? What is the need? Again and again, spiritual literature emphasizes the Master. It is not only in the

Bhagavad Gītā. In all integrated spiritual traditions, the living Master plays an important role. Why?

Especially in *Vedānta*, the Vedic system, the Master plays a major role. Why?

Unless we see someone continuously living in the consciousness and continuously expressing that consciousness, our unconscious refuses to believe it is possible. Whenever we read or hear about these truths, our conscious mind believes in them, but the unconscious says, 'All these things are old theories! Some crazy person might have written all these things!' Our unconscious mind won't accept the truth and possibility of Enlightenment. Our head and heart fight with each other because of this. When we see a living Enlightened Master, our emotions also automatically start experiencing it. Our unconscious, which continuously questions, becomes silent when we see a living Master. With books we learn through verbal language; with a Master we learn through his body language. He is a living example that proves the truth can become a reality for us in our life.

Listen. Three things happen when we meet an Enlightened Master:

First, we see in front of our own eyes that it is possible to live in eternal bliss or in bliss consciousness all 24 hours of the day. The assurance and inspiration to achieve that state is there. We understand the possibility.

Next we ask, 'All right, it is possible for the Master. But is it possible for me?' That assurance is also given when we reach the Master. The Master instills the confidence in us by showing us, 'If I can achieve, why not you?'

It is like this: the seed is afraid to sprout and thinks, 'I may die if I rupture and sprout.' But the tree says, 'No, you must break open. Only when you break open can I happen.' The tree within the seed is waiting for the seed to break so that it can come out, but the seed is waiting for the tree to happen! The seed thinks, 'Who knows whether the tree will happen?' The tree says, 'Open, only then can I happen,' and the seed tells the tree, 'No, let me see you happen and only then will I open.'

A Master represents the tree in the analogy. In our life too, we are afraid to jump because we look for a guarantee that Enlightenment is possible if we take the jump. We are afraid of being caught in an 'in-between situation'! Then neither would we become enlightened nor would we be able to return to our normal lives. We are afraid of the insecurity and uncertainty. But the Master offers this guarantee.

The Master has already become a tree. He gives confidence to the disciple. He says, 'Don't worry. I also struggled like you. Look at me, I have flowered. I have not died. I have become a tree. If you open, you will also become a tree.' He sits with us and assures us that he will take care. He creates the energy and gives confidence to open and become a tree. He reminds us, 'When I have achieved, why not you?'

Third, the Master creates the right space or technology for the tree to happen. He creates the right conditions, the right soil, water, etc. All that we need to do is trust the master and break open. That is why Masters create ashrams. An ashram is a space that allows the seed to open so that the tree can happen. The ashram is a space where the conditions are controlled, and in a secure and safe way we can enter into the consciousness.

The Master makes us experience the Truth which is in our very being. So first, he assures us of the possibility through his body language. Next, he makes us understand that it is possible for us also. Third, he creates a space in which it can happen. Fourth, he ensures that we are established in that consciousness. These are the responsibilities of an Enlightened Master. That is why the vedic way of life, insists that we reach a living Enlightened Master. This is what Kṛṣṇa calls *ācāryopāsana.* He gives the important guidelines for us to experiment with the technology.

Consciousness Is Eternal

13.13 *I shall give you the full understanding about the knowable,*
with which one can taste eternal bliss or the being or
the consciousness that has no beginning.
A life beyond the law of cause, effect and the material world.

13.14 *With hands and feet everywhere, with eyes, heads and mouths*
everywhere, with ears everywhere, He exists in the worlds,
enveloping all. The Paramātman (supreme spirit) is all pervading.
He exists everywhere.

13.15 *The Paramātman is the original source of all the senses.*
Yet, He is beyond all the senses. He is unattached.
Although the consciousness is the maintainer of all the
living beings, yet He transcends the modes of nature and at the
same time He is the master of the modes of our material nature.

13.16 *The Supreme Truth exists both internally and externally,*
in the moving and nonmoving. It is beyond the power
of the material senses to see or to know Him.
Although far, far away, He is also near to all.

13.17 *Although the Paramātman appears to be divided,*
He is indivisible Whole. He is situated as one. Though He is the
maintainer of every living entity, it is to be understood
that He consumes and creates all.

13.18 *He is the source of light in all-luminous objects.*
He is beyond the darkness of matter and is formless.
He is knowledge, He is the object of knowledge, and
He is the goal of knowledge. He is situated in everyone's heart.

Kṛṣṇa says, 'I shall explain the knowable, knowing which, you will taste the eternal Being, the beginning-less consciousness that lies beyond the causes and effects of this material world.'

In the previous verses, Kṛṣṇa talks about the qualities that happen with the flowering of the divine consciousness within. Now He reveals to Arjuna that this consciousness is eternal.

Please understand that our mind associates a time and space with every incident or event. The mind can only think chronologically. It is like an inner reference chart and all incidents are placed in this chart of time and space. Modern science asks questions like, 'How did this happen? What was there before this? What came after this? What triggered this?' When they asked about the creation of this Universe, they explained it with the Big Bang theory.

They said that a tiny mass of fire exploded and gave rise to our Universe. What they could not answer was, 'What existed before that?' Kṛṣṇa says that this universal energy, the ultimate consciousness, always existed. It manifested in various forms as planets, as humans and so on, but it is eternal. It will continue to manifest itself and return to the Source and it will always exist.

The concept of time and space that we have is based on our mind and senses. Whatever we perceive is a projection of our mind. This understanding of time is different from an enlightened Master's understanding. He measures time in terms of *kṣaṇa*. *Kṣaṇa* is the time between two thoughts. It is the space between two thoughts. Buddha referred to this time and space as *śūṇya*. Ādī Śaṅkarācārya referred to it as *pūrṇa*. It is the no-mind zone, the mindful zone, the space of completion in which we touch base with ourselves. It is the present moment, in which we come face to face with the divinity within, by which we recognize the Cosmic energy that is our essential nature.

When we are caught in chasing one material pleasure after another we have so much stress, tension and worry bombarding our heads every second. Our *kṣaṇa* is very small because of the high number of thoughts inside us. This is why we get a suffocated, panicking feeling. We constantly feel time is running out. We are greedy for more and more experiences before this body dies and we are afraid that we might lose whatever we have come to possess.

We feel this way because we associate ourselves with the *kṣetra,* the temporary body and mind. Please understand that the body and mind are made up of the five elements and they return to their source once they have served their purpose.

On the other hand, an enlightened Master knows he is *kṣetrajña.* He knows that he is not the body-mind system. He has realized that he is the ultimate consciousness. He has no urgency to run in the rat race because he knows that life goes on, even if this body perishes. He has become a witness to the mind. Any thought that springs up will be only an action-oriented authentic thought, never an unproductive thought. He expresses the power of words, *vāk śakti.* The moment the thought happens, it immediately expresses itself as an action. No thoughts accumulate inside him. He experiences eternity because of this thoughtless zone that he stays in. This is the beginninglessness of the consciousness that Kṛṣṇa explains here.

The Master Exists Everywhere

When we are in front of an Enlightened Master, one who is in a no-mind state of completion, the number of thoughts in us also comes down and our *kṣaṇa* becomes longer. The gaps between thoughts increase. So without even trying, we become calmer, more peaceful, and more aware!

The knowable that Kṛṣṇa explains is beyond any changes. It is eternal because it does not follow the laws of creation and destruction like other objects around us. It has always been there and will always continue to exist. Whatever physical matter we see around us follows a particular cause-effect relationship. However, our deepest core is untouched by these changes.

Please listen! Every thought inside us affects the functioning of the whole Cosmos. Whether we want to accept it or not, we do not operate as separate islands. Thoughts that are present in the space that we live in affect our mental setup, that is the way we think and operate.

This positivity and negativity, creation and destruction, are all properties of the changing world around us, of the *kṣetra* that we live in. The minute we know that we are not this changing *kṣetra* but the eternal and unmoving *kṣetrajñya* (the consciousness that runs the *kṣetra)*, we are liberated.

Kṛṣṇa calls this eternal bliss *jñeya*, knowable. When the knowing happens, the knowable (*jñeya*), knower *(jñātā)*, and the knowledge *(jñāna)* merge. In this experience, the knower, known, and knowledge become one. No separate experience, experiencer or object of experience exists. It is called *triputi*, where no difference between the three entities exists.

It is like this: Imagine that you love driving and are sitting in a nice new car with all automatic systems and you are driving on a highway at full speed. You are so immersed in that joy of driving the car that you forget yourself. After some time you suddenly realize you are not even driving; the driving is simply happening. You have become the experience of driving and there is no more a sense of you doing the driving. The car is moving forward on its own and you have become the experience. Similarly, if you are immersed and involved deeply in any other passion, the experience, experiencer and object of experience suddenly merge into the Eternal consciousness. You call it being in 'the space of completion.'

Kṛṣṇa explaines that His eternal nature, the eternal Self, is not bound by time. Now He says that He exists everywhere, *sarvam āvṛtya tiṣṭhati* and He is not bound by space. Normally we understand the presence or absence of an object or person in terms of physical attributes. We function in our lives based upon what we see, smell, touch, taste and hear. If our *pañca indriya*, five senses, cannot sense anything, we think nothing exists.

sarvataḥ pāṇi-pādaṁ tat sarvato 'kṣi-śiro-mukham /
sarvataḥ śrutimal loke sarvam āvṛtya tiṣṭhati // 13.14

One important and surprising thing is that an Enlightened Master is more present in his absence than in his physical presence. This means that his energy never dies nor does it know any barriers.

Many disciples in different parts of the world tell me, '*Swamiji*, we wish to be with you more often, please visit us.'

I tell them, 'Truly, sixty six percent of *Nithyananda* is in the mission and the message; only thirty three percent is in this body.' If we limit an enlightened Master to his form, we miss him completely. His energy transcends time and space and is always available everywhere, forever!

When you are in the energy field of an enlightened Master who is no longer in his body, as in a *jīva samādhi*, the final resting place of the Master's body, without even making an effort, you become calmer and experience that space of peace within. Many great temples such as Tirupati, Tiruvannamalai, Mantralaya and Pazhani in India are built around the final resting places of Enlightened Masters. That is why these places serve as powerful energy centers today, drawing millions of people every year. Although physically the Master is no longer in the body, we feel his presence. Why? Because he is not bound in space by the body. The cosmic energy that he manifests transcends space and time. Only we know physical barriers.

Here, Kṛṣṇa uses the phrase, 'Hands and feet everywhere, *sarvataḥ pāṇi-pādaṁ*, eyes, heads, faces, ears everywhere, *sarvato akṣi-śiro-mukham* (13.14).' What does He mean by this?

This is beyond the comprehension of the human mind and needs a little bit of internalization. We understand only one body—the physical body—because we associate ourselves with it completely. Let me explain with a small diagram:

This diagram shows the seven energy bodies or layers that we have in us. The outermost layer is the physical layer, with which we associate ourselves all the time. We know this body as having a pair of eyes, hands, legs, one nose, head, etc. Now let us take a few points on that layer. Let us call them 'you', 'me', 'your neighbor', 'Kṛṣṇa', 'Buddha' etc. So, at the gross layer, you are different from your neighbor; your neighbor is different from me and different from the various forms of God. You can see each point being distinct from the others. We are so rooted in this physical gross layer and so we see many barriers between us and everything around us, because everything appears to be different from the other in this layer.

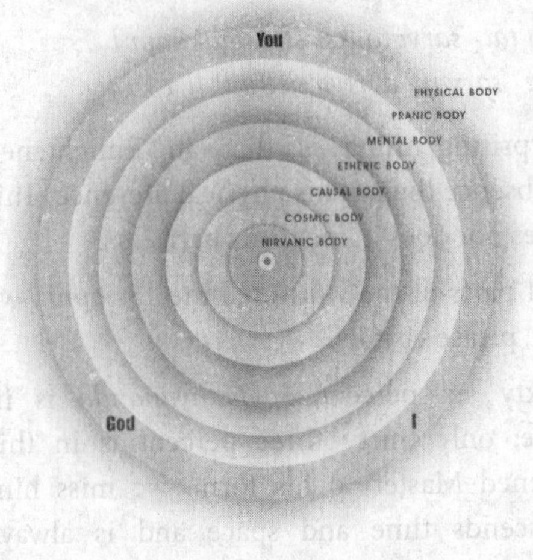

Now, for each point, if we follow the corresponding points in the inner layers, as we go deeper and deeper, we suddenly realize that we all merge in the nirvanic layer. It is here that the Universal Energy connects every being. There is no difference in this space between you and me. This is the space of consciousness that Kṛṣṇa talks about. Here, Kṛṣṇa and Buddha are no different. All are various forms of God, all are manifestations of the same divinity.

> The women who used to look after the cowherds during Kṛṣṇa's time, that is the gopīs, were great devotees of Kṛṣṇa. Despite their other household chores, they were soaked in devotion for Kṛṣṇa all the time.
>
> In the *Rās līlā*, divine play of Kṛṣṇa, He gave the experience of Universal consciousness to the gopīs; Kṛṣṇa danced with each of the hundred thousand gopīs in Brinḍāvan. Kṛṣṇa manifested a form for each of the gopis

in order to dance with them individually. It was not merely one form, one body of Kṛṣṇa, but one hundred thousand forms manifesting simultaneously.

Please understand the deeper meaning in this *līlā*. Each gopī was so deeply connected with that divine consciousness, the Kṛṣṇa consciousness, that each one felt His presence. When we go within, into our core, we see divinity in everything. The gopīs saw Kṛṣṇa everywhere and in everything they did. This universal consciousness knows no physical barriers. That is why Kṛṣṇa says He is 'all pervading, *sarvam āvṛtya tiṣṭhati*.' He is all enveloping. He is omnipresent.

That is why I say, 'All those who I ordain as healers are my hands, all our *ācāryas* (initiated teachers) are my *vāk* (energy of power of words), and all our organizers are my mind.' I can only heal a limited number of people with these two physical hands. I can only conduct a limited number of programs with this one mouth, and I can only organize a limited events with this one brain. That is why I operate through my healers, teachers and organizers. The Cosmic *Nithyananda* operates through them!

For a phone connection to happen from one country to another, we need to have the infrastructure: all the cables installed below the sea and so forth. But for this cosmic connection to happen, nothing is needed. If we simply connect to the Self within, suddenly there will be no barriers. We will simply fly!

Kṛṣṇa goes on to give further qualities of the Self. But understand that all this is said only to inspire us to experience it first hand ourselves. If somebody asks us, 'What does sugar taste like?' and if he has never tasted anything sweet before, how will you explain to him? You may tell him, 'It will be in the form of white cubes, transparent, very sweet.' When he asks, 'What does 'sweet' mean?' You can continue to tell him other things, 'Sugar is made from sugar cane, which is full of sugary syrup, it is fibrous, you can chew on it.' What is the use?

Instead if he puts a handful of sugar in his mouth, he will

automatically say, 'This is how sugar tastes! This is how something sweet tastes!' Unless he experiences what 'sweet' means, things will remain a theory for him, although the conviction about sugar might grow in him.

In Chapter 11, when Kṛṣṇa gives His Cosmic form vision, the *Viśvarūpa Darśan,* Arjuna feels intimidated within a few moments and cannot handle the energy. He pleads with Kṛṣṇa, 'I cannot understand You. I cannot withstand Your glory.' But Arjuna wants to know what Kṛṣṇa is talking about. So once again Kṛṣṇa gives all kinds of descriptions to penetrate Arjuna's doubts and fears.

The compassion of an Enlightened Master is so great. In spite of the doubts and skepticism, he quietly and patiently sits with the disciple until, one by one, all doubts are washed away. You see, our self-doubts and questions arise from our mind, forming a thick layer over us. A Master's grace gently dissolves this layer.

Kṛṣṇa says all life happens because of the thread of the Universal energy flowing through. You see, so many things are happening around us, on their own, beyond our awareness. The life force that conducts the whole show, that controls every breath we take, the same energy that maintains an order in the chaos of the Universe, is pure intelligence. In Saṃskṛit, there is a saying that means not even a blade of grass can move without the will of the Divine.

Kṛṣṇa is sending a message to us about how much we depend on Him, who is the Cosmic intelligence, for anything to happen. At the same time, without getting involved, the Universal energy is a witness to all activities and all life forms.

If we look deeper, we realize that whatever we see and perceive as objects, are creations of the mind along with the senses. We create a world of our own. Deep down, the true Self watches the whole thing without getting involved. The mind projects some people as good, some as bad, some incident as painful, others as joyful, etc. and then runs after or away from the people and experiences. For an enlightened being, a knower of the truth, everything is the same. He stops labeling because he has moved beyond names and forms, and beyond the dualities of good and bad.

Rāmakṛṣṇa Paramahamsa gives a beautiful analogy. When we stand in a valley, we see pits and depressions on the ground if we look down, and mountain cliffs when we look up. But when we climb up to the summit, we observe that all the ups and downs below no longer matter. We have transcended the ups and downs that we saw when we were on the ground. How to climb to the summit above all the ups and downs?

You must relax. You must realize that you are already on the summit. You are beyond the ups and downs. But no, we don't want to believe it. Our mind tells us, 'No. What is he saying? I have important things to do in life. How can I relax?' We love our tensions and problems too much. We like to clutch onto our lives. We do not want to let go because we think this is all there is. We do not realize that if we relax, we can fly.

A small story:

> A hunter in a forest came across a clearing where there were many birds. He took a twig and tied a rope at the center of the twig. Then he took the two ends of the rope and tied them firmly to a pole on each side. Now the twig was hanging by the rope. He sprinkled a few grains around the setup. He was a clever hunter. Happily, he went away for a nap.
>
> After some time, a bird was attracted by the grains and sat on the twig. The minute it sat on one side of the twig, the whole twig turned upside down due to the bird's weight. The bird now saw the whole world upside down and became frightened. It thought it was trapped! It clasped to the twig harder than ever and prayed to God to be set free.
>
> After an hour, the hunter returned leisurely and caught hold of the bird. After that, you know what happened.

This is what we do in our lives. The bird did not realize that it was always free! All it needed to do was let go of the twig and fly away. We do the same thing. We grasp and clutch onto our past. We clutch onto the pains and joys and keep missing the space of completion. We miss eternity. We miss our Consciousness inside.

The supreme truth is inside and outside all living entities. It is moving and non-moving on account of being subtle. It is near and far. Kṛṣṇa uses all these terms and concepts such as moving and non-moving, near and far, inside and outside because these are the only terms we can understand. He is giving us an idea to tell us that Supreme Consciousness is beyond these concepts and terms that we know.

The Indivisible Space Within

You see the world full of objects with different qualifiers because you associate yourself with a fixed entity. You say something is far or near based on the physical boundaries, with respect to the coordinates of your body. Whatever you do, what you think, is based on this reference point. You live in this space enclosed by your physical boundary called *ghaṭākāśa*.

There are three spaces we can live in: The space that is covered by the body, the space that is covered by the mind, and the space that cannot be covered by body and mind. The first is *ghaṭākāśa*, or the space enclosed by this physical body. Most of us live in this space nearly all the time. The next is *cidākāśa*, the space that you are aware and conscious of. Right now, if you are aware of this hall it is your *cidākāśa*. This is the space of the thoughts and mind. The third is *mahākāśa*. This is the whole space, cosmos, everything put together.

The *ghaṭākāśa* is made up of the five elements that are: earth, water, fire, air and ether. These elements become subtler as we move up, from earth, to water, to fire, to air, to ether. None of the first four reflect consciousness. Ether, the subtlest element, connects with consciousness. It reflects consciousness. And that is the reason why we are alive. The problem is, we think consciousness is bound by *ghaṭākāśa*. We think it is limited to this body.

That is why we make this body the reference when we view the outer world. We think this body is the 'I' that sees the rest of the world. You see, all science had this as its basic foundation: we are separate entities defined by physical boundaries. Enlightened Masters who have moved beyond *ghaṭākāśa* into *mahākāśa* understand that all this division of space is due to our ignorance.

Please understand that space can never be divided. Yet we divide it into boundaries and associate terms: within, inside, outside, near, far, etc. because of our limited understanding. This is the cause for our suffering. First of all, we divide the space because of our ignorance. Second, we try to possess the space that we think is in our control. And third, we fear that the space might be taken from us. All fears, including the fear of death, happen because we constantly try to protect the space covered by our body and mind.

Understand the basic truth that space cannot be divided. When we understand that we are *mahākāśa,* we transcend all boundaries. Whatever space we may be in, the possibility of achieving a higher space is available to every one of us. Man, as such, is only potentiality. He is not actuality. He is not what he is supposed to be. As of now we are in seed form and have not expressed our potential fully. We have not become trees yet. But that does not mean we cannot grow and become trees. When we transcend these relative boundaries we will understand through experience what Kṛṣṇa says.

Kṛṣṇa says that the supreme truth is inside and outside all living entities, *bahir antaś ca bhūtānām*. It is moving and non-moving on account of being subtle, *acaraṁ caram eva ca* (13.16). This is the space of *mahākāśa,* which includes the space of everything. This space is absolute. Everything is included in this space. When there is no 'two,' how can we compare? How can we say something is near or far when there is only one? The truth is absolute and one.

avibhaktaṁ ca bhūteṣu vibhaktaṁ iva ca sthitam /
bhūta-bhartṛ ca taj jñeyaṁ grasiṣṇu prabhaviṣṇu ca // 13.17

Although the supreme spirit appears to be divided as the Cosmic and individual entities, it is never divided, *avibhaktaṁ ca bhūteṣu.* It is the basis of generation, maintenance and destruction of life. When we pour water into containers of different shapes and sizes, it takes on their shapes. If we carefully examine their contents, all of them contain the same water. Similarly, the world of many forms and shapes, so many species of plants and animals, appears as though there is so much variety. Underlying them all is the same energy. The *prāṇa śakti,* life force, running in each of them is the same.

If we understand this simple *tattva* (principle) of life—that we came from the same Source and we return to it—we will realize that we are connected to something much greater than our individual self.

I AM THE SOURCE OF ALL LIGHT

The Universal consciousness manifests in numerous ways and is also responsible for destruction. When the same Universal energy is unmanifest, unexpressed, it exists in potential form. This is referred to as *puruṣa* in the scriptures. When this energy manifests itself in this world, taking various names, forms, and shapes, it expresses itself as prakṛti. *Prakṛti* is the creative expression of *puruṣa.*

The life force that caused us to be born also maintains us. Every little thing happening within us is carried out by the same intelligence that brought us into this world. Similarly, the same intelligence accompanies us when we leave the body.

The water of the ocean is the *puruṣa* and the waves that dance and play are *prakṛti.* The water appears to be divided in the form of waves of many shapes and sizes. In reality it is one mass of the same water. Similarly, Kṛṣṇa reminds Arjuna that the supreme spirit appears to be divided into *puruṣa* and *prakṛti* because of the different creations and expressions of *prakṛti*. However, He is beyond all this and exists undivided. At their core, all are creations of the universal energy.

Kṛṣṇa says, 'He is the Supreme Self, or witnessing consciousness that is the source of all light in all luminous objects. He is knowledge, He is the object of knowledge, and He is the goal of knowledge. He is situated in everyone's heart.'

jyotiṣām api taj jyotis tamasaḥ param ucyate |
jñanaṁ jñeyaṁ jñana-gamyaṁ hṛdi sarvasya viṣṭhitam || 13.18

The sources of light as we understand them are the sun, moon, lightning, fire or artificial means like electricity. All these produce light, which makes life possible. An object that is around us becomes visible because of the light energy. The *cakṣu,* the energy behind vision, can perceive that object when the surroundings are lit up. The light energy from the sun is responsible for the birth and growth of all living beings. All beings on planet Earth depend on the sun for their survival.

What gives these sources of light the energy to run? What drives them? The Universal consciousness gives energy to all sources of light. Kṛṣṇa calls this Self the 'Source of light—*jyotiṣam api taj jyotis*'. The sources of light—the sun, the moon and lightning derive their energy from that self-luminous Self. That is why there is a common adjective given to the Self as 'effulgent' or 'luminous'.

In a deeper sense, when the Self is referred to as luminous, it is not what we normally understand. The Self is pure intelligence and this knowledge dispels ignorance. An Enlightened Master sees everything with clarity. He sees truth as it is. You see, when you are in a dark room you are ignorant of what is present in that room. When the lights are switched on, you become aware of things around you.

An Enlightened Master uses the lamp of consciousness to see the truth *as it is,* without any filters. Using this lamp, he experiences his surroundings in totality, in completion with the whole. This lamp is not like any other lamp; it cuts the layers of ignorance, however deep they may be. That is why the Master sees 360 degrees around him. He does not filter what he sees like we do. Please understand, the filtering that we do is the cause of our problems, our incompletions. We do not see whatever exists *as it exists*. We distort it to suit our inadequate, limited ideas, that are born out of our root thought patterns.

The ego is like darkness; it has no positive existence. Just as darkness is the absence of light, the ego is the absence of awareness. To struggle to kill the ego is like struggling to push darkness out of the room. To expel the darkness, what you need to do is to forget about dealing with the darkness. Focus your energy on light instead.

Bring a small lamp into the room and the darkness will leave on its own! This lamp of Consciousness is available to all of us. It lies within us. Forget all about the ego. Instead, focus on bringing the lamp into your being. When your entire Consciousness has become a flame, the ego is no more.

Understanding The Energy

13.19 *Thus the field of activities, knowledge and the knowable*
has been summarily described by Me.
It is only when we can understand the true nature of
our Supreme Self and the material world with which we have
created false identities that we can go beyond this and attain the
Supreme Self itself.

13.20 *Prakṛti or the field and its attributes and Puruṣa or*
the knower or the Supreme Consciousness are both
without beginning.
All the transformations of nature that we see
are produced by the field or prakṛti.

13.21 *In the production of the body and the senses, prakṛti*
is said to be the cause; In the experience of pleasure and pain,
puruṣa is said to be the cause.

13.22 *The living entity in the material nature follows the way of life,*
enjoying the moods of nature.
Due to association with the material nature,
it meets the good or evil among various species.

13.23 *Yet, in this body there is a transcendental energy.*
He who is divine, who exists as an owner or the witness,
supporter, enjoyer and the pure witnessing consciousness,
is known as the Paramātman.

13.24 *One who understands this philosophy concerning material nature,*
the living entity and the interaction of the modes of nature is sure
to attain liberation. He will not take birth here again, regardless of
his present position.

Kṛṣṇa delivers this discourse of the *Bhagavad Gītā* to Arjuna standing in a chariot on the battlefield of kurukṣetra. If you look a little deeper, this is a beautiful picture of each of us. Kṛṣṇa represents the Self, the charioteer, knower of the field, *kṣetrajña*, the one who runs the show. If the charioteer does not know how to take charge, the horses start to pull the chariot in different directions.

These horses symbolize the senses and the mind pulling us to different places as they please, thus leaving us in a state of confusion in everything that we do. If we are not ready to control the horses, the horses will control us. This is what happens in our lives. Due to our lack of understanding about how to drive the chariot, we conveniently give the horses the authority.

The very understanding about the *kṣetra,* meaning the material things around us, teaches us how to control them. The minute we understand the *kṣetra*, the body-mind, we realize we are not the *kṣetra*! If we are the *kṣetra*, then how can we understand it? You see, we can read this book because we are not the book. There is a separation between the book and us. In the same way, only when we understand the *kṣetra*, do we understand that we are *not* the *kṣetra.* This understanding that we are not the *kṣetra* brings with it the understanding that *we* are the *kṣetrajña*. When we realize that we are the *kṣetrajña*, we have transcended the *kṣetra*.

How do we understand the *kṣetra?* It is important to gain knowledge about our material world. Until then, we are in ignorance. When we are in ignorance, our senses and societal conditioning drive us.

LIFE IS A DREAM

Actually, there is no such thing as *kṣetra*. It is a projection of the mind, just like a dream. You see, when we go to bed we know that we are so-and-so, husband or wife of so-and-so, working in such-and-such company, etc. We know our whole identity with solid clarity when we go to sleep. We know that even if we have dreams, they are not real. We will wake up the next day and continue our life at the office, with our children and so on.

But the minute we drift into the dream state, we start to think that the dream is real. The more we get into the dream, the more our identity completely changes to suit the role in the dream. What happens in the dream may not be related to what we do in real life. Yet we start to believe it all. If a lion in the dream attacks us, we feel fear and worry and we may even sweat as though it is really happening to us!

In the same way, we think this life is real. If I tell you now that the life that you are leading is nothing but a creation of your mind, will you believe me? No! You are so immersed in this dream that you think is real.

See, when we wake up from a dream, why do we suddenly understand that it was not real? It is because suddenly we perceive a separation between the dream and us. The understanding that it was merely a dream, puts us into reality. Similarly, the understanding that this world is nothing but a projection of the mind, the understanding that this is not our real identity, will put us into reality.

Let us say we dream of winning some award in front of thousands of people. The mind is so powerful that it can create the entire picture including every detail of the auditorium, all the thousand people sitting and clapping, the speeches, everything that we would normally see in an auditorium. The mind is so powerful to be able to give life to the scene around us and not just to our identity in the dream.

This is what the mind does in the so-called real world also. The only difference is that we wake up easily from our night dreams. However, we do not know how to wake up from this bigger day dream that we now think is reality. As long as we think this world is real, we suffer. The minute we realize this world is not real, we create a distance between the suffering and us. Only an enlightened Master who has experienced the truth can awaken us to reality. Out of their compassion, these masters descend on planet Earth to tell us that everything we see around us is a projection of our minds.

The understanding of the *kṣetra*, the illusory world created by our minds, is important in helping us to differentiate between reality and non-reality. Kṛṣṇa says that we need to understand what *kṣetra* and *kṣetrajña* to realize the truth. Until then we blindly believe that the projection of our mind, the drama, is reality. We have created our own drama and are acting in it. By and by, we forget that we created the drama. We forget that we are not the roles or characters we enact onstage. We start judging and reacting to everything about it.

If a child is constantly reminded about the divinity within right from birth, it grows up to be a *jīvan mukta*, liberated while still in the body. This is how children were brought up in the vedic tradition. That is why the level of consciousness was so high.

Prakṛti, the material world that we see, is without beginning. *Puruṣa* or supreme consciousness is also without beginning. All changes and transformations are produced by *prakṛti.*

All the transformations that we see, such as the change in seasons, concepts of time and space, our body, mind or anything that changes are different attributes of *prakṛti*. It is like the ebb and flow of the waves in an ocean. These attributes rise and fall. The time and space of the rise and fall is totally relative. The duration of the rise and fall of these attributes is also highly relative because it is purely a concept created by our senses. Our senses perceive time as moving. Our senses perceive the motion of time with respect to the material world, with relation to the speed of the planets, etc. We have created this concept of time for our sensory perceptions. We have created the space and location also with the concept of comparative reality.

For example, if we are sitting with someone we love, no matter how much time passes, we feel as if we were with that person for a short duration. We will not be aware how time passed so quickly. On the other hand, if we are sitting with a person who bores us or bothers us, we will feel like looking at our watch constantly. We would feel that time is not moving at all.

As long as our mind moves, time moves. When we look deeply, we realize that the mind is a constant movement between past and future.

The mind is a dilemma; it is constantly reviewing the past and planning for the future. We are constantly pulled towards the past or future and are never in the present moment.

When we fall into the present moment, we fall into eternity and that eternity is a combination of past, present and future. There is no distinction. In this state we become the witness of all time and space-related happenings. We become the witnessing consciousness. We become the knower and we witness the field or *kṣetra* with complete detachment. We realize that everything in the outer world is a drama or a dream, and anything that we attempt to do in our lives is housekeeping in this dream.

Any effort that we make is another act in this dream. The whole idea is to not become entangled or emotionally attached to the housekeeping in this dream. The idea is to enjoy it and watch it by becoming one with our true self.

Knowledge about the material world is necessary to help us step back from the dream and realize that we are unnecessarily attached and entangled in the field, *kṣetra.* All transformations in the field are related to time and space, which are in turn related to our mind. All transformations are the play of *prakṛti* or the field. Mind is a part of *prakṛti.*

'Nature is the source of all material causes and their effects, whereas the living entity is the source of things such as *sukha* (pleasure), *duḥkha* (pain) and everything that is of the world.'

Kṛṣṇa puts us back into our consciousness through these words. This contains the gist of what He has been saying in the previous verses. He makes a clear statement that whatever we see is not us.

He says, 'Go beyond and beyond and beyond and beyond. When you are able to see the body, move beyond. If you are able to witness your thoughts, go further beyond. If you are able to see your moods, go further beyond. If you are able to witness your emotions, go further beyond. You are not that either.'

Witness the consciousness that is witnessing. When you watch, detach from the thoughts, sit back, relax and watch. Do not try to create, nourish or destroy the thoughts. The ultimate consciousness that witnesses is beyond Brahma (Creator), Viṣṇu (Sustainer) or Śiva (Rejuvenator). When we learn to welcome thoughts and allow them to complete, they merely come and go.

It is like watching clouds in the sky. Even if there is a thought saying that you are witnessing, watch that thought also. Watch the witnessing until that thought also disappears. Go beyond and beyond, deep into your being. Go beyond the thought that you are witnessing. Please listen. As long as you think in your mind that you are witnessing, you are not witnessing. When the thought that you are witnessing exists, you are not witnessing. You are now caught in the thought, 'I am witnessing.' Drop that!

This last thought that you are witnessing is like a bridge between you and God, between you and the thoughtless space. Initially, when you try to witness your actions and your thoughts, it is natural to think that you are watching. Let it be. Having this thought is better than having a hundred incomplete thoughts bombarding your inner space. But go beyond. Do not stop there. Witness the thought that you are witnessing. Then the pure, uncorrupted and untouched complete inner space happens in you. It is only in the uncorrupted and pure inner space of completion that God manifests and the Divine consciousness is perceived. Understand, Completion is God.

Witnessing is the Master Key

Here Kṛṣṇa gives us a technique. As of now, we are like 18-carat gold, copper and gold mixed together. When we repeatedly put the 18-carat gold into the fire of witnessing consciousness, eventually it becomes 22-carat gold. If we continue to put that gold into the fire, the 22-carat gold becomes pure 24-carat gold. In the same way, if we put ourselves into the fire of witnessing consciousness, we become purified to a certain extent. Again and again, if we constantly put ourselves into this fire of witnessing consciousness, our inner space eventually becomes completely pure, like 24-carat gold.

The essence of all religions and all spirituality, the whole thing is contained in this single verse that Kṛṣṇa presents here. Kṛṣṇa presents the master key that opens all locks, in this chapter:

upadraṣṭānumantā ca bhartā bhoktā maheśvaraḥ |
paramātmeti cāpy ukto dehe 'smin puruṣaḥ paraḥ || 13.23

Witnessing the body and the mind, witnessing your being. Witnessing is the master key.

If we can enter the witnessing technique and experience the witnessing space of completion for at least a few minutes, we will get a taste of it. However much we hear about witnessing, however much we talk about witnessing or however much we analyze the art of witnessing, unless we experience it ourselves, it is of no use.

You must test it on yourself. You must test it with your being. Reading or listening will not transform you. Reading or listening is like reading the menu and leaving the restaurant without tasting the food on the menu! If you listen to what I say without testing, it is like going away from a restaurant without eating.

So now since we have read the menu card, it is time to taste the preparation.

YOUR COGNITION IS TRANSFORMABLE, BE COMPLETE

Kṛṣṇa goes one step further. All along He told us how to cleanse our inner space and how to realize the Divine consciousness within. Now, in the last verse He says that one who does so attains liberation, regardless of his present position, *sarvathā vartamāno 'pi na sa bhūyo 'bhijāyate* (13.24).

Every being is moving towards the Divine, whether or not the being is aware of it. We take on this body to fulfill certain desires. If we truly put our energies into dissolving these desires, we have no reason to take another birth to fulfill these desires. The incompletion happens when we start to lead somebody else's life and forget we are here to live our desires and not others' desires. We constantly borrow other people's desires and accumulate them in us.

Then, before we start realizing our true nature, it becomes time to leave this body. We take with us the entire baggage of unfulfilled desires and take another body again. The universe again and again tries to help us dissolve our desires so that we become free of them. But we resist by not feeling responsible for what happens within and around us.

Kṛṣṇa says that an understanding of *kṣetra* or *prakṛti* straightaway liberates us. We are caught up in pursuing sense pleasures and accumulating desires as long as we associate ourselves with this body. The minute we understand that we are beyond the body and mind, we suddenly realize, 'What stupidity to run in this rat race!'

All our problems, all our incompletions arise due to the ignorance of our true nature. The understanding that we are beyond all petty things like fighting for name, fame, money or power liberates us from them. A cognitive shift happens that transforms and frees us from the bondage of material things. This cognitive shift can happen at any time, to anyone. It is not necessary that you be brought up in an ashram, listening to God's name all the time. You could be anywhere, doing anything. And when it happens, it is a quantum jump in the level of consciousness. It does not happen gradually. It is spontaneous enlightenment. It is like pressing a switch and the whole room is lit up in one shot.

Understand, your cognition is changeable, transformable is the first cognition you need. Whenever people realize that they are beyond the bondages of body and mind, that their cognition is changeable, spontaneous Enlightenment happens. When people who go on doing completion, with their body and mind, along with the basic root-pattern that their cognition is *not* changeable; then finally, at one point, they break and understand that cognition is changeable, they become enlightened. That is called Enlightenment process, gradual

Enlightenment. People who immediately understand that cognition is changeable and awaken, are people who have become spontaneously enlightened, they have instant Enlightenment.

Please listen. You go on believing that because you are *seeing* from the time of your birth, seeing is hardware of you like the eyes. You don't separate eyes and seeing, you don't separate ears and hearing, you don't separate tongue and tasting. You don't separate *kṣetra* and *kṣetrajñya* , the one watching the *kṣetra*. You think that if it is there, it is there, which is not the truth. Cognition is changeable. Cognition is transformable. With this clarity that the cognition is transformable, now decide and be liberated. Just an understanding that our cognition is changeable and transformable, that we are beyond material pursuits is enough to liberate us.

I tell you, just know your incompletions with this clarity that cognition is changeable, the incompletions of *kṣetra* will lose power over you. Incompletions will have power over you as long as you feel cognition is not changeable. With this understanding of *kṣetrajña*, start living and thinking. Regardless of your present position, your very thinking will be completion. This is the science of spontaneous completion, instant completion.

Technique For Spontaneous Completion

Completion does not mean blindly accepting everything that happens in your life, in the *kṣetra*. It simply means not resisting life as it happens to us. The root of all our incompletions is the idea we carry—Life should not be this way.

That is why we spend our whole life asking, 'Why, why, why? Why is life so bad? Why did this happen to me? Why do bad things happen to good people?'

Spontaneous completion or instant completion means simply dropping the wrong understanding that is creating conflict for you in a particular situation.

It is possible! Next time you face a crisis or conflict in life, don't ask, 'Why is life this way? Instead, decide: this is life, so now what? Do I want to accept it and move on? Do I want to reject it and move on? Or do I change it the way I want?

Whatever decision you make out of this cognition will be right for you. When you act out of completion, you are empowered to resolve any conflict that happens inside you or outside you.

Manys People, Many Paths

13.25 *Some perceive the Paramātman in their inner psyche through mind and intellect that have been purified by meditation*
Or by metaphysical knowledge [sāṅkhya yoga], and others through working without fruitive desire [karma yoga].

13.26 *There are those who, although not conversant in spiritual knowledge, begin to worship the Supreme personality upon hearing about Him from others.*
Through the process of hearing about the Supreme Self, they also transcend the path of birth and death.

13.27 *Bhārata, know that whatever you see in Existence, both the movable or the immovable, comes into being only by the union of kṣetra, the field and kṣetrajña, the knower of the field.*

In this verse, Kṛṣṇa gives various techniques for the path to Self-realization. He says various methods or paths may be used to realize our true Self.

People say 'As many Masters, so many paths.' Actually it should be 'As many disciples, so many paths!' Each disciple can have his own path. This is what Kṛṣṇa says. We can attain the ultimate consciousness through different paths.

Kṛṣṇa says that through meditation or yoga or knowledge or contemplation or surrendering to the Divine, you can attain liberation. All the different methods lead to the same goal. Each chapter of the *Bhagavad Gītā* gives a different technique to realize the Self.

After our Inner Awakening meditation program, I give spiritual names to those who ask for it. I give the names based on the energies of the devotees. The names depend on how they connect to the Cosmic *Nithyananda*. If I see that individuals act at an emotional level like devotion, I give names that suit that particular energy. The second category is intellectual people. Intellectual people are those who connect at a mental level. They need logical explanations for everything. The third category is of those who connect at the being level.

When I ask for their names, I meditate on their energies and give them the spiritual names. The spiritual name gives them a path, and the path is different for each one. The name has significance. The name reminds you of your path. We generally associate ourselves with our name. So whenever you utter your name or when somebody calls you by your spiritual name, it rings a bell in your head. It guides you to the destination.

Kṛṣṇa tells Arjuna about the paths. He gives alternatives: meditation, yoga, chanting *mantra,* learning and acquiring knowledge and surrendering to the Cosmos.

FOLLOW YOUR OWN PATH

Listen. You should know which path is good for you. Lots of people take up a spiritual path without knowing what it is. You can have a starting point but you should find out if you are on the right path. You should not blindly follow someone because someone you know is following that guru or that path.

A small story:

> On a dark night, a man discovered that the headlights of his car had failed. He decided to follow the car in front of him. It was dark outside and he could not see anything. If the car in front took a turn, he also took that turn. He managed quite well using the light from the car ahead of him.
>
> After some time, the lights of the lead car switched off and

came to a sudden halt. The second driver bumped into the car and shouted at the driver of the first car, 'Why did you stop?'

'I've reached my house. What do you expect me to do?' replied the other driver.

You see, if you follow something or someone blindly, you will not reach the correct destination. You must know your own path.

There are different paths to realize the truth. However, we must understand what our path is. This is where a true Enlightened Master can enrich you. He knows exactly what the path is for you. He corrects you when you are on the wrong path.

In this verse Kṛṣṇa gives different techniques, like meditation, yoga, knowledge. Lots of people do these things. Some people ask, '*Swamiji,* I am meditating daily for 21 minutes. I am still unable to feel anything. Why is it?' I ask them, 'Tell me with integrity and authenticity, are you meditating with full intensity and full awareness? When you are meditating, is your mind with your body or are you thinking about the office?' Naturally, they do not say anything after that.

You see, all the techniques must be done out of completion. Meditation must be done with awareness. Everything you do can be meditation if you do it with awareness and intensity.

Kṛṣṇa gives it as a path to attain the Ultimate consciousness. In this verse Kṛṣṇa talks about *sāṅkhyena,* through knowledge or philosophical discussion. He says you can attain the goal using knowledge. Understand, gathering knowledge and philosophical discussions can be done in two ways. Many people read a lot of books. These people are the intellectuals. They collect knowledge like others collect stamps or coins. But if you look deeper, the knowledge will be just another manifestation of their ego. They would just show off. They would not have really assimilated the knowledge for themselves. If we discuss for the sake of showing our knowledge and ego, we have made no use of that knowledge.

At the end of the verse, Kṛṣṇa gives a wonderful technique. He gives the ultimate technique, the technique of surrendering. He says, '*Surrender the outcome of your actions to Me.*' This is the most effective technique. He talks about it throughout the Gītā.

Just surrender the fruits of your actions to Him, the Universal Consciousness. Most often, we take responsibility for the outcome of our actions. That is when our tensions and problems start. Just surrender everything to the Cosmic energy of Kṛṣṇa. Once we do, we will feel liberated. We will feel free. This is the easiest path to reach the truth.

Listen. A person need not have any spiritual knowledge to start on a particular path. There is no prerequisite. Even if the person is totally new to spirituality, he can follow a spiritual path. Only a cognitive shift must happen.

So many Enlightened Masters did not have any prior knowledge about spirituality. They just realized that their cognition is changeable. Let me tell you about the Enlightened Master, Maharṣi Vālmikī who wrote the great epic Rāmāyaṇa.

Before Enlightenment, he was a highway robber. Whenever wealthy people crossed that jungle, he robbed them.

> One day the sage Nārada was passing through that jungle. Nārada is cosmically known for his devotion to Viṣṇu. All Nārada had was a small stringed instrument that he played while constantly singing the praises of Viṣṇu.
>
> When Vālmikī saw him, he stopped him and said, 'Give me everything you have, otherwise I will kill you!'
>
> Nārada told him, 'I don't have anything with me except this small instrument and God's name. So I can't give you anything.'
>
> Vālmikī thought he was bluffing. He asked Nārada, 'How can you not have anything?'
>
> Nārada smiled and asked, 'What do you do with all these

things that you rob from others?' Vālmikī told him, 'These are for my family, my children, my wife and my parents.'

Nārada asked, 'You do all this for your children, wife and parents. Do you think they will stay with you forever?'

Vālmikī told Nārada, 'Yes, of course, they will be with me. I get them wealth and food. They will always be with me.'

Nārada once again asked him, 'Are you sure they will always be there for you?'

Vālmikī became irritated. He replied, 'Can't you understand? I am sure that they will always be there for me.'

Actually Nārada was only keeping Vālmikī engaged in a conversation and made him look at life from a different cognition. Finally Nārada asked, 'Okay, you have lots of trust that your family will always support you; they will always be there for you. Will they be there when you die? If you ask them to die with you, will they agree?'

Vālmikī confidently answered, 'I am sure at least one of them will come if I ask them. I am robbing people only to support them. They are surviving because I get them this wealth. I am sure if I ask, they will die with me.'

Nārada said, 'Okay, if you think they will do that for you, go and ask them and come back to me. If any one of them agrees, you can kill me. I will not go anywhere. I will stay here.'

Vālmikī agreed and went home. He asked his wife first if she would die with him. His wife said, 'Dear, it is true that I am your other half, but I don't think it is fair to ask me to die with you. When it comes to your death, it is your death only.'

Vālmikī was shocked. Anyway, he thought his children would surely go with him, as they loved him very much. They said, 'Father, we are young. We haven't seen the world

> yet. You have seen everything but we haven't. How can we die with you?'
>
> Vālmikī became depressed. His wife and children were saying they wouldn't be there with him when he died. He then thought his parents would surely go with him as they had taken care of him and had raised him. So he went up to them and to his surprise, they said, 'Why should we die with you? We are enjoying our life with our grandchildren.'
>
> This shocked him. He went back to Nārada and told him what had happened. Nārada listened and told him, 'The only person who can be with you always is God.'

This statement changed the whole life of Vālmikī. He realized the futility of what he was doing. He sat in the forest and meditated so deeply and for so long that an anthill formed on top of him. That is how he got his name '*Vālmikī*', which means 'born from an anthill'. When he came out of meditation, he was enlightened!

Vālmikī did not have any knowledge about spirituality. He was a robber. That one statement by Nārada made all the difference. He started looking inward after that, and became enlightened.

Please listen! Just because someone has spiritual knowledge, it does not mean that he is actually a seeker. Actually, all they have is intellectual knowledge, not spiritual knowledge. When they speak, they do not speak out of experience. That is the difference between an Enlightened Master and a normal person. When an enlightened master speaks about spirituality, he speaks from his experience of the truth. When a normal person speaks, it is his ego that is speaking.

That is what Kṛṣṇa says. You do not need prior knowledge about spirituality to embark on a path. Even if someone simply tells you about it and you start following a path, it is enough. But be very clear, you should know what you are doing. Don't do anything blindly. In the previous verse, we have talked about it. We should understand what our path is. That's all.

Whatever you see is a combination of matter and energy. The whole Universe is seen as *kṣetra* and *kṣetrajña*, *māyā* and *ātman*, *prakṛti* and *puruṣa*, matter and energy, body-mind and consciousness. Existence as we see it cannot be with only one of them. If we believe that what we see is simply matter, we are in illusion or *māyā*.

Kṣetra is the body that we associate ourselves with and *kṣetrajña* is the consciousness. What we see as a human body is a combination of both. If there is no consciousness, the body is useless. The matter that we call a body comes to life because of consciousness. Both must be there.

Prakṛti is the manifest and *puruṣa* is the unmanifest. *Kṣetra* is like *prakṛti*. It is the manifested, that which we can see. Along with what you see, there is something behind its existence. It is *puruṣa* or the unmanifest, the energy behind the matter, which we do not normally see.

We have seen in the earlier verses that all the millions of stars, planets and other celestial bodies exist in perfect harmony. How are they moving in such order? Look at our solar system. All the planets move in perfect paths. If we think they are rocks, dust or ice, if we think they are simply matter, how is such an order maintained in the Universe? They are not solely matter. There is something behind the existence of that matter. There is so much chaos; yet there is a beautiful order in that chaos. Order is present because of *kṣetrajña*. If it were solely matter or *kṣetra*, there would not be any intelligence. There is intelligence in that matter. That intelligence or consciousness creates this existence. So the combination of *kṣetra* and *kṣetrajña* is necessary.

Modern science has shown that matter and energy are the same. They are interchangeable. The outer-world scientists proved this recently. However, the inner-world scientists proved it thousands of years ago. Matter and energy coexist to create existence.

We should understand that *kṣetra* and *kṣetrajña* are not separate entities when we analyze them at a deeper level. *Kṣetra* and *kṣetrajña* are comprised of the same thing. *Kṣetra* is the gross form of the energy that also makes up the subtle form of the *kṣetrajña*. For existence to happen, both the subtle and gross forms must be there.

How we look at things around us defines our lifestyle. We again and again look at things as only matter. When we see only this gross level, fear and greed creep into us. We then want to get more and more of this matter. We live a materialistic life when we think that all we see is solely matter. When we live at the *kṣetra* level, we live in an illusion or *māyā*. We want to possess the matter.

But when we realize that it is energy also, we think, 'How can I possess energy? Is it possible to possess it?' No. We can't hold energy in a bag. When this realization happens, we recognize the futility of running after different things that we think are only matter.

We Are Brahman

13.28 *One who sees the Supreme Spirit accompanying the individual soul in all bodies, who understands that neither the individual soul nor the Supreme Spirit is ever destroyed, he actually sees.*

13.29 *When one does not get degraded or influenced by the mind and when he can see the Supreme Spirit in all living and non-living things, one reaches the transcendental destination.*

13.30 *One who can see that all activities are performed by the body, which is created of material nature,*
Sees that the Self does nothing, he actually sees.

13.31 *When a person can see the Supreme Self in all living entities, then he will cease to see the separateness among the living entities. He will see that the whole Universe (Brahman) is an expansion and expression of the same truth.*

Kṛṣṇa says, 'Anyone who has reached Self-realization or the ultimate consciousness sees that the Supreme Self is present in all living and non-living entities. He perceives the Supreme Self as the indestructible, beginning-less witnessing consciousness.'

The Existence that we see is not comprised of individual entities. We think that we are separate from others around us. In reality, we are all one. The same Supreme Self, *Parameśvara* that Kṛṣṇa speaks about is present in all of us and in everything we see around us.

As I tell everyone, 'I am not here to prove that I am God, I am here to prove that you are God.'

This is the truth. When I say this, people say, 'No, no, *Swamiji*. How can we be God? We have done many sins. We agree that you are God because you have healing powers. But how can we be God?'

Please understand one thing. It is not that you are not God because you have committed sins. Understand that you do not become a devil if you commit a sin. You are still God. Sins do not qualify or disqualify you from being a God. Your nature is Godliness. Sin is a concept developed by society to control people. The soul of a robber has the same qualification to reach the truth as that of a priest in a temple.

We create a barrier between God and us. We are not ready to believe that what we call God is inside us also. We happily accept someone else standing in front of us as God; however, we cannot accept that the same God is inside us.

Society would find it difficult to keep us under control if we were to call ourselves Gods!

Let me tell you an incident from my own life:

> I left home at seventeen with nothing, nothing at all, and traveled northwards in India. As I had vowed to carry no money, I traveled without a ticket on train. In the northern part of India, my saffron robe was a passport to free travel. No one bothered me.
>
> However, once when I was traveling towards Kolkata, a ticket examiner asked for my ticket. In my broken Hindi mixed with the local language of Bengali, I asked him, 'What ticket? I am Brahman (universal energy). This train is Brahman. You are Brahman. Why ticket?'
>
> He was a good man. Not only did he let me travel without a ticket, he also bought food for me!

Yes, we are all Brahman. God is everywhere. Divine energy fills and overflows in all places. The only problem is we do not see this. We only see one thing at a time. We see God as someone different and powerful. We create a big gap between God and us.

People in the West call Hindus 'idol worshippers'. They make fun of them. Actually there are people in India too who make fun of idol worship. All the so-called intellectuals and scientific people look down upon people who worship idols. Some so-called neo-vedantis preach *Vedānta* but consider idol worship unscientific. The same is true about performing rituals like *homa* (fire rituals) or *abhiṣekha* (water rituals).

We should understand there is more than an idol in front of us when we worship. When we worship, we worship ***through*** the idol. We do not worship the idol itself. When we see the energy behind the idol and worship that energy, that worship has value. That is the science also.

Let me ask you, why do we feel a great sense of relief after we pray to God sincerely? Why do we feel a sense of satisfaction when we come out of the temple after prayers? Why do we feel light? When we see the energy behind the idol and worship that energy, we connect to that energy. When I say we connect to that energy, we create a channel for the soul that is inside us to connect to the supreme Self. This brief time of connection relieves us from our burdens of duties. We see the Supreme Spirit in the idol and pour out our problems in the form of prayers.

We feel relieved because we have full faith in the Supreme Spirit, *Param Īśvara*. We have full confidence that the Supreme Spirit will take care of us. We believe in the supreme spirit but we do not believe that the soul that we see in us is also the supreme spirit! We are not able to internalize this truth.

Everything Is The Supreme Spirit, Parameśvara

Kṛṣṇa says the soul, *ātma* that is in us and the soul, *ātma* that is in others is the Supreme Spirit and the Supreme Soul. But what do we do? We isolate our soul. We define a boundary for our soul and separate it from the Supreme Spirit, *Parameśvara*. It is like this. There are ten pots of water and there is the reflection of the sun in all the ten pots. Each pot thinks that it holds the sun. All ten pots think that each one is holding a different sun.

In the same way, we think the soul inside us is different from the soul outside us. When we see the same soul everywhere in everything, when we break the pots, we see what the supreme Self is.

Kṛṣṇa says, 'When we see that the Supreme Soul that resides in us and in everything around us—*samaṁ sarveṣu bhūteṣu tiṣṭhaṁ parameśvara*, is indestructible—*avinaśyantam*, we see the truth.'

The only thing that lives forever is the soul. We should understand that. Everything else must die one day. When we realize this truth, when we understand that only the soul can remain forever, our whole race to get more and more becomes worthless. We realize, 'What is the use of running after things that we know are not going to be with us forever?'

When this is realized, we see the truth.

The mind is the only obstacle on the path to reach the ultimate goal. In the previous verse, Kṛṣṇa tells us how we can see the truth. Here Kṛṣṇa talks about the hurdle that we must cross. He says that when we are not degraded or influenced by the mind, we can see the supreme spirit in everything. Only when we can do that, can we reach the final destination.

We talk about the mind as separate from ourselves. We say, 'It is thinking a lot.' We do not understand what the mind is and we start talking about it. What is the mind actually? It is only an organized structure gifted by God as a tool. The mind is man's servant that helps satisfy his needs and necessities in order to lead a happy life.

The reason for the incompletions is that the mind, which should be under the control of man, has become a structure that controls man. If a servant behaves like a master, what will happen? An immature servant becoming a master is like catching a monkey and putting it on the throne. If we can keep the mind aside for a while, we see the truth as it is. Our mind cannot accept that the Supreme Soul is in everything around us. Our soul inside us knows that the Supreme Soul is everywhere. But our mind creates a strong sheath around it. Our mind takes control over us. It harbors past memories (*saṁskāras*) and creates an illusion that leads to wrong cognition.

When we were children, the mind did not have much power. When we were children, we did not build new root thought patterns, *saṁskāras*.

The conditioning by society builds layers and layers of these *saṁskāras* that give power to the mind. Actually when people say that a child is growing up, it only implies that the child is growing smaller and smaller, only the mind is growing up. The soul is being pushed into a corner and the mind, with its root thought patterns, is given more and more power. This mind prevents us from seeing the Supreme Soul in everything around us. Be very clear, if we are out of the clutches of the mind, we see reality.

We are safe as long as we can separate the Self from the body and watch as the body reacts to materialistic things. As long as we know that the soul is supreme and the body is a means to fulfill our worldly desires, we are safe. We are on the right path of completion. However, when we place the body over the soul, the incompletion starts.

We give so much importance to this body, but we don't really respect it. Instead we make use of it. We abuse our body. We consider our body to be a tool to experience the sense pleasures from the outside world. That is why we take care of our body. We want our body to be safe so that we can enjoy. We want our body to look good all the time.

We must understand why we assume this human body form and come to planet Earth. This birth that we have taken is to fulfill the carried-over desires of our previous births. These desires are called *prārabdha karma*. Our soul has taken this body to fulfill our *prārabdha karma*. When we die, our last thought decides our next birth. Our soul chooses the body that can fulfill the desires of our last birth. This is the truth.

Understand that we assume a body to fulfill the desires carried over from our previous life. However, what happens is that we create new desires in this life as well. We use our body to experience the sense pleasures and we create more and more desires. Because of this, we fall into the cycle of birth and death. Once we realize that our soul takes this body to complete a mission that it left unfinished in our previous birth, our attitude towards our whole body will change.

People ask me, '*Swamiji*, why do Enlightened Masters take human birth? Why do they need a body if they are already enlightened, if they have fulfilled all their desires?'

> There is a beautiful incident from Rāmakṛṣṇa Paramahamsa's life, the Enlightened Master, Incarnation. He told his disciples, 'Once when I was returning from my village in an ox cart, some robbers stopped us. I started repeating all the names of Gods so that at least one would work.'
>
> He then explains why even Enlightened Masters hold onto their body. He says beautifully, 'A little of my mind is attached to the body so that it can enjoy the love of God and the company of the devotees.'

See how beautifully he says it. Please listen. An Enlightened Master holds onto his body out of pure compassion for others. An Enlightened Master wants to see transformation in others and he can do it more effectively when he is in the body. He does not have any other desire. He can leave his body any time. He holds his body through a thin thread of ego for enriching others.

We always want to get more and more out of our body. We want our eyes to see more television; we want our stomach to hold more food; we want our ears to hear louder music. We do all this out of greed. We want to experience more and more sense pleasures. Instead, if we look at our body with gratitude, when we thank our body every moment for the support it has given us, we connect with our body at a deeper level.

THE SELF DOES NOTHING

Our body is the temple of our soul. We should respect our body. We should look at our body with gratitude, not greed. We should thank our body, *prakṛti* for holding our spirit, our soul, *ātma*. Then, we will see a different dimension of our body.

Here Kṛṣṇa says, whatever we think we are enjoying, actually it is the body that is enjoying—*prakṛtaiva ca karmāṇi kriyamāṇāni sarvaśaḥ*

(13.30). Our body enjoys all the material comforts. Our soul can live without them. Our soul is pure consciousness. It does not need anything external to keep it happy.

Actually our soul is always in a state of bliss. It is always ecstatic. Our body is an embodiment of bliss. Whatever material things we think we need, whatever material comforts we think we enjoy, they are needed and enjoyed only by our body. Our soul does not need any of them.

The problem starts when we think that our soul needs these material things. We associate the happiness from the external materials with our soul. This is where the problem begins. We think the happiness that we gain from material comforts is because our soul feels happy to have them. That is when we accumulate more and more of these material comforts. We run after them.

Kṛṣṇa gives us a technique here. He says, when we watch our body enjoying the sense pleasures, when we watch only our body being associated with the external material comforts and not our soul, we see the truth. Just witness the body. Be aware of your body. Observe the body when it reacts to external things. You will notice a sense of separation from the body. You will see what your body is. You will see that your soul has nothing to do with the pleasures you are enjoying.

When you do this, you witness your body and mind as if you are an outsider. It is like watching a movie. When you watch a movie, you watch what happens on the screen. In the same way, when you watch your body and mind, you understand what Kṛṣṇa says. Only when you witness that the body experiences material pleasures and it is the body that does everything and the soul does not need anything, you see the truth.

Kṛṣṇa gives the great truth of *advaita* in this verse. He talks about collective consciousness. He says when we see the Supreme Soul in all living beings, we no longer see the separateness. We see everything as one single entity. We see the whole Universe as one single body, as one entity expressing the same truth of oneness.

Please be very clear, we are all connected. Each and every living entity is connected to the other. Your thoughts affect the thoughts of the person sitting beside you. Whether or not you believe it, this is the truth.

We think we are individual consciousness. We think we are separate islands. We think our thoughts are limited to us. We think nobody watches our thoughts. Please listen. The whole Universe constantly responds to your thoughts. The whole Universe is made up of the same Universal consciousness.

Actually there is nothing but Universal consciousness. Individual consciousness is a piece of the hologram of the universal collective consciousness. What happens when you break a hologram into five pieces? Each piece becomes a hologram again. Each piece shows the same thing as the whole piece showed you before. Our individual consciousness is like that hologram. The Universal consciousness hologram is broken into many small holograms or individual living things. But each one of us has the same consciousness as the universal consciousness.

You see, your individual consciousness is like an onion. What do you see in an onion? There are layers over layers of skin. When you peel the onion layer by layer, what is there inside? Nothing! You are just like that onion. You think the onion is solid. Only when you peel, you see that there is nothing inside it. In the same manner, if you peel all the individual body-mind layers, you experience that you are the collective consciousness. Once you remove all the layers, you see that every entity around you has the same consciousness. Everything is the same.

From the beginning, from your birth, society starts creating new layers on you. In the process, the innocent, childlike nature that sees the Self in everything is slowly lost in us. As a child you do lots of things through which you connect to the Self. You do not know you are different from soil or earth. That is why you play with mud. But what do parents do? They scold you. 'Don't do this. Don't do that.' They say, 'You will get dirty. Your clothes will become dirty.'

We continuously impose societal conditions on the child. The child does not know what is dirty or what is clean. The child sees the soil just the same as the floor. He does not see any difference. He connects to the same energy when he plays on the dusty road or inside a clean house. Adults condition children to see the difference, the duality.

When we remove these conditionings caused by our body-mind association, we see that everything is pure consciousness. Only then we see that we are all the same. Only then we experience the space of non-duality, *Advaita*. That is what Krṣna says here. When we see that the Supreme Soul resides in each of us, we see that all of us are connected to each other. When we see this, we see the truth of living *Advaita*. We see that the whole Universe is the expansion of the same consciousness—*tata eva ca vistāraṁ brahma sampadyate tadā* (13.31). The whole Universe is the expression of the same truth.

Soul Situated in Body Does Nothing

13.32 *Those with the vision of eternity can see*
that the soul is transcendental, eternal, and
beyond the modes of nature.
Despite contact with the material body,
O Arjuna, the soul neither does anything nor is attached.

13.33 *The sky, due to its subtle nature, does not mix with anything,*
although it is all pervading. Similarly, the soul,
situated in Brahman, does not mix with the body,
though situated in that body.

13.34 *O son of Bhārata, as the sun alone illuminates*
the entire Universe, so does the living entity,
one within the body, illuminate the entire consciousness.

13.35 *Those, who see with the eyes of knowledge,*
the difference between the body-mind, kṣetra and
the Knower of the body-mind, kṣetrajña,
also can understand the process of liberation
from the bondages of material nature
and attain Paramātman.

Kṛṣṇa again and again talks about the true nature of the Self. He tells Arjuna that the soul is free from all entanglements. It is eternal and transcendental. Kṛṣṇa says that though the soul has come into contact with the material body, it still is free.

In the previous verses, we talked about how the body is the temple of our soul. We saw how the soul takes this body to fulfill the desires of our past birth. The soul actually does nothing. It does not entangle itself in the web of greed and fear. It is the mind that continuously adds new desires to the list and keeps the body running after them. Internally, the soul is always free. It has no bondage.

It is like the lotus plant in a lake. Water droplets that fall on the lotus leaves do not get attached to the leaves. They simply roll off and merge with the water again.

In the same way, the soul that rests inside this body is completely free from worldly joys and sorrows. It is like the drops of water. The soul, *Ātma* can simply merge into the Supreme Soul, *Paramātma*. Only the body is related to the worldly happenings. The soul is not involved at all.

Kṛṣṇa uses the word *nirguṇa* meaning beyond the three attributes—*nirguṇatvāt.* The three attributes of *satva* (calmness), *rajas* passion and *tamas* (inactivity) are related to the mind and body. The soul is free from these attributes. It is neither restless nor is it lazy. It is pure. Actually it is beyond purity. When we use the word pure, then it means that the soul can be associated with the attribute of calmness. But the soul is even beyond calmness. That is why I say it is beyond purity. Nothing can circumscribe it.

One important thing we should know. Only when something is seen by the mind, do words come out. Words are an expression of the chatter that happens in our mind. When there is no mind, there are no words. When you go to the Himālayas surrounded by mountains, the first thing that happens is awe. No words come out. We are silent. Our being enjoys the beauty. Our being does not try to relate it to anything. Our mind has not yet associated any word to it. After a few seconds we experience the 'wow' feeling; it cannot be expressed.

In the same way, Enlightenment cannot be expressed in words. There is no Enlightened Master who can adequately explain what Enlightenment is, in words.

Associating the soul with even the word calmness, requires the mind. But the soul is beyond this also. No word can describe it. It just IS, that's all. All Enlightened Masters are *triguṇa rahita* meaning residing in a state that is beyond the three attributes. They know that the soul is free from everything. They know that the body is the temple of the soul. They know that the body does not affect the soul.

Kṛṣṇa gives an example to make this point clear. He says the space that is everywhere is unaffected by anything that is in that space. The subtle energy, space or ether, is present everywhere. Every molecule and atom has this subtle energy. Though it is present in everything that we see, it does not inherit the properties of what it resides in. Even if it is in a flower, it does not take up the scent of the flower.

In the same way, the soul is not affected by where it resides. People think that their soul will go to hell if they have committed sins. They think if they have lived a pious life, their soul will go to heaven. They think that the soul is affected by the deeds of the body. Our sins do not affect the nature of our soul. Please understand that by infusing awareness into what we do, we realize that the body does whatever we do. The soul is completely free from it. The soul is not affected by it.

Kṛṣṇa says that just as the sun illuminates our whole world, one Supreme Self—*Paramātma*, that is one *kṣetrajña*, illuminates all beings in the Universe, whether they are animate or inanimate. He says everything has the same consciousness.

Kṛṣṇa gives more and more examples. The sun sheds light on the surrounding planets. The darkness on the planets is removed by the sun's light. In the same way, the Supreme Self, *kṣetrajña*, lights up all beings in the Universe. The ultimate consciousness lights up the entire Universe. All beings of the Universe have this consciousness.

We may wonder why Kṛṣṇa says the same thing over and over again. But He is trying to make the concept of *kṣetra* and *kṣetrajñya* clear to Arjuna. Kṛṣṇa knows that this is important and He wants Arjuna to understand it completely. Anyhow, Kṛṣṇa says something new here. He says that just as the sun illumines the Universe, the soul in this body illumines not only this body but also everything surrounding it, the entire Universe. He says:

yathā prakāśayaty ekaḥ kṛtsnaṁ lokaṁ imaṁ raviḥ |
kṣetraṁ kṣetrī tathā kṛtsnaṁ prakāśayati bhārata || 13.34

Kṣetri is the Self. This Self illumines all the *kṣetra*, all the bodies. Not just our body or *kṣetra* is illumined but all the *kṣetra* are illumined. The consciousness present in each of us is the hologram of the supreme Self. So there is no separation between the consciousness present in our body and the consciousness present in a plant or a rock. Everything is the same energy.

The sun lights up everything that is around. There is no partiality. It does not discriminate. Whatever comes its way, it removes the darkness from it. In the same way, the supreme Self present in us illuminates everything in the Universe. Our ignorance separates the soul from the Supreme Soul.

Actually to even use two different words—soul and Supreme Soul, *ātma and parmātma*—is not correct. There are no two separate entities called soul and Supreme Soul. There is only soul. There is only one. Everything in this Universe has the Supreme Soul. Our mind draws boundaries. It is like creating borders between two countries. So many countries fight over boundaries. One country fights with the other to acquire more land. They are drawing and erasing boundaries all the time.

We think we can draw boundaries between the Self, which is present in us, and the supreme Self. We try to put our soul in a tight container made of greed and fear. We close the lid and are afraid to open it. Actually, we fear losing our identity. We associate ourselves with our individual ego. We want to show others how different we are.

Our mind knows that if it opens the lid, the soul and the Supreme Soul will become one. Our mind knows that the soul in this body and the Supreme Soul are one and the same; there is no difference between the two. So our mind fears that if it opens the lid, our whole identity will be lost and we will become the same as everyone else. Our mind does not want this to happen.

So we continuously hold onto our individual ego. Only when we realize that we are all connected, that everything in this universe is the same universal consciousness, will we break open the container and merge with the Supreme Soul.

Here Kṛṣṇa ends by saying, 'If we can witness as pure consciousness, we will be liberated from the bondages of the body-mind and achieve the eternal consciousness.' Kṛṣṇa gives a technique to realize the eternal consciousness.

Witness and Be Liberated

Please know that becoming the witness of the *kṣetra* is the only way to keep us away from the bondages of the body-mind. We must witness as the *kṣetrajña,* consciousness. When we do that we will see the separation of the Self from the body and mind.

Understand that all our movements, reactions and emotions are related to the body-mind system. The way we move our body is a reaction by our body-mind system. Our emotions like anger, laughter, sadness and happiness are reactions of our mind. All of them are movements created by our body-mind system.

When we witness these movements happening in our system, we separate ourselves from the body-mind system. When we watch them like clouds in the sky, when we watch them like a movie on a screen, without getting attached, we see the truth.

Even the thought of witnessing our thoughts and our emotions is a thought that is controlled by our mind. Even that is our thought and implies that mind is still acting. Only when we go beyond that thought, do we experience the eternal consciousness.

Let me explain the technique. The technique may take at least ten minutes.

You are going to witness your body movements, breath movements and mind movements: movements of your body, movements of your breath and movements of your mind. You may ask what kind of body movements do we have? Understand that by inhaling and exhaling, your belly will be moving continuously up and down. There will be a slight movement of your belly during your breathing.

Witness that movement.

Next, watch the flow of your breath during inhaling and exhaling, without any attempt to control it.

Third, watch your mind. Thoughts will be going on. Please do not judge your thoughts as right or wrong. Don't be afraid of your thinking. For a few minutes, sit comfortably next to your mind, like a close friend. You can place a mirror in front of you and cognize that the person in the mirror is your incomplete half, your mind who is your close friend. Let it tell you whatever it wants to. Let it speak out loud whatever it wants. Without speaking, your thinking will not have its clarity, depth and strength. Allow your mind to talk, talk and talk and make it as part of you by befriending it.

Witness all these with no attachment. Do not stop, control or go behind anything. This is the self-completion process *(svapūrṇatva kriya)* with your mind.

We continuously fight with our body and mind. We cannot get rid of the body and mind by constantly fighting with them. We can only go beyond them through friendliness. Only if we feel deeply friendly towards them, will we be able to go beyond body and mind. If we have a negative emotion of fear or greed towards the body-mind, we will naturally abuse and only have a violent relationship with it. Be complete with the body and the mind.

Please listen, the Cosmos functions with a mutual law, *dharma* of—'*don't give onto others what should not be given to you.* If you don't give to others what should not be given to you, what should not be given to you, will not be given to you by others.' It is a cosmic law of life.

Listen. Please internalize! When you don't have fear of thinking, thinking will not give fear to you. Both of you, you and your thinking, you and your body and mind, come to a peace agreement—'till today, we had war. Let us stop the war. Let us come to an agreement. I will not be afraid of you and you don't be afraid of me.' **This agreement is what I call as Integrity. You not having fear of thinking and thinking not having fear of you, this agreement is Integrity.**

Witness the mind like a friend with integrity. Let whatever is inside come out with friendliness. There's nothing wrong. Neither support nor suppress. If we support, we will go after the garbage. If we suppress, we will end up analyzing the garbage and pushing it aside. Neither approach is going to work. Just witness and be complete.

Witnessing acts like fire. All the thoughts are burned away and what remains is the pure space of completion. Understand, neither suppressing nor supporting your thoughts will work. Only witnessing with integrity works.

When we go deep into our being, into our space of completion, the witnessing consciousness automatically creates intelligence. Understand that we don't need to be in that space all twenty-four hours of each day. Even if we get a few glimpses, that is enough. That energy will guide our whole life. If we understand the silence that happens to us when we are witnessing, even for a few seconds, we will taste it and start acting on it. Only out of these few moments does the energy of great creation and achievement happen.

Listen! When we do completion, creation simply happens. Enriching will just be our lifestyle. When we are in the space of completion, we will simply create and enrich everyone. All great things are achieved from the consciousness and intuition that is beyond the body-mind. They are products of the witnessing consciousness. This is true not only in the field of science but in arts, spirituality or any field. When we are beyond the body and mind, we bring the maximum powers out of our being. We start expressing the power of words through integrity, the power of thinking through authenticity, and ultimately the powers of feeling and living through responsibility and enriching.

The ultimate expression of our being happens when we are Whole. Whenever we are whole, we are holy. Understand that witnessing consciousness or being in the space of completion is the only path to Wholeness or Holiness.

Let us pray to the *Parabrahman*, Lord Śrī Kṛṣṇa, the ultimate Universal consciousness, to give us the inner space of completion or the pure witnessing consciousness; to give us the ultimate experience and establish us in eternal bliss, *Nityānanda.*

Thank you.

Thus ends the thirteenth chapter named ***Kṣetra Kṣetrajña Vibhāga Yogaḥ****, 'The Yoga of Discrimination of the kṣetra, the field and kṣetrajña, the knower of the field,' of the* ***Bhagavad Gītā Upaniṣad, Brahmavidyā Yogaśāstra****, the scripture of yoga dealing with the science of the Absolute in the form of* ***Śrī Kṛṣṇārjuna saṃvād****, dialogue between Śrī Kṛṣṇa and Arjuna.*

CHAPTER

14

Guṇatraya Vibhāga Yogaḥ

Find Your Root Pattern And Complete

Human Beings have the choice of being ignorant or enlightened, being incomplete or complete. Most often we exercise our freewill and choose to stay ignorant. Kṛṣṇa explains how to choose to be complete and enlightened!

Find Your Root Pattern And Complete

A small story:

On the last day of the school term, all the students brought gifts to their teacher. The first student presented the teacher with a nicely wrapped gift. The student's father owned the local bakery. The teacher looked at the package, shook it and asked, 'Is this a box of pastries?' The child said, 'Yes.'

Next, a student, whose father was the owner of a clothing store, presented a beautifully decorated gift and again the teacher shook it close to her ears. She then asked, 'Is it a dress?' The child said, 'Yes.'

Another girl came up with a nicely wrapped box. Her father owned a liquor store. The teacher shook the box. She noticed that the package was leaking. She dipped her finger in the leaking fluid and asked the girl curiously, 'Is this some kind of beer?' The child said, 'No.'

The teacher dipped her finger again in the fluid, tasted it carefully and asked, 'Ah, this tastes quite exotic. What is it? Is it some kind of wine?' The child again said, 'No.'

Then the teacher said, 'Alright, I give up. Please tell me, what is it?'

The child said in a worried tone, 'It is a puppy.'

The moral of this story is simple: Please don't put anything in your mouth unless you know what it is! What this really means is, don't make major decisions in your life based on your past experiences. Everything has roots. The way you behave, the way you think, the way you react, the way you respond, the way you cognize and why you behave the way you behave—everything has a root thought pattern!

Whether you feel unhealthy or helpless, or emotionally weak, tired, bored, lazy, agitated or irritated, all these put together is what I classify as powerlessness, feeling powerless. The good news is that you can live without any of these. The bad news is that you need to work for it! Our past experiences are stored in our unconscious as root thought patterns. They will only mislead you to a space of powerlessness, incompletion. In Saṃskṛit, the right technical word for these root thought patterns is *mūla vāsanā* or *mūla vichāra dhārā*.

We make incomplete decisions when we make the major decisions through root thought patterns or *mūla vāsanā*. The teacher thought that the gift was a bottle of wine since the student's father sold alcohol. In the same way, time and again, we make powerless decisions driven by our root thought patterns.

Before we put anything into our mouth, we should be sure to know what it is, else it can lead to a lot of trouble. Before we make any decisions, we should find the root of our incompletions and complete with it, else it will lead to more and more powerlessness, more and more suffering. When you are in the space of powerlessness, the only decision you have to take is to come out of powerlessness.

Let me define 'root thought pattern'.

> **The first strong cognition you receive in your life, which influences you to continue to function based on the same cognition, is a root thought pattern!** When the first attack of any strong emotion happens in you and imbalances your whole cognition of life, giving birth to your mind, the pattern you develop from that moment is the 'root thought pattern'. It is a pattern you develop when powerlessness takes you over for the first time in your life. Your pure cognition is imbalanced and that is the root on which the mind is born!

I will give you a simple example for root thought pattern.

In the young age, if your mother teaches you, 'Don't go in the rain. You will catch cold'. Naturally, at that age your immune system is yet to be developed. But even after you are twenty-five, when your immune system is at its peak, you don't even go in the rain, you just see the rain through the window and you start sneezing, 'hachoo'. What you internalized, what you cognized in the very young age, which has imbalanced your nature is root pattern. Your natural existence is root thought pattern. Get out of your root thought pattern and complete with it.

Please understand, it may be anything as simple as your mother not giving you the cake and giving it to your brother. It may be as simple as your mother making you sit on the dining table so that you will not run around and make a mess; or you trying your best and failing in your exam or some competition. It can be even that small!

Understand, what is a pattern? It is an action that is unfulfilled as per your fantasy, either because of an outside hindrance or an inside hindrance, and is in incompletion. If your expectations are not met by yourself or by others, it remains as an incompletion.

For example, you always wanted to wake up early in the morning and practice yoga, but you never succeeded in that, so it remains as an incompletion. You always wanted your father to be very loving and caring, and he never honored your expectations, this remains as an incompletion. I tell you, the incompletions embedded in you, go on creating more and more incompletions. So, first find the root of incompletions, the root pattern.

Please listen!

The moment a root pattern enters your system you are dead. After that only the root pattern lives through you. You don't live. Your life is over. Your body may be functioning but your life is over. The first thing any human being should do is—learn this science of discovering the root pattern. I tell you, anything you discover is yours. Anything you have not discovered is *not* yours. When you discover your root pattern and complete with it, your whole being will be filled, your being will have the space to live integrity, authenticity, responsibility and enriching.

This whole chapter called *Guṇatraya Vibhāga Yogaḥ*, is about the science of completion—discovering your root thought patterns, *mūla vichāra dhārā*, your *guṇas* (root attributes) and completing with them to experience the space of completion, *pūrṇatva*.

Please listen! What is Completion?

> **Completion means consciously reliving the same experience and relieving the powerful impact of the past, which makes you powerless in the present.**

The powerful impact of the past which makes you powerless in the present should be relieved from your system. Past should not bind you in the present. What we term perception is not the experience we perceive through our senses; perception is how we respond emotionally to the experience. This response is an incomplete, inadequate response based on our root thought patterns.

Modern psychology tells us that almost 90% of our mind is unconscious. This means that we typically use 10% of our conscious mind. In other words, our conscious mind drives only 10% of our thoughts, words and actions. The rest is driven by the unconscious. We have no control over how our unconscious mind functions. Many unconscious memories called root thought patterns are based on fear and pain. They rise up in moments of trauma or difficult situations. They influence decisions with no awareness on our part.

All that we perceive is not true; all that we do not perceive is not unreal. It is a simple truth that what you cognize is only a fraction of what our five senses perceive. The rest goes directly into the unconscious as a pattern. Yet this does not mean that these perceptions and the memories of these perceptions are forgotten. They remain as deep incompletions in us. And these memories strongly drive our actions.

You don't see what IS. You only see what you want. You create what you want. Human beings are in such an unfortunate space, they very strongly believe that only what 'IS' is perceived by them.

What is your reality? It is just your perception—your perception about what you feel as you —your *mamakāra*, what you project to others as you – your *ahaṁkāra*, and what others expect about you—*anyakāra*.

Please understand, all human beings need to know why you behave the way you behave, why you do the way you do, why you do what you do. You may be a doctor, an engineer in the corporate field, or a politician, or in the field of finance or religion—whatever you may be, whether you act with softness, peace, agitation or irritation, it is your root thought pattern that is responsible for the way you react, the way you function.

Understand this. The first strong cognition you go through in your life which influences you to continue to function based on the same cognition is root thought pattern.

For example, at the age of three or four, for some reason, somebody tries to attack you. Shivering and frightened, you run and hide yourself. The cognition was so deep in you that your whole inner space was filled with fear for a few minutes. The possibility for all other cognitions is shut down and this one cognition just fills you for a few moments. Even after that person has gone, you are still shivering in your hiding place. Please understand, if you had this kind of experience at that young age, you literally never came out of that hiding place after that! You may physically come out, but the suffering and shivering continue to happen. Even at the age of ninety-five, you will be shivering just like the three-year-old boy.

Once some root thought pattern starts in you, your growth stops. After that, only that pattern grows in you, not you! Listen! Only pattern grows in you, not you. If you had chosen to attack him back with whatever you got in your hand, even that will be a pattern.

FIND THE ROOT OF YOUR HAPPENING

Listen! How you behave, how you feel, how you respond—this means the cognition that happens in you and fills you at a very young age and overpowers you. Sometimes it is fear, sometimes it is greed, sometimes it is jealousy and sometimes it is the decision to prove yourself. Sometimes it is just being blocked out with confusion and worry!

The first thing you need to know is that only when you find your root thought pattern and complete with it, your life as a human being starts. Otherwise, you go on cheating yourself most of the time.

We tend to think that our actions are based on a logical sequence of thoughts. However, almost all our decisions have neither logic nor awareness. One of the worst things is that the root thought pattern becomes so much part of you that you don't even realize that the root thought pattern and you are two different things! You just listen to your root thought pattern and behave as if the decision is your own.

It is like some traitor becoming the power-center of that country! What will happen to that country? In the same way, root thought pattern is your traitor. It means that it is your enemy. If your enemy becomes part of your decision-making mechanism, your life will be destroyed!

Listen! Look in. Unless you find your root thought pattern and complete with it, your independent life does not start. Do not allow root patterns to get rooted in you. Look into the root patterns, into why you behave how you behave.

Everything in Existence has a root. Everything you do has a reason, a root. There is a reason for every happening in Existence. Find out the root of your happening. When you find your root pattern and complete with it, you will understand your *prārabdha,* the purpose of your happening.

In this chapter called *Guṇatraya Vibhāga Yogaḥ*, Kṛṣṇa explains the root of our happening; why we do the way we do, why we perceive the way we perceive. Kṛṣṇa explains the three different *guṇas* (attributes) to Arjuna. How we act—actually I can't say we 'act', I should say how we 'react' to every situation—is based on these three *guṇas*, the root patterns and how to complete with them.

Why Kṛṣṇa Repeats

14.1 *Bhagavān Kṛṣṇa says,*
I will declare to you again the Supreme wisdom,
The knowledge of which has helped all Sages
attain Supreme perfection.

14.2 *By becoming fixed in this knowledge,*
one can attain the transcendental nature, like My own,
And establish in his Eternal Consciousness, that one is not born
at the time of creation, or destroyed at the time of dissolution.

14.3 *The total material substance, called Brahman, is the source of birth,*
It is that Brahman that I impregnate, making possible the births
of all living beings, O son of Bhārata.

14.4 *Arjuna, understand that all species of life are made possible by*
birth in this material nature, and I am the seed-giving father.

By repeating the truth again and again, Kṛṣṇa tries to create the right inner space of completion in Arjuna. Please understand why Kṛṣṇa repeats Himself. He literally uses the same words again and again. Why? Why should Kṛṣṇa repeat?

Kṛṣṇa is a Master who is result-oriented. He persists with what He wants as if Arjuna is going to get enlightened today, but He is ready to wait until the last person gets enlightened. He is the embodiment of Enriching, which is the constitution of life. His whole life is a play from the space of enriching. He is radiating the power of not giving-up on people with His uncompromising compassion. He is not easily satisfied with the attitude, 'I said whatever I had to say; whether he wants to listen or not is up to him.'

No! Kṛṣṇa takes the responsibility to make Arjuna responsible. Again and again, He repeats Himself because He wants to create a bio-memory of His teachings, the space of completion in Arjuna's inner space. He does this so that even if Arjuna misses listening to the teaching the first time, perhaps he will give his authentic listening the next time. That is why He repeats the truth again.

Carry the Right Inner Space

Any transmission of knowledge, energy or experience happens between us only when you give your listening!

In the *Upaniṣads,* it is told that when the young seeker Śvetaketu was initiated by his Guru, his Guru said to him only nine times, '*Tat Tvam Asi! Tat Tvam Asi! Tat Tvam Asi!*' (You are That!) Śvetaketu became enlightened just by hearing those words! Then how come you don't become enlightened even if you listen to '*Tat Tvaṃ Asi!*' nine thousand times? You have to be carrying the right inner space!

Listen. On the rock, seed cannot sprout as a tree. In the right fertile ground only, the seed can become tree. In the right inner space only, the teachings can become reality.

Let me define exactly what is the right inner space!

> **Right inner space means where all the root thought patterns of suffering are destroyed. All the root thought patterns are destroyed where your inner space is fertile for experiencing the higher ideal and ideas.**

Listen! Inner space means when you close your eyes and look inside, how you feel and what you feel *as you*, that is your inner space. In that inner space, if you suddenly feel as if you have taken bath in the cold water and the whole thing inside is in eternal peace, and there is no agitation; it is all completely in peace, in restful awareness, in completion, that is what I call inner silence or the right inner space. It means the space where all your root patterns of suffering are destroyed.

You may wonder, 'When will I experience the right inner space or inner silence?' Whenever you want, that's all.

It is actually you who needs to feel tired of wandering around. Unless you feel tired of wandering around or if I have to use a strong term—fooling around, your mind will continue to go on fooling around, being in incompletion. Instead of the real source of joy, you will just go around and try to taste everything. When I say everything, I mean everything. I tell you, your mind needs to be little tired of roaming around, only then will it look in and decide to find and destroy the root patterns and create the fertile ground of the right space.

Here Kṛṣṇa says, 'I shall declare once more, I will speak to you about the ultimate Truth, through the knowledge of which all the Sages have attained Supreme perfection.'

śrī bhagavān uvāca
paraṁ bhūyaḥpravakṣyāmi jñānānāṁ jñānam uttamam I
yaj jñātvā munayaḥsarve parāṁ siddhim ito gatāḥ II 14.1

You need to have tremendous love and patience. I tell you, in any field, life happens to you, completion happens to you, only when there is tremendous love for people and a decision not to give-up on people. Kṛṣṇa is expressing the power of passion and the power of patience.

Listen. I am not tired of my own past. That is why I can repeat the same principles any number of times, without changing a word, without changing the tone, for any number of classes! When you are not tired of your own past, you are a *jīvan mukt*a, living enlightenment.

Whether we believe it or not, man by nature is a mechanism. Not only at the body level, he is a mechanism even at the level of the mind. At most, we can call it a bio-mechanism, yet he is still a mechanism. He works based on memories, the root patterns or what we call *mūla vāsanā* in Saṃskṛit.

If you have a certain pattern in you as a compulsive disorder, it is a bio-memory. It is just dead memory. If you get frightened, you will run away. If you have some thoughts or doubts that a person doesn't love you, that person doesn't care for you, all other thoughts will immediately wake up, and you will be in depression.

Please understand, memories which stay in you and make you continuously respond unconsciously in the same pattern again and again, is bio-memory. If you learn the essence of the lessons you need to catch from the bio-memory, and live spontaneously based on that essence, it becomes bio-energy.

Understand. For example, you see a snake and you know that you may die if the snake bites. This situation can become a bio-memory in you—that even if you see the photograph of a snake, you may step back. I have seen people who don't even touch a snake's photo on the TV screen or computer screen! This is bio-memory. See, I am not saying that you should not have bio-memory of snake fear or go and catch the snake! No! If you learn just the intelligence from that incident, you are clear that snake bite can lead to death, so you don't go near the snake, but you don't have the compulsive patterns related to snakes and snake fear. You only have the intelligence. Then, that same thing becomes bio-energy.

Understand, in every situation, if you catch bio-memory, you will miss the bio-energy. If you function on just bio-memories, you are a bound soul. You are a *baddha jīva*, entangled soul. Living in bondage! Not only that, when you are living here, you also accumulate more and more muscle-memory. All the patterns you accumulate and continue to accumulate are muscle-memory. The confusion between muscle-memory and bio-memory is a confused memory! So for every act, you will not know the right reason; if you know the reason, you do not know how to act. It is a kind of chaos.

Listen! Man is continuously caught in the web of these confused memories in his mind and his being, because he works based on root patterns that have been stored in his bio-memory, and accumulated as his muscle-memory.

So, you do not know the reasons for the act you performed! Muscle-memory is the memory you accumulate in this *janma* (lifetime). Bio-memory is the memory you bring from the past births. Even in this birth, the muscle-memory can become bio-memory. When you psychologically collapse, with whatever ideas you elevate yourself and stand up, those ideas will become bio-memory in you, even though you accumulated them in this body.

Does God exist?

Many religious rituals are designed to build the right muscle-memory and bio-memory in us. Going to a temple or a *satsang* (spiritual gathering) reinforces our desire to move forward spiritually. They create the right space—the environment, the mood for the right decision to happen. These actions cannot liberate or enlighten us. However, they can create the right inner space in us and program our unconscious mind, the muscle memory and bio-memory to work in a particular way. They can rewire us.

In the *Vedic* tradition, the power of sound is used. Vedic chanting is nothing but becoming It just by declarations. Every morning you declare, '*Aham Brahmāsmi Ahaṁ Brahmāsmi, Ahaṁ Brahmāsmi* (I Am That)! *Śivo'ham Śivo'ham Śivo'ham* (Śiva I Am).' Just the declaration! Such a powerful declaration. Especially the collective declarations. You are in that right inner space.

Science is about facts that can be recorded. Spirituality is about the truth that needs to be experienced. That is why our scriptures never bothered about historical accuracy and factual details. They dealt with issues that affected our consciousness. To understand our scriptures, we cannot use logic. Truth has nothing to do with our head. It has everything to do with our being.

People ask me, 'Can you prove the existence of God?'

Listen! Everything is experienced by you as per the space you carry. Everything—your reality of God, reality of yourself, reality of society and reality of Universe is experienced by you as per the space you carry. Whether it is the great realities of cosmos or the realities of life or the realities of mind, the space you create, creates your reality. God can only be experienced when we drop our root patterns and create the space of completion. How can we prove His existence through the logic of our mind? If we can comprehend Him through our mind, our patterns how can He be in any way superior to us? How can He then be God?

God can only be experienced. He cannot be proved or disproved. He cannot be believed or disbelieved. If you wish to experience God, come to me and be in the space of listening. If you have courage, find your root thought pattern and complete with it and I will show you God. You will experience Him in you.

Kṛṣṇa wants to take Arjuna there, to the space of completion. In fact, He already took him there when He revealed His cosmic form to Arjuna through *Viśvarūpa Darśan Yoga* (chapter 12). Now, Kṛṣṇa wants to take the rest of humanity to the same space of completion. So again and again, without giving up on us, He repeats the techniques of completion so we may realize our divinity. In His deep compassion He gives us a chance to catch the lifeline. He is throwing us so that we can be saved.

YOU CAN ACHIEVE MY STATE

For the first time, Kṛṣṇa says that we will reach His state. So far He said, 'Worship Me. Surrender unto Me.' Now He says, 'You will achieve the same state in which I am. Anyone can attain the transcendental nature like My own, *mama sādharmyam āgatāḥ*.'

idam jñānam upāśritya mama sādharmyam āgatāḥ I
sarge 'pi nopajāyante pralaye na vyatthanti ca II 14.2

We can achieve the state in which He is. Kṛṣṇa is the first Master courageous and bold enough to declare that Enlightenment is available to everybody; anybody can achieve it. Enlightenment is not an accident. It is an incident that we can create.

Until the time of Śrī Kṛṣṇa, *the Upaniṣads, Brahma Sutras* and other scriptures spoke as if Enlightenment was an accident. Some people became enlightened; however, nobody knew why. Nor did they know why others could not get it or how exactly to get it. Nobody knew. They merely knew that some people were blessed, almost as if God was sitting up there and reviewing applications, and to some, He said, 'Alright, yes, granted' and immediately that person became enlightened!

Kṛṣṇa is the first Master who showed how to write the application or present the resume for Enlightenment! He showed how to achieve Enlightenment. He showed the exact Science of Enlightenment. We can experience it through our conscious decision to create the space of completion.

He says that by being fixed in this knowledge, 'One can attain—*mama sādharmyam āgatāḥ.*' He doesn't say, 'You can attain it,' indicating only Arjuna. He says one can attain it, meaning that anybody can attain it.

Kṛṣṇa beautifully declares, 'By establishing yourself in this knowledge, you can achieve the experience, or you can establish yourself in the same state in which I am, like My own.' 'Mama' means 'My own'. Kṛṣṇa declares, 'This truth will directly lead you to the state in which I am established—*mama sādharmyam āgatāḥ.*'

There are very few concepts Kṛṣṇa repeats in *Bhagavad Gīta*. One concept is, 'understand me, you will become God'. It may look very arrogant for an onlooker. Kṛṣṇa says, 'understand my Divinity, you will become God'; 'understand Me you will become Me!'; 'understand My inner space, you will achieve that space'.

Please understand, it means that when you understand the inner space of Enlightened beings, without even missing a single step, now you know the method to reach that space.

See, when you look at the personality, the power, the valor, the courage of an Enlightened being, you take Him for granted and think, 'He is from a different plane. He will be like that only.' That is why when people say, 'I am God', I feel, 'No! Don't use that word and take me for granted.' The moment you use that word, you stop studying my personality which will make you as God!

Listen! Personality of the enlightened being is not a person, it is personification. When you grasp the personality of an enlightened being, suddenly you know why you are the way you are, why you think the way you think, why you behave the way you behave. You know all the possible confusions and incompletions. And you will see, you will simply know the methodology to experience completion, *pūrnatva*.

YOU ARE ETERNAL, NOT LIMITED BY BIRTH AND DEATH

Kṛṣṇa talks about the truth that one is eternal, and not limited by birth and death. The state of being eternal transcends creation and dissolution. It transcends the past and future. Eternal is to be here and now. Eternal is the present moment of completion.

He declares—*sarge api nopajāyante pralaye na vyathanti ca* (14.2).

Brahma is the Lord of creation. Creation is of the past. To exist in the physical plane, we need to have been created. To maintain is the job of Viṣṇu. Maintenance is about the future. It is about how we wish to be, what we wish to have, our desires, our expectations and everything related to the future. Śiva is the Lord of the present. He is the Destroyer of the future, making it flow into the past, by way of the present. He is the Master of the here and now.

Śiva is the Rejuvenator, not just the Destroyer. The present always rejuvenates. In Saṃskṛit, Śiva means 'causeless auspiciousness'. The present is the most auspicious; whatever happens in the present is auspicious. We should develop the attitude of accepting what happens in the present as auspicious.

Past, present and future, all three are in the same DNA seed of Kāla! Listen! If Kāla is the seed, past, present and future, all these three are in that seed, in the form of DNA. Your attitude towards the past and your attitude towards the future will be same. If you think that you are powerless, you were powerless in your past and you will be powerless in the future also. Understand, the impact of the past enters as a perverted inadequate cognition in your present and destroys your future.

Listen! Your inner space experiences the past and future in the same language, in the same way. I will tell you how your past is built. Incidents, your perceptions and your self-assessments are the pillars on which your past is built. If you complete yourself now, if you complete your perception and self-assessments, sixty percent of your past will be burnt! Then can your past stand as it is now? No! It will just be with facts. So, your past will lose its power over you. Your past will be transformed. That is the way your future will be transformed.

You need to catch it and live it! The words you utter inside and outside you is hundred percent you. It is not bad news. It is good news. Understand, because you can change now! If you utter the word now and complete, 'I drop the past; it has no power over me' 'I am declaring and committing to myself that I am a winner. I am a success. I am Śiva—*Mangalatva* (auspiciousness)!'

You can be complete now! By declaring that you are complete, just once in the present, you can finish off all your millions of declarations in the past. Because when time and space cross, the declarations you make are alive and powerful! Time and space always cross in the present moment. In any legal system, the latest order will be the order that will be executed. Even in your life, only your latest declaration will be executed.

Śiva is completion. Completion is auspiciousness. If you declare completion now, you are complete. When you complete, you transcend the past and the future. Wherever you go, you are going to be carrying this auspiciousness, radiating it. You will be a moving auspiciousness.

There are two kinds of people. The first type looks at everything suspiciously. They find everything unsatisfactory, incomplete. These people say, 'All very well, but...' They cannot say anything without 'butting'. Such people can never be happy. Their logic gets sealed in inadequate cognitions when incompletions drive them. They live with an idea of what life should be, rather than accepting it as it is. They are purely materialistic.

Please understand, when you are driving out of incompletion, you may have one dimension success in the life. But you will fail in life itself! Listen! One dimension success in life is not success.

Understand. For example, if you have a root thought pattern of fear or shivering in you, even if you make billions of dollars out of that root pattern, you will not achieve satisfaction. Because the reason why you are making money is to feel secured. You will feel secured only when you break that pattern, not my money! It is wrong strategy, for the wrong reason!

Life has no 'ifs' or 'buts'! But our fear does not even allow us to think that there is a space where there is no 'ifs' and 'buts'. This space of no 'ifs' or 'buts' is Enlightenment.

The second type finds everything to be auspicious! Whatever happens is as it should be. They welcome life as it is. They carry the space of completion. These are the people who Kṛṣṇa says transcend creation and dissolution, past and future—*sarge api nopajāyante pralaye na vyathanti ca.* They live in Kṛṣṇa consciousness.

THE GREAT 'WHY'

Kṛṣṇa is trying to answer philosophical questions that can never really be answered: How is the whole Universe created? If everything is God, why is the Universe created? How are we born? Whoever tried to answer these questions just created another philosophy.

Out of frustration, someone once asked me such questions, 'Why are we born? Why this whole drama of taking birth, meditating, then achieving enlightenment? Why? For whose sake is this drama? If we must end up working out our *karma*, why do we create karma in the first place? What is the reason for this?'

You need to know one important truth. When it comes to Cosmic questions, unless you discover your answer, you will never be in peace. 'Why', 'the why' related to the outer world can be answered by others. 'Why should I drive the vehicle from the left?'; 'why should I drive a vehicle at all?' 'Why' related to the outer world can be answered by the law of the land or the outer world science. But all the 'whys' related to cosmic law, all the 'whys' related to life can be answered only by yourself by discovering it. I tell you, the religion you discover is your religion, not the religion you are born in, is your religion. Answer you discover is your answer!

For this great 'why' you have to discover an answer. If you accept my answer for 'why', you will be living for my answer. At the most, my answer should be an inspiration for you to find out the answer for 'why'.

Kṛṣṇa tries to answer these questions as an inspiration for Arjuna to find his own answer for his 'why'. However, this answer is not the ultimate Truth. He says, 'Please wait until the teachings are over.' Normally when we don't receive an answer for our philosophical question, we will be stuck with that 'why'.

Kṛṣṇa says, 'I am the seed-giving father, the *pitā*, I am the root cause for everything—*ahaṁ bīja pradaḥ pitā* (14.4).'

'Why', this 'great why' is Kṛṣṇa's seed put inside you and sent, so that you won't rest until you become a tree. Understand, each seed has an energy called '*vīrya*' that does not rest until it produces more seeds. Until then, it cannot rest. Even if you destroy the seed or eat the seed, that *vīrya* goes into your body and does its job in some other way! Here, Arjuna also comes back to the same great 'why' again and again and gets stuck. For the sake of inspiration or just for the sake of giving him an understanding, Kṛṣṇa gives an answer.

Listen, Kṛṣṇa's words can be fully understood only when we experience the consciousness of Kṛṣṇa. Until then, it is just a cognition. Even if it is a cognition, it is okay. Proceed with this new cognition into the next chapters, into the next verse. Suddenly, when you see the result, we will understand that whatever you have cognized is the truth. Kṛṣṇa makes this declaration so that you can understand the truth. You can discover the root cause based on which you cognize your whole life, based on which your consciousness functions.

Natural Attributes, Guṇas

14.5 *Material nature consists of the three modes:*
goodness, passion and ignorance.
When the living entity comes in contact with nature,
it becomes conditioned by these modes.

14.6 *O Sinless One, the mode of goodness, satva, being purer than the others, is illuminating, and it frees one from all sinful reactions. Those situated in that mode develop knowledge, but they become conditioned by the concept of happiness.*

14.7 *Kaunteya, know that the mode of passion, rajas, is characterized by intense craving and is the source of desire and attachment. Rajas binds the living entity by attachment to work.*

14.8 *Know, O Arjuna, that the mode of ignorance, tamas, the deluder of the living entity, is born of inertia. Tamas binds the living entity by carelessness, laziness, and excessive sleep.*

Material nature consists of three modes or attributes: goodness, passion and ignorance. These are called *Guṇas* in Saṃskṛit. Kṛṣṇa explains how we are operate through three different types of root thought patterns. One is *satva*, the other is *rajas* and the third is *tamas*. These are translated as goodness, passion and ignorance; however, these are not exact translations.

Let me explain these concepts: *Satva* refers to the root patterns that lead us to bliss, the space of completion. These root patterns lead us to joy and ecstasy. *Rajas* refers to the root patterns that lead us to restlessness, excitement and to work intensely. They make us active and materially productive. The third attribute, *tamas*, refers to the root patterns that lead us to depression, laziness and to dullness. Root patterns that lead to ecstasy and bliss form *satva*. Root patterns that lead to restlessness, anger and emotional imbalance form *rajas*. Root patterns that lead to depression, dullness and low moods form *tamas*. Those root thought patterns that automatically arise and imbalance our cognition, and lead to depression are called *tamas*.

Sometimes a thought suddenly comes up, 'I will not let him off so easily. I will see that he learns a lesson. I will not let him go.' We may unexpectedly make an angry gesture with our hands while engrossed in this thought.

Patterns that make us active or cause anger or violence and imbalance our cognition are called rajas. We are normally caught between rajas and *tamas*. Very rarely do we get *sātvic* patterns. *Sātvic* patterns do not disturb us. They give rise to a memory of deep completion, bliss or joy that we have experienced. If we are pulled inwards, if we are made to do something good that leads to bliss, ecstasy and peace of mind, it is due to root patterns of *satva*, *sāvtic* memories.

For example: if we go to the Himalayas for a few days, we may experience joy and peace. Then later when we see pictures of a mountain, the memory of the Himalayan experience suddenly comes up and we think, 'Oh, I should spend a couple of months in the Himalayas again. It was so peaceful.' Patterns that lead us to peace, bliss and ecstasy are *sāvtic* patterns.

The Science of Completion

These three different types of root thought patterns or *saṁskāras* rule our entire life. Knowledge of these root patterns is the basic knowledge that must be possessed by anyone who wants to live successfully. Ayurveda, the *Vedic* science of health and wellness, is structured around the concept of *guṇas* and their effect on our body-mind system.

Understanding the three different root thought patterns or *saṁskāras* is the operating manual for the mind, the inner space. The science of completing with these roots thought patterns is the owner's manual for life. This is the basic life science! Kṛṣṇa calls it *Guṇatraya Vibhāga Yoga.*

When we don't comprehend this manual, we are not able to catch the whole understanding of life. We miss so many opportunities. We miss expansion in life, growth in life. We miss many possibilities in many dimensions. We miss the actual life itself! Because we have never learned or understood about the *guṇas,* we live only a very small fraction of what is possible in life.

Listen! At the outset, root patterns are not dead memories. *Mūla vāsanas* are living bio-memories and muscle-memories, not dead memories. The more we travel with these memories, the more we live with these memories, the more they become a part of our being. They take up residence in deeper levels of our consciousness. They get engraved into our brain structure.

Kṛṣṇa explains step-by-step how we become caught in these three levels of root patterns and how, we are pulled and pushed by these patterns. It is almost like having three wives. If we have one woman in our life, enlightenment is a luxury. If we have two women, enlightenment is an option. If we have three women, enlightenment is compulsory! With three wives or husbands, one cannot live without enlightenment.

Someone asked me, 'Why did Kṛṣṇa have so many girlfriends?' I answered, 'This is solid proof that He is enlightened! The fact that He survived despite having so many girlfriends is evidence of Enlightenment. No doubt, that is also solid proof that He is God!'

Here, He gives us an understanding of how to find these root thought patterns and complete with these bio-memories and muscle-memories. Another important point is that because these memories are living energies, they can be used for creating powerlessness, the space of incompletion or powerfulness, the space of completion.

Understand, the inner space you carry is such a powerful space. When a person has energies to do powerless acts out of incompletion, we can tap into those energies and make him do powerful acts out of completion. From my experiences of conducting meditation programs in prisons, no one puts in as much effort into meditation as a prisoner. When prisoners take up meditation, they really take it up. They are intense. When they are transformed, their whole life is transformed!

You are hypnotized to believe that your past has influence over your future. No! Till this moment if somebody is a sinner, in the next moment he can become a saint. Till this moment if somebody is a saint, next moment he can become a sinner! That is the beauty of Mahākāla, Time. If we look at the lives of Indian *Ṛsis* like Vālmikī or the great saint Aruṇāgirināthar, Pattināthar, Tulasidās and Angulimāla, they and many others were sinners.

Look at Vālmikī! What was his history? He just decided for a moment that he is disassociating from all the powerlessness space, he became a saint. See Aruṇāgirināthar, the great saint who lived in Tiruvannamalai. Till the age of thirty, he was a drunkard! In one moment he decided to live in the space of completion. The whole cognitive shift happened. He became a saint!

Same way, there are millions of stories where people decided to be in incompletion only for a moment and fell down. I can give a big list. Hṛdaya Cattopādhyaya in Śrī Rāmakṛṣṇa's life served him sincerely for almost twelve years. Only for one moment he decided to live in incompletion out of anger and disappeared from Śrī Rāmakṛṣṇa's life. Perumal Swami in Bhagavān Ramaṇa Mahaṛsi's life served him so much. Just for a moment he decided to be in incompletion and fell down. One moment of incompletion, you can vertically fall down. In one moment of completion, you can vertically fly up; because completion or incompletion does not work logically in a horizontal way, it works in a vertical way.

Please understand, how the science of completion and incompletion work, how powerfulness and powerlessness work, how the space of *satsaṇga* and *nissaṇga* work. When you associate yourself with powerfulness, you are in satsaṇga. When you associate yourself with powerlessness, the wrong association, you are in *nissaṅga.*

When you allow incompletion, you cannot say, 'Oh! I allowed incompletion only for three minutes, then how can thirty years of completion be destroyed?' You cannot say, 'Oh! I put only a drop of poison in the milk!' Same way, in one minute of deciding to be complete, your *janmas* (births) of sins will be washed away. You cannot say, 'What is this? It is unfair. This person was in completion space for only one minute! How can all his sins be washed away?'

When we entertain and associate ourselves with powerlessness, powerlessness is so powerful that it can destroy us. Powerlessness is worst than alcohol and poison. Poison destroys our physiology. Alcohol destroys our psychology. Powerlessness destroys both our physiology and psychology. If we entertain powerfulness, if we complete, the same way completion will raise us so quickly! See Aruṇāgirināthar! See Pattināthar! See Vālmikī! Please understand, even for a few minutes if we decide to be in incompletion, it can put us in a space where we will stoop so low, all the *janmas* (births) of spiritual achievement will be destroyed. And the same way, if we decide to be in the space of completion for a few minutes, it can open a new consciousness for us.

The powerfulness and powerlessness, completion and incompletion doesn't work logically, it works miraculously. Miraculous changes happened to these sinners and a cognitive shift took place in their being. The shift usually happens in the way that our mind receives data, processes it and delivers the result based on the root patterns.

Once the cognitive shift takes place, we receive data, process it and go inside instead of outside. We respond from the complete cognition we carry inside and create more and more completion outside also. As long as we operate from the incomplete cognition, we react externally and we work towards depression, powerlessness. However, once we go in and complete with our root patterns, and associate ourselves with powerfulness, we move into bliss.

HOW THE MIND AND SENSES WORK

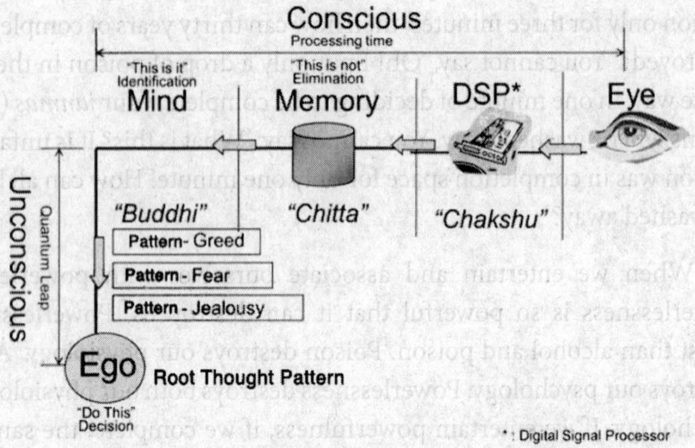

Kṛṣṇa explains how root thought patterns disturb our inner space and through this understanding, we can transform our being.

Before explaining these verses, let me present a small diagram through which we can understand how patterns affect our cognition, our decisions and how to come out of the influence of patterns.

Please understand how we receive information or data from the outer world, how we internally process it or cognize it, and how we make decisions.

I am defining Cognition.

> Cognition is the process of receiving information through our five senses, processing that information internally, relating with it based on our root patterns, and responding to life based on our patterns. This is known as cognition.

First, we see something through the eyes. I have taken the example of sight but we can replace it with any other sense: like hearing, smelling, tasting or touching. Among these five *jñānendriya* (senses of perception), any one can be used here.

There are five *jñānendriya* and five *karmendriya* (senses of action) that are the means of communication between the external world and us. *Jñānendriya* are the senses of perception, the five senses of smell, taste, sight, touch and hearing. The *karmendriya* are five actions of elimination, procreation, locomotion, grasping and speaking. Each sense is related to one of the energy centers (cakras) in our body-mind system.

Let us say we see this scene of this discourse happening. You see me talking to you. First your eye captures this whole scene like a picture and this picture goes to the *cakṣu* (the energy behind the eyes). Understand, we don't see with the eye, we see through the eye. There is an energy that is inside or behind the eye that actually sees. There is an energy inside or behind the ears that hears. The ears by themselves cannot hear. That is why when we are engrossed in a book, we may not hear the alarm or doorbell ring. So, there is an energy inside the eyes that sees. We call this energy *cakṣu*. The whole scene is converted into a file like in a digital signal processor in a computer so that our mind can process the data.

The *cakṣu* is almost like the digital signal processor or DSP in electronics. In a computer, whether it is an audio or visual file, it must be converted into a digital file. In the same way in our inner space whatever we see or hear is converted into a bio-signal file like a digital file.

Then the file starts moving up, step-by-step. The file goes to the part of the mind called *citta*. If we understand this, our whole life can be transformed. We will know why we do the way we do, and how we react. We will cognize how we make big decisions based upon our root thought patterns, and consequently suffer.

The file goes to *citta*, the place where past bio-memories are collected. *Citta* means mind, inner space. This area is where the work of excluding happens as—'*Na iti, Na iti*'—this is not, this is not. The process of *neti neti* (this is not, this is not) takes place in this area. Upon seeing his file, our *citta* starts eliminating whatever the object is not.

Take the example of this scene: First you see me, the whole scene is photographed. It goes to *cakṣu* and becomes a bio-signal file. The file is then taken to *citta*, bio-memory. *Citta* says, 'This is not a tree. This is not an animal. This is not a plant. This is not this. This is not that.' The excluding process happens in *citta*.

Next, the file goes to *manas*, another part of the mind. The manas tries to positively identify, 'This is a human being. He is wearing a saffron robe. He is standing on a stage.' The identification process, '*iti, iti*' (this is it, this is it) identification process happens in manas. In *citta*, '*neti, neti*' or the 'not this, not this' elimination happens.

Once this positive identification happens, the file goes to a third part of the mind called *buddhi* or intelligence. *Buddhi* is where the trouble starts. Here the analysis starts, 'How am I related to this file? How am I connected to this scene? How is it relevant to me? How should I respond to this scene?' If past bio-memories about me have been good or pleasant according to your intelligence, you cognize and respond in a positive way. You immediately refer to those past memories and review, 'It was so good at yesterday's discourse.'

Your intelligence refers to the past bio-memory and muscle-memory and makes a decision based upon your cognition of these experiences. If your cognition about the past experiences with me has been positive, your intelligence tells you to stay and listen. If your cognition of the past experiences has been inadequate, unpleasant and you felt bored, your intelligence tells you that this is not the place for you and that you should leave. These are logical decisions based on conscious memories retained by your mind.

Up to this point, your cognition, the transmission of what is perceived by the senses and what is the response based on that pattern is relatively straightforward. It is a conscious process.

From the conscious mind, the information is passed to the unconscious space of the mind, the ego. I call this unconscious space of the mind as the ego, not because it is arrogant, but because it provides you the identity of who you are.

Your identity stems from your unconscious incompletions which are your root patterns. You project who you wish to be, never who you are. You do not even know who you are. Who you are is deeply buried in your unconscious. All the major decisions that shape your life are consigned to this unconscious space. This is the repository of all those emotionally-filled memories, the root thought patterns and beliefs about yourself; which constitute what you believe as you, what you project as you, what others expect you to be, and what you expect others or life to be for you and therefore, create your identity. This is what I call the ego.

Identify your root pattern! Listen! I am defining 'root pattern' once more.

> Root pattern means the first time in your life when your cognitions were imbalanced, disturbed by some external force; and your terrorized being started defining yourself with a disempowering word and started defining the world in that disempowering powerless state; and to compensate from this death, the disempowering inner identity—the inner image, you create a pseudo alternative compensating cognition—the outer image. This is what I call root pattern.

When your root pattern starts, that is moment you feel yourself as an individual identity. If it starts in an accidental moment, your life will be an accident forever. It is an eternal accident. Till you complete with that root pattern, you will continue to have accidents in your life.

Completion takes away the agitated confusion and the alternative compensating image we create in our life. Understand, this example of your life.

Please listen! Because we have a very disempowering cognition about ourselves, we go on creating an alternative compensating cognition to compensate with our inadequate cognition. It is like you first declare you are a beggar, forgetting the billions of dollars you have in your bank balance, and then you yourself try to project the rich image to cover your belief that you are a beggar. But unfortunately, the final thing is you will project that your whole life—that you were a rich man, but lived as a poor man, but in reality you were the richest man.

Understand, you project and you try so hard to prove to the world that you are a rich man, but you always believed yourself and lived as a poor man; but in reality you are the richest man. You never knew about the wealth you had in your bank balance. It is like you kept all your money in some Swiss Bank and you forgot the number. To compensate the inadequate cognition which got created unconsciously inside you, which is your inner image, *mamakāra*, you create an alternative compensating cognition which is your outer image, *ahaṁkāra*.

Till the end you never feel satisfied, because you feel the guilt you showed, which is not true, without realizing your true identity is much more than what you can imagine and show. So, your whole life ends in deep incompletion and the trial and error methods you do with these incompletions.

If you complete now, the first thing you will realize is that the alternative compensating cognition is a lie and it will melt down. Second thing, your disempowering cognition about yourself will melt down. Third, you will realize that your original self is much more than what you projected as your outer image, the alternative compensating cognition. And you will have complete easeness between *what you feel* as you, *what you show* as you, and *what you are* as you.

The conscious mind does not make important decisions. It makes a few decisions that can be reached by its limited intellect. Anything important moves to the unconscious ego or root patterns. Our unconscious handles all life-threatening situations with the disempowering cognitions, the so-called fight-or-flight decisions. Our conscious mind is too slow to handle them.

For example, the file travels to the ego, and the ego makes the decision, and we execute it. If there are more incompletions, the file travels to every table like in a bureaucratic office. Each incompletion stamps, puts its signature and writes its opinion. Take the example of attending this discourse and seeing me. One conflicting pattern says, 'I had a master in my life. He was a blessing. He helped me a lot. I think I should sit here.' So this pattern signs, 'Yes, I will sit here.' The next conflicting pattern says, 'I read in the newspapers that these masters do this or do that.' So, the second conflicting pattern signs off saying, 'doubt'. Then the file goes to the next table, and the third conflicting pattern says, 'I attended his discourse yesterday. What he says makes sense, I think I should stay.' This conflicting pattern signs, 'yes'.

Listen. The effects of your root pattern are your conflicting patterns. Conflicting patterns are the branches which sprout from the root pattern.

When the file reaches the ego, the ego comes to a conclusion based on all the 'yes' responses and all the 'no' responses based out of your conflicting patterns. Yes or no is not a problem; however, we have wasted so much time and energy on this small decision. Not only that, any decision you take out of powerlessness, restlessness, will lead you to more and more powerless space. Understand, it is very important. Any decision, whether you get into some challenge, or you get into any relationship, or you get into a business decision, any decision, please see to it that you are in the space of powerfulness, completion!

You break relationships, you break businesses, you break partnerships, you break families, you break life itself when you are powerless, incomplete! Powerless moments in life create more and more powerless moments in life. For example, when we sit in our office, not doing anything, just sitting and worrying, we become stressed. Within fifteen minutes, we have pain in our shoulders. Worrying about simple decision-making leads to shoulder pain.

Continuously, again and again, look into the reasons for your powerlessness—why are you in conflict? Why are you in a powerless space? Whenever you are possessed by powerlessness, confusion, agitation, and you don't know what to do, please don't take any decisions in your life. All restlessness is powerlessness. The more patterns you have, the more powerless you feel, the more restless and *rājasic* you will be.

Take the example of smoking: According to the data collected at the conscious level, we know smoking is injurious to health. However, when the time comes, suddenly we decide to smoke. How does the file take such a quantum leap? How is the decision totally changed? When the file travels to the unconscious space, patterns say, 'No, no! The last time I smoked, I felt really good, I felt relieved from all the stress.'

We make countless decisions based upon root thought patterns. We repent and suffer later on. Suddenly we shout and after ten minutes, we repent, 'Why did I shout? I always wanted to keep a smiling face. Why did I shout?' We reacted suddenly due to these patterns.

We will see later how root thought patterns disturb and torture our decisions. Kṛṣṇa says that we should ask our being how we missed reality. Why are we deluded by root thought patterns?

Kṛṣṇa speaks of *satva guṇa saṁskāras* that lead us to bliss and peace, *rājasic guṇa* that lead to restlessness and violence, and *tamasic saṁskāras* that lead to depression. He further explains how these saṁskāras influence our decision-making process.

When we try to work with different types of conflicting patterns, *satva, rajas* and *tamas* and all three cross each other, they create hell in our lives. We need intelligence to even look into our lives to find our root pattern, and see how many times we have carried the same pattern. We usually react out of arrogance or guilt. We say, 'So what if I made a mistake?' We brush it under the carpet leaving it incomplete. This is one kind of attitude, the attitude of might is right. The other attitude is that of suffering from guilt.

Kṛṣṇa gives techniques on how be complete with these three *guṇas*. Before entering into these three layers of patterns—*satva, rajas* and *tamas*, let me illustrate how we are caught in these *guṇas* and how these patterns work. Then, we will enter into each technique.

Seven Energy Layers of the Body

These are the seven energy layers of our body-mind system. These are seven parts of our inner space, our being.

The first is the physical body, our flesh and bones. Next is the prāṇic layer, the energies of *prāna, vyāna, udāna, apāna* and *samāna* or the five air movements that take place in our body-mind system. The third is the mental body. This is where our mental inner chattering continuously takes place. This is inner chattering or the mental body or *cañcala,* which means inner movement. The fourth is the etheric body. This is the space where our intense emotions and painful experiences are stored. Usually intense emotions are of pain and suffering.

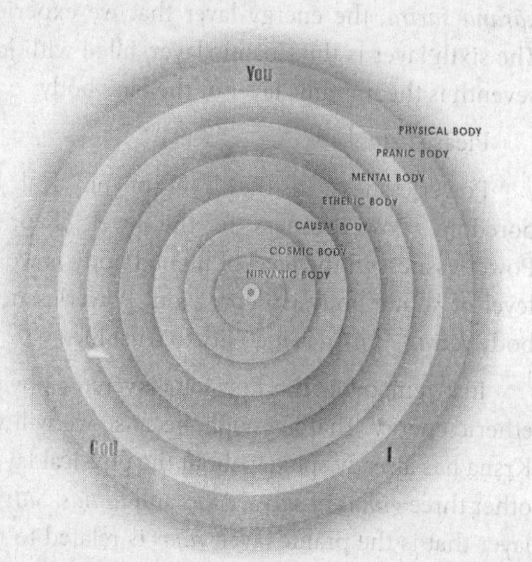

The prāṇic layer is the body filled with desires. The mental body is filled with 'I should have' or guilt feelings. The etheric body is pain. Understand these three. Desire, guilt and pain are the feelings or the experiences stored in these layers.

When emotions, desires and feelings arising out of these three attributes are pure, they are called *satva, rajas* and *tamas* depending on the quality of the emotion. Usually, they are impure. They are mixed with each other. We should know how to purify them. If we can purify our desires, we will be liberated. We cannot live without desires. We can only cleanse and purify the desires, directing them towards the right path. Without desires, we can't breathe. Desires must be handled properly. That's what we need to work towards, *satva.*

Next comes guilt or *rajas*. Our restlessness is created by thoughts like, 'I should have done that', 'I should have lived like that', 'Because I did not do it then, let me do it now', 'Let me teach him a lesson, I know what to do now.' This is how restlessness or *rajas* operates.

The third is pain. Whether we do right or wrong, we know how to make it painful. Whatever it is, we know how to create suffering through *tamas.*

The first four body-mind layers are influenced by the three *guṇas.* The mind cannot experience the remaining three layers beyond the fourth layer. They can be experienced only through meditation. In the fifth layer, the causal body, we sleep soundly without dreams. It is called *kāraṇa śarīra*, the energy layer that we experience during deep sleep. The sixth layer is the Cosmic layer, filled with joyful memories, and the seventh is the nirvāṇic layer or the bliss body.

Please listen!

Powerlessness in the level of physical body is tiredness and boredom. Powerlessness in the level of prāṇic body is dilemma. Powerlessness in the level of mental body is worry. Powerlessness in the level of subtle body is depression. Powerlessness in the level of causal body, *kārana śarira* is inability to trust life.

Just remember the first four layers of physical, prāṇic, mental and etheric energy. That's enough, because we will work only on these now. Kṛṣṇa has already spoken about the physical layer. Now He works on the other three *guṇas* of *satva, rajas* and *tamas. Satva* is related to the second layer that is the prāṇic layer, *rajas* is related to the third layer that is the mental body, and the fourth layer is the etheric layer of *tamas.*

As I was saying, *satva* is related to desires and the *prāṇa śarīra.* When our desires change, our prāna flow or our airflow changes. It is prāṇa that sustains life in us. This prāṇa is affected by the changing desires in us. For example, if we are caught in lust or an intense desire, our inhaling and exhaling becomes intense. The prāna going in and coming out increases. With any desire, the prāṇa flow totally changes. If we are in a silent, peaceful mood, the prāṇa flow will be so mild, we will not know prāṇa is flowing.

Understand that this prānic layer is filled with desires. What should we learn about *satva,* about this prānic layer? Let me explain.

YOUR INNER SPACE IS PURE CONSCIOUSNESS

Whether we believe it or not, accept it or not, we are God. We are pure consciousness. No matter how many millions of reasons you give, there are some things which cannot be changed. Our inner space is all-powerful! Our inner space is infinite and infinitely powerful! Our inner space carries the DNA of *Ahaṁ Brahmāsmi* (I Am That)!

How many ever arguments we may give, a country's constitution cannot be changed. In the same way, we may give a million reasons, many arguments to prove that we are not God, and we are not divine, and we are not powerful.

You think, 'I am not even able to get a cup of coffee when I want it. Then how can I be all-powerful? I don't even know what is happening in my spouse's mind. How can I be all-knowing?' You have very silly reasons to deny the possibility of your inner space. Please understand, you never tried to explore your inner space. How can you deny it before even trying?

Understand: if I am expressing the *aśṭa mahā siddhis*, extraordinary eight yogic powers, it is not to show that I am extraordinary; it is just to show that it is possible for you! It is possible for you! Nothing more is required than carrying the space, with the understanding—'When Swamiji can do it, I can do it!' That's all!

Please understand, the space you create inside is so powerful, it can straightaway affect the way you experience life and the way others around you experience life.

Let me define the term 'space'! How you feel things are going to be—that is what I call the 'space you create inside'.

If you are very clear that your space is already in a low energy, and you have thoughts like 'Anyhow, whatever I do is not going to work out, it is not going to be successful!,' then you have already dictated it. You have already given the plan to the Cosmos—'I want my life to be like this only, as a big failure. Please make it happen for me!' So Cosmos will stitch it and give it to you.

The space you carry inside is not the effect of the happenings of your life, it is the command you are giving to the Cosmos. You may put the blame somewhere else. You may say, 'No, no, no! I am in low mood because of the continuous failures that have happened in my life. If you were in my shoes, you would understand why I am like this!'

Please understand, the space is the order you give to the Cosmos to prepare your future. Listen! Just like how you place the order in the restaurants after looking at the menu card, the inner space you carry is also an order you give to the Cosmos, 'I want this, this, this in my life.'

Whatever you carry in your inner space is a possibility. If you are carrying sadness, you are ordering the Cosmos to bring greater sadness into your life. If you are carrying joy, you are waiting for more joy to come in your life. If you are carrying an inability, 'Yes, I have the wrong inner space. I am depressed, but I don't know how to change it,' that is one more inner space; it means you are ordering the Cosmos to give you more powerlessness.

Whatever thoughts we create in our pure consciousness gain power. This inner space exists in all of us and is called Self, *ātman*, or inner divinity. Whatever thoughts we create in this inner space, the deeper they are, the more power they get from this consciousness.

But, the problem is that we create self-conflicting desires. We suffer with our desires because of this. Whether our desires are fulfilled or not, the resulting suffering is inevitable. If the desires are fulfilled, there will be emptiness and if they are unfulfilled, there will be restlessness. In both cases, we move towards *tamas.* Why?

It is a subtle understanding. Many times people ask me, 'How can I complete just by declaring completion?' You can! You are nothing but the bunch of words you uttered, consciously or unconsciously to yourself and to others. Unfortunately, most of it is unconscious. That is where the problem starts. Many times, you do not recognize the power of the words you utter, especially towards yourself.

Whatever words we repeat unconsciously in our inner space become reality in our body, mind and in our world. It is because we have the power to give life to any word. If the words 'Let me get up and go', come to our mind, with those words, immediately our body will move, we will stand up and start going.

Understand, the first lesson you need to learn is the ability to trust the power of integrity.

If you say, 'I am free,' then, you are free! If you say, 'I am a liar,' then, you are a liar! If you say, 'I am powerful,' then, you are powerful! It is just you! The words you utter to yourself and others is life. What a big relief! It can be great news for you if you start living it. It can be good news for you if you start believing it. It can be bad news for you, if you start worrying about it. But the words you utter towards yourself and to others is you, you, you!

One word can make us do whatever we want. Words that appear in our inner space are mantra (sacred sounds). When put together, all the words that appear in our inner space form our life, especially the words that we repeat unconsciously.

Thoughts that we repeat unconsciously are more powerful than words we use consciously. Your inner space is nothing but the words you repeat, again and again within you. So, now decide consciously that you will repeat the right words within you. Whatever mantra or word we use in our inner space, that *dhyāna* or meditation automatically happens in our unconscious. If we use the word 'headache' again and again, we will be meditating on the headache. If we use the word 'health', again and again, we will be meditating on health.

That is why when we start to meditate upon God, we start with a *dhyāna śloka*—meditation verse. It is like the invocation verses that invoke god with the right words. In these verses we verbalize what good things we wish to visualize in our lives.

Verbalization of visualization is the *dhyāna śloka*. Whatever we visualize again and again will be inscribed in our memory, in our inner space, in our inner being. If we have a disease, please never create and repeat a word that carries the name of the disease. Always use these powerful words, 'Let me be wealthy'; never say, 'Let me be free from my poverty.' Declare, 'I create the space of completion'; not, 'I am working hard on my incompletions.'

Please do not abuse the inner space or *icchā śakti* (power of creation). The prānic layer is our *icchā śakti*. It has the energy to make things happen. It has the energy to fulfill our desires. Do not waste *icchā śakti* by creating self-conflicting or self-doubting patterns. Declare completion with all the self-doubting patterns.

COMPLETE WITH SELF-DOUBTING PATTERN

Understand, all of you have one important pattern of self-doubting. Please listen, along with your root-pattern and split-up of your personality, one more thing has entered into you—constantly doubting. This is because any part of your personality decides or does anything, the other part doubts that cognition. Whatever your right hand does, your left hand is doubting. Whatever your left hand does, your right hand is doubting! But, you have to do everything with both hands, only then it will be successful.

Self-conflicting and self-doubting patterns corrupt our whole *satva* space. The *satva* space, restful awareness with you is your basic right and I declare that it is possible for you to reclaim your basic right. I tell you, in the cosmic constitution, restful awareness is your basic right. Enlightened beings land on planet Earth to ensure that your basic right is restored to you.

We continuously allow ourselves to be exploited by what we hear and see. People who don't know the truth about how the mind and consciousness influences us. All these problems arise because we don't know that pure joy of inner space is possible.

Let me make a bold statement that no medicine or chemical can help our mind. All anti-anxiety medicines, all anti-depression medicines are consolations. First, we visualized that we suffered from depression and now we visualize that we have taken some medicine, that's all.

How many of you behave like a self-fulfilling negative astrologer for you? You go on telling yourself, 'My time is not good, I will not be able to do anything.' And even after you do it, you start believing it so strongly that you fulfill it. You are the astrologer, you are the trainer for you, and you are the judge for you. You first give the self-fulfilling prophecy, 'I am a failure'. Then you train yourself for that, so that even the Guru should not make you successful, even by mistake! And you wait for those kinds of responses from society. You do not bother about the support you receive, but you are haunted by the discouragement you get, because you are training yourself to be a failure!

So, who is the decision-maker for your life? First, you are an astrologer who declares that you are a failure. Then, you are a trainer who trains yourself to be a failure, and if failure does not come even then, you become a judge and you declare that you are a failure!

Listen. Don't be caught in that self-doubting game. We disturb the *satva*, the pure space of our being, by creating self-conflicting and self-doubting patterns. Sit with yourself. Complete with all the negative conflicting patterns. Complete with all the self-doubting patterns. Allow the grace to move in you. Create the right inner space by completing again and again with yourself by doing *svapūrṇatva*, self-completion. Create the right space, right mood, and right experience.

COMPLETION WITH RAJAS PATTERN

Next, let us see how two desires conflict one another. We want to lead a peaceful life and we want wealth. With wealth comes responsibility as well. If you actually analyze your attitude towards wealth with integrity, you will understand that you are actually afraid of wealth. You hate wealth!

The fear of responsibility and the greed for wealth always go hand in hand. If you look in, you have greed for wealth, but you are not ready to take responsibility that comes with wealth. This is the self-conflicting desire. Either decide to take responsibility or decide to relax from that desire and restore your integrity by completing with it and accept whatever happens.

Only one thought should be strengthened when two desires conflict. When we have both, we have a self-conflicting mental setup. In the *satva* space, when we create self-conflicting patterns, we are automatically thrown into *rajas*.

Let me describe what Kṛṣṇa says about *rajas*. The mode of passion is born of unlimited desires and longings. This is a beautiful verse.

Kṛṣṇa says, because of this *rajas*, mode of passion, born of unlimited desires and longings, the embodied living entity is bound to doing result-oriented actions.

rajo rāgātmakaṁ viddhi tṛṣṇā saṅga samudhavam |
tan nibadhnāti kaunteya karma saṅgena dehinam || 14.7

He talks about desires and longings. What is the difference? Desires and longings—*rāga* means desire; *tṛṣṇā* means craving, longing. Some memories have our emotional support whereas some memories have been inserted into our being by advertisements.

Advertisements are not only on the television or in a movie theatre. If our father repeats something time and again, that is an advertisement. If our mother says again and again, 'This is right, this is for us, this is for you,' that becomes an advertisement. Some desires have our mental support. We feel these will give us fulfillment; we feel these are our genuine needs. Some desires have been sold to us by someone else. That is the difference between desires and longings.

Desires, *rāga* are ours and longings, *tṛṣṇā* have been given to us by society. Desires are inborn. They are our nature. If we fulfill desires, we feel fulfilled, relaxed and complete. With longings, the moment we fulfill them, we feel empty, incomplete. This is the difference between desire and longing. Desire gives us fulfillment, completion. Longing gives us emptiness, incompletion.

Kṛṣṇa shows us how self-conflicting desires lead us to *rajas*. When desires contradict each other, we get confused. We fall into *rajas*, restlessness.

I have a small story for you.

> One barber asks a man, 'How did you lose your hair?'
>
> The man replies, 'Worry!'
>
> The barber asks, 'What did you worry about?'
>
> The man says, 'About losing my hair!'

Your worrying makes you lose your hair. And in turn, you are worrying about losing the hair. It is a vicious circle. The more patterns you have, the more time it takes to make a decision. We will suffer and be in a dilemma. Man is a dilemma. Continuously we think, 'I should have done this,' or 'I should have done that.' I tell you, life is a failure, if in your old age, you think that you should have done all this when you were young. Dilemma is due to too many conflicting patterns

Dilemma is what Kṛṣṇa calls *rajas* and restlessness. All restlessness is powerlessness.

In rajas, we have tremendous anger, violence and inner restlessness. A person caught in rajas shouts at others and experiences an irritable mood. He has a poisonous tongue. He waits to vomit out his irritation and anger on others. What is agitation? Not taking the responsibility for what you mean to others is agitation. When you don't take responsibility for your commitments to others, you get agitated. You get irritated. If you take the responsibility for your commitments, you will not be agitated or irritated.

Please listen. How to complete with the *rajas* patterns? The first truth you need to know about completion—do completion just to be in the space of completion. All other reasons lead to more and more incompletions. Completion done in the space of completion transforms your personality, transforms your being; the intense, constant agitated violence you carry towards you and others due to *rajas* patterns.

When you drop a stone in the water how the ripples are created; in the same way the moment incompletion is dropped in your consciousness, the ripples of violence towards you and others starts in your being. Worrying becomes your lifestyle. Worrying becomes the compulsive pattern in you. Not only worrying, because of worrying, the inability to handle life. At the most, you only push your life under the carpet. Pushing life under the carpet is not going to be the solution.

See, there are only three ways to handle your incompletions.

One, by pushing them under the carpet.

Second, by trying to forget them either by alcohol or by other entertainments.

Third, by completing them and liberating yourself.

Listen! Continuously completing for the sake of completion leads you to the experience of Enlightenment. I tell you, nothing can be done. When you try to push your incompletions into your unconscious mind, unfortunately, it reaches deeper and goes closer to your consciousness. Anything closer to consciousness becomes powerful. That is why a small incompletion that happened in your life when you are young or a small incompletion which you are suppressing without completing it, it explodes in you as a dangerous imbalance of your *rājasic guṇa* patterns.

Many times, your imbalance is such that you do not care about your destruction. You go on waiting in anger and expecting the other person's destruction. No! If you drink poison, how can the other person die? It is not possible. That is the biggest foolishness human beings get into. They drink the poison thinking the other person is dying.

No! I tell you, all vengeance is rooted in incompletion. Complete it. Trust the Cosmos and complete it. Once we do completion with the *rajas* patterns, we can make one thousand decisions without any stress, violence or suffering. That is why Kṛṣṇa says that when we don't expect the result, when we don't think of *karma phala* (result of the work done), we can do the work intensely.

When we don't expect or worry about the result, we work beautifully because there are fewer patterns. We will not suffer or be tortured by root thought patterns. We will be in the space of completion, which will lead to more and more completion.

Consciousness can never be tired

In the next verse Kṛṣṇa talks about *tamas.*

He addresses Arjuna, 'Oh son of Bhārata, know that the mode of darkness, *tamas,* is born out of ignorance . It is the delusion of all embodied living entities. The result of this mode is madness, indolence and sleep, which bind the conditioned soul.'

This is a beautiful explanation of *tamas.*

> *tamas tv ajñānajaṁ viddhi mohanaṁ sarva dehinām* ǀ
> *pramādālasya nidrābhis tan nibadhnāti bharāta* ǁ 14.8

If there are more *vāsanas* or patterns, the file does not reach the ego easily or even fully. A powerful pattern may make the decision on the way. Why does this happen? Why do you decide unconsciously and regret later?

This unconscious space is filled with negative bio-memories, and powerlessness, restlessness. All our past bio-memory or root thought patterns are stored in your inner space as files without any logical connection between them.

This is what happens. When the file takes a quantum leap to this space, it does not reach the ego properly for a decision. It is as if your computer hard disk is loaded with high-resolution photographs and there is no further scope to work on your hard disk. Like that, when your unconscious is loaded with past root thought patterns and memories, it becomes inadequate, inefficient, and incomplete and makes superficial, illogical decisions.

Take this example: Why does drinking alcohol become a pattern, but drinking water is not becoming a pattern? Both of them, people drink every day. Water people drink more! Then, why does drinking alcohol becomes a pattern and drinking water never becomes a pattern? Because drinking water gives you completion and you are not stuck. After drinking water, you are out of thirst and are more energetic. But unfortunately, all alcoholics are either stuck with elated mood or belated mood, or depressed mood. It is the mood associated with alcohol that makes people stuck, not alcohol itself. Please understand, when a person drinks alcohol, if he feels elated or belated, he wants that mood again and again. That is why he starts and continues drinking alcohol.

Sometimes, people start enjoying even the self-sympathy, the victim mood, the depression! Even for that reason they start drinking alcohol! How do you think I liberate so many people from alcohol and smoking just through meditation, through the Inner Awakening program? Because, first I attack that mood pattern. I make sure neither they feel that elated pattern nor they feel that depressed pattern. When you break the pattern, they don't feel inspired to drink. Then addiction disappears.

Listen. When there are no patterns, there will be no need for the file to drop into the unconscious inner space for a decision. It straightaway meets the *buddhi* and ego after the mind. There are no blocks. The time taken for the unconscious process will be less than the conscious process. We will be intuitive or at the level of God.

The level of an animal is the level of instinct; the level of man is the level of intellect; the level of God is the level of intuition. The level of instinct is the level of *tamas*; the level of intellect is the level of *rajas*; the level of intuition is the level of *satva*.

In *satva*, our mind works continuously and we make decisions, yet we do not become tired. We can be active for twenty-four hours and yet remain peaceful. This is what I call action in inaction and inaction in action. Kṛṣṇa says we will be centered when we are in *satva*. Though lots of activities go on around us, we will remain utterly relaxed in restful awareness.

The whole thing is dependent on one thing: our root thought patterns or bio-memories. The number of root thought patterns determines whether we are caught in *satva, rajas* or *tamas.* These three are not enlightened states. Enlightenment is beyond these three.

If we are caught in *tamas*, we need to move towards *rajas*. If we are caught in *rajas*, make the move towards *satva*. If we are caught in *satva*, it will automatically lead us to enlightenment. How do we do this?

For example, we create a self-conflicting desire at the *satva* level. Because of that we create restlessness, the powerless space in the *rajas* level. When we feel too restless, we drop everything. We decide not to take any responsibility and we sleep instead. We fall into *tamas.*

Tamas is not only tiredness, sleep or depression, not taking enough responsibility is also *tamas.* Work does not need to make you tired. It is the wrong idea taught to you by the society. The only two enemies human beings have are boredom and tiredness. When you entertain them, you build wrong patterns. When you are bored of doing some work, you invoke tiredness—'Om tiredness swāha! ihāgachha! ihāgachha! (chant to invoke the presence of a deity or a quality). Please come here! Come here! Reside here! Reside here!' You invoke tiredness! You invoke depression!

Scrutinize your inner space with integrity. You will see that whenever you don't want to take responsibility, you invoke boredom, tiredness, and fear. Sometime, even greed is used as a substitute for enjoyment. Greed and fantasy are used as substitutes for alcohol and drugs. Listen, when you have a pattern of addiction and drugs, you go for it. When you are afraid that they will spoil your health, you use fantasy and greed as a powerful substitute for alcohol.

For example, we are in tamas if we studied to become a doctor and we do not practice our profession out of laziness. If we don't practice for some other reason, that is fine. However, if we are avoiding because of laziness, we are in *tamas*.

If we drop out because of a spiritual reason such as to meditate, to go on a pilgrimage or to do spiritual work. That is fine. However, dropping out and giving up on you due to tamas means that we don't have enough energy and we cannot make a responsible decision. Why? Too many patterns block our decision process. By the time we make one decision, we feel tired and want to sleep. That is why we attempt to escape from life. Escapists are *tāmasic* people.

How many of you struggle with this *tāmasic* pattern of tiredness and laziness? It is just lack of integrity. Be integrated to your Soul. The Soul can never have tiredness, consciousness can never have tiredness. That is the truth. Whether you realize or not, you are Soul and Consciousness.

Guarding The Senses

14.9 *The mode of goodness conditions one to happiness,*
passion conditions him to fruits of action,
and ignorance to madness.

14.10 *Sometimes the mode of passion becomes prominent,*
defeating the mode of goodness, O son of Bhārata.
And sometimes the mode of goodness defeats passion, and
at other times the mode of ignorance defeats goodness and
passion. In this way there is always competition for supremacy.

14.11 *When the light of Self-knowledge illuminates all the senses*
(or gates) in the body,
Then it should be known that goodness is predominant.

14.12 *O Bharatarṣabha, chief of Bhārata, when there is an increase*
in the mode of passion, the symptoms of great attachment,
uncontrollable desire, hankering, and intense endeavor develop.

Kṛṣṇa further explains the three modes.

'O Bhārata, sometimes the mode of goodness, *satva*, becomes prominent, defeating the modes of passion and ignorance, and at other times, ignorance defeats goodness and passion. In this way, there is always competition for supremacy.'

All of us are not completely caught in *satva* or *rajas* or *tamas*. We swing between *satva, rajas* and *tamas.* Sometimes we get up in the morning and feel fresh. We feel as if all our questions are answered; we are fresh, alive and we think we have become almost enlightened! Everything goes beautifully until evening. Suddenly we become restless. The very next day, we are in *tamas.* We don't want to do anything. These mood swings take place continuously.

Obesity and mood swings are closely related. When we allow these mood swings to happen, we torture ourselves. Sometimes we are restless, sometimes we are peaceful and sometimes we are in *tamas*. When we are in *tamas* we don't want to do anything; we want to escape from everything and run away. We are caught in these three modes of nature: sometimes in instinct, sometimes in intellect and sometimes in intelligence.

WHY DO WE HAVE MOOD SWINGS?

Why? This happens if we have collected too many patterns about something over many years. For example, the pattern of drinking develops if, from a young age, you were repeatedly taught not to drink and that drinking is a sin. This raises your curiosity to taste alcohol at least once. Never give a law to children. Instead give them understanding and the spirit behind the law.

If we want to bring up children blissfully, we need to bring them up without guilt. Breaking rules creates guilt. To give understanding, we need two things. First we need to be intelligent enough to understand the meaning behind the rules we are trying to enforce. Next we need patience to explain it all to them. Even though it takes more time and energy, focus on giving them understanding.

People complain to me, '*Swamiji*, in these modern times, there is no time. My daughter goes to school. I have a job. How do we find time to make her understand?' I say, 'Why did you give birth to your child if you don't have time to bring her up? You should have decided earlier in life.'

Before deciding to have children, find your root thought pattern and become complete, enlightened. That is the only qualification we need. Unless we are in the space of completion, we will not have any clarity how to guide them, and we will go on creating more confusion, guilt and incompletion in them. Till we learn the science of completion, we should not plan to have children.

Understand, without completing your root thought pattern, your DNA layers are not awakened, mitochondria cell energy is not awakened. For common human beings, two layers of DNA are awakened. If you find your root thought pattern and complete, six layers of DNA, your *kuṇḍalinī* (potential energy) will be awakened in you. If six layers of DNA are awakened, your child will be an enlightened being! If you decide to have children, have the intelligence to give them the right cognition behind all that you tell them.

When parents bring their kids to me, they force them to touch my feet. I say, 'Never do that. This is your greed.' These parents think that they and their children get *puṇya* or good credits by touching my feet. They impose this idea on their kids, an idea based on their greed. I ask these parents not to force them. *Namaskār* (respectful salutation) is more than enough. By forcing them, they make the kids hate me. The next time these kids see the orange robe, they will grumble, 'Oh, now we must do that exercise.'

Never enforce rules on kids. We are suffering from rules given to us by our parents. The rules given by our parents are in our *rajas* and *tamas* layers. They lead us to restlessness and deep depression again and again. They create more and more incompletion, powerlessness for us.

DESIRE AND GUILT PATTERNS

Desire and guilt are two forms of the same energy. One is related to the future. The other is related to the past. Desire is related to the future. Guilt is related to the past. 'I should have done that' plays a major role in our 'I should do this.' 'I should do this' is determined by 'I should have done that.'

Guilt that is created by rules handed down to us by our elders creates hell in our life and leads us to *tamas*. Kṛṣṇa says we are led to *antaḥ* (the end). We fall into ignorance or into the end.

Kṛṣṇa says the manifestations of the modes of goodness can be experienced when all the gates of the body are illuminated by knowledge.

This is the technique. The gates of the body are the gates through which we cognize: we receive knowledge or information through the eyes, ears, nose, tongue and the sense of touch or physical pleasure. These are the files through which we receive information from outside. He says that we should keep these five carefully guarded by *prakāśa* (illuminated knowledge). We should ensure security at these gates and knowledge is that security.

We should have knowledge about what should be taken in and what should not be taken in. Knowing this, we will reside in *satva* forever. We will reside in bliss forever. He says we should appoint a guard for the gates of our body. There is no security system for our body. We have security for our home. If someone breaks in, automatically the call goes to 911. We reside twenty-four hours every day in this house called our body, yet we don't have a security system!

> Ramaṇa Mahaṛṣi sings in beautiful homage to the sacred Aruṇācala Hill in Tiruvannamalai in his famous song 'Aruṇācala Akśaramaṇamalai', 'When these thieves, the five senses, have entered into the house, Oh Aruṇācala, were you not at home? How did they enter?' He asks Śiva, 'When these five senses entered the house (body-mind), were you not there? Why did you let them enter?'

Kṛṣṇa says, let us have the security, the protection of knowledge at the five gates, and we will reside in continuous bliss. Completion is Bliss. This means that we should not allow the incomplete thoughts that create suffering to enter our inner space through the eyes and other senses.

This means, avoid the television or media. At least do not watch programs that create violence, depression, and powerlessness in you. We should only watch programs that give joy and make us complete, blissful. When we protect our senses with *satva,* we will not allow negative patterns to come in.

Please do not infuse your consciousness with powerless thoughts that create suffering in you. Continuously add thoughts of completion that give power, bliss and peace. We may think this is impractical. We may think, 'How can we live in society without knowing what's going on in the world?' Be very clear, knowing what's going on in the world is a disease. Collecting information is a disease.

The other day, someone said, '*Swamiji*, we should watch television to get an idea of the culture.' However these television shows are trash. They are nonsensical. The more we watch, the more negative patterns we imbibe. We simply suffer. We put ourselves into *rajas* and *tamas* again and again.

Life is much too valuable and too short to be spent worrying. Do not allow powerless thoughts that create depression, low mood and longing, into your system, especially at *sandhyā* time - the twilight time at which day and night meet. Our ancient masters knew that *sandhyā* time, when day and night meet, is a critical time. There are two *sandhyās*, dawn and dusk. Our masters knew that whatever thought-seeds are sown inside our being at *sandhyā* come out as full-blown trees. That is why the masters insisted that at *sandhyā* time, one should spend time in a temple, praying, listening to prayers, reading devotional material. Meditate or go to a temple and do something spiritual at this time. These spiritual ideas go inside as seeds and become a valuable complete tree in our life.

Protect your senses twenty-four hours a day. Do not entertain any form of powerlessness at any time of the day, in any level of the body, mind and consciousness. If you cannot guard your senses at all times, protect yourself at least during *sandhyā* time.

Kṛṣṇa gives one technique, one suggestion: Protect the five senses from negative ideas of powerlessness, the incompletions and infuse positive ideas of completion through the five senses. Whatever we feed upon becomes our being and we radiate that energy.

Next, Kṛṣṇa says that attachment, greed, craving, and restless actions are indications of *rājasic* behavior. This fits most people, but it fits most aptly anyone in business or a corporate career.

Greed is the corporate creed. People who recruit and train employees use motivation as their only tool. What is motivation? The whole idea of motivating someone is ill-motivated. To motivate someone, we must hold a carrot in front of him or her. Then the carrot becomes the goal. If we are donkeys, we follow the carrot. If we have any intelligence, we will realize that the carrot will always be dangled in front of us just out of reach!

The donkey powerlessly runs after the carrot in restless action. It cannot stay still. The carrot is so near and yet so far. So how can it stay still? This is the story of the corporate people.

Instead of enjoying the path, we worry about the goal and constantly live in incompletion. We worry about when we will reach, where we will reach. In the process, we do not notice how we are traveling. We miss the beauty of the path.

When we torture ourselves with worrying about quarterly results, how can we enjoy work? How can results be achieved? As long as we struggle, we suffer even if we make money. The goal that we are chasing will be a mirage, an illusion. As soon as we reach that goal, we will be forced to chase another goal. Acquisition becomes the goal, not enjoyment.

That is why people who are successful have both passion and patience for what they do. They do not care about what happens in the end as long as what they do is from the space of completion. If we are complete about what we do, we will enjoy what we do. Whatever we do will be wonderful and successful.

We can never be happy in *rajas*. It drives us like a donkey until we are exhausted and we collapse with our incompletion. We need to decide whether or not this is the way we want to live.

Ask: Do I wish to be a donkey driven by a carrot dangling in front of me all my life? When we decide, 'No, this is not what I want,' it is time to break away from *rajas* and move towards bliss, *nityānanda*.

The Depression Of Success

14.13 *O son of Kuru, when there is an increase in the mode of ignorance, madness, illusion, inertia and darkness are manifested.*

14.14 *When one dies in the mode of goodness [satva],*
He goes where the realized souls are.

14.15 *When one dies in the mode of passion [rajas],*
he takes birth among those engaged in activities.
When he dies in the mode of ignorance [tamas],
he takes birth in the space of the ignorant.

14.16 *By acting in the mode of goodness, one becomes purified.*
Work done in the mode of passion result in distress, and actions performed in the mode of ignorance result in foolishness.

14.17 *From the mode of goodness, real knowledge develops; from the mode of passion, greed develops; From the mode of ignorance develops foolishness, madness and illusion.*

We act like a wind-up toy when we are steeped in *rajas,* and like a battery-operated toy with a dead battery when we are in tamas.

Kṛṣṇa uses powerful words to drive home how desperate that state is: ignorance, madness, illusion, inertia and darkness.

aprakāśo 'pravṛttiś ca pramādo moha eva ca |
tamasy etāni jāyate vivṛddhe kuru-nandana || 14.13

It is surprising how quickly one can slip from *rajas* to *tamas.* To slip from restless activity into inactivity and inertia is simple.

Activity without meaning, activity with tension and stress and activity totally focused on sensual satisfaction quickly leads to deep fatigue. The activity without any meaning that we find in *tamas* is not the same as activity without a purpose and goal that we experience in *satva*. Please do not confuse the two.

The Purpose Of Life

I mentioned earlier that the real danger of *rajas* is that we are constantly focused on a goal and we forget to be in completion and enjoy the path as we pursue a meaningless purpose. Life has no purpose. It only has meaning. The meaning of life is to be in the space of completion; to be in restful awareness, to realize our inner Divinity. That is why I say that I am here not to prove my Divinity, but to prove your Divinity.

To be divine and to realize that inner divinity is our true meaning in life. Anything less than that is meaningless. Being aggressive, being restlessly active, or being constantly on the move does not help us understand or realize this meaning. We will be running after one thing or another. We are just plain greedy.

If we are driven by mere possessive obsession, we are bound to become tired sooner or later. Aggression results in deep depression. This is what I call the 'depression of success'. I see this often in countries like the USA. People struggle to increase their material wealth, disregarding everything else. People change cars every year, houses every third year and their spouses every fifth year!

People run after material possessions and trophies without knowing the right context of 'why they are doing, what they are doing'. One day when they have acquired and reacquired so many things and still feel incomplete, unhappy, uneasy and listless, they wonder why they acquired the things that they struggled for. They go into deep depression, deep incompletion what we call *tamas*.

The depression of success is difficult to address. To experience failure when we have always been successful and worked so hard is difficult to accept. What results then is depression, *tamas. Tamas* is generally born out of the ignorance of our true Self. Sometimes *tamas* can arise out of an effort to move out of that ignorance. A highly *rājasic* person, one who has been aggressively pursuing material gains, when moving into a spiritual path can easily move into *tamas* for a while.

Listen. Life happens to you inside and outside, both. If you think it is only inside and not outside, you don't know the outside. If you think it is only outside, you don't know the inside. If life is not happening to you inside, it is depression; if life is not happening to you outside, it is inefficiency. If life is happening to you inside, it is responsibility; if life is happening to you outside, it is success.

Tamas is darkness. It is negative. We can only remove darkness by bringing in light. In the same way, we dispel ignorance by bringing in awareness of the science of completion, *pūrṇatva*. The *Upaniṣad* says—*tamaso mā jyotirgamaya*—meaning, let my darkness be removed by light.

Let the light and wisdom of Kṛṣṇa, the Jagadguru, dispel your darkness and *tamas*.

In these verses, Kṛṣṇa tells us where the person goes after death when steeped in these attributes of *satva, rajas* and *tamas*. A *sātvic* person becomes divine. A *tāmasic* person chooses a lower life. A *rājasic* person continues to suffer due to greed.

In another verse in the Gītā, Kṛṣṇa tells Arjuna that a person is reborn based on the last thought before death. Here Kṛṣṇa explains how that last thought is not an accident. It is based on one's *guṇa*, nature, his patterns. The mental setup, the conditioning, the *mūla vāsanā* with which we led life and with which we leave our life as well. When we are reborn, our spirit finds another body to occupy.

BE REBORN WITH GODS

Please listen! Every birth is your declaration of completion. You decide, 'Come on! I declare completion. I will now work from the space of completion.' During the birth you declare completion and start the whole think anew; and if you fall from the space of completion, you bring some of those past incompletions back. That is what is *prārabdha karma*. *Karma* which you bring back from the past incompletions is *prārabdha*. Whatever bio-memory you brought with you when you assumed the body is *prārabdha*. The muscle-memory you are accumulating is *agāmya*, and all collective bio-memories is *sañcita*. If you come to planet Earth only with bio-energy, without bio-memory, you are an Incarnation.

In the Inner Awakening program, we study the root thought patterns in great detail. People sometimes ask me, 'What do you give during Inner Awakening?' I tell you, I give *you* your life. I give your 'life' to you in Inner Awakening!

Only when you have found your root thought pattern and removed it and regained your consciousness, you will understand, 'Oh, God! I have literally wasted my whole life!' Understand, in the Inner Awakening program, I give you your life, because I help you find your root patterns and destroy it! Many superficial and deep root thought patterns will be burnt out during the meditations that the participants go through in this program. Therefore, symbolically, I give them the option to take a new spiritual name at the end, signifying a rebirth.

Kṛṣṇa says that a person living in *satva* goes to higher spaces, the abodes of the realized sages. He becomes divine, *tadottama vidāṁ lokān amalān pratipadyate* (14.14). When we are steeped in *satva*, we live in restful awareness, the space of enlightenment. We live in the present moment. We are no longer attached to the results of our action and we are no longer controlled by fear and greed root patterns. We stop thinking about ourselves and we start living for others.

When one is in *tamas,* in deep ignorance and darkness, one sinks lower in rebirth. Kṛṣṇa says such a person is reborn as an animal. The lowest energy center of a human being is the *mūlādhāra cakra*, the root center. Human beings are provided with intelligence to move upward in consciousness. We have the freedom to make mistakes and we do make mistakes. When Kṛṣṇa talks about being reborn in ignorance and as animals, it is not to denigrate animals. He means, a human being who behaves instinctively, out of a blocked *mūlādhāra cakra*, and out of an animalistic nature, is ignorant of his potential as a human.

We are not human beings striving for a spiritual experience. We are spiritual beings enjoying a human experience. That is the truth. We can be in this state only when we are in *satva*. When we are in *tamas*, we forget our spiritual nature. When we are in *rajas,* we have a vague idea; however, even that spiritual experience becomes an attachment, another pattern, goal and desire. We become attached to something that is beyond attachment. Kṛṣṇa says that we are reborn into this human form, back into this cycle of life and death, this cycle of *saṁsāra*, with all its suffering.

It is our choice to be instinctive and unconscious, in deep *tamas*, like an animal, or to be logical and chasing objects out of *rajas.* The third choice is to be beyond attachments, in a super conscious state of completion, in an intuitive state, in tune with our sublime *satva* nature. This choice determines our next birth. In fact, it determines whether we will even be born again.

Kṛṣṇa, the Master psychologist is right on the mark: Purification and knowledge from *satva,* distress and greed from *rajas*, and foolishness, madness and illusion from *tamas*!

Your True Nature is Pūrṇa Beyond Triguṇa

Our center is our true nature. Our true nature is divine. We are one with the universal energy, God, *Parāśakti* or whatever we want to call it. We cannot describe it. We can just experience it. We experience bliss when our focus is in that central core and not out at the edges of our personality. Throughout life we run away from that center, that core of bliss, that space of completion.

Let me define Completion.

Completion is removing the delusion of incompletion, which makes you cognize the other is separate from you; the delusive cognizance, the delusive cognition.

Our senses lead us towards the periphery where incompletions are, where material objects are. Our inner core is empty: it is *śūṇya*. But it is also *pūrṇa*, complete by itself with nothing else needed to top off the bliss. However, the outer periphery of incompletions is forever changing. Nothing is eternal about it. Even when objects are the same, our perceptions keep changing. This periphery is *māyā*, illusion, *tamas*, ignorance. Understand, incompletion has no existence. Incompletion is the delusive cognition that stands between you and the Whole. Complete with everything.

Our *rājasic* nature, the restless activity that strives to introduce purpose into something that is essentially without purpose, keeps driving us away from the center of completion into this peripheral darkness of incompletions, *tamas* and *māyā. Rajas* always drives us into *tamas.* Aggression, passion, attachment and aversion eventually take us into delusion and ignorance.

But from time to time we get that spark of intelligence that says—there is more meaning to life than fantasies. We start searching. When we seek our true nature, we move towards our center, the core of bliss. Then something in the external space attracts us and we move out to the periphery. We keep moving in and out, from center to periphery, from periphery back to center. That is why I call human beings eccentric! They can neither be in the center nor in the periphery. They settle in between and keep oscillating. They are eccentric. They are neither in complete madness nor in completion with their divine consciousness.

The movement towards our core, our true self, *ātma* is driven by *satva.* The movement outwards is driven by *rajas.* When we are fully settled in the periphery, we are caught in *tamas.* We are no longer human. When we settle into the center which is the space of completion, we go beyond the three *guṇas.* We become the *triguṇa rahita,* the Divine one who is beyond the three attributes, who is *pūrṇa*—complete.

Where Do We Go From Here

14.18 *Those situated in the mode of goodness, gradually go upward to the higher planes; those in the mode of passion live on the earthly planets; and those in the mode of ignorance go down to the worlds below.*

14.19 *When you see that there is nothing beyond these modes of nature in all activities and that the Supreme Lord is transcendental to all these modes, then you can know, attain My spiritual nature.*

14.20 *When the embodied being is able to transcend these three modes, he can become free from birth, death, old age and their distresses and can enjoy nectar even in this life.*

Kṛṣṇa provides the key to liberation here. Those who go beyond the three *guṇas*, beyond the activity-producing attributes, beyond the root thought patterns and become complete, free of bondages, enjoy bliss in this world. This is the assurance of the Master. This is a guarantee.

These words are a great technique.

Step one is when we realize that each of our thoughts, words, and activities arises from one of the three root patterns, *guṇas—satva, rajas* and *tamas.*

Step two is the understanding about which *guṇa,* root pattern it is and exactly what that *guṇa* is doing to us; what disempowering cognition that *guṇa* is building about our inner image (*mamakāra),* our outer-image (*ahaṁkāra*), others' image (*anyakāra*), others' expectation about us, and life's image (*svānyakāra*).

Step three is to do the completion and the creation process; do completion with that *guṇa* or root pattern and do creation of the *satva guṇa*, the right inner space to create the reality that we want. Finally we transcend *satva guṇa* and enter into *nirguṇa* or 'no *guṇa* state'.

Whatever we are doing, whatever is happening to us, we need to become aware of the attribute, the *guṇa*, the pattern that is driving us and complete with it. If it is a fantasy, we work out of *tamas*. If it is fear and greed, we work out of *rajas*. And if we are complete, unattached and undisturbed by all that is happening in and around us, we act out of *satva guṇa*.

Here Kṛṣṇa assures, 'Those situated in the mode of goodness gradually go upward to the higher planes—*ūrdhvaṁ gacchanti sattva-sthā* (14.18).' A continuous tireless completion process creates the basis for higher level practices, for higher planes.

We have talked about the *saṁskāras* or root thought patterns that are buried in our unconscious. They drive us through one of these attributes (*guṇas*). Conscious, logical and analytical procedures cannot easily identify them, let alone remove or repair them. That is why so-called catharsis processes that aim to rid us of negative emotions give only temporary relief. The basic negativity remains buried.

ONLY ENLIGHTENED MASTER DISSOLVES GUṆAS

Visualizing consciously or unconsciously does not take us out of *rajas* and *tamas*. We can be dragged deeper into the fantasyland of *tamas*. Those moments are the most dangerous moments you are spiritually vulnerable.

Listen. Crying out of powerlessness due to *rajas* or *tamas* is *not* okay. When your immune system is down, any wrong negative spiritual concepts can infect you. Infection by the root pattern can happen in you during those powerless moments. When the infection of neative patterns happens in you, it is almost incurable. **Only an Enlightened Master can do the surgery and cure it. That surgery is called Inner Awakening.**

The only way to move into *satva* and dissolve *saṁskāras* is to move into a super-conscious state through powerful meditations processes on root pattern completion. There is no other way that we can achieve it ourselves. Only the presence of super-conscious energy, the Enlightened Master can dissolve *saṁskāras*, the root patterns and burn out our *vāsanas*, the conflicting patterns developed through these root patterns. It is the only way. All other techniques do only one thing; they make money for those who promote them and put those who are seeking help into deeper trouble.

So first bring integrity to your thoughts and actions. Identify which *guṇa* they come from. If it is a fantasy, rooted in *tamas*, complete and drop the fantasy and move into the present reality.

Please listen. Every one of you has a fantasy deep down about you becoming all-powerful, all-knowing, *sarvajña*, that's all. I tell you, living as per the expectations of you, behaving as you expected about you, is the greatest joy you can experience in life. Completion does that to you! I tell you, nothing else can do *that* to you.

This realization and awareness that completion helps you move out of the zone of fantasies and creates your reality *as you want*, can only come as a result of learning the Science of Completion.

Going Beyond The Guṇas

14.21 *Arjuna inquires:*
O my Lord, by what symptoms is one known
who is transcendental to those modes? What is his behavior?
And how does he transcend the modes of nature?

14.22,23,24,25 *Śrī Bhagavān says:*
He who does not hate illumination, attachment and delusion
when they are present, nor longs for them when they disappear;
who is seated like one unconcerned, being situated beyond these
material reactions of the modes of nature, who remains firm,
knowing that the modes alone are active;
He who regards alike pleasure and pain, and looks on a
lump of earth, a stone and a piece of gold with an equal eye;
who is wise and holds praise and blame to be the same;
who is unchanged in honor and dishonor, who treats friend
and foe alike, who has abandoned all result-based undertakings,
such a man is said to have transcended the modes of nature.

With great clarity the Master tells us what to do. He uses specific terms that cannot be misunderstood or misinterpreted. Kṛṣṇa explains the nature of one who has transcended the three *guṇas*, one who has gone beyond his natural attributes, one who has completed with his root patterns. He explains what we need to do to become a *triguṇa rahita*, to become liberated from the influence of the three *guṇas.*

One who is beyond the three *guṇas* is unaffected by their play. He is beyond the play of emotions. Whatever happens is right for him. Success and failure mean the same. Friend and foe make no difference. Poverty or richness has no influence.

Such an attitude of total detachment requires one thing: complete trust. When we trust that whatever happens is what needs to happen and we accept whatever happens as it arises, we are totally detached. Then whatever happens will be right. Such trust can only come from surrender.

I tell my disciples that because I have no home, every home that I visit is my home. Anywhere and everywhere I stay, whether it is under a tree or out in the open, is my home. Four walls, a door and a lock do not create a home for me. There is neither attraction nor aversion. Just as people admire the clothes or accessories on a mannequin, I admire the clothes and jewelry on this body. They have no connection to me.

Every movement I make is at the order of Existence. I cannot move a finger without the permission of that universal energy. When we are one with Existence, one with nature, nothing affects us. I walked tens of thousands of miles barefoot across the length and breadth of India. People ask, 'How is it your feet are so soft, not calloused and broken as ours would be, if we walked barefoot even ten miles?' I tell you: If we trust Nature, Nature looks after us.

We create pain and pleasure through association with powerlessness, through conditioning. We create greed and fear through association. Our root patterns, our conditioned muscle-memories and bio-memories, create pain and pleasure.

Light and darkness, good and bad, right and wrong are based on root patterns. Our inadequate cognitions, the civilized education and refinement tells us that a person dressed in a particular manner is acceptable in society and another dressed differently is not.

No scripture ever said that one person is inferior to another. All scriptures affirm that every human being is a spiritual being; all of us carry the seed of Divinity in us.

When you complete with everything, animate or inanimate, you will experience the space of non-duality, *Advaita*. Relationships are nothing but your own extensions. Relationships are not outside; they are just your own extensions. The *you* extended outside *you* are your relationships. Completing with all your extensions, you learn to complete the incomplete *you* present in the other. Your negative cognitions disappear and from the space of completion, all that one can see is the Divinity in others, the space of non-duality, *Advaita*.

Expression Of The Divine

14.26 *One who engages in full devotional service, who does not fall down in any circumstance, at once transcends the modes of material nature and thus comes to the level of Brahman.*

14.27 *And I am the basis of Brahman, which is the rightful state of ultimate happiness, and which is immortal, imperishable and eternal.*

Kṛṣṇa concludes the chapter by saying that the transcendental state beyond the three attributes of nature, *guṇas*, is *Brahman*, the ultimate Cosmic Consciousness, the ultimate space of Completion. He says you reach this through devotion. He says that He is that Brahman, the source of Eternal Bliss—*brahmaṇo hi pratiṣṭhāham*.

brahmaṇo hi pratiṣṭhāham amṛtasyāvyayasya ca |
śāśvatasya ca dharmasya sukhasyaikāntikasya ca || 14.27

Kṛṣṇa speaks as *Parabrahma* Kṛṣṇa, the supreme energy and not as Vāsudeva Kṛṣṇa, the individual. He is in the expanded consciousness of Brahman, and beyond the three *guṇas*. He is the Source of the *guṇas*.

Your Level of Completion Decides

What is the difference between *Parabrahma* Kṛṣṇa (Ultimate Consciousness) and Vāsudeva Kṛṣṇa (the physical person, son of Vāsudeva)? In the case of an ordinary human being, even though he has the potential of Divinity, he has not realized it. That is the difference between *you* and an Enlightened Master, an Incarnation. Both of you are Divine to the same extent. Yet you are unaware of your Divinity, whereas the Enlightened Master, the Incarnation is fully aware of it.

In the case of Śrī Kṛṣṇa, He is the Master, the Complete Incarnation. Why then the difference? The difference is not to do with Him. It is to do with us.

Listen! In *Vedic* tradition, we narrate hundreds of Purāṇas, the recorded historical happenings, where Māhadeva Himself comes, where Kṛṣṇa appears to give victory and protection, to their devotees.

What is the gap between the life during *Vedic* times and now? Surely, our Masters are very logical, scientific people, never spreading superstition. But, in the modern days, all these things are thought to be superstitious. Why is it that all which happened at that time, is not happening now? Why is there so much gap? I tell you, the only gap, why it was happening then and why it is not happening *now*, the answer is—incompletions!

When you complete, complete, and complete, then everything what you read in the *Vedic* tradition becomes reality. It can be reality. I tell you, completion is the bridge to reach the *Vedic* tradition, to reach extraordinary powers, to experience Divine expressions in your life.

Completion is life at every level. I can give you the whole list. The only difference between *you* and Śrīnivāsan Rāmānujan, the genius mathematician is the level of completion. The only difference between *you* and Ādī Śaṅkara is the level of completion. The only difference between Arjuna and *Parabrahma* Kṛṣṇa is the level of completion. I tell you, with completion you start living with God directly!

The frequency of *Parabrahma* Kṛṣṇa is not visible to and approachable by mortals. That is why Arjuna had to be given the Divine vision to perceive *Parabrahma rūpa* or *viśvarūpa*. In order for humans to perceive Him and interact with Him, *Parabrahma* Kṛṣṇa must become Vāsudeva Kṛṣṇa. To a certain extent He must subject Himself to the play of the *guṇas*. When an Enlightened being has merged with the Universal energy and incarnates in human form, that Incarnation must have some *satva guṇa* infused into Him in order to take human form. Within some time, this *satva guṇa* also disappears, leaving the being beyond the three *guṇas* and once again in an Enlightened state.

Each Enlightened Master, each Incarnation is unique in His expression of the experience as the Divine. Some express experiences and some don't. Our scriptures say that if two enlightened masters say the same thing, one is a fake! The experience is the same, yet the expression is different. Kṛṣṇa is different from Buddha and Śiva. Each has the same theme of compassion, yet the way the compassion is expressed is different. Buddha expressed it as contemplation and Kṛṣṇa in joyous loving completion. So we choose a Master based upon how we vibrate to His expression. If our path is devotion, we gravitate to Kṛṣṇa; He is lovable. If we are the meditative type, we go to Śiva, the Master who teaches in vibrating, alive silence.

SURRENDER OUT OF COMPLETION IS REAL SURRENDER

It does not matter who our Master is. What matters is our faith, trust and the attitude or space of surrender. Our Master can be an unenlightened being. If we trust him, we can become enlightened, even though he may not be. What matters more is our attitude and feeling connection based on the level of our completion, our *guṇa*, and not the Master's state. Even if we worship a stone and surrender to it from a complete inner space, cognizing it to be our ultimate savior, we will be liberated. It is true.

Please listen. When you practice the right reason, right results come. When you practice even the same values with smaller reasons, only the small results come. More than what actions you do, what matters is the space from which the actions are done. If you do not have the right context, even when you worship a deity or a God, it is useless. Listen, because even while you pray, if you strengthen the space that you are poor, you are weak, if that gets strengthened more and more, even your prayer will make you weak.

Surrendering not even bothering to whom you are surrendering, as a quality of surrendering is Enlightenment.

Understand, surrendering without even looking up to whom you are surrendering, like Lakṣman's surrender out of his completion is real Surrender.

In Rāmāyaṇa, the great Hindu epic history of Lord Śrī Rāma's incarnation, Lakṣman is the younger brother of Lord Rāma, who devoted his whole life in selflessly serving the feet of Śrī Rama and Mātā Sītā.

When Sītā is kidnapped by Rāvaṇa, some of the *vānaras* (monkeys) gathered some jewels thrown by her and brought it to Rāma for identifying them.

Lakṣman could only recognize the anklets of Sītā. Rāma asked, 'why are you not able to recognize the jewelry?'

Lakṣman said, 'No. I have never seen the Mother above the feet. I look at both of you only when I do *nāmaskār* (surrendering salutation), but I never looked directly or intensely.'

Lakṣman never even saw the upper jewelry of Mātā Sītā.

Whatever we understand, we understand; but it is true. I tell you, Lakṣman does not even know whose feet he is falling at, he just sees the feet. It means that you are very clear, you are not that big! It is the realization that you are not that big; that humbleness without the humility.

Understand, humbleness as a fact not as a quality is the right context, the right space. Humbleness as a quality can bring ego, incompletion. 'I am very humble, I am very humble.' No! Humbleness as an effect of the space of completion, this is the way—'I am in humbleness without feeling humiliated.' These are different qualities, *guṇas*.

So, don't even bother to whom you are surrendering. It is the joy of surrender, the celebration of surrender. I can surrender in front any stone, I have no problem at all. Not just here, at any temple, anywhere, any deity, any stone. You can see very clearly, that is one job I do very sincerely. Because I have the space of surrender, I can surrender to Śiva,

I can surrender to Viṣṇu. I can surrender to my own Pādukas (sacred foot-sandal of master). In *Vedic* tradition, we can surrender to even a tree or a tulasi plant (holy basil plant). In Indian houses, even door-frames are worshipped, one lamp is worshipped.

The faith and the surrender help us transcend the nature of all activities. We surrender the result of our actions to that Master, whomsoever *He* may be, whomsoever *It* may be. We do everything meditating on that Master and surrender it all at His feet. That space of completion alone liberates us.

This is what Kṛṣṇa means by devotion, *bhakti-yogena sevate* (14.26), which is unfailing in all circumstances. Nothing more is needed. Kṛṣṇa is not talking about the flute-playing, yellow-robed Kṛṣṇa. Anyone that we surrender to totally, is Kṛṣṇa and we then fall into Kṛṣṇa consciousness, the Consciousness of Completion.

Let us pray to *Parabrahma* Kṛṣṇa, the Universal Consciousness, the Ultimate Energy, to give us all this understanding in our life, to make us experience the truth that He teaches and to establish us in Completion, make us radiate Eternal Bliss, *Nityānanda.*

'Thus ends the fourteenth chapter named ***Guṇatraya Vibhāga Yogaḥ****, The Yoga of Division of the three Guṇas,' of the* ***Bhagavad Gītā Upaniṣad, Brahmavidyā Yogaśāstra****, the scripture of yoga dealing with the science of the Absolute in the form of* ***Śrī Kṛṣṇārjuna saṃvād****, dialogue between Śrī Kṛṣṇa and Arjuna.*

CHAPTER

15

Puruṣottama Yogaḥ

No Questions, Only Doubts

When we question, we show our arrogance and violence. When we doubt, we reveal our authentic quest for the truth and readiness to receive the master. Arjuna, now beyond questions, allows Kṛṣṇa to give the experience of the Supreme Being, Puruṣottama.

No Questions, Only Doubts

Only Kṛṣṇa speaks in chapter 15 of *Bhagavad Gītā.* Arjuna does not utter a word. Arjuna's inner space has been silenced. He is in the pure space of listening. As a result, his questions have disappeared. Arjuna, who is *Puruṣa,* is now established in *Upaniṣad*, mirroring the Superconscious Supreme Being or Self, *Puruṣottama* Bhagavān Śrī Kṛṣṇa.

Kṛṣṇa expounds upon who He is and what He is. This chapter is traditionally titled *Puruṣottama Yogaḥ*, Yoga of the Supreme Being. Kṛṣṇa unveils the reasons why He is *Puruṣottama*, Supreme amongst beings and explains that what He has imparted to Arjuna is the most profound secret. Kṛṣṇa is convinced that Arjuna is ready to receive the Truth.

Arjuna has settled into his Self. His confusions have disappeared; questions have dissolved due to his cosmic experience in *Viśvarūpa Darśan Yogaḥ*—having the vision of Kṛṣṇa's Cosmic form—and his direct spiritual experience. He has achieved the depth of knowledge and the complete cognition required to intranalyze and radiate whatever Kṛṣṇa has taught him so far. He has achieved the intensity of spiritual experience. He is a new being. He can no more be called Arjuna. **He is expressing the power of living with enriching, overflowing with devotion onto Śrī Kṛṣṇa present in everything and everything present in Kṛṣṇa!**

With the revelation of Kṛṣṇa's cosmic form, Arjuna has the awareness of his own part in the collective consciousness. This experience of completion has put him in a devotional mood, which is now overflowing as enriching. This devotion is not merely towards Kṛṣṇa, but through Kṛṣṇa, to all of humanity. Only for enriching others, Arjuna speaks and listens on behalf of humanity and not for himself.

From now on, everything that Arjuna does is enriching, enriching, enriching his own extension in others! He becomes the cause for creating the ultimate reality for humanity in the Cosmic play of the complete Incarnation, *Pūrṇavātar* Śrī Kṛṣṇa!

Arjuna doesn't have any more intellectual questions. He has reached a point where he is totally ready to receive and mirror Kṛṣṇa. He has moved forward from a state of thoughtfulness, where he is confused, incomplete and full of questions, to a no-mind state of completion where questions disappear.

Doubts Are Necessary

Masters convey their experience. It is an energy transmission that occurs. To convey an experience in words denies the experience. Once verbalized, the experience loses meaning. Kṛṣṇa is different. He is engaged in a dialogue with Arjuna for the benefit of enriching the mankind to resolve those conflicts and doubts that arise in all humans. After seeing Kṛṣṇa's cosmic form, Arjuna's questions are about the nature of the divine Kṛṣṇa and how to approach Him. Kṛṣṇa now explains to him what He is and how to reach Him.

Doubt means a person is ready to receive the Master, ready to live the Master, ready to express and radiate the Master. Whatever word comes out of the Master completes the doubt. Doubt makes the Master express himself. Questions make the Master close himself.

Man cannot handle too much truth. He can handle half-truths. Beyond that, truth starts transforming him. He feels that the ground he is standing on is slipping away. None of us wants to know the truth. If truth is given honestly, only a few will be willing to listen. People become frightened the moment honest truths are given. So, they question the truth. We feel that we cannot afford to be truthful in verbal language as well as body language. The truth straightaway gives us Enlightenment. It transforms us. The moment someone authentically intranalyzes or catches a single dimension of truth, it does wonders.

If we scan our whole day, we will find it is filled with lies and inauthenticities. Our smiles are false. When we smile, we don't want the other person to know what is in our mind; so we don't look into each other's eyes. Why? We fear that the other person will read our mind and our inauthenticity will be exposed to them. However, nothing can be hidden in our eyes. Eyes are the doorway to the soul. Straightaway we see the being in another person's eyes.

TRUTH SHINES BY ITSELF

Truth endures logical questions and arguments. It withstands the test of logical analysis. If someone needs to verify whether something is pure gold, we must put it in acid to test it. An acid test is required to test the truth of gold. In the same manner, if we wish to know whether something is pure truth, we must put it to an acid test of logical analysis. Our inauthenticity will simply burn out. Our logic will simply fall and fail. If it is the ultimate Truth, if it is authentic, it must stand the test of logical analysis and prove itself.

If the disciple is in the questioning mood, the Master must prove his words. He must be prepared to go through the acid tests demanded by the questioning disciple. It is a big load. If the disciple is in doubt, the Master will open up with the truth. He will not cover the truth with words. He will not play with words. The naked truth will be told directly. Any truth can be served and explained to a mind with doubt. To a questioning mind, nothing can be explained.

The disciple's mood decides whether the Master's words will be advice or a powerful transformation technique. If the disciple is completely feeling connected, the Master can enrich him. The Master need not even be enlightened.

A small story:

> A scholar lived on the banks of the sacred Yamuna river. Daily he offered ritual worship to Kṛṣṇa. A milkmaid brought milk for the scholar on a regular basis. One day, she did not

come because it had rained heavily the previous night and the river had flooded.

The following day when she arrived at the scholar's home, he asked, 'Why didn't you bring my milk yesterday?' She replied, 'The river was flooded and I was unable to cross it.'

The scholar told her, 'Many have crossed the *saṁsāra sāgar* (ocean of worldly life) by chanting Kṛṣṇa's name. Yet you can't cross a small river. Chant His name and cross!'

Like a typical scholar, he showed off his dry knowledge to impress the poor milkmaid while also scolding her for missing a day of service. The milkmaid received his words as absolute truth. From that day onwards, the milkmaid was on time.

Sometime later, the river flooded again. The milkmaid shocked the scholar by arriving at the usual hour. He asked her, 'How did you manage to cross the river?'

The milkmaid replied, 'Due to your guidance, master. I chanted Kṛṣṇa's name and walked upon the water as you told me.'

The scholar could not digest it. He demanded proof. The milkmaid agreed. They went down to the riverbank. The milkmaid chanted Kṛṣṇa's name and walked upon the water. She just floated and crossed the river.

The scholar could not believe what was happening. He thought, 'If an ignorant milkmaid can walk on water based on my teachings, why can't I, a great scholar?'

He started chanting Kṛṣṇa's name. But, as he approached the water, he lifted his waistcloth so as not to wet it. He stepped into the water and sank.

He didn't actually have any authentic belief in what he told the milkmaid. He just spoke those words to show off his knowledge. But his inner space felt the impossibility of crossing the water. And the milkmaid was so authentic, her space was filled with making the impossible, possible!

Listen, if the disciple is in a receptive mood of listening with integrity, even casual words of the Master can be techniques for his growth; it will enrich him. Even if the master is unenlightened or if the master has no belief or experience of his own words, the disciple's authentic belief in the possibility surmounts any obstacle.

Doubt and faith are two sides of the same coin. We cannot have faith without doubt. That is why, however much people wish to believe my words, they have doubts. I tell them it is okay to have doubts. They are going through a process, a cycle of faith and doubt. As doubt is cleared, a greater faith, the courage of authenticity develops. Then, the next level of doubt occurs. A new layer of understanding is revealed. Ultimately, the disciple transcends doubt and faith. He reaches the truth. Until such time, it is normal to have recurring doubt and faith.

Now, Arjuna has come to an understanding. Because of his first-hand spiritual experience, he has come to the level of doubt. No more questions. He does not ask what is beneficial for him. Those self-serving calculations have gone. No more questions like, *kim tad brahma kiṁ-adhyātmaṁ kim karma puruṣottama* (8.1)—What is Brahman? Which is duty? etc. He was playing with words then. Now everything has disappeared. In the first chapter, Kṛṣṇa was totally silent. Arjuna spoke at length. He quoted on *dharma*, righteousness and from ancient scriptures. In this chapter, Arjuna is completely silent.

This is the problem faced by every Master descending on planet Earth. An innocent disciple is better than an ignorant disciple.

UNLEARN TO LEARN

All Masters descending on planet Earth bring the same *śāstra*, the knowledge that is written down. But they also bring the life that is infused in this knowledge. No book can give the ultimate Truth. The problem is that some people take books and their intellect as the ultimate authority.

Instead of living the truth with integrity and authenticity, they take books as authority. They demand proof for the masters' words based on books and scriptures they have read.

The main problem is the meaning of words. For example, if a Master utters the word '*Ātman*,' he says it from the Saṃskṛit dictionary. But we look for '*ātman*' in our own Oxford dictionary! Naturally the problem starts.

When we are in the presence of a living Master, we can immediately seek clarification and can complete with doubts. A Master knows by seeing our faces and our inner space that we are unable to cognize. Never giving-up on us, he explains further till things fit together and we experience completion. If our search is real, if it is an urge, we will be seeking a living Master. On the other hand, if our search is an entertainment, just passing time, we feel comfortable with books and old masters' photographs. If our search is intense, we feel deeply connected with a living Master.

Facts and truth do not always go together. Facts are one-dimensional, relating only to time, whereas the truth is space and time; it is multidimensional. Here Arjuna has come to a level of maturity that is no longer satisfied with factual information. His quest is for truth. He has no more questions. Only doubts. Doubts are great. They are clear green signals that the disciple is ready to receive and live the Master.

A small story:

> A young man approached an elderly person sitting under a tree near his village and told him that he was in search of a Guru.
>
> The old man replied that he knew of a Guru. He described him in detail, how he looked, where to locate him and so forth. The young man thanked him and moved on. For thirty years, he searched. Unable to find the Guru, he gave up and headed back to his hometown.
>
> Before reaching home, he saw an old man who exactly

> matched the description of the Guru. Approaching closer, the young man realized that he was none other than the old man with whom he started his search.
>
> The young man asked, 'Why did you allow me to waste thirty years looking for you?'
>
> The old man replied, 'Those years were not wasted. They molded you. When you came to me thirty years ago, I described myself, including the tree under which I sat. You were unable to recognize me. You were in a hurry to travel, wander and satisfy your ego. Your searching was necessary in order to dissolve questions that arose from your ego. Now you are ripe and ready to receive me.'

If the disciple is not in a receptive state, he is even unable to recognize his Guru. Questions arise from ego. Doubts arise from consciousness.

Arjuna did everything. In the second chapter, when Kṛṣṇa spoke about *ātma*, saying: *nainaṁ chindanti śastrāṇi nainaṁ dahati pāvakaḥ* (2.23)—The soul cannot be touched by any weapon or be burned by fire—Arjuna immediately asks: How will an enlightened man speak?

Why? Why did he ask that question? It was out of pure ego, to judge Kṛṣṇa, to see whether Kṛṣṇa was enlightened. Arjuna was checking the authority of the Master. It started with violence, with questions.

Gradually, by chapter 9, when Kṛṣṇa revealed *Rājavidyā Rāja Guhyaṁ Yogaḥ,* royal knowledge and royal secret, that Existence is intelligence, that the cosmic energy is intelligence, Arjuna's questions very slowly settle down, and intelligence happened. In chapter 10, with *Vibhūti Yogaḥ*, yoga of Divine manifestation, devotion started flowering. When he heard the glory of Kṛṣṇa, love started flowering in him. In Chapter 11, with *Viśvarūpa Darśan Yogaḥ*, Arjuna had the experience. Now all questions are over. Arjuna experienced the Ultimate Consciousness.

> Rāmakṛṣṇa Paramahamsa says beautifully, 'In a party, until the food is served, conversations and noise happen. Once the food is served, only the noise of serving and

eating will be heard! Till the ultimate experience, questions will be there. After that, the expression of that experience alone will be there. All other noise will disappear.'

Here, Arjuna has finished everything. His calculations are over. He has come down to the level of doubts. With questions, the tone is different. Questions demand proof from the Master. Doubts are not like that. They are just asking for some tips, tips for enriching your own self in others. Arjuna has come to the level of complete acceptance of the Master. That is why, throughout this chapter, Arjuna is silent. He is ready to mirror the Master. He is now soaked in devotion, ready to powerfully live and blissfully radiate everything transmitted to him.

Journey Into The Causal Body

15.1 *Śrī Bhagavān says,*
The imperishable banyan tree of life, symbolized by the Aśvattha, has its roots above, with the leaves and branches spreading below the earth. The leaves are said to be the Vedic hymns.
One who knows this eternal tree becomes the knower of the Vedas.

15.2 *The branches of this tree extend below and above the earth, nourished by the three human attributes, guṇas.*
Its buds are the sense objects. This tree also has roots going down and these are bound to the resultant actions of humans.

Kṛṣṇa refers to the causal body as the banyan tree. This is a continuation of the previous chapter. Chapters 14 to 17 are connected discourses. In chapter 14, *Guṇatraya Vibhāga Yogaḥ*, yoga of the division of three *guṇa* (attributes), Kṛṣṇa speaks about the first four layers of our being. In this chapter, *Puruṣottama Yogaḥ*, yoga of the Supreme Being, He refers to the fifth layer.

The totality of the seven layers is our body-mind-spirit system. The second layer is the *prāṇic* body, the body that controls air movements inside our physical body. In the previous chapter, Kṛṣṇa explains that this *prāṇic* layer is filled with desires. He further explains how we create conflicting desires and suffer with *rajas* (restlessness) and forced into *tamas* (inactivity or depression).

The fifth layer is the causal body. It is where all *saṁskāras*, our root patterns, are stored in seed form. Every night we enter the causal body in deep sleep. We take *saṁskāras* out from this layer and create the world.

In this chapter, Kṛṣṇa reveals the secrets of this causal layer. In the previous chapter, Kṛṣṇa explained how to use the power of desire energy with the power of thinking and words. Desire is an energy. That energy is abused by creating self-conflicting desires and self-doubting patterns, which put us into restlessness. If we don't complete with our self-doubts (*ātma sandeḥ*), we fall into depression, into self-revenge (*ātma droha*). He gave techniques to clear self-conflicting desires.

THE SEED OF PATTERNS

Our own desires, born out of our *mūla vāsanās,* the root patterns, carry their own energy for fulfillment, as they are the basic needs and purpose with which we were born.

The Universe blesses us with the power to meet all our real needs. When we are born on this planet we are sent with all that we need. However, once here, we accumulate other desires. Because of our root patterns, these desires are the wants that we borrow from others by comparing, copying and envying others. Rāmaṇa Mahaṛṣi says, 'This Universe can fulfill the needs of all its inhabitants; but it cannot fulfill the wants of even a single person.' How true!

When desires are borrowed, when they are based on coveting other people's belongings, there will be a serious conflict between our wants and needs. Fulfillment of our needs gives happiness, true joy, and completion. That is why a poor man eats his simple meal of roti and dal (bread and curry) with such gusto.

Desires are caused by *saṁskāras*, root thought patterns or bio-memories of experiences and sense perceptions. *Saṁskāras* are stored in our unconscious mind layer. Root thought patterns, *saṁskāras*, drive our actions. The Bṛhadaranyaka Upaniṣad says, 'We are our desires. Desires shape our will. Our will shapes our actions. Actions make us what we are.'

Now, Kṛṣṇa moves on to the next layer, where *saṁskāras* are stored in the seed form. Even if we move beyond the three layers of desire, restlessness and depression, these root patterns, *saṁskāras* in seed form, called *bīja saṁskāra* (bīja meaning seed), need to be cleared and completed.

Kṛṣṇa speaks of techniques to destroy these *bīja saṁskāras*. These may not express themselves in us right now. Yet if they are allowed to be there in seed form, at one time or another, they will exploit us.

In an office, some files are on the table, some are in the archives, while others are in the safety vault. The previous three layers are like the office table and archived material. This causal layer is the office safety vault. The next two layers are the external vaults. In the previous chapter, Kṛṣṇa explains techniques to clear the table. Now He gives techniques to empty the office safety vault.

Kṛṣṇa says, 'The roots of the tree are on the outside; the branches are inside.' From the causal body, if the roots are taken to be outside, it should be in the earlier three layers ending with the physical body. In a tree, the roots feed nutrients to the tree. The tree takes water and minerals through the roots. The roots decide the condition and growth of a tree. That is why Kṛṣṇa says the roots of the tree are in the physical body. The tree of *saṁskāra* is watered by the five senses of the physical body and our actions. The *saṁskāras* in seed form in the causal body are formed and watered by the five senses of the physical body.

Your Words are Vedic Hymns

Kṛṣṇa further says that the leaves are the *vedic* hymns—*chandāṁsi yasya parṇani* and one who knows the tree is knower of the Vedas—*yas taṁ veda sa veda-vit*. He says *saṁskāras* are the vedic hymns, the *mantras*. Mantras are defined as *manasasya sthiraha iti mantraḥ*, whatever controls or stabilizes the mind, or *manaḥ trāyate iti mantraḥ*, that which reclaims and completes the life of man.

śri bhagavān uvāca
ūrdhva-mūlam adhaḥ -śākhaṁ aśvatthaṁ prāhur avyayam /
chandāṁsi yasya parṇāni yas taṁ veda sa veda-vit // 15.1

Words that are settled in our inner space form the bone structure of our life. Words expressed or coming out when we are alone, are the root patterns or *saṁskāras* printed in the causal body. Our lives revolve them. If we give conflicting, contradictory words, the bone structure of our life will be a circle put on a square and rectangle—all crooked perversions! So, if you start building your life on it, how will it be? Crooked, perverted, incomplete, and useless!

If you give a word, be very clear that you have started building your life. You have to fulfill it. It is your life! Dropping the word and completing is like pulling down the structure and rebuilding it. How many times do you pull down the structure and rebuild?

Words are double-edged swords. When we lack integrity, whatever words we use to offend others settle in our inner self. They emerge whenever they find a chance to push out of our inner self. No man is intelligent enough to use harsh words on others and smooth words inside. It is an unconscious action. That is why, in ancient Indian society, the usage of harsh words was controlled by various customs.

Our mind is constantly occupied in inner chatter. Eventually we express part of this chatter in words. Part of it we suppress for fear of societal repercussions. We do not express what we fear would hurt others or what might be unacceptable to others. All these words settle deep inside our *maṇipūraka cakra*, the navel energy center, which is the seat of words. Words that are harsh, whether expressed externally or internally, settle down within us. What goes out also goes in. These settle within our navel energy center. Both expressed and unexpressed words build our bank of root thought patterns, *saṁskāras*.

If you have given a word, it just has to be lived. Word is mantra! Brahma created the world out of the word. The integrity of Viṣṇu is the lotus from whose navel creation or Brahma happens; and the tongue of Brahma is the word 'Veda', out of which the world happens. Understand, integrity should be the root foundation from which the lotus of the word blooms. Out of that word, Creation happens. Creation happens out of the word from integrity. When a person with integrity says, 'Let there be a huge organization here,' it happens just like that!

Understand, when your words are rooted in integrity, the word is Brahma. If it is rooted in Viṣṇu or integrity, it just becomes reality. Integrity is capable of maintaining creation. Viṣṇu maintains creation. Creation is possible only when you are established in the state of integrity and utter your words. When you utter your words from the space of integrity, creation is possible, creation happens!

Life is built on commitments. If you do not have respect for your commitments, your commitments also will not have respect for you. Listen! If you are integrated to your commitment, your commitment can make it into reality. Even in your day-to-day life, if you are integrated to your integrity, your integrity will be integrated to you.

One who understands this can influence other people through his thoughts and words, perhaps more effectively than through his actions. Even we do not know how our thoughts and words influence and affect other people; they may not be as focused and effective, but they will still affect others and us.

For those in business and corporate life, communication is the key to success. Communication is not about our facility with language. It is not about the accent we cultivate or how fluently we speak. Communication is expressing and living what we feel with integrity and authenticity. If our feelings and thoughts are negative, when we lack taking the responsibility to be integrated, however much we try to hide these, our words or body language reveal the inner inauthentic feelings and motives.

However, if we constantly complete with the negative words that we use towards ourselves and others to express our feelings, we will get rooted in integrity—Viṣṇu, the space of positivity. From this positive space, we will express the power of words and Brahma, creation happens! With completion the creation of space happens for whatever we want to make as reality.

The Transient and The Permanent

Kṛṣṇa further states, 'One who knows this tree is the knower of the Vedas, *yas taṁ veda sa veda-vit* (15.1).' He says one who has the knowledge that the root patterns or *saṁskāras*, which constitute the causal body, are the result of the five senses, knows the *Vedas* or has the knowledge of life's guiding force.

The water a tree receives through its roots mainly decides the condition of the tree. If good water and manure are available, the tree flourishes. The leaves will be green. If poison is poured on it, the tree sheds its leaves and slowly dies.

This tree of *saṁskāras*, which is in the causal body, lives mainly due to the five senses. Kṛṣṇa uses the word *aśvattha* which also means that which is transient, that which is not today as it was yesterday and which will not be tomorrow as it is today. It refers to material life where nothing is what it seems to be. Everything is temporary.

Life, as people say, is not unreal. If it were truly unreal, we would not be able to experience it. The fact that we experience material life and seem to enjoy it, even if temporarily, means it is real. It is unreal to the extent that whatever we experience is transient and impermanent. Unreal does not mean nonexistent. If something is nonexistent, we cannot perceive it or experience it, even temporarily. Even a dream is real. We say dreams are unreal, but we cannot deny that we experience dreams. However, it is a fact that we do not have self-awareness while dreaming.

Once we become aware, we wake up from the dream. It has never happened that a lion or a murderer chasing a person has caught that person in a dream. As soon as we are threatened, as soon as we become aware of ourselves, we wake up and the dream ends.

Dreams are not unreal in the sense that they are nonexistent; they are unreal to the extent that we are unaware. In the same manner, sages tell us that we are unaware even when we are awake. '*Jāgrat, jāgrat,*' they say, 'wake up, wake up.' They do not ask us to wake up from sleep. They ask us to wake up from our unaware wakefulness into an aware wakefulness.

Aśvattha signifies this state of unawareness. To understand this unawareness produced by our senses and directed by our root patterns, *saṁskāras*, is to gain knowledge, the Vedas. Kṛṣṇa goes on to explain more about this state of unawareness.

Kṛṣṇa says the roots go upwards as well as downwards. He says the leaves of the tree are decided by the tricks of the five senses and the resultant action of mankind. The roots are not only in the physical body, but also in the action. Kṛṣṇa says the tree is deeply rooted because the action of the entire mankind is always result-oriented. It is always guided by greed and fear.

The *aśvattha* tree, the banyan tree, is like a human body. Its roots, like in a human being, are above, like our hair. The hair is said to be a channel to draw in cosmic energy. Our limbs, hands and legs are like branches of the banyan tree. The human system is truly upside down!

Kṛṣṇa gives a beautiful tip to be complete with the root patterns, *saṁskāras*. If we are not guided by greed and fear patterns, if our actions are not result-oriented, no root patterns will be created. If you enrich selflessly for at least half an hour a day, it will do you a lot of good. It will create the space of completion in you!

While enriching others and yourself, don't plan anything. Don't even plan to have a group of volunteers do the enriching service. Just do any work that you can do. It may seem silly and a waste of time. But at a later date, this time alone will be felt as purposeful and complete. If your enriching service is fueled by the patterns of greed or fear, you may end up in a mess and be a nuisance to others, too. You need to know, if you are enriching with a vested interest, you will give-up on people. Don't have any vested interest. Enrich just for the sake of enriching.

We have a very wrong idea, 'First, let me experience; then I will enrich!' It is like, 'First let me get cured; then I will take medicine!' Understand, enriching is the cure! Enriching is the experience! Enriching is *tapas*! It is enriching which unclutches you from your past incompletions. It is enriching which distances you from your past incompletions. It is enriching which makes you grow. If a child tries to unclutch from a toy car, he will be struggling. But if he just grows, the toy will automatically drop him! Enriching makes you just grow to the next level of you.

Enrich and Be Free from Kārmic Cycle

Listen Don't plan anything. Just do enriching service anywhere. Then the enriching you do will infuse enormous power into your being. Enriching is the power of your being.

Understand this truth: Whenever life energy expands in you, it happens only through enriching. Whenever you enrich, expansion in the life energy happens; not otherwise. Listen, even your breathing can be enriching, but real enriching does not stop just by breathing. Real enriching means—you transmitting the highest possible consciousness to others.

Listen, real enriching is helping everyone, making everyone live enlightenment. Without giving-up on people, day in and day out sit and continue to enrich people. If you have wealth, use the wealth to enrich everyone to live enlightenment. If you have intelligence, use intelligence to enrich everyone to live enlightened life. If you have orating capability, use your orating capability to enrich everyone to live enlightened life.

Bhagavān says, '*karmānubandhīni manuṣya loke.*' All our actions revolve around results. So, at least in enriching, don't think of dollars or fame. Don't plan to impress. Don't plan to make your presence felt. Do the work for its own sake.

Many times you enrich others as a selfish motive. You think, 'If I enrich, I may get this, this, this back.' Listen. Do not enrich with the small purpose. Listen! Now I am giving the right and complete reason for enriching. Because everyone is part of you, enriching every being is nothing but enriching some part of you.

Enrich others. Listen! Anything you see is extension of you.

Anything or anybody you experience is extension of you. So, when you enrich them, parts of you are enriched. When they feel completion, part of you will become complete.

Mostly we do charitable work based on notions of earning brownie points that will do us good in our afterlife, whether we believe in rebirth or not. Or we would like to see ourselves in the media and feel good. It fulfills our need for attention either in this world or in another world after death.

When you work, whether it is charitable as you and society define it, or commercial, as long you do it with no expectation of results, just enriching because others are your very own extension, your actions will be selfless. These actions are not motivated by fear and greed patterns. They will not result in the hangover of root patterns, *saṁskāras*.

When you enrich, you can define the process of your actions and not the results. When a defined process is followed, results naturally follow. If we follow the right path with the right reason, we reach the right destination. It takes courage of authenticity to create the space of possibility and implement this. It takes courage of your being to say that we will work only to enrich without expecting rewards. It takes a truly complete person to cognize the right reason for enriching; that what is important is 'doing' and not 'doership' and that status is not as important as the state of doing.

If we are able to create this right space of enriching, we will find a true liberation within ourselves. We will experience the power of living, constantly expanding! A load will be lifted from our shoulders. The anxiety of constantly looking over our shoulder to peep into the future will be gone. We look at past results to define what needs to be done for the future.

All what needs to be done is being in the space of completion in the present, define an enriching path in everything we do and take responsibility that the 'doing' happens with integrity and authenticity. If this is done with awareness, results will follow. Real enriching is making people live enlightenment. Take up this as a life. You will see all kinds of miracles happening in your life.

Cutting Down The Tree

15.3 *The real form of this tree cannot be perceived.*
No one can understand where it ends,
where it begins, or where its foundation is.
But with determination one must cut down
this strongly rooted tree with the weapon of detachment.

15.4 *One must then seek that place from which having gone,*
one never returns, and surrender to the Supreme Being
from whom all activities started in ancient times.

Kṛṣṇa speaks further about the causal body where *saṁskāras* are stored. He is an extraordinary scientist. A scientist can honestly search for the truth; he can give up his own faith and belief for the cause of this search and is courageous enough to express the secrets, which he discovers step-by-step.

We see these qualities in Kṛṣṇa. He is authentic in His expression or search. He is ready to give up yesterday's truth for today's updated intelligence.

Kṛṣṇa continuously updates Himself. Lastly, He is courageous to open up the secrets in public. He is not worried about copyright and intellectual property rights. The ancient vedic society in India believed that knowledge was free. The idea of copyright did not exist. Kṛṣṇa is courageous enough to open up all the secrets.

Bhagavān beautifully says, '*narūpamasyeha tathopalabhyate* (15.3).' No one can perceive the real form of this tree. No one can understand where it begins, where it ends or where its foundation is. However, with determination one should cut down this tree with the weapon of strong will and detachment, *asaṇga śastreṇa dṛdhena chittvā* (15.3).

No one can see what one has stored in one's causal body. It is like Pandora's Box. All the *saṁskāras* stored in the causal layer reveal themselves one by one. When we erase four of them, ten will surface. What is inside nobody knows. Only one thing is possible. All the *saṁskāras* can be cut by a strong will of detachment. With a strong will, with intelligence, the entire causal layer can be completed.

People ask the Master to show them how to get rid of root patterns, *saṁskāras*. Only strong will and intelligence can do that. Do we ask the Master's help to take our hands out of the fire? No! We know fire burns. So, we withdraw our hands immediately. We ask the Master only because the understanding is not there.

If the understanding is present, right action follows. If right action does not happen, be very clear that the understanding has not happened. Similarly, root patterns are dangerous. All that is needed is intelligence and a strong will of detachment.

Kṛṣṇa explains that after cutting the tree of root patterns, surrender to the space of eternal silence, from where there is no coming back, *tam eva cādyaṁ puruṣaṁ prapadye* (15.4). This is the space in which the whole of Existence is established.

One's identity is the collection of one's root patterns, *saṁskāras*, past bio-memories and incomplete desires that are stored in the unconscious mind. This is in the causal layer of our energy. Through deep and focused meditation, we can access this unconscious causal layer and dissolve the *saṁskāras* stored here. Once done, we no longer return as the same person. We are free of *saṁskāras* and liberated.

The spirit that leaves the body goes through a comatose state when it passes through this causal body layer. As long as the spirit has not crossed this layer, it can return to the body. This is the power of *saṁskāras*. These bio-memories or desires can pull the spirit back. That is why sometimes after many years in a coma, people return to consciousness. They are pulled back by unfulfilled desires. However, once the spirit crosses the causal layer, it cannot return to the body. It must move on to the next layer, the cosmic layer.

Once we access this point of dissolution of *saṁskāras* and move on to the cosmic layer, we no longer operate unconsciously at the behest of our stored bio-memories. We move into an intuitive state of completion, as opposed to our earlier instinctive state of incompletion. We are no longer in an ignorant wakeful state, but in the truly awakened state of consciousness. Bringing awareness into the unconscious through the super-conscious meditative route of completion is the only correct way to dissolve accumulated *saṁskāras*.

Completion And Creation Techniques

15.5 *Those who are free from pride, delusion, and attachment,*
those who dwell in the Self, who are complete with lust,
who are free from the dualities of joy and sorrow, not confused, and
who know how to surrender to the Supreme Person,
attain the eternal consciousness.

15.6 *That supreme space of eternal consciousness, My consciousness,*
is not illuminated by the Sun or the Moon, or by fire.
Those who enter that space never return to this material world.

Kṛṣṇa explains the same truth again at a deeper level. He had expressed the same idea in earlier chapters. But Arjuna was unable to understand. At that time, Arjuna was in the questioning mood. In the questioning mood, we miss the whole subject and are busy preparing questions. Now that mood has gone and there are only doubts, no questions.

Beyond Attachment, The Eternal Consciousness

nirmāna-mohā jita-saṇga-dośa
adhyātma-nityā vinivṛtta-kāmāḥ /
dvandair vimukhtāḥ sukha-duḥka-saṁjñair
gacchanty amūḍhāḥ padam avayayaṁ tat // 15.5

Here Kṛṣṇa says, "Those who are free from pride, delusion, and attachment, those who dwell in the Self, who are complete with lust, who are free from the dualities of joy and sorrow, who are not confused, and who know how to surrender to the supreme person, attain the eternal consciousness.'

What wonderful usage of words!

He does not say who have 'renounced' lust. No, because renunciation won't do. *Vairāgya* means beyond attachment and detachment. *Rāga* means attachment. *Arāga* means detachment. *Virāga* or *vairāgya* means beyond attachment and detachment. It is non-attachment.

Until the age of seven, we are attached to toys. By age eight or nine we are forced to be detached from these. By twenty, most people are complete with toys, beyond attachment or detachment to children's toys. With detachment, we might have renounced it externally. But the inner urge for it prevails.

That is why Kṛṣṇa uses fitting words: *vinivṛtta-kāmāḥ*, those who are 'complete' with lust. *Nivṛitti* is the completion you carry that leads to more and more completion. In this state, we know what we can afford. We know it is there at our disposal. We don't possess anything, we don't own anything, but everything is at our disposal. We can use it or drop it based on the need. Life is also like a toy. If this is fully understood, you will live like a king, not an ordinary materialistic king, but an enlightened king, a *Rājarṣi*.

This is a *tattva* (principle). This is not for understanding. This is to be meditated upon. On meditating upon this technique, these characteristics will start flowering in you and give you a clear-cut idea about the causal body.

Earlier, Kṛṣṇa explained ways to erase and complete with our root thought patterns, *saṁskāras*. Now He speaks on the creation of a proper layer. It is about re-programming your causal layer with the space of completion.

PROGRAMMING THE CAUSAL LAYER

Please listen! In two words I am giving you the gist: Completion and Creation of space. I can say, this is the essence of all the essence of my messages. As essence of the *Vedic* tradition, I have given so many messages. Now I can say, all their essence is this—

Using your *ātma jñāna*, using your conscious energy, using your peak possibility and making it into reality, making it into life.

Kṛṣṇa gives the essence of the most secret science, the science of completion and creation of space. He gives the technique for creation of the causal body.

Kṛṣṇa's words are *mantras*. Actually Kṛṣṇa uses the same words again. Not only words and expressions, He uses the same letters again. Earlier He used these words as advice. Now He uses same words as programming techniques for completion and creation. This chapter is about programming our causal layer; completing our root patterns, *saṁskāras*. This program creates the space in our causal layer to make our conscious energy into our reality; for life to happen in its peak energy!

As long as Arjuna was in the questioning mood, these same words were spelt out as advice. When he enters into the mood of doubts, he receives the same words as techniques. When the disciple is in a questioning mood, the Master's words will be taken as advice. Only when the disciple stops questioning and starts listening, these same words will be techniques. Listen, with advice, you need keys to open the door. Techniques are the keys themselves. They are ready to open the door.

Arjuna receives the gist of earlier chapters. He receives the juice in this chapter. In North Indian monasteries, this chapter is chanted before every meal. This 15th chapter must be chanted before meals, since this chapter is a programming tool of the inner space. The mere words of this chapter can do wonders in reprogramming your causal layer with the space of completion and creation.

It takes less than five minutes to chant it. Anybody can do it. Don't worry about the meaning. If you understand the meaning, it is good. Yet, it is highly useful even if chanted without understanding. Repeating these words can program your causal layer with the power of completion and creation. Especially, when you chant them in a mood of surrender, with due respect to the Master, it directly touches the causal layer.

Arjuna is completely in a receiving mood. He is fully connected to the Master. If the disciple is completely feeling connected to the Master, Existence helps him through the Master. Arjuna needs no explanations, no logic. He is ready to live the Master.

Hence, Kṛṣṇa utters the following words to program the causal layer. He gives techniques to create the space of completion and creation in Arjuna.

He says: 'Those who are free from pride, delusion, and attachment, those who dwell in the Self, who are complete with lust, who are free from the dualities of joy and sorrow, who are not confused, and who know how to surrender to the supreme person, attain eternal consciousness.'

Lust is difficult for a man to shed. Even the greatest of sages have succumbed to lust. Lust is of the body and as long as body consciousness remains, lust will stay. Only a person who has gone beyond body consciousness can drop lust.

A small story:

> A small boy went to a kids' movie with his parents. It was about a lion cub and other animals in a jungle. The boy was thoroughly enjoying it. Suddenly there was a scene where the lion cub was trapped by a hunter and became terrified.
>
> The boy was not able to bear this scene. He just jumped from his seat and ran down the hall towards the movie screen. He started throwing up his hands and legs as if in a fight with the hunter in the movie who was about to cage the lion cub. Soon the other animals in the jungle joined together and drove away the hunter and rescued the cub.
>
> The boy came back to his seat and proudly told his mother, 'See how I went first and all the animals followed me and we saved the cub!'

Just as the boy thought that the movie was real, we believe that the input perceived by our senses is also real. We are caught in the *māyā* or illusion created by our senses. The most powerful illusion is the lust within us.

Suppressing lust externally and not indulging in sex does not and will not make one enlightened. It only turns one insane. Celibacy of the body, without eliminating the fantasies of the mind, creates greater suffering than indulging in lust and sex. Enlightenment helps one transcend lust and sex by transcending the senses and attaining a no-mind state.

An Enlightened Master transcends sex. He is genderless. He becomes *ardhanārīśvara*, a man-woman, a person who expresses both traditionally male and female qualities or attributes. One key attribute of Enlightenment is genderlessness.

Kṛṣṇa is direct. He does not believe in giving brain candy to keep you happy. He is brutally direct. He says, 'He who has conquered lust.' Lust is a primal emotion provided by nature for continuation of the species. Going beyond lust, conquering by completing with lust, is the first major step in realizing Super-consciousness.

Human beings are forever confused between love and lust. They think only animals are lustful. Actually, only animals are capable of pure lust when they mate. Humans, with their rationalization, can neither be lustful nor loving. So, they are forever in the twilight zone, dissatisfied and unfulfilled.

In ancient times, lust and sex left the householder around the age of forty because they had enjoyed these fully. When a desire is fully experienced it leaves your system. Now marital relationship has become a business for security or material benefits. You may live in the same home, but not in a homely way. You have to remove the imagination and dreams from your lust, both about your partner's body and your own body.

Add friendliness to love. As of now, our love and lust are deep-rooted violence, to own the other person while he or she resists. It's a war. Instead, add friendliness to relationships. Welcome the partner as he or she is; do not just accept him or her. Welcome and accept the mind, body and being as it is.

Many of us are ashamed of our body. We hate it. All body pains and chronic skin diseases arise out of low self-esteem and disrespect to our body. We would like to be someone else. We would like to shape our body and dress like someone else. We stop staying within the boundary of our own skin, and fantasize about being someone else. Whenever we hear our name we think of our face, not our whole body, because we are not comfortable with our body. When we do not accept ourselves fully and copy someone else artificially, we can be beautiful at best, but never graceful. Grace comes from within.

For the next few days, watch your body with love. Feel comfortable. Our body oozes bliss all the time. Yet we feel only the pain. If we are relaxed with our body, our mind will not wander. Usually, when we are at home, our mind is in the office and when we are working, we wish we were at a party. Where our body is, our mind will not be.

Drop your imagination and dreams, and be complete. Add friendliness towards yourself and others, towards their body, mind and being. Carry words that heal others. Carry your body in a way that heals others. Carry friendliness with you always. This is a spiritual process. Carry the grace and goodwill of Lakṣmi instead of observing fasts and *pūjā*.

The first time you approach others with friendliness, they may not receive you openly because of your past inauthentic behavior. Persist and persevere. Complete with the idea of impossibility. Complete with your self-doubt. Stand up powerfully. Don't give up on you and others. Don't stop even if others do not reciprocate. Carry on till others feel enriched and reciprocate. Complete! Create the space of friendliness towards yourself and others, and persevere. Lust will turn to love. Your being will be in Eternal Bliss.

Kṛṣṇa says, 'That supreme space of eternal consciousness, My Consciousness, is not illuminated by the sun or the moon, or by fire. Those who enter that space never return to this material world.'

na tad bhāsayate sūryo na śaśāṇko na pāvakaḥ |
yad gatvā na nivartante tad dhāma paramaṁ mama || 15.6

These words are not advice. They are for contemplation. Advice is the only thing everybody gives and nobody takes! Kṛṣṇa gives these words to program our Causal layer with completion. These are words to contemplate, to meditate upon. They are the hymns to be meditated upon.

In the Inner Awakening program, participants are guided through a meditation upon darkness while working on the Causal layer. This darkness is not mere absence of light. It is Energy. The Causal layer of energy is the passage through which the spirit passes on its last leg before it leaves the material world. When the spirit is stuck in this Causal layer, one is in coma. One can be stuck in this layer for a long time.

Those who go past the causal layer, this layer of energetic darkness, where neither the sun nor the moon shines, nor fire warms, progress onwards to the Cosmic layer and then to the nirvanic layer, which signifies true liberation.

One can meditate upon this technique, upon this truth expounded by Kṛṣṇa, through the darkness meditation in some of our meditation programs. This meditation, which focuses on darkness, liberates one from the fear of death and the fear of loss of identity that causes the fear of death.

Death is not an option. Death of the body is certain. Separation of the spirit from the body-mind is painful. Vivekananda says it is like a thousand scorpions stinging at once.

At death the spirit leaves the body shell and merges into infinite energy. It then reappears in another shell, another body. It is like drawing circles on a whiteboard. The background is Universal energy and the perimeters of the circles drawn are the bodies that envelop the individual spirit. These circles separate individual spirit or self from Universal energy or Self.

When we erase these circles with the process of completion, the whiteness within the circles merges into the whiteness of the background. Individual self merges with universal Self. When the spirit is such that it has completed and created the space beyond attachment and lust and is constantly focused on the Self, then there is no return for that spirit into another body-mind complex. Else it returns.

Kṛṣṇa points out that the death of the body is a certainty, however, the death of the spirit is impossible. The spirit lives on. When the spirit is evolved it doesn't revert to a mental setup and root pattern that it transcended in the previous birth, that's all.

Mind Is the Conditioning

15.7 *The living entities in this conditioned material world*
are a portion of My eternal Self.
In this conditioned material world they are attracted
by the six senses, which include the mind, dwelling in prakṛti,
the active energy principle.

15.8 *The spirit in the body-mind living in this material world*
moves from one body to another carrying
these just as wind carries fragrance.

Jīva bhūtaḥ—conditioned living entity, 'conditioning' is the new word that Kṛṣṇa uses here.

Recent research tells us that human beings walk on two legs due to conditioning. A group of scientists recently found a seventeen-year-old boy in a forest. Wolves had raised him. The scientists tried to teach him how to walk on two legs and speak a few words. They were unable to do this and he died within a year. Man walking on two legs is due to conditioning.

Everything we consider as human nature is nothing but conditioning.

mamaivāṁśo jīva-loke jīva-bhūtaḥ sanātanaḥ I
manaḥ ṣaṣṭhānīndriyāṇi prakṛti sthāni karṣati II 15.7

Here Kṛṣṇa says, 'conditioned world, *jīva-loke*'. Everything is conditioning. Right and wrong, honor and dishonor, are all conditioning, all are patterns. We think of honor or dishonor because we are taught that way.

We are conditioned. If a group of people give us a certificate and clap their hands, we take it as an honor. That is the way we are taught. But never judge yourself by others' applause. This idea of honor drives many people mad. Never accept the judgment of the crowd.

Consciousness Carries the Mind

Here Kṛṣṇa gives these meditation hymns to re-program your causal layer for completion of your *saṁskāras* and creation of space.

After crossing the three layers and going beyond the causal layer, you enter a space where you are free from conditioning. This is the space of completion and creation! May you be free from all conditioning!

Kṛṣṇa says: 'They are attracted by the six senses that include the mind—*manaḥ ṣaṣthānīndriyāṇi prakṛti sthāni karṣati* (15.7).'

There are five physical senses and the sixth sense is the mind, *ṣaṣthānīndriyāṇi*. However, according to me, the mind is the only sense and the so-called five physical senses are slaves to it. The mind jumps around. If the mind can be handled, all the other five can be handled.

A small story:

> Queen Madalasa gave birth to seven children.
>
> Each child became enlightened by the age of seven and moved out of the kingdom. Their father, the king, was puzzled. How did seven children in a row become enlightened? He probed into the issue and found that Madalasa had taught them one phrase, *Tat Tvam Asi* (You are That).
>
> Just by internalizing '*Tat Tvam Asi*', their mental setup changed. They were complete with the root thought patterns, *saṁskāras* in the causal layer. They became enlightened.

Enlightenment is the removal of root thought patterns, *saṁskāras* and the dissolution of conditioning. We return to our pure original state. This is why enlightenment is referred to as *samādhi*. The Saṃskṛit word *samādhi* means 'returning to the original state'.

The spirit in the body-mind living in this material world, moves from one body to another carrying these root thought patterns just as the wind carries fragrance. *Saṁskāras* in one body quit that body and take shelter in another. This continuous vicious cycle of movement of *saṁskāras* is what Kṛṣṇa refers to as *saṁsāra*, the life-and-death cycle.

Kṛṣṇa says 'taking these, *gṛhītvā etāni saṁyati* (15.8)'. What does He mean by 'these, *etāni*'? In the previous verse, Kṛṣṇa talked about the six senses, including the mind. He refers to them here.

When the spirit leaves one body and moves to another body, it carries the six senses, *ṣaṣthānīndriyāṇi,* the five physical senses and the mind, in the same way as the wind carries fragrances, *vāyur gandhān ivaśayāt (*15.8). Just as the wind carries fragrances, consciousness carries *saṁskāras*, causal level imprints, from body to body.

Kṛṣṇa answers a frequently asked question about sin. People ask whether sins come with them from one birth to another. Sins never follow. Only imprints travel. For example, if a man commits one hundred murders, the quantity will not follow, but the basic mentality of violence accompanies and tortures him. Only the mental setup is carried.

The concept of *karma* is often used to justify actions, by saying, 'It is our *karma*,' 'It is our fate,' 'It is our destiny, what can be done?,' 'Whatever had to happen has happened.' This is pure fabrication and justification of our negative deeds.

We have the freedom to act: the free will to decide and act. Ironically, only an enlightened Master has no freedom. Enlightened Masters are driven by Parāśakti's will; they are guided by Her, that universal power, into doing what they must do. Understand: I cannot take a single step on my own. My limbs move in accordance with Her wishes.

The ordinary human being, *jīva bhūta* is in control of his destiny. All that nature provides are paths in our lives and we choose the path we travel by. We decide the path. What drives us into taking one fork or another is *vāsana*, the 'smell' that the spirit carries. It is the subtle imprint of our past actions, *saṁskāras* and *karmas*. It is not definitive or predestined.

We have the choice to redefine that *vāsana*, that smell, into either a stink or a wonderful fragrance. It is in our hands only. Whether we wish to travel in the same merry-go-round or decide to break out and walk free is our decision.

Rāmakṛṣṇa beautifully says that the soul travels from one body to another like we move from one room to another. When He left His physical body, His wife Sārada Devi was about to remove her jewelry. (Traditional Hindu families do not allow a widow to wear jewels, especially the sacred thread signifying marital status, and bracelets.)

Just as she was about to remove the sacred thread, Rāmakṛṣṇa appeared and told her not to remove it. He said, 'Where have I gone? Just to another room. Don't remove your jewelry.' From that time till her end, Sārada Devi followed His words. This may seem easier today. But in those days, in an orthodox Hindu family in a small village, it was not so. She was highly courageous.

Someone who completes with all social conditioning, who sheds all root patterns in his causal layer, moves from body to body as easily as moving from one room to another.

We create big buildings. We accumulate a good bank balance. We have friends. Just as we start enjoying life, suddenly death appears before us. We fear death only because it takes everything away from us. If we are unattached, if our causal layer is not filled with *saṁskāras*, if we are not gripped by social conditioning, we will not fear death. We know it is like moving from one room to another.

As Kṛṣṇa says in *Sāṅkhya Yogaḥ*, 'It is like changing one dress for another.'

The *saṁskāras* of this life are the result of *prārabdha karma*, the mindset and bio-memory, along with the spirit from the *vāsanas*, the imprints of the past birth that are carried into this birth. It is always a mix of pain and pleasure.

You Are Your Saṁskāras

15.9 *The living entity, the spirit, leaves one body, takes another body and gets new eyes, ears, nose, tongue and sensing body according to the saṁskāras it had in its causal layer and enjoys the new mental setup.*

15.10 *Fools in ignorance do not perceive the spirit being united with the guṇas or modes of nature, as it enters, enjoys and leaves the body. The one whose inner eyes of knowledge is open, can see everything.*

The living entity, the spirit, leaves one body, takes another body and gets new eyes, ears, nose, tongue and sensing body according to the *saṁskāras* it had in its causal layer and enjoys the new mental setup.'

Here Kṛṣṇa reveals another secret. He says, 'You create a body according to the root thought patterns or *saṁskāras* in the causal layer, *adhiṣṭhāya manaś cāyaṁ* (15.9).'

There is an Indian science called *sāmudrika lakṣaṇa śāstra*, the technique of studying body features. By observing our physical body structure, experts can read and reveal our mental setup. They know the relationship between mind and body.

Kṛṣṇa says that we create our sensory organs, according to *saṁskāras* in our causal layer. Kṛṣṇa says that living entities create all five senses through the mind or mental setup. This happens not only when we take another body. Every day when we wake up from deep sleep, our senses are recreated. If we change our mental setup, within a short time, our face changes.

You Create Yourself Every Moment

Our 'mind, manaś ' is the intelligence spread all over our body. It is the intelligence that resides in our cells. Each cell carries genetic intelligence. Body and mind are not separate entities. It is just body-mind or mind-body, one system. Within this body-mind system, scientists say that every moment of your life thousands of cells die and thousands of new cells are created. This is a constant process that Nature, the universal intelligence, dictates. It does not happen because of us; it happens in spite of us.

In a period of a little under two years, every part of our body, every cell in our body, gets renewed. Our body as it was a year ago is not the body it is today. This is not fiction; it is a proven scientific fact. Then why do we behave the same way as we have for years? Why do illnesses plague us for years, even though the cells are no longer the same?

Each cell as it dies, leaves behind a memory that the newly created cell follows. That is the bio-memories, *saṁskāras* within us. The *saṁskāras* ensures the continuation of a pattern despite complete changes in the body-mind system. These *saṁskāras* are more powerful than the rest of the body-mind system. It decides and drives.

The deep sleep we go into everyday is a rehearsal of our death process. We die and are reborn. Our subtle body leaves the gross body and returns reenergized if we allow it to. It is in our hands to maximize this process of rejuvenation that happens automatically everyday.

Through meditation we can clear our *saṁskāras* and be reborn. We can change our features, our character and behavior, all by reprogramming our *saṁskāras*.

That is why people radiate grace after they start meditation. Beauty is created by make-up. Grace is radiated by meditation. Grace makes the occupant feel at home. It soothes the atmosphere. Beauty creates excitement. Beauty moves the other person into *rajas* (restlessness). Grace creates calmness, *satva*. Grace puts the other person in energy.

People reminisce about great Masters like Rāmaṇa Mahaṛṣi and say that He imparted wisdom through silence. It is the Enlightened Master's grace that penetrates the other person's energy and changes that person's *saṁskāras.* All that we need to do in an Enlightened Master's presence is just be, be open and silent and allow the Master's eternal grace to penetrate us. There is nothing that we need to do. The Master's grace does whatever is needed.

One version of the great Indian epic Ramāyaṇa says that when princess Sītā, the incarnation of Devi Lakṣmi, entered the court of King Janaka, her father, all the great kings, monks and mystics stood up automatically. This was not a protocol. The grace she radiated caused this response in them. Beauty can create only temptation in the other person. Only grace can create respect. The grace radiating from Sītā's being made everybody stand up.

Zen Buddhism says that if we can walk on a lawn without killing the grass or creating a path with our footsteps, we are eligible for Sannyāsa. I doubted this. After all, the whole body weight is there. How can grass bear such a load and not leave imprints?

Once I went on a safari in South India.

I sat on an elephant and the caretaker came along with me. It was evening. It became dark. The caretaker had no torch or light. I asked him how he would find his way back home.

He replied, 'I have created a path by my daily walk that I can follow even in darkness.'

I asked about the elephant because it traveled with him everyday.

He said, 'The elephant's feet do not create a path. The elephant and other animals do not destroy grass as they walk over it.' I started calculating the load exerted by one foot of the elephant. At the least, it works out to four times that of an average man. However, it did not create a path. It did not kill a single blade of grass. In spite of the physical mass, there was no damage to the environment.

The negativity, arrogance, violence, negative *saṁskāras* in our causal layer, makes us feel heavy on earth. If we feel heavy around our navel area, we carry negative *saṁskāras*. The feeling of heaviness is not connected to our weight. It is due to imprints in our inner space. A person who feels light radiates grace from his being and he never creates a path on a lawn. He never kills a blade of grass by his walk.

We are spiritually evolved souls only when our feet do not create a path, when we float while we walk, when we do not go against nature.

Here Kṛṣṇa says, we create our senses according to our root patterns, *saṁskāras.* This happens not only when we die and take birth; we redesign our senses to suit our root patterns everyday, when we wake up too. If we wake up with the right mental setup, we will have our senses accordingly and for the whole day we can enjoy it. If on the other hand, we get up with negativity, we suffer.

The few moments immediately after we wake up are crucial. Whatever we feel will be reflected the rest of the day. If we radiate joy, our whole day will be joyful. If we are irritable, our whole day will be irritable.

Do this with the space of completion everyday at least for twenty-one days. You will be amazed at the changes that happen within your body-mind. You will develop grace and equally important, you will learn to love yourself, which means that you can love others without difficulty.

Kṛṣṇa further says, the type of senses we create determines the type of sensory objects we enjoy. If we create positive senses, we enjoy a positive life. If we create negative senses, we suffer a negative life. The type of senses we create determines what type of objects or pleasures attract us, and we experience that.

Our senses, intelligence and our body-mind system create the energy field around us. This energy field attracts similar energy fields. If we are negative, if our perceptions are negative, we attract people with negative mindsets and descend into a vicious cycle. However, if we do completion with all our negativity, sufferings of the past and do the creation of a space of positive emotions and positive perceptions, we attract like-minded, positive people and situations.

Completion, Completion, Completion! The energy field of completion. I tell you, just by completing with your past lifestyle, you can get out of all your sufferings of the past. Just by declaring completion with all the past mental setup, you can get out of all the side effects, after-effects, and impact of the past over you. So, completion forms the basic truth, the basic principle. The whole energy field supports you to fulfill your life as you want.

This space is extremely important in spiritual progress. It is easy to make progress and evolve when we are with a Master. However, when we get into the company of people who are not following the path, it is easy to slip from our path.

Only Eyes of Knowledge can See

Kṛṣṇa provides a wonderful punchline in the middle of this chapter.

'Fools, *vimūḍhā*' He says. Kṛṣṇa uses the Saṃskṛit word '*mūḍhaḥ*' that means 'fool'. Fools can neither understand how a living entity can quit his body nor what sort of a body he enjoys under the spell of *guṇa*, the attributes and moods of nature. Only those whose eyes are trained by knowledge can see these things.

The first thought with which we get up from our bed plays a major role in our enrichment throughout the day. What is our first thought usually? First we feel awake. We feel our body. Then it may be the fear that we must go to our office or it may be the greed to finish some work. At the stroke of the thought, fear or greed, our body jumps out of bed. We connect to our body through fear or greed.

Kṛṣṇa says that if we catch our body with fear or greed, we attract more and more fear or greed throughout the day.

There are many gates to enter the body. Never enter through the fear or greed gate. Get up with a spiritual thought that brings completion in you. Remember your Master or favorite God and thank Him. Thank Him for the extended life. Everyday that you wake up is an extension to your life on planet Earth. Thank Divinity for the grace, for the extension.

Let your first thought be spiritual. Practice it consciously for a few days. Then it will become your routine. Don't connect to your body with fear or greed; you will attract more and more greed or fear.

Listen. Waking up from bed is not our birthright. Of course, birth itself is not our right. It is a pure gift from Existence. Be grateful to the Divine for this day and extension here. Completion forms the basic rule for gratitude, enlightenment, and liberation.

Please listen to these basic truths!

Grace is flowing in you forever! Life is flowing in you just to make your life as you want! Life is not sadistic. God is not sadistic. And God is not enjoying your conflicts and complications. Don't think that! Please listen, if you are able to wake up in the morning and if you are able to breathe, understand that His Grace is there on you. He wants you to fulfill your life as you want.

If we wake up from bed with spiritual thoughts of completion, that consciousness stays with us the whole day. If we are made to get up from bed by incomplete material thoughts, we start our day with incompletions—irritation, worry, and agitation. The entire day we carry the same irritated mood.

When we are in deep sleep, we are in touch with the causal layer. While waking up, we travel along the other three layers and reach the physical body. The three layers are like a shopping mall with various *saṁskāras*. According to our causal layer, we pick up the related *saṁskāras* and contact our physical body and design our senses accordingly.

Just for twenty-one days, every night before sleeping do self-completion with all your incompletions for at least forty-two minutes; reliving and relieving your past sufferings and root patterns. This completion process will directly work on your causal layer. Always sleep in the space of completion. And wake up with a spiritual thought of completion. Then, check your face. It will be changed. Your eyes will have a new look. Your body will have the grace.

One more thing, understand, if you have dreams, whatever type of dreams it may be, whether it is good or bad, or whatever; if you have dreams, then you have incompletions in you. When you start doing completions every night, your dreams will reduce.

Listen. I am defining dreams. Incompletions expressing when you are unconscious is dreams. Incompletions expressing when you are conscious is thinking. If you have a dreamless sleep, I guarantee, you will have birthless life! If you have dream-free sleep, you will have birth-free, death-free life! That's all.

I am not putting forward a theory. I have experienced this. A few hundred thousand people around the world practice these words. From that authority, I tell you, this process of completion is a vibrant technique.

Don't contact the body with *tamas* or *rajas* (depression or restlessness). If you get up with greed or fear, you design a body that radiates greed or fear and thereby attracts incidents that put you in greed or fear.

When you travel from the causal layer to the physical body, pick up completion, the *satva* (peaceful or blissful) *saṁskāras*. Have a spiritual thought of completion as the first thought. Think of your Master or God or anything that gives you a spiritual memory. That is why in India, ancient Mystics tell us to meditate early in the morning. At least for a few seconds be in a blissful mood. Your inner space will be fresh and new.

Kṛṣṇa says, 'Only those whose eyes are trained by knowledge can see the truth of this science, *paśyanti jñāna cakṣuṣaḥ* (15.10)'. The whole science of completion is before you. He says fools cannot understand and only those with eyes of knowledge, can see. The choice of being a fool or a man with eyes of knowledge, *jñāna-cakṣu* is left to us. The choice is completely ours.

Awareness Not Achievement

15.11 *The serious practitioner of Yoga, with an understanding of his Self, can see all this clearly.*
But those who do not have an understanding of the Self, however much they try, cannot see.

15.12 *The light of the Sun, the light of the Moon and the light of fire, all their radiance is also from Me.*

15.1 *Entering into earth, I support all beings with My energy; becoming the watery Moon, I nourish all plant life.*

15.14 *I am the fire of digestion in every living body and*
I am the breath of life, exhaled and inhaled,
with which I digest the four-fold food.

Kṛṣṇa uses the word '*yoginaḥ*' in this verse. It is important to understand what He means by this. *Yoga* has become a buzzword; a trendy, fashionable word for cool people.

Yoga is the link, the union, between the individual self, *ātman*, and universal Self, cosmic consciousness, *Brahman*. Awareness of this link, awareness that the self is the same as the Self, leads to liberation. The understanding happens in an instant; however, the practice leading to it requires a disciplined approach.

In today's world, my opinion is that *dhyāna*, meditation, is best suited for spiritual progress and for the realization that one's self is part of that cosmic Self.

Kṛṣṇa says that until that awareness happens, however much one may strive, one will not reach Him.

Understand, here we are talking about awareness, not achievement. The truth is that our individual self is an integral part of the Universal consciousness, the Self. This truth is not something that we need to work towards. It exists. It is. We are blinded by individual ego, māyā, the illusion of our individual identity, in forgetting that we are part of the Collective consciousness.

Yogis, sincere spiritual practitioners, lift this veil of *māyā,* destroy the illusion, to see beyond into the truth of their oneness with the Divine. Meditation is the path and technique to lift this veil. Meditation enables the practitioner to go deeper and deeper into himself. Meditation brings about awareness of what is.

MASTER—THE DISPELLER OF DARKNESS

Light is awareness. Light is the sustainer of life. Light is one of the first manifestations of the Divine in creation. Without light and heat from the sun, life as we know it would be impossible. Everything in this world revolves around energy received from the sun in the form of light and heat.

The sun is also the dispeller of darkness. Not only does Kṛṣṇa establish that He is the creator of this Universe—the solar system, sun, moon and the fire which sustain our lives, but He also tells us that He is the Dispeller of darkness.

Kṛṣṇa, as the Master, as the Guru, is the Dispeller of darkness. Guru means one who dispels darkness. As the sun, moon and the fire, Kṛṣṇa is the ultimate Master who leads us into awareness of our natural state of completion.

Please listen! Come to the listening space. You are vibrating a magnetic field. There are two frequencies inside you.

There is a *self* in you which has a frequency of its own, this is what I call the energy of possibility of enlightenment. In Saṃskṛit we use the word *jīvātma*—individual soul. Then, there is the mind in you which it has the frequency of its own, this is the energy of the pattern and suffering present in you, which derived energy from the *ātman*.

Please listen! You need to understand: there is a mirror in front of me. I always saw the mirror only reflecting these lights. Because, I have always seen this mirror lit up, I forgot that it only reflects, it does not have its own radiation, its own natural light! In the same way, because you always see the Moon reflecting the Sun, you forget Moon does not have its own light!

Same way, your mind does not have its own energy. But, from the time you saw your mind, it was always reflecting the consciousness. Because of that you started thinking, you started feeling your mind as independent energy, which is not! So, the patterns you carry inside you have no independent energy or power. At any given point in time, you are either used by the frequency of your *self* or the frequency of your mind.

Please listen to the truths. First, you have a frequency of consciousness in you. Second, you have the frequency of mind in you. The frequency of the mind is the pattern, incompletion, suffering present in you. Third, at any given point in time, you are either used by the frequency of your soul, *ātman,* consciousness or the frequency of your mind, the patterns.

Kṛṣṇa is the destroyer of our root thought patterns, *saṁskāras*. *Saṁskāras* are products of darkness, our unconscious. Darkness is not a positive entity. It cannot be shifted from point to point. However, it can be destroyed by light. The presence of light dissolves darkness. The presence of awareness of completion, our frequency of consciousness destroys *saṁskāras*. Darkness has no existence of its own. It only exists when there is no light. We cannot create darkness. It is the absence of something.

When someone cannot see, he is not bothered by darkness. He is not afraid of darkness. To a blind man, darkness is his nature. A blind man will not say that he sees ghosts and spirits in darkness. Darkness is the state that he exists in.

A truly courageous man established in completion is also not disturbed by darkness. Someone who is not afraid of anything does not fear the loss of ego, loss of identity and death. To him, darkness poses no fear as well. He can equally handle darkness and light, without fear or attraction.

Other than these two classes of people, darkness poses problems and presents fears for everyone else. In this sense, Kṛṣṇa is not only the Lord of light, but of darkness as well.

FROM ME COMES LIGHT, FIRE, LIFE ENERGY

Kṛṣṇa further expands on His pervasiveness. In the form of light and heat, He is the Sustainer of all beings within this Universe. He says that He is the energy of the watery moon and through this energy He is the life energy within plant life, *puṣṇāmi cauṣadhīḥ sarvāḥ somo bhūtvā rasātmakaḥ* (15.13)'.

Kṛṣṇa affirms that He is Brahman and through His manifestation of the various natural elements of space, air, fire, water and earth, He is responsible for plant life and therefore for food and human beings.

Without plant life, there is no food. Without food, there is no body and mind. Body and mind become food for others after death. Food is an expression of divinity. The energy behind food is both the creator and destroyer of *saṁskāras*.

Most of us treat food as a basic necessity or an object of sensual pleasure. We ignore it or become addicted to it. We need to be aware of what we eat. Before eating, offer gratitude to the Universe for what you have received and meditate upon the food. Traditionally Hindus offer oblations to the Divine and chant prayers before eating. Major changes happen when you follow these customs with awareness.

A person who can be so settled in the present is one who is aware and complete. He is one with Kṛṣṇa.

The role of the sun as the giver of light and heat energies is obvious. It is also obvious that without the sun, all life forms will cease to exist. However, the fact that the moon is a nourishing energy providing life energy to plants and therefore to humans is not that well appreciated. The moon controls our behavior, moods and minds. *Soma*, the name for the moon, refers to its fluidity and the transient nature of waxing and waning.

Kṛṣṇa then talks about *vaiśvānara*, *prāṇa* and *apāna*.

ahaṁ vaiśvānaro bhūtvā prāṇināṁ deham āśritaḥ |
prāṇapāna samāyuktaḥ pacāmy annaṁ catur-vidham || 15.14

The *Bṛhadāraṇyaka Upaniṣad* says:

> 'This fire that is within the human being and which digests the food that he eats is *vaiśvānara*. The sound of this fire *vaiśvānara* is that which one hears by closing the ears. When death nears and the spirit is about to leave the body, he no longer hears this sound.'

This *Upaniṣad* goes on to say that neither *āhāra* (food), nor *prāṇa* (breath), can function alone, one without the other. Food will decay without breath and breath will dry up without food. Together, when the awareness of their union happens, true consciousness results.

Food is also related to the four elements other than space: air, fire, water and earth. The ancient Hindu traditional medicine system, Ayurveda, works on this principle of *vaiśvānara*. The quality of this inner fire determines our state of hunger or lack of hunger as well as the state of health.

What Kṛṣṇa implies here as well is that food is divine since it has His imprint on it. We tend to take food for granted. Offering food to other living beings, has been considered a form of worship in Hindu tradition. Food has always been considered the repository of the Divine.

From Me Comes Memory And Knowledge

15.15 *I am seated in everyone's heart and from Me came memory, knowledge and their loss. I am known by the Vedas; indeed, I am the creator of Vedānta and I am the knower of the Vedas.*

15.16 *There are two things, the perishable and the imperishable, in this world. There are the living beings who are perishable while there is the unchangeable, the imperishable.*

Kṛṣṇa says that He is seated in everyone's heart, *sarvasya ca aham hṛdi sanniviṣto.* He is memory, He is knowledge, He is forgetfulness, *mattaḥ smṛtir jñānaṁ apohanaṁ ca* (15.15). What does this mean? How does our mind work? How does it invent beliefs? We don't even know where our mind is. If I ask you where your mind is, you will point to your head. That's not your mind.

Every cell in our body has inbuilt intelligence. These cells constantly regenerate themselves. These cells present everywhere make up our body-mind system. Therefore, there is no one place where our mind is definitely located; certainly it is not in our head!

Intellect and Intuition

All our decisions are influenced by our past experiences that are stored as root thought patterns in our unconscious mind.

This unconscious area or the root where the mind is born is powerful enough to make you feel powerless or powerful. It can be used in three ways: at the instinct level, intellect level or intuition level. As long as the unconscious is overloaded with negative memories and restlessness, it works at the instinct level. We decide instinctively, unconsciously, just like an animal does.

Next is the intellect level. Here, we are conscious; we make decisions logically, but we don't have extra enthusiasm or energy. We are not creative or innovative; we don't take big steps; we don't grow. We don't experience the space of possibility and expansion. We make decisions in a logical and conscious way, that's all.

When we are at the intellect level, we are not tired; yet we are not energetic either. We are in a break-even state. At this level, we do not use our potential to the maximum. Constant completion with our root thought patterns, and bringing integrity in our words, authenticity in our actions melts the intellect layer.

The level where we can actualize our entire potential with power of thinking, power of words, power of feeling and power of living is the intuition level. This is the space of completion and creation. If we can infuse deep silence and completion into the unconscious zone and replace root thought patterns, then we are at the intuition level.

Please listen, if you come to a decision without a thought, you are living in the space of intuition. If you come to a decision after multiple thoughts, it is ignorance. If you come to a decision after one clear flow of thoughts, it is called intelligence. If you come to a decision without any thought, it is called intuition.

Please understand, I really tell you, completion is equivalent to inner cleansing. All your muscle-memories come to peace and rest in peace.

The greatest wealth lies within, not outside. The greatest joy lies within, not outside. In the outside world, every experience of joy is followed by sorrow. Joy creates expectations and when expectations are not fulfilled, they lead to sorrow. When the search begins inside, expectations drop, attachments drop and a new joy of completion happens. That joy is eternal, never ending. It is *Ānanda, Nityānanda,* eternal bliss.

Because we are unaware of this, we search outside for happiness, because that is the only way we know.

In his commentary on the Gītā, Ādī Śaṅkara says that memory and knowledge come from Kṛṣṇa to those who do good enriching deeds and loss of memory and knowledge to those who do evil deeds. The reference to memory and knowledge here is to the understanding of our true nature, the understanding and realization that we are one with the Divine, that Kṛṣṇa is seated in our hearts.

Perishable and Imperishable Puruṣa

Kṛṣṇa takes Arjuna into a deeper understanding. Kṛṣṇa talks about *puruṣa*, the principle of energy that underlies our existence. *Sāṅkhya* philosophy talks about *puruṣa* and *prakṛti. Puruṣa,* in one sense is energy, and *prakṛti* is matter. *Puruṣa* is the unmoving, passive energy principle, whereas *prakṛti* is the active material principle. *Puruṣa* is the male principle; *prakṛti* is the female principle. *Puruṣa* is Śiva and *prakṛti* is Śakti.

Kṛṣṇa goes beyond that philosophy. He says *Puruṣa* is twofold, one imperishable and the other perishable. He says all living beings are the perishable *puruṣa* and they are situated in the imperishable energy.

dvāv imau puruṣau loke kṣaraś cākṣara eva ca /
kṣaraḥ sarvāṇi bhūtani kūṭa-stho 'kṣara ucyate // 15.16

In earlier chapters, Kṛṣṇa has covered in depth, these aspects of *prakṛti*, which operate through the mind, senses and the attributes, the three types of *guṇa*. Here, He expands upon *puruṣa*.

Puruṣa is the Ultimate Energy from which all emanates. *'īśā vāsyaṁ idaṁ sarvaṁ'* says the Īśāvāsya Upaniṣad , 'All that exists is energy.'

When Einstein read this verse from the Upaniṣads, written possibly tens of thousands of years ago, he said, 'I felt proud that I had discovered that matter is energy. Many thousand years ago, these Sages knew this, and also knew that matter arises from energy. The last step in science is the first step in spirituality.'

More and more, scientists are beginning to sound like the Eastern Mystics. They no longer have the attitude of scientists of a hundred years ago who felt that they were rewriting the laws of Nature.

Our *Vedic* scriptures said this over thousands of years ago. Śaṅkara has said again and again that the *Seer* influences what is *seen*. That was over a thousand years ago.

The primal energy principle, *puruṣa* is like potential energy. It is energy, but passive. It is the operating principle behind the entire Universe. Without this energy, nothing will exist. Nothing will live.

Kṛṣṇa says that there are two kinds of *puruṣa*: one is eternal, *akṣara* and one perishes, *kṣara*. The *puruṣa* that perishes is the body-mind energy embedded in all beings, including humans. This energy has a definite, limited lifetime. It is always changing. There is nothing permanent about it. It is programmed for deterioration and destruction.

The *puruṣa* that is *kūṭastha* is the imperishable aspect of this energy. It is the energy of the spirit that is indestructible, *akṣara*. It is the Soul that is forever, that which cannot be destroyed.

Kṛṣṇa points out that primal energy manifests in different ways, as perishable and imperishable. Both are aspects of primal energy. One is destroyed and the other lives. One who realizes this difference and understands the true nature of puruṣa is liberated.

Rāmakṛṣṇa Paramahamsa beautifully narrates:

> An arrogant scholar was very proud of his learning. He was a great Advaitic (non-dualitistic) scholar and did not believe in the various forms of God.
>
> Then, God came to him one day.
>
> The mother goddess appeared before him in all Her splendor. She came as the primal energy, *Parāśakti*. The scholar was in a swoon for a long time.
>
> When he woke up, he shouted, 'Ka, Ka, Ka.' He could not

fully pronounce 'Kāli,' the name of the goddess whom he had seen. Words cannot describe the Divine!

Scholars argue endlessly about the nature of *puruṣa*, the various aspects of *puruṣa*, the difference between *prakṛti* and *puruṣa*. It strengthens their ego. When the Divine presents itself before them, they cannot recognize or cognize what they see.

Collective Consciousness

15.17 *Besides these two, there is the Supreme Puruṣa, the Lord Himself, who pervades and sustains these three worlds.*

15.18 *As I am transcendental, beyond both the perishable and the imperishable, and the best, I am declared both in the world and in the Vedas as that Supreme Person, Puruṣottama.*

15.19 *Whoever knows Me as the Supreme, without a doubt, is to be understood as the knower of everything, and he worships Me with all his being, O son of Bhārata.*

15.20 *This is the most confidential teaching disclosed by Me, O Sinless One, and whoever knows this will become wise and his actions will bear fruit.*

Kṛṣṇa says that beyond these two aspects of *puruṣa*, the perishable body-mind energy and the imperishable spirit energy, there lies another level of energy that is the Supreme *puruṣa*. He goes on to say that He is that Supreme puruṣa, *Puruṣottama.*

Puruṣa is the energy that pervades us. *Puruṣottama* is the energy that pervades the entire Universe. *Puruṣottama* in that sense is no different from *Parāśakti*, the cosmic energy. It is only a play of words to separate *Puruṣa* as male and *śakti* as female, while describing the ultimate Cosmic Consciousness.

All-pervading Energy Behind Life

The Universe is imperishable. The energy behind the Universe is imperishable. Kṛṣṇa says that He is that energy, the *Puruṣottama,* that drives the Universe eternally—*prathitaḥ puruṣottamaḥ* (15.18).

Modern astrophysicists speak about many universes, not just one. They say there are millions of galaxies in each universe, millions of stars and planets in each galaxy. Even with the aid of advanced equipment, we cannot determine where the universe starts and where it ends. It will never be possible with material aids. The energy behind the Universe is spiritual. It is intangible, invisible and immeasurable.

Kṛṣṇa says, 'Beyond the perishable and imperishable, I am *Puruṣottama*.' He is not talking about the Yādava king Kṛṣṇa, *Vāsudeva* Kṛṣṇa, son of Vāsudeva and Devaki. He is talking about *Parabrahma* Kṛṣṇa, the *Īśvara*. He is *saguṇa*, the universal form and *nirguṇa*, the formless energy. He is that Brahman into whom both the soul, the individual imperishable Self and the perishable body-mind, merge.

He is the Brahman into whom the six-billion humans and countless billion living beings on planet Earth as well as countless trillion upon trillion entities in all the Universes merge. He is *Puruṣa*, the energy, and *Prakṛti*, the matter. Without Him, nothing moves.

We see *Puruṣottama* in different ways, depending upon our upbringing and capabilities. We see Him as the six-headed, twelve-handed Kārtikeya or Murugā, or the two-handed Rāma or the two-handed, peacock-feather-adorned, flute-playing Kṛṣṇa. We see Him in a way that is comfortable for us to see Him, so that we can reach Him.

What difference does it make whether we call Kṛṣṇa '*Brahman, Puruṣottama, Parabrahma, Prakṛti*,' or any other name? By whatever name He is called, He is the supreme energy who causes us to move.

It is the unbounded authority of Kṛṣṇa, with which He declares Himself as *Puruṣottama*, that makes Gītā a scriptural authority. It is not the wisdom contained in it, nor the eternal truths, but the courage of that *one* person, who declared Himself to be the Transcendental Being, that defines this work as an eternal scriptural truth. May that *Puruṣottama*, that *Parabrahma* Kṛṣṇa, bless us all!

Know Me as the Supreme and Know Everything

Now, Kṛṣṇa presents the great truths about His true representation as the collective consciousness, the Supreme Self.

This may surprise you or it may be something you already know. Irrespective of whether this concept is new or old, analyze this Truth for the sake of internalizing, until your logic fails.

The first Truth:

All our minds are not individually separated pieces of the Universe. They are all one and the same. All our minds are interlinked. Not only interlinked, they directly affect each other. This is what I call collective consciousness. Anything we think affects people around us. Not only are those near us touched by our thoughts, so is everyone living on planet Earth.

Listen. We are not individual islands, separated from each other and uninfluenced by each other. Only one truth called collective consciousness links all of us.

The next Truth:

Not only at the mental level, even at the deeper level of consciousness, the deeper we go, the deeper we are connected. In Existence, there is no such thing as a separate individual identity. Once we know this truth, we will go beyond pain, suffering, depression and disease.

Understand that as long as we hold onto the concept of individual consciousness, we will be continuously suffering, physically or mentally or on the being level. Why do we continuously resist Nature? Whatever Nature offers, we resist. When the weather is cold, we resist. We think we are different from Existence. I never thought that I was different from the atmosphere, never had the feeling of separation from Nature. It is only when we think that we are different from the atmosphere, from the air around us that we resist it.

You see, we are a part of the Whole. If we fall in tune with the Whole, the Whole behaves as a friend. The moment we think, discriminate or behave with the Whole in the opposite way, it acts like an enemy. Be very clear, the Whole is not here to kill or destroy us.

An example is what happens when a person dies of drowning. The dead body floats. The dead body is heavier than water. Yet, it floats. But, a living body that is lighter than water, does not float. It drowns. Why is this so? As long as we are living, we are unable to relate with water. Our ego prevents that. Our mind prevents that. In the dead body, there is no mind and no ego. It is the mind and ego that causes our heaviness.

When we are in completion with the collective consciousness, when we become a part of collective consciousness, Nature is our friend and Nature protects us. When we think that we are different from Nature, as long as we think that we are an individual consciousness, Nature protests against us.

If we disappear into the collective consciousness, we are protected and taken care of. We attain complete success, not only socially and economically, but we experience it as well. It will be a feeling of fulfillment, an experience of complete completion.

A small story:

> Once there were two ants sitting on the rim of a cup that contained *amṛta*, the nectar of immortality. As they were talking, one of the ants lost his balance and was about to fall into the cup. He somehow managed to get back on the rim.
>
> The other ant asked him, 'Why don't you want to fall into the cup? Even if you drown in this, you will become only immortal.'
>
> The first ant replied, 'But I don't want to drown!'

We don't realize that merging with the collective consciousness will liberate us in totality. We resist and hold on to ourselves. As long as we do not disappear into the collective consciousness, we continuously create hell for ourselves and for others.

The third Truth:

At the ultimate level, at the spiritual level, the moment we understand that we are deeply connected, totally connected to the whole group, to the whole Universe, not only do we experience bliss, but we really live, opening many dimensions of our being.

Right now we are stressed out and disturbed continuously. With our separate body-mind, we need to think too much, we need to try too hard to enjoy life. If we disappear into collective consciousness, we open many dimensions, many possibilities. See, now with only this one body we have, we can enjoy so much. Imagine what we can do when we have many bodies! If the multitudes of bodies increase, so does the joy, the bliss. This is our experience when we realize we are a part of the collective consciousness.

When we experience that we are boundariless consciousness, we experience the infinity. It is difficult to imagine. When we experience the feeling of non-duality, *Advaita* or collective consciousness, when we experience the bliss of collective consciousness, we forget differences of name, wealth, social status and prestige; whatever we think of ourselves disappears. The truth of who we are is revealed.

Life is not restricted to inanimate forms. Life is happening in everything; may be in a frequency where it is not realized, recognized by you. But, everything has life. Learn to complete with everything! I tell you, the state of completion is the best way to prepare yourself for life; and completion is the best way to prepare for death. For anything, just the completion!

When we complete with everything, animate and inanimate, we experience the space of non-duality, *Advaita,* where each one is infinitely powerful and infinitely intelligent. Completion should be carried till we become enlightened. Understand, till we feel we are one with the space of *Nithyānando'ham* (I am *Nithyānanda*, Eternal Bliss); till we experience the space of *Nityānando'ham.*

Kṛṣṇa declares, 'whoever knows Me as the Supreme, *Puruṣottama*, without a doubt, is to be understood as the knower of everything, and worships Me with all his being.'

yo mām evam asammūḍho jānāti puruṣottamam /
sa sarva-vid bhajati māṁ sarva-bhāvena bhārata // 15.19

The difference between the *puruṣa*, self and the *Puruṣottama*, *Self*, the difference between the perishable and the imperishable, are for the 'deluded' and 'confused' as Kṛṣṇa says. Once one has the awareness of collective consciousness, he becomes the knower of everything. Everyone merges into the collective consciousness, the space of oneness, *Advaita*.

The wave thinks that it is separate from the ocean. It does not realize that it comes from the ocean and goes back to the ocean, that *it is the ocean*. Just as the wave is part of the ocean, we are part of Existence. How can we attain or reach *Puruṣottama*, when we are already a part of Him? We can only gain awareness that we are a part of Him.

This is the profound secret teaching of Kṛṣṇa. In this chapter, Kṛṣṇa becomes the ultimate Master. Arjuna is completely in silence, the best way to imbibe the Master.

What is the difference between a Master and a teacher?

A teacher knows intellectually; a Master knows experientially. A Master has experienced what he is speaking, the truth. If Indian kings wanted to learn archery, they went to a master. You may wonder what enlightened persons know about agriculture, archery or business. Every art and science has a technique. In the *gurukul*, the Vedic education system, everyone was happy because they were properly guided by Enlightened Masters to live the life best suited to them. A teacher teaches through verbal language; a Master teaches through his body language. It is known now that ninety percent of our communication is through non-verbal communication, through the body language. The direct touch and presence of a Master transforms and awakens a person by creating such a space.

We don't have to become something new; we need to wake up and realize what we already are. The Master never allows us to stop at any step before the full flowering. Again and again, he inspires and takes us to higher levels of conscious experience, until we realize we are that eternal consciousness; our true potentiality.

Masters use these techniques only with those who feel completely connected with them. They operate on disciples who have devotion for them. This is the ultimate technique that is used in the most loving, caring way. To the outsider, it may look harsh; however, the disciple understands the love and care behind it when the Master uses it on him and is eternally grateful for such surgery.

The Master never allows anyone to get stuck with ordinary experiences. Even though we call it a spiritual experience, it is only when we stop experiencing anything that we enter into a real spiritual experience. Only in such an experience, the Experiencer, the Experienced and the Experience, disappear into *one*; all three merge into the experience. Only 'we' remain, even the word 'we' can't be used since there is no other, all boundaries are lost!

Unless that experience of '*Tat Tvam Asi, That Are Thou*,' happens, unless the experience of '*Nithyānandoham, I Am Nīthyananda*,' happens, the Master never rests.

The Master is the ultimate Master surgeon who removes the ego at all levels, the ordinary or the spiritual. People have spiritual ego when they have a 'holier than thou' attitude. The Master will never allow us to be stuck in that area. He pushes us forward until we experience the Ultimate.

The more we allow His surgery, the more we realize the Truth. A few people run away from the operating table during surgery; that's dangerous. Before surrendering, do all the checking, verifying, window-shopping. But once you surrender, allow Him to work on you.

Let us pray to *Puruṣottama* Kṛṣṇa, the Ultimate Energy, the Universal Consciousness, the Cosmic intelligence, to give us the experience of Eternal Consciousness; to make us beings with *jñāna cakṣu*, eyes of knowledge, and establish us in *Nityānanda*, eternal bliss.

Thank you!

Thus ends the fifteenth chapter named ***Puruṣottama Yogaḥ****, 'The Yoga of the Supreme Being,' of the* ***Bhagavad Gītā Upaniṣad****,* ***Brahmavidyā Yogaśāstra****, the scripture of yoga dealing with the science of the Absolute in the form of* ***Śrī Kṛṣṇārjuna saṃvād****, dialogue between Śrī Kṛṣṇa and Arjuna.*

CHAPTER

16

Daivāsura Sampad Vibhāga Yogaḥ

YOU AND ME

HUMAN BEINGS ARE BORN WITH INNATE DIVINE NATURE; THEY ARE NOT SINNERS! WHETHER WE ACT DIVINE (DAIVIC) OR DEMONIC (ASURA), OUR INNER SPACE IS DIVINE. HOW DO WE AWAKEN THE SPACE OF DIVINITY WITHIN US AGAIN? KRSNA REVEALS! . . .

You And Me

This chapter is traditionally called *Daivāsura Sampad Vibhāga Yogaḥ*, or the Yoga of divine and demonic nature. Here Kṛṣṇa explains the concept of *saṁskāras* (root thought patterns) from an even deeper level.

In the 14th chapter, *Guṇatraya Vibhāga Yoga*, He spoke on *satva, rajas* and *tamas,* the three attributes of nature in which all living beings exist. He also explains the three layers of the body-mind system: *prāṇa śarīra, manaḥ śarīra* and *sūkṣma śarīra,* which are the physical, mental and subtle bodies, respectively. In the 15th chapter, Kṛṣṇa speaks extensively about deeper body-mind layer, the causal body. That chapter is called the *Puruṣottama Yogaḥ* or the Yoga of the perfected being. Kṛṣṇa points out how the body-mind system is like a unique tree, with its roots in the physical world, and the branches in the causal world. Here, in the 16th chapter, He moves into the deeper energy layers of the body-mind system and takes us to the Cosmic layer.

Kṛṣṇa speaks about the qualities of the divine, *daiva* and the demonic, *asura*. The beauty is that both these words have the same root. Of course, it is not accidental; both qualities are rooted in the same energy. It is just a simple decision. When you choose the word 'you', you become divine, and when you choose the word 'me', you become a demon. That's all.

Śrī Rāmakṛṣṇa Paramahamsa speaks beautifully of the same energy. No energy can be destroyed; your love can never be destroyed. It can only be converted. He says that as long as the calf says, *'ahaṁ, ahaṁ'* ('me, me') it must work, suffer, get beaten and tortured. Once it is killed, musical instruments are made out of its skin; then when we beat the instrument, it says, '*tumi, tumi*' or '*tum*' ('you, you'). As long as it says, '*ahaṁ, ahaṁ*' it suffers, when it says, '*tuṁ, tuṁ*,' it starts being used for wonderful purposes like singing the glory of the divine!

The moment the cognitive shift happens in us, that is when the '*tumi, tumi*' ('you, you') happens, we will be a blessing for ourselves and for others.

All the root thought patterns or bio-memories, *saṁskāras*, are stored in the causal layer. They operate without our control. Decisions are made without our knowledge. However, at the deeper level, in the cosmic layer, we decide consciously: *you* or *me*, divine or demon, *daiva* or *asura*.

When we make the decision of 'You,' we radiate divine qualities. When we make the decision of 'me,' we radiate demonic qualities.

The decision about 'You' or 'me' is made in the Cosmic layer. If we decide with the attitude of 'you,' the whole thing becomes divine; if we decide with the attitude of 'me,' the whole thing becomes demonic. The mind or *citta*, the inner space is neither negative nor positive. None of these, including the *guṇa* (attributes) are negative or positive. Even *tāmasic* qualities, such as laziness, are neither negative nor positive. Many Enlightened Masters seem passive, not doing anything at all. We cannot differentiate between their attitude and laziness. For instance, Bhagavān Ramaṇa Maharṣi sat throughout his life in one little town, Tiruvannamalai. He never moved out of there. He was mostly in silence. Yet we cannot say he was in *tamas* since he never made any decision out of 'me.' The whole process was happening with 'you' as a center, not 'me.'

We cannot call the *citta*, the mind or *samskāra*, the root pattern good or bad. In the superficial layers, they are neither. However, the decisions we make in the cosmic layer, in the deeper layer, determine whether they are good or bad. The energy behind passion and compassion is really one and the same. When we decide based on 'me', it is passion; when we decide based on 'You', it is compassion.

We need to understand one important thing.

If we feel passion strongly in our being, but our compassion has only a little intensity, then our compassion is just a pseudo-expression, perhaps for the sake of name and fame, not for anything else. If we are not integrated to compassion as intensely as our passion, all our activities are based on ego. Even this *Gītā* discourse can become food for the ego, if the decision is taken out of 'I' and 'me'. When the decision happens out of 'You,' even ordinary daily activities can become divine, not just *Gītā* discourses.

We need not work on the 'doing'; we need to work on the 'being'. Doing can never lead us to anything. As long as we believe that *doing* can lead us to the Ultimate, we have *karma*. This is called *Pūrva Mimāṁsi* (those who interpret the *Vedic* rituals literally). Only when we understand that only *being* can lead us to the Ultimate, we are called *Uttara Mimāṁsi* (those who interpret the *Vedic* scriptures according to vedānta-based non-duality).

According to the *Vedas,* there are two major types of people: People who believe in *doing* and people who believe in *being*. People who believe in transforming the 'Being' are *Vedāntins*, people who believe that the transformation to the Ultimate can be achieved by 'doing' are *karmakāndis*.

Of course, the Ultimate can be achieved only by working on the *being*, not by working on the *doing*. If we work on the *doing*, we either suppress or express. We continuously fight with ourselves; nothing else is achieved. Only a man who transforms his *being* can achieve the Ultimate.

Whether to be a demon or divine, we decide at that one point. When we receive the data through our senses, process it and deliver the result or command, how is the command delivered? If the command comes out with the thinking, 'What is there for *me?*' then whatever we do, including meditation, will be only ego satisfying, not enriching.

Many people ask, '*Swamiji*, at some point, I felt such deep ecstasy in meditation, such beautiful bliss. But suddenly, within two hours it disappeared, it never came back! Why is this so? How can we get it back?'

Please understand that bliss is choicelessness. When we are absent, when our identity disappears, we experience bliss. The moment we want the bliss back, we have already chosen. We have made the choice! The moment we choose, we will always choose suffering. All choices are suffering, because choice is based on the mind. It is based on duality. Bliss is choicelessness. It is beyond duality, it is *Advaita*, therefore there is nothing to choose 'between'. The moment the space of 'me' or 'mine' appears and decides, it destroys the bliss. We can no longer be Divine. When we are blissful, we have said, 'No' to 'me'; we are relaxed in the 'You' idea. The moment we want to possess bliss, we have said, 'Yes' to 'me'.

'You' and 'me'

Listen. We need to understand 'You' and 'me' properly. The word 'me' means ego; the word 'You' means the whole of Existence. When our identity evaporates, when our ego dissolves, whatever is left is Existence; it is Divine, *daivic*. We create the demon by bringing in the idea of 'me'. The moment we bring in the idea of 'me,' whatever is there, is demonic. The moment the 'me' idea is removed, whatever there is, is Divine.

With the 'me' idea, whatever we do, be it meditation, rituals, learning, or knowledge, it will only strengthen the ego. Anything done to strengthen the idea of 'me', naturally leads to more ignorance and suffering. Anything done with the attitude of 'You,' whatever it is, naturally becomes Divine and leads to Bliss.

In Saṁskṛit, we have two words: *nivṛitti* and *pravṛitti*. *Nivṛitti*—looking inwards or liberation or completion—is centered on the idea of 'You'. *Pravṛitti*—looking outwards or bondage or incompletion—is centered on the idea of 'me'. Whatever is done out of 'You', leads to liberation; whatever we do out of the idea of 'me', leads to bondage.

As long as we are centered in ourselves, we are in the bondage of attraction and aversion, greed and fear. Most people are centered in their *mūlādhāra cakra,* the energy center in our body associated with the emotion of greed, or in the *svādiṣṭhāna cakra*, the energy center in our body associated with fears and insecurity.

The *mūlādhāra* is all about 'me'—our possessions: 'What is in it for me? Where do I go from here?' The *svādiṣṭhāna* is about 'I', our identity, insecurity and fear arising from our need to protect the body-mind system. Both these bind us, block us, and keep us firmly locked in the material world.

As our higher centers of energy get energized and unblocked, and our energy rises from the *mūlādhāra* and *svādiṣṭhāna*, to *anāhata* (heart center) and beyond, we look beyond ourselves. The 'me' starts dropping. When the *ājñā cakra* (energy center between the eyebrows) becomes energized, the ego, the identity, the 'I' and 'me', disappear and the 'you' takes over. The demon becomes the Divine.

When we shed our ego, we become boundary-less. We are no longer limited by selfish thoughts about 'me' and 'mine', our kith and kin. The whole world is ours to care for. Kṛṣṇa refers to this as *Vasudaiva Kuṭuṁbakaṁ*, 'the whole world is one family'. As long as we feel that our body-mind is our boundary, that we are separate from the rest of the Universe, we will continuously fight with Existence, with the nature, with the Whole. Understand, the part can never succeed when it fights with the Whole.

Whatever we think, speak or do based upon the idea 'me', it leads to more and incompletions, more and more suffering.

This whole Universe is God's will and so are we. However, God has willed that we use our free will. That is why He has given us consciousness, so that we are aware of what we do. If we truly believed in God's will, we would do our very best and leave the result to Him. This is what Kṛṣṇa declared earlier—*karmaṇy evādhikāraste mā phaleṣu kadācana* (2.47). Do what you have to do without bothering about the results.

When we move into the space of 'You', we move into the attitude Kṛṣṇa speaks about. When we are no longer worried about ourselves and we think of everyone else's needs as our own, results lose meaning. There is no selfish pressure. There is no identity that directs us towards success instead of failure, based upon how we imagine success looks. Success and failure lose their meaning.

Whether we act demonic or Divine, the inner space in all of us is Divine. The inner space is pure; it is uncontaminated. Whether we are tuned inwards towards that purity or tuned outwards towards gratification is the choice we make through our free will. A Rāvaṇa had the choice of being a Rāma, and a Duryodhana had the choice of being an Arjuna. Through their own free will, they did not exercise that choice.

Here, Kṛṣṇa beautifully explains the demonic and Divine natures. Now in the 15th and 16th chapters, only Kṛṣṇa speaks, Arjuna is practically silent; he is in the space of pure listening, *Upaniṣad.* All the questions have disappeared and only small doubts are left, which are a means to enrich others. He is asking for clarifications on this sacred science from his Master.

Qualifications Of Divinity

16.1,2,3 *Bhagavān Kṛṣṇa says,*
Fearlessness, purification of the being, cultivation of spiritual knowledge, charity, and being centered on the being, performance of sacrifices, and accumulation of knowledge, austerity, simplicity, non-violence, truthfulness, freedom from anger, renunciation, tranquility, aversion to fault finding, compassion for all living entities, freedom from covetousness, gentleness, modesty, studied determination, vigor, more forgiveness, fortitude, cleanliness, freedom from envy and from the passion for honor, these transcendental qualities, O Son of Bharata (Arjuna), belong to Divine men, endowed with Divine nature.'

Kṛṣṇa lists a number of qualities that take us to a higher plane of consciousness; qualities that make us divine.

Qualities of the Heart not the Mind

Now when we listen to these things with the space of 'me', what do we usually do? We start practicing all these virtues. Be clear that if we try to practice all of these qualities, one thing is sure: we will become mad. We will not be able to do anything because we will be fighting with ourselves. We will be controlling our senses to strengthen our ego. When we try to understand these ideas with our ego, with the space of 'me', we practice them to strengthen the idea of 'me', to improve ourselves and become better beings. Again and again, Masters prove that they are not better beings; they are totally transformed beings. There is a difference between better beings and transformed beings.

The other day, I shared the story of the lion and the sheep-lion told by Swami Vivekananda. It is a beautiful story. The sheep-lion does not want to realize that he is a lion. He wants to be a good, strong sheep. He asks the lion to give him a technique for becoming a strong sheep.

Similarly, if we start practicing these qualities listed by Kṛṣṇa, we may have a stronger ego. That is why so-called tapasvi (ascetics, people performing penances), people who repress themselves, have a strong ego. People who perform penances or repress desires, radiate ego. We clearly see that they do these things to strengthen their ego.

When we are in the space of completion, completely blissful and relaxed, austerity, *tapaḥ* happens. I have seen many Sannyāsais (ascetics), especially in India, who blame householders for not being pure, for being sinners. When we force ourselves to do penance, we continuously burn inside with incompletions; as a side effect we often have self-doubts about our path and ourselves. This self-doubt makes us continuously do something; we then make others guilty about the path that they are following.

Penance is supposed to happen naturally out of completion, joy and bliss. Just as a natural thing. Anything done by force is not going to enrich us or society.

Society teaches us that we are sinners. First of all, this is not true. No enlightened Master who has realized the divinity within is capable of saying this. Secondly, who gains anything at all by calling everyone a sinner?

Kṛṣṇa tells us to be without fear and greed. He also says to be without anger. He says to be truthful, simple, meek, gentle, non-violent, and to be without expectations and to renounce. These are qualities of the Divine; these are qualities that you express when you are focused not on your own self but on others. These are qualities that arise from the heart and not from the mind. These are qualities that arise from love and not from desire. These are enriching qualities that naturally express from completion not compulsion.

God, the very idea of God, should evoke love not fear. God in any religion should be portrayed as compassionate. No Enlightened Master has experienced otherwise or expressed otherwise. The concept of a fearsome God with vengeance is a manmade myth. It is created by man, to set one man against another, to divide, control and conquer. We are conditioned to believe in them because this is the easiest way to control us, through fear and greed. The greatest fear of any religion is that we might start thinking for ourselves. Worse still, they are afraid that we may stop thinking, and drop our mind!

The very lack of awareness that we are divine, in my opinion, is a sin. When we got into thinking and started clutching onto our thoughts, we became ignorant. If at all there is an original sin, it is that—the clutching onto our thoughts, associating with our incompletions.

God resides in you and me. We know everything that we do. When we do wrong, we know. No one has to tell us. That becomes our sin. The guilt makes our life hell, nothing else.

When we are complete, free and liberated, we are in sheer enjoyment and we are in heaven. If we focus on enriching others, on 'You', we expand with the power of living. In fact, the more we focus to create the inner space of completion, the more we open up to enrich others. We move from the 'me' to 'You.' As we move inwards, our higher intelligence awakens. Our higher intelligence is nothing but the Divine. That completion alone makes us God. Completion is God! Completion is Divinity!

Please understand that what we think of as God is not an old bearded man sitting on the clouds, playing on a harp! God is merely that energy of inner and higher intelligence. That same intelligent energy that is within us also drives the entire Universe. The energy that powers us is the same energy that powers the sun. There is no difference at all.

As human beings we have the opportunity to expand into this energy, into this higher intelligence. Unfortunately, animals do not have this ability, this consciousness. Humans do. To ignore this gift, this opportunity, this consciousness, is our original sin. The entire meaning of our life is to discover this truth and become divine. That is why, if we die without realizing this truth, we are born again.

We go through this cycle of life and death again and again because we do not recognize who we are. As Buddha says, that is the cause of our suffering. When we realize our own Self, our true divine potential, we realize the meaning of our life, and there is no need to be born again. We become liberated.

LIVING THE DIVINE

Here Kṛṣṇa gives all the divine qualities, one by one. It is not necessary to explain all the qualities. Let us take a few. Let us take fearlessness, *abhayaṁ* for example.

As long as we carry the instinct to survive, we have fear. Fear can never be taken away from our being, as long as we want to survive. Surrendering to Existence, surrendering to death is the one and only way to achieve fearlessness.

In the *Kaṭhopaniṣad*, the beautiful *Upaniṣad*, which comes from the wonderful system of *Vedānta*, the essence of the *Vedas*, they have gone deep into the science of death. The West has dedicated its entire energy to understand life, whereas the East has dedicated its energy to understanding death! That is why *Ṛṣis* live even after they die. They exist; they discovered the science of living even after death. However, people who are caught in the material world die each moment, even as they live. This *Kaṭhopaniṣad* is the science of death.

> A young boy, Naciketa, who goes to the abode of Yama, the Lord of death. Yama was not there when Naciketa went to meet Him. Yama receives him after three days. Yama welcomes him.

At this point, we must understand that no one goes to Yama's abode; always it is He who comes! When we try to escape from Him, He is death as we know it ordinarily; He will take away our 'I' and 'mine'—all our possessions and relationships; we cannot sign our check or drive our car once He takes us. Whatever we think is ours will be taken away: wealth, relationships, bank balance, everything. What we think is 'I'—the body, even that will be taken away. When death comes to us, everything is taken away. On the contrary, when we go to death like Naciketa did, fearlessly, death welcomes us! Yama becomes our host!

> Here, Yama receives Naciketa with love and care. First thing: He becomes a loving host. Next, He offers him three boons. Naciketa first asks for good relationships.
>
> He says, 'When I go back to my family, my father should accept me, love me and take me back.' Yama blesses him with good relationships, completion with others. After that Yama blesses him with completion with wealth, and shows him how to create wealth, pleasure and comforts. Now, Yama is behaving like a God.
>
> Ultimately, Yama gives him *ātmajñāna*—knowledge of the Self, completion with the Self. Now, He is behaving like an enlightened Master himself! The third boon He gives because Naciketa asks Him for the secret of death.
>
> Understand, Naciketa is the embodiment of authenticity. Pleased with the boy's integrity and courageous authenticity, *Śraddha*, Yama blesses him with Enlightenment itself.

Look at the paradox of life: When we run away from death, Death or Yama chases us, wherever we are. Death takes away all our wealth, our relationships, whatever we think of as 'I' and 'mine'. But here, with Naciketa, the whole situation is just the opposite! When we surrender to Yama, when we go to Him, He is a loving host. He is not something terrible as we imagine Him to be. He says, 'Welcome! You are the form of Agni, fire.' A guest is considered to be the form of fire that we worship.

> Yama tells Naciketa, 'You are my guest and you have come to my house in the form of '*vaiśvānarāgni*' (the fire

> that we worship).' The *vaiśvānara* (priest) is considered to be the embodiment of the divine *Agni*. 'You have come to my house as the embodiment of the Divine. Let me pay my respects to you. Please forgive me for not being here for three days to receive you.'

Usually we postpone Yama (death). Usually we try to escape from Him. But when we go in search of Him, He will not be there, as we feared! That is the essence of this whole history. Understand this important point. It has a tremendous truth. When Naciketa went to death, death was not there. Whatever imagination we have about death will not be there when we surrender to death. Now, because of our fear, we try to escape; because we try to escape, He chases us.

THINKING ABOUT FEAR, LIBERATES YOU FROM IT

Please listen! Listen, I am making a very important statement. Most of your sufferings are because you are afraid to think about some parts of your life, some components of your life. You are afraid of thinking. You always think that because you are thinking, you are getting fear. No! You are actually afraid of thinking. That is why those thoughts may cause fear in you, you think and then you stop thinking!

Listen! Fear of thinking! I am giving an example. Please get it. I am unlocking some of the important self-doubting structures of your being. I am giving you the formulae of life algebra.

If you are afraid of poverty, but you don't want to think about it logically, it is not that you are not going to think about poverty. You will constantly be afraid of poverty and you will be brooding over poverty unconsciously, wasting all your energy; because that is going to be sitting in your unconscious space as a big tumor. Thinking about fire and its after-effects is not going to burn your body! When you have that clarity, you will know how not to be afraid of thinking.

Ironing out your thinking and not being afraid of thinking about anything, taking any thinking to the logical conclusion is Integrity.

Whenever you want to think about poverty or death, you are always afraid that if you think about all that, it may come true in your life. But whenever you want to think about being rich to fulfill your desires, you always have the fear, 'Even if I think about it, I won't get it.' See the funny way your brain functions! See, all the things that *you want* in your life, you think that you won't get them, even if you work for it. But all the things that you *don't want*, you are afraid that you will get them, even if you just think about them.

Please listen! Life is not *that* unfair with you. Anything happens only when you take the responsibility of inviting it and making it happen. You should know very clearly and see your own hypocrisy. What a funny belief space we create about life and then we go on blaming life! If you create this kind of space, will life respond to you?

Ironing out your thinking to the logical flow of your thinking, needs to be done as the first step for awakening the divine qualities. First thing you need to do—sit with yourself and list out all the areas of your life that you are afraid of. Whatever you are afraid of, write it down and logically think about it. Allow all of them to surface. Let your mind face the fears. Let your mind speak everything. Think intensely and logically about the fears. Give it half an hour. You may feel afraid, tears may roll and your whole body may shake. Let everything come out. What can be done? If you could do anything, you would have done it. Allow the fear come up to your conscious layer without being suppressed.

Whatever you are afraid of, sit in a very cool and comfortable way and know very clearly that just because you are thinking, you are not going to have it. Millions of things about which you thought, you didn't have them. You also wanted a private jet, but did you get it? No! So, know very clearly, mere thinking is not going to get you the results. Only creating the space is going to get you the results. Creating the space means, taking the responsibility and thinking.

Accept that there is a possibility for all these fears to come true: your wealth may be stolen, you may have an accident, a near or dear one may die, or you may die. All these possibilities are real. Yes. What can be done? This is life. This is what is called facing reality as it is. So, sit comfortably and tell yourself clearly, 'Now I am going to allow myself to think to the extreme conclusions, the logical conclusions of any thought-trend which I am afraid of. If I am afraid of poverty, let me sit and think about the extreme possibility of poverty.

I tell you, anything that stays in your unconscious as a weight and makes you brood over it, bring all of them out and consciously think through them to the logical conclusion. With integrity, fear of thinking will disappear, and once fear of thinking disappears, they cannot cause fear to you.

When you lose fear of thinking, thinking loses fear of you. When both of you lose fear of each other, you live happily, blissfully, ever after. Having eternal romance with your thinking is integrity. Integrity takes away the fear component in your thinking. You can think about anything; you will take responsibility for the right thing.

You Are A Demon If...

16.4 *Pride, arrogance, conceit, anger, harshness or cruelty, and ignorance—these qualities belong to those born with demonic nature, O Pātha (son of Prithā).*

16.5 *The transcendental qualities are conducive to liberation,*
whereas the demonic qualities make for bondage.
Do not worry, Pāṇḍava, you are born with Divine qualities.

16.6 *Pārtha, in this world there are two kinds of created beings,*
one is divine and the other, demonic.
I have explained at length to you the Divine qualities.
Now hear about the demonic qualities also, so that
you will understand and live your life blissfully and happily.

16.7 *Persons with demonic nature do not know*
what is bondage and what is liberation;
nor what is cleanliness; truthful behavior is not in them.

What is demonic nature? Kṛṣṇa says that all actions done out of arrogance, out of pride, out of ego, for name and fame, and for power, are demonic in nature. As in the case of Rāvaṇa, they benefit neither the person himself nor others. Their actions are performed out of ignorance, and ultimately lead to their own downfall.

I have seen many people do penance like Rāvaṇa (King of Lankā who abducted Rāma's wife Sītā, in the Indian epic, the Ramāyaṇa). Rāvaṇa did penance; however, his powers neither helped him nor others. He became a demon for others and for himself. He killed others, and finally destroyed himself. His penance was done with the attitude of 'me' and 'what is there in it for me?' The whole history happened to strengthen the 'I' and 'mine'.

Please understand that whatever we do, whether we study the scriptures, do charity or social service, or perform *pūjā* (prayer), rituals or meditation, if they are done to strengthen the 'I' and 'mine', they always lead to suffering.

Focusing on the 'I' is instinctive. It is a call for survival. It is a call for our survival based on our conditioning and insecurities. The instinct to survive is what is called 'I', and the instinct to possess is what is referred to as 'mine'. The person who understands that both are illusions is a complete person. Such a person realizes that the instinct to survive does not help, and no matter what one may have, one still cannot survive forever.

The instinct to survive is pure illusion. At the most we can survive perhaps for 70 to 80 years. Sometimes a person lives to be 90 to 100 years with the same identity. Yet the instinct to survive tries to extend itself. It wants to make life eternal. No one wants to die. Naturally we are then walking towards suffering. As long as we carry this instinct to survive, we repeatedly hurt ourselves.

One morning an ashramite complained that she is hurt by small and well-meaning criticisms from others. She said she is sensitive. I asked her to stop using that word. I said, 'You are not sensitive. A sensitive person is porous; he allows the words to pass through him. Only arrogant people get hurt. If we are hurt, please understand that we are arrogant. We are impenetrable like stone, which is why words come and hit us. Don't say that you are sensitive.'

A sensitive person lets words pass through him. He never suffers. Suffering is from arrogance, never from sensitivity. A person who is sensitive never suffers. We suffer from words when we stop them, when we resist them, when we make our own meaning out of them. When we do not make meanings out of words, we do not suffer. It is like playing with words. We choose nice words to support our ego. We do not say, 'I am hurt because I am arrogant.' We use polished words such as, 'I am hurt because I am sensitive.'

Please don't cheat yourself with words that lack integrity. Let straight integrated words be used. Let us be integrated about what we mean. Let us use the same integrated words to express what we really are and what we really feel. Rāmakṛṣṇa says, 'Let your words and mind be straightened.'

FROM SURVIVAL TO GRATITUDE

In our Inner Awakening program, we have a meditation replicating the 'death experience'. It is based on my personal experience of death. People feel frightened to enter into the meditation, but on coming out of the experience, they feel completely reborn and complete.

They say, 'I have been postponing many things; now I have decided that when I go back, I will complete those things.' Naturally these people become integrated and authentic when they come out of the death meditation. They understand the value of relationships and do completion with others. Many people report that after that meditation, they began respecting their spouses; they do not take them for granted anymore. When we think of the possibility of death, we will never take life or our spouse for granted. We will start really living an enriching life.

Similarly, when there is a possibility that our good health may be taken away from us, after this meditation, we will not take our health for granted; we will start living life with integrity and authenticity. We will realize the gift of life that Existence has bestowed upon us.

Yama gave relationships, wealth, and finally Enlightenment to Naciketa. When people come out of the darkness or death meditation in the program, they tell me that they understand the real meaning of relationships; this means Yama has blessed them completion with others! They know the value of their wealth now; it means Yama has blessed them completion with wealth. They realize that life is the ultimate blessing. They understand that the body may die and that there is something beyond the body and mind that exists in them; that is what I call *ātmajñāna* (Self-knowledge).

Here, when Kṛṣṇa speaks of fearlessness, He means, 'Face it, face the fear, only then fearlessness can happen.' Only when we face the instinct to survive and the instinct to possess and experience completion, will we enter the space of fearlessness. Until then it can never happen. You can face and complete with the instinct for survival or the instinct for possession only by making decisions based on the concept of 'You', not on the concept of 'me'.

As long as you act, speak and think centered on 'me, me, me', you will be a demon; you will work out of the instinct for survival and possession. When you work based on the space of 'You, you, you,' you will radiate a new energy, the energy of enriching.

Try this simple experiment: Try living for others' sake out of gratitude for just one week. Try to live with the new root-cognition of 'You'. I am not asking you to give away your property or any such thing. Please catch this principle of root cognition. Basically, what you strongly believe as you is root cognition.

Usually we think, 'What is there in this for me?' For example, if your wife calls you up to see a movie, you say, 'No, I want to go to the beach.' You always force your preference. Just for one week, in your office, in your house, wherever you go, decide and be with the new root cognition of 'you' instead of 'me'. Try this with simple, day-to-day life decisions. Immediately the mind thinks, 'If I start thinking based on 'you', people will take me for granted, people may exploit me, people may cheat me.'

Alright, that is fine. Now nobody is cheating you. You are living centered on the idea of 'me'. You are protecting yourself. Are you happy? Come on, be frank, are you happy? Not really!

So why not then give a chance to be centered on the root cognition of 'You'? We live all our life with this '*āsuri sampat,*' what Kṛṣṇa calls demonic nature, the inauthentic attitude of 'me, me, me'.

LIVING BEYOND 'ME'

Now, for just one week, put that 'You' into your being. You will not know from where the bliss suddenly comes! Suddenly you will feel that your whole being is relaxed. When you don't give attention to 'me', you will never be 'in tension'.

When you replace your root cognition of 'me' with 'You', a deep inner healing, a deep completion happens in you. Please understand, completing with the root cognition is completing with self-doubt.

What I am talking about is not morality. Please don't think I am teaching you how to live happily. I am not the person to teach 'How-to stuff.' I am giving this as a spiritual practice.

Listen. I am not just teaching you the science of success; I am teaching you the science of deathlessness! I am not just teaching you the science of *Ānanda* (bliss). I am teaching you the science of *Nithya* (immortality).

If you thing you are really a seeker, then do this one spiritual practice for seven days. If you think there is any way I can enrich you, take this single statement and forget about everything else. Work based on this single statement: instead of deciding based on the default root cognition of '*me, me, me*', decide based on the new root cognition of '*You, You, You*'.

You will become a hollow bamboo. Whenever you become a hollow bamboo, you are a flute in the hands of the Divine. Whatever happens through you will be divine; you will imbibe the divine nature.

Kṛṣṇa further explains step-by-step how to imbibe Divine nature: How to cause the cognitive shift at the deep, subtle level of our root cognitions.

Please understand that working at the level of *satva* (equanimity), *rajas* (aggression), or *tamas* (slothfulness) is difficult. It is akin to changing all the servants in order to change the master. We will never be able to do that. Just change the master and all the servants will be transformed.

Here, Kṛṣṇa gives the technique to change the master, the ego or the root patterns that makes decisions. He gives the straight technique for the cognitive shift to happen. At present, the root cognition happens in us keeping the 'I' as the center; He gives a simple technique to replace the 'I' with 'You' so that the cognitive shift happens. This same system will be used for the Divine nature.

Rāma and Rāvaṇa in the Hindu epic Rāmāyaṇa, are both energetic; both have the *brahmāstra* (high energy weapon). The only difference is that one is centered on the root cognition of 'I'; the other one is centered on the root cognition of 'you.' That is the only thing that makes one person Divine and the other demonic. Rāma is Divine, Rāvaṇa is demonic.

Please understand, first you need to find out whether your thinking is acting as divine inside you or as a demon inside you. Whether your thinking is acting as a god inside you or as a ghost inside you! Sometimes, many of you are possessed by a ghost. What is that ghost? '*me, me, me*'.

Kṛṣṇa goes further to give subtle techniques to experience the consciousness of 'You', the ultimate consciousness, the consciousness of the Whole, the '*daivika saṁpat*' or divine nature of your being through this root cognitive shift.

Step-by-step Kṛṣṇa explains all these great qualities. As I mentioned, please don't try to practice these qualities as a separate effort. The more we try to practice these separately, the more schizophrenic we will become. We will be fighting with ourselves.

Enrich others with the space of 'You' which will naturally make you express these divine qualities in life. Enriching will be just your lifestyle. You will understand that enriching the 'You' enriches the 'I' back. Enriching others enriches you back. Experientially you will understand that 'you' is one with others, others are one with you. Automatically you will become blissful, free from anger and full of *dhārmic* (righteous) qualities.

Ramaṇa Maharṣi says beautifully, 'When you don't ask, you will be given.' I tell people, 'When you don't tell what good things you do, I will tell.' When people do things for the āśram but do not tell anyone about them, I tell the whole world about them. However, when they tell, I keep quiet. When you don't do from the 'I', you won't feel like something is being taken away from you. Above all, you will feel tremendous fulfillment, what I call the space of completion. Anything you do with the space of 'you' will make you radiate these beautiful, divine qualities.

Serving is not always Devotion

Even Yaśodā (the foster mother of Kṛṣṇa) had the idea of 'I'.

Let me tell you a lovely history. It is about a great Kṛṣṇa devotee named Taraṅgiṇi. It is a wonderful expression of love; the 'I' and 'you' are expressed truly here.

> The history goes that within twelve hours of Kṛṣṇa's birth, He was handed over to Yaśodā. He took birth at midnight, and before sunrise, He was brought to Yaśodā. This was because of a prophecy that Kamsa, His uncle, would come to kill Him at sunrise. Yaśodā brought Him up until He left his home, Vrindāvan. Despite her bringing Him up, when Yaśodā asked Him to sing or play the flute, He would not play.
>
> However, when Taraṅgiṇi, a devotee of Kṛṣṇa from a lower caste asked Kṛṣṇa to play, He would play for her. She would stand in a corner and would not come in front of Him. She would quietly enjoy His presence and music from a distance. Once Kṛṣṇa had gone, Taraṅgiṇi would touch the dust in the place where He had stood and played.
>
> One day Kṛṣṇa forgot the flute and went away. Of course, He did not forget, He must have pretended to have forgotten it. Would Kṛṣṇa forget? He would make others forget, but He would never forget anything! He pretended to have forgotten the flute. Taraṅgiṇi noticed the flute and with love and care, kept it in her home to hand over to Kṛṣṇa.
>
> The next day Kṛṣṇa said, 'Someone has taken My flute.'

He pretended to search for it. He learned that Taraṅgiṇi had the flute and went to her house. Since He was from a higher caste, He needed a reason to go to the area of the lower community people. Yaśodā would ask Him why he had gone there. She would punish Him, since higher caste people did not go to that area. Kṛṣṇa went to the area which was full of mud, dirty roads, and a hut in which a thousand suns were shining, meaning that there were a thousand holes in the hut! Kṛṣṇa entered the house and asked for His flute.

Taraṅgiṇi was totally shaken to see Kṛṣṇa in her house. She was overwhelmed; she was unable to speak. She ran and brought the flute to Him. Kṛṣṇa continued His divine act, *līlā,* asking if He should play the flute. And who can refuse when Kṛṣṇa asks?

She replied, 'My Lord, even Gods and *Ṛṣis* come down to listen to Your music, how can I say no?'

He sat on the steps, and started playing; she sat in a corner filled with ecstasy. Yaśodā arrived at that moment. She felt terribly upset because He had never played the flute for her.

She said, 'I take care of you; I give you food and look after you completely. You never play for me. Yet you come and play here for this urchin girl!'

Please understand that the space of Taraṅgiṇi is 'you' and the space of Yaśodā is 'me'. Due to this, all Yaśodā's enriching service had no positive result for her. Since Yaśodā disturbed him, Kṛṣṇa stopped playing. The tune that Kṛṣṇa played to Taraṅgiṇi is known as *punnagavarali,* 'the broken tune'.

Kṛṣṇa told Yaśodā, 'You served Me, no doubt, but with the space of 'I'. Taraṅgiṇi is devoted to Me; you are devoted to yourself. As long as I am *your* Kṛṣṇa, you take care of Me;

that means you are devoted to *yourself*, you are centered on *yourself* and not on *Me*. That is why you are unable to digest five minutes of separation.'

This is the instinct to possess.

Kṛṣṇa continued, 'You have come all the way here; you are not even giving five minutes of My space to her. Taraṅgiṇi never asked Me to come to her house. She never expected that I would play for her. She is totally dedicated, with only the space of 'you'.'

Then Kṛṣṇa blessed Taraṅgiṇi uttering, 'You will have *sāmīpya mukti;* you will become a *shanbaga* flower and reside in My garland. You will stay with Me forever.'

There are four *muktis* or levels of liberation:

sālokya mukti, *sārūpya mukti*, *sāmīpya mukti* and *sāyujya mukti*. *Sālokya* means 'same place'; it means we will be allowed to stay in Vaikunṭa, Viṣṇu's abode. We will have a residence in heaven. *Sārūpya* means we will have the same form as the Lord. For example, we can see Jaya-Vijaya, the gatekeepers of heaven; they have the same *ṣankh* (conch), *cakra* (discus), *gadā* (mace), *padma* (lotus)—all the accessories of Viṣṇu in the same *svarūpa* (form).

Sāmīpya (being near) is being in the inner circle; the *cakra* that Viṣṇu is carrying has achieved *sāmīpya mukti*! Becoming enlightened oneself is *sāyujya mukti*. *Sāmīpya mukti* is the best Enlightenment because we can enjoy Him forever! It is like an ant forever enjoying the sugar candy.

Sāyujya mukti is like becoming the sugar candy. This is for all the *ṛṣis.* For devotees, the ultimate state is *sāmīpya mukti*. So Kṛṣṇa blessed Taraṅgiṇi with *sāmīpya mukti.*

He said, 'May you become a flower in My garland and be on My body. May you be on Me.'

He then turned to Yaśodā and said, 'Because you served with the cognition of 'me, me, me', may you not have any temple on planet Earth.'

Yaśodā served Kṛṣṇa so much, but have you seen a single Yaśodā temple? No! Everywhere you see Rādhā temples. If you go to Vrindāvan, Rādhā is worshipped more than Kṛṣṇa. Even a milkman when selling milk will call out, 'Rādhe, Rādhe,' not 'Kṛṣṇa, Kṛṣṇa.' Despite all her service, since it was centered on 'me', Yaśodā was unable to achieve Enlightenment.

On the other hand, Taraṅgiṇi, being born of a lower community, was never even close to Kṛṣṇa. She was not allowed to serve Him; however, because she lived with the enriching space of 'you, you, you', Kṛṣṇa went to her home, blessed her with eternal closeness to Him, and gave her liberation.

Even if they run after the Divine, people with the root cognition of 'I' can never reach the Divine, because the Divine runs away from them. If we live with the root cognition of 'you', even if we live in a hut with a thousand holes, Kṛṣṇa waits for us at our doorstep.

Many stories illustrate how the 'I' drives the Divine away, and the 'you' attracts the Divine. One small shift in our inner space, can take care of the cognitive shift. How we are centered and where our inner space is focused is what makes our life demonic or divine. Divine or demon is determined only by one concept: 'You' or 'me'.

Are you Divine or Demonic?

Now, here is another important point. After hearing about 'You' and 'me', the next thought that may come to our mind is, '*Swamiji*, I do not know whether I am working based on root cognition of 'You' or based on 'me'. I am worried about whether I am a demon or divine. Please guide me, tell me, based on which quality I am working.'

Let me assure you that if this fear arises in you, you are divine. The person who is ready to look into his mind, the person who is afraid about whether he is living rightly or wrongly, always lives rightly. Only the person who is arrogant is demonic. The person who is demonic never considers whether he does right or wrong. He thinks that he is always right.

Arjuna also has that fear, '*Bhagavān*, am I living with Divine or demonic nature?' He is not expressing that feeling, but his face reveals his fear.

daivī sampad vimokṣāya nibandāyāsuri matā |
mā śucaḥ sampadaṁ daivīm abhijāto 'si pāṇḍava || 16.5

Now Lord Kṛṣṇa explains that living with transcendental qualities, that is the right space of 'you', one achieves liberation or Enlightenment—*nivṛitti*. By living with the space of 'I' we create more bondage. The demonic qualities make for bondage, meaning *pravṛitti*.

Lord Kṛṣṇa assures Arjuna that he is born with Divine qualities.

If we have ever contemplated whether we were living with 'You' or 'I', if the doubt ever arose, if we have suffered, if we have felt fear or guilt, be clear that we are born with divine nature. On the other hand, if we feel that we are living properly, and that we came here because we had no other entertainment, with the thought, 'Let me listen to whatever master is saying,' if we have that attitude, then we know our nature!

If we have looked once into our being, considered and thought, 'Am I living with demonic nature? Or am I living with divine nature? What is my nature?' If we looked even once into our being and tried to measure ourselves with this scale, we are in the position of Arjuna. Be very clear that we too are born with divine qualities. So if you are worried after hearing the qualities, then be sure, you are born with divine qualities and you don't need to worry about it any further.

When a person who is righteous listens to such words, he will try to verify his own nature, since he is centered on *dharma*, righteousness. People who are *adhārmic,* non-righteous, even if they listen to such discourses, think, 'Oh, *Swamiji* speaks about all these things as though he lives them. Let us see how he lives them.' A person who is divine tries to chisel or correct himself, whereas a person who is demonic tries to correct others. With demonic nature, the person holds the hammer and chisel towards others, whereas with the divine nature, he holds the hammer and chisel towards himself.

When we carve ourselves, we become God. If we have ever looked within ourselves, then we are born with the Divine nature. Now Arjuna has become mature; the moment he hears these truths, he looks into his being. Naturally then Lord Kṛṣṇa tells him that he is born with Divine nature.

Kṛṣṇa describes the qualities of a person who lives based on 'I, I, I.' I don't think we need to understand these qualities because we already have these qualities which is why we still feel we are suffering. There is no need to read these qualities, because we know enough of them. All that we need to know is how to live with the attitude of 'You, You, You'.

Please understand that when we live with the root cognition of 'You, You, You', we completely forget ourselves; we disappear into Existence. We are in bliss.

TECHNIQUE TO EXPERIENCE DIVINITY

Pleaae listen.

Let me share an important technique that Lord Kṛṣṇa speaks about.

For three days, create a space and think you are somebody else. It may seem funny! For instance, if you are a doctor, for three days think you are a sports person or a divine being with whom you feel connected. Clearly visualize yourself as that divine being, not as a doctor. The moment you change the idea, the root cognition about yourself, a tremendous freedom happens to you. Your tension disappears.

For three days try this meditation. For three days, create the space and think you are somebody else. Whatever you think of as your property, forget it; whatever you think are your problems, throw them out; whatever you think of as your profession, give it up. You can pick it up later, but for three days throw it all away.

You will see a new consciousness rising in you. If you throw away the 'me', that alone liberates you, and if you start working on 'You', you experience tremendous bliss. When you drop 'me', you experience peace and completion; when you start working with 'You', you experience peace and bliss. This is the straight path to peace and bliss.

A demon is not one with horns on his head, with protruding teeth, with six hands and a fearsome look. Kṛṣṇa says that one with a demonic nature is not aware of what bondage is and what liberation is. People of this nature are so deeply immersed in their attachment and aversion that they no longer feel themselves separated from these qualities. They are so much in bondage to their senses that they can no longer know they are in bondage.

pravṛttiṁ ca nivṛttiṁ ca jанā na vidur āsurāḥ |
na śaucam nāpi cācāro na satyam teṣu vidyate || 16.7

Even if you start with the doubt, 'Perhaps I'm not Divine,' you start moving into that default Divine nature. Caring for enriching others, focusing on the 'you' instead of 'I,' automatically takes you to the path of the Divine. The problem with most people however, is that their caring is a business transaction. They care when there is something in it for them. Whether the transaction is with mother, father, spouse, son, daughter, relative or friend, there is a 'What's in it for me?' attitude.

When the focus is on 'you,' as in caring for enriching someone with no expectation, with no conditions, we slip into a state of bliss. This state of bliss is our natural state. When you are focused on 'I', you invite suffering and misery.

Remember one thing: God is closest when we are blissful; when we are in misery we are farthest from God. The dilemma is that most of us remember God when we are in misery and that is the moment when we are farthest away also! Even if we shout from a place of misery, our voice cannot reach Him. When we are blissful, we need not even whisper. Without saying a single word, our prayer is understood. Even our silence is eloquent.

When we are in a blissful moment, when we feel blessed by Existence, let us be enriched that moment. That is when we are closest to God. Let that moment be of gratitude, prayer, and meditation. In that moment, remember God existentially, not verbally. Let your whole being feel the vibration and become overwhelmed with the beyond. Don't lose that moment. It is precious.

Everybody is born ready for divinity. If we miss it, it is totally our responsibility. We miss it because we never look within. We miss it because we never use the opportunity that life gives us. We miss it because we are lazy and we give up on our ourselves. We miss it because we are unconscious, sleepy. We miss it because we are not aware of the great blessing that life is.

How To Save Our Planet?

16.8 *People with such demonic qualities think there is no ultimate energy or intelligence, which is running this planet Earth, which is running the Universe, and that this whole creation is produced out of lust and desire, and is unreal.*

16.9 *Following this material view of creation, these degraded souls with small intellect, lost in themselves and committing cruel deeds, are engaged in the destruction of the world.*

Please understand, the energy that is within us, the energy that drives us is the same energy that drives this Universe, this solar system and planet Earth. This energy is intelligence, the highest intelligence.

Kṛṣṇa says that when we are unable to recognize this energy, we are demonic. We do not believe everything operates out of this energy; instead we believe we make things happen with our greed, lust and desires. We believe we run this world with our puny intellect that we consider intelligence.

For years, many religious institutions believed planet Earth was the center of this Universe. They killed millions for believing otherwise. They assumed that they ruled earth, and that there was nothing beyond them. We need not even be irreligious to be demonic. We just need to be so self-centered that even our God is at our disposal. Then we are demonic.

Such a belief is different from the concept of believing that *you are God* and that God resides in you. This belief arises from deep awareness and completion instead of dark ignorance and is totally selfless. Once you become God, the rest of the world is part of you and you are part of that world. There is no longer the duality of 'I' and 'You'. Both merge into the non-duality of either 'I' or 'You'; it does not matter.

People who think the world is pure chemistry become demons. Naturally, if we think this whole world is just inert matter, we try to acquire more and more by killing everybody, by right or wrong means, and we do what we want to. Only when we understand that this Universe is intelligence, and that it responds to our thoughts and actions, will we live in the space of completion, and start really living.

A small story:

> A group of scientists thought they could do anything and everything. They challenged God, 'Now you are unnecessary. Whatever you do, we can do. We can even clone human beings. What do you say? Now we can also develop whatever you have created on earth. Our department has developed everything.'
>
> God was surprised to see all the scientists' creations—the sizes of the bananas, and other fruits they had created, and so forth! The scientists then challenged God to a competition. 'Come face us. We will do whatever you do. We are better than you; you can go and rest. We don't need you anymore.'
>
> God agreed to face the scientists. God created a plant, and immediately the scientists created the same plant in a better way. One by one, they created the same thing God created. Suddenly, God took a little dust and created a man.
>
> The scientists said, 'This is not a big deal, now that we have the ability to clone.' They took some dust and were about to create a man.
>
> God said 'Stop. Bring your own dust and create. Don't use My dust!'

Whatever we may achieve, wherever science may go, the Divine is alive. God exists and the Cosmic intelligence runs this whole Universe.

We cannot create dust! It has to be God's dust! Listen. There is a pure energy and intelligence that is the Source, the thread of the whole Universe.

When a person is living within the limits of the intellect and 'me', he cannot experience the Whole. He knows only logic and calculation and with that arrogance thinks he knows everything.

People with demonic qualities say the world is produced out of sexual desire and lust. Please be clear that lust cannot be the reason. Intelligence, the divine energy is the cause and effect of this whole Universe; the cause and effect is the Divine that is responsible for the Universe. However, when we think it is lust or that we are responsible, we live with the idea of 'me, me, me'.

Kṛṣṇa says firmly that when we believe that we are the cause of this Universe, this Existence, we are so deluded and locked in our own little identities, with small intelliegence, we destroy the world and ourselves as well.

Our ancient sages, the great *ṛṣis*, were not fools. They did not retire to forests because they had nowhere else to go. Many were great kings, rulers of this planet, and they voluntarily left behind all that they had, so that they could understand where they came from. It was not enough for them to read and listen to the experiences of others; they chose to experience the truth themselves.

In the process, they realized themselves and became liberated. As many others over thousands of years have discovered, they discovered that they were part of this cosmic Existence. They realized and experienced that *they too were Gods.* They found that the same energy that operated in this Universe operated within them. They experienced that every living being on earth came from the same Source, and is the same Source.

Now, what do we do when we need water? We dig a well and, as if by magic, water appears. Now our neighbor wants water; he too digs a well and finds water. Yet are these waters different? The locations are at two ends, but the source is the same. Not merely the source, the water is also the same. Yet, we fight over common resources, thinking that we created them and therefore we own them.

This cognition of selfishness leads only to destruction of everything, *kṣayāya jagato 'hitaḥ* (16.9)—the environment, the world and all living beings. One part of this world, perhaps with less than one-sixth of the world's population, the so-called developed world, the so-called Western world, consumes more than half of the natural resources of this world. What right do they have to do this?

When we are not in the present, we are in a state of low intelligence, *alpabuddhi;* we become demons. Low intelligence leads to cruel deeds, *prabhavanty ugra karmāṇaḥ* (16.9). When we have no awareness of who we are, we do not care about anyone else.

All this can be changed. All that is needed is the cognitive shift from the demon to the Divine, from 'I' to 'You'. The environment we live in, the oxygen we breathe, the water we drink, the soil that gives the food we eat, all this is energy. This is what we call *pañca bhūta* in Saṁskṛit, the five elemental energies that sustain us. When these are destroyed by our low intelligence, out of our selfishness, the world around us collapses.

How To Save Ourselves

16.10 *Filled with insatiable desires, hypocrisy, pride, and arrogance; holding wrong views due to delusion, they act with impure motives and for impermanent objectives.*

16.11,12 *Obsessed with endless anxiety lasting until death,*
considering sense gratification their highest aim, and
convinced that sense pleasure is everything;
bound by hundreds of ties of desire and enslaved and filled
with anger, they strive to obtain wealth by unlawful means
to fulfill sensual pleasures.

What Kṛṣṇa says here is applicable to a vast majority of people today.

Times have changed since the days of the Vedic educational system where, from childhood, one was guided toward self-completion. Modern day education is based upon logic, science and rules, and is short on self-completion and *dharma*, righteousness.

When we are caught in the material world, focused on 'I' and 'me', we are stuck in the *mūlādhāra* and *svādiṣṭhāna cakras*. Greed and fear rule us and we are forever in the bondage of attachment and aversion. Whatever we do is with selfish and impure motives, and results in consequences that are mostly illusionary.

In the earlier verse, Kṛṣṇa explained how a person with demonic nature could destroy this world. Here, He shows how such a person can destroy himself. Out of pride, arrogance and hypocrisy, such a person moves in a path directed by purely selfish and material objectives, and derives results that produce suffering.

When we focus on matter, we tend to lose sight of the energy inherent in matter. When we focus on the form, we cannot see the formless that enables the form. What is permanent in both cases is the formless energy that drives the form and matter.

Science has moved a long way from the Newtonian model based on matter and form. This model is no longer relevant. From the days of Einstein, when matter and energy were linked inextricably, the concept has changed. Today all sciences accept that matter and energy not only co-exist, but also that the same object or event can be perceived or experienced by the observer as matter or energy or both.

So, we are back to the Indian master Ādī Śaṅkarācarya's theory that the observer determines what is being observed. We may think this is fanciful. However, this is an accepted theory in the most advanced form of Quantum Physics today. Elementary subatomic particles, when observed in identical conditions with identical tools, appear differently to different observers. As yet there is no explanation for this phenomenon.

Our ancient Sages, Ṛṣis explained that this happens based on our deep root cognitions, which colors our perceptions. When science is sufficiently advanced, it will accept this truth.

Listen! Just as the army tanker has teeth in its wheels, and leaves its footprint when it goes on the road, in the same way, you leave the imprint of the guilt from your past, when you plan your future with fantasy, without responsibility. When you take responsibility, it is no more a fantasy. But when you don't take responsibility, it is a fantasy. When you plan for your future without responsibility, you leave the imprint of the guilt from your past!

Once we know how to lead our life without fantasies with responsibility, the fear of death disappears. Then suffering and misery dissolve automatically. We move from the demonic into the divine realm.

Here Lord Kṛṣṇa explains the same concept in a deeper way, and gives a beautiful punchline.

Many take shelter in pleasures and pain that end only with their death. With some, even at that time, it doesn't end. They think of the money they paid for insurance, casket, marble gravestone, etc. They regard gratification of desires as the sole objective in life.

The nature of the unconscious mind is to react to the senses. We may think we respond consciously. But almost all the time our reactions are instinctive, decided by *vāsanās* and *saṁskāras*, conflicting patterns and root patterns, rather than by conscious application of our rational mind. This is what Kṛṣṇa refers to as the nature of a demonic person. Instinct is the nature of animals, and because it is their nature, it works well for them. They flow with nature.

Instinct is not the nature of humans. Human consciousness can rise to the intuitive level, in which awareness results in high action. This is the potential of the Divine inherent in all of us. Instead of rising to the intuitive level, the super conscious level, most people find it easier to descend into the instinctive or unconscious level.

The problem is that we do not know how to fulfill desires. We go through peaks of emotions goaded by our desires and then slip into valleys of depression and guilt. Our emotions are not authentic because they do not touch our inner core. If we intensely experience these events born out of desires and perceived by our senses, we find that neither the peaks thrill us nor the valleys sadden us. We don't need to suppress or ignore these emotions; we can experience them fully without differentiation and move on.

We rush towards pleasure and away from pain. We are so eager to fulfill our desires that we go to any length to amass wealth and do any deed, however questionable it may seem. As Kṛṣṇa says, this goes on until we die. If we expect that we will suddenly be filled with thoughts of the Divine at death, even though our whole life we chased only pleasures, this is another foolish fantasy.

If all our life we have been chasing money, at the point of death also, we will be obsessed with money, even if we realize that we can't take it with us. If all our life we have been obsessed with lust, we will die in lust. If we live as a demon, focused on 'me', we cannot suddenly take the leap to 'You' at the point of death. That does not happen.

Only if man blossoms in his consciousness, he is God; he is Bliss. He is in *Nityānanda.*

Sensory Traps

16.13 *They think: This has been gained by me today;*
I shall fulfill this desire; I have this much wealth
and will have more wealth in the future;

16.14 *That enemy has been slain by me,*
and I shall slay others also. I am the Lord.
I am the enjoyer. I am successful, powerful, and happy.

16.15 *I am rich and born in a noble family. Who is equal to me?*
I shall perform sacrifice, I shall give charity, and I shall rejoice.
Thus deluded by ignorance;

16.16 *Thus confused by various anxieties and*
caught in a net of illusions, one becomes
too deeply attached to sensory pleasures and falls into hell.

Kṛṣṇa does not let go. He wants Arjuna and mankind to understand how deeply the human psyche is damaged by the ego.

Śaṅkara defines *āhāra* or food, in one of his commentaries, to mean all sensory inputs, whereas traditionally *āhāra* is translated as food. Food, as we normally understand it, is what the mouth consumes. This is the sustenance upon which the physical body feeds and grows. Many live only to eat, but a few aware ones eat only enough to sustain them, so that they can live.

Every sensory organ has its own *āhāra*, inputs, upon which it feeds. Based on these inputs, the eye, ear, tongue, nose and skin develop their desires and convey these desires to the body-mind system. Control of these senses and the desires that they weave is what Sage Patañjali prescribed as *pratyāhāra*, one of the eight methods of his *Aṣṭāṅga Yoga*.

Pratyāhāra is not suppression or starving the senses. Just as we need to eat in order to live, the senses need inputs to function. However, these inputs can be regulated so that the fantasies they weave are kept in control.

The average human is led by his senses; he does not lead his senses. His *karmendriya*, the organs of action that are responsible for movements are driven by these senses without the need for input from the conscious mind. Instinctively, they avoid pain and welcome pleasure.

A small story:

> Two friends met in the street. One of them looked sad and almost on the verge of tears. The other one asked, 'What happened? Why do you look so sad?'
>
> He replied, 'My uncle passed away three weeks ago. He left me fifty thousand dollars.' His friend said, 'That's not bad.'
>
> He continued, 'Two weeks ago my cousin died and he left me ninety thousand dollars.'
>
> His friend cried, 'This is great!' He went on, 'Last week my grandfather died. He left me a million.'
>
> His friend asked, 'Then why are you so sad? He replied, 'Because this week, nobody died.'

Understand: Once we allow our mind to get driven away by the senses, there is no stopping. We won't know how to make it stop either. So we continue with our fantasies. We fantasize about accumulating wealth. Unfortunately for us, the purpose of gaining wealth is rarely to enjoy it. If that was the reason, all we need to do is to gain some wealth and then spend it on enjoyment. In most cases, the joy of acquisition becomes the drive for the person rather than the joy of using the wealth. It has nothing to do with what one can do with the wealth. It has to do with how much more we have than all the other people that we know.

The day our neighbor buys a new air-conditioner, the temperature in our house goes up! The day our neighbor buys a new car, our car, which till that day ran well, will stall. As soon as we see another woman wearing the latest style shoes, our shoes that had fit absolutely fine, start pinching.

We are driven by comparison and envy. We are not merely fulfilling our needs, we are actually fulfilling other people's wants and desires. From childhood, we are taught to grab. Nothing we have is enough. Nothing fulfills us. Until death, we are driven by greed.

Existence is waiting to shower us with all that we need. The problem is that we never stop to understand what we need. All the time we are caught in the web of our sensory fantasies, and we run after what others own; we let our senses lead us. After doing the meditation programs and becoming healers, people spend more time meditating, doing completion processes and being aware of *who they are* and *the reality they want to create.* They develop an understanding of their real needs. It is no longer necessary to run after empty wants. What they need comes to them; their needs follow them.

I tell them again and again, 'Do not get stuck in my form. Do not run after me. Do not chase me. Just devote yourself to enrich the mission, which is for enriching the Universe with Enlightenment. Focus only on enriching the mission. Then, I will run after you. I shall chase you to be with you.' Many quickly understand this. To them it makes no difference where they are and where I am physically. Wherever they are, I am with them. It is not a mere theory or illusion. Ask them. It is real.

Once we move from the 'me' focused demonic state into the 'you' based Divine state, we no longer need to worry about creating wealth, developing a power base, establishing relationships or whatever else we have focused attention upon all our lives. Existence takes care of all this. Existence takes care of us.

If instead, we are focused on our own self, 'me,' be sure, we are moving in a downward spiral that Kṛṣṇa says takes us into hell.

Cast Into Suffering

16.17 *Self-complacent and always conceited, deluded by wealth and false pride, they perform superficial sacrifices in name only, without following the vedic rules or regulations.*

16.18 *The demonic person, consumed by ego, power, pride, lust and anger, becomes envious of Me (Supreme Divine),*
who is situated in his own body and in the bodies of others,
and blasphemies against Him.

16.19 *Those who are envious (of Him) and cruel, who are the lowest among men, I repeatedly cast into the ocean of material existence, into various lowly, demonic forms of life.*

16.20 *These foolish beings attain repeated birth*
amongst the species of demonic life.
Without ever achieving Me, O Kaunteya,
they sink into the most abominable existence.

Kṛṣṇa has said in other verses that He will receive anyone with compassion and liberate them. Here He says He will cast them aside into suffering. How do we reconcile these two positions?

Both positions are true! After all, every word that an enlightened Master utters is true. It is our understanding that needs to evolve.

Kṛṣṇa is compassion Incarnate. Anyone who surrenders to Him is liberated. That is the absolute truth. The problem is that we only pretend to surrender. What we have are mere words with no integrity and no authenticity. Our thoughts do not match our words, and our words do not match our actions.

People come to me and say, '*Swamiji*, we surrender to you. Please help us and relieve us of our suffering.' When I tell them to attend the meditation program the following week, they say they need to check their appointment book!

Is this surrender? Does this have any meaning? It is sheer hypocrisy, trying to involve the Master in a conspiracy of our own making.

As human beings we have free will. The problem is that we feel free, yet we are unwilling to exercise our will. People ask whether they are controlled by destiny or free will. I tell them that no destiny binds them; they are free to exercise their will.

The *Bṛhadāraṇyaka Upaniṣad* puts it so well:

As are your thoughts, so is your will; as is your will, so your action, as are your actions, so is your destiny.

Destiny is nothing but the end result of how we exercise our free will. The problem is, we have no will; in the morning we want to do one thing, by noon it is something different, by night it is totally different. So, if our will keeps changing, how can it ever be converted into action?

CREATE THE SPACE OF SURRENDER

People tell me, '*Swamiji,* you say creating the space by visualizing it in the present helps make things happen in reality; we have tried: nothing happens.'

Nothing happens because you are full of self-contradiction, self-doubt, self-hatred and impossibilities. If we wish to get rid of back pain, and we keep saying, 'Let this back pain go,' it will never go. Every time we utter the words back pain, our mind latches more firmly onto the past hangover of pain. If we want to get rid of pain, we must complete with all self-doubts and create the space for health visualizing it in the present; not pain, not getting rid of pain, but feeling healthy.

When you create the space to make something into reality, complete with all the doubts, complete with all the impossible ideas that come to you, complete with your ability to even create the space. Stand up powerfully without listening to any form of impossible shouted by your mind towards you.

When you create a space, first thing itself you will face is depression of past failures and complete distrust. 'How can this be reality? I suffered too much! I know it is not possible!' This is the first thing you go through, and two days you get depressed and lock yourself in the bedroom. So, understand, when you create a space, this is the first thing you face. So, complete with that first. Completion with that is the most important thing.

Listen! I am defining Space Creation.

Bringing your past hangover into the present is incompletion. Bringing your future possibility into the present is Space. Please listen! Bringing your past hangover into the present is incompletion. Bringing your future possibility into the present is Space Creation.

Bring your future possibility into the present and decide you will not challenge the power of the space, but you will take the responsibility to fulfill that space.

When we surrender to Kṛṣṇa, our surrender must be total. We must take the responsibility to fulfill the space of surrender. There can be nothing between Him and us. Then, He surely liberates us. Because then we are already liberated, we are in Kṛṣṇa consciousness.

Here, He talks about people who feel no need to surrender to Him. They are so full of ego, that they feel He is their competitor. He says He will cast them into the material world. In this material world, they can follow their senses, sense objects and what they consider to be sensual pleasures till death. As I said before, it is our decision. Even Kṛṣṇa is helpless to change it, because He has given us the power to decide. He has handed over the decision to us; to decide whether we want to be 'me' or 'You' focused: demonic or divine.

'YOU'—THE FOUNDATION OF SURRENDER

Saying again and again, 'I believe in what Kṛṣṇa says,' has no meaning. It does not help. Faith does not mean belief. Belief is not trust.

Belief is a pseudo-trust, imposed, cultivated out of fear. It is not something that has grown from within us. Rather, it is something that has been implanted by others: society, religion, the state. Believers remain stupid; they never grow in intelligence. And society does not want people to be intelligent.

The 'yes' of a man who cannot say 'no' is always powerless. First a man must learn to say 'no,' only then does his 'yes' have meaning.

Faith is different from belief. With faith we grow. We grow in love to a Master and to God. Most of us look to God as a person to pray to, to worship. We feel God is a third person. He is not us. Prayer and worship become important pathways to reach this form. The moment we drop the idea of a person, prayer disappears; instead, meditation becomes significant.

Meditation is going inwards. So, it is more difficult for many who are educated rationally. That's why meditation never became the central core of religion in the West. In the East all the great masters founded their teachings on meditation. They taught followers to turn inwards. They taught them to *be God, not to worship God.*

Meditation leads us to surrender. Meditation is the process of creation of the space of completion. Completion is the knowledge that we are one with the Universe. It is then about 'you' instead of 'me'. The feeling of 'you' and the absence of 'me' dissolve the idea of 'I' as identity. This is the foundation of surrender.

Become a servant of love. You then become a master of humanity. One begins as a servant. However, one ends as a master. In this world, you often begin as a master and you end up as a servant. That is the law of the external world. In the inner world there is a totally different law. You begin as a servant and you can end up as a master. You surrender *to* love, you surrender *and* love and you shall certainly conquer the world.

Buddha has said: In the outer world everything is sweet in the beginning and bitter in the end; in the inner world, everything is bitter in the beginning and sweet in the end. Only the end matters. Where you begin is not in your control.

Once you understand how to love the people around you, only then can you love God. You cannot hate your neighbor, brother or spouse and love only God. This is impossible. When you start loving those around you, you start loving yourself more. Strangely, you start thinking less about yourself. In your defeat, you win others.

This is what surrender is about: It is asking for your defeat. Let me repeat: Surrender, renunciation of the self, or sannyāsa is a defeat, a defeat of the ego. God is realized the moment the ego is dissolved.

Surrender is the search for the Divine principle. Call it God, truth, freedom, or *nirvāṇa.* They mean the same thing. The search is for something that is missing in life. We are alive but unaware of what life is about. We exist, but we are completely oblivious to the fact of who we are.

This is what Kṛṣṇa talks about in this chapter. The courage to move from 'me' to 'You' is the courage to trust, love and surrender. When that happens there is nothing else but Him. We become Kṛṣṇa.

When we are one with the Universe, one with Kṛṣṇa, there is nothing else we need to look up to. There is nothing else to look for. We have reached eternal bliss—*Nityānanda*.

Of Gold And Women

16.21 *There are three gates leading to this hell: lust, anger and greed. As they lead to the degradation of the soul, these three are to be abandoned.*

16.22 *Those who have escaped these three gates of hell, O Kaunteya, behave in a manner beneficial to the (evolution of the) soul, and thus (gradually) attain the supreme destination.*

16.23 *But he who discards scriptural injunctions and acts according to his base impulses attains neither perfection, nor happiness, nor the supreme destination.*

16.24 *By the regulations of the scriptures, one should understand what is duty and what is not duty. After being versed in scriptural injunctions, one should act accordingly.*

Kṛṣṇa ends the chapter with this advice: Shed anger, greed and lust and we will be saved. He calls them gates to hell. These are the qualities of the blocked *mūlādhāra cakra*. These are attributes that bind us to 'me' and 'mine'. We mistakenly believe that these qualities are essential for our life on this planet. Nothing can be more wrong.

tri-vidhaṁ narakasyedaṁ dvāraṁ nāśanam ātmanaḥ /
kāmaḥ krodhas tathā lobhas tasmād etat trayam tyajet // 16.21

As long as we are bound by anger, lust and greed, *kāmaḥ krodhas tathā lobhas*, what He calls the three gateways to hell, we are in bondage; we are in suffering. We do not need to die and be escorted to someplace called hell. We live in it day after day and suffer.

Kāma, krodha and *lobha*: lust, anger and greed—when we shed these we are liberated. Rāmakṛṣṇa says again and again, drop *kāñcana* and *kāminī*, gold and women, greed and lust, and we will be liberated. Lust for women, and greed for gold, these two desires more than anything else, cause all our sufferings.

Krodha, anger, arises out of the suffering. We feel thwarted and we feel angry. The cycle goes on. When these three combine, they create moha, or delusion. At one level these emotions are desires. Anger, greed and lust are expressions related to desires. Desires are energy. Lust is what drives us into reproduction and it is essential for the survival of species. Greed is the extreme expression of our survival needs. Anger is often the driving force to get things done. They achieve positive results, too.

However, Kṛṣṇa refers to the expression of these emotions in the context of self-gratification. He refers to the gratification of base impulses. The baseness of the impulse is related to the intention, the context. As long as these are expressed with the cognition of 'me,' they are base and demonic impulses. There are no liberating features.

Lust can be transformed when it is expressed in an unselfish and unattached way. Lust will then totally disappear. Compassion and caring will be in its place. Lust is one aspect of the broad spectrum of desires. Unending desire is greed. When a desire is truly fulfilled, it leaves us. *Karma* is unfulfilled desires that goad us into action. We can never fulfill our desires because many of these desires are not truly ours. We borrow these desires from other people. There is never conten'tment. Each desire is the seed of suffering. That is why Kṛṣṇa calls it a gateway to hell. But how do we get rid of these desires?

This is what we teach experientially at the twenty-one days Inner Awakening program. We enrich you in completing with your lust, anger, greed, conflicting desires, and help you identify true desires, the *prārabdha karma*, with which you are born into this world. You are intiated into the science of creating the space to have the energy to fulfill them. Our *karma* dissolves. Above all, all the non-mechanical parts of your brain are awakened. Many powers which you have inside and you don't know, are awakened. People who attend this program say that they cannot hate or even dislike anyone. The 'I' blossoms into 'you' effortlessly.

At this stage, we shed anger as well. Anger and guilt are byproducts of desires. What we cannot acquire makes us angry. Anger produces guilt. Being angry towards a person is fruitless. Much of the negativity expressed towards others comes back to us. It depletes our energy. Anger or even guilt is also often an expression of one's inability to do something. It is a self-centered emotion born of one's weakness, powerlessness.

Suppression of anger does not help. It can actually lead to chronic diseases like cancer. When we learn to complete with the emotion of anger instead of controlling it, it becomes energy instead of a disability. Anger needs to be completed with and transformed into the positive energy of authentic action.

What Kṛṣṇa asks us to do is to complete with the negative emotions like lust, greed and anger and create the space, with responsibility, to transform them into positive energies. He tells us that these are gateways to hell so long as we use them from the root cognition of 'me.' When we do completion and transform these emotions into energy, by creating the space of 'you', these same emotions become gateways to heaven, gateway to bliss.

Bliss comes with total trust in Existence

Bliss is never an achievement on our part. Whatsoever we do to achieve bliss is doomed to fail. Bliss always comes from the beyond as a gift. We must be passively receptive to it. We are not to be aggressively active for it, just be receptive like a womb. We must be feminine to receive bliss. We must become pregnant with God. When ego or 'I' disappears, anger, greed and lust also disappear. What is left is bliss.

Bliss is a by-product of total trust in Existence or in God. God is not a person but the impersonal presence. The very life or Existence is God and the living energy is God. And to trust in it means to stop struggling against it. Struggling against it creates misery; it is trying to go upstream.

Trust means surrender, going with the stream. And going with the stream is bliss. All misery is because of the ego and its struggle, its resistance. Trust means that resistance has been dropped. You don't think of yourself as separate from the Whole; you are just an intrinsic part of the great harmony of Existence. Then bliss is natural.

My whole effort here is to help you move towards bliss. The way to bliss is through the heart and through devotion. The real transformation happens when your energy moves from the head to the heart. When you reach the heart, you reach the core of your consciousness.

> Listen, remember the most important thing!
>
> God loves us: He has not given up on us, He is not indifferent to us and He is continuously concerned about us, He cares. The deeper this idea enters your heart, the better, because when you feel more *loved by God*, you will be able to have *love for God*, and you will have *love for others.* That's how we are able to love: if we are loved, we can love. If we are not loved, we don't know how to love; we don't know what love is.

God is our substance, our very being. He is not something outside us; He is our innermost core. We do not need to seek and search for Him. Only this has to be remembered: we have forgotten it. God is not lost; only we have forgotten who we are.

Don't be identified with the body. Don't be identified with your mind, country, race or religion. Don't be identified with anything. Don't think, 'I am this' or 'I am that'. Remember, neither 'this' nor 'that'. That is one of the secret teachings of the mystics: *neti-neti*, neither 'this' nor 'that'. If you can avoid both polarities, day and night, life and death, body and mind, then slowly a third energy arises in you, a third force arises in you. That is consciousness. That's your reality. That is freedom—freedom from fear, anxiety, misery, freedom from the world, freedom from the wheel of life and death. Then you are a witness, watching, a mirror reflecting but not getting caught in any reflection.

When you are a witness, the 'me' and 'mine' drop. What remains is identification with your energy, with your *state,* not your *status.* In that state, you are one with all. You are in the space of *Living Advaita,* oneness—living the truth that everything is 'you' and 'you' are everything. Because 'you' is 'me', 'me' is 'you', 'you' 'me' becomes 'you-me'. It is 'you-me' that becomes the center, no longer 'me'. You become Divine, *daivic.*

Let us pray to the ultimate energy, *Parabrahma* Kṛṣṇa, the Divine Consciousness, to bless us all with *'daiva sampat'* and establish us in eternal bliss, *nityānanda*.

Thank You.

Thus ends the sixteenth chapter named ***Daivāsura Sampad Vibhāga Yogaḥ****, 'The Yoga of Divine and Demonic Nature,' of the* ***Bhagavad Gītā Upaniṣad, Brahmavidyā Yogaśāstra****, the scripture of yoga dealing with the science of the Absolute in the form of* ***Śrī Kṛṣṇārjuna saṃvād****, dialogue between Śrī Kṛṣṇa and Arjuna.*

CHAPTER

17

Śraddhatraya Vibhāga Yogaḥ

AUTHENTICITY: STRAIGHT WAY TO LIBERATION

LIVING IS ABOUT HAVING SRADDHA, COURAGE OF AUTHENTICITY TO LIVE THE TRUTH. JUST READING OR LISTENING AND THINKING ONE HAS UNDERSTOOD IT, IS MEANINGLESS. NOT HAVING A GAP BETWEEN YOUR CONVICTIONS AND YOUR DAY-TO-DAY LIFE IS WHAT I CALL LIVING!

Authenticity: Straight Way To Liberation

In the seventeenth chapter, Kṛṣṇa straightaway gives the methodology or technique to imbibe whatever He speaks in *Śraddhatraya Vibhāga Yogaḥ*, the Yoga of Discerning the Three-Fold Faith. After all the words that Kṛṣṇa expressed in earlier chapters, no new teaching is given here. All that Kṛṣṇa has spoken and taught so far is a prelude to what He is speaking now. Here, Kṛṣṇa speaks about authenticity, *śraddha.*

Let me explain the meaning of the word *śraddha*. Please understand that *śraddha* is not faith; always the word *śraddha* is translated as faith. This is not correct.

Authenticity to Live the Truth

Listen, human beings do not suffer because they don't get to *listen* to the truths. They suffer because they don't *live* the truth. Śraddha means faith plus the courage of authenticity to live the truth. Śraddha means the courage of authenticity to live your peak possibility. With authenticity, *śraddha* you awaken the power of thinking, *mano siddhi* to live the truth.

With authenticity, there is no more space for unconscious thinking, because we will always be aware of the causes and effects that are playing in our life. With *śraddha* we will never fail. Understand that there is a possibility that we may fail with faith alone. When we have faith without the courage of authenticity to experiment, to live the truth, it is like going to a restaurant, reading the menu card and just leaving. We miss eating. We never taste the food. We never experience the great powers of thinking and living the truth. However, when we have *śraddha*, authenticity, there is no chance of missing the truth. A person never misses when he has *śraddha*.

Lord Kṛṣṇa explains and now puts all His emphasis on *śraddha*. After sixteen chapters of teachings, He has nothing new to add. He has said whatever can be said. He has explained all the seven layers of energy. In the fourteenth chapter, He started with *Guṇatraya Vibhāga Yoga*—the three *guṇas* (attributes) of *satva, rajas* and *tamas*, the three-folds of root thought patterns. Then in the *Puruṣottama Yoga,* He explained the causal layer, where the root thought patterns are stored in seed form. The deeper layers of the cosmic and nirvāṇic bodies are explained in the sixteenth chapter. Kṛṣṇa elaborates on the attributes of the Divine and the demon, the no-ego and ego, 'you' or 'me'. The root cause of our identity that separates us from our core space of completion, which is Divine, is explained in the sixteenth chapter.

Now Kṛṣṇa comes to the seventeenth chapter, *Śraddhatraya Vibhāga Yogaḥ*. Nothing more needs to be added. Whatever can be said has been said. Now all we need is *śraddha.* If somebody has had a good feast, his stomach is full. All he needs is an antacid, 'Digene'. Throughout the chapters Lord Kṛṣṇa has given Arjuna a beautiful spiritual feast. All Arjuna needs is 'Digene' to digest the whole thing and enjoy. This chapter is 'Digene'. The whole emphasis is on *śraddha*: authenticity, integrity, truthfulness and straightforwardness.

We may question, 'Why would He devote one full chapter for *śraddha*?' Please understand that we invariably miss Enlightenment because of lack of understanding and intranalyzing of this subject, *śraddha*. Let me be very clear, it is not that we don't know the truth that Lord Kṛṣṇa speaks. We know whatever Lord Kṛṣṇa speaks of and all that He has spoken so far. We know it all. It's not that we don't know. Yet why have we not become Kṛṣṇa?

We miss one thing—*Śraddha*. That's the only thing we need. Our problem is not that we don't know. Our problem is that we know too much and we are unable to digest and live it.

Swami Vivekananda says beautifully that instead of knowing the whole library, we should know just five concepts. We should experiment to live with these five concepts with *śraddha*, authenticity. Let the five concepts become your life. That is enough. Nothing else is necessary. Instead of having the whole library in your head, have the five concepts in your heart.

Please understand, you might have struggled, spent money, time and energy, and finally passed your driving test to get your driving license, but it will be useful to you, only if you are regularly driving. In the same way, Śrī Kṛṣṇa's song, His words will directly be useful to you, only if you are living them. Use all the principles. Use all the truths. Don't deny them in the name of practicality or convenience. No! Be very clear, once you are convinced, you will live the spiritual truths.

Listen. Living has nothing to do with some hard and strict rules. Wherever you can, pull the truths into your thinking. **Not having gap between your spiritual understandings and your day-to-day life is what I call Living.**

Here, Kṛṣṇa emphasizes the importance of *śraddha*: how *śraddha* and only *śraddha* can transform your whole life. Understand, whatever you believe, if you have *śraddha*, if you have authenticity in aligning that belief in all your identities—inner image, outer image, others' image and life's image, you will achieve the Ultimate.

Understand, *Śraddha,* Authenticity. I am giving you deeper definition.

Authenticity is nothing but being sincere to the four aspects of you: what you feel as you—inner image; what you project you to others—outer image; what you think about others and life—others' image, and what others hold you as—life image. Being sincere to all these four is authenticity.

Please listen, being sincere in all these four identities! What does this mean? Having the best inner image, having the best outer image, having the best idea about others and life; and being very sincere about what others hold as *you*. Just create the best image, the most sincere image that you wanted to feel, think and project about you.

Again and again, align your thinking to authenticity. See very clearly: Are you functioning towards the best inner image by constantly developing liberated thinking?

Liberated thinking means your thinking should not have or should not lead you towards powerlessness. Constantly your thinking should be leading you to being in a powerful space.

Listen. It is neither difficult nor easy, but *you* have to do it! It is nothing but tuning yourself to a certain frequency. How tuning or changing a channel is neither difficult nor easy, it is a simple technique; same way, go on tuning your thinking to *śraddha*, authenticity. Always think about your thinking and align your thinking to authenticity.

Kṛṣṇa declares earlier, '*śraddhāvān labhate jñānaṁ* (4.39)—the person who is established in authenticity, experiences the true wisdom, Enlightenment.' Listen, *śraddha*, authenticity will become reality in you, only when you live it.

Live authenticity! Many people have achieved God, experienced Enlightenment and attained the Truth through the path of living authenticity. Buddha never spoke of God. Yet not only did He become enlightened, thousands attained Enlightenment because of Him. What you believe is not important, how intense you are is important; how integrated and authentic you are in living all the four identities is important.

Working with the truth and creating the most sincere inner image, outer image, others' image and life's image based on that truth is what I call Authenticity. Authenticity is not just listening, reading or believing in the truth. Authenticity is working with the truths with responsibility. It is straightaway executing them to your peak possibility, experimenting with them and having the courage to play with them.

Just listening to these truths is not enough; start living them by taking up higher responsibilities. Only then you pull the *tattvas* into your life, and the *tattvas* pull you into their life. That is the only way any growth is possible.

POSSIBLE TO LIVE THE GĪTĀ

Both meditation and gambling require courage. We need courage for gambling. And we also need courage for meditation. Meditation is the ultimate gamble we take up with higher responsibility. With ordinary gambling, we gamble with money out of irresponsibility. In meditation we take the responsibility to gamble with our ego. We take the highest responsibility to gamble with our whole being to experience the space of possibility, authenticity, *śraddha*. But one thing is for sure in the gamble of meditation: if we lose, we win. Only losers win in this game!

Spiritual life needs the courage of authenticity. That is why Swami Vivekananda calls his spiritual disciples '*dhīraḥ*'. *Dhīra* means someone who is courageous, who is courage personified. We might ask, 'Why do spiritual people need courage? For spiritual life, don't we need to be silent?' No! Spiritual life calls for courage to declare completion and live it with integrity, authenticity, responsibility and enriching. We need the courage of authenticity. We need to take the responsibility!

Listen! When you landed on planet Earth, so much energy and power is deposited in your bank balance, and the cheque book is available in your hand. You just need to sign it! The signature is authenticity, *śraddha*. Reclaim it!

In the past sixteen chapters we have heard many different teachings, different understandings and so many different techniques directly from the Master of masters, Śrī Kṛṣṇa. We have heard everything. All of this can help transform our life only if we have the courage to live them. Otherwise they add more weight to our head, that's all.

Please understand that if we receive these teachings and store them in our head, we gain more head weight, nothing else. Now we think, 'I know the *Gītā*.' However, we need to create the space of possibility in our heart and live the *Gītā*. We need authenticity to live *Gītā*.

For example, if we eat too much food and we are unable to digest it, what happens? We have a stomach ache and we vomit. Similarly, if we hear all these things and we don't experience it, we will get a headache.

We will catch people and vomit all these things on them. Please be very clear that unless we have authenticity, unless we experiment to live these truths to our peak possibility, listening to these truths is dangerous.

Everything that we listened in the *Gītā,* all that we cognized inside our minds, should be responded with the idea 'Possible'! Possible! Possible! That should be the word, the *mantra* ringing in our heart, our inner space. Kṛṣṇa's words are possible! Possible! Possible!

Now I am giving one more step. As I said, 'If you don't practice, listening to these truths is dangerous.' We may ask, 'Why?' Because now, by and by, even after so many days of listening or reading these great truths, we will start hallucinating that we know, without knowing. That is the most dangerous game. Never ever get caught in that game!

When you bring yourself to the peak of you, there is no wastage of inner powers. I tell you, when you waste your love, it becomes lust. When you waste your responsibility, it becomes jealousy. The lower dimensions of you are nothing but rejected parts of your higher dimension. When your higher dimension is not materialized, when it is not realized, your lower dimension is empowered!

Bring yourself to the peak possibility. Listen, it happens! It can happen only when you practice living the truth of Gītā every moment. Spiritual life needs courage to harness the power of words by integrity, power of thinking by authenticity, power of feeling by responsibility, power of living by enriching; and the consciousness of *dhīraḥ,* courage.

BHARAṆI—KILLER OF THOUSAND MINDS

A beautiful history:

The great saint, Dakśināmūrti Swamigal, lived in Tamil Nadu, South India, near a place called Tiruvaroor. Let me share a historical incident from his life.

> A poet from the king's court met Dakśināmūrti Swamigal and was inspired by his presence. Consequently, the poet wrote one thousand songs in the

Bharaṇi style in the saint's honor. Bharaṇi is a special style of poetry involving one thousand verses. The rule is that only someone who shows courage and power and kills one thousand elephants in war is qualified to have such a song written about him. Here, this poet was so inspired by the saint's presence that he simply wrote the songs on him on the spot.

The king also considered himself to be Bharaṇi. I don't know if he killed one thousand elephants in war. Anyway, suddenly, one day in court, out of ego and pride, the king announced, 'I am the only Bharaṇi in this whole country, in this whole region!' One of his poets stood up and said, 'No O king, you are wrong. Dakśināmūrti Swamigal is also a Bharaṇi. One of your court poets has sung a Bharaṇi about him.'

The king's ego was hurt. He said, 'What? Who is this person deserving Bharaṇi? Bring him here.'

The poet said, 'No, no, he is a beggar. He will not come here.'

Beggars can never be forced. We can force anybody but a homeless person to do what we want, because he has no desire. As long as someone has some desire, he obeys the social system. But, the one beyond desire does not care for name, home, fame or security. In this case, this man was a beggar and a saint. They could not bring him to the king.

The king felt deeply offended. He said, 'What? For a beggar, Bharaṇi! Which fool sang the songs? Call him to me right now.'

The poet was summoned to the court. The king said, 'Fool, how dare you sing bharaṇi for a beggar.' The poet replied, 'O King, please forgive me. Before you say anything, before you abuse that Master, it would be nice if you would go to see him.'

The king said, 'What kind of advice are you giving me? Tomorrow morning your head will be cut off.'

That was the king's usual trend, direct violence. Only foolish people immediately express violence. When they can't behave in an intelligent way, when they don't know the truth and they don't have enough energy to convince the other person of the truth, they take to the sword.

Take for example the history of Buddhism or Hinduism. They never converted anyone with the sword. They had intelligence. They transformed through logic, analysis and enriched the other person with the Truth.

For example, great Masters like Ādī Śaṅkarācārya and Maṇḍana Miśra had different views on a particular subject, still they did not fight with each other. Śaṅkara did not say, 'If you don't convert to *Vedānta*, I will kill you.' They sat together and analyzed what they knew. It was a loving discussion. It was a beautiful scene. Śaṅkara and Maṇḍana Miśra sorted out their philosophical differences with a deep respect through *khandana-mandana*, positive discussions and expositions without rancor.

The person who acted as judge in the discussion was Maṇḍana Miśra's wife. What a beautiful, loving atmosphere it must have been! Can you believe that the wife of one of the competitors was the judge? Never! And here, Śaṅkara appointed Maṇḍana Miśra's wife, Bhārati as the judge. And finally, she passed judgment of the debate in favor of Śaṅkara. The whole thing happened out of love. There was no violence, no cutting, no killing, nothing. It was just a simple discussion.

Throughout the history of Eastern religions, there was never any cutting or killing. They never converted through the sword because they did not believe in killing. They had enough intelligence to express the concept. And one more thing, the loser automatically joined the group which expressed the truth more clearly!

When Śaṅkara convinced Maṇḍana Miśra, Miśra dropped everything and surrendered his life to Śaṅkara! He became a disciple of Śaṅkara and took the spiritual name 'Sureśvarācārya.' He followed the path of Śaṅkara's teachings. We can never achieve anything by the sword. Only destruction is possible through the sword, never construction.

> This king, foolish as he was, straightaway said, 'Kill him. Tomorrow morning the poet should be killed.' The poet replied, 'I have no problem. I have experienced Truth through this master. I am ready to die; however, if you are really intelligent, meet this master at least once. Don't punish me until you have seen him. Then I will be ready to die.'
>
> The king agreed, 'Alright, I will see him. If he is not a real Bharaṇi, we will kill him also.'

The king set off to meet the Master with all his paraphernalia: chariots, foot soldiers, elephants, armies and all his warriors. Kings always travel with their paraphernalia because they lose their identity without their paraphernalia. In contrast, Dakśināmūrti Swamigal was a *Paramahamsa*, an enlightened Master. Masters always live by themselves. They do not need any paraphernalia. This Master was an *Avadhūta*, which means he never wore clothes. The king found him sitting under a big banyan tree, without any paraphernalia.

This was the scene: This simple beggar sat in a corner without any clothes. He was in bliss and peace, completely soaked in Existence, in *brahmajñāna* (knowledge of the Supreme). He sat in intense silence and peace. This silence penetrated anyone in his presence. The king appeared with his warriors and entire army to confront this yogi.

The king jumped down from his chariot and advanced towards the Master. The Master did not move. There was no movement in him even after seeing the king and his army and hearing all the commotion. He opened his eyes and looked straight into the king's eyes. It was the first time that someone looked straight into the king's eyes. The king had always looked at others straight in their eyes and they had always put their heads down. For the first time somebody looked straight into the eyes of the king. After a few seconds, the king put his head down. The king clearly felt something happening inside his being. He felt like a mere beggar in the Master's presence. He did not know how to act or react. It was a strange situation. He was at a loss. He could not decide what to do. He felt overwhelmed.

Dakśināmūrti Swamigal signaled to the king to sit down. There were no words from him. He simply made a sign asking the king to sit. All the ministers and the army dropped their weapons and also sat in silence. In ten minutes the whole army was sitting down. It is impossible to make an army sit. Even the leader of the army can't make the army sit. But here the whole army sat in silence.

One hour passed. Then three hours passed; then the evening also passed; one day got over. The Master, the king and the entire army sat in silence. Not a single word was exchanged. There were no instructions, nothing. They did not even greet each other. They were merely sitting.

Three days got over. Now the Master thought, 'This is too much. The poor man and his entire army have been simply sitting for three days without food and even without toilet visits! These people must return to their kingdom, to the palace. The king must take care of the country.

The Master opened his eyes and said, 'Now you can go.' The king fell flat at the Master's feet, did *namaskār* (obeisance) and came out of the forest.

Then the king summoned the poet and said, 'Leave alone thousand elephants... You may sing for the Master praises that you usually sing for the one who has killed ten thousand elephants!'

The poet made a beautiful statement, 'Killing ten thousand elephants is easy. It is not a big deal. You don't need any powers for it. You just need the weapons and you can simply kill; however, killing one's mind is the real achievement.'

This Master had killed the king's mind. Not only had Dakṣināmūrti Swamigal killed his own mind, he could kill anybody else's mind if they sat in his presence. He made the impossible into 'i m possible' with his power of authenticity, the space of possibility. Killing ten thousand elephants doesn't take courage, but killing your mind requires the courage of authenticity.

COURAGE OF AUTHENTICITY, THE ONLY PRE-REQUISITE

All we need for real spiritual life is courage of authenticity to experiment with the truth. We typically lack that quality. We listen to everything. Wherever there are discourses and lectures, we go and listen to anyone who speaks. We read all the books. When it comes to facing the reality of putting this knowledge to test, there is no action. Then you tell me, 'For practical purposes, *Swamiji,* we must have our possessions. Otherwise how can we survive in this world?...' You just compromise cunningly.

Compromising is cowardice. Please understand that the person who compromises never experiences anything in his life; not only in the spiritual life, even in the outer world life. He can never experience life itself.

Authenticity to experience a single truth is enough. Nothing else is necessary. We don't need to do big things. Please be very clear, we can't call somebody 'a big person' if he does something big. What he does is unimportant; *how* he does it is important.

As an example, the great saint Nammalvar, who lived in Tamil Nadu, made garlands for Viṣṇu throughout his life. He did nothing else. He picked flowers from a garden, made garlands and gave it to God. He became enlightened. So many enlightened Masters did not do big things. They did small things in a big way. They had deep trust.

Another enlightened being did not even do that. He did not make garlands to offer God. Instead he threw a stone towards the *Śiva liṅga* everyday. His name was Sakyanayanar (Sakya refers to the clan of the Buddha, and Nayanar is a name for devotees of Śiva). Somehow he became a Buddhist monk. Because he was a Buddhist monk, he could not worship the *Śiva liṅga* in public. Yet he had tremendous respect and devotion for Śiva.

> In Buddhism, at least one son from every family is given to the monastery at a young age. They bring him up and make him a Buddhist monk.
>
> Like that, Sakyanayanar was given away to a Buddhist monastery. Still, he had a deep devotion to Śiva.
>
> Everyday he went near the Śiva temple. It was not even a regular temple, it was just a small *Śiva liṅga* under a tree. From a distance he took a stone, visualized it as a flower and threw the stone at the *Śiva liṅga*. If someone observed him and asked, 'What are you doing?' he would say, 'I am only throwing stones at the *Śiva liṅga*.' He would throw the stones and leave that place.
>
> One day when he threw a stone, an old man suddenly appeared and asked, 'What are you doing?'
>
> He replied, 'I am only throwing stones at the *liṅga*.'
>
> The old man said, 'No, the way in which you throw shows your devotion. You may be throwing stones, but the way in which you are throwing shows devotion. Tell me who are you?'
>
> Sakyanayanar replied, 'Somehow I was born in a Buddhist family, yet I am deeply devoted to Śiva. Everyday I come and offer my being to him by throwing a stone.
>
> Immediately the old man turned around, gave *darśan* (vision) as Śiva and blessed him with Enlightenment.

Understand that what we *do* is unimportant; what we *think* is important. Even if we just clean our house, it is okay as long as we do it with complete and intense authenticity in our thinking in that moment.

Listen! Authenticity is the power of thinking. In one moment we can make anything look like God; within the next moment, we can make anything look like a demon in our lives. Please understand, if we bow down to even a small stone, it can become a God. If we are afraid of that, even God will look like demon.

Live the Truth Through Words, Mind And Body

Understand that spiritual practice does not mean you need to go into a deep forest, hold your nose ten times, and breathe this way and that way. You will only torture yourself. Do anything, but do it with intensity, with authenticity. Have courage to express whatever you believe.

Don't bother whether the truth you believe is the ultimate Truth. You will never know whether it is ultimate unless you have the courage to authenticity to live it. Without living it, you cannot conclude. If you conclude without living it, it is prejudice. You cannot conclude without living it to your peak possibility. All you need is authentic courage to experiment living the truth that you believe.

Tamil has three words for *satya* (truth). One word is *vaaimai,* which means speaking the truth through the mouth. Another word is *unmai*, which is speaking the truth through your mind or heart. The third beautiful word is *meimai,* which means living the truth through your body.

In Tamil, '*mai*' means body. Truth means living the truth through the body. All of us understand speaking the truth through the mouth and speaking the truth through the mind. However, what does 'living the truth through the body' mean? We have never heard this before.

This is where we miss the boat. We continuously think about the truth. We go on contemplating on the truth from morning till night. We speak what we think is the truth. Nonetheless, we forget one important thing: executing the truth in life, living the truth in life. That is where we miss. Living the truth in life is the essence.

Patañjali gives *satya* as the first instruction in his *Aṣṭāṅga Yoga.* This *satya* refers to truth in thought, word and action. It is *vaaymai, unmai* and *maimai*, all the three combined.

The authenticity with which we practice leads us to Enlightenment. That is why I have said time and again that it is not necessary to have an enlightened Master as our Guru to become enlightened. Any master whom we follow sincerely with integrity and authenticity can lead to Enlightenment. Even if we truly believe a stone idol will deliver us into liberation, it will do so. Our approach, our conviction, our courage and our trust elevate us.

Śraddha is total conviction in what we are feeling, thinking, speaking and doing. There should be no doubt in our mind about the path that we are following and why we are following it. All great Masters had undivided integrity and authenticity in their thinking and words in whatever they did. They never swerved from their chosen path no matter what challenges and problems they faced, including threats to their lives.

Śraddha, authenticity has to be practiced in every dimension of your life, at every level of your thinking, and at every level of your cognizance. I tell you, bring yourself to the peak, whether it is related to your body, profession or relationships.

> When you bring yourself to your peak possibility relating to your body, it becomes health. When you bring yourself to your peak possibility relating to your profession, it becomes success. When you bring yourself to your peak possibility relating to others, it becomes happy relationships. When you bring yourself to your peak possibility relating to your whole life, it becomes Enlightenment!

Understand that the ultimate step or the straight way to Enlightenment is—authenticity to live the truth.

Way To Worship

17.1 *Arjuna says:*
What is the mode of devotion of those who perform
spiritual practices with authenticity [śraddha],
but without following the scriptural injunctions, O Kṛṣṇa?
Is it in the mode of goodness [satva], aggression [rajas] or
ignorance [tamas]?

Arjuna asks a beautiful question.

Arjuna asks: 'Kṛṣṇa, those who discard the ordinances of the scriptures, *śāstras* and perform sacrifices, what is their position? Is it *sātvic, rājasic* or *tāmasic*? What is the state of people who don't follow the instructions of the scriptures, the ancient books, and instead worship with *śraddha*, authenticity according to their own beliefs? Is it *rajas, tamas* or *satva*? Are they in a peaceful (*sātvic*) state, restless (*rājasic*) state or an ignorant (*tāmasic*) state?'

ye śāstra-vidhim utsṛjya yajante śraddhayānvitāḥ |
teṣāṁ niṣṭhā tu kā kṛṣna sattvam āho rajas tamaḥ || 17.1

Please listen. Worship can occur at many levels. Arjuna's question is based upon the three attributes or *guṇas*. Worship is also dependent on our energy levels. Many people are comfortable worshipping at the physical level, the gross level, through techniques such as *pūjā*, going to temples to worship the deities, bathing in holy rivers, etc. From an energy point of view, these are linked to the earth energy and the water energy.

At another level of energy, one may perform fire sacrifices such as *yajña* or homa. These are related to the fire energy. Typically the energy of the fire is transferred to water pots that are placed around the sacrificial fireplace. This water, which is energized by the ritual, is then poured over idols, or sprinkled over people or upon the earth to energize them.

The energy of air, *vāyu* can be accessed through breathing techniques such as *prāṇāyāma* or chanting of verses. In the first nine verses of *Śiva Sutra*, Lord Śiva explains these types of techniques to Devi, His disciple.

It is possible to access the etheric energy, *ākāśa* through meditation, though this requires understanding and awareness.

Each form of worship or sacrifice is based upon one's aptitude and inclination. Each of these is guided by scriptural instructions on how to perform the worship, when and where, etc.

Arjuna asks, 'How important is it to follow these instructions? What happens when one follows one's own inclinations and worships?'

This is an interesting question.

A saint named Kannappan in Tamil Nadu worshipped Śiva with such intensity that he cut out his eyes and placed them on the *Śiva liṅga*. Other Masters placed all kinds of material at the altar including raw meat. Rāmakṛṣṇa placed a thread under the nose of Kāli's deity to check whether She was breathing before he offered Her the ritual food!

Many Masters have followed their inclination when worshipping their favorite deity god, *Iśṭa Devatā*. Scriptures never stood in their way of worship. However, these Masters were completely authentic in what they were doing. They had *śraddha*. That is important.

Arjuna's query is in this connection.

Don't Torture Me

17.2 *The Supreme Lord Kṛṣṇa says:*
The natural authenticity (faith) of embodied beings is of three
kinds: Goodness, aggression, and ignorance.
Now listen about these from Me.

17.3 *O Arjuna, the authenticity of each is in accordance*
with one's own natural disposition.
One is known by one's authenticity, śraddha.
One can become whatever one wants to be.

17.4 *Men in the nature of goodness worship the deities; those in the*
nature of aggression worship the demons and
those in the nature of ignorance worship ghosts and spirits.

17.5, 6 *Ignorant persons of demonic nature are those*
who practice severe austerities without following
the prescription of the scriptures, who are full of hypocrisy and
egotism, who are impelled by the force of desire and attachment and
who senselessly torture the elements in their body and
also Me who dwells within the body.

Kṛṣṇa explains that the way we worship depends upon our natural disposition, the *guṇa*, attributes that we are born with.

When we are born, we carry within us the *vāsanā*, the essence of the mental cognition or bio-memory from our past lives. This comes with the *prārabdha karma* (unfulfilled actions from past lives) and the *saṁskāras* (root thought patterns), that drive our mental makeup and actions throughout our present lives. In turn, *guṇas* or the attributes we are born with are determined.

Our being, our undying spirit, keeps an account of every thought we have and every move that we make. There is no escape from this account keeper. When we reach the end of the road, when our body dies, the spirit plays back all that happened during the journey of life and goes through the pains and pleasures. According to Kṛṣṇa, the attitude, the space or the last thought with which we left our body carries over to our next birth and the next body that our spirit moves into.

Hence we are born with a natural inclination based upon our last life and attitude. Depending on the attitude, we may have the attribute of *satva*, goodness, *rajas*, aggression, or *tamas*, ignorance as our driving nature.

All societies, religions, faiths, castes or creeds are simply translations of these basic natures or root thought patterns or mental conditionings; nothing more. After taking birth on planet Earth, we adopt the nature into which we are born that is according to our past bio-memories. In our new birth, we settle into a religious belief dictated by that natural attribute.

However, we do not realize that we are a part of the Whole, a fragment of Existence or the supreme consciousness. We do not realize that our true nature transcends all material associations and conditionings. When this relationship with Existence is forgotten, we give energy to our inauthentic associations in material life. We develop allegiance to the blind rules of some religion. Such an existence is purely materialistic and the association itself is artificial, inauthentic. To come out of this, we must do completion and break out of our material bonds and enter authenticity, the path of Self-realization.

Śraddha here refers to the faith that comes out of authenticity in action or good work. Yet pure goodness goes beyond all material acts. It is transcendental. Hence there is nothing like fully good, completely good in material life.

Listen! If you don't bring authenticity, inauthenticity is waiting to take you over. Because you trained yourself for so many years with inauthenticity, inauthenticity is waiting to take you over. Bring authenticity continuously; go on expanding, go on expanding. Authenticity is the possibility of Life in you.

One of the biggest mistakes you make in your life is thinking that you are still a possibility, but your life is a reality! That is why you feel weak. Your life is not a stone wall that is already built. It is a wax model that is getting ready! Understand, the reality you experience is not a stone wall that is already built. It is only a wax model that is getting ready. Authenticity is the intelligence to alter your possibility consciously, in the right way. Authenticity is a great possibility for you to alter your life in the right way.

Whatever you perceive about you is only a possibility. If you think you are a good person, a *Swami* (saint), even that is only a possibility for a greater saint to happen. If you think that you are filled with jealousy, dirt, disease, depression and what not, that is also not reality. It is a possibility for greater disease, depression, and disorder to happen!

Now, almost all of us experience our *self* as a mixture of both. You experience your *self* as a mixture of both—a little health and a little disease, a little goodness and a little badness, a little *satva, rajas* and a little *tamas*, a little joy and a little depression, a little fight and a little reconciliation, a little wealth and a little poverty.

So you are a possibility for any extreme. You are a possibility for any possibility. When you are in the state of possibility for any possibility, you are called a seeker.

Please be very clear, only a person whose nature is pure goodness can connect with the Divine, with Existence—*yajante sāttvikā devān* (17.4).

An Enlightened Master goes beyond the three *guṇas* of *satva, rajas* and *tamas.* He transcends these attributes because he burns out all his *vāsanās, saṁskāras* and *karmas,* of which these *triguṇas* are a product. An Enlightened Master has no bondages. He is not bound by desires, greed, fear or attachment. He is beyond the illusion of material existence. He dissolves into the cosmic energy when he chooses to leave the body and it perishes.

When the energy of an enlightened Master is reborn on this planet, when it takes human form, it is imbued with some *satva guṇa*, since all beings in physical form must by nature have an attribute. Such a being is an Incarnation, an *Avatār.* Upon realization of the being's enlightened state, that Incarnation reverts to its transcendental state of being without attributes or *guṇa.* In some cases, the Incarnation continues upon this planet to fulfill the mission that Existence has sent it to accomplish. In other cases, upon realization of its true nature, the Incarnation reverts to its original cosmic state.

The classic examples of these two different events are Rāmākṛṣṇa and Vivekananda. Both were Incarnations who reappeared upon this planet on the mission of Existence, *Parāśakti.* Rāmakṛṣṇa continued after realization of His state of enlightenment. However, Vivekananda, as predicted by his master Rāmakṛṣṇa, left his mortal body once He realized his enlightened state.

If a *tāmasic* person becomes enlightened, he goes through the stages of *rajas* and *satva* before the realization happens. The transition may happen quickly but it must happen. Vālmīki, the great sage, was once a robber who terrorized and killed people. His nature was deep *tamas* with a layer of *rajas.* When he caught hold of Nārada and demanded money, Nārada offered him the name Nārāyaṇa. The moment Vālmīki uttered the name of the Lord, he was transformed. He shifted to *satva* and became the enlightened Master who wrote the Ramāyaṇa epic.

Kṛṣṇa says that our style of worship depends upon our nature—*sattvānurūpā sarvasya śraddhā bhavati bhārata* (17.3). A person established in *satva* worships *devatas* (deities, gods) who are peaceful—*yajante sāttvikā devān.* A person established in *rajas* worships *yakṣas* (supernatural beings) and *rākṣasas* (demons)—*yakṣa-rakṣāṁsi rājasāḥ.* A person established in *tamas* (ignorance) worships *pretas* (spirits of the dead) and *bhūtas* (ghosts)—*pretān bhūta-gaṇāṁś cānye yajante tāmasā janāḥ* (17.4).

Please understand, whatever is your ideal, whatever you hold in high esteem, whoever you feel connected to, whatever you worship, that is your nature and that decides your quality. If we worship the right ideal, we are established in *satva*. If we have Swami Vivekananda's poster or Śiva's photo in our room, we are in *satva*. If we have an actor's photo or poster in our room, we are in *rajas* and *tamas*. Tamas is like watching a violent fighting show. If you continuously sit in front of the television and watch fighting, you are established in *tamas*.

Kṛṣṇa says that based upon our ideal, our *guṇas* (attributes) can be described.

Do not abuse your body, I reside in you

In the last verse, He says, 'Please do not punish your body. You not only punish yourself, but you also punish Me because I reside in you—*mām caiva antaḥ śarīra-stham*'.

karṣayantaḥ śarīra-sthaṁ bhūta-grāmam acetasaḥ |
māṁ caivāntaḥ śarīra-sthaṁ tān viddhy āsūra-niścayān || 17.6

The scriptures do not recommend severe austerities and penances. Walking on fire and such other things are unnecessary. When I make you do these things once in a while, it is to make you break the pattern with which you have always lived your life. But you should not subject yourself to these as daily rituals, 'Every morning when I wake up, I should walk on ten feet of fire...' No!

Kṛṣṇa says there is no need for all these things. People perform them out of pride and ego, merely to show, 'I did all these things.' They are done out of pride and egoism. They are done out of lust and attachment. Some people, for example, sit for years on a bed of nails or sit with one hand raised. All these painful contortions are foolish. These people torture their bodies and the material elements as well as the *Paramātman* (supreme consciousness) dwelling inside them.

Beautifully Bhagavān Kṛṣṇa says, 'Please do not torture the Soul inside your body. Don't abuse your body. The body is the temple of God. By torturing the temple of God, you torture the Supreme Consciousness residing inside—*mām caiva antaḥ śarīra-stham*.' He says that those who torture the supreme consciousness inside the body are certainly demons—*tān viddhy āsura niścayān* (17.6).

Rāvaṇa did penance. He cut off his heads and put them into the fire. This is a demon's penance, torturing the body and torturing the supreme consciousness residing in the body. There is no need to do self-torture. Kṛṣṇa says, 'Don't torture yourself.' God never asked you to torture yourself. These people wanted to destroy somebody all the time. That is why they did these violent things even to themselves. The entire purpose of this penance and self-torture was to boost the ego, to seek power.

No scripture expects or teaches us how to kill others, torture others or do black magic to others. The other day I spoke to somebody about *yantras* as a remedy. Yantra is a metal plate with a diagrammatic representation of powerful *mantra* (chant) that is sanctified through rituals. After that lecture someone told me, 'I bought a *yantra*, but when I wanted to return it to the person I bought it from, he threatened to curse me.'

You need to understand that only an Enlightened being can curse. Only he has that power. But an Enlightened person will never curse. It is not that anybody can curse and it will become reality. No, only an enlightened person can curse, and an enlightened person will *never* curse. If he curses, he is not enlightened. Nobody can curse you. If he is not enlightened, don't be concerned about it. It will never work because for a curse you need *satya-saṅkalpa*, the backing of Truth.

Only the words of a person who has achieved the ultimate energy can become reality. Because the enlightened person is in Universal Consciousness, cursing another person is the same as cursing himself! One thing is sure, if someone curses, he hurts himself more than he hurts others. So never be afraid of curses.

Spiritual relationships can never exist out of fear or greed. Never be obedient to somebody out of fear. Simply throw things out if it is forced on you out of fear. Never be afraid of anything.

Here Kṛṣṇa says that there is no need for all this penance. You cheat yourself with all this penance out of pride and ego but you never really achieve anything. The person who does these things out of ego and pride is a demon, a *rākṣasa*. A demon is in deep *tamas*, in ignorance. All that drives such a person is the boost to his ego, his inauthenticities without consideration for himself and others. Such a person is a spiritual cipher.

Trust And Practice Authenticity

17.7 *Food that we consume is of three kinds,*
according to the three types of material nature.
These are the sacrifice, austerity and charity.
Listen to the difference between these three.

Kṛṣṇa now speaks about food. Three different types of people enjoy three different types of food. Before we discuss these verses, let me explain the three different types of śraddha based on what we are.

āhāras tv api sarvasya tri-vidho bhavati priyaḥ |
yajñas tapas tathā dānaṁ teśāṁ bhedam imaṁ sṛṇu || 17.7

Please understand that one group of people is completely negative. They lack integrity, the space of positivity. They only doubt, doubt and doubt. They doubt themselves and others. They have decided not to believe in anything. They have decided not to raise themselves in their lives. They remain dumb in self-doubt. We can't do anything with them. This is the first group.

The second group consists of people who positively believe, who are integrated, but do not practice authenticity, the space of possibility. They build the pattern of impossibility. They continuously resist expansion. Understand, while on the surface they believe that they are confronted by patterns and limitations imposed by their patterns, deep down inside them, they actually resist expansion. Just see, look around the society. Everything is nothing but the resistance to expansion.

The third group of people believes and practices authenticity, the space of possibility with responsibility. They know that nothing is impossible. For them, life is all about making the impossible into I-M-Possible.

There are three groups. One group is in self-doubt. Even the word doubt is too good to describe it. They are in self-denial. They are prejudiced. This group is in *tamas*. The next group is the believers. They are in *rajas*. The third group is authentic. This group is in *satva*. Kṛṣṇa beautifully explains the differences between the prejudiced group in self-denial, the believers with positivity and the authentic group with possibility. He then talks about their ways of life, character and how we can achieve the authenticity of *satva* and imbibe the truths explained in the Gītā.

He gives a beautiful step-by-step explanation and the teachings on how to raise ourselves from the prejudiced level to the believing level, and from the believing level to the authenticity level. All those here are already at the believing level.

If you are prejudiced, you will not sit here everyday. You would merely stand there, listen to two or three words and go away. Many people come just to check out what is going on. They stand here for two or three minutes and look at their watch. And even in those few minutes, their feet will shuffle ten times this way and that, and they will say, 'Alright, enough. I think he is just a young *Swami*. What can he say that I do not already know?' They just walk out in self-denial.

If you are not at least at the level of belief, you will not sit here. Coming regularly and sitting through these satsangs shows that you are at least at the level of belief. You are integrated, living in the space of positivity. Now, all you need to do is jump into the level of authenticity, the space of possibility. The moment we jump into the level of authenticity, *śraddha*, we experience the truth. We become Kṛṣṇa. We experience Kṛṣṇa consciousness.

Technology to Experience Authenticity

Now, we will enter into the technology of experiencing the authenticity, the technology of Kṛṣṇa consciousness.

You see, there is an important choice that you must make. Either you should be completely sincere and trust what I say as the truth, or be very clear that whatever I am saying is just lies.

If you can't practice what I am saying, whatever I am saying is a lie. If you are unable to practice, what is the use of this truth? Whether I am saying the truth or not, you will decide. Only *you* can decide that. No one else can decide for you. I cannot decide for you. If you can execute what I tell you with authenticity in your thinking and actions, if you are able to commit to live the great principle of authenticity, I am speaking the truth. If you are unable to do it, what is the use of the whole thing? Nothing, there's no use. For eighteen days, it's a waste of your time and my time, that's all. If you don't have the cognitive shift, if it does not transform your life to its highest possibility, then it is only wastage of time; and whatever has happened here is not the truth.

Please listen. The result of my words on your consciousness decides whether what I spoke is the truth or a lie. Understand, you don't need to do it completely or perfectly. Having the courage of authenticity to experiment with a clear decision that you will expand your possibility is enough. After my talking all these days, if you consciously say, 'Why not test for two or three days?', if you have that much courage, that is enough.

Practicing integrity creates the space of positivity in you, and practicing authenticity creates the space of possibility in you. The clear decision that you will continuously expand your possibility for you and you will not be satisfied with what you are now, is more than enough! You do not need any other separate practice. That is the good news I have for you! A conscious decision is enough!

The cognitive shift itself will make you live the principles. It is unfortunate that we do not understand the importance of cognitive shift. We think that some form of practice is required. I do promote spiritual practices like kriya, yoga and praṅāyāma, for the purpose of purifying your bio-memory, purifying your body and to cure some diseases. But I tell you, that is not the first priority in spiritual life. It may be like a pickle, but it is not the main meal! The main meal is cognitive shift! Shift in your cognition, shift in your perception, shift in your decision!

You need to know the power of your authenticity. Even if it looks like inauthenticity in the initial level, stand by it. It will rise and rise to the next-next levels of authenticity. When you are authentic towards your inauthenticity, it will lead to authenticity. Like, any number, any equation multiplied with zero, becomes zero. In the same way, however much your inauthenticity may be, if you are authentic towards your inauthenticity, you will become authentic.

Please understand, the gap between your desire and your responsibility is your inauthenticity. Bring more and more authenticity. Take more and more responsibility. So, when you take responsibility, sit by creating the space and be ready to sacrifice. The world will simply move based on your word! The world will move as you want!

Please understand, our meeting will become just one more meeting, if you don't have the courage to consciously decide to live the truth learned here. If you don't practice integrity and authenticity with responsibility, if you don't allow Kṛṣṇa's words to work on you, this meeting will be another polite meeting. Let these words penetrate you. May you consciously decide to experiment with the truths of *Bhagavad Gītā*. If you don't experiment, at least it will be mentally clear to you that this is not the truth.

You might think, '*Swamiji* was simply saying what he has read somewhere.' But if you believe this is the truth, you *will* be here. If you think this is not the truth, you will *not* be here. You will not come everyday and sit for three hours, even if you do not have any other work to do. You could have sat in front of the television at home. There are many other places to go to, yet you chose to be here. You chose to listen. This shows that you think there is truth behind these words. So, when you think there is some truth, never allow inauthenticity in you, never wait to experiment living the truth.

COURAGEOUSLY DECIDE TO EXPAND YOUR POSSIBILITY

Have the courage of authenticity and experiment with the space of possibility. Life starts with the space of possibility! I tell you, bliss or *Ānanda* means 'the space of possibility, where life oozes out of you'. Everything should create a space of possibility in you. Take one single idea. You don't need to experiment with the whole *Gītā*. Take one single principle and intranalyze that to the core. Let your whole being vibrate with that single thought.

Swami Vivekananda says, 'When you commit to a single idea, your blood should boil with that single idea. Even your hair should stand in that direction. Your bones, your thoughts, your body and your mind should all stand for it. Your whole being should be directed towards that concept. Only then success is certain.'

Please understand, take one life principle and work with it to the peak of your possibility. The peak of possibility should be realized in every human being so that you become empty. You are nothing but a NO. When the NO's disappear, you disappear and the truths, *satya* start living through you. Your personality is made of NO's and your identity is made of YES. Let your personality be dropped and identity be awakened. Your personality is given by society but identity is natural.

If you fail, there is nothing wrong. But have courage to work with it. If you succeed, you will know it is the truth and you will be liberated. You will be in the space of completion. You will have bliss. If it fails, you will know that it is not the truth and you will be clear. You can continue your search elsewhere. So be very clear about it. The basic truth Kṛṣṇa is telling you is about integrity and authenticity.

THREE GROUPS OF PEOPLE

Please listen. There are three groups of people—*tāmasic* group, *rājasic* group, and *satva* group.

The *tāmasic* group is prejudiced, meaning negative and lacks integrity. Understand, it is due to the fear of your possibilities you get into the space of impossibility. Your patterns, fears, everything is directed only in one line—fear of your possibilities. Lack of integrity is nothing but fear of confrontation. See, the moment I present the truth of integrity, everyone thinks, 'Oh! I can do this may be for two days or four days.' But no one, no one thinks or understands, realizes, why you are afraid of integrity.

You strongly believe that the manipulativeness of your mind has saved you, helped you in many situations. I tell you, a lion not realizing it is the lion and thinking it is a sheep, is also not that big crime. But the lion thinking it may need the help of a fox in its life and keeping the fox as a friend and companion, is the biggest crime.

Please understand, deciding not to declare integrity in your whole life, itself is nothing but the lion believing strongly it may need the help of a fox and keeping it with himself continuously and pampering it, 'No, no! Please don't go away. There may be some time when I may need your help.' Slap the wolf. If needed slap yourself once.

Realize you are the lion who does not need the help of the wolves and foxes. Realize you are the being who does not need the help of the manipulative mind. So, integrity is your strength. Lion's roar is enough. No animal will even stand in that area. Your integrity is enough. No problems can even stand in your breathing space.

Next, the *rājasic* group believes intellectually but lacks authenticity in action, which is the space of possibility. They carry self-doubt and the space of impossible. Understand, why do you feel you can't commit to live the great principle of authenticity? It is because you have an innate fear, innate pattern, self-doubt about your laziness; self-doubt that your laziness may overpower your consciousness. That's the biggest enemy for authenticity, *śraddha*.

You have to complete with the pattern of laziness and with the greed for vacation. You have to complete with the desire for being in non-doing physically, but lot of doing mentally. Please understand, non-doing physically. See, if you love non-doing mentally, that is great. That is all I wanted. But you love non-doing physically, but lot of doing mentally. A lot of doing happens mentally. I tell you, authenticity brings life in you. Authenticity is Life! Life is the possibility of expansion.

Please understand. Even your ignorance is nothing but fear of expansion. Many times you continue to be in ignorance, because of your fear of failure.

Listen! Expansion is possible when we are ready to become responsible to have it. Why do we feel the fear of responsibility? Because it brings more and more of our possibilities to our light. This means that we can't continue to be asleep, we have to wake up. Wealth wakes us up to more responsibility. Health wakes us up to more responsibility. Happy relationships wake us up to more responsibility. Everything we love wakes us up to more responsibility which we don't like that.

Listen! You love many things in your life, but you don't like the path to achieve them. See the conflict. Complete with the laziness, the tiredness, the boredom pattern continuously. I tell you, then starts life; then starts something in your life. I call that as Life.

The third group, the *satva* group has the power of authenticity. They not only believe, but they have the courage to create the space of possibility and play with the words and ideas as well. They don't settle with the patterns of 'impossible'. They go on expanding their possibilities.

There is nothing impossible! Listen! Actually what separates you from the Cosmos? The skin and the identity that you are only up to your skin! What separates your mind from the Cosmic mind? It is just the borders you made that separates your mind from the Cosmic mind. Just as the wall separates the ocean from the boat jetty, your 'Impossible' separates your individual mind from the Cosmic mind! Break that wall! After that, for anything that happens in your individual mind, the Cosmic mind will say '*tathāstu*—so be it!'

Go on making impossibilities into possibilities. What is Life? Continuously making impossibilities into possibilities is Life. When you accept that impossibility as impossibility in your life, you are dead! After that, where is life? Life is life as long as you are making all 'Impossible' into 'I-M Possible,' all 'Impossible' into 'I Am Possible'!

Please do not miss authenticity, the fragrance of courage. Let these words penetrate you. The work that a disciple enters into is with the unknown, the uncharted, and the unmapped territory; so fear of expansion will be there. That is the only barrier. In spite of it, we should go on expanding. Let fear be there. It will hang around for a while. When we do not listen to it, it will leave us. It is a great day when fear of the unknown leaves us. From then on growth becomes simple, easy and spontaneous.

This committed journey leads to bliss, eternal bliss, *Nityānanda.*

We Are What We Eat

17.8 *The foods that promote longevity, virtue, strength, health, happiness and joy are juicy, smooth, substantial and nutritious.* Such foods are liked by persons in the mode of goodness.

17.9 *People in the mode of aggression like foods that are very bitter, sour, salty, hot, pungent, dry, and burning, and which cause pain, grief and disease.*

17.10 *People in the mode of ignorance like foods that are stale, tasteless, putrid, rotten, refuse and of impure energy.*

Kṛṣṇa talks about the nature of food consumed by people of *satva, rajas* and *tamas* temperaments.

He explains what kind of food these people like, what kind of lives these people lead and what kind of understanding these people experience in their lives. The most important thing is what kind of understanding they acquire. See, the same words can be cognized in many different ways.

We need to understand the word in the context of its spirit. Words can easily be misunderstood! Please don't miss the essence of the words. It is easy to miss the spirit, the true meaning behind the words. Experiment with courage. And if you can't, if this is not the truth for you, forget about it. At least you will be free to search somewhere else.

Experiment and Experience

If you think that it is the truth and you don't execute it or experiment with it in your life, then drop it! Otherwise it will become a habit to listen to the truth and not practice it. It will become an inauthentic mental setup. It is the most dangerous mental setup.

People ask me, '*Swamiji*, should I renounce everything to become enlightened? Should I become a Sannyāsi, a monk?'

I tell them, 'No. There is no need. Just do one thing. Don't have the inauthentic mental setup of receiving the truth and not taking the responsibility of practicing it. Complete with all your self-doubting, 'impossible' patterns and create the space for authenticity, which is creating your best inner image, outer image, others' image and life's image, that's all.'

Inauthenticity is the most dangerous thing that can happen to any being. Please be very clear, receiving the truth and understanding it intellectually without having the courage of authenticity to live it is the worst possible mental setup. That is the worst devil or demon that can catch hold of you. So at least have the courage to decide, 'This is not for me because this is not the truth.' If you believe this is the truth, then have the courage of authenticity to experiment with it.

That is all I am saying. Don't come back to me like a beggar with a powerless mood, 'How can I have my own mind under my control, how can I be complete, how can I be authentic, can you tell me?' Once you are married, you don't go around and ask, 'How can I have kids?' You are a man! You know it! Once you are initiated, you don't go around and ask, 'How can I practice integrity and authenticity?' It is a simple decision!

Weakness is death which you give to yourself. Nobody can save you. Vivekananda is right when he says, 'Nobody can save a person filled with weakness!' You don't need to swim and save yourself. If I come in the ship and throw the rope, you can at least hold the rope so that I can lift you! If you don't have the power even for that, then nobody can save you!

You have heard many things. Kṛṣṇa does not say anything new in this chapter. He says only one thing, 'Be authentic.' Authenticity is the straight way. I tell people, 'Authenticity is the basic spiritual virtue. Authenticity is the basic spiritual virtue.' First be a gentleman, then you can be a spiritual man. Gentleman means to be authentic to what you feel as you, what you project as you, what others' expect from you, and what you expect from life—being aligned and truthful to the core to all these four identities.

Never do anything without being clear and complete about the truth, and never stop doing anything if you know it is the truth. The scientist is courageous enough to authentically go after the truth. Wherever the research takes him, he is ready to experiment. The brain which is established in integrity and authenticity can read any book and understand the truths from that book. It can.

Just like how the *Paramahamsa* swan can separate the water from the milk in a mixture of milk and water, the brain established in integrity can separate truth from untruth. The brain established in integrity and authenticity is *Paramahamsa*.

In the same way, you must become an inner scientist, a spiritual scientist. You must have the courage of authenticity to go behind the experience within the words. You must be able to play with them.

A small story:

> An Enlightened Master and his disciple went to the river to bathe.
>
> Suddenly, the disciple fell into the river and shouted, 'Master, save me, save me!'
>
> The Master said, 'You are ātman (soul), save yourself. You are God, save yourself.'
>
> The disciple shouted, 'Master, first save me, then you can teach me philosophy. Then you can teach me meditation. First, please save me.'
>
> The Master replied, 'Stand up and save yourself.'
>
> The disciple shouted, 'No, No, Master, save me first. Then you can teach me.'
>
> The Master shouted back, 'Fool, I am telling you to stand up.'

> The disciple became frightened. Just out of fear, he simply stood up, and realized that the water was only up to his knees!

When you stand up, you understand the whole *saṁsāra sāgara*, the ocean of Life. Whatever you consider to be the great worries of your life are not even up to your knee level. They are just up to the ankle level. Because you are lying down, because you never stand up, you think you are drowning; you think you are going to die.

I tell you from my personal experience, if you stand up with the power of authenticity, you will realize that the water is only knee-deep. Whatever you regard as the *saṁsāra sāgar* (ocean of life) is only knee deep. It is nothing. There is no way it can affect you. But you need courage of authenticity to stand up.

For example, if the disciple had decided, 'No, no, I am drowning and instead of pulling me out and helping me, Master is teaching me impractical and impossible things. What kind of a Master is he?' If he simply blamed the Master, doubting the Master and doubting himself, he would have gone with the river.

He had the courage of authenticity, he just decided to complete and drop his doubts and impossibilities, and in a minute, he got the power of possibility to experiment with the master's words and was saved. You need the power. Stand up with the courage of authenticity as your bone marrow. You need the courage to stand up with authenticity and see the truth by yourself. Nothing will be lost. If something can be lost, it is better to lose it as soon as possible. May you be rid of that thing or situation. If something can be lost by practicing the truth, may it be lost as early as possible. The earlier it is lost, the better for you.

May you flood your being with the Truth. Whatever cannot stand, whatever is washed away, let it be washed away. May it be lost from your being as early as possible.

Kṛṣṇa explains here about the energy of various food substances. Generally, all food that is not from plants i.e., from animal origin, has negative energy. Food that is hot and spicy tends to aggravate desires. Vegetarian food that is fresh and not spicy is ideal for spiritual practices.

In our *Nithya Spiritual Healing* system, it is essential that the healers become vegetarians and give up substances such as alcohol, tobacco, drugs, etc. I have nothing against alcohol or meat. I have no theories about cruelty to animals and so on. Plants also have life, just perhaps not at the same frequency. So if one argues from the point of cruelty to animals, eating vegetables also is cruelty to plants. This system is based on deep meditative techniques. For the meditative energy to be effective, negative energy substances should not be used. I have seen that these meditations do not go together with meat as well as with tobacco and alcohol. If healers eat meat, smoke or drink, they are affected physiologically and psychologically.

Any serious meditation technique requires one to be in the energy field. The word *āhāra* used by Kṛṣṇa can be expanded to mean food for all senses, not merely for the tongue. All sensory inputs need to be of the same description that Kṛṣṇa uses here, promoting 'longevity, virtue, strength, health, happiness and joy' to aid one's progress in one's spiritual path by the *sātvic* route.

Ayurveda recommends different foods for each constitutional type based upon tastes such as sweet, sour, bitter, pungent, etc. These are specific recommendations as to what tastes would be healthy for which constitutions and based on this what kind of vegetables and fruits one should eat and so on. Even cooking methods are specified that can be used to provide wholesome ayurvedic food.

Kṛṣṇa outlines a more general classification based upon the purity and nature of food. Kṛṣṇa explains that *tāmasic* food, putrid and stale, is forbidden for consumption by *vedic* tradition. The injunction is to eat food within a few hours of cooking. Beyond that, the food should be discarded.

Eat fresh food in silence and with completion and gratitude. Pay attention to each morsel of food and eat with gratitude and love. Eating does not need to be a social occasion. It should not be. Enjoy your social interactions before and after meals, not while eating. Be in the present moment while you eat.

What Kṛṣṇa says makes pure sense for wellness. Natural foods contain their own flavor and goodness. You do not need to add spices and flavoring agents to corrupt their taste. He says eat food as it comes, fresh from the earth, and cooked with the energy of fire. Eat it while it is fresh. You will be in *satva*. You will be in bliss.

Enriching Without Expectation

17.11 *Sacrifice without expectation of results, as stipulated in the scriptures, with a firm belief and conviction that it is a duty, is in the mode of goodness.*

17.12 *O Arjuna, that sacrifice that is performed with expectation of result or for show out of pride, is of the nature of aggression.*

17.13 *Sacrifice that is performed without following the scripture, in which no food is distributed, which is devoid of mantra, authenticity, and gift, is said to be in the mode of ignorance.*

Kṛṣṇa talks about how to give, how to sacrifice and how to enrich others.

In the vedic tradition, enriching sacrifices such as fire rituals (yajña and homa) were not mere rituals to worship celestial beings. They had a far deeper meaning of enriching for the benefit of the living and the poor.

Every ritualistic offering had a major element of gifting the deserving poor. Whoever came to such a ritual never went away empty-handed. When the great Ṛṣis, the Masters, performed rituals, they had nothing to seek. They performed these in line with the truth of their experiences, which were the scriptural understandings. They expected nothing. They performed rituals as a day-to-day living expression. These rituals were conducted so that the celestial beings and nature were pleased and humanity benefited. These were selfless offerings of *satva guṇa* (good nature).

Great kings also practiced these rituals. Kings performed fire rituals to display power and to show that they controlled other kings. These were a display of ego. Kings such as Yudhiṣtra performed the horse sacrifice, *Aṣvamedha Yāga*, and the *Rājasūya Yāga* to announce their supremacy over other kings. However, these were required of kings and were also occasions to give their wealth away generously. These were performed in the mode of aggression, *rajas*.

Other extreme sacrifices were also performed by demonic creatures with no concern except to show their brute strength. These did not involve any enriching, any charity or generosity. These did not follow the scriptural guidelines. These were carried out purely for selfish reasons.

> In Kaṭhopaniṣad, when young Naciketa's father gave away useless old cows that no longer produced milk as fire offerings, the young lad protested his father's inauthenticity.
>
> 'What are you doing?' he asked his father. 'Why are you giving away useless things in a sacrifice that is meant for giving away valuable material offerings? If you want to give nothing else, give me away,' Naciketa said.
>
> In deep ignorance and anger, his father offered his son to Yama, god of death, as a result.

Please understand that an enriching sacrifice is not measured by how much we give. It is measured by how much we give that we cannot afford to give. It is measured by how much we give when it hurts us to give and that too without any expectation in return. Such an enriching sacrifice straightaway leads to liberation.

Many people give with wonderful intent. It is not charity if they give part of their wealth without it affecting their lifestyle. It is no sacrifice. Many people tell me, '*Swamiji*, I am writing a legal will leaving all my possessions to this ashram, temple or your mission.' What is the big deal in giving away after death? You cannot carry it with you anyway.

An enriching sacrifice must hurt to be genuine. It must cause you discomfort and yet be given with total completion, pleasure and without expectations. That is the spirit of genuine surrender. That is the spirit of doing things without expectation of the fruits of action.

I am not denouncing the wonderful charity that many wealthy people do without posing for photographs. They do it with good intentions of helping the disadvantaged. That mental attitude of giving and sharing what they have with the needy, benefits them. That *vāsanā* of generosity stays with their spirit. There is no doubt in this.

However, that charity will be in the mode of *rajas*, not *satva*. When people move from this *rajas* state of giving to the *satva* state of giving, wealth seeks them out. Lakṣmī, the goddess of wealth comes to them without being asked! She knows these people will be the route for enriching mankind.

There is nothing degrading about wealth and power. They are great energies. Like all great energies, the problem is handling them with responsibility without letting them go to one's head. As an example, look at the difference between Rāvaṇa and Janaka. Janaka was a *Rājarṣi*, the king who was also a sage, a complete being. He ruled a kingdom, but treated the power and wealth as if they belonged to someone else. He was a mere keeper, a mere witness. He ruled from the space of enriching others. On the other hand, Rāvaṇa, although highly gifted and a great *tapasvi*, who undertook many severe penances, was ruled by his ego, incompletions and senses. That brought about his ruin.

The Universe operates on the principle of abundance. There is no shortage of anything in the Universe. What we need, we get. The trouble is that we are dissatisfied with what we need. Our wants are immeasurable. Great Masters have said that it is possible for the Universe to fulfill the needs of all the people on planet Earth, but not the wants of one single person. Our greed has no limits.

May your desire to enrich others and give away be limitless. May your desire to acquire become zero. You will be amazed at how wealth seeks you.

Austerity Of Deeds, Words, And Thoughts

17.14 *The worship of deities, the priest, the Guru, and the wise;*
purity, honesty, living in reality, and nonviolence
are said to be austerity of deed.

17.15 *Speech that is non-offensive, truthful, pleasant, beneficial,*
and is used for the regular study of scriptures
is called austerity of word.

17.16 *Serenity of mind, gentleness, equanimity, self-control,*
and purity of thought are called austerity of thought.

17.17 *The above mentioned threefold austerity (of thought, word*
and deed), practiced by Yogīs with supreme authenticity,
without a desire for the fruit,
is said to be in the mode of goodness.

17.18 *Austerity that is performed for gaining respect, honor, reverence,*
and for the sake of show, yielding an uncertain and temporary
result, is said to be in the mode of aggression.

17.19 *Austerity performed with foolish stubbornness or*
with self-torture or for harming others,
is said to be in the mode of ignorance.

Kṛṣṇa defines austerity of deeds, words and thoughts.

Tapas or penance is the austere, simple way of living, the mode of *aparigraha* (simplicity). It is based upon what one needs and not what one craves for. One who successfully practices this is a *tapasvi*.

Kṛṣṇa explained earlier and repeats here that *tapasya*, austerity or penance, doesn't mean inflicting pain or torturing oneself and others. This includes not merely physical torture and pain, but also takes into account pain through words and thoughts. Penance undertaken in this manner is abusing oneself and the God who resides within, forgetting that the body is a temple of God.

Penance performed out of foolishness and self-torture destroys or injures others. Please understand, such acts are done out of ignorance. That's what I explained earlier with regard to black magic. No black magic can be done. No evil spirit can be sent to you. No one but an Enlightened Master can curse, and an Enlightened Master cannot curse. He can only bless.

Bhagavan Kṛṣṇa says that the people who are in *rajas* carry out sacrifices for the sake of respect, honor and worship. When they do penance or sacrifice in this manner, it is unstable. When people don't respect them, they stop doing it. They do it as long as people fall at their feet. If the respect is lost, they stop their *tapasyā*.

Penance performed with the view of obtaining any result, even a noble ideal like Enlightenment is a result...is in the mode of *rajas*, aggression or passion. Only when it is in the nature of total surrender, with no expectation of any results, it is in *satva* and of spiritual value.

> When I talk about my *tapas* during my days of wandering all over India, I did difficult things. I realize now that many of these could have been dispensed with. I experimented with ten thousand keys before I found the key to unlock the door to Enlightenment. I tell my disciples that they do not need to go through that. There is an easier, faster and simpler way!
>
> As long as I struggled towards Enlightenment in my spiritual practices, it eluded me. I was able to realize myself only when I threw away my *rudrākśa* (energy beads) and the photograph of Śrī Rāmakṛṣṇa Paramahamsa that I had with me all those years, and sat down in meditation, with the feeling, 'let what may happen, happen.'

Here, Kṛṣṇa uses the word *Saumyatvaṁ* beautifully.

We have no exact English translation for this word *Saumyatva*; *manaḥ prasādaḥ saumyatvaṁ* (17.16). *Saumyatvaṁ* refers to satisfaction and a feeling that is so comfortable. It refers to one whose presence makes you feel totally relaxed, complete and induces thoughts that calm and center the mind. Please understand *saumyatva* and pleasing words are basic qualities to be practiced by a spiritual person.

Some people become enlightened, yet they can't enrich others. For example, I saw a great, enlightened Swami living in the Himalayas who spent the whole day smoking *gañja.* No doubt he was enlightened. He put a copper coin in the *chillum* pipe with which he smoked *gañja.* You will be surprised that when he emptied the chillum pipe, a gold coin fell out! I witnessed this happen many times. He sold that coin to buy more *gañja*. He lived in Uttarkashi (in Uttaranchal, North India). Of course, I had great respect for him because he was a *tapasvi*, and he never wore any clothes. He was a *nāga-sādhu*.

Nāga means a Sannyāsi who does not wear clothes. In that cold weather they lived without clothes. They are also called *Paramahamsa*. *Paramahamsa* Sannyāsis do not wear clothing except to go into the city to spread the Divine mission. Otherwise they are not supposed to wear clothes.

Paramahamsas live like children. When this *Swami*, a great *Paramahamsa*, emptied his *chillum*, there would be a gold coin in it. I asked him, 'Bābā, you are a great *tapasvi*, an *atmajñāni* (one who has attained Self-knowledge) and a *brahmajñāni* (knower of Brahman), why are you smoking *gañja*?'

He said, 'A big elephant cannot be tied to a small hut. We must make it a little dull and silent. Only then can the elephant stay in the small hut. After enlightenment, the soul cannot stay in this small body. I must bring it down and make it dull. Then it can stay in this body. To bring it down, I do these things.' Of course, their smoking is different from an ordinary man's smoking.

Someone asked me, '*Swamiji,* Swami Vivekananda and Rāmakṛṣṇa Paramahamsa used to smoke. Why can't I smoke?'

I explained to him, 'Swami Vivekananda became enlightened before he started smoking. Become enlightened and then you can smoke and do whatever you want. Without achieving what they achieved, doing what they did is wrong.' Please understand that whatever Enlightened Masters do is totally different from what you are supposed to do. Actually, they do things opposite of what you are supposed to do. You must do things to elevate yourself. They must do things to bring themselves down!

This *nāga-sādhu* in Uttarkashi is enlightened; however, he cannot enrich everybody. His type is such that he will not enrich people. He is a mystic. He will not teach anybody and he will not make anybody enlightened. He does not work with people. He is that type.

On the other hand, some people who experience the truth share the truth with the world. Swami Vivekananda and Paramahamsa Yogananda were great souls who shared their experiences for the benefit of enriching others. That was their mission. Their power was the space of completion they carried.

Bhāgavatam says that people who explain or enrich others by sharing the Truth, such as Śrī Kṛṣṇa, are Incarnations. Incarnations still landing on planet Earth to make all of you enlightened is nothing but the Universe practicing responsibility. Even after so much torture and abuse by human beings, enlightened beings and Incarnations are continuing to enrich planet Earth; this is nothing but the cosmos deciding to do whatever it takes to enrich all of you.

Listen, only my integrity and authenticitymakes me an Enlightened being. Only my commitment to taking responsibility and enriching all of you, makes me an Incarnation!

Sukha Brahma was the son of Vyāsa, the compiler of the Vedas and author of Bhāgavatam and Mahābhārat. Sukha Brahma Ṛṣi is an Enlightened Master who wore no clothes.

Sukha Brahma was questioned, 'What is the difference between Enlightened people and *Avatārs* or Incarnations?'

Sukha Brahma says beautifully: *Soundaryatva, Tejavastva, Sārasvatya,* and the power, *lakṣmitva. Soundaryatva* means that if we see them, we will automatically feel like sitting and listening to them. We will automatically feel like turning around once more to capture their grace! That which simply attracts our mind is *soundaryatva.*

The next attribute is *tejas*, a sharp radiating energy and clarity. The third is *sārasvatya.* This means that no matter how difficult a concept or idea is, they can explain it in a simple way. It merely flows from their tongue where *Sarasvatī* (goddess of knowledge) resides.

Above all is *Lakṣmītva.* This means that just by their thought, wealth and work will happen. Everything happens according to how they want it to happen. When somebody radiates all four of these qualities, he is an Incarnation.

Austerity of Body, Words and Mind

Here, Kṛṣṇa says the same thing. *Saumyatva...* Please understand, even for Incarnations, *Soundaryatva* and *Saumyatva* are necessary qualities. Now surely we should imbibe these qualities in our lives.

The penance that is supposed to be done by words, is speaking the truth and speaking pleasing words—*satyaṁ priyahitaṁ ca yat* (17.15). Please understand, creating a healing effect through words is important. Creating a healing effect through our words is basic for a spiritual practitioner who is established in integrity. We should not utter words that hurt others—*anuvega karaṁ vākyaṁ.* Our presence should be healing and enriching others. Based on the words we utter, people can find out what kind of a space we are carrying.

Always use pleasing words. Never use sharp or disturbing words. One more thing, sometimes we don't understand how our words disturb others. We do not know how our words disrespect or emotionally disturb other beings. We must bring integrity in the words we utter to ourselves and to others, and bring completion to our speech. Kṛṣṇa calls this austerity of words, *vān-mayaṁ tapa ucyate* (17.15).

Please be very clear, the words you utter are *you*. If you constantly utter the words, 'I am this, I am this', you will become that! Constantly utter right words about you, inside you and outside you. Please listen about the power of words. Unfortunately, we don't harness the power of words. And as per the law, when we don't use any power properly and play with it without the knowledge about it, it destroys us! It is like electricity, we can use electricity for the best things in our lives. But, if we don't want to use it properly and misbehave with it, it destroys us. It kills us straightaway! That is why I am saying that learn to harness every power available to you.

Please understand, I am defining Integrity.

Understand, aligning yourself more and more, deeper and deeper into your completion, aligning your words, internal and external, towards the space of completion is Integrity.

When you start practicing integrity, you will harness the power of words. The words you utter will have so much power that just through the words you will be able to change your life and others' life, for the better! Please understand, from the time I know myself I am doing this only. I am using the right words to transform people's lives.

When we sit with somebody, that person should feel, 'Can I sit for longer time with him? Can I meet him tomorrow? Will I see him again?' We should create that healing feeling in the other person. People should wait for us rather than run away from us. Usually we create a negative effect. We create an uncomfortable feeling. People just run away from us. A simple, single word if used improperly, can destroy a whole relationship.

Bhagavān Kṛṣṇa says a spiritual person should use pleasing words and not agitate others. When we do not agitate others, we will not be arrogant. See, this is not even a social morality. This is a spiritual practice.

As I explained the other day, the same words that we use to hurt others will hurt us as well. We will use these same words towards ourselves as well. This truth is embedded in the science of energy and vibration. So, we must be in integrity to harness the power of words. The ability to speak, the ability to utter words towards yourself, and the ability to utter words towards others—each one of us has this powerful ability. We can use it either to make our life or break our life. Right words that we utter in right time will make our life. Wrong words uttered in the wrong moment can break our life. Especially, the words we are uttering towards our self and towards others.

Kṛṣṇa says to study spiritual literature regularly. By regularly studying scriptural literature, these ideas go again and again into our brain. Consequently, we acquire the courage to experiment and live the truth.

I ask you to take up any truth and practice it at least a few times. For example, yesterday I told you not to continuously function based on the idea 'me, me, me.' Instead try the idea 'you, you, you.' Try that at least ten times and see the effect in your life. If it does not work out, you throw can it away, it's up to you, but at least try it out ten times. You will get a glimpse of the truth expressed by Kṛṣṇa.

Intellectuals have two weapons: words and logic. They can be helpful teaching tools if properly used or they can be frightening weapons. It is up to us to choose how to use them: whether in the mode of ignorance, aggression or goodness.

Kṛṣṇa talks about austerity in action, *śarīraṁ tapa* as well. He speaks about the five conditions that are also in Patañjali's *Aṣṭāṅga Yoga* as the five disciplines of yama: *satya, ahiṁsā, asteya, aparigṛha* and *brahmacarya*. These mean truth in thoughts, words and deeds embodying nonviolence, non-covetousness, simplicity and living in reality with the focus on the Supreme as the ultimate in any kind of penance.

Many feel that the truth must be told even if it hurts. Please understand that if it hurts someone, it cannot be the truth. It is only our perception of the truth. It is only a reflection of our ego presented by our minds as the truth. We are not in the truth if we perceive something with our senses and we draw conclusions with our limited knowledge based upon those perceptions, and then express these as our truth and hurt someone. If we do this, be very clear, we are in aggression and ignorance. We are not in the truth. We are not in goodness.

Truth is a reflection of compassion. Truth is an expression of compassion. Truth and compassion always go together. For that reason, truth can never hurt.

How To Give?

17.20 *Charity that is given at the right place and time,*
as a matter of duty to a deserving candidate
who does nothing in return,
is considered to be in the mode of goodness.

17.21 *Charity that is given unwillingly or to get something in return*
or to gain some result is in the mode of aggression.

17.22 *Charity that is given at a wrong place and time*
to unworthy persons or without paying respect
to the receiver or with ridicule is in the mode of ignorance.

Kṛṣṇa speaks about the concept of *dāna*, enriching charity, which I explained earlier.

Dāna, charity is sharing out of the space of enriching. It is not done with the attitude of giving. It is done with the attitude of sharing and not expecting good results because of it or some easy route into heaven because of it. Charity is done out of love and gratitude.

'O God, you have given me so much, now let me share a little bit with society and with the world.' Charity is the attitude of sharing and enriching. Charity that is done out of the responsibility to enrich others, without any expectation means feeling complete and committed to the Whole, to God, and with that feeling giving as a natural commitment. It is given with the enriching attitude that it is my quality and I have to do it. Only then it becomes real *dāna*. Sharing at the proper time and place and with a worthy person is charity in the mode of goodness, *satva*.

There are three kinds of *dāna*.

Understand, *annadāna* means giving to enrich with food, clothes and whatever is related to someone's physical needs.

Next is *vidyādāna*. This means giving to enrich with education and also whatever someone needs for mental growth. For example, when somebody is depressed, if you enrich him with some consoling ideas, this is *vidyādāna*. If somebody does not know how to clean a room and you teach him, this is *vidyādāna*. If somebody does not know how to cut grass and you teach him, this is *vidyādāna*.

And the third kind is *jñānadāna*, giving to enrich with spiritual knowledge.

If we give *annadāna*, we satisfy a person for three hours. After three hours, again he needs food. If we give *vidyādāna*, education or knowledge, he will have food for himself for one life. If we give education, he can earn food for himself. He will make money and buy food for himself. If we give *jñānadāna*, we will satisfy that person birth after birth!

Annadāna satisfies for three hours. *Vidyādāna* satisfies the receiver for one life. If we give *jñānadāna*, it fulfills that person for life after life. He will never fall into depression or the ocean of material world, birth after birth.

THE ULTIMATE ENRICHING CHARITY, JÑĀNADĀNA

Jñānadāna is the ultimate sharing of enriching with knowledge.

The common expression says, 'If a person needs fish and we feed or buy him a fish, he can be satisfied for one meal.' This is *annadāna*. 'If we teach him how to fish, he can manage his whole life without hunger.' This is *vidyādāna*. This is where the expression stops. In our Healer's Initiation Program, we tell them to stop eating fish! That solves their problem for many cycles of birth. This is *jñānadāna*!

Understand one thing, even if you have come and sat here accidentally after looking at my pictures saying, 'I saw a cutout or poster. He is so young. The poster says that he is speaking on *Bhagavad Gītā*. Let me see what he is saying...'

Even if you have come just to check it out and you land up listening to the whole *Gītā*, it will enrich you. At some point in time, you will remember these truths and live them. Naturally you cannot be the same person again. You will be enriched! At some point in time when you are about to make a mistake or you fall into powerlessness, you will remember these truths. These thoughts have gone inside you. They will make you complete with yourself choicelessly and lead you to completion. This is *jñānadāna*.

The knowledge that you have received now will transform your whole life even if you don't practice it. These words are so powerful that automatically they will start working on you. You will not remain the same person. Your depth of depression will be reduced. Your depth of suffering will be reduced. You will feel that you are entering a new life. You will become courageous and a new confidence will enter your life. This is *jñānadāna*. This is the ultimate *puṇya* (virtuous deed) of giving knowledge. No other good deed is equivalent to giving spiritual knowledge.

Giving food bestows three hours of satisfaction. Giving education gives satisfaction for this one life. Giving spiritual knowledge satisfies souls life after life. Kṛṣṇa says when charity is done purely out of a feeling of sharing to enrich others, it is *sātvika*, the ultimate good, the ultimate purity—*tad dānaṁ sāttvikaṁ smṛtam* (17.20).

One more point is that the person who gives loses nothing with *jñānadāna*. With all other *dāna*, the person who gives has a little less. In *annadāna*, he who gives will lose and he who receives will gain. In *vidyādāna*, the giver does not lose. He retains the same level. In *jñānadāna*, I tell you a secret, the more you share, the more it grows in you! The more you enrich others with the science of completion, the more you grow in completion. It is a win-win situation. Here, you receive automatically. It grows in the person who shares and enriches.

I tell you another important secret: Don't think you are the only one being enriched by listening to me now. By expressing these truths, even I am being enriched. Enriching others enriches you back! Listen! Enriching others enriches you back!

A simple analogy will help explain how this happens. When a woman gives birth to a child, not only is the child born, the woman too takes birth, as a mother. Until then she is only a woman. Once she gives birth, she is called 'mother'. When a child takes birth, not only does the child take birth, even the mother takes birth. Before that she is not a mother. She is only a woman. The moment she gives birth to a child, both the child and the mother are born.

In the same way, when you receive spiritual knowledge from me, I also grow! That is why in the *Vedic* system, we recite the following *mantra* before spiritual lessons:

Oṁ sahanāvavatu sahanau bhunaktu
saha vīryam karavāvahai
tejasvi nāvadhītamastu mā vidviśāvahai
Oṁ śānti śānti śāntiḥ

This *śānti* or peace *mantra* means: may we both (master and disciple) achieve perfection or completion. May both of us grow. May both of us enrich each other. May we not have enmity towards each other.

Understand, the *mantra* doesn't say, 'May you learn.' It says, 'May both of us learn.' The *vedic* system is so humble. To tell you the truth, when I speak, I also learn. Somebody asked me, '*Swamiji*, what are you going to speak about?' I said, 'Who knows? Just like you, I also sit and listen!'

Here all I have in front of me are saṃskṛit verses. I read the verse and speak whatever comes forth spontaneously; that's all. Just like you, I also sit and listen. Just as you are enriched, I am also enriched. Both of us grow. Only an egoistic person thinks that the disciple is benefited. No! The Master also benefits, he is also enriched. He can become a Master only when a disciple happens!

Only when a child is given birth, the woman is called a mother.

Only when a disciple becomes enlightened, the *Guru* becomes a Master. Otherwise, he is not a Master.

If the woman is unable to give birth to a child, she cannot be a mother. Similarly, until you become enlightened, I cannot be called a Master. Be very clear, by sharing this knowledge, I also grow. The person who shares with simplicity and humility, who is very clear, very integrated and authentic about the whole truth of sharing and is not caught in the false ego, his *dāna*, his sharing of thoughts is *sātvika* and is related to *satva guṇa*—attribute of goodness.

When you ask questions, if I don't know the answer, I say I don't know the answer. People ask, 'What is this? *Swamiji*, you are enlightened and you say you don't know.'

I tell them, 'Only an Enlightened Master says I don't know. Only he has the courage to speak the truth. If a normal person doesn't know, he minces words. He puts some words here and there and confuses the audience.'

Confusing the audience is not a complicated job. It is easy because they are already confused! There is nothing more to be done. Just use some words, that's all. And it's not a big thing. Only an Enlightened person is courageous enough to say, 'I don't know' when he doesn't know. To answer a question without knowledge doesn't require Enlightenment. It needs foolish hypocrisy. The straightforward, integrated and authentic approach to the truth is what Kṛṣṇa calls *sātvika dāna*.

Here, in whatever way I experience the truth, I simply express it and share it—authentically, without reservation. That is *sātvika dāna* according to Kṛṣṇa.

And He goes on to explain *rajas dāna* and *tamas dāna*. Many times, the *dāna* is not given voluntarily. Or they may give something away as a part of a ritual. For example, in a Hindu wedding the giving away of a bride is called *kanyā dāna*.

Earlier I spoke about people who give their property for charitable purposes in their will. What choice do they have? They cannot carry it with them. In many cases they may have fought with their children and decided not to leave them anything. So instead of giving away the wealth to their children, these people give it away as charity. Such acts are not acts of charity. They are done with ulterior motives.

There are others whose charity it is better not to accept. Kṛṣṇa refers to this as giving in ignorance, *tamas*. People will come with money not declared for tax as earned income and gift that to the ashram. They will use it as a tax saving strategy. What for?

Often, disciples ask why I am not accepting donations from very wealthy people who come to the ashram seeking help. Unless the person stays with me for a year or more and shows his integrity, authenticity and responsibility towards enriching the mission, it is difficult to accept anything from that person. Why become bonded to people whose motives are not merely selfish but self-defeating?

Parāśakti (Existence) guides the mission and She takes care. What She cannot give, no one else can give. What She decides not to give, who else can give?

Oṁ Tat Sat

17.23 *'Oṁ Tat Sat' is said to be the threefold name*
of the Eternal Being (Brahma).
Persons with good (brahmanic) qualities, the Vedas,
and the selfless service (seva, yajña) were created
by and from Brahma in the ancient times.

17.24 *Therefore, acts of sacrifice, charity, and austerity*
prescribed in the scriptures are always commenced
by uttering 'Oṁ' by the knowers of the supreme being.

17.25 *Various types of sacrifice, charity, and austerity are performed*
by the seekers of liberation by uttering 'Tat' (or He is all)
without seeking a reward.

17.26 *The word 'Sat' is used in the sense of Reality and goodness.*
The word 'Sat' is also used for an auspicious act, O Pārtha
(Arjuna).

17.27 *Authenticity in sacrifice, charity, and austerity*
is also called 'Sat'. Selfless enriching
for the sake of the Supreme is, in truth, termed as 'Sat'.

17.28 *Whatever is done without authenticity, whether it is sacrifice,*
charity, austerity, or any other act is called 'Asat'.
It has no value here or hereafter, O Pārtha (Arjuna).

In conclusion, Kṛṣṇa moves on to a different plane altogether.

So far He explained the distinctions between sacrifice, austerity and charity—*yajñas tapas tathā dānaṁ teṣāṁ bhedam imaṁ śṛṇu* (17.7). He clarified what needs to be done and how. He spelled out the different modes based on the nature of people in relation to performing sacrifice, austerity and charity.

Please understand that all kinds of food, penance, sacrifice or charity fall into the basic three categories explained by Kṛṣṇa—*sātvic, rājasic* and *tāmasic.* These translate as the modes of goodness, passion and ignorance. But the important thing is that as long as they are done in the materialistic world, they are conditioned. When they are done from the space of completion with the attitude of gratitude to the Divine and Existence, only then you encounter spiritual progress or spiritual elevation. Our scriptures explain that anything done in the nature of *rajas* or *tamas* cannot give the ultimate result. Only the act done from the space of *satva* or goodness gives the final result. One who does such acts without this awareness has temporary results but not the final result.

In the days of Mahābhārat, sacrificial rituals were a part and parcel of daily life. This is not the case today. The *brāhmaṇas* (highly learned sect of people) were the keepers of the sacred knowledge that connected the physical ritual with the metaphysical truth expressed by the great sages in the *Vedas*. They were the keepers of the flame, in a real sense, since most *vedic* rituals invoked and addressed the fire energy.

Sacrifices or *yajña* were directed towards enriching the elemental energies and celestial beings. Austerity or *tapas* was directed towards enriching your own self. Charity or *dāna* was directed towards enriching those around you.

The brāhmaṇas were expected to lead an austere and charitable life in keeping with the spirit of their profession. In this chapter Kṛṣṇa elaborates on these concepts so that everyone can move forward on the path to completion or liberation. It is not only for the *brāhmaṇas,* it is also for *kṣatriyas, vaiśyas* and *śūdras*—the other castes. Any member of any caste is qualified for completion if he follows these principles. Completion has nothing to do with birth.

The prime requirement is authenticity, *śraddha*. Śraddha refers as well to the understanding that the enriching act of sacrifice, austerity or charity, *yajña, tapas or dāna* is not directed towards oneself or a material goal. They are directed to the enrichment of Supreme consciousness.

Commit to complete with yourself and others. When I say 'others', I don't mean only the friends and family and relatives who are present in your life. Complete with your *kula devatā (*family deity), complete with your *kula guru* (family guru), complete with your house, complete with the plants with which you are living, complete with your pet, complete with the different energies of the Cosmos, complete with everything! Continuously complete and continuously enrich others!

The real scale and measure of your completion is whether you are able to move the others' space and enrich others and life continuously. If you are not enriching constantly, be very clear, the completion has not yet happened in you.

I tell you, when completion happened in me, I just realized the authentic selflessness, *śraddha.* All our selflessness is also packed in our selfishness. All our selflessness is packed in our selfishness. When I completed, I discovered the authentic selflessness and enriching which never tires me. If you are getting tired, please be very clear, still you have incompletions in you. You have to complete! You have to complete!

Listen! This is the scale—having a tireless mind. The being happened in me is just because my enriching is out of pure selflessness. I tell you, once you complete, you will suddenly realize, 'Why should I live now?'—'For enriching! Nothing else...Nothing else!' Complete! Complete! Complete!

In the last three verses Kṛṣṇa provides the technique to achieve this space of completion that expresses as the space of enriching, the shift of space from self to *Self*. He provides the method by which anyone can surrender the results of his activities, the fruits of his action called *karma phala* to the Divine. He provides the tool in the form of the invocation, *Oṁ Tat Sat.*

oṁ tat sad iti nirdeśo brahmaṇas tri-vidhaḥ smṛtaḥ |
brāhmaṇās tena vedās ca yajñāś ca vihitāḥ purā || 17.23

The three words 'Oṁ Tat Sat 'are the words of the Divine.

- '*Oṁ iti etat brahmano nedisthaṁ namaḥ*', shows the first goal, the beginning.
- '*Tat tvam asi*' indicates the second goal, the continuation.
- '*Sat eva saumya*' is the third goal or final result.

All three combined give the words: *Oṁ Tat Sat.*

This is why these words have such great importance or significance. Any person doing enriching or working with the space of addressing *Oṁ Tat Sat* will be with Existence, the Divine consciousness.

These three words simply imply: 'I offer all to that Truth. I surrender everything to that Divine. Let that be the Truth.' This is the *Mahā-vākya*, the great truth, handed down by the Master to Arjuna as the technique to ensure *śraddha*, authenticity in all activities of sacrifice, austerity and charity.

Please understand that any action, whether penance, charity or sacrifice, has no meaning when the purpose is not to achieve the Ultimate, the Divine.

The final aim in all the *Vedas* is to gain the experience of Kṛṣṇa or the supreme consciousness. No success, completion, fulfillment or happiness is possible without following this principle.

The Guru or spiritual Master is the only being who can enrich you and guide you into the space of completion to make your life successful and fulfilled.

Understand, people are conditioned to worship all kinds of deities or demi-gods or spirits right from birth. This is simply because their nature is from one of the three *guṇas*. Among the three *guṇas*, *satva guṇa* is considered the best and higher than the other *guṇas*, namely *rajas* and *tamas*. But the path of achieving the ultimate consciousness, the understanding of Kṛṣṇa, goes beyond and transcends all three *guṇas.*

This is where the role of a Guru or a spiritual Master is important. He directs and leads you on the path of complete cognition for an experience of the ultimate consciousness. Such an understanding, such a perception, leads to faith and ultimately to love for the Divine. This is the purpose and final goal of life.

Let us all pray to *Parabrahma* Kṛṣṇa with all authenticity to give us the experience of this chapter of the *Gītā* that leads to attainment of the ultimate consciousness, *Nityānanda*!

Let us all experience *Śraddha*, the authenticity and imbibe and experience the truths of *Parabrahma* Kṛṣṇa.

Let us pray to Him to give us all the authenticity and experience of the truth that He is teaching through the *Gītā,* to all of us, and let Him make us experience and establish ourselves in Eternal Bliss, *Nityānanda*!

Thus ends the seventeenth chapter named ***Śraddhatraya Vibhāga Yogaḥ****, 'The Yoga of Discerning the Three-Fold Faith,' of the* ***Bhagavad Gītā Upaniṣad, Brahmavidyā Yogaśāstra****, the scripture of yoga dealing with the science of the Absolute in the form of* ***Śrī Kṛṣṇārjuna saṃvād****, dialogue between Śrī Kṛṣṇa and Arjuna.*

CHAPTER

18

Mokṣa Sannyāsa Yogaḥ

Drop Everything And Surrender

Do not worry. There is nothing to surrender except the 'I' and 'mine.' Kṛṣṇa reveals the final secret to experience and become Him — 'Drop everything you know as dharma and surrender onto Me. I promise you liberation, mokṣa.'

Drop everything And Surrender

Drop everything and surrender. This is the gist not only of this final chapter of *Bhagavad Gītā*, but it is also the essence of the entire *Bhagavad Gītā*. In addition, throughout the ages it has been the basis of the teachings of all the spiritual Masters.

Kṛṣṇa concludes the *Bhagavad Gītā* with one subject: drop everything and surrender. Beautifully He says:

sarvadharmān parityajya mām ekaṁ śaraṇaṁ vraja |
ahaṁ tvām sarvapāpebhyo mokṣayiṣyāmi mā sucaḥ || 18.65

Drop everything, whatever you know as *dharma*, whatever you know as life, whatever you think you know, just drop it. Drop everything and surrender. Whatever you know is only your knowledge, it is just what *you* know. It is not what *is*.

Knowledge does not prove Existence

In fact, wisdom and truth are about what we do not know. That is all! What we know cannot lead us to the ultimate Truth. Knowledge of the mind, that we take so much pride in, functions like blinkers that we wear to shut out the truth of Existence. The mind is not the scale of measure of Existence. What we are has nothing to do with our thoughts. What we are is beyond our thoughts. If our thoughts alone could define what we are, we would be nothing more than a biomechanical machine.

Humans think. That is the problem. Our great Sages, the ancient *Ṛṣis* declare, 'Drop your mind and you will be complete. You will realize your true potential as a human.'

Ādī Śaṅkarācārya, one of the greatest Masters and Hindu philosophers, proclaims this so beautifully in the verses of his *Ātma*

Ṣaṭakam. To define what He truly is, Śaṅkara negates his body, mind, senses, emotions and all his relationships. By negating all this, he declares his inner divinity boldly and beautifully.

Understand, we are spiritual beings in human form, and not human beings striving to be spiritual. Our potential is infinite. Our intelligence is unlimited. But our intellect is limited.

When we started the *Bhagavad Gītā* series, we learned what *śāstras, stotras* and *sūtras* are. *Śāstra* is knowledge of the intellect. It is acquired by reading and understanding. *Stotra* is knowledge acquired through learning, through the heart, that is through devotion. *Sūtra* is learning through the being, that is through meditative techniques that cut to the core of what is essential.

Even knowledge about God creates bondage when it is merely intellectual because we will only know about God. That is all! We will not know God. Please understand this. Knowing *about* God is not the same as *knowing* God. When we completely surrender everything, we will not even have the idea that we know God. When that idea does not exist in us, we know God. Otherwise we may know about God but we do not know exactly what the Divine is.

Words do not express God. No expressions can lead to the experience of God. God is when expressions cease. Masters say that the finger pointing to the moon is not the moon. It is only a pointer, a reminder. Words about God in any form, however sincere they may be, are mere pointers and reminders. The problem with religions is that they teach us *about* God. They do not teach us how to know God. Religions tell us a few things about God and instill fear and greed in us.

No spiritual Master preached violence. If he did, he would be no master! Great spiritual Masters and Incarnations happen with the mission to raise us to a super conscious state. They aim to cause our Inner Awakening, awakening the individual consciousness, so that we realize that we are one with the collective consciousness of this Universe. They come with a mission to make us understand that we must move from the space of 'I' to 'you' and 'us.' Unlike spirituality that spreads love among people, religion fosters violence.

Understand: Enlightenment is a gift. It makes no difference what effort we put in. We may have stood on one leg for hundreds of years. We may have fasted for thousands of years. We may have practiced meditation or yoga or some other technique. These are equivalent to buying the one-dollar lottery ticket. Anything we put in is comparable to that one-dollar lottery ticket. What we receive in return is a pure gift. Whatever we do is within the dream. How can that get us something beyond the dream?

Śrī Kṛṣṇa says, 'Drop everything and surrender—*sarvadharmān parityajya mām ekaṁ śaraṇaṁ vraja*.' First let us understand the word 'surrender'. The word itself frightens people. We must understand that we are not going to lose anything when we surrender. We are only going to gain everything. However, for lack of a better word, we must use this word.

Surrender and Understand

Realize first of all that we have nothing of any value to surrender! We only think we have something to surrender. The truth is that we have nothing to surrender. We simply need to open our eyes and see that everything that *is,* is divine. It is Existence. Whatever we think is ours does not exist! The 'I' and 'mine' that we hold onto are mere lies. The moment we understand this, we surrender. The moment we surrender, we understand.

When we call something 'mine', legally it may belong to us, but existentially, it does not. Legally we can fence off a piece of land and call it ours. Legally we can own things. But Nature or Existence does not know that it is ours. When a cyclone hits, it does not care whose property it is. It does not know the law! It does not know that legally a cyclone is not allowed on someone's property! For Existence there is no law.

Your idea of 'mine' is protected by the laws of society. You cannot truly use the term 'law of the land.' The land has no laws. Only society has laws. The land can have an earthquake at any time. We cannot have laws to govern Nature. The law of the land is beyond your comprehension. As long as you are caught with the concept of 'I' and 'mine', you will not understand the truth about Existence. You are caught in thinking that something is 'you' and something is 'yours'.

When Kṛṣṇa tells us to drop everything and surrender, He asks us to open our eyes and see the foolishness of the drama we play with our possessions and expectations. Listen! It is one thing if you play the game to cheat others; but, do not cheat yourself.

Please understand, there is no 'I', there is no 'mine.' The person who is intelligent and willing to open his eyes and see reality, will sooner or later wake up to the truth that there is no 'I' or 'mine'. Can whatever you think of as 'I,' either your body or mind, function without air? Can you say that the air belongs to you? This basic energy, *prāṇa*, which goes in and comes out, does not belong to you. If *prāṇa* stops happening, what you think of as 'you' disappears.

It is like saying that the foundation does not belong to me, but the first floor of the house is mine! You can do that legally. But it is impossible existentially. In the same way, the building may belong to you, but the earth that it sits on does not belong to you. The earth can give one small shake, and whatever you thought was yours just disappears!

The very foundation of whatever you think is 'you' does not belong to you. It belongs to the Whole. It belongs to Existence. It belongs to the Universe. It belongs to Nature with whom you are continuously fighting. The base or root of what you think of as 'you' does not belong to you.

We take for granted the air that continuously goes in and comes out. We believe that the air belongs to us. There is no break in this natural supply. Maybe if God called a strike, like a workers' union strike, we would understand that we cannot take even the air for granted. Suppose He called a strike for a minute, then we would understand that it did not belong to us. But He is a *Karuṇāmūrti*, god of mercy. Out of His compassion, He never goes on strike! That is why we take life for granted. Just because certain things belong to us legally, we think that the concept 'mine' is solid. The truth is that both the 'I' and 'mine' have no base.

Anybody who is intelligent enough to open his eyes and see, realizes that 'I' and 'mine' are a drama. The moment the air that goes in does not come out, it is over. 'I' disappears. Immediately your name will be taken from the nameboard outside your house and put on your tombstone. You will be called a dead body! You will be taken to the place where you can rest forever! Your house and car will be useless. So, whatever we think is 'I' and 'mine' is baseless.

Sometimes even the piece of land that we think belongs to us we may find doesn't, when we see the papers of that land! Our life itself is built on paper. The moment we have the intelligence to see this, the moment we wake up to this reality, we achieve the state of surrender. The moment we understand that in Existence nothing called 'I' or 'mine' exists, we immediately experience tremendous relief from the need to continuously protect ourselves.

These two instincts of holding onto 'I' and 'mine' are the reason for physical and mental problems. The instinct to survive and the instinct to possess are the root cause of our problems. On the other hand, when we realize that the 'I' and 'mine' do not exist, we realize how we have cheated ourselves and how foolish we have been in spending our whole life and energy in building sandcastles. The whole thing is pure fun! We must understand that whatever way we live and whatever we may build, does not belong to us. If we do not internalize the outer incidents and if we treat them with the indifference they deserve, we experience what I call surrender.

There is only one thing to remember: Do not internalize sensory inputs and do not take things too seriously. When you take life too seriously, you can be sure of one thing, and that is sickness. All seriousness is a form of sickness. When you think the 'I' or 'mine' is the truth, you create trouble for yourself. The moment you believe that there is an 'I' in your being, you start moving away from life.

The idea that you have of yourself has no base, whatever you may think of as you. Sometimes you think you are the body. Sometimes you think you are the mind. And other times, you think you are the senses. No matter what you identify yourself with, it is baseless.

Please listen. There is another critical aspect to understand in this regard. Whatever aspect you think of as 'you' will not grow. If you think you are the body, you stop the growth of the body because you do not like change. When you think you are the mind, you stop the growth of the mind. You stop the inputs to the mind.

That is the reason egoistic people cannot listen to new ideas or read about them. They cannot learn because learning is against their vested interests. They think that they already know and have nothing more to learn. When you think that your mind is you, the very attitude of learning, the beginner's mind, is lost. Wherever you cling, you destroy that.

If you think you are the body, you do not let the body rejuvenate itself. You do not let your body do its regular work. If you think you are the mind, you do not let it learn anything new. You do not allow anything new to enter. That is a sure way of destroying it. The same applies to what you consider as 'mine'. This is based on the laws of society. In no way is it related to the laws of Existence.

You are not who you think you are

It is well known to science that of the trillions of cells in our body-mind system, millions of cells die each day and millions of cells are reborn. After a few years, there isn't a single cell in our body which existed two years earlier. Every single entity in the body is new. This means that there is really no constant 'I' as we imagine. Yet, we carry that label proudly.

All we are is a bunch of memories, root patterns, collectively known as *saṁskāras*. Our root patterns define us. Our root patterns rule us and make decisions for us. That is what this 'I' is all about. When we complete with our root thought patterns and give up our possessions and attachment to possessions, we feel liberation. When I walked out of my home for spiritual wandering, I felt no loss. Today, the whole world is my home! This does not mean that all of you need to become monks, renunciates and Sannyāsis. You can happily continue your normal life, but drop your attachments, fantasies, speculations, greed and fear about the past or the future.

So, you need not renounce what you already have. All you need to do to achieve the space of completion is to renounce what you *do not* have.

Renunciation does not mean sitting cross-legged with a tense look and eyes closed. If Enlightenment could happen by shutting off our senses, it would be easy. We would just need to sit in soundproof rooms and wear blindfolds. Renunciation, *tyāga* is a state of mind and not a mere state of the body. It is even more than a state of mind; it is a space of being. We can renounce attachments to relationships and possessions while being involved in material life. On the other hand, we could take Sannyāsa, go to the distant Himalayas, and every time we close our eyes, our inner television would switch on.

The surrender that Kṛṣṇa talks about involves completing and dropping fantasies of the future, incompletions of the past, and surrendering to the reality of the present. The true reality, the only truth is that we are part of the universal energy. We are part of the collective consciousness. When we have this awareness, there is no room for the individual 'I' and 'mine' to rule our actions.

Throughout *Bhagavad Gītā*, Kṛṣṇa talks about renunciation. Śrī Rāmakṛṣṇa Paramahamsa said that the Gītā is nothing but '*Tā Gī*', meaning *tyāga*, or renunciation. Śrī Rāmakṛṣṇa said, 'Keep repeating '*Tā Gī*' and you will understand '*Gī Tā*.'

Again and again Kṛṣṇa speaks about renunciation: How we should surrender the fruits of action to Him, without renouncing the action itself, and how all knowledge and action should be surrendered at His feet. He prepares Arjuna for this final moment when He tells him that all that needs to be done is surrender. That is all.

Surrender is of three kinds. The first step is the surrender of the intellect. For most people, especially intellectuals, this is the easiest. Your ego must be ripe before it can fall. The more stuff you pack into your thick skull, the more bloated it becomes. You become intoxicated with your own knowledge. You become intellectually arrogant. You are then ripe for surrender. When someone appears on the scene and proves that intellectual knowledge is a pile of garbage, a person with a truly ripe intellectual ego understands and accepts the truth. Only those with half-baked knowledge who pretend to have intellectual status have a problem in understanding such a truth. A true intellectual can understand that all acquired knowledge is a mirage, an illusion.

When this happens, such a person surrenders his intellect to the Master who shows him the way. Many intellectual seekers and spiritual shoppers come to me with loads of questions. After spending time with me, most of them tell me with great surprise that they no longer have questions. I don't take the trouble to answer their questions. No one can answer such questions. All I do is add more words to them. They struggle with the new words and ultimately find the right answers themselves!

When I do answer, I answer the questioner. I address the person, not his question. I look into his being and provide the solution.

The next step in surrender is the surrender of the heart. People ask how they will remember me when they go away from the ashram. I tell them that if I am their Master, they will have trouble forgetting me! Remembering me is not an issue, forgetting me is.

The thought of the Master will melt your heart. You will become emotional. You do not need to be in the Master's physical presence. The mere thought is enough. Tears will flow from your eyes. This is a powerful form of surrender. Rāmakṛṣṇa says, 'Know this for sure: When the mere thought of your *iṣṭadevatā* (favorite deity) or your Master reduces you to tears, you are in your final *janma*, your final birth.'

What an Enlightened Master says is always true. So powerful is this surrender that it can liberate you, complete you, enlighten you. This is the power of devotion, *bhakti*. Kṛṣṇa keeps repeating that this is the easiest way to reach Him. Do not worry about learning scriptures or performing rituals. Do not worry about techniques. He says, 'Just be devoted to Me and Me alone, and I shall save you.'

The third and final form of surrender is the surrender of the senses. When the surrender of senses happens, Enlightenment happens, and when Enlightenment happens, the surrender of the senses happens.

> Walking with Arjuna after the Mahābhārat war, Kṛṣṇa points to a bird on a tree and remarks, 'Arjuna, look at that green crow!'
>
> Arjuna responds, 'Yes, Kṛṣṇa, I see the green crow.'
>
> Kṛṣṇa says, 'What a fool you are! How can a crow be green?'
>
> Arjuna simply says, 'Kṛṣṇa, when you told me to look at that green crow, what I saw was indeed a green crow.'

Such was the state of Arjuna's surrender to his Master, whatever He said was what Arjuna's eyes saw. This is the final state of surrender.

The master-disciple relationship is the most mysterious phenomenon in Existence. It is not intellectually comprehensible. It cannot be proved in a logical way. Those who become Sannyāsis out of a logical conviction by listening to Masters and becoming convinced that what the Masters say is true, are only on the periphery. The true disciple has nothing to do with what the Master is saying; the true disciple has something to do with what the Master IS.

The true disciple rises in love. It is not a question of conviction. It is something more mysterious and transcendental. Hence, a real disciple cannot explain to anybody what has happened. Everybody will think that he has gone mad, that he has been hypnotized and that he is no longer in control of his senses.

People who think like that are not to blame. Certain things are beyond explanation. They elude rationalization. And in fact, life begins when you come in contact with something incomprehensible, inexplicable, indefinable and unprovable; yet somewhere deep down, your heart says it is so. It is falling totally in love, and it is a love of an entirely new quality.

This love is not limited to the Master but it is experienced towards the entire world. You no longer think in terms of 'I,' but in terms of 'you'. This is compassion. This feeling of unconditional, uncalled for and uncontrollable love is compassion. This happens when your ego surrenders.

It may surprise you that an enlightened Master has no freedom to do what he wishes. His surrender to the cosmic energy is so total that every move he makes is dictated by that energy. Ordinary people have the freedom to do what they wish. All this talk about destiny has no meaning. Each of you has full freedom to do what you wish. After doing what you want and suffering, you claim it was because of your destiny! Whatever you do is within your power. In contrast, I have no power to move on my own. Every word I utter is at the command of Parāśakti, the Cosmic energy.

Śrī Kṛṣṇa's message to enrich Arjuna and to all seekers is to be complete, drop everything and surrender unto Him—*mām ekaṁ śaraṇaṁ vraja* (18.65). That is the only and final solution.

The Act And The Actor

18.1 *Arjuna says,*
'O mighty armed Kṛṣṇa, I wish to understand
what is the essence, tattva of renunciation, tyāga and
the renounced order of life, sannyāsa, and the difference
between the two, O Hriśikeṣa, O Killer of the demon Keśī.'

Arjuna speaks now after being silent for a long time. He will stop speaking soon. He has just a few words. He is not questioning. He just expresses a few doubts. The arrogance or violence in Arjuna's being has disappeared. He has become like a flower due to the experience of the cosmic vision that Kṛṣṇa showered on him. I cannot even call these words doubts. He just wants to hear the truth from Kṛṣṇa again and again.

Sometimes after listening to the whole discourse, disciples ask me to repeat a joke or a story once more! They have heard it once but want to hear it again. Especially from the master, listening to certain things again and again gives great joy. The words of a Master are energy. These words drill deep into you and transform you. At the time of listening, you may not realize their impact. But they never fail to impact and enrich you. Arjuna asks some of these questions to listen to Kṛṣṇa again.

arjuna ūvāca
sannyāsasyā mahā-bāho tattvam icchāmi veditum |
tyāgasya ca hṛṣīkeśa pṛthak keśi-niṣūdana || 18.1

Arjuna says, 'O Mighty One, I wish to understand the purpose of renunciation and of the monastic life of Sannyāsa. O Hriśikesa (another name of Kṛṣṇa, one who is in complete control of His senses), please tell me the truth.'

As I told you, it is not that Arjuna does not know. He has just heard the whole thing. Still, he wants to listen to it once more. Sometimes we enjoy listening to the same thing over and over. It is not that we do not understand, but it gives us great joy to listen to the same thing again and again! Like that, Arjuna wants to listen to the same truth again and again.

Arjuna wants to know why a person would want to sacrifice everything and what is the process of renunciation.

In India it is often difficult to distinguish a renunciate, a Sannyāsi, from a common beggar. Both seek alms. Both possess very little. And both are homeless. Many people take the easy path and treat the Sannyāsi like a beggar and shoo him off.

I tell my disciples, 'When in doubt treat the beggar as if he were a monk. If you have money to give, what harm is there if you give it to enrich another person?' Some people tell me, 'But *Swamiji*, they are cheating us!' So what? Get cheated, that's all. When you give, give out of completion, give unconditionally or don't give at all. When you give out of completion, not expecting anything in return, what difference does it make whether you give to a monk or a beggar. If you expect that a monk will bless you if you give and that the blessing will have effect, why can't the blessing of a beggar have the same effect? And how do you know that a person wearing a monk's garb is truly leading a monk's life?

So, giving alms to a Sannyāsi is like taking out insurance. You expect that your merits are getting noted down in a Cosmic record to decide whether you go to hell or heaven.

Make it simple. Give out of your completion. Give unconditionally if you can afford it. Give even if you cannot afford it. That is when giving becomes truly enriching. When you sacrifice what you cannot afford to sacrifice, by the mere act of giving, you become a renunciate, a Sannyāsi. How noble it is!

Arjuna is confused about the act and the actor. What is important is the act. Anyone can be the actor.

Never Give Up Selfless Enriching

18.2 *Bhagavān Kṛṣṇa says,*
the renouncing of all selfish work based on desire, is what the
learned ones call as sannyāsa, the renounced order of life.
And renunciatig the attachment to fruit or result of one's actions
is what the wise ones call as tyāga, renunciation.

18.3 *Some learned men say that all kinds of result-based activities*
are faulty and should be given up, but there are yet other sages
who maintain that acts of enriching sacrifice [yajña],
charity [dāna] and austerity [tapaḥ] should never be given up.

18.4 *Arjuna, best of Bhāratas, now listen from Me certainly*
about renunciation or tyāga; O tiger among men,
renunciation or tyāga is declared to be of three kinds.

18.5 *Acts of enriching sacrifice [tyāga], charity [dāna]*
and austerity [tapaḥ] are not to be given up;
they should be performed. Indeed, even the Sages
are purified by enriching sacrifice, charity and penance.

18.6 *O Pārtha (Arjuna), all these activities must also be performed*
without any attachment or any expectation of fruit or result.
They should be done as an act of responsibility.
That is My final and ultimate opinion.

Kṛṣṇa replies: 'Bhārata, now hear my judgment about renunciation. Renunciation is of many types. Let me explain the truth.'

And then Bhagavān starts.

Bhagavān says that some learned masters say that giving up activities based on material desires is renunciation, *tyāga*. Others say that giving up the results is renunciation. Hence some say that giving up activity is renunciation whereas others say that it is giving up the results.

No other master is as compassionate as Kṛṣṇa. He is the ultimate Master. He does not merely teach. He knows it is difficult for people to believe. It takes time to believe. So He gives logic to support His teachings. Again and again, He tries His best to convince Arjuna. Considering the level that He is at, there is no need for Him to come down to the level of Arjuna. He can say, 'This is the truth. If you want you can follow it, otherwise get out!' But He does not do that. He is compassionate. Again and again, He comes down and explains the truths step-by-step.

Some learned people recommend ritualistic actions, such as killing an animal for a sacrifice. Other learned people denounce that act. Thus there are different opinions regarding the same action by different Sages. Kṛṣṇa clarifies these opinions now.

ENRICHING SACRIFICE IS THE PATH OF COMPLETION

After all, it is Śrī Kṛṣṇa in the form of the Ultimate who originally created the scriptures and laws. Therefore any explanation from Him should be considered the last word. He says that any process of renunciation should be considered within the context in which it is performed. Renunciation can be of three types: enriching sacrifice, charity and penance; *yajña, dāna, tapaḥ*. These purify even those who are already evolved and pure.

It must be understood that the purpose of performing *yajña*, enriching sacrifices is the purification or upliftment or completion of the human being on the spiritual path. They link cosmic energy with individual energy.

Kṛṣṇa says that any sacrifice done for the welfare or enrichment of humanity is not to be given up. As enriching sacrifices, *yajñas* are meant to achieve the supreme, performing charity, *dāna* is recommended to purify one's heart and put one on the path of spiritual progress. Sacrifice is normally understood to be rituals such as *yajña* and *homa*, etc. These are the fire rituals prescribed in *Vedic* literatures to propitiate the deities. When carried out with integrity and authenticity, these powerful techniques link us to the Cosmic energy.

Here you must understand that Kṛṣṇa talks about the reality of what existed more than five thousand years ago when these rituals were performed with awareness, integrity and authenticity. In performing an *aśwamedha yajña*, a powerful king let loose his prize horse to roam as it pleased in enemy territory and waged war with anyone who dared stop the horse. All the land that the horse covered became his vassal territory and those kings accepted the sovereignty of the owner of the horse.

This is what we know from the epics Mahābhārat and Rāmāyaṇa that detail these sacrifices. The *Upaniṣads* talk about the metaphorical significance of these rituals. In the scriptures, reference is made to the inner *aśwamedha yajña*, meditating upon the sun that is identified with *aśwamedha*.

In our times, sacrifice refers to any selfless enriching service that enriches others and enriches you. Whatever enriching we do for others out of completion, without expecting anything in return is a sacrifice, an enriching sacrifice or *yajña*. Unfortunately, many people engaged in sacrifice are more interested in seeing their pictures on the television or in newspapers than in the service.

Charitable enriching, *dāna* is giving out of overflowing completion with no expectation in return. Charity is not giving while posing for a picture that will be published in tomorrow's newspaper. That is business. Those who are truly charitable never allow others to know what they are doing. That is why it is said that your left hand should not know what your right hand is giving. Only then charity achieves its authentic purpose of enriching others.

Charity should also involve pain. You can call it charity when you cannot afford to give something away and yet you give it away. Charity must become a penance, *tapaḥ* and lead to austerity if it is to be real.

Penance, *tapaḥ* is denying oneself sense pleasures and being complete with the senses. Ultimately, the purpose of all spiritual exercise is to be complete with the mind, body and senses and thereby controlling the mind and senses. Penance, *tapaḥ* is turning inwards whereas sacrifice, *yajña* and charity, *dāna* are focused outwards.

'All these enriching activities should be performed without attachment or expectation of results. They should be performed as a matter of responsibility, and this is My final opinion,' says the Master.

Only by enriching others does your life get enriched. Don't be selfish. Understand, responsibility is the fruit. Enriching is sowing the seed for the fruit to happen. Enriching is sharing the fruit to create more fruits. Every person who eats the fruit is responsible for sowing the seed for more fruits to happen.

Kṛṣṇa gives His ultimate opinion. Earlier He explained what others said about renunciation, as either giving up the activity itself or the results of the activity. Now He says that His opinion on renunciation is living without attachment, *etāny api tu karmāṇi saṅgaṁ tyaktvā phalāni ca* (18.6).

This must be understood in depth. Listen! Whether it is spiritual or worldly activity, as long as you struggle with a purpose and a goal, you can never relax. Whether it is the act of purifying your inner space by doing self-completion or purifying your outer space by enriching others, as long as you struggle, you will be in incompletion. Please be very clear about this. The person who surrenders to the flow of life, experiences the inner space and outer space at the same time. He enjoys the inner and the outer space at the same time. Whatever Kṛṣṇa has spoken in these seventeen chapters, He is now giving its gist.

SURRENDER BOTH INNER AND OUTER SPACE

Let me explain what I mean by the word surrender. Then you can understand better. Think of two intersecting lines, axes.

The vertical axis is spiritual life. The horizontal axis is

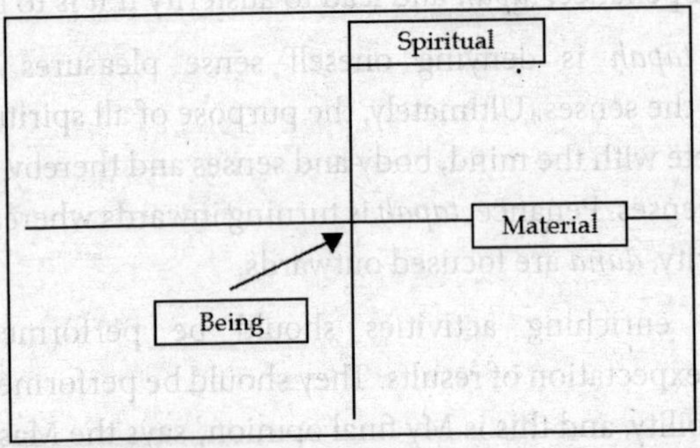

material life. The point of intersection is your being. This is the goal you have. You have some goal in your material life and also in your spiritual life. To achieve your goal in your material life, you are continuously struggling and working. You are somewhere on the horizontal axis. To achieve your spiritual goal, you are again working intensely doing *yoga, prāṇāyāma, pratyāhāra*, etc. You practice spiritual techniques. You are somewhere on the vertical axis. So when you struggle with material goals, you are on the horizontal line whereas when you struggle with spiritual goals, you are on the vertical line.

As long as you are struggling, you can struggle either in this direction or that direction. As long as you struggle in material life, you avoid spiritual life. As long as you struggle in spiritual life, you avoid material life. Listen! As long as you struggle with completion, you don't enrich. As long as you struggle with enriching, you are not complete! Both are a struggle.

Kṛṣṇa says, 'Relax from both.' You may think, 'What is this funny instruction He is giving!' You think that if you relax in both you will lose both. However, the truth is that when you relax in both, you fall into your inner consciousness, your being or your inner space. When you experience this inner space, this inner consciousness, you will suddenly realize that you can explode in all directions. You do not need to choose between horizontal and vertical lines. You can travel on both lines at the same time!

Not only that, you can explode in all directions. The only difficulty is that you must surrender at least to your own being. You do not need to surrender to somebody else. To whom you surrender is unimportant. Just relax into your own being. Just relax into your inner space, into your inner consciousness. Just surrender to your own inner space. Stop your struggle in the material world and the spiritual world.

In the material world or my world, the world of 'mine', your properties are your goal. You struggle to achieve these goals, such as enriching with wealth, career, success, etc. In the spiritual world also you have certain goals, such as Enlightenment, living in the space of completion, being integrated and authentic, etc. And you constantly run to attain that goal. Actually, spiritual goals create more ego than material goals. At least with material goals, at some point, you realize that you cannot achieve real happiness by running behind them. It can be tiring. But with spiritual goals you do not even understand what you are doing. Both goals take your being away from your being. When you surrender and relax into your being, you suddenly realize you are neither the body nor the mind, to choose between the horizontal and the vertical lines.

As long as you believe you are the mind, you will be forced to choose between the vertical and horizontal lines. You will be in a dilemma because the mind wants to choose. The mind and dilemma are the same thing. The mind ceases to exist once dilemmas vanish. The mind exists as long as you have dilemma. As long as you have confusion, the mind exists. Has your mind existed without dilemmas? No, never! You may be in a dilemma even to answer this question; that is all! The mind continues to exist only in dilemma. You continuously worry about whether to choose this or that.

Whenever you choose something, someday you will definitely wonder and your mind will create self-doubt about the choice you made. The mind only exists because of dilemma. As long as you are based in your mind, you will be choosing between material and spiritual goals. The people who choose material goals will feel that they are missing spiritual life. And those who pick spiritual goals will feel they are missing material life. This is because you choose between the two.

For the first time, Kṛṣṇa gives the ultimate technique for Quantum Spirituality. He is the first quantum scientist of the inner world. He says relax and surrender and you will experience the completion of your inner consciousness. You will understand that you do not need to choose between the horizontal and vertical lines. You can explode in all 360 degrees. You need not make a choice. You experience choicelessness. Choicelessness does not mean that you do not choose anything. When you stop choosing, you will choose everything.

Listen! I am asked by my disciples, 'Should we not become completely complete from our root patterns and only then enrich others? Should we choose to do one?'

Please listen! Enriching and completion, both should be practiced simultaneously. Listen! With more and more completion, more and more enriching will happen. With more and more enriching, completion will happen. Actually, when you complete with somebody, you already started enriching that person. You can explode in all 360 degrees with completion and enriching, both!

Enriching starts happening with completion. Without enriching, completion cannot happen. Without completion, enriching cannot happen. When we stop choosing, both start together, one supports the other. You cannot say, 'First I will operate my heart; and then once the heart starts functioning completely, then I will start operating the lungs.' No! Lungs are completion. Heart is enriching. Both have to happen simultaneously. Lungs remove the carbon dioxide—incompletions from your system, and infuse oxygen—completion into your system. Heart circulates that whole oxygen into your blood and enriches your whole body. You cannot separate enriching and completion. If you are not enriching, please be very clear, completion is not happening. You are only fantasizing about completion. When you stop choosing between completion and enriching, your completion will be so powerful that you will simply enrich!

Similarly, surrender does not mean passive surrender or pretending, fantasizing to give up. Many people claim, '*Swamiji*, I have surrendered everything to God.' It is mere lip service only. It is not reality.

People come up with odd statements. They tell me, '*Swamiji*, I have given up everything, I have surrendered everything to God. Bless me so that I get a better paying job!' We sometimes make statements without knowing what the reality is.

A small story:

> A journalist saw a crowd gathered around an accident on the road. He tried to find out what had happened, but could not get through the crowd.
>
> He shouted, 'Oh! My son has been hurt in the accident. Please move out of the way.' The people gave way. He moved forward, only to see that a car had hit a donkey!

Before making any statement, look in, know your thoughts and words, know the situation. Bring integrity and authenticity! Otherwise, you will suffer! With the word surrender you make that mistake.

With real surrender you do not exclude anything. You include everything. You experience everything at once. You do not need to choose between horizontal and vertical lines. You can experience both and something more. You can explode! You experience something beyond your imagination. You experience different dimensions of your being.

Again, when I say surrender, you do not need to surrender to any God or Guru. God or Guru are symbols or representations. Just surrender to your own being, to your own consciousness, to your own inner space. The problem is you do not respect your inner space. That is why in the initial level you need an entity called God or Guru.

Duty Without Delusion

18.7 *Prescribed duties should never be renounced. If one gives up his prescribed duties through the illusion of renunciation [tyāga], this is said to be in the state of ignorance or tamas.*

18.8 *Anyone who gives up prescribed duties as troublesome, or out of fear of bodily discomfort, his renunciation [tyāga] is said to be in state of aggression [rajas], Such action never leads to gaining the fruit of renunciation.*

18.9 *But he who performs what is prescribed, as a matter of responsibility, without expectation or attachment to the results, his renunciation [tyāga] is said to be in the nature of satva, goodness, O Arjuna.*

18.10 *One who neither hate disagreeable work nor is attached to pleasant work, is in a state of intelligence, goodness and renunciation, having cut-off all doubts.*

18.11 *Embodied beings cannot give up all activities. Therefore, the one who has renounced the fruits of action is called the tyāgī, one who has truly renounced.*

18.12 *For one who has not renounced, the three kinds of fruits of action, desirable, undesirable and mixed, accrue after death, but those who are in renounced order of life, sannyāsa, have no such result to suffer or to enjoy.*

Kṛṣṇa says that *nitya karma* or obligatory responsibilities must be followed with discipline and consistency. Not doing these takes us into the state of tamas, inaction born out of ignorance and laziness.

Nitya karmas vary from person to person. The duties of a householder are different from those of a monk or a student. Each has clear guidelines in terms of what they should and should not do.

Many times the idea of dropping our responsibilities and taking up a different role is more attractive than growing in completion so that we can perform our own responsibilities well and without attachment. Be very clear, without the right cognition of completion, no role that we take up will work out for us.

Instead of taking up responsibility and expanding you and your life around you, watching television, sleeping or daydreaming seems much more pleasant and easy. We would rather do that than meditate or perform pūjā or whatever is our prescribed duty.

Please listen! I am talking something very important and very mystical! It takes just four days for your muscle-memory to taste laziness, boredom and tiredness and settle down with it! I tell you, never ever take vacation for four days continuously in your life. The very frequency in which you function is reduced. Because, in four days, your muscle-memory gets settled with tiredness, boredom and laziness! Even if you are without job for four days, be active in something. Go and meet your friends, family. Take up some voluntary service. Do not be without responsibility for four days.

You may ask, 'Why four days?' Listen! It takes four days for anything to become part of your muscle-memory. For four days in the morning, if you don't come for yoga, don't come for satsang, fifth-sixth day your muscle-memory will start proposing alternatives to you at that time. What are the alternatives? Sleeping, rolling on the bed, TV, so many things are there.

FEEL RESPONSIBLE IN YOUR BEING

One of the biggest diseases that people suffer physically is unable to be active, having incompletions with being active. Giving up the responsibility for what needs to be done because it is uncomfortable is not renunciation! That is convenient inaction born out of *rajas*.

Please listen! I am defining Sannyāsa.

When you don't take responsibility for anything, you live as slave, śūdra. When you take the responsibility for the money of the society, you become vaiśya. When you take the responsibility for weapon of the society, you become kṣatriya.When you take the responsibility for knowledge of the society, you become brāhmaṇa. When you take responsibility for everything, you become Sannyāsi.

Only when you take responsibility, life happens to your body. If you have any disease, take responsibility for it; so that you can heal and then take care that you don't attract that disease again back.

In the same way, if you have broken a relationship because of your irresponsibility, unconsciousness, now take the responsibility that next time you don't do it. Life does not end by breaking one relationship. You don't need to be depressed or you don't need to start being in that same space of powerlessness. When you take the responsibility you can even patch up with the relationship you broke. You can approach the person and rebuild the relationship.

Listen. One of the biggest problem we have is—'let me have the power first, let me have the status first, let me have the position first, then I will take the responsibility.' No! That does not happen in life. Take the responsibility to build the state inside you. Then, after you are tested by the Cosmos, it gives you the status. That status can never be taken away.

I took the responsibility for teaching the science of Enlightenment. I started living, I started building the state, then human society has tested me enough. Now I can simply see many powerful positions are automatically coming towards me. Listen, I am not going in search of them. Responsibility attracts more responsibility. The problem is we are afraid of more responsibility, so we deny even the responsibility that we have in our hand. But more and more responsibility adds more and more life energy into you.

Understand, because Siddharth took the responsibility and he became Buddha, the whole of Buddhism is built on responsibility and enriching. Integrity leads to authenticity. Responsibility leads to enriching. Take responsibility for everything happening around you. Buddha did not make that man old. Buddha did not make that man diseased. Buddha did not kill that man. But he took the responsibility for that state of affairs! He did not say, 'Oh! I don't know why he became sick. I don't know why he became old. I didn't kill him.' Had he thought in that manner, Siddharth would have been Siddharth; Buddha would never have happened! Fortunately, he thought that he is responsible for it. He cognized His responsibility. Siddharth became Buddha when He applied the truth that the science of life is responsibility!

After attending a course many ask how many meditation techniques they can do each day. I tell them, 'Do at least one properly.' A week later, after the fervor has cooled down, if I ask, they sheepishly say, 'I do not have time to practice even one meditation, *Swamiji*.' All of us find time for everything except meditation. We find time to give appointments to everyone else except ourselves! Who is the loser?

Kṛṣṇa says that doing what needs to be done because that is what is our responsibility, without attachment to the action and without desire is the ideal condition of *satva*.

Kṛṣṇa has said this many times in the *Gītā*. He repeats it again so that the message sinks in our muscle-memory and bio-memory. Do what must be done. Do what your responsibility is, based on your societal or religious beliefs and codes. However, do it with integrity and authenticity without attachment and expectation of results.

The consciousness of 'I' and 'mine', in terms of the performance of the activity should be absent. The consciousness of 'feeling responsible in your being' should be present. Restricting your being in feeling responsible is what I call conditioning. Responsibility in your being means the space from which you cognize, from where you make decisions, carrying responsibility in that zone.

Please listen! If you don't feel you are responsible for something, you don't even think in that line. If you feel you are responsible for something, only then will you even look into that part of your life. When you feel responsible in your being, for any problem, or anything, you find solution for that problem or that situation.

You don't need to do any action, you don't need to do any thinking. Decide from your being that you will feel responsible for the whole world. You will take actions towards your immediate responsibility as per your prescribed duty , but you will feel responsible for the whole.

Suddenly, you will see all your actions will have authenticity, your thinking will have integrity! Mainly, whatever you are doing, if you take responsibility for the world, even if you are a doctor, you will become a better doctor. If you are a lawyer, you will become a better lawyer. If you are an engineer, you will become a better engineer, If you are a politician, you will become a better politician.

If you are a doctor, know that you are responsible for the whole world. So you are responsible for your patients also! With this context when you start functioning, even you attending to your patients will become a spiritual practice leading you to enlightenment, because in any context you do any action, that context will become your bio-memory and reality.

If you are a cook and you are cooking with the responsibility that only if you cook you will have money, and with that money only you can take care of your needs and your family, then you may be a good family man, you may be a head of family, you may be a good cook, nothing more than that! But, if you do the same job with the cognition of 'I will enrich the world with the food! I am responsible for the whole world. So this cooking and enriching the world is the immediate action I will do, but I am responsible for the whole world.'

I tell you, just with this shift in your cognition, you will be a *karma yogi*; because innumerable right things will be added to your thinking, to your being, to your action and to your life.

It is the amount of responsibility you bring into your being that makes your life juicy. I tell you, if you bring more responsibility into your cognition, your life becomes exciting! Understand, if your cognition shrinks, you also shrink, your actions shrink, your integrity shrinks. If your cognition expands with more responsibility, authenticity happens in your action, integrity happens in your thinking and your words.

Kṛṣṇa says that a person in the *sātvic* space of completion, calmness and awareness is undisturbed by external conditions. He is not bothered whether someone appreciates or condemns what he does. He just feels responsibility in his being. He is clear what he should do and he carries on with excitement.

Renunciation is in the true spirit of completion and is done out of goodness, only when a person renounces the expectation of result.

It is natural that a human being cannot remain still without doing some work. Man must be doing something, anything, all the time. If not physically, at least mentally he does something. Even in sleep, he dreams. If we close our eyes, we watch our inner television. Mentally we think the whole day, but it is not directed in one direction, we are not useful to ourselves and to others. Please understand, when you lack integrity, when you have incompletions mentally, even if you think, it will not be useful thinking.

Only an Enlightened person truly keeps his body and mind still. So the normal man is never without activity. This being the case, the only way man can be comfortable and at peace with himself is by not having any expectation of the result of his thoughts or words or actions. This can be achieved by every one of us. Kṛṣṇa says that one who is not concerned about the fruits of his action has truly renounced.

Attachment to action and to the results of action creates more desires. Even when an action has been completed and the expected result achieved, as long as one is attached to that action and its result, another desire crops up. Even when one desire is fulfilled, another unfulfilled desire rises. This is a constant, consistent sequence of incompletions. This is what I call *karma*.

Karma is nothing but unfulfilled, incomplete desires. As long as we have attachment to the action as 'doer', which in turns creates an expectation of reward or punishment, we are caught in the cycle of *karma* and *saṁsāra*. Our concern about whether an action or the result is good, bad or a mix of both, follows us as our mental patterns or *vāsanā* after death.

Please understand that no one is 'up there' keeping an account of our deeds and misdeeds. Our own spirit does that job. So we can never escape! No amount of propitiation or contribution to 'noble' causes will erase the knowledge from our inner Self of what we have done. When we die, the body perishes but the spirit moves on to another body. That spirit carries its earlier mental patterns, its *vāsanā.* There is no exception to this rule. Saṁskāras or root patterns are the carried-over incomplete desires and they cause the cycle of saṁsāra, birth, death and rebirth.

However, we have no unfulfilled desires, *karma*, *saṁskāra* or *vāsanā* left when we renounce attachment to 'doership' and become a mere witness to both the action and the result. This means we act without expectation and attachment to the result of our action. Such a person breaks out of this cycle of *saṁsāra*.

Technology Of Surrender

18.13,14 *Learn from Me Arjuna, there are five causes that bring*
about the accomplishment of all action, as described in Sāṅkhya
philosophy. These are: physical body that is the seat of action,
the attributes of nature or guṇa that are the Doer, the eleven
organs of perceptions [illegible] action by the life forces and
finally the Divine.

18.15 *These five factors are responsible for whatever right or wrong*
actions a man performs by deed, word and thought.

18.16 *Therefore, one who thinks himself, his body and spirit,*
as the only doer [kartā], is certainly ignorant and
foolishly does not see things as they are.

In these verses, Kṛṣṇa gives the exact technology of surrender. These two verses can be called techniques.

Kṛṣṇa lists five factors from *Sāṅkhya* philosophy responsible for our activities. These are the body-mind system, the operator of the body-mind system (that is the individual), the senses, different efforts causing the activities and finally the ultimate power of God. All activities, right or wrong, good or bad, are caused by these five factors. If however, the individual considers himself to be the doer, his body and mind, he is not aware.

Kṛṣṇa uses the word *ātman* while saying that one who perceives one's spirit or Self as the agent, the doer, or the performer, does not see and is not aware. Kṛṣṇa draws a distinction between the individual Self and the cosmic energy. He differentiates between ātman and Brahman, mānava and Deva, nara and Nārāyaṇa, self and Parāśakti.

Kṛṣṇa concludes that while philosophical discussion mentions five players in all activities, the ultimate controller is the Divine. We are immersed in our body-mind-spirit system and caught in our sensory perceptions and believe that we are the power behind all that we do. So long as we have this deluded belief, we are rooted in ignorance.

Whatever you may understand as yourself, your body-mind-spirit system is the totality of many things. And individually each is responsible for something. In spite of this, you think that 'you' are responsible for the whole thing. That is where the trouble starts. Kṛṣṇa gives the technology for the deeper levels of surrender.

As we saw earlier, there are three levels of surrender. The first is intellectual surrender. This means you accept that the Master's intellect is sharper than your intellect; His intellect is of a higher order than yours. This is intellectual surrender. Next is emotional surrender. This is trusting that the Master's guidance on the emotional plane is more intelligent than your emotions. The third is surrendering the senses, your cognition or the root of cognition itself.

Surrendering the intellect is easy because it continuously tortures you. You have suffered with the intellect for many years. You want to get rid of it. So you surrender it. When you see somebody more intelligent and with clearer thinking, you just surrender. For example, when you hire a consultant, you surrender to his ideas. When you take on a lawyer, you surrender to his ideas because you know his intellect is sharper than yours in that field. In the spiritual field also, when you see a person who knows more, you surrender your intellect to that person. That is not a big thing. Surrendering intellectually happens easily. Most of the time you want to get rid of your intellect. Finding somebody to dump your intellect on allows you to relax from it.

Next comes emotional surrender. This happens when you feel deeply connected to the Master after experiencing some meditation or understanding. You respect his emotions more than your own. The Master's emotions mean the things he guides you in, the way he wants you to live. You give more importance to these things than what you think of as life. Slowly he becomes the center of your life. You respect him more than other emotional attachments. Priorities shift. The Master becomes the number one priority at the emotional level. Emotional surrender is when you feel totally connected at the emotional level.

DEEPER LEVEL OF SURRENDER—MIND OR MASTER?

Next is a deeper level of surrender.

After listening to these seventeen days of discourses, you can understand this deeper level of surrender. This is the level of the senses. The surrender of the senses means that your senses listen to what he says. Normally, when you listen to me, a filter in your mind discounts what you do not agree with. You hear what you want to hear. However, when intellectual and emotional surrender happen, you are ready to surrender this disbelief and unblock your senses.

> Once a disciple asked his Master, 'Why should I surrender?'
>
> The Master asked, 'How do you know whatever you think you know about yourself?'
>
> The disciple replied, 'I know myself through my senses.'
>
> The Master asked, 'Who do you think you are according to your senses?'
>
> The disciple said, 'As far as I know, I am the body and mind.'
>
> His Master responded, 'You are God, not just body and mind.'
>
> The Master said, 'Only when you surrender your senses, will you realize the truth of what I am saying. The moment you trust me more than your senses, you experience that you are God. You then understand the meaning of *Tat Tvam Asi* (literally 'You Are That', meaning 'you are divine').'

The Master again and again tries to show that you are God. I keep saying, 'I am not here to prove that I am God. I am here to prove that you are God.'

The Master stands for the idea that you are the infinite. He shows you various dimensions of your inner self that you have not explored or experienced. He shows you so many dimensions of your being. The Master stands for your multi-dimensional being. He tries to show you that it is possible. He shows that if it is possible for him, it is possible for you also. But as long as you believe your senses, you think that you are the body and mind.

When you trust the Master more than your senses, you understand that the Master's words are the truth and not your senses. Then you experience the truth of the Master's words. When the Master says you are God, you suddenly realize the truth for yourself. You understand that you are God. You realize that you are not the body or mind as your senses have led you to believe. When you believe the Master's words more than your senses, you experience this truth.

Two voices are speaking from two different levels. On the one hand, your senses tell you that you are the body and mind. On the other hand, the Master tells you that you are God; you are divine and have many dimensions to your being. He tells you to enjoy and experience everything. As long as you listen to your senses, you will not even listen to what the Master says. When you move away from your senses and come to the Master, you listen to Him and experience the truth that you are Divine.

Final Surrender Itself is Enlightenment

In the inner world, the first and last tool you need is complete surrender. Only then can you wake up to the Truth. If Arjuna had trusted only his senses, he would have been at best a good warrior and king. Instead he trusted Kṛṣṇa more than his senses and became enlightened. He experienced the truth of Kṛṣṇa. When Kṛṣṇa said that the crow was green, he saw a green crow. Such was his faith.

You can experience Kṛṣṇa consciousness not just by surrendering the intellect and emotions but also by surrendering the root of the intellect and emotions, that is the senses. The senses supply the data. When you surrender them, the source of the data is surrendered.

When you surrender your senses, the root cognition of yourself, you lose your identification with the body and mind. As long as you believe your senses, you think that you are the body and mind. Only when you believe the Master's words more than your senses, do you realize the truth that you are divine. On one hand, your senses say you are the body and mind. On the other hand, the Master tells you that you are divine and in eternal bliss. He tells you that you are the consciousness beyond body and mind.

It is up to you to choose. If you believe the senses, you cannot believe the Master. And if you believe the Master, you cannot believe your senses. Your way of life decides whether you surrender to your senses or your Master. It is for you to decide.

Kṛṣṇa says that only when you surrender at all three levels do you have the ultimate experience. Let me tell you this, surrender itself is Enlightenment. Please do not think Enlightenment will be issued to you after surrendering. No! It is not a paycheck you receive by courier. Surrender itself is Enlightenment. At that moment, you experience the Truth.

Usually we play with words. At least be aware of the moments when you play with words. People tell me that they have surrendered their life to Kṛṣṇa, Venkateśvara or Śiva. Then they say that their only wish is to be happy. If they have truly surrendered, surrender is enough. They will not need to ask for anything else. Sometimes people ask if they need to meditate since they have surrendered to God. If they have surrendered, they will have no doubts, nor will they need meditation! If they have doubts, they need meditation. As long as doubts remain, surrender has not happened, because the moment you surrender, *you* disappear.

A beautiful verse in Tamil says, 'When you give your 'I' and 'mine' to Existence, Parāśakti or Existence gives Her 'I' and 'Mine' to you.' Both bank accounts merge and become one. It becomes a joint account! You have nothing to lose.

When you think of yourself as body and mind, you have *śariram rogamayam* and *manam sohamayam*. *Śariram rogamayam* means that the body is filled with diseases. *Manam sohamayam* means that the mind is filled with sorrows or depression. Since that is the case, what can we surrender? Absolutely nothing, except a body full of diseases and a mind full of sorrows. When you drop these two at the feet of the Divine, He gives you His body and mind! And it becomes, *śariram devamayam, manam sukhamayam, atma anandamayam*—meaning, you get in exchange a Divine body, a mind in happiness as well as a third thing: a Soul in bliss! A 'give one, get three free' offer!

> Manickavasagar, the great Enlightened Master, sings a beautiful Tamil song to Śaṅkara (Lord Śiva): *tandadu entanai, kondadu untanai, sankara yaarkolo saturar*? He says, 'I gave myself to You and received You in return. Who benefited most from this bargain? Who is more intelligent, O Śaṅkara?'

In surrender, you have nothing to lose and everything to gain. Surrendering does not mean giving up everything. It does not mean giving up your property. Keep everything; however, take care that you do not internalize them. Do not judge yourself based on your properties. You are far greater than you think. Do not judge yourself based on your bank balance. Do not judge yourself based on your relationships. Do not judge yourself based on name and fame. Do not judge yourself based on your friends. You are greater than all these things put together.

As long as you judge yourself based on these things, you internalize these into your being. These become the central points in your life. They push and pull you in all directions. You will not have yourself for your being. As long as these are the major factors in your life, these things will rule you. Even so, you are greater than all these things put together.

Understand that you are something beyond these things. The moment you wake up to this truth, you will not allow yourself to be put into any frame based upon bank balance, relationships, attitudes or name and fame. These things cannot be used to judge you. The moment you wake up to this truth, you have surrendered. I simply ask you to surrender these small ideas you have about yourself.

On the surface of the vast ocean, small bubbles are formed. One bubble starts thinking that it is an individual long lasting entity. It thinks that it must become strong. It lasts only for a few moments. Yet within those few moments, it collects other bubbles around it. One bubble is its wife, another bubble is its son and so on. Some are called parents or relatives, still others are friends, and so on. It collects bubbles on all sides to protect itself.

It collects a few grains of sand from the beach and thinks it is its property. It thinks one grain of sand is its bank balance, another is its jewelry and treasures and so on. Then it builds a fence to protect its property. How long can the bubble play this game? Only for a few seconds! Before it can complete its game, it disappears back into the ocean.

The bubble was part of the ocean in all three instances: when it was created, when it existed and when it disappeared. Even though it claimed to be different from the ocean, even though it thought it was an individual, and even though it thought many people and things belonged to it, it was always part of the ocean and very soon disappeared into it also!

In the same way, for a few moments you think you exist as an individual being in this universal consciousness. Within those few moments you catch hold of a few people as your relatives and friends. This makes you feel safe. You collect a few things as possessions. You feel secure with these things around you. With these things you form an opinion about yourself. You play the same game as the bubble.

Waking up to the Truth is Surrender

Suddenly the whole thing disappears. Before the game started, while the game is going on and when the game ends, whether you understand it or not, realize it or not, experience it or not, you belong to the ocean. You are God. You are one with Existence.

You are playing a game. You register your marriage to another bubble. You register some grains of sand as your property. The registrar is another bubble! A larger bubble is the ruler of the land or that bit of the ocean! And there is an understanding among the bubbles, 'You will not hit me and I will not hit you! You will not take my bubble and I will not take yours!' The whole game goes on in this way. Suddenly within one moment the whole thing is part of the ocean again.

When I say surrender, I mean wake up to the truth that you are in the ocean. When you are born, when you think you are an individual or when you become enlightened, you are always in the ocean. Just wake up! Waking up to this ultimate Truth is surrender. Surrender these small ideas about yourself and wake up to reality. As a result, surrender automatically happens in your inner space, your inner Consciousness. Otherwise you just play with the word surrender.

We use inflated words when we define ourselves. We do not realize that we are beyond these descriptions. One day a follower used exaggerated words about himself in front of me. After he left I told my disciple that he seemed to be suffering from an inferiority complex. My disciple was perplexed. He asked how it could be called an inferiority complex when he boasted so much. I told him, 'Understand, each of us is God. Hence anything we say about ourselves that is lesser than that, is an inferiority complex!'

Any estimation you have of yourself except that *you are God* is an underestimation! You suffer from an inferiority complex if you think of yourself as anything other than God. Drop your ideas about yourself. Wake up to the Truth that you are the ocean.

Some fish swim along with the current and others swim against the current. Whether they go with or against the current, all the fish are in the water. Whether you flow with Existence or fight it, you are one with it. Whether or not you have realized you are Divine, *you* are Divine. There is no choice in this. There is only one choice, realize and enjoy or continue to struggle and suffer; that's all! You may try to create stronger fences around yourself or collect more bubbles around you, but can you ask the wave not to come? Whatever you may do, the whole thing is only a drama of a few seconds.

The next problem is what to do if you cannot surrender. Some people tell me, '*Swamiji*, I am unable to surrender. What can I do?'

Do not worry, because you have nothing to surrender. By understanding that you have nothing to surrender, you have already surrendered. Just relax. Whether you surrender or not, this is the truth. Whether you surrender or not, Existence takes care. Automatically life continues and you will relax. That relaxation itself is surrender.

Relax into the flow of life and wake up to the truth that you are something greater than your body and mind as suggested by your senses. You are led by society to think that you are something. Now wake up to the truth that you are greater than what you can imagine. You are beyond any imagination you can have of yourself. Surrendering will give you a new consciousness. You will not be the same person. One single moment of surrender will transform your whole life. You will be a new being.

Receive this truth of surrender and work on it. Suddenly you will wake up and give birth to yourself as an enlightened being. The moment you understand you belong to the ocean, that you are from it, that you are in it and that you will disappear into it, you will realize that you will never die, because you are the ocean.

As long as you identify with the bubble, you feel insecure. The instinct to survive and the instinct to possess torture you. The moment you realize that you are the ocean, the instinct to survive disappears because there is no death for you. There is nothing to fear, nothing to feel insecure about. Death creates fear as long as you think you are the bubble.

The moment you realize that you are the ocean, there is nothing to possess because everything belongs to you. There is nothing to lose and nothing to acquire. Hence, the instinct to possess disappears. I am not asking you to legally throw away your possessions. You do not need to throw away whatever you have done for your 'I' and 'mine'. You do not need to throw away whatever you have. Just do not internalize them. Within yourself be aware and be complete that you are something greater than anything you can possibly possess.

At the age of seven, your toys are important to you. Do they hold the same importance today? You have neither renounced them nor are you attached to them. They are just there. Do you feel that you must return home because the toys are there? No! Do you feel the toys make your life a torture and that you must renounce them? No! You feel neither attached nor detached. You have grown beyond them.

Rāga means attachment. *Arāga* means detachment. *Virāga* (or *vairāgya*) means beyond attachment and detachment. As you grew up, *vairāgya* naturally happened towards your toys. So also, when you realize that you are the ocean, *vairāgya* will happen towards the few sand particles and bubbles that you have collected and gathered around yourself. You will have gone beyond these things.

The instincts to survive and possess would no longer be relevant to you. Your property does not suddenly disappear. They are there, but you live them and enjoy them more intensely. You do not take them for granted. You do not feel bored with them. You do not think: same house, same wife and same life! You take them for granted only when you think they are your properties.

When you realize that they may be taken from you at any moment, you do not take them for granted. When you realize that you are the ocean and that they are also of the same ocean, you value them more. When you realize this, you are transformed at the level of body, mind and consciousness. When consciousness is transformed, you give birth to a new you.

Kṛṣṇa goes much deeper than these three levels of surrender: surrender of the intellect, surrender of the emotions and surrender of the senses. He gives Arjuna a glimpse of the greatest surrender. He gives Arjuna a glimpse of the ultimate experience itself. Kṛṣṇa already gave Arjuna the experience during *Viśvarūpa darśan*, the vision of His Cosmic form. Even so, Arjuna was unable to establish himself in that experience due to fear.

Always you miss the first experience because of fear. Now Arjuna is more mature and capable of being established in the experience. Kṛṣṇa gives Arjuna the experience that will stay with him forever. In the next few verses Kṛṣṇa puts Arjuna into the experience of Enlightenment. He wakes him up to the ultimate Truth.

Kṛṣṇa is waking Arjuna up from the long slumber called *saṁsāra sāgara*. This can also be called unconsciousness or *tamas*. Kṛṣṇa gives him a good shake by giving him the ultimate experience and puts him in that state forever. I was telling you about the three levels of surrender. Kṛṣṇa puts Arjuna into that final level or highest level of surrender.

Extreme Statement

18.17 *One who is egoless, whose intelligence is not of attachment, though he may kill, is not the slayer and is never bound by his actions.*

A very dangerous statement! Kṛṣṇa goes to the extreme.

No master except Kṛṣṇa can make such a courageous statement. Kṛṣṇa makes a bold statement here. One who is not motivated by ego, whose intelligence is not based on attachment, though he may kill many men in this world, he does not kill, nor is he bound by his actions.

Of course, one who has reached that level of completion does not think of killing. As long as we have the idea of 'I' and 'mine', we attack or kill. When we exclude, we kill. On the other hand, when we surrender, we learn to include everything.

One thing we need to understand. We kill others only when we feel insecure. We do not need courage to make war. We only need cowardice. Only cowards go to war. They are afraid for themselves and kill others. To kill others, we do not need courage. We simply need cowardice. The person who is courageous never kills others. He is established in non-violence. Only cowards continuously try to hurt others. A courageous person does not try to hurt others. That is the reason Kṛṣṇa makes this bold statement—one who is not entangled in ego, even if he kills, does not kill.

Kṛṣṇa emphasizes here: May you be liberated from entanglement. May you liberate yourself from ego, *yasya nāhaṅkṛto bhāvo*. He does not ask Arjuna to kill. One problem is that people give their own meaning to words. They have their own delusive cognition.

A small story:

> Once there was a little boy in a Zen monastery training to be a monk. One day, when he was cleaning his master's room he accidentally broke his master's favorite teacup. He wanted to confess to his master about the teacup, but was scared that he would punish him.
>
> He approached the Master and asked him, 'Master, isn't it true that everything that was born has to die someday?'
>
> The master replied, 'Yes.'
>
> The boy then showed him the fragments of the broken cup and said, 'It was time for your teacup to die.'

Do not give your own meaning to what Kṛṣṇa has said! He is asking you to be liberated from ego. He is asking you to be complete with your root patterns. The person who has realized that he is part of a whole will not kill even if he kills. Grasp the proper meaning of this. Kṛṣṇa asks you to experience the truth about yourself. He does not ask you to kill people. Recognize the correct meaning. Kṛṣṇa inspires you to realize the truth of your natural space of completion, not to kill.

Understand, only if you start living completion, you will understand the quality of life. I tell you, when there is incompletion, your life is stolen away from you! When the completion happens in you, you regain your life!

Kṛṣṇa asks you to complete yourself from your delusory cognition of ego. He does not ask you to go around killing people. Understand the truth behind the words. Only a Master like Kṛṣṇa can make such a courageous statement.

Kṛṣṇa uses killing as an extreme example to make Arjuna think. The focus is on non-attachment arising out of egolessness, which is the space of completion. You need to know, completion done to be in the space of completion transforms your personality, transforms your being, heals the intense, constant, agitāted violence you carry towards you and others.

When one no longer feels the need to survive, anything that one does is without attachment and without expectation. When a person is in that state, he is truly in completion with Existence. If such a person destroys, it is similar to the destruction caused by Nature, which happens at a different frequency and understanding level as I explained earlier.

Kṛṣṇa makes this statement to drive the point home to Arjuna that it is his responsibility to stand up and fight instead of running away from the battlefield.

Components Of Action

18.18 *Knowledge, the object of the knowledge and the subject of the knowledge, the knower, are the three factors that stimulate action; the senses, the action and the performer comprise the three components of action.*

18.19 *According to the science of guṇa or attributes in Sāṅkhya, there are three types in knowledge, action, and performers of action. Now Listen as I describe them.*

18.20 *That knowledge by which the one imperishable reality is seen in all Existence, undivided in the divided, you should undrestand to be the knowledge in the state of goodness.*

18.21 *The knowledge by which one sees different realities of various types among all beings as separate from one another, such knowledge is in the mode of aggression.*

18.22 *The irrational, baseless, and worthless knowledge by which one clings to one single effect as if it is everything; such knowledge is in the mode of darkness or ignorance.*

18.23 *Obligatory duty performed without likes and dislikes and without selfish motives and attachment to the fruit, is in the mode of goodness.*

18.24 *Action performed with ego, with selfish motives, and with too much effort, is in the mode of aggression.*

18.25 *Action that is undertaken because of delusion, disregarding consequences, loss, injury to others, as well as one's own ability, is in the mode of ignorance.*

18.26 *The performer who is free from attachment, non-egoistic, endowed with resolve and enthusiasm, and unperturbed in success or failure is called good.*

18.27 *The performer who is impassioned, who desires the fruits of work, who is greedy, violent, impure, and affected by joy and sorrow, is called aggressive.*

18.28 *The performer who is indisciplined, vulgar, stubborn, wicked, malicious, lazy, depressed, and procrastinating is called ignorant.*

In these verses Kṛṣṇa explains the nature of man, the human.

Kṛṣṇa has already said that the final performer is not man, *nara*, but the Divine, *Nārāyaṇa*. Even so the human is still the subject, the medium that we are dealing with. All the frailties that we have are inherent in our nature. These are the guṇas or attributes that define our behavior. These attributes control our thoughts, words and actions. One is not all the time, from birth to death, in one *guṇa* or attribute.

The *guṇas* are of three kinds: *satva*, *rajas* and *tamas. Satva* is defined as calm, peaceful, spiritual and good, etc. This is generally the attribute of spiritually inclined persons. *Rajas* is translated as aggressive, passionate and active, etc. This is the primary attribute of kings, warriors and business people. *Tamas* is lazy, ignorant and passive, etc. Tamas is seen as the inactive component that many of us experience at times. It is the active component of those who live to eat and sleep.

In these verses Kṛṣṇa beautifully defines in detail the qualities and effects of these guṇas upon us. His purpose in doing this is to make us aware of what happens within us. Majority of the time we are ignorant of 'why' we react the way we do. As the Master explains in these words, and once we understand and cognize how we react, we can move to the next level of completion and shift to a superior attribute. If we find our own answer for the 'why' we will become spiritually enlightened!

Yes, all of us must be *rājasic* or aggressive, part of the time to accomplish things. Even so, if we can act aggressively without greed, anger or fear affecting us, as well as acting without attachment, we are in the *sātvic* space, although superficially we seem to be in the *rājasic* space.

Swami Vivekananda says beautifully, 'First of all, the beaten and broken consciousness which has fallen into *tamas,* inertia, let it come to the awakening state of *rajas,* activism. Then it can be guided into *sātvic,* spiritual balance.'

Kṛṣṇa defines a *sātvic* person as one who sees the collective consciousness, the whole, in parts. He understands that he is not alone and not an island, rather he is linked with everyone and everything in this Universe. He understands his connection with the cosmic energy.

A satvic person is not focused on himself, he is focused on enriching others. Because he completes with his root patterns, He realizes that his survival and possessions, the 'I' and 'mine', are meaningless. His activities are selfless, without expectation of praise or reward, and without attachment to the process or result. Such a person is not affected by the seeming success or failure of what he undertakes because there is no feeling of 'I' and 'mine' involved in his actions.

It is not that difficult to move into a *sātvic* state. True, you may not be able to stay there all the time, but once you understand how this state completes you, you try more and more to stay there.

To be in the *sātvic* state is to understand that past and future are mere illusions. They do not exist. Past is gone, never to return. Why worry? Future is a mirage. All you can do is activate your present moment. That is all you can do. The present moment determines your future. Once you focus on the present, your space of completion increases manifold and you drop expectations and attachment. You just do what is needed. You respond to reality. You respond to the now. You are in *satva.*

You fall into a *rājasic* state when you distinguish between 'you' and 'I', between this and that. There is no differentiation. Your mind, the ego, creates this differentiation. Your root thought patterns, saṁskāras overpower your complete cognition and bring up this delusory cognition of differentiating between you and others. A *rājasic* person does everything expecting a reward. He is selfish, aggressive and impatient. When he does not get what he wants, he is upset. Failure is a blow to his ego.

A *rājasic* person can never be happy and complete. Please understand, almost all of you are driven by *rajas*. This is the predominant attribute in modern society. Rich or poor, intelligent or foolish, educated or uneducated, almost everyone compares himself with the next person and wants what the other person has. As long as you are driven by your desires, and not complete with what you have, you are in *rajas*.

Too much of society has entered into human beings. You all have become social beings, you are no more human beings. You just have a set of manuals – at what age what is expected of you, at what age what are you supposed to do, and where are you supposed to be, how are you supposed to be talking, what are you supposed to be thinking, how are you supposed to be behaving. See, by default society is incomplete. So you are put in that *rājasic* space. Only if you are conscious, you can attract the space of completion.

Please listen! The pure space, *satva* seems to be a little heavy, little too much of joy! You feel you can't afford it. It is like you don't want to own the whole ocean, you want to own only the beach. Because only in the beach you can put a fence and ensure that others can't enter into it. Ocean you can own, but not possess. Please understand, owning is different and possessing is different.

All of us can own the whole world; that is not a problem at all. But we can't possess it, that is where the problem starts. Owning is different and possessing is different. The whole village owns the village temple, but you possess your house. We not only own our house, we possess it and make sure that others don't enter. We don't want to own the ocean, we want to possess the ocean. When we want to possess, we know that we can't possess the ocean. Not only we can't deny entry to other human beings, we can't deny entry to other animals. There are millions of animals below.

When we want to possess that is where the problem starts.

Rajas corrodes you. It eats up your soul. There is no boundary to possessing, no end to greed and no limit to fear. These are the driving forces of *rajas. Rajas* is about trying to attain what you don't have, trying to eliminate and possess what you want to have, not being complete with what you have, not being complete about where you are and not being complete and happy when you are in the present moment. You are either constantly in the future, imagining what you would like to be and what you would like to possess, or you are in the past thinking about how you could have done better. *Rajas* is living in a fantasy world of possessing. *Satva* is living in a reality world of owning and also letting others own.

Listen! If you want to own, you can own the whole world. See, unfortunately, only if you eliminate others, you feel that you are victorious, which is not right. This is a basic wrong understanding. Please get it! I want you to know a very important fact. Never, ever will you be free by your efforts to be free. Freedom will happen to you only by the right knowledge about freedom, never by your efforts towards freedom. Listen! Never your effort towards freedom is going to give you freedom. It is only the knowledge about the freedom that will give you freedom. Get it!

So, the basic mistake that eliminating others is the only way you can possess or own is wrong! To own, you don't need to eliminate others. But because of this pattern, just because you want to eliminate others, you are ready to settle down with a few acres of beach. You are ready to forego the whole ocean! It is exactly with the same patterns, it is only with these patterns you define your identity. Without patterns, it is like you in the ocean.

In *tamas* one is fully in delusion, in the delusory cognition of incompletion. One sticks to root thought patterns, incomplete knowledge or inadequate cognition and conditions without making an effort to verify the answer of the 'why', whether they are right or wrong, appropriate or not, harmful or not. Listen! If one does not find the answer for 'why' and eats somebody else's answer, one can even be made as a religious terrorist. Religious zealots are in *tamas*. There is no difference between them; only their objectives are different. Both are dogmatic, violent and totally selfish. They adopt any means, even criminal, to achieve their objectives.

Tamas does not just mean inactivity, laziness and procrastination. Yes, it is all that; however, it also includes mindless action performed without realizing that one is part of a whole. The ego is so enlarged that it believes it is the whole. It believes nothing else of significance exists; others are of no consequence.

Meanings Of Life

18.29 *Now hear Me explain, fully and separately, the threefold division of intellect and resolve, based on modes of material nature, O Dhanañjaya.*

18.30 *O Arjuna, that intellect is in the mode of goodness that understands the path of work and the path of renunciation, right and wrong action, fear and fearlessness, bondage and liberation.*

18.31 *That intellect is in the mode of passion that cannot distinguish between principles of right conduct and wrongdoing, and right and wrong action, O Pārtha (Arjuna).*

18.32 *That intellect is in the mode of ignorance that accepts unrighteousness as righteousness and thinks everything to be that which it is not, O Arjuna.*

18.33 *Consistent and continuous determination in controlling mind, breath and senses for uniting with the Divine is goodness, Pārtha*

18.34 *Craving for results of action while clinging to goals of proper conduct, pleasure and wealth is the state of passion., Arjuna.*

18.35 *Ignorant resolve that cannot go beyond dreaming, fear, grief, despair and delusion—such is in darkness, Pārtha.*

Here Kṛṣṇa refers to the approach known as defining the *puruṣārtha* or meanings of life.

Dharma, artha, kāma and *mokṣa* are the four *puruṣārtha.* These can be translated as righteousness, wealth, desire or lust and liberation. These are the four-fold meanings of life. I prefer not to call them the purposes of life. There is no purpose to life. Once we fix a purpose to life, it becomes a goalpost and attachments and expectations result.

Life is a path without a destination. Once we assume there is a destination, we hurry. The future becomes a stress-inducing factor. Let us say we travel from New York to Washington. Once we fix Washington as our destination, the next issue is, 'When will we reach there?' From then on, we are constantly tormented by, 'When will we reach there?' It is a different matter that we may have nothing to do in Washington once we arrive, and therefore there is no need to hurry! In the process we do not enjoy the journey. The journey becomes an irritation that we must cross in order to reach our destination.

In life, do not fix a destination. Each journey must be enjoyed being in the space of completion. The path and the journey are what life is. Life is completion. I tell you, have the space of completion for yourself. That will attract all the right experiences. Completion is power! Completion is Life! Enjoy the people you meet, the experiences you have and what you pick up on the way, without being greedy to acquire more. The journey, the path, becomes so enjoyable that whatever destination you reach is the right destination. Completion gets you all the best things of life! Completion is the basic need of life.

People who attach a purpose to life are disturbed. Philosophers who have no other work create false purposes to life. Philosophers exist to confuse people whereas mystics solve problems and provide guidance to awaken intelligence. When we let life lead us, when we let life enrich us, when we take life as it comes, we enjoy every moment. We truly live with completion in the present, like a God. We realize and manifest our potential, possibility and reality! As of now, man is only a possibility. A human being has everything in him to become the ultimate reality, the divine reality.

Puruṣārtha provides four meanings to life:

Dharma is right conduct or virtue. Dharma means the natural law of the cosmos. Buddha preached this as the middle path. It is an independent intelligence. The very DNA structure with which human consciousness is built, the natural law of human life, the dharma are these four principles.

Constantly give life to the four *dharmas* of authenticity, integrity, responsibility and enriching. When you protect *dharma*, it protects you. When you are integrated to it, it is integrated to you. When you are authentic with it, it is authentic with you. When you take responsibility for it, it takes responsibility for you. When you enrich *dharma*, it enriches you. Only then it is possible that your energy is awakened. Only then is your energy awakened.

Artha is the stuff that we pick up on our path and journey, the material things that we need to sustain ourselves.

Kāma is the pleasure of the senses we experience and enjoy on this journey. These are rightful acquisitions and pleasurable experiences. Do not feel disturbed by the need for these. But do not become caught up in them and forget to move on the path with completion and enjoy the journey to the fullest.

Mokṣa or liberation is the ultimate meaning to life. The meaning of human life is you experiencing completion, and working, radiating, showering others also with the same space of completion. This is the culmination of the liberation from expectation, desires, greed and fear, and liberation from attachment to desires. This understanding that experiencing completion with non-attachment and absence of expectation leads to liberation can fill us with bliss.

Here Kṛṣṇa gives the essence of how we should lead our lives to make it meaningful with completion. He says that goodness or *satva* is the state of completion in which there is clarity about right and wrong, and whatever we do with our body, mind and senses is done with a view to liberate ourselves from attachment and desires in order to realize that we are Divine.

Delusion Of Senses

18.36,37 *And now hear from Me, O Arjuna, about three kinds of pleasure. The pleasure that one enjoys from spiritual practice results in cessation of all sorrows.*
The pleasure that appears as poison in the beginning, but is like nectar in the end, comes by the grace of Self-knowledge and is in the mode of goodness.

18.38 *Sensual pleasures that appear as nectar in the beginning, but become poison in the end, are in the mode of passion.*

18.39 *Pleasure that is delusion from beginning to end and born out of sleep, laziness and illusion is said to be of the nature of ignorance.*

18.40 *No one, either here or among the celestials in the higher planetary systems, is free from these three states [triguṇa] of material nature.*

Earlier Kṛṣṇa spoke about the influence of *guṇas* (attributes) on the intellect, that in turn defines the way we act. Now He talks about how we respond as a result of our root patterns.

Kṛṣṇa says that spiritual practice, that is the state of *satva*, is difficult in the beginning, and it is like poison; however, it becomes life-giving nectar in the end.

Sensual pleasures born out of *rajas*, on the other hand, seem like nectar in the beginning but become poisonous. In the *tamasic* state, Kṛṣṇa says, one is deluded as if in sleep, laziness and illusion. Every human is in one state or another. Not merely humans, even the celestials who are supposedly more evolved are in the same mode. No one can escape the effect of the *guṇas*, the attributes of Nature.

How beautifully the Master summarizes how we become deluded by our senses! It is not easy to begin spiritual practice. In the vedic tradition, in the Gurukul schools, from a young age children were brought up in an environment of spirituality. They learned to live in the pure space of completion and control their mind and senses at an early age and to focus upon Self-realization. They understood by the example of their Masters that there was something more pleasurable than sensory pleasures. This gave them courage.

In today's age, this education system is considered impractical. Invading Moghuls and the colonizing British destroyed the *Vedic* culture, especially the *Gurukul* tradition. This was not accidental or incidental. It was a deliberate strategy. British rulers identified the educational system of *Gurukul* as the key to India's tremendous intelligence and targeted its destruction so that they could rule.

What we have today is a mass of literate Indians who are uneducated. The whole country, the whole civilization, the whole spiritual tradition is suffering now just because of not having completion with one another. They are totally unaware that the great tradition of our *Vedic* culture is established on completion. They think rituals are meaningless. We have lost the knowledge of the connection between these rituals and spirituality. Rituals, when carried out meaningfully, are the basis of spirituality.

Please understand, the biggest asset a man can acquire is the space of completion. I am so happy I am getting that wealth for my *Gurukul* kids. The biggest asset for any man, the best thing a human being can have in his life is completion, the space of completion.

We are behind our sensory pleasures now. When we are in the *rājasic* mode, only sensory pleasures of the body matter. In the *tamasic* mode, we don't even know we are in deep ignorance. The sensory organs are powerful. They are our windows to the external world. They are trained to run away from pain and chase pleasure. Bodily pleasure gives mental pleasure and therefore emotional satisfaction. Once we experience the mental pleasure, we constantly rewind and replay that pleasure. Our past drives our future. Attachments and expectations drive our actions.

We try to keep on experiencing pain and pleasure alternately. Either way it is only an illusion. If you lead your life with completion, you won't get caught in the illusions of attachment and expectations driving your actions.

> Kaṭhopaniṣad says, 'The good and the pleasant approach man. The wise examines both and discriminates between them. The wise prefers the good to the pleasant. But the foolish man chooses the pleasant through love of bodily pleasure.'

'If you are given the option of 'right or pleasant', 'right thing, good thing or very pleasant, convenient and happy thing', always choose the 'right thing', not the 'pleasant' one, not the convenient one.' Understand, when you choose the pleasant, your destruction is inevitable.

Your Space of Completion is Kṛṣṇa

Look for the right, not for light. Your whole life is nothing but Mahābhārat.

I tell you, the Kauravas' birth, what is it? One child, Duryodhana is born who is unconscious, dead, aborted. So, that was broken into hundred pieces. This means what? When you are born, you are unconscious and you are broken into hundreds of root-patterns, and all hundred grow as demons. It means that all your root-patterns are growing as demons! When you are tired of being a demon, you also encourage some good qualities in you just for a change. Please understand, there is nobody who is hundred percent demon, because being hundred percent demon makes you feel bored.

Otherwise, why should Rāvaṇa do Śiva Puja? You cannot be hundred percent demon or hundred percent saint till you become enlightened. Till you become an enlightened soul, both sides will be there because you need choice. Life is all about just jumping from one side to another.

Choice! Choice! Choice!

Listen. A few good patterns which you develop in you just as a choice, as an alternative, those few good patterns are the Pāṇḍavas. The space of completion which you have inside you, which cannot be destroyed by any root pattern is Kṛṣṇa.

Once in a while, Kṛṣṇa comes out and says, 'Hey! All you root patterns, you guys are doing wrong things! Don't do it!'

Then, all hundreds of your patterns stand and laugh at Kṛṣṇa, 'Ha, Ha! Can you can stop us? Do what you want!'

Every time, every day, every moment, the struggle between the Pāṇḍavas and the Kauravas goes on. Kṛṣṇa also comes to the scene once in a while. But He comes for such a short time that you forget His Existence. He goes back to Dwārika (the capital city that Kṛṣṇa ruled), He goes back to His space, the space where you push your completion. All of us have the space of completion, but we push it under the ocean like Dwārika. We don't want to interact with that space every day, because that takes away many of our vested interests. Many things which we forcibly imagine as joyful and pleasurable do not look good with the space of completion.

Understand, your whole life is a Mahābhārat. Then, when your weight becomes too much for your own body, when Bhū Devī, the Earth Goddess, is unable to hold the weight, Kṛṣṇa comes and reduces the *bhū bhāra*, the weight of the Earth. It means that when your incompletions become too much even for yourself, Kṛṣṇa comes and destroys all your incompletions.

Kṛṣṇa describes the *tāmasic* person with great insight. He does not use the word poison in describing the state of such a person. A *tāmasic* person is like a drug addict, He says. At least a *rājasic* person enjoys the experience now and suffers later. A *tāmasic* person has no enjoyment. He suffers without knowing that he is suffering. His delusion is so deep. That is why he passes his suffering on to others. That is how ignorant people who rise to become leaders act.

Rightful Conduct, Not To Perfection

18.41 *Brāhmaṇas, kṣatriyas, vaiśyas and sūdras are divided in the work they do based on their nature, Parantapa (Arjuna).*

18.42 *The nature of Brāhmaṇa is characterized by calmness, discipline, austerity, tolerance, honesty, knowledge, wisdom and belief in God.*

18.43 *Kṣatriya are characterized by their qualities of heroism, vigor, firmness, dexterity, and steadfastness in battle, leadership and generosity.*

18.44 *Those who are good at cultivation, cattle rearing and trade are known as Vaiśya. Those who are very good in service are classified as Sūdra.*

18.45 *One can attain the highest perfection [saṁsiddhi] by devotion to one's natural work. Listen to Me how one attains perfection while engaged in one's natural work.*

18.46 *One attains perfection by worshipping the Supreme Being, from whom all beings originate and by whom this entire Universe is pervaded, through performance of one's natural duty for Him.*

18.47 *It is better to engage in one's rightful conduct [svadharma], even though one may not perform it to perfection, than to accept another's conduct and perform it perfectly. Responsibility prescribed according to one's nature is never affected by sinful reactions.*

18.48 *Every work has some defect, just as fire is covered by smoke. One should not give up the work that is born of his own nature, even if such work is full of fault, O Kaunteya (Arjuna).*

Sreyān svadharmo viguṇaḥ paradharmāt svanuṣṭhitāt—says Śrī Kṛṣṇa.

So-called scholars have interpreted this verse in a very inappropriate way compared to the other verses of the Gītā. The uneducated have also used this verse in order to condemn the *Vedic* culture.

First of all, one must understand how the caste system originated, as well as realize how it became corrupted. In the *Vedic* culture, under the *Gurukul* tradition, young children were left in the care of the Master. This is how Arjuna grew up with Aśvattama, Drona's son. No caste was considered inferior or superior to another. No caste was hereditary. The selection and training was scientific and done impartially. It enriched society well since everyone was living and expressing themselves according to their aptitudes, their peak possibility and their unique path towards liberation.

This is why Kṛṣṇa says it is better to do one's assigned work imperfectly rather than do another's work perfectly. It is possible that one can perform elements of another's work well. A *brāhmaṇa*, being a schoar, may excel as a *vaiśya* in commercial calculations; however, he will have neither the heart nor the head to be a businessman. In this *Gurukul* system, along with the Master, the child also was allowed to select his vocation. The child could express its passion and decide.

Over time, this classification of selection and training became corrupted. Those who were *brāhmaṇa* wanted their children to be brāhmaṇa and so on. The *varṇa* or caste system that had originally been a selection and training system in education led to the stratification of society based upon birth.

Before we condemn the caste system, realize that every society has stratification. Wherever equality has been forced on society, it has been a failure. Each person is unique and when similar people form groups, there will be stratification and classification. In *Vedic* India this classification was based upon talents and intelligence. In modern society it is based on money and power. Which is better?

Without the *brāhmaṇa* being the keepers of knowledge, our *Vedic* treasures would have disappeared thousands of years ago. Do you know that there is a group of scholars in Chidambaram, the *dīkśitars* even today, and similarly in other places, who take their traditional job of preserving *Vedic* wisdom so seriously that they will not travel out of their town limits? They have made this sacrifice for generations and for thousands of years so that this knowledge could be preserved for posterity. We make fun of them, revile them and denounce the system.

The people who denounce the system do it for power and money, not for any selfless reasons. They recommend no alternative means of preserving traditional knowledge.

I am not a *brāhmaṇa*. *Brāhmaṇas* have come to me and hinted at their discomfort at being termed *brāhmaṇas*. They are well-educated people. I tell them, 'Be proud of your culture, your tradition. Without *brāhmaṇas*, the *vedic* tradition would have died long ago.' This praise is for those *brāhmaṇas* who have remained true to their scholarship. Those who have succumbed to the lure of wealth have no right to be called *brāhmaṇas*.

This is where the *varṇa* system has failed. From a scientific and efficient work system, it has deteriorated into a power broking system. We need to fix that. Those who are true to their tradition are poor and disrespected. Only those who use their scholarly skills to become *kṣatriyas* and *vaiśyas* have gained power, money and respect. It is better they continue to be where they are respected and happy!

The problem with society and the societal structure is that they become exclusive; good societies should be inclusive. Today in the West as well as in other places including India, if we have money or power, we are respected. Does anyone rebel against that? No! How can we call a society advanced or progressive when its main criterion for respect is money?

By that logic, I would have been denounced had I been born in any country other than India. For nearly ten years I was homeless! For nine years I traveled the length and breadth of India without carrying money.

I never bought train tickets and never paid for meals or lodging. People welcomed me and offered me transport, shelter and food. In the West I would have been locked up in a jail or a shelter!

When you see a homeless person approaching your car in the USA, you instinctively raise your windows and lock your doors. You are so afraid. In India, is anyone afraid of a beggar coming and standing in front of them? Why? There is acceptance. People in the West say that acceptance is weakness, not violence. How strange societal values have become! You respect a person only when you are afraid of him.

We cannot evolve unless there is a fundamental change in our thinking. We have come to a stage where negative qualities are the hallmark of respectability. Violence and aggression never win. Acceptance and compassion do.

Instructions For Enlightenment

18.49 *One whose intelligence is always free from selfish attachment,*
who has controlled the mind and who is free from desires,
by practicing renunciation [sannyāsa], attains the ultimate state
of perfection of selfless work or actionlessness [naiṣkarma siddhi].

18.50 *Understand from Me, how one who has achieved this perfection,*
can attain the Supreme state of Truth, Brahman,
by acting in the way I shall now summarize, Kaunteya.

18.51,52,53 *Endowed with purified intellect; subduing the mind with firm resolve; turning away from objects of the senses; giving up likes and dislikes; living in solitude; eating lightly;*
controlling the mind, speech, and organs of action;
being ever absorbed in meditation; taking refuge in detachment,
and relinquishing egotism, violence, pride, lust, anger, and proprietorship, one becomes peaceful, free from the notion of 'I' and 'mine', and fit for attaining oneness with the Supreme Being.

These verses are the ultimate *sūtra*, the technique to liberate oneself and realize *Brahman*, ultimate Truth. Kṛṣṇa describes how to reach the ultimate Truth. He tells us to just follow His instructions.

The beauty of Kṛṣṇa's advice in *Bhagavad Gītā* is that He makes no assumptions. He goes to the depths of Arjuna's stated and unstated doubts and tells him in such clear words that there can be no ambiguity. *Bhagavad Gītā* is primarily a *śāstra*, a scripture that gives knowledge. Even though the author who is the Divine Himself, He must bring Himself down to the level of Arjuna, a mortal. Kṛṣṇa's compassion drives Him to repeat the same words to ensure that Arjuna listens and understands.

As long as we question why, we never get a clear answer. Especially with Existence, the question 'Why?' has no relevance. As I said earlier, we operate at a different frequency from the Divine, so even if it is explained, we will not understand. Listen! Spirituality is an inner science, not an outer science, and that is fortunate! In the outer sciences, we keep asking 'Why?' and when we cannot get answers, we get stuck. 'Why?' is about logic. 'How?' is about realism. *Śāstras* answer the 'Why?' *Sūtras* answer the 'How?' Once in a while, the Master delivers the *Sūtra* amidst the *śāstra* that He must deliver to keep Arjuna quiet.

He says, 'Settle the mind and control the senses.' Can you do that while sitting in the middle of a traffic junction? No. That is why He says go into solitude and cut yourself off from disturbances. Go into meditation and shut your senses to external objects. These are the clearest instructions on how to meditate. Prepare yourself to be away from potential sensory disturbances. There is no point in meditating when you are sure the phone will ring or a guest will be arriving. Fix a time and place when you will be alone, undisturbed. Closing the eyes is insufficient. Your eyeballs will still move and inner television will still play. Mentally freeze your eyeballs, think they are made of stone and still them. At the same time place your tongue on your upper palate and lock it. If there is movement of the tongue, that creates verbalization, then visualization is difficult. These two tools of mentally freezing your eyeball movement and locking your tongue, substantially reduce the wandering of the mind due to sensory disturbances.

Meditate on an empty stomach or eat little. A full stomach makes us sleepy. Ideally one should meditate in the same location regularly to preserve the energy raised in meditation. These are the physical requirements. Next Kṛṣṇa repeats what He has been emphasizing all along.

Complete and drop your personality, He says, drop your ego or root patterns, your attachments, your ideas of 'I' and 'mine' as well as the emotions that bind you to survival and possession. Then you will be liberated, you will be in the space of completion and ready to reach the Supreme Being.

Work Always Under My Protection

18.54 *Absorbed in the Supreme Brahman, the serene one neither grieves nor desires. Becoming equally disposed to all living beings, one obtains My highest pure devotional love [madbhakti].*

18.55 *Only by devotion one truly understands Me as I am and My tattva, essence. Having known Me in Truth in full consciousness of Me, one immediately merges with Me.*

18.56 *My pure devotee, though occupied in all kinds of activities of everyday life, under My protection, still reaches the eternal, imperishable ultimate abode through My Grace [mad-prasād].*

18.57 *While being engaged in activities, just depend upon Me, and being fully conscious of Me, work always under My protection [matparaḥ].*

18.58 *When your mind and inner-space becomes fixed on Me, you shall overcome and cross all difficulties by My Grace. But if due to ego, you do not listen to Me, you shall perish.*

Kṛṣṇa explains how devotion is reached and how He protects the devotee.

Developing the state of non-attachment, being equally disposed to all beings, being unconcerned by success and failure, fully absorbed in Godhood, one becomes His devotee. In that state alone does one understand the essence of Kṛṣṇa. Once one understands this, one merges into Kṛṣṇa consciousness. When one is in Kṛṣṇa consciousness, the devotee, even if he is engaged in worldly activities, is protected by the grace and compassion of Kṛṣṇa. Without any difficulty such a devotee reaches the ultimate reality.

Recently I expressed this concept to some devotees. When we relax from the instinct that constantly works to protect us, the space created allows the power of extraordinary possibilities, coincidence to happen. Kṛṣṇa says that even though we may be engaged in the activities of the world, if we are His devotees, under His protection we experience Eternal consciousness. If Kṛṣṇa only wanted to give us the spiritual experience, He would not have used the word 'protection, *mad-vyapāśrayaḥ*.' So Kṛṣṇa is referring to both the outer and inner worlds. The person who surrenders gets the best experience in both worlds. We simply need to get out and He will get in. Just get out and let Him get in.

A small story:

> One day Śrī Viṣṇu was resting on Ādīśeśa, His bed that is actually a big serpent. Lakṣmī, His consort, was pressing His feet. This is known as *pādasevā*—service to the feet.
>
> Suddenly Śrī Viṣṇu called for His vehicle, Garuḍa. He stood up, ran a few steps, stopped and then walked back. Lakṣmī was puzzled and asked what had happened.
>
> Śrī Viṣṇu explained that He had seen a man throwing stones at one of His devotees who was meditating. He jumped up, intending to protect him. However, He saw the devotee open his eyes and pick up a stone to defend himself. When Viṣṇu saw that the man could protect himself, He decided not to go!

Thus, when you protect yourself and your property, He withdraws. To protect does not mean that you should not lock your house. It means that you should drop the instinct of survival. The instinct of survival constantly tortures you. It is the greatest killer. If somebody kills you, you can only be killed once. But the instinct to survive kills you every moment. When you surrender this instinct, Kṛṣṇa will protect you. Intellectually you cannot understand this.

You think, 'How can somebody who made a statement thousands of years ago give me protection?' You think that only you can protect and look out for yourself. You are wrong!

You think that the survival instinct is essential in order to exist. You will realise the futility of the survival instinct only when you surrender. After that, you will automatically realize that you can live without the instinct to survive or the instinct to possess. You will realize that you can live in the material world without these instincts ruling you. This is what Kṛṣṇa means when He says that He will protect you. His energy takes care. When you surrender, a space is created that allows the power of coincidence, the power of extraordinary possibilities to happen. Automatically things fall into place. Automatically you are taken care of by the energy of Śrī Kṛṣṇa.

When you believe that you are intelligent enough to use your mind and go your own way, you are asking for trouble. Kṛṣṇa says you will perish if you follow your mind and senses instead of listening to Him.

Understand Surrender

We must understand two things. The first is about listening to one's mind and the second is about not listening to the Master.

Many people have an issue about accepting another human as superior, as someone to whom they should defer, let alone surrender. They think that prostrating at another person's feet is disrespecting themselves and quite uncivilized.

When I heal someone, if the pain is in the leg, I normally bend down and touch the person's feet. Once someone asked me, '*Swamiji*, how can you touch someone's feet? You are lowering yourself.'

I said, 'When I touch someone's feet, I am raising them to my level. When they fall at my feet, they surrender their ego!'

When you fall at someone's feet, you surrender your ego. It is good for you. It does not matter to whom you surrender. Whether you surrender to a stone or a human being, surrendering your ego raises you spiritually. This is the absolute Truth. You do not need to discriminate, search, filter and go through a lot of effort and time to surrender to an enlightened Master.

> Someone asked me, 'What do you mean by surrender?' Surrender is when you find someone whom you can unconditionally love and you have no problem if it is obvious that you are in love with that person. Your identity then merges with that person.
>
> I tell them, 'Think of the person whom you would like to be with if God told you that the entire earth is about to be destroyed. Only you and one other person will survive and you can choose that person. Who will that person be? That person is the one you have surrendered to!'

Vedic chants end with the word *namaḥ*. What does this mean? It means 'I surrender to You.' Each time you utter a *vedic* prayer, you say, 'I surrender to You, my Lord.' Is there another system of prayer that so thoroughly destroys your ego?

So, just because you do not surrender to a Master or a favorite deity, because one is human and the other is stone, do you think you are the Master, free and independent? You surrender to someone else for money, power or lust. One of these will surely happen. How much more sensible it is to follow and surrender to someone out of intelligence, because that person is more aware and complete, and can guide you on the path to completion?

Why are we reluctant to surrender to another person? It is because we have been captured by our mind and senses. We are in a jail and we are captive. We fear losing the identity that our mind and senses have created for us. We fear letting go of that identity. Our mind fights against shifting our allegiance from that ego and identity to someone else.

Realize that you are a slave to your senses and *not* the master of your destiny as you imagine. Be aware that your pains and sorrows arise from the mistaken belief that you are the master of your destiny. Once you realize this, you will look for an alternative.

You then understand what the greatest Master of all, Śrī Kṛṣṇa, says:

mac-cittaḥ sarva durgāṇi mat-prasādāt tariṣyasi I
atha cet tvam ahaṅkārān na śroṣyasi vinaṅkṣyasi II 18.58

'If you listen to Me, I shall protect you, whatever may happen. If you do not, and you follow your mind, you shall perish.'

Devotion and Knowledge are not Separate

Kṛṣṇa says that 'having known Me in essence, one merges in Me' and refers to this as devotion.

bhaktyā mām abhijānāti yāvān yaś c'āsmi tattvataḥ I
tato māṁ tattvato jñātvā viśate tad-anantaram II 18.55

Please understand that *bhakti* (devotion) and *jñāna* (knowledge) are not separate. Where there is devotion, there is knowledge and where there is true knowledge, there is devotion.

Kṛṣṇa does not refer to dry intellectual knowledge, even if such knowledge is of the scriptures. Thousands of scholars and philosophers waste their time and everybody else's time by analyzing *Bhagavad Gītā* word by word and comparing it with other scriptures. What is the point? This is a pointless, foolish exercise that serves only to boost one's ego.

The entire purpose of Gītā is to enrich you to complete with your root patterns and drop the ego! All you need to do is understand one verse of Gītā, one statement of Kṛṣṇa, in its entirety. That is enough to enlighten you. This is what Vivekananda meant when he said that the study of one handful of earth can teach you about the entire earth. You need depth, not breadth of knowledge.

Every word of Gītā, every word of Kṛṣṇa, is energy. That is the knowledge that you need to imbibe and experience. This is what the 'knowing, *tattvato jñātva*' that Kṛṣṇa refers to. Once you 'know' this energy, you reach this energy. You become Kṛṣṇa. You are not only devoted to Kṛṣṇa, *you* become *Kṛṣṇa*.

There are two paths. One way is to 'know' the truth so clearly and completely that there is absolutely no doubt about your trust in the Master. There is no doubt that you are the same consciousness as the Master. Once you know this, there is no duality, there is the space of *advaita*, non-duality. You and the Master are the same. This is the height of devotion.

The other way is the deep surrender that happens within, the unbridled love that arises within you and through which you merge with the Master. Along with the merger, comes the knowledge that you are no different. Seemingly, knowledge comes from devotion; *jñāna* comes from *bhakti*.

The truth is that both happen simultaneously. Do you think Mīrā did not know that she was one with Kṛṣṇa? Do you think she could have drunk poison without knowing that whatever she consumed was being consumed by her Lord and Master, Kṛṣṇa? Do you feel Śaṅkara was just a dry philosopher when he beheld the form of Devi and sang the verses of *Soundarya Lahiri*? He is possibly the greatest philosopher the world has ever seen, and he melted in front of Her in devotion.

All this talk about the three approaches to Divinity as *dvaita* (duality), *viśiṣṭādvaita* (qualified duality) and *advaita* (non-duality) are best left to philosophers to argue about.

Duality happens when you are *open* to that Cosmic energy but you still feel separate. You are like the ocean drop that knows it is part of the ocean but sees itself as separate. To reach this stage, you need to be open. When you are closed, you do not even accept that there is this huge ocean of which you are a part. You are ignorant. Duality or *dvaita* is the first step.

Next, you become *available*. Not only do you know that there is this huge energy around you, but you become aware that you are part of it. You are a part of the Whole. You realize that as a drop, you are a part of the ocean. This is qualified duality, *viśiṣṭādvaita*. Then you suddenly realize and know that you *are* the ocean. There is no difference or barrier between you and the energy. You are the energy. You are God. This is non-duality, *advaita*. You just *are*. From being *open*, to being *available*, you just *are*.

When you 'know' Kṛṣṇa, there is nothing else to know. Then, you become Kṛṣṇa.

Root Patterns Will Drive You

18.59 *If, due to ego you thus think: 'I shall not fight,' your resolve*
is useless, and your own nature will compel you.

18.60 *O Kaunteya, you are controlled by your own natural conditioning.*
Therefore you shall do, even against your will,
what you do not wish to do out of delusion.

18.61 *The Supreme Lord resides in everyone's heart, O Arjuna,*
and is directing the activities of all living entities,
who are placed on a machine under His illusive material power.

Kṛṣṇa delivers an ultimatum to Arjuna.

'Whether you like it or not, Arjuna,' He says, 'you will fight. In seeming intelligence, your ego tells you that you should not fight. You are under the illusion of your superficial knowledge that it is not right to wage war against friends, relatives and teachers. But you forget that your nature and your conditioning as a warrior drive you. You are a puppet in the hands of Existence, *prakṛtis tvāṁ niyokṣyati*. You will fight.'

These are extraordinary words. Whether we like it or not, whatever our intelligence may be, and whatever our will may be, Kṛṣṇa says we will be driven by our root patterns, *saṁskāras*. The Divine power drives the machine that is the *kārmic cycle.* There is no escape.

Nothing can be clearer. The law of nature drives us to fulfill our unfulfilled desires. Our past conditioning invokes these desires. Even though they may be in our unconscious, inaccessible to us, they determine what we do. The Master sees this even if we cannot. That is why Kṛṣṇa makes this bold statement.

The mind creates and stores the root patterns, *saṁskāras*. You can refuse to bow down to your mind and refuse to accept these *saṁskāras* that control you.

All meditation techniques bring you into the space of completion, being in the present moment. When you are in the present moment, you renounce attachment to fantasies about the future. You detach yourself from the results of your action. This alone leads you into liberation from the bondage of *saṁskāra*.

Surrender to the Master, surrender to the Universe, is the ultimate technique to do completion and rid oneself of all bondages—*karma*, *vāsanā* and *saṁskāra*, of the past, present and future. When people come to me for help, I usually say one of two things. To those who come purely for material assistance, health and wealth, I say, 'I shall pray to Nithyānandeśvara (presiding deity of Śiva at Nithyananda temples) to help you.' To those who come as sincere seekers, connected to me at the being level, my disciples and devotees, I say 'I will take care.' Ask my disciples about the power of these words.

I say this to those who come in a mode of total surrender. They have such absolute trust in me that they tell me, 'Please say you will take care.' They know at their being level that once they have downloaded their problems and pain to me, it is no longer their burden. It is mine. They know it so deeply that there is not an iota of doubt in their minds that the problem has disappeared.

I do nothing with them. All I do is pass their problems onto *Parāśakti*, the Universal feminine cosmic energy; that is all. I have already surrendered to Her. Not one finger of mine can move without Her command. So, what can I do? But such is Her compassion that She responds every time. When the being surrenders, when the ego and mind surrender, She takes over. On the other hand, if you are filled with your ego, there is no place for Her.

This is what Kṛṣṇa, the greatest Master of all, the *Parama Guru*, the *Jagat Guru*, has repeated throughout the *Gītā*. He does not ask you to surrender to Him out of His ego. He asks you to surrender to Him out of His deep compassion. What can you give Him that He does not have? Where else would you want to go since *only* He can grant everything you want? More importantly, only He can grant you what you need to free you from your suffering forever. Who else can do this for you? No one.

Don't lose hope. There is no need to do that. Kṛṣṇa is situated in everyone's heart. All you need is trust in Him.

Surrender To Him Completely

18.62 Surrender unto Him completely with all your being, O Bhārata. By His Grace you will attain supreme peace and the eternal abode.

Kṛṣṇa switches gears and starts giving Arjuna the experience. He starts radiating eternal consciousness. He is putting Arjuna into that consciousness, into the experience of enlightenment.

Just relax for a few minutes. Relax from all the thoughts and ideas going on in your head. There is every possibility that you can also glimpse what Arjuna received by His grace. We always miss due to our instinct to survive and possess. For a few minutes, relax from thoughts. You can pick them up later. There is no problem in that. Just for a few moments keep them away from your consciousness. Drop them from your inner space so that you may glimpse that consciousness. There is a distinct possibility that you may experience what Arjuna experienced by the grace of Kṛṣṇa.

tam eva śaranaṁ gaccha   sarva-bhāvena bhārata |
tat-prasādāt parāṁ śāntiṁ   sthānaṁ prāpsyasi śāśvatam || 18.62

Throughout *Bhagavad Gītā*, Śrī Kṛṣṇa has been saying, surrender to *Me*. He has been saying 'I' and 'Me', meaning that *He* represents the Divine. Now, suddenly, He changes that and says surrender *unto Him* (*tam*) as a third person. For the first time He refers to the Divine in this way. This means that He has expanded beyond the body. He now speaks as *Parabrahma* Kṛṣṇa, the universal Kṛṣṇa. He speaks from the eternal consciousness. That is the reason He says surrender unto Him and not surrender unto Me. Earlier He used the word 'I' or 'Me'. This change means that He is in an expanded state to put Arjuna into the experience. In order to give a disciple the experience, the Master must be in the same state, too. That is why Śrī Kṛṣṇa went into that expanded state.

Before a *pūjā*, the priest chants the *aṅganyāsa karanyāsa* mantra—*anguṣṭhābhyām daśadibhyāṁ*—these mantras are chanted in order to expand and go beyond body consciousness. These purify the body and help us go beyond the body. Actually, purifying and going beyond are the same thing.

So now Kṛṣṇa says 'Surrender unto Him, *tam eva śaranaṁ gaccha*' since He has expanded and He cannot use the word 'Me'. He says, 'Bhārata, surrender unto Him utterly. By His grace you will attain eternal consciousness and supreme peace.'

He has expanded into that consciousness and is about to give *energy darśan*. He is ready to shower His energy on Arjuna.

Surrender To Me, I Will Liberate You

18.63 *Thus, I have explained to you, the knowledge that is*
the most secret of secrets. After fully reflecting on this,
do as you wish.

18.64 *Because you are My dear friend, I am speaking My Ultimate*
words with you. This is the most confidential of all knowledge.
Hear this from Me. It is for your benefit.

18.65 *Always think of Me and become My devotee.*
Worship Me and offer your homage unto Me.
Thus you will certainly attain Me.
This I promise you because you are My very dear friend.

18.66 *Abandon all principles and concepts of right conduct*
and simply surrender unto Me.
I shall liberate you from all sinful reactions. Have no worry.

What powerful words! Only the Divine can speak these words of absolute authority.

'Always think of Me, become My devotee, worship Me and offer your homage unto Me. This is the way you will come to Me without fail. I promise this because you are My great *bhakta* (devotee) and very dear to Me.'

man-manā bhava mad-bhakto mad-yāji māṁ namaskuru |
māṁ ev'aiṣyasi satyaṁ te pratijāne priyo'si me || 18.65

Now He comes to the ultimate teaching. This is the essence of all His teachings, the quintessence of *Bhagavad Gītā*. He wakes up Arjuna with this verse and puts him into Kṛṣṇa consciousness, the Eternal consciousness or Enlightenment.

Kṛṣṇa showers Himself on Arjuna, waking him up to the experience of the Whole.

sarvadharmān parityajya māṁ ekaṁ śaraṇaṁ vraja |
ahaṁ tvāṁ sarvapāpebhyo mokṣayiṣyāmi mā śucaḥ || 18.66

He says, 'Give up everything, whatever you know as *dharma*, the rules and regulations of the outer life and of the inner life. Drop everything that you know and surrender unto Me. I shall liberate you from everything. Do not fear.' Kṛṣṇa gives him *abhaya*, complete protection.

He liberates Arjuna with these words. He gives the ultimate experience to Arjuna. With this verse, Kṛṣṇa makes Arjuna drop everything and liberates him. He gives him a conscious experience of the ocean. He asks Arjuna to drop his ideas about being a separate bubble, relax and realize the truth. Even the idea of the ocean or of God are simply our ideas. Kṛṣṇa makes Arjuna drop those ideas and makes him explode into Kṛṣṇa consciousness, the eternal consciousness.

Now Kṛṣṇa enters into the actual experience.

Kṛṣṇa liberates Arjuna and gives him the ultimate experience permanently. We cannot call him Arjuna any longer because he has become Kṛṣṇa. He has achieved Kṛṣṇa consciousness. Now only Kṛṣṇa exists. As long as Kṛṣṇa and Arjuna existed, there were two entities. But now that they have become one, neither exists. There is no name for it. It is only energy.

Forget about *dharma*, the codes of conduct laid down by religions, and turn to Me. I shall be your savior, says Kṛṣṇa.

Do not misunderstand, misquote and misuse these words. You will do yourself the greatest disservice. The Divine does not care whether you are good or evil. The Divine does not care whether you are a saint or sinner. A saint and a sinner, a celibate monk and a prostitute have equal chances of reaching the Divine. This is the truth. Of course, when you come close to the Divine, the energy transforms you. Negativities will be dissolved. Root patterns will be completed. They will be burnt and you will be pure as you were at birth.

Religion is the creation of men. Spirituality is the creation of enlightened Masters who live in the energy of the Divine with total completion. Kṛṣṇa, Śiva, Buddha, Mahāvira and Jesus are Enlightened Masters. They related to no religion. The followers who interpreted them to the best or worst of their understanding created religions. The followers established *dharma*, the codes of righteous conduct. No God or Master is interested in coming down to tell you how you should behave. They tell you to be in the space of completion and that will put you on the right path to live *advaita*, the space of non-duality.

Thus, Kṛṣṇa says with absolute conviction and authority: Forget all codes of conduct, give up all religions and come to Me with completion. This is your enlightenment.

Śrī Kṛṣṇa is *triguṇa rahita*: beyond the attributes of nature and *kārmic* influence. Merging with Him, surrendering to Him takes you beyond all *kārmic* bondages.

If you understand this verse and act accordingly, you will be liberated. That is Kṛṣṇa's promise.

Take a few moments now to pray to *Parabrahma* Kṛṣṇa, the universal Kṛṣṇa, who showered enlightenment on Arjuna and gave him the ultimate experience. Pray that He may shower the same experience on us or give us a glimpse of the ultimate Truth. Take a few moments to pray. Please close your eyes and pray intensely to Him. Do not think that He is unavailable now. He is always available to everybody on planet Earth. He may not have the body, but He is available in the form of energy. The deities in the temples are called *arcāvatār*. That means 'incarnation of the Divine'. He is available to us all the time, whenever we call Him. Close your eyes and pray intensely to Him to shower us with the same experience He showered on Arjuna.

Relax in silence and listen to the words of Śrī Kṛṣṇa.

Without A Doubt, He Comes Back To Me

18.67 *This knowledge should never be spoken by you*
to one who is devoid of austerity, who is without devotion,
who does not desire to listen, or who speaks ill of Me.

18.68 *One who communicates the supreme secret to the devotees*
performs the highest devotional service to Me,
and, at the end he will without doubt, come back to Me.

18.69 *No other person shall do a more pleasing service to Me,*
and no one on the earth shall be more dear to Me.

18.70 *I declare that one who studies this sacred dialogue of ours,*
worships Me with the sacrifice of his intelligence [jñāna-yajña].

18.71 *One who listens with faith and without envy becomes*
free from sinful reactions and attains to the planets
where those of merit dwell.

18.72 *O Pārtha, did you listen to this with single-minded attention?*
Has your delusion born of ignorance been completely destroyed,
Dhanañjaya?

These words are meant not merely for Arjuna, but for all of humanity.

Kṛṣṇa says here that we should read, listen and understand this dialogue between Arjuna and Kṛṣṇa, between *Nara* and *Nārāyaṇa*. Nothing more needs to be read or listened to. Everything we need is here.

ya idam paramaṁ guhyaṁ mad-bhateṣv abhidhāsyati |
bhaktiṁ mayi parāṁ kṛtvā mām ev'aiṣyaty asaṁśayaḥ || 18.68

Only one who is in deep devotion to Me should read this. I have conveyed here that which is most beneficial, the secret of how to live and how to reach Me. One who understands this and drops his mind with his focus entirely upon Me, shall reach Me without a doubt.

This is Kṛṣṇa's promise.

He blesses the whole Universe with His grace and compassion. He showered His blessing on Arjuna and made him merge with Him. The same consciousness is being showered on the whole Universe.

He declares that whoever studies this sacred conversation will achieve His eternal consciousness. He blesses us with His grace and assures us that we can achieve Him through this *jñāna yajña*, sacrifice of intellect. That is, by offering ourselves into that knowledge, by completely purifying ourselves in that knowledge, we can achieve Him. We can disappear into Him. When we put anything into the fire, it disappears. In the same way, when we immerse ourselves in the study of *Gītā*, we will not remain as we are. We will disappear into Him. Only He remains, only He exists.

adhyeṣyate ca ya imaṁ dharmyaṁ saṁvādam āvayoḥ |
jñāna-yajñena ten'āham iṣṭaḥ syām iti me matiḥ || 18.70

The whole experience of the Truth has descended on Arjuna. Kṛṣṇa's blessings are upon us also. Let us pray to the ultimate consciousness to put us into that same energy. Relax into that energy. May the grace and compassion of Kṛṣṇa that was showered on Arjuna, be showered on us.

Earlier Kṛṣṇa said that He would appear again and again whenever He is needed to restore equilibrium between good and bad. He is the only great Master who has the courage to say, 'I am not the last Master, it is not that there will be no one after Me.' Instead He says, 'I shall appear again and again, *sambhavāmi yuge yuge*.'

Kṛṣṇa will not reappear in His *Vāsudeva* Kṛṣṇa form with peacock feathers and a flute! That is the mistake we make in our assumption. His energy will reappear. He will reappear in the form of enlightened Masters and Incarnations, time and again. He will come again and again to restore the balance, liberate the good and destroy the evil.

This is the last time Śrī Kṛṣṇa speaks in the *Bhagavad Gītā*. He asks, 'Arjuna, have you listened to Me with attention? Has your delusion disappeared?'

kaccid etac chrutaṁ pārtha tvayaikāgreṇa cetasā /
kaccid ajñāna-sammohaḥ praṇaṣtas te dhanañjaya // 18.72

Until the end He is the teacher. He is full of compassion. His concern is only for Arjuna and the rest of humanity. 'Have you understood?' He asks. 'Have your doubts disappeared? Do you need anything more?'

This is the greatness of Masters. Nothing concerns them except the deliverance of their disciples. That is why they have come here. Otherwise why should they waste their time on planet Earth? They can be immersed in the blissful energy that they are part of without disturbance.

My disciples understand when I tell them that the only time I feel anything like sadness is when a disciple leaves me. It saddens me because he is losing a great opportunity. His spirit brought him to me for completion. If the body-mind does not cooperate, the spirit must live again and again until it gets the opportunity to be liberated. Each cycle of birth that the spirit undertakes, it suffers and regrets not having taken that final step.

No one who has crossed my ashram gates can ever leave me. Even if they leave, I shall not leave them. I shall be with them. That one moment of intelligence that brought them in is enough for me to care for them. Those who have understood the formless form that resides in Me know that I am part of them. Wherever they are, I am part of them.

This is Śrī Kṛṣṇa's promise: Listen to Me, understand Me and come to Me; then you are a part of Me.

Kṛṣṇa Is Present

18.73 *Arjuna says: O dear Acyuta (infallible lord), my illusion is now gone. I have regained my memory by Your Grace, and I am now firm and free from doubt, and ready to act as per your instructions.*

18.74 *Sañjaya said: Thus have I heard the conversation of two great souls, Kṛṣṇa and Arjuna. And so wonderful is that message that my hair stands on end.*

18.75 *By the mercy of Vyāsa, I have heard these most confidential words directly from Yogeśvara Kṛṣṇa, the Master of all mysticism, who was speaking personally to Arjuna.*

18.76 *O King, as I repeatedly recall this wondrous and holy dialogue between Kṛṣṇa and Arjuna, I take pleasure, being thrilled at every moment.*

18.77 *O King, when I remember the wonderful form of Lord Kṛṣṇa, I am struck with even greater wonder, and I rejoice again and again.*

18.78 *Wherever there is Yogeśvara Kṛṣṇa, the Master of all mystics, and wherever there is Pārtha, the supreme carrier of bow and arrow, there will certainly be opulence, victory, extraordinary power, and morality. That is my opinion.*

In these last verses Arjuna and Sañjaya take over.

Arjuna bows down to the *JagadGuru,* Master of Cosmos, and says, 'All my doubts are gone and by Your grace, my memory is regained, O Acyuta; I understand. I am ready. I shall obey whatever you say and I shall fight.'

arjuna uvāca
naṣṭo mohaḥ smṛtir labhā tvat-prasādān mayā'cyuta |
sthito'smi gata-sandehaḥ kariṣye vacanaṁ tava || 18.73

The rest is history. Under the guidance of Arjuna, the Kaurava army is annihilated. All the Kaurava brothers, all the great teachers and all the great warriors perish. The Pāṇḍava brothers win and Yudhiṣṭira conducts the *rājasūya* and other fire sacrifices to signify his ascendance to the throne.

It is also history that in due course all the Pāṇḍava brothers die, as does the great Master Kṛṣṇa. He gives up His mortal form. This is the story of life. As long as you are in any form, the form will perish. The energy lives on. That is what Kṛṣṇa taught in these chapters and verses. Sacrifice your form and gain the formless.

Now Sañjaya comes back into the picture. Neither Kṛṣṇa nor Arjuna can speak since both of them are in a different mood. Arjuna has disappeared and Kṛṣṇa is in ecstasy. Both are in no mood to speak. Sañjaya started speaking when Arjuna was in depression and Kṛṣṇa had nothing to say at that time. Then when Kṛṣṇa was giving the first experience to Arjuna, Kṛṣṇa was in the higher consciousness and Arjuna was in ecstasy. Sañjaya came in to speak at that time because both were not in a mood to speak. Now Sañjaya comes back again. Not only are Kṛṣṇa and Arjuna not in a mood to speak, they are both no longer there. Arjuna has disappeared into the pure consciousness of *Parabrahma* Kṛṣṇa. They have nothing to say.

Sañjaya addresses Dhṛitarāṣṭra, 'O King, as I repeatedly recall this wondrous spiritual dialogue between Kṛṣṇa and Arjuna, I feel a great joy or ecstasy at every moment.'

Sañjaya is expressing his joy and bliss and says, '*muhurmuhuḥ*, again and again, whenever I recall it, I am filled with ecstasy. This truth fills my being completely. I am showered with divine grace.'

Sañjaya says, 'By the mercy of Vyāsa, I heard these confidential talks directly from the Master of all mysticism, Yogeśvara Śrī Kṛṣṇa.'

vyāsa prasādāc chrutavān etad guhyam ahaṁ param |
yogaṁ yogeśvarāt kṛṣṇāt sākṣāt kathayataḥ svayam || 18.75

Sañjaya expresses gratitude and joy at hearing this by the grace of Vyāsa, *Vyāsa-prasād.* Vyāsa refers to the Guru (Master) here. In North India, wherever the scriptures are studied, that place is called a *Vyāsa Pīṭha*. Vyāsa is the *Ādi Guru* (first Master). So he expresses gratitude to the Master for giving him the opportunity to listen to the conversation between Kṛṣṇa and Arjuna. Vyāsa is also the author of the epic Mahābhārat, of which *Bhagavad Gītā* is a part.

Sañjaya says, 'O King, as I remember the wonderful form of Lord Kṛṣṇa, I am awestruck and I rejoice again and again.' He has nothing much to say! He overflows with ecstasy. He ends the whole thing beautifully with this verse.

'Wherever there is Kṛṣṇa, the Master of all mystics, and wherever there is Arjuna, the supreme archer, there will certainly be opulence, victory, extraordinary power and morality. This is my opinion.'

yatra yogeśvaraḥ kṛṣṇo yatra pārtho dhanurdharaḥ |
tatra śrīrvijayo bhūtir dhrūvānītir matir mama || 18.78

He ends the whole thing with a beautiful auspicious blessing. Wherever the name of Kṛṣṇa, the divine energy of Kṛṣṇa is present and wherever Arjuna dwells, there will also be victory, prosperity, wealth and morality. All the divine positive energy will shower there. He concludes with this beautiful blessing, this beautiful verse.

Whenever we read, teach or listen to Bhagavad Gītā, Kṛṣṇa and Arjuna are present. They are present in their formless form. Make no mistake, they are here. They have been here throughout these eighteen days. You are the fortunate listeners and readers of this mystic dialogue between the two great souls, the Master and the disciple. You are blessed with wealth, health and success in whatever you undertake.

Go with this Kṛṣṇa consciousness and you will be in *Nityānanda*, eternal bliss.

SURRENDER—MOST SECRET, ULTIMATE, FINAL TECHNIQUE

Through out the *Bhagavad Gītā*, Kṛṣṇa gives Arjuna many meditation techniques or methods to evolve from the ordinary level to the higher level of completion. Every chapter, every verse, is a technique or method to reach the Divine consciousness. After listening to so many techniques, Arjuna is totally confused.

He asks the Master, 'O Lord, after listening to thousands of techniques, after hearing about each and every method, I am more confused. Please tell me, what is the ultimate technique? What is the right technique?'

Even today, we are totally confused because we listen to many methods and techniques. Every Master declares his own technique as the best. When Arjuna was confused, he asked, 'What is the ultimate technique? I have listened to so many methods from you.' At least Arjuna received all the meditations from the same Master, but today, people listen from thousands of sources.

A confused Arjuna asks Kṛṣṇa. 'What is the way? Tell me the final way, the final method, the ultimate technique.'

Finally, Kṛṣṇa says very beautifully, 'This is the last technique, the ultimate technique: Dropping all the *dharma*, dropping all the confusions, surrendering at My feet. I will take care and give you liberation.'

This is the gist of the whole *Bhagavad Gītā.* This is a beautiful verse:

sarvadharmān parityajya māṁ ekaṁ śaraṇaṁ vraja /
ahaṁ tvām sarvapāpebhyo mokṣayiṣyāmi mā śucaḥ // 18.66

Let me again translate it word by word. 'Drop all techniques, all methods and all the roots.' *Dharma* means the way of living in the space of completion. 'Drop all roots, all methods and all ways of living. Drop everything. Don't bother about anything. Surrender everything at My feet.'

sarvadharmān parityajya māmekaṁ śaraṇaṁ vraja—'Don't carry even a bit; just complete and drop everything, surrender your whole being to Me.'

ahaṁ tvām sarvapāpebhyo mokṣayiṣyāmi mā sucaḥ—'I will remove all darkness, all negativities, all incompletions, and all sin from your being. I will liberate you. I will give you the ultimate enlightenment. I will complete you. Do not grieve.'

It's the final word given by Kṛṣṇa. It's the last word anyone could give. In every Master's life, the final teaching is surrender. What is the meaning of surrender?

As soon as we hear the word 'surrender,' we think: Oh, this is the easiest technique. For surrendering, we don't need to do anything. In any other method or meditation, we must do something. If it is a *pūjā* or a fire ritual, we need to do something. For every technique, we must do something. For surrender, we don't need to do anything.' Hence everyone feels surrendering means doing nothing.

> Many people tell me, '*Swamiji*, I've surrendered everything, but nothing is happening in me. What should I do?'
>
> The statement, I've surrendered everything, but nothing is happening inside me, is wrong. If you have really surrendered, you will not expect that anything should or should not happen. When you say, nothing is happening, be very clear, you have *not* surrendered. Most of the time, people use the word 'surrender'. They never understand what it means.
>
> Now, let us look into the sacred secrets of surrender.

Deeper Meanings of Surrender

What actually is surrender? What do the Masters mean by the word surrender? The way they use the word 'surrender, *śaraṇaṁ*' is totally different from the way people normally use it.

Let us see what the Masters mean by surrender.

There are three levels of surrender:

First: Surrendering the I. Second: Surrendering the Mine. Third: Surrendering the I and Mine, both. Let me explain step-by-step.

First: Surrendering the I

Surrendering the 'I' is surrendering the ego, the mind, the root thought patterns, the mental setup. This is surrendering your conditions, your cognitions.

> Somebody asked Rāmakṛṣṇa Paramahamsa, 'Master, I am addicted to alcohol. How can I give it up?'
>
> He said, 'Surrender it to goddess Kāli. You will automatically give it up. You will become all right.'
>
> The disciple asked, 'How can I surrender this to Kāli?'
>
> He replied, 'Before you drink, remember Kāli. Offer the drink to Kāli first, and then drink.'
>
> This is a strange situation. Even so, the man followed the Master's advice. Before drinking, he offered the drink to Kāli, and said, 'O Kāli, this belongs to you.' After that, he drank it as prasād (sacred offering).
>
> According to the record, three days later the man said, 'I am unable to drink anymore. I have totally forgotten such things.'

Of course, when you authentically surrender, a deep transformation happens. The change from mind and matter to energy happens in you. It's a deep transformation and difficult to explain. You can understand only when you have the taste, when you have at least one glimpse of surrender.

You may be surprised that a man could give up an addiction by offering alcohol to God, to a deity. But when he offered it, his heart began to wonder, 'How can I offer this alcohol to Devi, the Goddess whom I love?' Next he began to question, 'If I cannot offer alcohol to the Goddess, how can I drink it? After all, the same Goddess resides in my body, in my system. How can I offer that to myself?' Once he realized that he could not give the alcohol to God and that the same God resided in him, he naturally questioned, 'How can I pour it into myself and disturb the system?'

Surrender gave him intelligence. Surrender gave him understanding. This natural understanding made him complete and drop what he had been doing.

One more thing, when you really, intensely offer your mental setup, or root thought patterns at the feet of the Master or God, it gets totally disintegrated. The mind in itself is a pattern, a habit. Your 'I' is a set of habits. Your ego is a set of conditions. When you offer that at the Master's feet, when you surrender the 'I', it becomes totally disintegrated.

Understand, your thoughts are patterns or conditioning. Even your moods are patterns. Even your mind is a record. Just as you have the coffee habit, you also have the habit of worrying. You have the habit of having an excited mood. You have the habit of reacting to every situation. Even if you understand this one example, you can cognize what I mean.

If somebody criticizes you, you immediately choose to react. You become disturbed. After that, you criticize him in return or you rebuke him. If somebody praises you, you choose to be flattered. You give him a good smile and feel great. Even this choice is your root thought pattern. It is your mental cognition.

When you surrender the 'I', your root thought patterns, to the Divine, you can't choose. When you really surrender, even if somebody criticizes you, you can't choose to be offended or feel disturbed. Whenever you bring in your root thought patterns, you react in accordance with your mental patterns. When this is still the case, you cannot say you have surrendered. Real surrender can and will transform your life.

When you really surrender, whatever you choose is not really your choice. When you have surrendered, you are immune to criticism. After being criticized, you cannot choose to be disturbed. You do not feel that you have been criticized. If you feel disturbed after some criticism, you have not surrendered. Again and again check whether you have surrendered or not.

Surrender is such a beautiful word that you can be easily cheated by it. We always say, 'I have surrendered everything to my Master, to God. He will take care.' But all our surrender is only skin deep. Scratch a little bit to see whether you have really surrendered or not.

When you have really surrendered your 'I', the root thought pattern is totally disintegrated. The egocentric mind becomes God-centric. Egocentric means eccentric. When you surrender your 'I', your mind to God, your ego to God, your thinking system to God, it will be continuously bubbling with joy, because the Divine is always bliss, eternal bliss, *Nitya ānanda*. Whenever you surrender your root thought patterns, you will be bubbling with joy, life and vibrancy.

As long as we are not conditioned, we don't have a mind. We don't have an ego. We have a special grace around us. We have joy and ecstasy. We have innocence and simplicity. A man who has surrendered becomes a small child once again. That is why there is a beautiful word in Saṃskrit, *dvijā* meaning reborn. When you surrender, you are re-born. Our first birth is *janma,* which happens from the mother and father. Our second birth happens from the Guru and God. When you surrender your ego at the feet of the Guru or God, you take the next *janma*, the second birth. You are then called *dvijā*.

When you surrender the 'I,' the root pattern, you experience the space of completion with immense pleasure, joy and ecstasy. Pleasure, joy and ecstasy are different layers. Pleasure happens because of sensory objects. Joy happens because of seeing nature, such as a beautiful mountain, snow, ocean or a forest. Ecstasy or bliss is whenever joy happens for no reason; it happens from your inner being. Pleasure, joy, and bliss continuously happen in you, whenever you surrender your 'I', your ego.

When you surrender your ego, your mind becomes alive and

spontaneously joyful. As of now, every moment you are preparing to live tomorrow. When you surrender, you move without a script! Whenever you move like that, in such a simple way, tremendous courage and trust walks through you. When we really surrender the 'I', the ego, we surrender the mind that continuously prepares the script for our life. We will live in the space of completion with tremendous spontaneity and courage. We will trust our intelligence. We will live our life as it is. We will accept, welcome and enrich life as it flows into us.

A beautiful verse in the Gītā says:

ananyāś-cintayanto māṁ ye janāḥ paryupāsate /
teṣāṁ nity'ābhiyuktānāṁ yogakṣemaṁ vahāmy aham // 9.22

'Continuously merge in Me. Merge in the Divine and all your needs and necessities will be taken care of by Me. Bringing them to you and taking care of them is My responsibility.'

Kṛṣṇa assures us that He will manage both. We may think, 'How can this be?' Just by our surrendering to Him, how can He take care of our needs? What He means by, *'I'll take care,'* is that He will activate or He will let you have the intelligence and courage to have everything and to love everything.

Surrendering 'I', surrendering the root thought patterns, totally changes your being. It shifts you from thinking to the energy, from the mind to no-mind, from incompletion to completion, and from *mithya* (the temporal) to *nithya* (the eternal).

Second: Surrendering the Mine

Here comes the big trouble. Mine means possessiveness, to possess the things that we have.

We can surrender the mind, but never our possessions. We always think our ego comes before our possessions. On the contrary, Tantra says, 'Your ego is only based upon your possessions.' This is a strange statement but I analyzed it carefully. It is true. Your ego is a byproduct of your possessions, of your 'mine'. It is from whatever you think of as 'mine', that is from your possessions, that your sense of identity as 'I' originates. If we look a little deeply, we can understand that our idea of 'mine' creates our idea of 'I.' Our mind, even our body is our possession. So whatever we think of as ours, if we think, 'this is mine, that is mine,' from that root our ego starts growing.

If ego is akin to a tree, the root is 'mine.' The tree is 'I.' From the root 'mine', the 'I', the ego starts growing. If your 'mine' is growing, if your possessions are growing, you feel expanded. You become solid. You become somebody. You feel you have become free. By the expansion of comforts, the outer world possessions, by the expansion of the 'mine', you experience freedom. However, this is only freedom to choose your sufferings, and not to choose between joy and suffering!

To have the freedom to choose between suffering and joy comes from dropping the 'mine' and 'I.' It does not result from possessing the 'mine'. Even if you enjoy your possessions, underneath the enjoyment and joy, you have a deep fear. It is the fear, 'I do not know when it will be lost.' The fear of losing your possessions will not allow you to enjoy those things or relationships. I have seen that the man who is not possessive enjoys the same object more deeply because he does not fear when he might lose it. The person who continuously possesses it, who feels it is 'mine', will only own it, never enjoy it.

Listen. There are two *devatas*, Hindu deities, related to this: Kubera and Lakṣmī. Wealth has two aspects: wealth with possessiveness and wealth without possessiveness. Wealth with possessiveness is Kubera or yakṣa. Kubera means the person who possesses and never enjoys. Yakṣa is a being that owns wealth, but never enjoys it. He feels so satisfied with possessing that he can never enjoy.

Kubera represents richness, whereas another deity, Lakṣmī, stands for wealth. Richness means you have but you never enjoy and enrich yourself. That is Kubera. Wealth means something that not only do you have, but you also enjoy and enrich joyously!

Lakṣmī means abundance. The abundance or wealth is there

without possessiveness. There is no possessiveness, no sense of 'mine, mine, mine'. That feeling is absent. When that feeling is not there, we really enjoy and enrich our life. We can really live life. We each decide whether we are a Lakṣmī or a Kubera. If we surrender our possessiveness, the feeling of 'mine', we will be continuously joyful, ecstatic and enjoying. Whenever we complete and drop possessiveness, whenever we relax from the feeling of 'mine', we live even with the material comforts and enjoy life.

Please listen. Whenever you surrender the 'I' to the Existence, understand this one thing. Never think that the world is running because of you. It is running in spite of you! Fifty years from now, none of us will be here. Do you think the world will stop? No! Even so, we think the whole world is running only because of us. Understand that not only *you* but your whole 'I' and 'mine' are taken care of by the Divine. It takes care in its own way. But we, out of our ego, keep all our headaches, all the loads, upon our own heads.

When you rest, when you really relax, when you surrender at the feet of the Divine, your space of completion awakens the space of creation. Ninety-nine percent of your energy is available for expressing your positive creativity and power, and for living and celebrating. You harness the power of words through integrity, power of thinking through authenticity, power of feeling through responsibility and power of living through enriching! Until then that entire ninety-nine percent is wasted in unnecessarily worrying, self-doubting and struggling with incompletions.

Continuous self-doubting with worrying, fear and greed creates incompletions in your life. When you surrender, when you trust in the Divine, when you relax in the name of the Divine, the energy and powers that you had been wasting on worrying turns towards the power of creation with positivity and possibility.

Ninety-nine percent of your worries, fears and greed never come true. Whatever one percent comes true is always good for you! When you surrender your 'I,' your suffering is transformed into the space of completion bringing intelligence, love, joy, and ecstasy. When you surrender your 'mine,' your richness becomes the space of creation for wealth, power, and celebration.

You start really living to enrich others and yourself with your possessions. You enjoy and celebrate whatever you have. You start living it, and really feel ecstasy and joy from the things that you have. You go beyond the fear of 'When will I lose them?'

Third: Surrender both I and Mine

Listen. When I say both 'I' and 'mine,' I mean surrendering your whole life unconditionally, completely.

When you surrender both 'I' and 'mine,' your whole life is totally transformed. It becomes completely different. The proof that you have surrendered is that you no longer worry and suffer. If you have really surrendered, you will not have worry or suffering.

To whom you surrender is immaterial. I have been speaking of surrender but I have not said 'to whom'. You don't need to bother about to whom to surrender to. It is immaterial whether you surrender to God, the Guru, Śiva or Kṛṣṇa. It is unimportant and has nothing to do with liberation. Surrender itself has the power to transform and complete you.

Surrendering itself will do the miracle. Surrender has the energy and the capacity to transform you and to bring completion to you. Don't bother about which form or name you surrender to. It does not matter.

JUST SURRENDER! DON'T DOUBT, DON'T YOU WORRY

There is no need to worry about what will happen thereafter, or what will be the effect or next step after the surrender. Most of the time, before surrendering itself, we calculate logically, 'After surrendering, what will happen to this or that?' Can we logically calculate what will happen? Never. If we do so, we project our mind beyond surrender.

If you know what will happen after death, only then will you know what will happen after surrender. Surrender and death are the same.

When you surrender, psychologically you die. You are re-born. Can you say what will happen after your death? No. In the same way, you can never imagine or visualize what will happen after surrender. If you are imagining, visualizing, be very clear, you are not surrendering.

> Somebody asked me, '*Swamiji*, I have surrendered to you. What should I do?'
>
> I told him, 'If you really surrender, you will not have that question! You will be guided from within. When you fully surrender, intuition or divine intelligence automatically guides you. As long as you have doubts, you have not surrendered.'

This question, whether you have surrendered or not, will disappear. You will have no doubt about whether you have surrendered or not. Your whole being will be flooded and will be bubbling with ecstasy and joy. There is just a feeling of surrendering, utter relaxation and utter bliss. You will not bother about what happens next. You will be totally relaxed from your duties, pains, suffering and responsibilities. The responsibilities will be fulfilled effortlessly. Your body, your mind will be doing the right action effortlessly. It's not that you won't go to your office tomorrow because you have surrendered. You will go—the body will carry on. Everything will be happening. But you will see utter relaxation in your being, the utter bliss in your 'mind' and the utter 'IS ness' in your life.

When you surrender the 'I', there is utter bliss. When you surrender the 'mine,' there is utter relaxation. When you surrender the 'I' and 'mine', there is a beautiful 'IS ness' in your life. This is the scale to measure whether your surrender is merely lip service or it is real. With this scale you can measure whether you have surrendered or not.

> **Listen. Surrender is nothing but a clear, conscious decision to be complete. Nothing else.** You will conclude, 'Why can't the energy that can move my body, this sun, this moon and this planet Earth, move and complete my life?'

Understand: The bread that we eat becomes blood. It is not an insignificant process. Still, scientists have not succeeded in converting bread into blood. And such a big process happens inside our body! Just six feet tall—in such a small system, this big process is happening! Air is taken in, the prāṇa (life force) is separated out, the air goes out—the process is happening inside us. If the Divine can manage so much inside our body, if the Divine can manage so much in this Universe, it can well manage and complete our life, too.

Understand. Existence is intelligence. The Divine is intelligence.

I've seen people ask God, 'O God, please give me this. O God, please give me a million dollars.' Let me ask you this. Why do you pray? You pray because you think that God has the capacity to give, that God has the *śakti* (power) to give. But when you insist, 'O God, give me *now*, give me right *now*,' it means you believe that He has *śakti*, but you don't believe that he has *buddhi*, the intelligence to decide when to give. That is what it means! You believe He has energy, but you don't believe He has intelligence. That is what your prayer means!

When you surrender, you understand that not only does He have *śakti*, He has *buddhi* also. Every moment, something will be taught to you. When you surrender, you will not have any pain. You will feel complete and liberated.

So whenever you relax and complete, you transform your life from *mithya* (illusion) to *nitya ānanda* (eternal bliss). You transform your suffering to a space of bliss. You move from depression to expression, from self-doubt to Self, from 'me' to 'you' , from worrying to wondering. The genesis of identity is transformed with the process of completion.

The knowledge of *advaita*—the space of non-duality, becomes a living reality in you with completion. You conquer all fears with completion. You conquer all wrong self-identification of 'I' and 'mine' with your completion. I tell you, the feeling you have—that you are inadequate, that you are incomplete, that you are not capable, that you can't—all the impossibilities will just disappear and melt down with completion. Do completion and surrender. Everything, the wrong, inadequate cognitions you have will melt down, you will become complete.

So may you decide consciously to declare your completion with everything and surrender. Don't question or doubt once the conscious decision is made. Once you surrender, even after the decision, you will have the feeling, you will have the self-doubt whether you really did surrender or not.

Listen. Let me tell you one thing.

First just decide consciously to be complete and surrender. Surrender everything at the feet of God who runs this world. You don't even need to have any name or form in your mind, 'Oh, I surrendered to this god. So what will happen?' Don't worry. Just surrender to the energy that runs the whole world. Then everybody is included under that title—God, Guru, Divine, energy of this whole Universe. Just decide to let this run your life.

After that, naturally, you will have a self-doubt whether you have surrendered or not. Then just say, 'Even this doubt is a gift from the Divine, the same Divine that is running the world. The Divine gives this doubt also. The intelligence to surrender and to doubt my surrender are both His gifts. Let me offer my doubt also to Him. Let Him take care.'

Surrender your doubt also. Then you will see the transformation happens in you just as you are. Don't think, 'First I will change, and then I will surrender.' No. You cannot do that. Surrender as you are, consciously, totally. Whatever is in your hands, whatever 'mine' is in your hands, whatever position is in your hands, surrender completely. Your being will be flooded with a new feeling, a new life, a new energy and a new bliss.

So, may you surrender at the feet of the Divine. May you enter the space of completion. May you be in the energy. May you enter into the Divine energy. May this happen to you. May you be in and may you become eternal bliss, *Nitya ānanda*.

Here ends the ultimate teaching of Śrī Kṛṣṇa and here starts our enlightened life! Let us take a few minutes to offer our gratitude to the great Masters.

First, offer gratitude to the great Master Śrī Kṛṣṇa who showered these great truths upon the whole Universe. Let us give our gratitude to Him.

Then come all the Masters who preserved these truths so that we can enjoy and experience these truths in our life.

Let us give our gratitude to the entire *Guru Paramparā*, the lineage of Gurus.

Please close your eyes and remain in silence for a while.

I bless you all. Let you all radiate with completion. And, let you all radiate with integrity, authenticity, responsibility and enriching with Eternal bliss, *Nitya ānanda*.

Thank you.

*Thus ends the eighteenth chapter named **Mokṣa-Sannyāsa Yogaḥ**, 'The Yoga of Liberation by Renunciation,' of the **Bhagavad Gītā Upaniṣad, Brahma-vidyā Yogaśāstra**, the scripture of yoga dealing with the science of the Absolute in the form of **Śrī Kṛṣṇārjuna saṃvād**, dialogue between Śrī Kṛṣṇa and Arjuna.*

Bhagavad Gītā Śloka

Bhagavad Gita Verses

Invocation Verses

ॐ पार्थाय प्रतिबोधितां भगवता नारायणेन स्वयं
व्यासेन ग्रथितां पुराणमुनिना मध्ये महाभारतम्
अद्वैतामृतवर्षिणीं भगवतीं अष्टादशाध्यायिनीं
अम्ब त्वमनुसन्दधामि भगवद्गीते भवद्वेषिणीम्

Oṁ pārthāya pratibodhitāṁ bhagavatā nārāyaṇena svayaṁ
vyāsena gratitāṁ purāṇa muninā madhye mahābhāratam /
advaitāmṛtavarṁiṇīṁ bhagavatīṁ aṣṭāśdaśādhyāyinīṁ
amba tvām anusandadhāmi bhagavadgīte bhavadveṁiṇīm //

Oṁ, I meditate upon you, ***Bhagavad Gītā*** *the affectionate Mother,*
the Divine Mother showering the ***nectar of Advaita*** *(non-duality)*
and destroying rebirth, (who was)
incorporated into the ***Mahābhārat*** *of eighteen chapters*
by sage ***Vyāsa****, the author of the purāṇas and*
imparted to ***Arjuna*** *by* ***Lord Nārāyaṇa****, Himself.*

वसुदेवसुतं देवं कंसचाणूरमर्दनम् ।
देवकीपरमानन्दं कृष्णं वन्दे जगद्गुरुम् ॥

vasudeva sutaṁ devaṁ kamsa cāṇūra mardanam /
devakī paramānandaṁ kṛṣṇam vande jagadgurum //

I bow down to you Lord Kṛṣṇa, Jagadguru (Master to the world),
son of Vasudeva, Supreme Bliss of Devakī,
destroyer of Kaṁsa and Cāṇūra.

CHAPTER

1

अथ प्रथमोऽध्याय:

अर्जुनविषादयोग:

Arjunaviṣāda Yogaḥ

धृतराष्ट्र उवाच

धर्मक्षेत्रे कुरुक्षेत्रे समवेता युयुत्सव: ।
मामका: पाण्डवाश्चैव किमकुर्वत सञ्जय ॥ १.१

dhṛtarāṣṭra uvāca
dharmakṣetre kurukṣetre samavetā yuyutsavaḥ /
māmakāḥ pāṇḍavāś caiva kim akurvata sañjaya // *1.1*

dhṛtarāṣṭra: Dhṛtarāṣṭra; uvāca: said; dharmakṣetre: in the place of righteousness; kurukṣetre: in this location of kurukṣetra; samavetāḥ: gathered; yuyutsavaḥ: desiring to fight; māmakāḥ: my people; pāṇḍavāḥ: the sons of Pāṇḍu; ca: and; eva: also; kiṃ: what; akurvata: did they do; sañjaya: O Sañjaya

1.1 Dhṛtarāṣṭra said: O Sañjaya, assembled on this righteous holy land of pilgrimage at Kurukṣetra, what did my sons and those of Pāṇḍu, eager and ready to fight, do?

सञ्जय उवाच

दृष्ट्वा तु पाण्डवानीकं व्यूढं दुर्योधनस्तदा ।
आचार्यमुपसङ्गम्य राजा वचनमब्रवीत् ॥ १.२

sañjaya uvāca

dṛṣṭvā tu pāṇḍavānīkaṃ vyūḍhaṃ duryodhanas tadā |

ācāryam upasaṅgamya rājā vacanam abravīt || 1.2

sañjaya: Sañjaya; uvāca: said; dṛṣṭvā: having seen; tu: indeed; pāṇḍavānīkaṃ: the Pāṇḍava army; vyūḍhaṃ: arranged in formation; duryodhanaḥ: Duryodhana; tadā: then; ācāryam: the teacher; upasaṅgamya: approaching; rājā: the king; vacanam: words; abravīt: said

1.2 Sañjaya said: O king, looking at the Pāndava army in full formation, Duryodhana went to his teacher and spoke.

पश्यैतां पाण्डुपुत्राणामाचार्य महतीं चमूम् ।

व्यूढां द्रुपदपुत्रेण तव शिष्येण धीमता ॥ १.३

pasyai 'tāṃ pāṇḍuputrānām ācārya mahatīṃ camūm |

vyūḍhām drupada putreṇa tava śiṣyeṇa dhīmatā || 1.3

pasya: behold; etāṃ: this; pāṇḍuputrānām: of the sons of Pāṇḍu; ācārya: O teacher; mahatīṃ: great; camūm: army; vyūḍhām: formed; drupada-putreṇa: by the son of Drupada; tava śiṣyeṇa: by your disciple; dhīmatā: intelligent

1.3 O my teacher, behold the great army of the sons of Pāndu, arrayed for battle by your intelligent disciple, the son of Drupada.

अत्र शूरा महेष्वासा भीमार्जुनसमा युधि ।

युयुधानो विराटश्च द्रुपदश्च महारथ: ॥ १.४

atra śūrā maheṣvāsā bhīmārjunasamā yudhi |

yuyudhāno virāṭaś ca drupadaś ca mahā rathaḥ || 1.4

atra: here; śūrāḥ: heroes; maheṣvāsāḥ: mighty archers; bhīmārjuna: Bhīma and Arjuna; samāḥ: equal; yudhi: in battle; yuyudhānaḥ: Yuyudhana; virāṭaḥ: Virāṭa; ca: and; drupadaḥ: Drupada; ca: and; mahārathaḥ: great charioteers

1.4 Here in this army there are many heroes wielding mighty bows, and equal in military prowess to Bhīma and Arjuna—

Yuyudhāna, Virāṭa, and the great chariot warrior Drupada.

धृष्टकेतुश्चेकितानः काशिराजश्च वीर्यवान् ।
पुरुजित् कुन्तिभोजश्च शैब्यश्च नरपुङ्गवः ॥ १.५

dhṛśṭaketuś cekitānaḥ kāśirājaś ca vīryavān I
purujit kuntibhojaś ca śaibyaś ca narapuṅgavaḥ II 1.5

dhṛṣṭaketuḥ: Dṛṣṭhtaketu; cekitānaḥ: Cekitāna; kāśirājaḥ: Kāśirāja; ca: and; vīryavān: courageous; purujit: Purujit; kuntibhojaḥ: Kuntibhoja; ca: and; śaibyaḥ: Śaibya; ca: and; narapuṅgavaḥ: best of men

1.5 There are courageous warriors like Dṛṣṭaketu, Cekitāna, the couragious Kāśīrāja, Purujit, Kuntibhoja and Śaibya, the best of men.

युधामन्युश्च विक्रान्त उत्तमौजाश्च वीर्यवान् ।
सौभद्रो द्रौपदेयाश्च सर्व एव महारथाः ॥ १.६

yudhāmanyuś ca vikrānta uttamaujāś ca vīryavān I
saubhadro draupadeyāś ca sarva eva mahārathāḥ II 1.6

yudhāmanyuḥ: Yudhāmanyu; ca: and; vikrāntaḥ: mighty; uttamaujāḥ: Uttamauja; ca: and; vīryavān: brave; saubhadraḥ: the son of Subhadrā; draupadeyāḥ: the sons of Draupadī ; ca: and; sarva: all; eva: certainly; mahārathāḥ: great chariot fighters.

1.6 There are the mighty Yudhāmanyu, the brave Uttamauja, Abhimanyu, the son of Subhadrā and the sons of Draupadī, all of them great chariot warriors.

अस्माकं तु विशिष्टा ये तान्निबोध द्विजोत्तम ।
नायका मम सैन्यस्य संज्ञार्थं तान् ब्रवीमि ते ॥ १.७

asmākaṃ tu viśiṣṭā ye tān nibodha dvijottama I
nāyakā mama sainyasya saṃjñārthaṃ tān bravīmi te II 1.7

asmākaṃ: our; tu: also; viśiṣṭāḥ: important; ye: who; tān: those; nibodha: know; dvijottama: the best of the brāhmaṇas; nāyakāḥ: leaders; mama: my; sainyasya: of the army; saṃjñārthaṃ: for information; tān: them; bravīmi: I speak; te: to you.

1.7 O best of the brāhmaṇas, let me tell you, who are the powerful warriors on our side—the generals of my army; for your information, I mention them.

भवान् भीष्मश्च कर्णश्च कृपश्च समितिञ्जय: ।
अेशत्थामा विकर्णश्च सौमदत्तिस्तथैव च ॥ १.८

bhavān bhīṣmaś ca karṇaś ca kṛ paś ca samitiṃjayaḥ |
aśvatthāmā vikarṇaś ca saumadattis tathai 'va ca || 1.8

bhavān: your self; bhīṣmaḥ: grandfather Bhīṣma; ca: and; karṇaḥ: Karṇa; ca: and; kṛpaḥ: Krpa; ca: and; samitiṃjayaḥ: victorious in war; aśvatthāmā: Aśvattāma; vikarṇaḥ: Vikarṇa; ca: and; saumadattiḥ: the son of Somadatta; tathā: thus as; eva: only; ca: and

1.8 Your goodself, Bhīṣma, Karṇa, Kṛpa, who are ever victorious in battle, an even so Aśvatthāma, Vikarṇa and the son of Somadatta.

अन्ये च बहव: शूरा मदर्थे त्यक्तजीविता: ।
नानाशस्त्रप्रहरणा: सर्वे युद्धविशारदा: ॥ १.९

anye ca bahavaḥ śūrā mad arthe tyakta jīvitāḥ |
nānā śastra praharaṇāḥ sarve yuddha viśāradāḥ || 1.9

anye: many others; ca: also; bahavaḥ: in great numbers; śūrāḥ: heroes; mad arthe: for my sake; tyakta jīvitāḥ: prepared to risk life; nānā: many; śastra: weapons; praharaṇāḥ: equipped with; sarve: all of them; yuddha: battle; viśāradāḥ: experienced in military science.

1.9 Many other heroes there are who are prepared to lay down their lives for my sake; all are well-equipped with different weapons, and well experienced in warfare science.

अपर्याप्तं तदस्माकं बलं भीष्माभिरक्षितम् ।
पर्याप्तं त्विदमेतेषां बलं भीमाभिरक्षितम् ॥ १.१०

aparyāptaṃ tad asmākaṃ balaṃ bhiṣmābhi rakṣitam /
paryāptaṃ tvidam eteṣāṃ balaṃ bhīmābhi rakṣitam // 1.10

aparyāptaṃ: unlimited; tat : that; asmākaṃ: of ours; balaṃ: strength; bhīṣmābhi rakṣitam: presided over and protected by Bhīṣma; paryāptaṃ: limited; tu: but; idaṃ: all this; eteṣāṃ: their; balaṃ: strength; bhīmābhi rakṣitam: presided over and protected by Bhīma

1.10 The strength of army of ours, protected by Bhīṣma, is invincible whereas the strength of their army carefully protected by Bhīma is limited.

अयनेषु च सर्वेषु यथाभागमवस्थिताः ।
भीष्ममेवाभिरक्षन्तु भवन्तः सर्व एव हि ॥ १.११

ayaneṣu ca sarveṣu yathā bhāgam avasthitāḥ /
bhīṣmam evā bhirakṣantu bhavantaḥ sarva eva hi // 1.11

ayaneṣu: in the divisions; ca: and; sarveṣu: everywhere; yathā bhāgam: as per the divisions; avasthitāḥ: situated; bhiṣmam: to Bhisma; eva: alone; abhi rakṣantu: protect; bhavantaḥ: you; sarva: all; eva: only; hi: indeed

1.11 Stationed in your respective divisions on all fronts, all of you must give full protection to Bhīṣma.

तस्य सञ्जनयन् हर्षं कुरुवृद्धः पितामहः ।
सिंहनादं विनद्योच्चैः शङ्खं दध्मौ प्रतापवान् ॥ १.१२

tasya sañjanayan harṣaṃ kuru vṛddhaḥ pitāmahaḥ /
siṃha nādaṃ vinadyoccaiḥ śaṅkhaṃ dadhmau pratāpavān // 1.12

tasya: his; sañjanayan: causing; harṣaṃ: joy; kuru vṛddhaḥ: old man of the

Kuru dynasty; pitāmahaḥ: the grandfather; siṃha nādaṃ: lion's roar; vinadya: causing to sound; uccaiḥ: loudly; śaṇkhaṃ: conch; dadhmau: blew; pratāpavān: mighty

1.12 Then Bhīṣma, the mighty patriarch of the Kuru dynasty, their glorious grandfather, roared like a lion and blew his conch, giving Duryodhana joy.

ततः शङ्खाश्च भेर्यश्च पणवानकगोमुखाः ।
सहसैवाभ्यहन्यन्त स शब्दस्तुमुलोऽभवत् ॥ १.१३

tataḥśaṇkhāś ca bheryaś ca paṇavānaka gomukhāḥ |
sahasaivābhyahanyanta sa śabdas tumulo 'bhavat || 1.13

tataḥ: then; śaṇkhāḥ: conches; ca: and; bheryaś ca paṇavānaka: drums, bugles, horns and trumpets; gomukhāḥ: cow horns; sahasā eva: quite suddenly abhyahanyanta: blared; saḥ: that; śabdaḥ: sound; tumulaḥ: tumultuous; abhavat: became

1.13 Then, conches, bugles, trumpets, drums and horns were all suddenly sounded, and the combined sound was tumultuous.

ततः शङ्खाश्च भेर्यश्च पणवानकगोमुखाः ।
माधवः पाण्डवश्चैव दिव्यौ शङ्खौ प्रदध्मतुः ॥ १.१४

tataḥ śvetair hayair yukte mahati syandane sthitau |
mādhavaḥ pāṇḍavaś caiva divyau śaṇkhau pradadhmatuḥ || 1.14

tataḥ: then; śvetaiḥ: by white; hayaiḥ: horses; yukte: being yoked; mahati: magnificent; syandane: chariot; sthitau: seated; mādhavaḥ: Mādhava, Śrī Kṛṣṇa; pāṇḍavaḥ: son of Pāṇḍu; ca: and; eva: only; divyau: divine; śaṇkhau: conches; pradadhmatuḥ: blew

1.14 Then, seated on a magnificent chariot drawn by white horses, both Mādhava (Kṛṣṇa) and Arjuna sounded their divine conches.

पाञ्चजन्यं हृषीकेशो देवदत्तं धनञ्जयः ।
पौण्ड्रं दध्मौ महाशङ्खं भीमकर्मा वृकोदरः ॥ १.१५

pāñcajanyaṃ hṛṣīkeśo devadattaṃ dhanañjayaḥ I
pauṇḍraṃ dadhmau mahā śaṅkhaṃ bhīma karmā vṛkodaraḥ II 1.15

pāñcajanyaṃ: the conch named Pāñcajanya; hṛṣīkeśaḥ: One who has mastered the senses (Kṛṣṇa) ; devadattaṃ: the conch named Devadatta; dhanañjayaḥ: Dhañanjaya, the winner of wealth; pauṇḍraṃ: the conch named Pauṇḍra; dadhmau: blew; mahā-śaṅkhaṃ: the great conch; bhīma karmā: one who performs terrible tasks; vṛkodaraḥ: one with the belly of a wolf

1.15 Then, Hṛṣikeśa (Kṛṣṇa) blew His conch, called Pāñcajanya; Dhanañjaya (Arjuna) blew his conch, called Devadatta; and Bhīma blew his mighty conch called Pauṇḍra.

अनन्तविजयं राजा कुन्तीपुत्रो युधिष्ठिरः ।
नकुलः सहदेवश्च सुघोषमणिपुष्पकौ ॥ १.१६

anantavijayaṃ rājā kuntī putro yudhiṣṭhiraḥ I
nakulaḥ sahadevaś ca sughoṣa maṇipuṣpakau II 1.16

काश्यश्च परमेष्वासः शिखण्डी च महारथः ।
धृष्टद्युम्नो विराटश्च सात्यकिश्चापराजितः ॥ १.१७

kāśyaś ca parameṣvāsaḥ śikhaṇḍī ca mahā rathaḥ I
dhṛṣṭadyumno virāṭaś ca sātyakiś cāparājitaḥ II 1.17

द्रुपदो द्रौपदेयाश्च सर्वशः पृथिवीपते ।
सौभद्रश्च महाबाहुः शङ्खान् दध्मुः पृथक् पृथक् ॥ १.१८

drupado draupadeyāś ca sarvaśaḥ pṛthivī pate I
saubhadraś ca mahābāhuh śaṅkhān dadhmuḥ pṛthak-pṛthak II 1.18

anantavijayaṃ: the conch named Ananta-vijaya; rājā: the king; kuntī putraḥ: the son of Kuntī; yudhiṣṭhiraḥ: Yudhistra; nakulaḥ: Nakula; sahadevaḥ: Sahadeva; ca: and; sughoṣa maṇipuṣpakau: the conches named Sughośa and Maṇipuṣpaka; kāśyaḥ: the king of Kāśī (Vāraṇāsi); ca: and; parameṣvāsaḥ: the great archer; śikhaṇḍī: Śikhaṇḍī; ca: and; mahā rathaḥ: great chariot warrior; dhṛṣṭadyumnaḥ: Dhṛṣṭadyumna; virāṭaḥ: Virāṭa; ca: and; sātyakiḥ: Sātyaki; ca: and; aparājitaḥ: invincible; drupadaḥ: Drupada; draupadeyāḥ: the sons of Draupadī ; ca: also; sarvaśaḥ: all; pṛthivīpate: O' king of earth; aubhadraḥ: the son of Subhadrā (Abhimanyu); ca: and; mahā bāhuḥ: mighty-armed; śaṅkhān: conches; dadhmuḥ blew; pṛthak pṛthak: severally

1.16, 17, 18 King Yudhiṣṭra, the son of Kuntī, blew his conch, the Anantavijaya, and Nakula and Sahadeva blew theirs known as Sughośa and Maṇipuṣpaka. The excellent archer, the king of Kāśī, the great chariot-fighter Śikhaṇḍī, Dhṛṣṭadyumna, Virāṭa and the invincible Sātyaki, Drupada, the sons of Draupadī , and the mighty-armed Abhimanyu, son of Subhadrā, all of them, O king, blew their own conches.

स घोषो धार्तराष्ट्राणां हृदयानि व्यदारयत् ।
नभश्च पृथिवीं चैव तुमुलो व्यनुनादयन् ॥ १.१९

sa ghoṣo dhārtarāṣṭrāṇāṃ hṛdayāni vyadārayat /
nabhaś ca pṛthivīṃ caiva tumulo vyanunādayan // 1.19

saḥ: that; ghoṣaḥ: uproar; dhārtarāṣṭrāṇām: of the sons of Dhṛtarāṣṭra; hṛdayāni: hearts; vyadārayat: broke; nabhaḥ: the sky; ca: and; pṛthivīm: the earth; ca: and; eva: only; tumulaḥ: tumultous; vyanunādayan: resounding

1.19 The terrible sound echoing through the sky and the earth rent the hearts of the sons of Dhṛtarāṣṭra.

अथ व्यवस्थितान्दृष्ट्वा धार्तराष्ट्रान् कपिध्वजः ।
प्रवृत्ते शस्त्रसम्पाते धनुरुद्यम्य पाण्डवः ।
हृषीकेशं तदा वाक्यमिदमाह महीपते ॥ १.२०

atha vyavasthitān dṛṣṭvā dhārtarāṣṭrān kapidhvajaḥ /

pravṛtte śastrasaṃpāte dhanur udyamya pāṇḍavaḥ |
hṛṣīkeśaṃ tadā vākyam idam āha mahīpate || 1.20

atha: then; vyavasthitān: stationed; dṛṣṭvā: seeing; dhārtarāṣṭrān: the sons of Dhṛtarāṣtra; kapidhvajaḥ: one whose flag is marked with the ape; pravṛtte: about to begin; śastrasaṃpāte: the arrows released; dhanuḥ: bow; udyamya: after taking up; pāṇḍavaḥ: the son of Pāṇḍu; hṛṣīkeśaṃ: to Kṛṣṇa; tadā: then; vākyam: words; idaṃ: this; āha: said; mahī pate: O Lord of the earth

1.20 Seeing the sons of Dhṛtarāṣṭra arrayed in the battle field, Arjuna, the son of Pāṇḍu, who was seated in his chariot, bearing the flag marked with Hanumān, took up his bow.

अर्जुन उवाच
सेनयोरुभयोर्मध्ये रथं स्थापय मेऽच्युत ।
यावदेतान्निरीक्षेऽहं योद्धुकामानवस्थितान् ॥ १.२१
कैर्मया सह योद्धव्यमस्मिन् रणसमुद्यमे ॥ १.२२

arjuna uvāca
senayor ubhayor madhye rathaṃ sthāpaya me 'cyuta |
yāvad etān nirīkṣe 'haṃ yoddhu kāmān avasthitān || 1.21
kair mayā saha yoddhavyam asmin raṇasamudyame || 1.22

arjuna: Arjuna; uvāca: said; senayoḥ: of the armies; ubhayoḥ: of both; madhye: in between; rathaṃ: the chariot; sthāpaya: position; me: my; acyuta: O infallible one; yāvat: while; etān: all these; nirīkṣe: behold; ahaṃ: I; yoddhu kāmān: desiring to fight; avasthitān: standing; kaiḥ: with whom; mayā: by me; saha: with; yoddhavyam: to be fought; asmin: in this; raṇasamudyame: situation of war;

1.21, 22 Arjuna said: O Acyuta (Infallible One), please place my chariot between the two armies while I may observe these warriors arrayed for battle and with whom I have to engage in fight.

योत्स्यमानानवेक्षेऽहं य एतेऽत्र समागताः ।
धार्तराष्ट्रस्य दुर्बुद्धेर्युद्धे प्रियचिकीर्षवः ॥ १.२३

yotsyamānān avekṣe 'haṃ ya ete 'tra samāgatāḥ |
dhārtarāṣṭrasya durbuddher yuddhe priyacikīrṣavaḥ || 1.23

yotsyamānān: those who wish to fight; avekṣe: see; ahaṃ: I; yaḥ: who; ete: these; atra : here; samāgatāḥ: assembled; dhārtarāṣṭrasya: the son of Dhṛtarāṣṭra; durbuddheḥ: evil-minded; yuddhe: in the fight; priyacikīrṣavaḥ: wishing to please

1.23 Let me see these well wishers in this war of the evil-minded Duryodhana, who have come together here to fight.

सञ्जय उवाच
एवमुक्तो हृषीकेशो गुडाकेशेन भारत ।
सेनयोरुभयोर्मध्ये स्थापयित्वा रथोत्तमम् ॥ १.२४
भीष्मद्रोणप्रमुखत: सर्वेषां च महीक्षिताम् ।
उवाच पार्थ पश्यैतान्समवेतान्कुरूनिति ॥ १.२५

sañjaya uvāca
evam ukto hṛṣīkeśo guḍākeśena bhārata |
senayor ubhayor madhye sthāpayitvā rathottamam || 1.24
bhīṣma droṇa pramukhataḥ sarveṣāṃ ca mahīkṣitām |
uvāca pārtha paśyaitān samavetānkurūniti || 1.25

sañjaya: Sañjaya; uvāca: said; evaṃ: thus; uktaḥ: addressed; hṛṣīkeśaḥ: Kṛṣṇa (Lord of senses); guḍākeśena: Arjuna (one who has conquered sleep); bhārata: O Bhārata; senayoḥ: of armies; ubhayoḥ: of both; madhye: in the middle of; sthāpayitvā: having placed; rathottamam: the finest chariot bhīṣma: grandfather Bhīṣma; droṇa: the teacher Droṇa; pramukhataḥ: in front of; sarveṣāṃ: of all; ca: and; mahīkṣitām: of rulers of the world; uvāca: said; pārtha: O Pārtha; paśyai: see; etān: these; samavetān: assembled; kurūn: the Kurus; iti: thus

1.24, 25 Sañjaya said: O descendant of Bhārata, being thus addressed by Guḍākeśa (Arjuna), Hṛṣīkeśa (Kṛṣṇa) then drew up the fine chariot to the middle of both the armies in front of Bhīṣma, Droṇa and all the kings and said, 'Arjuna, behold the Kauravas assembled here.'

तत्रापश्यत् स्थितान् पार्थः पितॄनथ पितामहान् ।
आचार्यान्मातुलान्भ्रातॄन् पुत्रान्पौत्रान्सखींस्तथा ।
षवशुरान्सुहृदश्चैव सेनयोरुभयोरपि ॥ १.२६

tatrā paśyat sthitān pārthaḥ pitṛ-n atha pitāmahān |
ācāryān mātulān bhrātṛ-n putrān pautrān sakhīṃs tathā |
śvaśurān suhṛdaś caiva senayorubhayorapi || 1.26

tatra: there; apaśyat: saw; sthitān: positioned; pārthaḥ: Arjuna; pitṛ-n: fathers; atha: also; pitāmahān: grandfathers; ācāryān: teachers; mātulān: maternal uncles; bhrātṛ-n: brothers; putrān: sons; pautrān: grandsons; sakhīn: friends; tathā: too; śvaśurān: fathers-in-law; suhṛdaḥ: well-wishers; ca: and; eva: only; senayoḥ: of the armies; ubhayoḥ: of both ; api: also

1.26 There Arjuna saw, stationed there in both the armies his uncles, grand uncles, teachers, maternal uncles, brothers, sons, grandsons, and friends, as well as his fathers-in-law and well-wishers.

तान् समीक्ष्य स कौन्तेयः सर्वान्बन्धूनवस्थितान् ।
कृपया परयाऽऽविष्टो विषीदन्निदमब्रवीत् । १.२७

tān samīkṣya sa kaunteyaḥ sarvān bandhūn avasthitān |
kṛpayā parayā 'viṣṭo viṣīdann idam abravīt || 1.27

tān: those; samīkṣya: after seeing; sa: he; kaunteyaḥ: kaunteya; sarvān: all; bandhūn: relatives; avasthitān: standing; kṛpayā: by pity; parayā: deep; āviṣṭaḥ: filled; viṣīdan: lamenting; idaṃ: thus; abravīt: spoke

1.27 Seeing all those relatives present there, Arjuna was overwhelmed with deep pity and spoke in sadness.

अर्जुन उवाच
दृष्ट्वेमं स्वजनं कृष्ण युयुत्सुं समुपस्थितम्
सीदन्ति मम गात्राणि मुखं च परिशुष्यति ॥ १.२८

arjuna uvāca
dṛṣṭvemaṃ svajanaṃ kṛṣṇa yuyutsuṃ samupasthitam |
sīdanti mama gātrāṇi mukhaṃ ca pariśuṣyati || 1.28

arjuna: Arjuna; uvāca: said; dṛṣṭvā: after seeing; imaṃ: all these; svajanaṃ: kinsmen; kṛṣṇa: Kṛṣṇa; yuyutsuṃ: all eager to do battle; samupasthitam: arranged in form; sīdanti: fail; mama: my; gātrāṇi: limbs; mukhaṃ: mouth; ca: and; pariśuṣyati: is parching

वेपथुश्च शरीरे मे रोमहर्षश्च जायते ।
गाण्डीवं स्रंसते हस्तात्त्वक्चैव परिदह्यते ॥ १.२९

vepathuś ca śarīre me romaharṣaś ca jāyate |
gāṇḍīvaṃ sraṃsate hastāt tvak caiva paridahyate || 1.29

vepathuḥ: trembling; ca: and; śarīre: in body; me: my; romaharṣaḥ: hair standing on end; ca: and; jāyate: happens; gāṇḍīvaṃ: Gāṇḍīva; sraṃsate: slips; hastāt: from the hands; tvak: skin; ca: and; eva: only; paridahyate: is burning

1.28, 29 Arjuna said: Kṛṣṇa, seeing my friends and relatives present before me, eager to wage war, my limbs are giving way, my mouth is parching and a shiver is running through my body, my hair is standing on end.

न च शक्नोम्यवस्थातुं भ्रमतीव च मे मनः ।
निमित्तानि च पश्यामि विपरीतानि केशव ॥ १.३०

na ca śaknomy avasthātuṃ bhramatīva ca me manaḥ |
nimittāni ca paśyāmi viparī tāni keśava || 1.30

na: not; ca: and; śaknomi: am able; avasthātuṃ: to stand; bhramatīva: as if whirling; ca: and; me: my; manaḥ: mind; nimittāni: portents; ca: also; paśyāmi: I see; viparī tāni: just the opposite; keśava: O Keśava, killer of demon Kesin

1.30 My bow gāṇḍīva is slipping from my hands and my skin is burning all over. My mind is whirling as it were, and I am now unable to stand here any longer.

न च श्रेयोऽनुपश्यामि हत्वा स्वजनमाहवे ।
न काङ्क्षे विजयं कृष्ण न च राज्यं सुखानि च ।

na ca śreyo 'nupaśyāmi hatvā svajanam āhave /
na kāṅkṣe vijayaṃ krṣṇa na ca rājyaṃ sukhāni ca // 1.31

na: not; ca: and; śreyaḥ: good; anupaśyāmi: I see; hatvā: after killing; svajanam: own kinsmen; āhave: in battle; na: not; kāṅkṣe: I desire; vijayaṃ: victory; kṛṣṇa: O Kṛṣṇa; na: not; ca: and; rājyaṃ: kingdom; sukhāni: pleasures; ca: and

1.31 I foresee only evil omens, O Kṛṣṇa, I do not see any good coming out of killing one's own kinsmen [svajanam] in this battle. I do not covet my dear Kṛṣṇa, victory or kingdom or pleasures.

किं नो राज्येन गोविन्द किं भोगैर्जीवितेन वा ।
येषामर्थे काङ्क्षितं नो राज्यं भोगाः सुखानि च ॥ १.३१
त इमेऽवस्थिता युद्धे प्राणांस्त्यक्त्वा धनानि च ।
आचार्याः पितरः पुत्राः तथैव च पितामहाः ॥ १.३३
मातुलाः श्शुराः पौत्राः श्यालाः संबन्धिनस्तथा ।
एतान्न हन्तुमिच्छामि घ्नतोऽपि मधुसूदन ॥ १.३४
अपि त्रैलोक्यराज्यस्य हेतोः किं नु महीकृते ।
निहत्य धार्तराष्ट्रान्नः का प्रीतिः स्याज्जनार्दन ॥ १.३५

kiṃ no rājyena govinda kiṃ bhogair jīvitena vā /
yeṣām arthe kāṅkṣitaṃ no rājyaṃ bhogāḥ sukhāni ca // 1.32

ta ime 'vasthitā yuddhe prāṇāṃs tyaktvā dhanāni ca /
ācāryāḥ pitaraḥ putrāḥ tathaiva ca pitāmahāḥ // 1.33

mātulāḥ śvaśurāḥ pautrāḥ śyālāḥ saṃbandhinas tathā /
etān na hantum icchāmi ghnato 'pi madhusūdana // 1.34

api trailokyarājyasya hetoḥ kiṃ nu mahīkṛ te /

nihatya dhārtarāṣṭrān naḥ kā prī tiḥ syāj janārdana || 1.35

kiṃ: what; no: to us; rājyena: by kingdom; govinda: Govinda; kiṃ: what; bhogaiḥ: by pleasures; jīvitena: life; vā: or; yeṣām: for whose; arthe: sake; kāṅkṣitaṃ: desired; no: by us; rājyaṃ: kingdom; bhogāḥ: enjoyment; sukhāni: happiness; ca: and; te: they; ime: these; avasthitāḥ: stand; yuddhe: in battle; prāṇān: lives; tyaktvā: giving up; dhanāni: wealth; ca: and; ācāryāḥ: teachers; pitaraḥ: fathers; putrāḥ: sons; tathā eva: like that; ca: and; pitāmahāḥ: grandfathers; mātulāḥ: maternal uncles; śvaśurāḥ: fathers-inlaw; pautrāḥ: grandsons; śyālāḥ: brothers-in-law; saṃbandhinaḥ: relatives; tathā: as well as; etān: these; na: not; hantum: for killing; icchāmi: I wish; ghnataḥ: killed; api: even; madhusūdana: O killer of the demon Madhu; api: even; trailokya: of the three worlds; rājyasya: of the kingdoms; hetoḥ: in exchange; kiṃ: what; nu: then; mahīkṛte: for the sake of the earth; nihatya: after slaying; dhārtarāṣṭrān: sons of Dhṛtarāṣṭra; naḥ: to us; kā: what; prītiḥ: pleasure; syāt: may be; janārdana: Janārdana; pāpaṃ: sins; eva: only; āśrayet: will take hold; asmān: us; hatvā: after killing; etān: these; ātatāyinaḥ: wrong-doers

1.32—1.36 Of what use will kingdom or happiness or even life be to us? For whose sake we desire this kingdom, enjoyment and happiness, they stand in battle staking their lives and property. Teachers, fathers, sons as well as grandfathers, maternal uncles, fathers-inlaw, grandsons, brothers-in-law and other relatives. Madhusūdana (Kṛṣṇa), even if I am killed (by them) I do not want to kill these ones even to gain control of all three worlds, much less for the earthly lordship. What pleasure will we get by destroying the sons of Dhṛtarāṣṭra, Janārdana? Only sin will overcome us if we slay these wrong doers.

पापमेवाश्रयेदस्मान्हत्वैतानाततायिनः

तस्मान्नार्हा वयं हन्तुं धार्तराष्ट्रान्स्वबान्धवान् ।

स्वजनं हि कथं हत्वा सुखिनः स्याम माधव ॥ १.३७

pāpam evāśrayed asmān hatvaitān ātatāyinaḥ |

tasmān nārhā vayaṃ hantuṃ dhārtarāṣṭrān svabāndhavān |
svajanaṃ hi kathaṃ hatvā sukhinaḥ syāma mādhava || 1.37

tasmāt: therefore; na: not; arhāḥ: justified; vayaṃ: we; hantuṃ: to kill; dhārtarāṣṭrān: the sons of Dhṛtarāṣṭra; svabāndhavān: our friends; svajanaṃ: kinsmen; hi: for; kathaṃ: how; hatvā: after killing; sukhinaḥ: happy; syāma: may be; mādhava: O Mādhava (Kṛṣṇa)

1.37 Therefore, it is not proper for us to kill the sons of Dhṛtarāṣṭra and our relations, for how could we be happy after killing our own kinsmen, Mādhava?

यद्यप्येते न पश्यन्ति लोभोपहतचेतसः ।
कुलक्षयकृतं दोषं मित्रद्रोहे च पातकम् ॥ १.३८

yadyapyete na paśyanti lobhopahata cetasaḥ |
kulakṣayakṛtaṃ doṣaṃ mitradrohe ca pātakam || 1.38

yadyapi: even if; ete: these; na: not; paśyanti: see; lobhopahata: greed overtaken; cetasaḥ: intelligence; kulakṣayakṛtaṃ: in killing the race done; doṣaṃ: fault; mitradrohe: treason to friends; ca: and; pātakam: sin

1.38 O Janārdana, these men, blinded by greed, see no fault in killing one's family or being treasonable to friends, incur sin.

कथं न ज्ञेयमस्माभिः पापादस्मान्निवर्तितुम् ।
कुलक्षयकृतं दोषं प्रपश्यद्भिर्जनार्दन ॥ १.३९

kathaṃ na jñeyam asmābhiḥ pāpād asmān nivartitum |
kulakṣaya kṛ taṃ doṣaṃ prapaśyadbhir janārdana || 1.39

kathaṃ: why; na: not; jñeyam: to be understood; asmābhiḥ: by us; pāpāt: from sins; asmāt: from this; nivartitum: to turn away; kulakṣaya kṛtaṃ: destruction of a dynasty; doṣaṃ: evil; prapaśyadbhiḥ: by the witnessing; janārdana: Janārdana (Kṛṣṇa)

1.39 Why should we, who clearly see the sin in the destruction of a dynasty, not turn away from this crime?

कुलक्षये प्रणश्यन्ति कुलधर्माः सनातनाः ।
धर्मे नष्टे कुलं कृत्स्नमधर्मोऽभिभवत्युत ॥ १.४०

kulakṣaye praṇaśyanti kuladharmāḥ sanātanāḥ |
dharme naṣṭe kulaṃ kṛ tsnam adharmo 'bhibhavatyuta || 1.40

kulakṣaye: in destroying the family; praṇaśyanti: perish; kuladharmāḥ: the family traditions; sanātanāḥ: age-old; dharme: virtue; naṣṭe: destroyed; kulaṃ: family; kṛtsnam: whole; adharmaḥ: non-righteousness; abhibhavati: overtakes; uta: and

1.40 With the destruction of the dynasty, the age-old family traditions die and virtue having been lost, vice overtakes the entire race.

अधर्माभिभवात्कृष्ण प्रदुष्यन्ति कुलस्त्रियः ।
स्त्रीषु दुष्टासु वार्ष्णेय जायते वर्णसङ्करः ॥ १.४१

adharmābhibhavāt krṣna praduṣyanti kula striyaḥ |
strīṣu duṣṭāsu vārṣṇeya jāyate varṇasaṃkaraḥ || 1.41

adharma: non-righteousness; abhi bhavāt: from the preponderance; kṛṣṇa: O Kṛṣṇa; praduṣyanti: become corrupt; kula striyaḥ: family women; strīṣu duṣṭāsu: when women become corrupt; vārṣṇeya: O Vārṣṇeya (Kṛṣṇa); jāyate: arises; varṇasaṃkaraḥ: intermixture of castes

1.41 When non-righteous practices become common, O Kṛṣṇa, the women of the family become corrupt, and with the degradation of womanhood, O Descendant of Vṛṣṇi, ensues intermixture of castes.

सङ्करो नरकायैव कुलघ्नानां कुलस्य च ।
पतन्ति पितरो ह्येषां लुप्तपिण्डोदकक्रियाः ॥ १.४२

saṃkaro narakāyaiva kulaghnānāṃ kulasya ca |
patanti pitaro hyeṣāṃ lupta piṇḍodaka kriyāḥ || 1.42

saṃkaraḥ: mixture; narakāya: for hell; eva: only; kulaghnānāṃ: of the killers of the family; kulasya: of the family; ca: and; patanti: fall; pitaraḥ : forefathers; hi: also; eṣāṃ: their; lupta: deprived; piṇḍodaka: offering of rice and water to the departed souls; kriyāḥ: performances

दोषैरेतैः कुलघ्नानां वर्णसङ्करकारकैः ।
उत्साद्यन्ते जातिधर्माः कुलधर्माश्च शोशताः ॥ १.४३

doṣair etaiḥ kulaghnānāṃ varṇa saṃkarakārakaiḥ |
utsādyante jātidharmāḥ kuladharmāś ca śāśvatāḥ || 1.43

doṣaiḥ: faults; etaiḥ: these; kulaghnānāṃ: of the destroyer of the family; varṇa saṃkara: mixture of castes; kārakaiḥ : by the doers; utsādyante: are destroyed; jāti dharmāḥ: caste rituals; kula dharmāḥ: family traditions; ca: and; śāśvatāḥ: age-old

1.42, 43 A mixture of blood damns the destroyers of race and the race itself. Deprived of offering of oblations of rice and water the departed souls of the race also fall, the age-long caste traditions and family customs of the killers of kinmen become extinct.

उत्सन्नकुलधर्माणां मनुष्याणां जनार्दन ।
नरकेऽनियतं वासो भवतीत्यनुशुश्रुम ॥ १.४४

utsannakula dharmāṇāṃ manuṣyāṇāṃ janārdana |
narake 'niyataṃ vāso bhavatītyanuśuśruma || 1.44

utsanna: spoiled; kula dharmāṇāṃ: of those who have the family traditions; manuṣyāṇāṃ: of such men; janārdana: O Kṛṣṇa; narake: in hell; aniyataṃ: always; vāsaḥ: residence; bhavati: becomes; iti: thus; anuśuśruma: we hear

1.44 O Janārdana, we hear that those who have lost family traditions dwell in hell for an indefinite period of time.

अहो बत महत् पापं कर्तुं व्यवसिता वयम् ।
यद्राज्यसुखलोभेन हन्तुं स्वजनमुद्यताः ॥ १.४५

aho bata mahat pāpaṃ kartuṃ vyavasitā vayaṃ /
yad rājya sukha lobhena hantuṃ svajanam udyatāḥ // 1.45

aho bata: alas; mahat: great; pāpaṃ: sins; kartuṃ: to do; vyavasitā: prepared; vayaṃ: we; yat: that; rājya: kingdom; sukha lobhena: by greed for kingdom; hantuṃ: to kill; svajanaṃ: kinsmen; udyatāḥ: prepared

1.45 Alas, we are prepared to commit greatly sinful acts of killing our kinsmen, driven by the desire to enjoy royal happiness.

यदि मामप्रतीकारमशस्त्रं शस्त्रपाणयः ।
धार्तराष्ट्रा रणे हन्युस्तन्मे क्षेमतरं भवेत् ॥ १.४६

yadi mām apratīkāram aśastraṃ śastrapāṇayaḥ /
dhārtarāṣṭrā raṇe hanyuḥ tan me kṣemataraṃ bhavet // 1.46

yadi: if; māṃ: me; apratīkāraṃ: not resistant; aśastraṃ: unarmed; śastrapāṇayaḥ: with weapons in hand; dhārtarāṣṭrāḥ: the sons of Dhṛtarāṣṭra; raṇe: in the battle; hanyuḥ: may kill; tat: that; me: mine; kṣemataraṃ: better; bhavet: will be

1.46 It would be better if the sons of Dhṛtarāṣṭra, armed with weapons, killed me in battle while I am unarmed and unresisting.

सञ्जय उवाच

एवमुक्त्वार्जुनः सङ्ख्ये रथोपस्थ उपाविशत् ।
विसृज्य सशरं चापं शोकसंविग्नमानसः ॥ १.४७

sañjaya uvāca
evam uktvārjunaḥ saṃkhye rathopastha upāviśat /
visṛ jya saśaraṃ cāpaṃ śokasaṃvignamānasaḥ // 1.47

sañjaya: Sañjaya; uvāca: said; evaṃ: thus; uktvā: having said; arjunaḥ: Arjuna; saṃkhye: in the battle field; rathopastha: chariot at the rear side; upāviśat: sat down; visṛ jya: having cast aside; saśaraṃ: with the arrow; cāpaṃ: the bow; śoka: sorrow; saṃvigna: distressed; mānasaḥ: with a mind

1.47 Sañjaya said: Arjuna, whose mind was agitated by grief on the battle field, having spoken thus, cast aside his bow along with the arrow and sat down at the rear portion of the chariot.

इति श्रीमद्भगवद्गीतासूपनिषत्सु ब्रह्मविद्यायां योगशास्त्रे
श्रीकृष्णार्जुनसंवादे अर्जुनविषादयोगो नाम प्रथमोऽध्यायः ॥

iti śrī mad bhagavadgītāsūpaniṣatsu brahmavidyāyām
yogaśāstre śrīkṛṣṇārjuna saṃvāde arjuna visāda yogo nāma
prathamo 'dhyāyaḥ ॥

In the ***Upaniṣad*** of ***Śrimad Bhagavad Gītā***, the scripture of yoga dealing with the science of Brahman, the Supreme Absolute, ***Brahmavidyā Yogaśāstra***, in the form of ***Śrī Kṛṣṇārjuna saṁvād,*** dialogue between Śrī Kṛṣṇa and Arjuna, this is the first chapter named, ***Arjunaviṣāda Yogaḥ***, *'The Yoga of Arjuna's Dilemma'*

CHAPTER 2

अथ द्वितीयोऽध्यायः

सांख्य योगः

Sāṅkhya Yogaḥ

सञ्जय उवाच ।
तं तथा कृपयाविष्टमश्रुपूर्णाकुलेक्षणम् ।
विषीदन्तमिदं वाक्यमुवाच मधुसूदनः ॥ २.१ ॥

sañjaya uvāca
taṁ tathākṛpayāviṣṭamaśrupūrṇākulekṣaṇam /
viṣīdantaṁidam vākyamuvāca madhusūdanaḥ // 2.1

sañjaya uvāca: Sañjaya said; taṁ: to him; tathā: thus; kṛpayā: by pity; āviṣṭam: overcome; aśrupūrṇā: full of tears; ākula: agitated; īkṣaṇam: (one with) eyes; viṣīdantaṁ: sorrowing; idaṁ: this; vākyam: word; uvāca: said; madhu-sūdanaḥ: the killer of Madhu

2.1 Sañjaya said: As Arjuna's eyes overflowed with tears of pity and despair, Madhusūdana (Kṛṣṇa) spoke to him thus.

श्री भगवानुवाच
कुतस्त्वा कश्मलमिदं विषमे समुपस्थितम् ।
अनार्यजुष्टमस्वर्ग्यमकीर्तिकरमर्जुन ॥ २.२

śrībhagavānuvāca

kutastvā kaśmalamidaṁ viṣame samupasthitam |
anārya-juṣṭam asvargyam akīrti-karam arjuna || 2.2

śrī bhagavān uvāca: Lord says; kutaḥ: why; tvā: upon you; kaśmalam: delusion; idaṁ: this; viṣame: in this critical time; samupasthitam: arrived; anārya juṣṭam: unworthy of a noble soul; asvargyam: not leading to heaven; akīrtikaram: disgraceful; arjuna: O Arjuna

2.2 Bhagavān Kṛṣṇa says: Where from has this impurity, dejection descended on you at this critical time, Arjuna! You behave unlike a noble man and this will keep you away from realization.

क्लैब्यं मा स्म गमः पार्थ नैतत्त्वय्युपपद्यते ।
क्षुद्रं हृदयदौर्बल्यं त्यक्त्वोत्तिष्ठ परन्तप ॥ २.३

klaibyaṁ mā sma gamaḥ pārtha naitattvayyupapadyate |
kṣudraṁ hṛdayadaurbalyaṁ tyaktvottiṣṭha parantapa || 2.3

klaibyaṁ: impotence; mā: do not; sma gamaḥ: yield; pārtha: son of Pritā; na: not; etat: this; tvayi: in you; upapadyate: is fitting; kṣudraṁ: mean; hṛdaya daurbalyaṁ: weakness of heart; tyaktvaa: after abandoning; uttiṣṭha: get up; paraṁtapa: O destroyer of enemies

2.3 Do not yield to fear, Pārtha! It does not befit you. Drop this powerlessness of the heart and stand up, O Parantapa, destroyer of enemies!

अर्जुन उवाच
कथं भीष्ममहं सङ्ख्ये द्रोणं च मधुसूदन ।
इषुभिः प्रतियोत्स्यामि पूजार्हावरिसूदन ॥ २.४

arjuna uvāca

katham bhīṣmamahaṁ saṅkhye droṇaṁ ca madhusūdana |
iṣubhiḥ pratiyotsyāmi pūjārhāvarisūdana || 2.4

arjuna uvāca: Arjuna said; katham: how; bhīṣmam: Bhīṣma; ahaṁ: I; saṁkhye: in battle; droṇaṁ: Droṇa; ca: also; madhusūdana: O killer of Madhu; iṣubhiḥ: with arrows; pratiyotsyāmi: shall counterattack; pūjārhāu: the two worthy of worship; arisūdana: O killer of the enemies

2.4 Arjuna said: O Madhusūdana (killer of Madhu), how can I oppose, in battle, Bhīṣma and Droṇa who are worthy of my worship?

गुरूनहत्वा हि महानुभावान्
श्रेयो भोक्तुं भैक्ष्यमपीह लोके ।
हत्वाऽर्थकामांस्तु गुरूनिहैव
भुञ्जीय भोगान् रुधिरप्रदिग्धान् ॥ २.५

gurūnahatvā hi mahānubhāvān
śreyo bhoktuṁ bhaikṣyam apīha loke |
hatvārtha-kāmāṁs tu gurūnihaiva
bhuñjīya bhogān rudhira-pradigdhān || 2.5

gurūn: the elders; ahatvā: not having killed; hi: indeed; mahānubhāvān: great souls; śreyah: it is better; bhoktuṁ: to enjoy life; bhaikṣyam: begging; api: even; iha: in this life; loke: in this world; hatvā: after killing; arthakāmān: wealth and enjoyment; tu: but; gurūn: elders; iha: in this world; eva: only; bhuñjīya: has to enjoy; bhogān: enjoyable things; rudhira: blood; pradigdhān: tainted with

2.5 I would rather beg for my food in this world than kill the most noble of teachers. If I kill them, all my enjoyment of wealth and desires will be stained with blood.

न चैतद्विद्मः कतरन्नो गरीयो
यद्वा जयेम यदि वा नो जयेयुः ।
यानेव हत्वा न जिजीविषाम-
स्तेऽवस्थिताः प्रमुखे धार्तराष्ट्राः ॥ २.६

na caitadvidmaḥ kataranno garīyo
yadvā jayema yadi vā no jayeyuḥ |
yān eva hatvā na jijīviṣāmas
te'vasthitāḥ pramukhe dhārtarāṣṭrāḥ || 2.6

na: nor; cha: also; etat: this; vidmaḥ: do know; katarat: which; naḥ: us; garīyah: better; yat: what; vā: either; jayema: shall conquer; yadi: if; vā: or; naḥ: us; jayeyuḥ: shall conquer; yān: those whom; eva: only; hatvā: after killing; na: never; jijīviṣāmaḥ: want to live; te: all of them; avasthitāḥ: assembled; pramukhe: in front of; dhārtarāṣṭrāḥ: the sons of Dhṛtarāṣṭra

2.6 I cannot say which is better; their defeating us or us defeating them. We do not wish to live after slaying the sons of Dhṛtarāṣṭra who stand before us.

कार्पण्यदोषोपहतस्वभाव:
पृच्छामि त्वां धर्मसम्मूढचेता: ।
यच्छ्रेय: स्यान्निश्चितं ब्रूहि तन्मे
शिष्यस्तेऽहं शाधि मां त्वां प्रपन्नम् ॥ २.७

kārpaṇya-doṣopahata-svabhāvaḥ
pṛcchāmi tvāṁ dharma-saṁmūḍha-cetāḥ |
yacchreyaḥ syānniścitaṁ brūhi tan me
śiṣyaste'ham śādhi māṁ tvāṁ prapannam || 2.7

kārpaṇya: miserly; doṣa: weakness; upahata: being inflicted by; svabhāvaḥ: characteristics; pṛcchāmi: I am asking; tvāṁ: you; dharma: religion; saṁmūḍha cetāḥ: bewildered mind; yat: what; śreyaḥ: good; syāt: may be; niścitaṁ: decidedly; brūhi: tell; tat: that; me: unto me; śiṣyaḥ: disciple; te: your; aham: I am; śādhi: just instruct; māṁ: me; tvāṁ: you; prapannam: surrendered

2.7 My heart is overwhelmed with pity and my mind is confused about what my duty is. I beg of you, please tell me what is best for me. I am your disciple. Instruct me as I seek refuge in you.

न हि प्रपश्यामि ममापनुद्याद्यच्छोकमुच्छोषणमिन्द्रियाणाम् ।
अवाप्य भूमावसपत्नमृद्धं राज्यं सुराणामपि चाधिपत्यम् ॥ २.८

na hi prapaśyāmi mamāpanudyād
yac chokam ucchoṣaṇam indriyāṇām /
avāpya bhūmāva-sapatnam-ṛddhaṁ
rājyaṁ surāṇām api cādhipatyam // 2.8

na: do not; hi: indeed; prapaśyāmi: I see; mama: my; apanudyāt: can drive away; yat: that; śokam: lamentation; ucchoṣaṇam: drying up; indriyāṇām: of the senses; avāpya: after achieving; bhūmau: on the earth; asapatnam: without rival; ṛddhaṁ: prosperous; rājyam: kingdom; surāṇām: of the demigods; api: even; ca: also; ādhipatyam: supremacy

2.8 Even if I were to attain unrivalled dominion and prosperity on earth or even lordship over the Gods, how would that remove this sorrow that burns my senses?

सञ्जय उवाच
एवमुक्त्वा हृषीकेशं गुडाकेश: परन्तप ।
न योत्स्य इति गोविन्दमुक्त्वा तूष्णीं बभूव ह ॥ २.९

sañjaya uvāca
evamuktvā hṛṣīkeśaṁ guḍākeśaḥ parantapa /
na yotsya iti govinda muktvā tūṣṇīṁ babhūva ha // 2.9

sañjaya uvācha: Sañjaya said; evam: thus; uktvā: after speaking; hṛṣīkeśam: unto Kṛṣṇa, the master of the senses; guḍākeśaḥ: one who has won over sleep (Arjuna); parantapa: destroyer of the enemies; na yotsye: I shall not fight; iti: thus; govindam: unto Kṛṣṇa, the giver of pleasure; uktvā: having said; tūṣṇīṁ: silent; babhūva: became; ha: clearly

2.9 Sañjaya said: Guḍākeśa (Arjuna) then said to Hṛṣīkeśa (Kṛṣṇa), 'Govinda, I shall not fight,' and fell silent.

तमुवाच हृषीकेश: प्रहसन्निव भारत ।

सेनयोरुभयोर्मध्ये विषीदन्तमिदं वचः ॥ २.१०

tam uvāca hṛṣīkeśaḥ prahasanniva bhārata /
senayor ubhayor madhye viṣīdantamidaṁ vacaḥ // 2.10

tam: unto him; uvācha: said; hṛṣīkeśaḥ: the master of the senses, Kṛṣṇa; prahasan: smiling; iva: as if; bhārata: O Dhṛtarāṣṭra, descendant of Bhārata; senayoḥ: of the armies; ubhayoḥ: of both; madhye: between; viṣīdantam : unto the lamenting one; idaṁ: the following; vachaḥ: words

2.10 Kṛṣṇa, Hṛṣikeśa, smilingly spoke the following words to the grief-stricken Arjuna, as they were placed in the middle of both armies.

श्री भगवानुवाच ।
अशोच्यानन्वशोचस्त्वं प्रज्ञावादांश्च भाषसे ।
गतासूनगतासूंश्च नानुशोचन्ति पण्डिताः ॥ २.११

śrībhagavānuvāca
aśocyān anvaśocas tvaṁ prajñāvādāṁś ca bhāṣase /
gatāsūn agatāsūṁś ca nānuśocanti paṇḍitāḥ // 2.11

śrī bhagavān uvāca: the Lord says; aśocyān: those not worthy of lamentation; anvaśocas: you are lamenting; tvaṁ: you; prajñāvādaṁ: learned talks; ca: also; bhāṣase: you are speaking; gatāsūn: lost life; agatāsūn: not past life; ca: also; na: never; anuśocanti: lament; paṇḍitāḥ: the learned

2.11 Bhagavān says: You grieve for those that should not be grieved for and yet, you speak words of wisdom. The wise grieve neither for the living nor for the dead.

न त्वेवाहं जातु नासं न त्वं नेमे जनाधिपाः ।
न चैव न भविष्यामः सर्वे वयमतः परम् ॥ २.१२

na tvevāhaṁ jātu nāsaṁ na tvaṁ neme janādhipāḥ /
na caiva na bhaviṣyāmaḥ sarve vayam ataḥ param // 2.12

na: not; tu: but; eva: only; ahaṁ: I; jātu: at any time; na: not; āsaṁ: existed; na: it is not so; tvaṁ: yourself; na: not; ime: all these; janādhipāḥ: kings; na: never; ca: also; eva: only; na: not like that; bhaviṣyāmaḥ: shall exist; sarve: all of us; vayaṁ: we; ataḥ paraṁ: hereafter

2.12 It is not that at anytime in the past I did not exist. So did you and these rulers exist, and we shall not ever cease to be hereafter.

देहिनोऽस्मिन्यथा देहे कौमारं यौवनं जरा ।
तथा देहान्तरप्राप्तिर्धीरस्तत्र न मुह्यति ॥ २.१३

dehino'sminyathā dehe kaumāraṁ yauvanaṁ jarā /
tathā dehāntara prāptir dhīras tatra na muhyati // 2.13

dehinaḥ: of the embodied soul; asmin: in this; yathā: as; dehe: in the body; kaumāraṁ: boyhood; yauvanaṁ: youth; jarā: old age; tathā: similarly; dehāntara: transference of the body; prāptiḥ: achievement; dhīraḥ: the brave; tatra: thereupon; na: never; muhyati: is deluded

2.13 Just as the spirit in this body passes through childhood, youth and old age, so does it pass into another body; the man centered in himself does not fear this.

मात्रास्पर्शास्तु कौन्तेय शीतोष्णसुखदुःखदाः ।
आगमापायिनोऽनित्यास्तांस्तितिक्षस्व भारत ॥ २.१४

mātrā-sparśāśtu kaunteya śītoṣṇa-sukha-duḥka-dāḥ /
āgamāpāyino'nityās tāṁs titikṣasva bhārata // 2.14

mātrā: of the senses; spārśāḥ: contact; tu: only; kaunteya: O son of Kuntī; śīta: cold; uṣṇa: hot; sukha: pleasure; dukkha-dah: giving pain; āgama: appearing; apāyinaḥ: disappearing; anityāḥ: nonpermanent; tān: all of them; titikṣasva: tolerate; bhārata: O descendant of the Bhārata dynasty

2.14 O Kaunteya (son of Kuntī), contact with sense objects causes heat and cold, pleasure and pain, and these have a beginning and an end. O Bhārata, these are not permanent; endure them bravely.

यं हि न व्यथयन्त्येते पुरुषं पुरुषर्षभ ।
समदु:खसुखं धीरं सोऽमृतत्वाय कल्पते ॥ २.१५

yaṁ hi na vyathayanty ete puruṣam puruṣarṣabha I
samaduḥkhasukhaṁ dhīraṁ so'mṛtatvāya kalpate II 2.15

yaṁ: whom; hi: indeed; na: never; vyathayanti: are distressing; ete: all these; puruṣam: to a person; puruṣarṣabha: O best among men; sama: equal; duḥkha: sorrow; sukhaṁ: happiness; dhīraṁ: brave; saḥ: he; amṛtatvāya: for liberation; kalpate: is fit

2.15 O Puruṣarṣabha, chief among men, the brave person to whom all these are not distressing, for whom sorrow and happiness are equal, is fit for liberation.

नासतो विद्यते भावो नाभावो विद्यते सत: ।
उभयोरपि दृष्टोऽन्तस्त्वनयोस्तत्त्वदर्शिभि: ॥ २.१६

nāsato vidyate bhāvo nābhāvo vidyate sataḥ I
ubhayorapi dṛṣṭontas tv anayos tattva-darśibhiḥ II 2.16

na: never; asataḥ: of the nonexistent; vidyate: there is; bhāvaḥ: existence; na: never; abhāvaḥ: non existence; vidyate: there is; sataḥ: of the eternal; ubhayoḥ: of the two; api: verily; dṛṣṭaḥ: observed; antaḥ: essence; tu: but; anayoḥ: of them; tattvadarśibhiḥ: truth by the seers

2.16 The nonexistent has no being; that which exists never ceases to exist. This truth about both is perceived by those who know the Truth.

अविनाशि तु तद्विद्धि येन सर्वमिदं ततम् ।
विनाशमव्ययस्यास्य न कश्चित्कर्तुमर्हति ॥ २.१७

avināśi tu tadviddhi yena sarvamidaṁ tatam I

vināśamavyayasyāsya na kaścitkartumarhati // *2.17*

avināśi: imperishable; tu: but; tat: that; viddhi: know it; yena: by whom; sarvaṁ: all of the body; idaṁ: this; tataṁ: pervaded; vināśaṁ: destruction; avyayasya: of the imperishable; asya: of it; na kaścit: no one; kartuṁ: to do; arhati: is able

2.17 Know It to be indestructible by which all this body is pervaded. Nothing can destroy It, the Imperishable.

अन्तवन्त इमे देहा नित्यस्योक्ताः शरीरिणः ।
अनाशिनोऽप्रमेयस्य तस्माद्युध्यस्व भारत ॥ २.१८

antavanta ime dehā nityasyoktāḥ śarīriṇaḥ /
anāśino 'prameyasya tasmād-yudhyasva bhārata // *2.18*

antavantaḥ: perishable; ime: all these; dehāḥ: bodies; nityasya: eternal in existence; uktāḥ: it is so said; śarīriṇaḥ: of the embodied soul; anāśinaḥ: never to be destroyed; aprameyasya: immeasurable; tasmāt: therefore; yudhyasva: fight; bhārata: O descendant of Bhārata

2.18 These bodies of the material energy are perishable. The energy itself is eternal, incomprehensible and indestructible. Therefore, fight, O Bhārata.

य एनं वेत्ति हन्तारं यश्चैनं मन्यते हतम्
उभौ तौ न विजानीतो नायं हन्ति न हन्यते ॥ २.१९

ya enaṁ vetti hantāraṁ yaścainaṁ manyate hatam /
ubhau tau na vijānīto nāyaṁ hanti na hanyate // *2.19*

yaḥ: anyone; enaṁ: this; vetti: knows; hantāraṁ: the killer; yaḥ: anyone; ca: also; enaṁ: this; manyate: thinks; hatam: killed; ubhau: both of them; tau: they; na: not; vijānītaḥ: know; na: never; ayaṁ: this; hanti: kills; na: nor; hanyate: be killed

2.19 Neither understands; he who takes the Self to be the slayer nor he who thinks he is slain. He who knows the truth understands that the Self does not slay, nor is It slain.

न जायते म्रियते वा कदाचित्
नायं भूत्वा भविता वा न भूयः ।
अजो नित्यः शोशतोऽयं पुराणो
न हन्यते हन्यमाने शरीरे ॥ २.२०

na jāyate mriyate vā kadācit
nāyaṁ bhūtvā bhavitā vā na bhūyaḥ |
ajo nityaḥ śāśvato 'yaṁ purāṇo
na hanyate hanyamāne śarīre || 2.20

na: never; jāyate: takes birth; mriyate: dies; vā: either; kadācit: at any time (past, present or future); na: never; ayaṁ: this; bhūtvā: having come into being; bhavitā: will come to be; vā: or; na: not; bhūyaḥ: after; ajaḥ: unborn; nityaḥ: eternal; śāśvataḥ: permanent; ayaṁ: this; purāṇaḥ: the oldest; na: never; hanyate: is killed; hanyamāne śarīre: when the body is killed

2.20 The Self is neither born nor does It ever die. After having been, It never ceases not to be. It is unborn, eternal, changeless and ancient. It is not killed when the body is killed.

वेदाविनाशिनं नित्यं य एनमजमव्ययम् ।
कथं स पुरुषः पार्थ कं घातयति हन्ति कम् ॥ २.२१

vedāvināśinaṁ nityaṁ ya enamajamavyayam |
kathaṁ sa puruṣaḥ pārtha kaṁ ghātayati hanti kam || 2.21

veda: knows; avināśinaṁ: indestructible; nityaṁ: permanent; yaḥ: one who; enaṁ: this (soul); ajam: unborn; avyayam: immutable; kathaṁ: how; saḥ: he; puruṣaḥ: person; pārtha: O Pārtha (Arjuna); kaṁ: whom; ghātayati: hurts; hanti: kills; kaṁ: whom

2.21 O Pārtha, how can man slay or cause others to be slain, when he knows It to be indestructible, eternal, unborn, and unchangeable?

वासांसि जीर्णानि यथा विहाय नवानि गृह्णाति नरोऽपराणि ।
तथा शरीराणि विहाय जीर्णान्यन्यानि संयाति नवानि देही ॥ २.२२

vāsāṁsi jīrṇāni yathā vihāya
navāni gṛhṇāti naro 'parāṇi I
tathā śarīrāṇi vihāya jīrṇā
nyanyāni saṁyāti navāni dehī II 2.22

vāsāṁsi: garments; jīrṇāni: old and worn out; yathā: as; vihāya: after giving up; navāni: new garments; gṛhṇāti: does accept; naraḥ: a man; aparāṇi: others; tathā: in the same way; śarīrāṇi: bodies; vihāya: after giving up; jīrṇāni: old and useless; anyāni: different; saṁyāti: accepts; navāni: new sets; dehī: the embodied soul

2.22 Just as man casts off his worn out clothes and puts on new ones, the Self casts off worn out bodies and enters newer ones.

नैनं छिन्दन्ति शस्त्राणि नैनं दहति पावकः ।
न चैनं क्लेदयन्त्यापो न शोषयति मारुतः ॥ २.२३

nainaṁ chindanti śastrāṇi nainaṁ dahati pāvakaḥ I
na cainaṁ kledayantyāpo na śoṣayati mārutaḥ II 2.23

na: not; enaṁ: this (soul); chindanti: cut to pieces; śastrāṇi: weapons; na: not; enaṁ: this soul; dahati: burns; pāvakaḥ: fire; na: not; ca: also; enaṁ: this soul; kledayanti: moistens; āpaḥ: water; na: not; śoṣayati: dries; mārutaḥ: wind

2.23 Weapons do not cleave the Self, fire does not burn It, water does not moisten It and wind does not dry It.

अच्छेद्योऽयमदाह्योऽयं अक्लेद्योऽशोष्य एव च ।
नित्यः सर्वगतः स्थाणुः अचलोऽयं सनातनः ॥ २.२४

acchedyo'yamadāhyo'yam akledyo'śoṣya eva ca I
nityaḥ sarvagataḥ sthāṇur acalo'yaṁ sanātanaḥ II 2.24

acchedyaḥ: incapable of being cut; ayaṁ: this soul; adāhyaḥ: cannot be burned; ayaṁ: this soul; akledyaḥ: insoluble; aśoṣyaḥ: cannot be dried; eva: certainly; ca: and; nityaḥ: everlasting; sarvagataḥ: all-pervading; sthāṇuḥ: unchangeable; acalaḥ: immovable; ayaṁ: this soul; sanātanaḥ: eternally the same

2.24 The Self cannot be broken nor burnt nor dissolved nor dried up. It is eternal, all-pervading, stable, immovable and ancient.

अव्यक्तोऽयमचिन्त्योऽयं अविकार्योऽयमुच्यते ।
तस्मादेवं विदित्वैनं नानुशोचितुमर्हसि ॥ २.२५

avyakto'yamacintyo'y amavikāryo'yamucyate |
tasmādevaṁ viditvainaṁ nānuśocitumarhasi || 2.25

avyaktaḥ: unmanifest; ayaṁ: this; acintyaḥ: unthinkable; ayaṁ: this; avikāryaḥ: immutable; ayaṁ: this; ucyate: is spoken of; tasmāt: therefore; evaṁ: as such; viditvā: having known; enaṁ: this; na: not; anuśocituṁ arhasi: (you) should not grieve

2.5 The Self is said to be unmanifest, unthinkable and unchangeable and able. Knowing this to be such, you should not grieve.

अथ चैनं नित्यजातं नित्यं वा मन्यसे मृतम् ।
तथापि त्वं महाबाहो नैवं शोचितुमर्हसि ॥ २.२६

atha cainaṁ nityajātaṁ nityaṁ vā manyase mṛtam |
tathāpi tvaṁ mahābāho naivaṁ śocitum arhasi || 2.26

atha: however; ca: also; enaṁ: this soul; nityajātaṁ: always born; nityaṁ: forever; vā: either; manyase: think; mṛtaṁ: dead; tathā api: still; tvaṁ: you; mahābāho: O mighty-armed one; na: not; enaṁ: like this ; śocituṁ arhasi: you lament

2.26 O mighty-armed, even if you should think of the soul as being constantly born and constantly dying, even then, you should not lament.

जातस्य हि ध्रुवो मृत्यु र्ध्रुवं जन्म मृतस्य च ।
तस्मादपरिहार्येऽर्थे न त्वं शोचितुमर्हसि ॥ २.२७

jātasya hi dhruvo mṛtyur dhruvaṁ janma mṛtasya ca |
tasmādaparihārye'rthe na tvaṁ śocitumarhasi || 2.27

jātasya: one who has taken his birth; hi: indeed; dhruvo: certain; mṛtyuḥ: death; dhruvaṁ: certain; janma: birth; mṛtasya: of the dead; ca: also; tasmāt: therefore; aparihārye: for that which is unavoidable; arthe: in the matter of; na: do not; tvaṁ: you; śocituṁ arhasi: you lament

2.27 Indeed, death is certain for the born and birth is certain for the dead. Therefore, you should not grieve over the inevitable.

अव्यक्तादीनि भूतानि व्यक्तमध्यानि भारत ।
अव्यक्तनिधनान्येव तत्र का परिदेवना॥ २.२८

avyaktādīni bhūtāni vyaktamadhyāni bhārata |
avyakta-nidhanāny eva tatra kā paridevanā || 2.28

avyaktādīni: unmanifest in the beginning; bhūtāni: living beings; vyakta: manifest; madhyāni: in the middle; bhārata: O descendant of Bhārata; avyakta nidhanāni: unmanifest after death; eva: like that; tatra: therefore; kā: what; paridevanā: lamentation

2.28 O Bhārata, being intangible in the beginning, being intangible again in their end, seemingly tangible in the middle, what are we grieving about?

आश्चर्यवत्पश्यति कश्चिदेन
आश्चर्यवद्वदति तथैव चान्यः ।
आश्चर्यवच्चैनमन्यः शृणोति
श्रुत्वाप्येनं वेद न चैव कश्चित् ॥ २.२९

āścaryavatpaśyati kaścidenam
māścaryavadvadati tathaiva cānyaḥ /
āścaryavaccainamanyaḥ śṛṇoti
śṛutvāpyenaṁ veda na caiva kaścit // 2.29

āścaryavat: amazingly; paśyati: see; kaścit: some one; enaṁ: this soul; āścaryavac: amazingly; vadati: speaks; tathā: like that; eva: only; ca: also; anyaḥ: another; āścaryavat: amazingly; ca: also; enaṁ: this soul; anyaḥ: another; śṛṇoti: hear; śrutvā: having heard; api: even; enaṁ: this soul; veda: do know; na: not; ca: and; eva: only; kaścit: someone

2.29 One sees It as a wonder, another speaks of It as a wonder, another hears of It as a wonder. Yet, having heard, none understands It at all.

देही नित्यमवध्योऽयं देहे सर्वस्य भारत ।
तस्मात्सर्वाणि भूतानि न त्वं शोचितुमर्हसि ॥ २.३०

dehī nityamavadhyo 'yaṁ dehe sarvasya bhārata /
tasmātsarvāni bhūtāni na tvaṁ śocitumarhasi // 2.30

dehī: the soul; nityaṁ: eternally; avadhyaḥ: cannot be killed; ayaṁ: this soul; dehe: in the body; sarvasya: of everyone; bhārata: O descendant of Bhārata; tasmāt: therefore; sarvāṇi: all; bhūtāni: living entities (that are born); na: not; tvaṁ: yourself; śocituṁ arhasi: should grieve

2.30 O Bhārata, this that dwells in the body of everyone can never be destroyed; do not grieve for any creature.

स्वधर्ममपि चावेक्ष्य न विकम्पितुमर्हसि ।
धर्म्याद्धि युद्धाच्छ्रेयोऽन्यत्क्षत्रियस्य न विद्यते ॥ २.३१

svadharmamapi cāvekṣya na vikampitumarhasi /
dharmyāddhi yuddhācchreyo'nyat kṣatriyasya na vidyate // 2.31

svadharmaṁ: one's own responsibility; api: also; ca: and; avekṣya: considering; na: not; vikampitum: to hesitate; arhasi: you deserve; dharmyāt hi yuddhāt:

from righteous war indeed; śreyaḥ: better; anyat: anything else; kṣatriyasya: of the kṣatriya; na: does not; vidyate: exist

2.31 You should look at your own responsibility [svadharma] as a kṣatriya. There is nothing higher for a kṣatriya than a righteous war. You ought not to hesitate.

यदृच्छया चोपपन्नं स्वर्गद्वारमपावृतम् ।
सुखिनः क्षत्रियाः पार्थ लभन्ते युद्धमीदृशम् ॥ २.३२

yadṛcchayā copapannaṁ svargadvāramapāvṛtam |
sukhinaḥ kṣatriyāḥ pārtha labhante yuddhamīdṛśam || 2.32

yadṛcchayā: by its own accord; ca: also; upapannaṁ: arrived; svargadvāraṁ: gate of heaven; apāvṛtaṁ: wide open; sukhinaḥ: happy; kṣatriyāḥ: the members of the royal order; pārtha: O son of Pritā; labhante: achieve; yuddhaṁ: war; īdṛśaṁ: like this

2.32 O Pārtha, happy indeed are the kṣatriyas who are called to fight in such a battle without seeking. This opens for them the door to heaven.

अथ चेत्त्वमिमं धर्म्यं सङ्ग्रामं न करिष्यसि ।
ततः स्वधर्मं कीर्तिं च हित्वा पापमवाप्स्यसि ॥ २.३३

atha cettvamimaṁ dharmyaṁ saṅgrāmaṁ na kariṣyasi |
tataḥ svadharmaṁ kīrtiṁ ca hitvā pāpamavāpsyasi || 2.33

atha: therefore; cet: if; tvaṁ: you; imaṁ: this; dharmyaṁ: righteous; saṅgrāmaṁ: war; na: do not; kariṣyasi: you will perform; tataḥ: then; svadharmaṁ: your duty; kīrtiṁ: reputation; ca: also; hitvā: having lost; pāpaṁ: sin; avāpsyasi: do gain

2.33 If you will not fight this righteous war, then you will incur sin having abandoned your own responsibility [svadharma], and you will lose your reputation.

अकीर्तिंचापि भूतानि कथयिष्यन्ति तेऽव्ययाम् ।
संभावितस्य चाकीर्तिः मरणादतिरिच्यते ॥ २.३४

akīrtiṁ cāpi bhūtāni kathayiṣyanti te'vyayām |
saṁbhāvitasya cākīrtir maraṇādatiricyate || 2.34

akīrtiṁ: infamy; ca: also; api: also; bhūtāni: all people; kathayiṣyanti: will speak; te: of you; avyayāṁ: undying; saṁbhāvitasya: of a respectable man; ca: also; akīrtiḥ: ill-fame; maraṇāt: than death; atiricyate: becomes more than

2.34 People too will remember your everlasting dishonor and to one who has been honored, dishonor is worse than death.

भयाद्रणादुपरतं मंस्यन्ते त्वां महारथाः ।
येषां च त्वं बहुमतो भूत्वा यास्यसि लाघवम् ॥ २.३५

bhayādraṇāduparataṁ maṁsyante tvāṁ mahārathāḥ |
yeṣāṁ ca tvaṁ bahumato bhūtvā yāsyasi lāghavam || 2.35

bhayāt: out of fear; raṇāt: from war; uparataṁ: retired; maṁsyante: will consider; tvāṁ: you; mahārathāḥ: the great generals; yeṣāṁ: of those who; ca: also; tvaṁ: you; bahumataḥ: in great estimation; bhūtvā: having become; yāsyasi: will get; lāghavaṁ: decreased in value

2.35 The great generals will think that you have withdrawn from the battle because you are a coward. You will be looked down upon by those who had thought much of you and your heroism in the past.

अवाच्यवादांश्च बहून्वदिष्यन्ति तवाहिताः ।
निन्दन्तस्तव सामर्थ्यं ततो दुःखतरं नु किम् ॥ २.३६

avācyavādāṁśca bahūn vadiṣyanti tavāhitāḥ |
nindantastava sāmarthyaṁ tato duḥkhataraṁ nu kim || 2.36

avācyavādān: unspeakable words; ca: also; bahūn: many; vadiṣyanti: will say; tava : your; ahitāḥ: enemies; nindantaḥ: while vilifying; tava : your; sāmarthyaṁ: ability; tataḥ: than that; duḥkhataraṁ: more painful; nu: of course; kiṁ: what

2.36 Many unspeakable words would be spoken by your enemies reviling your power. Can there be anything more painful than this?

हतो वा प्राप्स्यसि स्वर्गं जित्वा वा भोक्ष्यसे महीम् ।
तस्मादुत्तिष्ठ कौन्तेय युद्धाय कृतनिश्चयः ॥ २.३७

hato vā prāpsyasi svargaṁ jitvā vā bhokṣyase mahīm |
tasmāduttiṣṭha kaunteya yuddhāya kṛtaniścayaḥ || 2.37

hataḥ: being killed; vā: either; prāpsyasi: you will gain; svargaṁ: heaven; jitvā: after conquering; vā: or; bhokṣyase: you will enjoy; mahīṁ: the world; tasmāt: therefore; uttiṣṭha: get up; kaunteya: O son of Kuntī; yuddhāya: for war; kṛta niścayaḥ: determined

2.37 Slain, you will achieve heaven; victorious, you will enjoy the earth. O Kaunteya (son of Kuntī), stand up determined to fight.

सुखदुःखे समे कृत्वा लाभालाभौ जयाजयौ ।
ततो युद्धाय युज्यस्व नैवं पापमवाप्स्यसि ॥ २.३८

sukhaduḥkhe same kṛtvā lābhālābhau jayājayau |
tato yuddhāya yujyasva naivaṁ pāpamavāpsyasi || 2.38

sukha duḥkhe: in happiness as well as in distress; same: equal; kṛtvā: doing so; lābhālābhau: gain and loss; jayājayau: victory and defeat; tataḥ: thereafter; yuddhāya: for war; yujyasva: get ready; na: not; evaṁ: in this way; pāpaṁ: sin; avāpsyasi: you will gain

2.38 Pleasure and pain, gain and loss, victory and defeat–treat them all the same. Do battle for the sake of battle and you shall incur no sin.

एषा तेऽभिहिता सांख्ये बुद्धिर्योगे त्विमां श्रृणु ।
बुद्ध्या युक्तो यया पार्थ कर्मबन्धं प्रहास्यसि ॥ २.३९

eṣā tebhihitā sānkhye buddhiryoge tvimāṁ śṛṇu /
buddhyā yukto yayā pārtha karmabandhaṁ prahāsyasi // 2.39

eṣā: all these; te: you; abhihitā: described; sāṁkhye: in the Sāṅkhya Yoga (yoga of knowledge); buddhiḥ: intelligence; yoge: in the Karma Yoga of selfless action; tu: but; imāṁ: this; śṛṇu: hear; buddhyā: by intelligence; yuktaḥ: equipped; yayā: by which; pārtha: O son of Pritā; karma bandhaṁ: bondage of action; prahāsyasi: you shall throw off

2.39 Thus far, what has been taught to you concerns the wisdom of Sāṅkhya. Now, listen to the wisdom of yoga [buddhiyoga]. Having known this, O Pārtha, you shall cast off the bonds of action.

नेहाभिक्रमनाशोऽस्ति प्रत्यवायो न विद्यते ।
स्वल्पमप्यस्य धर्मस्य त्रायते महतो भयात् ॥ २.४०

nehābhikrama-nāśo 'sti pratyavāyo na vidyate /
svalpamapyasya dharmasya trāyate mahato bhayāt // 2.40

na: there is not; iha: in this path of yoga (of selfless action); abhikramanāśaḥ: loss of effort; asti: there is; pratyavāyaḥ: contrary result; na: not; vidyate: there is; svalpaṁ: a little; api: also; asya: of this discipline; dharmasya: of this occupation; trāyate: releases; mahataḥ: of very great; bhayāt: from fear

2.40 There is no wasted effort or dangerous effect in this path of yoga. Even a little knowledge of this, even a little practice of this dharma, protects and releases one from very great fear.

व्यवसायात्मिका बुद्धिरेकेह कुरुनन्दन ।
बहुशाखा ह्यनन्ताश्च बुद्धयोऽव्यवसायिनाम् ॥ २.४१

vyavasāyātmikā buddhir ekeha kurunandana /

bahuśākhā hyanantāś ca buddhayovyavasāyinām || 2.41

vyavasāyātmikā: fixed resolve; buddhiḥ: intelligence; ekā: only one; iha: in this (Karma Yoga); kuru nandana: O son of the Kurus; bahuśākhāḥ: various branches; hi: indeed; anantāḥ: unlimited; ca: also; buddhayaḥ: intelligence; avyavasāyinām: of the undecided (ignorant men moved by desires)

2.41 Joy of the Kurus, on this path (of yoga), the intelligence is resolute with a single-pointed determination. Thoughts of the irresolute are many, branched and endlsess.

यामिमां पुष्पितां वाचं प्रवदन्त्यविपश्चितः ।
वेदवादरताः पार्थ नान्यदस्तीतिवादिनः ॥ २.४२

yāmimāṁ puṣpitāṁ vācaṁ pravadantyavipaścitaḥ |
vedavādaratāḥ pārtha nānyadastīti vādinaḥ || 2.42

yāṁ imāṁ: all these; puṣpitāṁ: flowery; vācaṁ: words; pravadanti: say; avipaścitaḥ: ignorant men; vedavādaratāḥ: devoted to the letter of the Veda; pārtha: O son of Pārtha; na: not; anyat: anything else; asti: there is; iti: thus; vādinaḥ: advocates

कामात्मानः स्वर्गपरा जन्मकर्मफलप्रदाम् ।
क्रियाविशेषबहुलां भोगैशर्यगतिं प्रति ॥ २.४३

kāmātmānaḥ svargaparā janmakarmaphalapradām |
kriyā-viśeṣa-bahulāṁ bhogaiśvarya-gatiṁ prati || 2.43

kāmātmānaḥ: desirous of sense gratification; svargaparāḥ: aiming at heaven as supreme goal; janma karma phala pradām: resulting in rebirth as the fruit; kriyā viśeṣa bahulāṁ: many rituals of various kinds; bhogaiśvarya: sense enjoyment opulence; gatiṁ: way; prati: towards

2.43 Men of little knowledge, who are very much attached toeulogizing the flowery words of the Vedas, O Pārtha, argue that, 'there is nothing else'; these advocates of Vedas (vādīna) look upon and recommend various fruitful actions for elevation to heavenly planets, resulting in high birth, power, and so forth.

Thus being desirous of sense gratification and opulent life, they say that there is nothing more than this to living.

भोगैश्वर्यप्रसक्तानां तयापहृतचेतसाम् ।
व्यवसायात्मिका बुद्धिः समाधौ न विधीयते ॥ २.४४

bhogaiśvarya-prasaktānāṁ tayāpahṛtacetasām /
vyavasāyātmikā buddhiḥ samādhau na vidhīyate // 2.44

bhogaiśvarya: material enjoyment opulence; prasaktānāṁ: of those who are so attached; tayā: by such words; apahṛta cetasāṁ: bewildered in mind; vyavasāyātmikā: fixed determination; buddhiḥ: intellect; samādhau: in the supreme goal; na: not; vidhīyate: centers on

2.44 Those whose minds are attached to sense pleasures and lordship, who are diverted by such teachings, for them, the determination for steady meditation and samādhi, fixed intelligence does not happen.

त्रैगुण्यविषया वेदा निस्त्रैगुण्यो भवार्जुन ।
निर्द्वन्द्वो नित्यसत्त्वस्थो निर्योगक्षेम आत्मवान् ॥ २.४५

traiguṇyaviṣayā vedā nistraiguṇyo bhavārjuna /
nirdvandvo nityas-attva-stho niryogakṣema ātmavān // 2.45

traiguṇya viṣayā: pertaining to the three modes of material nature and the means of achieving them; vedā: Vedic literature; nistraiguṇyaḥ: indifferent to the material enjoyments and their means; bhava: be; arjuna: O Arjuna; nirdvandvaḥ: free from the pairs of opposites; nitya sattvasthaḥ: ever remaining in satva (eternal existence); niryogakṣemaḥ: free from (the thought of) acquisition and preservation; ātmavān: established in the Self

2.45 O Arjuna! Be you above the three guṇas (attributes) that the Vedas deal in: free yourself from the pairs-of-opposites and be always in satva (goodness), free from all thoughts of acquisition (yoga) or preservation (kṣema), and be established in the Self.

यावानर्थ उदपाने सर्वतः सम्प्लुतोदके ।
तावान्सर्वेषु वेदेषु ब्राह्मणस्य विजानतः ॥ २.४६

yāvānartha udapāne sarvataḥ saṁplutodake |
tāvānsarveṣu vedeṣu brāhmaṇasya vijānataḥ || 2.46

yāvān: how much; arthaḥ: means; udapāne: in a well of water; sarvataḥ: on all sides; saṁplutodake: in a great reservoir of water; tāvān: that much; sarveṣu: in all; vedeṣu: in the Veda; brāhmaṇasya: of the man who knows the supreme Brahman; vijānataḥ: of one who has achieved enlightenment

2.46 The Brāhmaṇa (sage), who has known the Self, has little use for the vedic scriptures, as these are like a pool of water in a place that is already in flood, overflowing with a great water reservoir.

कर्मण्येवाधिकारस्ते मा फलेषु कदाचन ।
मा कर्मफलहेतुर्भूर्मा ते सङ्गोऽस्त्वकर्मणि ॥ २.४७

karmaṇyevādhikāraste mā phaleṣu kadācana |
mā karmaphalaheturbhūr mā te saṅgo 'stvakarmaṇi || 2.47

karmaṇi: in the duties; eva: only; adhikāraḥ: right; te: of you; mā: never; phaleṣu: in the fruits; kadācana: at any time; mā: do not; karma phala: in the result of action; hetuḥ: cause; bhūḥ: let be; mā: never; te: of you; saṅgaḥ: attachment; astu: be there; akarmaṇi: in inaction

2.47 You have a right only to work, but never to the fruits (outcome) of action. Never let the fruit of action be your motive; and never let your attachment be to inaction.

योगस्थः कुरु कर्माणि सङ्गं त्यक्त्वा धनञ्जय ।
सिद्ध्यसिद्ध्योः समो भूत्वा समत्वं योग उच्यते ॥ २.४८

yogasthaḥ kuru karmāṇi saṅgaṁ tyaktvā dhanañjaya |
siddhyasiddhyoḥ samo bhūtvā samatvaṁ yoga ucyate || 2.48

yogasthaḥ: steadfast in yoga; kuru: perform; karmāṇi: duties; saṅgaṁ: attachment; tyaktvā: having abandoned; dhañajaya: O Dhanañjaya; siddhyasiddhyoḥ: success and failure; samaḥ: the same; bhūtvā: having become; samatvaṁ: evenness of mind; yoga: yoga; ucyate: is called

2.48 O Dhanañjaya! Do your actions dropping all attachment to the outcome, being centered and complete in Yoga. Be balanced in success and failure. Such evenness of mind is Yoga.

दूरेण ह्यवरं कर्म बुद्धियोगाद्धनञ्जय ।
बुद्धौ शरणमन्विच्छ कृपणाः फलहेतवः ॥ २.४९

dūreṇa hyavaraṁ karma buddhiyogād dhanañjaya /
buddhau śaraṇamanviccha kṛpaṇāḥ phalahetavaḥ // 2.49

dūreṇa hi avaraṁ: far superior; karma: activities; buddhiyogāt: based on the yoga of knowledge; dhanañjaya: O conqueror of wealth; buddhau: in such wisdom; śaraṇam: full surrender; anviccha: desire; kṛpaṇāḥ: wretched; phalahetavaḥ: those desiring fruit of action

2.49 O Dhanañjaya, beyond the action with selfish motive is Yoga (of action) in wisdom [buddhiyoga]. Wretched are those whose motive is the fruit (outcome); Surrender yourself fully to the wisdom of completion.

बुद्धियुक्तो जहातीह उभे सुकृतदुष्कृते ।
तस्माद्योगाय युज्यस्व योगः कर्मसु कौशलम् ॥ २.५०

buddhiyukto jahātīha ubhe sukṛtaduṣkṛte /
tasmādyogāya yujyasva yogaḥ karmasu kauśalam // 2.50

buddhiyuktaḥ: even minded person; jahāti: gives up; iha: in this life; ubhe: both; sukṛta duṣkṛte: good and bad results; tasmāt: therefore; yogāya: for the sake of yoga; yujyasva: be so engaged; yogaḥ: yoga; karmasu: in all activities; kauśalam: art (of freeing the Self from the bondage of action)

2.50 Endowed with the wisdom of evenness of mind, move

away from both good and evil deeds in this life. Devote yourself to yoga. Authenticity in action is yoga.

कर्मजं बुद्धियुक्ता हि फलं त्यक्त्वा मनीषिणः ।
जन्मबन्धविनिर्मुक्ताः पदं गच्छन्त्यनामयम् ॥ २.५१

karmajaṁ buddhiyuktā hi phalaṁ tyaktvā manīṣiṇaḥ |
janmabandhavinirmuktāḥ padaṁ gacchantyanāmayam || 2.51

karmajaṁ: born of action; buddhiyuktā: even minded ones; hi: indeed; phalaṁ: results; tyaktvā: after giving up; manīṣiṇaḥ: sages; janma bandha vinirmuktāḥ: free from the bondage of birth; padaṁ: position; gacchanti: reach; anāmayaṁ: without ills

2.51 The wise, having abandoned the outcome of their actions and possessed of knowledge of completion, are freed from the cycle of birth and death. They go to the state that is beyond all sorrow.

यदा ते मोहकलिलं बुद्धिर्व्यतितारिष्यति ।
तदा गन्तासि निर्वेदं श्रोतव्यस्य श्रुतस्य च ॥ २.५२

yadā te mohakalilaṁ buddhirvyatitariṣyati |
tadā gantāsi nirvedaṁ śrotavyasya śrutasya ca || 2.52

yadā: when; te : they; moha kalilaṁ: slough of delusion; buddhiḥ: understanding; vyatitariṣyati: will pass through; tadā: at that time; gantāsi: you shall attain; nirvedaṁ: cheerlessness; śrotavyasya: all that is to be heard; śrutasya: all that is already heard; ca: also

2.52 When your wisdom takes you beyond delusion, you shall be indifferent to what has been heard and what is yet to be heard.

श्रुतिविप्रतिन्ना ते यदा स्थास्यति निश्चला ।
समाधावचला बुद्धिस्तदा योगमवाप्स्यसि ॥ २.५३

śrutivipratipannā te yadā sthāsyati niścalā /
samādhāvacalā buddhis tadā yogamavāpsyasi // 2.53

śrutivipratipannā: confused by much hearing; te: this; yadā: when; sthāsyati: rests; niścalā: steady; samādhau: on God; acalā: unflinching; buddhiḥ: intellect; tadā: at that time; yogaṁ: self-realization; avāpsyasi: you will achieve

2.53 When you are not confused by what you have heard and your wisdom stands steady and unmoving in the Self, you shall attain Self–realization.

अर्जुन उवाच
स्थितप्रज्ञस्य का भाषा समाधिस्थस्य केशव ।
स्थितधीः किं प्रभाषेत किमासीत व्रजेत किम् ॥ २.५४

arjuna uvāca
sthitaprajñasya kā bhāṣā samādhisthasya keśava /
sthitadhīḥ kiṁ prabhāṣeta kimāsīta vrajeta kim // 2.54

arjuna uvāca: Arjuna said; sthitaprajñasya: of one who is of secure mind; kā: what; bhāṣā: language; samādhisthasya: of one established in the tranquility of mind; keśava: O Kṛṣṇa; sthitadhīḥ: one with stable mind; kiṁ: how; prabhāṣeta: speak; kim: how; āsīta: sits; vrajeta: walks; kim: how

2.54 O Keśava! What is the description of one who stays in the space of completion in present moment and is merged in the restful awareness of truth and wisdom? How does one of steady wisdom speak, how does he sit, how does he walk?

श्री भगवानुवाच ।
प्रजहाति यदा कामान्सर्वान्पार्थ मनोगतान् ।
आत्मन्येवात्मना तुष्टः स्थितप्रज्ञस्तदोच्यते ॥ २.५५

śrībhagavānuvāca
prajahāti yadā kāmān sarvānpārtha manogatān /

ātmanyevātmanā tuṣṭaḥ sthitaprajñastadocyate // 2.55

śrī bhagavān uvāca: The Lord says; prajahāti: gives up; yadā: when; kāmān: desires; sarvān: of all varieties; pārtha: O son of Pritā; manogatān: existing in mind; ātmani: in the soul; eva: only; ātmanā: by the self; tuṣṭaḥ: satisfied; sthitaprajñaḥ: one of secure understanding; tadā: at that time; ucyate: is said

2.55 Śrī Bhagavān says: O Pārtha, a man who casts off completely all the desires of the mind and is satisfied in the Self by the Self, He is said to be Sthhitaprajña, one of steady wisdom in completion.

दुःखेष्वनुद्विग्नमनाः सुखेषु विगतस्पृहः ।
वीतरागभयक्रोधः स्थितधीर्मुनिरुच्यते ॥ २.५६

duḥkheṣv anudvigna-manāḥ sukheṣu vigataspṛhaḥ /
vītarāgabhayakrodhaḥ sthitadhīrmunirucyate // 2.56

duḥkheṣu: in sorrow; anudvignamanāḥ: without being agitated in mind; sukheṣu: in happiness; vigataspṛhaḥ: without being interested; vīta: free from; rāga: passion; bhaya: fear; krodhaḥ: anger; sthitadhīḥ: one who is steady in mind; muniḥ: a sage; ucyate: is called

2.56 He whose mind is not disturbed by adversity and who, in prosperity, does not go after other pleasures, he who is free from attachment, fear or anger is called a sage of steady wisdom.

यः सर्वत्रानभिस्नेहस्तत्तत्प्राप्य शुभाशुभम् ।
नाभिनन्दति न द्वेष्टि तस्य प्रज्ञा प्रतिष्ठिता ॥ २.५७

yaḥ sarvatrānabhisnehas tat tat prāpya śubhāśubham /
nābhinandati na dveṣṭi tasya prajñā pratiṣṭhitā // 2.57

yaḥ: one who; sarvatra: everywhere; anabhisnehaḥ: without affection; tat: that; tat: that; prāpya: after achieving; śubhāśubhaṁ: good evil; na: not; abhinandati: rejoices; na: not; dveṣṭi: resents; tasya: his; prajñā: knowledge; pratiṣṭhitā: fixed

2.57 His wisdom is fixed who is everywhere without attachment, meeting with anything good or bad and who neither rejoices nor hates.

यदा संहरते चायं कूर्मोऽङ्गानीव सर्वशः ।
इन्द्रियाणीन्द्रियार्थेभ्यस्तस्य प्रज्ञा प्रतिष्ठिता ॥ २.५८

yadā saṁharate cāyaṁ kūrmo 'ṅgānīva sarvaśaḥ |
indriyāṇīndriyārthebhyas tasya prajñā pratiṣṭhitā || 2.58

yadā: when; saṁharate: withdraws; ca: also; ayaṁ: this; kūrmaḥ: tortoise; aṅgānī: limbs; iva: like; sarvaśaḥ : altogether; indriyāṇi : senses; indriyārthebhyaḥ: from the sense objects; tasya: his; prajñā: consciousness; pratiṣṭhitā: fixed

2.58 As the tortoise withdraws its limbs from all sides, when a person withdraws his senses from the sense-objects, his wisdom becomes steady in completion.

विषया विनिवर्तन्ते निराहारस्य देहिनः ।
रसवर्जं रसोऽप्यस्य परं दृष्ट्वा निवर्तते ॥ २.५९

viṣayā vinivartante nirāhārasya dehinaḥ |
rasavarjaṁ raso'pyasya paraṁ dṛṣṭvā nivartate || 2.59

viṣayāḥ: sense objects; vinivartante: turn away; nirāhārasya: of one who does not enjoy them with his senses; dehinaḥ: of the embodied; rasavarjaṁ: yearning, persisting; rasaḥ: yearning; api: although there is; asya: his; paraṁ: the supreme; dṛṣṭvā: after seeing; nivartate: returns

2.59 From the body, the sense objects turn away, but the desires remain; his desires also leave him on seeing the Supreme.

यततो ह्यपि कौन्तेय पुरुषस्य विपश्चितः ।
इन्द्रियाणि प्रमाथीनि हरन्ति प्रसभं मनः ॥ २.६०

yatato hyapi kaunteya puruṣasya vipaścitaḥ |

indriyāṇi pramāthīni haranti prasabhaṁ manaḥ // 2.60

yatataḥ: while endeavoring; hi: indeed; api: also; kaunteya: O son of Kuntī; puruṣasya: of the man; vipaścitaḥ: the wise; indriyāṇi: the senses; pramāthīni: turbulent; haranti: carry away; prasabhaṁ: by force; manaḥ: the mind

2.60 O Kaunteya (son of Kuntī), the turbulent senses carry away the mind of a wise man, though he is striving to be in control.

तानि सर्वाणि संयम्य युक्त आसीत मत्परः ।
वशे हि यस्येन्द्रियाणि तस्य प्रज्ञा प्रतिष्ठिता ॥ २.६१

tāni sarvāṇi saṁyamya yukta āsīta matparaḥ /
vaśe hi yasyendriyāṇi tasya prajñāpratiṣṭhitā // 2.61

tāni: those senses; sarvāṇi: all; saṁyamya: keeping under control; yuktaḥ: yogi; āsīta: sitting; matparaḥ: devoted to Me; vaśe: in full subjugation; hi: indeed; yasya: one whose; indriyāṇi: senses; tasya: his; prajñā; mind; pratiṣṭhitā: stable

2.61 Having restrained them all, he should sit steadfast, intent on Me. His mind is steady in the present whose senses are under control.

ध्यायतो विषयान्पुंसः सङ्गस्तेषूपजायते।
सङ्गात् सञ्जायते कामः कामात्क्रोधोऽभिजायते ॥ २.६२

dhyāyato viṣayānpuṁsaḥ saṅgasteṣūpajāyate /
saṅgātsañjāyate kāmaḥ kāmātkrodhobhijāyate // 2.62

dhyāyataḥ: contemplating; viṣayān: sense objects; puṁsaḥ: of the person; saṅgaḥ: attachment; teṣu: in these sense objects; upajāyate: develops; saṅgāt: from attachment; saṁjāyate: develops; kāmaḥ: desire; kāmāt: from desire; krodhaḥ: anger; abhijāyate: ensues

2.62 When a man thinks of objects, it gives rise to attachment for them. From attachment, desire arises; from desire, anger is born.

क्रोधाद्भवति संमोह: संमोहात्स्मृतिविभ्रम: ।
स्मृतिभ्रंशाद् बुद्धिनाशो बुद्धिनाशात्प्रणश्यति ॥ २.६३

krodhād bhavati saṁmohaḥ saṁmohāt smṛtivibhramaḥ |
smṛtibhraṁśād buddhināśo buddhināśātpraṇaśyati || 2.63

krodhāt: from anger; bhavati: takes place; saṁmohaḥ: illusion; saṁmohāt: from illusion; smṛti: of memory; vibhramaḥ: loss; smṛti bhraṁśāt: from loss of memory; buddhi nāśaḥ: loss of reason; buddhināśāt: from loss of reason; praṇaśyati: perishes

2.63 From anger arises delusion, from delusion, loss of memory, from loss of memory, the destruction of discrimination, from destruction of discrimination, he perishes.

रागद्वेषवियुक्तैस्तु विषयानिन्द्रियैश्चरन्।
आत्मवश्यैर्विधेयात्मा प्रसादमधिगच्छति ॥ २.६४

rāgadveṣaviyuktaistu viṣayānindriyaiścaran |
ātmavaśyairvidheyātmā prasādamadhigacchati || 2.64

rāga dveṣa: likes and disklikes; viyuktaiḥ: by those free from such things; tu: but; viṣayān: sense objects; indriyaiḥ: by the senses; caran: enjoying; ātmavaśyaih: by the disciplined; vidheyātmā: self controlled; prasādaṁ: placidity of mind; adhigacchati: attains

2.64 The self-controlled man, moving among objects with his senses under control, free from both attraction and repulsion, attains peace.

प्रसादे सर्वदु:खानां हानिरस्योपजायते ।
प्रसन्नचेतसो ह्याशु बुद्धि: पर्यवतिष्ठते ॥ २.६५ ॥

prasāde sarvaduḥkhānāṁ hānirasyopajāyate |
prasannacetaso hyāśu buddhiḥ paryavatiṣṭhate || 2.65

prasāde: with achieving peace of mind; sarva: of all; duḥkhānāṁ: of miseries; hāniḥ: destruction; asya: his; upajāyate: takes place; prasannacetasaḥ:

of the happy-minded; hi: indeed; āśu: very soon; buddhiḥ: intelligence; paryavatiṣṭhate: firmly established

2.65 All pains are destroyed in that peace, for the intellect of the tranquil-minded soon becomes steady.

नास्ति बुद्धिरयुक्तस्य न चायुक्तस्य भावना ।
न चाभावयतः शान्तिरशान्तस्य कुतः सुखम् ॥ २.६६ ॥

nāsti buddhirayuktasya na cāyuktasya bhāvanā |
na cābhāvayataḥ śāntir aśāntasya kutaḥ sukham || 2.66

na asti : there is not; buddhiḥ: wisdom; ayuktasya: of one who is not connected to Self; na: neither; ca: and; ayuktasya: of one devoid of Self awareness; bhāvanā: devotion; na: neither; ca: and; abhāvayataḥ: for the indisciplined; śāntiḥ: peace; aśāntasya: of the indisciplined; kutaḥ: how; sukhaṁ: happiness

2.66 A person not in self awareness cannot be wise or happy or peaceful. How can there be happiness to one without peace?

इन्द्रियाणां हि चरतां यन्मनोऽनुविधीयते ।
तदस्य हरति प्रज्ञां वायुर्नावमिवांभसि ॥ २.६७ ॥

indriyāṇāṁ hi caratāṁ yanmano 'nuvidhīyate |
tadasya harati prajñāṁ vāyurnāvamivāmbhasi || 2.67

indriyāṇāṁ: of the senses; hi: indeed; caratāṁ: moving among objects; yat: that; manaḥ: mind; anu: with; vidhīyate: joined; tat: that; asya: his; harati: takes away; prajñāṁ: discrimination; vāyuḥ: wind; nāvaṁ: a boat; iva: like; ambhasi: on the water

2.67 He loses his awareness of the present moment when his mind follows the wandering senses, just as the wind carries away a boat on the waters.

तस्माद्यस्य महाबाहो निगृहीतानि सर्वशः ।
इन्द्रियाणीन्द्रियार्थेभ्यस्तस्य प्रज्ञा प्रतिष्ठिता ॥ २.६८ ॥

tasmādyasya mahābāho nigṛhītāni sarvaśaḥ |
indriyāṇīndriyārthebhyas tasya prajñā pratiṣṭhitā || 2.68

tasmāt: therefore; yasya: of one's; mahābāho: O mighty-armed one; nigṛhītāni: so curbed down; sarvaśaḥ: in all respects; indriyāṇi: the senses; indriyārthebhyaḥ: from the sense objects; tasya: his; prajñā: intelligence; pratiṣṭhitā: fixed

2.68 O Mahābāho (mighty-armed one), his knowledge is therefore steady whose senses are completely detached from sense objects.

या निशा सर्वभूतानां तस्यां जागर्ति संयमी ।
यस्यां जाग्रति भूतानि सा निशा पश्यतो मुनेः ॥ २.६९ ॥

yā niśā sarvabhūtānāṁ tasyāṁ jāgarti saṁyamī |
yasyāṁ jāgrati bhūtāni sā niśā paśyato muneḥ || 2.69

yā: what; niśā: is night; sarva: all; bhūtānāṁ: of living entities; tasyāṁ: in that; jāgarti: wakeful; saṁyamī: the self-controlled; yasyāṁ: in which; jāgrati: awake; bhūtāni: all beings; sā: that is; niśā: night; paśyataḥ: for the seer; muneḥ: for the sage

2.69 The self–controlled man lies awake in that which is night to all beings. That in which all beings are awake is the night for the sage who sees.

आपूर्यमाणमचलप्रतिष्ठं समुद्रमापः प्रविशन्ति यद्वत् ।
तद्वत्कामा यं प्रविशन्ति सर्वे स शान्तिमाप्नोति न कामकामी ॥ २.७० ॥

āpūryamāṇ amacala-pratiṣṭhaṁ
samudramāpaḥ praviśanti yadvat |
tadvatkāmā yaṁ praviśanti sarve
sa śāntimāpnoti na kāmakāmī || 2.70

āpūryamāṇaṁ: always filled; acalapratiṣṭhaṁ: steadily established; samudraṁ: the ocean; āpaḥ: water; praviśanti: enter; yadvat: as; tadvat: so; kāmāḥ: desires;

yaṁ: one; praviśanti: enter; sarve: all; saḥ: that person; śāntiṁ: peace; āpnoti: achieves; na: not; kāmakāmī: one who cherishes longings

2.70 Just as all waters enter the ocean, he attains peace into whom all desires enter, which when filled from all sides, remains unmoved; not the desirer of desires.

विहाय कामान्यः सर्वान् पुमांश्चरति निःस्पृहः ।
निर्ममो निरहङ्कारः स शान्तिमधिगच्छति ॥ २.७१ ॥

vihāya kāmānyaḥ sarvān pumāṁścarati niḥspṛhaḥ |
nirmamo nirahaṅkāraḥ sa śāntimadhigacchati || 2.71

vihāya: after giving up; kāmān: desires for sense gratification; yaḥ: the person; sarvān: all; pumān: a person; carati: moves; niḥspṛhaḥ: desireless; nir mamaḥ: without a sense of proprietorship; nir ahaṁkāraḥ: without false ego; saḥ: he; śāntiṁ: peace; adhigacchati: attains

2.71 The man who moves about abandoning all desires, without longing, without the sense of I and mine, attains peace.

एषा ब्राह्मी स्थितिः पार्थ नैनां प्राप्य विमुह्यति ।
स्थित्वाऽस्यामन्तकालेऽपि ब्रह्मनिर्वाणमृच्छति ॥ २.७२ ॥

eṣā brāhmī sthitiḥ pārtha naināṁ prāpya vimuhyati |
thitvāsyāmantakāle'pi brahmanirvāṇamṛcchati || 2.72

eṣā: this; brāhmī: God-realised soul; sthitiḥ: situation; pārtha: O son of Pritā; na: not; enāṁ: this; prāpya: after achieving; vimuhyati: get deluded; sthitvā: being so situated; asyāṁ: in this state; antakāle: at the end of life; api: also; brahma nirvāṇaṁ: passing into one with the ultimate Reality; ṛcchati: attains

2.72 O Pārtha, this is the state of Brahman, Brāhmī-sthiti; none is deluded after attaining this. Even at the end of life, one attains Brahmanirvāṇa, oneness with Brahman when established in this state.

इति श्रीमद्भगवद्गीतासूपनिषत्सु ब्रह्मविद्यायां योगशास्त्रे
श्रीकृष्णार्जुनसंवादे साङ्ख्ययोगो नाम द्वितीयोऽध्यायः ॥

iti śrī mad bhagavadgītāsūpaniṣatsu brahmavidyāyām yogaśāstre śrīkṛṣṇārjuna saṁvāde sāṅkhya yogo nāma dvitīyo'dhyāyaḥ ||

In the ***Upaniṣad*** of ***Śrimad Bhagavad Gītā***, the scripture of yoga dealing with ***Brahmavidyā Yogaśāstra,*** the science of Brahman, the Supreme Absolute, in the form of ***Śrī Kṛṣṇārjuna saṁvād,*** dialogue between Śrī Kṛsna and Arjuna, this is the third chapter named, ***Karma Yogaḥ,*** *'The Yoga of Action.'*

CHAPTER 3

अथ तृतीयोऽध्यायः

कर्मयोगः

Karma Yogaḥ

अर्जुन उवाच

ज्यायसी चेत्कर्मणस्ते मता बुद्धिर्जनार्दन ।
तत्किं कर्मणि घोरे मां नियोजयसि केशव ॥ ३.१

arjuna uvāca

jyāyasī cetkarmaṇaste matā buddhirjanārdana /
tatkiṁ karmaṇi ghore māṁ niyojayasi keśava // *3.1*

arjuna: Arjuna; uvāca: says; jyāyasī: speaking highly; cet: although; karmaṇaḥ: action; te: your; matā: opinion; buddhir: knowledge; janārdana: Janārdana; tat: therefore; kiṁ: why; karmaṇi: in action; ghore: terrible; māṁ: me; niyojayasi: engaging me; keśava: Keśava (slayer of the demon Keśi)

3.1 Arjuna says: O Janārdana, O Keśava, Why do You make me engage in this terrible war if You think that knowledge is superior to action?

व्यामिश्रेणेव वाक्येन बुद्धिं मोहयसीव मे ।
तदेकं वद निश्चित्य येन श्रेयोऽहमाप्नुयाम् ॥ ३.२

vyāmiśreṇeva vākyena buddhiṁ mohayasīva me /
tadekaṁ vada niścitya yena śreyohamāpnuyām // *3.2*

vyāmiśreṇa: by ambiguous; iva: as; vākyena: words; buddhiṁ: intelligence; mohayasi: confusing; iva: as; me: my; tat: therefore; ekaṁ: one; vada: tell; niśc-itya: for certain; yena: by which; śreyaḥ: benefit; ahaṁ: I; āpnuyāṁ: may have

3.2 My intelligence is confused by Your conflicting words. Tell me clearly what is best for me.

श्रीभगवानुवाच
लोकेऽस्मिन्द्विविधा निष्ठा पुरा प्रोक्ता मयानघ ।
ज्ञानयोगेन साङ्ख्यानां कर्मयोगेन योगिनाम् ॥ ३.३

śrībhagavānuvāca
loke'smindvividhā niṣṭhā purā proktā mayānagha /
jñānayogena sāṁkhyānāṁ karmayogena yogināṁ // 3.3

śrī bhagavān uvāca: the Lord says; loke: in the world; asmin: this; dvividhā: two kinds of; niṣṭhā: faith; purā: before; proktā: were said; mayā: by Me; anagha: O sinless one; jñānayogena: by the yoga of knowledge; sāṁkhyānāṁ: of the Sāṅkhya; karmayogena: by the yoga of action; yoginām: of the yoga practitioners

3.3 The Lord says, 'O sinless Arjuna, as I said before, in this world there are two paths; Self knowledge for the intellectual and the path of action of the knowing.

न कर्मणामनारम्भान्नैष्कर्म्यं पुरुषोऽश्नुते ।
न च सन्न्यसनादेव सिद्धिं समधिगच्छति ॥ ३.४

na karmaṇāmanārambhānnaiṣkarmyaṁ puruṣo'śnute /
na ca sannyasanādeva siddhiṁ samadhigacchati // 3.4

na: without; karmaṇām: of the actions; anārambhāt: abstaining; naiṣkarmyaṁ: freedom from action; puruṣaḥ: man; aśnute: achieve; na: not; ca: also; sanny-asanāt: by renunciation; eva: surely; siddhiṁ: success; samadhigacchati: attain

3.4 A person does not attain freedom from action by abstaining from work, nor does he attain fulfillment by giving up action.

न हि कश्चित्क्षणमपि जातु तिष्ठत्यकर्मकृत् ।
कार्यते ह्यवशः कर्म सर्वः प्रकृतिजैर्गुणैः ॥ ३.५

na hi kaścitkṣaṇamapi jātu tiṣṭhatyakarmakṛt |
kāryate hyavaśaḥ karma sarvaḥ prakṛtijairguṇaiḥ || 3.5

na: not; hi: surely; kaścit: anyone; kṣaṇam: for a moment; api: also; jātu: even; tiṣṭhati: stands; akarmakṛt: without doing something; kāryate: forced to work; hi: surely; avaśaḥ: helplessly; karma: action; sarvaḥ: all; prakṛtijaih: of the modes of material nature; guṇaiḥ: by the attributes

3.5 Surely, not even for a moment can anyone stand without doing something. He is always in action, despite himself, as this is his very nature.

कर्मेन्द्रियाणि संयम्य य आस्ते मनसा स्मरन् ।
इन्द्रियार्थान्विमूढात्मा मिथ्याचारः स उच्यते ॥ ३.६

karmendriyāṇi saṁyamya ya āste manasā smaran |
indriyārthānvimūḍhātmā mithyācāraḥ sa ucyate || 3.6

karmendriyāṇi: the five working sense organs; saṁyamya: restraining; ya: who; āste: remains; manasā: mentally; smaran: recollecting; indriyārthān: objects of the senses; vimūḍha: foolish; atma: soul; mithyācāraḥ: hypocrite; saḥ: he; ucyate: is called

3.6 He who restrains the sense organs, but who still thinks of the objects of the senses is deluded and is called a hypocrite.

यस्त्विन्द्रियाणि मनसा नियम्यारभतेऽर्जुन ।
कर्मेन्द्रियैः कर्मयोगमसक्तः स विशिष्यते ॥ ३.७

yastvindriyāṇi manasā niyamyārabhate 'rjuna |
karmendriyaiḥ karmayogamasaktaḥ sa viśiṣyate || 3.7

yaḥ: who; tu : but; indriyāṇi : senses; manasā: by the mind; niyamya: controlling; ārabhate: begins; arjuna: O Arjuna; karmendriyaiḥ: by the active sense organs; karmayogam: work of devotion; asaktaḥ: without attachment; saḥ: he; viśiṣyate: superior

3.7 He who begins controlling the senses by the mind and performs selfless work through the sense organs is superior, O Arjuna.

नियतं कुरु कर्म त्वं कर्म ज्यायो ह्यकर्मण:
शरीरयात्रापि च ते न प्रसिद्ध्येदकर्मण: ॥ ३.८

niyataṁ kuru karma tvaṁ karma jyāyo hyakarmaṇaḥ |
śarīrayātrāpi ca te na prasiddhyedakarmaṇaḥ || 3.8

niyataṁ: prescribed; kuru: do; karma: work; tvaṁ: you; karma: work; jyāyaḥ: better; hi: than; akarmaṇaḥ: without work; śarīra: body; yātrā: maintenance; api: even; ca: also; te: your; na: never; prasiddhyet: possible; akarmaṇaḥ: without work

3.8 Do your prescribed work, as doing work is better than being idle. Even your own body cannot be maintained without work.

यज्ञार्थात्कर्मणोऽन्यत्र लोकोऽयं कर्मबन्धन: ।
तदर्थं कर्म कौन्तेय मुक्तसङ्ग: समाचर ॥ ३.९

yajñārthātkarmaṇo'nyatra loko'yam karmabandhanaḥ |
tadarthaṁ karma kaunteya mukta saṅgaḥ samācara || 3.9

yajñārthāt: sacrifice for; karmaṇaḥ: work done; anyatra: otherwise; lokaḥ: world; ayaṁ: this; karma bandhanaḥ: bondage by work; tad: that; arthaṁ: for; karma: work; kaunteya: O son of Kuntī; mukta: liberated; saṅgaḥ: attachment; samācara: do perfectly

3.9 Work has to be performed selflessly; otherwise, work binds one to this world. O son of Kuntī, perform your work for Me and you will do it authentically, liberated and without attachment.

सहयज्ञाः प्रजाः सृष्ट्वा पुरोवाच प्रजापतिः ।
अनेन प्रसविष्यध्वमेष वोऽस्त्विष्टकामधुक् ॥ ३.१०

sahayajñāḥ prajāḥ sṛṣṭvā puro'vāca prajāpatiḥ /
anena prasaviṣyadhvameṣa vo'stviṣṭakāmadhuk // 3.10

sah: along with; yajñāḥ: sacrifices; prajāḥ: people; sṛṣṭvā: creating; purā: before; uvāca: said; prajāpatiḥ: the lord of creation; anena: by this; prasaviṣyadhvaṁ: be more and more prosperous; eṣaḥ: certainly; vaḥ: your; astu: let it be; iṣṭa: desired; kāma dhuk: bestower of gifts

3.10 Brahma, the lord of creation before creating human kind as selfless sacrifice said, 'By this selfless enriching, be more and more prosperous and let it bestow all the desired gifts.'

देवान्भावयतानेन ते देवा भावयन्तु वः ।
परस्परं भावयन्तः श्रेयः परमवाप्स्यथ ॥ ३.११

devān bhāvayatā'nena te devā bhāvayantu vaḥ /
parasparaṁ bhāvayantaḥ śreyaḥ paramavāpsyatha // 3.11

devān: celestial beings; bhāvayata: having pleased; anena: by this sacrifice; te: those; devāḥ: demigods; bhāvayantu: will please; vaḥ: you; parasparaṁ: mutual; bhāvayantaḥ: pleasing one another; śreyaḥ: prosperity; paraṁ: supreme; avāpsyatha: achieve

3.11 The celestial beings, being pleased by this sacrifice, will also nourish you; with this mutual nourishing of one another, you will achieve supreme prosperity.

इष्टान्भोगान्हि वो देवा दास्यन्ते यज्ञभाविताः ।
तैर्दत्तानप्रदायैभ्यो यो भुङ्क्ते स्तेन एव सः ॥ ३.१२

iṣṭānbhogān hi vo devā dāsyante yajñabhāvitāḥ /
tairdattānapradāyaibhyo yo bhuṅkte stena eva saḥ // 3.12

iṣṭān: desired; bhogān: necessities of life; hi: certainly; vaḥ: to you; devāḥ:

demigods; dāsyante: award; yajña: sacrifice; bhāvitāḥ: satisfied; taiḥ: by them; dattān: things given; apradāya: without offering; ebhyaḥ: to the celestial beings; yaḥ: who; bhuṅkte: enjoys; stenaḥ: thief; eva: certainly; saḥ: he

3.12 Satisfied with the selfless enriching service, the celestial beings certainly award you the desired necessities of life. He who enjoys the things given by them without offering to the celestial beings is certainly a thief.

यज्ञशिष्टाशिनः सन्तो मुच्यन्ते सर्वकिल्बिषैः ।
भुञ्जते ते त्वघं पापा ये पचन्त्यात्मकारणात् ॥ ३.१३

yajñaśiṣṭāśinaḥ santo mucyante sarvakilbiṣaiḥ |
bhuñjate te tvaghaṁ pāpā ye pacantyātmakāraṇāt || 3.13

yajñaśiṣṭāśinaḥ: those who eat the food remnants of sacrifice; santaḥ: devotees; mucyante: get relief from; sarva: all; kilbiṣaiḥ: sins; bhuñjate: enjoy; te: they; tu: but; aghaṁ: grievous; pāpāḥ: sins; ye: those; pacanti: prepare food; ātmakāraṇāt: for sense enjoyment

3.13 Those who eat food after selfless enriching service are free of all sins. Those who prepare food for sense enjoyment do grievous sin.

अन्नाद्भवन्ति भूतानि पर्जन्यादन्नसम्भवः ।
यज्ञाद्भवति पर्जन्यो यज्ञः कर्मसमुद्भवः ॥ ३.१४

annādbhavanti bhūtāni parjanyādannasaṁbhavaḥ |
yajñādbhavati parjanyo yajñaḥ karmasamudbhavaḥ || 3.14

annāt: from grains; bhavanti: grow; bhūtāni: beings; parjanyāt: from rains; anna: food grains; saṁbhavaḥ: possible; yajñāt: from sacrifice; bhavati: becomes possible; parjanyaḥ: rains; yajñaḥ: sacrifice; karma: work; samudbhavaḥ: born of

3.14 All beings grow from food grains, from rains the food grains become possible, the rains become possible from selfless sacrifice of enriching.

कर्म ब्रह्मोद्भवं विद्धि ब्रह्माक्षरसमुद्भवम् ।
तस्मात्सर्वगतं ब्रह्म नित्यं यज्ञे प्रतिष्ठितम् ॥ ३.१५

karma brahmodbhavaṁ viddhi brahmākṣarasamudbhavam |
tasmātsarvagataṁ brahma nityaṁ yajñe pratiṣṭhitam || 3.15

karma: work; brahmodbhavaṁ: Creator born of; viddhi: know; brahma: Creator; akṣarasamudbhavaṁ: Supreme born of; tasmāt: therefore; sarvagataṁ: all-pervading; brahma: Supreme; nityaṁ: eternally; yajñe: in sacrifice; pratiṣṭhitaṁ: situated

3.15 Know that work is born of the Creator and He is born of the Supreme. The all-pervading Supreme is eternally situated in sacrifice of enriching.

एवं प्रवर्तितं चक्रं नानुवर्तयतीह यः ।
अघायुरिन्द्रियारामो मोघं पार्थ स जीवति ॥ ३.१६

evaṁ pravartitaṁ cakraṁ nānuvartayatīha yaḥ |
aghāyurindriyārāmo moghaṁ pārtha sa jīvati || 3.16

evaṁ: prescribed; pravartitaṁ: established; cakraṁ: cycle; na: not; anuvartayati: adopt; iha: in this; yaḥ: who; aghāyuḥ: life full of sins; indriyārāmaḥ: satisfied in sense gratification; moghaṁ: useless; pārtha: O son of Pritā; saḥ: he; jīvati: lives

3.16 O Pārtha, he who does not adopt the prescribed, established cycle lives a life full of sins. Rejoicing in sense gratification, he lives a useless life.

यस्त्वात्मरतिरेव स्यादात्मतृप्तश्च मानवः ।
आत्मन्येव च सन्तुष्टस्तस्य कार्यं न विद्यते ॥ ३.१७

yastvātmaratireva syādātmatṛptaśca mānavaḥ |
ātmanyeva ca santuṣṭastasya kāryaṁ na vidyate || 3.17

yaḥ: who; tu: but; ātmaratiḥ: takes pleasure; eva: certainly; syāt: remains;

ātmatṛptaḥ: satisfied in self; ca: and; mānavaḥ: man; ātmani: in oneself; eva: certainly; ca: and; saṁtuṣṭaḥ: satiated; tasya: his; kāryaṁ: work; na: not; vidyate: exist

3.17 One who takes pleasure in the Self, who is satisfied in the Self and who is content in one's Self, for him certainly, no work exists.

नैव तस्य कृतेनार्थो नाकृतेनेह कश्चन ।
न चास्य सर्वभूतेषु कश्चिदर्थव्यपाश्रय: ॥ ३.१८

naiva tasya kṛtenārtho nākṛteneha kaścana I
na cāsya sarvabhūteṣu kaścidarthavyapāśrayaḥ II 3.18

na: never; eva: certainly; tasya: his; kṛtena: by doing duty; arthaḥ: purpose; na: not; akṛtena: without doing duty; iha: in this world; kaścana: whatever; na: never; ca: and; asya: of him; sarvabhūteṣu: all living beings; kaścit: any; artha: purpose; vyapāśrayaḥ: taking shelter of

3.18 Certainly, he never has any purpose for doing his duty or for not doing his duty in this world. He does not depend on any living being.

तस्मादसक्त: सततं कार्यं कर्म समाचर ।
असक्तो ह्याचरन्कर्म परमाप्नोति पूरुष: ॥ ३.१९

tasmādasaktaḥ satataṁ kāryaṁ karma samācara I
asakto hyācaran karma paramāpnoti pūruṣaḥ II 3.19

tasmāt: therefore, asaktaḥ: without attachment, satataṁ: always, kāryaṁ: work, karma: work, samācara: perform, asaktaḥ: not attached, hi: certainly, ācaran: performing, karma: work, paraṁ: supreme, āpnoti: achieves, pūruṣaḥ: man

3.19 Therefore, one should work always without attachment. Performing work without attachment, certainly, man achieves the Supreme.

कर्मणैव हि संसिद्धिमास्थिता जनकादय: ।
लोकसंग्रहमेवापि संपश्यन्कर्तुमर्हसि ॥ ३.२०

karmaṇaiva hi saṁsiddhimāsthitā janakādayaḥ I
lokasaṁgrahamevāpi sampaśyankartumarhasi II 3.20

karmaṇā: by work; eva: also; hi: certainly; saṁsiddhiṁ: perfection; āsthitāḥ: situated; janakādayaḥ: Janaka and other kings; lokasaṁgrahaṁ: educating people; eva: also; api: therefore; saṁpaśyan: considering; kartuṁ: act; arhasi: deserve

3.20 King Janaka and others attained perfection by selfless enriching. To guide others you too must act selflessly.

यद्यदाचरति श्रेष्ठस्तत्तदेवेतरो जन: ।
स यत्प्रमाणं कुरुते लोकस्तदनुवर्तते ॥ ३.२१

yad yad ācarati śreṣṭhas tat tad evetaro janaḥ I
sa yatpramāṇaṁ kurute lokastadanuvartate II 3.21

yad-yat: what; ācarati: act; śreṣṭhaḥ: great; tat-tat: that; eva: certainly; itaraḥ: common; janaḥ: persons; saḥ: he; yat: what; pramāṇaṁ: evidence; kurute: perform; lokaḥ: world; tat: that; anuvartate: follow in footsteps

3.21 Whatever action is performed by a great person, others follow. They follow the example set by him.

न मे पार्थास्ति कर्तव्यं त्रिषु लोकेषु किञ्चन ।
नानवाप्तमवाप्तव्यं वर्त एव च कर्मणि ॥ ३.२२

na me pārthāsti kartavyaṁ triṣu lokeṣu kiñcana I
nānavāptamavāptavyaṁ varta eva ca karmaṇi II 3.22

na: not; me: mine; pārtha: O son of Pritā; asti: is; kartavyaṁ: duty; triṣu: in the three; lokeṣu: worlds; kiṁcana: anything; na: no; anavāptaṁ: in want; avāptavyaṁ: to be gained; varte: engaged; eva: only; ca: and; karmaṇi: work

3.22 O Pārtha, there is nothing that I must do in the three worlds. Neither am I in want of anything nor do I have anything to gain. Yet, I am always in action.

यदि ह्यहं न वर्तेयं जातु कर्मण्यतन्द्रितः ।
मम वर्त्मानुवर्तन्ते मनुष्याः पार्थ सर्वशः ॥ ३.२३

yadi hyahaṁ na varteyaṁ jātu karmaṇyatandritaḥ I
mama vartmānuvartante manuṣyāḥ pārtha sarvaśaḥ II 3.23

yadi: if; hi: certainly; ahaṁ: I; na: not; varteyaṁ: engage; jātu : ever; karmaṇi: work; atandritaḥ: with care; mama: My; vartma: path; anuvartante: follow; manuṣyāḥ: persons; pārtha: Pārtha; sarvaśaḥ: in all respects

3.23 If I did not engage in work with care, O Pārtha, certainly, people would follow My path in all respects.

उत्सीदेयुरिमे लोका न कुर्यां कर्म चेदहम् ।
सङ्करस्य च कर्ता स्यामुपहन्यामिमाः प्रजाः ॥ ३.२४

utsīdeyurime lokā na kuryāṁ karma cedaham I
sakarasya ca kartā syāmupahanyāmimāḥ prajāḥ II 3.24

utsīdeyuḥ: ruin; ime: these; lokāḥ: worlds; na: not; kuryāṁ: do; karma: work; cet: if; ahaṁ: I; sakarasya: confusion of species; ca: and; kartā: doer; syāṁ: shall be; upahanyāṁ: destroy; imāḥ: these; prajāḥ: beings

3.24 If I do not work, then these worlds would be ruined. I would be the cause of creating confusion and destruction.

सक्ताः कर्मण्यविद्वांसो यथा कुर्वन्ति भारत ।
कुर्याद्विद्वांस्तथासक्तश्चिकीर्षुर्लोकसंग्रहम् ॥ ३.२५

saktāḥ karmaṇyavidvāṁso yathā kurvanti bhārata I
kuryādvidvāṁstathāsaktaścikīrṣurlokasaṁgraham II 3.25

saktāḥ: attached; karmaṇi: work; avidvāṁsaḥ: ignorant; yathā: as; kurvanti: do; bhārata: Bhārata; kuryāt: do; vidvān: wise; tathā: and; asaktaḥ: without attachment; cikīrṣuḥ: desiring; lokasaṁgrahaṁ: leading people

3.25 As the ignorant do their work with attachment to the results, O Bhārata, the wise do so without attachment, for the enrichment (welfare) of people.

न बुद्धिभेदं जनयेदज्ञानां कर्मसङ्गिनाम् ।
जोषयेत्सर्वकर्माणि विद्वान्युक्तः समाचरन् ॥ ३.२६

na buddhi bhedaṁ janayedajñānāṁ karmasaginām |
joṣayetsarvakarmāṇi vidvānyuktaḥ samācaran || 3.26

na: not; buddhi: intelligence; bhedaṁ: disrupt; janayet: do; ajñānāṁ: ignorant; karma: work sagināṁ: attached; joṣayet: engaged; sarva: all; karmāṇi: work; vidvān: wise; yuktaḥ: balanced; samācaran: practising

3.26 Let not the wise disturb the minds of the ignorant who are attached to the results of work. They should encourage them to act without attachment.

प्रकृतेः क्रियमाणानि गुणैः कर्माणि सर्वशः ।
अहङ्कारविमूढात्मा कर्ताहमिति मन्यते ॥ ३.२७

prakṛteḥ kriyamāṇāni guṇaiḥ karmāṇi sarvaśaḥ |
ahakāravimūdhātmā kartāhamiti manyate || 3.27

prakṛteḥ: of material nature; kriyamāṇāni: all being done; guṇaiḥ: by the attributes; karmāṇi: work; sarvaśaḥ : all kinds of; ahaṁkāra: ego; vimūdhātmā: confused being; kartā: doer; ahaṁ: I; iti: thus; manyate: thinks

3.27 People, confused by ego, think they are the doers of all kinds of work while it is being done by the energy of nature.

तत्त्ववित्तु महाबाहो गुणकर्मविभागयोः ।
गुणा गुणेषु वर्तन्त इति मत्वा न सज्जते ॥ ३.२८

tattvavittu mahābāho guṇakarmavibhāgayoḥ /
guṇā guṇeṣu vartanta iti matvā na sajjate // 3.28

tattvavit: one who knows the truth; tu: but; mahābāho: mighty-armed one; guṇa: attributes; karma: work; vibhāgayoḥ: differences; guṇāḥ: attributes; guṇeṣu: in sense gratification; vartante: engaged; iti: thus; matvā: thinking; na: never; sajjate: becomes attached

3.28 One who knows the Truth, O mighty-armed one, knows the differences between the attributes of nature and work. Knowing well about the attributes and sense gratification, he never becomes attached.

प्रकृतेर्गुणसंमूढा: सज्जन्ते गुणकर्मसु ।
तानकृत्स्नविदो मन्दान्कृत्स्नविन्न विचालयेत् ॥ ३.२९

prakṛterguṇasaṁmūḍhāḥ sajjante guṇa karmasu /
tānakṛtsnavido mandānkṛtsnavinna vicālayet // 3.29

prakṛteḥ: by the material nature; guṇa: attributes; saṁmūḍhāḥ: fooled; sajjante: become engaged; guṇa: attributes; karmasu: actions; tān: those; akṛtsnavidaḥ: persons with less wisdom; mandān: lazy; kṛtsnavit: who has wisdom; na: not; vicālayet: unsettle

3.29 Fooled by the attributes of nature, those people with less wisdom or who are lazy become engaged in actions driven by these attributes. But, the wise should not unsettle them.

मयि सर्वाणि कर्माणि संन्यस्याध्यात्मचेतसा ।
निराशीर्निर्ममो भूत्वा युध्यस्व विगतज्वर: ॥ ३.३०

mayi sarvāṇi karmāṇi sannyasyādhyātmacetasā /
nirāśīrnirmamo bhūtvā yudhyasva vigatajvaraḥ // 3.30

mayi: to Me; sarvāṇi: all kinds of; karmāṇi: work; saṁnyasya: renouncing; adhyātma: spiritual knowledge; cetasā: consciousness; nirāśīḥ: without desire for gain; nir mamaḥ: without sense of ownership; bhūtvā: being; yudhyasva:

fight; vigatajvaraḥ: without being lazy

3.30 Dedicating all actions to Me, with consciousness filled with spiritual knowledge of Self, without desire for gain and without sense of ownership, without being lazy, fight.

ये मे मतमिदं नित्यमनुतिष्ठन्ति मानवा: ।
श्रद्धावन्तोऽनसूयन्तो मुच्यन्ते तेऽपि कर्मभि: ॥ ३.३१

ye me matamidaṁ nityamanutiṣṭhanti mānavāḥ I
śraddhāvanto 'nasūyanto mucyante tepi karmabhiḥ II 3.31

ye: who; me: My; matam: teaching; idaṁ: these; nityaṁ: always; anutiṣṭhanti: execute regularly; mānavāḥ: persons; śraddhāvantaḥ: with faith; anasūyantaḥ: without envy; mucyante: become free; te: all of them; api: even; karmabhiḥ: from the bondage of fruitive actions

3.31 Those persons who execute their duties according to My teaching and who follow these teachings faithfully with authenticity, without envy, become free from the bondage of fruitive actions.

ये त्वेतदभ्यसूयन्तो नानुतिष्ठन्ति मे मतम् ।
सर्वज्ञानविमूढांस्तान्विद्धि नष्टानचेतस: ॥ ३.३२

ye tvetad abhyasūyanto nānutiṣṭhanti me matam I
sarvajñānavimūḍhāṁstānviddhi naṣṭānacetasaḥ II 3.32

ye: those; tu: but; etat : this; abhyasūyantaḥ: out of envy; na: not; anutiṣṭhanti: regularly perform; me: My; mataṁ: teaching; sarvajñāna: all kinds of knowledge; vimūḍhān: fooled; tān: they; viddhi: know; naṣṭān: ruined; acetasaḥ: without Consciousness

3.32 But those who do not regularly perform their duty according to My teaching, are ignorant, senseless and ruined.

सदृशं चेष्टते स्वस्याः प्रकृतेर्ज्ञानवानपि ।
प्रकृतिं यान्ति भूतानि निग्रहः किं करिष्यति ॥ ३.३३

sadṛśaṁ ceṣṭate svasyāḥ prakṛterjñānavānapi |
prakṛtiṁ yānti bhūtāni nigrahaḥ kiṁ kariṣyati || 3.33

sadṛśaṁ: according to; ceṣṭate: tries; svasyāḥ: by one's nature; prakṛteḥ: modes; jñānavān: wise; api: even; prakṛtiṁ: nature; yānti: goes through; bhūtāni: living beings; nigrahaḥ: suppression; kiṁ: what; kariṣyati: can do

3.33 Even the wise person tries to act according to the modes of his own nature, for all living beings go through their nature. What can restraint of the senses do?

इन्द्रियस्येन्द्रियस्यार्थे रागद्वेषौ व्यवस्थितौ ।
तयोर्न वशमागच्छेत्तौ ह्यस्य परिपन्थिनौ ॥ ३.३४

indriyasyendriyasyārthe rāgadveṣau vyavasthitau |
tayorna vaśamāgacchet tau hyasya paripanthinau || 3.34

indriyasya: of the senses; indriyasya arthe: for sense objects; rāga: attachment; dveṣau: repulsion; vyavasthitau: put under control; tayoḥ: of them; na: never; vaśaṁ: control; āgacchet: come; tau: those; hi: certainly; asya: his; paripanthinau: stumbling blocks

3.34 Attachment and repulsion of the senses for sense objects should be put under control. One should never come under their control as they certainly are the stumbling blocks on the path of self-realization.

श्रेयान्स्वधर्मो विगुणः परधर्मात्स्वनुष्ठितात् ।
स्वधर्मे निधनं श्रेयः परधर्मो भयावहः ॥ ३.३५

śreyānsvadharmo viguṇahparadharmātsvanuṣṭhitāt |
svadharme nidhanaṁ śreyaḥ paradharmo bhayāvahaḥ || 3.35

śreyān: better; svadharmaḥ: own duty; viguṇaḥ: in a faulty manner; paradharmāt: other's duty; svanuṣṭhitāt: perfectly done; svadharme: in one's duty; nidhanaṁ: death; śreyaḥ: better; paradhamaḥ: other's duty; bhayāvahaḥ: dangerous

3.35 Better it is to do one's own responsibility, even if it is in a faultily, than to do someone else's responsibility perfectly. Death in the course of performing one's own responsibility is better than doing another's responsibility, as this can be dangerous.

अर्जुन उवाच

अथ केन प्रयुक्तोऽयं पापं चरति पूरुषः ।

अनिच्छन्नपि वार्ष्णेय बलादिव नियोजितः ॥ ३.३६

arjuna uvāca

atha kena prayukto'yaṁ pāpaṁ carati pūruṣaḥ /

anicchannapi vārṣṇeya balādiva niyojitaḥ // 3.36

arjuna uvāca: Arjuna said; atha: then; kena: by what; prayuktaḥ: forced; ayaṁ: this (person); pāpaṁ: sins; carati: acts; pūruṣaḥ: man; anicchan: without desiring; api: though; vārṣṇeya: O descendant of Vrishni; balāt: by force; iva: as if; niyojitaḥ: engaged

3.36 Arjuna says, 'O descendant of Vṛṣṇi, then, by what is man forced to sinful acts, even without desiring, as if impelled by force?'

श्री भगवानुवाच

काम एष क्रोध एष रजोगुणसमुद्भवः ।

महाशनो महापाप्मा विद्ध्येनमिह वैरिणम् ॥ ३.३७

śrībhagavānuvāca

kāma eṣa krodha eṣa rajoguṇasamudbhavaḥ /

mahāśano mahāpāpmā viddhyenamiha vairiṇam // 3.37

śrī bhagavān uvāca: the Lord said; kāma: lust; eṣa: these; krodha: anger; eṣa: these; rajoguṇa: attribute of passion; samudbhavaḥ: born of; mahāśanaḥ: all-devouring; mahāpāpmā: greatly sinful; viddhi: know; enaṁ: this; iha: in the world; vairiṇaṁ: greatest enemy

3.37 The Lord says, 'It is lust and anger born of the attribute of passion, alldevouring and sinful, which is one's greatest enemy in this world.'

धूमेनाव्रियते वह्निर्यथादर्शो मलेन च ।
यथोल्बेनावृतो गर्भस्तथा तेनेदमावृतम् ॥ ३.३८

dhūmenāvriyate vanhiryathādarśo malena ca |
yatholbenāvṛto garbhastathā tenedamāvṛtam || 3.38

dhūmena: by smoke; āvriyate: covered; vahniḥ: fire; yathā: as; ādarśaḥ: mirror; malena: by dust; ca: also; yathā: as; ulbena: by the womb; āvṛtaḥ: covered; garbhaḥ: embryo; tathā: so; tena: by that; idaṁ: this; āvṛtaṁ: covered

3.38 As fire is covered by smoke, as a mirror is covered by dust, or as the e bryo is covered by the womb, so also, the living being is covered by lust.

आवृतं ज्ञानमेतेन ज्ञानिनो नित्यवैरिणा ।
कामरूपेण कौन्तेय दुष्पूरेणानलेन च ॥ ३.३९

āvṛtaṁ jñānametena jñānino nityavairiṇā |
kāmarūpeṇa kaunteya duṣpūreṇānalena ca || 3.39

āvṛtaṁ: covered; jñānam: knowledge; etena: by this; jñāninaḥ: of the knower; nitya: eternal; vairiṇā: enemy; kāma: desire; rū peṇa: in the form of; kaunteya: O son of Kuntī; duṣpūreṇa: never satisfied; analena: by fire; ca: and

3.39 The knowledge of the knower is covered by this eternal enemy in the form of lust, which is never satisfied and burns like fire, O son of Kuntī

इन्द्रियाणि मनो बुद्धिरस्याधिष्ठानमुच्यते ।
एतैर्विमोहयत्येष ज्ञानमावृत्य देहिनम् ॥ ३.४०

indriyāṇi mano buddhirasyādhiṣṭhānamucyate |
etairvimohayatyeṣa jñānamāvṛtya dehinam || 3.40

indriyāṇi: senses; manaḥ: mind; buddhiḥ: intelligence; asya: of; adhiṣṭhānaṁ: sitting place; ucyate: called; etaiḥ: by these; vimohayati: confuses; eṣaḥ: this; jñānaṁ: knowledge; āvṛtya: covering; dehinam: embodied being

3.40 The senses, the mind and the intelligence are the locations of this lust, which confuses the embodied being and covers the knowledge.

तस्मात्त्वमिन्द्रियाण्यादौ नियम्य भरतर्षभ ।
पाप्मानं प्रजहि ह्येनं ज्ञानविज्ञाननाशनम् ॥ ३.४१

tasmāttvamindriyāṇyādau niyamya bharatarṣabha |
pāpmānaṁ prajahi hyenaṁ jñānavijñānanāśanam || 3.41

tasmāt: therefore; tvam: you; indriyāṇi: senses; ādau: in the beginning; niyamya: by controlling; Bharata ṛṣabha: O chief amongst the descendants of Bhārata; pāpmānaṁ: symbol of sin; prajahi: curb; hi: certainly; enaṁ: this; jñāna: knowledge; vijñāna: consciousness; nāśanaṁ: destroyer

3.41 Therefore, O Bharatarṣabha, chief amongst the descendants of Bhārata, in the very beginning, control the senses and curb the symbol of sin, which is certainly the destroyer of knowledge and consciousness.

इन्द्रियाणि पराण्याहुरिन्द्रियेभ्यः परं मनः ।
मनसस्तु परा बुद्धिर्यो बुद्धेः परतस्तु सः ॥ ३.४२

indriyāṇi parāṇyāhurindriyebhyaḥ paraṁ manaḥ |
manasastu parā buddhiryo buddheḥ paratastu saḥ || 3.42

indriyāṇi: senses; parāṇi: superior; āhuḥ: is said; indriyebhyaḥ: more than the senses; paraṁ: superior; manaḥ: mind; manasaḥ: more than the mind; tu: also; parā: superior; buddhiḥ: intelligence; yaḥ: who; buddheḥ: more than intelligence; parataḥ: superior; tu: but; saḥ: he

3.42 It is said that the senses are superior to the body. The mind is superior to the senses. The intelligence is still higher than the mind and the consciousness is even higher than intelligence.

एवं बुद्धेः परं बुद्ध्वा संस्तभ्यात्मानमात्मना ।
जहि शत्रुं महाबाहो कामरूपं दुरासदम् ॥ ३.४३

evaṁ buddheḥ paraṁ buddhvā saṁstabhyātmānamātmanā I
jahi śatruṁ māhābāho kāmarūpaṁ durāsadam II 3.43

evaṁ: and; buddheḥ: of intelligence; paraṁ: superior; buddhvā: knowing; saṁstabhya: by steadying; ātmānaṁ: of the mind; ātmanā: by intelligence; jahi: conquer; śatruṁ: enemy; māhābāho: O mighty-armed one; kāma: lust; rūpaṁ: in the form of; durāsadaṁ: insatiable

3.43 Knowing the Self to be superior to mind and intelligence, by steadying the mind by intelligence, conquer the insatiable enemy in the form of lust, O Mahābāho, mighty-armed one.

इति श्रीमद्भगवद्गीतासूपनिषत्सु ब्रह्मविद्यायां योगशास्त्रे
श्रीकृष्णार्जुनसंवादे कर्मयोगो नाम तृतीयोऽध्यायः ॥

iti śrī mad bhagavadgītāsūpaniṣatsu brahmavidyāyām
yogaśāstre śrīkṛṣṇārjuna saṁvāde karmayogo nāma
tṛtīyo'dhyāyaḥ II

*Thus ends the third chapter named **Karma Yogaḥ**, 'The Yoga of Action,' of the **Bhagavad Gītā Upaniṣad, Brahmavidyā Yogaśāstra**, the scripture of yoga dealing with the science of the Absolute in the form of **Śrī Kṛṣṇārjuna saṃvād**, dialogue between Śrī Kṛṣṇa and Arjuna.*

CHAPTER

4

अथ चतुर्थोऽध्याय:

ज्ञानकर्मसंन्यासयोग:

Jñānakarmasannyāsa Yogaḥ

श्री भगवानुवाच ।
इमं विवस्वते योगं प्रोक्तवानहमव्ययम् ।
विवस्वान्मनवे प्राह मनुरिक्ष्वाकवेऽब्रवीत् ॥ ४.१

śrībhagavānuvāca
imaṁ vivasvate yogaṁ proktavānaham avyayaṁ I
vivasvānmanave prāha manurikṣvākave'bravīt II *4.1*

śrī bhagavān uvāca: the Lord says; imaṁ: this; vivasvate: to the Sun god; yogaṁ: the science of yoga; proktavān: instructed; ahaṁ: I; avyayaṁ: imperishable; vivasvān: sun god; manave: to Manu, the father of mankind; prāha: told; manuḥ: Manu; ikṣvākave: to King Ikṣvāku; abravīt: said

4.1 Bhagavān says: 'I taught the sun god, Vivasvān, the imperishable science of yoga and Vivasvān taught Manu, the father of mankind and Manu in turn taught Ikṣvāku.'

एवं परम्पराप्राप्तमिमं राजर्षयो विदुः ।
स कालेनेह महता योगो नष्टः परन्तप ॥ ४.२

evaṁ paramparāprāptamimaṁ rājarṣayo viduḥ I
sa kāleneha mahatā yogo naṣṭaḥ parantapa II *4.2*

evaṁ: thus; paraṁparā: Master-disciple succession; prāptaṁ: received; imaṁ: this science; rājarṣayaḥ: the saintly kings; viduḥ: understood; saḥ: that knowledge; kālena: in the course of time; iha: in this world; mahatā: by great; yogaḥ: the science of yoga; naṣṭaḥ: lost; paraṁtapa: subduer of the enemies

4.2 The supreme science was thus received through the chain of master-disciple succession and the saintly kings understood it in that way. In the course of time, the succession was broken and therefore the science as it was appears to have been lost.

स एवायं मया तेऽद्य योगः प्रोक्तः पुरातनः ।
भक्तोऽसि मे सखा चेति रहस्यं ह्येतदुत्तमम् ॥ ४.३

sa evāyaṁ mayā te'dya yogaḥ proktaḥ purātanaḥ |
bhakto 'si me sakhā ceti rahasyaṁ hyetaduttamam || 4.3

saḥ: that; eva: only; ayaṁ: this; mayā : by Me; te: to you; adya: today; yogaḥ: the science of yoga; proktaḥ: spoken; purātanaḥ: very old; bhaktaḥ: devotee; asi: you are; me: My; sakhā : friend; ca: also; iti: therefore; rahasyaṁ: mystery; hi: because etat: this; uttamaṁ: supreme

4.3 That ancient science of Enlightenment, or entering into eternal bliss, is today taught by me to you because you are my devotee as well as my friend. You will certainly understand the supreme mystery of this science.

अर्जुन उवाच ।
अपरं भवतो जन्म परं जन्म विवस्वतः ।
कथमेतद्विजानीयां त्वमादौ प्रोक्तवानिति ॥ ४.४

arjuna uvāca
aparaṁ bhavato janma paraṁ janma vivasvataḥ |
kathametad vijānīyāṁ tvamādau proktavāniti || 4.4

arjuna uvāca: Arjuna says; aparaṁ: of recent origin; bhavataḥ: Your; janma: birth; paraṁ: very old; janma: birth; vivasvataḥ: of the Sun god; kathaṁ: how;

etat: this; vijānīyāṁ: can I understand; tvaṁ: You; ādau: in the beginning; proktavān: instructed; iti: thus

4.4 Arjuna says: 'Oh Kṛṣṇa, you are younger to the sun god Vivasvān by birth. How am I to understand that in the beginning you instructed this science to him?'

श्री भगवानुवाच
बहूनि मे व्यतीतानि जन्मानि तव चार्जुन ।
तान्यहं वेद सर्वाणि न त्वं वेत्थ परन्तप ॥ ४.५

śrībhagavānuvāca
bahuni me vyatītāni janmāni tava cārjuna ।
tānyahaṁ veda sarvāṇi na tvaṁ vettha parantapa ॥ 4.5

śrī bhagavān uvāca: The Lord says; bahūni: many; me: of Mine; vyatī tā ni: have passed; janmāni: births; tava: yours; ca: also; arjuna: O Arjuna; tā ni: all of those; ahaṁ: I; veda: do know; sarvāṇi: all; na: not; tvaṁ: yourself; vettha: know; paraṁtapa: O scorcher of the foes

4.5 Bhagavān says: Many many births both you and I have passed. I can remember all of them, but you cannot, O Parantapa!

अजोऽपि सन्नव्ययात्मा भूतानामीशरोऽपि सन् ।
प्रकृतिं स्वामधिष्ठाय संभवाम्यात्ममायया ॥ ४.६

ajo 'pi sannavyayātmā bhūtānām īśvaro 'pi san ।
prakṛtiṁ svāmadhiṣṭhāya saṁbhavāmyātmamāyayā ॥ 4.6

ajaḥ: unborn; api: also; san: being so; avyaya: instructible; atmā: spirit; bhūtānāṁ: living entities; īśvaraḥ: supreme Lord; api: also; san: being so; prakṛtiṁ: nature; svāṁ: of Myself; adhiṣṭhāya: keeping under control; saṁbhavāmi: I come into being; ātmamāyayā: by My divine potency.

4.6 Although I am unborn, imperishable and the lord of all living entities, by ruling my nature I reappear by my own māyā.

यदा यदा हि धर्मस्य ग्लानिर्भवति भारत ।
अभ्युत्थानमधर्मस्य तदात्मानं सृजाम्यहम् ॥ ४.७

yadā yadā hi dharmasya glānirbhavati bhārata |
abhyutthānam adharmasya tad ātmānaṁ sṛjāmyaham || 4.7

yadā -yadā : whenever; hi: well; dharmasya: of righteousness; glāniḥ: decline; bhavati: takes place; bhārata: O descendant of Bhārata; abhyutthānaṁ: predominance; adharmasya: of unrighteousness; tadā : at that time; ātmānaṁ: self; sṛjāmi: bring forth; ahaṁ: I

4.7 Whenever positive consciousness declines, when collective negativity rises, O Bhārat, again and again, at these times, I happen Myself.

परित्राणाय साधूनां विनाशाय च दुष्कृताम् ।
धर्मसंस्थापनार्थाय संभवामि युगे युगे ॥ ४.८

paritrāṇāya sādhūnāṁ vināśāya ca duṣkṛtām |
dharma-saṁsthāpanārthāya saṁbhavāmi yuge-yuge || 4.8

paritrāṇāya: for the protection of; sādhūnāṁ: of the pious; vināśāya: to destroy; ca: also; duṣkṛtāṁ: of the wicked; dharma: righteousness; saṁsthāpanārthāya: to establish; saṁbhavāmi: I manifest; yuge-yuge: age after age

4.8 To protect the pious and to annihilate the wicked, to re-establish righteousness I Myself appear, age after age.

जन्म कर्म च मे दिव्यमेवं यो वेत्ति तत्त्वतः ।
त्यक्त्वा देहं पुनर्जन्म नैति मामेति सोऽर्जुन ॥ ४.९

janma karma ca me divyamevaṁ yo vetti tattvataḥ |
tyaktvā dehaṁ punarjanma naiti māmeti so 'rjuna || 4.9

janma: birth; karma: work; ca: and; me: of Mine; divyaṁ: divine; evaṁ: so also; yaḥ: anyone whoever; vetti: knows; tattvataḥ: in reality; tyaktvā: after leaving aside; dehaṁ: body; punaḥ: again; janma: birth; na: never; eti: attains; māṁ:

unto Me; eti: does attain; saḥ: he; arjuna: Arjuna

4.9 One who knows or experiences My divine appearance and activities does not take birth again in this material world after leaving the body but attains Me, o Arjuna.

वीतरागभयक्रोधा मन्मया मामुपाश्रिता: ।
बहवो ज्ञानतपसा पूता मद्भावमागता: ॥ ४.१०

vītarāgabhayakrodhā manmayā māmupāśritāḥ /
bahavo jñānatapasā pūtā madbhāvamāgatāḥ // 4.10

vīta: free from; rāga: passion; bhaya: fear; krodhāḥ: anger; manmayā: fully absorbed in Me; māṁ: unto Me; upāśritāḥ: taking refuge; bahavaḥ: many beings; jñāna: wisdom; tapasā: by penance; pūtāḥ: sanctified; mad bhāvaṁ: My nature; āgatāḥ: attained

4.10 Being freed from attachment, fear and anger, being filled with me and by taking refuge in me, many beings in the past have become sanctified by the knowledge of me and have realized me.

ये यथा मां प्रपद्यन्ते तांस्तथैव भजाम्यहम् ।
मम वर्त्मानुवर्तन्ते मनुष्या: पार्थ सर्वश: ॥ ४.११

ye yathā māṁ prapadyante tāṁstathaiva bhajāmyaham /
mama vartmānuvartante manuṣyāḥ pārtha sarvaśah // 4.11

ye: whoever; yathā: whatever way; māṁ: unto Me; prapadyante: seek; tān: unto them; tathā eva: in the same way; bhajāmi : I approach; ahaṁ: I; mama: My; vartma: of the path; anuvartante: follow; manuṣyāḥ: people; pārtha: son of Pritā; sarvaśaḥ: in all respects

4.11 I reward everyone, I show Myself to all people, according to the manner in which they surrender unto me, in the manner that they are devoted to me, O Pārtha!

काङ्क्षन्तः कर्मणां सिद्धिं यजन्त इह देवताः ।
क्षिप्रं हि मानुषे लोके सिद्धिर्भवति कर्मजा ॥ ४.१२

kāṅkṣantaḥ karmaṇāṁ siddhiṁ yajanta iha devatāḥ I
kṣipraṁ hi mānuṣe loke siddhirbhavati karmajā II 4.12

kāṅkṣantaḥ: desiring; karmaṇāṁ: of activities; siddhiṁ: success; yajante: worship; iha: in this world; devatāḥ: gods; kṣipraṁ: quickly; hi: for; mānuṣe loke: in human society; siddhiḥ bhavati: success comes; karmajā : born of action

4.12 Men in this world desire success from activities and therefore they worship the gods. Men get instant results from active work in this world.

चातुर्वर्ण्यं मया सृष्टं गुणकर्मविभागशः।
तस्य कर्तारमपि मां विद्ध्यकर्तारमव्ययम् ॥ ४.१३

cāturvarṇyaṁ mayā sṛṣṭaṁ guṇakarma vibhāgaśaḥ I
tasya kartāram api māṁ viddhyakartāramavyayam II 4.13

cāturvarṇyaṁ: the four divisions of human society; mayā: by Me; sṛṣṭaṁ: created; guṇa: attribute; karma: work; vibhāgaśaḥ: in terms of division; tasya: of that; kartāraṁ: doer; api: although; māṁ: Me; viddhi: know; akartāraṁ: as the non-doer; avyayaṁ: immortal

4.13 Depending upon the distribution of the three attributes or guṇas and action, I have created the four castes. Yet, I am to be known as the non-doer, the unchangeable.

न मां कर्माणि लिम्पन्ति न मे कर्मफले स्पृहा ।
इति मां योऽभिजानाति कर्मभिर्न स बध्यते ॥ ४.१४

na māṁ karmāṇi limpanti na me karmaphale spṛhā I
iti māṁ yo'bhijānāti karmabhirna sa badhyate II 4.14

na: never; māṁ: Me; karmāṇi: work; limpanti: affect; na: not; me: My; karmaphale: in fruits of action; spṛhā : longing for; iti: thus; māṁ: Me; yaḥ: one who; abhijānāti: understands; karmabhiḥ : by the action; na: never; saḥ: he; badhyate: is bound.

4.14 I am not affected by any work; nor do I long for the outcome of such work. One who understands this truth about me also does not get caught in the bondage of work.

एवं ज्ञात्वा कृतं कर्म पूर्वैरपि मुमुक्षुभिः ।
कुरु कर्मैव तस्मात्त्वं पूर्वैः पूर्वतरं कृतम् ॥ ४.१५

evaṁ jñātvā kṛtaṁ karma pūrvairapi mumukṣubhiḥ I
kuru karmaiva tasmāttvaṁ pūrvaiḥ pūrvataraṁ kṛtam II 4.15

evaṁ: thus; jñātvā: knowing well; kṛtaṁ: performed; karma: work; pūrvaiḥ: by the ancient people; api: also; mumukṣubhiḥ: by those seeking liberation; kuru: perform; karma: prescribed duty; eva: only; tasmāt: therefore; tvaṁ: you; pūrvaiḥ: by the predecessors; pūrvataraṁ: as in the past; kṛtaṁ: as performed

4.15 All the wise and liberated souls of ancient times have acted with this understanding and thus attained liberation. Just as the ancients did, perform your duty with this understanding.

किं कर्म किमकर्मेति कवयोऽप्यत्र मोहिताः ।
तत्ते कर्म प्रवक्ष्यामि यज्ज्ञात्वा मोक्ष्यसेऽशुभात् ॥ ४.१६

kiṁ karma kimakarmeti kavayo'pyatra mohitāḥ I
tat te karma pravakṣyāmi yaj jñātvā mokṣyase'śubhāt II 4.16

kiṁ: what; karma: action; kiṁ: what; akarma: inaction; iti: thus; kavayaḥ: the wise; api: also; atra: in this matter; mohitāḥ: confused; tat: that; te: unto you; karma: action; pravakṣyāmi: I shall explain; yat: which; jñātvā: after knowing; mokṣyase: be liberated; aśubhāt: from ills

4.16 What is action and what is inaction, even the wise are confused. Let me explain to you what action is, knowing which you shall be liberated from all ills.

कर्मणो ह्यपि बोद्धव्यं बोद्धव्यं च विकर्मण: ।
अकर्मणश्च बोद्धव्यं गहना कर्मणो गति: ॥ ४.१७

karmaṇo hyapi boddhavyaṁ boddhavyaṁ ca vikarmaṇaḥ |
akarmaṇaśca boddhavyaṁ gahanā karmaṇo gatiḥ || 4.17

karmaṇaḥ: of action; hi: for; api: also; boddhavyaṁ: should be understood; boddhavyaṁ: to be understood; ca: also; vikarmaṇaḥ: wrong action; akarmaṇaḥ: inaction; ca: also; boddhavyaṁ: should be understood; gahanā: mysterious; karmaṇaḥ: of action; gatiḥ: way.

4.17 The complexities of action are very difficult to understand. Understand fully the nature of proper action by understanding the nature of wrong action and inaction.

कर्मण्यकर्म य: पश्येदकर्मणि च कर्म य: ।
स बुद्धिमान्मनुष्येषु स युक्त: कृत्स्नकर्मकृत् ॥ ४.१८

karmaṇyakarma yaḥ paśyedakarmaṇi ca karma yaḥ |
sa buddhimān manuṣyeṣu sa yuktaḥ kṛtsnakarmakṛt || 4.18

karmaṇi: in action; akarma: inaction; yaḥ: one who; paśyet: sees; akarmaṇi: in inaction; ca: also; karma: action; yaḥ: one who; saḥ: he; buddhimān: wise; manusyeṣu: among men; saḥ: he; yuktaḥ: yogi; kṛtsnakarmakṛt: engaged in all activities

4.18 He who sees inaction in action and action in inaction, is wise and a yogi, Even if engaged in all activities.

यस्य सर्वे समारम्भा: कामसङ्कल्पवर्जिता: ।
ज्ञानाग्निदग्धकर्माणं तमाहु: पण्डितं बुधा: ॥ ४.१९

yasya sarve samārambhāḥ kāmasaṅkalpavarjitāḥ |
jñānāgnidagdhakarmāṇaṁ tam āhuḥ paṇḍitaṁ budhāḥ || 4.19

yasya: one whose; sarve: all kinds of; samārambhāḥ: in all situations; kāma:

desire for sense gratification; saṅkalpa: purpose; varjitāḥ: devoid of; jñāna: of perfect knowledge; agni: fire; dagdhakarmāṇaṁ: whose actions have been burnt; taṁ: him; āhuḥ: declare; paṇḍitaṁ: wise; budhāḥ: the wise.

4.19 He who is determined and devoid of all desires for sense gratification, he is of perfect knowledge. The sages declare such a person wise whose actions are burnt by the fire of knowledge.

त्यक्त्वा कर्मफलासङ्गं नित्यतृप्तो निराश्रयः ।
कर्मण्यभिप्रवृत्तोऽपि नैव किञ्चित्करोति सः ॥ ४.२०

tyaktvā karmaphalāsaṅgaṁ nityatṛpto nirāśrayaḥ |
karmaṇyabhipravṛtto'pi naiva kiñcitkaroti saḥ || 4.20

tyaktvā : having given up; karmaphalāsaṅgaṁ: attachment to results of action; nitya: always; tṛptaḥ: satisfied; nirāśrayaḥ: without shelter; karmaṇi: in action; abhipravṛttaḥ: being fully engaged; api: although; na: does not; eva: verily; kiñcit: anything; karoti: does; saḥ: he

4.20 Having given up all attachment to the results of his action, always satisfied and independent, the wise man does not act, though he is engaged in all kinds of action.

निराशीर्यतचित्तात्मा त्यक्तसर्वपरिग्रहः ।
शारीरं केवलं कर्म कुर्वन्नाप्नोति किल्बिषम् ॥ ४.२१

nirāśī ryatacittātmā tyaktasarvaparigrahaḥ |
śārīraṁ kevalaṁ karma kurvannāpnoti kilbiṣam || 4.21

nirāśīḥ: without desire for the result; yata: controlled; cittātmā: mind and consciousness; tyakta: giving up; sarva: all; parigrahaḥ: sense of ownership; śārīraṁ: bodily effort; kevalaṁ: only; karma: work; kurvan: doing so; na: never; āpnoti: acquire; kilbiṣaṁ: sin

4.21 The person who acts without desire for the result; with his consciousness controlling the mind, giving up all sense of ownership over his possessions and body and only working, incurs no sin.

यदृच्छालाभसन्तुष्टो द्वन्द्वातीतो विमत्सरः ।
समः सिद्धावसिद्धौ च कृत्वापि न निबध्यते ॥ ४.२२

yadṛcchālābhasantuṣṭo dvandvātī to vimatsaraḥ /
samaḥ siddhāvasiddhau ca kṛtvāpi na nibadhyate // 4.22

yadṛcchā lābha: what is obtained unsought; santuṣṭa: satisfied; dvandva: pairs of opposites; atī taḥ: surpassed; vimatsaraḥ: free from envy; samaḥ: equal; siddhau: in success; asiddhau: in failure; ca: also; kṛtvā: after doing; api: even; na: never; nibadhyate: bound

4.22 He who is satisfied with profit which comes of its own accord and who has gone beyond duality, who is free from envy, who is in equanimity both in success and failure, such a person though doing action, is never affected.

गतसङ्गस्य मुक्तस्य ज्ञानावस्थितचेतसः ।
यज्ञायाचरतः कर्म समग्रं प्रविलीयते ॥ ४.२३

gatasaṅgasya muktasya jñānāvasthitacetasaḥ /
yajñāyācarataḥ karma samagraṁ pravilī yate // 4.23

gatasaṅgasya: unattached to the modes of material nature; muktasya: of the liberated; jñānā: knowledge; avasthita: established; cetasaḥ: of such spirit; yajñāya: for the sake of sacrifice; ācarataḥ: practice; karma: work; samagraṁ: in total; pravilī yate: melts away.

4.23 The work of a liberated man who is unattached to the modes of material nature and who is fully centered in the ultimate knowledge, who works totally for the sake of sacrifice, merges entirely into the knowledge.

ब्रह्मार्पणं ब्रह्महविर्ब्रह्माग्नौ ब्रह्मणा हुतम् ।
ब्रह्मैव तेन गन्तव्यं ब्रह्मकर्मसमाधिना ॥ ४.२४

brahmārpaṇaṁ brahmahavir brahmāgnau brahmaṇā hutam |
brahmaiva tena gantavyaṁ brahmakarmasamādhinā || 4.24

brahma: supreme; arpaṇaṁ: offering; brahma: supreme; haviḥ: oblation; brahma: supreme; agnau: in the fire of; brahmaṇā: by the supreme; hutaṁ: offered; brahma: supreme; eva: only; tena: by him; gantavyaṁ: to be reached; brahma: supreme; karma: action; samādhinā: by complete absorption

4.24 The offering, the offered butter to the supreme in the fire of the supreme is offered by the supreme. Certainly, the supreme can be reached by him who is absorbed completely in action.

दैवमेवापरे यज्ञं योगिनः पर्युपासते ।
ब्रह्माग्नावपरे यज्ञं यज्ञेनैवोपजुह्वति ॥ ४.२५

daivamevāpare yajñaṁ yoginaḥ paryupāsate |
brahmāgnāvapare yajñaṁ yajñenaivopajuhvati || 4.25

daivaṁ: gods; eva: only; apare: others; yajñaṁ: sacrifices; yoginaḥ: yogis; paryupāsate: worship; brahma: supreme; agnau: in the fire; apare: others; yajñaṁ: sacrifice; yajñena: by sacrifice; eva: only; upajuhvati: offer as sacrifice.

4.25 Some yogis worship the gods by offering various sacrifices to them, While others worship by offering sacrifices in the fire of the supreme.

श्रोत्रादीनीन्द्रियाण्यन्ये संयमाग्निषु जुह्वति ।
शब्दादीन्विषयानन्य इन्द्रियाग्निषु जुह्वति ॥ ४.२६

śrotrādī nīndriyāṇyanye saṁyamāgniṣu juhvati |
śabdādī nviṣayānanya indriyāgniṣu juhvati || 4.26

śrotrādīnī : organ of hearing; indriyāṇi: senses; anye: others; saṁyama : self discipline; agniṣu: in the fire; juhvati: offer as sacrifice; śabdādī n: sound vibrations; viṣayān: objects of sense gratification; anye: others; indriya: of sense organs; agniṣu: in the fire; juhvati: sacrifice

4.26 Some sacrifice the hearing process and other senses in the fire of equanimity and others offer as sacrifice the objects of the senses, such as sound in the fire of the sacrifice.

सर्वाणीन्द्रियकर्माणि प्राणकर्माणि चापरे ।
आत्मसंयमयोगाग्नौ जुह्वति ज्ञानदीपिते ॥ ४.२७

sarvāṇīndriyakarmāṇi prāṇakarmāṇi cāpare /
ātmasaṁyamayogāgnau juhvati jñānadī pite // 4.27

sarvāṇi: all; indriya: senses; karmāṇi: actions; prāṇakarmāṇi: activities of the life breath; ca: also; apare: others; ātmasaṁyama: self control; yoga: yoga; agnau: in the fire of; juhvati: offer; jñāna dīpite: kindled by wisdom.

4.27 One who is interested in knowledge offers all the actions due to the senses, including the action of taking in the life breath into the fire of Yoga and is engaged in the yoga of the equanimity of the mind.

द्रव्ययज्ञास्तपोयज्ञा योगयज्ञास्तथापरे ।
स्वाध्यायज्ञानयज्ञाश्च यतयः संशितव्रताः ॥ ४.२८

dravyayajñāstapoyajñā yogayajñāstathāpare /
svādhyāyajñānayajñāśca yatayaḥ saṁśitavratāḥ // 4.28

dravya: material wealth; yajñāḥ : sacrifice; tapo: penance; yajñāḥ : sacrifice; yoga: yoga; yajñāḥ: sacrifice; tathā : and; apare: others; svādhyāya: self-study; jñāna: knowledge; yajñāḥ: sacrifice; ca: and; yatayaḥ: striving souls; saṁśita vratāḥ: those of strict vows.

4.28 There is the sacrifice of material wealth, sacrifice through penance, sacrific through yoga and other sacrifices while there is sacrifice through self-study and through strict vows.

अपाने जुह्वति प्राणं प्राणेऽपानं तथापरे ।
प्राणापानगती रुद्ध्वा प्राणायामपरायणाः ॥ ४.२९

apāne juhvati prāṇaṁ prāṇe 'pānaṁ tathāpare /
prāṇāpānagatī ruddhvā prāṇāyāmaparāyaṇāḥ // 4.29

apāne: in the out going breath; juhvati: sacrifice; prāṇaṁ: life energy; prāṇe: in the life energy; apānaṁ: the outgoing breath; tathā : thus; apare: others; prāṇa: inhaling; apāna: exhaling; gatī : movement; ruddhvā : after restraining; prāṇāyāma: breath control; parāyaṇāḥ : so inclined

4.29 There are others who sacrifice the life energy in the form of incoming breath and outgoing breath, thus checking the movement of the incoming and outgoing breaths and controlling the breath.

अपरे नियताहाराः प्राणान्प्राणेषु जुह्वति ।
सर्वेऽप्येते यज्ञविदो यज्ञक्षपितकल्मषाः ॥ ४.३०

apare niyatāhārāḥ prāṇānprāṇeṣu juhvati /
sarve'pyete yajñavido yajñakṣapitakalmaṣāḥ // 4.30

apare: others; niyata: controlled; āhārāḥ: eating; prāṇān: vital energy; prāṇeṣu: in the vital energy; juhvati: sacrifice; sarve api ete: all of these; yajñavidaḥ: those knowing sacrifice; yajña kṣapita kalmaṣāḥ: those destroying their sins through sacrifice.

4.30 There are others who sacrifice through controlled eating and offering the outgoing breath, life energy. All these people know the meaning of sacrifice and are purified of sin or karma.

यज्ञशिष्टामृतभुजो यान्ति ब्रह्म सनातनम् ।
नायं लोकोऽस्त्ययज्ञस्य कुतोऽन्यः कुरुसत्तम ॥ ४.३१

yajñaśiṣṭāmṛtabhujo yānti brahma sanātanam /
nāyaṁ loko'styayajñasya kuto'nyaḥ kurusattama // 4.31

yajñaśiṣṭa: left over of sacrifice; amṛta: nectar; bhujaḥ: one who enjoys; yānti: attain; brahma: supreme; sanātanaṁ: eternal; na: not; ayaṁ: this; lokah: world; asti: is; ayajñasya: to one who does not sacrifice; kutaḥ: where; anyaḥ: other;

kuru sattama: O best among the Kurus

4.31 Having tasted the nectar of the results of such sacrifices, they go to the supreme eternal consciousness. This world is not for those who have not sacrificed. How can the other be, Arjuna?

एवं बहुविधा यज्ञा वितता ब्रह्मणो मुखे ।
कर्मजान्विद्धि तान्सर्वानेवं ज्ञात्वा विमोक्ष्यसे ॥ ४.३२

evaṁ bahuvidhā yajñā vitatā brahmaṇo mukhe |
karmajānviddhi tānsarvānevaṁ jñātvā vimokṣyase || 4.32

evaṁ: thus; bahu: many; vidhāḥ: kinds of; yajñāḥ: sacrifices; vitatā : explained; brahmaṇaḥ mukhe: in the words of the Veda; karmajān: born of actions of mind, sense and body; viddhi: know; tān: those; sarvān: all; evaṁ: thus; jñātvā: after knowing; vimokṣyase: will be liberated

4.32 Thus, there are many kinds of sacrifices born of work mentioned in the Vedas. Thus, knowing these, one will be liberated.

श्रेयान्द्रव्यमयाद्यज्ञाज्ज्ञानयज्ञः परंतप ।
सर्वं कर्माखिलं पार्थ ज्ञाने परिसमाप्यते ॥ ४.३३

śreyān-dravya-mayād yajñāj jñāna-yajñaḥ parantapa |
sarvaṁ karmā'khilaṁ pārtha jñāne parisamāpyate || 4.33

śreyān: superior; dravyamayāt: material wealth; yajñāt: sacrifice; jñāna yajñaḥ: sacrifice in wisdom; paraṁtapa: O subduer of foes; sarvaṁ: all; karma: activities; akhilaṁ: in totality; pārtha: O son of Pritā; jñāne: in wisdom; parisamāpyate: ends in

4.33 O Parantapa (conqueror of foes), the sacrifice of wisdom is superior to the sacrifice of material wealth. After all, all activities totally end in wisdom.

तद्विद्धि प्रणिपातेन परिप्रश्नेन सेवया ।

उपदेक्ष्यन्ति ते ज्ञानं ज्ञानिनस्तत्त्वदर्शिनः ॥ ४.३४

tadviddhi praṇipātena paripraśnena sevayā /
upadekṣyanti te jñānaṁ jñāninastattvadarśinaḥ // 4.34

tat: that; viddhi: understand; praṇipātena: by approaching a spiritual master; paripraśnena: by questioning; sevayā: by offering service; upadekṣyanti: will advise; te: unto you; jñānaṁ: knowledge; jñāninaḥ : the enlightened; tattva darśinaḥ: the spiritual seers.

4.34 Understand these truths by approaching a spiritual Master, by asking him your questions, by offering service. The enlightened person can initiate the wisdom unto you because he has seen the truth

यज्ज्ञात्वा न पुनर्मोहमेवं यास्यसि पाण्डव ।
येन भूतान्यशेषेण द्रक्ष्यस्यात्मन्यथो मयि ॥ ४.३५

yajjñātvā na punar moham evaṁ yāsyasi pāṇḍava /
yena bhūtāny aśeṣeṇa drakṣyasy ātmanyatho mayi // 4.35

yat: which; jñātvā: after knowing; na: not; punaḥ: again; mohaṁ: desire; evaṁ: thus; yāsyasi: shall attain; pāṇḍava: O son of Pāṇḍu; yena: by which; bhūtāni: living entities; aśeṣeṇa: totally; drakṣyasi: will see; ātmani: within yourself; atho: then; mayi: in Me

4.35 O Pāṇḍava, knowing this you will never suffer from desire or illusion, you will know that all living beings are in the supreme, in Me.

अपि चेदसि पापेभ्यः सर्वेभ्यः पापकृत्तमः ।
सर्वं ज्ञानप्लवेनैव वृजिनं संतरिष्यसि ॥ ४.३६

api cedasi pāpebhyaḥ sarvebhyaḥ pāpakṛttamaḥ /
sarvaṁ jñānaplavenaiva vṛjinaṁ santariṣyasi // 4.36

api: even; cet: if; asi: you are; pāpebhyaḥ: of sinners; sarvebhyaḥ: of all; pāpakṛttamaḥ: greatest sinner; sarvaṁ: all; jñāna plavena: by the boat of knowledge; eva: only; vṛjinaṁ: the ocean of miseries; santariṣyasi: you will cross.

4.36 Even if you are the most sinful of all sinners, you will certainly cross completely the ocean of miseries through the boat of knowledge.

यथैधांसि समिद्धोऽग्निर्भस्मसात्कुरुतेऽर्जुन ।
ज्ञानाग्निः सर्वकर्माणि भस्मसात्कुरुते तथा ॥ ४.३७

yathaidhāṁsi samiddho'gnir bhasmasātkurute'rjuna |
jñānāgniḥ sarvakarmāṇi bhasmasātkurute tathā || 4.37

yathā: as; edhāṁsi: firewood; samiddhaḥ : blazing; agniḥ: fire; bhasmasāt: ashes; kurute: does; arjuna: O Arjuna; jñāna: knowledge; agniḥ: fire; sarva: all; karmāṇi: actions; bhasmasāt: ashes; kurute: does; tathā: in the same way.

4.37 Just as a blazing fire turns firewood to ashes, O Arjuna, so does the fire of wisdom burn to ashes all actions, all your karma.

न हि ज्ञानेन सदृशं पवित्रमिह विद्यते ।
तत्स्वयं योगसंसिद्धः कालेनात्मनि विन्दति ॥ ४.३८

na hi jñānena sadṛśaṁ pavitramiha vidyate |
tatsvayaṁ yogasaṁsiddhah kālenātmani vindati || 4.38

na: not; hi: certainly; jñānena: with knowledge; sadṛśaṁ: similar; pavitraṁ: pure; iha: here; vidyate: exists; tat: that; svayaṁ: himself; yoga: in devotion; saṁsiddhaḥ: purified; kālena: in course time; ātmani: within self; vindati: acquires.

4.38 Truly, in this world, there is nothing as pure as wisdom. One who has matured to know this enjoys in himself in due course of time.

श्रद्धावाँल्लभते ज्ञानं तत्परः संयतेन्द्रियः ।
ज्ञानं लब्ध्वा परां शान्तिमचिरेणाधिगच्छति ॥ ४.३९

śraddhāvāllabhate jñānaṁ tatparaḥ saṁyatendriyaḥ |
jñānaṁ labdhvā parāṁ śāntimacireṇādhigacchati || 4.39

śraddhāvān: faithful person; labhate: achieves; jñānaṁ: knowledge; tatparaḥ: attached; saṁyata: controlled; indriyaḥ: senses; jñānaṁ: knowledge; labdhvā: having achieved; parāṁ: supreme; śāntiṁ: peace; acireṇa: without delay; adhigacchati: attains

4.39 A person with śraddhā (courageous faith) achieves wisdom and has control over the senses. Achieving wisdom, without delay, he attains supreme peace.

अज्ञश्चाश्रद्दधानश्च संशयात्मा विनश्यति ।
नायं लोकोऽस्ति न परो न सुखं संशयात्मनः ॥ ४.४०

ajñaś cāśraddadhānaś ca saṁśayātmā vinaśyati |
nāyaṁ loko 'sti na paro na sukhaṁ saṁśayātmanaḥ || 4.40

ajñaḥ: ignorant; ca: and; aśraddadhānaḥ: one having no faith; ca: and; saṁśayātmā: doubting soul; vinaśyati: perish; na: not; ayaṁ: this; lokah: world; asti : is; na: not; paraḥ: next; na: not; sukhaṁ: happiness; saṁśayātmanaḥ: of the doubting soul.

4.40 Those who have no wisdom and faith, who always have doubts, are destroyed. There is no happiness in this world or the next.

योगसंन्यस्तकर्माणं ज्ञानसंछिन्नसंशयम् ।
आत्मवन्तं न कर्माणि निबध्नन्ति धनञ्जय ॥ ४.४१

yoga-sannyasta-karmāṇaṁ jñānas-aṁchinna-saṁśayam |
ātmavantaṁ na karmāṇi nibadhnanti dhañanjaya || 4.41

yogasannyastakarmāṇaṁ: one who has dedicated his actions to god according to Karma yoga; jñānasaṁchinna saṁśayaṁ: whose doubts have been cleared by knowledge; ātmavantaṁ: self possessed; na: not; karmāṇi: actions; nibadhnanti: bind; dhañanjaya: O Dhañanjaya

4.41 O Dhanañjaya (winner of riches), one who has renounced the fruits of his actions, whose doubts are destroyed, who is well-situated in the Self, is not bound by his actions.

तस्मादज्ञानसंभूतं हृत्स्थं ज्ञानासिनात्मनः ।
छित्त्वैनं संशयं योगमातिष्ठोत्तिष्ठ भारत ॥ ४.४२

tasmād ajñāna saṁbhūtaṁ hṛtsthaṁ jñānāsinātmanaḥ /
chittvainaṁ saṁśayaṁ yogam ātiṣṭhottiṣṭha bhārata // 4.42

tasmāt: therefore; ajñāna: ignorance; saṁbhūtaṁ: born of; hṛtsthaṁ: situated in the heart; jñānāsinā: by the sword of knowledge; ātmanaḥ: of the self; chittvā: having cutting off; enaṁ: this; saṁśayaṁ: doubt; yogaṁ: in yoga; ātiṣṭha: be firm; uttiṣṭha: stand up; bhārata: O descendant of Bhārata

4.42 O descendant of Bhārata, therefore, stand up, be situated in yoga. Armed with the sword of knowledge; cut the doubt born of ignorance that exists in your heart.

इति श्रीमद्भगवद्गीतासूपनिषत्सु ब्रह्मविद्यायां योगशास्त्रे
श्रीकृष्णार्जुनसंवादे ज्ञानकर्मसंन्यासयोगो नाम चतुर्थोऽध्याय: ॥

iti śrī mad bhagavadgītāsūpaniṣatsu brahmavidyāyām
yogaśāstre śrī kṛṣṇārjuna saṁvāde jñānakarmasannyāsa yogo nāma
caturtho'dhyāyaḥ //

In the ***Upaniṣad*** of ***Śrimad Bhagavad Gītā***, the scripture of yoga dealing with ***Brahmavidyā Yogaśāstra,*** the science of Brahman, the Supreme Absolute, in the form of ***Śrī Kṛṣṇārjuna saṁvād,*** dialogue between Śrī Kṛṣṇa and Arjuna, this is the fourth chapter named, ***Jñānakarmasannyāsa Yogaḥ***, *'The Yoga of Action in Knowledge and Renunciation.'*

CHAPTER

5

अथ पञ्चमोऽध्यायः

संन्यासयोगः

Sannyāsa Yogaḥ

अर्जुन उवाच ।
सन्न्यासं कर्मणां कृष्ण पुनर्योगं च शंससि ।
यच्छ्रेय एतयोरेकं तन्मे ब्रूहि सुनिश्चितम् ॥ ५.१

arjuna uvāca
sannyāsaṁ karmaṇāṁ kṛṣṇa punaryogaṁ ca śaṁsasi /
yacchreya etayorekaṁ tanme brūhi suniścitaṁ // 5.1

arjuna uvāca: Arjuna says; sannyāsaṁ: renunciation; karmaṇāṁ: of all actions; kṛṣṇa: O Kṛṣṇa; punaḥ: again; yogaṁ: devotion; ca: also; śaṁsasi: praising; yat: which; śreyaḥ: beneficial; etayoḥ: of the two; ekaṁ: one; tat: that; me: to me; brūhi: please tell; suniścitaṁ: definitely

5.1 Arjuna says: Oh Kṛṣṇa, you asked me to renounce work first and then you asked me to work with devotion. Will you now please tell me, definetely, which of the two will be more beneficial to me?

श्री भगवानुवाच ।
सन्न्यासः कर्मयोगश्च निःश्रेयसकरावुभौ ।
तयोस्तु कर्मसंन्यासात्कर्मयोगो विशिष्यते ॥ ५.२

śrībhagavānuvāca

sannyāsaḥ karmayogaś ca niḥśreyasakarāvubhau |
tayostu karma-sannyāsāt karmayogo viśiṣyate || 5.2

śrī bhagavān uvāca: Lord Kṛṣṇa says; sannyāsah: renunciation; karmayogaḥ: work in devotion; ca: also; niḥśreyasakarāv: for liberation; ubhau: both; tayoḥ: of the two; tu: but; karmasannyāsāt: between work and renunciation; karmayogaḥ: work in devotion; viśiṣyate: better

5.2 Bhagavān says: The renunciation of work [sannyāsa] and work in devotion [karmayoga] are both good for liberation. But, of the two, work in devotional service is better than renunciation of work.

ज्ञेयः स नित्यसंन्यासी यो न द्वेष्टि न काङ्क्षति ।
निर्द्वन्द्वो हि महाबाहो सुखं बन्धात्प्रमुच्यते ॥ ५.३

jñeyaḥ sa nityasannyāsī yo na dveṣṭi na kāṅkṣati |
nirdvandvo hi mahābāho sukhaṁ bandhātpramucyate || 5.3

jñeyaḥ: should be known; saḥ: he; nitya: always; saṁnyāsī : renouncer; yaḥ: who; na: never; dveṣṭi: hates; na: never; kāṅkṣati: desires; nirdvandvaḥ: free from all dualities; hi: certainly; mahābāho: mighty-armed one; sukham: easily; bandhāt: from bondage; pramucyate: completely liberated

5.3 He who neither hates nor desires the fruits of his activities has renounced. Such a person, free from all dualities, easily overcomes material bondage and is completely liberated, Oh Arjuna!

साङ्ख्ययोगौ पृथग्बालाः प्रवदन्ति न पण्डिताः ।
एकमप्यास्थितः सम्यगुभयोर्विन्दते फलम् ॥ ५.४

sāṅkhyayogau pṛthagbālāḥ pravadanti na paṇḍitāḥ |
ekamapyāsthitaḥ samyag ubhayorvindate phalam || 5.4

sāṁkhyayogau: sāṁkhya system and yoga; pṛthak: different; bālāḥ: less intelligent; pravadanti: say; na: not; paṇḍitāḥ: learned; ekaṁ: one; api: even; āsthitaḥ: situated; samyak: complete; ubhayoḥ: of both; vindate: enjoys; phalaṁ: result

5.4 Only the ignorant, not the wise, speaks of the path of action [karma-yoga] to be different from the path of renunciation [sāṅkhya yoga]. Those who are actually learned say that one who is firmly established in either of the paths, achieves the fruit of both.

यत्साङ्ख्यैः प्राप्यते स्थानं तद्योगैरपि गम्यते ।
एकं साङ्ख्यं च योगं च यः पश्यति स पश्यति ॥ ५.५

yat sāṅkhyaiḥ prāpyate sthānaṁ tad yogairapi gamyate /
ekaṁ sāṅkhyaṁ ca yogaṁ ca yaḥ paśyati sa paśyati // 5.5

yat: what; sāṅkhyaiḥ: by Sāṅkhya system; prāpyate: get; sthānaṁ: position; tat: that; yogaiḥ: by work in devotion; api: also; gamyate: can reach; ekam: one; sāṅkhyaṁ: Sāṅkhya system; ca: and; yogaṁ: work in devotion; ca: and; yaḥ: who; paśyati: sees; saḥ: he; paśyati: sees

5.5 He who knows, knows that the state reached by renunciation [sāṅkhya] and action [karma] are one and the same. State reached by renunciation can also be achieved by action, know them to be at same level and see them as they are.

संन्यासस्तु महाबाहो दुःखमाप्तुमयोगतः ।
योगयुक्तो मुनिर्ब्रह्म नचिरेणाधिगच्छति ॥ ५.६

sannyāsastu mahābāho duḥkhamāptumayogataḥ /
yogayukto munirbrahma na cireṇādhigacchati // 5.6

sannyāsaḥ: renunciation; tu: but; mahābāho: mighty-armed one; duḥkham . : misery; āptuṁ: afflicts with; ayogataḥ: without devotion; yogayuktaḥ: engaged in devotion; muniḥ: wise; brahma: supreme; nacireṇa: without delay; adhigacchati: attains

5.6 Renunciation without devotional service afflicts one with misery, Oh mighty-armed one. The wise person engaged in devotional service attains the Supreme without delay.

योगयुक्तो विशुद्धात्मा विजितात्मा जितेन्द्रियः ।
सर्वभूतात्मभूतात्मा कुर्वन्नपि न लिप्यते ॥ ५.७

yogayukto viśuddhātmā vijitātmā jitendriyaḥ I
sarva-bhūtātma-bhūtātmā kurvannapi na lipyate II 5.7

yogayuktaḥ: engaged in work with devotion; viśuddhātmā : a man of purified mind; vijita: self-controlled; atma: soul; jitendriyaḥ: conquered the senses; sarvabhūtātma: to all living beings; bhūtātma: compassionate; kurvan api: though engaged in work, na: never; lipyate: entangled

5.7 The person engaged in devoted service, beyond concepts pure and impure, self-controlled and who has conquered the senses is compassionate and loves everyone, although engaged in work, he is never entangled.

नैव किञ्चित्करोमीति युक्तो मन्येत तत्त्ववित् ।
पश्यञ्श्रुण्वन्स्पृशञ्जिघ्रन्नश्नन्गच्छन्स्वपञ्श्वसन् ॥ ५.८

naiva kiñcitkaromīti yukto manyeta tattvavit I
paśyan śṛṇvan spṛśañ jighrann aśnan gacchan svapañ śvasan II 5.8

na: never; eva: certainly; kiṁcit: anything; karomi: I do; iti: thus; yuktaḥ: engaged; manyeta: thinks; tattvavit: one who knows the truth; paśyan: seeing; śṛṇvan: hearing; spṛśan: touching; jighran: smelling; aśnan: eating; gacchan: going; svapan: dreaming; śvasan: breathing

प्रलपन्विसृजन्गृह्णन्नुन्मिषन्निमिषन्नपि ।
इन्द्रियाणीन्द्रियार्थेषु वर्तन्त इति धारयन् ॥ ५.९

pralapan visṛjan gṛhṇann unmiṣannimiṣannapi I
indriyāṇīndriyārtheṣu vartanta iti dhārayan II 5.9

pralapan: talking; visṛjan: giving up; gṛihṇan: accepting; unmishan: opening;

nimiṣan: closing; api: though; indriyāṇi: the senses; indriyārtheṣu: in gratifying senses; vartanta: are engaged; iti: thus; dhārayan: considering

5.8, 9 One who knows the truth, though engaged in seeing, hearing, touching, smelling, eating, going, dreaming, and breathing, always knows within himself that—'I never do anything at all.' While talking, letting go, receiving, opening, closing, he considers that the senses are engaged with their sense objects.

ब्रह्मण्याधाय कर्माणि सङ्गँ त्यक्त्वा करोति य: ।
लिप्यते न स पापेन पद्मपत्रमिवाम्भसा ॥ ५.१०

brahmaṇy ādhāya karmāṇi saṅgaṁ tyaktvā karoti yaḥ /
lipyate na sa pāpena padma-patram ivāmbhasā // 5.10

brahmaṇi: Eternal Consciousness; ādhāya: surrendering to; karmāṇi: actions; saṅgaṁ: attachment; tyaktvā : giving up; karoti: does; yaḥ: who; lipyate: affected; na: never; saḥ: he; pāpena: by sin; padma: lotus; patraṁ: leaf; iva: like; ambhasā: water

5.10 He, who acts without attachment, giving up and surrendering to the eternal consciousness, He is never affected by sin, in the same way that the lotus leaf is not affected by water.

कायेन मनसा बुद्ध्या केवलैरिन्द्रियैरपि ।
योगिन: कर्म कुर्वन्ति सङ्गं त्यक्त्वात्मशुद्धये ॥ ५.११

kāyena manasā buddhyā kevalairindriyairapi /
yoginaḥ karma kurvanti saṅgaṁ tyaktvātmaśuddhaye // 5.11

kāyena: by the body; manasā: by the mind; buddhyā: by the intellect; kevalaiḥ: only; indriyaiḥ: by the senses; api also: yoginaḥ: yogis; karma: action; kurvanti: perform; saṅgaṁ: attachment; tyaktvā; having abandoned; ātmaśuddhaye: for the purification of the self

5.11 The yogis, giving up attachment, act with the body, mind, intelligence, even with the senses for the purpose of self-purification.

युक्तः कर्मफलं त्यक्त्वा शान्तिमाप्नोति नैष्ठिकीम् ।
अयुक्तः कामकारेण फले सक्तो निबध्यते ॥ ५.१२

yuktaḥ karmaphalaṁ tyaktvā śāntimāpnoti naiṣṭhikīm |
ayuktaḥ kāma-kāreṇa phale sakto nibadhyate || 5.12

yuktaḥ: one steadfast in devotion; karma: action; phalaṁ: fruit: tyaktvā: giving up; śāntiṁ: peace; āpnoti: achieves: naiṣṭhikīṁ: established; ayuktaḥ: one not steadfast in devotion; kāmakāreṇa: for enjoying the fruits of the action; phale: fruit; saktaḥ: attached; nibadhyate: becomes entangled

5.12 One who is engaged in devotion, gives up attachment to outcome of one's actions and is centered, is at peace. One who is not engaged in devotion, attached to the outcome of one's action becomes entangled.

सर्वकर्माणि मनसा संन्यस्यास्ते सुखं वशी ।
नवद्वारे पुरे देही नैव कुर्वन्न कारयन् ॥ ५.१३

sarvakarmāṇi manasā sannyasyāste sukhaṁ vaśī |
navadvāre pure dehī naiva kurvanna kārayan || 5.13

sarva: all; karmāṇi: activities; manasā: by the mind; sannyasya: giving up; āste: remains; sukhaṁ: in happiness; vaśī : who is controlled; navadvāre: of nine gates; pure: in the city; dehī : body; na: never; eva: surely; kurvan: doing; na: never: kārayan: causing to be done

5.13 One who is controlled, giving up all the activities of the mind, surely remains in happiness in the city of nine gates (body), neither doing anything nor causing anything to be done.

न कर्तृत्वं न कर्माणि लोकस्य सृजति प्रभुः ।
न कर्मफलसंयोगं स्वभावस्तु प्रवर्तते ॥ ५.१४

na kartṛtvaṁ na karmāṇi lokasya sṛjati prabhuḥ |
na karmaphalasaṁyogaṁ svabhāvas tu pravartate || 5.14

na: never; kartṛtvaṁ: of doing; na: not; karmāṇi: activities; lokasya: of the people; sṛjati: creates; prabhuḥ: master; na: not; karma: activities; phala: fruit; saṁyogaṁ: connection; svabhāvaḥ: nature; tu: but; pravartate: act

5.14 The master does not create activities nor makes people do nor connects with the outcome of the actions. All this is enacted by the material nature.

नादत्ते कस्यचित्पापं न चैव सुकृतं विभुः ।
अज्ञानेनावृतं ज्ञानं तेन मुह्यन्ति जन्तवः ॥ ५.१५

nādatte kasyacitpāpaṁ na caiva sukṛtaṁ vibhuḥ |
ajñānenāvṛtaṁ jñānaṁ tena muhyanti jantavaḥ || 5.15

na: never; ādatte: accepts; kasyacit: anyone's; pāpaṁ: sins; na: not; ca: and; eva: surely; sukṛtaṁ: good deeds; vibhuḥ: lord; ajñānena: by ignorance; āvṛtaṁ: covered; jñānaṁ: knowledge; tena: by that; muhyanti: are confused; jantavaḥ: living beings

5.15 The Lord, surely, neither accepts anyone's sins nor good deeds. Living beings are confused by the ignorance that covers the knowledge.

ज्ञानेन तु तदज्ञानं येषां नाशितमात्मनः ।
तेषामादित्यवज्ज्ञानं प्रकाशयति तत्परम् ॥ ५.१६

jñānena tu tadajñānaṁ yeṣāṁ nāśitamātmanaḥ |
teṣāmādityavajjñānaṁ prakāśayati tatparam || 5.16

jñānena: by knowledge; tu : but; tad: that; ajñānaṁ: ignorance; yeṣāṁ: whose; nāśitaṁ: destroyed; ātmanaḥ: of the self; teṣām: their; ādityavat: like the rising sun; jñānaṁ: knowledge; prakāśayati: throws light on; tat param: that supreme consciousness

5.16 Whose ignorance is destroyed by the knowledge, their knowledge, like the rising sun, throws light on the supreme consciousness.

तद्बुद्धयस्तदात्मानस्तन्निष्ठास्तत्परायणाः ।
गच्छन्त्यपुनरावृत्तिं ज्ञाननिर्धूतकल्मषाः ॥ ५.१७

tadbuddhayas tad-ātmānas tan-niṣṭhās tat parāyaṇāḥ I
gacchanty apunar-āvṛttiṁ jñāna-nirdhūta-kalmaṣāḥ II 5.17

tad buddhyaḥ: one whose intelligence is in the supreme; tad ātmānaḥ: whose mind is in the supreme; tanniṣṭhāḥ: whose faith is in the supreme; tat parāyaṇāḥ: who has surrendered to the supreme; gacchanti : go; apunarāvṛittiṁ: liberation; jñāna: knowledge; nirdhūta: cleansed; kalmaṣāḥ: sins

5.17 One whose intelligence, mind, faith are in the Supreme and one who has surrendered to the Supreme, his misunderstandings are cleansed through knowledge and he goes towards liberation.

विद्याविनयसंपन्ने ब्राह्मणे गवि हस्तिनि ।
शुनि चैव शपाके च पण्डिताः समदर्शिनः ॥ ५.१८

vidyā-vinaya-sampanne brāhmaṇe gavi hastini I
śuni caiva śvapāke ca paṇḍitāḥ samadarśinaḥ II 5.18

vidyā: knowledge; vinaya: compassion; sampanne: full with; brāhmaṇe: in the brahmana; gavi: in the cow; hastini: in the elephant; śuni: in the dog; ca: and; eva: surely; śvapāke: in the dog-eater; ca: and; paṇḍitāḥ: learned; sama: equal; darśinaḥ: see

5.18 One who is full of knowledge and compassion sees equally the learned brāhmaṇa, the cow, the elephant, the dog and the dog-eater.

इहैव तैर्जितः सर्गो येषां साम्ये स्थितं मनः ।
निर्दोषं हि समं ब्रह्म तस्माद्ब्रह्मणि ते स्थिताः ॥ ५.१९

ihaiva tairjitaḥ sargo yeṣāṁ sāmye sthitaṁ manaḥ |
nirdoṣaṁ hi samaṁ brahma tasmād brahmaṇi te sthitāḥ || 5.19

iha: in this life; eva: surely; taiḥ: by them; jitaḥ: conquered; sargaḥ: birth and death; yeṣāṁ: of whose; sāmye: in equanimity; sthitaṁ: situated; manaḥ: mind; nir doṣaṁ: flawless; hi: surely; samaṁ: in equanimity; brahma: supreme; tasmāt: therefore; brahmaṇi: in the supreme; te: they; sthitāḥ: situated

5.19 In this life, surely, those whose minds are situated in equanimity have conquered birth and death. They are flawless like the Supreme and therefore, are situated in the Supreme.'

न प्रहृष्येत्प्रियं प्राप्य नोद्विजेत्प्राप्य चाप्रियम् ।
स्थिरबुद्धिरसंमूढो ब्रह्मविद्ब्रह्मणि स्थितः ॥ ५.२०

na prahṛṣyetpriyaṁ prāpya nodvijet prāpya cāpriyam |
sthirabuddhir asaṁmūḍho brahmavid brahmaṇi sthitaḥ || 5.20

na: never; prahṛṣyet: rejoice; priyaṁ: like; prāpya: achieving; no: not; udvijet: agitated; prāpya: achieving; ca: and; apriyaṁ: the unpleasant; sthirabuddhiḥ: steady intelligence; asaṁmūḍhaḥ: undeluded; brahmavid: one who knows the Supreme; brahmaṇi: in the Supreme; sthitaḥ: situated

5.20 One who does not rejoice at achieving something he likes nor gets agitated on getting something he does not like, who is of steady intelligence, who is not deluded, one who knows the Supreme, is situated in the Supreme.

बाह्यस्पर्शेष्वसक्तात्मा विन्दत्यात्मनि यत्सुखम् ।
स ब्रह्मयोगयुक्तात्मा सुखमक्षयमश्नुते ॥ ५.२१

bāhyasparśeṣvasaktātmā vindatyātmani yatsukham |
sa brahma-yoga-yuktātmā sukhamakṣayamaśnute || 5.21

bāhya: outer; sparśeṣu: sense pleasures; asaktātmā : not attached; vindati: enjoys; ātmani: in the Self; yat: that; sukhaṁ: happiness; saḥ: he; brahma yoga: engaged in the Supreme; yuktātmā: self-connected; sukhaṁ: happiness;

akṣayaṁ: unlimited; aśnute: enjoys

5.21 One who is not attached to the outer world sense pleasures, who enjoys in the Self, in that happiness, he, having identified with his Self by engaging in the Supreme [brahma-yoga], enjoys unlimited happiness.

ये हि संस्पर्शजा भोगा दुःखयोनय एव ते ।
आद्यन्तवन्तः कौन्तेय न तेषु रमते बुधः ॥ ५.२२

ye hi saṁsparśajā bhogā duḥkhayonaya eva te /
ādyantavantaḥ kaunteya na teṣu ramate budhaḥ // 5.22

ye: those; hi: surely; saṁsparśajāḥ: by contact with the senses; bhogāḥ: enjoyments; duḥkha: misery; yonayaḥ: sources of; eva: surely; te: they are; ādya: beginning; antavantaḥ: subject to end; kaunteya: son of Kuntī; na: not; teṣu: in those; ramate: enjoys; budhaḥ: intelligent person

5.22 The intelligent person surely does not enjoy the sense pleasures, enjoyments which are sources of misery and which are subject to beginning and end.

शक्नोतीहैव यः सोढुं प्राक्शरीरविमोक्षणात् ।
कामक्रोधोद्भवं वेगं स युक्तः स सुखी नरः ॥ ५.२३

śaknotīhaiva yaḥ soḍhuṁ prākśarīravimokṣaṇāt /
kāma-krodhodbhavaṁ vegaṁ sa yuktaḥ sa sukhī naraḥ // 5.23

śaknoti: able to do; iha eva: in this body; yaḥ: one who; soḍhuṁ: tolerate; prāk: before; śarīra: body; vimokṣaṇāt: give up; kāma: desire; krodha: anger; udbhavaṁ: generated from; vegaṁ: urge; sa: he; yuktaḥ: well-situated; saḥ: he; sukhī : happy; naraḥ: man

5.23 Before leaving this present body, if one is able to tolerate the urges of material senses and check the force of desire and anger, he is well situated and he is happy in this world.

योऽन्तःसुखोऽन्तरारामस्तथान्तर्ज्योतिरेव यः ।
स योगी ब्रह्मनिर्वाणं ब्रह्मभूतोऽधिगच्छति ॥ ५.२४

yo'ntaḥsukho'ntarārāmas tathāntar-jyotir eva yaḥ |
sa yogī brahman-irvāṇaṁ brahmabhūto'dhigacchati || 5.24

yaḥ: who; antaḥ sukhaḥ: happy from within; antarārāmaḥ: active within; tathā : as well as; antarjyotiḥ: illumined within; eva: surely; yaḥ: who; saḥ: he; yogī : mystic; brahma nirvāṇaṁ: liberated in the Supreme; brahma bhūtaḥ: self realized; adhigacchati: attains

5.24 One who is happy from within, active within as well as illumined within, surely, is a Yogi and he is liberated in the Supreme [brahma-nirvāṇa], is Self-realized and attains the Supreme.

लभन्ते ब्रह्मनिर्वाणमृषयः क्षीणकल्मषाः ।
छिन्नद्वैधा यतात्मानः सर्वभूतहिते रताः ॥ ५.२५

labhante brahma-nirvāṇam ṛṣayaḥ kṣīṇakalmaṣāḥ |
chinn-advaidhā yatātmānaḥ sarvabhūtahite ratāḥ || 5.25

labhante: achieve; brahma nirvāṇaṁ: liberation in the Supreme; ṛṣayaḥ: who are active within; kṣīṇakalmaṣāḥ: devoid of sins; chinna: torn off; dvaidāḥ: duality; yatātmānaḥ: engaged in self-realization; sarva: all; bhūta: living beings; hite: for the welfare; ratāḥ: engaged

5.25 Those, whose sins have been destroyed, who have dispelled the dualities arising from doubts, whose minds are engaged within, and who are working for the welfare of other beings, attain the eternal liberation in the Supreme [brahma-nirvāṇa].

कामक्रोधवियुक्तानां यतीनां यतचेतसाम् ।
अभितो ब्रह्मनिर्वाणं वर्तते विदितात्मनाम् ॥ ५.२६

kāmakrodhaviyuktānāṁ yatīnāṁ yatacetasām |

abhito brahmanirvāṇaṁ vartate viditātmanām // 5.26

kāma: desire; krodha: anger; viyuktānām; one freed from; yatīnāṁ; of the ascetics; yata cetasāṁ: with the thoughts controlled; abhitaḥ: on all sides; brahma nirvāṇaṁ: absolute freedom; vartate: exists; viditātmanāṁ: of those who have realized the Self

5.26 They who are free from lust and anger, who have subdued the mind and senses, and who have known the Self, easily attain liberation [brahma-nirvāṇa].

स्पर्शान्कृत्वा बहिर्बाह्यांश्चक्षुश्चैवान्तरे भ्रुवोः ।
प्राणापानौ समौ कृत्वा नासाभ्यन्तरचारिणौ ॥ ५.२७

sparśān kṛtvā bahir bāhyāṁś cakṣuś caivāntare bhruvoḥ /
prāṇāpānau samau kṛtvā nāsābhyantara-cāriṇau // 5.27

sparśān: external sense objects; kṛtvā : keeping; bahiḥ: external; bāhyān: external; cakṣuḥ: eyes; ca: and; eva: surely; antare: within; bhruvoḥ: eyebrows; prāṇāpānau: inward and outward breath; samau: suspending; kṛtvā : doing; nāsābhyantara: within the nostrils; cārinau: moving

यतेन्द्रियमनोबुद्धिर्मुनिर्मोक्षपरायणः ।
विगतेच्छाभयक्रोधो यः सदा मुक्त एव सः ॥ ५.२८

yatendriya-mano-buddhir munir mokṣaparāyaṇaḥ /
vigatecchā-bhaya-krodho yaḥ sadā mukta eva saḥ // 5.28

yata: controlled; indriya: senses; mano: mind; buddhiḥ: intelligence; muniḥ: the sage; mokṣa: liberation; parāyaṇaḥ: aiming; vigata: free from; icchā: desires; bhaya: fear; krodah: anger; yaḥ: one who; sadā: always; muktaḥ: liberated; eva: certainly; saḥ: he is

5.27,28 Shutting out all external sense objects, keeping the eyes and vision concentrated between the two eyebrows, suspending the inward and outward breaths within the nostrils and thus controlling the mind, senses and intelligence, the transcendental who is aiming at liberation, becomes free from desire, fear and the by-product of desire and fear, anger all three. One who is always in this state is certainly liberated.

भोक्तारं यज्ञतपसां सर्वलोकमहेशरम् ।
सुहृदं सर्वभूतानां ज्ञात्वा मां शान्तिमृच्छति ॥ ५.२९

bhoktāraṁ yajñatapasāṁ sarva-loka-maheśvaram /
suhṛdaṁ sarvabhūtānāṁ jñātvā māṁ śāntimṛcchati // 5.29

bhoktāraṁ: one who enjoys; yajña: sacrifice; tapasāṁ: penance; sarva: all; loka: worlds; maheśvārāṁ: lord; suhṛdaṁ: benefactor; sarva: all; bhūtānāṁ: living beings; jñātvā: knowing; māṁ: me; śāntiṁ: peace; ṛcchati: achieves

5.29 One who knowing Me as the purpose of sacrifice and penance, as the lord of all the worlds and the benefactor of all the living beings, achieves peace.

इति श्रीमद्भगवद्गीतासूपनिषत्सु ब्रह्मविद्यायां योगशास्त्रे
श्रीकृष्णार्जुनसंवादे संन्यासयोगो नाम पञ्चमोऽध्यायः ॥

iti śrīmad bhagavadgītāsūpaniṣatsu brahmavidyāyām
yogaśāstre śrīkṛṣṇārjuna saṁvāde sannyāsayogo nāma
pañcamo 'dhyāyaḥ //

In the ***Upaniṣad*** of ***Śrimad Bhagavad Gītā***, the scripture of yoga dealing with ***Brahmavidyā Yogaśāstra,*** the science of Brahman, the Supreme Absolute, in the form of ***Śrī Kṛṣṇārjuna saṁvād,*** dialogue between Śrī Kṛṣṇa and Arjuna, this is the fifth chapter named, ***Sannyāsa Yogaḥ***, *'The Yoga of Renunciation.'*

CHAPTER

6

अथ षष्ठोऽध्याय:

ध्यानयोग:

Dhyāna Yogaḥ

श्री भगवानुवाच
अनाश्रित: कर्मफलं कार्यं कर्म करोति य: ।
स संन्यासी च योगी च न निरग्निर्न चाक्रिय: ॥ ६.१

śrībhagavānuvāca
anāśritaḥ karmaphalaṃ kāryaṃ karma karoti yaḥ /
sa sanyāsī ca yogī ca na niragnirna cā'kriyaḥ // 6.1

śrī bhagavān uvāca: the Lord says; anāśritaḥ: without shelter; karma: action; phalaṃ: fruit; kāryaṃ: obligated; karma: work; karoti: performs; yaḥ: who; saḥ: he; sannyāsī: ascetic; ca: and; yogī: one engaged in yoga; ca: and; na: not; nir: without; agniḥ: fire; na: not; ca: and; akriyaḥ: without work

6.1 Bhagavān says: One who performs his actions without being attached to their fruit (outcome) of his work is a Sannyāsi, and he is truly an ascetic; a Yogi also.; not the one who renounces to light the fire and performs no action.

यं संन्यासमिति प्राहुर्योगं तं विद्धि पाण्डव ।
न ह्यसंन्यस्तसङ्कल्पो योगी भवति कश्चन ॥ ६.२

yaṃ sannyāsamiti prāhur yogaṃ taṃ viddhi pāṇḍava |
na hyasannyastasaṅkalpo yogī bhavati kaścana || 6.2

yaṃ: what; sannyāsam: renunciation; iti: thus; prāhuḥ: they say; yogaṃ: linking with the Supreme; taṃ: that; viddhi: you should know; pāṇḍava: O son of Pāṇḍu; na: never; hi: certainly; asannyasta: without renouncing; saṅkalpaḥ: self interest; yogī: one engaged in yoga; bhavati: becomes; kaścana: anyone

6.2 O Pāṇḍava, what is called renunciation, or sannyāsa, you must know to be the same as yoga, or uniting oneself with the Supreme., for never can anyone become a yogī, until he renounces the desire for self-gratification [saṅkalpa].

आरुरुक्षोर्मुनेर्योगं कर्म कारणमुच्यते ।
योगारूढस्य तस्यैव शमः कारणमुच्यते ॥ ६.३

āruruksormuner yogaṃ karma kāraṇamucyate |
yogārūḍhasya tasyaiva śamaḥ kāraṇamucyate || 6.3

āruruksoḥ: one wishing to ascend to the state of yoga (no-mind state); muneḥ: of the sage; yogaṃ: yoga system; karma: work; kāraṇaṃ: cause; ucyate: is said to be; yoga: yoga; arūḍhasya: of one who has attained; tasya: his; eva: certainly; śamaḥ: cessation of all activities; kāraṇaṃ: cause; ucyate: is said to be

6.3 A one desirious of achieving the state of yoga or no-mind state, action is said to be the means and for the one who is already elevated in yoga, cessation from all actions is said to be the means.

यदा हि नेन्द्रियार्थेषु न कर्मस्वनुषज्जते ।
सर्वसङ्कल्पसंन्यासी योगारूढस्तदोच्यते ॥ ६.४

yadā hi nendriyārtheṣu na karmasvanuṣajjate |
sarvasankalpasannyāsī yogārūḍhastadocyate || 6.4

yadā: when; hi: certainly; na: not; indriyārtheṣu: in sense gratification; na: never; karmasu: in fruitive activities; anuṣajjate: does necessarily engage; sarva sankalpa: all material desires; sannyāsī: renouncer; yogārūḍhaḥ: elevated in yoga; tadā: at that time; ucyate: is said to be

6.4 Any one is said to have attained the state of yoga when, having renounced all material desires, he neither acts for sense gratification nor engages in result focused activities.

उद्धरेदात्मनात्मानं नात्मानमवसादयेत्
आत्मैव ह्यात्मनो बन्धुरात्मैव रिपुरात्मनः ॥ ६.५

uddhared ātmanātmānaṃ natmānam avasādayet /
ātmaiva hyātmano bandhur ātmaiva ripurātmanaḥ // 6.5

uddharet: one must deliver; ātmanā: by the mind; ātmānaṃ: the conditioned soul; na: never; ātmānaṃ: the conditioned soul; avasādayet: put into degradation; ātmā: mind; eva: certainly; hi : surely; ātmanaḥ: of the conditioned soul; bandhuḥ: friend; ātmā: mind; eva: certainly; ripuḥ: enemy; ātmanaḥ: of the conditioned soul

6.5 You are your own friend; you are your own enemy. Evolve yourself through the Self and do not degrade yourself.

बन्धुरात्मात्मनस्तस्य येनात्मैवात्मना जितः ।
अनात्मनस्तु शत्रुत्वे वर्तेतात्मैव शत्रुवत् ॥ ६.६

bandhur ātmātmanas tasya yenātmaivātmanā jitaḥ /
anātmanastu śatrutve vartetātmaiva śatruvat // 6.6

bandhuḥ: friend; ātmā: the Self; ātmanaḥ: of the living entity; tasya: of him; yena: by whom; ātmā: the Self; eva: certainly; ātmanā: by the living entity; jitaḥ: conquered; anātmanaḥ: of one who has failed to control the Self; tu: but; śatrutve: because of enmity; varteta: remains; ātmā eva: the very mind; śatruvat: as an enemy

6.6 For him who has conquered the Self, the Self is the best of friends; for one who has failed to do so, his Self will remain the greatest enemy.

जितात्मनः प्रशान्तस्य परमात्मा समाहितः ।
शीतोष्णसुखदुःखेषु तथा मानापमानयोः ॥ ६.७

jitātmanaḥ praśāntasya paramātmā samāhitaḥ |
śītoṣṇa-sukha duḥkheṣu tathā mānāpamānayoḥ || 6.7

jitātmanaḥ: of one who has conquered his self; praśāntasya: who has attained tranquility; paramātmā: Supreme; samāhitaḥ: approached completely; śītoṣṇa: in cold heat; sukha: happiness; duḥkheṣu: and distress; tathā: also; māna: in honor; apamānayoḥ: dishonor

6.7 For one who has conquered the self, who has attained tranquility, the Supreme is already reached. Such a person remains in this state in happiness or distress, heat or cold, honor or dishonor.

ज्ञानविज्ञानतृप्तात्मा कूटस्थो विजितेन्द्रियः ।
युक्त इत्युच्यते योगी समलोष्टाश्मकाञ्चनः ॥ ६.८

jñāna-vijñāna-tṛptātmā kūṭastho vijitendriyaḥ |
yukta ityucyate yogī sama-loṣṭāśma-kāñcanaḥ || 6.8

jñāna: acquired knowledge; vijñāna: realized knowledge; tṛptātmā: contented self; kūṭasthaḥ: established in Self-realization; vijitendriyaḥ: one who has subdued his senses; yukta: competent for self-realization; iti: thus; ucyate: is said; yogī: one established in yoga; sama: equipoised; loṣṭāśma: lump of earth, stone; kāñcanaḥ: gold

6.8 A person whose mind is contented because of spiritual knowledge, who has subdued his senses and to whom stone and gold are same and who is satisfied with what he is having, is said to be established in Self-realization and is called an enlightened being.

सुहृन्मित्रार्युदासीन मध्यस्थद्वेष्यबन्धुषु ।
साधुष्वपि च पापेषु समबुद्धिर्विशिष्यते ॥ ६.९

suhṛn-mıtrāry-udāsīna madhyastha-dveṣya bandhuṣu |
sadhuṣvapi ca pāpeṣu sama-buddhir viśiṣyate || 6.9

suhṛt: to well-wishers by nature; mitra: affectionate benefactors; ari: enemies; udāsīna: neutral; madhyastha: mediators; dveṣya: envious; bandhuṣu: friends; sādhuṣu: pious; api: also; ca: and; pāpeṣu: sinners; sama: equal buddhiḥ: with equal mind; viśiṣyate: is further advanced

6.9 A person is considered truly advanced when he regards honest well-wishers, affectionate benefactors, the neutral, mediators, the envious, friends and enemies, the pious and the sinners all with an equal mind.

योगी युञ्जीत सततमात्मानं रहसि स्थितः ।
एकाकी यतचित्तात्मा निराशीरपरिग्रहः ॥ ६.१०

yogī yuñjīta satatam ātmānaṃ rahasi sthitaḥ |
ekākī yatachittātmā nirāśīraparigrahaḥ || 6.10

yogī: yogi; yuñjīta: concentrate; satataṃ: always; ātmānaṃ: himself; rahasi: in a secluded place; sthitaḥ: situated; ekākī : alone; yatachittātmā : careful in mind; nir āśīḥ: without being attracted by anything else; aparigrahaḥ: free from the feeling of possessiveness

6.10 A Yogī should always try to concentrate his mind on the Supreme Self; situated in a secluded place, he should carefully control his mind without being attracted by anything and should be free from the feeling of possessiveness.

शुचौ देशे प्रतिष्ठाप्य स्थिरमासनमात्मनः ।
नात्युच्छ्रितं नातिनीचं चैलाजिनकुशोत्तरम् ॥ ६.११

śucau deśe pratiṣṭhāpya sthiram āsanam ātmanaḥ |
nātyucchritaṃ nātinīcaṃ cailājina-kuśottaram || 6.11

śucau: in a clean state; deśe: land; pratiṣṭhāpya: placing; sthiraṃ: stable; āsanaṃ: seat; ātmanaḥ: own; na: not; ati: very low; ucchritaṃ: high; na: not; nīcaṃ:

low; caila ajina: of soft cloth and deerskin; kuśa: kuśa grass; uttaraṃ: covering

6.11 On a clean and pure place, one should establish his seat by laying kuśa grass, a deer skin and a cloth, one over another, neither too high nor too low.

तत्रैकाग्रं मनः कृत्वा यतचित्तेन्द्रियक्रियः ।
उपविश्यासने युञ्ज्याद्योगमात्मविशुद्धये ॥ ६.१२

tatraikāgraṃ manaḥ kṛtvā yata-cittendriya-kriyaḥ I
upaviśyāsane yuñjyād yogamātmaviśuddhaye II 6.12

tatra: then; ekāgraṃ: with one focus; manaḥ: mind; kṛtvā: making; yata cittendriya kriyaḥ: having restrained the functions of the mind and senses; upaviśya: sitting; āsane: on the seat; yuñjyāt: should execute; yogaṃ: yoga; ātma: oneself; viśuddhaye: to purify

6.12 Sitting firmly on that pure seat, the yogi should practice the purification of the self by controlling the activities of mind and the senses

समं कायशिरोग्रीवं धारयन्नचलं स्थिरः
सम्प्रेक्ष्य नासिकाग्रं स्वं दिशश्चानवलोकयन् ॥ ६.१३

samaṃ kāyaśirogrīvaṃ dhārayannacalaṃ sthiraḥ I
sampreksya nāsikāgraṃ svaṃ diśaścānavalokayan II 6.13

samaṃ: straight; kāya: body; śiraḥ: head; grīvaṃ: neck; dhārayan: holding; acalaṃ: steady; sthiraḥ: still; saṃprekṣya: looking; nāsika: nose; agraṃ: at the tip; svaṃ: own; diśaḥ: directions; ca: and; anavalokayan: not looking

6.13 Holding the body, head and neck steady, look at the tip of your nose without looking in any other direction.

प्रशान्तात्मा विगतभीर्ब्रह्मचारिव्रते स्थितः ।
मनः संयम्य मच्चित्तो युक्त आसीत मत्परः ॥ ६.१४

praśāntātmā vigatabhīr brahmacārivrate sthitaḥ |
manaḥ saṃyamya maccitto yukta āsī ta matparaḥ || 6.14

praśāntātmā: unagitated mind; vigatabhīḥ: free from fear; brahmachārivrate: in the vow of living with Existence; sthitaḥ: situated; manaḥ: mind; saṃyamya: controlling; maccittaḥ: mind fixed in Me; yuktaḥ: balanced; āsīta: sit; matparaḥ: Me supreme goal

6.14 Sit with an unagitated mind, free from fear and in tune with Existence, controlling the mind, focusing it on Me and make Me the supreme goal.

युञ्जन्नेवं सदात्मानं योगी नियतमानसः ।
शान्तिं निर्वाणपरमां मत्संस्थामधिगच्छति ॥ ६.१५

yuñjannevaṃ sadātmānaṃ yogī niyatamānasaḥ |
śāntiṃ nirvāṇa paramāṃ mat-saṃsthām adhigacchati || 6.15

yuñjan: practicing; evaṃ: thus; sadā: always; ātmānaṃ: Self; yogī : yogi; niyata: controlled; mānasaḥ: mind; śāntiṃ: peace; nirvāṇa: liberation; paramāṃ: supreme; matsaṃsthāṃ: My kingdom; adhigacchati: attain

6.15 Always practising control over the mind and situated in the Self, the yogi attains peace, the supreme liberation and My kingdom.

नात्यश्नतस्तु योगोऽस्ति न चैकान्तमनश्नतः ।
न चाति स्वप्नशीलस्य जाग्रतो नैव चार्जुन ॥ ६.१६

nātyaśnatastu yogosti na caikāntamanaśnataḥ |
na cāti svapnaśīlasya jāgrato naiva cārjuna || 6.16

na: never; atyaśnataḥ: too much eats; tu: but; yogaḥ: yoga; asti: is; na: not; ca: and; ekāntaṃ: on the one side; anaśnataḥ: not eat; na: not; ca: and; ati: too much; svapna śīlasya: sleep; jāgrataḥ: awake; na: not; eva: also; ca: and; arjuna: Oh Arjuna

6.16 Yoga is neither eating too much nor eating too little; it is neither sleeping too much nor sleeping too little, Oh Arjuna.

युक्ताहारविहारस्य युक्तचेष्टस्य कर्मसु ।
युक्तस्वप्नावबोधस्य योगो भवति दुःखहा ॥ ६.१७

yuktāhāra vihārasya yuktaceṣṭasya karmasu |
yukta-svapnāvabodhasya yogo bhavati duḥkhahā || 6.17

yukta: regulated; āhāra: food; vihārasya: rest; yukta: regulated; ceṣṭasya: exertion; karmasu: work; yukta: regulated; svapna avabodhasya: sleep and wakefulness; yogaḥ: yoga; bhavati: becomes; duḥkhahā : reduced misery

6.17 One who is regulated in food, rest, recreation and work, sleep and wakefulness, can reduce misery.

यदा विनियतं चित्तमात्मन्येवावतिष्ठते ।
निःस्पृहः सर्वकामेभ्यो युक्त इत्युच्यते तदा ॥ ६.१८

yadā viniyataṃ cittam ātmanyevāvatiṣṭhate |
niḥspṛhaḥ sarvakāmebhyo yukta ityucyate tadā || 6.18

yadā: when; viniyataṃ: disciplined; cittaṃ: mind; ātmani: situated in the Self; eva: certainly; avatiṣṭhate: situated; niḥspṛhaḥ: free of desire; sarva: all; kāmebhyaḥ: material desires; yuktaḥ: situated; iti: thus; ucyat : said to be; tadā : then

6.18 When the mind is disciplined and one is situated in the Self, free from all desires, then one is said to be situated in yoga.

यथा दीपो निवातस्थो नेङ्गते सोपमा स्मृता ।
योगिनो यतचित्तस्य युञ्जतो योगमात्मनः ॥ ६.१९

yathā dīpo nivātastho neṅgate sopamā smṛ tā |
yogino yatacittasya yuñjato yogamātmanaḥ || 6.19

yathā: as; dīpaḥ: lamp; nivātasthaḥ: in a place without wind; na: not; iṅgate:

waver; sā: this; upamā: comparison; smṛtā: is considered; yoginaḥ: of the yogi; yata cittasya: whose mind is controlled; yuñjataḥ: engaged; yogaṃ: in yoga; ātmanaḥ: in the Self

6.19 As a lamp in a place without wind does not waver, so also the yogi, whose mind is controlled remains steady, engaged in yoga, in the Self.

यत्रोपरमते चित्तं निरुद्धं योगसेवया ।
यत्र चैवात्मनात्मानं पश्यन्नात्मनि तुष्यति ॥ ६.२०

yatroparamate cittaṃ niruddhaṃ yogasevayā |
yatra caivātmanātmānaṃ paśyannātmani tuṣyati || 6.20

yatra: there; uparamate: quietened; cittaṃ: mind; niruddhaṃ: stop; yoga: yoga; sevayā: work; yatra: there; ca: and; eva: certainly; ātmanā: by the Self; ātmānaṃ: Self; paśyan: seeing; ātmani: in the Self; tuṣyati: satisfied

6.20 In yoga, the mind becomes quiet and the Self is satisfied by the Self in the Self.

सुखमात्यन्तिकं यत्तद्बुद्धिग्राह्यमतीन्द्रियम् ।
वेत्ति यत्र न चैवायं स्थितश्चलति तत्त्वत: ॥ ६.२१

sukhamātyantikaṃ yat tad buddhigrāhyamatīndriyam |
vetti yatra na caivāyaṃ sthitaścalati tattvataḥ || 6.21

sukhaṃ: happiness; ātyantikaṃ: supreme; yat: which; tad: that; buddhi: intelligence; grāhyaṃ: grasped; atīndriyaṃ: beyond the senses; vetti: know; yatra: where; na: not; ca: and; eva: certainly; ayaṃ: he; sthitaḥ: situated; calati: moves; tattvataḥ: from truth

6.21 Supreme bliss is grasped by intelligence transcending the senses. The person who knows this is based in reality.

यं लब्ध्वा चापरं लाभं मन्यते नाधिकं तत:
यस्मिन्स्थितो न दु:खेन गुरुणापि विचाल्यते ॥ ६.२२

yaṃ labdhvā cāparaṃ lābhaṃ manyate nādhikaṃ tataḥ |
yasminsthito na duḥkhena guruṇāpi vicālyate || 6.22

yaṃ: that which; labdhvā: by attaining; ca: and; aparaṃ: any other; lābhaṃ: gain; manyate: considers; na: not; adhikaṃ: more; tataḥ: than that; yasmin: in which; sthitaḥ: situated; na: not; duḥkhena: by misery; guruṇā api: though difficult; vicālyate: becomes shaken

6.22 By attaining that Supreme, one does not consider any other gain as being greater. By being situated in the Supreme, one is not shaken by the greatest of misery.

तं विद्याद् दुःखसंयोगवियोगं योगसंज्ञितम् ।
स निश्चयेन योक्तव्यो योगोऽनिर्विण्णचेतसा ॥ ६.२३

taṃ vidyād duḥkhasaṃ yogaviyogaṃ yoga-saṃjñitam |
sa niścayena yoktavyo yogo'nirviṇṇacetasā || 6.23

taṃ: that; vidyāt: know; duḥkha: misery; saṃyoga: contact; viyogaṃ: removal; yoga: yoga; saṃjñitaṃ: is termed as; saḥ: he; niśchayena: with determination; yoktavyaḥ: practiced; yogaḥ; yoga; anirviṇṇa cetasā: without deviating

6.23 When yoga is practiced with determination without deviating, the misery by contact with material senses is removed.

सङ्कल्पप्रभवान्कामांस्त्यक्त्वा सर्वानशेषत:
मनसैवेन्द्रियग्रामं विनियम्य समन्तत: ॥ ६.२४

saṅkalpa-prabhavān kāmāṃs tyaktvā sarvānaśeṣataḥ |
manasaivendriya-grāmaṃ viniyamya samantataḥ || 6.24

saṃkalpa: thought; prabhavān: born of; kāmān: desires; tyaktvā: give up; sarvān: all; aśeṣataḥ: completely; manasā: mind; eva: certainly; indriya grāmaṃ: all senses; viniyamya: regulating; samantataḥ: from all sides

6.24 Giving up completely all the fantasies born of the mind, one can regulate all the senses from all the sides by the mind.

शनैः शनैरुपरमेद् बुद्ध्या धृतिगृहीतया ।
आत्मसंस्थं मनः कृत्वा न किञ्चिदपि चिन्तयेत् ॥ ६.२५

śanaiḥ śanairuparamed buddhyā dhṛtigṛhītayā |
ātmasaṃsthaṃ manaḥ kṛtvā na kiñcidapi cintayet || 6.25

śanaiḥ: gradually; śanaiḥ: step by step; uparamet: hold; buddhyā: by intelligence; dhṛti gṛhītayā: held by conviction; ātma: Self; saṃsthaṃ: established; manaḥ: mind; kṛtvā: doing; na: not; kiṃcit: other; api: also; cintayet: thinking of

6.25 Gradually, step by step, one should become established in the Self, held by the conviction of intelligence, with the mind not thinking of anything else.

यतो यतो निश्चरति मनश्चञ्चलमस्थिरम् ।
ततस्ततो नियम्यैतदात्मन्येव वशं नयेत् ॥ ६.२६

yato yato niścarati manaś cañcalamasthiram |
tatas tato niyamyaitad ātmanyeva vaśaṃ nayet || 6.26

yataḥ-yataḥ: wherever; niścarati: becomes agitated; manaḥ: mind; cañcalaṃ: moving; asthiraṃ: not steady; tataḥ-tataḥ: there; niyamya: control; etat: this; ātmani: in the Self; eva: certainly; vaśaṃ: under control; nayet: must bring under

6.26 From wherever the mind becomes agitated due to its wandering and unsteady nature, from there, one must certainly bring it under the control of the Self.

प्रशान्तमनसं ह्येनं योगिनं सुखमुत्तमम् ।
उपैति शान्तरजसं ब्रह्मभूतमकल्मषम् ॥ ६.२७

praśānta-manasaṃ hy enaṃ yoginaṃ sukhamuttamam |
upaiti śāntarajasaṃ brahma-bhūtam akalmaṣam || 6.27

praśānta: peaceful; manasaṃ: mind; hi: certainly; enaṃ: this; yoginaṃ: yogi; sukhaṃ: happiness; uttamaṃ: highest; upaiti: attains; śānta rajasaṃ: passion pacified; brahma bhūtaṃ: liberated by the Supreme; akalmaṣaṃ: free from sins

6.27 The yogi whose mind is peaceful attains the highest happiness; his passion is pacified and he is free from sins as he is liberated by the Supreme.

युञ्जन्नेवं सदात्मानं योगी विगतकल्मषः ।
सुखेन ब्रह्मसंस्पर्शमत्यन्तं सुखमश्नुते ॥ ६.२८

yuñjannevaṃ sadātmānaṃ yogī vigatakalmaṣaḥ |
sukhena brahma-saṃspars amatyantaṃ sukhamaśnute || 6.28

yuñjan: being engaged; evaṃ: in this way; sadā : always; ātmānaṃ: Self; yogī : yogi; vigata: free from; kalmaṣaḥ: material contamination; sukhena: in happiness; brahma saṃsparśaṃ: in touch with the Supreme; atyantaṃ: highest; sukhaṃ: happiness; aśnute: attains

6.28 The yogi always engaged in the Self and free from material contamination, is in touch with the Supreme and attains the highest happiness.

सर्वभूतस्थमात्मानं सर्वभूतानि चात्मनि ।
ईक्षते योगयुक्तात्मा सर्वत्र समदर्शनः ॥ ६.२९

sarvabhūtastham-ātmānaṃ sarvabhūtāni cātmani |
īkṣate yogayuktātmā sarvatra samadarśanaḥ || 6.29

sarva: all; bhūta: living beings; sthaṃ: situated; ātmānaṃ: Supreme; sarva: all; bhūtāni: living beings; ca: and; ātmani: in the Supreme; īkṣate: sees; yoga: yoga; yuktātmā: engaged Self; sarvatra: everywhere; sama: equal; darśanaḥ: seeing

6.29 The Yogī sees the Supreme situated in all beings and also all beings situated in the Supreme. One established in the Self sees the Supreme everywhere.

यो मां पशयति सर्वत्र सर्वं च मयि पश्यति ।
तस्याहं न प्रणश्यामि स च मे न प्रणश्यति ॥ ६.३०

yo māṃ paśyati sarvatra   sarvaṃ ca mayi paśyati |
tasyāhaṃ na praṇaśyāmi   sa ca me na praṇaśyati || 6.30

yaḥ: who; māṃ: Me; paśyati: sees; sarvatra: everywhere; sarvaṃ: everything; ca: and; mayi: in Me; paśyati: sees; tasya: for him; ahaṃ: I; na: not; praṇaśyāmi: lost; saḥ: he; ca: and; me: Me; na: not; praṇaśyati: lost

6.30 For one who sees Me everywhere and who sees everything in Me, for him I am never lost nor is he lost to Me.

सर्वभूतस्थितं यो मां भजत्येकत्वमास्थितः ।
सर्वथा वर्तमानोऽपि स योगी मयि वर्तते ॥ ६.३१

sarvabhūtasthitaṃ yo māṃ   bhajatyekatvamāsthitaḥ |
sarvathā vartamānopi   sa yogī mayi vartate || 6.31

sarva: all; bhūta: beings; sthitaṃ: situated; yaḥ: who; māṃ: Me; bhajati: worships; ekatvaṃ: in oneness; āsthitaḥ: situated; sarvathā : in all respects; vartamānaḥ: present; api: though; saḥ: he; yogī : yogi; mayi : in Me; vartate: remains

6.31 He who is in oneness with Me in all respects, worships Me situated in all beings and remains present in Me.

आत्मौपम्येन सर्वत्र समं पश्यति योऽर्जुन ।
सुखं वा यदि वा दुःखं स योगी परमो मतः ॥ ६.३२

ātmaupamyena sarvatra   samaṃ paśyati yorjuna |
sukhaṃ vā yadi vā duḥkhaṃ   sa yogī paramo mataḥ || 6.32

ātmaupamyena: self by comparison; sarvatra: everywhere; samaṃ: equal; paśyati: see; yaḥ: who; arjuna: Oh Arjuna; sukhaṃ: happiness; vā: or; yadi: if; vā: or; duḥkhaṃ: misery; saḥ: such; yogī : yogi; paramaḥ: supreme; mataḥ: opinion

6.32 One who, by comparision to his own Self, sees the true oneness of all beings, in both their happiness or misery, is Supreme Yogi in My opinion, Arjuna.

अर्जुन उवाच।

योऽयं योगस्त्वया प्रोक्तः साम्येन मधुसूदन ।
एतस्याहं न पश्यामि चञ्चलत्वात्स्थितिं स्थिराम् ॥ ६.३३

arjuna uvāca

yoyaṃ yogastvayā proktaḥ sāmyena madhusūdana |
etasyāhaṃ na paśyāmi cañcalatvātsthitiṃ sthirām || *6.33*

arjuna uvāca: Arjuna says; yaḥ: this; ayaṃ: system; yogaḥ: yoga; tvayā : by You; proktaḥ: said; sāmyena: generally; madhusūdana: O killer of Madhu; etasya: of this; ahaṃ: I; na: not; paśyāmi: see; cañcalatvāt: due to being restless; sthitiṃ: situation; sthirāṃ: steady

6.33 Arjuna says: O Madhusūdana, I am not able to see this system of yoga as told by You in the situation of the mind being restless and not steady.

चञ्चलं हि मनः कृष्ण प्रमाथि बलवद्दृढम् ।
तस्याहं निग्रहं मन्ये वायोरिव सुदुष्करम् ॥ ६.३४

cañcalaṃ hi manaḥ kṛṣṇa pramāthī balavad dṛḍham |
tasyāhaṃ nigrahaṃ manye vāyoriva suduṣkaram || *6.34*

cañcalaṃ: wavering; hi: certainly; manaḥ: mind; kṛṣṇa: O Kṛṣṇa; pramāthī : agitating; balavat: strong; dṛḍhaṃ: firm; tasya: its; ahaṃ: I; nigrahaṃ: controlling; manye: think; vāyoḥ: of the wind; iva: like; suduṣkaraṃ: difficult

6.34 O Kṛṣṇa, the wavering mind is agitated, strong and firm. I think it is difficult to control the mind like it is difficult to control the wind.

श्री भगवानुवाच

असंशयं महाबाहो मनो दुर्निग्रहं चलम् ।
अभ्यासेन तु कौन्तेय वैराग्येण च गृह्यते ॥ ६.३५

śrībhagavānuvāca

asaṃśayaṃ mahābāho mano durnigrahaṃ calam /
abhyāsena tu kaunteya vairāgyeṇa ca gṛhyate // 6.35

śrī bhagavān uvāca: the Lord says; asaṃśayaṃ: without doubt; mahābāho: O mighty-armed one; manaḥ: mind; durnigrahaṃ: difficult to control; calaṃ: wavering; abhyāsena: by practice; tu : but; kaunteya: O son of Kuntī; vairāgyeṇa: by detachment; ca: and; gṛhyate: is controlled

6.35 Bhagavān says: O mighty-armed Kaunteya (son of Kuntī), it is undoubtedly difficult to control the wavering mind but by practice and detachment, it can be controlled.

असंयतात्मना योगो दुष्प्राप इति मे मतिः ।
वश्यात्मना तु यतता शक्योऽवाप्तुमुपायतः ॥ ६.३६

asaṃyatātmanā yogo duṣprāpa iti me matiḥ /
vaśyātmanā tu yatatā śakyo vāptum upāyataḥ // 6.36

asaṃyatātmanā: uncontrolled by the mind; yogaḥ: yoga; duṣprāpaḥ: difficult to attain; iti: thus; me: My; matiḥ: opinion; vaśyātmanā: controlled by the mind; tu: but; yatatā: by one engaged in practise; śakyaḥ: practical; avāptuṃ: to achieve; upāyataḥ: by appropriate means

6.36 For one whose mind is uncontrolled, it is difficult to attain yoga in My opinion. But, it is practical to achieve control over the mind by appropriate means.

अर्जुन उवाच
अयतिः श्रद्धयोपेतो योगाच्चलितमानसः ।
अप्राप्य योगसंसिद्धिं कां गतिं कृष्ण गच्छति ॥ ६.३७

arjuna uvāca
ayatiḥ śraddhayopeto yogāc calita mānasaḥ /
aprāpya yoga-saṃsiddhiṃ kāṃ gatiṃ kṛṣṇa gacchati // 6.37

arjuna uvāca: Arjuna says; ayatiḥ: the uncontrolled person; śraddhyā: with faith; upetaḥ: engaged; yogāt: from yoga; calita: wavered; mānasaḥ: mind; aprāpya: not getting; yoga: yoga; saṃsiddhiṃ: achieve; kāṃ: which; gatiṃ: destination; kṛṣṇa: O Kṛṣṇa; gacchati: achieve

6.37 Arjuna says: O Kṛṣṇa, if a person is engaged in yoga with faith but does not attain yoga because of the wavering mind, what destination does he achieve

कच्चिन्नोभयविभ्रष्टश्छिन्नाभ्रमिव नश्यति ।
अप्रतिष्ठो महाबाहो विमूढो ब्रह्मणः पथि ॥ ६.३८

kaccinnobhayavibhraṣṭaś chinnābhramiva naśyati |
apratiṣtho mahābāho vimūḍho brahmaṇaḥ pathi || 6.38

kaccit: whether; na: not; ubhaya: both; vibhraṣṭaḥ: deviated from; chinna: torn; abhraṃ: cloud; iva: like; naśyati: perish; apratiṣṭhaḥ: without any position; mahābāho: O mighty-armed one; vimūḍhaḥ: confused; brahmaṇaḥ: Supreme; pathi: on the path

6.38 O mighty-armed Kṛṣṇa, does the person who deviated from the path perish, torn like a cloud without any position?

एतन्मे संशयं कृष्ण छेत्तुमर्हस्यशेषतः ।
त्वदन्यः संशयस्यास्य छेत्ता न ह्युपपद्यते ॥ ६.३९

etanme saṃśayaṃ kṛṣṇa chettumarhasyaśeṣataḥ |
tvadanyaḥ saṃśayasyāsya chettā na hyupapadyate || 6.39

etat: this; me: My; saṃśayaṃ: doubt; kṛṣṇa: O Kṛṣṇa; chettuṃ: dispel; arhasi: deserve; aśeṣataḥ: completely; tvat: than You; anyaḥ: another; saṃśayasya: of the doubt; asya: of this; chettā : remover; na: not; hi: certainly; upapadyate: to be found

6.39 This is my doubt, O Kṛṣṇa and I request You to dispel it completely. Certainly, there is no one to be found other than You who can remove this doubt.

श्री भगवानुवाच ।
पार्थ नैवेह नामुत्र विनाशस्तस्य विद्यते ।
न हि कल्याणकृत्कश्चिद् दुर्गतिं तात गच्छति ॥ ६.४०

śrībhagavānuvāca
pārtha naiveha nāmutra vināśastasya vidyate |
na hi kalyāṇakṛtkaścid durgatiṃ tāta gacchati || 6.40

śrī bhagavān uvāca: the Lord says; pārtha: O son of Prithā; na: not; eva: thus; iha: in this; na: not; amutra: in the next life; vināśaḥ: destruction; tasya: his; vidyate: exists; na: not; hi: certainly; kalyāṇakṛt: doing activities for the good; kaścit: anyone; durgatiṃ: degradation; tāta: then; gacchati: goes

6.40 Bhagavān says: O Pārtha, the person engaged in activities for good does not meet with destruction either in this world or the next life; he never faces degradation.

प्राप्य पुण्यकृतां लोकानुषित्वा शोशतीः समाः ।
शुचीनां श्रीमतां गेहे योगभ्रष्टोऽभिजायते ॥ ६.४१

prāpya puṇyakṛtāṃ lokān uṣitvā śāśvatiḥ samāḥ |
śucīnāṃ śrī matāṃ gehe yogabhraṣṭo'bhijāyate || 6.41

prāpya: after achieving; puṇyakṛtāṃ: one who has done virtuous deeds; lokān: worlds; uṣitvā : after living; śāśvatīḥ: many; samāḥ: years; śucīnāṃ: of the virtuous; śrī matāṃ: of the prosperous; gehe: in the house; yoga bhraṣṭaḥ: one who has fallen from yoga; abhijāyate: takes birth

6.41 The person who has fallen from yoga {yogabṛasṭa] after many years of living in the planets of the pious and doing virtuous deeds, takes birth in the house of the virtuous and prosperous.

अथवा योगिनामेव कुले भवति धीमताम् ।
एतद्धि दुर्लभतरं लोके जन्म यदीदृशम् ॥ ६.४२

athavā yogināmeva kule bhavati dhī matām I
etaddhi durlabhataraṃ loke janma yadīdṛśam II 6.42

athavā : or; yogināṃ: yogis'; eva: certainly; kule: in the family; bhavati: becomes; dhīmatāṃ: wise; etat: this; hi: certainly; durlabhataraṃ: rare; loke: in the world; janma: birth; yat: which; īdṛśaṃ: like this

6.42 Or the Yogī certainly takes birth in a family of wise people. Certainly, such a birth is rare in this world.

तत्र तं बुद्धिसंयोगं लभते पौर्वदेहिकम् ।
यतते च ततो भूयः संसिद्धौ कुरुनन्दन ॥ ६.४३

tatra taṃ buddhisaṃyogaṃ labhate paurva dehikam I
yatate ca tato bhūyaḥ saṃsiddhau kurunandana II 6.43

tatra: then; taṃ: that; buddhi: intelligence; saṃyogaṃ: united with; labhate: gains; paurva: previous; dehikaṃ: body; yatate: try; ca: and; tataḥ: then; bhūyaḥ: again; saṃsiddhau: for attaining; kuru nandana: O son of Kuru

6.43 O son of Kuru, on taking such a birth, he revives the intelligence, consciousness of the previous body, and tries again to attain complete success [yoga].

पूर्वाभ्यासेन तेनैव ह्रियते ह्यवशोऽपि सः ।
जिज्ञासुरपि योगस्य शब्दब्रह्मातिवर्तते ॥ ६.४४

pūrvābhyāsena tenaiva hriyate hyavaśo'pi saḥ I
jijñāsurapi yogasya śabda-brahmātivartate II 6.44

pūrva: previous; abhyāsena: by practice; tena: by that; eva: certainly; hriyate: is attracted; hi: certainly; avaśaḥ: automatically; api: also; saḥ: he; jijñāsuḥ: inquisitive; api: also; yogasya: about yoga; śabda brahma: scriptures; ativartate: transcends

6.44 Due to the practice in his previous life, he certainly gets attracted automatically to yoga and he is inquisitive about yoga and transcends the scriptures.

प्रयत्नाद्यतमानस्तु योगी संशुद्धकिल्बिषः ।
अनेकजन्मसंसिद्धस्ततो याति परां गतिम् ॥ ६.४५

prayatnādyatamānastu yogī saṃśuddhakilbiṣaḥ |
aneka-janmasaṃ-siddhas tato yāti parāṃ gatim || 6.45

prayatnat: by trying; yatamānaḥ: endeavor; tu: and; yogī: yogi; saṃśuddha: cleaned; kilbiṣaḥ: sins; aneka: many; janma: births; saṃsiddhaḥ: achieved; tataḥ: then; yāti: achieves; parāṃ: highest; gatiṃ: state

6.45 And when the Yogī engages himself with sincere endevour in progressing fruther, being cleansed of all incompletions, then ultimately, achieving perfection [saṁsiddhi] after many births of practice, he attains the highest state [parām-gati].

तपस्विभ्योऽधिको योगी ज्ञानिभ्योऽपि मतोऽधिकः ।
कर्मिभ्यश्चाधिको योगी तस्माद्योगी भवार्जुन ॥ ६.४६

tapasvibhyodhiko yogī jñānibhyo'pi mato 'dhikaḥ |
karmibhyaścādhiko yogī tasmādyogī bhavārjuna || 6.46

tapasvibhyaḥ: than the ascetic; adhikaḥ: greater; yogī : yogi; jñānibhyoḥ: than the wise; api: also; mataḥ: opinion; adhikaḥ: greater; karmibhyaḥ: than person who works for the fruit of action; ca: and; adhikaḥ: greater; yogī : yogi; tasmāt: so; yogī : yogi; bhava: become; arjuna: O Arjuna

6.46 A Yogī is greater than the ascetic [tapasvi], greater than the wise [jñāni] and greater than the fruitive worker. Therefore, Arjuna, do become a Yogī.

योगिनामपि सर्वेषां मद्गतेनान्तरात्मना ।
श्रद्धावान्भजते यो मां स मे युक्ततमो मतः ॥ ६.४७

yogināmapi sarveṣāṃ madgatenāntarātmanā |
śraddhāvān bhajate yo māṃ sa me yuktatamo mataḥ || 6.47

yogināṃ: yogis; api: also; sarveṣāṃ: all kinds of; madgatena: living in Me; antarātmanā: thinking of Me; śraddhāvān: in full faith; bhajate: worship; yaḥ: who; māṃ: Me; saḥ: he; me: Me; yuktatamaḥ: engaged; mataḥ: opinion

6.47 Of all Yogīs, one who always lives in Me, thinking of Me within himself, who worships Me in full faith, he is the most intimately united with Me in Yoga and is the highest of all Yogīs; that is My opinion.

इति श्रीमद्भगवद्गीतासूपनिषत्सु ब्रह्मविद्यायां योगशास्त्रे
श्रीकृष्णार्जुनसंवादे ध्यानयोगो नाम षष्ठोऽध्यायः ॥

iti śrīmad bhagavadgītāsūpaniṣatsu brahmavidyāyām
yogaśāstre śrīkṛṣṇārjuna saṃvāde dhyānayogo nāma
ṣaṣtho'dhyāyaḥ //

In the ***Upaniṣad*** of ***Śrimad Bhagavad Gītā,*** the scripture of yoga dealing with ***Brahmavidyā Yogaśāstra,*** the science of Brahman, the Supreme Absolute, in the form of ***Śrī Kṛṣṇārjuna saṁvād,*** dialogue between Śrī Kṛṣṇa and Arjuna, this is the sixth chapter named, ***Dhyāna Yogaḥ,*** *'The Yoga of the Path Of Meditation.'*

CHAPTER

7

अथ सप्तमोऽध्याय:

ज्ञानविज्ञानयोग:

Jñānavijñāna Yogaḥ

श्री भगवानुवाच।

मय्यासक्तमना: पार्थ योगं युञ्जन्मदाश्रय: ।
असंशयं समग्रं मां यथा ज्ञास्यसि तच्छृणु ॥ ७.१

śrībhagavānuvāca
mayyāsaktamanāḥ pārtha yogaṃ yuñjanmadāśrayaḥ |
asaṃśayaṃ samagraṃ māṃ yathā jñāsyasi tacchṛṇu || 7.1

śrībhagavānuvāca: Kṛṣṇa says; mayi: in Me; āsaktamanāḥ: mind attached; pārtha: Arjuna, O son of Pritā; yogaṃ: union; yuñjan: so practising; madāśrayaḥ: in My shelter; asaṃśayaṃ: without doubt; samagraṃ: completely; māṃ: to Me; yathā: how, in what manner; jñāsyasi: you can know; tat: that; śṛṇu: hear

7.1 Bhagavān Kṛṣṇa says, Arjuna, Listen to Me, you can know Me completely and without doubt by practicing yoga in true consciousness of Me, with your mind attached to Me.

ज्ञानं तेऽहं सविज्ञानमिदं वक्ष्याम्यशेषत: ।
यज्ज्ञात्वा नेह भूयोऽन्यज्ज्ञातव्यमवशिष्यते ॥ ७.२

jñānaṃ te'haṃ savijñānam idaṃ vakṣyāmyaśeṣataḥ |
yajjñātvā neha bhūyo'nyaj jñātavyamavaśiṣyate || 7.2

jñānaṃ: phenomenal knowledge; te: unto you; ahaṃ: I; sa: with; vijñānaṃ: absolute knowledge; idaṃ: this; vakṣyāmi: shall explain; aśeṣataḥ: in full; yat: which; jñātvā: knowing; na: not; iha: in this world; bhūyaḥ: further; anyat: anything more; jñātavyaṃ: knowable; avaśiṣyate: remains to be known

7.2 Let Me explain to you in detail this phenomenal and absolute knowledge along with its realization; by knowing which, there shall remain nothing further to be known.

मनुष्याणां सहस्रेषु कश्चिद्यतति सिद्धये ।
यततामपि सिद्धानां कश्चिन्मां वेत्ति तत्त्वत: ॥ ७.३

manuṣyāṇāṃ sahasreṣu kaścidyatati siddhaye |
yatatāmapi siddhānāṃ kaścinmāṃ vetti tattvataḥ || 7.3

manuṣyāṇāṃ: of men; sahasreṣu: out of many thousands; kaścit: hardly one; yatati: endeavors; siddhaye: for perfection of self-realization; yatatāṃ: of those so endeavoring; api: indeed; siddhānāṃ: of those who have achieved perfection; kaścit: hardly one; māṃ: Me; vetti: does know; tattvataḥ: in truth

7.3 Out of many thousands of men, hardly one endeavors or strives to achieve perfection of self-realization; of those so endeavoring, hardly one achieves the perfection of self-realization and of those, hardly one knows Me in truth or reaches that state of oneness with Me.

भूमिरापोऽनलो वायु: खं मनो बुद्धिरेव च ।
अहङ्कार इतीयं मे भिन्ना प्रकृतिरष्टधा ॥ ७.४

bhūmirāpo'nalo vāyuḥ khaṃ mano buddhireva ca |
ahankāra itīyaṃ me bhinnā prakṛtiraṣṭadhā || 7.4

bhūmiḥ: earth; āpaḥ: water; analaḥ: fire; vāyuḥ: air; khaṃ: ether; manaḥ: mind; buddhiḥ: intelligence; eva: certainly; ca: and; ahaṃkāraḥ: ego; iti: thus; iyaṃ:

all these; me: My; bhinnā: separated, various; prakṛtiḥ: external energies; aṣṭadhā: total eight

7.4 Earth, water, fire, air, ether, mind, intelligence and false ego all together these eight constitute My separated external energies.

अपरेयमितस्त्वन्यां प्रकृतिं विद्धि मे पराम् ।
जीवभूतां महाबाहो ययेदं धार्यते जगत् ॥ ७.५

apare'yamitastvanyāṃ prakṛtiṃ viddhi me parām /
jīvabhūtāṃ mahābāho yayedaṃ dhāryate jagat // 7.5

aparā: inferior; iyaṃ: this; itaḥ: besides this; tu : but; anyāṃ: another; prakṛtiṃ: energy; viddhi: understand; me: my; parāṃ: superior; jīvabhūtāṃ: the living entities; mahā-bāho: O mighty armed one; yayā: by whom; idaṃ: this; dhāryate: bearing; jagat: the material world

7.5 Besides these external energies, which are inferior in nature, O mighty-armed Arjuna, there is a superior energy of Mine. This comprises all the embodied souls of all the living entities by which this material world is being utilized or exploited.

एतद्योनीनि भूतानि सर्वाणीत्युपधारय ।
अहं कृत्स्नस्य जगत: प्रभव: प्रलयस्तथा ॥ ७.६

etadyonī ni bhūtāni sarvāṇītyupadhāraya /
ahaṃ kṛ tsnasya jagataḥ prabhavaḥ pralayastathā // 7.6

etad: these two natures; yonīni: source of birth; bhūtāni: everything created; sarvāṇī: all; iti: thus; upadhāraya: know; ahaṃ: I; kṛtsnasya: all-inclusive; jagataḥ: of the world; prabhavaḥ: source of manifestation; pralayaḥ: annihilation; tathā: as well as

7.6 Know for certain that everything living is manifested by these two energies of Mine. I am the Creator, the Sustainer and the Destroyer of them.

मत्तः परतरं नान्यत्किञ्चिदस्ति धनञ्जय ।
मयि सर्वमिदं प्रोतं सूत्रे मणिगणा इव ॥ ७.७

mattaḥ parataraṃ nānyat kiñcidasti dhanañjaya /
mayi sarvamidaṃ protaṃ sūtre maṇigaṇā iva // 7.7

mattaḥ: beyond Myself; parataraṃ: superior; na: not; anyat kiñcit: anything else; asti: there is; dhanañjaya: O conqueror of wealth; mayi: in Me; sarvaṃ: all that be; idaṃ: which we see; protaṃ: strung; sūtre: on a thread; maṇigaṇāḥ: pearls; iva: likened

7.7 O Dhanañjaya (conqueror of wealth), there is no truth superior to Me. Everything rests upon Me, as pearls are strung on a thread.

रसोऽहमप्सु कौन्तेय प्रभास्मि शशिसूर्ययोः ।
प्रणवः सर्ववेदेषु शब्दः खे पौरुषं नृषु ॥ ७.८

raso'hamapsu kaunteya prabhāsmi śaśisūryayoḥ /
praṇavaḥ sarvavedeṣu śabdaḥ khe pauruṣaṃ nṛṣu // 7.8

rasaḥ: taste; ahaṃ: I; apsu: in water; kaunteya: O son of Kuntī; prabhā: light; asmi: I am; śaśisūryayoḥ: in the sun and the moon; praṇavaḥ: the letters a-u-m; sarva: in all; vedeṣu: in the Vedas; śabdaḥ: sound vibration; khe: in the ether; pauruṣaṃ: virility, manliness; nṛṣu: in man

7.8 O Kaunteya (son of Kuntī), I am the taste of water, the radiance of the sun and the moon, the sacred syllable 'Om' in the vedic mantras. I am the sound in ether and ability in man.

पुण्यो गन्धः पृथिव्यां च तेजश्चास्मि विभावसौ ।
जीवनं सर्वभूतेषु तपश्चास्मि तपस्विषु ॥ ७.९

puṇyo gandhaḥ pṛthivyāṃ ca tejaścāsmi vibhāvasau /
jīvanaṃ sarvabhūteṣu tapaścāsmi tapasviṣu // 7.9

puṇyaḥ: original; gandhaḥ: fragrance; pṛthivyāṃ: in the earth; ca: also; tejaḥ:

temperature; ca: also; asmi: I am; vibhāvasau: in the fire; jīvanaṃ: life; sarva: all; bhūteṣu: living entities; tapaḥ: penance; ca: also; asmi: I am; tapasviṣu: in those who practice penance.

7.9 I am the original fragrance of the earth, and I am the heat in fire. I am the life of all living beings, and I am the penances of all ascetics.

बीजं मां सर्वभूतानां विद्धि पार्थ सनातनम् ।
बुद्धिर्बुद्धिमतामस्मि तेजस्तेजस्विनामहम् ॥ ७.१०

bījaṃ māṃ sarvabhūtānāṃ viddhi pārtha sanātanam I
buddhirbuddhimatāmasmi tejastejasvināmaham II 7.10

bī jaṃ: the seed; māṃ: Me; sarvabhūtānāṃ: of all living entities; viddhi: understand; pārtha: O son of Prithā; sanātanaṃ: original, eternal; buddhiḥ: intelligence; buddhimatāṃ: of the intelligent; asmi: I am; tejaḥ: prowess; tejasvināṃ: of the powerful; ahaṃ: I am

7.10 O Pārtha (son of Prithā), I am the eternal source of all creatures, the intelligence of the intelligent, and the brilliance of all those who are brilliant.

बलं बलवतां चाहं कामरागविवर्जितम् ।
धर्माविरुद्धो भूतेषु कामोऽस्मि भरतर्षभ ॥ ७.११

balaṃ balavatāṃ cāhaṃ kāmarāgavivarjitaṃ I
dharmāviruddho bhūteṣu kāmo'smi bharatarṣabha II 7.11

balaṃ: strength; balavatāṃ: of the strong; cāham: I am; kāma: desire; rāga: attachment; vivarjitaṃ: devoid of; dharma: religious principle; aviruddhaḥ: not against the religious principles; bhūteṣu: in all beings; kāmaḥ: lust; asmi: I am; Bhārata ṛṣabha: O Lord of the Bhāratas

7.11 I am the strength of the strong, and I am procreative energy in living beings, devoid of lust and in accordance with religious principles, O Bharatarṣabha (Lord of Bhārata).

ये चैव सात्त्विका भावा राजसास्तामसाश्च ये ।
मत्त एवेति तान्विद्धि न त्वहं तेषु ते मयि ॥ ७.१२

ye caiva sāttvikā bhāvā rājasāstāmasāśca ye |
matta eveti tānviddhi na tvahaṃ teṣu te mayi || 7.12

ye: all those; ca: and; eva: certainly; sāttvikāḥ: in goodness; bhāvāḥ: states of being; rājasāḥ: mode of passion; tāmasāḥ: mode of ignorance; ca: and; ye: although; mattaḥ: from Me; eva: certainly; iti: thus; tān: those; viddhi: try to know; na: not; tu: but; ahaṃ: I; teṣu: in those; te: they; mayi: unto Me

7.12 All states of being—be they of goodness, passion or ignorance—all emanate from Me. I am independent of them but they are dependent on Me.

त्रिभिर्गुणमयैर्भावैरेभिः सर्वमिदं जगत् ।
मोहितं नाभिजानाति मामेभ्यः परमव्ययम् ॥ ७.१३

tribhirguṇamayair bhāvairebhiḥ sarvamidaṃ jagat |
mohitaṃ nābhijānāti māmebhyaḥ paramavyayam || 7.13

tribhiḥ: three; guṇamayaiḥ: by the three gunas; bhāvaiḥ: state of being; ebhiḥ: all these; sarvaṃ: the whole world; idaṃ: this; jagat: universe; mohitaṃ: deluded; nābhijānāti: do not know; māṃ: Me; ebhyaḥ: above these; paraṃ: the Supreme; avyayaṃ: immutable

7.13 The whole world is deluded by the three modes (goodness, passion and ignorance), and thus does not know Me. I am above the modes and unchangeable

दैवी ह्येषा गुणमयी मम माया दुरत्यया ।
मामेव ये प्रपद्यन्ते मायामेतां तरन्ति ते ॥ ७.१४

daivī hyeṣā guṇamayī mama māyā duratyayā |
māmeva ye prapadyante māyāmetāṃ taranti te || 7.14

daivī: transcendental; hi: certainly; eṣā: this; guṇamayī: consisting of the three modes of material nature; mama: My; māyā: energy; duratyayā: very difficult to overcome; māṃ: unto Me; eva: certainly; ye: those; prapadyante: surrender; māyāmetāṃ: this illusory energy; taranti: overcome; te: they

7.14 My divine energy, consisting of the three modes of material nature, is difficult to overcome. But those who surrender unto Me can cross beyond it with ease.

न मां दुष्कृतिनो मूढाः प्रपद्यन्ते नराधमाः ।
माययापहृतज्ञाना आसुरं भावमाश्रिताः ॥ ७.१५

na māṃ duṣkṛ tino mūḍhāḥ prapadyante narādhamāḥ I
māyayāpahṛtajñānā āsuraṃ bhāvamāśritāḥ II 7.15

na: not; māṃ: unto Me; duṣkṛtinaḥ: miscreants; mūḍhāḥ: foolish; prapadyante: surrender; nara adhamāḥ: lowest among mankind; māyayā : by the illusory energy; apahṛta: stolen by illusion; jñānāḥ: knowledge; āsuraṃ: demonic; bhāvaṃ: nature; āśritāḥ: accepting.

7.15 Those miscreants who are foolish, lowest among mankind, whose knowledge is stolen by māyā (that which is not real), and who have taken shelter in demonic nature, do not surrender unto Me.

चतुर्विधा भजन्ते मां जनाः सुकृतिनोऽर्जुन ।
आर्तो जिज्ञासुरर्थार्थी ज्ञानी च भरतर्षभ ॥ ७.१६

caturvidhā bhajante māṃ janāḥ sukṛtino'rjuna I
ārto jijñāsurarthārthī jñānī ca bharatarṣabha II 7.16

caturvidhāḥ: four kinds of; bhajante: render services; māṃ: unto Me; janāḥ: persons; sukṛtinaḥ: those who are pious; arjuna: O Arjuna; ārtaḥ: the distressed; jijñāsuḥ: the inquisitive; arthārthī : one who desires material gain; jñānī: one who knows things as they are; ca: also; bharatarṣabha: O great one amongst the descendants of Bhārata.

7.16 O Bharatarṣabha, best among Bhārata, four kinds of pious men begin to render devotional service unto Me. They are: the distressed, the desirer of wealth, the inquisitive, and those searching for knowledge of the Absolute.

तेषां ज्ञानी नित्ययुक्त एकभक्तिर्विशिष्यते ।
प्रियो हि ज्ञानिनोऽत्यर्थमहं स च मम प्रियः ॥ ७.१७

teṣāṃ jñānī nityayukta eka-bhaktir viśiṣyate |
priyo hi jñānino'tyartham ahaṃ sa ca mama priyaḥ || 7.17

teṣāṃ: of them; jñānī: the wise; nityayuktaḥ: ever steadfast; eka bhaktiḥ: whose devotion is to the one; viśiṣyate: better; priyaḥ: dear; hi: verily; jñāninaḥ: of the wise; atyarthaṃ: exceedingly; ahaṃ: I; saḥ: he; ca: and; mama: to me; priyaḥ: dear

7.17 Of these, the wise one who is in full knowledge and ever united with Me through single-minded devotion is the best. I am very dear to him, and he is dear to Me

उदाराः सर्व एवैते ज्ञानीत्वात्मैव मे मतम् ।
आस्थितः स हि युक्तात्मा मामेवानुत्तमां गतिम ॥ ७.१८

udārāḥ sarva evaite jñānītvātmaiva me matam |
āsthitaḥ sa hi yuktātmā māmevānuttamāṃ gatim || 7.18

udārāḥ: noble; sarve: all; eva: certainly; ete: these; jñānī: one who is in knowledge; tu: but; ātmā eva: just like Myself; me: My; mataṃ: opinion; āsthitaḥ: situated; saḥ: he; hi: certainly; yuktātmā: engaged in devotional service; māṃ: unto Me; eva: certainly; anuttamāṃ: the highest goal; gatiṃ: destination

7.18 All these devotees are indeed noble; one who knows Me, dwells in Me. Being engaged in My mission, he attains Me.

बहूनां जन्मनामन्ते ज्ञानवान्मां प्रपद्यते ।
वासुदेवः सर्वमिति स महात्मा सुदुर्लभः ॥ ७.१९

bahūnāṃ janmanām ante jñānavānmāṃ prapadyate |
vāsudevaḥ sarvamiti sa mahātmā sudurlabhaḥ || 7.19

bahūnāṃ: many; janmanāṃ: births; ante: after; jñānavān: he possessing knowledge; māṃ: unto Me; prapadyate: surrenders; vāsudevaḥ: cause of all causes; sarvaṃ: all; iti: thus; saḥ: such; mahātmā : great soul; sudurlabhaḥ: very rare.

7.19 After many births and deaths, he who knows Me surrenders to Me, knowing Me to be the cause of all causes and all that is. Such a great soul is very rare.

कामैस्तैस्तैर्हृतज्ञाना: प्रपद्यन्तेऽन्यदेवता: ।
तं तं नियममास्थाय प्रकृत्या नियता: स्वया ॥ ७.२०

kāmais tais tair hṛta-jñānāḥ prapadyante'nyadevatāḥ |
taṃ taṃ niyamamāsthāya prakṛtyā niyatāḥ svayā || 7.20

kāmaiḥ: by desires; taiḥ: by those; taiḥ: by those; hṛta: distorted; jñānāḥ: knowledge; prapadyante: surrender; anya: other; devatāḥ: deities; taṃ-taṃ: that; niyamaṃ: rules; āsthāya: following; prakṛtyā: by nature; niyatāḥ: controlled; svayā: by their own.

7.20 Those whose discrimination has been distorted by various desires, surrender unto deities. They follow specific rules and regulations of worship according to their own nature.

यो यो यां यां तनुं भक्त: श्रद्धयार्चितुमिच्छति ।
तस्य तस्याचलां श्रद्धां तामेव विदधाम्यहम् ॥ ७.२१

yo yo yāṃ yāṃ tanuṃ bhaktaḥ śraddhayārcitumicchati |
tasya tasyācalāṃ śraddhāṃ tāmeva vidadhāmyaham || 7.21

yaḥ: that; yaḥ: that; yāṃ: which; yāṃ: which; tanuṃ: form of the deities; bhaktaḥ: devotee; śraddhayā: with faith; arcituṃ: to worship; icchati: desires; tasya: of that; tasya: of that; acalāṃ: steady; śraddhāṃ: faith; tāṃ: him; eva: surely; vidadhāmi: give; ahaṃ: I

7.21 I am in everyone's heart as the super soul. As soon as

one desires to worship some deity, I make his faith steady so that he can devote himself to that particular deity.

स तया श्रद्धया युक्तस्तस्याराधनमीहते ।
लभते च ततः कामान्मयैवविहितान्हि तान् ॥ ७.२२

sa tayā śraddhayā yuktas tasyārādhanamīhate /
labhate ca tataḥ kāmān mayaiva vihitānhi tān // 7.22

saḥ: he; tayā: with that; śraddhayā: with faith; yuktaḥ: endowed; tasya: his; ārādhanaṃ: worship; īhate: endeavors; labhate: obtains; ca: and; tataḥ: from that; kāmān: desires; mayā: by Me; eva: alone; vihitān: bestowed; hi: for; tān: those.

7.22 Endowed with such a faith, he endeavors to worship a particular demigod and obtains his desires; In reality, these benefits are granted by Me alone.

अन्तवत्तु फलं तेषां तद्भवत्यल्पमेधसाम् ।
देवान्देवयजो यान्ति मद्भक्ता यान्ति मामपि ॥ ७.२३

antavattu phalaṃ teṣāṃ tadbhavatyalpamedhasām /
devāndevayajo yānti madbhaktā yānti māmapi // 7.23

antavat tu: limited and temporary; phalaṃ: fruits; teṣāṃ: their; tat: that; bhavati: becomes; alpa medhasāṃ: of those of small intelligence; devān: demigods' planets; devayajaḥ: worshipers of demigods; yānti: achieve; mad: My; bhaktāḥ: devotees; yānti: attain; māṃ: to Me; api: surely

7.23 Men of limited intelligence worship the demigods and their fruits are limited and temporary. Those who worship the demigods go only to the planets of the demigods, but My devotees reach My supreme planet.

अव्यक्तं व्यक्तिमापन्नं मन्यन्ते मामबुद्धयः ।
परं भावमजानन्तो ममाव्ययमनुत्तमम् ॥ ७.२४

avyaktaṃ vyaktimāpannaṃ manyante māmabuddhayaḥ I
paraṃ bhāvamajānanto mamāvyayam anuttamam II 7.24

avyaktaṃ: nonmanifested; vyaktiṃ: personality; āpannaṃ: achieved; manyante: think; māṃ: unto Me; abuddhayaḥ: less intelligent persons; paraṃ: supreme; bhāvaṃ: state of being; ajānantaḥ: without knowing; mama: My; avyayaṃ: imperishable; anuttamaṃ: the finest.

7.24 Unintelligent men, who do not know Me perfectly, think that I, the supreme personality of godhead, the Bhagavān, who was impersonal before, have become a human being now. They do not know that I am imperishable and supreme, even when I assume the body.

नाहं प्रकाशः सर्वस्य योगमायासमावृतः ।
मूढोऽयं नाभिजानाति लोको मामजमव्ययम् ॥ ७.२५

nāhaṃ prakāśaḥ sarvasya yogamāyāsamāvṛtaḥ I
mūḍhoyaṃ nābhijānāti loko māmajamavyayam II 7.25

na: nor; ahaṃ: I; prakāśaḥ: manifest; sarvasya: to everyone; yoga māyā: internal potency; samāvṛtaḥ: covered; mūḍhaḥ: foolish; ayaṃ: this; na: not; abhijānāti: can understand; lokaḥ: such less intelligent persons; māṃ: Me; ajaṃ: unborn; avyayaṃ: immutable.

7.25 I am never revealed to the foolish and unintelligent, covered as I am by My divine power ; the ignorant do not know Me, unborn and eternal.

वेदाहं समतीतानि वर्तमानानि चाऽर्जुन ।
भविष्याणि च भूतानि मां तु वेद न कश्चन ॥ ७.२६

vedāhaṃ samatī tāni vartamānāni cārjuna I
bhaviṣyāṇi ca bhūtāni māṃ tu veda na kaścana II 7.26

veda: know; ahaṃ: I; sama: equally; atītāni: past; vartamānāni: present; ca: and; arjuna: O Arjuna; bhaviṣyāṇi: future; ca: also; bhūtāni: living entities;

māṃ: Me; tu: but; veda: knows; na: not; kaścana: anyone

7.26 O Arjuna, as the supreme personality of Godhead, I know all that has happened, all that is happening, and all that is to happen. I also know all living entities; but no one knows Me.

इच्छाद्वेषसमुत्थेन द्वन्द्वमोहेन भारत ।
सर्वभूतानि संमोहं सर्गे यान्ति परन्तप ॥ ७.२७

icchādveṣasamutthena dvandvamohena bhārata /
sarvabhūtāni saṃmohaṃ sarge yānti parantapa // 7.27

icchā: desire; dveṣa: hate; samutthena: born; dvandva: duality; mohena: overcome; bhārata: O scion of Bhārata; sarva: all; bhūtāni: living entities; saṃmohaṃ: into delusion; sarge: in creation; yānti: go; parantapa: O conqueror of enemies.

7.27 O scion of Bhārata (Arjuna), O conqueror of the foe, Parantapa, all living entities are born into delusion, overcome by the dualities of attachment and aversion.

येषां त्वन्तगतं पापं जनानां पुण्यकर्मणाम् ।
ते द्वन्द्वमोहनिर्मुक्ता भजन्ते मां दृढव्रताः ॥ ७.२८

yeṣāṃ tvantagataṃ pāpaṃ janānāṃ punyakarmaṇām /
te dvandvamohanirmuktā bhajante māṃ dṛḍhavratāḥ // 7.28

yeṣāṃ: whose; tu : but; antagataṃ: completely eradicated; pāpaṃ: sin; janānāṃ: of the persons; punya: pious; karmanām: previous activities; te: they; dvandva: duality; moha: delusion; nirmuktāḥ: free from; bhajante worship; māṃ: Me; dṛḍhavratāḥ: with determination.

7.28 Persons who have acted virtuously, whose sinful actions are completely eradicated and who are freed from the duality of reality and unreality, engage themselves in My worship with firm resolve.

जरामरणमोक्षाय मामाश्रित्य यतन्ति ये ।
ते ब्रह्म तद्विदुः कृत्स्नमध्यात्मं कर्म चाखिलम् ॥ ७.२९

jarāmaraṇa mokṣāya māmāśritya yatanti ye /
te brahma tadviduḥ kṛtsnam adhyātmaṃ karma cākhilam // 7.29

jarā: old age; maraṇa: death; mokṣāya: for the purpose of liberation; māṃ: unto Me; āśritya: taking shelter of; yatanti: endeavor; ye: all those; te: such persons; brahma: Brahman; tat: actually that; viduḥ: they know; kṛtsnaṃ: everything; adhyātmaṃ: transcendental; karma: activities; ca: and; akhilaṃ: entirely

7.29 Persons who are striving for liberation from the cycle of birth, old age and death, take refuge in Me. They are actually Brahman because they comprehend everything about activities that transcend these.

साधिभूताधिदैवं मां साधियज्ञं च ये विदुः ।
प्रयाणकालेऽपि च मां ते विदुर्युक्तचेतसः ॥ ७.३०

sādhibhūtādhidaivaṃ māṃ sādhiyajñaṃ ca ye viduḥ /
prayāṇakāle 'pi ca māṃ te vidur yuktacetasaḥ // 7.30

sādhibhūta: the governing principle of the material manifestation; adhidaivaṃ: underlying all the demigods; māṃ: Me; sādhiyajñaṃ: sustaining all sacrifices; ca: and; ye: those; viduḥ: know; prayāṇa: of death; kāle: at the time; api: even; ca: and; māṃ: Me; te : they; viduḥ: know; yukta cetasaḥ: with steadfast minds.

7.30 Those who know Me as the Supreme Lord, as the governing principle of the material manifestation, who know Me as the one underlying all the demigods and as the one sustaining all sacrifices, can with steadfast mind, understand and know Me, even at the time of death.

इति श्रीमद्भगवद्गीतासूपनिषत्सु ब्रह्मविद्यायां योगशास्त्रे
श्रीकृष्णार्जुनसंवादे ज्ञानविज्ञानयोगो नाम सप्तमोऽध्यायः ॥

iti śrīmad bhagavadgītāsūpaniṣatsu brahmavidyāyāṃ yogaśāstre śrīkṛṣṇārjuna saṃvāde jñānavijñāna yogo nāma saptamo'dhyāyaḥ ||

In the ***Upaniṣad*** of ***Śrimad Bhagavad Gītā***, the scripture of yoga dealing with ***Brahmavidyā Yogaśāstra,*** the science of Brahman, the Supreme Absolute, in the form of ***Śrī Kṛṣṇārjuna saṁvād,*** dialogue between Śrī Kṛṣṇa and Arjuna, this is the seventh chapter named, ***Jñānavijñāna Yogaḥ,*** *'The Yoga of Knowledge and Conscious Realization of the Absolute.'*

CHAPTER

8

अथ अष्टमोऽध्यायः
अक्षरब्रह्मयोगः

Akṣarabrahma Yogaḥ

अर्जुन उवाच ।
किं तद् ब्रह्म किमध्यात्मं किं कर्म पुरुषोत्तम ।
अधिभूतं च किं प्रोक्तमधिदैवं किमुच्यते ॥ ८.१

arjuna uvāca
kiṃ tadbrahma kimadhyātmaṃ kiṃ karma puruṣottama |
adhibhūtaṃ ca kiṃ proktam adhidaivaṃ kimucyate || 8.1

arjuna uvāca: Arjuna said; kiṃ: what; tat: that; brahma: Brahman; kiṃ: what; adhyātmaṃ: the self; kiṃ: what; karma: fruitive activities; puruṣottama: O Supreme Person; adhibhūtaṃ: the material manifestation; ca: and; kiṃ: what; proktaṃ: is called; adhidaivaṃ: the demigods; kiṃ: what; ucyate: is called.

8.1 Arjuna says: O my Lord, O supreme person, what is Brahman? What is the Self? What are result-based actions? What is this material manifestation? And what are the demigods? Please explain all this to me.

अधियज्ञः कथं कोऽत्र देहेऽस्मिन्मधुसूदन ।
प्रयाणकाले च कथं ज्ञेयोऽसि नियतात्मभिः ॥ ८.२

adhiyajñaḥ kathaṃ ko'tra dehe'smin madhusūdana |

prayāṇakāle ca kathaṃ jñeyo'si niyatātmabhiḥ // 8.2

adhiyajñaḥ: the Lord of sacrifice; kathaṃ: how; kaḥ: who; atra: here; dehe: in the body; asmin: in this; madhusūdana: O Madhusudana; prayāṇakāle: at the time of death; ca: and; kathaṃ: how; jñeyaḥ: be known; asi: You can; niyatātmabhiḥ: by the self-controlled.

8.2 How does this Lord of sacrifice live in the body, and in which part does He live, O Madhusūdana? How can those engaged in devotional service know You at the time of their death?

श्री भगवानुवाच ।
अक्षरं ब्रह्म परमं स्वभावोऽध्यात्ममुच्यते ।
भूतभावोद्भवकरो विसर्गः कर्मसंज्ञितः ॥ ८.३

śrībhagavānuvāca
akṣaraṃ brahma paramaṃ svabhāvo'dhyātmamucyate /
bhūta-bhāvodbhava-karo visargaḥ karmasañjñitaḥ // 8.3

śrībhagavānuvāca: Bhagavān said; akṣaraṃ: indestructible; brahma: Brahman; paramaṃ: transcendental; svabhāvaḥ: eternal nature; adhyātmaṃ: the self; ucyate: is called; bhūtabhāva-udbhavakaraḥ: action producing the material bodies of the living entities; visargaḥ: creation; karma: fruitive activities; saṃñitaḥ: is called.

8.3 Bhagavān says: The indestructible, transcendental living entity is called Brahman and his eternal nature is called the self. Action pertaining to the development of the material bodies is called karma, or result based activities.

अधिभूतं क्षरो भावः पुरुषश्चाधिदैवतम् ।
अधियज्ञोऽहमेवात्र देहे देहभृतां वर ॥ ८.४

adhibhūtaṃ kṣaro bhāvaḥ puruṣaś cādhidaivatam /
adhiyajño'ham evātra dehe dehabhṛtāṃ vara // 8.4

adhibhūtaṃ: the physical manifestation; kṣaraḥ: constantly changing; bhāvaḥ: nature; puruṣaḥ: the universal form; ca: and; adhidaivataṃ: including all demigods like the sun and moon; adhiyajñaḥ: the Supersoul; ahaṃ: I (Kṛṣṇa); eva: alone; atra: in this; dehe: body; dehabhṛtāṃ: of the embodied; vara: the Supreme.

8.4 Physical nature is known to be endlessly changing. The universe is the cosmic form of the supreme Lord, and I am that Lord represented as the super soul, dwelling in the heart of every being that dwells in a body.

अन्तकाले च मामेव स्मरन्मुक्त्वा कलेवरम् ।
यः प्रयाति स मद्भावं याति नास्त्यत्र संशयः ॥ ८.५

antakāle ca māmeva smaranmuktvā kalevaram |
yaḥ prayāti sa madbhāvaṃ yāti nā'styatra saṃśayaḥ || 8.5

antakāle: at the end of life; ca: also; māṃ: unto Me; eva: only; smaran: remembering; muktvā: quitting; kalevaraṃ: the body; yaḥ: he who; prayāti: goes; saḥ: he; madbhāvaṃ: My nature; yāti: achieves; na: not; asti: there is; atra: here; saṃśayaḥ: doubt.

8.5 Whoever, at the time of death, quits his body, remembering Me alone, attains My nature immediately. Of this there is no doubt.

यं यं वापि स्मरन्भावं त्यजत्यन्ते कलेवरम् ।
तं तमेवैति कौन्तेय सदा तद्भावभावितः ॥ ८.६

yaṃ yaṃ vāpi smaranbhāvaṃ tyajatyante kalevaram |
taṃ taṃ evaiti kaunteya sadā tadbhāvabhāvitaḥ || 8.6

yaṃ yaṃ: whatever; vā: either; api: also; smaran: remembering; bhāvaṃ: nature; tyajati: give up; ante: at the end; kalevaraṃ: this body; taṃ taṃ: similar; eva: certainly; eti: gets; kaunteya: O son of Kuntī; sadā: always; tat: that; bhāva: state of being; bhāvitaḥ: remembering.

8.6 Whatever state of being one remembers when he quits his body, it is that state one will attain without fail.

तस्मात्सर्वेषु कालेषु मामनुस्मर युध्य च ।
मय्यर्पितमनोबुद्धिर्मामेवैष्यस्यसंशयम् ॥ ८.७

tasmāt sarveṣu kāleṣu mām anusmara yudhya ca |
mayy arpita-mano-buddhir mām evaiṣy asyasaṃśayam || 8.7

tasmāt: therefore; sarveṣu: always; kāleṣu: time; māṃ: unto Me; anusmara: go on remembering; yudhya: fight; ca: also; mayi: unto Me; arpita : surrender; manaḥ: mind; buddhiḥ: intellect; māṃ: unto Me; eva: alone; eṣyasi: will attain; asaṃśayaḥ: beyond a doubt.

8.7 Arjuna, think of Me in the form of Kṛṣṇa always, while continuing with your prescribed duty of fighting. With your activities dedicated to Me and your mind and intelligence fixed on. Me, you will attain Me without doubt.

अभ्यासयोगयुक्तेन चेतसा नान्यगामिना ।
परमं पुरुषं दिव्यं याति पार्थानुचिन्तयन् ॥ ८.८

abhyāsa yoga yuktena cetasā nānyagāminā |
paramaṃ puruṣaṃ divyaṃ yāti pārthānucintayan || 8.8

abhyāsa: practice; yoga yuktena: being engaged in meditation; cetasā: by the mind and intelligence; nā 'nyagāminā: without their being deviated; paramaṃ: the Supreme; puruṣaṃ: personality of godhead; divyaṃ: transcendental; yāti: achieves; pārtha: O son of Pritā; anucintayan: constantly thinking of

8.8 He who meditates on the supreme person, his mind constantly engaged in remembering Me, not deviating from the path, O Pārtha, He is sure to reach Me.

कविं पुराणमनुशासितार-
मणोरणीयांसमनुस्मरेद्यः

सर्वस्य धातारमचिन्त्यरूप-
मादित्यवर्णं तमसः परस्तात् ॥ ८.९

kaviṃ purāṇaṃ anuśāsitāram
aṇoraṇī yām sam anusmared yaḥ /
sarvasya dhātāram acintya-rūpam
ādityavarṇaṃ tamasaḥ parastāt // 8.9

kaviṃ: one who knows everything; purāṇaṃ: the oldest; anuśāsitāraṃ: the controller; aṇoḥ: of the atom; aṇīyāṃsaṃ: smaller than; anusmaret: always thinking; yaḥ: one who; sarvasya: of everything; dhātāraṃ: the maintainer; acintya: inconceivable; rūpaṃ: form; āditya varṇaṃ: illuminated like the sun; tamasaḥ: of the darkness; parastāt: transcendental

8.9 One should meditate on the Supreme as the one who knows everything, as He is the most ancient, who is the controller, who is smaller than the smallest, who is the maintainer of everything, who is beyond all material conception, who is inconceivable, and who is always a person.

प्रयाणकाले मनसाऽचलेन
भक्त्या युक्तो योगबलेन चैव ।
भ्रुवोर्मध्ये प्राणमावेश्य सम्यक्
स तं परं पुरुषमुपैति दिव्यम् ॥ ८.१०

prayāṇakāle manasācalena
bhaktyā yukto yogabalena caiva /
bhruvor madhye prāṇam āveśya samyak
sa taṃ paraṃ puruṣam upaiti divyam // 8.10

prayāṇa kāle: at the time of death; manasā: by the mind; acalena: without being deviated; bhaktyā: in full devotion; yuktaḥ: engaged; yoga balena: by the power of mystic yoga; ca: also; eva: certainly; bhruvoḥ: between the two eyebrows;

madhye: in; prāṇaṃ: the life air; āveśya: establishing; samyak: completely; saḥ: he; taṃ: that; paraṃ: transcendental; puruṣaṃ: personality of godhead; upaiti: achieves; divyaṃ: in the spiritual kingdom.

8.10 One, who at the time of death, fixes his mind and life air between the eyebrows without being distracted, by the power of yoga and in full devotion, engages himself in dwelling on Me, He will certainly attain Me.

यदक्षरं वेदविदो वदन्ति
विशन्ति यद्यतयो वीतरागाः ।
यदिच्छन्तो ब्रह्मचर्यं चरन्ति
तत्ते पदं संग्रहेण प्रवक्ष्ये ॥ ८.११

yad akṣaraṃ vedavido vadanti
viśanti yadyatayo vītarāgāḥ I
yad icchanto brahmacaryaṃ caranti
tatte padaṃ sangraheṇa pravakṣye II 8.11

yat: that which; akṣaraṃ: inexhaustible; vedavidaḥ: a person conversant with the Vedas; vadanti: say; viśanti: enters; yat: in which; yatayaḥ: great sages; vītarāgāḥ: in the renounced order of life; yat: that which; icchanṭaḥ: desiring; brahmacaryaṃ: celibacy; caranti: practices; tat: that; te: unto you; padaṃ: situation; sangraheṇa: in summary; pravakṣye: I shall explain.

8.11 Persons who are learned in the Veda and who are great sages in the renounced order, enter into Brahman. Desiring such perfection, one practices brahmacarya. I shall now explain to you this process by which one may attain liberation.

सर्वद्वाराणि संयम्य मनो हृदि निरुध्य च ।
मूर्ध्न्याधायात्मनः प्राणमास्थितो योगधारणाम् ॥ ८.१२

sarva-dvārāṇi saṃyamya mano hṛdi nirudhya ca I
mūrdhny ādhāyātmanaḥ prāṇam āsthito yogadhāraṇām II 8.12

sarva dvārāṇi: all the doors of the body; saṃyamya: controlling; manaḥ: mind; hṛdi: in the heart; nirudhya: confined; ca: also; mūrdhni: on the head; ādhāya: fixed; ātmanaḥ: soul; prāṇaṃ: the life air; āsthitaḥ: situated; yoga dhāraṇāṃ: the yogic situation

8.12 Closing all the doors of the senses and fixing the mind on the heart and the life air at the top of the head, one establishes himself in yoga.

ओमित्येकाक्षरं ब्रह्म व्याहरन्मामनुस्मरन् ।
यः प्रयाति त्यजन्देहं स याति परमां गतिम् ॥ ८.१३

om ity ekākṣaraṃ brahma vyāharan mām anusmaran |
yaḥ prayāti tyajandehaṃ sa yāti paramāṃ gatiṃ || 8.13

om: the combination of letters om (omkāra); iti: thus; ekākṣaraṃ: supreme indestructible; brahma: absolute; vyāharan: vibrating; māṃ: Me (Kṛṣṇa); anusmaran: remembering; yaḥ: anyone; prayāti: leaves; tyajan: quitting; dehaṃ: this body; saḥ: he; yāti: achieves; paramāṃ: supreme; gatiṃ: destination

8.13 Centered in this yoga practice and vibrating the sacred syllable OM, the supreme combination of letters, if one dwells in the Supreme and quits his body, he certainly achieves the supreme destination.

अनन्यचेताः सततं यो मां स्मरति नित्यशः ।
तस्याहं सुलभः पार्थ नित्ययुक्तस्य योगिनः ॥ ८.१४

ananyacetāḥ satataṃ yo māṃ smarati nityaśaḥ |
tasyāhaṃ sulabhaḥ pārtha nityayuktasya yoginaḥ || 8.14

ananyacetāḥ: without deviation; satataṃ: always; yaḥ: anyone; māṃ: Me (Kṛṣṇa); smarati: remembers; nityaśaḥ: regularly; tasya: to him; ahaṃ: I am; sulabhaḥ: very easy to achieve; pārtha: O son of Pritā; nitya: regularly; yuktasya: engaged; yoginaḥ: of the devotee.

8.14 I am always available to anyone who remembers Me

constantly Pārtha, because of his constant engagement in devotional service.

मामुपेत्य पुनर्जन्म दुःखालयमशाश्वतम् ।
नाप्नुवन्ति महात्मानः संसिद्धिं परमां गताः ॥ ८.१५

māmupetya punarjanma duḥkhālayam aśāśvatam |
nāpnuvanti mahātmānaḥ saṃsiddhiṃ paramāṃ gatāḥ || 8.15

māṃ: unto Me; upetya: achieving; punaḥ: again; janma: birth; duḥkhālayaṃ: a place of miseries; aśāśvataṃ: temporary; na: never; āpnuvanti: attain; mahātmanaḥ: the great souls; saṃsiddhiṃ: perfection; paramāṃ: ultimate; gatāḥ: achieved.

8.15 After attaining Me, the great souls who are devoted to Me in yoga are never reborn in this world. This world is temporary and full of miseries and they have attained the highest perfection.

आब्रह्मभुवनाल्लोकाः पुनरावर्तिनोऽर्जुन ।
मामुपेत्य तु कौन्तेय पुनर्जन्म न विद्यते ॥ ८.१६

ā-brahma-bhuvanāl lokāḥ punarāvartinorjuna |
māmupetya tu kaunteya punarjanma na vidyate || 8.16

ābrahmabhuvanātlokāḥ: upto the world of Brahma; punarāvartinaḥ: again returning; arjuna: O Arjuna; māṃ: unto Me; upetya: arriving; tu: but; kaunteya: O son of Kuntī; punar janma: rebirth; na: never; vidyate: takes to

8.16 From the highest planet in the material world down to the lowest, all are places of misery wherein repeated birth and death take place. One who reaches My abode, O Kaunteya, is never reborn.

सहस्रयुगपर्यन्तमहर्यद् ब्रह्मणो विदुः ।
रात्रिं युगसहस्रान्तां तेऽहोरात्रविदो जनाः ॥ ८.१७

sahasrayuga-paryantam aharyad brahmaṇo viduḥ /
rātriṃ yuga-sahasrāntāṃ te'ho-rātravido janāḥ // 8.17

sahasra: thousand; yuga: millenniums; paryantaṃ: including; ahaḥ: day; yat: that; brahmaṇaḥ: of Brahma; viduḥ: they know; rātriṃ : night; yuga: millenniums; sahasrāntāṃ: similarly, at the end of one thousand; te: that; aho rātra: day and night; vidaḥ: understand; janāḥ: people

8.17 By human calculation, a thousand ages taken together is the duration of Brahma's one day. His night is just as long.

अव्यक्ताद् व्यक्तय: सर्वा: प्रभवन्त्यहरागम ।
रात्र्यागमे प्रलीयन्ते तत्रैवाव्यक्तसंज्ञके ॥ ८.१८

avyaktād vyaktayaḥ sarvāḥ prabhavanty aharāgame /
rātryāgame pralīyante tatraivāvyakta-saṃjñake // 8.18

avyaktāt: from the unmanifest; vyaktayaḥ: living entities; sarvāḥ: all; prabhavanti: come into being; aharāgame: at the beginning of the day; rātryāgame: at the fall of night; pralīyante: are annihilated; tatra: there; eva: certainly; avyakta: the unmanifest; saṃjñake: called

8.18 From the intangible all living entities come into being at the beginning of Brahma's day. During Brahma's night all that are called intangible are annihilated.

भूतग्राम: स एवायं भूत्वा भूत्वा प्रलीयते ।
रात्र्यागमेऽवश: पार्थ प्रभवत्यहरागमे ॥ ८.१९

bhūtagrāmaḥ sa evāyaṃ bhūtvā bhūtvā pralīyate /
rātryāgame'vaśaḥ pārtha prabhavaty ahārāgame // 8.19

bhūtagrāmaḥ: the aggregate of all living entities; saḥ: they; eva: certainly; ayaṃ: this; bhūtvā bhūtvā : taking birth; pralī yate: annihilate; rātri: night; āgame: on arrival; avaśaḥ: automatically; pārtha: O son of Pritā; prabhavati: manifest; ahar: during daytime; āgame: on arrival.

8.19 Again and again the day comes, and this host of beings

is active; and again the night falls, O Pārtha (son of Prithā), and they are automatically annihilated.

परस्तस्मात्तु भावोऽन्योऽव्यक्तोऽव्यक्तात्सनातन: ।
य: स सर्वेषु भूतेषु नश्यत्सु न विनश्यति ॥ ८.२०

paras tasmāttu bhāvo'nyo 'vyakto'vyaktātsanātanaḥ |
yaḥ sa sarveṣu bhūteṣu naśyatsu na vinaśyati || 8.20

paraḥ: transcendental; tasmāt: from that; tu: but; bhāvaḥ: nature; anyaḥ: another; avyaktaḥ: unmanifest; avyaktāt: from the unmanifest; sanātanaḥ: eternal; yaḥ: that; saḥ: which; sarveṣu: all; bhūteṣu: manifestation; naśyatsu: being annihilated; na: never; vinaśyati: annihilated.

8.20 Yet there is another nature, which is eternal and is beyond this tangible and intangible matter. It is supreme and is never annihilated. When all in this world is annihilated, that part remains the same.

अव्यक्तोऽक्षर इत्युक्तस्तमाहु: परमां गतिम् ।
यं प्राप्य न निवर्तन्ते तद्धाम परमं मम ॥ ८.२१

avyakto'kṣara ity uktas tamāhuḥ paramāṃ gatim |
yaṃ prāpya na nivartante tad dhāma paramaṃ mama || 8.21

avyaktaḥ: unmanifested; akṣaraḥ: infallible; iti: thus; uktaḥ: said; taṃ: that which; āhuḥ: is known; paramāṃ: ultimate; gatiṃ: destination; yaṃ: that which; prāpya: gaining; na: never; nivartante: comes back; tat dhāma: that abode; paramaṃ: supreme; mama: Mine

8.21 That Supreme abode is said to be intangible and infallible and is the Supreme destination. When one gains this state one never comes back. That is My supreme abode.

पुरुष: स पर: पार्थ भक्त्या लभ्यस्त्वनन्यया ।
यस्यान्त:स्थानि भूतानि येन सर्वमिदं ततम् ॥ ८.२२

puruṣaḥ sa paraḥ pārtha bhaktyā labhyas tv ananyayā /
yasyāntaḥ sthāni bhūtāni yena sarvam idaṃ tatam // 8.22

puruṣaḥ: that supreme power; saḥ: He; paraḥ: the Supreme, than whom no one is greater; pārtha: O son of Pritā; bhaktyā: by devotional service; labhyaḥ: can be achieved; tu: but; ananyayā: unalloyed, undeviating devotion; yasya: whom; antaḥ sthāni: within; bhūtāni: all of this material manifestation; yena: by whom; sarvaṃ: all; idaṃ: whatever we can see; tataṃ: distributed

8.22 O Pārtha (son of Prithā), the supreme person, who is greater than all, is attainable by undeviating devotion. Although He is present in His abode, He is all-pervading, and everything is situated within Him.

यत्र काले त्वनावृत्तिमावृत्तिं चैव योगिनः ।
प्रयाता यान्ति तं कालं वक्ष्यामि भरतर्षभ ॥ ८.२३

yatra kāle tv anāvṛttim āvṛttim caiva yoginaḥ /
prayātā yānti taṃ kālaṃ vakṣyāmi bharatarṣabha // 8.23

yatra: in that; kāle: time; tu: but; anāvṛttiṃ: no return; āvṛttiṃ: return; ca: also; eva: certainly; yoginaḥ: of different kinds of mystics; prayātāḥ: one who goes; yānti : departs; taṃ: that; kālaṃ: time; vaksyāmi: describing; bharatarṣabha: O best of the Bhāratas.

8.23 O best of the Bhārata, I shall now explain to you the different times when passing away from this world, one returns or does not return.

अग्निर्जोतिरहः शुक्लः षण्मासा उत्तरायणम् ।
तत्र प्रयाता गच्छन्ति ब्रह्म ब्रह्मविदो जनाः ॥ ८.२४

agnir-jyotir ahaḥ śuklaḥ ṣaṇmāsā uttarāyaṇam /
tatra prayātā gacchanti brahma brahmavido janāḥ // 8.24

agniḥ: fire; jyotiḥ: light; ahaḥ: day; śuklaḥ: white; ṣaṇmāsāḥ: six months; uttarāyaṇaṃ: when the sun passes on the northern side; tatra : there; prayātāḥ:

one who goes; gacchanti: passes away; brahma: to the Absolute; brahmavidah: one who knows the Absolute; janāḥ: person

8.24 Those who pass away from the world during the influence of the fire god, during light, at an auspicious moment, during the fortnight of the moon ascending and the six months when the sun travels in the north, and have realized the supreme Brahman do not return.

धूमो रात्रिस्तथा कृष्णः षण्मासा दक्षिणायनम् ।
तत्र चान्द्रमसं ज्योतिर्योगी प्राप्य निवर्तते ॥ ८.२५

dhūmo rātristathā kṛṣṇaḥ ṣaṇmāsā dakṣiṇāyanam /
tatra cāndramasaṃ jyotir yogī prāpya nivartate // 8.25

dhūmaḥ: smoke; rātriḥ: night; tathā: also; kṛṣṇaḥ: the fortnight of the dark moon; ṣaṇmāsāḥ: the six months; dakṣiṇāyanaṃ: when the sun passes on the southern side; tatra: there; cāndramasaṃ: the moon planet; jyotiḥ: light; yogī: the mystic; prāpya: achieves; nivartate: comes back.

8.25 The mystic who passes away from this world during the smoke, the night, the moonless fortnight, or the six months when the sun passes to the south, have done good deeds go to the cosmic layer and again comes back.

शुक्लकृष्णे गती ह्येते जगतः शाशते मते ।
एकया यात्यनावृत्तिमन्ययावर्तते पुनः ॥ ८.२६

śukla kṛṣṇe gatī hy ete jagataḥ śāśvate mate /
ekayā yāty anāvṛttim anyayāvartate punaḥ // 8.26

śukla: light; kṛṣṇe: darkness; gatī: passing away; hi: certainly; ete: all these; jagataḥ: of the material world; śāśvate: of the Vedas; mate: in the opinion; ekayā: by one; yāti: goes; anāvṛttiṃ: no return; anyayā: by the other; āvartate: comes back; punaḥ: again

8.26 According to the Vedas, there are two ways of passing

from this world: one in the light and one in darkness. When one passes in light, he does not return; but when one passes in darkness, he again comes back.

नैते सृती पार्थ जानन्योगी मुह्यति कश्चन ।
तस्मात्सर्वेषु कालेषु योगयुक्तो भवार्जुन ॥ ८.२७

naite sṛtī pārtha jānan yogī muhyati kaścana I
tasmātsarveṣu kāleṣu yogayukto bhavārjuna II 8.27

na: never; ete: all these; sṛtī : different paths; pārtha: O son of Pritā; jānan: even if they know; yogī : the devotees of the Lord; muhyati: bewildered; kaścana: anyone; tasmāt: therefore; sarveṣu kāleṣu: always; yoga yuktaḥ: being engaged in Kṛṣṇa consciousness; bhava: just become; arjuna: O Arjuna

8.27 O Pārtha (son of Prithā), the devotees who know these different paths are never bewildered. O Arjuna, be always fixed in devotion.

वेदेषु यज्ञेषु तपःसु चैव
दानेषु यत्पुण्यफलं प्रदिष्टम् ।
अत्येति तत्सर्वमिदं विदित्वा
योगी परं स्थानमुपैति चाद्यम् ॥ ८.२८

vedeṣu yajñeṣu tapaḥsu caiva
dāneṣu yat puṇyaphalaṃ pradiṣṭam I
atyeti tat sarvam idaṃ viditvā
yogī paraṃ sthānam upaiti cādyam II 8.28

vedeṣu: in the study of the Vedas; yajñeṣu: in the performances of yajna, sacrifice; tapaḥsu: undergoing different types of austerities; ca: also; eva: certainly; dāneṣu: in giving charities; yat: that which; puṇya phalaṃ: the result of pious work; pradiṣṭaṃ: directed; atyeti: surpasses; tat: all those; sarvam idaṃ: all those described above; viditvā: knowing; yogī: the devotee; paraṃ: supreme; sthānaṃ: abode; upaiti: achieves peace; ca: also; ādyaṃ: original.

8.28 A person who accepts the path of devotional service is not denied the results derived from studying the Vedas, performing austerities and sacrifices, giving charity or pursuing pious and result based activities. At the end he reaches the supreme abode.

इति श्रीमद्भगवद्गीतासूपनिषत्सु ब्रह्मविद्यायां योगशास्त्रे
श्रीकृष्णार्जुनसंवादे अक्षरब्रह्मयोगो नाम अष्टमोऽध्यायः ॥

iti śrīmad bhagavadgītāsūpaniṣatsu brahmavidyāyāṃ
yogaśāstre śrīkṛṣṇārjuna saṃvāde akṣarabrahmayogo
nāma aṣṭamo'dhyāyaḥ ||

In the ***Upaniṣad*** of ***Śrimad Bhagavad Gītā***, the scripture of yoga dealing with ***Brahmavidyā Yogaśāstra,*** the science of Brahman, the Supreme Absolute, in the form of ***Śrī Kṛṣṇārjuna saṁvād,*** dialogue between Śrī Kṛṣṇa and Arjuna, this is the eight chapter named, ***Akṣarabrahma Yogaḥ,*** *'The Yoga of Imperishable Brahma.'*

CHAPTER

9

अथ नवमोऽध्यायः
राजविद्याराजगुह्ययोगः

Rājavidyā Rājaguhya Yogaḥ

श्री भगवानुवाच
इदं तु ते गुह्यतमं प्रवक्ष्याम्यनसूयवे ।
ज्ञानं विज्ञानसहितं यज्ज्ञात्वा मोक्ष्यसेऽशुभात् ॥ ९.१

śrī bhagavānuvāca
idaṁ tu te guhyatamaṁ pravakṣyāmy anasūyave /
jñānaṁ vijñāna-sahitaṁ yajjñātvā mokṣyase'śubhāt // *9.1*

śrī bhagavān uvāca: the supreme personality of godhead says; idaṁ: this; tu: but; te: unto you; guhyatamaṁ: the most confidential; pravakṣyāmi: I am speaking; anasūyave: to the non-envious; jñānaṁ: knowledge; vijñāna: realized knowledge; sahitaṁ: with; yat: which; jñātvā: knowing; mokṣyase: be released; aśubhāt: from this miserable material existence.

9.1 Kṛṣṇa says: Dear Arjuna, because you trust Me and you are not envious of Me; I shall therefore impart to you this profound and secret wisdom and experience; This will free you of all miseries of material existence.

राजविद्या राजगुह्यं पवित्रमिदमुत्तमम् ।
प्रत्यक्षावगमं धर्म्यं सुसुखं कर्तुमव्ययम् ॥ ९.२

rājavidyā rājaguhyaṁ pavitram idam uttamam |
pratyakṣāvagamaṁ dharmyaṁ su-sukhaṁ kartum avyayam || 9.2

rājavidyā: the king of education; rājaguhyaṁ: the king of confidential knowledge; pavitraṁ: the purest; idaṁ: this; uttamaṁ: transcendental; pratyakṣa: directly experienced; avagamaṁ: understood; dharmyaṁ: the principle of religion; susukhaṁ: very happy; kartuṁ: to execute; avyayaṁ: everlasting.

9.2 This knowledge is king of all knowledge and the most secret of all secrets. It is the purest knowledge, sacred, and because it gives direct perception of the Self by Self-realization, it is the perfection of religion, dharma. It is eternal, easy and it is very joyfully performed.

अश्रद्दधानाः पुरुषा धर्मस्यास्य परन्तप ।
अप्राप्य मां निवर्तन्ते मृत्युसंसारवर्त्मनि ॥ ९.३

aśraddadhānāḥ puruṣā dharmasyāsya parantapa |
aprāpya māṁ nivartante mṛtyu-saṁsāra-vartmani || 9.3

aśraddadhānāḥ: those who are faithless; puruṣāḥ: such persons; dharmasya: of this process of religion; asya: of it; parantapa: O killer of the enemies; aprāpya: without obtaining; māṁ: Me; nivartante: come back; mṛtyu: death; saṁsāra: material existence; vartmani: on the path of.

9.3 Those who have no faith in this knowledge cannot attain Me, O Parantapa, conqueror of foes. They will return to the path of birth and death in this material world.

मया ततमिदं सर्वं जगदव्यक्तमूर्तिना ।
मत्स्थानि सर्वभूतानि न चाहं तेष्ववस्थितः ॥ ९.४

mayā tatam idaṁ sarvam jagadavyakta mūrtinā |
matsthāni sarvabhūtāni na cahaṁ teṣv-avasthitaḥ || 9.4

mayā: by Me; tataṁ: spread; idaṁ: all these manifestations; sarvaṁ: all; jagat: cosmic manifestation; avyakta mūrtinā: unmanifested form; matsthāni: unto

Me; sarvabhūtāni: all living entities; na: not; ca: also; ahaṁ: I; teṣu: in them; avasthitaḥ: situated.

9.4 By Me, the entire Universe is pervaded in My formless form. All beings are based in Me, but I am not in them.

न च मत्स्थानि भूतानि पश्य मे योगमैश्वरम् ।
भूतभृन्न च भूतस्थो ममात्मा भूतभावनः ॥ ९.५

na ca matsthāni bhūtāni paśya me yogam aiśvaram |
bhūtabhṛnna ca bhūtastho mamātmā bhūtabhāvanaḥ || 9.5

na: never; ca: also; matsthāni: situated in Me; bhūtāni: all creations; paśya: just see; me: My; yogaṁ aiśvaraṁ: inconceivable mystic power; bhūtabhṛt: maintainer of all living entities; na: never; ca: also; bhūtasthaḥ: in the cosmic manifestation; mama: My; ātmā: Self; bhūtabhāvanaḥ: is the source of all manifestations.

9.5 And yet everything that is created does not rest in Me. Look at My mystic powers! Although, I am the Creator and Sustainer of all living entities, I do not depend the Cosmic manifestation; for My Self is the very source of all creation.

यथाकाशस्थितो नित्यं वायुः सर्वत्रगो महान् ।
तथा सर्वाणि भूतानि मत्स्थानीत्युपधारय ॥ ९.६

yathākāśasthito nityaṁ vāyuḥ sarvatrago mahān |
tathā sarvāṇi bhūtāni matsthānīty upadhāraya || 9.6

yathā: as much as; ākāśasthitaḥ: situated in space; nityaṁ: always; vāyuḥ: wind; sarvatragaḥ: blowing everywhere; mahān: mighty; tathā: similarly; sarvāṇi: everything; bhūtāni: created beings; matsthānī: situated in Me; iti: thus; upadhāraya: try to understand.

9.6 As the mighty wind, blowing everywhere, always rests in eternal space, all beings rest in Me.

सर्वभूतानि कौन्तेय प्रकृतिं यान्ति मामिकाम् ।
कल्पक्षये पुनस्तानि कल्पादौ विसृजाम्यहम् ॥ ९.७

sarvabhūtāni kaunteya prakṛtiṁ yānti māmikām |
kalpakṣaye punas tāni kalpādau visṛjāmyaham || *9.7*

sarva bhūtāni: all created entities; kaunteya: O son of Kuntī; prakṛtiṁ: nature; yānti: enter; māmikām: unto Me; kalpakṣaye: at the end of the millennium; punaḥ: again; tāni: all those; kalpādau: in the beginning of the millennium; visṛ jāmi: I create; ahaṁ: I.

9.7 O Kaunteya (son of Kuntī), at the end of every age all beings merge into Me, at the beginning of every new age I create them again.

प्रकृतिं स्वामवष्टभ्य विसृजामि पुनः पुनः ।
भूतग्राममिमं कृत्स्नमवशं प्रकृतेर्वशात् ॥ ९.८

prakṛtiṁ svāmavaṣṭabhya visṛjāmi punaḥ punaḥ |
bhūtagrāmam imaṁ kṛtsnam avaśaṁ prakṛtervaśāt || *9.8*

prakṛtiṁ: material nature; svāṁ: of My personal Self; avaṣṭabhya: enter in; visṛjāmi: create; punaḥ punaḥ: again and again; bhūta grāmaṁ: all these cosmic manifestations; imaṁ: this; kṛtsnaṁ: total; avaśaṁ: automatically; prakṛteḥ: by the force of nature; vaśāt: under obligation.

9.8 The whole Cosmic order is under Me and My material nature creates the beings again and again, and it is controlled by My material nature.

न च मां तानि कर्माणि निबध्नन्ति धनञ्जय ।
उदासीनवदासीनमसक्तं तेषु कर्मसु ॥ ९.९

na ca māṁ tāni karmāṇi nibadhnanti dhanañjaya |
udāsīna-vad āsīnam asaktaṁ teṣu karmasu || *9.9*

na: never; ca: also; māṁ: Me; tāni: all those; karmāṇi: activities; nibadhnanti:

bind; dhanañjaya: O conqueror of riches; udāsī navat: as neutral; āsīnaṁ: situated; asaktaṁ: without attraction; teṣu: in them; karmasu: in activities.

9.9 O Dhanañjaya, all this work does not bind Me. I am ever unattached from these activities, seated as though neutral.

मयाध्यक्षेण प्रकृतिः सूयते सचराचरम् ।
हेतुनानेन कौन्तेय जगद्विपरिवर्तते ॥ ९.१०

mayādhyakṣeṇa prakṛtiḥ sūyate sacarācaram |
hetunānena kaunteya jagad viparivartate || 9.10

mayā: by Me; adhyakṣeṇa: by superintendence; prakṛtiḥ: material nature; sūyate: manifests; sacarācaraṁ: with the moving and the nonmoving; hetunā: for this reason; anena: this; kaunteya: O son of Kuntī; jagat: the cosmic manifestation; viparivartate: is working.

9.10 The material nature or prakṛti works under My direction, O Kaunteya, and creates all moving and unmoving beings through My energies. By its cause, this manifestation is created and annihilated again and again.

अवजानन्ति मां मूढा मानुषीं तनुमाश्रितम् ।
परं भावमजानन्तो मम भूतमहेशरम् ॥ ९.११

avajānanti māṁ mūḍhā mānuṣīṁ tanumāśritam |
paraṁ bhāvam ajānanto mama bhūta-maheśvaram || 9.11

avajānanti: deride; māṁ: Me; mūḍhāḥ: foolish men; mānuṣīṁ: in human form; tanuṁ: body; āśritaṁ: assuming; paraṁ: transcendental; bhāvaṁ: nature; ajānantaḥ: not knowing; mama: Mine; bhūta: everything that be; maheśvaraṁ: the supreme proprietor.

9.11 Fools deride Me when I descend in the human form. They do not know My transcendental nature as the Supreme Lord [maheśavara] of the entire creation.

मोघाशा मोघकर्माणो मोघज्ञाना विचेतसः ।
राक्षसीमासुरीं चैव प्रकृतिं मोहिनीं श्रिताः ॥ ९.१२

moghāśā moghakarmāṇo moghajñānā vicetasaḥ |
rākṣasīmāsurīṁ caiva prakṛtiṁ mohinīṁ śritāḥ || 9.12

moghāśāḥ: baffled hope; moghakarmāṇaḥ: baffled in fruitive activities; mogha jñānāḥ: baffled in knowledge; vicetasaḥ: bewildered; rākṣasīṁ: demonic; āsurīṁ: atheistic; ca: and; eva: certainly; prakṛtiṁ: nature; mohinīṁ: bewildering; śritāḥ: taking shelter of.

9.12 Those who are thus deluded are demonic and atheistic. In their deluded condition, their hopes for liberation, their result oriented actions and their culture of knowledge become false and useless.

महात्मानस्तु मां पार्थ दैवीं प्रकृतिमाश्रिताः ।
भजन्त्यनन्यमनसो ज्ञात्वा भूतादिमव्ययम् ॥ ९.१३

mahātmānastu māṁ pārtha daivīṁ prakṛtimāśritāḥ |
bhajanty ananya-manaso jñātvā bhūtādim avyayam || 9.13

mahātmānaḥ: the great souls; tu: but; māṁ: unto Me; pārtha: O son of Pritha; daivīṁ: divine; prakṛtiṁ: nature; āśritāḥ: taken shelter of; bhajanti: render service; ananya manasaḥ: without deviation of the mind; jñātvā: knowing; bhūta: creation; ādiṁ: original; avyayaṁ: inexhaustible.

9.13 O Pārtha (son of Prithā), the great souls, who are not deluded, are under the protection of My Divine nature. They are fully devoted to Me with a single-pointed mind as they know Me as the origin of all creation, the unchangeable.

सततं कीर्तयन्तो मां यतन्तश्च दृढव्रताः ।
नमस्यन्तश्च मां भक्त्या नित्ययुक्ता उपासते ॥ ९.१४

satataṁ kīrtayanto māṁ yatantaśca dṛḍhavratāḥ |
namasyantaśca māṁ bhaktyā nityayuktā upāsate || 9.14

satataṁ: always; kīrtayantaḥ: chanting; māṁ: Me; yatantaḥ ca: fully endeavoring also; dṛḍha vratāḥ: with determination; namasyantah ca: offering obeisance; māṁ: unto Me; bhaktyā: in devotion; nitya yuktā: perpetually engaged; upāsate: worship.

9.14 Always chanting My names and glories, fully striving with great determination, bowing down onto Me, these great devotees of firm resolve, perpetually worship Me with devotion.

ज्ञानयज्ञेन चाप्यन्ये यजन्तो मामुपासते ।
एकत्वेन पृथक्त्वेन बहुधा विशतोमुखम् ॥ ९.१५

jñānayajñena cāpyanye yajanto māmupāsate |
ekatvena pṛthaktvena bahudhā viśvatomukham || 9.15

jñāna yajñena: by cultivation of knowledge; ca: also; api: certainly; anye: others; yajantaḥ: worshiping; māṁ: Me; upāsate: worship; ekatvena: in oneness; pṛthaktvena: in duality; bahudhā: diversity; viśvato mukhaṁ: in the universal form.

9.15 Some worship Me by acquiring and spreading wisdom of the Self [jñāna-yajña]. Others worship Me in My non-dual form in oneness, in My infinite form as many, and in My Universal form.

अहं क्रतुरहं यज्ञः स्वधाहमहमौषधम् ।
मन्त्रोऽहमहमेवाज्यमहमग्निरहं हुतम् ॥ ९.१६

ahaṁ kraturahaṁ yajñaḥ svadhāham ahamauṣadham |
mantro 'hamahamevājyaṁ aham agnir ahaṁ hutam || 9.16

ahaṁ: I; kratuḥ: ritual; ahaṁ: I; yajñaḥ: sacrifice; svadhā: oblation; ahaṁ: I; auṣadhaṁ: healing herb; mantraḥ: transcendental chant; ahaṁ: I; eva: certainly; ājyaṁ: melted butter; ahaṁ: I; agniḥ: fire; ahaṁ: I; hutaṁ: offering.

पिताहमस्य जगतो माता धाता पितामहः ।
वेद्यं पवित्रमोङ्कार ऋक्साम यजुरेव च ॥ ९.१७

pitāhamasya jagato mātā dhātā pitāmahaḥ |
vedyaṁ pavitram oṁkāra ṛksāma yajureva ca || 9.17

pitā: father; ahaṁ: I; asya: of this; jagataḥ: of the universe; mātā: mother; dhātā: supporter; pitāmahaḥ: grandfather; vedyaṁ: what is to be known; pavitraṁ: that which purifies; oṁkāraḥ: the syllable om; ṛk: the Rig Veda; sāma: the Sama Veda; yajuḥ: the Yajur Veda; eva: certainly; ca: and

गतिर्भर्ता प्रभुः साक्षी निवासः शरणं सुहृत् ।
प्रभवः प्रलयः स्थानं निधानं बीजमव्ययम् ॥ ९.१८

gatirbhartā prabhuḥ sākṣī nivāsaḥ śaraṇaṁ suhṛt |
prabhavaḥ pralayaḥ sthānaṁ nidhānaṁ bījamavyayam || I 9.18

gatiḥ: goal; bhartā: sustainer; prabhuḥ: Lord; sākṣī: witness; nivāsaḥ: abode; śaraṇaṁ: refuge; suhṛt: most intimate friend; prabhavaḥ: creation; pralayaḥ: dissolution; sthānaṁ: ground; nidhānaṁ: resting place; bījaṁ: seed; avyayaṁ: imperishable.

तपाम्यहमहं वर्षं निगृह्णाम्युत्सृजामि च ।
अमृतं चैव मृत्युश्च सदसच्चाहमर्जुन ॥ ९.१९

tapāmy aham ahaṁ varṣaṁ nigṛhṇāmy utsṛjāmi ca |
amṛtaṁ caiva mṛtyuśca sadasac cāham arjuna || 9.19

tapāmi: give heat; ahaṁ: I; ahaṁ: I; varṣaṁ: rain; nigṛhṇāmi: withhold; utsṛjāmi: send forth; ca: and; amṛtaṁ: immortality; ca: and; eva: certainly; mṛtyuḥ: death; ca: and; sat: being; asat: nonbeing; ca: and; ahaṁ: I; arjuna: O Arjuna.

9.16, 17, 18, 19 I am the ritual, I am the sacrifice, I am the offering, I am the herb, I am the mantra, I am the clarified butter, I am the fire, and I am the oblation. I am the supporter of the universe, the father, the mother, and the grandfather. I am the object of knowledge, the sacred syllable "OM", and also the Ṛg, the Yajur, and the Sāma Vedas. I am the goal, the supporter, the Lord, the witness, the abode, the refuge, the friend, the origin, the dissolution, the foundation, the substratum, and the immutable seed. I give heat. I send, as well as withhold, the rain. I am immortality, as well as death. I am also both the Eternal and the temporal, O Arjuna.

त्रैविद्या मां सोमपाः पूतपापा
यज्ञैरिष्ट्वा स्वर्गतिं प्रार्थयन्ते ।
ते पुण्यमासाद्य सुरेन्द्रलोक-
मश्नन्ति दिव्यान्दिवि देवभोगान् ॥ ९.२०

traividyā māṁ somapāḥ pūtapāpā
yajñairiṣṭvā svargatiṁ prārthayante |
te puṇyam āsādya surendra-lokam
aśnanti divyāndivi devabhogān || 9.20

traividyāḥ: the knowers of the three Vedas; māṁ: unto Me; somapāḥ: drinkers of soma juice; pūta: purified; pāpāḥ: sins; yajñaiḥ: with sacrifices; iṣṭvā: after worshiping; svargatiṁ: passage to heaven; prārthayante: pray; te: they; puṇyaṁ: virtue; āsādya: enjoying; surendra: of Indra; lokaṁ: the world; aśnanti: enjoy; divyān: celestial; divi: in heaven; devabhogān: pleasures of the gods.

9.20 Those who practice the vedic rituals and drink the soma juice worship Me indirectly seeking the heavenly pleasures. They go to heaven and enjoy sensual delights.

ते तं भुक्त्वा स्वर्गलोकं विशालं
क्षीणे पुण्ये मर्त्यलोकं विशन्ति।
एवं त्रयीधर्ममनुप्रपन्ना
गतागतं कामकामा लभन्ते ॥ ९.२१

te taṁ bhuktvā svargalokaṁ viśālaṁ
kṣīṇe puṇye martyalokaṁ viśanti |
evaṁ trayīdharmam anuprapannā

gatāgataṁ kāmakāmā labhante || 9.21

te: they; taṁ: that; bhuktvā: enjoying; svargalokaṁ: heaven; viśālaṁ: vast; kṣīṇe: being exhausted; puṇye: merits; martya lokaṁ: mortal earth; viśanti: fall down; evaṁ: thus; trayī: three Vedas; dharmaṁ: doctrines; anuprapannāḥ: following; gatāgataṁ: death and birth; kāma kāmāḥ: desiring sense enjoyments; labhante: attain

9.21 Once they have thus enjoyed heavenly sense pleasure, they are reborn on this planet again. By practicing vedic rituals as result oriented actions, they are bound by the cycle of birth and death.

अनन्याश्चिन्तयन्तो मां ये जनाः पर्युपासते ।
तेषां नित्याभियुक्तानां योगक्षेमं वहाम्यहम् ॥ ९.२२

ananyāścintayanto māṁ ye janāḥ paryupāsate |
teṣāṁ nityābhiyuktānāṁ yogakṣemaṁ vahāmy aham || 9.22

ananyāḥ: no other; cintayantaḥ: concentrating; māṁ: unto Me; ye: who; janāḥ: persons; paryupāsate: properly worship; teṣāṁ: their; nityābhiyuktānāṁ: always fixed in devotion; yogakṣemaṁ: requirements; vahāmi: carry; ahaṁ: I.

9.22 When you reside in My consciousness, always fixed in undivided remembrance, whatever you lack I give [yoga]. And whatever you have, I preserve [kṣema].

येऽप्यन्यदेवता भक्ता यजन्ते श्रद्धयान्विताः ।
तेऽपि मामेव कौन्तेय यजन्त्यविधिपूर्वकम् ॥ ९.२३

ye'pyanyadevatā bhaktā yajante śraddhayā'nvitāḥ |
te'pi mām eva kaunteya yajanty avidhipūrvakam || 9.23

ye: those; api: also; anya: other; devatāḥ: demigods; bhaktāḥ: devotees; yajante: worship; śraddhayā anvitāḥ: with faith; te: they; api: also; māṁ: Me; eva: even; kaunteya: O son of Kuntī; yajanti: sacrifice; avidhi pūrvakaṁ: in an improper manner.

9.23 Even those who worship other deities, they too worship Me, O Kaunteya (son of Kuntī), but without true understanding.

अहं हि सर्वयज्ञानां भोक्ता च प्रभुरेव च ।
न तु मामभिजानन्ति तत्त्वेनातश्च्यवन्ति ते ॥ ९.२४

ahaṁ hi sarvayajñānāṁ bhoktā ca prabhureva ca |
na tu mām abhijānanti tattvenātaścyavanti te || 9.24

ahaṁ: I; hi: surely; sarva: of all; yajñānāṁ: sacrifices; bhoktā: enjoyer; ca: and; prabhuḥ: Lord; eva: also; ca: and; na: not; tu: but; māṁ: Me; abhijānanti: know; tattvena: in reality; atah: therefore; cyavanti: fall down; te: they

9.24 I am the only enjoyer [bhokta] and the only Lord [prabhu] of all sacrifices. Those who do not recognize My true transcendental nature are born again and again.

यान्ति देवव्रता देवान्पितृन्यान्ति पितृव्रताः ।
भूतानि यान्ति भूतेज्या यान्ति मद्याजिनोपि माम् ॥ ९.२५

yānti devavratā devān pitṛān yānti pitṛ vratāḥ |
bhūtāni yānti bhūtejyā yānti madyājino'pi mām || 9.25

yānti: achieve; deva vratāḥ: worshipers of demigods; devān: to demigods; pitṛĀn: to ancestors; yānti: go; pitṛ vratāḥ: worshipers of the ancestors; bhūtāni: to ghosts and spirits; yānti: go; bhūtejyāḥ: worshippers of ghosts and spirits; yānti: go; mad: My; yājinaḥ: devotees; api: also; māṁ: unto Me.

9.25 Those who worship the deities will take birth among the deities; those who worship ghosts and spirits will take birth among such beings; those who worship ancestors go to the ancestors; those who worship Me will live with Me.

पत्रं पुष्पं फलं तोयं यो मे भक्त्या प्रयच्छति ।
तदहं भक्त्युपहृतमश्नामि प्रयतात्मनः ॥ ९.२६

patraṁ puṣpaṁ phalaṁ toyaṁ yo me bhaktyā prayacchati |
tad ahaṁ bhakty-upahṛtam aśnāmi prayatātmanaḥ || 9.26

patraṁ: a leaf; puṣpaṁ: a flower; phalaṁ: a fruit; toyaṁ: water; yaḥ: whoever; me: unto Me; bhaktyā: with devotion; prayacchati: offers; tat: that; ahaṁ: I; bhaktyupahṛtaṁ: offered in devotion; aśnāmi: accept; prayatātmanaḥ: of one in pure consciousness.

9.26 Whoever offers Me with love and devotion a leaf, a flower, fruit or water, I will accept and consume what is offered by the pure-hearted.

यत्करोषि यदश्नासि यज्जुहोषि ददासि यत् ।
यत्तपस्यसि कौन्तेय तत्कुरुष्व मदर्पणम् ॥ ९.२७

yat karoṣi yad aśnāsi yaj juhoṣi dadāsi yat |
yat tapasyasi kaunteya tat kuruṣva madarpaṇam || 9.27

yat: whatever; karoṣi: you do; yat: whatever; aśnāsi: you eat; yat: whatever; juhoṣi: you offer; dadāsi: you give away; yat: whatever; tapasyasi: austerities you perform; kaunteya: O son of Kuntī; tat: that; kuruṣva: make; mat: unto Me; arpaṇaṁ: offering.

9.27 O Kaunteya (son of Kuntī), all that you do, all that you eat, all that you offer and give away, as well as all austerities that you may perform, give them as an offering to Me.

शुभाशुभफलैरेवं मोक्ष्यसे कर्मबन्धनैः ।
संन्यासयोगयुक्तात्मा विमुक्तो मामुपैष्यसि ॥ ९.२८

śubhāśubha-phalair evaṁ mokṣyase karma-bandhanaiḥ |
sannyāsa-yoga-yuktātmā vimukto māmupaiṣyasi || 9.28

śubha: good; aśubha: evil; phalaiḥ: results; evaṁ: thus; mokṣyase: free; karma: action; bandhanaiḥ: bondage; sannyāsa: of renunciation; yoga: the yoga; yuktātmā: having the mind firmly set on; vimuktaḥ: liberated; māṁ: to Me; upaiṣyasi: you will attain.

9.28 You will be freed from all reactions to good and evil deeds by this renunciation, You will be liberated and come to Me.

समोऽहं सर्वभूतेषु न मे द्वेष्योऽस्ति न प्रिय: ।
ये भजन्ति तु मां भक्त्या मयि ते तेषु चाप्यहम् ॥ ९.२९

samo'haṁ sarvabhūteṣu na me dveṣyo'sti na priyaḥ |
ye bhajanti tu māṁ bhaktyā mayi te teṣu cā'pyaham || 9.29

samaḥ: equally disposed; ahaṁ: I; sarva bhūteṣu: to all living entities; na: no ne; me: Mine; dveṣyaḥ: hateful; asti: is; na: nor; priyaḥ: dear; ye: those; bhajanti: render transcendental service; tu: yet; māṁ: unto Me; bhaktyā: in devotion; mayi: unto Me; te: such persons; teṣu: in them; ca: also; api: certainly; ahaṁ: I.

9.29 I am equal to all beings. No one to Me is hateful or dear. But, whoever worships, offers enriching service onto Me in devotion, is in Me and I am also indeed in him.

अपि चेत्सुदुराचारो भजते मामनन्यभाक् ।
साधुरेव स मन्तव्य: सम्यग्व्यवसितो हि स: ॥ ९.३०

api cet sudurācāro bhajate māmananyabhāk |
sādhureva sa mantavyaḥ samyag vyavasito hi saḥ || 9.30

api: in spite of; cet: although; sudurācāraḥ: one committing the most abominable actions; bhajate: engaged in devotional service; māṁ: unto Me; ananyabhāk: without deviation; sādhuḥ: saint; eva: certainly; saḥ: he; mantavyaḥ: to be considered; samyak: completely; vyavasitaḥ: situated; hi: certainly; saḥ: he.

9.30 Even if the most sinful person engages himself in devotional service, He is to be considered saintly because he is properly situated in his determination.

क्षिप्रं भवति धर्मात्मा शेशच्छान्तिं निगच्छति ।
कौन्तेय प्रतिजानीहि न मे भक्त: प्रणश्यति ॥ ९.३१

kṣipraṁ bhavati dharmātmā śaśvacchāntiṁ nigacchati |
kaunteya pratijānīhi na me bhaktaḥ praṇaśyati || 9.31

kṣipraṁ: very soon; bhavati: becomes; dharmātmā: righteous; śaśvat śāntiṁ: lasting peace; nigacchati: attains; kaunteya: O son of Kuntī; pratijānīhi: justly declare; na: never; me: Mine; bhaktaḥ: devotees; praṇaśyati: perishes.

9.31 He quickly becomes righteous and attains lasting peace. O Kaunteya (son of Kuntī), declare it boldly that My devotee never perishes.

मां हि पार्थ व्यपाश्रित्य येऽपि स्युः पापयोनयः ।
स्त्रियो वैश्यास्तथा शूद्रास्तेऽपि यान्ति परां गतिम् ॥ ९.३२

mām hi pārtha vyapāśritya ye'pi syuḥ pāpayonayaḥ |
striyo vaiśyāstathā śūdrās te'pi yānti parāṁ gatim || 9.32

māṁ: unto Me; hi: certainly; pārtha: O son of Pṛtha; vyapāśritya: particularly taking shelter; ye: anyone; api: also; syuḥ: becomes; pāpayonayaḥ: born of a lower family; striyaḥ: women; vaiśyāḥ: mercantile people; tathā: also; śūdrāḥ: people considered low-born; te api: even they; yānti: go; parāṁ: supreme; gatiṁ: destination.

9.32 O Pārtha (son of Prithā), anyone who takes shelter in Me, women, traders, workers or even sinners can approach the Supreme destination.

किं पुनर्ब्राह्मणाः पुण्या भक्ता राजर्षयस्तथा ।
अनित्यमसुखं लोकमिमं प्राप्य भजस्व माम् ॥ ९.३३

kiṁ punar brāhmaṇāḥ puṇyā bhaktā rājarṣayas tathā |
anityam asukhaṁ lokam imaṁ prāpya bhajasva mām || 9.33

kiṁ: how much; punaḥ: again; brāhmaṇāḥ: brahmanas; puṇyāḥ: righteous; bhaktāḥ: devotees; rājarṣayaḥ: saintly kings; tathā: also; anityaṁ: temporary; asukhaṁ: sorrowful; lokaṁ: planet; imaṁ: this; prāpya: gaining; bhajasva: are engaged in loving service; māṁ: unto Me.

9.33 How easier then it is for the learned, the righteous, the devotees and saintly kings who in this temporary miserable world engage in loving service unto Me.

मन्मना भव मद्भक्तो मद्याजी मां नमस्कुरु ।
मामेवैष्यसि युक्त्वैवमात्मानं मत्परायणः ॥ ९.३४

manmanā bhava madbhakto madyājī māṁ namaskuru |
māmevaiṣyasi yuktvaivam ātmānaṁ matparāyaṇaḥ || 9.34

manmanāḥ: always thinking of Me; bhava: become; mad: My; bhaktaḥ: devotee; madyājī: My worshiper; māṁ: unto Me; namaskuru: offer obeisances; māṁ: unto Me; eva: completely; eṣyasi: come; yuktvā evaṁ: being absorbed; ātmānaṁ: your soul; matparāyaṇaḥ: devoted to Me.

9.34 Fix your mind on Me, be devoted to Me, worship Me, and bow down to Me. Thus, uniting yourself with Me by setting Me as the supreme goal and the sole refuge, you shall certainly come to Me.

इति श्रीमद्भगवद्गीतासूपनिषत्सु ब्रह्मविद्यायां योगशास्त्रे
श्रीकृष्णार्जुनसंवादे राजविद्याराजगुह्ययोगो नाम नवमोऽध्यायः ॥

iti śrīmad bhagavadgītāsūpaniṣatsu brahmavidyāyām
yogaśāstre śrīkṛṣṇārjuna saṁvāde rājavidyā rājaguhyayogo nāma
navamo'dhyāyaḥ ||

In the ***Upaniṣad*** of ***Śrimad Bhagavad Gītā***, the scripture of yoga dealing with ***Brahmavidyā Yogaśāstra,*** the science of Brahman, the Supreme Absolute, in the form of ***Śrī Kṛṣṇārjuna saṁvād,*** dialogue between Śrī Kṛṣṇa and Arjuna, this is the ninth chapter named, ***Rājavidyā Rājaguhya Yogaḥ,*** *'The Yoga of Supreme Knowledge and Supreme Secret.'*

CHAPTER

10

अथ दशमोऽध्यायः

विभूतियोगः

Vibhūti Yogaḥ

श्री भगवानुवाच ।

भूय एव महाबाहो शृणु मे परमं वचः ।
यत्तेऽहं प्रीयमाणाय वक्ष्यामि हितकाम्यया ॥१

śrībhagavānuvāca

bhūya eva mahābāho śṛṇu me paramaṁ vacaḥ /
yatte'haṁ prīyamāṇāya vakṣyāmi hitakāmyayā // 10.1

śrī bhagavān uvāca: Lord Kṛṣṇa says; bhūyaḥ: again; eva: surely; mahābāho: mighty-armed; śṛṇu: hear; me: My; paramaṁ: supreme; vacaḥ: words; yat: that which; te: to you; ahaṁ: I; prīyamāṇāya: dear to Me; vakṣyāmi: say; hita-kāmyayā: with the desire for your benefit.

10.1 Lord Kṛṣṇa says: Listen carefully again, Oh mighty-armed Arjuna! Because you are My dear friend, I shall speak further on the Supreme knowledge for your welfare.

न मे विदुः सुरगणाः प्रभवं न महर्षयः ।
अहमादिर्हि देवानां महर्षीणां च सर्वशः ॥ २

na me viduḥ suragaṇāḥ prabhavaṁ na maharṣayaḥ /
ahamādirhi devānāṁ maharṣīṇāṁ ca sarvaśaḥ // 10.2

na: not; me: My; viduḥ: know; suragaṇāḥ: demigods; prabhavaṁ: glories; na: not; maharṣayaḥ: great sages; ahaṁ: I; ādiḥ: origin; hi: certainly; devānāṁ: of the gods; maharṣīṇāṁ: of the great sages; ca: and; sarvaśaḥ: in all respects.

10.2 Neither the hosts of deities nor the great sages know My origin, My opulence. I am the source of the deities and the sages.

यो मामजमनादिं च वेत्ति लोकमहेशरम् ।
असंमूढः स मर्त्येषु सर्वपापैः प्रमुच्यते ॥ ३

yo māmajamanādiṁ ca vetti lokamaheśvaram /
asaṁmūḍhaḥ sa martyeṣu sarvapāpaiḥ pramucyate // *10.3*

yo: who; mām: to Me; ajaṁ: unborn; anādiṁ: without beginning; ca: and; vetti: know; loka: worlds; maheśvaram: supreme lord; asaṁmūḍhaḥ: without doubt; sa: he; martyeṣu: mortal; sarva: all; pāpaiḥ: sins; pramucyate: delivered.

10.3 He who knows Me as the unborn, without beginning, and supreme Lord of all the worlds, Only he, who has this clarity, is wise and freed from all bondage.

बुद्धिर्ज्ञानमसम्मोहः क्षमा सत्यं दमः शमः ।
सुखं दुःखं भवोऽभावो भयं चाभयमेव च ॥ ४

buddhirjñānam asaṁmohaḥ kṣamā satyaṁ damaḥ śamaḥ /
sukhaṁ duḥkhaṁ bhavo 'bhāvo bhayaṁ cābhayameva ca // *10.4*

buddhih: intelligence; jñānam: knowledge; asaṁmohaḥ: free from doubt; kṣamā: forgiveness; satyaṁ: truthfulness; damaḥ: control of senses; śamaḥ: control of mind; sukhaṁ: happiness; duḥkhaṁ: distress; bhavo 'bhāvo: birth and death; bhayaṁ: fear; cā: and; abhayaṁ: fearlessness; eva: also; ca: and

अहिंसा समता तुष्टिस्तपो दानं यशोऽयशः ।
भवन्ति भावा भूतानां मत्त एव पृथग्विधाः ॥ ५

ahiṁsā samatā tuṣṭis tapo dānaṁ yaśo 'yaśaḥ /

bhavanti bhāvā bhūtānāṁ matta eva pṛthagvidhāḥ || 10.5

ahiṁsā: non-violence; samatā: equanimity; tuṣṭis: satisfaction; tapo: austerity; dānaṁ: charity; yaśo: fame; ayaśaḥ: infamy; bhavanti: become; bhāvā: nature; bhūtānāṁ: living beings; matta: from me; eva: surely; pṛthagvidhāḥ: in various forms

10.4,5 Intelligence, knowledge, freedom from doubt and delusion, forgiveness, truthfulness, control of the senses, control of the mind, happiness, distress, birth, death, fear, fearlessness, non-violence, equanimity, satisfaction, austerity, charity, fame and infamy, all these various qualities of living beings are created by Me alone.

महर्षयः सप्त पूर्वे चत्वारो मनवस्तथा।
मद्भावा मानसा जाता येषां लोक इमाः प्रजाः ॥ ६

maharṣayaḥ sapta pūrve catvāro manavastathā |
madbhāvā mānasā jātā yeṣāṁ loka imāḥ prajāḥ || 10.6

maharṣayaḥ: great sages; sapta: seven; pūrve: before; catvāro: four; manavas: Manus; tathā: and; madbhāvā: endowed with My power; mānasā: from the mind; jātā: born; yeṣāṁ: of them; loka: worlds; imāḥ: all this; prajāḥ: living beings.

10.6 The seven great sages and before them, the four great Manus, endowed with My power, They arose from My mind and all the living beings populating the planet descend from them.

एतां विभूतिं योगं च मम यो वेत्ति तत्त्वतः ।
सोऽविकम्पेन योगेन युज्यते नात्र संशयः ॥ ७

etāṁ vibhūtiṁ yogaṁ ca mama yo vetti tattvataḥ |
so 'vikampena yogena yujyate nātra saṁśayaḥ || 10.7

etāṁ: all this; vibhūtiṁ: glory; yogaṁ: powers; ca: and; mama: My; yo: who; vetti: knows; ta tvataḥ: truth; so: he; 'vikampena: without distraction; yogena:

in yoga; yujyate: engaged; nā: not; atra: here; saṁśayaḥ: doubt.

10.7 He who knows all this glory and powers of mine, truly, he is fully united in Me; Of that there is no doubt.

अहं सर्वस्य प्रभवो मत्तः सर्वं प्रवर्तते ।
इति मत्वा भजन्ते मां बुधा भावसमन्विताः ॥ ८

ahaṁ sarvasya prabhavo mattaḥ sarvaṁ pravartate /
iti matvā bhajante māṁ budhā bhāvasamanvitāḥ // 10.8

ahaṁ: I; sarvasya: all; prabhavo; source; mattaḥ: from Me; sarvaṁ: all; pravartate: emanates; iti: thus; matvā: knowing; bhajante: pray; māṁ: to Me; budhā: wise; bhāvasamanvitāḥ: surrender

10.8 I am the source of all the spiritual and material worlds. Everything arises from Me. The wise who know this are devoted to Me and surrender their heart to Me.

मच्चित्ता मद्गतप्राणा बोधयन्तः परस्परम् ।
कथयन्तश्च मां नित्यं तुष्यन्ति च रमन्ति च ॥ ९

maccittā madgataprāṇā bodhayantaḥ parasparam /
kathayantaśca māṁ nityaṁ tuṣyanti ca ramanti ca // 10.9

maccittā: with mind engaged in Me; madgataprāṇā: lives absorbed in Me; bodhayantaḥ: enlightening; parasparam: one another; kathayantaḥ: talkin about My glories; ca: and; māṁ: about Me; nityaṁ: always; tuṣyanti: satisfied; ca: and; ramanti: enjoy bliss; ca: and

10.9 With mind and lives absorbed on Me, always enlightening one another and talking about My glories, the wise are content and blissful.

तेषां सततयुक्तानां भजतां प्रीतिपूर्वकम् ।
ददामि बुद्धियोगं तं येन मामुपयान्ति ते ॥ १०

teṣāṁ satatayuktānāṁ bhajatāṁ prītipūrvakam |
dadāmi buddhiyogaṁ taṁ yena māmupayānti te || 10.10

teṣāṁ: to them; satatayuktānāṁ: always engaged; bhajatāṁ: praying; prītipūrvakam: with love; dadāmi: I give; buddhiyogaṁ: intelligence; taṁ: that; yena: by which; mām: to Me; upayānti: come; te: they

10.10 To those who are always engaged in Me with love, I give them enlightenment by which they come to Me.

तेषामेवानुकम्पार्थमहमज्ञानजं तमः ।
नाशयाम्यात्मभावस्थो ज्ञानदीपेन भास्वता ॥ ११

teṣāṁ evānukampārtham aham ajñānajaṁ tamaḥ |
nāśayāmy ātma-bhāvastho jñānadīpena bhāsvatā || 10.11

teṣāṁ: to them; evā: also; anukampārtham: out of compassion; aham: I; ajñānajaṁ: born of ignorance; tamaḥ: darkness; nāśayāmi: destroy; ātma: within; bhāvasthaḥ: themselves; jñānadīpena: lamp of knowledge; bhāsvatā: shining

10.11 Out of compassion to them, I destroy the darkness born out of their ignorance by the shining lamp of knowledge.

अर्जुन उवाच
परं ब्रह्म परं धाम पवित्रं परमं भवान् ।
पुरुषं शोशतं दिव्यमादिदेवमजं विभुम् ॥ १२

arjuna uvāca
paraṁ brahma paraṁ dhāma pavitraṁ paramaṁ bhavān |
puruṣaṁ śāśvataṁ divyam ādidevamajaṁ vibhum || 10.12

Arjuna uvāca: Arjuna says; paraṁ: supreme; brahman: truth; paraṁ: supreme; dhāma: light; pavitraṁ: pure; paramaṁ: supreme; bhavān: yourself; puruṣaṁ: person; śāśvataṁ: original; divyam: godly; ādidevam: original god; ajaṁ: unborn; vibhum: glorious

10.12 Arjuna says: You are the supreme truth, supreme sustenance, supremely purifier, the primal, eternal and glorious Lord.

आहुस्त्वामृषयः सर्वे देवर्षिर्नारदस्तथा ।
असितो देवलो व्यासः स्वयं चैव ब्रवीषि मे ॥ १३

āhustvāmṛṣayaḥ sarve devarṣirnāradastathā /
asito devalo vyāsaḥ svayaṁ caiva bravīṣi me // 10.13

āhuh: say; tvām: to you; ṛṣayaḥ: sages; sarve: all; devarṣiḥ: sage of gods; nāradaḥ: Nārada; tathā: and; asitaḥ: Asita; devalaḥ: Devala; vyāsaḥ: Vyāsa; svayaṁ: personally; ca: and; eva: surely; bravīṣi: explain; me: to me

10.13 All the sages like Nārada, Asita, Devala, and Vyāsa have explained this. Now you are personally explaining to me.

सर्वमेतदृतं मन्ये यन्मां वदसि केशव ।
न हि ते भगवन्व्यक्तिं विदुर्देवा न दानवाः ॥ १४

sarvametadṛtaṁ manye yanmāṁ vadasi keśava /
na hi te bhagavanvyaktiṁ vidurdevā na dānavāḥ // 10.14

sarvam: all; etad: these; ṛtaṁ: truths; manye: accept; yan: which; māṁ: to me; vadasi: say; keśava: Keshava; na: not; hi: surely; te: your; bhagavan: lord; vyaktiṁ : express; viduḥ: know; devā: gods; na: nor; dānavāḥ: demons

10.14 Oh Keśava, I accept all these truths that You have told me. Oh Lord, neither he gods nor the demons know You.

स्वयमेवात्मनात्मानं वेत्थ त्वं पुरुषोत्तम ।
भूतभावन भूतेश देवदेव जगत्पते ॥ १५

svayamevātmanātmānaṁ vettha tvaṁ puruṣottama /
bhūtabhāvana bhūteśa devadeva jagatpate // 10.15

svayam: own; evā: surely; atmanā: by yourself; atmānaṁ: yourself; vettha: know; tvaṁ: you; puruṣottama: perfect man; bhūtabhāvana: origin of beings; bhūteśa: lord of beings; devadeva: god of gods; jagatpate: lord of the world

10.15 Surely, You alone know Yourself by Yourself, Oh Perfect One, the origin of beings, Oh Lord of beings, Oh God of gods, Oh Lord of the world.

वक्तुमर्हस्यशेषेण दिव्या ह्यात्मविभूतयः ।
याभिर्विभूतिभिर्लोकानिमांस्त्वं व्याप्य तिष्ठसि ॥ १६

vaktumarhasyaśeṣeṇa divyā hyātmavibhūtayaḥ /
yābhirvibhūtibhirlokān imāṁstvaṁ vyāpya tiṣṭhasi // 10.16

vaktum: say; arhasi: deserve; aśeṣeṇa: in detail; divyā: divine; hi: surely; ātma: Your; vibhūtayaḥ: glories; yābhir: by which; vibhūtibhiḥ: glories; lokān: worlds; imān: these; tvaṁ: You; vyāpya: pervade; tiṣṭhasi: remain

10.16 Only You can describe in detail Your divine glories by which You pervade this universe.

कथं विद्यामहं योगिंस्त्वां सदा परिचिन्तयन् ।
केषु केषु च भावेषु चिन्त्योऽसि भगवन्मया ॥ १७

kathaṁ vidyāmahaṁ yogiṁs tvāṁ sadā paricintayan /
keṣu keṣu ca bhāveṣu cintyo'si bhagavanmayā // 10.17

kathaṁ: how; vidyām: know; ahaṁ: I; yogins: yogi; tvāṁ: you; sadā: always; paricintayan: contemplation; keṣu-keṣu: in which; ca: and; bhāveṣu: nature; cintyo'si: contemplated; bhagavan: lord; mayā: by me

10.17 How may I know You by contemplation? In which forms should I contemplate on You, Oh Lord?

विस्तरेणात्मनो योगं विभूतिं च जनार्दन ।
भूयः कथय तृप्तिर्हि शृण्वतो नास्ति मेऽमृतम् ॥ १८

vistareṇātmano yogaṁ vibhūtiṁ ca janārdana /
bhūyaḥ kathaya tṛptirhi śṛṇvato nāsti me'mṛtam // 10.18

vistareṇā: in detail; atmano: of Yourself; yogaṁ: powers; vibhūtiṁ: glories; ca: and; janārdana: Janārdana; bhūyaḥ: again; kathaya: say; tṛptiḥ: satisfaction; hi:

surely; śṛṇvato: hear; nā: not; asti: is; me: my; amṛtam: nectar

10.18 Tell me in detail of your powers and glories, Oh Janārdana. Again, please tell for my satisfaction as I do not tire of hearing your sweet words.

श्री भगवानुवाच ।
हन्त ते कथयिष्यामि दिव्या ह्यात्मविभूतय: ।
प्राधान्यत: कुरुश्रेष्ठ नास्त्यन्तो विस्तरस्य मे ॥ १९

śrībhagavānuvāca
hanta te kathayiṣyāmi divyā hyātmavibhūtayaḥ /
prādhānyataḥ kuruśreṣṭha nāstyanto vistarasya me // 10.19

śrī bhagavān uvāca: The Lord says; hanta: yes; te: to you; kathayiṣyāmi: I will talk; divyā: divine; hi: surely; ātma: My; vibhūtayaḥ: glories; prādhānyataḥ: main; kuruśreṣtha: great among the Kurus; na: not; asti: there; antaḥ: end; vistarasya: detail; me: My

10.19 Kṛṣṇa says, 'Yes, Oh kuruśreṣtha, I will talk to you surely of My divine glories; but only of the main ones as there is no end to the details of My glories.

अहमात्मा गुडाकेश सर्वभूताशयस्थित: ।
अहमादिश्च मध्यं च भूतानामन्त एव च ॥ २०।

ahamātmā guḍākeśa sarvabhūtāśayasthitaḥ /
ahamādiśca madhyaṁ ca bhūtānāmanta eva ca // 10.20

aham: I; ātmā: soul; guḍākeśa: Arjuna; sarva: all; bhūtā: living beings; aśayasthitaḥ: situated in; aham: I; ādiḥ: beginning; ca: and; madhyaṁ: middle; ca: and; bhūtānām: of living beings; anta: end; eva: also; ca: and

10.20 I am the Spirit, Oh Guḍākeśā, situated in all living beings. I am surely the beginning, middle and end of all beings.

आदित्यानामहं विष्णुर्ज्योतिषां रविरंशुमान् ।
मरीचिर्मरुतामस्मि नक्षत्राणामहं शशी ॥ २१

ādityānāmahaṁ viṣṇur jyotiṣāṁ raviraṁśumān |
marīcirmarutāmasmi nakṣatrāṇāmahaṁ śaśī || 10.21

ādityānām: of the Ādityas; ahaṁ: I; viṣṇuḥ: Viṣṇu; jyotiṣāṁ: of the luminaries; raviḥ : the sun; aṁśumān: bright; marīciḥ: Marīcī; marutām: of the Maruts; asmi: am; nakṣatrāṇāṁ: of the Nakṣatras; ahaṁ: I; śaśī: the moon

10.21 Of the Ādityas, I am Viṣṇu. Of the luminaries, I am the bright sun. Of the Maruts, I am Marīcī. Of the Nakṣatras, I am the moon.

वेदानां सामवेदोऽस्मि देवानामस्मि वासवः ।
इन्द्रियाणां मनश्चास्मि भूतानामस्मि चेतना ॥ २२

vedānāṁ sāmavedo'smi devānāmasmi vāsavaḥ |
indriyāṇāṁ manaścāsmi bhūtānāmasmi cetanā || 10.22

vedānāṁ: of the Vedas; sāmavedaḥ: Sāma Veda; asmi: I am; devānām: of the gods; asmi: I am; vāsavaḥ: Vasava; indriyāṇāṁ: of the senses; manaḥ: mind; ca: and; asmi: I am; bhūtānām: of living beings; asmi: I am; cetanā: consciousness

10.22 Of the Vedas, I am the Sāma Veda. Of the gods, I am Indra. Of the senses, I am the mind and in living beings, I am the consciousness.

रुद्राणां शङ्करश्चास्मि वित्तेशो यक्षरक्षसाम् ।
वसूनां पावकश्चास्मि मेरुः शिखरिणामहम् ॥ २३

rudrāṇāṁ śaṅkaraścāsmi vitteśo yakṣarakṣasām |
vasūnāṁ pāvakaścāsmi meruḥ śikhariṇāmaham || 10.23

rudrāṇāṁ: of the rudras; śaṅkaraḥ: Shankara; ca: and; asmi: I am; vitteśaḥ: god of wealth; yakṣa: demigods; rakṣasām: demons; vasūnāṁ: of the Vasus; pāvakaḥ: fire; ca: and; asmi: I am; meruḥ: Meru; śikhariṇām: of the peaks; aham: I

10.23 Of the Rudras, I am Sankara and of the Yakṣas and Rākṣasas, I am Kubera, god of wealth. Of the Vasus, I am fire and of the peaks, I am Meru.

पुरोधसां च मुख्यं मां विद्धि पार्थ बृहस्पतिम् ।
सेनानीनामहं स्कन्दः सरसामस्मि सागरः ॥ २४

purodhasāṁ ca mukhyaṁ māṁ viddhi pārtha bṛhaspatim /
senānīnāmahaṁ skandaḥ sarasāmasmi sāgaraḥ // 10.24

purodhasāṁ: of the priests; ca: and; mukhyaṁ: main; māṁ: Me; viddhi: understand; pārtha: Pārtha; bṛhaspatim: Brihaspati; senānīnām: of the warriors; ahaṁ: I am; skandaḥ: Skanda; sarasām: of the water bodies; asmi: I am; sāgaraḥ: the ocean

10.24 Of the priests, understand, O Pārtha, that I am the chief Brihaspati. Of the warriors, I am Skanda. Of the water bodies, I am the ocean.

महर्षीणां भृगुरहं गिरामस्म्येकमक्षरम् ।
यज्ञानां जपयज्ञोऽस्मि स्थावराणां हिमालयः ॥ २५

maharṣīṇāṁ bhṛgurahaṁ girāmasmyekamakṣaram /
yajñānāṁ japayajño'smi sthāvarāṇāṁ himālayaḥ // 10.25

maharṣīṇāṁ: of the great sages; bhṛguḥ: Bhrigu; ahaṁ: I; girām: of the vibrations; asmi: I am; ekam akṣaram: single letter (Om); yajñānāṁ: of the yajnas (sacrifices); japayagñaḥ: chanting of holy names; asmi: I am; sthāvarāṇāṁ: of the immovables; himālayaḥ: Himalayas

10.25 Of the great sages, I am Bhrigu. Of the vibrations, I am the OM. Of the sacrifices, I am the chanting of holy names. Of the immovable objects, I am the Himālayas.

अश्वत्थः सर्ववृक्षाणां देवर्षीणां च नारदः ।
गन्धर्वाणां चित्ररथः सिद्धानां कपिलो मुनिः ॥ २६

aśvatthaḥ sarvavṛkṣāṇāṁ devarṣīṇāṁ ca nāradaḥ |
gandharvāṇāṁ citrarathaḥ siddhānāṁ kapilo muniḥ || 10.26

aśvatthaḥ: banyan tree; sarva: all; vṛkṣāṇām: of the trees; devarṣīṇāṁ: of the sages of the gods; ca: and; nāradaḥ: Nārada; gandharvāṇāṁ: of the Gandharvas; citrarathaḥ: Chitraratha; siddhānāṁ: of the Siddhas; kapilaḥ: Kapila; muniḥ: sage

10.26 Of all the trees, I am the Banyan tree and of all the sages of the gods, I am Nārada. Of the Gandharvas, I am Chitraratha. Of the realized souls, I am the sage Kapila.

उच्चैःश्रवसमेशानां विद्धि माममृतोद्भवम् ।
ऐरावतं गजेन्द्राणां नराणां च नराधिपम् ॥ २७

uccaiḥśravas amaśvānāṁ viddhi mām amṛtodbhavam |
airāvataṁ gajendrāṇāṁ narāṇāṁ ca narādhipam || 10.27

uccaiḥśravasaṁ: Ucchaishravas; aśvānāṁ: of the horses; viddhi: know; māṁ: Me; amṛtodbhavam: Born of nectar produced from the churning of the ocean; airāvataṁ: Airavata; gajendrāṇāṁ: of the elephants; narāṇāṁ: of men; ca: and; narādhipam: king

10.27 Of the horses, know me to be Ucchaiṣravas born of the nectar generated from the churning of the ocean; Of the elephants, Airāvata and of men, the king.

आयुधानामहं वज्रं धेनूनामस्मि कामधुक् ।
प्रजनश्चास्मि कन्दर्पः सर्पाणामस्मि वासुकिः ॥ २८

āyudhānāmahaṁ vajraṁ dhenūnāmasmi kāmadhuk |
prajanaścāsmi kandarpaḥ sarpāṇāmasmi vāsukiḥ || 10.28

āyudhānām: of the weapons; ahaṁ: I am; vajraṁ: thunderbolt; dhenūnām: of the cows; asmi: I am; kāmadhuk: Kamadhenu; prajanaḥ: for begetting children; cā: and; asmi: I am; kandarpaḥ: god of love; sarpāṇāṁ: of the snakes; asmi: I am; vāsukiḥ: Vasuki

10.28 Of the weapons, I am the thunderbolt. Of the cows, I am Kamadhenu; For begetting children, I am the god of love. Of the snakes, I am Vasuki.

अनन्तश्चास्मि नागानां वरुणो यादसामहम् ।
पितॄणामर्यमा चास्मि यमः संयमतामहम् ॥ २९

anantaścāsmi nāgānāṁ varuṇo yādasām aham /
pitṛṇāmaryamā cāsmi yamaḥ saṁyamatāmaham // 10.29

anantaḥ: Ananta; ca: and; asmi: I am; nāgānāṁ: of the serpents; varuṇaḥ: Varuṇa; yādasām: of the water deities; aham: I am; pitṛṇām: of the ancestors; aryamā: Aryama; ca: and; asmi: I am; yamaḥ: Yama; saṁyamatām: of the ones who ensure discipline; aham: I

10.29 Of the serpents, I am Ananta. Of the water deities, I am Varuṇa. Of the ancestors, I am Aryama and of the ones who ensure discipline, I am Yama.

प्रह्लादश्चास्मि दैत्यानां कालः कलयतामहम् ।
मृगाणां च मृगेन्द्रोऽहं वैनतेयश्च पक्षिणाम् ॥ ३०

prahlādaścāsmi daityānāṁ kālaḥ kalayatāmaham /
mṛgāṇāṁ ca mṛgendro'haṁ vainateyaśca pakṣiṇām // 10.30

prahlādaḥ: Prahlada; ca: and; asmi: I am; daityānāṁ: of the Daityas; kālaḥ: time; kalayatām: of the subduers; aham: I; mṛgāṇāṁ: of the animals; ca: and; mṛgendraḥ: king of animals; ahaṁ: I; vainateyaḥ: Garuda; ca: and; pakṣiṇām: of the bird

10.30 Of the Daitya (demons), I am Prahlad and of the reckoners, I am time. Of the animals, I am the king of animals (lion) and of the birds, I am Garuda.

पवनः पवतामस्मि रामः शस्त्रभृतामहम् ।
झषाणां मकरश्चास्मि स्रोतसामस्मि जाह्नवी ॥ ३१

pavanaḥ pavatāmasmi rāmaḥ śastrabhṛtāmaham |
jhaṣāṇāṁ makaraścāsmi srotasāmasmi jānhavī || 10.31

pavanaḥ: wind; pavatāṁ: that which purifies; asmi: I am; rāmaḥ: Rama; śastrabhṛitām: wielders of weapons; ahaṁ: I; jhaṣāṇāṁ: of the water beings; makaraḥ : fish; cā: and; asmi: I am; srotasām: of the flowing rivers; asmi: I am; jānhavī: Jahnavi (Ganga)

10.31 Of the purifiers, I am the wind. Of the wielders of weapons, I am Rāma. Of the water beings, I am the shark and of the flowing rivers, I am Jahnavi (Gaṅgā).

सर्गाणामादिरन्तश्च मध्यं चैवाहमर्जुन ।।
अध्यात्मविद्या विद्यानां वादः प्रवदतामहम् ।। ३२

sargāṇāmādirantaśca madhyaṁ caivāhamarjuna |
adhyātmavidyā vidyānāṁ vādaḥ pravadatāmaham || 10.32

sargāṇāṁ: of all creations; ādiḥ: beginning; antaḥ: end; ca: and; madhyaṁ: middle; ca: and; eva: surely; aham: I; arjuna: Arjuna; adhyātmavidyā: spiritual knowledge; vidyānāṁ: of all knowledge; vādaḥ: logic; pravadatām: of arguments; aham: I

10.32 Of all creations, I am surely the beginning and end and the middle, O Arjuna. Of all knowledge, I am the spiritual knowledge of the Self. Of all arguments, I am the logic.

अक्षराणामकारोऽस्मि द्वन्द्वः सामासिकस्य च ।
अहमेवाक्षयः कालो धाताहं विशतोमुखः ।। ३३

akṣarāṇāmakāro'smi dvandvaḥ sāmāsikasya ca |
ahaṁevākṣayaḥ kālo dhātāhaṁ viśvatomukhaḥ || 10.33

akṣarāṇām: of the letters; akāraḥ: The letter A; asmi: I am; dvandvaḥ: of the dual words; sāmāsikasya: compounds; ca: and; ahaṁ: I; evā: surely; akṣayaḥ: never-ending; kālo: time; dhātā: creator; ahaṁ: I; viśvatomukhaḥ: faces facing the world (Brahma)

10.33 Of the letters, I am the 'A'. Of the dual words, I am the compounds and surely I am the never-ending time. I am the Omniscient who sees everything.

मृत्यु: सर्वहरश्चाहं उद्भवश्च भविष्यताम् ।
कीर्ति: श्रीर्वाक्च नारीणां स्मृतिर्मेधा धृति: क्षमा ॥ ३४

mṛtyuḥ sarva-haraś cāham udbhavaśca bhaviṣyatāï /
kīrtiḥ śrīrvākca nāriṇāṁ smṛtirmedhā dhṛtiḥ kṣamā // 10.34

mṛtyuḥ: death; sarvaharaḥ: all-devouring; ca: and; aham: I; udbhavaḥ: creation; ca: and; bhaviṣyatāï: of the future; kīrtiḥ: fame; śrīr vāk: wealth of words; ca: and; nāriṇāṁ: of the feminine; smṛtiḥ: memory; medhā: intelligence; dhṛtiḥ: faithfulness; kṣamā: patience

10.34 I am the all-devouring death and I am the creator of all things of the future. Of the feminine, I am fame, fortune, beautiful speech, memory, intelligence, faithfulness and patience.

बृहत्साम तथा साम्नां गायत्री छन्दसामहम् ।
मासानां मार्गशीर्षोऽहं ऋतूनां कुसुमाकर: ॥ ३५

bṛhatsāma tathā sāmnāṁ gāyatrī chandasām aham /
māsānāṁ mārgaśīrṣo'ham ṛtūnāṁ kusumākaraḥ // 10.35

bṛhatsāma: Bṛhat Sāma; tathā: and; sāmnāṁ: of the Sāma Veda; gāyatri: Gāyatrī; chandasām: of all poetry; aham: I; māsānāṁ: of the months; mārgaśīrṣaḥ: Mārgaśīrṣa; aham: I; ṛtūnāṁ: of the seasons; kusumākaraḥ: spring

10.35 Of the Sāma Veda hymns, I am the Bṛhat Sāma and of all poetry, I am the Gāyatrī. Of the months, I am Mārgaśīrṣa and of the seasons, I am Spring.

द्यूतं छलयतामस्मि तेजस्तेजस्विनामहम् ।
जयोऽस्मि व्यवसायोऽस्मि सत्त्वं सत्त्ववतामहम् ॥ ३६

dyūtaṁ chalayatām asmi tejas tejasvinām aham /
jayo'smi vyavasāyo'smi sattvaṁ sattvavatām aham // 10.36

dyūtaṁ: gambling; chalayatām: of all cheating; asmi: I am; tejaḥ: effulgence; tejasvinām: of all the effulgent things; aham: I; jayaḥ: victory; asmi: I am; vyavasāyaḥ: of all adventure; asmi: I am; sattvaṁ: the satvic nature; sattvavatām: of those who are tranquil; aham: I

10.36 Of all the cheating, I am Gambling. Of the effulgent things, I am the Effulgence. I am Victory, I am Effort, I am the Goodness (sattva) of those who are with satva (good) quality.

वृष्णीनां वासुदेवोऽस्मि पाण्डवानां धनञ्जयः ।
मुनीनामप्यहं व्यासः कवीनामुशना कविः ॥ ३७

vṛṣṇīnāṁ vāsudevo'smi pāṇḍavānāṁ dhanañjayaḥ /
munīnāmapyahaṁ vyāsaḥ kavīnāmuśanā kaviḥ // *10.37*

vṛṣṇīnāṁ: of the Vṛṣṇis; vāsudevaḥ: Vāsudeva; asmi: I am; pāṇḍavānāṁ: of the Pāṇḍavas; dhanañjayaḥ: Dhanañjaya; munīnām: of the sages; api: also; ahaṁ: I; vyāsaḥ: Vyāsa; kavīnām: of the thinkers; uśanā: Uśāna; kaviḥ: seer

10.37 Of the descendants of Vṛṣṇi, I am Vāsudeva Kṛṣṇa. Of the Pāṇḍavas, I am Arjuna. Of the sages, I am also Vyāsa and of the seer, I am Uśāna.

दण्डो दमयतामस्मि नीतिरस्मि जिगीषताम् ।
मौनं चैवास्मि गुह्यानां ज्ञानं ज्ञानवतामहम् ॥ ३८।

daṇḍo damayatām asmi nītirasmi jigīṣatām /
maunaṁ caivāsmi guhyānāṁ jñānaṁ jñānavatāmaham // *10.38*

daṇḍaḥ: rod of punishment; damayatām: of all punishments; asmi: I am; nītiḥ: morality; asmi: I am; jigīṣatām: of the victorious; maunaṁ: silence; ca: and; evā: also; asmi: I am; guhyānāṁ: of the secrets; jñānaṁ: knowledge; jñānavatāṁ: of the wise; aham: I

10.38 Of rulers, I am their Sceptre. Of the victorious, I am Statesmanship. Of all secrets, I am also Silence. Of the wise, I am Wisdom.

यच्चापि सर्वभूतानां बीजं तदहमर्जुन ।
न तदस्ति विना यत्स्यान्मया भूतं चराचरम् ॥ ३९॥

yaccāpi sarvabhūtānāṁ bījaṁ tadahamarjuna |
na tadasti vinā yat syān mayā bhūtaṁ carācaram || 10.39

yat: what; cā: and; api: also; sarva: all; bhūtānāṁ: beings; bījaṁ: seed; tat: that; aham: I; arjuna: Arjuna; na: not; tat: that; asti: is; vinā: without; yat: that; syān: exists; mayā: by Me; bhūtaṁ: created; cara: moving; acaram: unmoving

10.39 Also, of whatever beings exist, I am the seed, O Arjuna. There is nothing that exists without Me in all creations, moving and unmoving.

नान्तोऽस्ति मम दिव्यानां विभूतीनां परन्तप ।
एष तूद्देशतः प्रोक्तो विभूतेर्विस्तरो मया ॥ ४०॥

nānto'sti mama divyānāṁ vibhūtīnāṁ parantapa |
eṣa tūddeśataḥ prokto vibhūtervistaro mayā || 10.40

na: not; antaḥ: end; asti: is; mama: My; divyānāṁ: divine; vibhūtīnāṁ: glories; parantapa: Supreme Lord; eṣa: all this; tu: that; uddeśataḥ: examples; proktaḥ: says; vibhūteḥ: glories; vistaraḥ: detailed; mayā: by Me

10.40 There is no end to My Divine glories, Oh Parantapa. What have been says by Me are examples of My detailed glories.

यद्यद्विभूतिमत्सत्त्वं श्रीमदूर्जितमेव वा ।
तत्तदेवावगच्छ त्वं मम तेजोंशसंभवम् ॥ ४१

yad yad vibhūtimat sattvaṁ śrīmad ūrjitameva vā |
tat tad evā'vagaccha tvaṁ mama tejoṁśa saṁbhavam || 10.41

yad-yad: whatever; vibhūtimat: glorious; sattvaṁ: existence; śrīmad: beautiful; ūrjitam: glorious; eva: also; vā: or; tat-tad: all that; eva: surely; avagaccha: you should know; tvaṁ: you; mama: My; tejaḥ: splendour; aṁśa: part; saṁbhavam: born of

10.41 You should know that whatever glories exist or whatever beautiful and glorious exists, all that surely is born of just a portion of My splendour.

अथवा बहुनैतेन किं ज्ञातेन तवार्जुन ।
विष्टभ्याहमिदं कृत्स्नमेकांशेन स्थितो जगत् ॥ ४२

athavā bahunaitena kiṁ jñātena tavārjuna |
viṣṭabhyāhamidaṁ kṛtsnam ekāṁśena sthito jagat || 10.42

athavā: or; bahunā: many; etena: of this kind; kiṁ: what; jñātena: know; tava: you; arjuna: Arjuna; viṣṭabhya: full; aham: I; idaṁ: this; kṛtsnam: of all manifestations; eka: one; amśena: part; sthito: situated; jagat: world

10.42 Of what use is to know about the many manifestations of this kind, O Arjuna? I pervade this entire world with just a part of Myself.

इति श्रीमद्भगवद्गीतासूपनिषत्सु ब्रह्मविद्यायां योगशास्त्रे
श्रीकृष्णार्जुनसंवादे विभूतियोगो नाम दशमोऽध्यायः ॥

iti śrīmad bhagavadgītāsūpaniṣatsu brahmavidyāyām
yogaśāstre śrīkṛṣṇārjuna saṁvāde vibhūtiyogo nāma
daśamo'dhyāyaḥ ||

In the ***Upaniṣad*** of ***Śrimad Bhagavad Gitā***, the scripture of yoga dealing with ***Brahmavidyā Yogaśāstra,*** the science of Brahman, the Supreme Absolute, in the form of ***Śrī Kṛṣṇārjuna saṁvād,*** dialogue between Śrī Kṛṣṇa and Arjuna, this is the tenth chapter named ***Vibhūti Yogaḥ,*** *'The Yoga of Divine Manifestations.'*

CHAPTER

11

अथ एकादशोऽध्यायः

विश्वरूपदर्शनयोगः

Viśvarūpa Darśan Yogaḥ

अर्जुन उवाच

मदनुग्रहाय परमं गुह्यमध्यात्मसंज्ञितम्।

यत्त्वयोक्तं वचस्तेन मोहोऽयं विगतो मम ॥ १

arjuna uvāca

madanugrahāya paramaṁ guhyaṁ adhyātma-saṁjñitam /

yat tvayoktaṁ vacas tena moho'yaṁ vigato mama // 11.1

Arjuna uvāca: Arjuna says; madanugrahāya: out of compassion for me; paramaṁ: supreme; guhyaṁ: confidential; adhyātma: spiritual; saṁjñitam: in the matter of; yat: what; tvayā: by You; uktaṁ: says; vacaḥ: words; tena: by that; mohaḥ: delusion; ayaṁ: this; vigataḥ: removed; mama: my

11.1 Arjuna says: 'O Lord! By listening to Your wisdom on the supreme secret of Existence and your glory, I feel that my delusion has disappeared.'

भवाप्ययौ हि भूतानां श्रुतौ विस्तरशो मया ।

त्वत्तः कमलपत्राक्ष माहात्म्यमपि चाव्ययम्॥ २

bhavāpyayau hi bhūtānāṁ śrutau vistaraśo mayā /

tvattaḥ kamalapatrākṣa māhātmyamapi cāvyayam // 11.2

bhava: creation; apyayau: dissolution; hi: certainly; bhūtānāṁ: of all living entities; śrutau: have heard; vistaraśaḥ: detail; mayā: by me; tvattaḥ: from You; kamalapatrākṣa: O lotus-eyed one; māhātmyam: glories; api: also; cā: and; avyayam: inexhaustible

11.2 O Lotus-eyed Kṛṣṇa! I have listened from You in detail about the creation and destruction of all living beings, also Your inexhaustible greatness.

एवमेतद्यथात्थ त्वमात्मानं परमेशर।
द्रष्टुमिच्छामि ते रूपमैशरं पुरुषोत्तम ॥ ३

evaṁetadyathāttha tvam ātmānaṁ parameśvara /
draṣṭumicchāmi te rūpam aiśvaraṁ puruṣottama // 11.3

evaṁ: thus; etat: this; yathā: as it is; āttha: have spoken; tvaṁ: You; ātmānaṁ: the soul; parameśvara: the Supreme Lord; draṣṭuṁ: to see; icchāmi: I wish; te: You; rūpaṁ: form; aiśvaraṁ: divine; puruṣottama: best of manifested forms

11. O Parameśvara, Lord Supreme, though You are here before Me as You have declared Yourself, I wish to see the Divine Cosmic Form of Yours, Puruṣottama, Supreme Being.

मन्यसे यदि तच्छक्यं मया द्रष्टुमिति प्रभो।
योगेशर ततो मे त्वं दर्शयात्मानमव्ययम् ॥ ४

manyase yadi tacchakyaṁ mayā draṣṭumiti prabho /
yogeśvara tato me tvaṁ darśayātmānamavyayam // 11.4

manyase: You think; yadi: if; tat: that; śakyaṁ: able; mayā: by me; draṣṭum: to see; iti: thus; prabho: O Lord; yogeśvara: O Lord of all mystic power; tataḥ: then; me: unto me; tvaṁ: You; darśaya: show; ātmānaṁ: Yourself; avyayaṁ: imperishable

11.4 O Prabhu, my Lord, if You think it is possible for me to see Your Cosmic Form, then please, O Yogeśvara, Lord of Yoga and all mystic power, kindly show me that Imperishable Universal Self.

श्री भगवानुवाच
पश्य मे पार्थ रूपाणि शतशोऽथ सहस्रशः।
नानाविधानि दिव्यानि नानावर्णाकृतीनि च ॥ ५॥

śrībhagavānuvāca
paśya me pārtha rūpāṇi śataśo'tha sahasraśaḥ I
nānāvidhāni divyāni nānāvarṇākṛtīni ca II 11.5

śrī bhagavān uvāca: Kṛṣṇa says; paśya: behold; me: Mine; pārtha: arjuna; rūpāṇi: forms; śataśaḥ: hundreds; atha: also; sahasraśaḥ: thousands; nānāvidhāni: of different nature; divyāni: divine; nānā: various; varṇa: colors; ākṛtīni: shapes; ca: also

11.5 Bhagavān says: O My dear Pārtha, behold now My hundreds and thousands of forms, of infinite divine sorts, of infinite colors and shapes.

पश्यादित्यान्वसून्रुद्रानश्विनौ मरुतस्तथा।
बहून्यदृष्टपूर्वाणि पश्याश्चर्याणि भारत॥ ६

paśyādityān vasūn rudrān aśvinau marutastathā I
bahūny adṛṣṭa-pūrvāṇi paśyāścaryāṇi bhārata II 11.6

paśya: see; adityān: the twelve sons of Aditi; vasūn: the eight Vasus; rudrān: the eleven forms of Rudra; aśvinau: the two Aśvinis; marutaḥ: the forty-nine Maruts (wind deities); tathā: also; bahūni: many; adṛṣṭa: that you have never seen; pūrvāṇi: before; paśya: see; āścaryāṇi: wonderful; bhārata: O best of the Bhāratas

11.6 O Bhārata, see here the different manifestations of the Ādityas, the Vasus, the Rudras, the Aśvins, the Māruts and all other gods. Behold the many wonderful forms which noone has ever seen before.

इहैकस्थं जगत्कृत्स्नं पश्याद्य सचराचरम् ।
मम देहे गुडाकेश यच्चान्यद्द्रष्टुमिच्छसि ॥ ७

ihaikasthaṁ jagat kṛtsnaṁ paśyādya sacarācaram |
mama dehe guḍākeśa yac cānyad draṣṭumicchasi || 11.7

iha: in this; ekasthaṁ: situated in one; jagat: the universe; kṛtsnaṁ: whole; paśya: see; adya: now; sa: with; carā: moving; acaram: not moving; mama: My; dehe: in this body; guḍākeśa: O Arjuna; yat: that; ca: also; anyat: other; draṣṭum: to see; icchasi: you like

11.7 O Arjuna, see at once now in this body of Mine, the whole Universe completely in this one place, all the moving and the unmoving, and see everything else you desire to see also.

न तु मां शक्यसे द्रष्टुमनेनैव स्वचक्षुषा ।
दिव्यं ददामि ते चक्षुः पश्य मे योगमैशरम् ॥ ८

na tu māṁ śakyase draṣṭum anenaiva svacakṣuṣā |
divyaṁ dadāmi te cakṣuḥ paśya me yogamaiśvaram || 11.8

na: never; tu: but; māṁ: Me; śakyase: able; draṣṭum: to see; anena: by this; eva: certainly; svacakṣuṣā: with your own eyes; divyaṁ: divine; dadāmi: I give; te: to you; cakṣuḥ: eyes; paśya: see; me: My; yogam aiśvaram: divine powers

11.8 But you cannot see Me with your own physical eyes. Let Me give you the Divine eye; Behold My Divine power and opulence!

सञ्जय उवाच
एवमुक्त्वा ततो राजन्महायोगेशरो हरिः ।
दर्शयामास पार्थाय परमं रूपमैशरम ॥ ९

sañjaya uvāca
evamuktvā tato rājan mahāyogeśvaro hariḥ |
darśayāmāsa pārthāya paramaṁ rūpamaiśvaram || 11.9

Sañjaya uvāca: Sañjaya said; evam: thus; uktvā: having says; tataḥ: thereafter; rājan: O King; mahāyogeśvaraḥ: the great Lord of Yoga; hariḥ: Kṛṣṇa; darśayāmāsa: showed; pārthāya: to Arjuna; paramaṁ: divine; rūpam: form; aiśvaram: opulences

11.9 Sañjaya said: O King, having spoken thus, the great Lord of Yoga, Mahā Yogeśvara Hari (Kṛṣṇa), showed to Arjuna His supreme Cosmic form.

अनेकवक्त्रनयनमनेकाद्भुतदर्शनम्।
अनेकदिव्याभरणं दिव्यानेकोद्यतायुधम्॥ १०

aneka-vaktra-nayanam anekādbhuta darśanam /
aneka-divyābharaṇaṁ divyānekodyatāyudham // 11.10

aneka: various; vaktra: mouths; nayanam: eyes; aneka: various; adbhuta: wonderful; darśanam: sights; aneka: many; divya: divine; ābharaṇaṁ: ornaments; divya: divine; aneka: various; udyata: uplifted; āyudham: weapons

11.10 Infinite mouths and eyes, with infinite wonderful sights, infinite divine ornaments, with numerous divine weapons uplifted.

दिव्यमाल्याम्बरधरं दिव्यगन्धानुलेपनम्।
सर्वाश्चर्यमयं देवमनन्तं विशतोमुखम्॥ ११

divya-mālyāmbara-dharaṁ divya-gandhānulepanam /
sarvāścarya-mayaṁ devam anantaṁ viśvatomukham // 11.11

divya: divine; mālya: garlands; ambaradharaṁ: covered with the dresses; divya: divine; gandha: fragrance; anulepanam: smeared; sarva: all; aścaryamayaṁ: wonderful; devaṁ: shining; anantaṁ: endless; viśvatomukham: with faces on all sides

11.11 Arjuna saw this Universal form wearing divine garlands and clothing, anointed with celestial fragrances, wonderful, resplendent, endless, with faces on all sides.

दिवि सूर्यसहस्रस्य भवेद्युगपदुत्थिता।
यदि भा: सदृशी सा स्याद्भासस्तस्य महात्मनः॥ १२

divi sūryasahasrasya bhaved yugapad utthitā |
yadi bhāḥ sadṛśī sā syād bhāsastasya mahātmanaḥ || 11.12

divi: in the sky; sūrya: sun; sahasrasya: of many thousands; bhaved: there were; yugapad: simultaneously; utthitā: present; yadi: if; bhāḥ: splendor; sadṛśī: like; sā: that; syād: may be; bhāsaḥ: effulgence; tasya: there is; mahātmanaḥ: of the great Lord

11.12 If the splendor of a thousand suns were to blaze all together in the sky, it would be like the splendor of that mighty Being.

तत्रैकस्थं जगत्कृत्स्नं प्रविभक्तमनेकधा।
अपश्यद्देवदेवस्य शरीरे पाण्डवस्तदा॥ १३

tatraikasthaṁ jagat kṛtsnaṁ pravibhaktamanekadhā |
apaśyad devadevasya śarīre pāṇḍavastadā || 11.13

tatra: there; ekasthaṁ: in one place; jagat: universe; kṛtsnaṁ: completely; pravibhaktam: divided in; anekadhā: many groups; apaśyat: saw; devadevasya: God of gods; śarīre: in the body; pāṇḍavaḥ: Arjuna; tadā: at that time

11.13 There, in the body of the God of gods, the Pāṇḍava then saw the whole universe resting in one, with all its infinite parts.

ततः स विस्मयाविष्टो हृष्टरोमा धनञ्जयः।
प्रणम्य शिरसा देवं कृताञ्जलिरभाषत॥ १४

tataḥ sa vismayāviṣṭo hṛṣṭaromā dhanañjayaḥ |
praṇamya śirasā devaṁ kṛtāñjalirabhāṣata || 11.14

tataḥ: thereafter; saḥ: he; vismayāviṣṭaḥ: being overwhelmed with wonder; hṛṣṭaromā: with his bodily hair standing on end; dhanañjayaḥ: Arjuna; praṇamya: offering obeisances; śirasā: with the head; devaṁ: to God; kṛtāñjaliḥ:

with folded palms; abhāṣata: says

11.14 Dhanañjaya, filled with wonder, his hair standing on end, then bowed his head to the God and spoke with joined palms.

अर्जुन उवाच।
पश्यामि देवांस्तव देव देहे
सर्वांस्तथा भूतविशेषसङ्घान्।
ब्रह्माणमीशं कमलासनस्थम्
ऋषींश्च सर्वानुरगांश्च दिव्यान्॥ १५

arjuna uvāca
paśyāmi devāṁstava deva dehe
sarvāṁstathā bhūta-viśeṣa-saṅghān /
brahmāṇam īśaṁ kamalāsana-sthaṁ
ṛṣīṁś ca sarvān uragāṁśca divyān // 11.15

arjuna uvāca: Arjuna says; paśyāmi: I see; devān: all the gods; tava: Your; deva: O Lord; dehe: in the body; sarvān: all; tathā: also; bhūta: living entities; viśeṣa saṅghān: specifically assembled; brahmāṇam: Brahma; īśaṁ: Lord; kamalāsanastham: sitting on the lotus flower; ṛṣin: great sages; ca: also; sarvān: all; uragān: serpents; ca: also; divyān: divine

11.15 Arjuna says; O God, I see all the gods in Your body and many types of beings. Brahma, the Lord of creation seated on the lotus, all the sages and celestial serpents.

अनेक बाहूदरवक्त्रनेत्रं
पश्यामि त्वां सर्वतोऽनन्तरूपम् ।
नान्तं न मध्यं न पुनस्तवादिं
पश्यामि विशेशर विशरूप॥ १६

aneka-bāhūdara-vaktranetraṁ
paśyāmi tvām sarvato'nantarūpam /

nāntaṁ na madhyaṁ na punastavādiṁ
paśyāmi viśveśvara viśvarūpa || *11.16*

aneka: many; bāhu: arms; udara: bellies; vaktra: mouths; netraṁ: eyes; paśyāmi: I see; tvām: unto You; sarvataḥ: from all sides; anantarūpam: endless form; nā 'ntaṁ: there is no end; na madhyaṁ: there is no middle; na punaḥ: nor again; tava: Your; ādiṁ: beginning; paśyāmi: I see; viśveśvara: O Lord of the universe; viśvarūpa: in the form of the universe

11.16 I see Your infinite form on every side, with many arms, stomachs, mouths and eyes; Neither the end, nor the middle nor the beginning do I see, O Lord of the Universe, O cosmic form.

किरीटिनं गदिनं चक्रिणं च
तेजोराशिं सर्वतो दीप्तिमन्तम्।
पश्यामि त्वां दुर्निरीक्ष्यं समन्ता-
द्दीप्तानलार्कद्युतिमप्रमेयम्॥ १७

kirīṭinaṁ gadinaṁ cakriṇaṁ ca
tejorāśiṁ sarvato dīptimantam |
paśyāmi tvāṁ durnirīkṣyaṁ samantād
dīptānalārka-dyutim-aprameyam || *11 .17*

kirīṭinaṁ: with helmets; gadinaṁ: with maces; cakriṇaṁ: with discs; ca: and; tejorāśiṁ: radiance; sarvataḥ: all sides; dīptimantam: glowing; paśyāmi: I see; tvāṁ: You; durnirīkṣyaṁ: difficult to see; samantāt: spreading; dīptānala: blazing fire; arka: sun; dyutiṁ: sunshine; aprameyam: immeasurable

11.17 I see You with crown, club and discus; a mass of radiance shining everywhere, difficult to look at, blazing all round like the burning fire and sun in infinite brilliance.

त्वमक्षरं परमं वेदितव्यं
त्वमस्य विशस्य परं निधानम्।
त्वमव्यय: शोशतधर्मगोप्ता
सनातनस्त्वं पुरुषो मतो मे॥ १८

tvamakṣaraṁ paramaṁ veditavyaṁ
tvamasya viśvasya paraṁ nidhānam |
tvamavyayaḥ śāśvata-dharma-goptā
sanātanastvaṁ puruṣo mato me || 11.18

tvaṁ: You; akṣaraṁ: inexhaustible; paramaṁ: supreme; veditavyaṁ: to be understood; tvaṁ: You; asya: of this; viśvasya: of the universe; paraṁ: supreme; nidhānam: basis; tvaṁ: You are; avyayaḥ: inexhaustible; śāśvata dharma goptā: maintainer of the eternal religion; sanātanaḥ: eternal; tvaṁ: You; puruṣaḥ: supreme personality; mato me: is my opinion

11.18 You are the imperishable; the supreme being worthy to be known. You are the great treasure house of this Universe. You are the imperishable protector of the eternal order. I believe You are the eternal being.

अनादिमध्यान्तमनन्तवीर्यं
अनन्तबाहुं शशिसूर्यनेत्रम्।
पश्यामि त्वां दीप्तहुताशवक्त्रं
स्वतेजसा विशमिदं तपन्तम्॥ १९

anādi-madhyāntam ananta-vīryam
ananta-bāhuṁ śaśisūrya netram |
paśyāmi tvāṁ dīpta-hutāśavaktraṁ
svatejasā viśvam idaṁ tapantam || 11.19

anādi: without beginning; madhya: middle; antaṁ: end; ananta: unlimited; vīryaṁ: glorious; ananta: unlimited; bāhuṁ: arms; śaśi: moon; sūrya: sun;

netram: eyes; paśyāmi: I see; tvāṁ: You; dīpta: blazing; hutāśa vaktraṁ: fire coming out of Your mouth; svatejasā: by Your; viśvam: this universe; idaṁ: this; tapantaṁ: scortching

11.19 I see you without a beginning, middle or end, infinite in power and many arms, The sun and the moon being Your eyes, the blazing fire your mouth, the whole universe scorched by Your radiance.

द्यावापृथिव्योरिदमन्तरं हि
व्याप्तं त्वयैकेन दिशश्च सर्वाः।
दृष्ट्वाद्भुतं रूपमुग्रं तवेदं
लोकत्रयं प्रव्यथितं महात्मन्॥ २०

dyāvāpṛthivyor idam antaraṁ hi
vyāptaṁ tvayaikena diśaśca sarvāḥ I
dṛṣṭvādbhutaṁ rūpamugraṁ tavedaṁ
lokatrayaṁ pravyathitaṁ mahātman II 11.20

dyāvā: in outer space; pṛthivyoḥ: of the earth; idaṁ: this; antaraṁ: unlimited; hi: certainly; vyāptaṁ: pervaded; tvaya : by You; ekena: by one; diśaḥ: directions; ca: and; sarvāḥ: all; dṛṣṭvā: by seeing; adbhutaṁ: wonderful; rūpaṁ: form; ugraṁ: terrible; tava: Your; idaṁ: this; loka: three world; trayaṁ: three; pravyathitaṁ: perturbed; mahātman: O great one

11.20 This space between earth and the heavens and everything is filled by You alone O great Being, having seen Your wonderful and terrible form, the three worlds tremble with fear.

अमी हि त्वां सुरसङ्घा विशन्ति
केचिद्भीताः प्राञ्जलयो गृणन्ति।
स्वस्तीत्युक्तवा महर्षिसिद्धसङ्घाः
स्तुवन्ति त्वां स्तुतिभिः पुष्कलाभिः॥ २१

amī hi tvāṁ surasaṅghā viśanti
kecidbhītāḥ prāñjalayo gṛṇanti |
svastī tyuktvā maharṣisiddhasaṅghāḥ
stuvanti tvāṁ stutibhiḥ puṣkalābhiḥ || 11.21

amī: all those; hi: certainly; tvāṁ: unto You; surasaṁghā: groups of celestials; viśanti: entering; kecit: some of them; bhītāḥ: out of fear; prāñjalayaḥ: with folded hands; gṛṇanti: offering prayers unto; svastī: all peace; iti: thus; uktvā: speaking like that; maharṣi: great sages; siddhasaṁghāḥ: realized sages; stuvanti: singing hymns; tvāṁ: unto You; stutibhiḥ: with hymns; puṣkalābhiḥ: sublime

11.21 Many celestials enter into You; some praise You in fear with folded hands; many great masters and sages hail and adore you.

रुद्रादित्या वसवो ये च साध्या
विश्वेऽश्विनौ मरुतश्चोष्मपाश्च ।
गन्धर्वयक्षासुरसिद्धसङ्घा
वीक्षन्ते त्वां विस्मिताश्चैव सर्वे ॥ २२

rudrādityā vasavo ye ca sādhyā
viśve'śvinau marutaś coṣmapāśca |
gandha-rvayakṣāsura siddhasaṅghā
vīkṣante tvaṁ vismitāś caiva sarve || 11.22

rudra: manifestations of Lord Śiva; ādityāḥ: the Āditya; vasavaḥ: the Vasu; ye: all those; ca: and; sādhyāḥ: the Sādhyā; viśve: the Visvedeva; aśvinau: the aśvini-kumāra; marutaḥ: the Marut; ca: and; ūṣmapāḥ: the forefathers; ca: and; gandharva: of the Gandharva; yakṣa: the Yakṣa; asura siddha: the demons and the perfected demigods; saṅghāḥ: assemblies; vīkṣante: are seeing; tvāṁ: You; vismitāḥ: in wonder; ca: also; eva: certainly; sarve: all

11.22 The Rudra, Āditya, Vasu, Sādhyā, Viśvedeva, aśvin, Marut, Ūṣmapa and a host of Gandharva, yakṣa, Asura and Sidhha are all looking at You in amazement.

रूपं महत्ते बहुवक्त्रनेत्रं
महाबाहो बहुबाहुरुपादम् ।
बहूदरं बहुदंष्ट्राकरालं दृष्ट्वा
लोकाः प्रव्यथितास्तथाहम् ॥ २३

rūpaṁ mahatte bahuvaktranetraṁ
mahābāho bahubāhūrupādam /
bahūdaraṁ bahu-daṁṣṭrā-karālaṁ dṛṣṭvā
lokāḥ pravyathitās tathāham // *11.23*

rūpaṁ: form; mahat: very great; te: of You; bahu: many; vaktra: faces; netraṁ: eyes; mahābāho: O mighty-armed one; bahu: many; bāhu: arms; ūru: thighs; pādam : legs; bahūdaraṁ: many bellies; bahu daṁṣṭrā: many teeth; karālaṁ: horrible; dṛṣṭvā: seeing; lokāḥ: all the world; pravyathitāḥ: perturbed; tathā: similarly; aham: I

11.23 Having seen Your immeasurable form with many mouths and eyes, with many arms, thighs and feet, with many stomachs and frightening tusks, O mighty-armed, the worlds are terrified and so am I.

नभःस्पृशं दीप्तमनेकवर्णं
व्यात्ताननं दीप्तविशालनेत्रम् ।
दृष्ट्वा हि त्वां प्रव्यथितान्तरात्मा
धृतिं न विन्दामि शमं च विष्णो ॥ २४

nabhaḥspṛśaṁ dīptamanekavarṇaṁ
vyāttānanaṁ dīptaviśāla netram /
dṛṣṭvā hi tvāṁ pravyathitāntarātmā
dhṛtiṁ na vindāmi śamaṁ ca viṣṇo // *11.24*

nabhaḥ spṛśaṁ: touching the sky; dīptaṁ: glowing; aneka: many; varṇaṁ: color; vyāttā: open; ānanaṁ: mouth; dīpta: shining; viśāla: very great; netraṁ: eyes; dṛṣṭvā : by seeing; hi: certainly; tvāṁ: You; pravyathita: perturbed; antarātmā: soul; dhṛtiṁ: steadiness; na: no; vindāmi: find; śamaṁ: peace; ca: also; viṣṇo: O Lord Viṣṇu

11.24 Seeing You, Your form touching the sky, flaming in many colors, mouths wide open, large fiery eyes, O Viṣṇu, I find neither courage nor peace; I am frightened.

दंष्ट्राकरालानि च ते मुखानि
दृष्ट्वैव कालानलसन्निभानि ।
दिशो न जाने न लभे च शर्म
प्रसीद देवेश जगन्निवास ॥ २५

daṁṣṭrākarālāni ca te mukhāni
dṛṣṭvaiva kālānalasannibhāni /
diśo na jāne na labhe ca śarma
prasīda deveśa jagannivāsa // 11.25

daṁṣṭrā: teeth; karālāni: ferocious; ca: also; te: Your; mukhāni: faces; dṛṣtvā: seeing; eva: thus; kālānala: the fire of death; sannibhāni: as if blazing; diśaḥ: directions; na jāne: do not know; na labhe: nor obtain; ca śarma: and grace; prasīda: be pleased; deveśa: O Lord of all lords; jagannivāsa: refuge of the worlds

11.25 Having seen your fearsome mouths with blazing tusks like the fire of the end of the universe, I know not the four directions nor do I find peace. O Lord of the Deva, O refuge of the Universe, be gracious.

अमी च त्वां धृतराष्ट्रस्य पुत्राः
सर्वे सहैवावनिपालसङ्घैः ।
भीष्मो द्रोणः सूतपुत्रस्तथासा
सहास्मदीयैरपि योधमुख्यैः ॥ २६

amī ca tvāṁ dhṛtarāṣṭrasya putrāḥ
sarve sahaivāvanipālasaṅghaiḥ |
bhīṣmo droṇaḥ sūtaputrastathāsau
sahāsmadīyairapi yodhamukhyaiḥ || 11.26

amī: all those; ca: also; tvāṁ: You; dhṛtarāṣṭrasya: of Dhṛtarāṣṭra; putrāḥ: sons; sarve: all; sahaiva: along with; avanipāla: warrior kings; saṁghaiḥ: the groups; bhīṣm: Bhīṣma; droṇaḥ: Droṇācārya; sūtaputraḥ: Karṇa; tathā: also; asau: that; saha: with; asmadīyaiḥ: our; api: also; yodhamukhyaiḥ: chief among the warriors

11.26 All the sons of Dhṛtarāṣṭra with many kings of the earth, Bhīṣma, Droṇa, the son of the charioteer, Karṇa, with our warrior chieftains.

वक्त्राणि ते त्वरमाणा विशन्ति
दंष्ट्राकरालानि भयानकानि ।
केचिद्विलग्ना दशनान्तरेषु
संदृश्यन्ते चूर्णितैरुत्तमाङ्गैः ॥ २७

vaktrāṇi te tvaramāṇā viśanti
daṁṣṭrā-karālāni bhayānakāni |
kecidvilagnā daśanāntareṣu
sandṛśyante cūrṇitair uttamāñgaiḥ || 11.27

vaktrāṇi: mouths; te: Your; tvaramāṇḥ: hurrying; viśanti: entering; daṁṣṭrā: teeth; karālāni: terrible; bhayānakāni: very fearful; kecit: some of them; vilagnā: being attacked; daśanāntareṣu: between the teeth; saṁdṛśyante: found; cūrṇitaiḥ: crushed; uttamāñgaiḥ: by the head

11.27 Into Your mouths with terrible tusks, fearful to behold, they enter. Some are seen caught in the gaps between the tusks and their heads crushed.

यथा नदीनां बहवोऽम्बुवेगाः
समुद्रमेवाभिमुखा द्रवन्ति।
तथा तवामी नरलोकवीरा
विशन्ति वक्त्राण्यभिज्वलन्ति॥ २८

yathā nadīnāṁ bahavo'mbuvegāḥ
samudram evābhimukhā dravanti /
tathā tavāmī naralokavīrā
viśanti vaktrāṇy abhivijvalanti // *11.28*

yathā: as; nadīnāṁ: of the rivers; bahavaḥ: many; ambuvegāḥ: waves of the waters; samudram: ocean; eva: certainly; abhimukhāḥ: towards; dravanti: gliding; tathā; similarly; tava: Your; amī: all those; naralokavīrāḥ: the human kings; viśanti: entering; vaktrāṇi: into the mouths; abhivijvalanti: blazing

11.28 Even as many torrents of rivers flow towards the ocean, so too these warriors in the world of men enter Your flaming mouths.

यथा प्रदीप्तं ज्वलनं पतङ्गा
विशन्ति नाशाय समृद्धवेगाः।
तथैव नाशाय विशन्ति लोका-
स्तवापि वक्त्राणि समृद्धवेगाः॥ २९

yathā pradīptaṁ jvalanaṁ pataṅgā
viśanti nāśāya samṛddhavegāḥ /
tathaiva nāśāya viśanti lokās
tavāpi vaktrāṇi samṛddhavegāḥ // *11.29*

yathā: as; pradīptaṁ: blazing; jvalanaṁ: fire; pataṅgāḥ: moths; viśanti: enters; nāśāya: destruction; samṛddha: full; vegāḥ: speed; tathai 'va: similarly; nāśāya: for destruction; viśanti: entering; lokāḥ: all people; tava: unto You; api: also; vaktrāṇi: in the mouths; samṛddhavegāḥ: with full speed

11.29 Just as moths hurriedly rush into the fire for their own destruction, So too these creatures rush hastily into Your mouths of destruction.

लेलिह्यसे ग्रसमान: समन्ता-
ल्लोकान्समग्रान्वदनैर्ज्वलद्भि: ।
तेजोभिरापूर्य जगत्समग्रं
भासस्तवोग्रा: प्रतपन्ति विष्णो ।। ३०

lelihyase grasamānaḥ samantāl
lokān samagrān vadanair jvaladbhiḥ /
tejobhir āpūrya jagatsamagraṁ
bhāsastavo'grāḥ pratapanti viṣṇo // *11.30*

lelihyase: licking; grasamānaḥ: devouring; samantāt: from all directions; lokān: people; samagrān: completely; vadanaiḥ: by the mouth; jvaladbhiḥ: with blazing; tejobhiḥ: by effulgence; āpūrya: covering; jagat: the universe; samagraṁ: all; bhāsas: illuminating; tava: Your; ugrāḥ: terrible; paratapanti: scorching; viṣṇo: O all pervading Lord

11.30 Swallowing all worlds on every side with your flaming mouths You lick in enjoyment. O Viṣṇu, Your fierce rays are burning, filling the whole world with radiance.

आख्याहि मे को भवानुग्ररूपो
नमोऽस्तु ते देववर प्रसीद ।
विज्ञातुमिच्छामि भवन्तमाद्यं
न हि प्रजानामि तव प्रवृत्तिम् ।। ३१

ākhyāhi me ko bhavānugrarūpo
namo'stu te devavara prasīda /
vijñātum icchāmi bhavantam ādyaṁ
na hi prajānāmi tava pravṛttim // *11.31*

ākhyāhi: please explain; me: unto me; kaḥ: who; bhavān: You; ugrarūpaḥ: fierce form; namaḥ astu: obeisances; te: unto You; devavara: the great one amongst the gods; prasīda: be gracious; vijñātum: just to know; icchāmi: I wish; bhavantaṁ: You; ādyaṁ: the original; na: never; hi: certainly; prajānāmi: do I know; tava: Your; pravṛttim: purpose

11.31 Tell me who You are, so fierce in form; salutations to You, O Supreme; have mercy. Indeed I know not Your purpose but I desire to know You, the Original Being.

श्री भगवानुवाच
कालोऽस्मि लोकक्षयकृत्प्रवृद्धो
लोकान् समाहर्तुमिह प्रवृत्तः।
ऋतेऽपि त्वां न भविष्यन्ति सर्वे
येऽवस्थिताः प्रत्यनीकेषु योधाः॥ ३२

śrī bhagavānuvāca
kālo'smi loka-kṣaya-kṛt pravṛddho
lokān samāhartumiha pravṛttaḥ |
ṛte'pi tvāṁ na bhaviṣyanti sarve
ye'vasthitāḥ pratyanīkeṣu yodhāḥ || 11.32

śrī bhagavān uvāca: Kṛṣṇa says; kālaḥ: time; asmi: I am; loka: the worlds; kṣayakṛt: destroyer; pravṛddhaḥ: to engage; lokān: all people; samāhartuṁ: to destroy; iha: in this world; pravṛttaḥ: to engage; ṛte 'pi: without even; tvāṁ: you; na: never; bhaviṣyanti: will be; sarve: all; ye: who; avasthitāḥ: situated; pratyanīkeṣu: on the opposite side; yodhāh: the soldiers

11.32 Śrī Bhagavān says: I am the mighty world-destroying Time, I am now destroying the worlds. Even without you, none of the warriors standing in the hostile armies shall live.

तस्मात्त्वमुतिष्ठ यशो लभस्व
जित्वा शत्रून् भुङ्क्ष्व राज्यं समृद्धम्।

मयैवैते निहता: पूर्वमेव
निमित्तमात्रं भव सव्यसाचिन् ॥ ३३

tasmāt tvamuttiṣṭha yaśo labhasva
jitvā śatrūn bhuṅkṣva rājyaṁ samṛddham /
mayaivaite nihatāḥ pūrvameva
nimittamātraṁ bhava savyasācin // 11.33

tasmāt: therefore; tvaṁ: you; uttiṣṭha: get up; yaśaḥ: fame; labhasva: gain; jitvā: conquering; satrūn: enemies; bhuṅkṣva: enjoy; rājyaṁ: kingdom; samṛddham: flourishing; maya: by Me; eva: certainly; ete: all these; nihatāḥ: already killed; pūrvameva: by previous arrangement; nimittamātraṁ: just an instrument; bhava: become; savyasācin: O Arjuna (one who can use both the hands equally)

11.33 Get up and gain glory. Conquer the enemies and enjoy the prosperous kingdom. I have slain all these warriors; you are a mere instrument, Arjuna.

द्रोणं च भीष्मं च जयद्रथं
च कर्णं तथान्यानपि योधवीरान्।
मया हतांस्त्वं जहि मा व्यथिष्ठा
युध्यस्व जेतासि रणे सपत्नान् ॥ ३४

droṇaṁ ca bhīṣmaṁ ca jayadrathaṁ
ca karṇaṁ tathānyānapi yodhavīrān /
mayā hatāṁstvaṁ jahi mā vyathiṣṭā
yudhyasva jetāsi raṇe sapatnān // 11.34

droṇaṁ ca: also Droṇa; bhīṣmaṁ ca: also Bhisma; jayadrathaṁ ca: also Jayadratha; karṇaṁ: also Karṇa; tathā: also; anyān: others; api: certainly; yodhavīrān: great warriors; mayā: by Me; hatān: already killed; tvaṁ: you; jahi: becomes victorious; mā: never; vyathiṣṭā: be disturbed; yudhyasva: just fight; jetāsi: just conquer; raṇe: in the fight; sapatnān: enemies

11.34 Droṇa, Bhīṣma, Jayadratha, Karṇa and other brave warriors have already been slain by Me; destroy them. Do not be be afraid; fight and you shall conquer your enemies in battle.

सञ्जय उवाच
एतच्छ्रुत्वा वचनं केशवस्य
कृताञ्जलिर्वेपमानः किरीटी।
नमस्कृत्वा भूय एवाह कृष्णं
सगद्गदं भीतभीतः प्रणम्य॥ ३५

sañjaya uvāca
etacchrutvā vacanaṁ keśavasya
kṛtāñjalirvepamānaḥ kirīṭī /
namaskṛtvā bhūya evāha kṛṣṇaṁ
sagadgadaṁ bhītabhītah praṇamya // 11.35

sañjaya uvāca: Sañjaya said; etat: thus; śrutvā: hearing; vacanaṁ: speech; keśavasya: of Kṛṣṇa; kṛtāñjaliḥ: with folded hands; vepamānaḥ: trembling; kirīṭī: Arjuna; namaskṛtvā: offering obeisances; bhūya: again; eva: also; āha kṛṣṇaṁ: says unto Kṛṣṇa; sagadgadaṁ: faltering; bhītabhītaḥ: fearful; praṇamya: offering obeisances

11.35 Sañjaya said: Having heard this speech of Keśava, the crowned Arjuna with joined palms, trembling, prostrating himself, again addressed Kṛṣṇa, voice choking, bowing down, overwhelmed with fear.

अर्जुन उवाच
स्थाने हृषीकेश तव प्रकीर्त्या
जगत्प्रहृष्यत्यनुरज्यते च।
रक्षांसि भीतानि दिशो द्रवन्ति
सर्वे नमस्यन्ति च सिद्धसङ्घाः॥ ३६

arjuna uvāca
sthāne hṛṣīkeśa tava prakīrtyā
jagat prahṛṣy atyanurajyate ca |
rakṣāṁsi bhītāni diśo dravanti
sarve namasyanti ca siddhasaṅghāḥ || 11.36

arjuna uvāca: Arjuna says; sthāne: rightly; hṛṣīkeśa: O master of all senses; tava: Your; prakīrtyā: glories; jagat: the entire world; prahṛṣyati : rejoicing; anurajyate: becoming attached; ca: and; rakṣāṁsi: the demons; bhītāni: out of fear; diśaḥ: directions; dravanti: fleeing; sarve: all; namasyanti: offering respect; ca: also; siddhasaṅghāḥ: the perfect human beings

11.36 Arjuna says: O Hṛṣīkeśā, it is but right that the world delights and rejoices in Your praise. Rākṣasas fly in fear in all directions and all hosts of sages bow to You.

कस्माच्च ते न नमेरन्महात्मन्
गरीयसे ब्रह्मणोऽप्यादिकर्त्रे।
अनन्त देवेश जगन्निवास
त्वमक्षरं सदसत्तत्परं यत्॥ ३७

kasmācca te na nameran mahātman
garīyase brahmaṇo'pyādikartre |
ananta deveśa jagan-nivāsa
tvam akṣaraṁ sad-asat tat paraṁ yat || 11.37

kasmāt: why; ca: also; te: unto You; na: not; nameran: offer proper obeisances; mahātman: O great one; garīyase: You are better than; brahmaṇaḥ: Brahma; api: although; ādikartre: the supreme creator; ananta: unlimited; deveśa: God of the gods; jagannivāsa: O refuge of the universe; tvaṁ: You are; akṣaraṁ: imperishable; sadasat: cause and effect; tat paraṁ: transcendental; yat: because

11.37 And why should they not bow to Thee, O great soul, greater than all else, the Creator of even Brahma the Creator. O Lord of Lords, O infinite Being, O Abode of the Universe,

You are the imperishable, that which is beyond both seen and the unseen.

त्वमादिदेवः पुरुषः पुराण-
स्त्वमस्य विशस्य परं निधानम्।
वेत्तासि वेद्यं च परं च धाम
त्वया ततं विशमनन्तरूप॥ ३८

tvamādidevaḥ puruṣaḥ purāṇas
tvamasya viśvasya paraṁ nidhānam |
vettāsi vedyaṁ ca paraṁ ca dhāma
tvayā tataṁ viśvam ananta rūpa || 11.38

tvaṁ: You; ādidevaḥ: the original supreme God; puruṣaḥ: the supreme being; purāṇaḥ: old; tvaṁ: You; asya: this; viśvasya: universe; paraṁ: transcendental; nidhānam: refuge; vettā: knower; asi: You are; vedyaṁ ca: and the knowable; paraṁ ca: and transcendental; dhāma: refuge; tvayā: by You; tataṁ: pervaded; viśvaṁ: universe; anantarūpa: unlimited form

11.38 You are the primal God, the ancient Being, the supreme refuge of the universe. You are the knower and the One to be known. You are the supreme abode. O Being of infinite forms, by You alone is the universe pervaded.

वायुर्यमोऽग्निर्वरुणः शशाङ्कः
प्रजापतिस्त्वं प्रपितामहश्च।
नमो नमस्तेऽस्तु सहस्रकृत्वः
पुनश्च भूयोऽपि नमो नमस्ते॥ ३९

vāyur yamo'gnir varuṇaḥ śaśāṅkaḥ
prajāpatis tvaṁ prapitāmahaś ca |
namo namaste'stu sahasrakṛtvaḥ
punaśca bhūyo'pi namo namaste || 11.39

vāyuḥ: air; yamaḥ: controller; agniḥ: fire; varuṇaḥ: water; śaśāṅkaḥ: moon; prajāpatiḥ: Brahma; tvaṁ: You; prapitāmahaḥ: grandfather; ca: also; namaḥ: offering respects; namas te: again my respects unto You; astu : be; sahasrakṛt-vaḥ: a thousand times; punaḥ ca: and again; bhūyaḥ: again; api: also; namaḥ: offer my respects; namas te: offering my respects unto You

11.39 You are Vāyu, Yama, Agni, Varuṇa, the moon, Prājapati and the greatgrandfather of all. Salutations unto You a thousand times and again, salutations unto You!

नम: पुरस्तादथ पृष्ठतस्ते
नमोऽस्तु ते सर्वत एव सर्व।
अनन्तवीर्यामितविक्रमस्त्वं
सर्वं समाप्नोषि ततोऽसि सर्व॥ ४०

namaḥ purastādatha pṛṣṭataste
namo'stu te sarvata eva sarva |
ananta-vīryāmita-vikramas tvaṁ
sarvaṁ samāpnoṣi tato'si sarvaḥ || 11.40

namaḥ: offering obeisances; purastāt: from the front; atha: also; pṛṣṭhataḥ: from behind; te: You; namo 'stu: offer my respects; te: unto You; sarvata: from all sides; eva sarva: because You are everything; ananta vīrya: unlimited potency; amita vikramaḥ: unlimited force; tvaṁ: You; sarvaṁ: everything; samāpnoṣi: cover; tato 'si: therefore You are; sarvaḥ : everything

11.40 Salutations to You, before and behind! Salutations to You on every side! O All! Infinite in power and Infinite in prowess, You are everything and everywhere.

सखेति मत्वा प्रसभं यदुक्तं
हे कृष्ण हे यादव हे सखेति।
अजानता महिमानं तवेदं
मया प्रमादात्प्रणयेन वापि॥ ४१

sakheti matvā prasabhaṁ yaduktaṁ
he kṛṣṇa he yādava he sakheti |
ajānatā mahimānaṁ tavedaṁ
mayā pramādāt praṇayena vāpi || 11.41

sakha: friend; iti: thus; matvā: thinking; prasabhaṁ: easy familiarity; yat: whatever; uktaṁ: says; he Kṛṣṇa: O Kṛṣṇa; he yādava: O Yadava; he sakhe 'ti: O my dear friend; ajānatā: without knowing; mahimānaṁ: glories; tava: Your; idaṁ: this; mayā: by me; pramādāt: out of foolishness; praṇayena: out of love; vā 'pi: either

11.41 Whatever I have rashly says from carelessness or love, addressing You as Kṛṣṇa, Yādava, my friend regarding You merely as a friend, unaware of this greatness of Yours.

यच्चावहासार्थमसत्कृतोऽसि
विहारशय्यासनभोजनेषु ।
एकोऽथवाप्यच्युत तत्समक्षं
तत्क्षामये त्वामहमप्रमेयम् ॥ ४२

yac cāvahāsārtham asatkṛto'si
vihāraśayyāsana bhojaneṣu |
eko'tha va'py acyuta tat samakṣaṁ
tat kṣāmaye tvām aham aprameyam || 11.42

yat: whatever; ca: also; avahāsārthum: for joking; asatkrtaḥ: dishonor; asi: have been done; vihāra: in relaxation; śayyā: while lying on the bed; āsana: in a sitting place; bhojaneṣu: or while eating together; ekaḥ: alone; athava: or; api: others; acyuta: O infallible one; tatsamakṣaṁ: in their presence; tat: all those; kṣāmaye: excuse; tvām: from You; aham: I; aprameyam: immeasurable

11.42 In whatever way I may have insulted You in fun, while at play, resting, sitting or at meals, when alone with You or in company, O Acyuta, O immeasurable One, I implore You to forgive me.

पितासि लोकस्य चराचरस्य
त्वमस्य पूज्यश्च गुरुर्गरीयान्।
न त्वत्समोऽस्त्यभ्यधिकः कुतोऽन्यो
लोकत्रयेऽप्यप्रतिमप्रभाव॥ ४३

pitāsi lokasya carācarasya
tvamasya pūjyaśca gururgarīyān |
na tvatsamo'sty abhyadhikaḥ kuto'nyo
lokatraye'py apratima-prabhāva || 11.43

Pitā: father; asi: You are; lokasya: of all the world; cara: moving; acarasya: nonmoving; tvaṁ: You are; asya: of this; pūjyaḥ: worshipable; ca: also; guruḥ: master; garīyan: glorious; na: never; tvatsamaḥ: equal to You; asti: there is; abhyadhikaḥ: greater; kutaḥ: how is it possible; anyo: other; lokatraye: in three planetary systems; api: also; apratima: immeasurable; prabhāva: power

11.43 You are the father of this world, moving and unmoving. You are to be adored by this world. You are the greatest guru; there is none who exists equal to You. O Being of unequalled power, how then can there be another, superior to You in the three worlds?

तस्मात्प्रणम्य प्रणिधाय कायं
प्रसादये त्वामहमीशमीड्यम्।
पितेव पुत्रस्य सखेव सख्युः
प्रियः प्रियायार्हसि देव सोढुम्॥ ४४

tasmātpraṇamya praṇidhāya kāyaṁ
prasādaye tvāṁaham īśam īḍyam |
pite'va putrasya sakhe'va sakhyuḥ priyaḥ
priyāyārhasi deva soḍhum || 11.44

tasmāt: therefore; praṇamya: after offering obeisances; praṇidhāya: laying down; kāyaṁ: body; prasādaye: to beg mercy; tvāṁ: unto You; ahaṁ: I; īśaṁ:

unto the Supreme Lord; īḍyam: who is worshipable; pite 'va: like a father; putrasya: of a son; sakhe 'va: like a friend; sakhyuḥ: of a friend; priyaḥ: lover; priyāya: of the dearmost; arhasi: You should; deva: my Lord; soḍhum: tolerate

11.44 Therefore, bowing down, I prostrate my body before You and crave Your forgiveness, adorable Lord. Even as a father forgives his son, a friend his friend, a lover his beloved, You should, O Deva, forgive me.

अदृष्टपूर्वं हृषितोऽस्मि दृष्ट्वा
भयेन च प्रव्यथितं मनो मे।
तदेव मे दर्शय देव रूपं
प्रसीद देवेश जगन्निवास॥ ४५

adṛṣṭa-pūrvaṁ hṛṣito'smi dṛṣṭvā
bhayena ca pravyathitaṁ mano me /
tadeva me darśaya devarūpaṁ
prasīda deveśa jagannivāsa // *11.45*

adṛṣṭapūrvaṁ: never seen before; hṛṣito: gladdened; asmi: I am; dṛṣṭvā: by seeing; bhayena: out of fear; ca: also; pravyathitaṁ: perturbed; mano: mind; me: my; tad: therefore; eva: certainly; me: unto me; darśaya: show; deva: O Lord; rūpaṁ: the form; prasīda: just be gracious; deveśa: O Lord of lords; jagannivāsa: the refuge of the universe

11.45 After seeing this form that I have never seen before, I am filled with gladness but at the same time I am disturbed by fear. Please bestow Your grace upon me and show me Your form as the supreme personality, O Lord of Lords, O refuge of the Universe.

किरीटिनं गदिनं चक्रहस्त-
मिच्छामि त्वां द्रष्टुमहं तथैव।

तेनैव रूपेण चतुर्भुजेन
सहस्रबाहो भव विश्वमूर्ते ॥ ४६

kirīṭinaṁ gadinaṁ cakra-hastam
icchāmi tvāṁ draṣṭumahaṁ tathaiva /
tenaiva rūpeṇa caturbhujena
sahasrabāho bhava viśvamūrte // 11.46

kirīṭinaṁ: crowned; gadinaṁ: with club; cakrahastam: disc in hand; icchāmi: I wish; tvāṁ: You; draṣṭum: to see; ahaṁ: I; tathai'va: in that form; tenai 'va: by that; rūpeṇa: with form; caturbhujena: four-handed; sahasrabāho: O thousand-handed one; bhava: just become; viśvamūrte: O universal form

11.46 O thousand armed Universal Form! I wish to see Your form with crown, fourarmed with mace, disc in Your hand. I yearn to see You in that form.

श्रीभगवानुवाच
मया प्रसन्नेन तवार्जुनेदं
रूपं परं दर्शितमात्मयोगात् ।
तेजोमयं विश्वमनन्तमाद्यं
यन्मे त्वदन्येन न दृष्टपूर्वम् ॥ ४७

śrī bhagavānuvāca
mayā prasannena tavārjunedaṁ
rūpaṁ paraṁ darśitam ātma-yogāt /
tejo-mayaṁ viśvamam anantamādyaṁ
yanme tvad anyena na dṛṣṭa-pūrvam // 11.47

śrī bhagavān uvāca: Śrī bhagavan says; mayā: by Me; prasannena: happily; tava: unto you; arjuna: O Arjuna; idam: this; rūpaṁ: form; paraṁ: transcendental; darśitaṁ: shown; ātmayogāt: by My internal power; tejomayaṁ: full of effulgence; viśvaṁ: the entire universe; anantaṁ: unlimited; ādyaṁ: original;

yan me: that which is Mine; tvad anyena: besides you; na dṛṣṭapūrvam: no one has previously seen

11.47 Bhagavān says: Dear Arjuna, I happily show you this transcendental form within the material world of My internal power. No one before you has seen this unlimited, brilliant form.

न वेदयज्ञाध्ययनैर्न दानैः
न च क्रियाभिर्न तपोभिरुग्रैः ।
एवं रूपः शक्य अहं नृलोके
द्रष्टुं त्वदन्येन कुरुप्रवीर ॥ ४८

na veda-yajñādhyayanairna dānaiḥ
na ca kriyābhir na tapobhir ugraiḥ /
evaṁ-rūpaḥ śakya ahaṁ nṛ-loke
draṣṭuṁ tvadanyena kuru-pravīra // *11.48*

na: never; veda: by Vedic study; yajña: sacrifice; ādhyayanaiḥ: study; na dānaiḥ: not by charity; na: never; ca: also; kriyābhiḥ: by pious activities; na tapobhiḥ: by serious penances; ugraiḥ: severe; evaṁ: thus; rūpaḥ: form; śakyaḥ: can be seen; ahaṁ: I; nṛloke: in this material world; draṣṭuṁ: to see; tvad: you; anyena: by another; kurupravīra: O best among the Kuru warriors

11.48 O best among Kuru warriors, no one had ever before seen this Universal form of mine, for neither by studying the Vedas nor by performing sacrifices or charities, can this form be seen. Only you have seen this form.

मा ते व्यथा मा च विमूढभावो
दृष्ट्वा रूपं घोरमीदृङ्ममेदम् ।
व्यपेतभीः प्रीतमनाः पुनस्त्वं
तदेव मे रूपमिदं प्रपश्य ॥ ४९

mā te vyathā mā ca vimūḍhabhāvo

dṛṣṭvā rūpaṁ ghoramīdṛṅmamedam |
vyapetabhīḥ prītamanāḥ punastvaṁ
tadeva me rūpamidaṁ prapaśya || 11.49

mā: let it not be; te: unto you; vyathā: trouble; mā: let it not be; ca: also; vimūḍhabhāvaḥ: bewilderment; dṛṣṭvā: by seeing; rūpaṁ: form; ghoraṁ: terrible; īdṛk: like this; mama: My; idaṁ: as it is; vyapetabhīḥ: just become free from all fear; prītamanāḥ: be pleased in mind; punaḥ: again; tvaṁ: you; tat: that; eva: thus; me: My; rūpam: form; idaṁ: this; prapaśya: just see

11.49 Do not be disturbed any longer by seeing this terrible form of Mine. Dear devotee, be free from all disturbances. With a peaceful mind, you can now see the form you wish to see.

सञ्जय उवाच ।
इत्यर्जुनं वासुदेवस्तथोक्त्वा
स्वकं रूपं दर्शयामास भूयः ।
ओशसयामास च भीतमेनं
भूत्वा पुनः सौम्यवपुर्महात्मा ॥ ५०

sañjaya uvāca
ityarjunaṁ vāsudevastatho'ktvā
svakaṁ rūpaṁ darśayāmāsa bhūyaḥ |
āśvasayām āsa ca bhītam enaṁ
bhūtvā punaḥ saumya-vapur-mahātmā || 11.50

sañjaya uvāca: Sañjaya said; iti: thus; arjunaṁ: unto Arjuna; vāsudevaḥ: Kṛṣṇa; tathā: that way; uktvā: saying; svakaṁ: His own; rūpaṁ: form; darśayāmāsa: showed; bhūyaḥ: again; āśvāsayāmāsa: also convinced him; ca: also; bhītam: fearful; enaṁ: him; bhūtvā punaḥ: becoming again; saumyavapuḥ: beautiful form; mahātmā: the great one

11.50 Sañjaya said: Kṛṣṇa, while speaking to Arjuna, revealed His form with four arms, Then assuming His human form He consoled the terrified Arjuna.

अर्जुन उवाच।
दृष्ट्वेदं मानुषं रूपं तव सौम्यं जनार्दन।
इदानीमस्मि संवृत्तः सचेताः प्रकृतिं गतः॥ ५१

arjuna uvāca
dṛṣṭvedaṁ mānuṣaṁ rūpaṁ tava saumyaṁ janārdana |
idānīmasmi saṁvṛttaḥ sacetāh prakṛtiṁ gataḥ || I 11.51

arjuna uvāca: Arjuna says; dṛṣṭvā: seeing; idaṁ: this; mānuṣaṁ: human being; rūpam: form; tava: Your; saumyaṁ: very beautiful; janārdana: O chastiser of the enemies; idānīm: just now; asmi: I am; saṁvṛttaḥ: settled; sacetāh: in my consciousness; prakṛtiṁ: my own; gataḥ: I

11.51 Arjuna says: Seeing this wonderful human form, My mind is now calm and I am restored to my original nature.

श्री भगवानुवाच
सुदुर्दर्शमिदं रूपं दृष्टवानसि यन्मम।
देवा अप्यस्य रूपस्य नित्यं दर्शनकाङ्क्षिण॥ ५२

śrībhagavānuvāca
sudurdarśamidaṁ rūpaṁ dṛṣṭavānasi yanmama |
devā apyasya rūpasya nityaṁ darśanakāṅkṣiṇaḥ || 11.52

śrī bhagavān uvāca: Kṛṣṇa says; sudurdarśaṁ: very difficult to be seen; idaṁ: this; rūpaṁ: form; dṛṣṭavān asi: you have seen; yat: which; mama: of Mine; devāḥ: the celestials; apyasya: also this; rūpasya: form; nityaṁ: eternally; darśana kāṅkṣiṇaḥ: always aspire to see

11.52 Bhagavān says: The four-armed form that you have seen is rare to behold. Even the celestials are forever aspiring to see this form.

नाहं वेदैर्न तपसा न दानेन न चेज्यया।
शक्य एवंविधो द्रष्टुं दृष्ट्वानसि मां यथा॥ ५३

nāhaṁ vedairna tapasā na dānena na cejyayā |
śakya evaṁvidho draṣṭuṁ dṛṣṭavānasi māṁ yathā || 11.53

nā: never; ahaṁ: I; vedaiḥ: by study of the Vedas; na: never; tapasā: by serious penances; na: never; dānena: by charity; na: never; ca: also; ijyayā: by worship; śakyaḥ: it is possible; evaṁvidhaḥ: like this; draṣṭuṁ: to see; dṛṣṭavān: seeing; asi: you are; māṁ: Me; yathā: as.

11.53 The four armed form which you have seen with your transcendental eyes cannot be understood simply by study of the Vedas, nor by undergoing penances or charity or worship; one cannot see Me as I am by these means.

भक्त्या त्वनन्यया शक्य अहमेवंविधोऽर्जुन।
ज्ञातुं द्रष्टुं च तत्त्वेन प्रवेष्टुं च परन्तप॥ ५४

bhaktyā tvananyayā śakya aham evaṁ vidho'rjuna |
jñātuṁ draṣṭuṁ ca tattvena praveṣṭuṁ ca parantapa || 11.54

bhaktyā: by devotional service; tu: but; ananyayā: without being mixed with fruitive activities or speculative knowledge; śakyaḥ: possible; aham: I; evaṁvidhaḥ: like this; arjuna: O Arjuna; jñātuṁ: to know; draṣṭuṁ: to see; ca: and; tattvena: in fact; praveṣṭuṁ: and to enter into; ca: also; paraṁtapa: O mighty-armed one

11.54 My dear Arjuna, only by undivided devotional service can you understand Me as I am, standing before you, be seen directly. Only in this way can you reach Me, O Parantapa.

मत्कर्मकृन्मत्परमो मद्भक्तः संङ्गवर्जितः।
निर्वैरः सर्वभूतेषु यः स मामेति पाण्डव॥ ५५

mat-karma-kṛn mat-paramo mad-bhaktaḥ saṅgavarjitaḥ |
nirvairaḥ sarvabhūteṣu yaḥ sa māmeti pāṇḍava || 11.55

matkarmakṛt: engaged in doing My work; matparamaḥ: considering Me the Supreme; madbhaktaḥ: engaged in My devotional service; saṅgavarjitaḥ:

freed from the contamination of previous activities and mental speculation; nirvairaḥ: without an enemy; sarvabhūteṣu: to every living entity; yaḥ: one who; sa: he; mām: unto Me; eti: comes; pāṇḍava: O son of Pāṇḍu

11.55 My dear Arjuna, one who is engaged entirely in My devotional service, free from attachment, full of love for every entity, surely comes to Me.

इति श्रीमद्भगवद्गीतासूपनिषत्सु ब्रह्मविद्यायां योगशास्त्रे
श्रीकृष्णार्जुनसंवादे विश्वरूपदर्शनयोगो नाम एकादशोऽध्याय: ॥

iti śrīmad bhagavadgītāsūpaniṣatsu brahmavidyāyām
yogaśāstre śrīkṛṣṇārjuna saṁvāde viśvarūpadarśanayogo
nāmaekādaśo'dhyāyaḥ //

In the ***Upaniṣad*** of ***Śrimad Bhagavad Gītā***, the scripture of yoga dealing with ***Brahmavidyā Yogaśāstra,*** the science of Brahman, the Supreme Absolute, in the form of ***Śrī Kṛṣṇārjuna saṁvād,*** dialogue between Śrī Kṛṣṇa and Arjuna, this is the eleventh chapter named, ***Viśvarūpa Darśan Yogaḥ,*** *'Yoga of the Vision of the Cosmic Form.'*

CHAPTER

12

अथ द्वादशोऽध्याय:

भक्तियोग:

Bhakti Yogaḥ

अर्जुन उवाच
एवं सततयुक्ता ये भक्तास्त्वां पर्युपासते ।
ये चाप्यक्षरमव्यक्तं तेषां के योगवित्तमा: ॥ १

arjuna uvāca
evaṁ satata-yuktā ye bhaktāstvāṁ paryupāsate |
ye cā'py akṣaram avyaktaṁ teṣāṁ ke yoga-vittamāh || 12.1

arjuna uvāca: Arjuna says; evaṁ: thus; satata: always; yuktāḥ: engaged; ye: those; bhaktāḥ: devotees; tvāṁ: you; paryupāsate: worship; ye: those; cā: and; api: also; akṣaraṁ: imperishable; avyaktaṁ: the unmanifest; teṣāṁ: of these; ke: who; yogavittamāḥ: perfect in knowledge of yoga

12.1 Arjuna asked: Who are considered perfect, those who are always engaged sincerely in Your worship in form, or those who worship the imperishable, the unmanifest formless You?

श्री भगवानुवाच
मय्यावेश्य मनो ये मां नित्ययुक्ता उे।
श्रद्धया परयोपेतास्ते मे युक्ततमा मता: ॥ २

śrī Bhagavānuvāca
mayyāveśya mano ye māṁ nityayuktā upāsate |
śraddhayā parayo'petās te me yuktatamā matāḥ || 12.2

śrī bhagavān uvāca: Lord Kṛṣṇa says; mayi: on Me; āveśya: fixing; manaḥ: the mind; ye: those; māṁ: Me; nitya: eternally; yuktāḥ: engaged; upāsate: worship; śraddhayā: with faith; parayā: supreme; upetāḥ: endowed; te: these; me: by Me; yuktatamāḥ: perfect in yoga; matāḥ: opinion

12.2 Lord Kṛṣṇa says: Those, who by fixing their mind on Me eternally, and those who are steadfast in worshipping Me with supreme faith, I consider them to be perfect in Yoga, ready to be united with Me.

ये त्वक्षरमनिर्देश्यमव्यक्तं पर्युपासते ।
सर्वत्रगमचिन्त्यं च कूटस्थमचलं ध्रुवम् ॥ ३

ye tv akṣaram anirdeśyam avyaktaṁ paryupāsate |
sarvatragam acintyaṁ ca kūṭa-stham acalaṁ dhruvam || 12.3

ye: those; tu: but; akṣaraṁ: imperishable; anirdeśyaṁ: indefinable; avyaktaṁ: unmanifest; paryupāsate: worship; sarvatragaṁ: all pervading; acintyaṁ: inconceivable; ca: also; kūṭasthaṁ: unchanging; achalaṁ: immovable; dhruvam: fixed

सन्नियम्येन्द्रियग्रामं सर्वत्र समबुद्धयः ।
ते प्राप्नुवन्ति मामेव सर्वभूतहिते रताः ॥ ४

sanniyamyendriya-grāmaṁ sarvatra samabuddhayaḥ |
te prāpnuvanti mām eva sarvabhūta-hite ratāḥ || 12.4

sanniyamya: restrained; indriyagrāmaṁ: all the senses; sarvatra: everywhere; samabuddhayaḥ: equally disposed; te: they; prāpnuvanti: achieve; mām: Me; eva: only; sarvabhūta hite: for the welfare of all living beings; ratāḥ: engaged

12.3,4 But those who worship with awareness the imperishable, the unmanifest, that which lies beyond the perception of senses, the all pervading, inconceivable, unchanging, the non-moving and permanent, those who worship by restraining their senses, and are working with even mind for the benefit of mankind, they too attain Me.

क्क्लेशोऽधिकतरस्तेषामव्यक्तासक्तचेतसाम्।
अव्यक्ता हि गतिर्दुःखं देहवद्भिरवाप्यते॥ ५

kleśo'dhikatarasteṣām avyaktāsakta-cetasām /
avyaktā hi gatir duḥkhaṁ dehavadbhir avāpyate // 12.5

kleśaḥ: trouble; adhikataraḥ: greater; teṣām: of those; avyaktāsaktacetasām: whose minds are set on the unmanifest; avyaktā: unmanifest; hi: for; gatiḥ: goal; duḥkhaṁ: sorrow; dehavadbhiḥ: for the embodied; avāpyate: is attained

12.5 For those whose minds are set on the unmanifest, the formless, it is more difficult to advance; attaining the formless unmanifest is difficult for the embodied.

ये तु सर्वाणि कर्माणि मयि संन्यस्य मत्पराः।
अनन्येनैव योगेन मां ध्यायन्त उपासते॥ ६

ye tu sarvāṇi karmāṇi mayi sannyasya matparāḥ /
ananyenaiva yogena māṁ dhyāyanta upāsate // 12.6

ye: who; tu: but; sarvāṇi: all; karmāṇi: actions; mayi: in me; saṇnyasya: renouncing; matparāḥ: regarding me as the supreme goal; ananyena: focussed; eva: even; yogena: with yoga; māṁ: me; dhyāyantaḥ: meditating; upāsate: worship

तेषामहं समुद्धर्ता मृत्युसंसारसागरात्।
भवामि नचिरात्पार्थ मय्यावेशितचेतसाम्॥ ७

teṣām ahaṁ samuddhartā mṛtyu-saṁsāra-sāgarāt /
bhavāmi na cirātpārtha mayy āveśita cetasām // 12.7

teṣām: for them; ahaṁ: I; samuddhartā: the savior; mṛtyu saṁsāra sāgarāt: from the ocean of life and death cycle; bhavāmi: become; na cirāt: before long; pārtha: Arjuna; mayi: in me; āveśita cetasām: of those whose minds are set

12.6,7 But those who worship me with single minded devotion, renouncing all activities unto Me, regarding Me as their supreme goal, whose minds are set in Me, I shall deliver them soon from their ocean of the birth and death cycle.

मय्येव मन आधत्स्व मयि बुद्धिं निवेशय।
निवसिष्यसि मय्येव अत ऊर्ध्वं न संशयः॥ ८

mayyeva mana ādhatsva mayi buddhiṁ niveśaya |
nivasiṣyasi mayyeva ata ūrdhvaṁ na saṁśayaḥ || 12.8

mayi: upon Me; eva: only; manaḥ: mind; ādhatsva: fix; mayi: upon Me; buddhiṁ: mind; niveśaya: apply; nivasiṣyasi: you will live; mayi: in Me; eva: alone; ata ūrdhvaṁ: thereafter; na: no; saṁśayaḥ: doubt

12.8 You fix your mind on Me alone, establish your mind in Me. You will live in Me always. There is no doubt in it.

अथ चित्तं समाधातुं न शक्नोषि मयि स्थिरम्।
अभ्यासयोगेन ततो मामिच्छाप्तुं धनञ्जय॥ ९

atha cittaṁ samādhātuṁ na śaknoṣi mayi sthiram |
abhyāsayogena tato mām icchāptuṁ dhanañjaya || 12.9

atha: if; cittaṁ: mind; samādhātuṁ: to fix; na: not; śaknoṣi: you are able; mayi: upon Me; sthiram: steadily; abhyāsa yogena: by the practice of yoga; tataḥ: then; mām: Me; iccha: desire; āptuṁ: to get; dhanañjaya: Arjuna

12.9 If you are not able to fix your mind upon Me then Arjuna, with the constant practice of Yoga, you try to attain Me.

अभ्यासेऽप्यसमर्थोऽसि मत्कर्मपरमो भव।
मदर्थमपि कर्माणि कुर्वन्सिद्धिमवाप्स्यसि॥ १०

abhyāse'pyasamartho'si matkarmaparamo bhava |
madarthamapi karmāṇi kurvan-siddhim avāpsyasi || 12.10

abhyāse: in practice; api: even if; asamarthaḥ: unable; asi: you are; matkarma: My work; paramaḥ: dedicated to; bhava: become; madarthaṁ: for Me; api: even; karmāṇi: work; kurvan: performing; siddhim: perfection; avāpsyasi: you will achieve

12.10 If you are not able to practice even this yoga then performing your duties and surrendering all your actions to Me, you will attain perfection.

अथैतदप्यशक्तोऽसि कर्तुं मद्योगमाश्रितः।
सर्वकर्मफलत्यागं ततः कुरु यतात्मवान्॥ ११

athaitad apy aśakto'si kartuṁ madyogamāśritaḥ |
sarva-karma-phalatyāgaṁ tataḥ kuru yatātmavān || 12.11

atha: even though; etad: this; api: also; aśaktaḥ: unable; asi: you are; kartuṁ: to perform; madyogam: My yoga; āśritaḥ: taking refuge in; sarva karma: of all activities; phala: of the results; tyāgaṁ: renunciation; tataḥ: then; kuru: do; yatātmavān: self controlled.

12.11 If you are not able to work even this way, surrendering unto Me, give up all the results of your actions to Me without ego.

श्रेयो हि ज्ञानमभ्यासात् ज्ञानाद्ध्यानं विशिष्यते।
ध्यानात्कर्मफलत्यागस्त्यागाच्छान्तिरनन्तरम्॥ १२

śreyo hi jñānamabhyāsāj jñānāddhyānaṁ viśiṣyate |
dhyānāt karma-phala-tyāgas tyāgāc chāntir anantaram || 12.12

śreyo: better; hi: indeed; jnānam: knowledge; abhyāsāt: than practice; jñānāt:

than knowledge; dhyānaṁ: meditation; viśiṣyate: superior; dhyānāt: than meditation; karmaphala tyāgaḥ: renunciation of the fruits of action; tyāgāt: than such renunciation; śāntiḥ: peace; anantaram: thereafter

12.12 Knowledge is better than mere practice. Meditation is superior to knowledge. Renunciating the fruit of actions is better than meditation. After renouncing of fruits of actions, one immediately attains peace.

अद्वेष्टा सर्वभूतानां मैत्रः करुण एव च।
निर्ममो निरहङ्कारः समदुःखसुखः क्षमी॥ १३

adveṣṭā sarvabhūtānāṁ maitraḥ karuṇa eva ca |
nirmamo nirahaṅkāraḥ samaduḥkhasukhaḥ kṣamī || 12.13

adveṣṭā: non envious; sarvabhūtānāṁ: toward all living entities; maitraḥ: friendly; karuṇa: kindly; eva: certainly; ca: also; nirmamaḥ: with no sense of proprietorship; nirahankāraḥ: without false ego; sama: equal; duḥkha: in distress; sukhaḥ: and happiness; kṣamī: forgiving.

सन्तुष्टः सततं योगी यतात्मा दृढनिश्चयः।
मय्यर्पितमनोबुद्धिर्यो मद्भक्तः स मे प्रियः॥ १४

santuṣṭaḥ satataṁ yogī yatātmā dṛḍhaniścayaḥ |
mayy arpita-mano-buddhir yo madbhaktaḥ sa me priyaḥ || 12.14

santuṣṭaḥ: satisfied; satataṁ: always; yogī: one engaged in yoga; yatātmā: self controlled; dṛḍhaniścayaḥ: with determination; mayi: upon Me; arpita: engaged; manaḥ: mind; buddhiḥ: and intelligence; yaḥ: one who; madbhaktaḥ: My devotee; saḥ: he; me: to Me; priyaḥ: dear.

12.13,14 One who has no dislike or envy for any being, who is friendly and compassionate to everyone, free from the sense of I and mine, the ego, maintains equanimity of mind both in joy and sorrow, forgiving, ever satisfied, united with Yoga, has a strong commitment to Me and has fixed his mind and intellect upon Me, such a devotee of Mine is very dear to Me.

यस्मान्नोद्विजते लोको लोकान्नोद्विजते च यः ।
हर्षामर्षभयोद्वेगैर्मुक्तो यः स च मे प्रियः ॥ १५

yasmānnodvijate loko lokānnodvijate ca yaḥ |
harṣāmarṣabha-yodvegair mukto yaḥ sa ca me priyaḥ || 12.15

yasmāt: from whom; na: not; udvijate: is agitated; lokaḥ: the world; lokāt: from the world; na: not; udvijate : is agitated; ca: and; yaḥ: who; harṣāmarṣabhayodvegaiḥ: from joy; envy; fear and anxiety; muktaḥ: freed; yaḥ: who; sa: he; ca: and; me: to me; priyaḥ: dear

12.15 He, by whom the world is not affected adversely, and who in turn does not affect the world adversely, and he, who is free from joy, anger, and anxiety, he is dear to Me.

अनपेक्षः शुचिर्दक्ष उदासीनो गतव्यथः ।
सर्वारम्भपरित्यागी यो मद्भक्तः स मे प्रियः ॥ १६

anapekṣaḥ śucirdakṣaḥ udāsīno gatavyathaḥ |
sarvārambhaparityāgī yo madbhaktaḥ sa me priyaḥ || 12.16

anapekṣaḥ: free from expectations; śuciḥ: pure; dakṣa: expert; udāsīnaḥ: unconcerned; gatavyathaḥ: untroubled; sarvārambha parityāgī: renouncing all undertakings; yo: who; madbhaktaḥ: my devotee; saḥ: he; me: to me; priyaḥ: dear

12.16 He, who is free from wants, who is pure and skilled, unconcerned, untroubled, who is selfless in whatever he does, he who is devoted to Me, he is dear to Me.

यो न हृष्यति न द्वेष्टि न शोचति न काङ्क्षति ।
शुभाशुभपरित्यागी भक्तिमान्यः स मे प्रियः ॥ १७

yo na hṛṣyati na dveṣṭi na śocati na kāṅkṣati |
śubhāśubhaparityāgi bhaktimānyaḥ sa me priyaḥ || 12.17

yaḥ: who; na: not; hṛṣyati: rejoices; na: not; dveṣṭi: hates; na: not; śocati: grieves; na: not; kāṅkṣati: desires; subhāśubha parityāgī: renouncing good and evil; bhaktimān: full of devotion; yaḥ: who; sa: he; me: to me; priyaḥ: dear

12.17 He who does not rejoice or hate or grieve or desire, renounces both good and evil and who is full of devotion, he is dear to Me.

समः शत्रौ च मित्रे च तथा मानापमानयोः।
शीतोष्णसुखदुःखेषु समः सङ्गविवर्जितः॥ १८

samaḥ śatrau ca mitre ca tathā mānāpamānayoḥ |
śītoṣṇasukhaduḥkheṣu samaḥ saṅgavivarjitaḥ || 12.18

samaḥ: equal; śatrau: to an enemy; ca: also; mitre: to a friend; ca: also; tathā: so; māna: in honor; apamānayoḥ: and dishonour; śīta: in cold; uṣṇa: heat; sukha: happiness; duḥkheṣu: and sorrow; samaḥ: same; saṅgavivarjitaḥ: free from all association

तुल्यनिन्दास्तुतिर्मौनी संतुष्टो येन केनचित्।
अनिकेतः स्थिरमतिर्भक्तिमान्मे प्रियो नरः॥ १९

tulyanindāstutir maunī santuṣṭo yena kenacit |
aniketaḥ sthira-matir bhaktimānme priyo naraḥ || 12.19

tulya: equal; nindā: in defamation; stutiḥ: and repute; maunī: silent; santuṣṭaḥ: satisfied; yena kenacit: with anything; aniketaḥ: having no residence; sthira: fixed; matiḥ: mind; bhaktimān: engaged in devotion; me: to Me; priyaḥ: dear; naraḥ: a man

12.18,19 One who treats friends and enemies the same, who faces in the same manner honor and dishonor, heat and cold, happiness and sorrow, fame and infamy, one who is always free from attachment, always silent and satisfied with anything, without a fixed home, who is fixed in mind and who is devoted to Me, such a person is very dear to Me.

ये तु धर्म्यामृतमिदं यथोक्तं पर्युपासते।
श्रद्दधाना मत्परमा भक्तास्तेऽतीव मे प्रियाः॥ २०

ye tu dharmyāmṛtam idaṁ yathoktaṁ paryupāsate /
śraddadhānā matparamā bhaktās te 'tīva me priyāḥ // 12.20

ye: who; tu: indeed; dharmya: righteous path; amṛtam: nectar; idaṁ: this; yathā: as; uktaṁ: says; paryupāsate: follow; śraddadhānā: with faith; matparamā: taking Me as the Supreme Lord; bhaktāḥ: devotees; te: they; atīva: very much; me: to Me; priyāḥ: dear

12.20 Those who truly follow this imperishable path of righteousness with great faith, making Me the supreme goal, are very dear to Me.

इति श्रीमद्भगवद्गीतासूपनिषत्सु ब्रह्मविद्यायां योगशास्त्रे
श्रीकृष्णार्जुनसंवादे भक्तियोगो नाम द्वादशोऽध्यायः॥

iti śrīmad bhagavadgītāsūpaniṣatsu brahmavidyāyām
yogaśāstre śrīkṛṣṇārjuna saṁvāde bhaktiyogo nāma
dvādaśo'dhyāyaḥ //

In the ***Upaniṣad*** of ***Śrimad Bhagavad Gītā,*** the scripture of yoga dealing with ***Brahmavidyā Yogaśāstra,*** the science of Brahman, the Supreme Absolute, in the form of ***Śrī Kṛṣṇārjuna saṁvād,*** dialogue between Śrī Kṛṣṇa and Arjuna, this is the twelfth chapter named, ***Bhakti Yogaḥ***, *'Union Through Devotional Love.'*

CHAPTER

13

अथ त्रयोदशोऽध्यायः

क्षेत्रक्षेत्रज्ञविभागयोगः

Kṣetra Kṣetrajña Vibhāga Yogaḥ

अर्जुन उवाच
प्रकृतिं पुरुषं चैव क्षेत्रं क्षेत्रज्ञमेव च।
एतद्वेदितुमिच्छामि ज्ञानं ज्ञेयं च केशव॥ १

arjuna uvāca
prakṛtiṁ puruṣaṁ caiva kṣetraṁ kṣetrajñameva ca /
etad veditum icchāmi jñānaṁ jñeyaṁ ca keśava // 13.1

arjuna uvāca: Arjuna says; prakṛtiṁ: nature; puruṣaṁ: the enjoyer; ca: also; eva: certainly; kṣetraṁ: body; kṣetrajñam: knower of the body; eva: certainly; ca: also; etad: all this; vedituṁ: to understand; icchāmi: I wish; jñānaṁ: knowledge; jñeyaṁ: the object of knowledge; ca: also; keśava: O Kṛṣṇa.

13.1 Arjuna says: O Keśava, I wish to know and understand about prakṛti and puruṣa, passive and active energies. The field [kṣetra] and the knower of the field [kṣetrajña], and of knowledge [jñānaṁ] and of the end of knowledge [jñeyaṃ].

श्री भगवानुवाच।
इदं शरीरं कौन्तेय क्षेत्रमित्यभिधीयते।
एतद्यो वेत्ति तं प्राहुः क्षेत्रज्ञ इति तद्विदः॥ १

śrībhagavānuvāca
idaṁ śarīraṁ kaunteya kṣetram ity abhidhīyate /
etadyo vetti taṁ prāhuḥ kṣetrajña iti tadvidaḥ // 13.2

śrī bhagavān uvāca: the personality of God says; idaṁ: this; śarīraṁ: body; kaunteya: O son of Kuntī; kṣetraṁ: the field; iti: thus; abhidhīyate: is called; etat: this; yaḥ: anyone; vetti: knows; taṁ: he; prāhuḥ: is called; kṣetrajña: knower of the body; iti: thus; tadvidaḥ: one who knows

13.2 Bhagavān Kṛṣṇa replies: This body, O Kaunteya, is called the field, kṣetra. Anyone who knows this body is called the knower of the field, kṣetrajña.

क्षेत्रज्ञं चापि मां विद्धि सर्वक्षेत्रेषु भारत।
क्षेत्रक्षेत्रज्ञयोर्ज्ञानं यत्तज्ज्ञानं मतं मम॥ २

kṣetrajñaṁ cāpi māṁ viddhi sarvakṣetreṣu bhārata /
kṣetra-kṣetrajñayor jñānaṁ yat taj jñānaṁ mataṁ mama // 13.3

kṣetrajñaṁ: the knower; ca: also; api: certainly; māṁ: Me; viddhi: know; sarva: all; kṣetreṣu: in bodily fields; bhārata: O son of Bhārata; kṣetra: field of activities (the body); kṣetrajñayoḥ: the knower of the field; jñānaṁ: knowledge; yat: that which is taught; tat: that; jñānaṁ: knowledge; mataṁ: opinion; mama: that

13.3 O Bhārata, know that I am the Knower in all bodies [kṣetrajña], the witness. In my opinion knowledge means the understanding of this body or the field of activity as well as the Knower of this field.

तत्क्षेत्रं यच्च यादृक्च यद्विकारि यतश्च यत्।
स च यो यत्प्रभावश्च तत्समासेन मे श्रृणु॥ ३

tat kṣetraṁ yac ca yādṛk ca yadvikāri yataś ca yat /
sa ca yo yat prabhāvaś ca tat samāsena me sṛṇu // 13.4

tat: that; kṣetraṁ: field of activities; yah: as; ca: and; yādṛk: as it is; ca: and; yat: what is; vikāri: changes; yataḥ: from which; ca: and; yat: which; sa: he; ca: also; yaḥ: one; yat: which; prabhāvaśca: influence also; tat: that; samāsena: in summary; me: from Me; sṛṇu: understand

13.4 Understand my summary of this field of activity and how it is constituted, what its changes are, how it is produced, who that knower of the field of activities is, and what his influences are.

ऋषिभिर्बहुधा गीतं छन्दोभिर्विविधैः पृथक्।
ब्रह्मसूत्रपदैश्चैव हेतुमद्भिर्विनिश्चितैः॥ ४

ṛṣibhir bahudhā gītaṁ chandobhir vividhaiḥ pṛthak /
brahma-sūtra padaiś caiva hetumadbhir viniścitaiḥ // 13.5

ṛṣibhir: by the wise sages; bahudhā: in many ways; gītaṁ: described; chandobhiḥ: Vedic hymns; vividhaiḥ: in various; pṛthak: variously; brahmasūtra: the Vedanta; padaiḥ: aphorisms; ca: also; eva: certainly; hetumadbhir: with cause and effect; viniścitaiḥ: ascertained

13.5 That knowledge of the field of activities and of the knower of activities is described by various sages with chants in the scriptures It is presented with all reasoning as to cause and effect.

महाभूतान्यहङ्कारो बुद्धिरव्यक्तमेव च।
इन्द्रियाणि दशैकं च पञ्च चेन्द्रियगोचराः॥ ५

mahā-bhūtāny ahaṅkāro buddhir avyaktam eva ca /
indriyāṇi daśaikaṁ ca pañca cendriya gocarāḥ // 13.6

इच्छा द्वेषः सुखं दुःखं सङ्घातश्चेतना धृतिः।
एतत्क्षेत्रं समासेन सविकारमुदाहृतम्॥ ६

icchādveṣaḥ sukhaṁ duḥkhaṁ saṅghātaścetanā dhṛtiḥ I
etatkṣetraṁ samāsena savikāram udāhṛtam II 13.7

mahābhūtāni: great elements; ahaṅkāraḥ: ego; buddhiḥ: intelligence; avyaktaṁ: the unmanifested; eva: certainly; ca: also; indriyāṇi: senses; daśaikaṁ: eleven; ca: also; pañca: five; ca: also; indriyagocarāḥ: objects of the senses; icchā: desire; dveṣaḥ: hatred; sukhaṁ: happiness; duḥkhaṁ: distress; saṅghātaḥ: the aggregate; cetanā: living symptoms; dhṛtiḥ: conviction; etat: all this; kṣetraṁ: the field of activities; samāsena: in summary; savikāraṁ: with its modifications; udāhṛtam: exemplified

13.6,7 The field of activities and its interactions are said to be: the five elements of nature, ego, intelligence, the mind, the formless, the ten senses of perception and action, as well as the five objects of senses and desire, hatred, happiness, distress, the aggregate, the life symptoms, and convictions.

अमानित्वमदम्भित्वमहिंसा क्षान्तिरार्जवम् ।
आचार्योपासनं शौचं स्थैर्यमात्मविनिग्रहः ॥ ७

amānitvam adambhitvam ahimsā kṣāntir ārjavam I
ācāryopāsanaṁ śaucaṁ sthairyam ātma-vinigrahaḥ II 13.8

amānitvaṁ: humility; adambhitvaṁ: pridelessness; ahimsā: nonviolence; kṣāntiḥ: tolerance; ārjavam: simplicity; ācāryopāsanaṁ: approaching a bonafide spiritual master; śaucaṁ: cleanliness; sthairyaṁ: steadfastness; ātma-vinigrahaḥ: control

इन्द्रियार्थेषु वैराग्यमनहङ्कार एव च ।
जन्ममृत्युजराव्याधिदुःखदोषानुदर्शनम् ॥ ८

indriyārtheṣu vairāgyam anahaṁkāra eva ca I
janma-mṛtyu-jarā-vyādhi- duḥkha-doṣānudarśanam II 13.9

indriyārtheṣu: in the matter of the senses; vairāgyaṁ: renunciation; anahaṁkāra: being without egoism; eva: certainly; ca: also; janma: birth; mṛtyu:

death; jarā: old age; vyādhi: disease; duḥkha: distress; doṣa: fault; anudarśanam: observing

असक्तिरनभिष्वङ्गः पुत्रदारगृहादिषु ।
नित्यं च समचित्तत्वमिष्टानिष्टोपपत्तिषु ॥ ९

asaktir anabhiṣvaṅgaḥ putra-dāra-gṛhādiṣu |
nityaṁ ca sama-cittatvam iṣṭāniṣṭopapattiṣu || 13.10

asaktiḥ: without attachment; anabhiṣvaṅgaḥ: without association; putra: sons; dāra: wife; gṛhādiṣu: home, etc.; nityaṁ: eternal; ca: also; samacittatvaṁ: equilibrium; iṣṭā: desirable; aniṣṭa: undesirable; upapattiṣu: having obtained

मयि चानन्ययोगेन भक्तिरव्यभिचारिणी ।
विविक्तदेशसेवित्वमरतिर्जनसंसदि ॥ १०

mayi cānanya-yogena bhaktir avyabhicāriṇī |
vivikta-deśa-sevitvam aratirjana saṁsadi || 13.11

mayi: unto Me; ca: also; ananyayogena: by devotional service; bhaktiḥ: devotion; avyabhicāriṇī: constant, unalloyed; vivikta: solitary; deśa: place; sevitvaṁ: resorting to; aratiḥ: without attachment; jana: to people in general; saṁsadi: mass

अध्यात्मज्ञाननित्यत्वं तत्त्वज्ञानार्थदर्शनम् ।
एतज्ज्ञानमिति प्रोक्तमज्ञानं यदतोऽन्यथ ॥ ११

adhyātma-jñāna-nityatvaṁ tattva-jñānārtha-darśanam |
etaj-jñānam iti proktam ajñānaṁ yad atonyathā || 13.12

adhyātma: pertaining to the self; jñāna: knowledge; nityatvaṁ: eternity; tattva jñānā: knowledge of the truth; artha: for the purpose of; darśanam: philosophy; etat: all this; jñānam: knowledge; iti: thus; proktam: declared; ajñānaṁ: ignorance; yat: that which; ataḥ: from this; anyathā: others

13.8,9,10,11,12 Humility, absence of pride, nonviolence, tolerance, simplicity, service to an enlightened spiritual

Master, cleanliness, steadiness and self-control; renunciation of the objects of sense gratification; absence of ego, the perception of the pain of the cycle of birth and death, old age and disease; nonattachment to children, wife, home and the rest and even-mindedness amid pleasant and unpleasant events; constant and unalloyed devotion to Me, resorting to solitary places, detachment from the general mass of people; accepting the importance of self realization, and philosophical search for the absolute truth: All these I thus declare to be knowledge and anything contrary to these is ignorance.

ज्ञेयं यत्तत्प्रवक्ष्यामि यज्ज्ञात्वामृतमश्नुते।
अनादिमत्परं ब्रह्म न सत्तन्नासदुच्यते॥ १२

jñeyaṁ yat tat pravakṣyāmi yaj jñātvāmṛtam aśnute |
anādi matparaṁ brahma na sat tan nāsad ucyate || 13.13

jñeyaṁ: knowable; yat: that; tat: which; pravakṣyāmi: I shall now explain; yat: which; jñātvā: knowing; amṛtaṁ: nectar; aśnute: taste; anādimat: that which has no beginning; paraṁ: the supreme; brahma: spirit; na: neither; sat: cause; tat: that; nā: nor; asat: effect; ucyate: is called

13.13 I shall fully give you the understanding about the knowable with which one can taste eternal bliss or the being or the consciousness that has no beginning. A life beyond the cause and effect and the material world.

सर्वत: पाणिपादं तत्सर्वतोऽक्षिशिरोमुखम्।
सर्वत: श्रुतिमल्लोके सर्वमावृत्य तिष्ठति॥ १३

sarvataḥ pāṇipādaṁ tat sarvato 'kṣiśiromukham |
sarvataḥ śrutimalloke sarvamāvṛtya tiṣṭhati || 13.14

sarvataḥ: everywhere; pāṇi: hands; pādaṁ: legs; tat: that; sarvataḥ: everywhere; akṣi: eyes; śiro: head; mukham: face; sarvataḥ: everywhere; śrutimat: hearing; loke: in the world; sarvaṁ: everything; āvṛtya: covering; tiṣṭhati: exists

13.14 With hands and feet everywhere, with eyes, heads and mouths everywhere, with ears everywhere, He exists in the worlds, enveloping all. The Paramātman (supreme spirit) is all pervading.

सर्वेन्द्रियगुणाभासं सर्वेन्द्रियविवर्जितम्।
असक्तं सर्वभृच्चैव निर्गुणं गुणभोक्तृ च॥ १४

sarvendriya-guṇābhāsaṁ sarvendriya-vivarjitam /
asaktaṁ sarva-bhṛccaiva nirguṇaṁ guṇabhoktṛ ca // 13.15

sarva: all; indriya: senses; guṇa: qualities; ābhāsaṁ: original source; sarva: all; indriya: senses; vivarjitam: being without; asaktaṁ: without attachment; sarvabhṛt: maintainer of everyone; ca: also; eva: certainly; nirguṇaṁ: without material qualities; guṇabhoktṛ: simultaneously master of the gunas; ca: also

13.15 The Paramātman is the original source of all the senses. Yet, He is beyond all the senses. He is unattached. Although the consciousness is the maintainer of all the living beings, yet He transcends the modes of the nature and at the same time He is the master of the modes of our material nature.

बहिरन्तश्च भूतानामचरं चरमेव च।
सूक्ष्मत्वात्तदविज्ञेयं दूरस्थं चान्तिके च तत्॥ १६

bahir antaśca bhūtānām acaraṁ carameva ca /
sūkṣmatvāt tad avijñeyaṁ dūrasthaṁ cāntike ca tat // 13.16

bahiḥ: outside; antaḥ: inside; ca: also; bhūtānām: of all living entities; acaraṁ: not moving; caraṁ: moving; eva: also; ca: and; sūkṣmatvāt: on account of being subtle; tat: that; avijñeyaṁ: unknowable; dūrasthaṁ: far away; ca: also; antike: near; ca: and; tat: that

13.16 The supreme truth exists both within and without, it is present in everything mobile or immobile. It is not knowable through the senses as it is very subtle. Though far, yet it is the nearest.

अविभक्तं च भूतेषु विभक्तमिव च स्थितम्।
भूतभर्तृ च तज्ज्ञेयं ग्रसिष्णु प्रभविष्णु च॥ १६

avibhaktaṁ ca bhūteṣu vibhaktamiva ca sthitam |
bhūta-bhartṛ ca tajjñeyaṁ grasiṣṇu prabhaviṣṇu ca || 13.17

avibhaktaṁ: without division; ca: also; bhūteṣu: in every living being; vibhaktaṁ: divided; iva: as if; ca: also; sthitam: situated; bhūta bhartṛ: maintainer of all living entities; ca: also; tat: that; jñeyaṁ: to be understood; grasiṣṇu: devours; prabhaviṣṇu: develops; ca: also

13.17 Though appearing fragmented it is indivisible whole. Though He is the maintainer of every living entity, it is to be understood that He consumes and creates all.

ज्योतिषामपि तज्ज्योतिस्तमसः परमुच्यते।
ज्ञानं ज्ञेयं ज्ञानगम्यं हृदि सर्वस्य विष्ठितम्॥ १७

jyotiṣām api tajjyotis tamasaḥ paramucyate |
jñānaṁ jñeyaṁ jñāna-gamyaṁ hṛdi sarvasya viṣṭhitam || 13.18

jyotiṣām: in all luminous objects; api: also; tat: that; jyotiḥ: source of light; tamasaḥ: of the darkness; paraṁ: beyond; ucyate: is said; jñānaṁ: knowledge; jñeyaṁ: to be known; jñānagamyaṁ: to be approached by knowledge; hṛdi: in the heart; sarvasya: of everyone; viṣṭhitam: situated

13.18 He is the source of light in all luminous objects. He is beyond the darkness of matter and is formless. He is knowledge, He is the object of knowledge, and He is the goal of knowledge. He is situated in everyone's heart.

इति क्षेत्रं तथा ज्ञानं ज्ञेयं चोक्तं समासतः।
मद्भक्त एतद्विज्ञाय मद्भावायोपपद्यते॥ १८

iti kṣetraṁ tathā jñānaṁ jñeyaṁ co 'ktaṁ samāsataḥ |
madbhakta etadvijñāya madbhāvāyopapadyate || 13.19

iti: thus; kṣetraṁ: the field of activities (the body); tathā: also; jñānaṁ: knowledge; jñeyaṁ: the knowable; ca: also; uktaṁ: described; samāsataḥ: in summary; madbhaktaḥ: My devotee; etad: all this; vijñāya: after understanding; madbhāvāya: My nature; upapadyate: attains

13.19 Thus the field of activities, knowledge and the knowable has been summarily described by Me. It is only when we can understand the true nature of our supreme Self and the material world with which we have created false identities that we can go beyond this and attain the supreme Self itself.

प्रकृतिं पुरुषं चैव विद्ध्यनादी उभावपि।
विकारांश्च गुणांश्चैव विद्धि प्रकृतिसंभवान्॥ १९

prakṛtiṁ puruṣaṁ caiva viddhyanādī ubhāvapi /
vikārāṁś ca guṇāṁś caiva viddhi prakṛti saṁbhavān // 13.20

prakṛtiṁ: material nature; puruṣaṁ: living entity; ca: also; eva: certainly; viddhi: must know; anādī: without beginning; ubhāu: both; api: also; vikārān: transformations; ca: also; guṇān: three modes of nature; ca: also; eva: certainly; viddhi: know; prakṛti: material nature; saṁbhavān: produced of

13.20 Prakṛti or the field and its attributes and the puruṣa or the knower or the supreme consciousness are both without beginning. All the transformations of nature that we see are produced by the field or prakṛti.

कार्यकारणकर्तृत्वे हेतुः प्रकृतिरुच्यते।
पुरुषः सुखदुःखानां भोक्तृत्वे हेतुरुच्यते॥ २०

kārya-kāraṇa-kartṛtve hetuḥ prakṛtirucyate /
puruṣaḥ sukha-duḥkhānāṁ bhoktṛtve heturucyate // 13.21

kārya: effect; kāraṇa: cause; kartṛtve: in the matter of creation; hetuḥ: instrument; prakṛtiḥ: material nature; ucyate: is said to be; puruṣaḥ: the living entity; sukha: of happiness; duḥkhānāṁ: and distress; bhoktṛtve: in enjoyment; hetuḥ:

the instrument; ucyate: is said to be

13.21 In the production of the body and the senses, prakṛti is said to be the cause; In the experience of pleasure and pain, puruṣa is said to be the cause.

पुरुषः प्रकृतिस्थो हि भुङ्क्ते प्रकृतिजान्गुणान ।
कारणं गुणसङ्गोऽस्य सदसद्योनिजन्मसु ॥ २१

puruṣaḥ prakṛtistho hi bhuṅkte prakṛti-jān-guṇān /
kāraṇaṁ guṇasaṇgosya sadasadyonijanmasu // 13.22

puruṣaha: the living entity; prakṛtisthaḥ: being situated in the material energy; hi: certainly; bhuṅkte: enjoys; prakṛtijān: produced by the material nature; guṇān: modes of nature; kāraṇaṁ: cause; guṇasaṅgaḥ: association with the modes of nature; asya: of the living entity; sadasad: good and bad; yoni: species of life; janmasu: births

13.22 The living entity in the material nature follows the way of life, enjoying the moods of nature. Due to association with the material nature it meets the good or evil among various species.

उपद्रष्टानुमन्ता च भर्ता भोक्ता महेशरः।
परमात्मेति चाप्युक्तो देहेऽस्मिन्पुरुषः परः॥ २३

upadraṣṭānumantā ca bhartā bhoktā maheśvaraḥ /
paramātmeti cāpyukto dehe'sminpuruṣaḥ paraḥ // 13.23

upadraṣṭā: overseer; anumantā: permitter; ca: also; bhartā: master; bhoktā: supreme enjoyer; maheśvaraḥ: the supreme Lord; paramātmā: supersoul; iti: also; ca : and; apyuktaḥ: is said; dehe: in this body; asmin: this; puruṣaḥ: enjoyer; paraḥ: transcendental

13.23 Yet, in this body there is a transcendental energy. He who is divine, who exists as a owner or the witness, supporter, enjoyer and the pure witnessing consciousness, is known as the Paramātman.

य एवं वेत्ति पुरुषं प्रकृतिं च गुणैः सह।
सर्वथा वर्तमानोऽपि न स भूयोऽभिजायते॥ २४

ya evaṁ vetti puruṣaṁ prakṛtiṁ ca guṇaiḥ saha I
sarvathā vartamānopi na sa bhūyobhijāyate II 13.24

yaḥ: he who; evaṁ: thus; vetti: understands; puruṣaṁ: the living entity; prakṛtiṁ: material nature; ca: and; guṇaiḥ: modes of material nature; saha: with; sarvathā: by all means; vartamānaḥ: situated; api: in spite of; na: never; saḥ: he; bhūyaḥ: again; abhijāyate: takes his birth

13.24 One who understands this philosophy concerning material nature, the living entity and the interaction of the modes of nature is sure to attain liberation. He will not take birth here again, regardless of his present position.

ध्यानेनात्मनि पश्यन्ति केचिदात्मानमात्मना।
अन्ये साङ्ख्येन योगेन कर्मयोगेन चापरे॥ २५।

dhyānenātmani paśyanti kecidātmānamātmanā I
anye sāṅkhyena yogena karmayogena cāpare II 13.25

dhyānena: by meditation; ātmani: in one self; paśyanti: see; kecit: some; ātmānam: Supersoul; ātmanā: by the mind; anye: others; sāṅkhyena: by philosophical discussion; yogena: by the yoga system; karmayogena: by activities without fruitive desire; ca: also; apare: others

13.25 Some perceive the Paramātman in their inner psyche through mind and intellect that have been purified by meditation or by metaphysical knowledge or by karma yoga.

अन्ये त्वेवमजानन्तः श्रुत्वान्येभ्य उपासते।
तेऽपि चातितरन्त्येव मृत्युं श्रुतिपरायणाः॥ २६

anye tv evam ajānantaḥ śrutvānyebhya upāsate I
te 'pi 'cātitaranty eva mṛtyuṁ śrutiparāyaṇāḥ II 13.26

anye: others; tu: but; evaṁ: thus; ajānantaḥ: without spiritual knowledge; śrutvā: by hearing; anyebhyaḥ: from others; upāsate: begin to worship; te: they; api: also; ca: and; atitaranti: transcend; eva: certainly; mṛtyuṁ: the path of death; śrutiparāyaṇāḥ : inclined to the process of hearing

13.26 There are those who, although not conversant in spiritual knowledge, begin to worship the supreme personality upon hearing about Him from others. Through the process of hearing about the supreme Self, they also transcend the path of birth and death.

यावत्सञ्जायते किञ्चित्सत्त्वं स्थावरजङ्गमम्।
क्षेत्रक्षेत्रज्ञसंयोगात्तद्विद्धि भरतर्षभ॥ २७

yāvatsañjāyate kiñcit sattvaṁ sthāvarajaṅgamam |
kṣetra-kṣetrajña-saṁyogāt tadviddhi bharatarṣabha || 13.27

yāvat: whatever; sañjāyate: takes place; kiñcit: anything; sattvaṁ: existence; sthāvara: not moving; jaṅgamam: moving; kṣetra: the body; kṣetrajña: knower of the body; saṁyogāt: union between; tadviddhi: you must know it; bharatarṣabha: O chief of the Bhāratas

13.27 Bhārata, know that whatever that is movable or immovable is born, It comes into existence by combination of kṣetra and kṣetrajña

समं सर्वेषु भूतेषु तिष्ठन्तं परमेशरम्।
विनश्यत्स्वविनश्यन्तं यः पश्यति स पश्यति॥ २८

samaṁ sarveṣu bhūteṣu tiṣṭhantaṁ parameśvaram |
vinaśyatsvavinaśyantaṁ yaḥ paśyati sa paśyati || 13.28

samaṁ: equally; sarveṣu: in all; bhūteṣu: living entities; tiṣṭhantaṁ: residing; parameśvaram: the supersoul; vinaśyatsu: in the destructible; avinaśyantaṁ : not destroyed; yaḥ: anyone; paśyati: sees; saḥ: he; paśyati: actually sees

13.28 One who sees the supreme Spirit accompanying the

individual soul in all bodies, who understands that neither the individual soul nor the supreme Spirit is ever destroyed, actually sees.

समं पश्यन्हि सर्वत्र समवस्थितमीशरम्।
न हिनस्त्यात्मनात्मानं ततो याति परां गतिम्॥ २९

samaṁ paśyanhi sarvatra samavasthitamīsvaram /
na hinastyātmanā 'tmanaṁ tato yāti parāṁ gatim // 13.29

samaṁ: equally; paśyan: seeing; hi: certainly; sarvatra: everywhere; samavasthitam: equally situated; īsvaraṁ: Supersoul; na: does not; hinasti: degrade; ātmanā: by the mind; atmanaṁ: the soul; tato yāti: then reaches; parāṁ: the transcendental; gatim: destination

13.29 When one does not get degraded or influenced by the mind and when he can see the Supreme Spirit in all living and non-living things, One reaches the transcendental destination.

प्रकृत्यैव च कर्माणि क्रियमाणानि सर्वशः।
यः पश्यति तथात्मानमकर्तारं स पश्यति॥ ३०॥

prakṛtyaiva ca karmāṇi kriyamāṇāni sarvaśaḥ /
yaḥ paśyati tathātmānam akartāraṁ sa paśyati // 13.30

prakṛtyā: by material nature; eva: certainly; ca: also; karmāṇi: activities; kriyamāṇāni: engaged in performing; sarvaśaḥ: in all respects; yaḥ: anyone who; paśyati: sees; tathā: so also; atmānaṁ: himself; akartāraṁ: non-doer; saḥ: he; paśyati: sees perfectly

13.30 One who can see that all activities are performed by the body, which is created of material nature, sees that the Self does nothing, actually sees.

यदा भूतपृथग्भावमेकस्थमनुपश्यति।
तत एव च विस्तारं ब्रह्म सम्पद्यते तदा॥ ३१

yadā bhūta-pṛthag-bhāvam ekasthamanupaśyati |
tata eva ca vistāraṁ brahma saṁpadyate tadā || 13.31

yadā: when; bhūta: living entities; pṛthagbhāvaṁ: separated identities; ekasthaṁ: situated in one; anupaśyati: tries to see through authority; tata eva: thereafter; ca: also; vistāraṁ: expanded; brahma: the Absolute; saṁpadyate: attains; tadā: at that time

13.31 When a person can see the supreme Self in all living entities then he will cease to see the separateness among the living entities. He will see that the whole universe is an expansion and expression of the same truth.

अनादित्वान्निर्गुणत्वात्परमात्मायमव्ययः।
शरीरस्थोऽपि कौन्तेय न करोति न लिप्यते॥ ३२

anāditvānnirguṇa tvāt paramātmāyamavyayaḥ |
śarīrastho'pi kaunteya na karoti na lipyate || 13.32

anāditvāt: due to eternity; nirguṇatvāt: due to transcendental; paramātmā: supreme soul; ayaṁ: this; avyayaḥ: inexhaustible; śarīrastho 'pi: though dwelling in the body; kaunteya: O son of Kuntī; na karoti: never does anything; na lipyate : nor is he entangled

13.32 Those with the vision of eternity can see that the soul is transcendental, eternal, and beyond the modes of nature. Despite contact with the material body, O Arjuna, the soul neither does anything nor is attached.

यथा सर्वगतं सौक्ष्म्यादाकाशं नोपलिप्यते।
सर्वत्रावस्थितो देहे तथात्मा नोपलिप्यते॥ ३३

yathā sarvagataṁ saukṣmyād ākāśaṁ nopalipyate |
sarvatrāvasthito dehe tathātmā nopalipyate || 13.33

yathā: as; sarvagataṁ: all-pervading; saukṣmyād: due to being subtle; ākāśaṁ: the sky; na: never; upalipyate: mixes; sarvatra: everywhere; avasthitaḥ: situated;

dehe: in the body; tathā: such; ātmā: the self; na: never; upalipyate: mixes.

13.33 The sky, due to its subtle nature, does not mix with anything, although it is all-pervading. Similarly, the soul, situated in Brahman, does not mix with the body, though situated in that body.

यथाप्रकाशयत्येक: कृत्स्नं लोकमिमं रवि:।
क्षेत्रं क्षेत्री तथा कृतस्नं प्रकाशयति भारत॥ ३४

yathā prakāśayatyekaḥ kṛtsnaṁ lokamimaṁ raviḥ /
kṣetraṁ kṣetrī tathā kṛtsnaṁ prakāśayati bhārata // 13.34

yathā: as; prakāśayati: illumines; ekaḥ: one; kṛtsnaṁ: the whole; lokaṁ: universe; imaṁ: this; raviḥ: the sun; kṣetraṁ: this body; kṣetrī: the soul; tathā: similarly; kṛtsnaṁ: all; prakāśayati: illumines; bhārata: O son of Bhārata

13.34 O son of Bhārata, as the Sun alone illumines the entire Universe, so does the living entity, one within the body, illumines the entire consciousness.

क्षेत्रक्षेत्रज्ञयोरेवमन्तरं ज्ञानचक्षुषा।
भूतप्रकृतिमोक्षं च ये विदुर्यान्ति ते परम्॥ ३५

kṣetrakṣetrajñayor evam antaraṁ jñāna-cakṣuṣā /
bhūta-prakṛti-mokṣaṁ ca ye viduryānti te param // 13.35

kṣetra: body; kṣetrajñayoḥ: of the proprietor of the body; evaṁ: that; antaraṁ: difference; jñānacakṣuṣā: by vision of knowledge; bhūta: living entity; prakṛti: material nature; mokṣaṁ: liberation; ca: also; ye: one who; viduḥ: knows; yānti: approaches; te: they; param: supreme

13.35 Those, who see with the eyes of knowledge the difference between the body-mind, kṣetra and the knower of the body-mind, kṣetrajña, can understand the process. Are liberated from the bondages of the material nature and attain the Paramātman.

इति श्रीमद्भगवद्गीतासूपनिषत्सु ब्रह्मविद्यायां योगशास्त्रे
श्रीकृष्णार्जुनसंवादे क्षेत्रक्षेत्रज्ञविभागयोगो नाम
त्रयोदशोऽध्यायः ॥

iti śrīmad bhagavadgītāsūpaniṣatsu brahmavidyāyām
yogaśāstre śrīkṛṣṇārjuna saṁvāde
kṣetra kṣetrajña vibhāgayogo nāma
trayodaśo'dhyāyaḥ ||

In the ***Upaniṣad*** of ***Śrimad Bhagavad Gītā***, the scripture of yoga dealing with ***Brahmavidyā Yogaśāstra,*** the science of Brahman, the Supreme Absolute, in the form of ***Śrī Kṛṣṇārjuna saṁvād,*** dialogue between Śrī Kṛṣṇa and Arjuna, this is the thirteenth chapter named, ***Kṣetra Kṣetrajña Vibhāga Yogaḥ,*** *'The Yoga of Discrimination of the Kṣetra, the Field and Kṣetrajña, the Knower of the Field ."*

CHAPTER

14

अथ चतुर्दशोऽध्यायः

गुणत्रयविभागयोगः

Guṇatraya Vibhāga Yogaḥ

श्री भगवानुवाच।

परं भूयः प्रवक्ष्यामि ज्ञानानां ज्ञानमुत्तमम्।
यज्ज्ञात्वा मुनयः सर्वे परां सिद्धिमितो गताः॥ १

śrībhagavānuvāca

paraṁ bhūyaḥ pravakṣyāmi jñānānāṁ jñānamuttamam /
yajjñātvā munayaḥ sarve parāṁ siddhimito gatāḥ // *14.1*

śrī bhagavān uvāca: Kṛṣṇa says; paraṁ: supreme; bhūyaḥ: again; pravakṣyāmi: I shall speak; jñānānāṁ: of all knowledge; jñānaṁ: knowledge; uttamam: the supreme; yat: which; jñātvā: knowing; munayaḥ: the sages; sarve: all; parāṁ: supreme; siddhiṁ: perfection; itaḥ: from this world; gatāḥ: attained

14.1 Bhagavān Śrī Kṛṣṇa says: I will declare to you again the Supreme wisdom, The knowledge of which has helped all sages attain Supreme perfection.

इदं ज्ञानमुपाश्रित्य मम साधर्म्यमागताः।
सर्गेऽपि नोपजायन्ते प्रलये न व्यथन्ति च॥ २

idaṁ jñānamupāśritya mama sādharmyamāgatāḥ /
sarge'pi nopajāyante pralaye na vyathanti ca // *14.2*

idaṁ: this; jñānam: knowledge; upāśritya: taking shelter of; mama: My; sādharmyam: nature; āgatāḥ: attained; sarge 'pi: even in the creation; na: never; upajāyante: comes in; pralaye: in the annihilation; na: nor; vyathanti: disturbed; ca: also

14.2 By becoming fixed in this knowledge, one can attain the transcendental nature, like my own, and establish in his Eternal Consciousness, that one is not born at the time of creation, or disturbed at the time of dissolution.

मम योनिर्महद्‌ब्रह्म तस्मिन्गर्भं दधाम्यहम्।
संभवः सर्वभूतानां ततो भवति भारत॥ ३

mama yonir-mahad-brahma tasmingarbhaṁ dadhāmyahaṁ /
saṁbhavaḥ sarvabhūtānāṁ tato bhavati bhārata // 14.3

mama: My; yoniḥ: source of birth; mahad brahma: material cause of the entire creation called mahat brahma; tasmin: in that; garbhaṁ: pregnancy; dadhāmi: create; ahaṁ: I; saṁbhavaḥ: possibility; sarvabhūtānāṁ: of all living entities; tataḥ: thereafter; bhavati: becomes; bhārata: O son of Bhārata

14.3 The total material substance, called Brahman, is the source of birth, It is that Brahman that I impregnate, making possible the births of all living beings, O son of Bhārata.

सर्वयोनिषु कौन्तेय मूर्तयः सम्भवन्ति याः।
तासां ब्रह्म महद्योनिरहं बीजप्रदः पिता॥ ४

sarvayoniṣu kaunteya mūrtayaḥ saṁbhavanti yāḥ /
tāsāṁ brahma mahad yonir ahaṁ bījapradaḥ pitā // 14.4

sarva yoniṣu: in all species of life; kaunteya: O son of Kuntī; mūrtayaḥ: forms; saṁbhavanti: as they appear; yāḥ: which; tāsāṁ: all of them; brahma: supreme; mahad yoniḥ: the source of birth in the material substance; ahaṁ: Myself; bījapradaḥ: seed-giving; pitā: father

14.4 Arjuna, understand that all species of life are made possible by birth in this material nature, and I am the seed-giving father.

सत्त्वं रजस्तम इति गुणाः प्रकृतिसंभवाः ।
निबध्नन्ति महाबाहो देहे देहिनमव्ययम् ॥ ५

sattvaṁ rajastama iti guṇāḥ prakṛtisaṁbhavāḥ /
nibadhnanti mahābāho dehe dehinamavyayam // *14.5*

sattvaṁ: mode of goodness; rajaḥ: mode of passion; tamaḥ: mode of ignorance; iti: thus; guṇāḥ: qualities; prakṛti: material nature; saṁbhavāḥ: produced of; nibadhananti: does condition; mahābāho: O mighty-armed one; dehe: in this body; dehinaṁ: the living entity; avyayaṁ: eternal

14.5 Material nature consists of the three modes—goodness, passion and ignorance. When the living entity comes in contact with nature, it becomes conditioned by these modes.

तत्र सत्त्वं निर्मलत्वात्प्रकाशकमनामयम् ।
सुखसङ्गेन बध्नाति ज्ञानसंङ्गेन चानघ ॥ ६

tatra sattvaṁ nirmalatvāt prakāśakamanāmayam /
sukhasaṅgena badhnāti jñānasaṅgena cānagha // *14.6*

tatra: thereafter; sattvaṁ: mode of goodness; nirmalatvāt: being purest in the material world; prakāśakaṁ: illuminating; anāmayam: without any sinful reaction; sukha: happiness; saṅgena: association; badhnāti: conditions; jñāna: knowledge; saṅgena: association; ca: also; anagha: O sinless one

14.6 O Sinless One, the mode of goodness, satva, being purer than the others, is illuminating, and it frees one from all sinful reactions. Those situated in that mode develop knowledge, but they become conditioned by the concept of happiness.

रजो रागात्मकं विद्धि तृष्णासङ्गसमुद्भवम् ।
तन्निबध्नाति कौन्तेय कर्मसङ्गेन देहिनम् ॥ ७

rajo rāgātmakaṁ viddhi tṛṣṇāsaṅgasamudbhavam |
tannibadhnāti kaunteya karmasaṅgena dehinam || 14.7

rajaḥ: the mode of passion; rāgātmakaṁ: born of desire or lust; viddhi: know; tṛṣṇā: with craving; saṅga: association; samudbhavam: produced of; tan: that; nibadhnāti: binds; kaunteya: O son of Kuntī; karmasaṅgena: by association with fruitive activity; dehinam: the embodied

14.7 Kaunteya, know that the mode of passion, rajas, is characterized by intense craving and is the source of desire and attachment. Rajas binds the living entity by attachment to work.

तमस्त्वज्ञानजं विद्धि मोहनं सर्वदेहिनाम् ।
प्रमादालस्यनिद्राभिस्तन्निबध्नाति भारत ॥ ८

tamas tv ajñānajaṁ viddhi mohanaṁ sarvadehinām |
pramādālasya-nidrābhis tannibadhnāti bhārata || 14.8

tamaḥ: mode of ignorance; tu: but; ajñānajaṁ: products of ignorance; viddhi: know; mohanaṁ: delusion; sarvadehinām: of all embodied beings; pramāda: madness; ālasya: indolence; nidrābhiḥ: sleep; tat: that; nibadhnāti: binds; bhārata : O son of Bhārata

14.8 Know, O Arjuna, that the mode of ignorance, tamas, the deluder of the living entity is born of inertia. Tamas binds the living entity by carelessness, laziness, and excessive sleep.

सत्त्वं सुखे सञ्जयति रजः कर्मणि भारत ।
ज्ञानमावृत्य तु तमः प्रमादे सञ्जयत्युत ॥ ९

sattvaṁ sukhe sañjayati rajaḥ karmaṇi bhārata |
jñānamāvṛtya tu tamaḥ pramāde sañjayatyuta || 14.9

sattvaṁ: mode of goodness; sukhe: in happiness; sañjayati: develops; rajaḥ: mode of passion; karmaṇi: fruits of activities; bhārata: O son of Bhārata; jñānam: knowledge; āvṛtya: covering; tu: but; tamaḥ: the mode of ignorance; pramāde: in madness; sañjayati: develops; uta: it is said

14.9 The mode of goodness conditions one to happiness, passion conditions him to fruits of action, and veiling the knowledge, tamas binds one to carelessness.

रजस्तमश्चाभिभूय सत्त्वं भवति भारत।
रज: सत्त्वं तमश्चैव तम: सत्त्वं रजस्तथा॥ १०

rajas tamaś cābhibhūya sattvaṁ bhavati bhārata /
rajaḥ sattvaṁ tamaścaiva tamaḥ sattvaṁ rajastathā // 14.10

rajaḥ: mode of passion; tamaḥ: mode of ignorance; ca: also; abhibhūya: also surpassing; sattvaṁ: mode of goodness; bhavati: becomes prominent; bhārata: O son of Bhārata; rajaḥ: mode of passion; sattvaṁ: mode of goodness; tamaḥ: mode of ignorance; ca: also; eva: like that; tamaḥ: mode of ignorance; sattvaṁ: mode of goodness; rajaḥ: mode of passion; tathā: as in this

14.10 Sometimes the mode of passion becomes prominent, defeating the mode of goodness, O son of Bhārata. And sometimes the mode of goodness defeats passion, and at other times the mode of ignorance defeats goodness and passion. In this way there is always competition for supremacy.

सर्वद्वारेषु देहेऽस्मिन्प्रकाश उपजायते।
ज्ञानं यदा तदा विद्याद्विवृद्धं सत्त्वमित्युत॥ ११

sarvadvāreṣu dehesmin prakāśa upajāyate /
jñanaṁ yadā tadā vidyād vivṛddhaṁ sattvamityuta // 14.11

sarvadvāreṣu: all the gates; dehe 'smin: in this body; prakāśaḥ: quality of illumines; upajāyate: develops; jñanaṁ: knowledge; yadā: when; tadā: at that time; vidyāt: must know; vivṛddhaṁ: increased; sattvam: the mode of goodness; iti: thus; uta: said

14.11 When the light of Self-knowledge illumines all the senses (or gates) in the body, then it should be known that goodness is predominant.

लोभः प्रवृत्तिरारम्भः कर्मणामशमः स्पृहा।
रजस्येतानि जायन्ते विवृद्धे भरतर्षभ॥ १२

lobhaḥ pravṛttirārambhaḥ karmaṇāmaśamaḥ spṛhā /
rajasyetāni jāyante vivṛddhe bharatarṣabha // 14.12

lobhaḥ: greed; pravṛttiḥ: hankering; ārambhaḥ: endeavor; karmaṇām: of activities; aśamaḥ: uncontrollable; spṛhā: desire; rajasi: in the mode of passion; etāni: all this; jāyante: develop; vivṛddhe: when there is excess; bharatarṣabha: O chief of the descendants of Bhārata

14.12 O Bharatarṣabha, chief of the Bhārata, when there is an increase in the mode of passion, the symptoms of great attachment, uncontrollable desire, hankering, and intense endeavor develop.

अप्रकाशोऽप्रवृत्तिश्च प्रमादो मोह एव च।
तमस्येतानि जायन्ते विवृद्धे कुरुनन्दन॥ १३

aprakāśo'pravṛttiś ca pramādo moha eva ca /
tamasyetāni jāyante vivṛddhe kurunandana // 14.13

aprakāśaḥ: darkness; apravṛttiḥ: inactivity; ca: and; pramādaḥ: madness; mohaḥ: illusion; eva: certainly; ca: and; tamasi: in the mode of ignorance; etāni: these; jāyante: are manifested; vivrddhe: is developed; kurunandana: O son of Kuru

14.13 O son of Kuru, when there is an increase in the mode of ignorance, madness, illusion, inertia and darkness are manifested.

यदा सत्त्वे प्रवृद्धे तु प्रलयं याति देहभृत्।
तदोत्तमविदां लोकानमलान्प्रतिपद्यते॥ १४

yadā sattve pravṛddhe tu pralayaṁ yāti dehabhṛt /
tadottamavidāṁ lokānam alānpratipadyate // 14.14

yadā: when; sattve: mode of goodness; pravṛddhe: in development; tu: but; pralayaṁ: dissolution; yāti: goes; dehabhṛt: embodied; tadā: at that time; uttamavidāṁ: of the great sages; lokān: the planets; amalān: pure; pratipadyate: attains.

14.14 When one dies in the mode of goodness [satva], He goes to the highest of worlds.

रजसि प्रलयं गत्वा कर्मसङ्गिषु जायते।
तथा प्रलीनस्तमसि मूढयोनिषु जायते॥ १५

rajasi pralayaṁ gatvā karmasaṅgiṣu jāyate |
tathā pralīnas tamasi mūḍhayoniṣu jāyate || 14.15

rajasi: in passion; pralayaṁ: dissolution; gatvā: attaining; karmasaṅgiṣu: in the pursuit of activities; jāyate: takes birth; tathā: thereafter; pralīnaḥ: being dissolved; tamasi: in ignorance; mūḍha: ignorant; yoniṣu: species; jāyate: take birth

14.15 When one dies in the mode of passion [rajas], he takes birth among those engaged in activities. When he dies in the mode of ignorance [tamas], he takes birth in the space of the ignorant.

कर्मण: सुकृतस्याहु: सात्त्विकं निर्मलं फलम्।
रजसस्तु फलं दु:खमज्ञानं तमस: फलम्॥ १६

karmaṇaḥ sukṛtasyāhuḥ sāttvikaṁ nirmalaṁ phalam |
rajasastu phalaṁ duḥkham ajñānaṁ tamasaḥ phalam || 14.16

karmaṇaḥ: of work; sukṛtasya: in the mode of goodness; āhuḥ: said; sāttvikaṁ: mode of goodness; nirmalaṁ: purified; phalam: result; rajasaḥ: of the mode of passion; tu: but; phalaṁ: result; duḥkham: misery; ajñānaṁ: nonsense; tamasaḥ: of the mode of ignorance; phalam: result

14.16 By acting in the mode of goodness, one becomes

purified. Work done in the mode of passion results in distress, and actions performed in the mode of ignorance result in foolishness.

सत्त्वात्सञ्जायते ज्ञानं रजसो लोभ एव च।
प्रमादमोहौ तमसो भवतोऽज्ञानमेव च॥ १७

sattvātsañjāyate jñānaṁ rajaso lobha eva ca |
pramādamohau tamaso bhavato'jñānameva ca || 14.17

sattvāt: from the mode of goodness; sañjāyate: develops; jñānaṁ: knowledge; rajasaḥ: from the mode of passion; lobhaḥ: greed; eva: certainly; ca: also; pramāda: madness; mohau: illusion; tamasaḥ: from the mode of ignorance; bhavataḥ: develops; ajñānam: ignorance; eva: certainly; ca: also

14.17 From the mode of goodness, real knowledge develops; from the mode of passion, greed develops; from the mode of ignorance develops foolishness, madness and illusion.

ऊर्ध्वं गच्छन्ति सत्त्वस्था मध्ये तिष्ठन्ति राजसाः।
जघन्यगुणवृत्तिस्था अधो गच्छन्ति तामसाः॥ १८

ūrdhvaṁ gacchanti sattvasthā madhye tiṣṭhanti rājasāḥ |
jaghanyaguṇavṛttisthā adho gacchanti tāmasāḥ || 14.18

ūrdhvaṁ: upwards; gacchanti: go; sattvasthāḥ: one who is situated in the mode of goodness; madhye: in the middle; tiṣṭhanti: dwell; rājasāḥ: those who are situated in the mode of passion; jaghanya: abominable; guṇa: quality; vṛttisthāḥ: occupation; adhaḥ: down; gacchanti: go; tāmasāḥ: people in the mode of ignorance

14.18 Those situated in the mode of goodness gradually go upward to the higher world; those in the mode of passion live on the earthly planets; and those in the mode of ignorance go down to the worlds below.

नान्यं गुणेभ्यः कर्तारं यदा द्रष्टानुपश्यति।
गुणेभ्यश्च परं वेत्ति मद्भावं सोऽधिगच्छति॥ १९

nānyaṁ guṇebhyaḥ kartāraṁ yadā draṣṭānupaśyati /
guṇebhyaśca paraṁ vetti madbhāvaṁ so'dhigacchati // 14.19

na: never; anyaṁ: other than; guṇebhyaḥ: from the qualities; kartāraṁ: the performer; yadā: when; draṣṭā'nupaśyati: he who sees properly; guṇebhyaśca: from the modes of nature; paraṁ: transcendental; vetti: know; madbhāvaṁ: My spiritual nature; saḥ: he; adhigacchati: is promoted

14.19 When we see that there is nothing beyond these modes of nature in all activities and that the supreme Lord is transcendental to all these modes, the seeker can know My spiritual nature.

गुणानेतानतीत्य त्रीन्देही देहसमुद्भवान्।
जन्ममृत्युजरादुःखैर्विमुक्तोऽमृतमश्नुते॥ २०

guṇānetānatītya trīn dehī dehasamudbhavān /
janma-mṛtyu-jarā-duḥkhair vimukto'mṛtamaśnute // 14.20

guṇān: qualities; etān: all these; atītya: transcending; trīn: three; dehī: embodied; deha: body; samudbhavān: produced of; janma: birth; mṛtyu: death; jarā: old age; duḥkhaiḥ: distresses; vimuktaḥ: being freed from; amṛtam: nectar; aśnute: enjoys

14.20 When the embodied being is able to transcend these three modes, he can become free from birth, death, old age and their distresses and can enjoy nectar even in this life.

अर्जुन उवाच
कैर्लिङ्गैस्त्रीन्गुणानेतानतीतो भवति प्रभो।
किमाचारः कथं चैतांस्त्रीन्गुणानतिवर्तते॥ २१

arjuna uvāca
kair liṅgais trīnguṇān etān atīto bhavati prabho |
kim ācāraḥ kathaṁ caitāṁs trīnguṇānativartate || 14.21

arjuna uvāca: Arjuna says; kaiḥ: by which; liṅgaiḥ: symptoms; trīn: three; guṇān: qualities; etān: all these; atītaḥ: having transcended; bhavati: become; prabho: my Lord; kim: what; ācāraḥ: behavior; kathaṁ: what; ca: also; etāṁ: these; trīn: three; guṇān: qualities; ativartate: transcend

14.21 Arjuna inquires: O my Lord, by what symptoms is one known who is transcendental to those modes? What is his behavior? And how does he transcend the modes of nature?

श्री भगवानुवाच
प्रकाशं च प्रवृत्तिं च मोहमेव च पाण्डव।
न द्वेष्टि सम्प्रवृत्तानि न निवृत्तानि काङ्क्षति॥ २२

śrībhagavānuvāca
prakāśaṁ ca pravṛttiṁ ca mohameva ca pāṇḍava |
na dveṣṭi saṁpravṛttāni na nivṛttāni kāṅkṣati || 14.22

śrībhagavānuvāca: the supreme personality of Divine says; prakāśaṁ ca: and illumination; pravṛttiṁ ca: and attachment; mohaṁ: illusion; eva ca: also; pāṇḍava: O son of Pāṇḍu; na dveṣṭi: does not hate; saṁpravṛttāni: although developed; na nivṛttāni: nor stop development; kāṅkṣati: desires

उदासीनवदासीनो गुणैर्यो न विचाल्यते।
गुणा वर्तन्त इत्येव योऽवतिष्ठति नेङ्गते॥ २३

udāsīnavadāsīno guṇairyo na vicālyate |
guṇā vartanta ityeva yo'vatiṣṭhati neṅgate || 14.23

udāsīnavat: as if neutral; āsīnaḥ: situated; guṇaiḥ: by the qualities; yaḥ: one who; na: never; vicālyate: is agitated; guṇāḥ: the qualities; vartante: is situated; ityeva: knowing thus; yaḥ: one who; avatiṣṭhati: remains; na: never; eṅgati: flickering

समदुःखसुखः स्वस्थः समलोष्टाश्मकाञ्चनः।
तुल्यप्रियाप्रियो धीरस्तुल्यनिन्दात्मसंस्तुतिः॥ २४

sama-duḥkha-sukhaḥ svasthaḥ sama-loṣṭāśma-kāñcanaḥ /
tulya-priyāpriyo dhīras tulya-nindātma-saṁstutiḥ // 14.24

sama: equal; duḥkha: in distress; sukhaḥ: in happiness; svasthaḥ: being situated himself; sama: equally; loṣṭa: a lump of earth; aśma: stone; kāñcanaḥ: gold; tulya: equally disposed; priya: dear; apriyo: undesirable; dhīraḥ: steady; tulya: equally; nindā: in defamation; ātmasaṁstutiḥ: in praise of himself

मानापमानयोस्तुल्यस्तुल्यो मित्रारिपक्षयोः।
सर्वारम्भपरित्यागी गुणातीतः स उच्यते॥ २५।

mānāpamānyos tulyastulyo mitrāri-pakṣayoḥ /
sarvārambha-parityāgī guṇātitaḥ sa ucyate // 14.25

māna: in honor; apamānyoḥ: dishonor; tulyaḥ: equally; tulyaḥ: equally; mitra: friend; ari: enemy; pakṣayoḥ: in parties; sarva: all; ārambha: endeavor; parityāgī: renouncer; guṇātītaḥ: transcendental to the material modes of nature; saḥ: he; ucyate: is said to be

14.22,23,24,25 The Blessed Lord says: He who does not hate illumination, attachment and delusion when they are present, nor longs for them when they disappear; who is seated like one unconcerned, being situated beyond these material reactions of the modes of nature, who remains firm, knowing that the modes alone are active; He who regards alike pleasure and pain, and looks on a lump of earth, a stone and a piece of gold with an equal eye; who is wise and holds praise and blame to be the same; who is unchanged in honor and dishonor, who treats friend and foe alike, who has abandoned all result based undertakings—such a man is said to have transcended the modes of nature.

मां च योऽव्यभिचारेण भक्तियोगेन सेवते।
स गुणान्समतीत्यैतान्ब्रह्मभूयाय कल्पते॥ २६

maṁ ca yo'vyabhicāreṇa bhaktiyogena sevate |
sa guṇān-samatītyaitān brahmabhūyāya kalpate || 14.26

maṁ: unto Me; ca: also; yaḥ: person; avyabhicāreṇa: without fail; bhaktiyogena: by devotional service; sevate: renders service; saḥ: he; guṇān: all the modes of material nature; samatītya: transcending; etān: all this; brahmabhūyāya: to be elevated to the Brahman; kalpate: is considered.

14.26 One who engages in full devotional service, who does not fall down in any circumstance, at once transcends the modes of material nature and thus comes to the level of Brahman.

ब्रह्मणो हि प्रतिष्ठाहममृतस्याव्ययस्य च।
शाश्वतस्य च धर्मस्य सुखस्यैकान्तिकस्य च॥ २७

brahmaṇo hi pratiṣṭhāham amṛtasyāvyayasya ca |
śāśvatasya ca dharmasya sukhasyaikāntikasya ca || 14.27

brahmaṇaḥ: of the impersonal brahma; hi: certainly; pratiṣṭhā: the rest; aham: I am; amṛtasya: of the immortal; avyayasya: of the imperishable; ca: also; śāśvatasya: of the eternal; ca: and; dharmasya: of the rightful state; sukhasya: happiness; aikāntikasya: ultimate; ca: also.

14.27 And I am the basis of Brahman, which is the rightful state of ultimate happiness, and which is immortal, imperishable and eternal.

इति श्रीमद्भगवद्गीतासूपनिषत्सु ब्रह्मविद्यायां योगशास्त्रे
श्रीकृष्णार्जुनसंवादे गुणत्रयविभागयोगो नाम चतुर्दशोऽध्यायः ॥

iti śrīmad bhagavadgītāsūpaniṣatsu brahmavidyāyām
yogaśāstre śrīkṛṣṇārjuna saṁvāde
Guṇatraya-vibhāgayogo nāma
caturdaśo'dhyāyaḥ ||

In the ***Upaniṣad*** of ***Śrimad Bhagavad Gītā***, the scripture of yoga dealing with ***Brahmavidyā Yogaśāstra,*** the science of Brahman, the Supreme Absolute, in the form of ***Śrī Kṛṣṇārjuna saṁvād,*** dialogue between Śrī Kṛṣṇa and Arjuna, this is the fourteenth chapter named, ***Guṇatraya Vibhāga Yogaḥ,*** *'The Yoga of the Division of the three Guṇas.'*

CHAPTER 15

अथ पञ्चदशोऽध्यायः

पुरुषोत्तमयोगः

Puruṣottama Yogaḥ

श्री भगवानुवाच
ऊर्ध्वमूलमधःशाखमेशत्थं प्राहुरव्ययम्।
छन्दांसि यस्य पर्णानि यस्तं वेद स वेदवित्॥ १

śrī bhagavan uvāca
ūrdhvamūlamadhaḥ śākham aśvatthaṁ prāhuravyayam /
chandāṁsi yasya parṇāni yastaṁ veda sa vedavit // 15.1

śrī bhagavan uvāca: the Lord says; ūrdhvamūlam: with roots above; adhaḥ: downwards; śākham: branches; aśvatthaṁ: banyan tree; prāhuḥ: is said; avyayam: eternal; chandāṁsi: the vedic hymns; yasya: of which; parṇāni: leaves; yaḥ: anyone who; taṁ: that; veda: knows; saḥ: he; vedavit: knower of the Vedas

15.1 Śrī Bhagavān says, The imperishable banyan tree of life, symbolized by the Aśvattha, has its roots above, with the leaves and branches spreading below the earth. The leaves are said to be the Vedic hymns. One who knows this eternal tree becomes the knower of the Vedas.

अधश्चोर्ध्वं प्रसृतास्तस्य शाखा
गुणप्रवृद्धा विषयप्रवालाः।
अधश्च मूलान्यनुसंततानि
कर्मानुबन्धीनि मनुष्यलोके॥ २

adhaś cordhvaṁ prasṛtās tasya śākhā
guṇa-pravṛddhā viṣaya-pravālāḥ /
adhaśca mūlāny anusaṁtatāni
karmānubandhīni manuṣya-loke // 15.2

adhaḥ: below; ca: and; urdhvaṁ: above; prasṛtāḥ: extended; tasya: its; śākhāḥ: branches; guṇa: by the human attributes; pravṛddhāḥ: nourished; viṣaya: sense objects; pravālāḥ: buds; adhaḥ: downward; ca: and; mūlani: roots; anusaṁtatāni: extended; karma: action; anubandhīni: bound; manuṣyaloke: in the world of men

15.2 The branches of this tree extend below and above the earth, nourished by the three human attributes, guṇa. Its buds are the sense objects. This tree also has roots going down and these are bound to the resultant actions of humans.

न रूपमस्येह तथोपलभ्यते
नान्तो न चादिर्न च संप्रतिष्ठा।
अश्वत्थमेनं सुविरूढमूल-
मसङ्गशस्त्रेण दृढेन छित्त्वा॥ ३

na rūpam asyeha tathopalabhyate
nānto na cādirna ca saṁpratiṣṭhā /
aśvatthamenaṁ su-virūḍha-mūlam
asaṅga-śastreṇa dṛḍhena chittvā // 15.3

na: not; rūpam: form; asya: its; iha: here; tathā: as such; upalabhyate: can be perceived; na: not; antaḥ: end; na: not; ca: and; ādiḥr: beginning; na: not; ca: and; saṁpratiṣṭhā: foundation; aśvatthaṁ: banyan tree; enaṁ: this; suvirūḍha:

strongly; mūlaṁ: rooted; asaṅgaśastreṇa: by the weapon of detachment; dṛḍhena: strong; chittvā: cut down

15.3 The real form of this tree cannot be perceived. No one can understand where it ends, where it begins, or where its foundation is. But with determination one must cut down this strongly rooted tree with the weapon of detachment.

ततः पदं तत्परिमार्गितव्यं
यस्मिन्गता न निवर्तन्ति भूयः ।
तमेव चाद्यं पुरुषं प्रपद्ये
यतः प्रवृत्तिः प्रसृता पुराणी ॥ ४

tataḥ padaṁ tat parimārgitavyaṁ
yasmingatā na nivartanti bhūyaḥ /
tameva cādyaṁ puruṣaṁ prapadye
yataḥ pravṛittiḥ prasṛtā purāṇī // 15.4

tataḥ: thereafter; padaṁ: goal; tat: that; parimārgitavyaṁ: has to be searched out; yasmin: where; gatāḥ: going; na: not; nivartanti: return; bhūyaḥ: again; taṁ: in that; eva: even; ca: and; ādyaṁ: original; puruṣaṁ: supreme; prapadye: surrender; yataḥ: from whom; pravṛittiḥ: activity; prasṛtā: began; purāṇī: ancient

15.4 One must then seek that place from which having gone, one never returns and surrender to the Supreme Being from whom all activities started from ancient times.

निर्मानमोहा जितसङ्गदोषा
अध्यात्मनित्या विनिवृत्तकामाः ।
द्वन्द्वैर्विमुक्ताः सुखदुःखसंज्ञै-
र्गच्छन्त्यमूढाः पदमव्ययं तत् ॥ ५

nirmāna-mohā jita-saṅga-doṣā
adhyātma-nityā vinivṛitta-kāmāḥ /

dvandvair vimuktāḥ sukha-duḥkha-sañjñair
gacchanty amūḍhāḥ padam avyayaṁ tat // 15.5

nirmāna: without pride; mohāḥ: delusion; jita: having conquered; saṅga: attachment; doṣāḥ: defects; adhyātma: in the Self; nityāḥ: eternally; vinivṛitta: detached; kāmāḥ: from desires; dvandvaiḥ: from the dualities; vimuktāḥ: liberated; sukha: happiness; duḥkha: sorrow; sañjñaiḥ: known; gacchanti: reach; amūḍhāḥ: not confused; padam: goal; avyayaṁ: eternal; tat: that

15.5 Those who are free from pride, delusion, and attachment, those who dwell in the Self, who are done with lust, who are free from dualities of joy and sorrow, not confused and those who know how to surrender to the supreme person, attain the eternal consciousness.

न तद्भासयते सूर्यो न शशाङ्को न पावकः।
यद्गत्वा न निवर्तन्ते तद्धाम परमं मम ॥ ६

na tadbhāsayate sūryo na śaśāṅko na pāvakaḥ /
yadgatvā na nivartante taddhāma paramaṁ mama // 15.6

na: not; tat: that; bhāsayate: illuminates; sūryaḥ: the sun; na: not; śaśāṅkaḥ: the moon; na: not; pāvakaḥ: fire; yat: where; gatvā: going; na: not; nivartante: return; tad dhāma: that abode; paramaṁ: supreme; mama: My

15.6 That supreme space of eternal consciousness, My consciousness, is not illumined by the Sun or the Moon, or by fire. Those who enter that space never return to this material world.

ममैवांशो जीवलोके जीवभूतः सनातनः।
मनःषष्ठानीन्द्रियाणि प्रकृतिस्थानि कर्षति ॥ ७

mamai'vā'ṁśo jīvaloke jīvabhūtaḥ sanātanaḥ /
manaḥ ṣasḍhānī'ndriyāṇi prakṛitisthāni karṣati // 15.7

mama: My; eva: even; aṁśaḥ: portion; jīvaloke : in the world of life; jīvabhūtaḥ:

the living entity; sanātanaḥ: eternal; manaḥ: with the mind; ṣaṣḍāni: six; indriyāṇi: senses; prakṛiti: active principle; sthāni: staying; karṣati: attract

15.7 The living entities in this conditioned material world are a portion of My eternal Self; in this conditioned material world they are attracted by the six senses, which include the mind, dwelling in prakṛti, the active energy principle.

शरीरं यदवाप्नोति यच्चाप्युत्क्रामतीशरः।
गृहीत्वैतानि संयाति वायुर्गन्धानिवाशयात्॥ ८

śarīraṁ yadavāpnoti yaccāpyutkrāmatīśvaraḥ |
grihītvai'tāni saṁyāti vāyurgandhānivāśayāt || 15.8

śarīraṁ: body; yat: when; avāpnoti: gets; yat: when; cāpi: and also; utkrāmati: leaves; īśvaraḥ: the lord of the mind body; grihītvā: taking; etāni: all these; saṁyāti: goes away; vāyuḥ: the wind; gandhān: smells; iva: like; āśayāt: from their source

15.8 The spirit in the mind-body living in this material world moves from one body to another carrying these just as air carries aroma.

श्रोत्रं चक्षुः स्पर्शनं च रसनं घ्राणमेव च।
अधिष्ठाय मनश्चायं विषयानुपसेवते॥ ९

śrotraṁ cakṣuḥ sparśanaṁ ca rasanaṁ ghrāṇaṁ eva ca |
adhiṣṭhāya manaścāyaṁ viṣayānupasevate || 15.9

śrotraṁ: ears; cakṣuḥ: eyes; sparśanaṁ: touch; ca: and; rasanaṁ: tongue; ghrāṇaṁ: smelling power; eva: even; ca: and; adhiṣṭhāya: presiding over; manaḥ: mind; ca: and; ayaṁ: he; viṣayān: sense objects; upasevate: enjoys

15.9 The living entity, the spirit, leaves one body, takes some other body and gets new eyes, ears, nose, tongue and sensing body according to the samskāras it had in its causal layer and enjoys the new mental setup.

उत्क्रामन्तं स्थितं वापि भुञ्जानं वा गुणान्वितम्।
विमूढा नानुपश्यन्ति पश्यन्ति ज्ञानचक्षुषः॥ १०

utkrāmantaṁ sthitaṁ vāpi bhuñjānaṁ vā guṇānvitam |
vimūḍhā nānupaśyanti paśyanti jñānacakṣuṣah || 15.10

utkrāmantaṁ: departing; sthitaṁ: staying; vāpi: or also; bhuñjānaṁ: enjoying; vā: or; guṇānvitam: united with attributes; vimūḍhā: foolish persons; na: not; anupaśyanti: see; paśyanti: see; jñānacakṣuṣah: those who have the eyes of knowledge

15.10 Fools in ignorance do not perceive the spirit being united with the guṇās as its enters, enjoys and leaves the body. The one whose inner eye is open clearly perceives everything.

यतन्तो योगिनश्चैनं पश्यन्त्यात्मन्यवस्थितम्।
यतन्तोऽप्यकृतात्मानो नैनं पश्यन्त्यचेतसः॥ ११

yatanto yoginaścainaṁ paśyantyātmanyavasthitam |
yatanto'pyakṛtātmāno nainaṁ paśyantyacetasaḥ || 15.11

yatantaḥ: trying; yoginaḥ: those who practice yoga; ca: and; enaṁ: this; paśyanti: can see; ātmani: in the self; avasthitam: situated; yatantaḥ: trying; api: also; akṛtātmānaḥ: without an understanding of the self; na: not; enaṁ: this; paśyanti: see; acetasaḥ: unintelligent

15.11 The serious practitioner of Yoga, with an understanding of his self, can see all this clearly. But those who do not have an understanding of the self, however much they try, cannot see.

यदादित्यगतं तेजो जगद्भासयतेऽखिलम्।
यच्चन्द्रमसि यच्चाग्नौ तत्तेजो विद्धि मामकम्॥ १२

yad āditya-gataṁ tejo jagad bhāsayate'khilam
yac candramasi yaccāgnau tattejo viddhi māmakam || 15.12

yat: which; ādityagataṁ: residing in the sun; tejaḥ: light; jagat: world; bhāsayate: lights up; akhilam: completely; yat: which; candramasi: in the moon; yat: which; ca: and; agnau: in the fire; tat: that; tejaḥ: light; viddhi: know; māmakam: from me

15.12 The light of the sun, the light of the moon and the light of fire, all their radiance is also from Me.

गामाविश्य च भूतानि धारयाम्यहमोजसा।
पुष्णामि चौषधीः सर्वाः सोमो भूत्वा रसात्मकः॥ १३

gāmāviśya ca bhūtāni dhārayāmy aham ojasā |
puṣṇāmi cauṣadhīḥ sarvāḥ somo bhūtvā rasātmakaḥ || 15.13

gām: the earth; āviśya: entering; ca: and; bhūtāni: living beings; dhārayāmi: sustaining; aham: I; ojasā: by energy; puṣṇāmi: nourishing; ca: and; oṣadhīḥ: plant life; sarvāḥ: all; somaḥ: the Moon; bhūtvā: becoming; rasātmakaḥ: watery

15.13 Entering into earth, I support all beings with My energy; becoming the watery moon I nourish all plant life.

अहं वैशानरो भूत्वा प्राणिनां देहमाश्रितः।
प्राणापानसमायुक्तः पचाम्यन्नं चतुर्विधम्॥ १४

ahaṁ vaiśvānaro bhūtvā prāṇināṁ dehamāśritaḥ |
prāṇāpāna-samāyuktaḥ pacāmy annaṁ caturvidham || 15.14

ahaṁ: I; vaiśvānaro: as the digestive fire; bhūtvā: becoming; prāṇinām: of all living beings; dehaṁ: body; āśritaḥ: situated; prāṇā: exhaled breath; apāna: inhaled breath; samāyuktaḥ: associated; pacāmi: digest; annaṁ: food; caturvidham: fourfold

15.14 I am the fire of digestion in every living body and I am the breath of life, exhaled and inhaled, with which I digest the four-fold food.

सर्वस्य चाहं हृदि सन्निविष्टो मत्तः स्मृतिर्ज्ञानमपोहनं च।
वेदैश्च सर्वैरहमेव वेद्यो वेदान्तकृद्वेदविदेव चाहम्॥ १५

sarvasya cāhaṁ hṛdi sanniviṣṭo
mattaḥ smṛtir jñānam apohanaṁ ca /
vedaiśca sarvairahameva vedyo
vedānta-kṛd vedavid eva cāham // 15.15

sarvasya: of all; ca: and; ahaṁ: I; hṛdi: in the heart; sanniviṣṭo: seated; mattaḥ: from Me; smṛtiḥ: memory; jñānaṁ: knowledge; apohanaṁ ca: and loss; vedaiḥ: by the Vedas; ca: also; sarvaiḥ: all; aham: I; eva: even; vedyaḥ: to be known; vedāntakṛt: creator of the Vedānta; vedavit: the knower of the Veda; eva: even; ca: and; aham: I

15.15 I am seated in everyone's heart and from Me came memory, knowledge and their loss. I am known by the Vedas; indeed, I am the Creator of Vedānta and I am the knower of the Vedas.

द्वाविमौ पुरुषौ लोके क्षरश्चाक्षर एव च।
क्षर: सर्वाणि भूतानि कूटस्थोऽक्षर उच्यते॥ १६

dvāvimau puruṣau loke kṣaraścākṣara eva ca /
kṣaraḥ sarvāṇi bhūtāni kūṭasthokṣara ucyate // 15.16

dvāu: two; imau: these; puruṣau: puruṣa; loke: in the world; kṣaraḥ: perishable; ca: and; akṣara: imperishable; eva: even; ca: and; kṣaraḥ: the perishable; sarvāṇi: all; bhūtāni: living being; kūṭasthaḥ: unchangeable; akṣara: imperishable; ucyate: is said

15.16 There are two things, the perishable and the imperishable, in this world. There are the living beings who are perishable while there is the unchangeable, the imperishable.

उत्तम: पुरुषस्त्वन्य: परमात्मेत्युदाहृत:।
यो लोकत्रयमाविश्य बिभर्त्यव्यय ईशर:॥ १७

uttamaḥ puruṣastv anyaḥ paramātmetyudāhṛtaḥ /
yo lokatrayamāviśya bibhartyavyaya īśvaraḥ // 15.17

uttamaḥ: the best; puruṣaḥ: puruṣa; tu: but; anyaḥ: another; paramātmā: the Supreme Self; iti: thus; udāhṛtaḥ: is said; yaḥ: who; lokatrayaṁ: the three worlds; āviśya: pervading; bibharti: sustaining; avyayaḥ: indestructible; īśvaraḥ: the Lord

15.17 Besides these two, there is the supreme Puruṣa the Lord Himself, who pervades and sustains these three worlds.

यस्मात्क्षरमतीतोऽहमक्षरादपि चोत्तमः।
अतोऽस्मि लोके वेदे च प्रथितः पुरुषोत्तमः॥ १८

yasmāt kṣaram atīto'ham akṣarād api cottamaḥ I
atosmi loke vede ca prathitaḥ puruṣottamaḥ II 15.18

yasmāt: from which; kṣaram: the perishable; atītaḥ: transcendental; aham: I; akṣarāt: from the impersishable; api: also; ca: and; uttamaḥ: the best; ataḥ: therefore; asmi: I am; loke: in the world; vede: in the Veda; ca: and; prathitaḥ: declared; puruṣottamaḥ: as the Supreme Purusha

15.18 As I am transcendental, beyond both the perishable and the imperishable, and the best, I am declared both in the world and in the Vedas as that supreme person, Puruṣottama.

यो मामेवमसंमूढो जानाति पुरुषोत्तमम्।
स सर्वविद्भजति मां सर्वभावेन भारत॥ १९

yo mām evam asammūḍho jānāti puruṣottamam I
sa sarva-vidbhajati mām sarvabhāvena bhārata II 15.19

yaḥ: who; mām: Me; evam: thus; asammūḍhaḥ: without a doubt; jānāti: knows; puruṣottamam: the supreme Puruṣa; saḥ: he; sarvavid: knower of everything; bhajati: worships; mām: Me; sarva bhāvena: with all being; bhārata: O son of Bhārata

15.19 Whoever knows Me as the supreme without a doubt, is to be understood as the knower of everything and he worships Me with all his being, O son of Bhārata.

इति गुह्यतमं शास्त्रमिदमुक्तं मयाऽनघ ।
एतद्बुद्ध्वा बुद्धिमान्स्यात्कृतकृत्यश्च भारत ॥ २०

iti guhyatamaṁ śāstram idam uktaṁ mayānagha /
etad buddhvā buddhimān syāt kṛtakṛtyaśca bhārata // 15.20

iti: thus; guhyatamaṁ: secret; śāstraṁ: science; idaṁ: this; uktaṁ: taught; mayā: by Me; anagha: O sinless one; etat: this; buddhvā: knowing; buddhimān: wise; syāt: becomes; kṛtakṛtyaḥ: accomplished all actions; ca: and; bhārata: O son of Bhārata

15.20 This is the most profound teaching taught by Me, O Sinless One and whoever knows this will become wise and his actions will bear fruit.

इति श्रीमद्भगवद्गीतासूपनिषत्सु ब्रह्मविद्यायां योगशास्त्रे
श्रीकृष्णार्जुनसंवादे पुरुषोत्तमयोगो नाम पञ्चदशोऽध्यायः ॥

iti śrīmad bhagavadgītāsūpaniṣatsu brahmavidyāyām
yogaśāstre śrīkṛṣṇārjuna saṁvāde puruṣottamayogo nāma
pañcadaśo 'dhyāyaḥ //

In the ***Upaniṣad*** of ***Śrimad Bhagavad Gītā***, the scripture of yoga dealing with ***Brahmavidyā Yogaśāstra,*** the science of Brahman, the Supreme Absolute, in the form of ***Śrī Kṛṣṇārjuna saṁvād,*** dialogue between Śrī Kṛṣṇa and Arjuna, this is the fifteenth chapter named, ***Puruṣottama Yogaḥ,*** *'The Yoga of the Supreme Being'.*

CHAPTER

16

अथ षोडशोऽध्यायः

दैवासुरसम्पद्विभागयोगः

Daivāsura Saṁpad Vibhāga Yogaḥ

श्री भगवानुवाच
अभयं सत्त्वसंशुद्धिर्ज्ञानयोगव्यवस्थितिः।
दानं दमश्च यज्ञश्च स्वाध्यायस्तप आर्जवम्॥ १

śrī bhagavan uvāca
abhayaṁ sattva-saṁśuddhir jñānayogavyavasthitiḥ /
dānaṁ damaśca yajñaś ca svādhyāyastapa ārjavam // 16.1

अहिंसा सत्यमक्रोधस्त्यागः शान्तिरपैशुनम्।
दया भूतेष्वलोलुप्त्वं मार्दवं ह्रीरचापलम्॥ २

ahiṁsā satyam akrodhas tyāgaḥ śāntir apaiśunam /
dayā bhūteṣv aloluptvaṁ mārdavaṁ hrīracāpalam // 16.2

तेजः क्षमा धृतिः शौचमद्रोहो नातिमानिता।
भवन्ति संपदं दैवीमभिजातस्य भारत॥ ३

tejaḥ kṣamā dhṛtiḥ śaucam adroho nātimānitā /
bhavanti saṁpadaṁ daivīm abhijātasya bhārata // 16.3

śrī bhagavan uvāca: Lord Kṛṣṇa says; abhayaṁ: fearlessness; sattvasaṁśuddhiḥ: purification of one's existence; jñāna: knowledge; yoga: of linking up; vyavasthitiḥ: remaining engaged in; dānaṁ: charity; damaś ca: and controlling the mind; yajñaś ca: and performance of sacrifice; svādhyāyaḥ: study of vedic literature; tapaḥ: austerity; ārjavam: simplicity;

ahiṁsā: nonviolence; satyaṁ: truthfulness; akrodhaḥ: freedom from anger; tyāgaḥ: renunciation; sāntiḥ: tranquillity; apaiśunaṁ: aversion to fault-finding; dayā: mercy; bhūteṣu: towards all living entities; aloluptvaṁ: freedom from greed; mārdavaṁ: gentleness; hrīḥ: modesty; acāpalam: determination;

tejaḥ: vigor; kṣamā: forgiveness; dhṛtiḥ: fortitude; śaucaṁ: cleanliness; adrohaḥ: freedom from envy; na: not; atimānitā: expectation of honor; bhavanti: become; saṁpadaṁ: qualities; daivīṁ: transcendental; abhijātasya: of one who is born of; bhārata: O son of Bhārata (Arjuna).

16.1,2,3 Bhagavān Kṛṣṇa says: Fearlessness, purification of the being, cultivation of spiritual knowledge, charity and being centered on the being, performance of sacrifices, and accumulation of knowledge, austerity, simplicity, non-violence, truthfulness, freedom from anger, renunciation, tranquility, aversion to fault finding, compassion for all living entities, freedom from covetousness, gentleness, modesty, studied determination, vigor, more forgiveness, fortitude, cleanliness, freedom from envy, and from the passion of honor, these transcendental qualities, O Son of Bhārata (Arjuna), belong to divine men, endowed with divine nature.

दम्भो दर्पोऽभिमानश्च क्रोधः पारुष्यमेव च।
अज्ञानं चाभिजातस्य पार्थ सम्पदमासुरीम्॥ ४

dambho darpo'bhimānaś ca krodhaḥ pāruṣyameva ca |
ajñānaṁ cābhijātasya pārtha sampadamāsurīm || 16.4

dambhaḥ: pride; darpaḥ: arrogance; abhimānaḥ: conceit; ca: and; krodhaḥ: anger; pāruṣyaṁ: harshness; eva: certainly; ca: and; ajñānaṁ: ignorance; ca: and; abhijātasya: one who is born of; pārtha: O son of Prithā; saṁpadaṁ: nature; āsurīm: demonic.

16.4 Pride, arrogance, conceit, anger, harshness or cruelty, and ignorance—these qualities belong to those born with demonic nature, O Pārtha (Arjuna).

दैवी सम्पद्विमोक्षाय निबन्धायासुरी मता।
मा शुचः सम्पदं दैवीमभिजातोऽसि पाण्डव।। ५

daivī sampadvimokṣāya nibandhayāsuri matā /
mā śucāḥ sampadaṁ daivīm abhijātosi pāṇḍava // *16.5*

daivī: transcendental, divine; saṁpat: nature; vimokṣāya: for liberation; nibandhaya: for bondage; asuri: demonic qualities; matā: it is considered; mā: do not; śucāḥ: worry; saṁpadaṁ: nature; daivīm: transcendental, divine; abhijātaḥ: born; asi: you are; pāṇḍava: O son of Pāṇḍu.

16.5 The transcendental qualities are conducive to liberation, whereas the demonic qualities make for bondage. Do not worry, Pāṇḍava (Arjuna), you are born with Divine qualities.

द्वौ भूतसर्गौ लोकेऽस्मिन्दैव आसुर एव च।
दैवो विस्तरशः प्रोक्त आसुरं पार्थ मे श्रृणु।। ६।

dvau bhūtasargau loke'smin daiva āsura eva ca /
daivo vistaraśaḥ prokta āsuraṁ pārtha me śṛṇu // *16.6*

dvau: two; bhūtasargau: created living beings; loke: in the world; asmin: in this; daiva: godly; āsura: demonic; eva: certainly; ca: and; daivaḥ: divine; vistaraśaḥ: in great detail; proktaḥ: said; āsuraṁ: demonic; pārtha: O son of Pritā; me: from Me; śṛṇu: hear.

16.6 Pārtha (Arjuna), in this world there are two kinds of created beings, one is divine and the other, demonic. I have explained at length to you the Divine qualities, now understand the demonic qualities also, so that you will understand and live your life blissfully and happily.

प्रवृत्तिं च निवृत्तिं च जना न विदुरासुराः ।
न शौचं नापि चाचारो न सत्यं तेषु विद्यते ॥ ७॥

pravṛttiṁ ca nivṛttiṁ ca janā na vidurāsurāḥ I
na śaucaṁ nāpi cācāro na satyaṁ teṣu vidyate II 16.7

pravṛttiṁ: bondages; ca: also; nivṛttiṁ: liberation; ca: and; janāḥ: persons; na: never; viduḥ: know; āsurāḥ: demoniac qualities; na: never; śaucaṁ: cleanliness; na: nor; api: also; ca: and; ācāraḥ: behavior; na: never; satyaṁ: truth; teṣu: in them; vidyate: there is.

16.7 Persons with demonic nature do not know what is bondage and what is liberation; not what is cleanliness; truthful behavior is not in them.

असत्यमप्रतिष्ठं ते जगदाहुरनीशरम् ।
अपरस्परसंभूतं किमन्यत्कामहैतुकम् ॥ ८

asatyamapratiṣṭhaṁ te jagad āhura nīśvaram I
aparaspara-saṁbhūtaṁ kim anyat kāmahaitukam II 16.8

asatyaṁ: unreal; apratiṣṭhaṁ: without foundation; te: they; jagat: the cosmic manifestation; āhuḥ: is said; anīśvaram: with no controller; aparasparasaṁbhūtaṁ: born of mutual union; kimanyat: there is no other cause; kāmahaitukam: it is due to lust only.

16.8 People with such qualities think there is no ultimate energy or intelligence that is running this planet earth, that is running the universe, and that this whole creation is produced out of lust and desire, and is unreal.

एतां दृष्टिमवष्टभ्य नष्टात्मानोऽल्पबुद्धयः।
प्रभवन्त्युग्रकर्माणः क्षयाय जगतोऽहिताः॥ ९

etāṁ dṛṣṭimavaṣṭabhya naṣṭātmāno'lpabuddhayaḥ |
prabhavanty ugra-karmāṇaḥ kṣayāya jagato'hitāḥ || 16.9

etāṁ: thus; dṛṣṭim: vision; avaṣṭabhya: accepting; naṣṭa: lost; ātmānaḥ: self; alpabuddhayaḥ: less intelligent; prabhavanti: come forth; ugrakarmāṇaḥ: in painful activities; kṣayāya: for the destruction; jagataḥ: of the world; ahitāḥ: unbeneficial.

16.9 Following this material view of creation, these degraded souls with small intellect, lost in themselves and committing cruel deeds are engaged in the destruction of the world.

काममाश्रित्य दुष्पूरं दम्भमानमदान्विताः।
मोहाद्गृहीत्वाऽसद्ग्राहान्प्रवर्तन्तेऽशुचिव्रताः॥ १०

kāmamāśritya duṣpūraṁ dambhamānamadānvitāḥ |
mohādgṛhītvā 'sadgrāhān pravartante'śucivratāḥ || 16.10

kāmaṁ: lust; āśritya: taking shelter of; duṣpūraṁ: insatiable; dambha: pride; māna: false prestige; madānvitāḥ: absorbed in conceit; mohāt: by illusion; gṛhītvā: taking; asat: nonpermanent; grāhān: things; pravartante: flourish; aśuci: unclean; vratāḥ: avowed.

16.10 Filled with insatiable desires, hypocrisy, pride, and arrogance; holding wrong views due to delusion, they act with impure motives and for impermanent objectives.

चिन्तामपरिमेयां च प्रलयान्तामुपाश्रिताः।
कामोपभोगपरमा एतावदिति निश्चिताः॥ ११

cintāmaparimeyāṁ ca pralayāntāmupāśritāḥ |
kāmopabhogaparamā etāvaditi niścitāḥ || 16.11

आशापाशशतैर्बद्धाः कामक्रोधपरायणाः।
ईहन्ते कामभोगार्थमन्यायेनार्थसञ्चयान्॥ १२

āśāpāśaśatairbaddhāḥ kāmakrodhaparāyaṇāḥ I
īhante kāmabhogārtham anyāyenā'rthasañcayān II 16.12

cintāṁ: fears and anxieties; aparimeyāṁ: unmeasurable; ca: and; pralayāntāṁ: unto the point of death; upāśritāḥ: having taken shelter of them; kāmopabhoga: sense gratification; paramāḥ: the highest goal of life; etavad: thus; iti: in this way; niścitāḥ: ascertained; āśāpāśa: entanglements in the network of hope; śataiḥ: by hundreds; baddhāḥ: being bound; kāma: lust; krodha: anger; parāyaṇāḥ: always situated in that mentality; īhante: desire; kāma: lust; bhogā: sense enjoyment; arthaṁ: for that purpose; anyāyenā: illegally; artha: wealth; sañcayān: accumulate.

16.11,12 Obsessed with endless anxiety lasting until death, considering sense gratification their highest aim, and convinced that sense pleasure is everything; bound by hundreds of ties of desire and enslaved and filled with anger, they strive to obtain wealth by unlawful means to fulfill sensual pleasures.

इदमद्य मया लब्धमिमं प्राप्स्ये मनोरथम्।
इदमस्तीदमपि मे भविष्यति पुनर्धनम्॥ १३

idamadya mayā labdham imaṁ prāpsye manoratham I
idamastīdamapi me bhaviṣyati punardhanam II 16.13

idaṁ: this; adya: today, now; mayā: by me; labdhaṁ: attained; imaṁ: this; prāpsye: I shall gain; manoratham: according to my desires; idaṁ: this; asti: there is; idaṁ: this; api: also; me: mine; bhaviṣyati: will increase in the future; punaḥ: again; dhanaṁ: wealth.

16.13 They think: This has been gained by me today; I shall fulfill this desire; I have this much wealth and will have more wealth in the future;

असौ मया हतः शत्रुर्हनिष्ये चापरानपि।
ईशरोऽहमहं भोगी सिद्धोऽहं बलवान्सुखी॥ १४

asau mayā hataḥ śatrur hanişye cāparānapi |
īśvaro'hamahaṁ bhogī siddho'haṁ balavānsukhī || 16.14

आढयोऽभिजनवानस्मि कोऽन्योऽस्ति सदृशो मया।
यक्ष्ये दास्यामि मोदिष्य इत्यज्ञानविमोहिताः॥ १५

āḍhyo'bhijanavānasmi ko'nyo'sti sadṛśo mayā |
yakṣye dāsyāmi modiṣya ity ajñānavimohitāḥ || 16.15

asau: that; mayā: by me; hataḥ: has been killed; śatruḥ: enemy; haniṣye: I shall kill; ca: also; aparān: others; api: certainly; īśvaro: the lord; ahaṁ: I am; ahaṁ: I am; bhogī: the enjoyer; siddhaḥ: complete, perfect; ahaṁ: I am; balavān: powerful; sukhī: happy; āḍhyaḥ: wealthy; abhijanavān: surrounded by aristocratic relatives; asmi: I am; kaḥ: who else; anyaḥ: other; asti: there is; sadṛśo: like; mayā: me; yakṣye: I shall sacrifice; dāsyāmi: I shall give charity; modiṣya: I shall rejoice; iti: thus; ajñāna: by ignorance; vimohitāḥ: misled, deluded by.

16.14, 15 That enemy has been slain by me, and I shall slay others also. I am the Lord. I am the enjoyer. I am successful, powerful, and happy; I am rich and born in a noble family. Who is equal to me? I shall perform sacrifice, I shall give charity, and I shall rejoice. Thus deluded by ignorance.

अनेकचित्तविभ्रान्ता मोहजालसमावृताः।
प्रसक्ताः कामभोगेषु पतन्ति नरकेऽशुचौ॥ १६

aneka-citta-vibhrāntā mohajālasamāvṛtāḥ |
prasaktāḥ kāmabhogeṣu patanti narake'śucau || 16. 16

aneka: many; citta vibhrāntāḥ: perplexed by anxieties; moha jāla: by a net of illusions; samāvṛtāḥ: surrounded; prasaktāḥ: attached; kāma: lust; bhogeṣu: sense gratification; patanti: slides down; narake: into hell; aśucau: unclean.

16.16 Thus confused by various anxieties and caught in a net of illusions, one becomes too deeply attached to sensory pleasures and falls into hell.

आत्मसम्भाविताः स्तब्धा धनमानमदान्विताः ।
यजन्ते नामयज्ञैस्ते दम्भेनाविधिपूर्वकम् ॥ १७

ātmasaṁbhāvitāḥ stabdhā dhana-māna-madānvitāḥ /
yajante nāma-yajñais te dambhenā'vidhipūrvakam // 16.17

ātmasaṁbhāvitāḥ: self-complacent; stabdhāḥ: conceited; dhanamāna: wealth and false pride; madānvitāḥ: absorbed in pride; yajante: perform sacrifices; nāma: in name only; yajñaiḥ: with such a sacrifice; te: they; dambhena: out of pride; avidhipūrvakaṁ: without following regulations.

16.17 Self-complacent and always conceited, deluded by wealth and false pride, they perform superficial sacrifices in name only, without following the vedic rules or regulations.

अहंकारं बलं दर्पं कामं क्रोधं च संश्रिताः ।
मामात्मपरदेहेषु प्रद्विषन्तोऽभ्यसूयकाः ॥ १८

ahaṁkāraṁ balaṁ darpaṁ kāmaṁ krodhaṁ ca saṁśritāḥ /
mām-ātma-paradeheṣu pradviṣanto'bhyasūyakāḥ // 16.18

ahaṁkāraṁ: false ego; balaṁ: power, strength; darpaṁ: arrogance, pride; kāmaṁ: lust; krodhaṁ: anger; ca: also; saṁśritāḥ: having taken shelter; mām: of Me; ātma: one's own; paradeheṣu: in other bodies; pradviṣantaḥ: blasphemes against God; abhyasūyakāḥ: envious.

16.18 The demonic person, consumed by ego, power, pride, lust and anger, becomes envious of the supreme personality of godhead, who is situated in his own body and in the bodies of others, and blasphemes against Him.

तानहं द्विषतः क्रूरान्संसारेषु नराधमान्।
क्षिपाम्यजस्रमशुभानासुरीष्वेव योनिषु॥ १९

tānahaṁ dviṣataḥ krūrān saṁsāreṣu narādhamān /
kṣipāmy ajasram aśubhān āsurīṣveva yoniṣu // 16.19

tān: those; ahaṁ: I; dviṣataḥ: envious; krūrān: cruel, wicked; saṁsāreṣu: into the ocean of material existence; narādhamān: the lowest of mankind; kṣipāmi: put; ajasraṁ: repeatedly; aśubhān: inauspicious; āsurīṣu: demonic; eva: certainly; yoniṣu: in the wombs.

16.19 Those who are envious (of Him) and cruel, who are the lowest among men, I repeatedly cast into the ocean of material existence, into various lowly, demonic forms of life.

आसुरीं योनिमापन्ना मूढा जन्मनि जन्मनि।
मामप्राप्यैव कौन्तेय ततो यान्त्यधमां गतिम्॥ २०

āsurīṁ yonimapannā mūḍhā janmani janmani /
māmaprāpyaiva kaunteya tato yāntyadhamāṁ gatim // 16.20

āsurīṁ: demonic; yoniṁ: species; apannā: gaining; mūḍhāḥ: the foolish; janmani janmani: in birth after birth; mām: unto Me; aprāpya: without achieving; eva: certainly; kaunteya: O son of Kuntī; tataḥ: thereafter; yānti: goes; adhamāṁ: condemned; gatim: destination.

16.20 These foolish beings attain repeated birth amongst the species of demoniac life. Without ever achieving Me, O Kaunteya (Son of Kuntī), they sink into the most abominable existence.

त्रिविधं नरकस्येदं द्वारं नाशनमात्मनः।
कामः क्रोधस्तथा लोभस्तस्मादेतत्त्रयं त्यजेत्॥ २१

trividhaṁ narakasyedaṁ dvāraṁ nāśanamātmanaḥ /
kāmaḥ krodhastathā lobhas tasmādetattrayaṁ tyajet // 16.21

trividhaṁ: three kinds of; narakasya: hellish; idaṁ: this; dvāraṁ: gate; nāśanaṁ: ruin, destruction; ātmanaḥ: of the self; kāmaḥ: lust; krodhaḥ: anger; tathā: as well as; lobhaḥ: greed; tasmāt: therefore; etat: these; trayaṁ: three; tyajet: give up.

16.21 There are three gates leading to this hell: lust, anger and greed. As they lead to the degradation of the soul, these three are to be abandoned.

एतैर्विमुक्तः कौन्तेय तमोद्वारैस्त्रिभिर्नरः।
आचरत्यात्मनः श्रेयस्ततो याति परां गतिम्॥ २२

etairvimuktaḥ kaunteya tamodvāraistribhirnaraḥ |
ācaratyātmanaḥ śreyas tato yāti parāṁ gatim || 16.22

etaiḥ: by these; vimuktaḥ: escaped; kaunteya: O son of Kuntī; tamodvāraiḥ: the gates of darkness; tribhiḥ: three kinds of; naraḥ: a person; ācarati: acts, behaves; ātmanaḥ: self; śreyaḥ: benediction; tataḥ: thereafter; yāti: goes; parāṁ: supreme; gatim: destination

16.22 Those who have escaped these three gates of hell, O Kaunteya, behave in a manner beneficial to the (evolution of the) soul, and thus (gradually) attain the supreme destination.

यः शास्त्रविधिमुत्सृज्य वर्तते कामकारतः।
न स सिद्धिमवाप्नोति न सुखं न परां गतिम्॥ २३

yaḥ śāstravidhimutsṛjya vartate kāmakārataḥ |
na sa siddhimavāpnoti na sukhaṁ na parāṁ gatim || 16.23

yaḥ: anyone; śāstravidhiṁ: the injunctions of the scriptures; utsṛjya: giving up; vartate: remains; kāmakārataḥ: acting whimsically in lust; na: never; saḥ: he; siddhiṁ: perfection; avāpnoti: achieves; na: never; sukhaṁ: happiness; na: never; parāṁ: the supreme; gatim: destination.

16.23 But he who discards scriptural injunctions and acts according to his base impulses attains neither perfection, nor happiness, nor the supreme destination.

तस्माच्छास्त्रं प्रमाणं ते कार्याकार्यव्यवस्थितौ।
ज्ञात्वा शास्त्रविधानोक्तं कर्म कर्तुमिहार्हसि ॥ २४

tasmācchāstraṁ pramāṇaṁ te kāryākāryavyavasthitau |
jñātvā śāstravidhānoktaṁ karma kartumihārhasi || 16.24

tasmāt: therefore; śāstraṁ: scriptures; pramāṇaṁ: evidence; te: your; kārya: duty; akārya: forbidden activities; vyavasthitau: in determining; jñātvā: knowing; śāstra: of scripture; vidhāna: regulations; uktaṁ: as declared; karma: work; kartuṁ: to do; ihā'rhasi: you should do it

16.24 By the regulations of the scriptures, one should understand what is duty and what is not duty. After being versed in scriptural injunctions, one should act accordingly.

इति श्रीमद्भगवद्गीतासूपनिषत्सु ब्रह्मविद्यायां योगशास्त्रे
श्रीकृष्णार्जुनसंवादे दैवासुरसम्पद्विभागयोगो नाम षोडशोऽध्यायः ॥

iti śrīmad bhagavadgītāsūpaniṣatsu brahmavidyāyām
yogaśāstre śrīkṛṣṇārjuna saṁvāde
daivāsurasaṁpad vibhāgayogo nāma
ṣoḍaśo'dhyāyaḥ ||

In the ***Upaniṣad*** of ***Śrimad Bhagavad Gītā***, the scripture of yoga dealing with ***Brahmavidyā Yogaśāstra,*** the science of Brahman, the Supreme Absolute, in the form of ***Śrī Kṛṣṇārjuna saṁvād,*** dialogue between Śrī Kṛṣṇa and Arjuna, this is the sixteenth chapter named, ***Daivāsura Saṁpad Vibhāga Yogaḥ***, *'The Yoga of Divine and Demonic Nature.'*

CHAPTER

17

अथ सप्तदशोऽध्यायः

श्रद्धात्रयविभागयोगः

Śraddhatraya Vibhāga Yogaḥ

अर्जुन उवाच

ये शास्त्रविधिमुत्सृज्य यजन्ते श्रद्धयान्विताः।

तेषां निष्ठा तु का कृष्ण सत्त्वमाहो रजस्तमः॥ १

arjuna uvāca

ye śāstravidhiṁ utsṛjya yajante śraddhayānvitāḥ /

teṣāṁ niṣṭhā tu kā kṛṣṇa sattvamāho rajastamaḥ // 17.1

arjuna uvāca: Arjuna says; ye: those; śāstravidhiṁ: the regulations of scripture; utsṛjya: giving up; yajante: worship; śraddhayā: authenticity; anvitāḥ: possessed of; teṣāṁ: of them; niṣṭhā: faith; tu: but; kā: what is that; Kṛṣṇa: O Kṛṣṇa; sattvaṁ: in goodness; āho: said; rajas: in aggression; tamaḥ: in ignorance.

17.1 Arjuna says: What is the mode of devotion of those who perform spiritual practices with authenticity, but without following the scriptural injunctions, O Kṛṣṇa? Is it in the mode of goodness, aggression or ignorance?

श्री भगवानुवाच।

त्रिविधा भवति श्रद्धा देहिनां सा स्वभावजा।

सात्त्विकी राजसी चैव तामसी चेति तां श्रृणु ॥ २

śrībhagavānuvāca

trividhā bhavati śraddhā dehināṁ sā svabhāvajā |
sāttvikī rājasī caiva tāmasī ceti tāṁ śṛṇu || 17.2

śrī bhagavan uvāca: Kṛṣṇa says; trividhā: three kinds; bhavati: become; śraddhā: authenticity; dehināṁ: of the body; sā: that; svabhāvajā: according to his nature; sāttvikī : nature of goodness; rājasī: nature of aggression; ca: also; eva: certainly; tāmasī: nature of ignorance; ca: and; iti: thus; tāṁ: that; śṛṇu: hear from Me.

17.2 The Supreme Lord says: The natural authenticity (faith) of embodied beings is of three kinds: goodness, aggression, and ignorance. Now hear about these from Me.

सत्त्वानुरूपा सर्वस्य श्रद्धा भवति भारत।
श्रद्धामयोऽयं पुरुषो यो यच्छ्रद्धः स एव सः ॥ ३

sattvānurūpā sarvasya śraddhā bhavati bhārata |
śraddhāmayo'yam puruṣo yo yacchraddhaḥ sa eva saḥ || 17.3

satvānurūpā: according to the existence; sarvasya: of everyone; śraddhā: authenticity; bhavati: becomes; bhārata: O son of Bhārata; śraddhā: authenticity; mayaḥ: full; ayam: this; puruṣaḥ: living entity; yaḥ: anyone; yat: that; śraddhaḥ: sincerity; saḥ: that; eva: certainly; saḥ: he.

17.3 O Arjuna, the authenticity of each is in accordance with one's own natural disposition. One is known by one's authenticity. One can become whatever one wants to be.

यजन्ते सात्त्विका देवान्यक्षरक्षांसि राजसाः।
प्रेतान्भूतगणांश्चान्ये यजन्ते तामसा जनाः ॥ ४

yajante sāttvikā devān yakṣarakṣāṁsi rājasāḥ |
pretān-bhūta-gaṇāṁś cānye yajante tāmasā janāḥ || 17.4

yajante: worship; sāttvikāḥ: those who are in the mode of goodness; devān: deities; yakṣarakṣāṁsi rājasāḥ: those who are in the mode of aggression worship demons; pretān: dead spirits; bhūtagaṇān: ghosts; cā 'nye: and others; yajante: worship; tāmasāḥ: in the mode of ignorance; janāḥ: people.

17.4 Men in the nature of goodness worship the deities; those in the nature of aggression worship the demons and those in the nature of ignorance worship ghosts and spirits.

अशास्त्रविहितं घोरं तप्यन्ते ये तपो जनाः ।
दम्भाहङ्कारसंयुक्ताः कामरागबलान्विताः ॥ ५॥

aśāstravihitaṁ ghoraṁ tapyante ye tapo janāḥ I
dambhāhaṅkārasamyuktāḥ kāmarāgabalānvitāḥ II 17.5

कर्शयन्तः शरीरस्थं भूतग्राममचेतसः ।
मां चैवान्तः शरीरस्थं तान्विद्ध्यासुरनिश्चयान् ॥ ६॥

karśayantaḥ śarīrasthaṁ bhūtagrāmamacetasaḥ I
mām caivāntah śarīrasthaṁ tān viddhy āsura-niścayān II 17.6

aśāstra: not mentioned in the scriptures; vihitaṁ: directed; ghoraṁ: harmful to others; tapyante: undergo penances; ye: those; tapaḥ: austerities; janāḥ: persons; dambha: pride; ahaṁkāra: egoism; samyuktāḥ: engaged; kāma: lust; rāga: attachment; bala: force; anvitāḥ: impelled by; karṣayantaḥ: tormenting; śarīrasthaṁ: situated within the body; bhūtagrāmaṁ: combination of material elements; acetasaḥ: by such a misled mentality; mām: to Me; ca: also; eva: certainly; antaḥ: within; śarīrasthaṁ: situated in the body; tān: them; viddhi: understand; āsura: demons; niścayān: certainly.

17.5,6 Ignorant persons of demonic nature are those who practice severe austerities without following the prescription of the scriptures, who are full of hypocrisy and egotism, who are impelled by the force of desire and attachment and who senselessly torture the elements in their body and also Me who dwells within the body.

आहारस्त्वपि सर्वस्य त्रिविधो भवति प्रियः।
यज्ञस्तपस्तथा दानं तेषां भेदमिमं श्रृणु॥ ७॥

āhārastvapi sarvasya trividho bhavati priyaḥ /
yajñastapastathā dānaṁ teṣāṁ bhedamimaṁ śṛṇu // 17.7

āhāra: eating; tu: certainly; api: also; sarvasya: of everyone; trividhaḥ: three kinds; bhavati: there are; priyaḥ: dear; yajñaḥ: sacrifice; tapaḥ: austerity; tathā: also; dānaṁ: charity; teṣāṁ: of them; bhedaṁ: differences; imaṁ: thus; śṛṇu: hear.

17.7 Food that we consume is of three kinds, according to the three types of material nature. So are the sacrifice, austerity and charity. Hear the difference between these three.

आयुःसत्त्वबलारोग्यसुखप्रीतिविवर्धनाः।
रस्याः स्निग्धाः स्थिरा हृद्या आहाराः सात्त्विकप्रियाः॥ ८

āyuḥsattvabalārogy- asukhaprītivivardhanāḥ /
rasyāḥ snigdhāḥ sthirā hṛdyā āhārāḥ sāttvikapriyāḥ // 17.8

āyuḥ: duration of life; sattva: existence; bala: strength; ārogya: health; sukha: happiness; prīti: satisfaction; vivardhanāḥ: increasing; rasyāḥ: juicy; snigdhāḥ: fatty; sthirāḥ: enduring; hṛdyāḥ: pleasing to the heart; āhārāḥ: food; sāttvika: goodness; priyāḥ: palatable.

17.8 The foods that promote longevity, virtue, strength, health, happiness, and joy are juicy, smooth, substantial, and nutritious. Such foods are liked by persons in the mode of goodness.

कट्वम्ललवणात्युष्णतीक्ष्णरूक्षविदाहिनः।
आहारा राजसस्येष्टा दुःखशोकामयप्रदाः॥ ९॥

kaṭv-amla-lavaṇāty-uṣṇa- tīkṣṇa rūkṣa vidāhinaḥ /
āhārā rājasasyeṣṭā duḥkha-śokāmaya-pradāḥ // 17.9

kaṭu: bitter; amla: sour; lavaṇa: salty; atyuṣṇa: very hot; tīkṣṇa: pungent; rūkṣa: dry; vidāhinaḥ: burning; āhārāḥ: food; rājasasya: in the mode of aggression; iṣṭāḥ: palatable; duḥkha: distress; śoka: misery; āmaya pradāḥ: causing disease.

17.9 People in the mode of aggression like foods that are very bitter, sour, salty, hot, pungent, dry, and burning, and cause pain, grief, and disease.

यातयामं गतरसं पूति पर्युषितं च यत्।
उच्छिष्टमपि चामेध्यं भोजनं तामसप्रियम्॥ १०

yātayāmaṁ gatarasaṁ pūti paryuṣitaṁ ca yat /
ucchiṣṭam api cā medhyaṁ bhojanaṁ tāmasapriyam // 17.10

yātayāmaṁ: food cooked three hours before being eaten; gatarasaṁ: tasteless; pūti: bad smelling; paryuṣitaṁ: decomposed; ca: also; yat: that which; ucchiṣṭam: remnants of food eaten by others; api: also; ca: and; amedhyaṁ: untouchable; bhojanaṁ: eating; tāmasa: in the mode of darkness; priyam: dear

17.10 People in the mode of ignorance like foods that are stale, tasteless, putrid, rotten, refuse, and of impure energy.

अफलाकाङ्क्षिभिर्यज्ञो विधिदृष्टो य इज्यते ।
यष्टव्यमेवेति मनः समाधाय स सात्त्विकः॥ ११

aphalākāṅkṣibhir yajño vidhidṛsto ya ijyate /
yaṣṭavyam eveti manaḥ samādhāya sa sāttvikaḥ // 17.11

aphalākāṅkṣibhiḥ: without desire for result; yajñaḥ: sacrifice; vidhi : accordingly; dṛstaḥ: direction; yaḥ: anyone; ijyate: performs; yaṣṭavyaṁ: must be performed; eva: certainly; iti: thus; manaḥ: mind; samādhāya: fixed in; saḥ: he; sāttvikaḥ: in the nature of goodness

17.11 Sacrifice without expectation of results, as stipulated in the scriptures, with a firm belief and conviction that it is a duty, is in the mode of goodness.

अभिसन्धाय तु फलं दम्भार्थमपि चैव यत्।
इज्यते भरतश्रेष्ठ तं यज्ञं विद्धि राजसम्॥ १२

abhisandhāya tu phalaṁ dambhārthamapi caiva yat /
ijyate Bhāratasreṣṭha taṁ yajñaṁ viddhi rājasam // 17.12

abhisandhāya: desiring; tu: but; phalaṁ: the result; dambha: pride; arthaṁ: for the sake of; api: also; ca: and; eva: certainly; yat: that which; ijyate: is offered; bharataśreṣṭha: O chief of the Bhāratas; taṁ: that; yajñaṁ: sacrifice; viddhi: know; rājasam : in the mode of aggression

17.12 O Arjuna, that sacrifice that is performed with expectation of result or for show out of pride, is of the nature of aggression.

विधिहीनमसृष्टान्नं मन्त्रहीनमदक्षिणम्।
श्रद्धाविरहितं यज्ञं तामसं परिचक्षते॥ १३

vidhihīnam asṛṣṭānnaṁ mantrahīnamadakṣiṇam /
śraddhā-virahitaṁ yajñaṁ tāmasaṁ paricakṣate // 17.13

vidhihīnaṁ: without scriptural direction; asṛṣṭānnaṁ: without distribution of prasadam; mantrahīnaṁ: with no chanting of the vedic hymns; adakṣiṇam: with no remunerations to the priests; śraddhā: authenticity; virahitaṁ: without; yajñaṁ: sacrifice; tāmasaṁ: in the mode of ignorance; paricakṣate: is to be considered

17.13 Sacrifice that is performed without following the scripture, in which no food is distributed, which is devoid of mantra, authenticity, and gift, is said to be in the mode of ignorance.

देवद्विजगुरुप्राज्ञपूजनं शौचमार्जवम्।
ब्रह्मचर्यमहिंसा च शारीरं तप उच्यते॥ १४

deva-dvija-guru-prājña- pūjanaṁ śaucamārjavam /
brahmacaryamahiṁsā ca śārīraṁ tapa ucyate // 17.14

deva: deities; dvija: the priest; guru: the master; prājña: worshipable personalities; pūjanaṁ: worship; śaucaṁ: cleanliness; ārjavam: simplicity; brahmacaryaṁ: living in reality; ahiṁsā: nonviolence; ca: also; śārīraṁ: pertaining to the body; tapa: austerity; ucyate: is said to be

17.14 The worship of deities, the priest, the guru, and the wise; purity, honesty, living in reality, and nonviolence are said to be austerity of deed.

अनुद्वेगकरं वाक्यं सत्यं प्रियहितं च यत्।
स्वाध्यायाभ्यसनं चैव वाङ्मयं तप उच्यते॥ १५

anudvegakaraṁ vākyaṁ satyaṁ priyahitaṁ ca yat |
svādhyāyābhyasanaṁ caiva vāṅmayaṁ tapa ucyate || 17.15

anudvega: not agitating; karaṁ: producing; vākyaṁ: words; satyaṁ: truthful; priya: dear; hitaṁ: beneficial; ca: also; yat: which; svādhyāya: vedic study; abhyasanaṁ: practice; ca: also; eva: certainly; vāṅmayaṁ: of the voice; tapa: austerity; ucyate: is said to be

17.15 Speech that is non-offensive, truthful, pleasant, beneficial, and is used for the regular study of scriptures is called austerity of word.

मनः प्रसादः सौम्यत्वं मौनमात्मविनिग्रहः।
भावसंशुद्धिरित्येतत्तपो मानसमुच्यते॥ १६

manaḥ prasādaḥ saumyatvaṁ maunamātmavinigrahaḥ |
bhāva-saṁśuddhir ity etat tapo mānasam ucyate || 17.16

manaḥ prasādaḥ: fulfillment of the mind; saumyatvaṁ: satisfied; maunaṁ: gravity; ātma: self; vinigrahaḥ: control; bhāva: nature; saṁśuddhiḥ: purification; iti: thus; etat: that is; tapaḥ: austerity; mānasaṁ: of the mind; ucyate: is said to be.

17.16 Serenity of mind, gentleness, equanimity, self-control, and purity of thought are called austerity of thought.

श्रद्धया परया तप्तं तपस्तत्त्रिविधं नरैः।
अफलाकाङ्क्षिभिर्युक्तैः सात्त्विकं परिचक्षते॥ १७

śraddhayā parayā taptaṁ tapastattrividhaṁ naraiḥ |
aphalākāṅkṣibhiryuktaiḥ sāttvikaṁ paricakṣate || 17.17

śraddhayā: with authenticity; parayā: transcendental; taptaṁ: execution; tapaḥ: austerity; tat: that; trividhaṁ: three kinds; naraiḥ: by men; aphalākāṅkṣibhiḥ: without desires for fruits; yuktaiḥ: engaged; sāttvikaṁ: in the mode of goodness; paricakṣate: is called

17.17 The above mentioned threefold austerity (of thought, word, and deed), practiced by yogis with supreme authenticity, without a desire for the fruit, is said to be in the mode of goodness.

सत्कारमानपूजार्थं तपो दम्भेन चैव यत्।
क्रियते तदिह प्रोक्तं राजसं चलमध्रुवम्॥ १८

satkāra-māna-pūjārthaṁ tapo dambhena caiva yat |
kriyate tadiha proktaṁ rājasaṁ calamadhruvam || 17.18

satkāra: respect; māna: honor; pūjārthaṁ: for worship; tapaḥ: austerity; dambhena: pride; ca: also; eva: certainly; yat: which is; kriyate: performed; tat: that; iha: in this world; proktaṁ: is said; rājasaṁ: in the mode of aggression; calaṁ: flickering; adhruvam: temporary

17.18 Austerity that is performed for gaining respect, honor, reverence, and for the sake of show, yielding an uncertain and temporary result, is said to be in the mode of aggression.

मूढग्राहेणात्मनो यत्पीडया क्रियते तपः।
परस्योत्सादनार्थं वा तत्तामसमुदाहृतम्॥ १९

mūḍhagrāheṇātmano yat pīḍayā kriyate tapaḥ |
parasyotsādanārthaṁ vā tattāmasamudāhṛtam || 17.19

mūḍha: foolish; grāheṇā: with endeavor; atmanaḥ: of one's own self; yat: which; pīḍayā: by torture; kriyate: is performed; tapaḥ: penance; parasya: to others; utsādanārthaṁ: causing annihilation; vā: or; tat: that; tāmasaṁ: in the mode of darkness; udāhṛtam: is said to be

17.19 Austerity performed with foolish stubbornness or with self-torture or for harming others, is said to be in the mode of ignorance.

दातव्यमिति यद्दानं दीयतेऽनुपकारिणे।
देशे काले च पात्रे च तद्दानं सात्त्विकं स्मृतम्॥ २०

dātavyamiti yaddānaṁ dīyate'nupakāriṇe /
deśe kāle ca pātre ca tad dānaṁ sāttvikaṁ smṛtam // 17.20

dātavyaṁ: worth giving; iti: thus; yat: that which; dānaṁ: charity; dīyate: given; anupakāriṇe: to person who does no service in return; deśe: in place; kāle: in time; ca: also; pātre: suitable person; ca: and; tat: that; dānaṁ: charity; sāttvikaṁ: in the mode of goodness; smṛtam: consider

17.20 Charity that is given at the right place and time as a matter of duty to a deserving candidate who does nothing in return, is considered to be in the mode of goodness.

यत्तु प्रत्युपकारार्थं फलमुद्दिश्य वा पुनः।
दीयते च परिक्लिष्टं तद्दानं राजसं स्मृतम्॥ २१

yattu pratyupakārārthaṁ phalamuddiśya vā punaḥ /
dīyate ca parikliṣṭaṁ tad dānaṁ rājasaṁ smṛtam // 17.21

yat: that which; tu: but; pratyupakārārthaṁ: for the sake of getting some return; phalaṁ: result; uddiśya: desiring; vā: or; punaḥ: again; dīyate: is given in charity; ca: also; parikliṣṭaṁ: grudgingly; tat: that; dānaṁ: charity; rājasaṁ: in the mode of aggression; smṛtam: is understood to be

17.21 Charity that is given unwillingly or to get something in return or to gain some result is in the mode of aggression.

अदेशकाले यद्दानमपात्रेभ्यश्च दीयते।
असत्कृतमवज्ञातं तत्तामसमुदाहृतम्॥ २२

adeśa-kāle yad dānam apātrebhyaś ca dīyate /
asat-kṛtam avajñātaṁ tat tāmasamudāhṛtam // 17.22

adeśa: unpurified place; kāle: unpurified time; yat: that which; dānaṁ: charity; apātrebhyaḥ: to unworthy persons; ca: also; dīyate: is given; asatkṛtaṁ: without respect; avajñātaṁ: without proper attention; tat: that; tāmasaṁ: in the mode of darkness; udāhṛtam: is said to be

17.22 Charity that is given at a wrong place and time to unworthy persons or without paying respect to the receiver or with ridicule is in the mode of ignorance.

ॐ तत्सदिति निर्देशो ब्रह्मणस्त्रिविधः स्मृतः।
ब्राह्मणास्तेन वेदाश्च यज्ञाश्च विहिताः पुरा॥ २३

Oṁ tat sad iti nirdeśo brahmaṇastrividhaḥ smṛtaḥ /
brāhmaṇās tena vedās ca yajñāśca vihitāḥ purā // 17.23

Oṁ: indication of the Supreme; tat: that; sat: eternal; iti: that; nirdeśaḥ: indication; brahmaṇaḥ: of the Supreme; trividhaḥ: three kinds; smṛtaḥ: consider; brāhmaṇāḥ: the brahmaṇas; tena: therefore; vedāḥ: the vedic literature; ca: also; yajñāḥ: sacrifice; ca: also; vihitāḥ: used; purā: formerly

17.23 'OṀ Tat Sat' is said to be the threefold name of the eternal Being (Brahma). Persons with good (brahminic) qualities, the Vedas, and the selfless service (seva, yajña) were created by and from Brahma in the ancient time.

तस्मादोमित्युदाहृत्य यज्ञदानतपःक्रियाः।
प्रवर्तन्ते विधानोक्ताः सततं ब्रह्मवादिनाम्॥ २४

tasmād oṁ ity udāhṛtya yajña-dāna-tapaḥ-kriyāḥ I
pravartante vidhānoktāḥ satataṁ brahmavādinām II 17.24

tasmāt: therefore; Om: beginning with om; iti: thus; udāhṛtya: indicating; yajña: sacrifice; dāna: charity; tapaḥ: penance; kriyāḥ: performances; pravartante: begin; vidhānoktāḥ: according to scriptural regulation; satataṁ: always; brahmavādinām: of the transcendentalists

17.24 Therefore, acts of sacrifice, charity, and austerity prescribed in the scriptures are always commenced by uttering 'OM' by the knowers of the supreme Being.

तदित्यनभिसंधाय फलं यज्ञतपःक्रियाः।
दानक्रियाश्च विविधाः क्रियन्ते मोक्षकाङ्क्षिभिः॥ २५।

tad ity anabhisandhāya phalaṁ yajñatapaḥkriyāḥ I
dāna-kriyāś ca vividhāḥ kriyante mokṣak-āṅkṣibhiḥ II 17.25

tat: that; iti: they; anabhisandhāya: without fruitive result; phalaṁ: result of sacrifice; yajña: sacrifice; tapaḥ: penance; kriyāḥ: activities; dāna: charity; kriyāḥ: activities; ca: also; vividhāḥ: varieties; kriyante: done; mokṣakāṅkṣibhiḥ: those who actually desire liberation.

17.25 Various types of sacrifice, charity, and austerity are performed by the seekers of liberation by uttering 'Tat' (or He is all) without seeking a reward.

सद्भावे साधुभावे च सदित्येतत्प्रयुज्यते।
प्रशस्ते कर्मणि तथा सच्छब्दः पार्थ युज्यते॥ २६

sadbhāve sādhubhāve ca sad ity etat prayujyate I

praśaste karmaṇi tathā sac-chabdaḥ pārtha yujyate II 17.26

यज्ञे तपसि दाने च स्थितिः सदिति चोच्यते।
कर्म चैव तदर्थीयं सदित्येवाभिधीयते॥ २७

yajñe tapasi dāne ca sthitiḥ sad iti cocyate |
karma caiva tad arthīyaṁ sadityevābhidhīyate || 17.27

sadbhāve: in the sense of the nature of the Truth; sādhubhāve: in the sense of the nature of devotion; ca: also; sat: the Truth; iti: thus; etat: this; prayujyate: is used; praśaste: auspicious; karmaṇi: activities; tathā: also; sacchabdaḥ: the sound sat; pārtha: O son of Prithā; yujyate: is used; yajñe: sacrifice; tapasi: in penance; dāne: charity; ca: also; sthitiḥ: situated; sat: the Truth; iti: thus; ca: and; ucyate: pronounced; karma: work; ca: also; eva: certainly; tad: that; arthīyaṁ: are meant; sat: Truth; iti: thus; eva: certainly; abhidhīyate: is called.

17.26,27 The word 'Sat' is used in the sense of reality and goodness. The word 'Sat' is also used for an auspicious act, O Pārtha (Arjuna). Authenticity in sacrifice, charity, and austerity is also called 'Sat'. Selfless service for the sake of the Supreme is, in truth, termed as 'Sat'.

अश्रद्धया हुतं दत्तं तपस्तप्तं कृतं च यत्।
असदित्युच्यते पार्थ न च तत्प्रेत्य नो इह॥ २८

aśraddhayā hutaṁ dattaṁ tapastaptaṁ kṛtaṁ ca yat |
asadityucyate pārtha na ca tatpretya no iha || 17.28

aśraddhayā: without authenticity; hutaṁ: offered in sacrifice; dattaṁ: given; tapaḥ: penance; taptaṁ: executed; kṛtaṁ: performed; ca: also; yat: that which; asat: not Truth; iti: thus; ucyate: is said to be; pārtha: O son of Prithā; no: never; ca: also; tat: that; pretya: after death; na: nor; iha: in this life.

17.28 Whatever is done without authenticity whether it is sacrifice, charity, austerity, or any other act is called 'asat.' It has no value here or hereafter, O Pārtha (Arjuna).

इति श्रीमद्भगवद्गीतासूपनिषत्सु ब्रह्मविद्यायां योगशास्त्रे
श्रीकृष्णार्जुनसंवादे श्रद्धात्रयविभागयोगो नाम सप्तदशोऽध्यायः ॥

iti śrīmad bhagavadgītāsūpaniṣatsu
brahmavidyāyām yogaśāstre
śrīkṛṣṇārjuna saṁvāde
śraddhātraya-vibhāgayogo nāma
saptadaśodhyāyaḥ //

In the ***Upaniṣad*** of ***Śrimad Bhagavad Gītā***, the scripture of yoga dealing with ***Brahmavidyā Yogaśāstra,*** the science of Brahman, the Supreme Absolute, in the form of ***Śrī Kṛṣṇārjuna saṁvād,*** dialogue between Śrī Kṛṣṇa and Arjuna, this is the seventeenth chapter named, ***Śraddhātrayā Vibhāga Yogaḥ***, *'The Yoga Discerning the Three-Fold Faith.'*

CHAPTER 18

अथ अष्टादशोऽध्यायः

मोक्षसंन्यासयोगः

Mokṣa Sannyāsa Yogaḥ

अर्जुन उवाच
सन्न्यासस्य महाबाहो तत्त्वमिच्छामि वेदितुम् ।
त्यागस्य च हृषीकेश पृथक्केशिनिषूदन ॥ १

arjuna uvāca

sannyāsasya mahābāho tattvamicchāmi veditum I
tyāgasya ca hṛṣīkeśa pṛthak keśiniṣūdana II 18.1

arjuna uvāca: Arjuna says; sannyāsasya: monkhood; mahābāho: O mightyarmed one; tattvaṁ: truth; icchāmi: I wish; veditum: to understand; tyāgasya: of renunciation; ca: also; hṛṣīkeśa : O master of the senses; pṛthak: differently; keśiniṣūdana: O killer of the Kesi demon

18.1 O mighty armed Kṛṣṇa, I wish to understand what is the essence, tattva of renunciation, tyāga and the renounced order of life, sannyāsa, and the difference between the two, O Hriśikeṣa, O Killer of the demon Keśī.'

श्री भगवानुवाच
काम्यानां कर्मणां न्यासं सन्न्यासं कवयो विदुः।
सर्वकर्मफलत्यागं प्राहुस्त्यागं विचक्षणाः॥ २

śrībhagavānuvāca
kāmyānāṁ karmaṇāṁ nyāsaṁ sannyāsaṁ kavayo viduḥ |
sarvakarmaphalatyāgaṁ prāhus tyāgaṁ vicakṣaṇāḥ || 18.2

śrībhagavānuvāca: Śrī Bhagavān says; kāmyānāṁ: with desire; karmaṇāṁ: activities; nyāsaṁ: renunciation; sannyāsaṁ: renounced order of life; kavayaḥ: the learned; viduḥ: know; sarva: of all; karma: activities; phala: of results; tyāgaṁ: renunciation; prāhuḥ: call; tyāgaṁ: renunciation; vicakṣaṇāḥ: the experienced

18.2 Bhagavān Kṛṣṇa says, the renouncing of all selfish work based on desire, is what the learned ones call as sannyāsa, the renounced order of life. And renunciatig the attachment to fruit or result of one's actions is what the wise ones call as tyāga, renunciation.

त्याज्यं दोषवदित्येके कर्म प्राहुर्मनीषिणः।
यज्ञदानतपःकर्म न त्याज्यमिति चापरे॥ ३

tyājyaṁ doṣavadity eke karma prāhurmanīṣiṇaḥ |
yajña-dāna-tapaḥ-karma na tyājyamiticāpare || 18.3

tyājyaṁ: must be given up; doṣavad: like sins; iti: thus; eke: one group; karma: work; prāhuḥ: said; manīṣiṇaḥ: of great thinkers; yajña: sacrifice or service; dāna: charity; tapaḥ: penance or austerity; karma: work; na: never; tyājyaṁ: is to be given up; iti: thus; ca: certainly; apare: others

18.3 Some learned men say that all kinds of result-based activities are faulty and should be given up, but there are yet other sages who maintain that acts of enriching sacrifice [yajña], charity [dāna] and austerity [tapaḥ] should never be given up.

निश्चयं श्रृणु मे तत्र त्यागे भरतसत्तम ।
त्यागो हि पुरुषव्याघ्र त्रिविधः सम्प्रकीर्तितः ॥ ४

niścayaṁ śṛṇu me tatra tyāge bharatasattama |
tyāgo hi puruṣavyāghra trividhaḥ samprakīrtitaḥ || 18.4

niścayaṁ: certainty; śṛṇu: hear; me: from Me; tatra: there; tyāge: in the matter of renunciation; bharata sattama: O best of the Bhāratas; tyāgaḥ: renunciation; hi: certainly; puruṣavyāghra: O tiger among human beings; trividhaḥ: three kinds; samprakīrtitaḥ : is declared

18.4 Arjuna, best of Bhāratas, now listen from Me certainly about renunciation or tyāga; O tiger among men, renunciation or tyāga is declared to be of three kinds.

यज्ञदानतपःकर्म न त्याज्यं कार्यमेव तत् ।
यज्ञो दानं तपश्चैव पावनानि मनीषिणाम् ॥ ५

yajñadānatapaḥ karma na tyājyaṁ kāryameva tat |
yajño dānaṁ tapaścaiva pāvanāni manīṣiṇām || 18.5

yajña: sacrifice; dāna: charity; tapaḥ: penance; karma: activities; na: never; tyājyaṁ: to be given up; kāryaṁ: must be done; eva: certainly; tat: that; yajñaḥ: service; dānaṁ: charity; tapaḥ: austerity; ca: also; eva: certainly; pāvanāni: purifying; manīṣiṇām: even of the great souls

18.5 Acts of enriching sacrifice [tyāga], charity [dāna] and austerity [tapaḥ] are not to be given up; they should be performed. Indeed, even the Sages are purified by enriching sacrifice, charity and penance.

एतान्यपि तु कर्माणि सङ्गं त्यक्त्वा फलानि च ।
कर्तव्यानीति मे पार्थ निश्चितं मतमुत्तमम् ॥ ६

etānyapi tu karmāṇi saṅgaṁ tyaktvā phalāni ca |
kartavyānīti me pārtha niścitaṁ matamuttamam || 18.6

etāni: all this; api: certainly; tu: must; karmāṇi: activities; saṅgaṁ: association; tyaktvā: renouncing; phalāni: results; ca: also; kartavyāni: as duty; iti: thus; me: My; pārtha: O son of Pritā; niścitaṁ: definite; mataṁ: opinion; uttamam: the best

18.6 O Pārtha (Arjuna), all these acts of responsibility must also be performed without any expectation of result. That is My final and ultimate opinion.

नियतस्य तु संन्यासः कर्मणो नोपपद्यते।
मोहात्तस्य परित्यागस्तामसः परिकीर्तितः॥ ७

niyatasya tu sannyāsaḥ karmaṇo nopapadyate |
mohāttasya parityāgas tāmasaḥ parikīrtitaḥ || 18.7

niyatasya: prescribed duties; tu: but; sannyāsaḥ: renunciation; karmaṇaḥ: activities; na: never; upapadyate: is deserved; mohāt: by illusion; tasya: of which; parityāgaḥ: renunciation; tāmasaḥ: in the mode of ignorance; parikīrtitaḥ: is declared

18.7 Prescribed duties should never be renounced. If one gives up his prescribed duties through the illusion of renunciation, this is said to be in the state of ignorance.

दुःखमित्येव यत्कर्म कायक्लेशभयात्त्यजेत्।
स कृत्वा राजसं त्यागं नैव त्यागफलं लभेत्॥ ८

duḥkhamityeva yat karma kāyakleśabhayāttyajet |
sa kṛtvā rājāsaṁ tyāgaṁ nai'va tyāgaphalaṁ labhet || 18.8

duḥkhaṁ: unhappy; iti: thus; eva: certainly; yat: that which; karma: work; kāya: body; kleśa: troublesome; bhayāt: out of fear; tyajet: gives up; sa: that; kṛtvā: after doing; rājāsaṁ: in the mode of aggression; tyāgaṁ: renunciation; nai'va: certainly not; tyāga: renounced; phalaṁ: results; labhet: gain

18.8 Anyone who gives up prescribed duties as troublesome, or out of fear, is said to be in the state of aggression, does not benefit from renunciation.

कार्यमित्येव यत्कर्म नियतं क्रियतेऽर्जुन।
सङ्गं त्यक्त्वा फलं चैव स त्यागः सात्त्विको मतः॥ ९

kāryam ity eva yat karma niyataṁ kriyate'rjuna |
saṅgaṁ tyaktvā phalaṁ caiva sa tyāgaḥ sāttviko mataḥ || 18.9

kāryaṁ: must be done; iti: thus; eva: thus; yat: that which; karma: work; niyataṁ: prescribed; kriyate : performed; arjuna: O Arjuna; saṅgaṁ: association; tyaktvā: giving up; phalaṁ: result; ca: also; eva: certainly; saḥ: that; tyāgaḥ: renunciation; sāttvikaḥ: in the mode of goodness; mataḥ: in My opinion.

18.9 But he who performs what is prescribed, as a matter of duty, without expectation or attachment to the results, his renunciation is of the nature of satva, goodness, O Arjuna.

न द्वेष्ट्यकुशलं कर्म कुशले नानुषज्जते।
त्यागी सत्त्वसमाविष्टो मेधावी छिन्नसंशयः॥ १०

na dveṣṭyakuśalaṁ karma kuśale nā'nuṣajjate |
tyāgī sattvasamāviṣṭo medhāvī chinnasaṁśayaḥ || 18.10

na: never; dveṣti: hates; akuśalaṁ: inauspicious; karma: work; kuśale: in the auspicious; na: nor; anuṣajjate: becomes attached; tyāgī: the renouncer; sattva: goodness; samāviṣṭaḥ: absorbed in; medhāvī: intelligent; chinna: cut up; saṁśayaḥ: all doubts

18.10 Those who neither hate disagreeable work nor are attached to pleasant work are in a state of intelligence, goodness and renunciation, free of all doubts.

न हि देहभृता शक्यं त्यक्तुं कर्माण्यशेषतः।
यस्तु कर्मफलत्यागी स त्यागीत्यभिधीयते॥ ११

na hi dehabhṛtā śakyaṁ tyaktuṁ karmāṇyaśeṣataḥ |

yastu karma-phala-tyāgī sa tyāgītyabhidhīyate || 18.11

na: never; hi: certainly; dehabhṛtā: of the embodied; śakyaṁ: possible; tyaktuṁ: to renounce; karmāṇi: activities of; aśeṣataḥ: altogether; yastu: anyone who; karma: work; phala: results; tyāgī: renouncer; sa tyāgī: the renouncer; iti: thus; abhidhīyate : it is said

18.11 Human beings cannot give up all activities. Therefore the one who has renounced the fruits of such activity is one who has truly renounced.

अनिष्टमिष्टं मिश्रं च त्रिविधं कर्मण: फलम्।
भवत्यत्यागिनां प्रेत्य न तु सन्न्यासिनां क्वचित्॥ १२

aniṣṭamiṣṭaṁ miśraṁ ca trividhaṁ karmaṇaḥ phalam |
bhavatyatyāgināṁ pretya na tu sannyāsināṁ kvacit || 18.12

aniṣṭaṁ: undesirable; iṣṭaṁ: desirable; miśraṁ ca: or mixture; trividhaṁ: three kinds; karmaṇaḥ: work; phalam: result; bhavati: becomes; atyāgināṁ: of the non-renouncer; pretya: after death; na tu: but not; sannyāsināṁ: of the renounced order; kvacit: at any time

18.12 For one who is not renounced, the three kinds of fruits of action—desirable, undesirable and mixed—acrue after death, but not to one who has renounced.

पञ्चैतानि महाबाहो कारणानि निबोध मे।
साङ्ख्ये कृतान्ते प्रोक्तानि सिद्धये सर्वकर्मणाम्॥ १३

pañcai'tāni mahābāho kāraṇāni nibodha me |
sāṅkhye kṛtānte proktāni siddhaye sarvakarmaṇām || 18.13

अधिष्ठानं तथा कर्ता करणं च पृथग्विधम्।
विविधाश्च पृथक्चेष्टा दैवं चैवात्र पञ्चमम्॥ १४

adhiṣṭhānaṁ tathā kartā karaṇaṁ ca pṛthagvidham |

vividhāśca pṛthakceṣṭā daivaṁ caivātra pañcamam || 18.14

pañca: five; etāni: all these; mahābāho: O mighty-armed one; kāraṇāni: causes; nibodha: just understand; me: from Me; sāṁkhya: in the Sāṅkhya philosophy; kṛtānte: after performance; proktāni: said; siddhaye: perfection; sarva: all; karmaṇām: actuated. adhiṣṭhānaṁ: place; tathā : also; kartā: worker; karaṇaṁ ca: and instruments; pṛthagvidham: different kinds; vividhāś ca: varieties; pṛthak: separately; ceṣṭā: endeavor; daivaṁ: the supreme; ca: also; eva: certainly; atra: here; pañcamam: five

18.13,14 Learn from Me Arjuna, the five causes that bring about the accomplishment of all action, as described in Sāṅkhya philosophy. These are: physical body that is the seat of action; the attributes of nature or guṇa, which is the doer; the eleven organs of perception and action by the life forces and finally the Divine.

शरीरवाङ्मनोभिर्यत्कर्म प्रारभते नरः।
न्याय्यं वा विपरीतं वा पञ्चैते तस्य हेतवः॥ १५

śarīra-vāṅ-manobhir yat karma prārabhate naraḥ |
nyāyyaṁ vā viparītaṁ vā pañcai 'te tasya hetavaḥ || 18.15

śarīra: body; vāk: speech; manobhiḥ: by the mind; yat: anything; karma: work; prārabhate: begins; naraḥ: a person; nyāyyaṁ: right; vā: or; viparītaṁ: the opposite; vā: or; pañca: five; ete: all these; tasya: its; hetavaḥ: causes

18.15 These five factors are responsible for whatever right or wrong actions a man performs by deed, word and thought.

तत्रैवं सति कर्तारमात्मानं केवलं तु यः।
पश्यत्यकृतबुद्धित्वान्न स पश्यति दुर्मतिः॥ १६

tatraivam sati kartāram ātmānaṁ kevalaṁ tu yaḥ |
paśyatyakṛtabuddhitvān na sa paśyati durmatiḥ || 18.16

tatra: there; evaṁ: certainly; sati: being; kartāraṁ: of the worker; ātmānaṁ:

the self; kevalaṁ: only; tu: but; yaḥ: anyone; paśyati: sees; akṛta buddhitvāt: due to unintelligence; na: never; saḥ: he; paśyati: sees; durmatiḥ: foolish

18.16 Those who think they, their spirit, are the doers, are ignorant and do not see things as they are.

यस्य नाहङ्कृतो भावो बुद्धिर्यस्य न लिप्यते।
हत्वाऽपि स इमाँल्लोकान्न हन्ति न निबध्यते॥ १७

yasya nāhaṅkṛto bhāvo buddhir yasya na lipyate /
hatvā 'pi sa imāl lokān na hanti na nibadhyate // 18.17

yasya: of one who; nā: never; ahaṁkṛtaḥ: ego; bhāvaḥ: nature; buddhiḥ: intelligence; yasya: one who; na: never; lipyate: is attached; hatvā 'pi: even killing; saḥ: he; imān: this; lokān: world; na: never; hanti: kills; na: never; nibadhyate: becomes entangled

18.17 One who is egoless, whose intelligence is not of attachment, though he may kill, is not the slayer and is never bound by his actions.

ज्ञानं ज्ञेयं परिज्ञाता त्रिविधा कर्मचोदना।
करणं कर्म कर्तेति त्रिविधः कर्मसंग्रहः॥ १८

jñānaṁ jñeyaṁ parijñātā trividhā karmacodanā /
karaṇaṁ karma karteti trividhaḥ karmasaṁgrahaḥ // 18.18

jñānaṁ: knowledge; jñeyaṁ: objective; parijñātā: the knower; trividhā: three kinds; karma: work; codanā: impetus; karaṇaṁ: the senses; karmā: work; kartā: the doer; iti: thus; trividhaḥ: three kinds; karma: work; saṁgrahaḥ: accumulation

18.18 Knowledge, object of the knowledge and the subject of the knowledge, the knower, are the three factors that stimulate action; the senses, the action and the performer comprise the three components of action.

ज्ञानं कर्म च कर्ता च त्रिधैव गुणभेदतः।
प्रोच्यते गुणसङ्ख्याने यथावच्छृणु तान्यपि॥ १९

jñānaṁ karma ca kartā ca tridhaiva guṇabhedataḥ /
procyate guṇa-sañkhyāne yathāvac chṛṇu tānyapi // 18.19

jñānaṁ: knowledge; karma: work; ca: also; kartā: worker; ca: also; tridha: three kinds; eva: certainly; guṇabhedataḥ: in terms of different modes of material nature; procyate: is said; guṇasañkhyāne: in terms of different modes; yathāvat: as they act; śṛṇu: hear; tāni: all of them; api: also

18.19 According to the science of guṇas, there are three types in knowledge, action, and performers of action. Listen as I describe them.

सर्वभूतेषु येनैकं भावमव्ययमीक्षते।
अविभक्तं विभक्तेषु तज्ज्ञानं विद्धि सात्त्विकम्॥ २०

sarvabhūteṣu yenaikaṁ bhāvamavyayamīkṣate /
avibhaktaṁ vibhakteṣu taj jñānaṁ viddhi sāttvikam // 18.20

sarvabhūteṣu: in all living entities; yena: by whom; ekaṁ: one; bhāvaṁ: situation; avyayaṁ: imperishable; īkṣate: does see; avibhaktaṁ: undivided; vibhakteṣu: in the numberless divided; tat: that; jñānaṁ: knowledge; viddhi: know; sāttvikam: in the mode of goodness

18.20 That knowledge by which one imperishable reality is seen in all Existence, undivided in the divided, is knowledge in the state of goodness.

पृथक्त्वेन तु यज्ज्ञानं नानाभावान्पृथग्विधान्।
वेत्ति सर्वेषु भूतेषु तज्ज्ञानं विद्धि राजसम्॥ २१

pṛthaktvena tu yajjñānaṁ nānābhāvān pṛthagvidhān /
vetti sarveṣu bhūteṣu taj jñānaṁ viddhi rājasam // 18.21

pṛthaktvena: because of division; tu: but; yajjñānaṁ: which knowledge; nānābhāvān: various situations; pṛthagvidhān: differently; vetti: one who knows; sarveṣu: in all; bhūteṣu: living entities; tajjñānaṁ: that knowledge; viddhi: must be known; rājasam: in terms of aggression

18.21 The knowledge by which one sees different realities of various types among all beings as separate from one another; such knowledge is in the mode of aggression.

यत्तु कृत्स्नवदेकस्मिन्कार्ये सक्तमहैतुकम्।
अतत्त्वार्थवदल्पं च तत्तामसमुदाहृतम्॥ २२

yat tu kṛtsnavad ekasmin kārye saktaṁ ahaitukam |
atattvārthavadalpaṁ ca tat tāmasamudāhṛtam || 18.22

yat: that which; tu: but; kṛtsnavat: all in all; ekasmin: in one; kārye: work; saktaṁ: attached; ahaitukam: without cause; atattvārthavat: without reality; alpaṁ: very meager; ca: and; tat: that; tāmasaṁ: in the mode of darkness; udāhṛtam: is spoken

18.22 The irrational, baseless, and worthless knowledge by which one clings to one single effect as if it is everything, such knowledge is in the mode of darkness of ignorance.

नियतं सङ्गरहितमरागद्वेषतः कृतम्।
अफलप्रेप्सुना कर्म यत्तत्सात्त्विकमुच्यते॥ २३

niyataṁ saṅgarahitam arāgadveṣataḥ kṛtam |
aphalaprepsunā karma yat tat sāttvikamucyate || 18.23

niyataṁ: regulative; saṅgarahitaṁ: without attachment; arāgadveṣataḥ: without love or hatred; kṛtam: done; aphalaprepsunā: without fruitive result; karma: acts; yat: which; tat: that; sāttvikaṁ: in the mode of goodness; ucyate: is called

18.23 Obligatory duty performed without likes and dislikes and without selfish motives and attachment to the fruit, is in the mode of goodness.

यत्तु कामेप्सुना कर्म साहङ्कारेण वा पुन: ।
क्रियते बहुलायासं तद्राजसमुदाहृतम् ॥ २४

yat tu kāmepsunā karma sāhaṁkāreṇa vā punaḥ |
kriyate bahulāyāsaṁ tad rājasamudāhṛtam || 18.24

yat: that which; tu: but; kāmepsunā: with fruitive result; karma: work; sāhaṁkāreṇa: with ego; vā: or; punaḥ: again; kriyate: performed; bahulāyāsaṁ: with great labor; tat: that; rājasaṁ: in the mode of passion; udāhṛtam: is said to be

18.24 Action performed with ego, with selfish motives, and with too much effort, is in the mode of aggression.

अनुबन्धं क्षयं हिंसामनपेक्ष्य च पौरुषम् ।
मोहादारभ्यते कर्म यत्तत्तामसमुच्यते ॥ २५

anubandhaṁ kṣayaṁ hiṁsām anapekṣya ca pauruṣam |
mohād ārabhyate karma yat tat tāmasamucyate || 18.25

anubandhaṁ: future bondage; kṣayaṁ: destruction; hiṁsām: violence; anapekṣya: without consideration of consequences; ca: also; pauruṣam: ability; mohāt: by illusion; ārabhyate: begun; karma: work; yat: which; tat: that; tāmasaṁ: in the mode of ignorance; ucyate: is said to be

18.25 Action that is undertaken because of delusion, disregarding consequences, loss, injury to others, as well as one's own ability, is in the mode of ignorance.

मुक्तसङ्गोऽनहंवादी धृत्युत्साहसमन्वित: ।
सिद्ध्यसिद्ध्योर्निर्विकार: कर्ता सात्त्विक उच्यते ॥ २६

muktasaṅgo'nahaṁvādī dhṛtyutsāhasamanvitaḥ |
siddhyasiddhyor nirvikāraḥ kartā sāttvika ucyate || 18.26

muktasaṅgaḥ: liberated from all material association; anahaṁvādī: without false ego; dhṛtyutsāha: with great enthusiasm; samanvitaḥ: qualified in that way; siddhi: perfection; asiddhyoḥ: failure; nirvikāraḥ: without change; kartā: worker; sāttvikaḥ: in the mode of goodness; ucyate: is said to be

18.26 The performer who is free from attachment, non-egotistic, endowed with resolve and enthusiasm, and unperturbed in success or failure is called sātvika.

रागी कर्मफलप्रेप्सुर्लुब्धो हिंसात्मकोऽशुचिः।
हर्षशोकान्वितः कर्ता राजसः परिकीर्तितः॥ २७

rāgī karmaphalaprepsur lubdho hiṁsātmako 'śuciḥ I
harṣaśokānvitaḥ kartā rājasaḥ parikīrtitaḥ II 18.27

rāgī: very much attached; karmaphala: to the fruit of the work; prepsuḥ: desiring; lubdhaḥ: greedy; hiṁsātmakaḥ: and always envious; aśuciḥ: unclean; harṣaśokānvitaḥ: complicated, with joy and sorrow; kartā: such a worker; rājasaḥ: in the mode of passion; parikīrtitaḥ: is declared

18.27 The performer who is impassioned, who desires the fruits of work, who is greedy, violent, impure, and affected by joy and sorrow, is called aggressive.

अयुक्तः प्राकृतः स्तब्धः शठोऽनैष्कृतिकोऽलसः।
विषादी दीर्घसूत्री च कर्ता तामस उच्यते॥ २८

ayuktaḥ prākṛtaḥ stabdhaḥ śaṭho naiṣkṛtiko 'lasaḥ I
viṣādī dīrghasūtrī ca kartā tāmasa ucyate II 18.28

ayuktaḥ: without reference to scriptural injunctions; prākṛtaḥ: materialistic; stabdhaḥ: obstinate; śaṭhaḥ: deceitful; naiṣkṛtikaḥ: expert in insulting others; alasaḥ: lazy; viṣādī: morose; dīrghasūtrī: procrastinating; ca: also; kartā: worker; tāmasa: in the mode of ignorance; ucyate: is said to be

18.28 The performer who is undisciplined, vulgar, stubborn, wicked, malicious, lazy, depressed, and procrastinating is called ignorant or tamasic.

बुद्धेर्भेदं धृतेश्चैव गुणतस्त्रिविधं शृणु।
प्रोच्यमानमशेषेण पृथक्त्वेन धनञ्जय॥ २९

buddherbhedaṁ dhṛteś cai 'va guṇatastrividhaṁ śṛṇu /
procyamānamaśeṣeṇa pṛthaktvena dhanañjaya // 18.29

buddheḥ: of intelligence; bhedaṁ: differences; dhṛteḥ: of steadiness; ca: also; eva: certainly; guṇataḥ: by the modes of material nature; trividhaṁ: the three kinds of; śṛṇu: just hear; procyamānaṁ: as described by Me; aśeṣeṇa: in detail; pṛthaktvena: differently; dhanañjaya: O winner of wealth

18.29 Now hear Me explain, fully and separately, the threefold division of intellect and resolve, based on modes of material Nature, O Dhanañjaya.

प्रवृत्तिं च निवृत्तिं च कार्याकार्ये भयाभये।
बन्धं मोक्षं च या वेत्ति बुद्धिः सा पार्थ सात्त्विकी॥ ३०

pravṛttiṁ ca nivṛttiṁ ca kāryakārye bhayābhaye /
bandhaṁ mokṣaṁ ca yā vetti buddhiḥ sā pārtha sāttvikī // 18.30

pravṛttiṁ: the path of work; ca: also; nivṛttiṁ: the path of renunciation; ca: and; kārya: work that is to be done; akārye: prohibited action; bhaya: fearful; abhaye: fearlessness; bandhaṁ: obligation; mokṣaṁ ca: and liberation; yā: that which; vetti: knows; buddhiḥ: understanding; sā: that; pārtha: O son of Pritā; sāttvikī: in the mode of goodness

18.30 O Arjuna, that intellect is in the mode of goodness which understands the path of work and the path of renunciation, right and wrong action, fear and fearlessness, bondage and liberation.

यया धर्ममधर्मं च कार्यं चाकार्यमेव च।
अयथावत्प्रजानाति बुद्धिः सा पार्थ राजसी॥ ३१

yayā dharmamadharmaṁ ca kāryaṁ cākāryam eva ca /
ayathāvat prajānāti buddhiḥ sā pārtha rājasī // 18.31

yayā: by which; dharmaṁ: right conduct; adharmaṁ: what is not right conduct; ca: and; kāryaṁ: work; ca: also; akāryaṁ: what ought not to be done; eva: certainly; ca: also; ayathāvat: not perfectly; prajānāti: knows; buddhiḥ: intelligence; sā: that; pārtha: O son of Pritā; rājasī: in the mode of passion

18.31 That intellect is in the mode of passion that cannot distinguish between principles of right conduct and wrong doing, and right and wrong action, O Pārtha (Arjuna).

अधर्मं धर्ममिति या मन्यते तमसावृता।
सर्वार्थान्विपरीतांश्च बुद्धिः सा पार्थ तामसी॥ ३२

adharmaṁ dharmamiti yā manyate tamasā 'vṛtā /
sarvārthānviparītāṁśca buddhiḥ sā pārtha tāmasī // 18.32

adharmaṁ: what is not right conduct; dharmaṁ: right conduct; iti: thus; yā: which; manyate: thinks; tamasā: by ignorance; avṛtā: covered; sarvārthān: all things; viparītāṁ: the wrong direction; ca: also; buddhiḥ: intelligence; sā: that; pārtha: O son of Pritā; tāmasī: the mode of ignorance

18.32 That intellect is in the mode of ignorance that accepts unrighteousness as righteousness and thinks everything to be that which it is not, O Pārtha.

धृत्या यया धारयते मनःप्राणेन्द्रियक्रियाः।
योगेनाव्यभिचारिण्या धृतिः सा पार्थ सात्त्विकी॥ ३३

dhṛtyā yayā dhārayate manaḥ-prāṇendriya-kriyāḥ /
yogenāvyabhicāriṇyā dhṛtiḥ sā pārtha sāttvikī // 18.33

dhṛtyā: determination; yayā: by which; dhārayate: continued; manaḥ: mind; prāṇa: life energy; indriya: senses; kriyāḥ: activities; yogena: uniting with God; avyabhicāriṇyā: without any break; dhṛtiḥ: such determination; sā: that; pārtha: O son of Pritā; sāttvikī: in the mode of goodness

18.33 Consistent and continuous determination in controlling the mind, breath and senses for uniting with the Divine is goodness, Pārtha.

यया तु धर्मकामार्थान्धृत्या धारयतेऽर्जुन।
प्रसङ्गेन फलाकाङ्क्षी धृतिः सा पार्थ राजसी॥ ३४

yayā tu dharma kāmārthān dhṛtyā dhārayate 'rjuna |
prasaṅgena phalākāṅkṣī dhṛtiḥ sā pārtha rājasī || 18.34

yayā: by which; tu: but; dharma kāmārthān: for the three goals in life, right conduct, sense pleasure and wealth; dhṛtyā: by determination; dhārayate: continuously; arjuna: O Arjuna; prasaṅgena: for that; phalākāṅkṣī: desiring fruitive results; dhṛtiḥ: determination; sā: that; pārtha: O son of Pritā; rājasī: in the mode of passion

18.34 Craving for results of action while clinging to goals of proper conduct, pleasure and wealth is the state of passion, Arjuna.

यया स्वप्नं भयं शोकं विषादं मदमेव च।
न विमुञ्चति दुर्मेधा धृतिः सा पार्थ तामसी॥ ३५

yayā svapnaṁ bhayaṁ śokaṁ viṣādaṁ madameva ca |
na vimuñcati durmedhā dhṛtiḥ sā pārtha tāmasī || 18.35

yayā: by which; svapnaṁ: dream; bhayaṁ: fearfulness; śokaṁ: lamentation; viṣādaṁ: moroseness; madaṁ: delusion; eva: certainly; ca: also; na: never; vimuñcati: is liberated; durmedhā: unintelligent; dhṛtiḥ: determination; sā: that; pārtha: O son of Pritā; tāmasī: in the mode of ignorance

18.35 Ignorant resolve which cannot go beyond dreaming, fear, grief, despair and, delusion—such is in darkness, Pārtha.

सुखं त्विदानीं त्रिविधं श्रृणु मे भरतर्षभ।
अभ्यासाद्रमते यत्र दुःखान्तं च निगच्छति॥ ३६

sukhaṁ tvidānīṁ trividhaṁ śṛṇu me bharatarṣabha |
abhyāsād ramate yatra duḥkhāntaṁ ca nigacchati || 18.36

यत्तदग्रे विषमिव परिणामेऽमृतोपमम्।
तत्सुखं सात्त्विकं प्रोक्तमात्मबुद्धिप्रसादजम्॥ ३७

yat tad agre viṣaṁ iva pariṇāme 'mṛtopamam |
tat sukhaṁ sāttvikaṁ proktaṁ ātma-buddhi-prasādajam || 18.37

sukhaṁ: happiness; tu: but; idānīṁ: now; trividhaṁ: three kinds; śṛṇu: hear; me: from Me; bharatarṣabha: O best amongst the Bhāratas; abhyāsāt: by practice; ramate: enjoyer; yatra: where; duḥkha: distress; antaṁ: end; ca: also; nigacchati: gains; yat: that which; tat: that; agre: in the beginning; viṣaṁ iva: like poison; pariṇāme: at the end; amṛta: nectar; upamam: compared to; tat: that; sukhaṁ: happiness; sāttvikaṁ: in the mode of goodness; proktaṁ: is said; ātma: self; buddhi: intelligence; prasādajam: satisfactory

18.36,37 And now hear from Me, O Arjuna, about three kinds of pleasure. The pleasure that one enjoys from spiritual practice results in cessation of all sorrows. The pleasure that appears as poison in the beginning, but is like nectar in the end, comes by the grace of Self-knowledge and is in the mode of goodness.

विषयेन्द्रियसंयोगाद्यत्तदग्रेऽमृतोपमम्।
परिणामे विषमिव तत्सुखं राजसं स्मृतम्॥ ३८

viṣayendriya-saṁyogadyat tad agre 'mṛtopamam |
pariṇāme visam iva tat sukhaṁ rājasaṁ smṛtam || 18.38

viṣaya: objects of the senses; indriya: senses; saṁyogat: combination; yat: which; tat: that; agre: in the beginning; amṛtopamam: just like nectar; pariṇāme: at the end; visamiva: like poison; tat: that; sukhaṁ: happiness; rājasaṁ: in the mode of passion; smṛtam: is considered

18.38 Sensual pleasures that appear as nectar in the beginning, but become poison in the end, are in the mode of passion.

यदग्रे चानुबन्धे च सुखं मोहनमात्मनः।
निद्रालस्यप्रमादोत्थं तत्तामसमुदाहृतम्॥ ३९

yadagre cānubandhe ca sukhaṁ mohanamātmanaḥ /
nidrālasyapramādotthaṁ tat tāmasamudāhṛtam // 18.39

yat: that which; agre: in the beginning; ca: also; anubandhe: by binding; ca: also; sukhaṁ: happiness; mohanaṁ: illusion; ātmanaḥ: of the self; nidrā: sleeping; ālasya: laziness; pramāda: illusion; utthaṁ: produced of; tat: that; tāmasaṁ: in the mode of ignorance; udāhṛtam: is said to be

18.39 Pleasure that is delusion from beginning to end and born out of sleep, laziness and illusion is said to be of the nature of ignorance.

न तदस्ति पृथिव्यां वा दिवि देवेषु वा पुनः।
सत्त्वं प्रकृतिजैर्मुक्तं यदेभिः स्यात्त्रिभिर्गुणैः॥ ४०

na tad asti pṛthivyāṁ vā divi deveṣu vā punaḥ /
sattvaṁ prakṛti-jair-muktaṁ yad ebhiḥ syāt tribhirguṇaiḥ // 18.40

na: not; tad: that; asti: there is; pṛthivyāṁ: within the universe; vā: or; divi: in the higher planetary system; deveṣu: amongst the demigods; vā: or; punaḥ: again; sattvaṁ: existence; prakṛtijaiḥ: under the influence of material nature; muktaṁ: liberated; yat: that; ebhiḥ: by this; syāt: so becomes; tribhiḥ: by three; guṇaiḥ : modes of material nature

18.40 No one, either here or among the celestials in the higher planetary systems, is free from these three states of material nature.

ब्राह्मणक्षत्रियविशां शूद्राणां च परन्तप।
कर्माणि प्रविभक्तानि स्वभावप्रभवैर्गुणैः॥ ४१

brāhmaṇa-kṣatriya-viśāṁ śūdrāṇāṁ ca parantapa /
karmāṇi pravibhaktāni svabhāva-prabhavair-guṇaiḥ // 18.41

brāhmaṇa: the brāhmaṇas; kṣatriya: the kṣatriyas; visāṁ: the vaiśyas; śūdrāṇāṁ: the śūdras; ca: and; parantapa: O subduer of the enemies; karmāṇi: activities; pravibhaktāni: are divided; svabhāva: own nature; prabhavaiḥ: born of; guṇaiḥ: by the modes of material nature

18.41 Brāhmaṇas, kṣatriyas, vaiśyas and śūdras are divided in the work they do based on their nature, Parantapa (Arjuna).

शमो दमस्तप: शौचं क्षान्तिरार्जवमेव च।
ज्ञानं विज्ञानमास्तिक्यं ब्रह्मकर्म स्वभावजम्॥ ४२

śamo damastapaḥ śaucaṁ kṣāntirārjavameva ca /
jñānaṁ vijñānam āstikyaṁ brahmakarma svabhāvajaṁ // *18.42*

śamaḥ: peacefulness; damaḥ: self-control; tapaḥ: austerity; śaucaṁ: purity; kṣāntiḥ: tolerance; ārjavaṁ: honesty; eva: certainly; ca: and; jñānaṁ: knowledge; vijñānaṁ: wisdom; āstikyaṁ: belief in God; brahma: of a brahmana; karma: duty; svabhāvajaṁ: born of his own nature

18.42 The nature of Brāhmaṇa is characterized by their calmness, discipline, austerity, tolerance, honesty, knowledge, wisdom and belief in God.

शौर्यं तेजो धृतिर्दाक्ष्यं युद्धे चाप्यपलायनम्।
दानमीशरभावश्च क्षात्रं कर्म स्वभावजम्॥ ४३

śauryaṁ tejo dhṛtir dākṣyaṁ yuddhe cāpyapalāyanam /
dānamīśvarabhāvaś ca kṣātraṁ karma svabhāvajam // *18.43*

śauryaṁ: heroism; tejaḥ: power; dhṛtir: determination; dākṣyaṁ: resourcefulness; yuddhe: in battle; ca: and; api: also; apalāyanam: not fleeing; dānam: generosity; īśvara: leadership; bhāvaḥ: nature; ca: and; kṣātraṁ: kṣatriya; karma: duty; svabhāvajam: born of his own nature

18.43 Kṣatriya are characterized by their qualities of heroism, vigor, firmness, dexterity, steadfastness in battle, leadership and generosity.

कृषिगौरक्ष्यवाणिज्यं वैश्यकर्म स्वभावजम्।
परिचर्यात्मकं कर्म शूद्रस्यापि स्वभावजम्॥ ४४

kṛṣi gaurakṣya vāṇijyaṁ vaiśya-karma svabhāvajam I
paricaryātmakaṁ karma śūdrasyā api śvabhāvajam II 18.44

kṛṣi: plowing; gaurakṣyaṁ: protecting cows; vāṇijyaṁ: trade; vaiśya: vaiśyas; karma: duty; svabhāvajam: born of his own nature; paricaryā: service; atmakaṁ: nature; karma: duty; śūdrasyā: of the śūdra; api: also; svabhāvajaṁ: born of his own nature

18.44 Those who are good at cultivation, cattle rearing, and trade are known as Vaiśya. Those who are very good in service are classed as śūdra.

स्वे स्वे कर्मण्यभिरत: संसिद्धिं लभते नर:।
स्वकर्मनिरत: सिद्धिं यथा विन्दति तच्छृणु॥ ४५

sve svẹ karmaṇy abhirataḥ saṁsiddhiṁ labhate naraḥ I
svakarmaniratạḥ siddhiṁ yathā vindati tacchṛṇu II 18.45

sve: own; sve: own; karmaṇi: in work; abhirataḥ: following; saṁsiddhiṁ: perfection; labhate: achieves; naraḥ: a man; svakarma: by his own duty; nirataḥ: engaged; siddhiṁ: perfection; yathā: as; vindati: attains; tat: that; śṛṇu: listen

18.45 One can attain the highest perfection by devotion to one's natural work. Listen to Me how one attains perfection while engaged in one's natural work.

यत: प्रवृत्तिर्भूतानां येन सर्वमिदं ततम्।
स्वकर्मणा तमभ्यर्च्य सिद्धिं विन्दति मानव:॥ ४६

yataḥ pravṛttirbhūtānāṁ yena sarvamidaṁ tatam I
svakarmaṇā tamabhyarcya siddhiṁ vindati mānavaḥ II 18.46

yataḥ: from whom; pravṛttiḥ: the emanation; bhūtānāṁ: of all living entities;

yena: by whom; sarvaṁ: all; idaṁ: this; tatam: is pervaded; svakarmaṇā: in his own duties; taṁ: Him; abhyarcya: by worshiping; siddhiṁ: perfection; vindati: achieves; mānavaḥ: a man

18.46 One attains perfection by worshipping the supreme Being from whom all beings originate and by whom all this universe is pervaded through performance of one's natural duty for Him.

श्रेयान्स्वधर्मो विगुण: परधर्मात्स्वनुष्ठितात् ।
स्वभावनियतं कर्म कुर्वन्नाप्नोति किल्बिषम् ॥ ४७

śreyān svadharmo viguṇaḥ paradharmāt svanuṣṭhitāt |
svabhāva-niyataṁ karma kurvannāpnoti kilbiṣam || 18.47

śreyān: better; svadharmaḥ: one's own rightful conduct; viguṇaḥ: imperfectly performed; paradharmāt: another's conduct; svanuṣṭhitāt: perfectly done; svabhāvaniyataṁ: prescribed duties according to one's nature; karma: work; kurvan: performing; na: never; āpnoti: achieve; kilbiṣam: sinful reactions

18.47 It is better to engage in one's rightful conduct [svadharma], even though one may not perform it to perfection, rather than to accept another's conduct and perform it perfectly. Responsibility prescribed according to one's nature, are never affected by sinful reactions.

सहजं कर्म कौन्तेय सदोषमपि न त्यजेत् ।
सर्वारम्भा हि दोषेण धूमेनाग्निरिवावृता: ॥ ४८

sahajaṁ karma kaunteya sadoṣamapi na tyajet |
sarvārambhā hi doṣeṇa dhūmenā gnirivā vṛtāḥ || 18.48

sahajaṁ: born simultaneously; karma: work; kaunteya: O son of Kuntī; sadoṣaṁ: with fault; api: although; na: never; tyajet: to be given up; sarvārambhāḥ: any venture; hi: certainly; doṣeṇa: with fault; dhūmenāgniḥivāvṛtāḥ: being covered like the smoke around the fire

18.48 Every work has some defect, just as fire is covered by smoke. One should not give up the work that is born of his own nature, even if such work is full of fault, O Kaunteya (Arjuna).

असक्तबुद्धिः सर्वत्र जितात्मा विगतस्पृहः ।
नैष्कर्म्यसिद्धिं परमां सन्न्यासेनाधिगच्छति ॥ ४९

asaktabuddhiḥ sarvatra jitātmā vigataspṛhaḥ |
naiṣkarmyasiddhiṁ paramāṁ sannyāsenādhigacchati || 18.49

asaktabuddhiḥ: unattached intelligence; sarvatra: everywhere; jitātmā: control of the mind; vigataspṛhaḥ: without material desires; naiṣkarmyasiddhiṁ: perfection through the realisation of state of Brahman; paramāṁ: supreme; saṁyāsena: by the renounced order of life; adhigacchati: attains

18.49 One whose intelligence is always free from selfish attachment, who has controlled the mind and who is free from desires, by practicing renunciation [sannyāsa], attains the ultimate state of perfection of selfless work or actionlessness [naiṣkarma siddhi].

सिद्धिं प्राप्तो यथा ब्रह्म तथाप्नोति निबोध मे ।
समासेनैव कौन्तेय निष्ठा ज्ञानस्य या परा॥ ५०

siddhiṁ prāpto yathā brahma tathāpnoti nibodha me |
samāsenaiva kaunteya niṣṭhā jñānasya yā parā || 18.50

siddhiṁ: perfection; prāptaḥ: achieving; yathā: as; brahma: the supreme; tathā: so; apnoti: achieves; nibodha: try to understand; me: from Me; samāsena: summarily; eva: certainly; kaunteya: O son of Kuntī; niṣṭhā: stage; jñānasya: of knowledge; yā: which; parā: transcendental

18.50 Understand from Me, how one who has achieved this perfection, can attain the Supreme state of Truth, Brahman, by acting in the way I shall now summarize, Kaunteya.

बुद्ध्या विशुद्धया युक्तो धृत्यात्मानं नियम्य च।
शब्दादीन्विषयांस्त्यक्त्वा रागद्वेषौ व्युदस्य च॥ ५१

buddhyā viśuddhayā yukto dhṛtyātmānaṁ niyamya ca /
śabādīnviṣayāṁstyaktvā rāgadveṣau vyudasya ca // 18.51

विविक्तसेवी लघ्वाशी यतवाक्कायमानसः।
ध्यानयोगपरो नित्यं वैराग्यं समुपाश्रितः॥ ५२

viviktasevī laghvāśī yat-avāk-kāyamānasaḥ /
dhyāna-yoga-paro nityaṁ vairāgyaṁ samupāśritaḥ // 18.52

अहङ्कारं बलं दर्पं कामं क्रोधं परिग्रहम्।
विमुच्य निर्ममः शान्तो ब्रह्मभूयाय कल्पते॥ ५३

ahaṁkāraṁ balaṁ darpaṁ kāmaṁ krodhaṁ parigraham /
vimucya nirmamaḥ śānto brahmabhūyāya kalpate // 18.53

buddhyā: by the intelligence; viśuddhayā: fully purified; yuktaḥ: such engagement; dhṛtyā: determination; atmānaṁ: self; niyamya: regulated; ca: also; śabdādīn: the sense objects, such as sound, etc.; viṣayān: sense objects; tyaktvā: giving up; rāga: attachment; dveṣau: hatred; vyudasya: having laid aside; ca: also; viviktasevī: living in a secluded place; laghvāśī: eating a small quantity; yatavāk: control of speech; kāya: body; mānasaḥ: control of the mind; dhyānayogaparaḥ: always absorbed in trance; nityaṁ: twenty-four hours a day; vairāgyaṁ: detachment; samupāśritaḥ: taken shelter of; ahaṁkāraṁ: false ego; balaṁ: false strength; darpaṁ: false pride; kāmaṁ: lust; krodhaṁ: anger; parigraham: acceptance of material things; vimucya: being delivered; nirmamaḥ: without proprietorship; sāntaḥ: peaceful; brahmabhūyāya: to become self-realized; kalpate: is understood

18.51,52,53 Endowed with purified intellect; subduing the mind with firm resolve; turning away from the objects of senses; giving up likes and dislikes; living in solitude; eating lightly; controlling the mind, speech, and organs of action; ever absorbed in meditation; taking refuge in detachment; and relinquishing egotism, violence, pride, lust, anger, and proprietorship, one becomes peaceful, free from the notion of "I" and "mine", and fit for attaining oneness with the Supreme Being.

ब्रह्मभूत: प्रसन्नात्मा न शोचति न काङ्क्षति।
समः सर्वेषु भूतेषु मद्भक्तिं लभते पराम्॥ ५४

brahmabhūtaḥ prasannātmā na śocati na kāṅkṣati |

samaḥ sarveṣu bhūteṣu madbhaktiṁ labhate parāṁ || 18.54

brahmabhūtaḥ: being one with the Absolute; prasannātmā: fully joyful; na: never; śocati: laments; na: never; kāṅkṣati: desires; samaḥ: equally disposed; sarveṣu: all; bhūteṣu: living entities; madbhaktiṁ: My devotion; labhate: gains; parāṁ: transcendental

18.54 Absorbed in the supreme Being, the serene one neither grieves nor desires. Becoming impartial to all beings, one obtains My highest devotional love.

भक्त्या मामभिजानाति यावान्यश्चास्मि तत्त्वत:।
ततो मां तत्त्वतो ज्ञात्वा विशते तदनन्तरम्॥ ५५

bhaktyā mām abhijānāti yāvān yaścāsmi tattvataḥ |

tato māṁ tattvato jñātvā viśate tad-anantaram || 18.55

bhaktyā: by pure devotional service; mām: Me; abhijānāti: one can know; yāvān: as much as; yaścāsmi: as I am; tattvataḥ: in truth; tataḥ: thereafter; māṁ: Me; tattvataḥ: by truth; jñātvā: knowing; viśate: enters; tadanantaram: thereafter

18.55 By devotion one truly understands what and who I am in essence. Having known Me in essence, one immediately merges with Me.

सर्वकर्माण्यपि सदा कुर्वाणो मद्व्यपाश्रयः।
मत्प्रसादादवाप्नोति शाश्वतं पदमव्ययम्॥ ५६

sarvakarmāṇy api sadā kurvāṇo madvyapāśrayaḥ |
mat-prasādād avāpnoti śāśvataṁ padamavyayam || 18.56

sarva: all; karmāṇi: activities; api: although; sadā: always; kurvāṇaḥ: performing; mat: under My; vyapāśrayaḥ: protection; mat: My; prasādāt: mercy; avāpnoti: achieves; śāśvataṁ: eternal; padaṁ: abode; avyayam: imperishable

18.56 My devotee occupied in everyday life still reaches under My protection the imperishable ultimate abode through my mercy, through devotion to Me.

चेतसा सर्वकर्माणि मयि सन्न्यस्य मत्परः।
बुद्धियोगमुपाश्रित्य मच्चित्तः सततं भव॥ ५७

cetasā sarvakarmāṇi mayi sannyasya matparaḥ |
buddhiyogam upāśritya maccittaḥ satataṁ bhava || 18.57

cetasā: by intelligence; sarvakarmāṇi: all kinds of activities; mayi: unto Me; sannyasya: giving up; matparaḥ: My protection; buddhiyogaṁ: devotional activities; upāśritya: taking shelter of; maccittaḥ: consciousness; satataṁ: always; bhava: just become

18.57 While being engaged in activities just depend upon Me, and being fully conscious of Me, work always under My protection.

मच्चित्तः सर्वदुर्गाणि मत्प्रसादात्तरिष्यसि।
अथ चेत्त्वमहङ्कारान्न श्रोष्यसि विनङ्क्ष्यसि॥ ५८

maccittaḥ sarvadurgāṇi matprasādāt tariṣyasi |
atha cet tvam ahaṁkārān na śroṣyasi vinaṅkṣyasi || 18.58

mat: My; cittaḥ: consciousness; sarva: all; durgāṇi: impediments; mat: My;

prasādāt: My mercy; tariṣyasi: you will overcome; atha: therefore; cet: if; tvaṁ: you; ahaṁkārāt: by false ego; na: not; śroṣyasi: do not hear; vinaṅkṣyasi: then lose yourself

18.58 When your mind becomes fixed on Me, you shall overcome all difficulties by My grace. But if you do not listen to Me due to ego, you shall perish.

यदहङ्कारमाश्रित्य न योत्स्य इति मन्यसे।
मिथ्यैष व्यवसायस्ते प्रकृतिस्त्वां नियोक्ष्यति॥ ५९

yad ahaṁkāram āśritya na yotsya iti manyase /
mithyaiṣa vyavasāyas te prakṛtis tvāṁ niyokṣyati // 18.59

yat: therefore; ahaṁkāram: false ego; āśritya: taking shelter; na: not; yotsye: shall fight; iti: thus; manyase: think; mithyaiṣa: this is all false; vyavasāyaste: your determination; prakṛtiḥ: material nature; tvāṁ: you; niyokṣyati: will engage you

18.59 If due to ego you think: 'I shall not fight,' your resolve is useless, and your own nature will compel you.

स्वभावजेन कौन्तेय निबद्धः स्वेन कर्मणा।
कर्तुं नेच्छसि यन्मोहात्करिष्यस्यवशोऽपि तत्॥ ६०

svabhāvajena kaunteya nibaddhaḥ svena karmaṇa /
kartuṁ necchasi yan mohāt kariṣyasyavaśo 'pi tat // 18.60

svabhāvajena: by one's own nature; kaunteya: O son of Kuntī; nibaddhaḥ: conditioned; svena: by one's own; karmaṇa: activities; kartuṁ: to do; na: not; icchasi: like; yat: that; mohāt: by illusion; kariṣyasi: you will act; avaśo: imperceptibly; api: even; tat: that

18.60 O Kaunteya, you are controlled by your own natural conditioning. Therefore, you shall do even against your will, what you do not wish to do out of delusion.

ईशरः सर्वभूतानां हृद्देशेऽर्जुन तिष्ठति।
भ्रामयन्सर्वभूतानि यन्त्रारूढानि मायया॥ ६१

īśvaraḥ sarvabhūtānāṁ hṛddeśe 'rjuna tiṣṭhati /
bhrāmayan sarvabhūtāni yantrārūḍhāni māyayā // 18.61

īśvaraḥ: the Supreme Lord; sarvabhūtānāṁ: of all living entities; hṛddeśe: in the heart; arjuna: O Arjuna; tiṣṭhati: resides; bhrāmayan: causing to travel; sarvabhūtāni : all living entities; yantra: machine; ārūḍhāni: being so placed; māyayā: under the illusion

18.61 The Supreme Lord resides in everyone's heart, O Arjuna, and is directing the activities of all living entities who are acting as machines under the illusion of the material world.

तमेव शरणं गच्छ सर्वभावेन भारत।
तत्प्रसादात्परां शान्तिं स्थानं प्राप्स्यसि शोशतम्॥ ६२

tameva śaraṇaṁ gaccha sarvabhāvena bhārata /
tatprasādātparāṁ śāntiṁ sthānaṁ prāpsyasi śāśvatam // 18.62

taṁ: unto Him; eva: certainly; śaraṇaṁ: surrender; gaccha: go; sarvabhāvena: in all respects; bhārata: O son of Bhārata; tatprasādāt: by His grace; parāṁ: supreme; śāntiṁ: in peace; sthānaṁ: abode; prāpsyasi: you will get; śāśvatam: eternal

18.62 Surrender to Him completely with all your being. By His grace you will attain supreme peace and the eternal abode.

इति ते ज्ञानमाख्यातं गुह्याद्गुह्यतरं मया।
विमृश्यैतदशेषेण यथेच्छसि तथा कुरु॥ ६३

iti te jñānamākhyātaṁ guhyād guhyataraṁ mayā /
vimṛśyai tadaśeṣeṇa yathecchasi tathā kuru // 18.63

iti: thus; te: unto you; jñānaṁ: knowledge; ākhyātaṁ: described; guhyāt:

confidential; guhyataraṁ: still more confidential; mayā: by Me; vimṛśya: by deliberation; etat: that; aśeṣeṇa: fully; yathā: as you; icchasi: you like; tathā: that; kuru: perform

18.63 I have explained the knowledge that is the secret of secrets. After fully reflecting on this, do as you wish.

सर्वगुह्यतमं भूयः शृणु मे परमं वचः।
इष्टोऽसि मे दृढमिति ततो वक्ष्यामि ते हितम्॥ ६४

sarva-guhyatamaṁ bhūyaḥ śṛṇu me paramaṁ vacaḥ |
iṣṭo 'si me dṛḍhamiti tato vakṣyāmi te hitam || 18.64

sarvaguhyatamaṁ: the most confidential of all; bhūyaḥ: again; śṛṇu: just hear; me: from Me; paramaṁ: the supreme; vacaḥ: instruction; iṣṭo 'si: you are very dear to Me; me: of Me; dṛḍhaṁ: very; iti: thus; tataḥ: therefore; vakṣyāmi: I am speaking; te: for your; hitam: benefit

18.64 Because you are My dear friend, I express this truth to you. This is the most confidential of all knowledge. Hear this from Me. It is for your benefit.

मन्मना भव मद्भक्तो मद्याजी मां नमस्कुरु।
मामेवैष्यसि सत्यं ते प्रतिजाने प्रियोऽसि मे॥ ६५

manmanā bhava madbhakto madyājī māṁ namaskuru |
māmevaiṣyasi satyaṁ te pratijāne priyo 'si me || 18.65

manmanāḥ: thinking of Me; bhava: just become; madbhaktaḥ: My devotee; madyājī: My worshiper; māṁ: unto Me; namaskuru: offer your obeisances; mām: unto Me; eva: certainly; eṣyasi: come; satyaṁ: truly; te: to you; pratijāne: I promise; priyaḥ: dear; asi: you are; me: Mine

18.65 Always think of Me and become My devotee. Worship Me and offer your homage unto Me. Thus you will certainly attain to Me. This I promise you because you are My very dear friend.

सर्वधर्मान्परित्यज्य मामेकं शरणं व्रज।
अहं त्वां सर्वपापेभ्यो मोक्षयिष्यामि मा शुचः॥ ६६

sarvadharmān parityajya mām ekaṁ śaraṇaṁ vraja |
ahaṁ tvāṁ sarvapāpebhyo mokṣayiṣyāmi mā śucaḥ || 18.66

sarvadharmān: all principles of right conduct; parityajya: abandoning; mām: unto Me; ekaṁ: only; śaraṇaṁ: surrender; vraja: go; ahaṁ: I; tvāṁ: you; sarva: all; pāpebhyaḥ: from sinful reactions; mokṣayiṣyāmi: deliver; mā: not; śucaḥ: worry

18.66 Abandon all principles and concepts of right conduct and simply surrender unto Me. I shall deliver you from all sinful reaction. Have no worry.

इदं ते नातपस्काय नाभक्ताय कदाचन।
न चाशुश्रूषवे वाच्यं न च मां योऽभ्यसूयति॥ ६७

idaṁ te nā 'tapaskāya nā 'bhaktāya kadācana |
na cā 'śuśrūṣave vācyaṁ na ca māṁ yo 'bhyasūyati || 18.67

idaṁ: this; te: you; na: never; atapaskāya: one who is not austere; na: never; abhaktāya: one who is not a devotee; kadācana: at any time; na: never; ca: also; aśuśrūṣave: one who is not engaged in devotional service; vācyaṁ: to be spoken; na: never; ca: also; māṁ: unto Me; yaḥ: anyone; abhyasūyati: envious

18.67 This knowledge should never be spoken by you to one who is devoid of austerity, who is without devotion, who does not desire to listen, or who speaks ill of Me.

य इमं परमं गुह्यं मद्भक्तेष्वभिधास्यति।
भक्तिं मयि परां कृत्वा मामेवैष्यत्यसंशयः॥ ६८

ya idaṁ paramaṁ guhyaṁ mad-bhakteṣv abhidhāsyati |
bhaktiṁ mayi parāṁ kṛtvā māmevaiṣyaty asaṁśayaḥ || 18.68

yaḥ: anyone; idaṁ: this; paramaṁ: most; guhyaṁ: confidential; mat: Mine; bhakteṣu: amongst devotees of; abhidhāsyati: explains; bhaktiṁ: devotional service; mayi: unto Me; parāṁ: transcendental; kṛtvā: having done; mām: unto Me; eva: certainly; eṣyati: comes; asaṁśayaḥ: without doubt

18.68 One who communicates the supreme secret to the devotees performs the highest devotional service to Me, and at the end he will without doubt, come back to Me.

न च तस्मान्मनुष्येषु कश्चिन्मे प्रियकृत्तमः।
भविता न च मे तस्मादन्यः प्रियतरो भुवि॥ ६९

na ca tasmānmanuṣyeṣu kaścin me priya kṛttamaḥ I
bhavitā na ca me tasmād anyaḥ priyataro bhuvi II 18.69

na: never; ca: and; tasmāt: therefore; manuṣyeṣu: among mankind; kaścit: anyone; me: My; priyakṛttamaḥ: more dear; bhavitā: will become; na: nor; ca: and; me: My; tasmāt: than him; anyaḥ: other; priyataraḥ: dearer; bhuvi: in this world

18.69 No other person shall do a more pleasing service to Me, and no one on the earth shall be more dear to Me.

अध्येष्यते च य इमं धर्म्यं संवादमावयोः।
ज्ञानयज्ञेन तेनाहमिष्टः स्यामिति मे मतिः॥ ७०

adhyeṣyate ca ya imaṁ dharmyaṁ saṁvādamāvayoḥ I
jñānayajñena tenāham iṣṭaḥ syāmiti me matiḥ II 18.70

adhyeṣyate: will study; ca: also; yaḥ: he; imaṁ: this; dharmyaṁ: sacred; saṁvādaṁ: conversation; āvayoḥ: of ours; jñāna: knowledge; yajñena: by sacrifice; tena: by him; ahaṁ: I; iṣṭaḥ: worshiped; syām: shall be; iti: thus; me: My; matiḥ: opinion

18.70 I declare that One who studies this sacred dialogue worships Me by sacrifice of his intelligence.

श्रद्धावाननसूयश्च शृणुयादपि यो नरः।
सोऽपि मुक्तः शुभाँल्लोकान्प्राप्नुयात्पुण्यकर्मणाम्॥ ७१

śraddhāvānanasūyaś ca śṛṇuyādapi yo naraḥ |

so 'pi muktaḥ śubhāṁl lokān prāpnuyāt puṇyakarmaṇām || 18.71

śraddhāvān: faithful; anasūyaś ca: and not envious; śṛṇuyāt: does hear; api: certainly; yaḥ: who; naraḥ: a man; saḥ: he; api: also; muktaḥ: being liberated; śubhān: auspicious; lokān: planets; prāpnuyāt: attains; puṇyakarmaṇām: of those with merit

18.71 One who listens with faith and without envy becomes free from sinful reactions and attains to the planets where those of merit dwell.

कच्चिदेतच्छ्रुतं पार्थ त्वयैकाग्रेण चेतसा।
कच्चिदज्ञानसम्मोहः प्रनष्टस्ते धनञ्जय॥ ७२

kaccid etac chrutaṁ pārtha tvayaikāgreṇa cetasā |

kaccid ajñāna-saṁmohaḥ pranaṣṭaste dhanañjaya || 18.72

kaccit: whether; etat: this; śrutaṁ: heard; pārtha: O son of Prithā; tvaya: by you; ekāgreṇa: with full attention; cetasā: by the mind; kaccit: whether; ajñāna: ignorant; saṁmohaḥ: illusion; pranaṣṭaḥ: dispelled; te: of you; dhanañjaya: O conqueror of wealth (Arjuna)

18.72 O Pārtha, did you listen to this with single-minded attention? Has your delusion born of ignorance been completely destroyed, Dhanañjaya?

अर्जुन उवाच

नष्टो मोहः स्मृतिर्लब्धा त्वत्प्रसादान्मयाऽच्युत।
स्थितोऽस्मि गतसन्देहः करिष्ये वचनं तव॥ ७३

Arjuna uvāca

naṣṭo mohaḥ smṛtirlabdhā tvat-prasādān mayā'cyuta |

sthito 'smi gata-sandehaḥ kariṣye vacanaṁ tava || 18.73

Arjuna uvāca: Arjuna says; naṣṭaḥ: dispelled; mohaḥ: illusion; smṛtiḥ: memory; labdhā: regained; tvatprasādāt: by Your mercy; mayā: by me; acyuta: O infallible Kṛṣṇa; sthitaḥ: situated; asmi: I am; gata: removed; sandehaḥ: all doubts; kariṣye: I shall execute; vacanaṁ: order; tava: Your

18.73 Arjuna says: O dear Acyuta (infallible lord), my illusion is now gone. I have regained my memory by Your Grace, and I am now firm and free from doubt, and ready to act as per your instructions.

संजय उवाच

इत्यहं वासुदेवस्य पार्थस्य च महात्मनः।

संवादमिममश्रौषमद्भुतं रोमहर्षणम्॥ ७४

Sañjaya uvāca

ityahaṁ vāsudevasya pārthasya ca mahātmanaḥ |

saṁvādam imam aśrauṣam adbhutaṁ roma-harṣaṇam || 18.74

Sañjaya uvāca: Sañjaya said; iti: thus; ahaṁ: I; vāsudevasya: of Kṛṣṇa; pārthasya: of Arjuna; ca: also; mahātmanaḥ: two great souls; saṁvādaṁ: discussion; imaṁ: this; aśrauṣaṁ: heard; adbhutaṁ: wonder; romaharṣaṇam: hair standing on end

18.74 Sañjaya said: Thus have I heard the conversation of two great souls, Kṛṣṇa and Arjuna. And so wonderful is that message that my hair stands on end.

व्यासप्रसादाच्छ्रुतवानेतद्गुह्यमहं परम्।

योगं योगेश्वरात्कृष्णात्साक्षात्कथयतः स्वयम्॥ ७५।

vyasā-prasādāc chrutavān etad guhyam ahaṁ param |

yogaṁ yogeśvarāt kṛṣnāt sākṣāt kathayataḥ svayam || 18.75

vyasāprasādāt: by the mercy of Vyāsadeva; śrutavān: heard; etat: this; guhyaṁ: confidential; ahaṁ: I; param: the supreme; yogaṁ: mysticism; yogeśvarāt: from the master of all mysticism; kṛṣnāt: from Kṛṣṇa; sākṣāt: directly; kathayataḥ: speaking; svayam: personally

18.75 By the mercy of Vyāsa, I have heard these most confidential words directly from Kṛṣṇa, the master of all mysticism, who was speaking personally to Arjuna.

राजन्संस्मृत्य संस्मृत्य संवादमिममद्भुतम्।
केशवार्जुनयोः पुण्यं हृष्यामि च मुहुर्मुहुः॥ ७६

rājan saṁsmṛtya-saṁsmṛtya saṁvādam imam adbhutam |
keśavārjunayoḥ puṇyaṁ hṛṣyāmi ca muhur-muhuḥ || 18.76

rājan: O King; saṁsmṛtya: remembering; saṁsmṛtya: remembering; saṁvādaṁ: discussion; imaṁ: this; adbhutam: wonderful; keśava: Lord Kṛṣṇa; arjunayoḥ: and Arjuna; puṇyaṁ: pious; hṛṣyāmi: taking pleasure; ca: also; muhurmuhuḥ: always, repeatedly

18.76 O King, as I repeatedly recall this wondrous and holy dialogue between Keśava (Kṛṣṇa) and Arjuna, I take pleasure, being thrilled at every moment.

तच्च संस्मृत्य संस्मृत्य रूपमत्यद्भुतं हरेः।
विस्मयो मे महान् राजन्हृष्यामि च पुनः पुनः॥ ७७

tacca saṁsmṛtya-saṁsmṛtya rūpam atyadbhutaṁ hareḥ |
vismayo me mahān rājan hṛṣyāmi ca punaḥ-punaḥ || 18.77

tat: that; ca: also; saṁsmṛtya: remembering; saṁsmṛtya: remembering; rūpaṁ: form; ati: great; adbhutaṁ: wonderful; hareḥ: of Lord Kṛṣṇa; vismayaḥ: wonder; me: my; mahān: great; rājan: O King; hṛṣyāmi: enjoying; ca: also; punaḥ-punaḥ: repeatedly

18.77 O King, when I remember the wonderful form of Lord Kṛṣṇa, I am struck with even greater wonder, and I rejoice again and again.

यत्र योगेश्वरः कृष्णो यत्र पार्थो धनुर्धरः।
तत्र श्रीर्विजयो भूतिर्ध्रुवा नीतिर्मतिर्मम॥ ७८॥

yatra yogeśvaraḥ kṛṣṇo yatra pārtho dhanurdharaḥ |
tatra śrīrvijayo bhūtir dhruvā nītirmatirmama || 18.78

yatra: where; yogeśvaraḥ: the master of mysticism; kṛṣṇaḥ: Lord Kṛṣṇa; yatra: where; pārthaḥ: the son of Pritā; dhanurdharaḥ: the carrier of the bow and arrow; tatra: there; śrīḥ: opulence; vijayaḥ: victory; bhūtiḥ: exceptional power; dhruvā: certain; nītiḥ: morality; matirmama: is my opinion.

18.78 Wherever there is Yogeśvara Kṛṣṇa, the Master of all mystics, and wherever there is Pārtha, the supreme carrier of bow and arrow, there will certainly be opulence, victory, extraordinary power, and morality. That is my opinion.

इति श्रीमद्भगवद्गीतासूपनिषत्सु ब्रह्मविद्यायां योगशास्त्रे
श्रीकृष्णार्जुनसंवादे मोक्षसंन्यासयोगो नाम अष्टादशोऽध्यायः ॥

iti śrīmadbhagavadgītāsūpaniṣatsu
brahmavidyāyāṁ yogaśāstre
śrī kṛṣṇārjunasaṁvāde
mokṣasaṁnyāsa yogo nāma
aṣṭādaśo 'dhyāyaḥ ||

In the ***Upaniṣad*** of ***Śrimad Bhagavad Gītā***, the scripture of yoga dealing with ***Brahmavidyā Yogaśāstra,*** the science of Brahman, the Supreme Absolute, in the form of ***Śrī Kṛṣṇārjuna saṁvād,*** dialogue between Śrī Kṛṣṇa and Arjuna, this is the eighteenth chapter named, ***Mokṣa Sannyāsa Yogaḥ***, *'The Yoga of Liberation by Renunciation.'*

Appendix

Scientific Research On Bhagavad Gītā

Several institutions have conducted experiments using scientific and statistically supported techniques to verify the truth behind Bhagavad Gītā. Notable amongst them is the work carried out by Mahṛṣi Mahesha yogi, whose findings are published through Mahaṛṣi ved vijñāna viśva vidyāpīṭaṁ.

Studies conducted using meditation techniques related to truths expressed in the verses of *Bhagavad Gītā* have shown that the quality of life is significantly improved through meditation. These studies have found that meditators experience a greater sense of peace resulting in a reduced tendency towards conflict.

Meditators gain greater respect for and appreciation of others. Their own inner fulfillment increases resulting in improved self-respect and self-reliance, leading to Self Realization.

One's ability to focus along with brain function integration is enhanced. These have resulted in greater comprehension, creativity, faster response time in decision-making and superior psychomotor coordination.

Stress levels have been shown to decrease with enhanced sensory perception and overall health. The tendency towards depression has been clearly shown to decrease.

There is enough evidence to show that as a result of meditation, individuals gain a better ethical lifestyle that in turn improves their interaction with others in the community, resulting in less conflict and crime. Group meditation of 7000 people (square root of 1% of world population at the time of the study) was significantly correlated to a reduction in conflict worldwide.

Meditation leads to higher levels of consciousness. Through the research tools of Applied Kinesiology, Dr. David Hawkins (author of the book *Power vs. Force*) and others have shown that human consciousness has risen in the last few decades, crossing a critical milestone for the first time in human history. Dr. Hawkins' research also documents that Bhagavad Gītā is at the very highest level of Truth conveyed to humanity.

We acknowledge with gratitude the work done by the Mahṛṣi Mahesha yogi institutions and Dr. David Hawkins in establishing the truth of this great scripture.

KURU FAMILY TREE

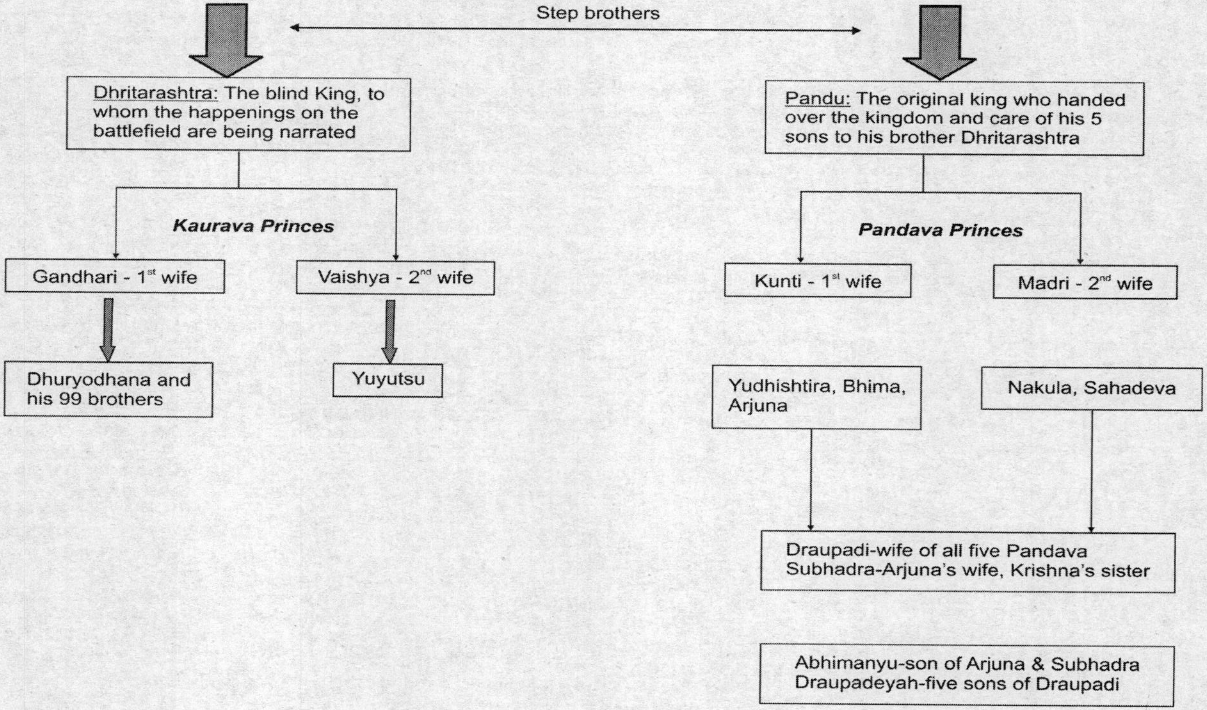
Step brothers
Dhritarashtra: The blind King, to whom the happenings on the battlefield are being narrated
Kaurava Princes
Gandhari - 1st wife
Vaishya - 2nd wife
Dhuryodhana and his 99 brothers
Yuyutsu
Pandu: The original king who handed over the kingdom and care of his 5 sons to his brother Dhritarashtra
Pandava Princes
Kunti - 1st wife
Madri - 2nd wife
Yudhishtira, Bhima, Arjuna
Nakula, Sahadeva
Draupadi-wife of all five Pandava
Subhadra-Arjuna's wife, Krishna's sister
Abhimanyu-son of Arjuna & Subhadra
Draupadeyah-five sons of Draupadi

Key Characters in Bhagavad Gītā

Kṛṣṇa	:	God Incarnate, Nārāyaṇa; eighth incarnation of Śrī Viṣṇu; complete Incarnation, Pūrnāvatar; Superconscious Divine, Parabrahma Kṛṣṇa; related to both Kauravas and Pāṇḍavas, Vāsudeva Kṛṣṇa; Arjuna's charioteer in the war; Master of the Universe, Jagadguru—revivor of the sacred, secret science of enlightenment through the Bhagavad Gītā to his disciple Arjuna; removes *bhū bhāra*, the weight of *adharma*, collective unconsciousness from the earth through the Mahābhārat war and re-establishes *dharma*.
Arjuna	:	the most illustrious of the Pāṇḍava brothers; divine son of Indra, the God of Devatas; expert wielder of the bow; the warrior leader amongst all warriors; human incarnate, Nara (reflection of Nārāyaṇa)
Veda Vyāsa	:	author of Mahābhārat, Brahma Sūtras; grandfather to the Pāṇḍavas; lord of Enlightened Masters; compiler of Vedas, the sacred texts of Truth.

Pañcha Pāṇḍavas : The 5 Pāṇḍava brothers, Yudhiṣṭra, Bhīma, Arjuna, Nakula, Sahadeva, who are immaculate conceptions of Exitence, born from Nature and Divine energies; embodiment of *dharma;* cousins of Vāsudeva Kṛṣṇa.

Yudhiṣṭra : eldestofPāṇḍavas,divineonofYamaDharma, the God of time and righteusness; renowned for his unflinching adherence to truth and righteousness which earned him the title 'Dharmarāja—king of Dharma'

Bhīma : The 2nd of the Pāṇḍava brothers; divine son of Vāyu, the wind God; blessed by energy of Hānuman; distinguished from his brothers by his great stature and unimaginable strength.

Nakula, Sahadeva : twin sons of Mādri; divine sons of Aśvini Kumāras, the Divine physicians; expert swordsmen; high wisdom and war skills; experts in Astrology and Ayurveda.

Draupadī : wife of all Pāṇḍavas; daughter of Drupad; emerged from the fire-sacrifice energy also named 'Yagñaseni'—born of fire' and 'Kṛṣṇa'; dear friend of Śrī Kṛṣṇa; perfectly faultless, chaste and virtous wife; embodied the energy of fighting injustice and *adharma*; incarnation of eight goddesses in one form.

Duryodhana :	son of Dhṛtarāṣṭra, the Kaurava King
Karṇa :	son of Kuntī from the Sun god; eldest of the Pāṇḍavas, renowned for his sacrifice and generosity; Duryodhana's close friend
Duśśāsana :	brother of Duryodhana, is killed by Bhīma in the war; committed the infamous act of attempting to disrobe Draupadī (wife of Pāṇḍavas)
Bhīṣma :	great grandfather of the Kaurava & Pāṇḍava; great warrior
Droṇa :	a great archer and teacher of both Kauravas and Pāṇḍavas
Pāṇḍu :	father of Pāṇḍavas, husband of Kuntī
Kuntī :	wife of Pāṇḍu, mother of Pāṇḍavas (along with Karṇa); embodiment of patience and penance.
Mādrī :	2nd wife of Pāṇḍu; mother of Sahadeva and Nakula; died after her husband left his body.
Gāndhārī :	mother of Kauravas; voluntarily blindfolded herself throughout her married life since her husband Dhṛtarāṣṭra was born blind.
Śakuni :	brother of Gāndhārī; prince of Gāndhāra kingdom. Duryodhana's maternal uncle; mastermind of inciting enmity between Kauravas and Pāṇḍavas.; attempted evil strategies to destroy Kuru dynasty, such as the dice game against Pāṇḍavas.

Drupad : a great warrior and father of Draupadī

Dṛṣṭadyumna : son of king Drupada and brother of Draupadī

Dṛṣṭaketu : king of Chedis, an ally of the Pāṇḍavas.

Śikhaṇḍi : a mighty archer and a transsexual person; responsible for bringing down Grandsire Bhīsma Pitāmaha from war. Was Ambā, princess of Kāshi, in previous birth.

Virāṭa : Abhimanyu's father-in-law; king of a neighboring kingdom; ally and host of Pāṇḍavas during their secret stay.

Yuyudhāna : Kṛṣṇa's charioteer and a great warrior

Kāśirāja : king of the neighboring kingdom of Kāśī

Cekitāna : an ally of the Pāṇḍavas, a great warrior

Kuntībhoja : adoptive father of Kuntī, the mother of the first three Pāṇḍava princes

Purujit : brother of Kuntibhoj

Śaibya : a ruler friendly to the Pāṇḍavas, leader of the Śibi tribe

Uttamouja : a great warrior

Sañjaya : minister and narrator of events to Dhṛtarāṣṭra

Vikarṇa : third of the Kaurava brothers

Aśvattāma : Droṇa's son and Achilles heel; said to always speak the truth; ally of Duryodhana

Kṛpācārya : teacher of martial arts to both Kauravas and Pāṇḍavas.

Śalya	:	king of neighboring kingdom and brother of Mādri, Nakula and Sahadeva's mother
Somadatta	:	king of Bahikas
Śāntanu	:	Arjuna's great grandfather
Subhadrā	:	Lord Kṛṣṇa's sister; wife of Arjuna; mother of Abhimanyu.
Abhimanyu	:	son of Arjuna and Subhadrā; nephew of Lord Kṛṣṇa and Lord Balarāma; most brave and illustrious warrior in entire Kuru and Pāṇḍava lineage; inherited the great courage, skills and valour from his father Arjuna and Uncle Kṛṣṇa; engaged in war at the age of 16 and defeated many Mahārathis, great warriors by himself; willingly fought and left his body in warfield proving his loyalty and love to his family; Abhimanyu's son, Parikśit became the sole survivor and heir to Pāṇḍava empire and throne.
Vicitravīrya	:	Śikhaṇḍi's step brother
Yudhāmanyu	:	an ally of Pāṇḍavas, prince of Pāñcāla
Yuyudhāna	:	another name for Sātyaki

SAMSKRIT PRONUNCIATION GUIDE

Saṃskṛit is *Devabhāśa*, meaning the language of the Gods. It is the sacred and sophisticated language or *bhāśā*, the source of all languages and vocal expressions from time eternal. Spoken by the Gods, it is the first langauge of the world, which flourished in the land of Bhāratavarśa (India).

Saṃskṛitaṃ is a perfect language of the perfect or enlightened ones, used by the learned sages and divine beings to express the inexpressible energy of the sacred Truths. The roots of vedic Saṃskṛit source directly to Lord Śiva, from His Cosmic sound creations (like *aiun rilrik* etc.), which were later concieved by Sage Pāṇani, who created the entire saṃskṛit grammar called Aṣṭādhyāyī. No one in the world could create perfect grammar just from a few sounds, and this is pure evidence that Saṃskṛit is a Divine literal manifestation. The word **Saṃskṛtaṁ** means—**'that which is perfectly, well done or refined or elaborate speech.'**

It is a phonetic language, for it is phonetically precise and natural, where every sound truly represents what it means by a unique symbol. For example, the sound 'ga' expresses motion or the saṃskṛit root 'gam.' The uniqueness of Saṃskṛit is that it is unchanged in every age in every Veda or in other Saṁskṛit literatures as it is Divinely created grammar. It uses 2200 verbal roots (dhātu) that combine to create an entire vocabulary of millions of words with precise and elaborate verbalization in short syllables. Its sophistication lies in its sacred meanings hidden in saṃskṛit texts, formed with its well-defined combinations (sandhi) of sounds.

In the **Vedic tradition,** the power of sound is used. **Vedic chanting** is nothing but 'becoming It' by creating the right space just by declarations. Each sound is a *mantra,* which invokes that specific energy when chanted with the right phonetic sound; perfect for expressing the power of words, *vāk śakti.* To retain the original Vedic tradition, as it is spoken, and to experience the energy of sacred sounds or *mantras,* the right pronunciation or chanting has utmost value in Saṃskṛit.

Bhagavad Gītā is the direct speech of the Divine—Bhagavān, Parabrahma Śrī Kṛṣṇa sung in His own sound, in the most-refined and kingly Saṃskṛit poetry. Just by chanting the Gītā, we can experience the pure space and energy of Śrī Kṛṣṇa and His teachings; the most confidential, sacred Truths. Ādī Śankaracārya, the great Enlightened Master sings in *Bhaja Govindaṁ,* 'Even a little chanting of the Bhagavad Gītā will liberate you from death.'

The *chanda* or the vedic meter for chanting the Gītā is '*anuśtubh chandaḥ*'—a meter of 32 syllables in a *shloka* (verse stanza) or 8 syllables in a 4 *pada (metrical foot)*; and the only other meter is '*trishubh chandaḥ*' of 4 padas of 11 syllables or 44 syllables in each *shloka* (e.g. most of chapter 11-Viśvarūpa Darśan Yoga). It is recommended to understand the *chanda* as the verse meter structure is directly related to the right listening and internalizing the meaning.

Saṃskṛit is now mostly written in Devanāgiri script, meaning 'the city of Gods', which is also the Hindi language script. Throughout this book, the diacritical marks have been rendered to indicate the right pronunciation of each Saṃskṛit sound in the English letter as per the accepted saṃskṛit transliteration system. In the Devanāgari script, there are fourty-nine characters—fourteen vowels and thirty-five consonants.

(स्वराः) Vowels

Simple Vowels	अ a	आ ā	इ i	ई ī	उ u	ऊ ū
	ऋ ṛ	ॠ ṝ	ऌ l̤	ॡ l̤̄		
Diphthongs	ए e	ऐ ai	ओ o	औ au		

Numerals

० - 0 १ - 1 २ - 2 ३ - 3 ४ - 4 ५ - 5
६ - 6 ७ - 7 ८ - 8 ९ - 9

(व्यञ्जनानि) Consonants

	Hard	**Hard Aspirate**	**Soft**	**Soft Aspirate**	**Soft Nasal**	**Soft Semi vowels**	**Hard Sibilants**
Guttural	क ka	ख kha	ग ga	घ gha	ङ ṅa	ह ha	: ḥ
Palatal	च ca	छ cha	ज ja	झ jha	ञ ña	य ya	श śa
Lingual	ट ta	ठ ṭa	ड ḍa	ढ ḍha	ण ṇa	र ra	ष ṣa
Dental	त ta	थ tha	द da	ध dha	न na	ल la	स sa
Labial	प pa	फ pha	ब ba	भ bha	म ma	व va	: ṁ

Consonant Pronuncations

- **Gutteral: ka, kha, ga, gha, ṅa**—pronounced from the throat.
- **Palatal: ca, cha, ja, jha, ña**—pronounced with the middle of the tougue against the palate
- **Lingual or Cerebral: ṭa, ṭha, ḍa, ḍha, ṇa**—pronounced from the tip of the tougue against the roof of the mouth
- **Dental: ta, tha, da, dha, na**—pronounced like the cerebrals but with the tongue against the teeth
- **Labial: pa, pha, b, bh, m**—pronounced with the lips
- **Semivowel:** ya, ra, la, va
- **Anusvara:** ṁ—a resonant nasal sound (mm)
- **Visarga:** ḥ—an outbreath h-sound like aḥ (aha), iḥ (ihi)
- **Aspirate:** h—a short h-sound (h)

ॐ	oṁ	home	ॐ	oṁ	Rome
अ	a	fun	ट	ṭa	touch
आ	ā	car	ठ	ṭha	ant-hill
इ	i	pin	ड	ḍa	duck
ई	ī	feen	ढ	ḍha	godhook
उ	u	put	ण	ṇa	thunder
ऊ	ū	pool	त	ta	(close to) think
ऋ	ṛ	rig	थ	tha	(close to) pathetic
ॠ	ṝ	(long r)	द	da	(close to) father
ऌ	ḷ	*	ध	dha	(close to) breathe hard
ए	e	play	न	na	numb
ऐ	ai	high	प	pa	purse
ओ	o	over	फ	pha	sapphire
औ	au	cow	ब	ba	but
अं	aṁ	**	भ	bha	abhor
अः	aḥ	***	म	ma	mother
क	ka	kind	य	ya	young
ख	kha	blockhead	र	ra	run
ग	ga	gate	ल	la	luck
घ	gha	log-hut	व	va	virtue
ङ	ṅa	sing	श	śa	shove
च	ca	chunk	ष	ṣa	bushel
छ	cha	match	स	sa	sir
ज	ja	jug	ह	ha	house
झ	jha	hedgehog	ळ	(Note 1)	(close to) world
ञ	ña	bunch	क्ष	kṣa	worksheet
त्र	tra	three	ज्ञ	jña	*
ऽ		unpronounced (a)	ऽऽ	″	Unpronounced (a)

note: * no English equivalent

** nasalisation of the preceding word

*** aspiration of preceding vowel

GLOSSARY

A

Abhaya: complete protection

Ābharaṇa: adornment

Abhin: an opium variant

Abhiṣeka: water rituals involving pouring of water on the deity

Abhaya hasta: the hand of the deity showing protection and grace

Abhyāsa yoga: practise of yoga of holding the mind in a state of union with divinity

Āditya: the Sun

Advaita: non-duality; the space of experiencing oneness, infinity with Cosmos where each one is infinitely powerful and infinitely intelligent. Advaita truth integrates the Self and Creator into one non-dual entity, where everything is 'you' and 'you' are everything.

Advaita anubhava: Non-duality experience where you experience everything animate and inanimate as 'you.'

Añjana: collyrium, black pigment used to paint the eye lashes

Aśraya doṣa: defect related to reality

Āśirvāda: blessing

Aṣṭāṇga Yoga: eight fold path to enlightenment prescribed by Patañjali, the founding father of yoga, in his Yoga Sūtra

Āgāmya karma: karma we accumulate in the present birth

Agarbathis: incense Sticks

Agni: fire, also 'god of fire'

Aham: me

Ahaṁkāra: the Outer image—the identity or image or ego you project to others and the world

Āhāra: food

Āhāra śuddhi: purity of food

Ahimsā: non-violence

Ahirbudhnya: one of the Rudras or the celestial beings

Airāvata: the elephant of Indra, king of celestial beings

Aja: one of the Rudras or the celestial beings

Ājñā cakra: the sixth energy center located between the eyebrows. Means 'command' or 'will' in Saṃskṛit. This cakra is blocked by one's own ego.

Ākāśa: space, sky; subtlest form of energy of universe

Akṣaram: imperishable

Āḷvārs: Tamil poet saints of south India who lived between the sixth and ninth centuries and espoused emotional devotion or bhakti to Viṣṇu-Kṛṣṇa in their songs of longing, ecstasy and service.

Amānitvam: humility

Ambā: the eldest daughter of King of Kāśi

Amṛta dhāra: flow of nectar

Amṛta: divine nectar whose consumption leads to immortality

Amṛtatva: immortality

Anāhata cakra: subtle energy center in the heart region related to love.

Ānanda Gandha: literally means 'the fragrance of bliss.' Ānanda Gandha is a nāḍi, a subtle cosmic energy center just below the heart center (anahata cakra) and above the stomach center (maṇipuraka cakra), which is rarely awakened only by the initiation of an Incarnation. Paramahamsa Nithyananda initiates participants of the Inner Awakening program into the sacred Ānanda Gandha, by which they become the channels of pure cosmic energy as Nithya Spiritual Healers, transmitting healing energy to the world

Ānanda sabha: meditation hall at Nithyananda Ashram, Bidadi

Ānanda spuraṇa: fountain of bliss

Ānandamaya kośa: the fifth and final energy layer in the five layers known as kośas. A meditative journey through the five kośas.

Anantavijaya: Yudhiṣṭhira's conch

Anasūyanto: without enemy

Anitya: transient

Annadāna: donation of food

Annapūrna Devi: Cosmic Mother, Devi who is 'giver of food and nourishment.' She is embodiment of completion with food and supreme welfare. Avatar (incarnation) of Devi Pārvati, Cosmic Mother, divine consort of Lord Śiva. She is the presiding Goddess of the city of Kāshi (Varanasi).

Annāmalai Swamigal: enlightened disciple and personal assistant of enlightened Master Bhagavān Ramaṇa Maharṣi

Annamaya kośa: food or Physical sheath, the first of the five kośas or energy sheaths.

Antarikṣa: space

Anubhūti: inner experience

Anyakāra: the Others' image—the image or expectation that others carry about you

Āpas: water

Apyāyanam: tattva (principle) of enriching that awakens the power of living

Apāna: part of prāna that works downwards and is responsible for the excretory and reproductory organs

Aparājita: form of rudra; also means 'invincible' or 'unconquered'

Aparigraha: concept of non-possessiveness

Arāga: detachment

Āraṇyaka: part of the vedic literature which describes the significance of rituals. Since they are voluminous they are referred as āranyakas which means forest.

Ārati: a Hindu ritual, in which light from wicks soaked in ghee (purified butter) or camphor is offered to one or more deities.

Arcāvatara: descent of the divine into the deity for purpose of worship

Ardha Kumbhamela: spiritual gathering which happens once in three years in India at one of the four places of Prayāg, Haridwar, Ujjain and Nāsik on the banks of sacred rivers.

Ardhanārīśvara: a form of Lord Śiva that is half-man and half-woman

Artha: a person who is in distress and suffering

Aruṇācala hill: a holy hill in the city of Tiruvannamalai, Tamil Nadu, South India; direct embodiment of Lord Śiva

Aruṇācala akṣaramanamalai: the soul stirring hymn to Aruṇācala Śiva, composed by the enlightened master Bhagavān Śrī Ramaṇa Maharṣi

Aruṇagirināthar: a Tamil poet who lived in the 15th century in Tamil Nadu, India. Authored Tirupugazh, a book of hymns in praise of Lord Muruga, a Hindu god

Aryamā: one of the adityās

Āsana: physical posture

Ashramites: residents of the ashram

Astra: a thought or word that is given an enormous power to destroy by its creator

Āsurī sampat: demonic nature

Aśvatta: banyan tree

Aśtamahāsiddhis: the eight extraordinary mystical powers

Aśvinī: it is the very first of the 27th constellation of stars in Hindu astronomy

Aśvinī kumāras: divine twin horsemen who were also the physicians of the Devas

Atharva veda: the last of the vedas, which are ancient Hindu texts

Atithi devo bhava : 'consider the guest as God Himself.' In Bhārat (India), serving the unexpected guest is considered a great enriching act of 'dāna' The mantra appears in Taittreya Upaniṣad

Ātma Bhūti: state of Divine

Ātma sādhana: self effort

Ātma vicāraṇa: self enquiry

Ātma vidya: knowledge of the self

Ātma jñāna: Self realization

Ātma śakti: (or ātma siddhi) the power of living; ability to live and radiate the powers of thoughts, words and feeling to create the reality for others and for yourself. Awakened by the tattva of enriching (āpayāyanam)

Avyakta: unseen or unmanifest

Avatār: Incarnation, the Supreme Divine; formless energy, the Super-conscious energy that manifests in human or living form for a specific Cosmic mission to bless, protect and grace humanity; Avatār literally means 'the happening or the appearance or the descend' as they appear in human plane with complete consciousness. Avātars are partial (anṣa avatār) or complete Incarnations (Purṇāvatār like Kṛṣna and Mīnākṣi) depending on their divine mission. Kṛṣna promises in Bhagavad Gītā that incarnations or enlightened beings eternally happen again and again to protect their devotees (Sādhu), to destroy the *adhārmic* (wicked) forces and to re-establish *dharma,* the *Yoga,* sacred science of Enlightenment

Āzhwars: devotional saints of Tamil Nadu, India

B

Bālāji: one of the names of the presiding deity of Tirumala Tirupati

Bali: a king of the demon race

Beedi: local Indian cigarette

Bīja: seed; bīja-mantra refers to the single syllable mantras used to invoke certain deities

Bhaga: a form of Śiva; a form of the sun

Bhagavān: literally god who possesses fortune, divinity; the blessed one; often used for an incarnation, the Supreme God or embodiment of Absolute Truth

Bhāgavatam: also called 'Śrimad Bhāgavataṁ Mahā Purāṇa'. Literally means 'Divine eternal happenings of Supreme God'; the richest philosophy of God narrating the divine plays of all incarnations of Viṣṇu especially Lord Kṛṣṇa, celebrating the true Divine love of God as path and goal of life and Existence. It explains the scientific history of Brahmāṇda (Existence) and its creation; ultimate compilation by Śrī Veda Vyāsa. Considered the very essence of all Vedānta literatures and the purest, greatest of all Purāṇas; the text incarnation of Lord Kṛṣṇa, as Supreme God

Bhāvanā: visualization

Bhakti: devotion

Bhakta: a devotee

Bhagīratha: ruler of Kośala, a kingdom in ancient India. He performed intense tapas to bring river Ganges to the Earth from the Heavens

Bhaja govindam: collection of 32 (sometimes 34) devotional verses composed by the great enlightened master and incarnation Ādi Śaṅkarācarya. This is considered to be the essence of Vedānta and Advaita philosophy

Bharaṇi: a form of poetry in the Tamil Sangam literature

Bharata: brother of lord Rāma in Rāmāyaṇa

Bhāva roga: emotional diseases

Bhāvana: visualization

Bhū garbha: womb of the mother

Bhūta śarīra vāsa: life in the earlier body or the previous birth

Big Bang: one of the cosmological models of the Universe; proposed by Georges Lemaitre, a Roman Catholic priest

Bodhi Dharma: Bodhi Dharma was a Buddhist monk from southern India who lived during the early 5th century and is traditionally credited as the transmitter of Zen to China.

Brahma: the Lord of Creation; one of the sacred trinity—Brahma, Viṣṇu, Śiva

Brahmavidyā: the science of the spiritual knowledge of the Absolute Universal reality. Considered the highest ideal of knowledge to be known in Sanatana dharma. Another name to define Bhagavad Gītā

Brahmakapāla: begging bowl made of Lord Brahma's skull that is insatiable (refers to wordly pursuits that are unending)

Brahmān: refers to the Supreme Self

Brāhmaṇa: individuals engaged in attaining the highest spiritual knowledge; the class of the society involved in learning and spreading knowledge

Brahmanyam bahuputratām: the state of being the favorite inheritor of the cosmos

Brahma Jñāna: Self Realization; knowledge of the Self or Brahman

Brahma sūtra: ancient spiritual treatise authored by Veda Vyāsa or Badrāyaṇa

Brahmaloka: the highest of the celestial worlds

Brahmāṇḍa: cosmos, macrocosm (also see Pinḍāṇḍa)

Brahmāstra: divine nuclear weapon in Vedic history of Bhārat by great accomplished warriors and sages; invoked by the power of mantras, sound vibration frequency. Used in Mahābharat world war

Brahmacarya: the state of living without fantacies or living like God; the person who walks the path of Brahma (Divine)

Brahmins: priestly / scholarly class of Hindus responsible for preserving and propagating the scriptures

Bṛhadāranyaka Upaṇiṣad: one of the primary (mukhya) Upaṇiṣads contained within the Śatapatha Brahmana, a portion of the *Brahmana* text branch, associated with the Śukla Yajurveda ascribed to Yajñavalkya. Its name implies, 'the great forest of Absolute Knowledge.'; asserting the Truth of Advaita (non-duality) and contains the Mahāvākya of '*Ahaṁ Brahmāsi*—I am Brahman' '*Puṛnamada puṛnamidam...*' and mantra of '*Oṁ asato ma satgamaya..*' and commented on by Ādī Śaṅkarācārya

Bhū Bhāra: the weight (bhāra) on Mother earth (Bhū)—implies the weight on unconsciousness or collective negativity on earth)

Bhṛgu: great sage of the Vedic tradition

Brihat sāma: a part of the Chāndogya Upaniṣad

Brindāvan: or Vṛndāvan, sacred place where Kṛṣṇa grew up near present day Mathurā, U.P

C

Caitanya Mahāprabhu: a 15th century Enlightened Master from Bengal, India steeped in devotion to Lord Kṛṣṇa; An Incarnation of Kṛṣṇa Himself who appeared to teach the science of pure devotion (*prema bhakti*) to Kṛṣṇa in Mahā-bhāva. His followers are known as Gaudīya Vaiśṇavas; essence of His teachings is encapsulated in Śikṣāśtakam (8 verses)

Cakra: energy centers in the body. Literally means 'wheel' based on the experience of mystics who perceived these energy centers as whirlpools of energy. There are seven major chakras along the spine: Mūlādhāra, Svādhiṣṭhāna, Maṇipūraka, Anahata, Viśuddhi, Ājñā and Sahasrāra.

Catur veda: the four Vedas, namely—Ṛg Veda, Yajur Veda, Sāma Veda and Atharva Veda; the large body of spiritual texts of Truth organized around four canonical collections; directly revealed to the enlightened sages, as Śrutis ('what is heard'); Originally in 100,000 verses in total, now 20,379 verses in total are available. The latest reproduction of Vedas is by Bhagavān Veda Vyāsa, about 5000 years ago

Catur tattvas: the four sacred life principles namely—integrity, authenticity, responsibility, enriching as revealed by Paramahamsa Nithyananda. Each tattva represents the essence of all each of the *Catur Vedas*

Cakṣu: energy behind the power of sight.

Candāla: low caste person

Cār dhām: four sacred pilgrim centres in the Himalayas, namely—Haridwar, Rishikesh, Kedarnath and Badrinath

Candramā: moon

Charles Townes: an American Nobel Prize-winning physicist and educator; well-known for his work in Maser and Quantum electronics

Cidākāśa : the space in the surrounding(e.g. as in a room). The other two being ghaṭākāśa and mahākāśa. Mahākāśa is the third infinite space of Consciousness.

Citragupta: a Hindu god assigned with the task of keeping complete records of actions of human beings on the earth, and upon their death, deciding as regards sending them to the heaven or the hell,

Citraratha: a gandharva, a celestial being

Cidākāśa: the inner space; literally means 'the sky of inner space.'

D

Dadhīci: a great sage

Daityas: race of beings that fought against demi gods

Daivī sampat: divine nature

Dakṣiṇāmūrti swamigal: great south indian saint

Dakṣiṇāyanam: the six months in the year when the sun moves to the southern hemisphere

Dakṣiṇeśvar: a small town in West Bengal, famous for its Kālī temple where Rāmakṛṣṇa Paramahamsa lived

Dāna: sharing or imparting. Considered a sacred sacrifice to enrich others.

Dānava: a race of the asuras or deamons

Darśan: vision; usually referred to seeing divinity

Dāsa bhāva: feeling that you are a servant of the Master

Dasa graha: ten major heavenly bodies

Devaki: Lord Kṛṣṇa's birth mother

Devatas: demigods

Devī: supreme goddess in Hinduism, Cosmic Mother; Ādi Śakti, the primordial energy of Existence

Devī Gāyatrī: goddess of knowledge

Deśa: country or a region

Dharma: righteousness, the eternal path of living in righteousness or Truth

Dharmakṣetra: holy land of dharma

Dhanañjaya: the name of a vital air nourishing the body; the winner or conqueror of wealth—a name of Arjuna called by Kṛṣṇa in Mahābhārat

Dhāraṇa: collection or concentration of the mind (joined with the retention of breath)

Dharmo rakṣati rakṣitah: dharma protects the one who protects it

Dhī: intellect

Dhīraḥ: courageous person. Term used by Svami Vivekānanda in exhorting his followers

Dhyāna: meditation

Dhyāna yoga: path of meditation techniques

Dīkṣa: grace bestowed by the Master (Guru) and the energy transferred by the Master to the disciple as an initiation or any other time, through a mantra, a touch, a glance or even a thought.

Divya cakṣu: divine eye. Also called divya netra

Doṣa: defect

Dṛṣṭi: sight, seeing with mental eye

Dṛṣṭi Sṛṣṭi: [lit: sight (dṛṣṭi), world or creation (sṛṣṭi)] seeing the world as we wish to see it

Drupada: king of Pāñcāla, a great warrior, father of Draupadī

Duḥkha: pain

Dvaita: school of thought that says the individual self is separate from existence

Dveśa: aversion

Dvija: twice born. Refers to the state of awakening of individual Consciousness.

Durga: meaning 'the inaccessible or the invincible', Durga is a popular fierce form of the Hindu Goddess or Devi.

Dussanga: company or association of the wicked

E

Ekapāda: form of rudra

Ekādaśi: eleventh day of every lunar month in the Hindu calendar. Normally people fast on this day for spiritual benefits

Energy darśan: the blessing or transmission of energy given by enlightened Master or an Incarnation imparting the cosmic energy to the recipient.

Engram: the embedded smell of a past action leading one to commit the same act

G

Gadā: weapon similar to a mace; also gadhāyudaḥ

Gandharvas: celestial beings with superb musical skills; act as messengers between God and man

Gaṅgā: the most celebrated river in India, considered holy by all Hindus.

Gaṅgotri: a famous pilgrim town where the river Gaṅgā originates.

Garuḍa: eagle; Lord Viṣṇu's vehicle

Garbha mandir: sanctum sanctorum of a temple

Ghaṭākāśa: the space enclosed by our physical body

Ghee: clarified butter

Giriśa: a form of Rudra, Lord Śiva

Girivala: circumambulating Aruṇācala, the holy hill of Tiruvannamalai for spiritual benefits

Gomukh: holy place in Himālayas. River Gaṅgā originates from the snout of Gomukh glacier

Gongura chutney: spicy south indian side dish

Gopikas: cow herdess who were Kṛṣṇa's playmates

Gopura, gopuram: temple tower

Govinda: another name for Lord Kṛṣṇa

Govindapāda: the guru of enlightened Master Ādi Śaṅkara

Gṛhasta: a householder, a married person; coming from the word gṛha, meaning house

Guṇa: the three human behavioural characteristics or predispositions; satva, rajas and tamas.

Guru: Master; literally one who leads from gu (darkness) to ru (light)

Gurukul, Gurukulam: literally 'tradition of guru', refers to the ancient education system in which children were handed over to a

Guru at a very young age by parents for upbringing and education

Guḍākeśā: one who has transcended sleep by conquering his incompletions; refers to name of Arjuna

Gurudakṣiṇā: offering to the Guru

Guruji: Master

Guru Pūjā: ritual sacred worship of the Master. Tradition started by Devi in gratitude to Ādi Guru, Śiva

Guru Parampara: lineage of gurus

Guru Swami: a person who leads a holy trip to Śabrimala

H

Hanumān: the monkey god from the epic Rāmāyaṇa; energy of Lord Śiva; endowed with 8 mystic powers, Aṣtamahāsiddhis and exemplifies pure devotion in dāsa bhāva—serving Lord Rāma

Hara: a form of Rudra, Lord Śiva

Hare Kṛṣṇa: a holy chant on Lord Kṛṣṇa

Haridwār: or Hardvār; temple town in North India; one of the holiest places for Hindus on the banks of sacred river Gangā.

Hariścāndra: a famous king of the Solar dynasty renowned for his piety and justice. He sacrificed his wife and child to keep his word

Hastināpura: a town in the state of Uttar Pradesh. It was the capital of the kingdom of the Kauravas

Hṛd garbha: womb of the heart

Hiraṇyagarbha: literally means 'the golden womb' where gold means the space of completion and joy of creation.Upaniṣads calls it the source of creation of the Universe or the manifested cosmos. It finds its mention in a hymn in the Ṛg Veda named 'Hiraṇyagarbha

Sūkta,' suggesting a single creator deity; Paramahamsa Nithyananda defines Hiraṇyagarbha as our powerful inner space—the space where planets and worlds get created and destroyed

Hiraṇyakaśipu: a demonic king who wanted to rule the worlds as god; father of the great child devotee of Lord Nārāyaṇa, Prahlād; he got annihiliated by Nārāyaṇa in the incarnartion of Lord Nṛsimbha, half-man and half-lion avatār

Holi: Indian festival celebrated with colors

Homa: ritual to Agni, the god of fire; metaphorically represents the transfer of energy from the energy of Ākāśa (space), through Vāyu (Air), Agni (Fire), Āpas (Water), and Pṛthvī (Earth) to humans. Also yāga, yajña

Homa kuṇḍa: sacrificial fire pit

Homa: a fire ritual

Hṛṣīkeśa: controller of the senses and superconscious, refers to Lord Kṛṣṇa

Halāhala: (or Kālakootam); the most deadliest and venemous poison that emerged from the churning of the milky ocean, Samudra Manthan by Devas and Asuras (God and demons)—as narrated in Bhagavad Purāṇa, Mahābhārat. Signfies the collective negativity of Cosmos. Lord Śiva as Nīlakanṭha, drank this poison to save the mankind and Cosmos from the negativity and held it in His throat.

I

Icchā śakti: energy of desire. The other two are kriya śakti, energy of action and jñāna śakti, energy of knowledge.

Icchā: desire

Iḍā: along with piṅgala and suṣuṁna, the virtual energy pathway through which pranic energy flows awakening the Kuṇḍalini energy

Ikṣvāku: was the first king of the Ikṣvāku dynasty and founder of the Solar Dynasty of kṣatriyas in vedic civilization in ancient India.

Indra: god of all divine beings

Indra loka: the abode of Indra, heaven (or swarga)

Indraprastha: (lit: the city of Indra) 'the land of creation.' The capital kindgom of Pāṇḍavas in Mahābhārat. Was a barron un-inhabited land known as Khāndavaprasta. which the Pāṇḍavas turned into a prosperous city by the grace of Lord Indra and Kṛṣṇa; built by the divine architect, Viśvakarma.

Itihāsa: (lit: history); epic, historical happenings; also purāṇa; the Rāmāyaṇa and Mahābhārat are the 2 main Itihās in Vedic history; (common misnomer: mythology)

Iṣṭadevatā: favourite deity

Īśvara: Lord of the Universe

Īśvaratva: the space of leadership consciousness awakened by the tattva of responsibility; the dimension of being the Lord where one takes ownership and responsibility for the whole Universe

Īśa Vāsya Upaniṣad or Īṣopaniṣad: (lit: enveloped by Energy or Īśa, Lord) The first and one of the shortest Upaniṣads of the Hindu scriptures; appears in the Śukla Yajur Veda in a poetic form describing the nature of the Supreme Being. Starts with 'Īśa vāsya idaṃ sarvam—out of energy arises all matter'

Intranalyze: (intra-analyze) analyzing for the sake of internalizing the Truth, and not for rejecting it. Saṃskṛit term from Vedānta is 'Manana.' The term coined and gifted by Paramahamsa Nithyananda.

J

Jagat: Universe

Jagat guru: Master of the whole Universe

Jahnu: a sage

Janaka: a noble and benevolent king who ruled Mithila; father of princess Sītā in the epic Rāmāyaṇa.

Janārdana: another name for Lord Kṛṣṇa

Janmas: births

Japa: repetition of mantras either silently or loudly

Jāṭarāgni: digestive fire inside our body

Jayanti: the Saṃskrit word for birth anniversary

Jiḍḍu Kṛṣṇamurti: renowned Indian philosopher

Jāgrata: wakefulness

Jāti: birth

Jāti-doṣa: defect related to birth

Jīva samādhi: burial place and energy field of an enlightened Master or an Incarnation, where he decides to rest His mortal form and continues to radiate His living presence and super conscious energy.

Jīvātman: the ordinary soul

Jīvan mukta: a person who is liberated from the bondage even while living with a body

Jīvanmukta sambhāvana: the inner recognition of the state of enlightenment

Jīvan Mukti: the science of living enlightenment, living a liberated life while in the body

Jñāna: knowledge

Jñāna garbha: womb of the knowledge

Jñāna Yagña: the enriching sacrifice of knowledge; enriching oneself by offering the mind onto the highest knowledge

Jñānendriya: organs of knowledge

Jyotiṣa: Astrology; jyotiṣi is an astrologer

Jyoti stambha: infinite shaft of light; In Arunachala, Lord Śiva appeared as an infinite column of light to grace Lord Viṣṇu and Lord Brahma; unmanifest beginning of Cosmos, the Big Bang, from where the manifest Universe appears.

K

Kailāśa: A part of Himalayas in Tibet; the abode of Lord Śiva and His family and disciples; a place of eternal bliss

Kaivalya: liberation; same as mokṣa, nirvāṇa

Kāla: time

Kālī: (or Durga) a Hindu goddess, Mother of cosmic energy as Time; the powerful feminine aspects of goddess Pārvati, associated with power and courage

Kālabhairava or Mahā Kālabhairava: Supreme Lord of Time and Space, and beyond; independent energy of Lord Śiva who destroys the past to create the future. He destroys the ego of Brahma and holds his skull 'Kapāla' in His hand; the presiding guarding God of Kāśi Kṣetra or Varanasi; embodiment of power, joy and compassion. 52 forms of Kālabhairava protect each of the 52 Śakti Pīṭhas, the sacred temples of Devi Ādi Śakti.

Kapila Muni: the founder of Sāṅkhya philosophy in Sanatana dharma; the founding father of Mahānirvaṇi Pīṭha; Bhagavān Kapila is the celebrated incarnation as of Viṣṇu and Śiva in Śrimad Bhāgavataṁ; the first thinking being on earth who experienced completion

Kalpa: According to Vedic cosmology, one cycle of 4 Yugas is 4.32 million years. Brahma's 1 day is equal to 1,000 cycles of 4 yugas, called 1 Kalpa. (Yugas follow a timeline ratio of 4:3:2:1)

Kalpataru, kalpavṛkśa: a wish-fulfilling divine tree; sacred banyan tree embodying cosmic energy; associated with spiritual awakening

Kalpana: imagination

Kāma: sensory pleasures, also means lust

Kāmadhenu: sacred cow

Kāminī: women

Kāñcana: gold

Kanyādāna: giving away a bride

Kāraṇa śarīra: causal body

Karma: spiritual law of cause and effect, driven by vāsana and samskāra

Karma kāndis: seekers who follow the path to achieve the ultimate through action

Karmaphala : literally action (karma), fruit (phala). The outcome or fruit of action

Karmendriya: organs of action

Karmī: one driven by desire

Karṇa: son of Kuntī, also is a step brother to the Pāṇḍavas; renowned for his generosity

Kārthigai Deepam: Festival of lights celebrated on full moon day in month of November/December in South India

Karuṇāmūrti: god of mercy

Kāśī: holy place on the banks of river Ganges; the city of Lord Śiva; also called Ānanda Van

Kaśyapa: an ancient sage believed to be the father of devas (celestial beings), asuras (demons) and the humans

Kathāmṛtam: words of immortality (amṛta) describing the divine happenings (kathā) your life

Kaṭhopaniṣad: one of the principal Upaniṣads, gives the science of Death and liberation; chronicles the journey of a courageous boy named Naciketa who faces death and experiences liberation through Yama (MahāKāla)

Kavacham: shield

Kaurava: one of the two principal clans in the epic, Mahābhārat

Kāvi vastra: saffron cloth usually worn by mendicants

Keśava: another name for Lord Kṛṣṇa

Keśī: a demon, was slain by Lord Kṛṣṇa

Khadga : sword

Kīrtans: devotional songs

Koan: Zen parables, an anecdote or riddle without any solution to show the inadequacy of logical reasoning

Kośa: energy layer surrounding body; there are 5 such layers. These are: annamaya or body, prānamaya or breath, manomaya or thoughts, vijñānamaya or sleep and ānandamaya or bliss kośas

Kriya śakti: energy of action. Other two energies are energy of desire and energy of knowledge.

Krodha: anger

Kṛpā: grace

Kṛṣṇārjuna Saṃvād: the discussion or talk between Kṛṣṇa and Arjuna; another name for Bhagavad Gītā

Kṛpācārya: a great general who fought in the battle of Kurukṣetra on the side of the Kauravas

Kriya: technique or practice within a yoga discipline meant to achieve a specific result.

Kṣaṇa: moment in time; refers to time between two thoughts

Kṣatriya: warrior class

Kṣema: protection, protecting what one has

Kṣipram: instant

Kubera: Lord of Wealth

Kumbh Mela: large spiritual gathering on the planet that occurs four times every twelve years, attracting millions of people. The four locations of Kumbh Mela are Prayāg in Allahabad at the confluence of Gaṅgā, Yamuna and the underground Sarasvati river; Haridwar on the banks of Gaṅgā; Ujjain along the Kṣipra river and Nasik along the Godāvarī river.

Kuṇḍalinī: energy that resides at the root chakra 'mūlādhāra'

Kubera: the lord of wealth

Kuṇḍalini śakti: dormant potential energy at the base of the spine

Kurukṣetra: the sacred and where the great war of Mahābharat was fought between the Pāṇḍavas and the Kauravas in the Haryana state of India

Kuṣa grass: sacred grass used in the Vedic tradition for various religious ceremonies. The seat made of Kuṣa grass and covered with a skin and a cloth is considered ideal for meditation.

L

Lakṣmī: goddess of wealth and fortune; divine consort of Śrī Viṣṇu

Lakṣmī Yantra: the divine mystical drawing that bestows wealth

Lakṣman: younger brother of Lord Rāma in Rāmāyaṇa epic, who is devoted in unswerving loyalty, love and surrender to Rāma and Sitā; avatār (incarnation) of Ādi Śeśa, the original serpent

Līlā: divine play; acts of the Divine

Lobha: greed

M

Mādhava: another name for Lord Kṛṣṇa; means 'husband of the Goddess of fortune'; Arjuna calls Kṛṣṇa as Mādhava in Bhagavad Gītā (1.36)

Madhura bhāva: the relationship of beloved between Master and disciple

Madhusūdana: another name for Kṛṣṇa, slayer of the demon madhu

Mahā Samādhi: Attaining Enlightenment and leaving the body; the final Liberation

Mahā: great

Maharṣi: great perfected sage

Mahāvatar Bābā: the great avatār living in Himalayas in eternal youth for thousands of years. The Great Master who graced Paramahamsa Nithyananda with spiritual vision, experience during his Parivṛājaka, spiritual wanderings at Kedarnath and bestowed the name—*Paramahamsa Nithyananda*.

Mahābhārat: the Great Hindu epic happening; the Itihās-5th Veda along with Rāmāyaṇa; whose central characters are the five Pāṇḍava princes with their wife Draupadī, their hundred Kaurava cousins with the complete Incarnation, Bhagavān Śrī Kṛṣṇa ascribed by Bhagavān Veda Vyāsa. Mahābhārat is the personification of Bhagāvad Gītā's teachings that re-establishes Sanatanā Dharma, the eternal religion of Truth on earth

Mahākaśa: the whole cosmos

Mahāmaṇḍaleśvar: prestigious title given to the holy leader of a very large religious organization or Pīṭha or Akhādā; signifies the highest level of traditional spiritual Hindu guardianship.

Mahānirvaṇi Pīṭha: the most ancient apex official body of Sanatana Dharma (Hinduism). It traces its recorded roots to 8th century A.D revived by Ādī Śaṇkara. Lord Kapila Muni, incarnation of Viṣṇu and Mahādeva, who is glorified in the Śrimad Bhāgavatam, is the spiritual guiding force of this Pīṭha. Paramahamsa Nithyananda is the 1008th Mahāmaṇḍaleśvar of Mahānirvaṇi Pīṭha.

Mahāmeru: a mountain

Mahāparinirvāṇa: day of enlightened souls

Mahāvākya: great sayings from the Upaniṣads. There are four: *Aham Brahmāsmi, Tat Tvam Asi, Ayam Ātma Brahma* and *Prājñānam Brahma*. All four mean that You are the Divine.

Mahāvīra: Varthamana Mahāvira was the 24th and last tīrthaṅkara or enlightened one, and established the tenets of the religion of Jainism, founded in India and now practiced by millions worldwide.

Mahā Kālabhairava: see Kālabhairava

Makara: name of a fish

Mālā: a garland, a necklace; rudrākṣamālā is a garland made of the seeds of the rudrākṣa tree

Mama: my own

Mamakāra: inner image you carry about yourself, that constantly says that you are smaller than what you think you are

Mana śarīra: mental layer

Manana: thinking, contemplating or intranalyzing

Manas: mind

Mānava: humans

Mandir: temple

Maṇḍana Miśra: a contemporary of Ādi Śaṅkarā who later became his disciple named Śureśvarācārya.

Maṅgala: auspicious; maṅgala sūtra, literally auspicious thread, the yellow or gold thread or necklace, a married Hindu woman wears

Maṇipūraka cakra: subtle energy center located near the navel region, related to the emotion of worry.

Mānickavāsagar: one of the 63 Nāyanmars, authored Thiruvasagam, a collection of hymns in praise of Lord Śiva.

Manipuṣpaka: Sahādeva's conch

Manomaya Kośa: the third mental energy sheath in the five Kośas or energy sheaths

Mano śakti: (or manosiddhi) the power of thinking; ability to focus and align your thoughts with authenticity to make the thoughts happen as reality. Awakened by the tattva of authenticity (śraddha)

Mantra: a sound, a formula; sometimes a word or a set of words, which because of their inherent sounds, have energizing properties. Mantras are used as sacred chants to worship and invoke the Divine

Manu: father of mankind, son of Lord Brahma, the creator.

Manusmṛti: code of conduct written by Manu, the father of mankind for harmonious existence

Marut: storm dieties

Mārgazhi: refers to the month of January in Tamil

Mātṛ bhāva: feeling that the Master is like the mother

Māyā: that which is not reality, but gives the illusion that it is real—'*yā mā iti māya*'; all life is māyā according to Advaita

Māyā Śakti: power of illusion; phrase used in Tantra

Meimai: living the truth through your body

Melkote: holy town in Karnataka, India where Śrī Rāmānujacārya, the great saint lived

Menakā: a celestial maiden

Mīnākśi: The Cosmic Mother, Ādi Śakti. She is the complete incarnation of Devi; consort of Lord Śiva as Śundareśvara; Mīnākśi and Śundareśvara are the presiding deities and living presence at Madurai, Tamil Nadu.

Mīmāmsā: a system of ancient Indian philosophy

Mīrā: a great devotee of Lord Kṛṣṇa

Mithya: transient

Mohinī: the only female incarnation of Lord Viṣṇu with the most beautiful, attractive form

Mokṣa: liberation; same as nirvāṇa, samādhi, turīya etc.

Mṛtyuñjaya Homa: fire ritual done to avoid untimely death and improve longevity of life.

Muṇḍa : the shaven head

Muni: realized being

Mūdhaḥ: fool

Mūlādhāra cakra: energy center located at the base of the spine

Mula vichāra dhārā: the right Saṃskṛit word for 'root thought pattern'

Mula vāsana: root thought pattern; the behaviorial kārmic imprints that make us react to life and others based on past inadequate cognitions

Muṇḍaka Upaṇiṣad: or Muṇḍakopniṣad is one of the primary or Mukhya Upaṇiṣads associated with the Atharva Veda; a mantra Upaṇiṣad—it has the form of a mantra, teaching the knowledge of Brahman; as a dialogue between Ṛṣi Śaunaka and Angiras. The mantra, '*Satyamaiva Jayate*' (3.1.6) and '*Brahma Vid Brahmaiva Bhavati*' (3.2.9) appear in this Upaniṣad.

N

Nārī: woman

Nārada: a divine sage and the greatest devotee, bhakta of Lord Viṣṇu always chanting— 'Nārāyaṇa Nārāyaṇa'; he playfully causes quarrels among Gods; he has no definite place of stay and keeps traveling the Universe

Nāyanmārs: Tamil devotee saints of Lord Śiva, 63 in number, whose life stories are told in the book Peria Puranam

Nīlakaṇṭha: the one with the 'blue throat,' refers to Lord Śiva; attributed to His divine play of drinking the deadly posion, Hālahāla which emerged during Samudra Manthan, the churning of the milky ocean by Devas and Asuras (gods and demons).

Na iti: not this

Naciketa: lead character and boy hero in Kaṭhopaniṣad, believed to have learnt the secret of death from Lord Yama (god of death) himself.

Nadi: river

Nāḍī: nerve; also an energy pathway that is not physical

Nāga sādhu: ascetic who does not wear clothes

Nāga: a snake

Nakṣatrāṇi: stars

Namaḥ: I surrender to you

Namaskār: traditional greeting with raised hands, with palms brought together, denoting surrender of the self.

Nānta: without end

Nārāyaṇa: another name for Lord Viṣṇu

Nārāyaṇī Senā: the most powerful divine army of Lord Nārāyaṇa as Śrī Kṛṣna; Kṛṣna gave His army to Duyodhana in the great Mahābhārat war

Nara: man; also depicts the human aspect of lord Viṣṇu; reflection of Nārāyaṇa

Narmadā: a holy river in central India

Naṭarāja: a depiction of Lord Śiva as the cosmic dancer, main deity in the famous temple at Chidambaram

Navagraha: nine major heavenly bodies as defined in Hindu sacred history

Neeru: water in Kannada

Neti neti: this is not

Nididhyāsana: powerfully living and radiating the Truth; expressing in your life. One of the three concepts in Hinduism (Vedānta)—Śravana, Manana, Nididhyāsana.

Nirguṇa: formless

Nirguṇa brahman: consciousness that cannot be limited to a form

Nirmohatvam: non attachment to desires

Nirāhara Saṁyama: the science of living beyond food patterns, a breakthrough spiritual process designed and revived by Paramahamsa Nithyananda to live without food radiating peak health and energy, intaking energy directly from prāṇa (air energy) and cosmic source, through the power of initiation by Paramahamsa Nithyananda. (www.bfoodfree.org)

Nirāharī: A person initiated by Paramahamsa Nithyananda into the science of Nirāhāra Saṁyama, who is living beyond food patterns, without the need for food intake

Nirvāṇa : liberation; same as mokṣa, samādhi

Nirvāṇi akhāda: the Saṅgha of Nāga sādhus

Nirvikalpa samādhi: the state of deep meditation wherein one transcends the form of the deity and experiences the pure space of Advaita, infinite oneness with Cosmos and beyond.

Nisargadatta Mahāraj: an enlightened Master who lived in Mumbai. Passed away on 8th September 1981, at the age of 84.

Nissanga: beyond the state of the need of sanga (association)

Nissaṅgatvam: a state of being non-attached

Nityānanda: eternal (nitya) bliss (ānanda); name and state of Paramahamsa Nithyananda

Nithyānandeshwar: name of Lord Śiva as the main presiding deity at Nithyananda temples

Nithyānando'ham: 'Nithyananda I am'; means 'I am Nithya Ānanda. I am eternal bliss.'; the great mantra revealed by Paramahamsa Nithyananda to experience and live Advaita

Nithya kīrtans: holy hymns and bhajans sung in the Nithyananda Sangha in the space of devotion to Divine

Nithya dhyana yoga: the first level meditation program conducted by Nithyananda Sangha; also called Life Bliss Program (level 1) for intiation into the science of completion with self

Nithya kriya yoga: the second level meditation program conducted by Nithyananda Sangha; also called Life Bliss Program (level 2) for deeper initiation into the science of completion

Nithya yoga: The authentic science and system of Aṣṭānga Yoga, with the experiential insight of Patañjali's vision, revived by Paramahamsa Nithyananda; the path and purpose of Nithya yoga is bliss, where bliss arising out of the uniting of mind, body and spirit is experienced

Nivṛtti: inward looking; 'path of completion leading to more and more completion.'

Niyama: moral discipline, the second of eight paths of Patañjali's Aṣṭāṇga Yoga; refers to a number of day-to-day rules of observance for a spiritual path

Nṛsimha Avatār: incarnation of Lord Viṣṇu in which he is half-lion and half-human

Nyāya Śāstra: scripture of logic called Nyāya Darśan by Sage Gautam that gives the science of logical quest for God, the absolute Divinity. It establishes the fact that only Divinity is desirable, knowable, attainable, and not this world through 16 steps of logical discussions, 16 Padārtha

Nyāya: logic

O

Oṁ: sacred syllable; the primordial sound

Oṁ Śanti Śanti Śantihi: the peace chants at the end of meditation or prayer or religious activity

Oṁkāreśvar: a Hindu temple, located in Shivapuri island on Narmada river; shaped like the sacred symbol 'Om' with presiding deity of Lord Śiva.

P

Pāda: feet, also means quarter of a poem

Pādaseva: service to the feet; usually to that of the Master

Padā: the 'word'

Padārtha: the meaning or figure of the 'word'

Pāduka: sacred sandals

Pāṇḍavas: five brothers in Mahābharata, also sons of Pāṇḍu

Pāñcāla: an ancient region in North India, around the rivers Ganges and Yamuna

Pāñcāli: another name for Draupadī , the wife of the Pāṇḍavas

Pāni: water in hindi language

Paṇḍit: scholar

Pañca bhūta: five elemental energies that sustain us, namely, earth, water, fire, air and ether

Pañca indriya: five senses

Pāñcajanya: Lord Kṛṣṇa's conch

Pāpa: sin

Pārtha: (lit: son of Prithā or Kuntī); name of Arjuna called lovingly by Kṛṣṇa

Parantapa: another name of Arjuna; means the destroyer of enemies

Parabrahma Kṛṣṇa: Kṛṣṇa as the cosmic energy, the Supreme God

Parāśakti: the supreme cosmic energy; Devi Ādi Śakti, the source of existence

Paramahamsa: literally the 'supreme swan'; refers to an Enlightened being; title of honor applied to Hindu spiritual teachers who are regarded as having attained Enlightenment, the state of non-duality, Advaita; a brahmajñāni

Paramahamsa Upaniṣad: Fourth upaniṣad of Śukla Yajurveda that describes the space, state of an Enlightened Being as Supreme Divine Being (Veda Puruṣa), as a discussion between Nārada and Lord Brahma.

Paramahamsa Yogānanda: an enlightened master, advocated practice of Kriya Yoga to attain Self-realization.

Parikrama: the ritual of going around a holy location, such as a hill or water body

Parivrājaka: wandering by an ascetic monk

Patañjali: father and founder of Yoga, famous for his treatise on yoga called Patañjali's Yoga Sūtras

Pauṇḍra: Bhīma's conch

Paśupati: In Śaiva tradition, the pure soul and the soul that reflects on the body is Paśupati. The pure soul is *Pati* (lord or protector) and the reflection of the soul on the body is *Paśu* (living entity); Lord Śiva is called Paśupatināth

Pazhani: a famous pilgrim town in south india

Periyapurānam: A Tamil classic by Sekkizhar on the lives of the 63 Nāyanmārs, the devotee saints of Lord Śiva.

Phala: fruit; phalāśruti refers to the assumed benefits of worship

Piṇḍāṇḍa: individual microcosm as against Brahmānda or universe; the space enclosed in the form

Piṅgala: please see idā

Prāṇāyāma: lit: 'extension of the life energy force' through the breath modulation and control; the fourth limb of the Āṣṭāṅga Yoga of Patañjali Yoga Sutra.

Prāṇa śakti: bliss energy

Prāṇa Pratiṣṭha: installation of cosmic energy in the main diety

Prāṇa: life energy; also refers to breath; prāṇāyāma is control of breath

Prāṇamaya kośa: The second sheath of energy in the 5 layer kośa system

Prārabdha karma: karmas based on which this life has been assumed

Praṇava: mystic symbol 'Om'

Prahlād: a great devotee of lord Viṣṇu and son of Hiranyakaśīpu, the demon king

Prajāpati: a Hindu diety from whom all beings are believed to originate

Prakṛti: Nature

Prakāśa: illuminated knowledge

Prakaśānanda Sarasvati: a Rasik saint in the tradition of Caitanya Mahāprabhu, his teachings are mainly based on the Bhagavad Gītā.

Pralaya: the great deluge

Prasād: food offered to God and eaten by devotees with his blessings

Pratijānīhi: declare it boldly

Pratyāhāra: fifth limb of Patañjali's Aṣṭaṇga Yoga referring to turning away from sensory inputs

Pratyāhāra: literally 'staying away from food'; in this case refers to control of all senses as part of the eight fold Aṣṭaṇga Yoga

Pravṛitti: looking outward (the worldly life), 'path of incompletion leading to more incompletion.'

Prayāg: city in the North Indian state of Uttar Pradesh, one of four sites of the mass Hindu pilgrimage Kumbh Mela, the others being Haridwar, Ujjain and Nāsik. It is situated at the confluence of the three rivers Ganga, Yamuna and Sarasvati

Prema śakti: (or prema siddhi) the power of feeling; ability to feel and express the power of thoughts and words as reality. Awakened by the tattva of responsibility (upāyanam)

Prithā: another name for Kuntī

Pṛthvī: earth energy

Pūjā: form of ritual worship

Punnāgavarāli: a tune in carnatic music, believed to be a melody that can mesmerize snakes

Puṇya: merit, beneficence

Purāṇa: the great historical happenings and narrations that depict the glory of Divine and Its sacred plays, līlās. (common misnomer-mythology)

Purohit: priest

Puruṣa: the personification of the Supreme energy

Puruṣottama: means Supreme Being amongst all beings; one of the glorious names of Lord Viṣṇu. Lord Kṛṣṇa speaks a complete chapter (ādhyāya) on Puruṣottama Yoga in Gītā

Puṣpaka vimānam: historical Aircraft that functioned with the power of mantras, the energy of sound vibrations.

Pūrṇāvatār: complete, absolute Incarnation of God who appears in human plane of Existence in Its pure form with His infinite energies and qualities

Pūrṇa: literally 'complete'; refers in the advaita context to reality

Pūrnatva: the space or state of 'completion' that signifies the Truth that from completion (whole) comes the Whole.

Pūrva mīmāmsa: one of the six branches of vedic knowledge that accepts only the karma kāṇḍa as the supreme authority

Putra: son; putrī: daughter

R

Rāga: attachment

Rājarṣi: king who is also a sage

Rājasūya yāga: a great sacrifice performed to celebrate victory of a king who is declared as an emporer over many kingdoms, where a great king's inauguration as *Chakravartin Rāja Samrāt* is ceremonially perfomed. King Yudhiṣtra performed the Rāhasuya Yāga in Mahābhārata under the blessings of Lord Kṛṣṇa

Rājasannyāsi: king of saints

Rajas, rajasic: the second characteristic of the three human guṇa or behaviour modes, referring to passionate action

Rakta: blood

Rākṣasa: demon

Rāma: the Supreme God, the seventh avatār, Incarnation of Lord Viṣṇu who appeared in the Treta Yuga to re-establish dharma and destroy the demonic king Rāvaṇa for plundering the goodness from earth and its mankind. He is glorified in the Rāmāyaṇa epic and Śrimad Bhāgavataṁ; also called 'Maryādā Puruṣottama—the most pure, virtuous ideal Supreme Being'; husband of Sītā (Lakṣmī); Lord of Hanumān

Raghupati Yogi: the teacher responsible for preparing Paramahamsa Nithyananda's body and mind for enlightenment at a very young age through authentic Patañjali's Aṣtāṇga Yoga; spiritual name Yogirāj Yogānanda Puri

Ramaṇa Purānam: verses in praise of Ramaṇa Mahaṛṣi, the enlightened Master from Tiruvannamalai

Ramaṇa Maharshi: an enlightened Master and Incarnation from Tiruvannamalai

Rāmānuja: founder of the Viśiṣṭādvaita or qualified non-duality principle. One of the greatest teachers of Hindu philosophy

Rāmāyaṇa: the great Indian epic happening ascribed by Mahaṛṣi Vālmiki as a poetical composition ; considered as Itihās (the great history), it narrates the Divine play of Lord Rāma, Sītā along with His brothers and Hanumān in the Treta Yuga

Rāmakṛṣṇa Paramahamsa: The enlightenend Master and incarnation from Dakṣiṇeśvar, West Bengal, India.

Rāsa līlā: divine dance of the gopīs, Kṛṣṇa's devotees

Rātri: night

Rāvaṇa: mighty emperor of Lanka, the villain in Rāmāyaṇa, who abducted Devi Sītā, consort of Lord Rāma, in the Indian historical epic—Itihās, Rāmāyaṇa.

Responsibilism: term used by Paramahamsa Nithyananda denoting the dharma; the natural law of Existence or Cosmos is responsibilism, the leadership consciousness.

Ṛg Veda: (lit: *ṛc*-praise, *veda*-knowledge) the foremost of the 4 Vedas.; the most ancient scriptural texts of Hinduism. Considered the oldest written text on the planet. The sacred vedic hymns from Ṛg Veda are recited in sacrificial rituals; consists of 1017 hymns composed in Vedic Saṁskṛit mostly devoted in praise of God and His attributes.

Rotis: flat circular Indian bread made usually from wheat

Ṛṣīkeśa: pilgrimage energy center in Himalayas

Ṛṣi: a sage who are seers of Truth

Rudrākṣa: beads of the Rudrākṣa tree, literally means 'Śiva's tears'

Rudrākṣamāla: necklace of holy rudrākṣa seeds

Rudra: another name for Lord Śiva

Rudras: elemental powers

S

Śabarimala: a famous pilgrim centre in Kerala, India

Śabda tattva: principle of sound

Sadāśiva Brahmendra: 18th century Tamil saint and music composer

Śadhana Sadan: Śankar Mahāraj's ashram at Hardwar, North India

Sādhu: literally a 'good person'; refers to an ascetic; same as sannyāsī

Saguṇa: with form

Saguṇa brahman: the formless in form

Sahasranāma: 1000 names invoking a particular deity which devotees recite

Sahasrāra: lotus with thousand petals; the crown energy centre

Saivism: a sect that reveres Lord Śiva as the Supreme Being

Sakha bhāva: the relationship of friendship between the Master and the disciple

Śakti: energy; intelligent energy; Parāśakti refers to universal energy, divinity; considered feminine; masculine aspect of Śakti is Śiva

Sākyanāyanār: originally a Buddhist monk who became an ardent devotee of Śiva in the later part of his life

Sālokya mukti: residence in the same abode of the Lord

Sāma veda: one of the Vedas, the ancient core Hindu scriptures

Samādhi: state of no-mind, no-thoughts; literally, becoming one's original state; liberated, enlightened state.

Śambāla: place where one is in peace and security; space of ultimate freedom

Śambhu: form of rudra, Lord Śiva

Saṁśaya: doubt

Saṁskāra: Root thought patterns; the embedded past memories of unfulfilled desires stored in unconsious space that drive one into powerlessnessa and incomplete decisions, adding to kārmic action

Saṁyama: complete concentration

Samāna: part of prāṇa responsible for digestion and assimilation of food

Sāmīpya mukti: enlightenment whereby one is very near to the Lord

Saṁsāra Sāgara: ocean of wordly life, which can be crosses by the grace of the Guru

Saṁsāra māya: illusion of life

Sāmudrika lakṣana Śāstra: technique of studying body features

Sanātana dharma: eternal path of righteous living (later called Hinduism). The most powerful, most sophisticated, intelligent presentation of the Ultimate Truth with the possibility to evolve by enlightened Masters. It is not a religion but the complete science of living, leaving and beyond

Sañcita karma: our complete bank of unfulfilled karmas

Sandhyā: twilight; sandhyā kāl refers to evening

Sañjaya: the narrator who tells blind Dhṛtarāṣṭra the progress of the war from day to day.

Saṅkalpa: vow or promise; also means conscious decision

Śakti: energy; also name of Devi as primal energy of Cosmos

Śankar Maharāj: Lord Śiva as a young sannyāsi who graced Paramahamsa Nithyananda during His spiritual wanderings as Parivṛajika

Śaṅkha: conch

Śānti: peace

Śaṅkarā: an enlightened Master and Incarnation of Lord Śiva from Kālady, Kerala. Exponent of Advaita Vedānta, celebrated as the great revivor of Sanatana Dharma who lived just 32 years in form

Sāṅkhya philosophy: one of the six schools of classical system of Indian philosophy expounded by Kapila Muni. Sāṅkhya philosophy regards the Universe as consisting of two realities: puruṣa (self) and prakṛti (matter).

Sannyāsa: completing with worldly lif; living for enriching others; sannyāsi or sannyāsin, a monk, an ascetic initiated into the path of Sannyāsa.

Saptapadi: the seven steps taken by the couple after tying the wedding knot in Hindu marriages

Saptaṛṣīs: the 7 sages who control the world

Śāradā Devī: wife of Śrī Rāmakṛṣṇa

Sārasvatya: explain a difficult idea very simply

Sari: traditional attire of Indian women

Śarīra: body

Śāstra: sacred texts

Sāṣṭāṅga namskāra: full prostration salutation

Saraswatī: Goddess of wisdom

Sarvajña: the Knower of all

Sat-cit-ānanda: existence, knowledge, bliss

Satori: high state of consciousness

Śatrughna: brother of lord Rāma in the Hindu epic, Rāmāyaṇa

Satsang: spiritual gatherings; literally 'association (sanga) of the Truth (sat)'

Sātyaki: name of a great warrior

Satyavatī: Arjuna's great grandmother

Savikalpa samādhi: is one of the highest forms of minor state of samādhi meditation; in which the human consciousness is dissolved into infinity for a short period of time

Sāyujya mukti: becoming enlightened oneself; uniting into the Divine or Existence

Satva, satvic: the highest attribute or guṇa of spiritual calmness

Senāpati: the Commander-in-chief of army

Siddhi: extraordinary powers attained through spiritual practice

Śikhaṇḍi: daughter-son of King Drupada, a girl-turned-man, warrior on the Pāṇḍava side. He had been born in an earlier lifetime as a woman named Ambā, who was rejected by Bhīśma for marriage.

Siṁha: lion

Siṁha svapna: nightmare

Sītā: wife of Lord Rāma in Rāmāyaṇa; incarnation of Lakṣmī, Goddess of Fortune

Śiṣya: disciple

Śiva: rejuvenator in the trinity; devotees call Him, Mahādev, Bhole Bābā and Kālabhairava, Mahākāla. Śiva also means 'causeless auspiciousness—mangalatva'; 'The original substance of Existence is Śiva'—defines Paramahamsa Nithyananda.

Skanda: Another name for Lord Subrahmaṇya or Murugā.

Smaraṇa: remembrance; constantly remembering the Divine

Smṛti: (lit: 'that which is remembered'); refers to later day Hindu works which are rules, regulations, laws and epics, such as Manu's works, Purāṇas etc.

Śraddhā: tattva of authenticity; trust, courageous faith, confidence

Śravaṇa: authentic listening. One of the three concepts in Hinduism (Vedānta)—Śravana, Manana, Nididhyāsana.

Sṛṣṭi: creation, which is created

Śruti: (lit: that which is heard) refers to the ancient scriptures of Vedas, Upaniṣads and Bhagavad Gītā; they are the revealed scriptures retained by the sages just by one listening.

Sloka: a saṃskṛit poem; a verse stanza which is made of a group of *pada* and sllyables chanted in a meter rhythm style or *chanda*

Stotras: devotional verses, to be recited or sung

Śūdra: the class of people who contribute by physical work and by giving their time

Sūtra: (lit: 'thread') refers to epigrams, short verses which impart spiritual techniques

Śūnya: literally zero; however, Buddha uses this word to mean reality

Suryanamaskār: (lit: Sun salutation). A comprehensive and main sequence of Yogāsanas that enrich the body-mind and space with complete energy flow; nornally done in the morning absorbing the life-nourshing energy of Sun

Suṣuṁna: Please see 'iḍa'

Svādhiṣṭhāna: where Self is established; the groin or spleen energy centre

Svapna: dream

Svatantra: free

Soma: wine of the gods

Somadatta: a kinsman of the Kuru clan

Soundaryatva: that which attracts our mind

Śrimad Bhāgavataṁ: also called 'Śrimad Bhāgavataṁ Mahā Purāṇa'. See Bhāgavatam.

Sṛṣṭi dṛṣṭi: accept the world and life as it is Sthira: stable

Sthūla śarīra: physical Body

Subramanya: a Lord, also is son of Śiva; also named Skanda, Murugā, Kārtikeya

Sudarśana homa: fire ritual done for success in an undertaking

Śūdras: workers

Sūfi: sect of divine mystics in Islam

Sughoṣa: Nakula's conch

Sukha: happiness

Śukrācārya: guru of asuras

Sūkṣma śarīra: subtle body

Suptacittam: state of being aware even in sleep

Sūrya: the son god

Suṣupti: deep sleep

Sūtradhāra: controller and director of the technique

Svānyakāra: the Life image—the image and expectation you carry about life.

Svapna: dream state

Svajanam: means 'my people, my relatives'. Saṃskṛit term used by Arjuna in Arjunaviṣāda Yoga (chapter 1) of Bhagavad Gītā to state his untold grief in killing 'his people'

Svadharmam: means 'my dharma.' Saṃskṛit term uttered by Śri Kṛṣṇa to Arjuna in Bhagavad Gītā to teach him the true path of self-righteousness to be lived by an individual

Svapuṛnatva: literally means 'self-completion' in Saṃskṛit. The process of doing completion with the self or 'Svapuṛnatva Kriya' as taught by Paramahamsa Nithyananda to experience fulfillment, completion with yourself, by dropping the past karmas, incompletions

Svayaṁvara: choosing of the husband by a woman by her own choice

Svāti nakśatra: the star Svati

Swāmiji: address of respect to one's Master

Swāmi Brahmānanda: disciple of Śrī Rāmakṛṣṇa Paramahamsa

Svarūpa: form

Svayam Prakaśa: self effulgent

T

Tamas, tamasic: the guṇa or attribute of laziness, irresponsibility or inaction

Tantra: esoteric techniques used in spiritual evolution

Tapas: severe spiritual endeavour, penance done voluntarily for inner purification

Tapovan: a holy place in the Himalayas

Tapasvī: one who undertakes severe penance

Tārakāsura: a demon who was killed by Kārtikeya or Skanda, son of Lord Śiva.

Tarangini: great selfless devotee of Kṛṣṇa

Tattva: philosophy or realm

Tattva satya: the existential reality; the truth of the philosophy

Tat tvam asi: that art thou

Tataḥ kim: what next

Taittreya Upaniṣad: One of the main or Mukhya Upaniṣads associated with the Taittriya school of Yajur Veda; number 7 in the Muktika canon of 108 Upaniṣads; intrumental in spreading the Truth of Vedānta; its commentary by Ādī Śankarācārya forms a great Saṃskṛit literature.

Tejas: glow, grace

Tejavastva: sharp radiating energy and clarity

Thatāgata: Buddhahood, a pāli word

Tiruvannamalai: temple town in South India, the birth-place of Paramahamsa Nithyananda; home of most sacred Arunachala hill, which is the direct embodiment of Lord Śiva and is the spiritual nerve center of the Cosmos.

Tīrtha: water; tīrthaṁ is a holy river and a pilgrimage centre

Trikāla: all three time zones, past, present and future; trikālajñāni is one who can see all three at the same time; an enlightened being is beyond time and space

Tirupati: temple town in South India where the presiding diety is Lord Veṅkateśwara

Tiruvaroor: a place in Tamil Nadu, India where Lord Dakṣiṇāmūrti, an enlightened Master lived

Triguṇa rahita: beyond the three guṇas of rajas, tamas and satva

Triputi: the triad of knower, known and knowledge

Tṛṣṇa: craving or longing

Turīya: state of samādhi, no-mind

Turīya avastha: state that persists through all the 3 states of consciousness—waking, dream and deep sleep

Tyāga: renunciation

U

Ucchaiśravas: the legendary snow white horse in the Hindu historical happenings

Udāna: part of prāṇa that helps the soul leave the body at the time of death

Uṇmai: 'Truth' in Tamil

Upāsanā: literally means 'sitting near,' denotes a prescribed method for approaching a deity or God

Uśana: guru of asuras, Śukrācārya

Uttamauja: a Pāñcāla prince, son of subhadrā

Uttar kāśī: a town in North India

Uttarāyaṇam: six months that the sun travels in the north

Uttara mimāmsi: those who interpret vedic scriptures according to vedānta

Upāyanam: the tattva (principle) of responsibility that awakens the power of feeling

Upaniṣads: scriptures that form the essence of the ancient texts of the Vedas, which show the direct path to God or Self-realization. Upaniṣad literally means 'sitting with the Master'. There were 1,180 Upaniṣads, related to 1,180 branches of Vedas. 200 of them are still available; 11 main Upaniṣads are commented on by Incarnation, Bhagavān Ādi Śaṅkara.

V

Vaikuṇṭha: the abode of lord Viṣṇu

Vāimai: truth spoken through the mouth

Vairāgya: beyond attachment and detachment

Vaiśvānarāgni: fire that we worship

Vaiśyas: business community; the class of the society involved in business and merchandize

Vajra: thunderbolt

Vāli: monkey king in the Hindu epic Rāmāyaṇa who is killed by prince Rāma

Vālmīki: author of the famous epic, Rāmāyaṇa; revered as the Ādī

Kavi, the first poet who invented śloka (epic meter). Once a thief, he attained liberation by Lord Rāma's name.

Vāraṇasi: famous pilgrimage centre and temple town of North India; also called Kāśi, the city of Lord Śiva

Vāk śakti: (or vāk siddhi) the power of words; ability to utter the right words and make them occur as reality. Awakened by the tattva of integrity

Varṇa dharma: duty of one's caste; caste classification based on one's natural attributes an not on birth

Varada hasta: boon-giving hand

Varuṇa: god of the ocean

Vāsanā: mental set up

Vāstu Śāstra: an ancient vedic science related to the science of architecture

Vasu: means 'Dweller' or 'Dwelling'

Vasudeva: father of Lord Kṛṣṇa

Vāsudeva Kṛṣṇa: Kṛṣṇa, the mortal being, the son of Vāsudeva

Vāsuki: the serpent with which the Gods and the demons churned the milky ocean in the Hindu Purāṇa

Vāyu: lord of wind

Vedānta: (lit: the 'essence or end of the Vedas'); describes a group of philosophical traditions concerned with the Self-realization by which one understands the ultimate nature of reality (Brahman). Originally a word used in Hindu philosophy as a synonym for that part of the Veda texts known also as the Upaniṣads

Venkaṭeśvara: the presiding diety in Tirupati, a temple in South India. Incarnation of Lord Śrī Viṣṇu

Vidyādāna: giving education to meet someone's mental growth

Vijaya: another name of Arjuna; the undefeatable victorious warrior

Vijñānabhairava tantra: classical sacred text cast as a discourse between the god Śiva and his consort Devi or Śakti, it briefly presents 112 meditation methods or centering techniques

Vijñānamaya kośa: knowledge layer

Vijitendriya: one who has won over his senses; another name of Arjuna

Vikarṇa: a Kaurava warrior

Vīṇa: a musical stringed instrument

Vipāsana meditation: Buddhist meditation technique

Virāṭa rupa: true universal form of Kṛṣṇa

Virāṭa: king of Matsya region

Vīrabhadra: form of Rudra; independent energy of Lord Śiva that destroys ego of Lord Brahma.

Viṣṇu sahasranāma: the vedic hymn that glorifies the 'thousand names of Viṣṇu'

Viṣṇu: supreme god in the Vaiśnavite tradition of Sanatana Dharma; He is the energy that pervades the Universe and sustains it; also called Nārāyaṇa

Viśāda: grief, dilemma, deep sorrow

Viśiṣṭādvaita: school of thought that says the individual self is a part of existence with its own attributes

Viśvāmitra: great sage

Viśvanāth: literally means 'Lord of the Universe'; name of Lord Śiva as the presiding God at the Kāśi Viśvanāth temple in Varanasi

Vivekānanda: primary disciple of Rāmakṛṣṇa Paramahamsa and Founder of the Rāmakṛṣṇa Order. 19th century Eastern Enlightened Master considered a key figure in spreading awareness of Hinduism and Yoga in Europe and America.

Vivekachūḍamaṇi: (lit. the crest jewel of discrimination). A famous Saṃskṛit poem ascribed by Ādi Śaṅkaracārya in 8th century expounding on Advaita Vedanta philosophy with 580 verses

Vrajā homa: a fire ritual of purification

Vṛikodara: one with the stomach of the wolf; another name for Bhīma, one of the Pāṇḍava brothers

Vyādha Gītā: (lit: 'song of a butcher') Consists of the teachings imparted by Vyādh (a butcher) to a monk

Vṛṣṇi: king of the yadu dynasty

Vṛtrāsura: evil being

Vyāna: the energy that pervades the whole body. Its major function is circulation

Vyakta: seen or manifest

Y

Yādava: the clan to which Kṛṣṇa belongs

Yajur veda: one of the 4 vedas

Yakṣa: demigod who according to Hindu sacred history guards wealth.

Yama or Yama dharma: the lord of death; yama also refers to inner discipline

Yantra: a tool for liberation

Yamunā: the sacred river on the banks of Vṛndavān associated with devotion to Kṛṣna; it is the largest tributary of the river Ganges

Yayāti: an illustrious king mentioned in Śrīmad Bhāgavatam

Yogabhraṣṭha: fallen away from the path of Yoga

Yoga: Yoga in Saṁskṛit means to unite or to become 'one' with. Yoga refers to the process of 'uniting.'

Yoga Śāstra: the scripture of Yoga

Yogi: practitioner of yoga

Yogirāj Yogānanda Puri: the teacher responsible for preparing Paramahamsa Nithyananda's body and mind for enlightenment at a very young age through authentic Patañjali's Aṣṭāṇga Yoga; he is also called Raghupati Yogi

Yuga: period of time than spans millions of human years; in Vedic period, there are four yuga namely—Satya Yuga (Nithya Yuga), Treta Yoga, Dwāpar Yuga and Kali Yuga. Bhāgavatam says—one cycle of 4 Yugas is 4.32 million years. Brahma's 1 day is equal to 1,000 cycles of 4 yugas, called 1 Kalpa. 155.2 trillion years have passed since Brahma originally created the planetary system. Each yuga is associated with the appearance of an absolute incarnation in the human plane to re-establish Sanatana-Dharma, such as Bhagavān Rāma in Treta Yuga, Bhagavān Kṛṣṇa in Dvāpara Yuga, etc, along with unbroken chain of Enlightened Masters, eternal sages.

About His Holiness Paramahamsa Nithyananda

His Holiness Paramahamsa Nithyananda is recognized today as a clear, legitimate, apolitical voice of Sanatana Hindu Dharma, and revered as a living incarnation of superconsciousness by millions worldwide. He is a Maha Mandaleshwar (spiritual head) of Mahanirvani Peetha, the most ancient apex body of Hinduism. He is the most watched spiritual teacher on You Tube with over 17.5 million views, and the author of more than 300 books published in over 20 languages. His lectures are watched live every day on http://www.nithyananda.tv, as well as on multiple international television channels and via video conferencing.

Paramahamsa Nithyananda is considered the foremost authority in the world today in the field of Consciousness and Kundalini Awakening, who has successfully demystified yogic sciences like spiritual healing, levitation, teleportation, materialization, anti-ageing and going beyond food.

A spiritual genius with an enlightened insight into everything from management to meditation, relationships to religion, success to spirituality, Paramahamsa Nithyananda brings to us a wealth of practical wisdom and techniques for lasting inner change.

Paramahamsa Nithyananda is the spiritual head of several non-profit organizations worldwide which enrich lives through personal transformation programs and courses, publications, spiritual healing and humanitarian services.

As a global humanitarian, Paramahamsa Nithyananda is working to promoting global peace, through transformation of the individual. His spiritual mission includes ashrams and centres worldwide which serve as spiritual laboratories where inner growth is profound and outer growth is a natural consequence.

Service activities include conducting meditation and de-addiction camps worldwide, free medical camps and artificial limb donation for the needy, support to children in rural areas, conducting meditation camps for prisoners, relief work and disaster recovery management in flood hit areas.

Paramahamsa Nithyananda is also deeply committed to creating international awareness about Indian culture and the ancient Vedic tradition. As an enlightened mystic, a spiritual evolutionary, a trained yogi, a powerful healer and a siddha, Paramahamsa Nithyananda is an inspiring personality for millions of people worldwide. His authenticity, depth of experience and his rare gift for making spirituality both practical and enjoyable have allowed His teachings to reach far and wide. He has healed thousands of people of diseases ranging from depression to cancer, often with a single touch. Working and sharing with over 10 million people worldwide every year, Paramahamsa Nithyananda and His mission are committed to help humanity make the next big breakthrough: into Superconsciousness.

Programs

Inner Awakening
Awaken The Right Intelligence For Life!

A unique 21-day yoga and meditation retreat with Enlightened Master, Paramahamsa Nithyananda.

Imagine,

- Being the master of your destiny
- Being the leader that you know you are
- Having the successful life you deserve
- Falling in love with life again!

STOP IMAGINING. CREATE YOUR REALITY!

Learn,

the ancient science and secrets:

- to awaken your kundalini energy
- to heal your mind, body, soul & relationships
- to activate your hidden potential for greatness
- to hand-craft a successful future, and..
- to TASTE ENLIGHTENMENT!

KALPATARU—MANIFEST YOUR DESTINY!

The Kalpataru is a powerful workshop that aligns your actions with your true intentions. It is a simple method that allows you to awaken your innate power so that you can manifest your own destiny. Chronic diseases are miraculously healed, financial or relationship problems are sorted out effortlessly, miracles of transformation happen and a deep sense of fulfillment and joy is experienced.

Receive a personal blessing from a rare living incarnation H.H. Paramahamsa Nithyananda and empower your true intentions to transform into your reality!

NITHYA KRIYA YOGA—LIVE LIFE AT YOUR PEAK

Our ability to live life to its fullest is blocked as we engage with life in a very limited way. In this 2 day intensive program, we learn to apply the techniques from the essence of all spiritual wisdom: the four sacred principles that reveal the secrets of life and death. Not adapting these principles in our life is the root of all conflicts we face with life.

Through this program, you will be initiated into these four principles and learn powerful techniques to overcome—

- Any kind of fear, especially fear of death
- Unconscious conflicting desires
- Guilts due to social conditioning

- Past traumas and pains and
- Live your life at its peak!

Nithya Dhyana Yoga—Break Free Of Limitations!

Have you wondered why the experience we receive from life is always the same, no matter how much we strive to alter it?

Our endeavors to find happiness, success and better relationships may yield varied results, but at the end we are almost always left with the feeling that nothing has changed.

The reason for this limited experience of life is the behavioural patterns which are deeply engraved in us. Each pattern is associated with one of the seven major energy centres (chakras) in our system, which subtly influence our emotional behaviour.

In this intensive 2-day workshop, we learn to apply the four sacred principles of blissful living (integrity, authenticity, responsibility and enriching), to heal our chakras and go beyond the influence of these limiting behavioural patterns.

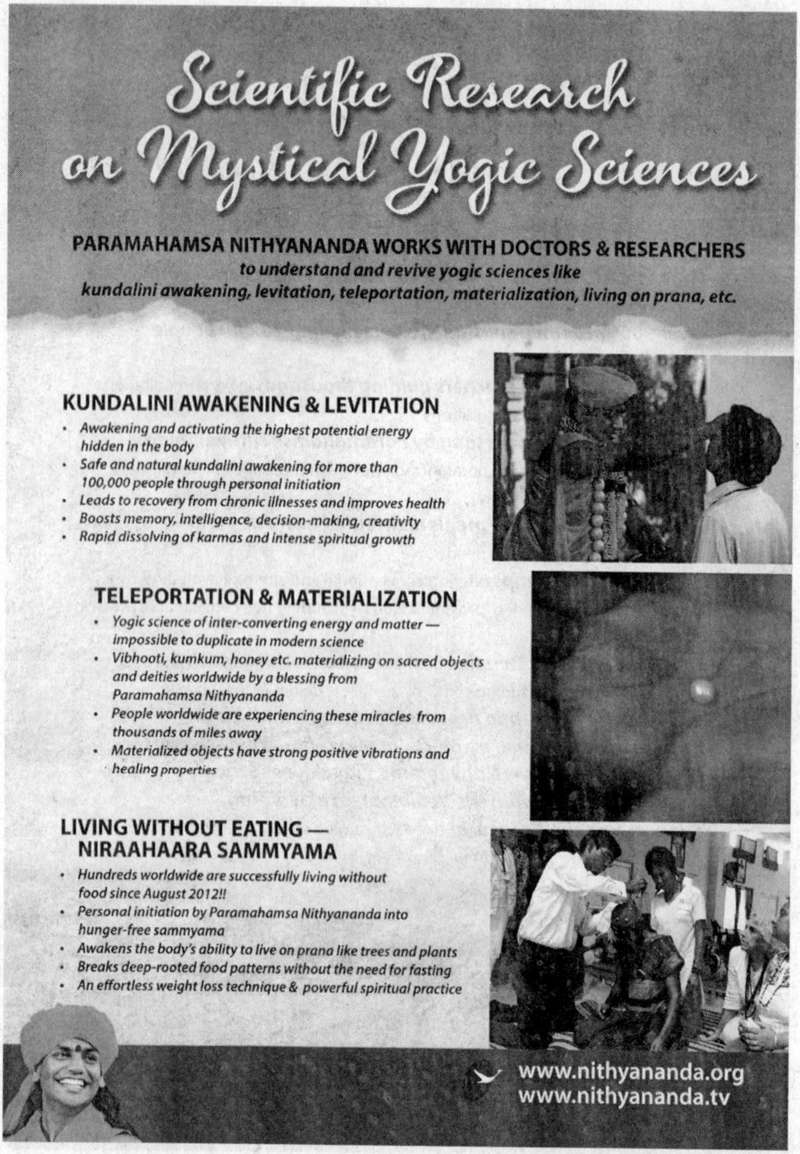
Scientific Research on Mystical Yogic Sciences
PARAMAHAMSA NITHYANANDA WORKS WITH DOCTORS & RESEARCHERS
to understand and revive yogic sciences like
kundalini awakening, levitation, teleportation, materialization, living on prana, etc.
KUNDALINI AWAKENING & LEVITATION
• Awakening and activating the highest potential energy hidden in the body
• Safe and natural kundalini awakening for more than 100,000 people through personal initiation
• Leads to recovery from chronic illnesses and improves health
• Boosts memory, intelligence, decision-making, creativity
• Rapid dissolving of karmas and intense spiritual growth
TELEPORTATION & MATERIALIZATION
• Yogic science of inter-converting energy and matter — impossible to duplicate in modern science
• Vibhooti, kumkum, honey etc. materializing on sacred objects and deities worldwide by a blessing from Paramahamsa Nithyananda
• People worldwide are experiencing these miracles from thousands of miles away
• Materialized objects have strong positive vibrations and healing properties
LIVING WITHOUT EATING — NIRAAHAARA SAMMYAMA
• Hundreds worldwide are successfully living without food since August 2012!!
• Personal initiation by Paramahamsa Nithyananda into hunger-free sammyama
• Awakens the body's ability to live on prana like trees and plants
• Breaks deep-rooted food patterns without the need for fasting
• An effortless weight loss technique & powerful spiritual practice
www.nithyananda.org
www.nithyananda.tv

Reaching Out to Serve the World

ANNADAAN : FREE FOOD FOR ALL

- *More than 10,000 free meals served each day in Nithyananda ashrams and centers worldwide.*
- *Nutritious vegetarian meals cooked using authentic sattvic methods in a hygienic environment*
- *Chanting of vedic mantras or keertans while cooking infuse high-energy vibrations into the food.*
- *Free meal schemes are also offered in schools, prisons and temples.*

FREE MEDICAL SERVICES : HEALTH WITH CARE

- *Fortnightly and monthly multispecialty medical camps offering all services*
- *Weekly mobile medical services including free consultation and medicines in rural areas*
- *A 100% free dialysis clinic with 47 dialysis machines catering to 250 patients per day in the pipeline*
- *Free 100-bed hospital with all amenities planned for the needy*

DISASTER RELIEF : HELPING TO HEAL

- *Emergency relief to victims of natural calamities such as tsunami, earthquake, floods etc*
- *Distribution of free through various relief measures, by offering clothes, food, water and most importantly, psychological support and trauma counseling.*

www.nithyananda.org
www.nithyananda.tv

INSPIRING A GLOBAL
Vedic Renaissance
Daily morning live satsang by Paramahamsa Nithyananda viewed online in over 40 countries through two-way video conferencing and Nithyananda TV.
Daily spiritual talks by Paramahamsa Nithyananda viewed on various TV channels
Over 20 different types of meditation programs at various levels offered in corporates, schools, prisons, etc.
Nithya Yoga & Nithya Kriya – authentic yogic solutions for 108 physical & mental disorders
Scientific & safe initiation into mystical yogic sciences like kundalini awakening, levitation, hunger-free Sammyama etc.
The Nithyananda Sannyas Order for spreading and continuing the sannyas parampara (tradition)
Nithyananda Gurukuls and eN-Vidyalayas offering holistic traditional and modern education in a healthy environment
Inspiring the youth to be the ambassadors of Vedic tradition by enriching them through scripture study, rituals and kriyas
www.nithyananda.org
www.nithyananda.tv

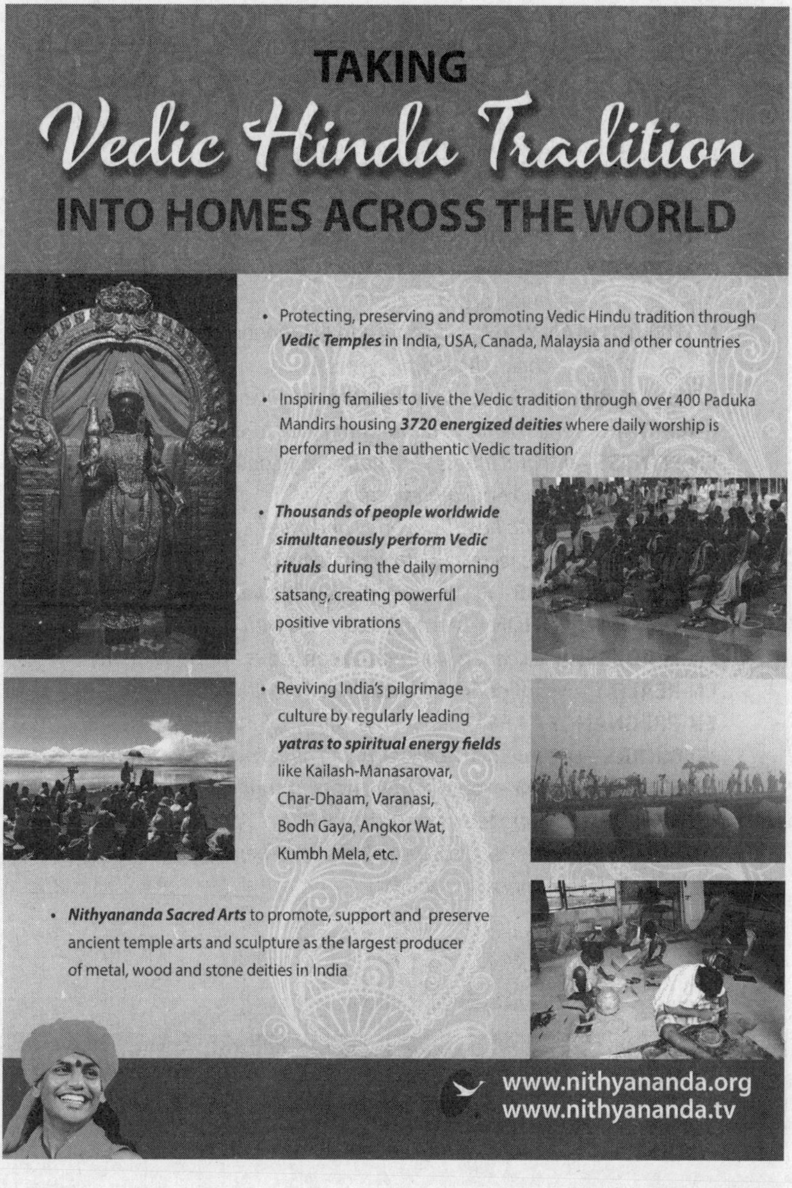
TAKING
Vedic Hindu Tradition
INTO HOMES ACROSS THE WORLD
• Protecting, preserving and promoting Vedic Hindu tradition through Vedic Temples in India, USA, Canada, Malaysia and other countries
• Inspiring families to live the Vedic tradition through over 400 Paduka Mandirs housing 3720 energized deities where daily worship is performed in the authentic Vedic tradition
• Thousands of people worldwide simultaneously perform Vedic rituals during the daily morning satsang, creating powerful positive vibrations
• Reviving India's pilgrimage culture by regularly leading yatras to spiritual energy fields like Kailash-Manasarovar, Char-Dhaam, Varanasi, Bodh Gaya, Angkor Wat, Kumbh Mela, etc.
• Nithyananda Sacred Arts to promote, support and preserve ancient temple arts and sculpture as the largest producer of metal, wood and stone deities in India
www.nithyananda.org
www.nithyananda.tv